Krista L. Wille

The Hornbook

Dr. Johnson described the hornbook as "the first book of children, covered with horn to keep it unsoiled." Pardon's New General English Dictionary (1758) defined it as "A leaf of written or printed paper pasted on a board, and covered with horn, for children to learn their letters by, and to prevent their being torn and daubed."

It was used throughout Europe and America between the late 1400s and the middle 1700s.

Shaped like an old-fashioned butter paddle, the first hornbooks were made of wood. The paper lesson the child was to learn was fastened to the wooden paddle and covered with a piece of horn. The transparent strip of horn was made by soaking a cow's horn in hot water and peeling it away at the thickness of a piece of celluloid. The horn was necessary to protect the lesson from the damp and perhaps grubby hands of the child. Hornbooks commonly contained the alphabet, the vowels, and the Lord's Prayer. Later hornbooks were made of various materials: brass, copper, silver, ivory, bronze, leather, and stone.

As the art of printing advanced, the hornbook was supplanted by the primer in the book form we know today. Subsequently West Publishing Company developed its "Hornbook Series", a series of scholarly and well-respected one volume treatises on particular areas of law. Today they are widely used by law students, lawyers and judges.

LAND USE PLANNING AND CONTROL LAW

By

Julian Conrad Juergensmeyer

Professor of Law, Gerald A. Sohn Research Scholar, and
Affiliate Professor of Urban and Regional Planning
University of Florida

and

Thomas E. Roberts

Professor of Law
Wake Forest University School of Law

HORNBOOK SERIES®

WEST
GROUP

ST. PAUL, MINN., 1998

COPYRIGHT © 1998 By WEST GROUP
                        610 Opperman Drive
                        P.O. Box 64526
                        St. Paul, MN 55164–0526
                        1–800–328–9352

Library of Congress Cataloging-in-Publication Data

Juergensmeyer, Julian Conrad.
    Land use planning and control law / Julian Conrad Juergensmeyer,
Thomas E. Roberts.
        p.   cm. — (Hornbook series)
    Includes index.
    ISBN 0–314–21203–5 (hc.)
    1. City planning and redevelopment law—United States.   2. Land
use—Law and legislation—United States.   3. Zoning law—United
States.   I. Roberts, Thomas E.   II. Title.   III. Series.
KF5692.J84   1998
346.7304'5—dc21   98–20943
                                                                          CIP

ISBN 0–314–21203–5

To the late Donald G. Hagman, whose enormous contributions to land use law have guided our work.

J.C.J and T.E.R.

To Ewa and Krissy.

J.C.J.

To Scott, Beth, and Mark.

T.E.R.

*

Preface

In Chapter One, we describe the scope of this Hornbook, give our views as to the issues that will dominate the field in, at least, the early years of the twentieth-first century, and provide an overview of the characteristics of land use planning and control law. We will not repeat that material here, but rather take a moment to explain the origin of this book and thank those who have helped us in this endeavor.

This Hornbook owes it origins to Hagman, Urban Planning and Land Development Control Law, originally published in 1971. Its author, Professor Donald Hagman, was, and no doubt will continue to be, one of the most important figures in the land use planning and control field. After Don's tragic and untimely death in 1982, Professor Juergensmeyer began the preparation of a second edition, which was published in 1986. Those with an interest in Professor Hagman's many accomplishments may wish to read the dedications to Don Hagman at 29 U.C.L.A.L.Rev. 772 (1982).

The original plan was for us to prepare a third edition of the Hagman book but when we began that task we came to realize that land use planning and control law changed so much in the 27 years since the first edition—and, in fact, so much in the 12 years since the second edition, that to represent the new book as a third edition with Don Hagman still listed as an author would be misleading. Since we have been able to retain so little from the first edition, we reluctantly decided to drop Don's name for fear of attributing ideas to him that he might not have agreed with or which were not even issues in the subject area at the time of his death. This decision gave us an opportunity to modernize the title of the book since the emphasis Don placed in the title and the content on *urban* planning is no longer appropriate. As we have suggested in our dedication, we nonetheless owe a great debt to Don's thoughts and approaches and have tried to retain his ideas as much as possible.

We have also benefited from the insights and comments of many colleagues. In particular, we thank Jim Nicholas of the University of Florida, James B. Wadley of Washburn University School of Law, Chris Nelson of the Georgia Institute of Technology, Jon W. Bruce of Vanderbilt University School of Law, David L. Callies, University of Hawaii School of Law, and Robert H. Freilich, University of Missouri-Kansas City School of Law.

We acknowledge a special debt of gratitude to Fred P. Bosselman and Clifford L. Weaver,—longtime and nationally renown practitioners of land use planning and control law. Fred Bosselman is now a professor at Chicago-Kent College of Law. Fred and Clif wrote four chapters in the practitioner's edition of the 1986 edition of this book's predecessor, the Hagman and Juergensmeyer book referred to above. With their permission, we have retained some of that material in this work. (See §§ 5.32-5.40.).

Professor Juergensmeyer wishes to acknowledge the personal, professional, and/or research assistance of the following people: Tom Pelham, Dan McIntyre, Roy Hunt, Thomas H. Roberts, Ray Young, Bob Rhodes, John Smitherman, Pam Smith, Ewa Gmurzynska, Conrad Juergensmeyer, Erik Juergensmeyer, Mike Ciccarone, Denis Calfee, Paul Fanning, Brian Leebrick, Sherri Johnson, Gerald Murphy, Steve Mench, Patrick Maraist, and Mark Dungan.

Professor Roberts acknowledges the support of Dean Robert Walsh of Wake Forest University School of Law and the Carl Holleman Research Fund for Real Estate and Property Law. He is also grateful to Wake Forest law students Scott M. Federoff, Steven R. Main, Rhapsody A. Paragas, Julian P. Robb, and R. Flint Crump for their research assistance.

JULIAN CONRAD JUERGENSMEYER
THOMAS E. ROBERTS

May, 1998

WESTLAW® Overview

Juergensmeyer and Roberts' *Land Use Planning and Control Law* offers a detailed and comprehensive treatment of basic rules, principles and issues relating to land use. To supplement the information contained in this book, you can access Westlaw, a computer-assisted legal research service of West Group. Westlaw contains an array of legal research resources, including case law, statutes, expert commentary, current developments and various other types of information.

Learning how to use these materials effectively will enhance your legal research. To help you coordinate your book and Westlaw research, this volume contains an appendix listing Westlaw databases, search techniques and sample problems.

THE PUBLISHER

*

Summary of Contents

*

Table of Contents

CHAPTER 5. ZONING "FORMS OF ACTION": OBTAINING OR RESISTING DEVELOPMENT PERMISSION

I. INTRODUCTION

II. LEGISLATIVE AND ADMINISTRATIVE ACTION

III. REZONINGS

IV. VARIANCES

CHAPTER 6. EXCLUSIONARY ZONING

II.   THE TAKING ISSUE

III.   DUE PROCESS AND EQUAL PROTECTION

II. TYPES OF PRIVATE CONTROLS

III. PUBLIC INTEREST IN, AND USE OF, PRIVATE CONTROLS

CHAPTER 16. THE POWER OF EMINENT DOMAIN

I. INTRODUCTION

II. PROPERTY, PUBLIC USE AND CONDEMNATION ISSUES

III. JUST COMPENSATION

LAND USE PLANNING AND CONTROL LAW

*

Chapter 1

AN INTRODUCTION TO LAND USE PLANNING AND CONTROL LAW

Analysis

---

§ 1.1 The Development of Land Use Planning and Control Law

The purpose of this Hornbook is to explicate the law of land use planning and control. Although instances of governmental and private regulation of the use of land can be found in virtually all legal systems and societies since the beginning of history, land use planning and control law is a relatively new area of the law in our legal system. Certainly, as just suggested, land regulation laws, court decisions, and private agreements can be found at the very beginning of our common law system. For example, the tenure and estates concepts which formed the basis of property law at the birth of our legal system in Norman England in 1066 were means of land use regulation as well as the conceptual foundations of property ownership. Even in the colonial period of the United States, governments and individuals used the legal system to regulate land use.

Land use planning and control law did not begin to emerge as a separate and distinct area of the law until the early zoning ordinances and judicial decisions concerning them in the 1920's. Even then, little evidence supported the recognition of land use control as a legal specialty or distinct area from a conceptual and subject matter viewpoint. Plan-

1

ners and municipal law specialists began to think of "zoning" as a "special" area in the 1930's, 40's and 50's, but few treatises, hornbooks, casebooks, manuals or law school courses were devoted to the subject before the 1960's. In the final quarter of the twentieth century the growth has been astounding.

The interest of the American public in land use regulation has expanded at least as rapidly. Today it is unusual to find a political campaign in which land use regulation and its cohort, environmental protection, are not crucial issues.

§ 1.2 Scope of This Hornbook

It is inevitable that there be uncertainty and disagreement over the scope of the subject matter of a new and rapidly changing and developing area of the law. Land use control law has matured enough for there to be general agreement that the core of this subject is planning and regulation of land use by governmental entities through the police power. Thus, zoning and subdivision control should make everyone's list of land use control law subtopics. The law on these is so vast—i.e. the court decisions; statutes, ordinances and regulations; and books, articles and manuals are so numerous that even if one confined land use control law to these two land regulatory approaches there would be more than enough law for courses and hornbooks.

No one, it seems, would confine land use control law to zoning and subdivision control. The uncertainty centers around how many related areas should be included.

The predecessor to this hornbook, as explained in the preface, was Urban Planning and Land Development Control Law by Donald Hagman, a giant in the field. That book, published originally in 1971, reflected Professor Hagman's interest in urban law developments.[1] While urban problems are as serious now as when as Professor Hagman wrote, significant changes have occurred to cause us to de-emphasize urban development in this book. One factor is the withdrawal of the federal government from significant participation in urban development, which began in the early 1970s and accelerated rapidly in the 1980s. A second factor is the growing realization of the environmental and social ills caused by sprawl development into the countryside. This book, in contrast to its predecessor, focuses predominantly on these issues.

The scope of this work is best analyzed on a chapter by chapter and topic by topic basis.

● *Planning Law* [Chapter 2]

Planning and land use control law have always been recognized as closely interrelated. Unfortunately, that recognition until recently was more theoretical than actual and plans had few legal consequences. The

---

§ 1.2

1. A second edition of Professor Hagman's book was prepared and published after his death: Hagman & Juergensmeyer, Urban Planning and Land Development Control Law (2d ed.1986).

recent advent of statutes requiring state, regional and local planning and the formulation of the consistency requirement, have created planning law as distinguished from planning theory. Since one of the principal tenets of planning law is that planning should precede any and all land use regulations this chapter is strategically located as the first substantive chapter. Discussion of planning principles are included in subsequent chapters in relation to particular land use control devices.

● *Zoning* [Chapters 3, 4, & 5]

The traditional "core" of land use control law is included within these chapters. They are critical to understanding the process by which land use development decisions are made.

● *Exclusionary Zoning* [Chapter 6]

One of the negative consequences of local governmental control of land use is that the power can be used to exclude persons and types of land uses that are perceived as threats to the homogeneity of the community. Exclusion may be based on any number of factors such as wealth, race, religion, political unpopularity, or stereotypes. Beyond the harm suffered by the excluded individual, there are widespread regional implications to parochial, selfish actions by local governments.

● *Subdivision Control* [Chapter 7]

Subdivision control law is almost as old as zoning law in this country and is a well recognized part of the land use control law "core."

● *Building and Housing Codes* [Chapter 8]

Building codes are even older than zoning and subdivision control laws. Housing codes are more recent but both are closely related to zoning. Their land use regulation consequences have traditionally been indirect. This promises to change because of their potential for being direct land use control devices through building specifications that make some uses impossible on certain types of tracts—for example coastal areas, flood plains, and environmentally sensitive and unstable land. Also, the issuance of building permits has increasingly become the regulatory stage at which many growth management techniques such as impact fees are imposed for developer funding of infrastructure.

● *Growth Management* [Chapter 9]

The present direction of land use planning and control law is its reformulation to fit and serve growth management. All land use planning concepts can be used as growth management tools. This chapter is designed to assimilate planning law, zoning law, subdivision control law, and, in fact, all aspects of land use planning and control law and focus it on growth management.

● *Constitutional Limitations* [Chapter 10]

The greatly increased frequency and severity of land use restrictions in recent years has made the limits of governmental power more important. For many years litigation over land use control regulations was confined almost exclusively to the state courts. In the past quarter-century, the interest of the Supreme Court and other federal courts in land use control law—an interest which was peacefully dormant for decades—awakened.

The limitation imposed on government by the Fifth Amendment's taking clause is the dominant constitutional issue in American land use law. There is a sharp debate over the Court's interpretation of the Fifth Amendment and the meaning of property in our legal system and our society. Beyond the taking issue, there are frequent issues of arbitrary and discriminatory government action in regulating land use, some of which affect speech, religion, and privacy rights.

- *Protection and Preservation of the Natural and Built Environment: Environmental Protection, Aesthetic Regulation, Historic Preservation, Farmland Preservation* [Chapters 11, 12 & 13]

Perhaps the fastest growing area of land use control law is that relevant to, and at times overlapping with that of, protection of the natural and built environments. Environmental law is even newer than land use law and in its early days it ran parallel to rather than intertwining with land use planning and control. Today, environmental protection and land use regulation overlap to such a great degree on many points that it is impossible to entirely separate the two. Chapter 11 attempts an explication of "basic" environmental law as it is most relevant to land use control law. Chapter 12 focuses on the "built environment" through consideration of aesthetic regulation and historic preservation. Chapter 13 treats farmland and open space preservation problems and the land use planning and control techniques for their accomplishment.

- *Nuisance Law* [Chapter 14]

Nuisance law was the earliest form of land use control, one effected by the courts, rather than the legislature. Though reliance on it diminished significantly throughout the twentieth century, it remains an important cog in the land use regulation machine. It is of particular relevance to the definition of property rights in the constitutional sense. There is no property right to conduct a nuisance and to the extent that land use directs itself to nuisance activities, no constitutional problem is present. Determining when that point is reached is, however, a point of difficulty.

- *Private Land Use Control* [Chapter 15]

Private individuals have for centuries regulated the use of land even absent governmental activities or interest. Privately created land use restrictions continue to function as significant and often effective means of controlling the use of land. Public land use regulation has in many regards made private methods more rather than less important and the ever frequent use of traditionally private devices (restrictive covenants for example) have revitalized the importance of "private" land use control techniques.

• *Power of Eminent Domain* [Chapter 16]

The power of eminent domain can be conceived of as the ultimate land use control power possessed by governmental entities since as long as the entity is willing to pay compensation, the government has the power to regulate land in virtually any way it wishes and even take title to it.

A few traditional techniques intentionally employ the power of eminent domain but usually governments, to protect the public interest and for practical fiscal reasons seek, to regulate land through the exercise of the police power. The close relationship and even overlap between the two powers necessitates an overview of eminent domain law.

§ 1.3   Issues for the Twenty–First Century

The chapters that follow focus on hundreds of issues. Some are old and have been discussed and disputed since the beginnings of land use control law. Others are quite recent in origin. Most if not all are interrelated so that it is difficult if not impossible to solve one without raising another. It would seem desirable to highlight the views of the authors concerning leading issues so that readers may reflect on what land use planning and control law will be like in the twenty-first century. The list that follows is not designed to be clever, exhaustive, or innovative. It is simply designed to establish greater rapport between the authors and readers so that the latter can read the balance of the Hornbook with some insight into what the authors "worried" about when the chapters which follow were written.[1]

• *What Will Become of Traditional Euclidean Zoning?*

Traditional zoning was indicted many years ago by Reps in a seminal analysis.[2] More recently, the abolition of zoning has been called for.[3] Certainly Euclidean zoning in its cumulative, static and negative sense should not and probably will not survive the next century. Even a more enlightened noncumulative and mixed use oriented zoning system is of questionable value. But, what will replace it? Will local governments—especially those with severe budget and staff limitations—be able to effectively, efficiently and equitably administer point systems, development order systems and performance standards?

• *Will Impact Analysis Become the Universal Antidote to Land Use Complaints and Will Land Use Regulatory Fees Based on That Analysis Rescue Local Governments From Their Infrastructure Funding Crisis?*

§ 1.3

1. For another list, see Netter, Land–Use Law: Issues for the Eighties (1981).

2. Reps, Pomeroy Memorial Lecture: Requiem for Zoning (Paper presented at the 1964 ASPO National Planning Conference. Planning 1964. American Society of Planning Officials).

3. Krasnowiecki, Abolish Zoning, 31 Syracuse L.Rev. 719 (1980). See also, Ziegler, The Twilight of Single–Family Zoning, 3 UCLA J. Envtl.L. & Policy 161 (1983).

Fred Bosselman raised the question in the mid 1980's.[4] Since then, conditioning development approval on impact analysis and the payment of impact, linkage and mitigation fees or participation in mitigation and transferable development rights programs have become common place. In an era in which tax revenues are less and less adequate to permit governments to pay for capital improvement needs, the revenue potential of land use regulation looms as a major fiscal resource for local governments and thereby a new function to be served by land use regulations.

- *Will the Coordination of Planning and Land Use Regulation and the Requirement That Land Use Regulations Be Consistent With Comprehensive Plans Become the Norm in All Jurisdictions?*

Nothing would seem more basic and essential than that land use regulations should be consistent with and implementations of comprehensive plans. Yet, only a few states have this requirement. Why is it taking so long to be accepted? Can there be any validity and long range effects to land use regulations not based upon comprehensive planning? Surely not.

- *Will the Quiet Revolution Continue?*

In 1972, Fred Bosselman and David Callies wrote of the revesting of land use control power in state government.[5] Will the trend continue or will there be a revitalization of local government home rule power?

- *Will Land Use Control Law Become a Step–Child of Constitutional Law? Will Governmental Liability and Taking Limitations Seriously Restrict the Future Exercise of the Land Use Control Power?*

The Supreme Court's land use decisions in recent years have tightened the reins on government regulation of land use by incorporating substantive due process into the protection afforded by the taking clause. Will this continue, and if so, how stringently will the courts limit government? Without detracting from the importance of constitutional guarantees of due process and of compensation for property that is taken for a public use, if governments are not allowed to effectively plan and regulate the use of land and resources, in the long run, society will suffer greater loss than some perceived freedoms and liberties. Rights to use real property should not be equated with essential freedoms such as speech, press, and religion.[6] Our common law system has always recognized that ownership of land carries with it both benefits and burdens. The so-called absolute right to use real property is inconsistent with our traditional legal concepts and is not supportive of our societal goals and values. Certainly individuals merit protection from inequitable, prejudi-

---

4. Bosselman, "Linkage, Mitigation and Transfer: Will Impact Analysis Become the Universal Antidote to Land Use Complaints?" (1985).

5. F. Bosselman and D. Callies, The Quiet Revolution in Land Use Control (1972).

6. Contrast the position taken in Ronald J. Krotoszynski, Fundamental Property Rights, 85 Georgetown L.J. 555 (1997).

cial and inefficient regulation of land but society merits protection from selfish, unreasonable use of private property.

• *Will Federal Control of Land Use Continue to Increase?*

In a wide array of areas, such as fair housing for the handicapped, telecommunications, clean water, and endangered species, Congress has stepped into areas traditionally the province of local government.

• *Will Environmental Regulation and Land Use Regulation Merge or Continue to Overlap and Conflict?*

In spite of considerable overlap in goals, principles and approaches, the land use and environmental regulatory systems often work at cross purposes to the great detriment of landowners and society. What should happen is that one permit-performance (or impact analysis) system should develop for the unified implementation of both systems.

• *Environmental Justice: What is it? Is there a solution?*

Many have charged that locally unwanted land uses, such as land-fills, are sited predominantly in minority and low-income communities. Numerous studies in recent years have attempted to determine whether the charge is true and, if so, what causes such disproportionate siting, and how more equitable sharing of the harms from such uses could be achieved.

• *Will Sustainable Development Become Integrated Into the Substance of Environmental and Land Use Law Thereby Emphasizing a "Land Ethic" Basis for Land Use and Environmental Law? Could Such a Development Counter the Private Property Rights Protection Movement?*

The importance placed on the concept and goal of global sustainable development by the United Nations publication OUR COMMON FUTURE[7] catapulted that concept into the forefront of the international political, social, economic and environmental agenda. Although the concept is no stranger to American land use and environmental law, the ramifications for domestic law are only beginning to be considered in the United States. The statutory and jurisprudential changes needed in our land use and environmental regulatory goals to implement the concept could be one of the headline stories for many years to come.

A small indication of a judicial awakening in this regard can be glimpsed in Minnesota where three judicial decisions consider that the Minnesota Legislature through its environmental legislation has given the "land ethic" of conservationist Aldo Leopold the "force of law."[8]

---

7. The World Commission on Environment and Development, Our Common Future (1987).

8. Freeborn County by Tuveson v. Bryson, 309 Minn. 178, 243 N.W.2d 316, 322 (Minn.1976); Application of Christenson, 417 N.W.2d 607 (Minn.1987); McLeod County Bd. of Com'rs as Drainage Authority for McLeod County Ditch No.8 v. State, Dept. of Natural Resources, 549 N.W.2d 630 (Minn.App.1996).

That "Land Ethic" adopted by the Minnesota courts merits quoting as a reference point for land use and environmental regulation in the twenty-first century:

All ethics so far evolved rest upon a single premise: that the individual is a member of a community of interdependent parts. His instincts prompt him to compete for his place in the community, but his ethics prompt him also to co-operate (perhaps in order that there be a place to compete for).

The land ethic simply enlarges the boundaries of the community to include soils, waters, plants, and animals, or collectively: the land.

In short, a land ethic changes the role of Homo sapiens from conqueror of the land community to plain member and a citizen of it. It implies respect for his fellow members, and also respect for the community as such.[9]

§ 1.4 Characteristics of Land Use Planning and Control Law

Several characteristics of land use planning and control law can be noted which assist in understanding the field.

- There are a relatively small number of very important cases which are constantly discussed and cited. No matter what the issues are in a controversy, there seems to always be something relevant in *Euclid*,[1] *Nectow*,[2] *Ramapo*,[3] *Penn Central*,[4] *Dolan*,[5] *Lucas*,[6] *Petaluma*,[7] *Mt. Laurel*,[8] *Nollan*,[9] *First English*,[10] or *Fasano*[11] or *all* of them! A well versed land use lawyer will be intimately familiar with these cases.

- There are a handful of leading and influential states. Traditionally land use planning and control law has been almost exclusively state as opposed to federal law. Although one can find interesting decisions throughout the country the list of most important states from a case decision and statutory perspective is not that long. New York and New Jersey were in the forefront of land use planning for many years and still are but most of the newer issues and approaches come from sunbelt and coastal states where development pressures generate controversies which in turn gen-

9. Aldo Leopold, A Sand County Almanac 203 (1949).

§ 1.4

1. 272 U.S. 365, 47 S.Ct. 114, 71 L.Ed. 303 (1926).

2. 277 U.S. 183, 48 S.Ct. 447, 72 L.Ed. 842 (1928).

3. 30 N.Y.2d 359, 334 N.Y.S.2d 138, 285 N.E.2d 291 (1972).

4. 438 U.S. 104, 98 S.Ct. 2646, 57 L.Ed.2d 631 (1978).

5. 512 U.S. 374, 114 S.Ct. 2309, 129 L.Ed.2d 304 (1994).

6. 505 U.S. 1003, 112 S.Ct. 2886, 120 L.Ed.2d 798 (1992).

7. 522 F.2d 897 (9th Cir.1975).

8. 67 N.J. 151, 336 A.2d 713 (1975).

9. 483 U.S. 825, 107 S.Ct. 3141, 97 L.Ed.2d 677 (1987).

10. 482 U.S. 304, 107 S.Ct. 2378, 96 L.Ed.2d 250 (1987).

11. 264 Or. 574, 507 P.2d 23 (1973).

erate cases and statutes. Within the sunbelt/coastal category, there are leaders. Note how many recent citations throughout the book are to material from California, Florida, and Oregon.

- The inter-disciplinary nature of land use law is increasingly important. Hardly any major land use regulation program or litigation is handled exclusively these day by lawyers or planners. Usually both are integrally involved as well as engineers and economists. The multi-disciplinary nature of the work is beginning to influence the content and subject matter of land use literature and consequently its study and practice.

- A standard list of issues are omnipresent regardless of the details of the controversy. It is hard to imagine a major land use controversy these days that does not raise at least most of the following issues:

    1. Does the action or proposed action of the governmental entity in question constitute an exercise of the police power?

    2. Has the police power been exercised reasonably?

    3. Has the governmental entity—if it is other than the State—been delegated the power to do what it has done or proposes to do?

    4. Has there been an unlawful delegation of legislative authority by the governmental entity?

    5. Has there been a denial of equal protection?

    6. Have notice and hearing requirements been respected?

    7. Is the action of the governmental unit legislative or quasi judicial? Will the fairly debatable standard or some stricter standard of review be applied to it?

    8. Has there been a taking?

§ 1.5   Research Sources

While we hope that this book will serve as a beginning step for research in land use law issues, in depth studies will require one to look at additional material. Fortunately, an array of sources is available.

A. *Westlaw*

An appendix to this book contains a guide on the research of land use law through Westlaw. This data base includes not only all state and federal cases and statutes, but also includes numerous recent law review articles, specialty journals, and daily newspapers that cover land use developments.

B. *One Volume Treatises*

There are several other one volume reference books available. Those with a primary focus on land use law include: Daniel R. Mandelker, *Land Use Law* (3d ed. Michie Co.1993) and Peter W. Salsich, *Land Use*

Regulation: Planning, Zoning, Subdivision Regulation, and Environmental Control (Shepard's/McGraw–Hill 1991).

A more limited focus on federal land use law is *Federal Land Use Law: Limitations, Procedures, and Remedies* by Daniel R. Mandelker, Jules B. Gerard and E. Thomas Sullivan (Clark Boardman 1986).

In the related area of environmental law, the leading book is by Professor William H. Rodgers, Jr. *Environmental Law* (2d ed. West Publishing Co. 1994). Professor Linda A. Malone also has an excellent book, *Environmental Regulation of Land Use* (Clark Boardman 1990–).

C. Multi–Volume Treatises

Several extensive multi-volume works are available. They include:

Edward H. Ziegler, Jr., *Rathkopf's the Law of Zoning and Planning* (4th ed.rev.1993 Clark Boardman Callaghan) (5 volumes);

Kenneth H. Young, *Anderson's American Law of Zoning* (4th ed. rev.1996 Lawyers Co-op. Publishing Co.) (4 volumes);

Patrick J. Rohan and Eric Damian Kelly, *Zoning and Land Use Controls* (Matthew Bender 1977–) (9 volumes); and

Norman Williams, Jr. and John M. Taylor, *American Planning Law: Land Use and the Police Power* (Callaghan 1974–) (6 volumes).

In the area of eminent domain the standard reference work is Julius Sackman and Patrick J. Rohan, *Nichols' The Law of Eminent Domain* (3rd ed. Matthew Bender 1976–) (14 volumes).

D. Law Reviews

Law school law reviews carry land use articles from time to time, and the frequency of coverage has significantly increased in recent years. Articles are available through Westlaw dating back to the mid 1980s with more complete coverage starting in the early 1990s. Among the law reviews carrying numerous land use articles are:

The Urban Lawyer, published four times a year by the Section of State and Local Government Law of the American Bar Association through the University of Missouri–Kansas City School of Law;

The *Journal of Land Use and Environment Law* published twice a year by Florida State University College of Law; and

The *Washington University Journal of Urban & Contemporary Law* published semi-annually by the Washington University School of Law.

E. Newsletters

The American Planning Association publishes a bi-monthly journal, *Land Use Law and Zoning Digest*, which contains a short lead article on a topic of current interest as well as briefs of recent cases and statutes.

A monthly newsletter, *Zoning and Planning Law Report*, is published by Clark Boardman Company. Like the APA digest noted above, it contains a short lead article on a topic of current interest as well as briefs of recent developments.

A bi-weekly newsletter, *Land Use Law Report,* is published by Business Publishers, Inc. The report contains case briefs as well as news of legislative developments around the country.

F.   *On–Line: Internet Sources*

Web sites, too numerous too list and ever growing, contain valuable information on land use topics.[1] A few of interest include:

The Section of State and Local Government Law of the American Bar Association has a web site *<http://www.abanet.org/statelocal/home.html>* with articles on land use. It also hosts an e-mail discussion group used by students, practitioners and academics.

The American Planning Association also has planning and land use information. It can be accessed at *<http://www.planning.org/index.html>*

The codes of hundreds of municipalities around the country are available through a site maintained by the Municipal Code Corporation *<http://www.municode.com/database.html>*

§ 1.5

1. See Martha Mann, Recommended Legal Web Sites for Land Use and Environmental Law, 12 J.Land Use & Envtl.L 425 (1997).

Chapter 2

COMPREHENSIVE PLANS AND
THE PLANNING PROCESS

Analysis

I.   **Planners and Planning**
II. **Antecedents of Local Government Planning**
III. **Relationship of Planning and Zoning**
IV. **The Process of Planning Comprehensively**
V.   **The Legal Status of the Comprehensive Plan**

I.   PLANNERS AND PLANNING

I. PLANNERS AND PLANNING

§ 2.1 The Practice of Planning

There is no universally-accepted definition of planning, nor is there a definition of "planner" which would be endorsed by all those who now practice urban planning. Currently, only two states have legislation concerned with defining or licensing the urban planner as a professional: New Jersey[1] and Michigan.[2] Nevertheless, those involved with urban planning would generally agree that the planner who deals with land use regulation has several principal characteristics.[3]

First, the planner has technical training at the undergraduate or graduate school level, often in one of the many university urban planning programs, or possibly in another discipline such as engineering, architecture or landscape architecture.

Second, the planner is future-oriented. The urban planner believes that by analyzing existing conditions, forecasting future trends, and establishing normative goals and policies, an optimum path for the development or redevelopment of a geographic area may be formulated. This process usually results in a "plan." In addition, many urban planners also perform independent projections, statistical analyses, studies of housing needs and conditions in blighted or underdeveloped areas, and draft municipal ordinances for zoning, aesthetic regulation, and environmental protection. These studies are often done in conjunction with the process of preparing a plan.

Third, the planner acts as a catalyst in the political process by which plans and land use regulations are developed, adopted, and implemented by a local government such as a county or city. This catalytic role arises from the planner's function as an analyst of conditions and trends in development or decline, and as a proponent of alternative means to guide the development, or redevelopment, of urban and rural areas. As the proponent of new regulations and of the plan, the planner exerts an influence through the legislative and administrative processes by which local governments plan for, and regulate, development.

Planners are most often employees of governmental agencies. According to a 1981 study of planners' employment trends performed by the American Planning Association, 63 percent of all planners responding to a nationwide survey were employed by governmental agencies as

§ 2.1

1. N.J. Statutes Annotated 45:14A–1 et seq.

2. Mich. Compiled Laws Annotated § 339.2301 et seq.

3. For information on the profession and practice of planning, see generally, Argyris and Schon, Theory in Practice: Increasing Professional Effectiveness (1974); Friedman, Planning in the Public Domain: From Knowledge to Action (1987); Michael, On Learning to Plan—And Planning to Learn (1973); Perloff, Education of Planning, City, State and Regional (1957); The Practice of Local Government Planning (So and Getzels eds.1998); see also Classic Readings in Urban Planning: An Introduction (Stein ed.1995).

permanent staff.[4] These agencies included city departments of planning, county planning departments, joint city-county planning agencies, metropolitan or regional planning agencies, state agencies, and federal government agencies. Those planners not employed by government work for consulting firms, business, colleges and universities, and nonprofit institutions, according to the study.

The planning profession has been seeking recognition as a profession for several decades. Engineers, architects, and landscape architects are often found in planning positions, but many colleges and universities now offer bachelor and masters degrees in urban planning. Curricula in these academic programs range from a technical, design-oriented approach, termed "physical planning" by planning theorists, to a more policy-oriented approach at the opposite extreme. Considerable intermixing of the two disciplines in planning occurs in practice.

In an effort to foster professionalism, the American Institute of Certified Planners (the professional component of the American Planning Association) administers an examination and certification program for urban planners. Passing the application and examination criteria entitles the planner to present himself as a "certified planner." Increasingly, government agencies seeking to fill positions request applicants with such certification. However, it has not yet become a thoroughly-established prerequisite for the practice of urban planning in either government or the private sector.

Thus, the planner may be educated in a field other than planning, and if so, is likely to be a licensed engineer, architect, or landscape architect. In truth, these professionals have not recently invaded the field of urban planning. Rather, the modern science of urban planning grew out of the efforts of individuals in these fields to design cities to accommodate the rapid growth that has consistently characterized the history of the United States. A debate continues to take place among these professions regarding their respective entitlements, and qualifications, to practice planning. Thus, when a state undertakes to regulate or register planners, litigation may ensue regarding the rights of other professionals to qualify as planners.[5]

A coming of age sign for the planning profession is the attention given by the United States Supreme Court in recent years. The attention, however, has not been benign. On several occasions, the Court has voiced concern over what it perceives as abusive treatment of property owners by planners acting for local government.[6] Exemplifying this is the

4. J. Getzels & G. Longhini, Planners' Salaries and Employment Trends, 1981 (American Planning Association Planning Advisory Service, Report No. 366).

5. See, e.g., New Jersey Chapter, Am. Inst. of Planners v. New Jersey State Bd. of Professional Planners, 48 N.J. 581, 227 A.2d 313 (1967) (state statute licensing planners did not violate equal protection clause by exempting, from examination requirements, any licensed engineer, land surveyor or registered architect of New Jersey), cert. denied 389 U.S. 8, 88 S.Ct. 70, 19 L.Ed.2d 8 (1967).

6. See Lucas v. South Carolina Coastal Council, 505 U.S. 1003, 112 S.Ct. 2886, 120 L.Ed.2d 798 (1992) (beach set back law suspected as pressing "private property into

rhetorical question posed by Justice Brennan in his San Diego Gas & Electric Co. v. City of San Diego dissent, that "[a]fter all if a policeman must know the Constitution, then why not a planner?"[7]

The consequence of this concern is that the Supreme Court and lower courts review the administration of land use regulatory programs with heightened scrutiny. This increases the likelihood that courts will find that municipalities have violated constitutional rights. When municipalities violate constitutional rights, planners, along with other government officials, may be held personally liable for money damages under federal law.[8]

The Court is not uniformly hostile to land use regulation; nor is it always skeptical of planners' motives. The Court has given wide latitude to government to enact laws protecting the environment, open space, and historic preservation. Indeed, in Dolan v. City of Tigard, the Court acknowledged that "[c]ities have long engaged in the commendable task of land use planning, made necessary by increasing urbanization...."[9] Still, the overall thrust of the Supreme Court's cases since 1987 is that the actions of government, and its planners, are less likely to be given the benefit of the doubt, particularly in cases challenging the means chosen to achieve admittedly legitimate public ends. More than in the past, courts today require planners to prove the reasonableness of regulations affecting private property.

II.   ANTECEDENTS OF LOCAL GOVERNMENT PLANNING[10]

§ 2.2   The Colonial Planning Era

Town planning in the United States, from early colonial days, resembled the modern science of subdivision design. At this stage in the

some form of public service under the guise of mitigating serious public harm"). See also Nollan v. California Coastal Commission, 483 U.S. 825, 107 S.Ct. 3141, 97 L.Ed.2d 677 (1987) (beach easement program labeled "extortion"), discussed infra §§ 10.5–6.

7. 450 U.S. 621, 661, 101 S.Ct. 1287, 1309, 67 L.Ed.2d 551 (1981). The point of the comment was that a monetary remedy was necessary to compel planners, as government officials, to abide by the Constitution. The Court subsequently decided that compensation was the mandatory remedy for a Fifth Amendment taking. See First English Evangelical Church v. County of Los Angeles, 482 U.S. 304, 107 S.Ct. 2378, 96 L.Ed.2d 250 (1987).

8. See discussion infra § 10.9 and §§ 10.23–26.

9. Dolan v. City of Tigard, 512 U.S. 374, 396, 114 S.Ct. 2309, 2322, 129 L.Ed.2d 304 (1994).

10. While planners are generally future oriented, the profession emphasizes the importance of history and several respected texts have been produced on the subject of planning and city building. See generally Boyer, Dreaming the Rational City (1983); Gottmann, Megalopolis (1961); Hall, Urban and Regional Planning (1975); Cities of Tomorrow: An Intellectual History of City Planning (1988); Krueckeberg, Introduction to Planning History in the United States (1983); Mumford, The Culture of Cities (1938); City Development (1945); The City in History (1961); The Urban Prospect (1968); Reps, The Making of Urban America: A History of City Planning in the United States (1965); Schuyler, The New Urban Landscape; Scott, American City Planning (1969).

early development of the American city, the planning of frontier settlements was dominated principally by civil engineers and land surveyors. The seminal town plan during the colonial era was the plan for the new City of Philadelphia, commissioned by William Penn and drawn up in 1681.[1] A site between two rivers was selected, and a gridiron system of streets was devised. Open spaces in the central area of the city were set aside, and uniform building spacings and setbacks were prescribed. Penn's engineer, Thomas Holme, prepared this plan, which became the model for most early city plans prepared for other colonial-era towns and cities. The Philadelphia Plan thus left its gridiron-street imprint on many cities planned later.

Such early town plans were invariably drawn by surveyors and engineers, and so the man-made aspects of cities took the rectilinear forms preferred by those professions. A notable departure from this approach was the first plan for Washington, D.C., commissioned in 1791 by the new federal government, and prepared by engineer Pierre L'Enfant that year. This plan superimposed an impressive diagonal-street and radial-thoroughfare system upon a traditional gridiron street system, thus incorporating elements of French civil design. Today, L'Enfant's plan can still be seen in the broad, sweeping vistas that characterize the nation's capital.

The Philadelphia and Washington plans are only two well-known examples of early town planning. Many other plans were prepared, some taking a different, smaller-scale approach.[2] Most of these city plans were no more than early forms of land subdivision control, since they were usually maps showing street right-of-way lines, parcel boundaries, open spaces and water bodies. The towns themselves were often no larger than modern tract subdivisions, but they accommodated that era's primitive technology and simple, agrarian economy.

After the American Revolution, power became more centralized in state governments, with a corresponding loss of autonomy by cities. With the adoption of state constitutions, cities henceforth derived powers of self-government usually by an act of the state legislature delegating that power. Thus, without a delegation of specific powers to control land uses, a municipality, the mere creature of the state, could not exert effective control over the use, and intensity of use, of private property. Land speculation became a new industry, and the practice of maximization of economic returns upon land investments made it difficult to implement the open space and civic design elements of city plans such as those for Philadelphia and the District of Columbia.

§ 2.3   The Sanitary Reform Movement

Along with the advent of widespread land speculation came the era of city-building. Factories were built in existing towns, attracting work-

§ 2.2

1. W. Goodman & E. Freund, Principles and Practice of Urban Planning 9–10 (1968).

2. Id. at 10–14.

ers from abroad and from agrarian areas. Slowly, American cities became aware that urbanization might be a contributing factor to disease and poor sanitation. Because their growth had been unplanned (and perhaps unanticipated), no American cities had ever comprehensively addressed the problems of drainage and disposal of wastes. The typical American city, by the 1840's, was characterized by filth, stench and stagnant water in the streets, backyard privies, dampness, and the absence of sunlight in residential space. As a result, deadly diseases such as yellow fever, cholera, typhoid, typhus, scarlet fever and diphtheria were commonplace.[1] Backyards, gullies, and even public streets became repositories of all kinds of waste matter, and drainage ditches became choked with debris, including fecal matter and animal carcasses.[2]

There was a remedy to this serious danger to the public health. English sanitary reformer Edwin Chadwick, commencing in 1842, began to champion the construction of "water-carriage sewerage systems." By use of an egg-shaped pipe, flushed with water, Chadwick learned, sewage and even the carcasses of animals could be carried away from homes and cities, and channeled into water bodies in which, presumably, they would disappear. The system required the construction of public potable water supply systems, and sewer lines to carry away wastes. Chadwick's ideas took root in the United States, during a brief period before the Civil War now referred to as the era of the Sanitary Reform Movement.

New York City opened its first public water piping system in 1842, recognizing early on the need to provide an adequate water supply system. Boston opened its first system in 1848. The delivery of water obviously led to the need to pipe it away again, laden with wastes. By 1865, New York City had constructed about 125 miles of sewerage pipelines; Boston completed about 100 miles of sewers by 1873.[3] These early systems were mostly unplanned, and constructed in response to pressures from landowners and political interest groups. Thus, a sort of incrementalist, project-by-project approach typified these early efforts at sanitation reforms.

Installation of sanitary sewers grew more widespread after the Civil War, and by 1875 sanitary engineering was firmly established as a profession in the United States. During this time period, there was also a virtual renaissance in the development of the design professions: in 1866, the American Institute of Architects was formed and in 1871 the engineering professions were first organized.[4] However, none of these professions engaged in comprehensive planning for the future, in the modern sense. The first major, comprehensive American effort to plan for future public health was spurred by the spread of a massive yellow-fever epidemic in the lower Mississippi River Valley in 1878. The

---

§ 2.3

1. J. A. Peterson, The Impact of Sanitary Reform upon American Urban Planning, 1840–1890, in Introduction to Planning History in the United States 13–17 (D. Krueckeberg ed.1983).

2. Id. at 17.

3. Id. at 19.

4. D. Krueckeberg, The Culture of Planning, id. at 1.

epidemic killed over 5,000 people in Memphis, Tennessee, then a city of only 45,000.

In 1879, in response to the plague, Congress created a National Board of Health to advise state governments and to regulate quarantines. The Board, at the request of Tennessee authorities, by 1880 completed an exhaustive, unprecedented study of physical and structural conditions in the City of Memphis, a study that filled 96 volumes and made over 12,000 recommendations for improvements of a remedial nature on property in Memphis—principally nuisance abatements.[5]

The recommendations also included major proposals for a new sanitary public water supply, a sewerage system, destruction of substandard buildings, enactment of a sanitary code for the entire city requiring elevation of buildings whose floors were less than two feet above the ground, repaving of many streets, ventilation of all city houses, and the appointment of a city sanitation officer to oversee all future sanitary work.[6]

This scheme is regarded by modern observers as the first major example of the modern "comprehensive" approach to urban problems, although limited to the goals of prevention of disease and sanitation problems caused by unregulated growth of an urban area. The Memphis scheme did not address many concerns now regarded as properly within the purview of urban planning, such as planning vehicular circulation, districting of incompatible land uses, and recreation space planning. But it was a sign of things to come.

A prophetic expression of the broad approach the planner of urban areas must take was expressed during this era by at least one writer. Horace Bushnell, in his essay "City Plans," observed in 1864 that

> Considering the immense importance of a right location, and a right planning for cities, no step should ever be taken by the parties concerned, without employing some person who is qualified by a special culture, to assist and direct. Our engineers are trained by a very different kind of service, and are partly disqualified for this by the habit of a study more strictly linear.... The qualifications of surveyors are commonly more meagre still.... We have cities for the new age that has come, adapted to its better conditions of use and ornament. So great an advantage ought not to be thrown away. We want, therefore, a city planning profession....[7]

§ 2.4 The City Beautiful Movement

The consciousness of a new age, with new opportunities for civic improvement, was not limited to those who advocated sanitary reforms. With the increasing congestion of urbanizing areas came a growing awareness that aesthetics also plays a role in the evolution of urban form and function.

---

5. Peterson, supra note 1, at 25.

6. Id.

7. H. Bushnell, Work and Play 196 (1864), reprinted, id. at 1.

American cities grew rapidly during the nineteenth century. In 1840, the census showed only twelve American cities with populations of over 25,000 and of these only three had populations of over 100,000. But as industry grew, so grew American cities. By 1880, seventy-seven cities had populations of over 25,000 and twenty cities had more than 100,000 residents. This rapid centralization of population in cities, where job opportunities were, led to an increased awareness of the need for civic beauty and amenities in America's unplanned urban areas.

The proponents of civic beauty would hardly have claimed the title, but their agitations for greater attention to aesthetics in city planning later became known as the City Beautiful Movement, the precursor to modern urban planning. The movement was really a groundswell, grass-roots concern with the physical appearance of towns and cities. Because they were largely the product of unrestrained private enterprise, towns across the United States were, before the advent of the twentieth century, largely unattractive, muddy, cluttered clusters of buildings. Individual residences sported trash-strewn alleys and yards, and there was little monumental civic architecture. But if sanitary reform could be planned, many believed, so could aesthetics.

The origin of the City Beautiful Movement is commonly traced to the Chicago World's Fair of 1893, a massive celebration of technology, art and architecture in which Americans were first introduced *en masse* to classical design via the Columbian Exposition. The exposition was an array of neo-classical structures and sculpture forming part of the Chicago World's Fair. But the World's Fair exposition was only a symbol of a growing consciousness of the importance of the physical appearance of towns.

In villages and towns across the country, "village improvement associations," usually ad-hoc committees of townspeople, were being created during the 1890s. The village improvement associations championed street lighting, paving of dirt streets and sidewalks, the cleaning up of private yards and alleys, planting of public and private gardens, and setting aside of public, urban parks. By 1901, over 1000 such improvement associations had sprung up across the United States, advocating both urban aesthetics and sanitation.[1]

The City Beautiful Movement, like the Sanitary Reform Movement, was oriented to physical improvements to rectify a perceived evil: the lack of order and cleanliness in American towns. Well-kept streets, beautiful parks, attractive private residences, fresh air and sanitary improvements became its hallmarks. Many of the village associations were persuaded to join the National League of Improvement Associations, which crusaded for these causes. Renamed the American League for Civic Improvement in 1901, the national association created advisory

§ 2.4   ed.1983).

1. Introduction to Planning History in the United States 46–49 (D. Krueckeberg

panels of experts in municipal art, sanitation, recreation and related concerns. To a great extent the City Beautiful Movement reflected the ideals of the Progressive Era of reform in which it flourished. But it also planted the seeds for a more comprehensive view of the science of planning urban spaces.

City Beautiful proponents caused a great deal of municipal expenditure for civic architecture and municipal improvements. But the proponents of beautification did not necessarily espouse comprehensive regulation of land uses and development. In fact, there was a fear of governmental regulation, rooted in a fundamental aversion to the limitation of private enterprise by local government. As one early commentator observed:

> In America it is the fear of restricting or injuring free and open competition that has made it so difficult for cities to exercise proper and efficient control over their development. The tendency therefore has been to promote those forms of civic improvement which can be carried out without interfering with vested interests.... [2]

§ 2.5 The Advent of Planning Commissions

Proponents of the City Beautiful advocated the creation of citizens' advisory planning commissions, which were the precursors to modern local government planning commissions. The early advisory planning commissions were composed, usually, of locally-prominent merchants and professionals who had an interest in civic beautification, the construction of parks, and the financing of municipal outdoor art. Frequently, these early planning commissions engaged prominent architects and landscape architects to prepare advisory "plans" for civic improvement. These early plans by consultants were non-legal documents, principally maps and lists of suggestions for civic improvements. Several of the early advisory plans, however, attempted to achieve a comprehensiveness of scope that was similar to the modern local government comprehensive plan.[1]

The citizens' advisory planning commissions, in some instances, achieved the status of organs of municipal government. Hartford, Connecticut in 1907 created the first city planning commission. Milwaukee, Wisconsin initiated its city planning commission in 1908. In 1909, Chicago, Illinois appointed a 328–member city planning commission. These commissions, without powers conferred by statute or ordinance, could only recommend the plans they produced as guidelines for decisionmaking by the local municipal legislative body.

In 1909, Chicago became the first city in the United States to voluntarily adopt, only as a non-legal, advisory document, a "comprehensive plan" for its future development. The plan was prepared by famed

2. J. Nolen, New Ideals in the Planning of Cities, Towns and Villages 133–34 (1919).

§ 2.5

1. J. Nolen, New Ideals in the Planning of Cities, Towns and Villages 133–34 (1919).

architect Daniel H. Burnham, who had been director of works for the Columbian Exposition at the 1893 Chicago World's Fair. Backed by wealthy commercial interests in Chicago, and with a budget of $85,000, Burnham prepared a long-range plan for the Chicago region more comprehensive in scope than any plan previously prepared for an American city.

The plan did not focus solely upon the civic beautification and sanitation concerns that had, until then, been the hallmark of the Sanitary Reform and City Beautiful Movements. Instead, Burnham made recommendations in the plan's maps and text for a host of planning considerations that have now become commonplace in local government comprehensive plans.

The Chicago plan addressed transportation and recommended a system of regional highways extending far outside the city. It made suggestions for improvement of traffic circulation within the city limits, including the development of new collector streets and consolidation of regional railroad terminals. It recommended new city shipping docks, new parks and beaches on Lake Michigan, and construction of a new city civic center. While the plan was to remain principally advisory in nature, it was nonetheless adopted as the official General Plan of Chicago, by the city's advisory planning commission, in 1911. Ultimately, implementation of its recommendations depended upon the degree of political influence over city government exercised by the businessmen who were members of the Chicago Planning Commission.

§ 2.6　Early Conceptions of the City Plan

In 1909, the First National Conference on City Planning and the Problems of Congestion was convened in Washington, D.C., and attended by many of the design professionals who were working, at that time, as consultants to advisory planning commissions across the United States. At this conference, Frederick Law Olmsted, a prominent landscape architect and planning consultant, described the city plan as a compendium of all regulations on building, physical development, "districting" of land, health ordinances, and "police rules" for the use and development of land. Olmsted drew many of his ideas on plans from earlier experiments in town planning in Germany and Switzerland.[1]

In 1911, Olmsted, again addressing the National Conference on City Planning, said the plan was a forecast of the best path for development to take, which should be followed by the local legislative body in making land use and development-related decisions:

> We must cultivate in our minds and in the minds of the people the conception of the city plan as a device or piece of . . . machinery for preparing, and keeping constantly up to date, a unified forecast and

§ 2.6　　　　　　　　　　Since 1890, at 97 (1969).

1. M. Scott, American City Planning

definition of all the important changes, additions, and extensions of the physical equipment and arrangement of the city which a sound judgment holds likely to become desirable and practicable in the course of time, so as to avoid as far as possible both ignorantly wasteful action and ... inaction in the control of the city's physical growth. It is a means by which those who become at any time responsible for decisions affecting the city's plan may be prevented from acting in ignorance of what their predecessors and their colleagues in other departments of city life have believed to be the reasonable contingencies.[2]

Olmsted's conception of the city plan was prophetic of today's plans, in focusing on the role of the plan as a rational, policy document by which development-related decisions by successive, elected city officials should be guided. Later, Alfred Bettman, a land use attorney from Cincinnati, reinforced the concept of the city plan as a master development guide for the city or town. Addressing the National Conference on City Planning in 1928, Bettman said:

A city plan is a master design for the physical development of the territory of the city. It constitutes a plan of the division of land between public and private uses, specifying the general location and extent of new public improvements, grounds and structures ... and, in the case of private developments, the general distribution [of land areas] amongst various classes of uses, such as residential, business and industrial uses.[3]

III. RELATIONSHIP OF PLANNING AND ZONING

§ 2.7 The Promulgation of Zoning Ordinances

The comprehensive plan's emphasis on setting the distribution of classes of land uses caused some confusion by many local governments over the difference between comprehensive *plans* and comprehensive *zoning ordinances*. Unlike the plans adopted during this era, which were advisory documents of a policy nature, zoning ordinances were local statutes establishing land-use districts for residential, commercial, industrial and agricultural activities, and usually prescribing standards within each district for building height and bulk, setbacks from lot lines, and density or intensity of the use of individual lots within each district. When faced with the choice of either preparing a comprehensive plan, followed by adoption of a zoning ordinance to implement the policies in the plan, or just preparing and adopting a "comprehensive zoning ordinance," most local governments opted for the latter alternative.

The first modern, comprehensive zoning ordinance was enacted by New York City in 1916. The ordinance classified land uses and created

2. Proceedings of the Third National Conference on City Planning, Philadelphia, Pennsylvania, 1911, as reprinted in W. Goodman & E. Freund, Principles and Practice of Urban Planning 352 (1968).

3. Planning Problems of Town, City and Region: Papers and Discussions of the Twentieth National Conference on City Planning, reprinted in W. Goodman & E. Freund, supra note 2, at 352–53.

zones for these uses, depicted on zoning maps. The purposes of zoning were to segregate residential uses from more intensive uses of land, such as industrial, and thereby to provide safer, more quiet areas for family life. By 1921, zoning had become fashionable: its advocates had persuaded almost half of the state legislatures to adopt zoning enabling acts, conferring upon municipalities the power to adopt and enforce zoning ordinances.

The popularity of zoning was given a boost by the preparation of a model zoning enabling act by the United States Department of Commerce. The Act, published in 1924, was entitled the Standard State Zoning Enabling Act.[1] It provided a ready-made model for legislatures to follow in delegating police power to municipalities to prepare, adopt, and administer zoning codes. The act authorized the appointment of zoning commissions by local governments, which would set district boundaries and regulations, hold a public hearing on the proposed zoning ordinance, and submit it to the city council for final hearings and enactment into law. Without such an enabling act, a municipal zoning ordinance was in danger of being invalidated as *ultra vires* if challenged in court.

By 1926, 564 cities and towns had adopted zoning ordinances, and several state courts had upheld zoning as a valid exercise of police powers delegated by states to their municipalities. In that year, the United States Supreme Court upheld the use of the police power to zone. In Village of Euclid v. Ambler Realty Co.,[2] the court heard a challenge by an Ohio landowner of a "comprehensive zoning plan" adopted by the city council of Euclid, Ohio. The ordinance established districts for land use, and district regulations for building heights and minimum lot sizes. The ordinance, the Supreme Court held, did not violate due process, and bore a rational relationship to valid governmental interests in preventing congestion and in segregating incompatible land uses.

But the attractiveness of zoning to the general public was due principally to the fact that a new zoning ordinance tended to validate existing land use patterns by including them on the zoning map, and also provided the opportunity to over-zone for profitable industrial and business uses. The comprehensive zoning ordinance of the City of New York, the first such ordinance in the nation, set aside enough land in business and industrial zones to accommodate an eventual city population of some 340 million persons.[3] Hence, zoning appeared to be a welcome device for facilitating land speculation and validating the existing pattern of land uses.

---

§ 2.7

1. Issued in draft form in 1922 and first published in mimeographed form in 1923, the Act was revised and printed for the first time in 1924, and reprinted in 1926. By the time the final version was released in 1926, 43 states had enacted it.

2. 272 U.S. 365, 47 S.Ct. 114, 71 L.Ed. 303 (1926).

3. R. Walker, The Planning Function in Urban Government 11 (1941).

§ 2.8   Zoning Displaces Planning

While "comprehensive zoning" proliferated, planning remained principally the province of advisory planning commissions. Few cities had created full-time planning staffs. By 1929, only forty-six cities had an annual city planning budget of more than $5,000.[1] Most city plans were prepared by consultants, and typically addressed a half-dozen principal elements of city design:

1. A land use plan or zoning plan.

2. A plan for streets.

3. A plan for public transit.

4. An element addressing rail and water transportation.

5. A plan addressing parks and public recreation.

6. An element addressing civic art or civic appearance.[2]

These plans exerted an influence upon the drafters of the first model act for planning, the Standard City Planning Enabling Act of 1928. The earlier Standard State Zoning Enabling Act had made little mention of planning. However, the Standard City Planning Enabling Act, also prepared by the U.S. Department of Commerce, addressed only city planning. The Act enabled local governments to prepare plans for five principal urban concerns (streets, public grounds, public buildings, utilities, and zoning) via a municipally-appointed planning commission:

> § 6.   General Powers and Duties—It shall be the function and duty of the commission to make and adopt a master plan for the physical development of the municipality ... [showing] the commission's recommendations for the development of said territory, including, among other things, the general location, character, and extent of streets, viaducts, subways, bridges, waterways, water fronts, boulevards, parkways, playgrounds, squares, parks, aviation fields, and other public ways ... [and] the removal, relocation, widening, narrowing, vacating, abandonment, change of use or extension of any of the foregoing ... as well as a zoning plan for the control of the height, area, bulk, location and use of buildings and premises. ...The commission may from time to time amend, extend, or add to the plan.
>
> § 7.   Purposes in View—In the preparation of such plan the commission shall make careful and comprehensive surveys and studies of present conditions and future growth of the municipality.... The plan shall be made with the general purpose of guiding and accomplishing a coordinated, adjusted, and harmonious development of the municipality ... as well as efficiency and economy in the process of development. ...

§ 2.8

1. Principles and Practice of Urban Planning 23 (W. Goodman & E. Freund, eds. 1968) [hereinafter cited as Principles].

2. M. Scott, American City Planning Since 1890, at 228 (1969).

Thus, the Standard City Planning Enabling Act envisioned a more comprehensive approach to regulating land uses and providing municipal services for future growth than zoning could attempt. Zones for land uses were to be only one concern in preparation of the plan, and efficient provision of utilities, transportation and other public services figured as prominently as land use districting.

The Act, however, contributed to the confusion over the differences between city plans and zoning ordinances, by stating that the plan should include a zoning element. As a result of this confusion and because of the growing interest in zoning, many communities prepared and adopted zoning ordinances without ever making the general, comprehensive plan upon which zoning was supposed to be based. This practice tended to divert attention from the future-oriented, general policies of city planning in favor of squabbles over the details which dominated individual zoning decisions and controversies.[3]

In addition, under the Act planning was not mandatory, but optional. While the Act implied that zoning was distinct from planning, it did not expressly state that zoning should be enacted in accordance with an existing comprehensive plan document. The Standard State Zoning Enabling Act did expressly state that zoning should be enacted "in accordance with a comprehensive plan,"[4] but in view of the fact that planning was optional under the Standard Planning Enabling Act, most courts addressing this question have held that the plan with which zoning must be in accord could be found in the entirety of the zoning ordinance. A separate plan was generally not required.[5] However, a growing number of states are requiring their municipalities to prepare comprehensive plans with specific "elements" therein, and in a growing minority of these jurisdictions zoning ordinances and other land use regulations are required to be "in accordance with," or consistent with, policies and provisions of the comprehensive plan.[6]

The federal government has also supplied strong incentives to municipalities to prepare comprehensive plans. Under the Housing Act of 1949,[7] municipalities applying for federal financial assistance in slum clearance were required to prepare a comprehensive plan before funds would be provided. Later, Congress provided federal funds to municipalities to finance preparation of such plans, under the Housing Act of 1954.[8] As a result of both federal and state initiatives, many local governments across the nation now maintain planning departments and routinely prepare and revise comprehensive plans.

---

3. Principles, supra note 1, at 353.

4. A Standard State Zoning Enabling Act, § 3 (1926): *"Purposes in view.* Such regulations shall be made in accordance with a comprehensive plan.... "

5. A minority of states require that plans be enacted and that zoning be in accordance with comprehensive plans. For a detailed discussion of this trend, see Man-

delker, The Role of the Comprehensive Plan in Land Use Regulation, 74 Mich.L.Rev. 899 (1976).

6. See generally id. See also § 2.13, infra.

7. 42 U.S.C.A. § 1441 et seq.

8. Id. §§ 1450–1469(c).

IV. THE PROCESS OF PLANNING COMPREHENSIVELY

§ 2.9 The Function of the Plan

Traditionally, land use regulations such as zoning and subdivision ordinances adopted by local governments were written and promulgated without reference to any prior comprehensive municipal plan. However, in a growing number of states, the adoption of such regulatory ordinances in the absence of a general comprehensive plan may cast doubts upon the validity of the ordinances. The comprehensive plan, once viewed as primarily an advisory document to the local legislative body, is in many states becoming a legal, binding document as well as a prescription for future development patterns.

The plan serves as an overall set of goals, objectives, and policies to guide land-use decisionmaking by the local legislative body. When particular regulatory decisions are made by the county commission or the city council, the comprehensive plan's policies, goals, and objectives may be invoked as the "rational basis" upon which local government exercises of the police power to zone must be based. Planners have encouraged the use of the comprehensive plan as a rational basis for land-use decisions, and, in an effort to promote planning as a new profession, have developed a theory of urban planning as a rational process of choice between different policy alternatives.[1]

§ 2.10 The Rational Planning Process

An overall definition of "comprehensive plan" has become necessary. The comprehensive plan is generally defined as an official public document, preferably (but often not) adopted as law by the local government, as a policy guide to decisions about the physical development of the community. Usually it sets forth, in a general way, using text and maps, how the leaders of local government want the community to develop in the future. The length of the future time period to be addressed by a comprehensive plan varies widely from locale to locale, and is often set by state legislation enabling or requiring local governments to plan.[1]

The growing importance of the comprehensive plan in local land-use decisions prompted urban planning practitioners and theorists to devel-

§ 2.9

1. For additional information on planning theory see generally Burchell and Sternlieb, Planning Theory in the 1980s (1978); A Reader in Planning Theory (Faludi ed., 1973). For comprehensive planning, see generally, Branch, Comprehensive City Planning, Introduction & Explanation (1985); Howard, Garden Cities of Tomorrow (1946); Kaiser, Godschalk, and Chapin, Ur-

ban Land Use Planning (4th ed. 1996); Kent, The Urban General Plan (1964); Nelson, Estimating Land Use and Facility Needs and Impacts (1998).

§ 2.10

1. Principles and Practice of Urban Planning 349 (W. Goodman & E. Freund, eds. 1968) [hereinafter cited as Principles].

op a theory of planning as a "rational process."[2] The rational, comprehensive planning process has four principal characteristics. First, it is *future-oriented,* establishing goals and objectives for future land use and development, which will be attained incrementally over time through regulations, individual decisions about zoning and rezoning, development approval or disapproval, and municipal expenditures for capital improvements such as road construction and the installation of municipal utilities.

Second, planning is *continuous,* in that the plan is intended not as a blueprint for future development which must be as carefully executed as the architect's design for a building or the engineer's plan for a sewer line, but rather as a set of policies which must be periodically reevaluated and amended to adjust to changing conditions. A plan that is written purely as a static blueprint for future development will rapidly become obsolete when circumstances change.

Third, the plan must be based upon a *determination of present and projected conditions* within the area covered by the plan. This requirement ensures that the plan is not simply a list of hoped-for civic improvements, as were many of the plans prepared during the era of the City Beautiful Movement. Substantial efforts have been made by public planning staffs, university planning departments, and planning consulting firms, to develop useful techniques for gathering data, analyzing existing conditions, and projecting future trends and conditions within the geographic area covered by a comprehensive plan. This body of methods, procedure and models is generally termed *planning methodology*.

Fourth, planning is *comprehensive*. In the past, architects, and engineers who became involved in solving urban problems, such as those attacked in the Sanitary Reform Movement, tended to identify one problem perceived to be solvable by one solution. Having targeted that problem, these early planners preferred to develop and advocate one solution, usually expressed as a static blueprint which, if fully implemented, would solve that problem. This problem—solution approach was the product of the project orientation that was typical of traditional civil engineering and architecture.

2. Planning is a comprehensive, coordinated and continuing process, the purpose of which is to help public and private decision makers arrive at decisions which promote the common good of society. This process includes: (1) Identification of problems or issues; (2) Research and analysis to provide definitive understanding of such problems or issues; (3) Formulation of goals and objectives to be attained in alleviating problems or resolving issues; (4) Development and evaluation of alternative methods (plans and programs) to attain agreed upon goals and objectives; (5) Recommendation of appropriate courses of action from among the alternatives; (6) Assistance in implementation of approved plans and programs; (7) Evaluation of actions taken to implement approved plans and programs in terms of progress towards agreed upon goals and objectives; and (8) A continuing process of adjusting plans and programs in light of the results of such evaluation or to take into account changed circumstances.

American Planning Association, Planning Policies, APA Action Agenda, APA News (in Planning) 24B (July 1979). See also Moore, Why Allow Planners to Do what They Do? A Justification from Economic Theory, 44 J.Am.Inst. of Planners 387 (1978).

Planning theorists over the past several decades have observed that this approach has led to a phenomenon termed "disjointed incrementalism," in which successive municipal problems such as drainage, traffic circulation, or sewage treatment might be incrementally "solved" without reference to related concerns of municipal government. For example, sewer systems in the era of the Sanitary Reform Movement were usually designed without reference to any overall plan for the optimum future locations, and densities, of different land uses to be served by them. Highways were often laid out without reference to any long-range plans for the types of land uses they were to serve in the future.

The recognition, starting after World War II, that the entire range of municipal land use, transportation, and growth problems were all interrelated, led to advocacy of comprehensive plans as a means of identifying the key problems in land use regulation, and recommending alternative solutions to these problems which were the product of a rational planning process. The courts have recognized this role of planning, in defining planning as concerned with

> the physical development of the community and its environs in relation to its social and economic well-being for the fulfillment of the rightful common destiny, according to a "master plan" based on "careful and comprehensive surveys and studies of present conditions and the prospects of future growth of the municipality," and embodying scientific teachings and creative experience.[3]

The rational planning process essentially subsumes four discrete steps: *data gathering and analysis, setting of policies, plan implementation,* and *plan re-evaluation.* Rather than resulting in a final plan effective for all time, the process is instead reiterative over a period of years: re-evaluation of the plan starts the process over again, resulting in a new set of policies to be implemented, and the success of the new plan is again evaluated at a future date. Thus the rational planning process is both reiterative and continuous.

During the first step of the process, the planner preparing the comprehensive plan performs research and analysis of a wide range of present and projected physical, economic, and sociological conditions of the municipality, aided by a wide variety of planning methodologies. Statistical surveying, population forecasting, mapping of existing conditions in land use, transportation, and environmentally-sensitive areas, mathematical modeling of economic trends, analysis of traffic flows on major highways, and techniques borrowed from other professions such as economics, geography, and engineering are some of the methods employed by planners in data gathering and analysis.[4]

The data-gathering and analysis phase of the process usually results in the identification of present and potential future concerns in land use,

---

3. Angermeier v. Borough of Sea Girt, 27 N.J. 298, 142 A.2d 624, 629 (1958).

4. For a detailed discussion of quantitative planning analysis methods, see gener-

ally D. Krueckeberg & A. Silvers, Urban Planning Analysis: Methods and Models (1974). See also Principles, supra note 1, at 49–242.

transportation, environment, utilities, housing, and other areas to be addressed in the plan. Thus, following the first stage of the process, the planner may identify and prioritize a range of municipal problems and opportunities which should be addressed in the policy-formation stage of the planning process.

Analysis of the data then leads naturally to the second phase, setting of policies for the plan. In this phase, the planner ceases being a data gatherer, and assumes a policy formation role.[5] Working closely with the planning commission and sometimes the local legislative body, the planner examines and proposes alternative means of solving or averting the problems identified in the first phase of the process. Through communication with the local legislative body and the planning commission (if one exists), the planner develops a set of policies, goals, and objectives which constitute the principal, future-oriented sections of the comprehensive plan. Thus, for example, the policies may include a provision that sewage-treatment services must be expanded to accommodate new development; that the legislative body should initiate a program to stimulate new economic development in the declining downtown; and that steps should be taken to prevent further flood-prone development in low-lying areas adjoining rivers and streams.

As a supplement to these general policies, or goals, of planning, the planner may suggest means of achieving these goals. In setting the goals and recommending alternative objectives, the planner may refer to standards and principles widely-accepted in the planning profession: that excessive use of septic tanks rather than public sewers tends to pollute groundwater; that decay of the central business district leads to devaluation of the tax base; that development in flood-prone areas is detrimental to public safety by exposing buildings and their occupants to flood hazards.

The mere statement of policies and objectives will not, in itself, ensure that action is taken. Thus, the third stage of the planning process, implementation of the plan, becomes the most important stage. Implementation involves three discrete steps: developing public support for the plan by means of various forms of citizen participation and a series of public hearings and media coverage; securing adoption of the plan, either as an advisory document (as in many states) or as a legally-binding ordinance (as in a growing number of states); and action by the legislative body to implement the policies and objectives.

Upon adoption of the plan, the adopting agency espouses the policies and objectives of the plan as guidelines for daily decision-making. Thus, to return to our three examples of policies, the local legislative body will undertake revisions of the municipal zoning map to bring it into accordance with the land-use recommendations of the plan. Similarly, the governing body may prepare plans for expansion of sewers and construc-

---

5. Planners, as a group, seem to share a number of biases that affect their approach to setting norms in the planning process. An interesting discussion of some of these biases is presented in H. Gans, People and Plans 57–75 (1968).

tion of new roads to serve new development. The legislative body may appoint a downtown revitalization authority to oversee efforts to attract new businesses back into the central business district. The governing body may authorize the city attorney to draft a new flood-plain protection ordinance prohibiting careless construction of new buildings in low-lying areas adjoining streams and rivers.[6]

V. THE LEGAL STATUS OF THE COMPREHENSIVE PLAN

§ 2.11 Plans as Optional Policy Documents

The majority of the states whose legislation enables the preparation of comprehensive plans do not require local governments to prepare plans, and comprehensive plans in these states are principally land use policy documents without the force of law. The justification frequently given for the lack of legal status is that urban planning has not yet proven itself capable of solving urban problems, and there is no consensus among the states over what elements of urban development plans should always address. Furthermore, some commentators believe that the comprehensive plan serves an important "visionary function," unlike the regulatory function of ordinances and statutes, and that to require the plan to be a painstakingly—drafted, regulatory document would prevent plans from being suggestive and boldly-innovative.[1]

The fact that plans are usually neither mandated by state laws nor given the force of law is traceable to the standard planning and zoning legislation promulgated by the United States Department of Commerce in the 1920's. The Standard State Zoning Enabling Act required that zoning regulations and zoning decisions be made "in accordance with the comprehensive plan," but failed to address the obvious question of what a comprehensive plan was. Later, the Standard City Planning Enabling Act of 1928, while boldly setting forth suggested "elements" of comprehensive plans, and the manner in which a city might prepare and adopt them, failed to strictly define the legal relationship between plans and zoning ordinances. In addition, plans were optional under the Standard City Planning Enabling Act.

Many states adopted these acts verbatim or only in slightly-altered form. The task of defining the relationship between local zoning statutes and local comprehensive plans (if one existed at all) naturally fell to the courts. In the majority of states, since a separate plan was not required, courts considering challenges to zoning ordinances as not "in accordance

---

6. This synopsis of the process represents a synthesis of current theories on the planning process. For a more detailed discussion, see F. Chapin & E. Kaiser, Urban Land Use Planning 68–104 (3d ed. 1979); Principles, supra note 1, at 327–48.

§ 2.11

1. See DiMento, The Consistency Doctrine: Continuing Controversy, F. Strom, ed., 1982 Zoning and Planning Law Handbook 77.

with a comprehensive plan" looked to the overall land-use policies of the zoning ordinance, if an optional comprehensive plan did not exist.

The best-known case taking this position is Kozesnik v. Montgomery Township.[2] The case arose before New Jersey enacted legislation requiring municipalities to prepare plans.[3] The existing zoning enabling legislation required zoning decisions to be "in accordance" with a plan, but the defendant township in the case had not prepared any plan. The state supreme court noted that New Jersey's zoning enabling legislation (like that of most states) pre-dated the adoption of its planning enabling legislation. Inferring from this that the legislature could not have possibly required zoning to be in accordance with non-existent "plans," the court concluded that the plan with which zoning had to accord could "readily be revealed in ... the zoning ordinance ... and no more is required by the statute."[4] Thus, although it appears to be a somewhat circular reasoning process, the court was willing to measure individual zoning decisions—even those that altered the community's zoning maps—for their "accordance" with the master zoning code for the municipality, which included the maps. This amounted to no more than a process of "discovering" a comprehensive plan and policies for land use within the dictates of a zoning code.

This process, which has been followed by the majority of states,[5] does not always result in a validation of rezoning decisions when challenged. Indeed, it may be no more than a reflection of the general requirement, under substantive due process, that exercises of municipal police powers be reasonable. However, the majority position appears to be largely the result of the historical accident of zoning becoming a widespread practice before the advent of comprehensive planning. The result of this doctrine, however, has been to perpetuate the "optional" nature of comprehensive plans in most states, because zoning codes so often became the "comprehensive plan" against which individual rezoning decisions had to be measured for conformity.

In a variation on this position, the New York Superior Court in Udell v. Haas required that "accordance" between rezoning and the overall zoning plan be "rational" as well. Reviewing a challenge to a zoning decision regarding an individual lot of land, the court observed that

> the comprehensive plan is the essence of zoning. Without it, there can be no rational allocation of land use. It is the insurance that the

2.   24 N.J. 154, 131 A.2d 1 (1957).

3.   N.J. Stat. Ann. § 40:55D–62 partially overrules *Kozesnik*, requiring elements of a formal plan and consistency unless set aside by a majority vote of the full membership of the governing body.

4.   24 N.J. at 166, 131 A.2d at 7.

5.   See 3 R. Anderson, American Law of Zoning § 21.01 et seq. (1977); but see Forestview Homeowners Ass'n v. County of Cook, 18 Ill.App.3d 230, 309 N.E.2d 763 (Ill.App.1974) (holding that the presumption of validity usually accorded zoning is shifted or weakened in the absence of a comprehensive plan).

public welfare is being served and that zoning does not become nothing more than just a Gallup poll.[6]

§ 2.12   Plans as Mandatory Policy Documents

The traditional position, that individual zoning decisions could be compared to the general zoning code to determine whether they are "in accordance with a comprehensive plan," had a circularity of reasoning which did not make sense to planning advocates. Many urged reform of the planning enabling statutes so as to clarify the role and status of the comprehensive, or master, plan. Thus, Harvard Law School Professor Charles Haar wrote in 1955:

> While the statutory references [to planning by municipalities] are cast in large and hopeful terms, they assign no clear legal position to the plan. The legal impact of planning is significant only as it imports governmental control of physical development ... [and] no consistent pattern of interpretation of the effect of the plan on the real world has yet emerged in the legislation or judicial opinions....
> The requirement in the Zoning Enabling Act that the zoning ordinance shall be made "in accordance with a comprehensive plan" has apparently carried the courts no further than requiring that the ordinance be reasonable and impartial so as to satisfy the *constitutional* conditions for the exercise of a state's police power.... Some acts do not even require the adoption of the master plan in order to exercise subdivision controls.[1]

Clearly, Haar said, the plan ought to have some legal significance, and it ought to be a separate document from zoning ordinances.[2] The states that have adopted this approach, by requiring a separate comprehensive plan, have escaped from the confusion, caused by the standard planning and zoning acts, over the role of the comprehensive plan.[3] In these jurisdictions, a zoning challenge does not draw the court into a process of "discovering" a comprehensive plan inside a general zoning ordinance. As a result, these states have also become laboratories for case law experimentation with the concept of "consistency" between comprehensive plan policies and individual zoning and development approval decisions.

6. 21 N.Y.2d 463, 469, 288 N.Y.S.2d 888, 893, 235 N.E.2d 897, 900 (1968); see also Palatine Nat'l Bank v. Village of Barrington, 177 Ill.App.3d 839, 127 Ill.Dec. 126, 532 N.E.2d 955 (Ill.App.1988).

§ 2.12

1. Haar, The Master Plan: An Impermanent Constitution, 20 Law & Contemp.Prob. 353, 366 (1955) (emphasis in original).

2. Id. at 367.

3. Those states, by statute or by court decision, include California, Delaware, Florida, Kentucky, Maine, Nebraska, Nevada, New Jersey, Oregon, South Dakota, and Vermont. See Edward J. Sullivan and Thomas G. Pelham, Comprehensive Planning and Growth Management, 28 Urb. Law. 819 (1996); Richard J. Roddewig, Recent Developments in Land Use, Planning and Zoning, 22 Urb. Law. 720–36 (1990); J. DiMento, The Consistency Doctrine and the Limits of Planning 18–21 (1980).

§ 2.13   The Consistency Requirement

In a broad sense, consistency refers to the relationship between planning and land use regulations. The concept can be traced back to the Standard State Zoning Enabling Act's (SZEA) requirement that zoning be "in accordance with a comprehensive plan."[1] Controversy regarding the term's precise meaning has existed for many years.[2] Much of this confusion stems from a difference in terminology used in the SZEA, referring to a comprehensive plan, and in the Standard City Planning Enabling Act (SPEA),[3] calling for a "master plan".[4] The SPEA provided for establishment of a local planning commission whose duty was to produce a master plan, to be used as a guide for orderly future development. The master plan was meant to serve as a substantive document, stating the goals of a locality to direct subsequent implementing legislation.[5] Because the SPEA's master plan was not considered binding, and because it has not traditionally been equated with the SZEA's comprehensive plan, implementation of the consistency mandate has been slow and controversial.

An unfortunate effect of this confusion has been a judicial tendency to interpret the "in accordance with" directive as meaning nothing more than that land use regulation ordinances be comprehensive or uniform in scope and coverage.[6] Thus many courts have looked to the zoning ordinance itself to fulfill the requirement and have regarded as sufficient elements of internal consistency and rationality within the ordinance.[7]

§ 2.13

1. U.S. Dep't of Commerce, A Standard State Zoning Enabling Act § 3 (rev. ed. 1926). See also § 2.11, supra.

2. See generally Haar, In Accordance With A Comprehensive Plan, 68 Harvard L.Rev. 1154, 1158 (1955).

3. U.S. Dep't of Commerce, Standard City Planning Enabling Act (rev. ed.1928).

4. An explanatory note to the SZEA indicated the comprehensive plan's purpose: "This will prevent haphazard or piecemeal zoning. No zoning should be done without such a comprehensive study." Id. § 3, note 22. Compare this with the SPEA's explication of master plan: "By this expression is meant a comprehensive scheme of development of the general fundamentals of a municipal plan. An express definition has not been thought desirable or necessary. What is implied in it is best expressed by the provisions of this section which illustrate the subject matter that a master plan should consider." Id. § 6, note 32. See generally Haar, The Master Plan: An Impermanent Constitution, 20 Law & Contemp.Probs. 353 (1955).

5. See J. DiMento, The Consistency Doctrine and the Limits of Planning, 9 n. 1 (1980). (Portions of this work are reproduced herein with the author's permission.)

6. See Haar, supra note 2 at 1157.

7. See Kozesnik v. Township of Montgomery, 24 N.J. 154, 131 A.2d 1 (1957) (finding that the zoning statutes' comprehensive plan is not identical with the planning act's master plan and that there is no requirement that the comprehensive plan exist in some physical form apart from the ordinance). This view of the consistency requirement is still prevalent in a number of jurisdictions. See e.g., Iowa Coal Mining Co. v. Monroe County, 494 N.W.2d 664 (Iowa 1993); American University Park Citizens Association v. Burka, 400 A.2d 737 (D.C.App.1979) (pending adoption of comprehensive plan, home rule act requires only that commission zone on a uniform and comprehensive basis); Town of Nottingham v. Harvey, 120 N.H. 889, 424 A.2d 1125 (1980) (subdivision regulations enacted without a comprehensive plan were valid where zoning ordinance constituted a comprehensive system for their application); Drake v. Craven, 105 Idaho 734, 672 P.2d 1064 (App.1983) (plan apparent in zoning regulations); McBride v. Town of Forestburgh, 54 A.D.2d 396, 388 N.Y.S.2d 940 (1976) (requirements of planning statute are met if implicit in zoning ordinance there is an element of planning which is both rational and consistent with community's basic land use policies).

This is a fairly common judicial response to the consistency requirement in those jurisdictions which do not statutorily mandate consistency.[8]

The scope of the consistency doctrine today is wide, and a number of different forms of the requirement have evolved. As noted above, consistency refers to the relationship between a comprehensive plan and its implementing measures. Not only does this mean that the plan and regulations promulgated under it must be consistent, it also means, in a growing number of jurisdictions, that any development orders and permits issued must be consistent with the local plan.[9] From a practical standpoint, the plan—implementation form is probably the most important type of consistency. It is from this relation that the bulk of inconsistency challenges are mounted.[10]

Jurisdictions that statutorily mandate planning frequently also require that the individual elements of the plan be consistent with one another. As one commentator has noted,

> [i]nternal consistency refers to compatibility within the general plan—that is, dimensions of planning are to be addressed with cognizance of other dimensions. Where several separate plan elements are mandated, for example, integration of elements is required.[11]

Thus, internal consistency requires coordination between the various elements of a plan so that they can operate in an effective and comprehensive manner.

Still another form of consistency, appearing with greater frequency, is the type mandated between local, regional, state, and even federal[12] comprehensive plans. A number of state planning acts now require this form of consistency.[13] This has caused a certain amount of controversy as

---

8. See generally, J. DiMento, supra note 5.

9. See e.g. West's Ann.Cal.Gov't Code § 65567 mandating that development requiring a building permit, subdivision approval, or open space zoning be consistent with the local open space plan. See generally the Florida Environmental Land and Water Management Act of 1972, West's Fla. Stats.Ann. ch. 380, in particular, §§ 380.04(1) (defining development) and 380.06 (mandating local and regional review of developments of regional impact and requiring that such projects be consistent with state and local comprehensive plans before development approval). See also West's Fla.Stat.Ann. § 163.3194(1)(b) (requiring consistency between land development regulations and the adopted comprehensive plan).

10. See generally J. DiMento, supra note 5. See also note 22, infra.

11. Id. at 16.

12. See e.g., The National Coastal Zone Management Act of 1972, 16 U.S.C.A. § 1456(c)(1), requiring that federal activity affecting coastal zones be consistent with state management programs. Section 1456(d) makes the act cut in both directions by requiring state and local coastal activities to be consistent with the federal plan as a prerequisite to receiving federal assistance.

13. See e.g. West's Ann.Cal.Gov't Code § 65030.1 (stating that local growth decisions should proceed within the framework of officially adopted statewide goals and policies); Or.Rev.Stat. 197.251 (creating an acknowledgement process wherein local plans are tested by a state agency for compliance with statewide planning goals); West's Fla. Stats.Ann. ch. 186 (the state and regional planning act, mandating state and regional plans with which local plans must be consistent). See also the 1985 amendments to Florida's Local Government Comprehensive Planning Act § 163.3177(9) (requiring the

some regard it as an affront on local land use autonomy.[14] Although the purpose of this form of consistency is to assure that individual local and regional plans operate in a rational and coordinated manner, the effect has been to place even greater control over local land use policy in the hands of state government.[15]

The consistency doctrine did not exist at common law and is purely a creature of statute and case law.[16] Attempts to define the concept precisely have proven largely unsuccessful. As Professor DiMento notes:

> [e]ven in those states where legislation has been passed to effect consistency, there is no generally accepted understanding of the term in affected local governments. This is certainly a common state of affairs in statutory interpretation; however, differences in terminology need to be addressed if other issues surrounding the legal effect of the comprehensive plan are to be resolved.

In California, for example, several attempts have been made to clarify the cryptic language in the consistency statutes. The major consistency mandate notes:

> A zoning ordinance shall be consistent with a city or county general plan only if:
>
> (i) The city or county has officially adopted such a plan, and
>
> (ii) The various land uses authorized by the ordinance are compatible with the objectives, policies, general land uses and programs specified in such a plan.[17]

This definition is neither very helpful nor clear, as zoning deals with more than just uses.[18] If consistency is limited to uses—as the definition suggests—then an ordinance permitting greater density than the plan might not be within the scope of the requirement, and as such might not be regarded as inconsistent with the plan.[19]

state land planning agency to establish guidelines for evaluation of local plans to ensure consistency with state and regional plans). For other examples of regionalism and federalization of comprehensive planning, see Mandelker, The Role of the Local Comprehensive Plan in Land Use Regulation, 74 Mich.L.Rev. 900, 915 (1976).

14. See, e.g., F. Bosselman & D. Callies, The Quiet Revolution in Land Use Controls (1971).

15. Id.

16. See e.g., *Fasano*, note 22 infra.

17. Cal.Gov't Code § 65860(a). See J. DiMento, supra note 5, at 18.

18. See Hagman & DiMento, The Consistency Requirement in California, 30:6 Land Use L. & Zoning Dig. 5, 6 (1978).

19. But see Twain Harte Homeowners Ass'n, Inc. v. County of Tuolumne, 138

Cal.App.3d 664, 188 Cal.Rptr. 233, 254 (1982), where the state planning act was held to require that population density be expressed numerically, and not merely in terms of uses (e.g., dwelling units per acre).

See generally City of Irvine v. Irvine Citizens Against Overdevelopment, 30 Cal. Rptr.2d 797, 25 Cal.App.4th 868, review denied (1994) (zoning ordinance is consistent with city's general plan, as statutorily required, where, considering all of its aspects, ordinance furthers objectives and policies of general plan and does not obstruct their attainment); A Local and Regional Monitor v. City of Los Angeles, 16 Cal. Rptr.2d 358, 12 Cal.App.4th 1773, rehearing denied (1993) (zoning ordinances must be consistent with city general plan, and to be consistent, they must be compatible with objectives, policies, general land uses, and programs specified in plan); Lesher Com-

The difficulty in defining consistency has undoubtedly been influenced by the use of similar terms; the "in accordance with" requirement of the SZEA, for example. Other synonymous terms include "substantially consistent with," "in conformity with," "in furtherance of," "closely attuned to," and "in basic harmony with" a comprehensive plan. None of these, however, has provided much in the way of progress toward an understanding of the term's meaning.

Another uncertain aspect of the doctrine concerns the phasing of consistency. Some jurisdictions might be willing to allow as consistent a less intensive use than the one contemplated by the plan on the theory that this type of development will lead toward achievement of the planned goal; for example, single family homes in an area with a plan designation approximating multi-family residential would be considered consistent. This holding zone approach reflects the planner's awareness of timing constraints, and recognizes the validity of interim development measures not inconsistent with the plan's long-term objectives.[20] Other jurisdictions might reject this as inconsistent, favoring instead a more literal one-to-one relationship between planning and zoning. A number of different approaches to the phasing problem have been suggested: i) requiring revision of the zoning ordinance to occur when the plan is adopted, ii) resolving the question through litigation on a case-by-case basis, iii) allowing a reasonable transition period, and iv) applying the comprehensive plan in a prospective manner only.[21]

Almost every zoning challenge contains an allegation that the contested action is inconsistent with some aspect of the comprehensive plan. Until recently, however, such challenges were seldom based solely on the grounds of inconsistency. In 1973, the Oregon Supreme Court in Fasano v. Board of County Commissioners[22] held that the state's planning act required that zoning ordinances and decisions be consistent with the adopted comprehensive plan. The court invalidated a rezoning which was determined to be inconsistent with the comprehensive plan. *Fasano* is

---

munications, Inc. v. City of Walnut Creek, 277 Cal.Rptr. 1, 52 Cal.3d 531, 802 P.2d 317 (1990) (municipal "Traffic Control Initiative" establishing building moratorium to combat traffic congestion was inconsistent with city's general plan which expressly recognized that anticipated development would lead to traffic congestion which residents would have to accept, and this inconsistency invalidated ordinance ab initio, and cities newly adopted general plan incorporating the initiative did not save the initiative); Sierra Club v. Kern County Bd. of Sup'rs, 179 Cal.Rptr. 261, 126 Cal.App.3d 698 (1981) (since county's general plan was internally inconsistent as regards open space and conservation elements on the one hand and land use element on the other hand, county zoning ordinance which was consistent with map of land use element but inconsistent with map of open space conservation element, could not be consistent with such plan and was invalid when passed).

20. See J. DiMento, supra note 5 at 22. But see Philippi v. Sublimity, 294 Or. 730, 662 P.2d 325 (1983) (plan favored agricultural designation until such time as needed for urban development, subdivision permit denial affirmed even though zoning permitted single family residential); Board of County Commissioners of Brevard County v. Snyder, 627 So.2d 469, 475 (Fla.1993) (local government should have discretion to decide that maximum development density should not be allowed provided government body approves some development that is consistent with the plan and government's decision is supported by substantial, competent evidence).

21. See J. DiMento, supra note 5 at 22.

22. 264 Or. 574, 507 P.2d 23 (1973).

seen by many as one of the earliest and strongest judicial endorsements of both consistency and comprehensive planning.[23]

As a practical matter, the meaning of consistency is in large part determined by what action courts will take for failure to meet the mandate. Remedies available include a reprimand,[24] injunctive relief, development moratoria,[25] and invalidation of the zoning ordinances.[26] It is clear that the impact of consistency will be greatly blunted unless an effective set of judicially enforceable remedies exists.[27] Thus the statutory remedies available for failure to meet the mandate will play an important role in defining consistency in a given jurisdiction.

Finally, an additional insight into the meaning of consistency can be gained by a consideration of some of the arguments for and against the doctrine. Proponents of consistency argue that the effectiveness of planning as a rational mechanism for allocating public resources will be weakened considerably by failure to mandate consistency. They additionally argue that planners can identify community objectives through a variety of means and present alternatives for rational and informed decisionmaking.[28] It has further been suggested that consistency helps prevent the taking challenge by putting landowners on notice well in advance as to what types of uses can be made of their property.[29] Thus proponents contend that only if consistency—the "missing link" between planning and zoning—is mandated can rational planning find any hope of successful implementation.

On the other hand, opponents of consistency argue forcefully that the doctrine creates more problems than it solves.[30] An interesting counter to one of the proponent's views is the argument that not only does mandatory consistency not prevent the taking challenge, it actually moves forward the point in time at which the taking occurs. Opponents suggest that if consistency really means that the plan controls, then planning is in reality regulatory, and such regulation results in "planning blight," potentially giving rise to claims of inverse condemnation.[31] They also contend that consistency does not prevent the spot zoning problem, but instead causes "spot planning".[32] Thus, rather than isolat-

---

23. The case is perhaps better known for the surprising approach it took in regard to judicial review of local land use decisions. See infra § 5.9.

24. See J. DiMento, supra note 5, at 24.

25. Allen v. Flathead County, 184 Mont. 58, 601 P.2d 399 (1979).

26. Manley v. Maysville, 528 S.W.2d 726 (Ky.1975).

27. See J. DiMento, supra note 5, at 23.

28. See generally Long, Making Urban Policy Useful and Corrigible, 10 Urb.Aff.Q. 379 (1975). See also J. DiMento, supra note 5, at 45.

29. See Housing for All Under Law: New Directions in Housing, Land Use and

Planning Law, Report of the A.B.A. Advisory Comm'n on Housing and Urban Growth, 379 (Fishman ed.1978).

30. See generally Tarlock, Consistency With Adopted Land Use Plans As A Standard of Judicial Review: The Case Against, 9 Urb.L.Ann. 69 (1975).

31. See generally DiMento, "But It's Only Planning": Planning and the Taking Issue in Land Development and Environmental Control Law, 1984 Zoning and Planning Law Handbook, ch. 5 (Clark Boardman 1984).

32. Spot planning occurs when instead of adhering to the existing plan designation, a locality allows both a comprehensive plan amendment and a zoning change to occur simultaneously without valid justification.

ing planning from outside forces, consistency in reality subjects planning to the pressures of political and economic influence.[33]

The consistency debate continues today. Although only a relatively small number of states currently have legally enforceable consistency requirements,[34] it is significant that several of these—California, Florida and Oregon—are regarded as innovators in land use and environmental law. Uncertainty about its true meaning will undoubtedly continue to plague the concept, but a growing number of statutory and judicial interpretations should help make a practical understanding of the concept possible.

Courts in states with mandatory local comprehensive planning and legally enforceable consistency requirements have begun to reexamine the traditional rules and procedures by which land use decisions are reached and judicially reviewed. Traditionally, courts have viewed zoning decisions as legislative decisions, subject to deferential review under the fairly debatable rule.[35] However, there is growing judicial recognition that local government decision-makers are not always equivalent to state and national legislatures, particularly where local governments are statutorily required to apply the standards and policies of the local plan in reaching land use decisions.[36] Challenges to the consistency of those decisions with the comprehensive plan have prompted some courts to characterize certain local land use decisions as quasi-judicial, subject to greater judicial scrutiny than legislative decisions.

In Board of County Commissioners of Brevard County v. Snyder,[37] the Florida Supreme Court held that while comprehensive rezonings affecting a large portion of the public are legislative in nature, rezoning actions which entail application of general rules or policies to specific individuals, interests, or activities are quasi-judicial, and subject to strict scrutiny review.[38] *Snyder* involved a landowner's request to rezone a one-half acre parcel in an area designated for residential use under the county's comprehensive plan. The parcel was zoned for single-family residences and the requested zoning classification would allow fifteen units per acre. While either classification was considered potentially consistent with the residential use designation under the comprehensive plan, the county denied the rezoning.

Another definition was recently suggested in an article on Florida's new growth management legislation; spot planning, the practice of post-hoc consistency by amending plans or planning maps to coincide with or follow individual rezoning approvals. Davidson, Florida Restructures State and Local Growth Management Laws, 9:5 APA Planning & Law Div. Newsletter 7, 10 (Sept. 1985). See e.g. Dalton v. City and County of Honolulu, 51 Haw. 400, 492, 462 P.2d 199 (1969) (purpose of plan was to prevent compromise of planning goals; simultaneous plan and zoning amendments declared void).

33. See generally J. DiMento, supra note 5, ch. 3.

34. See e.g., West's Ann.Cal.Gov't Code § 65860; D.C.Code 1981, § 5–414; West's Fla.Stat.Ann. § 163.3194; Ky.Rev. Stat. 100.213; Neb.Rev.Stat. § 23–114.03; N.J.Stat.Ann. 40:55D–62; Or.Rev.Stat. 197.010(1); West's Wash.Rev.Code Ann. §§ 36.70A.040.

35. See infra § 5.9.

36. See *Fasano*, supra note 22, at 580, 507 P.2d 23; § 5.9 infra.

37. 627 So.2d 469 (Fla.1993).

38. Id. at 474.

The court held that a landowner seeking to rezone property has the burden of proving the proposal is consistent with the comprehensive plan.[39] Upon demonstrating such consistency, however, the landowner is not presumptively entitled to such use.[40] Instead, the burden thereupon shifts to the local government to demonstrate that maintaining the existing zoning classification accomplishes a legitimate public purpose. [41]

In 1997, Florida courts shed further light on the distinction between planning and zoning explaining the scope of judicial review with respect to amendments of local comprehensive plans. In Martin County v. Yusem,[42] the Florida Supreme Court held that amendments to a comprehensive land use plan are legislative decisions subject to the fairly debatable standard of review.[43] The court further held that the fairly debatable standard applied even when such plan amendments are being sought as part of a rezoning application in respect to only one piece of property.[44] The court found that amendments to a comprehensive land use plan, like the adoption of the plan itself, result in formulation of policy, rather than application of policy, and, since amendments to comprehensive plans are legislative actions, the "fairly debatable" standard of review applies in these cases.[45]

As future opinions illuminate the extent of quasi-judicial land use decision making, the courts seem likely to confront and clarify the procedural responsibilities of local governments in reaching such decisions. At present, these procedural requirements are not well-developed in state law.

39. Id. at 476.

40. Id. at 475.

41. Although the local government is not required to make findings of fact in denying the application for rezoning, upon review the circuit court must be shown that there was competent substantial evidence presented to the local government to support its ruling. Id. at 476.

For a detailed discussion of the *Snyder* case and the historical evolution of quasi-judicial review of land use decisions in Flor-

ida, see Pelham, Quasi–Judicial Rezonings: A Commentary on the Snyder Decision and the Consistency Requirement, 9 J. Land Use & Envtl.L. 243 (1994); see also Jungreis, A Formal Affair: Land Use Decision-making, and Obstacles Thereto, in the Post–Snyder Era, 1996 Fla. B.J. 52 (Dec.).

42. 690 So.2d 1288 (Fla.1997).

43. Id. at 1293.

44. Id.

45. Id. at 1295.

Chapter 3

ZONING: HISTORY, SOURCES OF POWER, AND PURPOSES

Analysis

I.   INTRODUCTION

II.   THE HISTORY OF ZONING

III.   SOURCES OF ZONING POWER

IV.   PURPOSES OF ZONING

I.   INTRODUCTION

§ 3.1   Introductory Note

Zoning began early in the twentieth century, and, at the dawn of the twenty-first century, while it does not stand alone or unchanged, zoning remains the core tool of land use control.[1] While wholesale substitution of zoning by another system has not taken place, criticisms of zoning have had some effect. With the adoption of new control methods within zoning, the system today is significantly different from zoning in its original form. Though this chapter focuses primarily on zoning, other land use controls covered in other chapters, such as the planning process, building codes, subdivision control law, and growth management systems, are often so intertwined with zoning that drawing a clear division between them is difficult. Thus, much of what is said here relates not solely to zoning but to the land use control power in general.

Alternatives to zoning have been suggested over the years. The Model Land Development Code integrates zoning and subdivision controls and provides state oversight of local control of developments of regional impact.[2] Drawbacks from the parochial effects of localism have prompted greater use of state and regional controls.[3] Finally, and more fundamentally, use of the regulatory power to limit land use has been challenged. Some critics would simply, or essentially, omit government from the field,[4] while others would zone using the power of eminent

---

§ 3.1

1. See Charles M. Haar, The Twilight of Land–Use Controls: A Paradigm Shift? 30 U.Rich.L.Rev. 1011 (1996).

2. See infra § 3.23.

3. See supra § 2.13.

4. See Bernard Siegan, Land Use Without Zoning (1972); Douglas W. Kmiec, Deregulating Land Use, 130 U.Pa.L.Rev. 30 (1981); Robert C. Ellickson, Alternatives to Zoning: Covenants, Nuisance Rules, and

domain in combination with the police power.[5]

II. THE HISTORY OF ZONING

§ 3.2 Zoning's Predecessors

Land use regulations date back to colonial America, and earlier.[1] In the earliest days, colonists treated land as a community resource that was to be used in the public interest. For example, an ordinance passed January 7, 1632, in the Town of Cambridge, Massachusetts, provided that no buildings could be built in outlying areas until vacant spaces within the town were developed. Roofs had to be covered with slate or board rather than with thatch. Heights of all buildings had to be the same. Lots were forfeited if not built on in six months. Finally, buildings could only be erected with consent of the mayor.[2]

The Cambridge ordinance is typical of laws found throughout colonial America. Many restricted the location of dwellings, imposed affirmative obligations of use, compelled the fencing of agricultural land, required owners of wetlands to share the cost of drainage projects, and allowed the public to hunt on private land.[3] Over the following centuries, land use ordinances were enacted to deal with specific problems. For example, they excluded certain kinds of buildings and uses, such as wooden buildings, horse stables, and cemeteries, from particular areas of the city, imposed bulk requirements providing for setbacks and yards, and set height limits.

§ 3.3 Comprehensive Zoning

Zoning arrived in the twentieth century. The first comprehensive zoning ordinance was enacted in 1916 by New York City. It was comprehensive in the sense that it classified uses and created zones for all uses, which zones were then mapped, and it included height and bulk controls.[1] Four years after enactment, the ordinance was upheld in Lincoln Trust Co. v. Williams Building Corporation.[2]

Fines as Land Use Controls, 40 U.Chi. L.Rev. 681 (1973).

5. See infra §§ 3.24–3.28.

§ 3.2

1. See David L. Callies, Robert H. Freilich, and Thomas E. Roberts, Cases and Materials on Land Use 2–3 (2d.1994) (setting out ordinance from Elizabethan England).

2. The ordinance is reprinted in Gallagher, Report of Committee on Zoning and Planning, 18 NIMLO Mun.L.Rev. 373 (1955). With the exception of the compulsory forfeiture, the other controls find counterparts in today's growth management programs, safety and aesthetics ordinances. The power of mayoral control, a forerunner of the permitting process we now use, would be invalid today unless accompanied by adequate standards.

3. John F. Hart, Colonial Land Use Law and Its Significance for Modern Takings Doctrine, 109 Harv.L.Rev. 1252 (1996).

§ 3.3

1. On early zoning, particularly in New York, see E. Bassett, Zoning (1940); S. Makielski, The Politics of Zoning: The New York Experience (1966); J. McGoldrick, S. Graubard & R. Horowitz, Building Regulations in New York City (1944); S. Toll, Zoned American (1969); F. Williams, The Law of City Planning and Zoning (1922).

2. 229 N.Y. 313, 128 N.E. 209 (1920).

Zoning proved enormously popular and spread rapidly. By the time the Supreme Court upheld its constitutionality in 1926 in Village of Euclid v. Ambler Realty Co.,[3] some 564 cities and towns had enacted zoning.[4] After the *Euclid* decision, so-called Euclidean or use zoning swept the country. The zoning was Euclidean in two senses—the kind of zoning adopted was similar to that used in the Village of Euclid—and the landscape was divided into a geometric pattern of use districts.

While the Euclidean origins of most present-day zoning ordinances can be recognized, there have been many changes. Most of these provide flexibility in the development approval process. Basic use zoning and the flexibility devices used today are discussed in Chapter 4.

§ 3.4 Early Constitutional History of Zoning

A. *Pre–Comprehensive Zoning Cases*

A number of land use cases were decided by the Supreme Court on its way to sustaining comprehensive zoning. From 1885 to 1922, the Court upheld a San Francisco ordinance restricting the hours of operation of laundries in certain locations,[1] but invalidated another ordinance prohibiting laundries in wooden buildings unless permission was obtained from the Board of Supervisors, where it was applied exclusively against Chinese.[2] The Court upheld an ordinance designating certain areas of a city for prostitution,[3] a Massachusetts statute setting height limitations in the City of Boston,[4] and an ordinance precluding further burials in existing cemeteries.[5] The Court also invalidated an ordinance allowing neighbors to establish setback lines,[6] upheld an ordinance excluding stables from a commercial district,[7] upheld a Los Angeles regulation that precluded the operation of an existing brickyard within an area zoned to exclude them,[8] upheld an ordinance prohibiting signs in residential neighborhoods unless neighbors consented,[9] held invalid race-based zoning,[10] upheld an ordinance that precluded the storage of oil and gasoline within 300 feet of a dwelling house,[11] and invalidated a state statute that banned underground coal mining where it would cause

3. 272 U.S. 365, 47 S.Ct. 114, 71 L.Ed. 303 (1926).

4. See supra § 2.7.

§ 3.4

1. Barbier v. Connolly, 113 U.S. 27, 5 S.Ct. 357, 28 L.Ed. 923 (1884); Soon Hing v. Crowley, 113 U.S. 703, 5 S.Ct. 730, 28 L.Ed. 1145 (1885).

2. Yick Wo v. Hopkins, 118 U.S. 356, 6 S.Ct. 1064, 30 L.Ed. 220 (1886).

3. L'Hote v. New Orleans, 177 U.S. 587, 20 S.Ct. 788, 44 L.Ed. 899 (1900).

4. Welch v. Swasey, 214 U.S. 91, 29 S.Ct. 567, 53 L.Ed. 923 (1909).

5. Laurel Hill Cemetery v. San Francisco, 216 U.S. 358, 30 S.Ct. 301, 54 L.Ed. 515 (1910).

6. Eubank v. Richmond, 226 U.S. 137, 33 S.Ct. 76, 57 L.Ed. 156 (1912).

7. Reinman v. Little Rock, 237 U.S. 171, 35 S.Ct. 511, 59 L.Ed. 900 (1915).

8. Hadacheck v. Sebastian, 239 U.S. 394, 36 S.Ct. 143, 60 L.Ed. 348 (1915).

9. Cusack Co. v. Chicago, 242 U.S. 526, 37 S.Ct. 190, 61 L.Ed. 472 (1917).

10. Buchanan v. Warley, 245 U.S. 60, 38 S.Ct. 16, 62 L.Ed. 149 (1917).

11. Pierce Oil Corp. v. Hope, 248 U.S. 498, 39 S.Ct. 172, 63 L.Ed. 381 (1919).

subsidence of homes.[12]

In sum, the Court found that the police power was "one of the most essential powers of government-one that is the least limitable. * * * There must be progress, [said the Court,] and if in its march private interests are in the way, they must yield to the good of the community."[13] Regulations, however, did have a constitutional limit, and if they went "too far," they would be recognized as takings.[14]

B. Constitutional Parameters of Comprehensive Zoning: Euclid and Nectow

While the string of late nineteenth and early twentieth century cases noted above demonstrated the Court's view that the police power could be used to impose significant limitations on land use, there was still some doubt as to the validity of a comprehensive land use control system. In the early 1920s, several state courts addressed the issue, and, though most had upheld comprehensive zoning, some found it invalid.[15]

In 1926 the Court handed down the seminal land use decision of Village of Euclid v. Ambler Realty Co.,[16] where it upheld the general validity of an ordinance that set use, height, and bulk restrictions for an entire town. Key to the case was the use of a highly deferential standard of judicial review of municipal zoning. Urbanization, said the Court, had brought a set of problems that justified governmental intervention to protect the public. While there could be differences of opinion on the separation of residential, commercial, and industrial use in specific situations, as a general proposition the separation of uses made sense. Furthermore, said the Court, if all that could be said of a law was that it was "fairly debatable, the legislative judgment must be allowed to control."[17]

The Court tempered the reach of *Euclid* two years later in Nectow v. City of Cambridge,[18] when it held a zoning ordinance invalid as applied to a particular parcel because it found that the public good was not promoted by the zoning classification. In the end, though, it was the deferential review of *Euclid* rather than the closer scrutiny of *Nectow* that created the climate that allowed comprehensive zoning to flourish.[19]

C. The Current Generation of Cases

After setting constitutional guidelines for zoning in the 1920s, for almost fifty years the Court declined to address zoning issues. Since the early 1970s, however, the Court has acted on a wide array of land use

12. Pennsylvania Coal Co. v. Mahon, 260 U.S. 393, 43 S.Ct. 158, 67 L.Ed. 322 (1922).

13. Hadacheck v. Sebastian, 239 U.S. 394, 36 S.Ct. 143, 60 L.Ed. 348 (1915).

14. Pennsylvania Coal Co. v. Mahon, 260 U.S. 393, 415, 43 S.Ct. 158, 160, 67 L.Ed. 322 (1922). See infra Ch. 10 for discussion of constitutional issues.

15. Village of Euclid v. Ambler Realty Co., 272 U.S. 365, 390, 47 S.Ct. 114, 119, 71 L.Ed. 303 (1926).

16. 272 U.S. 365, 47 S.Ct. 114, 71 L.Ed. 303 (1926).

17. 272 U.S. at 388, 47 S.Ct. at 118.

18. 277 U.S. 183, 48 S.Ct. 447, 72 L.Ed. 842 (1928).

19. See discussion infra § 10.12.

and zoning controls under the First Amendment's speech clause, the Fifth Amendment's taking clause, and the Fourteenth Amendment's due process and equal protection clauses. These developments are covered in detail in Chapter 10.

III. SOURCES OF ZONING POWER

§ 3.5 In General

Public land use controls, including zoning, subdivision regulation, building codes and growth controls, are exercises of the police power. Though broad, this power to enact laws to promote the health, safety, morals, and general welfare is limited by the federal and state constitutions.[1] State legislatures can delegate their power to regulate land use and by and large have done so. In the early years, almost complete power was delegated to local governments, but over the past few decades, a number of state legislatures have limited local rule and instituted statewide controls.[2]

Among local governments, the delegated police power is distributed to municipal corporations—cities, villages and towns—and frequently to counties.[3] These terms generally are used interchangeably in this book to refer to any political subdivisions that have land use control power. Limited purpose governments, such as utility districts and school districts, are seldom given the power to zone or otherwise regulate land use.

Though the source of power to control land use in most states is by way of a zoning enabling act, the power may come from other sources. In a number of states, the state constitution provides for home rule to distribute state power to local governments. Home rule power is also sometimes granted by legislation. Land use control power can also be implied from a law generally authorizing the exercise of the police power by local government. Rarely, land use control power may also be based on a doctrine of inherent powers, meaning that the mere creation of a political subdivision confers power to do the kinds of things local governments need to do, such as zone.

Generally, the power to zone is delegated to the legislative bodies of local governments. When the source is the enabling act, the power is sometimes divided among legislative and administrative bodies, such as planning commissions and boards of adjustment.[4] In many states, the people retain the power of initiative and referendum and use them to control land use.

Finally, many states have enabling acts establishing or authorizing land use control systems for special situations, such as airport zoning,

§ 3.5

1. See infra Ch. 10.

2. See supra § 2.12.

3. "Town" may refer to a municipal corporation or to a subdivision of a county.

A county is not a municipal corporation but a subdivision of the state.

4. Boards of Adjustment are frequently called Boards of Appeal.

flood plain zoning, historic districting, landmark preservation, or watershed management. The following sections cover these matters in more detail.

§ 3.6 Standard Zoning Enabling Act

The popularity of Euclidean zoning was aided significantly by the fact that there was a good model: the Standard State Zoning Enabling Act (SZEA). Released in 1924, the SZEA resulted from the work of an Advisory Committee appointed by Herbert Hoover, then Secretary of Commerce.[1] Few model or uniform laws have enjoyed such widespread adoption or influence. All 50 states eventually adopted enabling acts substantially patterned on the Standard Act.[2] Many states still use the act today, having enacted piecemeal modifications over the years. Some commentators suggest more radical reform.[3]

The first three sections of the SZEA state the purposes of zoning and define its scope.[4]

> Sec. 1. Grant of Power.—For the purpose of promoting health, safety, morals, or the general welfare of the community, the legislative body of cities and incorporated villages is hereby empowered to regulate and restrict the height, number of stories, and size of buildings and other structures, the percentage of lot that may be occupied, the size of yards, courts, and other open spaces, the density of population, and the location and use of buildings, structures, and land for trade, industry, residence, or other purposes.

> Sec. 2. Districts.—For any or all of said purposes the local legislative body may divide the municipality into districts of such number, shape, and area as may be deemed best suited to carry out the purposes of this act; and within such districts it may regulate and restrict the erection, construction, reconstruction, alteration, repair, or use of buildings, structures, or land. All such regulations shall be uniform for each class or kind of buildings throughout each district, but the regulations in one district may differ from those in other districts.

> Sec. 3. Purposes in View.—Such regulations shall be made in accordance with a comprehensive plan and designed to lessen congestion in the streets; to secure safety from fire, panic, and other dangers; to promote health and the general welfare; to provide adequate light and air; to prevent the overcrowding of land; to avoid undue concentration of population; to facilitate the adequate provi-

---

§ 3.6

1. See Edward M. Bassett, Zoning: The Laws, Administration, and Court Decisions During the First Twenty Years 28–29 (1940).

2. See R. Anderson & B. Roswig, Planning Zoning & Subdivision: A Summary of Statutory Law in the 50 States (1966).

3. See, e.g., George W. Liebmann, The Modernization of Zoning: Enabling Act Revision as a Means to Reform, 23 Urb.Law. 1 (1991).

4. Dep't of Commerce (rev.ed.1926). The Act, with official commentary, is reprinted in full in 8 Zoning and Land Use Controls § 53.01 [1] (P. Rohan and E. Kelly eds.1997).

sion of transportation, water, sewerage, schools, parks, and other public requirements. Such regulations shall be made with reasonable consideration among other things, to the character of the district and its peculiar suitability for particular uses, and with a view to conserving the value of buildings and encouraging the most appropriate use of land throughout such municipality.

Subsequent sections provide a procedure for adopting zoning and making amendments, including provision for protest by neighbors. The Act calls for the establishment of a zoning commission or planning commission, which makes recommendations on zoning. The Act also permits the establishment of a Board of Adjustment to hear appeals from enforcement of the ordinance, to hear and decide special exceptions (i.e., special permits) and to give variances. Finally, the Act contains provisions for enforcement of the regulations.

In addition to ultra vires challenges to zoning enactments that fall outside the scope of the enabling act,[5] zoning can also be held invalid if the procedures established by the enabling act are not followed. For example, in Ellison v. Fort Lauderdale[6] a zoning ordinance was amended to exclude the keeping of horses in a residential zone. When the defendant was charged with violation of the ordinance he defended and won on the ground that notice and hearing were not provided as required by the statute. In City of Searcy v. Roberson,[7] business zoning was held invalid where it was not preceded by comprehensive study by the planning commission, as the statute required. In Holdredge v. Cleveland,[8] an amendment had not been submitted to the planning commission as required by the statute, so the rezoning was held invalid. However, an act that fails to meet the procedures dictated for zoning may be held valid under other authority, such as a building code that has more relaxed adoption requirements.[9]

§ 3.7 Home Rule

The courts of the various states are not in agreement as to whether home rule power authorized by state constitution or legislation is a source of zoning power. In California and Ohio, for example, power to make and enforce local regulations is interpreted as authorizing zoning,[1] whereas in New York, the constitutional power of municipalities to enact local laws does not authorize zoning.[2]

5. See infra § 3.13.

6. 183 So.2d 193 (Fla.1966).

7. 224 Ark. 344, 273 S.W.2d 26 (1954).

8. 218 Tenn. 239, 402 S.W.2d 709 (1966).

9. See infra § 8.3.

§ 3.7

1. Brougher v. Board of Pub. Works, 205 Cal. 426, 271 P. 487 (1928); Pritz v. Messer, 112 Ohio St. 628, 149 N.E. 30 (1925). See generally Janice C. Griffith, Connecticut's Home Rule: The Judicial Resolution of State and Local Conflicts, 4 U. Bridgeport L.Rev. 177 (1983).

2. Kenneth H. Young, Anderson's American Law of Zoning § 2.16 (1995).

Even where zoning power is authorized by home rule, it only applies to local matters not in conflict with state law.[3] In states with zoning enabling legislation, a conflict is possible, particularly on procedural issues due to a greater state interest in procedural uniformity. A state requirement that cities adopt plans has been held to be of such statewide concern that home rule cities must comply.[4] Local zoning measures often implicate substantial state interests.[5] Thus, the Colorado Supreme Court held that a town ordinance that totally prohibited oil and gas drilling was partially preempted by the state's oil and gas conservation act.[6] Mixed issues of state and local concerns with respect to oil and gas drilling permitted local regulation, but not exclusion.

§ 3.8 Charter

A charter is the basic document of a local government, akin to a constitution. The state legislature can confer power on a city in a charter, including zoning power.[1] Sometimes home rule powers can be obtained only by adopting a charter, that is, the zoning enabling act governs unless there is a charter.

§ 3.9 Inherent and Implied Powers

The power to zone does not arise from the mere creation of a municipal corporation.[1] Because zoning is a relatively new exercise of power, and having a city without having it zoned was possible historically (in fact Houston, Texas still has no zoning), a court is not likely to support zoning on the largely discredited theory that cities have inherent powers. Furthermore, the power to zone is usually not implied from typical legislation conferring general police power on a municipality.[2]

§ 3.10 Initiative and Referendum

In a few states, the people can enact legislation through use of the

3. Rispo Realty & Development v. City of Parma, 55 Ohio St.3d 101, 564 N.E.2d 425 (1990).

4. City of Los Angeles v. State of California, 138 Cal.App.3d 526, 187 Cal.Rptr. 893 (1982). But see Moore v. City of Boulder, 29 Colo.App. 248, 484 P.2d 134 (1971) (low cost housing a matter of purely local concern).

5. City of New Orleans v. Board of Commissioners of Orleans Levee District, 640 So.2d 237 (La.1994) (board required to prove that home rule city's zoning ordinance that barred construction by state of marina conflicted with vital interest of state as a whole).

6. Voss v. Lundvall Brothers, Inc., 830 P.2d 1061 (Colo.1992). See also National Advertising Co., v. Department of Highways, 751 P.2d 632 (Colo.1988) (outdoor advertising a matter of mixed local and state concern; where provisions conflict, the state's controls).

§ 3.8

1. Bartle v. Zoning Bd. of Adjustment, 391 Pa. 207, 137 A.2d 239 (1958).

§ 3.9

1. Detroit Osteopathic Hosp. v. Southfield, 377 Mich. 128, 139 N.W.2d 728 (1966) (no inherent authority).

2. City of Searcy v. Roberson, 224 Ark. 344, 273 S.W.2d 26 (1954); Stevens v. Salisbury, 240 Md. 556, 214 A.2d 775 (1965). See also Kline v. Harrisburg, 362 Pa. 438, 68 A.2d 182 (1949), which holds that a third-class city had no power to interim zone under the enabling act or under general police power or any other power, express, inherent or implied. But see Giger v. City of Omaha, 232 Neb. 676, 442 N.W.2d 182 (Neb.1989).

initiative, and in many states, can revoke legislative acts by referendum.[1] Use of the initiative for zoning is authorized by statute in some states.[2] Where the source of power to zone is the enabling act, complying with procedural requisites for zoning such as notice, hearing, and referral to the planning commission may be difficult, so the initiative process may not be possible.[3] Furthermore, some states have disallowed zoning by initiative reasoning that the comprehensiveness of zoning legislation would be destroyed.[4]

Since a referendum comes after the enactment of legislation, there are no procedural steps for zoning with which the referendum procedures may conflict.[5] Thus, a referendum on zoning legislation is possible in many states. Some states expressly authorize it,[6] in others the general authority to have referenda is sufficient.[7] Zoning referenda likewise have been disallowed to avoid piecemeal attacks on comprehensive plans.[8] The initiative and referendum are discussed in detail in Chapter 5.

§ 3.11 Special Enabling Acts

Authority for some kinds of zoning may be provided by a separate enabling act. Airport zoning and flood plain zoning, both of which were stimulated by federal legislation, are two examples. Enabling acts have also been amended, or special acts passed, to permit the creation of districts to preserve historic and architecturally significant areas.[1]

Peculiar aspects of airport operations have led to the passage in many states of specific airport zoning enabling legislation.[2] Airport zoning has also been encouraged by the federal government, which has helped fund airport construction provided that uses adjacent to the airport are so regulated as to preclude interference with airport operation.[3]

§ 3.10

1. Initiative and Referendum are discussed in detail infra § 5.5.

2. Ariz.Rev.Stat. § 11–826; Mich. Comp.Laws Ann. § 125.271; Ohio Rev.Code § 303.25.

3. City of Scottsdale v. Superior Court, 103 Ariz. 204, 439 P.2d 290 (1968). Contra, Associated Home Builders v. Livermore, 18 Cal.3d 582, 135 Cal.Rptr. 41, 557 P.2d 473 (1976).

4. Gumprecht v. Coeur D'Alene, 104 Idaho 615, 661 P.2d 1214 (1983).

5. But see San Pedro North, Ltd. v. San Antonio, 562 S.W.2d 260 (Tex.Civ.App. 1978), cert. denied 439 U.S. 1004, 99 S.Ct. 616, 58 L.Ed.2d 680 (1978), rehearing denied 439 U.S. 1135, 99 S.Ct. 1060, 59 L.Ed.2d 98 (1979). To allow a referendum would be to add a procedural step to zoning which is not required by the enabling act.

6. Mich.Comp.Laws Ann. § 125.282.

7. Florida Land Co. v. Winter Springs, 427 So.2d 170 (Fla.1983).

8. Township of Sparta v. Spillane, 125 N.J.Super. 519, 312 A.2d 154 (1973), cert. denied 64 N.J. 493, 317 A.2d 706 (1974).

§ 3.11

1. See, e.g., Mass.Gen.Laws Ann. c. 40c, § 2; Vernon's Ann.Mo.Ann.Stat. § 89.040; N.C.Gen.Stat. § 160A–400.1. See infra ch. 12.

2. See e.g., West's Ann.Cal.Gov't Code §§ 50485–50485.14; Ill.Rev.Stat. Ch. 15 1/2, § 48.13; Ohio Rev.Code § 4563.03; Utah Code Ann. § 2–4–6. See also infra § 4.29 for discussion on zoning for airports.

3. See Jeffrey Schoen, Comment, Airport Noise: How State and Local Governments Can Protect Airports from Urban Encroachments, 1986 Ariz.St.L.J. 309, 314.

A state's participation in the National Flood Insurance Program requires that certain regulatory measures be adopted to exclude or limit building on flood plains.[4] While some local governments implement these requirements through general zoning enabling legislation, a number of states have specific flood plain legislation.[5]

§ 3.12 Geographical Reach

A. *Extraterritorial Zoning*

The Standard Zoning Enabling Act did not provide for extraterritorial zoning.[1] The act also only empowered municipalities to zone. Counties were excluded, and without county power to zone, the fringes of city areas could be developed without zoning control. The power to zone eventually was extended to counties in most states, but extraterritorial concerns persisted.

Some states grant the power to zone extraterritorially.[2] Such power is frequently conferred only on larger cities and is limited in terms of miles from the city. It may be permitted only where the county does not zone or where the county approves.[3] In metropolitan areas, overlapping extraterritorial jurisdiction is usually solved by limiting power to points equidistant between the municipalities exercising the power. Regionalization of zoning in metropolitan areas remains a major problem, and the prospective loss of zoning power is one of the major reasons why municipalities in metropolitan areas resist metropolitan government.

B. *Annexation and Prezoning*

If extraterritorial zoning power is lacking, problems can arise upon annexation. Previous zoning regulations usually terminate upon annexation, leaving the land unzoned.[4] While the area can now be zoned, uses inconsistent with the plan for the area may become vested in the time that it takes to implement new zoning.

The Standard Zoning Enabling Act created no mechanism for zoning territory in advance of annexation, and states have handled the problem in a variety of ways. In California, cities are permitted to prezone territory to be annexed so that the zoning ordinance takes effect immedi-

4. 42 U.S.C.A. § 4001 et seq. See infra § 11.15.

5. See, e.g., Ala.Code § 22–3–100; Wyo. Stat. § 15–1–503. For a detailed breakdown of each state's program, see Richard Hamann and Alan C. Weinstein, Floodplain Regulation, Ch. 18, 2 Zoning and Land Use Controls (P.Rohan and E. Kelly eds.1996).

§ 3.12

1. A note suggested that power could be added. See SZEA, § 1, note 15a.

2. Extraterritorial power to plan and control subdivisions is more frequently conferred. See infra Ch. 7. See also Village of

DeForest v. County of Dane, 211 Wis.2d 802, 565 N.W.2d 296 (Wis.App.1997) (interim as well as permanent zoning authority applies extraterritorially).

3. See generally F. Sengstock, Extra–Territorial Powers in the Metropolitan Area (1962); Becker, Municipal Boundaries and Zoning: Controlling Regional Land Development, 1966 Wash.U.L.Q. 1; Cunningham, Land–Use Control—The State and Local Programs, 50 Iowa L.Rev. 367 (1965).

4. Louisville & Jefferson County Plan. & Zoning Comm'n v. Fortner, 243 S.W.2d 492 (Ky.1951).

ately upon annexation.[5] A zoning ordinance also may be part of the annexation ordinance.[6] Interim zoning also has been used.[7] In other states, statutes provide that upon annexation the area will remain as previously zoned for a period of time.[8] Ordinances sometimes provide that upon annexation the territory is automatically zoned to the most restrictive zone available under the zoning ordinance, pending reclassification.

IV.   PURPOSES OF ZONING

§ 3.13   In General

The purposes for which zoning may be enacted are as broad as the source of power from the state allows. Whether by enabling act or home rule, the power may extend to the full limits of the police power of the state, or it may be more limited.

Section 1 of the Standard Act broadly grants the power to zone to municipalities "for the purpose of promoting health, safety, morals, or the general welfare of the community." Section 3, set out above,[1] then lists various "purposes in view." Official commentary to the act observes that Section 1 "defined and limited the powers" conferred, while Section 3 "contain[ed] a direction from the [legislature] as to the purposes * * * [and] constitut[ed] the 'atmosphere' under which zoning [was] to be done."[2] The New York Court of Appeals has read Section 1 as merely providing the "constitutional predicate" for zoning, and not as conferring the full police power of the state. To be valid, says that court, a zoning ordinance must be authorized, expressly or implicitly, by Section 3.[3]

Zoning may be invalid because it is beyond the power conferred by the enabling act. The general language of the SZEA has led some courts to judge ultra vires challenges by reference to a reasonableness test that is the same as that used to determine whether an act is beyond the police power. This finds support not only in the fact that Section 1 of the SZEA provides a grant of power in language that equals the full reach of the police power, but in the long list of "purposes in view" of Section 3. Additional leeway exists since most courts will imply powers that are fairly related, or incident, to powers expressly granted.[4] As one court said, the legislature is "presumed never to have intended to authorize

5. West's Ann.Cal.Gov't Code § 65859.

6. Beshore v. Town of Bel Air, 237 Md. 398, 206 A.2d 678 (1965).

7. Williams v. Village of Deer Park, 78 Ohio App. 231, 69 N.E.2d 536 (1946). See infra §§ 5.28 and 9.5.

8. Ohio Rev.Code §§ 303.18, 519.08 & 711.14.

§ 3.13

1. See supra § 3.6.

2. SZEA, § 3, n. 21.

3. Golden v. Planning Bd. of Town of Ramapo, 30 N.Y.2d 359, 334 N.Y.S.2d 138, 285 N.E.2d 291, appeal dismissed 409 U.S. 1003, 93 S.Ct. 436, 440, 34 L.Ed.2d 294 (1972).

4. Giger v. City of Omaha, 232 Neb. 676, 442 N.W.2d 182, 193 (Neb.1989).

irrational classifications wholly unrelated to zoning objectives or violative of constitutional rights."[5] With that threshold, zoning authorities have room to operate. In some cases, courts may merge the enabling act question with the more fundamental police power question.[6]

Courts have upheld numerous ordinances that lack precise grounding in the "purposes in view" list. In Golden v. Planning Board of Town of Ramapo,[7] the court found that an ordinance that limited growth based on the availability of public services and infrastructure for an eighteen-year period was within the Standard Act's language that permits zoning "to avoid undue concentration of population [and] to facilitate the adequate provision of transportation, water, sewerage, schools, [and] parks, * * *."[8] Single-use zoning covering an entire municipality has been upheld even though a narrow reading of the enabling act arguably requires multiple districts.[9] Conditional zoning has also been upheld despite the lack of express language authorizing such a technique.[10]

Where a zoning ordinance is unrelated to the achievement of land use objectives, it will be invalidated. For example, a moratorium imposed on cellular telephone antennas enacted for the health of a village's residents was found to be outside the enabling act where there was not a scintilla of evidence to support the claim of a health hazard.[11] Zoning to quell community opposition[12] or to prevent riots[13] also has been held outside the enabling act.

Regardless of the breadth of the delegated power, zoning for a particular purpose may be invalid because the exercise of power constitutes an act that is beyond the scope of the police power. For example, if zoning is exercised to lower the market value of property so that a governmental body can acquire it more cheaply under eminent domain, exercise of the power for that purpose would be unconstitutional.

In the sections that follow, some of the purposes of zoning are considered in further detail. A particular zoning action often effectuates several purposes and the purposes often overlap.

§ 3.14 Preservation of Property Values

The preservation of property values is often cited as an important, if

5. Dinan v. Board of Zoning Appeals of Town of Stratford, 220 Conn. 61, 595 A.2d 864, 867 (1991).

6. See, e.g., Cellular Telephone Co. v. Village of Tarrytown, 209 A.D.2d 57, 624 N.Y.S.2d 170 (1995); Dinan v. Board of Zoning Appeals of Town of Stratford, 220 Conn. 61, 595 A.2d 864, 867 (1991) (defining family to include only related persons promotes general welfare, and regulates density within Standard Act).

7. 30 N.Y.2d 359, 334 N.Y.S.2d 138, 285 N.E.2d 291, appeal dismissed 409 U.S. 1003, 93 S.Ct. 436, 440, 34 L.Ed.2d 294 (1972).

8. SZEA § 3.

9. Valley View Village, Inc. v. Proffett, 221 F.2d 412, 416 (6th Cir.1955). See discussion infra § 6.9 for contrary authority.

10. Giger v. City of Omaha, 232 Neb. 676, 442 N.W.2d 182 (Neb.1989).

11. Cellular Telephone Co. v. Village of Tarrytown, 209 A.D.2d 57, 624 N.Y.S.2d 170 (1995).

12. Matter of Belle Harbor Realty Corp. v. Kerr, 35 N.Y.2d 507, 364 N.Y.S.2d 160, 323 N.E.2d 697 (1974).

13. De Sena v. Gulde, 24 A.D.2d 165, 265 N.Y.S.2d 239 (1965).

not primary, purpose of zoning.[1] While preservation is not an explicitly stated purpose,[2] none would likely quarrel with it as a legitimate factor in zoning. Whether it can stand alone is another question. Some courts say that it can. In a leading case in the area of aesthetic controls, the Wisconsin Supreme Court stated that "[a]nything that tends to destroy property values of the inhabitants of the village necessarily adversely affects the prosperity, and therefore the general welfare, of the entire village,"[3] is within the reach of the zoning power. The court's statement goes too far, and fails to recognize that one must ask what it is that affects value, and whether the regulation of that activity or occurrence is valid. That which causes the value to go down might be a commercial use in a residential neighborhood or the building of an architecturally unusual structure. It also might be the fact that a controversial radio talk show host plans to move into the neighborhood or that a non-mainstream religious group wishes to establish a place of worship in a neighborhood where other religious uses are located. The former, but not the latter, two could be restricted.[4]

Courts ought not allow a goal to preserve property values to obscure an unarticulated illegitimate motive. The Michigan Supreme Court recognized this when it held that the "conservation of property values is not by itself made a proper sole objective for the exercise of police power under the statute."[5] The court proceeded to invalidate an ordinance specifying a minimum house size enacted solely to preserve the value of existing homes.

If zoning depresses values of particular buildings or parcels, it is still valid.[6] Similarly, the zoning of a parcel can be valid though the value of neighboring property is adversely affected by the zoning.[7] In any event, to the extent zoning is effective, the sum total of real property values in a city should be increased by orderly rather than haphazard development.

The "maintenance of property values" purpose is sometimes used to support zoning that preserves the property tax base and to justify controls designed to preserve or promote aesthetics, or historic or natural areas. These matters are discussed separately.[8]

§ 3.14

1. See, e.g., City of Fargo v. Harwood Twp., 256 N.W.2d 694 (N.D.1977).

2. The Standard Act's only express reference to value is Section 3's provision that zoning should be done "with a view to conserving the value of buildings and encouraging the most appropriate use of land throughout such municipality." It may be wondered whether values should also be enhanced and whether land as well as building value should be conserved.

3. State v. Wieland, 269 Wis. 262, 69 N.W.2d 217, 224 (1955).

4. See infra §§ 10.12, 10.14, and 10.18.

5. Elizabeth Lake Estates v. Waterford Twp. 317 Mich. 359, 26 N.W.2d 788, 792 (1947).

6. Parking Ass'n of Georgia, Inc. v. City of Atlanta, 264 Ga. 764, 450 S.E.2d 200 (1994).

7. Braden v. Much, 403 Ill. 507, 87 N.E.2d 620 (1949).

8. See infra ch. 12.

§ 3.15 Preservation of Character

The Standard Act indicates that the zoning should take into consideration the character of the district. "Character" is a vague and loaded term. It may refer to the physical appearance of an area to justify architectural or other aesthetic controls.[1] It also may be "code" language to reflect "snob zoning," to exclude housing for persons of low and moderate income. The validity of such exclusionary ordinances is explored in Chapter 6.

Some ordinances indicate that zoning is to stabilize neighborhoods. Though the phrase is not in the Standard Act, perhaps the "character" language implies that zoning should not upset the status quo. Neighbors unhappy with a proposed zoning change often argue their right to have the zoning affecting them remain unchanged. While zoning should provide some stability, it is not a guarantee against change.[2]

§ 3.16 Traffic Safety

The Standard Act provides that regulations should be made to lessen congestion in the streets and to facilitate adequate provision of transportation. The location and dimension of streets are typically not controlled by zoning. However, there are several aspects of zoning related to traffic. The purpose is used to argue against nonresidential development in residential areas because of the danger to children in street crossing. The purpose is also effectuated by front yard and setback requirements, so that vision will not be impaired at street corners. Density controls, such as minimum lot sizes, can be used to lessen the amount of traffic generating activity.[1]

Off-street parking requirements are also justified to promote public safety and to maintain the traffic capacity of streets.[2] While generally held valid,[3] off-street parking requirements have been opposed because they add expense to construction and limit use of a lot for its primary purpose.[4] In one case, Ronda Realty Corp. v. Lawton,[5] the court held off-street parking requirements invalid on improper classification grounds when off-street parking requirements were imposed on apartment houses but not on hotels and rooming houses.

§ 3.15

1. See infra Ch. 12.

2. Lamb v. Monroe, 358 Mich. 136, 99 N.W.2d 566 (1959).

§ 3.16

1. Flora Realty & Inv. Co. v. Ladue, 362 Mo. 1025, 246 S.W.2d 771 (1952), appeal dismissed 344 U.S. 802, 73 S.Ct. 41, 97 L.Ed. 626 (1952) (large lot zoning upheld partially on traffic considerations).

2. Chambers v. Zoning Bd. of Adj., 250 N.C. 194, 108 S.E.2d 211 (1959).

3. Stroud v. City of Aspen, 188 Colo. 1, 532 P.2d 720 (1975) (citing other state authority and overruling prior case which had held off-street parking per se unconstitutional). In *Stroud*, the court adopts what regards as the universal rule that such laws are facially valid. 532 P.2d at 721–722.

4. See Margaret E. Vroman, Annot., Zoning: Residential Off–Street Parking Requirements, 71 A.L.R.4th 529 (1990).

5. 414 Ill. 313, 111 N.E.2d 310 (1953).

Subject to constitutional limitations,[6] municipalities may require the dedication of land for streets as a condition for the granting of development permission. Such dedications relate to the purpose of lessening congestion in the streets caused by the development.

Traffic relates to zoning in at least two other ways. First, a substantial increase in traffic along a street may be a change of condition making a rezoning of a residential area proper.[7] Second, parking is a use of land which, when not on public streets or areas, is a use of land subject to zoning regulation.[8]

§ 3.17 Regulation of Competition

The regulation of competition is often said to be an improper purpose of zoning.[1] In one case, when a city amended its zoning ordinance to allow new types of dry cleaners using particular solvents, it delayed the effective date of the ordinance to give existing businesses a chance to adjust to the new competition. Deeming the purpose improper, the court invalidated the portion of the ordinance that delayed the effective date of the new zoning.[2] Reasoning that zoning should not be used to create a monopoly, some courts also have held zoning invalid where there is no place in a community for a competitive business to be established.[3] On the other hand, the mere act of districting has some effect on competition,[4] and the fact that the control of competition was a factor in the zoning of an area will not necessarily be fatal.[5] The desire to achieve stability and balance in the provision of services is a legitimate goal, even though competition is suppressed.[6] Furthermore, a zoning ordinance enacted pursuant to a comprehensive plan will help shield it from attack.[7]

Improper regulation of competition is often argued with respect to spacing requirements between such uses as gasoline stations and bars.

6. See infra § 9.8.

7. Offutt v. Board of Zoning Appeals, 204 Md. 551, 105 A.2d 219 (1954). See also infra § 3.16.

8. City & County of San Francisco v. Safeway Stores, Inc., 150 Cal.App.2d 327, 310 P.2d 68 (1957) (traffic to and from store on private easement over land zoned residential held to be commercial use and therefore precluded by the zone).

§ 3.17

1. See, e.g., Pearce v. Village of Edina, 263 Minn. 553, 118 N.W.2d 659 (1962); Appeal of Lieb, 179 Pa.Super. 318, 116 A.2d 860 (1955). See generally Daniel R. Mandelker, Control of Competition as a Proper Purpose in Zoning, 14 Zoning Dig. 33 (1962).

2. Wyatt v. City of Pensacola, 196 So.2d 777 (Fla.App.1967).

3. In re White, 195 Cal. 516, 234 P. 396 (1925).

4. City of Columbia v. Omni Outdoor Advertising, Inc., 499 U.S. 365, 111 S.Ct. 1344, 113 L.Ed.2d 382 (1991).

5. Van Sicklen v. Browne, 15 Cal. App.3d 122, 92 Cal.Rptr. 786 (1971).

6. Id. See also Commercial Auto Wrecking Corp. v. Boyle, 20 Mich.App. 341, 174 N.W.2d 77 (1969). The vast majority of states hold that one whose goal is to prevent competition with an existing business lacks standing to challenge a zoning action. Earth Movers of Fairbanks, Inc. v. Fairbanks North Star Borough, 865 P.2d 741, 744 (Alaska 1993) (collecting cases).

7. Ensign Bickford Realty Corp. v. City Council, 68 Cal.App.3d 467, 137 Cal.Rptr. 304 (1977).

For example, in Mazo v. Detroit,[8] an ordinance that prohibited the establishment of a bar within 1,000 feet of another was upheld as applied to a "skid-row" area, which the legislative body thought would become worse if a large number of bars were permitted. Similarly, spacing requirements may be upheld for gasoline stations on the grounds of an undesirable increase of traffic or fire hazards,[9] or even on the ground that there are already a sufficient number of stations in the area to serve the public need.[10]

§ 3.18   Fiscal Zoning to Increase Tax Base

Fiscal zoning to increase the tax base, provide for employment, or otherwise plan the local economy has met with mixed reaction in the courts. In some states the enabling act provides that protecting or enhancing the tax base is a purpose of zoning.[1] In those states with the SZEA, which has no express provision regarding tax considerations, the purpose might be inferred from the preservation of property value purpose, though that purpose itself is not clearly set forth.[2] A non-fiscal purpose also may be found to support zoning that is alleged to be fiscally motivated.[3]

A number of courts have recognized the desire to stimulate the local economy as a valid purpose of zoning. In one case, a court upheld a rezoning based on the county's findings that the result would lead to the employment of eighty-seven people from the community and would produce tax revenues constituting 25 percent of the city's budget.[4]

For many courts, the goal of increasing the tax base and providing employment opportunities is not fatal, but it cannot stand alone. There must be other legitimate reasons.[5] Some courts, however, roundly condemn fiscal zoning, declaring it to be "totally violative of all the basic principles of zoning."[6]

Fiscal considerations often explain the use of exclusionary zoning devices, such as minimum lot sizes. The premise is that low density, high cost housing requirements protect a town from the burden of providing

---

8. 9 Mich.App. 354, 156 N.W.2d 155 (1968).

9. Mosher, Proximity Regulation of the Modern Service Station, 17 Syracuse L.Rev. 1 (1965); Williams, The Numbers Game: Gasoline Service Stations and Land Use Controls, 2 Urb.L.Ann. 23 (1969).

10. Turner v. Cook, 9 Misc.2d 850, 168 N.Y.S.2d 556 (1957). Contra, West Whiteland Township v. Sun Oil Co., 12 Pa. Cmwlth. 159, 316 A.2d 92 (1974).

§ 3.18

1. Utah Code Ann. § 17–27–102.

2. See supra § 3.15.

3. Putney v. Abington Township, 176 Pa.Super. 463, 108 A.2d 134 (1954).

4. See Watson v. Town Council of Bernalillo, 111 N.M. 374, 805 P.2d 641(App.1991). See also Chrismon v. Guilford County, 322 N.C. 611, 370 S.E.2d 579 (1988); Information Please, Inc. v. County Comm'rs of Morgan County, 42 Colo.App. 392, 600 P.2d 86 (1979); Goffinet v. County of Christian, 65 Ill.2d 40, 2 Ill.Dec. 275, 357 N.E.2d 442 (1976).

5. Griswold v. City of Homer, 925 P.2d 1015, 1023 (Alaska 1996). See also Oakwood at Madison, Inc. v. Township of Madison, 117 N.J.Super. 11, 283 A.2d 353, 357 (1971) (fiscal zoning per se is irrelevant to the statutory purposes of zoning).

6. Concerned Citizens for McHenry, Inc. v. City of McHenry, 76 Ill.App.3d 798, 32 Ill.Dec. 563, 395 N.E.2d 944, 950 (1979).

the public improvements, particularly schools, that must be constructed to accommodate high density development.[7] In some states, this is not a valid use of zoning.[8]

§ 3.19   Promotion of Morals

It is unusual for zoning ordinances to rely expressly on morals as a purpose, and the degree to which such a purpose is permissible is uncertain. Section 1 of the Standard Act provides that local government has the power to promote morals through zoning, but Section 3 does not list morals as an express purpose. Some early cases that authorized the banning of billboards did so on the rationale that immoral activities could be conducted behind them.[1] This presumably was a makeweight argument for courts that accepted, but were unwilling to acknowledge, the fact that aesthetics was the real purpose. This was necessary since aesthetics was once deemed an improper, or inadequate, purpose for which to exercise the police power.[2]

Some zoning ordinances provide that liquor stores and bars must be a certain distance from schools and churches. In one case, a town actually created an overlay "inebriate" district.[3] Other ordinances regulate the location of sexually oriented businesses. These are arguably based, at least in part, on a morals purpose, as well as directed at the secondary effects of such uses. Municipalities that regulate adult uses on "morals" grounds run some risk of running into First Amendment violations if the measure suppresses protected speech.[4]

§ 3.20   Managing Growth

The Standard Act makes no reference to timing and sequencing controls used today to manage growth. Enabling act problems can be encountered with respect to both short and long-term timing controls.

A.   Short-term Controls: Interim Zoning[1]

When an area is not zoned or is zoned but under comprehensive study for rezoning, a significant time delay may occur from the beginning of the planning process to the ultimate adoption of the zoning ordinance. Meanwhile, developers can emasculate the proposed controls by developing in a manner inconsistent with the proposed ordinance. In order to prevent such development, legislative bodies use temporary or

7. National Land & Investment Co. v. Kohn, 419 Pa. 504, 215 A.2d 597 (1965). See also Gruber v. Raritan Township, 39 N.J. 1, 186 A.2d 489 (1962) (proper to zone land exclusively industrial for the purpose of alleviating a heavy tax burden and harmful school congestion).

8. Id. See also infra § 6.6.

§ 3.19

1. St. Louis Gunning Advertisement Co. v. St. Louis, 235 Mo. 99, 137 S.W. 929 (1911), dismissed 231 U.S. 761, 34 S.Ct.

325, 58 L.Ed. 470 (1913). See also McCarthy v. Manhattan Beach, 41 Cal.2d 879, 264 P.2d 932 (1953), cert. denied 348 U.S. 817, 75 S.Ct. 29, 99 L.Ed. 644 (1954).

2. See infra Ch. 12.

3. Jachimek v. Superior Court, 169 Ariz. 317, 819 P.2d 487 (1991).

4. See discussion infra § 10.17.

§ 3.20

1. See related discussion infra §§ 5.28 and 9.5.

interim zoning to freeze or stringently limit land use. The need for speedy enactment of the interim control means that standard procedural safeguards of notice, hearing, referral to planning commissions and the like are usually not possible.

The SZEA did not provide for temporary or interim zoning. In earlier years, some courts invalidated interim zoning for lack of express authority.[2] Other courts, recognizing that proper zoning cannot be done quickly, found implied authority for interim ordinances and upheld it where the time delay was reasonable.[3] Several states now authorize interim zoning by special legislation.[4] The acts generally limit the period of time during which the interim ordinances are effective.

Where valid, the temptation is great to use interim zoning. Its availability, however, may lead the governmental body to adopt permanent regulations at too leisurely a pace, so that courts need to guard against its abuse.[5] It has also been misused to prevent development where the governmental body contemplates acquisition of the property and wants to keep compensation as low as possible.[6]

B. Long-term Growth Management

As is true with the short-term problem of stopping development pending completion of a planning process, municipalities face long-term growth concerns. In the leading case of Golden v. Planning Board of Town of Ramapo,[7] the New York Court of Appeals found that the state's enabling act, patterned after the SZEA, authorized controls on the timing and sequencing of development. A number of states specifically authorize growth management, which is covered in detail in Chapter 9.

§ 3.21   Zoning to Lower Condemnation Costs

Where zoning limits the use of land to fewer uses than those for which the market creates a demand, the value of the land is reduced. The effect of zoning on land is taken into account in determining just compensation in eminent domain proceedings.[1] If government yields to the temptation to use zoning to depress values to lower future condem-

---

2. Alexander v. Minneapolis, 267 Minn. 155, 125 N.W.2d 583 (1963); State ex rel. Kramer v. Schwartz, 336 Mo. 932, 82 S.W.2d 63 (1935).

3. Miller v. Board of Pub. Works, 195 Cal. 477, 234 P. 381 (1925).

4. See, e.g., Colo.Rev.Stat. § 30–28–121; Utah Code Ann. § 17–27–404 (authorizing six month ordinance without public hearing).

5. See discussion infra § 5.28 regarding the relationship between interim controls and vested rights and § 10.9 regarding interim controls as takings.

6. See Note, Stop-gap Measures to Preserve the Status Quo Pending Comprehensive Zoning or Urban Development Legisla-

tion, 14 Case W.Res.L.Rev. 135 (1962); Comment: Stop–Gap and Interim Legislation, A Device to Maintain the Status Quo of an Area Pending the Adoption of a Comprehensive Zoning Ordinance or Amendment Thereto, 18 Syracuse L.Rev. 837 (1967); Annot. 30 A.L.R.3d 1196 (1970).

7. 30 N.Y.2d 359, 334 N.Y.S.2d 138, 285 N.E.2d 291, appeal dismissed 409 U.S. 1003, 93 S.Ct. 436, 440, 34 L.Ed.2d 294 (1972).

§ 3.21

1. See infra § 16.12.

nation costs, the zoning will be held invalid.[2] Since courts do not generally inquire into motives, the circumstances surrounding the zoning must be considered before concluding that the purpose of zoning was to lower values rather than some legitimate purpose. An improper purpose may be evidenced when land that is rezoned is coextensive with land to be condemned, as distinguished from zoning that affects a large number of landowners or is part of a comprehensive rezoning.[3]

Zoning and condemnation proceedings that are substantially concurrent may reveal an improper purpose. When a court suspects that zoning is being used to depress values, it may hold the zoning invalid on other grounds without giving the real basis for its decision. For example, if an "island" is rezoned for agricultural uses in an area the government intends to acquire as an airport, the court may hold it invalid spot zoning.

Official maps, which restrict the right to build in the pathway of planned streets, parks and other public sites, and setback provisions,[4] imposed so that streets can be widened without the necessity of paying for buildings, are examples of other regulations that may limit costs of acquisition in some circumstances.[5]

V. ALTERNATIVES TO ZONING

§ 3.22 Alternatives to Euclidean Zoning and the Standard Act

The SZEA remains the basic enabling act in many states, but it, and its planning counterpart, the Standard Planning Enabling Act, are criticized as outdated. Many shortcomings in zoning enabling laws have been cured or improved upon by piecemeal changes to the SZEA.[1] There have been efforts at more revolutionary change, some more successful than others. As noted earlier, some call for deregulation, preferring to allow land use to be determined by market forces, limited only by the common law of nuisance.[2] Other alternatives are explored in the following sections.

§ 3.23 The Model Land Development Code

A major effort to modernize the land development process at one fell swoop began in 1963 when the Ford Foundation financed an American

---

2. State ex rel. Tingley v. Gurda, 209 Wis. 63, 243 N.W. 317 (1932); Board of Com'rs of State Inst. v. Tallahassee B. & T. Co., 108 So.2d 74 (Fla.App.1958), quashed 116 So.2d 762 (Fla.1959); Ventures in Property I v. Wichita, 225 Kan. 698, 594 P.2d 671 (1979).

3. Kissinger v. Los Angeles, 161 Cal. App.2d 454, 327 P.2d 10 (1958); Eldridge v. Palo Alto, 57 Cal.App.3d 613, 129 Cal.Rptr. 575 (1976).

4. See infra § 4.13.

5. Regarding official maps, see infra § 7.9.

§ 3.22

1. See, e.g., George W. Liebmann, The Modernization of Zoning: Enabling Act Revision as a Means to Reform, 23 Urb.Law. 1 (1991).

2. See supra § 3.1. See also Jan Krasnowiecki, Abolish Zoning, 31 Syr.L.Rev. 719 (1980).

Law Institute effort to develop a model code for land development. Completed in 1976,[1] the Model Land Development Code (MLDC) deals with the physical development of land, so as to maximize social and economic objectives.[2] The MLDC is based on the same assumptions underlying the Standard State Zoning Enabling Act, (SZEA) and its companion, the Standard City Planning Enabling Act (SPEA),[3] which provides powers for planning, control of subdivisions, official maps and regional planning. These assumptions are, first, that government should control privately initiated development rather than be the primary development agency itself as it is in some countries, and, second, that local government should exercise most of the control.

Nevertheless, the MLDC offers significant changes to the land development process. The drafters thought that changes were needed since land use was being regulated by standard acts,"product[s] of the twenties, that notwithstanding a mass of encrustations failed to provide the necessary guidance'"[4] to the legislators, administrators, planners, developers, judges, and lawyers involved in the process. Ad hoc rulings left parties unable to predict what would be allowed. The standard acts also were based on outdated views of lot by lot development that impeded growth.[5] The drafters intended to deal with these weaknesses and to reverse parochial decisionmaking that disregarded regional concerns.[6]

The MLDC integrates zoning and subdivision regulations under the concept of a development ordinance and streamlines the process of obtaining development permission. The most important definition in the MLDC is that of "development," which essentially is any material change in the appearance of a parcel of land or in its shape.[7] Under the MLDC, flexibility devices allow large scale development, which some courts held invalid under the strictures of the SZEA. Where subject to multiple permitting requirements, a developer is given the option of seeking a joint hearing.[8] The MLDC also addresses the legislative/administrative conundrum to clarify roles and provide clear rules of judicial review.[9]

Land development, not planning, is the focus of the act. The position of the drafters was that comprehensive planning was desirable, but was beyond the scope of the MLDC.[10] While the Code does not mandate planning, it encourages it by providing local governments with additional powers if a plan is adopted.[11] Regulation of the state and regional effects

---

§ 3.23

1. American Law Institute, A Model Land Development Code (1976).

2. Id., Art. 3, Commentary at 111–112.

3. U.S. Dep't of Commerce (1928).

4. Model Code, supra note 1, Foreword at x.

5. Id., Article 1, General Provisions, Commentary at 3.

6. Id.

7. Id., § 1–202.

8. Id., § 2–402.

9. Id., § 2–321 and § 9–101. See also commentary to Art. 9 at 365.

10. Id., Art. 3, Commentary at 114.

11. Id., § 3–101 and Note 3.

of local development practices is a major component of the MLDC. Article 7 uses two concepts, developments of regional impacts (DRIs) and areas of critical state concern (ACSC) to provide some state review and for override of local actions. DRIs, as the name suggests, are large scale developments such as airports, public utility transmission lines, major highways, shopping centers, and port facilities.[12] A state adjudicatory board has the power of review over local decisions affecting DRIs.[13] ACSCs are areas containing natural or historical resources of statewide significance or areas affected by, or having a significant effect upon, an existing or proposed public facility.[14] Examples include tidelands, and areas surrounding major highways or airports.[15]

In the more than twenty years that have passed since promulgation of the MLDC, there has been little in the way of direct adoption. Its greatest effect has been its approach to regional controls. Early on, Florida adopted Section 7 of the Model Code that deals with control over developments of regional impact and protection for areas of critical state concern.[16] A few other states have enacted provisions dealing with specific areas that use the MLDC approach.[17] The MLDC has also been influential as persuasive authority in several leading cases supporting growth management[18] and condemning exclusionary zoning.[19]

§ 3.24   Wipeout Mitigation and Windfall Recapture

Police power controls impose losses and create gains that generally go unrecognized. In recent years there has been a spate of legislative proposals around the country to compensate landowners who suffer economic loss from land use controls.[1] While only a few have been enacted, the concern with the losses sustained persists and deters the adoption of new controls needed to protect the public welfare. A notable omission from these proposals, and usually absent from the debate, is the question of recapturing for the public the gains conferred on land-owners by virtue of public improvements and government regulation. Recently, however, commentators have raised for consideration the equity of windfall recapture, often citing to the nineteenth century writings

---

12. See Thomas Pelham, Regulating Developments of Regional Impact: Florida and the Model Land Development Code, 29 U.Fla.L.Rev. 789 (1977).

13. Id., § 7–502. See also Manatee County v. Estech General Chemicals Corp., 402 So.2d 1251 (Fla.App.1981).

14. Id., § 7–201(3).

15. Id., § Art. 3, Commentary at 253.

16. See Thomas Pelham, Regulating Developments of Regional Impact: Florida and the Model Land Development Code, 29 U.Fla.L.Rev. 789 (1977).

17. See Colo.Rev.Stat. §§ 24–65–101 to 106 and the Cape Cod Commission Act, 1989 Mass. Acts 716, noted in Lee R. Epstein, Where Yards Are Wide: Have Land

Use Planning and Law Gone Astray ? 21 Wm. & Mary Envtl.L. & Pol'y Rev. 345, 379, n. 107 (1997).

18. Golden v. Planning Bd. of Town of Ramapo, 30 N.Y.2d 359, 334 N.Y.S.2d 138, 146, 285 N.E.2d 291, 297 n. 6, appeal dismissed 409 U.S. 1003, 93 S.Ct. 436, 440, 34 L.Ed.2d 294 (1972).

19. Southern Burlington County N.A.A.C.P. v. Township of Mt. Laurel, 67 N.J. 151, 210, 336 A.2d 713, 743 n. 132 (1975); Associated Home Builders v. City of Livermore, 18 Cal.3d 582, 557 P.2d 473, 497, 135 Cal.Rptr. 41, 65 (1976).

§ 3.24

1. See discussion of takings legislation infra § 10.11.

of Henry George, particularly his classic work Progress and Poverty, and to the late twentieth century work of Donald Hagman.[2]

Donald Hagman, coauthor of the precursor to this book,[3] was an ardent student and advocate of addressing the fairness of land use controls by systems of wipeout mitigation and windfall recapture. Hagman and Dean Misczynski published through the Planners Press of the American Planning Association a major collection of essays in 1978 entitled Windfalls For Wipeouts: Land Value Capture and Compensation that serves as a major resource in the area. The following sections are edited versions of chapters extracted from that work and other writings of Don Hagman.

§ 3.25 Wipeouts Defined and Illustrated[1]

A wipeout is any decrease in the value of real estate other than one caused by the owner or by general deflation. Decreases in value caused by the owner are not wipeouts. A pyromaniac burns down his house—that's not a wipeout; a farmer wastes his land by improper cultivation—that's not a wipeout; a speculator misjudges the market and pays too much for land or sells it too low—that's not a wipeout. Nor is it a wipeout if real estate decreases in value because of general deflation, because the property is still worth the same amount in real terms.

There remain a multitude of decreases that result from other factors that enter into the pool of wipeouts. For example, there may be wipeouts resulting from land-use controls implementing environmental protection measures. There are some who believe such wipeouts should be mitigated. If so, how about decreases caused by other types of regulations (e.g., traffic controls, prohibition of alcohol), or by planning, taxation, or government projects? The resulting decreases can be direct or indirect. For example, the opening of a new highway may indirectly decrease the value of property along the old route. These decreases may result from government action at all levels—local, regional, state, or federal.

Decreases can also be caused by natural disasters, such as earthquakes and floods. Finally, decreases can be caused by the actions of

2. Joan Williams, Recovering the Full Complexity of our Traditions: New Developments in Property Theory, 46 J.Legal Educ. 596, 606 (1996); J. Peter Byrne, Ten Arguments for the Abolition of the Regulatory Takings Doctrine, 22 Ecol.L.Q. 89, 126–127, n. 240 (1995); Patrick A. Parenteau, Who's Taking What? Property Rights, Endangered Species, and the Constitution, 6 Fordham Envtl.L.J. 619, 635 (1995); Marc N. Melnick, New Avenues for Special Assessment Financing, 25 Urb.Law. 539, 556–558 and n. 145 (1993); Thomas E. Roberts, Zoning by Condemnation and Assessment, 18 Wake For. J. 21 (1987).

3. Donald G. Hagman and Julian Conrad Juergensmeyer, Urban Planning and Land Development Law (2d ed.1986).

§ 3.25

1. This section is an edited extraction from Windfalls for Wipeouts: Land Value Capture and Compensation, ch. 1 (D. Hagman & D. Misczynski, eds. 1978). Changes and omissions are not marked with ellipses. Permission has been granted by the publisher: Planners Press, American Planning Association, Chicago, Ill.

others in the community (e.g., by a neighbor who builds a smoky factory next door), or by a change in community tastes. For example, if nobody goes skiing anymore, ski resort land would likely decrease in value. Many of these community actions and tastes are reflected in the property market as wipeouts.

Consider the following hypothetical example:

Mr. B bought a lot on Elm Street for $5,000 in 1965 which was zoned single family. He did nothing to his lot for 10 years. However, the city acquired an adjacent 20–acre site upwind of Mr. B's property for a garbage dump, which it later began using. Mr. C's property, on the sunny side of B's property, was rezoned for a 100–story skyscraper apartment which Mr. C then built. Mr. B sought a rezoning to 100–story skyscraper, too, but it was rejected by the planning commission because "it would be unhealthy to have apartment dwellers live near garbage dumps." Mr. B, however, appealed to the city council. The appeal drew attention to the property and it was discovered to be the only known habitat of the hexibilibus (a rare insect). A quickly formed Friends of the Hexibilibus Society packed the city council on the night of Mr. B's appeal and demanded that the property be placed in the CHA (conservation, historic, and antiquities) zone. Any land use can be made of the property in the CHA zone which is consistent with the reason for its designation, in this case, anything consistent with the health, safety, and welfare of hexibilibi.

The city council complied with the Friends' request and zoned CHA. In 1975, Mr. B agreed to sell the lot to the Friends of the Hexibilibus Society at its market value. The market value of hexibilibi sites downwind of garbage dumps and on the shady side of 100–story skyscrapers is $5. Five thousand dollars to $5 is a wipeout.

Note that B's wipeout could be said to be caused by government (project acquisition and use and regulation of Mr. B and Mr. C) and community action (Mr. C built his 100–story skyscraper and the market does not regard garbage dumps or high buildings as desirable neighbors).

The environmental decade of the 70s called forth a host of new tough wipeout-causing plans and controls. Traditional controls such as subdivision and zoning regulations became more restrictive. Planning became more pervasive and complicated. Plans took on regulatory effects, as statutes were amended to require consistency with plans.[2] Where statutes were not amended, courts began to give new weight to plans, thus giving them regulatory effects. Permit systems were overlaid on traditional controls so that development was often possible only after obtaining several permits from several different agencies. In short, nearly all land use regulations are potential progenitors of wipeouts.

2. See supra § 2.11.

§ 3.26 Windfalls Defined and Illustrated[1]

A windfall is an increase in the value of real estate—other than that caused by the owner—or by general inflation. As with wipeouts, windfalls are caused by a variety of factors. Some meanings of the British term betterment are roughly synonymous with windfall; some are not.

The best-known definition for betterment is:

any increase in the value of land (including the buildings thereon) arising from central or local government action, whether positive, e.g., by the execution of public works or improvements, or negative, e.g., by the imposition of restrictions on other land.

The term [betterment] is not, however, generally understood to include enhancement in the value of property arising from general community influences, such as the growth of urban populations.[2]

Consider the following hypothetical example:

Mr. A bought a lot on Elm Street for $5,000 in 1965 that was zoned for single-family use. He did nothing with the lot for 10 years, during which there was considerable high-class private development in the area. A millionaire who owned 20 acres of land adjoining Mr. A's lot died, his will leaving the acreage to the Horticultural Society of America with an endowment to establish a formal garden. Mr. A's lot thus received the enhancement of a park-like setting. The formal garden being the diadem of the city's aesthetic resources, it decided to enhance the approaches to it by downzoning the property around the formal gardens for open space use. The downzoning did not include Mr. A's lot, which the city rezoned for 100–story commercial residential uses to serve the needs of city dwellers who came seeking quiet in the garden. To minimize automobile congestion, the city also rerouted a planned subway, opening a station near the gardens and adjacent to Mr. A's lot. Mr. A sold his lot for $5,000,000 in 1975. Five thousand dollars to $5,000,000—that is a windfall, one that resulted from government regulation, a government project, and community action.

The following are reasons for recapturing windfalls: (1) Revenues would result. (2) The community is asking only for a return of wealth it creates. (3) The windfall recapture tax (charge, exaction, fee, levy, and so forth) would not raise land prices because supply is fixed. (4) When the public needs to acquire land it should not have to pay a price increased by its own activities. (5) It is a less socialistic scheme than public land ownership.

§ 3.26

1. This section is an edited extraction from Windfalls for Wipeouts: Land Value Capture and Compensation, ch. 2 (D. Hagman & D. Misczynski, eds. 1978). Changes and omissions are not marked with ellipses. Permission has been granted by the publisher: Planners Press, American Planning Association, Chicago, Ill.

2. English Expert Committee on Compensation and Betterment (Uthwatt Committee), Final Report, ¶ 260, Cmd. No. 6386 (1942).

Whether sufficient support exists to recapture windfalls depends on answers to questions similar to those asked about wipeout mitigation. Some will not be supportive because windfalls from personal property are not recaptured; others will not be supportive because windfall is defined too broadly; still others will be boggled by the measurement problem or the difficulty of drawing precise lines or by other administrative concerns.

There are five additional problems. First, while the argument is not made that there is a right to risk and lose, some argue that there is a right to keep if the risk-taker wins. Second, while some private property interests are strident in their call for wipeout mitigation, the public is not strident in its call for windfall recapture. Third, while government is often large and diverse enough to be able to distribute the cost of wipeout payments in a way that is not burdensome, especially if its accounts can be balanced by windfall recapture, the recapture of windfalls can run into resistance because of hardship. For example, if the windfall recapture technique selected is imposed on individuals and enterprises with small amounts of property and if it applies at the time there is only a paper windfall, i.e., no actual cash flow, the "little person" may have great difficulty meeting the windfall recapture payment. Fourth, windfall recapture might be most acceptable when capital gains taxes are not being used. Capital gains taxes have been in use in the United States as long as income has been taxed; capital gains have been taxed only recently in Canada and England and still are not taxed in Australia and New Zealand. If there were an expansion of capital gains taxes, there might be a tendency to view them as surrogate windfall recapture devices and dampen any tendency for further recapture. Fifth, there is some movement toward public land ownership as a way of keeping community-caused increments in the public treasury. England's Community Land Act, 1975, was partially so motivated and Australia and Canada are experimenting with land-banking.

§ 3.27 Implementing Land Value Capture and Compensation Programs[1]

Under a rational system of land-use controls, windfalls might roughly equal wipeouts on the theory that the price of land is largely determined by the demand for it.[2] If land-use controls prohibit a demand

§ 3.27

1. This section is an edited extraction from Windfalls for Wipeouts: Land Value Capture and Compensation, ch. 3 (D. Hagman & D. Misczynski, eds. 1978). Changes and omissions are not marked with ellipses. Permission has been granted by the publisher: Planners Press, American Planning Association, Chicago, Ill. Footnotes have been renumbered.

2. "The public control of the use of land * * * necessarily has the effect of shifting land values: in other words, it increases the value of some land and decreases the value of other land, but it does not destroy land values. Neither the total demand for development nor its average annual rate is materially affected, if at all, by planning ordinances." Expert Committee on Compensation and Betterment (Uthwatt Committee), Final Report, Cmd. 6386 E 26 (London: H.M.S.O., 1942). See also Freeman, Give and Take: Distributing Local Environmental Control Through Land Use Regulation, 60 Minn.L.Rev. 883 (1976).

from finding a supply in a particular place, the demand is shunted elsewhere. Indeed, under a rational planning system that reduces imperfections in the market, planning could be wealth-creative, that is, it could lead to more windfalls than wipeouts.

However, under the "Byzantine"—to use Fred Bosselman's phrase[3] —system of land use control in America, wipeouts may exceed windfalls. Developers must spend money learning the ropes and shepherding their projects through the chambers. Windfalls (which might otherwise be recaptured) are whittled away by administrative costs. Similarly, because of the bubbling cacophony of multitudinous edicts, it is unclear where the supply is. The demand goes around searching for it, the search being another high administrative cost. In short, strong controls produce both windfalls and wipeouts in significant quantities.

Under the existing system, windfalls and wipeouts are largely left to fall where they will. Failure to recapture windfalls and mitigate wipeouts leads to several deficiencies in the planning system. First, so long as we continue to have a nonsystem of planning, who gets the goodies and who gets deprived will be perceived as arbitrary and capricious.

Even if the Mr. Wipeoutee B's of the world could be persuaded that an offending regulator's action was justified by some brooding omniplanning in the sky, they are not likely to feel that they deserved their fate. And the Mr. Windfaller A's of the world are not likely to believe that they really earned theirs. Thus, even if planning is perceived to be in the public interest, the resulting windfalls and wipeouts may be regarded as arbitrary and capricious. It is another case of society pursuing otherwise laudable goals at the expense or profit of only a few of its members. If the burdened few could receive some relief, particularly if at the expense of unintended beneficiaries, one is hard disposed to understand why society doesn't go right out and do it.

Under the existing system the planner is often perceived as one who plans in the public interest without any concern for the benefits and costs to particular individuals. Indeed, there are some who fear that if the planner knew too much about the effect on individuals, planning might be inhibited. But one cannot make a positive rational case for crashing through with a plan entirely oblivious of effects on individuals. A windfalls for wipeouts system would identify the windfallers and the wipeoutees.

Further, to the extent that the planner has regard for citizen participation, the signals from the participants in the existing system may be wrong. Planners are often warmed by the support received for a plan, not realizing that the support may only be coming from those who are windfallers under the plan. Even if the plan were contrary to the overall public interest, the planner would still have their support. Similarly, the planner is often discouraged by opposition from those

---

3. Address by Fred Bosselman, ALI– ABA Land Planning and Regulation of De- velopment Course (Mar. 18, 1976).

"special interests," the wipeoutees, who fail to be sanguine about the public interest in the face of their impending financial loss.

Under a system of windfalls for wipeouts the planner is made aware of the windfalls and wipeouts yet need not be inhibited in the face of them. That is because the windfalls are partially recaptured and the wipeouts partially mitigated.

Even if the existing system is regarded as fair, as more than a fatalistic lottery, there are still those who will struggle mightily to disrupt a good plan because there are unrecaptured windfalls to be made and unmitigated wipeouts to be avoided.

Under the existing system, where great unrecaptured windfalls and unmitigated wipeouts can occur, manipulators sometimes urge the application of land-use control not because they believe in it but merely because they know how to manipulate it better than others (sometimes benefiting from shifting values from wipeouts caused others). For example, at least in times past when members of the real estate industry dominated local planning boards, land-use controls might be urged upon the city by members of the industry, who observed that "[w]ithout zoning you can have a gas station on a corner, an expensive house down the street, and a drive-in hamburger stand around the corner." Then, getting themselves appointed to the planning boards they so piously opined the need for, they do not resist the temptation to clothe their public duties with the private interests of themselves and their friends. No wonder then that "[i]n a zoned city, you can have a gas station on a corner, an expensive house down the street, and a drive-in hamburger stand around the corner."[4]

Under the present system, the most intense heat and participation from interested parties appears not at the comprehensive, policy-making level, but when that policy begins to affect and create windfalls or wipeouts for particular parcels. These controversies often involve the most narrow externalities problems, such as should a convenience store be permitted in this single-family residential neighborhood. Public decision-makers spend much of their time on these largely neighborhood squabble-resolving issues. Exhausted by these almost private concerns, many have little time or energy left to attend to the broader public interest.

Under some windfalls for wipeouts systems, these neighborhood externalities problems could be partially resolved by transfer payments, for example, the convenience store owner would be forced to share the windfall with those who are wiped out. There would be less incentive for making the change, less at stake if the change occurred. Neighborhood squabble resolving should therefore consume less time of public decision-makers.

---

4. Both quotations are taken from a cartoon appearing in Planning, Jan. 1973, at 22 (reproduced from the New York Times).

Under the present system, a city plans and zones some areas for intensive development; others for unintensive use. It places infrastructure accordingly. The result is that land prices are lower in the area scheduled for unintensive use. Where does the intensive (e.g., multiple-family) developer go to reap his windfall? He obtains a rezoning.

Thus, under the present system, planmaking invites its own destruction. Under a windfalls for wipeouts system, however, the multifamily developer will have less incentive to "break" the plan, for part of the windfall will be recaptured. Therefore, a windfalls for wipeouts system may lead to more consistent plan implementation.

Under the existing system, wipeouts are not generally mitigated, windfalls are not generally recaptured. There is now considerable pressure to pay compensation for wipeouts. When that step is considered, the first question that arises is, who will pay for it? While this seems to pose considerable difficulty, it needn't, for windfall recapture could fund wipeout mitigation. Certainly it is fair to do so. Landowners can hardly claim they should be paid for wipeouts but retain the right to keep windfalls.

There is no shortage of techniques if society has the will to apply a windfalls for wipeouts system. Some systems have already been tried. An English scheme still in effect in Australia recaptures betterment and mitigates worsenment from plans.[5] Zoning by special assessment financed eminent domain is the name for an early American scheme to pay off those damaged by zoning and assess those benefited.[6] It was used to make zoning constitutional and could still be used to make it fairer. Transferable development rights,[7] an American invention, is designed to "pay off" the wipeout from downzoning by allowing development rights to be used elsewhere. One or more of a variety of techniques could be used as a guide for wipeout mitigation, and windfall recapture.

§ 3.28 Zoning by Special Assessment Financed Eminent Domain (ZSAFED)

One windfalls and wipeouts technique goes by the name of zoning by special assessment financed eminent domain (ZSAFED). It was used in the early years of the twentieth century when there were doubts about validity of zoning under the police power.[1] Under this system, when the right to develop was restricted causing an economic loss, compensation was paid. Money to pay those restricted came from assessments that were levied on land benefited by the restrictions. The practice was never

---

5. See Windfalls for Wipeouts: Land Value Capture and Compensation, (D. Hagman & D. Misczynski, eds. 1978).

6. See infra § 3.28.

7. See infra § 9.9.

§ 3.28

1. Anderson, Zoning in Minnesota; Eminent Domain vs. Police Power, 16 Nat'l Mun.Rev. 624 (1927). See generally Erwin S. Barbee, Annot., Validity and Construction of "Zoning with Compensation" Regulation, 41 A.L.R.3d 636 (1972).

widespread, and not surprisingly, when the Supreme Court held zoning via the police power valid under the constitution, its use faded quickly. There are vestiges of the practice. Some parts of Minneapolis and St. Paul, and of Kansas City, Missouri are still zoned by eminent domain.[2]

A. A Hypothetical Example [3]

Nirvana is a mythical unspoiled island located just offshore of an expanding metropolis. Although it was zoned many years ago for single family residences, the island was never developed. The owners have recently announced plans to build on their property. Conservationists oppose the development, but the government does not have enough money to purchase the island.

A politically acceptable compromise would be to develop only the south half of the island, preserving the north half for conservation purposes. Accordingly, experts of zoning by special assessment financed eminent domain (ZSAFED) propose a plan to implement the compromise.[4] While the south half would be upzoned to multiple family use, the north half would be downzoned to conservation and recreation uses. The owners of the north half would be injured to the extent that their property has lost value. Under ZSAFED, damages would be paid to these owners since the right to develop the north half would be treated as if it had been taken by eminent domain.[5] Owners of the south half would enjoy an increase in the value of their property from the change in zoning not only because the supply of property in competition for sales would shrink but also because the south half could be developed more intensively. Therefore, a special assessment would be levied against the south half property, capturing the windfall to finance payment for damages to the north half.

B. History of ZSAFED in Missouri and Minnesota

ZSAFED was invented in 1893 by residents of Gladstone Boulevard in Kansas City who were attempting to preserve the residential charac-

---

2. Minn.Stat.Ann.   §§ 462.12–462.17. City of Kansas City v. Kindle, 446 S.W.2d 807 (Mo.1969) (upholding such zoning).

3. The balance of this section is an edited extract from Donald G. Hagman, Zoning by Special Assessment Financed Eminent Domain (ZSAFED), 28 U.Fla. L.Rev. 655 (1976). Changes and omissions are not marked with ellipses. Permission has been granted by the University of Florida Law Review. Comparable material can also be found in chapter 22 of Windfalls for Wipeouts: Land Value Capture and Compensation (D. Hagman & D. Misczynski, eds. 1978). Footnotes have been renumbered. See also Bosselman, The Third Alternative in Zoning Litigation, 17 Zoning Dig. 73 (1965).

4. For a discussion of alternative plans, see Carmichael, Transferable Development

Rights as a Basis for Land Use Control, 2 Fla.St.U.L.Rev. 35 (1975); Costonis, Development Rights Transfer: An Exploratory Essay, 83 Yale L.J. 75 (1973); Marcus, Mandatory Development Rights Transfer and the Taking Clause: The Case of Manhattan's Tudor City Parks, 24 Buff.L.Rev. 77 (1974); Rose, Transfer of Development Rights: A Preview of an Expanding Concept, 3 Real Estate L.J. 330 (1975); Rose, Proposal for the Separation and Marketability of Development Rights as a Technique to Preserve Open Space, 2 Real Estate L.J. 635 (1974).

5. The "as if" qualifier is important. ZSAFED's compensation scheme, though it carries an "eminent domain" label, is more an exercise of the police power than the eminent domain power.

ter of their street.[6] The Gladstonians petitioned to exclude business uses within 159 feet of the boulevard and offered to pay damages or assess benefits to affected property owners. Perhaps since experts opined that boulevard property would appreciate from the restriction and no damages would be paid, some disgruntled property owners brought suit seeking to invalidate the implementing ordinance. The basic question was whether the restriction constituted a taking for public use. The court had no trouble construing this restriction as a taking and found, in addition, that the city charter, which permitted the use of eminent domain for public purposes, was sufficient to authorize the ordinance.

ZSAFED did not surface in the Missouri appellate courts again until 1966.[7] Coleman Highlands, a residential area in Kansas City, had been restricted to single family dwellings. Most of the houses contained 1 to 14 rooms and were occupied by families with children. Some houses located along a major thoroughfare had been converted to apartment units. Recalling the 1893 ordinance, the vast majority of Coleman Highlands residents asked for the applications of ZSAFED, and it was instituted.

The application of ZSAFED resulted in a determination of damages of $37,588.88 and an assessment for benefits of the same amount. Most of the damages were to be paid to the landowners of apartment units located along the thoroughfare. These landowners, the primary group unhappy with the imposition of ZSAFED to enable the single family restriction to be enforced, attacked the ordinance in court.[8] ZSAFED was sustained, as the court applauded this zoning technique for its usefulness in preserving a residential neighborhood and for its method of compensating landowners for any demonstrably substantial damages that were suffered.[9]

In 1912, some residents of Minneapolis desired to live in areas undisturbed by apartment and commercial use. The city council met this demand by precluding the erection of commercial buildings and apartment houses over two and one-half stories on the exclusive Dupont Avenue South.[10] When questions were raised about the legality of a city's imposing such a restriction, the state legislature supplied the necessary authority.[11] Thus, zoning was instituted in Minnesota, and on this basis the Minneapolis building inspector began denying building permits for apartment buildings. The Minnesota courts, however, concluded that zoning was not a proper exercise of the police power.[12] In response to the invalidation of their authority, planners felt that payment of compensation for the taking of the right to develop for apartment and commercial

6. Kansas City v. Liebi, 298 Mo. 569, 252 S.W. 404 (1923).

7. Kindle v. Kansas City, 401 S.W.2d 385 (Mo.1966).

8. Id.

9. Id. at 816.

10. 38 Minneapolis Council Proceedings 1154 (1912).

11. Ch. 98, § 1, [1913] Minn.Laws 102; Ch. 420, §§ 1–4, [1913] Minn.Laws 618.

12. State ex rel. Roerig v. Minneapolis, 136 Minn. 479, 162 N.W. 477 (1917); State ex rel. Lachtman v. Houghton, 134 Minn. 226, 158 N.W. 1017 (1916).

use would overcome constitutional objections. This theory was based on cases that had upheld restriction on the right to develop if compensation was paid.[13] Therefore, "in great haste and with a minimum of consultation * * *,"[14] ZSAFED came to Minnesota, authorized by state statute.[15]

The Act, which applied to Minneapolis, St. Paul, and Duluth, permitted a city council to create restricted residential districts on petition of 50 percent of the owners of real estate in an area. The city was given the power of eminent domain to acquire the right to develop for anything but residential purposes. After notice to the record title holder of the property, a visit to the property, and a hearing, appointed appraisers determined the amount of damages to each parcel from the taking. They also assessed benefits in the district. These benefits were offset against damages, leaving a net damage or net benefit to each parcel. Net benefits were specifically assessed, although the total benefits assessed in the district could not exceed the total amount of damages plus costs.[16] The last step of the procedure fell to the city council, which confirmed the determination of damages and benefits. The damages were "a charge upon the city * * * [while] assessments [for benefits were] * * * a lien and charge upon the respective lands until paid."[17] If there was a delay in payments, interest was charged on the award of damages.

Maps of the restricted region were filed to establish the boundaries of the districts. The county auditor received a copy of the maps and the assessments on each parcel and collected them along with general property taxes. If nonresidential buildings were thereafter erected on restricted property, the structures were declared to be nuisances. After operating under this system for a short time, cities found that appraisals were becoming expensive; thus, the statute was amended to make it clear that appraisal costs would be assessed to the area rather than paid by the city.[18]

Thwarted by the ordinance, the owner of a three story apartment house in one of the restricted residence districts challenged the ZSAFED system in court. In a three to two decision, the Minnesota supreme court decided in favor of the landowner.[19] The court noted eminent domain may be used only to acquire property for public use. "A condemnation against an apartment house is not for a public use."[20] The court distinguished a series of other cases that had upheld the use of regulation with compensation to preserve aesthetic vistas around public facilities.[21]

13. Attorney Gen. v. Williams, 174 Mass. 476, 55 N.E. 77 (1899).

14. Rockwood, The Minnesota Residence District Act of 1915, 1 Minn.L.Rev. 487, 490–91 (1917).

15. Ch. 128, [1915] Minn.Laws 180 (now Minn.Stat. § 462.12–.17).

16. In re Establishment of Restricted Residence Dist., 151 Minn. 115, 186 N.W. 292 (1922).

17. Ch. 128, § 3, [1915] Minn.Laws 186.

18. Ch. 297, [1919] Minn.Laws 305.

19. State ex rel. Twin City Bldg. & Inv. Co. v. Houghton, 144 Minn. 1, 174 N.W. 885 (1919).

20. Id. at 12, 174 N.W. at 888.

21. United States v. Gettysburg Elec. Ry. Co., 160 U.S. 668, 16 S.Ct. 427, 40 L.Ed. 576 (1896); Attorney Gen. v. Williams, 174 Mass. 476, 55 N.E. 77 (1899);

As a commentator subsequently noted, the decision "seal[ed] one avenue of progress in the general program of the improvement of city life."[22] This criticism moved the court; when the case was reargued, one judge changed his mind and ZSAFED was found to be constitutional. The new majority analogized the public utilization of ZSAFED to the implementation of a drainage district and lauded the new act on policy grounds.[23]

At the same time ZSAFED was being refined, zoning under the police power was becoming well accepted and, in fact, Minneapolis had continued to zone without paying compensation. When ordinary zoning was challenged in 1925, the Minnesota supreme court upheld it, indicating a preference for zoning by exercise of the police power.

> [A]n award of damages to obtain a restricted residential district is largely theoretical, and, resulting in a possible incumbering of property with something akin to an easement, is practically objectionable. If restricted residential districts are to be established, there are substantial reasons why the result should be accomplished through the exercise of the police power.[24]

Fortunately, there had been enough districts established under ZSAFED by 1925 so that its merits could be subject to the crucible of experience. In one case, for example, a landowner in Duluth sold property by means of a contract calling for delivery of a deed without encumbrances.[25]

In State ex rel. Madsen v. Houghton,[26] a multiple dwelling building permit was denied to the owner of a lot that had been restricted under ZSAFED and subsequently zoned under the police power for multiple dwellings. Holding that ZSAFED restrictions were not eradicated when the property was zoned for multiple family housing, the court noted that a procedure for undoing the ZSAFED restrictions had been provided. The owner or his predecessors had been paid damages previously; therefore, he could not now reverse the restrictions except by persuading a sufficient number of the other owners to petition the city council and to accept a possible assessment when the restriction is removed.

C. *Modernizing ZSAFED*

ZSAFED was originally devised because zoning without compensation was thought to be constitutionally impermissible. The courts have since allowed governments to severely restrict usage of property through zoning under the police power without paying compensation.[27] Modern ZSAFED would be implemented for moral and political, rather than

Bunyan v. Commissioners, 167 A.D. 457, 153 N.Y.S. 622 (1915); In re New York, 57 App.Div. 166, 68 N.Y.S. 196 (1901).

22. Comment, The Failure of the Minnesota Residence District Act, 4 Minn. L.Rev. 50 (1919).

23. State ex rel. Twin City Bldg. & Inv. Co. v. Houghton, 144 Minn. 1, 19–20, 176 N.W. 159, 162 (1920).

24. State ex rel. Beery v. Houghton, 164 Minn. 146, 148, 204 N.W. 569, 569 (1925).

25. Summers v. Midland Co., 167 Minn. 453, 209 N.W. 323 (1926).

26. 182 Minn. 77, 233 N.W. 831 (1930).

27. There are limits on how severe the regulation may be. See infra §§ 10.2–9.

legal, reasons. First, a person whose property loses value because of government regulation would be entitled to receive payment for the damages as in an eminent domain proceeding. Second, a person whose property increases in value solely because of regulation by government should not be allowed to keep the unearned profit. To effectuate these goals today, ZSAFED must be modernized.

The fact that ZSAFED, as originally practiced, involved appraisals by specially appointed persons increased administrative costs. Tax assessors could do appraisals in a modern system, which would avoid duplication of costs. The assessor's present job is to measure the market value of property and to reassess property affected in value by a rezoning. ZSAFED would require only a computation of the change in value.

It would not be desirable to attempt to compensate 100 percent of damages or to recapture 100 percent of benefits because assessments are incapable of precisely reflecting true value. Furthermore, total elimination of risk could lead to stagnation and lack of change. ZSAFED should only minimize risk by moderating wipeout and windfall rather than excluding them entirely. Paying damages or assessing benefits of 50 to 75 percent of the change in value would move in the direction of equity without eliminating the risk inherent in a free market system. Similarly, slight changes in value should be ignored. Before ZSAFED would operate, a substantial change—for example more than ten percent—should occur.

In most instances benefits will equal damages. If property is downzoned, other property must become more valuable because competitive supply is reduced. ZSAFED should recapture benefit even though it is more than is necessary to pay damages from a particular change in zoning. Recapturing all ascertainable benefits would provide funds to pay damages in those instances when damages but not benefits can be determined. In addition, one goal of a modern ZSAFED should be to recapture windfalls. Sharing the benefit is the price of insurance against damage; moreover, planning may actually create wealth by imposing order.[28] Benefits should exceed damages in a community in which the planning is continually better; thus, the ZSAFED fund might show a profit. In such a case, the excess fund could be applied toward general government functions.

Whereas zoning under the police power has often been too easily changed, ZSAFED was almost impossible to change in Minnesota, but extreme rigidity is as undesirable as frequent rezoning. Under modern ZSAFED, the regulating government, landowners, or voter residents in the area should be permitted to initiate rezoning. Expanding the opportunity for change would not result in the upzoning pressures traditional

---

28. Chicago School economists argue to the contrary that wealth generation is greatest under free market conditions and that government control either dampens the increase or causes net loss. Bernard H. Siegan, Land Use Without Zoning (1972) (author makes the most elaborate case for the Chicago School in the context of land use).

to zoning under the police power since recapture eliminates much of the landowner's incentive to seek rezoning to a more intensive use.

Increasingly, it is no longer the case that zoning is the only control of land use. Local governments are shifting to permit systems of control, and control may also be exercised by one or more regional, state, or federal authorities. Therefore, a rezoning alone does not trigger realization of benefit or reception of damage. ZSAFED should be expanded to accommodate the changing kinds of controls on land use. Developers must usually obtain various permits before initiating a new project. This system of multiple permits from different levels of government complicates matters. A benefit is measured as the change in values before and after, but before and after *what* is the crucial issue. If, for example, five permissions are required before development can proceed, does the assessor make a determination of assessable benefits as each is obtained? Alternatively, since the project is not viable until all permits are obtained, should the "before" value be calculated as if no permit had been obtained and the "after" value as if all permits had been obtained?

The problem is a muddle of the first order. Perhaps the solution is as follows: if there is a governmental activity after which actual development would be possible when it was not previously possible, that activity is the event that triggers the determination of benefit or damage. The solution has problems, particularly if ZSAFED is built on an assessment system because the market will anticipate the benefit-damage triggering activity. When the first permit is issued, value may rise a bit; on the second permit value would increase a little more, and so on. The increase in value between the fourth and fifth permits may also be small, but under the suggested solution, the assessor will have to determine benefit or damage as if all five permits had been obtained at once.

The manner of multiple controls raises one other issue. Under a 1931 amendment to the Minnesota ZSAFED statute, other regulations were to be disregarded for the calculation of benefits and damages when ZSAFED was undone. This would not be the case under modernized ZSAFED since all land use controls would carry compensation and recapture incidents.

Benefits and damages from governmental development projects should also be included in a modernized ZSAFED. For example, if a government built a new causeway to Nirvana, making it more accessible, the benefits should be recaptured in part. ZSAFED would thus tax the cost of improvements in the same way as traditional special assessments[29] but with the difference that large projects would be included and recapture would not be limited to costs. Similarly, if the government built a regional garbage dump on the north end of Nirvana, owners of property on the south end could be compensated by a modernized ZSAFED.

---

29. For a more detailed discussion of the history of special assessments, see Windfalls for Wipeouts? Land Value Gains and Losses from Planning and a Catalog of Methods for Redistributing Them, ch. 13 (D. Hagman & D. Misczynski, eds. 1978).

Under ancient ZSAFED, each restricted residential district was a distinct entity. Because damages from restricting property to low density residential use were often offset to each landowner by the benefit of having neighboring property limited to residential use, little money was exchanged within a district and none could exchange hands outside the district for the law did not cover extradistrict benefits and damages. Under modern ZSAFED, there would be no districts. Damages and benefits would be identified by changes in value wherever they occurred. For example, if property was rezoned commercial for a shopping center and resulted in more than a 10 percent increase in value, a special assessment would be levied. Neighboring property might increase or decrease in value, and ZSAFED would assess benefits and pay damages accordingly. If the damage showed up far from the rezoned site, such as the location of an older shopping center, ZSAFED would pay compensation.

Separate accounting for the damage caused and the benefit resulting from each change would add an unnecessary complication. Rather, when an assessment is made, payments would go into a common fund; damage payments would be made from the same fund. Revolving funds are customarily used for local improvements that are funded partially by special assessments and partially by government. This obviates the need to issue bonds.

It may be necessary, for constitutional reasons, to pay damages when the damaging event occurs, but it will not be possible to recapture all benefits immediately. Suppose, for example, the property of a single family homeowner increases in value from $20,000 to $40,000 as the result of a rezoning. The assessment would be $10,000, and a lien would be imposed immediately on the property for that amount. For political reasons, however, immediate payment could not be exacted. The conventional practice of accepting payments for special assessments by installments would be followed. For example, the assessee might be given 18 years to pay at $500 per year plus interest. The amount would be added to the property tax bill and collected in the same way as other special assessments.

If damage payments also could be paid by installment, then it would not be necessary to issue bonds to make such payments before the ZSAFED revolving fund had been established. Damage payments could be used to offset property taxes. In actuality, while some property may remain unaffected, other land is likely to be buffeted by damages and benefits frequently, each canceling the other in a frenzy of activity that only computers could reconcile.

The administration of ZSAFED, although complicated, is essentially the same as conventional property tax and special assessment practices. Moreover, modern ZSAFED could replace many bodies of damage mitigation law that result in high administrative costs, such as nuisance, damages in eminent domain to severed parcels, inverse condemnation for regulatory and planning blight, and invalidation of land use regulation under the "taking" clause. It could also supplement or replace special assessments for particular projects, exactions on development permissions, and impact taxes.

It is not clear that ZSAFED is an answer to windfalls for wipeouts problems. However, precedent certainly has established that ZSAFED is valid, and this precedent should continue as ZSAFED is modernized. Armed with early experience and improved by the theory developed in connection with transferable development rights research, ZSAFED may well have a future as well as a past.

Chapter 4

TYPES OF ZONES AND USES

Analysis

I. INTRODUCTION

II. USE ZONES

III. HEIGHT, BULK, AND SETBACK CONTROLS

I. INTRODUCTION

§ 4.1 Types of Zones: In General

The Standard State Zoning Enabling Act empowers a legislative body to:

> regulate and restrict the height, number of stories, and size of buildings and other structures, the percentage of a lot that may be occupied, the size of yards, courts, and other open spaces, the density of population, and the location and use of buildings, structures and land for trade, industry, residence, or other purposes.[1]

To do so:

> [T]he local legislative body may divide the municipality into districts of such number, shape and area as may be * * * best * * * and within such districts it may regulate and restrict the erection, construction, alteration, repair, or use of buildings, structures, or land.[2]

The authority provided is the basis for four kinds of controls: use, height, bulk and density. Use zones for "trade, industry, residence or other purposes" are designated by an ordinance that either precisely describes the areas zoned in each category or incorporates a precise map showing the areas. Typically, there are several kinds of residential zones, e.g., single-family, two-family, and various multi-family classifications such as garden apartments and high-rise apartments, several kinds of commercial zones, and a few industrial categories. Frequently, there are also specialized use zones for institutional uses, historic areas, airports, and the like.[3]

An ordinance may establish a variety of height limitations for structures in the various use zones. Height regulations may be stated in terms of maximum permitted heights or number of stories or both. In some instances separate height zones may be adopted. Where this is done, the height zones generally have the same boundaries as the use zones.

While height regulations control building size by vertical measurement, bulk controls primarily deal with horizontal measurements such

---

§ 4.1

1. U.S. Dept. Commerce (rev.ed.1926).

2. Id. at § 2.

3. For a discussion of various specialized kinds of zones, see Edward H. Ziegler, Jr., Shaping Megalopolis: The Transformation of Euclidean Zoning by Special Zoning Districts and Site–Specific Development Control Techniques 15 Zon. & Plan.L.Rptr. 57 (1992); Richard Babcock and Wendy Larsen, Special Districts (1990).

as minimum lot size, percentage of a lot that may be occupied, and yard requirements. Ordinances also frequently tie bulk controls to use zones, so that the zone boundaries for all three are the same.

Use, height and bulk provisions can control population densities. Most zoning ordinances also control density by limiting areas to use by a specific number of families or living units per acre or per lot. Building or housing codes may also regulate density by establishing the number of persons who can occupy the habitable floor area based on its square footage.

II. USE ZONES

§ 4.2 Use Zoning

A. *In General*

Operating from the premise that everything has its place, zoning is the comprehensive division of a city into different use zones. Use zoning is also known as Euclidean zoning, taking the name from the leading case of Village of Euclid v. Ambler Realty Co.,[1] which upheld its validity. While use zoning has its detractors[2] and is supplemented in many jurisdictions by other techniques, it remains the primary tool that local governments use to regulate land use. In the typical zoning ordinance each zone has three varieties of uses: permitted, accessory and conditional. Ordinances may also specifically prohibit some uses.

B. *Permitted Uses*

There may be many permitted uses in a zone, any one of which may be engaged in as a matter of right within the zone. For example, the permitted uses list in the Office and Institution I District of the City of Raleigh, North Carolina contains thirty-four uses, beginning with accountant and ending with veterinary hospital.[3] The Buffer/Commercial District of that city allows forty-two uses, ranging from antique shops and banks to toy stores and variety stores.[4] There are five other commercial zones in the ordinance. Many city ordinances have lists that are longer.[5] The theory behind these groupings is that the uses are compatible and share reciprocal benefits or at least do not cast major external costs on other uses permitted in the zone.

Since it takes a long ordinance and an imaginative drafter to list every conceivable compatible use, in many ordinances the permitted use list will close with language such as "and any other similar uses." Even if the phrase is not in the ordinance, the building inspector or other

§ 4.2

1. 272 U.S. 365, 47 S.Ct. 114, 71 L.Ed. 303 (1926).

2. See Jan Krasnowiecki, Abolish Zoning, 31 Syr.L.Rev. 719 (1980). See also supra § 3.1.

3. Raleigh City Code § 10–2033 (as amended 1980).

4. Id. at § 10–2042.

5. The list is potentially quite long. The Southern Calif. Ass'n of Governments, Classification of Land Use (1968) lists about 6,100 different land uses.

administrator or administrative body may be given authority expressly or by practice to permit similar uses. Whether a particular use is similar to a use listed in the ordinance is frequently litigated.[6] Favoring free land use, courts generally construe similar use questions in favor of the least restrictive use.[7]

An ordinance may specifically prohibit a use to avoid the finding that it is similar to permitted uses. For example, if not specifically prohibited, a mobile home might be found to be a single-family dwelling allowable in a residential zone.[8] Occasionally, the lists of permitted and prohibited uses in the various zones are such that a particular use is not permitted anywhere in the city. Total exclusion of a use, however, may not be valid.[9]

There is some risk to the landowner who secures permission to develop on the basis that a proposed use is similar to expressly permitted uses. In one case, a building inspector issued a permit allowing a veterinary hospital in a zone where the ordinance permitted "hospitals." The veterinarian bought the lot and proceeded with construction. In response to an appeal by neighboring landowners, the Board of Appeals held that the term hospital did not include veterinary hospital. The veterinarian might have been forced to abandon his use but for the willingness of the court to protect him by applying equitable estoppel.[10] A safer course for a landowner in such a position is to apply for a textual amendment adding the use as expressly permitted, rather than rely on the "similar uses" provision.

C.　Regulating Use, Not Ownership

6. See, e.g., Appeal of Chatelain, 164 Vt. 597, 664 A.2d 269 (1995) (an emergency medical facility held not to be "meeting hall" permitted in residential zone because it was not like other uses such as museums, art galleries, and libraries in terms of impact on neighbors); County of Sonoma v. Rex, 231 Cal.App.3d 1289, 282 Cal.Rptr. 796 (1991) (whether a bed and breakfast inn comes within a roomer-boarder exemption: no); City of Lamoni v. Livingston, 392 N.W.2d 506 (Iowa 1986) (whether a sawmill is a "manufacturing enterprise": yes); Visionquest National, Ltd. v. Pima County Bd. of Adj., 146 Ariz. 103, 703 P.2d 1252 (App.1985) (whether a residential learning center for juvenile offenders is "private school": yes); Mouber v. City of Prairie Village, 6 Kan.App.2d 972, 637 P.2d 424 (1981) (whether a fast food restaurant is a "drive-in establishment": no).

7. Clout, Inc. v. Clinton County Zoning Hearing Bd., 657 A.2d 111, 114 (Pa. Cmwlth.1995). Where criminal sanctions may be imposed, the courts are particularly inclined to construe the ordinance strictly. State v. Nelson, 499 N.W.2d 512 (Minn. App.1993) (pet rooster not included within term "livestock" where defendant was prosecuted for a misdemeanor violation under a zoning ordinance that barred the raising of livestock).

8. See Puls v. Meyer, 195 Wis.2d 680, 538 N.W.2d 860 (App.1995) (mobile homes expressly excluded); Ciavarella v. Zoning Bd. of Adj. of Hazle Twp., 86 Pa.Cmwlth. 193, 484 A.2d 420 (1984) (mobile home once affixed to concrete slab deemed a single-family dwelling). As to the validity of excluding mobile homes, see infra § 6.5.

9. South Whitford Assoc., Inc. v. Zoning Hearing Bd. of West Whiteland Twp., 157 Pa.Cmwlth. 387, 630 A.2d 903 (1993) (the absence of a use from a list of prohibited uses does not mean it is permitted; the use will not be allowed unless it is specifically permitted since the listing of permitted uses implies that non-listed uses are not allowed). See infra § 6.9 as to the validity of total exclusion of particular uses.

10. Crow v. Board of Adjustment of Iowa City, 227 Iowa 324, 288 N.W. 145 (1939). See discussion of estoppel infra at § 5.29.

Zoning generally regulates how property is used, not who owns it or how title is held.[11] Thus, municipal claims that nonconforming use status is lost when the owner transfers title to the land have failed.[12] Distinguishing between owners and nonowners has also been held invalid.[13] Some courts also have rejected efforts to preserve rental housing by adopting ordinances that preclude condominiums.[14]

The bar, however, is not absolute. Some courts, for example, have upheld zoning ordinances that ban short term rentals in resort towns designed to preserve the residential character of areas for permanent residents.[15] Also, while zoning ordinances cannot normally be based on who owns the land, they often base them on who uses the land. Thus, an ordinance that zones land for single-family use and defines family regulates who can use the land.[16]

§ 4.3 Cumulative and Exclusive Zoning

A. *Higher and Lower Zones*

Euclidean or use zoning creates a pyramidal hierarchy of uses with the detached, single-family residence zone at the top. From the highest zone, the hierarchy moves down the pyramid, cumulatively adding zones of lower uses. The single-family zone is the highest zone in the sense that it is the most restricted area, the one needing and deemed deserving of protection from other uses. After single-family use, a Euclidean code permits other uses beginning with higher density residential uses (two-family, multi-family), moving through commercial uses, and ending with heavy industrial uses at the bottom.

The phrase "highest zone" is not the equivalent of the common appraisal phrase, "the highest and best use of land." The highest and best use of land is the use that will confer the highest market value on the land. A developer may argue that property should be rezoned from

---

11. FGL & L Property Corp. v. City of Rye, 66 N.Y.2d 111, 495 N.Y.S.2d 321, 485 N.E.2d 986 (1985) (city can neither require nor preclude condominium ownership through its zoning powers).

12. Town of Seabrook v. Tra–Sea Corp., 119 N.H. 937, 410 A.2d 240 (1979); O'Connor v. City of Moscow, 69 Idaho 37, 202 P.2d 401 (1949).

13. College Area Renters and Landlord Ass'n v. City of San Diego, 43 Cal.App.4th 677, 50 Cal.Rptr.2d 515 (1996) (challenged zoning ordinance violated equal protection due to fact that it irrationally distinguished between owner and nonowner occupied residences).

14. Appeal of Lowe, 164 Vt. 167, 666 A.2d 1178 (1995) (neither subdivision nor zoning permit was required to convert rental property to condominium ownership); McHenry State Bank v. City of McHenry,

113 Ill.App.3d 82, 68 Ill.Dec. 615, 446 N.E.2d 521 (1983); North Fork Motel, Inc. v. Grigonis, 93 A.D.2d 883, 461 N.Y.S.2d 414 (1983). But see Griffin Development Co. v. City of Oxnard, 39 Cal.3d 256, 703 P.2d 339, 217 Cal.Rptr. 1 (1985).

15. Ewing v. City of Carmel–By–The–Sea, 234 Cal.App.3d 1579, 286 Cal.Rptr. 382 (1991), cert. denied 504 U.S. 914, 112 S.Ct. 1950, 118 L.Ed.2d 554 (1992) (ban on rentals for fewer than 30 days held not to be a taking, not overly vague, and not violative of rights of privacy); Cope v. City of Cannon Beach, 317 Or. 339, 855 P.2d 1083 (1993) (ban on rentals for fewer than 14 days held not to constitute a facial taking); Farley v. Zoning Hearing Bd. of Lower Merion Twp., 161 Pa.Cmwlth. 229, 636 A.2d 1232 (1994) (upheld ban on rental to students in certain zones).

16. See infra § 4.5.

residential to commercial on the ground that commercial use is the highest and best use of land, but that generally is not persuasive. Planning and zoning focus on the appropriate use of the land from a community perspective, and are concerned with many factors beyond maximizing the market value for each parcel. The fact that it may have a higher market value zoned for more intensive uses does not compel its rezoning. Thus, viewing the single-family zone as the highest use does not reflect economic value. The reverse, in fact, is normally the case, in that land in the higher zone has a lower value than it would if zoned for a more intensive use.

Referring to a rezoning from residential to commercial as an upzoning is customary, since the value of the land usually increases when the number and intensity of allowable uses increase. A downzoning takes place when property loses market value in a change from a commercial zone to a residential zone. Strict adherence to the hierarchical value scheme that treats residential use as the highest use would require a reversal of terms.[1]

B. Intensive and Unintensive Zones

Zoning theorists and practitioners often speak of intensive and unintensive zones. While there are no precise meanings of the terms, an "intensive zone" is descriptive of those zones that permit heavy industry, or a large variety of activities or uses, high and large buildings, great densities, and require little open space. The large lot, single-family zone and agricultural zones[2] are generally the least intensive use zones.

C. Exclusive and Cumulative Zones

Historically, the single-family zone was an exclusive zone. Uses permitted in other zones were not permitted in the single-family zone. The theory of exclusive residential zones is that protecting homes from nonresidential intrusions is paramount. The latter uses simply do not belong in the former areas. As the Supreme Court said in Village of Euclid v. Ambler Realty Co., in analogizing zoning law to nuisance law, one does not put the "pig in the parlor instead of the barnyard."[3]

All other zones were cumulative, that is, they permitted all uses permitted in any higher, less intensive use zone and excluded uses permitted in lower, more intensive use zones.[4] For example, in a city with seven zones, the light commercial zone would permit those uses permitted in single-family, multi-family, and apartment zones and ex-

---

§ 4.3

1. A very few use the terms in this sense, calling a rezoning from commercial to residential an upzoning, see Munnelly v. Town of East Hampton, 173 A.D.2d 472, 570 N.Y.S.2d 93 (1991), but the almost universal practice labels such a rezoning as a downzoning.

2. Agricultural zones were not typical in early zoning. See infra § 4.8 and Chapter 13.

3. 272 U.S. 365, 38, 47 S.Ct. 114, 118, 71 L.Ed. 303 (1926).

4. For a description of such a scheme, see Cunningham v. Board of Aldermen of City of Overland, 691 S.W.2d 464, 468 (Mo. App.1985).

clude uses permitted in heavy commercial, light industrial and heavy industrial zones.

The anomaly of cumulative zoning is that it allows the people in the parlor to join the pigs in the barnyard. Since cumulative zoning does not preclude residences in commercial and industrial areas, it does not protect people from their own foibles. Perhaps the difference is explainable by reference to legal concerns prevalent when zoning originated. Zoning proponents knew that zoning was to be reviewed by courts who they feared would be inclined to declare it invalid on due process grounds.[5] These proponents recognized that they would more likely sustain such restrictions where strong and universally held values such as the sanctity of the home were involved. For all other uses, cumulative zoning represented less restraint on property, and thus was less offensive. Early zoners might also have assumed that since the land in low, intensive use zones would have high value, residential uses could not and would not compete with it. Further, to the extent that zoning was motivated by snobbery, as sometimes alleged, a scheme that kept commerce from upper and middle class residential enclaves, while permitting the poor and minorities to live near where they worked, was consistent with the allegation.[6]

By allowing uses with significantly different characteristics in the same zone, cumulative zoning causes several problems. Sensitive land uses permitted in intensive use districts may be harmed by locating there. In turn, the harmed sensitive use may claim the intensive use is a common law nuisance.[7] The possibility of this occurring may then deter the establishment of more intensive uses in the very zone where the community wants them. Consequently, the trend is against cumulative zoning and in favor of creating exclusive zones for uses beyond single-family residential.[8]

§ 4.4 Accessory Uses and Home Occupations

A. *Historical Basis and Modern Status*

Ordinances generally allow accessory activities that are necessary or convenient to principal, listed uses. Edward Bassett noted that "from time immemorial,"[1] people had used parts of their homes for office and other purposes, and from their inception, zoning codes acknowledged this tradition. There are accessory uses in all use zones. Examples include a garage or a part-time law office as accessory to a house in a single-family zone, a self-service gasoline pump as accessory to a conve-

---

5. For a typical case holding zoning invalid, see Goldman v. Crowther, 147 Md. 282, 128 A. 50 (1925).

6. See infra § 6.9 regarding environmental justice concerns.

7. See infra Ch. 14.

8. McDonough v. Apton, 48 A.D.2d 194, 200, 368 N.Y.S.2d 603, 608 (1975).

§ 4.4

1. Edward Bassett, Zoning 100 (2d ed.1940). Bassett has been described as the "father of zoning." Seymour Toll, Zoned American 143 (1969).

nience store in a commercial zone,[2] and a day care center as accessory to a religious use.[3] Though a code normally lists allowable accessory uses, where it fails to enumerate them, courts have implied such rights.[4] While accessory uses may be allowed in all zones, most disputes deal with three activities in residential areas: home occupations, recreational uses (e.g., tennis courts, swimming pools),[5] and accessory residential use (e.g., relatives, boarders, servant quarters).[6]

The predominant accessory use is the home occupation, and ordinances vary in what qualifies. They often allow such customary uses as sewing and clothing alterations, childcare, teaching music, and part-time offices for doctors, lawyers, real estate agents, and hairstylists. In addition to expectations based on customary use, considerations of personal liberty require concessions about what one can do at home.[7] Zoning codes that allow such uses recognize that the home is more than a place of shelter, that it is, as one court has said, a place for "private religious, educational, cultural, and recreational advantages of the family * * * ."[8] Still, there is disagreement as to what activities can be pursued without unduly harming neighbors, and the disputes are unlikely to wane. The revolution in communications that makes it easier for people to work at home and the concessions granted by employers allowing flexible employee work schedules mean increased use of the home for nontraditional purposes. The result is that communities must be concerned both with under-regulation, failing to adequately protect neighbors, and over-regulation, excessively restricting personal freedom.

B. Incidental and Customary Use

An accessory use must be subordinate or incidental to the principal use. If part-time business use is allowed as accessory to residential use, it is on the basis that the activity is incidental to the principal home use. If the business use predominates, it is disqualified. Typically, ordinances control the incidental requirement by limitations or prohibitions on

---

2. Borough of Fleetwood v. Zoning Hearing Bd. of Borough of Fleetwood, 538 Pa. 536, 649 A.2d 651 (1994).

3. City of Richmond Heights v. Richmond Heights Presbyterian Church, 764 S.W.2d 647 (Mo.1989).

4. Treisman v. Town of Bedford, 132 N.H. 54, 563 A.2d 786 (1989).

5. See Thomas v. Zoning Bd. of Adj. of City of University Park, 241 S.W.2d 955 (Tex.Civ.App.1951) (swimming pool was accessory use). See also Annot., Application of Zoning Regulations to Golf Courses, Swimming Pools, Tennis Courts, or the Like, 32 A.L.R.3d 424 (1971).

6. See, e.g., Township of Randolph v. Lamprecht, 225 N.J.Super. 236, 542 A.2d 36 (1988) (garage apartment for caretaker allowed); Kasper v. Town of Brookhaven,

142 A.D.2d 213, 535 N.Y.S.2d 621 (1988) (upholding ordinance that allowed only single-family homeowners who occupied their residences to apply for permits for accessory rental apartments); Rowatti v. Gonchar, 101 N.J. 46, 500 A.2d 381 (1985) (building addition intended for use by an elderly parent that had its own cooking facilities was not permitted). See also George W. Liebmann, Suburban Zoning: Two Modest Proposals, 25 Real Prop. Prob. & Tr. J. 1 (1990) (discussing need for accessory apartments).

7. See Thomas E. Roberts, The Regulation of Home Occupations Under Zoning Ordinances: Some Constitutional Considerations, 56 Temp. L.Q. 49 (1983).

8. Thomas v. Zoning Bd. of Adj. of City of University Park, 241 S.W.2d 955, 958 (Tex.App.1951).

outside employees, limits on the percentage of floor space the activity can occupy, and prohibitions on the sale of products.[9]

Typically, accessory uses must not only be incidental to the principal use. They also must be "customary," or "customarily incidental." The requirement should be eliminated since it is problematical to apply, does not rationally advance a legitimate interest, unfairly discriminates against some. Applying the requirement is difficult since a strict definition would preclude new uses from ever gaining legal status. For example, placing a large satellite dish in the sideyard would never qualify as customary.[10] That decision, of course, would elate some and distress others.

The "customary" requirement does not rationally achieve the goal of limiting non principal uses to avoid adverse impact on neighbors. New uses might be inoffensive and customary ones may have become offensive over time with changing tastes. While ordinances ought not use the limitation, if they do, one judicial method of liberalizing the requirement is to use a broad geographical area that reaches beyond the city to determine the customary nature of the use.[11]

The customary requirement also can operate unfairly. In one case, a court denied a barber a right to have a part-time shop in his home because it found that cutting hair in the home was not customary. Sewing and cooking would be fine, said the court, but not barbering.[12] In reaching that conclusion, the court failed to take note of the irrationality of the ordinance and the inequality of the result. Although the use was incidental, posing no harm to the neighbors, the court denied the barber the ability to work at home while anyone else in the neighborhood could operate a sewing or cooking business.

C. Professional Offices

Another troubling limitation in many ordinances is that they only allow offices for professional people. Who qualifies as a professional poses difficulties. While ordinances often expressly allow doctors, lawyers, and clergy, those who want to claim status as professionals, such as real estate or insurance agents, musicians, or artists must prove that they have specialized training, follow a code of ethics, and render a public service. A court held that a music teacher was a professional in one case,[13] while another court denied a management consultant that sta-

---

9. See, e.g., Town of Sullivans Island v. Byrum, 306 S.C. 539, 413 S.E.2d 325 (1992) (floor space limits); Levinson v. Montgomery County, 95 Md.App. 307, 620 A.2d 961 (1993) (prohibition on sale of products).

10. Local regulation of satellite dishes is partially preempted by FCC regulation. See Hunter v. City of Whittier, 209 Cal. App.3d 588, 257 Cal.Rptr. 559 (1989).

11. See, e.g., Atlantic Refining & Marketing Co. v. Whitpain Twp. Zoning Hearing Bd., 656 A.2d 598 (Pa.Cmwlth.1995) (examining incidence of gas stations with

convenience stores in the Delaware Valley and southeastern Pennsylvania to determine whether the practice was customary, and holding it was not). See also Note, Zoning: Accessory Uses and the Meaning of the "Customary" Requirement, 56 Boston Univ.L Rev. 542 (1976).

12. Gold v. Zoning Bd. of Adj., 393 Pa. 401, 403, 143 A.2d 59, 60 (1958).

13. People ex rel. Fullam v. Kelly, 255 N.Y. 396, 175 N.E. 108 (1931).

tus.[14] In all such cases, however, whether one is a professional is irrelevant to proper zoning considerations. The customer's car driven to the house of the part-time management consultant is no noisier than the car driven to the music teacher's or lawyer's house. Municipalities should eliminate the elitist and unnecessary requirement that the home occupation be that of a professional.[15]

§ 4.5 Single–Family Use

A. *The Single–Family Exclusive Zone*

In the early days of zoning the single-family detached home represented the American dream: the cottage in suburbia protected by zoning from multi-family, commercial and industrial uses. As the California Supreme Court said in Miller v. Board of Public Works, where it upheld the exclusion of multi-family buildings from a single-family zone,

> we do not wish to unduly emphasize the single-family residence as a means of perpetuating the home life of a people, [but] a single family home [is] more desirable for the promotion and perpetuation of family life than an apartment, hotel, or flat. * * * The establishment of such districts is for the general welfare because it tends to promote and perpetuate the American home. * * * The character and quality of manhood and womanhood are in a large measure the result of the home environment.[1]

Veneration of the single-family home continues in parts of the country, but it has many critics who point to its tendency to increase housing costs, to consume more land and destroy more of the natural environment than necessary, to unnecessarily mandate conformity in lifestyles, and to exclude persons on socioeconomic, and sometimes racial, grounds.[2] We explore these criticisms below.[3]

B. *Who Constitutes a Family?*

Who can legally live in a single-family zone turns on the ordinance's definition of the word "family." Ordinances usually define single-family use to require that persons live together as a "single housekeeping unit." If there is no statutory requirement that the persons be related, the test is a functional one. Some cases seem easy. In one case, a court found that a married couple, their two biological children, and their foster children did not violate the family definition of a zoning ordinance because they were found to "bear the generic character of a family."[4]

---

14. Simon v. Board of Appeals on Zoning of City of New Rochelle, 208 A.D.2d 931, 618 N.Y.S.2d 729 (1994).

15. See Roberts, supra note 7.

§ 4.5

1. 195 Cal. 477, 492–93, 234 P. 381, 386–87 (1925).

2. See, e.g., Edward H. Ziegler, The Twilight of Single–Family Zoning, 3 UCLA J.Envtl.L. & Policy 161 (1983); Richard F. Babcock, The Egregious Invalidity of the Exclusive Single–Family Zone, Land Use Law & Zoning Digest 4 (July 1983).

3. Some residential exclusionary zoning practices are invalid. See infra Ch. 6.

4. City of White Plains v. Ferraioli, 34 N.Y.2d 300, 357 N.Y.S.2d 449, 313 N.E.2d 756 (1974).

Cases involving groups of unrelated persons, such as college students, are more difficult. Thus, under an ordinance that allowed families of "one or more persons * * * who are living together as a stable and permanent living unit," ten unrelated college students were deemed a family upon proof that they ate together, shared household chores, paid expenses from a common fund, and intended to live together for three years.[5] In contrast, another court found seven unrelated college students who shared a house for convenience and economics did not meet the statutory requirement of a relationship of a "permanent and distinct character with a demonstrable and recognizable bond characteristic of a cohesive unit."[6] The court thought that a "ragtag collection of college roommates [could only be characterized as a family] in American society * * * by the most cynical."[7] College students are not alone in running the risk of violating family definitions. Depending on the definition employed, religious communities may or may not be families.[8] Groups of unrelated adults who live together for economics or convenience may also be challenged.[9]

The exclusion of non-traditional groups increases when municipalities define "family" to require that persons be related by blood, marriage, or adoption. In Village of Belle Terre v. Boraas,[10] the Supreme Court held that a municipal zoning ordinance limiting the occupancy of one-family dwellings to related persons or to groups of not more than two unrelated persons passed constitutional muster. Finding that the group of six unrelated college students presented no issue involving a fundamental right, such as association, privacy, or travel, the Court applied a relaxed standard of review, and upheld the restriction since it was conceivable that the village adopted it to secure the quality of the environment of single-family areas.

While the *Belle Terre* ordinance allowed two unrelated persons to constitute a family, there is little reason to believe an ordinance without that provision would be found unconstitutional.[11] At least one court has found that the state interest in marriage and in preservation of the biological or legal family justifies excluding unmarried couples.[12]

Critical to the validity of ordinances that ban the unrelated from living together is the determination that such laws do not affect a

5. Borough of Glassboro v. Vallorosi, 117 N.J. 421, 568 A.2d 888 (1990).

6. Stegeman v. City of Ann Arbor, 213 Mich.App. 487, 540 N.W.2d 724 (1995).

7. Id. at 492, 540 N.W.2d at 727.

8. Holy Name Hospital v. Montroy, 153 N.J.Super. 181, 379 A.2d 299 (1977); Carroll v. City of Miami Beach, 198 So.2d 643 (Fla.App.1967). See discussion infra § 4.27.

9. City of Santa Barbara v. Adamson, 27 Cal.3d 123, 164 Cal.Rptr. 539, 610 P.2d 436 (1980) (12 unrelated adults in 24 room, 10 bedroom, six bathroom house protected by state constitutional right of privacy).

10. 416 U.S. 1, 94 S.Ct. 1536, 39 L.Ed.2d 797 (1974). But compare Moore v. East Cleveland, 431 U.S. 494, 97 S.Ct. 1932, 52 L.Ed.2d 531 (1977).

11. Hollenbaugh v. Carnegie Free Library, 439 U.S. 1052, 99 S.Ct. 734, 58 L.Ed.2d 713 (1978) (Court denied review of a decision that found no constitutional violation where an unmarried man and woman were discharged from employment at a state library because they lived together).

12. City of Ladue v. Horn, 720 S.W.2d 745 (Mo.App.1986).

fundamental right. With some success, complainants have pressed state courts to reject the reasoning of *Belle Terre*, and use state constitutional provisions to offer more protection to alternate living arrangements. State courts divide fairly evenly on the question. Several have recognized a right of unrelated persons to live together as protected under their state constitutions, and have invalidated zoning ordinances restricting the size of unrelated families.[13] Other courts, however, have refused the request and, instead, follow the *Belle Terre* rationale.[14]

An ordinance that targets related persons is unlikely to survive judicial scrutiny. In Moore v. City of East Cleveland,[15] the Court struck down a housing code restriction that limited occupants of residences to individuals with specified degrees of consanguinity. The ordinance had the effect of making it a crime for a grandmother to have two of her grandsons live with her since the boys had different parents. In a 5–4 decision, a plurality of the justices found the definition of relatedness flawed on substantive due process grounds as an invasion of the sanctity of the family.

§ 4.6   Group Homes as Single–Family Use

Attempts to provide more normal living environments for persons in need of supervised care by placing them in group homes frequently lead to struggles with local zoning authorities. Often, group homes for mentally retarded persons, the elderly disabled, troubled teenagers, HIV infected persons, rehabilitation centers for persons recovering from drug abuse, and halfway homes for prisoners run afoul of "single-family" definitions found in zoning codes. Recent judicial and legislative intervention limits the ability of local government to exclude such homes.

Many single-family neighborhoods have refused to extend the welcome mat to group homes, and contentious zoning struggles often ensue when a group home seeks to "invade" a neighborhood. In some cases, the government has prosecuted neighbor-protesters, or threatened them with prosecution, on the basis that the neighbors are violating the federal Fair Housing Act's proscription against intimidating or interfering with the right of the handicapped to be free from discriminatory treatment in their pursuit of housing. Unsurprisingly, these prosecutions have raised First Amendment concerns.[1]

---

13. See McMinn v. Oyster Bay, 66 N.Y.2d 544, 498 N.Y.S.2d 128, 488 N.E.2d 1240 (1985); Charter Twp. of Delta v. Dinolfo, 419 Mich. 253, 351 N.W.2d 831(1984); City of Santa Barbara v. Adamson, 27 Cal.3d 123, 164 Cal.Rptr. 539, 610 P.2d 436 (1980); State v. Baker, 81 N.J. 99, 405 A.2d 368 (1979).

14. State v. Champoux, 252 Neb. 769, 566 N.W.2d 763 (1997); Dinan v. Board of Zoning Appeals of Town of Stratford, 220 Conn. 61, 595 A.2d 864 (1991); Rademan v. City and County of Denver, 186 Colo. 250, 526 P.2d 1325 (1974); Town of Durham v. White Enterprises, Inc., 115 N.H. 645, 348 A.2d 706 (1975); City of Ladue v. Horn, 720 S.W.2d 745 (Mo.App.1986).

15. 431 U.S. 494, 97 S.Ct. 1932, 52 L.Ed.2d 531 (1977).

§ 4.6

1. Michigan Protection and Advocacy Service v. Babin, 18 F.3d 337, 343, n. 2 (6th Cir.1994). See also discussion and cases infra § 5.2.

The argument in favor of allowing the mentally retarded to live in group homes in single-family areas is that society, whether government by zoning or private parties by covenant, ought not deny such persons the opportunity to enjoy at least a semblance of a way of life that is often characterized as "the American dream." The arguments against group homes vary. While the mere fact that the individuals in a home will be unrelated seems a petty objection, others are not necessarily so. These include the number of residents, the frequency of resident turn-over, whether the residents are likely to engage in antisocial behavior, and the traffic and activity that will be generated by outside supervisors or health providers. Whether or when these concerns justify relegating those who would live in the group homes to more crowded institutionalization arrangements elsewhere in town or to the streets is the issue.

Many states divest local authorities from using the zoning power to differentiate between residential use and certain types of group homes.[2] North Carolina, for example, provides that "family care homes," defined as adult care for not more than six handicapped persons, are residential uses for local zoning purposes. Under the statute cities cannot require that they obtain special permits, but they can prohibit new homes from locating within a one-half mile radius of an existing home.[3] Even where such a statute is lacking, group homes operated by a governmental entity or licensed by the state may be immune from local zoning.[4]

Differential zoning treatment of some group homes may be subject to exacting rational basis scrutiny.[5] In City of Cleburne v. Cleburne Living Center,[6] the Supreme Court held that a special permit requirement imposed on homes for the mentally retarded, but not imposed on similar uses, such as fraternity houses and nursing homes, violated the equal protection clause. The *Cleburne* Court refused to classify the mentally retarded as a "quasi-suspect class," which would have triggered intermediate scrutiny. Nonetheless, the Court invalidated the ordinance purportedly using the rational basis test.[7] The type of review used, however, was not the historically highly deferential conceivable basis standard, but one that required some degree of proof by the city that its treatment was justified. Numerous parties have unsuccessfully sought *Cleburne*-like review,[8] and for group homes courts have reached different

---

2. See Arlene S. Kanter, A Home of One's Own: The Fair Housing Amendments Act of 1988 and Housing Discrimination Against People with Mental Disabilities 925, 975 (1994).

3. N.C. Gen. Stat. § 168–22. See discussion infra § 6.8 regarding the validity of numerical limits and of such dispersal requirements under the Fair Housing Act.

4. See discussion of group home immunity infra §§ 4.23–24.

5. See infra § 10.14.

6. 473 U.S. 432, 105 S.Ct. 3249, 87 L.Ed.2d 313 (1985).

7. See infra § 10.14 regarding equal protection.

8. See Jacobs, Visconsi & Jacobs v. City of Lawrence, 927 F.2d 1111 (10th Cir. 1991) (shopping center); Pontarelli Limousine, Inc. v. City of Chicago, 929 F.2d 339 (7th Cir.1991) (airport livery services); Doe v. City of Butler, 892 F.2d 315 (3d Cir.1989) (shelter for battered women also refused such scrutiny). Courts have differed over whether halfway homes for prisoners deserve more exacting scrutiny. See Bannum, Inc. v. City of St. Charles, 2 F.3d 267 (8th Cir.1993) (no); Application of Freedom Ranch, Inc., 878 P.2d 380 (Okl.App.1994),

results using the *Cleburne* test.[9]

The holding of *Belle Terre*[10] survives the *Cleburne* decision. Nothing in *Cleburne* suggests that the equal protection clause prohibits municipalities from defining "family" to include related persons only.

The state court holdings noted above[11] offset the limited federal constitutional protection. In defining "family," these courts apply a higher level of scrutiny than *Belle Terre*, using their state constitutions. In one case, a lower New York court invalidated on state due process grounds an ordinance that excluded a group home for up to ten adolescents because a rotating professional staff, rather than house parents, supervised the residents.[12] The court said that whether such a home was the functional equivalent of a biological family was irrelevant, since no limit on the unrelated could stand if there was no corresponding limit on related persons.[13]

The need for group homes for the mentally retarded or other handicapped persons to seek constitutional protection from stringent zoning by trying to use or expand *Cleburne* receded in importance with the protection afforded the handicapped under the federal Fair Housing Amendments Act of 1988.[14]

§ 4.7 Federal Disabilities Laws and Use Zoning

A. *Fair Housing Amendments Act*

Federal law limits the exercise of the zoning power with respect to persons with disabilities. The primary restraint is the Fair Housing Amendments Act of 1988 (FHAA).[1] In that act, Congress extended the protection of the 1968 Fair Housing Act to the "handicapped," and significantly altered the legal environment for group homes. The Fair Housing Act, discussed in detail in Chapter 6,[2] has become the major vehicle used by group homes to challenge zoning ordinances that affect persons the act defines as handicapped.

B. *Americans With Disabilities Act*

The Americans With Disabilities Act (ADA)[3] may also limit local zoning. The ADA provides that no person with a qualifying disability

---

cert. denied, 513 U.S. 1043, 115 S.Ct. 636, 130 L.Ed.2d 543 (1994) (no); Bannum, Inc. v. City of Louisville, 958 F.2d 1354 (6th Cir.1992) (yes).

9. See, e.g., J.W. v. City of Tacoma, 720 F.2d 1126 (9th Cir.1983) and Burstyn v. City of Miami Beach, 663 F.Supp. 528 (S.D.Fla.1987), finding permit requirements invalid on basis of *Cleburne*. But see Thornton v. City of Allegan, 863 F.Supp. 504 (W.D.Mich.1993) and Howard v. City of Garland, 917 F.2d 898 (5th Cir.1990)(day care center for children validly denied special permit).

10. Discussed supra § 4.5.

11. See supra § 4.5, note 13.

12. Children's Village v. Holbrook, 171 A.D.2d 298, 576 N.Y.S.2d 405 (1991).

13. Id. One difficulty not addressed is the greater external impact on the neighborhood by a staff visiting daily from the outside compared to the possibly lesser burden from house parents.

14. 42 U.S.C.A. §§ 3610 et seq., discussed infra § 4.7 and § 6.8.

§ 4.7

1. 42 U.S.C.A. §§ 3610 et seq.

2. See infra § 6.8.

3. 42 U.S.C.A. §§ 12101 et seq.

shall, "by reason of such disability, * * * be denied the benefits of the services, programs, or activities of a public entity, or be subjected to discrimination by such entity."[4] A protected person under the ADA is "an individual with a disability who, with or without reasonable modifications * * *, meets the essential eligibility requirements for the receipt of services or the participation in programs or activities provided by a public entity."[5]

The leading case applying the ADA to zoning is Innovative Health Services v. City of White Plains.[6] An outpatient drug and alcohol rehabilitation treatment center obtained a permit to operate in a business district. Upon appeal by neighboring businesses, the board of adjustment set aside the permit, finding the center to be an unpermitted hospital use. The center challenged the permit denial as a violation of the ADA.[7] The city argued that zoning was not a service, program, or activity within the meaning of the ADA. The case law was on its side since several lower state and federal courts had taken that position. The district court, however, found the ADA applicable, and issued a preliminary injunction against the city barring it from interfering with the plaintiff's treatment center. The city appealed.

The Second Circuit affirmed the preliminary injunction. It disagreed with the lower court decisions from other circuits and found the plain meaning of the word "activity" to encompass zoning. Furthermore, the court held that the second and disjunctive phrase of the prohibitory section of the ADA plainly prohibits discrimination by a public entity, making it unimportant whether zoning is a program, activity or service.[8] The city argued that the plaintiff could not prevail on the merits since it had afforded the disabled with the benefits of zoning by allowing them to participate in the hearing. The issue, said the court, was the result, not the process. Examining the city's conduct in the permitting process, the court found it likely that the plaintiff could show that the city had discriminated based on the disabilities of the plaintiff's patients and, thus, would prevail on the merits. The court noted that the record was replete with negative comments about drug and alcohol users based on stereotypes and general unsupported fears.

While some courts agree with the Second Circuit that the ADA applies to zoning,[9] several courts disagree.[10] In Robinson v. City of

4. 42 U.S.C.A. § 12132.

5. 42 U.S.C.A. § 12131(2).

6. 117 F.3d 37 (2d Cir.1997).

7. Section 504 of the Rehabilitation Act of 1973, 29 U.S.C.A. § 794, was also raised.

8. 117 F.3d at 44.

9. Oak Ridge Care Center, Inc. v. Racine County, 896 F.Supp. 867 (E.D.Wis. 1995). See also City of Peekskill v. Rehabilitation Support Servs., Inc., 806 F.Supp. 1147, 1156 (S.D.N.Y.1992) (in dicta, suggesting ADA might apply).

10. United States v. City of Charlotte, 904 F.Supp. 482 (W.D.N.C.1995); Kessler Inst. for Rehabilitation, Inc. v. Borough of Essex Fells, 876 F.Supp. 641, 655 (D.N.J. 1995); Moyer v. Lower Oxford Twp., 1993 WL 5489 (E.D.Pa.1993); Oxford House, Inc. v. City of Albany, 155 F.R.D. 409 (N.D.N.Y. 1994); Burnham v. City of Rohnert Park, 1992 WL 672965 (1992) (holding implicit); Aquaro v. Zoning Bd. of Adj. of City of Philadelphia, 673 A.2d 1055 (Pa.Cmwlth. 1996).

Friendswood,[11] for example, the plaintiff resisted enforcement of a 25–foot front yard setback, which would require removal of a carport. Plaintiff claimed that his disability required him to continue to use the offending carport and he relied on the ADA for support. The court, however, held that zoning laws were not within the act's purview. The ADA was intended, said the court, to apply to employment and to assure access to places of public accommodation.

Section 504 of the Rehabilitation Act of 1973[12] may also be used to challenge zoning actions that deny permits to the disabled. The Rehabilitation Act, in language similar to the ADA, prohibits the denial of benefits or discrimination against the disabled. It differs in one significant respect from the ADA in that it applies only to "any program or activity receiving Federal financial assistance."[13] While all cities likely receive some federal funds, to prevail the plaintiff must show a nexus between the federal funds and the allegedly discriminatory program or activity.[14]

Remedies under these two federal acts are provided by reference to other acts. The ADA incorporates the remedies of the Rehabilitation Act.[15] That act, in turn, incorporates the remedies of the Civil Rights of 1964.[16]

§ 4.8 Agricultural Uses

Early zoning was urban oriented. Only cities and incorporated villages received the power to zone by the Standard Zoning Enabling Act and the use zones contemplated by the act were for "trade, industry, residence, or other purposes."[1] The country still had much open space, and prime agricultural land was not regarded as a limited resource. The phenomena of urban sprawl had not yet struck, and automobile and transit facilities were not so extensive as to allow the "leapfrogging" of urban development far out into the countryside. Agricultural use was not an issue of concern. In small towns, and in some areas of larger cities, the poor and those of moderate means often kept a garden and perhaps a few chickens. These modest agricultural uses were permissible since they were not considered industrial or commercial uses.

Over the years, this picture has changed in almost every respect. Farmland preservation is a major national concern,[2] and agricultural zoning is common.[3] Agricultural zoning is usually unintensive use zon-

---

11. 890 F.Supp. 616 (S.D.Tex.1995).

12. 29 U.S.C.A. § 794.

13. 29 U.S.C.A. § 794(a).

14. United States v. City of Charlotte, 904 F.Supp. 482, 486 (W.D.N.C.1995). See also Cleburne Living Center, Inc. v. City of Cleburne, 726 F.2d 191, 194 (5th Cir.1984), vacated on other grounds 473 U.S. 432, 105 S.Ct. 3249, 87 L.Ed.2d 313 (1985).

15. 42 U.S.C.A. § 12117.

16. 29 U.S.C.A. § 794(a).

§ 4.8

1. Standard State Zoning Enabling Act § 1 (rev.ed.1926).

2. Chapter 13 infra covers the topic in detail.

3. Teri E. Popp, A Survey of Agricultural Zoning: State Responses to the Farmland Crisis, 24 Real Prop. Prob. & Trust J. 371 (1989). See also infra Chapter 13 for a complete discussion of farmland preservation and agricultural zoning.

ing, though it will normally permit industrialized agriculture, such as intensive stock feeding, canneries and other uses compatible with an agricultural economy. Typically, it is also nonexclusive, allowing single-family homes on large lots. But, it will prohibit, or allow only as special uses,[4] conventional subdivisions and other urban uses that encroach upon the preservation of the prime agricultural resource. An agricultural zone may work as a holding zone[5] to contain urban areas and force denser development rather than allowing sprawl and destruction of agricultural areas.[6] Some communities make agricultural zones exclusive, prohibiting even low-density residential use.

The courts have upheld both exclusive and nonexclusive agricultural zoning, finding the preservation of farmland to be a legitimate exercise of the police power.[7] As-applied taking problems will arise if the permitted agricultural use is not economically viable, but typically the zoning does not have that effect and survives a takings challenge.[8]

The growth in agricultural zoning has been accompanied by a trend to ban certain agricultural uses from residential zones. Most residential zones ban commercial farming operations and the keeping of farm animals such as chickens, cows, goats and horses. It is not always clear, however, what "farm animal" includes. Pet Vietnamese pot-bellied pigs have been found not to be farm animals, allowing their owners to keep them in residential areas.[9] A horse, however, was found not to be a "household pet."[10] All zones, including residential zones, typically permit the growing of crops.[11]

§ 4.9 Industrial and Commercial Uses

Variations in industrial and commercial zones are considerable. The present complexity of zoning codes is exemplified by the numerous commercial districts found in many cities. Where an early zoning ordinance would have one general business district and one industrial district, today's ordinances often have separate districts for neighborhood retail businesses, office and institutional uses, and shopping centers. Industry is often divided into light and heavy use zones.

4. See, e.g., Henley v. Zoning Hearing Bd. of West Fallowfield Twp., 155 Pa. Cmwlth. 306, 625 A.2d 132 (1993) (special exception available from ten acre minimum lot size for small lot subdivisions); State ex. rel. Madison Landfills, Inc. v. Dane County, 183 Wis.2d 282, 515 N.W.2d 322 (App.1994) (government uses including landfills allowed as special uses).

5. See infra § 4.20.

6. See infra Chapter 9 on Growth Management and Planning.

7. See infra § 13.8.

8. See, e.g., Gardner v. New Jersey Pinelands Commission, 125 N.J. 193, 593 A.2d 251 (1991); Nelson v. Benton County, 115 Or.App. 453, 839 P.2d 233 (1992); Petersen v. Dane County, 136 Wis.2d 501, 402 N.W.2d 376 (1987).

9. City of Peoria v. Ohl, 262 Ill.App.3d 522, 201 Ill.Dec. 597, 636 N.E.2d 1029 (1994); Barnes v. City of Anderson, 642 N.E.2d 1004 (Ind.App.1994).

10. Kaeser v. Zoning Bd. of Appeals of the Town of Stratford, 218 Conn. 438, 589 A.2d 1229 (1991).

11. Farming is not always allowed outside agricultural zones. See Borough of Kinnelon v. South Gate Assoc., 172 N.J.Super. 216, 411 A.2d 724 (1980) (upholding exclusion of commercial farming).

In contrast to the early years of zoning, many industrial and commercial zones today are non-cumulative. Industrial zones commonly exclude residential uses for, just as industry can be a nuisance in residential zones, prime industrial land may be lost by the intrusion of residential uses. Furthermore, allowing homes in industrial zones may subject industry to nuisance actions.[1]

While cumulative zoning represented the early practice, the Standard Zoning Enabling Act did not require it, and exclusive industrial or commercial zoning does not conflict with a typical enabling act.[2] Litigation challenging exclusive districts has been based on arguments that it is beyond the police power to protect lower uses from higher uses and that exclusive industrial zoning is unreasonable as applied to particular property. The former ground has failed as courts have upheld commercial and industrial districts that exclude residential uses.[3] The courts reason that just as residential areas exclude industrial uses to promote the public welfare, people can be protected from themselves by precluding them from moving into industrial areas. Furthermore, courts may uphold exclusive industrial zoning to promote and protect industrial uses.[4] In states allowing fiscally-motivated zoning,[5] exclusive industrial zoning may also be justified as a measure to attract uses that will increase the tax base.[6]

Exclusive industrial or commercial zoning may be invalid as applied. Communities are frequently "overzoned" for commercial and industrial uses, that is, there is no demand for the quantity of land so zoned. Where the zoning is cumulative, it usually does not unreasonably burden the property owner, whose land can be devoted to some use for which there is a market. But when exclusive industrial zoning is used and there is no demand for using the property in that manner, it is in effect zoned for non-use, which is unreasonable and does not serve the public health, safety and welfare.[7]

Some communities exclude commercial as well as residential uses from industrial areas. In one case holding such zoning invalid, the court recognized that commercial uses could be excluded in theory, but held that there was not a sufficient distinction between commercial and industrial uses on the facts before it to justify such a classification.[8] The classification was thus unreasonable as applied.

§ 4.9

1. See infra Ch. 14.

2. Kozesnik v. Montgomery Township, 24 N.J. 154, 131 A.2d 1, 9 (1957).

3. See Grubel v. MacLaughlin, 286 F.Supp. 24, 27 (D.V.I.1968).

4. People ex rel. Skokie Town House Builders, Inc. v. Village of Morton Grove, 16 Ill.2d 183, 157 N.E.2d 33 (1959); State ex rel. Berndt v. Iten, 259 Minn. 77, 106 N.W.2d 366 (1960); Kozesnik v. Montgomery Township, 24 N.J. 154, 131 A.2d 1 (1957).

5. See supra § 3.18.

6. Mott & Wehrly, The Prohibition of Residential Developments in Industrial Districts, Urban Land Institute, Tech.Bull. No. 10 (Nov. 1948).

7. Corthouts v. Town of Newington, 140 Conn. 284, 99 A.2d 112 (1953). See also Gruber v. Raritan Township, 39 N.J. 1, 186 A.2d 489 (1962) (exclusive industrial zoning held invalid after residential development had been partially completed).

8. Katobimar Realty Co. v. Webster, 20 N.J. 114, 118 A.2d 824 (1955).

In addition, or as an alternative, to use zoning, performance standards may regulate industrial uses. A performance zoning ordinance provides standards to measure the external effects produced by industrial activities. Specific standards may be established for smoke, noise, dust, toxic emissions, glare, vibration, radioactivity, electrical disturbance, heat, and odors.[9] If the standards are met, the manufacturing use is permitted within the zone.[10]

§ 4.10 Enterprise Zones

Certain "zones," such as enterprise zones, are not zones at all in the Euclidean sense that refers to areas of land use classifications. Still, enterprise zones, as redevelopment tools, may override other planning concerns and may result in the intensification of land use.

Enterprise zones, which three-fourths of the states authorize,[1] are economically deteriorating areas into which government incentives attract commercial activity.[2] Though they have most often been directed toward urban renewal, enterprise zones increasingly target rural areas as well. Generally the enterprise zones contain reductions of tax rates or fees, attempts to increase the level and efficiency of local services,[3] provisions to streamline government regulation, and incentives to obtain commitments from the private sector to provide jobs and job training for low income residents. Income tax incentives for businesses may be split between employers and employees. Virginia's plan, for example, provides for tax incentives to encourage business participation in designated areas, and allows some regulatory flexibility at the local level by use of special zoning districts, ordinance exemption and permit process reform.[4]

While some 500 enterprise zones exist in cities around the country via state legislation,[5] there is federal involvement as well. Federal enterprise zone legislation was debated fairly continuously beginning in the early 1980s. Congress finally acted in 1993. Using the label "empowerment zones," Congress created nine zones: five in large urban centers, one in a medium size city, and three in rural areas.[6] Tax incentives

---

9. See, e.g., DeCoals, Inc. v. Board of Zoning Appeals of the City of Westover, 168 W.Va. 339, 284 S.E.2d 856 (1981), upholding absolute no dust standard against a substantive due process challenge.

10. See infra § 4.19 for a discussion of performance zoning.

§ 4.10

1. See David Williams, The Enterprise Zone Concept at the Federal Level: Are Proposed Tax Incentives the Needed Ingredient? 9 Va.Tax Rev. 711, 721–22 (1990), and Peter Dreier, America's Urban Crisis: Symptoms, Causes, and Solutions, 71 N.C.L.Rev. 1351, 1394 (1993).

2. See generally David Boeck, Enterprise Zone Debate, 16 Urb.Law. 71, 73–77

(1984); Sherman E. Unger, Enterprise Zones: Some Perspectives on Anglo–American Developments, 5 Urb.L. & Policy 129 (1982).

3. This is done by experimenting with contracts with private groups to provide the services, and trying to avoid monopoly problems. See Community Communications Co. v. City of Boulder, 455 U.S. 40, 102 S.Ct. 835, 70 L.Ed.2d 810 (1982).

4. Va. Code §§ 59.1–270 to 59.1–284.

5. See Williams, supra note 1, at 721–22 and Dreier, supra note 1, at 1394.

6. 26 U.S.C.A. § 1391.

amounting to $2.5 billion were provided as wage credits that entitled an employer to take credits equal to 20% of the first $15,000 of each employee's wages with a maximum of $3000. The legislation also provided $720 million for social service grants for child care, education, and job training. Finally, the zones were granted the power to use tax-exempt bonds to finance businesses. In addition to the empowerment zones, 95 "enterprise communities" (65 urban, 30 rural) received the tax-exempt bond powers of the empowerment zones and $280 million for social service grants.[7]

Though some question whether enterprise zones really attract business and revitalize an area and the British experience suggests that tax breaks and regulatory simplification alone are insufficient,[8] there is some evidence of success.[9] A 1987 study found that nationwide, enterprise zones had created 113,600 new jobs, retained 67,400 existing jobs, and provided a capital investment of $8.8 million.[10] Some dispute these numbers.[11] Another problem is that revitalization and redevelopment may lead to commercial gentrification, as rising property values drive out poorer residents and marginal businesses.[12]

Though not denominated a "zone," a related redevelopment tool is tax increment financing.[13] Authorized by enabling legislation in thirty-eight states,[14] tax increment financing uses the increase in value that results from the redevelopment. The *ad valorem* taxes levied on a redevelopment area are divided into two parts. That levied on the base value (assessed value at the time a project begins) is allocated to cities, counties, schools and other taxing districts, as usual. The tax levied on the increment (excess of assessed value over base value) goes to the redevelopment authority where the money may be used to finance the public costs of the redevelopment or to repay bonds previously issued to raise revenue for the redevelopment.

---

7. For data on the program, see "Empowerment Zones" Showing Progress, Wash. Post, March 8, 1997, 1997 WL 9338470.

8. Callies & Tamashiro, Enterprise Zones: The Redevelopment Sweepstakes Begins, 15 Urb.Law. 231 (1983). See also Abe L. Frank, Enterprise Zone Proposals: Incentives to Revive Our Decaying Inner Cities, 10 J.Legis. 425 (1983); Sherman E. Unger, Enterprise Zones, Some Perspectives on Anglo–American Developments, 5 Urb.L. & Policy 129 (1982).

9. Michael A. Wolf, An "Essay in Re–Plan": American Enterprise Zones in Practice, 21 Urb.Law. 29 (1989); Rubin & Trawinski, New Jersey's Urban Enterprise Zones: A Program That Works, 23 Urb. Law. 461 (1991).

10. See Williams, supra note 1.

11. Scott A. Tschirgi, Aiming the Tax Code at the Distressed Areas: An Examina-

tion and Analysis of Current Enterprise Zone Proposals, 43 Fla.L.Rev. 991, 1030 (1991).

12. See generally Ellen P. Aprill, Caution: Enterprise Zones, 66 S.Cal.L.Rev. 1341 (1993).

13. See Gary P. Winter, Tax Increment Financing: A Potential Redevelopment Financing Mechanism for New York Municipalities, 18 Fordham Urb.L.J. 655, 656, n.9 (1991); John S. Young, The Tax Increment Allocation Redevelopment Act: The "Blighted" Statute, 15 S.Ill.U.L.J. 145 (1990); Cardwell & Bucholtz, Tax–Exempt Redevelopment Financing in Florida, 20 Stetson L.Rev. 667 (1991); Hayes & Godec, Taxation Innovations: Enhanced Sales Tax Incentive Programs, 22 Urb.Law. 143 (1990).

14. See Winter, supra note 13, at 656.

§ 4.11 Buffer Zones

Land on the periphery of a zone may suffer adverse effects from neighboring uses in a more intensive zone. Euclidean zoning attempts to reduce these effects by transition or buffer zoning, which puts the next lower, more intensive zone as the adjacent zone. Thus, a single-family zone is in theory next to a two-family zone, which is next to a four-family zone and so on. Buffering is not always possible to that degree, but it is common for a multi-family zone to be placed between a single-family zone and an industrial zone to shield the single-family zone from industrial uses.[1] The result is anomalous in the sense that it places more people closer to the presumed harmful industrial use, but it is consistent with the zoning hierarchy that places single-family use at the top of the pyramid.

Buffer zones are valid so long as the property in the zone can be devoted to a profitable use.[2] If the buffer zone classification renders the land useless, the zoning may be found invalid or found to be a taking.[3]

Buffering is also achieved by height and bulk controls. For example, where commercial areas abut single-family residential areas, the commercial uses may be limited in height and greater than ordinary setbacks may be required.[4]

Buffer conditions are frequently imposed as part of the grant of development permission with rezonings, variances, or special permits. Typically, these conditions take the form of fencing, landscaping or open space requirements to protect neighbors from the external effects of noise and view of the new, more intensive development.[5]

III. HEIGHT, BULK, AND SETBACK CONTROLS

§ 4.12 Height Controls

Height regulations state maximum heights either in terms of feet or number of stories or both. The Supreme Court accepted their general validity long ago in Welch v. Swasey.[1] Today, most litigation questions their validity as applied. Height regulations effectuate purposes of the

---

§ 4.11

1. See Village of Arlington Heights v. Metropolitan Housing Dev. Corp., 429 U.S. 252, 97 S.Ct. 555, 50 L.Ed.2d 450 (1977), where the policy of the village was to only allow multi-family use where it served this buffering purpose.

2. Evanston Best & Co. v. Goodman, 369 Ill. 207, 16 N.E.2d 131 (1938).

3. Janesick v. City of Detroit, 337 Mich. 549, 60 N.W.2d 452 (1953) (found unreasonable). But see Quirk v. Town of New Boston, 140 N.H. 124, 663 A.2d 1328 (1995) (not a taking where economically viable use remained on balance of parcel).

4. Big Creek Lumber Co. v. County of San Mateo, 31 Cal.App.4th 418, 37 Cal. Rptr.2d 159 (1995) (1,000 foot buffer between lumber operations and residential area in part to mitigate erosion effects in the vicinity of residences valid; size of buffer was "fairly debatable").

5. Quirk v. Town of New Boston, 140 N.H. 124, 663 A.2d 1328 (1995) (upholding 200 foot buffer); Wellspring Zendo, Inc. v. Trippe, 211 A.D.2d 23, 625 N.Y.S.2d 334 (1995) (upholding a 50 foot buffer).

§ 4.12

1. 214 U.S. 91, 29 S.Ct. 567, 53 L.Ed. 923 (1909).

Standard Act, namely "to secure safety from fire," "to provide adequate light and air" and "to prevent the overcrowding of land." They may also promote aesthetics.[2] Denver, for example, has a height limitation in certain zones to preserve the view of the mountains from several city parks.[3]

Minimum height requirements are less common. Historically they have fared less well than maximum height limits. When courts first confronted minimum height requirements, they invalidated them. For example, where an ordinance required all facades of buildings to be at least 15 feet in height in a commercial area, the court held the regulation had no relation to the public health, safety and welfare.[4] These cases invalidating minimum height requirements, however, were decided in an era when courts refused to recognize aesthetics as a legitimate zoning aim. Today, the reverse is true,[5] and aesthetics may justify minimum height requirements.[6]

Problems with height controls may develop as applied to particular building features. Some ordinances anticipate this, by excepting roof top protrusions, such as elevator towers and heating and air-conditioning units and vents. Where height is measured by stories, the ordinance must be checked to determine whether a basement counts as a story. Cases construing ordinance provisions as to the level from which heights are measured are common.[7] Where practical difficulties or undue hardship will result from strict application of an ordinance, a variance may be sought. Height variances, as a type of area variance,[8] are usually less consequential than use variances and thus easier to obtain.[9]

§ 4.13 Bulk and Setback Controls

Bulk regulations provide a zoning envelope for buildings by horizontal measurement. They include such regulations as minimum lot size,

2. See infra § 4.14 (discussion of floor area ratios); supra § 3.11 and infra § 4.26 (discussion of airport/flight plane zoning); infra this section, note 6 and § 4.12 (other purposes of height restrictions).

3. Landmark Land Co. v. City and County of Denver, 728 P.2d 1281 (1986) (upholding act as legitimate effort to promote aesthetics).

4. City of North Miami v. Newsome, 203 So.2d 634 (Fla.App.1967). See also Frischkorn Const. Co. v. Lambert, 315 Mich. 556, 24 N.W.2d 209 (1946).

5. See infra Ch. 12.

6. Fiscal considerations may also be involved. See, e.g., Allright Auto Parks, Inc. v. Zoning Bd. of Adj. of City of Philadelphia, 107 Pa.Cmwlth. 448, 529 A.2d 546 (1987), holding that a minimum height requirement of 35 feet applied only to the north side of the street, thus exempting a pro-

posed eight foot kiosk on the south side. The city's apparent purpose in establishing a minimum height was to avoid a drag on development and investment by the "blighting influence of low, stunted one-story development." 107 Pa.Cmwlth. at 453, 529 A.2d at 549. See generally Landmark Land Co. v. City and County of Denver, 728 P.2d 1281 (1986) (upholding maximum height controls as legitimate effort to protect aesthetics).

7. Katcher v. Home Sav. & Loan Ass'n, 245 Cal.App.2d 425, 53 Cal.Rptr. 923 (1966) (height measured from finished grade level rather than original ground level); Opendack v. Madding, 69 Wash.2d 171, 417 P.2d 849 (1966) (height measured from average grade).

8. See infra § 5.15.

9. Wilcox v. Zoning Bd. of Appeals of Yonkers, 17 N.Y.2d 249, 270 N.Y.S.2d 569, 217 N.E.2d 633 (1966).

minimum frontage of lots, the area of a lot that may be covered, setbacks, and floor-area ratios (FARs).

A. Minimum Lots and Frontages

Minimum lot size and lot frontage requirements control densities and preserve view and open space. They are sometimes regulated by the subdivision ordinance instead of, or in addition to, the regulations in a zoning ordinance.[1] Reasonable frontage requirements are valid[2] as are minimum lot size requirements.[3] Both, however, by increasing housing costs, may be challenged as exclusionary zoning.[4] Details of application may also pose problems. Where the lot frontage is not straight, for example on a cul-de-sac, the proper construction of ordinances requiring minimum footage sometimes leads to litigation.[5]

B. Setback and Lot Coverage

The Standard Zoning Enabling Act provides that a community may regulate the percentage of a lot that may be occupied and the size of yards. A typical ordinance, for example, may provide that in a multi-family zone, not more than 60 percent of the lot shall be covered by buildings. Most ordinances go beyond regulating the percentage of the lot that is covered, and mandate building location by requiring minimum front, side and rear yards in residential districts. A 40,000 square foot minimum lot size in a residential zone may be accompanied by the requirement that any building on the lot be at least 40 feet from the front street, 30 feet from the rear line, and 10 feet from the side property lines.[6]

Setback and lot coverage requirements provide space, light and air, and safety from fire. Setbacks have several other purposes. They are used to reserve future street sites.[7] Flood plain zoning is a kind of setback provision,[8] as are provisions for setback of outdoor advertising signs and beachfront construction. In addition, setbacks may be used to keep buildings from active earthquake fault lines.[9]

In Gorieb v. Fox,[10] the United States Supreme Court upheld the general validity of setbacks to further the general goals of open space, light and air, and safety from fire.[11] Still, setbacks may be invalid as

---

§ 4.13

1. See infra Ch. 7.

2. Pitcher v. Heidelberg Twp. Bd. of Supervisors, 161 Pa.Cmwlth. 505, 637 A.2d 715, 717 (1994).

3. Trademark Homes v. Avon Lake Bd. of Zoning Appeals, 92 Ohio App.3d 214, 634 N.E.2d 685 (1993), app. denied, 69 Ohio St.3d 1449, 633 N.E.2d 543 (1994). But see Aronson v. Town of Sharon, 346 Mass. 598, 195 N.E.2d 341 (1964) (invalidating a 100,-000 square feet requirement).

4. See infra § 6.2.

5. See Annot., 96 A.L.R.2d 1367 (1964).

6. § 10–2062, Zoning Code of Raleigh, N.C.

7. See infra § 7.11.

8. See infra § 11.20.

9. See Better Alternatives For Neighborhoods v. Heyman, 212 Cal.App.3d 663, 260 Cal.Rptr. 758 (1989) (applying Cal.Resources Code § 2621.5, creating 50 foot setback).

10. 274 U.S. 603, 47 S.Ct. 675, 71 L.Ed. 1228 (1927).

11. In an earlier case the Court invalidated an ordinance that allowed neighbors to establish the setback. Eubank v. City of

applied, and if the property owner is left with no room to build, a Fifth Amendment taking may be found.[12] In Lucas v. South Carolina Coastal Council,[13] the Supreme Court examined a statute that prohibited building on a beachfront lot in front of a setback line established in part to prevent erosion. The Court held that where the effect of compliance with the setback prevented the property owner from engaging in any economically viable use of the lot, a taking had occurred. The state was required to pay compensation unless it could prove that state nuisance or property law justified the requirement.[14]

The rule of *Lucas* would pose problems for setbacks if the affected portion of the lot is used to judge the economic impact. Generally, however, a taking is not found since most courts measure the remaining economic viability by reference to the entire lot.[15] If courts were to focus on the affected strip alone, it would increase the likelihood that setbacks would be takings.

Construction of particular ordinances may be difficult with odd shaped lots,[16] unusual street patterns, or unanticipated uses. For example, should a tennis court or a satellite dish be considered a structure subject to a setback?[17] What if the front yard is on a corner lot? Does a balcony that overhangs a yard violate the yard requirements? A detailed ordinance may cover some of these matters.[18] If not, the problem must be solved by litigation.

Conventional yard requirements are measured from the building to the lot line and are a prime manifestation of the "cookie cutter" style of development. Development may not conform nicely to this pattern of lot by lot building. For example, in Akers v. Mayor and City Council of Baltimore[19] a builder planned a series of four-family buildings built in an offset pattern to touch only at the corners. The roof and foundation for the series of buildings were continuous. The ordinance required that each building have two side yards of ten feet or one side yard of 15 feet.

Richmond, 226 U.S. 137, 33 S.Ct. 76, 57 L.Ed. 156 (1912). This case turned on the impropriety of delegation of legislative power. See infra § 5.4.

12. Giambrone v. City of Aurora, 85 Ohio App.3d 758, 621 N.E.2d 475 (1993).

13. 505 U.S. 1003, 112 S.Ct. 2886, 120 L.Ed.2d 798 (1992), discussed infra § 10.6.

14. See discussion infra § 10.6.

15. See infra § 10.7 for a discussion of the issue of defining the relevant parcel. In connection with setbacks, see the comments of the Court in Keystone Bituminous Coal Association v. DeBenedictis, 480 U.S. 470, 497, 107 S.Ct. 1232, 1248, 94 L.Ed.2d 472 (1987). In a post-*Lucas* case, the court rejected use of a narrow definition of the relevant parcel in Zealy v. City of Waukesha, 201 Wis.2d 365, 548 N.W.2d 528 (1996).

16. Patricca v. Zoning Bd. of Adj. of City of Pittsburgh, 527 Pa. 267, 590 A.2d

744 (1991) (nearby boulevard and right of way providing access could not be used to determine front line for setbacks for irregular lot).

17. City of Ladue v. Zwick, 904 S.W.2d 470 (Mo.App.1995) (tennis court was a structure that could not be placed in rear or side yard); Township of Middletown v. New Jersey Dairies, 101 N.J.Super. 149, 243 A.2d 824 (1968) (vending machines were structures subject to front and side yard setbacks).

18. See Annot., 94 A.L.R.2d 398 (1964) (on side and rear yards); Annot., 93 A.L.R.2d 1223 (1964) (on front yards).

19. 179 Md. 448, 20 A.2d 181 (1941). See also Norwood Heights Improvement Ass'n v. Mayor and City Council of Baltimore, 191 Md. 155, 60 A.2d 192 (1948).

If the series was construed to be one building, it complied with the ordinance. However, if each four-family building was considered to be a separate building, the side yard requirement could not be met for any but two of the buildings.[20] The court construed the matter sensibly and held that the series of buildings was one building for setback purposes.

These conventional requirements reflect traditional housing patterns prevalent in zoning's early days. In many areas today there remains a deeply embedded preference for single-family detached homes surrounded by front, side, and back yards. Many have criticized excessive reliance on the single-family detached house for several reasons. It increases housing costs, consumes substantial open space, and limits personal choice.[21] Some have even questioned the legitimacy of mandating conformity to the single-family detached house style.[22] To avoid these kinds of problems and to offer options to developers, most ordinances provide for planned unit developments and cluster zoning.[23]

C. Setback Lines for Street Widening Purposes

Setback lines may facilitate the subsequent widening of streets, since the land can be acquired for less expense when buildings have not been erected on the site.[24] The validity of such a setback is suspect since the lowering of condemnation costs is not a proper purpose of zoning.[25] However, the courts are often not precise over the distinction between setbacks for street widening and setbacks for front yards, and the generally accepted validity of the latter has led to approval of the former under the police power, particularly if the setbacks are part of the zoning ordinance or a comprehensive plan.[26]

§ 4.14   Floor–Area Ratio (FAR)

FAR, meaning floor-area ratio, is a device that combines height and bulk provisions and provides an inducement to a developer to leave more open space by allowing a higher building. Under FAR, an ordinance designates a floor-area ratio for a particular zone. If the ratio is 1:1, a one story building can cover the entire buildable area of the lot, a two-story building can cover half the buildable area, a four-story building can cover one-fourth of the buildable area and so on. In commercial office

---

20. Each four-family building was closer than 10 feet to another. While two could be closer than 10 feet, they would have to be 15 feet from the third unit.

21. Edward H. Ziegler, Jr., The Twilight of Single–Family Zoning, 3 U.C.L.A. J.Envtl.L. & Policy 161 (1983).

22. Richard F. Babcock, The Egregious Invalidity of the Exclusive Single–Family Zone, Land Use Law & Zoning Digest 4 (July 1983).

23. See infra §§ 7.15–19.

24. A setback line used to reserve future street sites is similar to an official map provision, a distinction being that official maps reserve new street sites as well as

sites for widening existing streets. See infra § 7.11.

25. See supra § 3.21, regarding zoning to lower condemnation costs.

26. Palm Beach County v. Wright, 641 So.2d 50, 53 (Fla.1994) (emphasizing transportation regulations adopted as part of a comprehensive plan); Rochester Business Inst., Inc. v. City of Rochester, 25 A.D.2d 97, 267 N.Y.S.2d 274 (1966) (no taking found where property owner required to leave vacant a fourteen foot strip for a future road since the economic impact on the lot as whole was minimal).

areas in large cities the ratio may be 10:1, which allows a twenty-story building on half the buildable area of the lot. Some cities induce developers to leave more open space by offering increases in FAR in return for on-site public facilities, such as plazas.[1]

FAR may be used with maximum height limits and other bulk controls, so that in a 10:1 area, it may not be possible to build a 200–story building on ½₀th of the buildable area of a lot or to eliminate yards entirely and build a 10–story building up to all lot lines. Nevertheless, FAR does give the builder some flexibility.

FAR has been assumed to be valid,[2] but, as with other bulk controls, problems develop with specific applications. Where state law defined FAR as "the sum of the area of all floors of buildings or structures compared to the total area of the site," a municipality's attempt to exclude environmentally sensitive areas from calculations, thus reducing allowable development, was held ultra vires.[3] The statute, the court said, required use of the "total area." In contrast, a developer was unable to convince a court that the appropriate measure against which to calculate its building allowance included its fee interest in an abutting street.[4]

IV. ZONING WITH FLEXIBILITY

§ 4.15 The Need for Flexibility

Euclidean or use zoning[1] proved too rigid to adapt to changing community needs and development pressures.[2] Difficulties arose in determining the compatibility of different uses. Increased numbers of use districts with fewer permitted uses of right in each district, along with underzoning, limited developers' options.[3] This led to many rezoning requests, but change, at least in theory, was difficult.[4] Government approval involved an all or nothing decision to grant or deny development permission. A grant of permission left neighbors of the newly authorized use unprotected and allowed environmentally sensitive lands to be destroyed since the authorities lacked the capacity to impose site-specific controls. On the other hand, denial of permission left the land possibly underused.

Over the years governments developed a variety of techniques to

§ 4.14

1. See infra § 4.18 on bonus and incentive zoning.

2. The absence of direct challenges to the facial validity of FAR is unremarkable since the device is tied to height and lot coverage, matters expressly within the Standard Zoning Enabling Act.

3. Manalapan Builders Alliance, Inc. v. Township Committee of Manalapan, 256 N.J.Super. 295, 606 A.2d 1132 (1992).

4. Mall, Inc. v. City of Seattle, 108 Wash.2d 369, 739 P.2d 668 (1987).

§ 4.15

1. Use zoning is described supra §§ 4.1 to 4.9.

2. Another major deficiency was the lack of mandatory planning under the Standard Zoning Enabling Act, which meant that many codes were not based on a thoughtful assessment of the community's future needs. See supra Ch. 2.

3. Lane Kendig, Performance Zoning 9 (Planners Press 1980).

4. See infra Chapter 5 for methods of change.

inject flexibility into the process to remedy these deficiencies.[5] These include the use of floating zones, conditional zoning, increased reliance on the special permit process,[6] site review controls, performance zoning, planned unit developments,[7] interim zoning, and overlay zoning.

§ 4.16   Floating Zones

A floating zone is an unmapped district with detailed and conditional use requirements. Metaphorically, the zone "floats" over the city until affixed to a particular parcel. Floating zones generally involve predictable uses that have significant community impacts such as shopping centers and planned unit developments, or uses that the city wishes to encourage such as industrial parks, affordable housing, and housing for the elderly.

Use of the floating zone involves a two-step process. The city first creates a zone with listed characteristics, for example, a planned unit development with minimums set for acreage, open space, and a mix of uses. This ordinance provides that land meeting these characteristics may be so zoned by a second ordinance when a property owner applies for it, if the action will otherwise promote the public interest. Upon receipt of an application meeting the criteria of the initial ordinance, the zone floats down to the surface by enactment of the second ordinance. Once affixed, it is similar to any other zone, except that the invitation remains open to apply it wherever an applicant meets the conditions.

Rodgers v. Village of Tarrytown[1] upheld the floating zone technique. In that case, an ordinance provided that parcels of 10 acres or more could be rezoned to a BB district permitting multiple family dwellings if certain standards were met. The ordinance required a ten-acre minimum and imposed height, setback, and open space requirements. The BB zone floated since no parcel on the zoning map was so designated. At the request of a landowner, a tract zoned residential A was rezoned BB. When a neighbor challenged the rezoning, the court upheld it, noting that the village had acted to fill a need for multi-family housing to keep young families in the area. Thus, rather than being for the primary benefit of the owner, the zoning promoted the general welfare.[2] The court also held that the ordinance set sufficient standards for the zone, and exemplified a considered, comprehensive scheme.

---

5. Porter, Phillips & Lassar, Flexible Zoning: How It Works (1988); Sherman v. City of Colorado Springs Planning Comm'n, 763 P.2d 292, 296 (Colo.1988).

6. See infra § 5.24.

7. Discussed infra §§ 7.15–.19.

§ 4.16

1. 302 N.Y. 115, 96 N.E.2d 731 (1951).

2. For a case coming to the same result under a similar ordinance applied to a 2½ acre parcel, see Miss Porter's School, Inc. v. Town Plan & Zoning Comm'n of Farming-

ton, 151 Conn. 425, 198 A.2d 707 (1964). See also Floyd v. County Council of Prince George's County, 55 Md.App. 246, 461 A.2d 76 (1983). See generally Carol M. Rose, Planning and Dealing: Piecemeal Land Controls As a Problem of Local Legitimacy, 71 Cal.L.Rev. 837 (1983); Comment, Zoning—The Floating Zone: A Potential Instrument of Versatile Zoning, 16 Cath.U.L.Rev. 85 (1966); Herbert Goldman, Comment, Zoning Change: Flexibility vs. Stability, 26 Md. L.Rev. 48 (1966).

The floating zone's invitation to landowners to seek rezonings was the primary objection of Eves v. Zoning Board of Adjustment of Lower Gwynedd Township.,[3] the leading case invalidating floating zones. *Eves* involved a floating limited industrial zone applied to a 103–acre tract in a residential neighborhood. The court held the scheme invalid because, in the court's view, there was no plan. It viewed the failure of the legislative body to map land for industrial use in the first instance as an abdication of the power to zone. Development itself, as solicited by individuals, would become the plan. The court thought the process carried evils akin to spot zoning, and was particularly concerned with neighboring property owners who had no way of foreseeing changes resulting from floating zones. Perhaps the fact that the rezoned tract was to be used as a sewage treatment plant and that there were 300 neighbors who had objected accentuated the court's concern.

The objections of the *Eves* court have not troubled other courts, who recognize that the marketplace subjects zoning authorities to constant pressure to change. Even without floating zones, landowners and developers are usually the ones who initiate rezoning requests to intensify land use and neighboring property owners have no better chance of foreseeing that these types of changes may occur. Consequently, courts generally approve the idea of floating zones.[4]

The second or mapping step of the floating zone process, like any rezoning, can present problems. A floating zone may be held invalid as spot zoning.[5] There also may be contract-like features of the floating zone that make it invalid as contract zoning.[6] Or, if the ordinance lacks sufficient criteria to guide decisionmaking, it may be held unconstitutional as an invalid delegation of legislative authority.[7]

A floating zone also may be held invalid because it does not "accord with a comprehensive plan."[8] Floating zones may not be in accord where courts construe the comprehensive plan exclusively to mean the zoning plan as evidenced by the zoning map. In this instance, a floating zone appears as an "island" just as spot zoning. However, where zoning need accord only in the sense that it is not arbitrary, or may accord to a

---

3. 401 Pa. 211, 164 A.2d 7 (1960).

4. Treme v. St. Louis County, 609 S.W.2d 706 (Mo.App.1980); Sheridan v. Planning Bd. of City of Stamford, 159 Conn. 1, 266 A.2d 396 (1969); Huff v. Board of Zoning Appeals of Baltimore County, 214 Md. 48, 133 A.2d 83 (1957) (upheld the mapping of a floating light industrial zone into a residential area); Rodgers v. Village of Tarrytown, 302 N.Y. 115, 96 N.E.2d 731 (1951). Subsequent decisions in Pennsylvania have undermined *Eves* as well. See Donahue v. Zoning Bd. of Adj. of Whitemarsh Twp., 412 Pa. 332, 194 A.2d 610 (1963).

5. See infra § 5.10. See also Kristine Cordier Karnezis, Annot., 80 A.L.R.3d 95 (1977).

6. See infra § 5.11.

7. See infra § 5.4. See also City of Miami v. Save Brickell Ave., Inc., 426 So.2d 1100 (Fla.App.1983) (where legislative body acts in a quasi-judicial capacity, there must be standards to control its actions). See generally Margaret Marshall Prahl, Note, The Rezoning Dilemma: What May a Court Do with an Invalid Zoning Classification?, 25 S.D.L.Rev. 116 (1980).

8. See Eves v. Zoning Bd. of Adj. of Lower Gwynedd Twp., 401 Pa. 211, 164 A.2d 7 (1960).

master plan (and the master plan has embodied floating zones),[9] floating zones should be held valid.[10] Rather than showing a lack of planning, the mere creation of the floating zone is some evidence that the legislative body has thought the matter through. Furthermore, the fact that legislators take the first step in a neutral setting, without a specific rezoning request, eliminates the fear that private interests are driving the decision to invite applications for the particular use in question.

Use of a floating zone process may lead to greater judicial deference than is the case with the similar technique of the special use permit. The latter, an administrative process, is subject to close judicial review, while the former, a legislative act, traditionally enjoys a presumption of validity and more deferential review.[11] Also, a jurisdiction that requires proof of mistake or change in circumstances to uphold a standard rezoning may not apply that stringent rule to a floating zone.[12]

§ 4.17 Conditional Zoning

Conditional zoning provides flexibility to the basic use zoning system. While conditional zoning takes a variety of forms and lacks a precise definition, its use stems from the need to attach site-specific control to rezoned land.[1]

A. *Inadequacy of General Rezoning Process*

Zoning classifications typically contain many uses permitted of right.[2] A general rezoning of land allows all listed uses without regard to site-specific concerns that might suggest that some of those uses would be harmful to neighboring uses within the same zone or in adjacent zones. This is often the case as the theoretical compatibility of the uses may not accord with political reality and the needs of the specific area in question. Aware of this, zoning authorities have an unending interest in knowing a developer's specific plans. But, general rezonings leave the authorities with no commitment that the developer will use the land as indicated during the rezoning process.

A general rezoning request is an all or nothing proposition. When a city grants a general rezoning without limiting conditions, all permitted uses in the zoning classification are available. Assume that a developer says that it wishes to build a flower shop on a parcel and seeks rezoning to a commercial zone that allows numerous uses including flower shops, antique shops, banks, toy stores, and gas stations.[3] The legislative body of the city finds the idea of a flower shop unobjectionable and rezones

---

9. See supra Ch. 2 for discussion of relation of zoning to planning.

10. See Floyd v. County Council of Prince George's County, 55 Md.App. 246, 461 A.2d 76 (1983).

11. Homart Development Co. v. Planning & Zoning Comm'n of Town of Watertown, 26 Conn.App. 212, 600 A.2d 13, 15 (1991).

12. Rockville Crushed Stone v. Montgomery Co., 78 Md.App. 176, 552 A.2d 960, 962 (1989).

§ 4.17

1. See Chrismon v. Guilford County, 322 N.C. 611, 370 S.E.2d 579, 584 (1988).

2. See supra § 4.2.

3. Such a mixture of uses is common. See supra § 4.2.

the property to the general commercial use category. The property owner then builds a gas station. The neighbors have a fit, but the property is zoned for such use, and the gas station stays. Theoretically, a city should not rezone the parcel unless it is willing to permit any of the uses that are listed in the commercial zone. But, without the authority to impose conditions, a city must rezone for any listed commercial purpose or not rezone.

B. *Conditional Zoning as a Solution*

Conditional zoning is tailor-made zoning, designed to provide an escape from the dilemma of open-ended general rezonings. With conditional zoning, the property is rezoned to the more intensive zone, but a condition in the rezoning ordinance[4] or in a separate contract[5] limits the kinds of uses permitted. Using the example from above, if the legislative body is willing to permit any commercial uses at the site except gas stations, the land might be rezoned for commercial uses subject to the condition that the otherwise permitted gas station use is prohibited. If the city wishes to allow flower shops only, then the condition can preclude all other normally permitted uses. A condition requiring the planting and maintenance of a landscaped buffer may also be added. With this method, the legislative body can create an almost unlimited number of different kinds of zones.

Substantial, and some would say excessive, flexibility is obtained by combining the features of conditional zoning and floating zones. Floating above the general, and mapped, use districts, are special use districts created to parallel the general use districts. A property owner seeking a change in classification can apply for either general or special use rezoning. A general use rezoning allows all permitted uses of right, while a special use rezoning limits use to a specified, detailed project. For example, if R–2 zoning contains four permitted uses (say single-family, two-family, garden apartments, and institutional uses), an R–2–S special use, or floating zone, option exists so that a developer intending to build garden apartments can have its property specifically zoned for such use or can seek a general rezoning . .

In applying for general R–2 zoning the property owner may be precluded from making known its intended use, which is irrelevant since the rezoning will allow any of the four permitted uses, and the legislative body is obligated to find that any of the four uses are appropriate at the site. In contrast, for an R–2–S rezoning for garden apartments, the developer must submit to specific site plan review of its project by the legislative body. Protective conditions will also be imposed on the special use district to conform to site problems detected during the review process.[6] The fact that the city knows and can closely control the use to

---

4. Goffinet v. Christian County, 65 Ill.2d 40, 2 Ill.Dec. 275, 357 N.E.2d 442 (1976).

5. Sylvania Electric Products, Inc. v. City of Newton, 344 Mass. 428, 183 N.E.2d 118 (1962).

6. See Chrismon v. Guilford County, 322 N.C. 611, 370 S.E.2d 579 (1988), de-

take place in the special use district make a developer's chances of success much greater than with general rezonings.

Conditional zoning presents difficulties in some jurisdictions. The enabling act may not authorize it. It may be proscribed under the rubric of contract or spot zoning since it may appear to a court that private deal making, rather than the public interest, motivated the action. It also may violate the uniformity clause of the Standard Act. We explore these issues in detail elsewhere in this treatise.[7]

C. Automatic Zoning Conditions

Rezonings sometimes occur automatically. Like common law shifting and springing executory interests, property may be downzoned or upzoned upon the happening of a future event. Reversionary zoning is sometimes used where a community wishes to assure itself that a developer engages only in the use granted by a rezoning. To do so, it may provide that if no one develops the property for a specific use within a set time or if the newly allowed use ceases, the property's zoning classification will revert to its prior classification.

Reverter provisions pose problems. Since the property's classification moves automatically from one zoning classification to another, no notice is given and no hearing may be held. Some courts find this a violation of both due process and the enabling act requirement that a zoning enactment occur upon notice and public hearing.[8] Other courts uphold reversion conditions by implying an obligation on the zoning authorities to provide notice and a hearing.[9] Still, even if the authorities follow procedural safeguards, a substantive objection exists since the process assumes the prior classification, to which the land reverts, is still valid. With the passage of time and changing circumstances, however, that may not be the case. The reclassification should focus on current, not past, needs.[10]

Another automatic zoning process may be used to meet different community concerns. An ordinance might provide that the happening of certain events will reclassify the property for a different use. For example, the ordinance might provide that property zoned agricultural will be zoned residential upon the opening of a major street. This "potential classification zone" has the advantage of giving property owners and others some indication of the plans of the city. As with reverter provisions, substantive and procedural defects may exist with this technique. The new street may have opened, triggering the rezon-

---

scribing such a system authorized by special enabling legislation.

7. See infra § 5.11 discussing contract zoning and § 5.13 discussing uniformity.

8. Spiker v. City of Lakewood, 198 Colo. 528, 603 P.2d 130 (1979); Scrutton v. Sacramento County, 275 Cal.App.2d 412, 79 Cal.Rptr. 872 (1969).

9. Perry v. Planning Comm'n of Hawaii County, 62 Haw. 666, 619 P.2d 95

(1980); Goffinet v. Christian County, 65 Ill.2d 40, 2 Ill.Dec. 275, 357 N.E.2d 442 (1976).

10. See *Scrutton*, supra note 8, discussing this problem. But see Beyer v. Burns, 150 Misc.2d 10, 567 N.Y.S.2d 599 (1991), finding a reversion requirement valid as a timing control.

ing, but other intervening developments may have occurred that suggest uses other than residential would be preferable. There also may be no provision for notice and hearing.

§ 4.18 Incentive Zoning

Incentive zoning obtains public benefits or amenities from private developers.[1] A city may offer a developer an incentive, such as a density bonus, in return for the developer agreeing to provide a desired amenity. Typical amenities include public plazas, off-street parking, access sites to rapid transit, day care centers, and theaters.[2] New York City, for example, has granted incentives to development along the Fifth Avenue shopping area to provide hotel and residential uses above the street level commercial use.[3] Washington, D.C. granted a planned unit development on Dupont Circle an increase in height and density to provide a two-level pedestrian arcade and mini park.[4]

Incentive zoning is similar in some respects to conditional zoning, discussed in the previous section. As part of the development permission process, a condition is attached that grants added development rights and requires construction of, or payment for, some public facility. However, they have dissimilar goals and effects. Conditional zoning generally arises from the desire to accommodate development while protecting neighbors from a presumably more intense use. With incentive zoning, the acquisition of the amenity is the driving force, and while the neighbors might benefit from the amenity provided, it is acquired for the larger public. In fact, the neighbors may suffer more from the increased density allowed by the bonus.

One may attack the validity of incentive zoning on several fronts.[5] If authority from the state is not express,[6] a court may not imply the right to use it. The deal-making nature of incentive zoning may make it suspect as a species of spot or contract zoning.[7] Constitutional objections under the due process and taking clauses must be considered as well. If the incentive program is a voluntary option, a developer can hardly object to the consequences of its own choice. Even if participation in the program is mandatory, government typically designs the size of the bonus to more than offset the cost of the amenity, leaving the developer

---

§ 4.18

1. See generally Terry Lassar, Carrots and Sticks: New Downtown Zoning (1989).

2. See generally Alan C. Weinstein, Incentive Zoning, 2 Zoning and Land Use Controls, § 8.01 (Rohan ed.1994).

3. Id.

4. Dupont Circle Citizens Ass'n v. District of Columbia Zoning Comm'n, 431 A.2d 560 (D.C.App.1981).

5. See Weinstein, supra note 2, at § 8.04. Incentive zoning generally raises the same issues discussed infra § 6.7 regarding mandatory set-asides and density

bonuses. The latter, in fact, are essentially incentive zoning techniques with a particular purpose, namely affordable housing.

6. See New York–McKinney's Village Law § 7–703 authorizing incentive zoning.

7. See Municipal Art Society of New York v. City of New York, 137 Misc.2d 832, 522 N.Y.S.2d 800 (1987) (invalidating city's sale of land, which contained density bonus, finding it to be a "cash sale of a zoning bonus." Id. at 832, 522 N.Y.S.2d at 804). See also §§ 5.10–11.

better off economically with the incentive than without it.[8] This likely solves potential constitutional infirmities. This assumes, however, that the incentives are truly bonuses. If, in fact, the incentive zoning program is preceded by a downzoning of property, which is done to make the "incentive" attractive, the provision is an improper use of the police power.

An incentive program also may be vulnerable to the charge that it does not legitimately advance a public purpose. From one perspective incentive zoning is "zoning for sale",[9] as the city trades its zoning restrictions for the amenity. If the city allows the developer to build a larger building and the costs of the amenity are not too high, the developer wins. The city wins as well, since it acquires a free public amenity. The public does suffer harm from the greater building density, which exceeds the base zoning, and the city must still defend the base zoning as appropriate because it is the base zoning that creates the bonus that brings the developer to the bargaining table. Yet, if there is no such thing as a free lunch, then someone must be paying a cost. That "someone" may be the neighbors in the community surrounding the bigger building. For the neighbors the congestion from the more intensive use may outweigh any benefit they receive from the amenity, but the city is entitled to decide that the gain of the amenity for the public at large more than offsets the loss to the neighbors from congestion. If a legal challenge brought on due process or equal protection grounds by either a developer or a neighbor is tested by a deferential standard of judicial review, it would likely fail.[10]

Higher scrutiny may come by way of a nexus challenge under the taking clause. The Fifth Amendment requires that legislation substantially advance a legitimate state end. As applied by the Supreme Court this means there must be a connection between the public benefits sought and the use proposed. Thus, a developer constructing an office building will generate more traffic, and that likely justifies requiring the developer to provide off-street parking. No bonus or incentive is likely even necessary. But, if the office developer is told to build a performing arts center, the link or nexus to the office building is less clear, and the requirement to build the arts center may constitute a taking. We explore these constitutional arguments elsewhere.[11]

§ 4.19 Performance Zoning

An alternative to use zoning is performance or impact zoning.[1] Avoiding the rigidity of use classifications, performance zoning concerns

---

8. See Montgomery County v. Woodward & Lothrop, Inc., 280 Md. 686, 376 A.2d 483 (1977), cert. denied 434 U.S. 1067, 98 S.Ct. 1245, 55 L.Ed.2d 769 (1978).

9. See, e.g., Jerold Kayden, Zoning for Dollars: New Rules for an Old Game?, 39 Wash.U.J.Urb. & Contemp.L. 3 (1991).

10. See Asian Americans for Equality v. Koch, 72 N.Y.2d 121, 531 N.Y.S.2d 782,

527 N.E.2d 265 (1988). See generally infra §§ 10.12 and 10.14.

11. See § 9.8 regarding exactions and impact fees, and § 10.5 regarding the nexus test.

§ 4.19

1. See generally Christopher J. Duersken, Modern Industrial Performance Standards: Key Implementation and Legal

itself with the spillover effects of land use activities. Performance zoning establishes criteria to measure such effects, and if the criteria are met, the activity is allowed.

The most prevalent use of performance zoning involves industrial activities. First used in the 1950s, it is widespread today. Instead of, or in addition to, specifically listed uses, the industrial performance zoning ordinance provides standards to measure the external effects produced by industrial activities. It may establish specific standards for smoke, noise, dust, toxic emissions, glare, vibration, radioactivity, electrical disturbance, heat, and odors.[2] If the manufacturing operation meets the standards, it is permitted within the zone.

Performance standards are used increasingly in dealing with nonindustrial activities. Performance zoning even achieved the status of being "one of the trendiest topics"[3] of land use in the 1990s. Such natural resource features as floodplains, woodlands, steep slopes, and groundwater can be protected by performance standards. An ordinance might protect steep slopes by limiting the percentage of slopes of certain grades from being developed or stripped of vegetation. Topographical features may limit the density of development. These include such features as depth to bedrock and the seasonal high water table, factors that concern the possibility of sewage effluent polluting groundwater.[4] Set percentages of vegetation and trees that must remain on site are another example.[5] Noise controls also can be applied to any use.

Performance zoning has met with judicial approval so long as the standards are reasonably set.[6] While the enforcement of such standards may produce development lots of varying size, courts have held them not to violate the uniformity requirement because they treat similar property similarly.[7] As with any ordinance, overbreadth and vagueness may be concerns. For example, a noise standard of "plainly audible" was held invalid on these grounds.[8]

Whether performance standards do their job well is another matter. One commentator uses the scarcity of legal challenges as proof of their ineffectiveness.[9] Problems do exist. Performance zoning requires more

---

Issues, 18 Zoning and Planning Law Report 33 (May 1995); Martin Jaffe, Redesigning Industrial Performance Standards, 47 Land Use Law & Zoning Dig. 3 (Nov. 1995); Porter, Phillips & Lassar, Flexible Zoning: How It Works 82 (1988); Lane Kendig, Performance Zoning (1988); Frederick W. Acker, Note, Performance Zoning, 67 Notre Dame L.Rev. 363 (1991).

2. See, e.g., DeCoals, Inc. v. Board of Zoning Appeals of City of Westover, 168 W.Va. 339, 284 S.E.2d 856 (1981), upholding absolute no dust standard against a substantive due process challenge.

3. See Duersken, supra note 1.

4. Reimer v. Board of Supervisors of Upper Mount Bethel Twp., 150 Pa.Cmwlth. 323, 615 A.2d 938, 943 (1992).

5. Duerksen, supra note 1, at 35.

6. Jones v. Zoning Hearing Bd. of Town of McCandless, 134 Pa.Cmwlth. 435, 578 A.2d 1369 (1990); DeCoals, Inc. v. Board of Zoning Appeals of City of Westover, 168 W.Va. 339, 284 S.E.2d 856 (1981).

7. Reimer v. Board of Supervisors of Upper Mount Bethel Twp., 150 Pa.Cmwlth. 323, 615 A.2d 938, 943 (1992). See infra § 5.13 regarding uniformity.

8. Easy Way of Lee County, Inc. v. Lee County, 674 So.2d 863 (Fla.App.1996).

9. See Jaffe, supra note 1, at 3.

administrative time to administer than does use zoning. The systems are not as devoid of discretionary decisionmaking as theory envisions. Drafting workable standards can be difficult, and some standards are highly subjective, creating concerns of arbitrary application.

Still, performance zoning is viable as an alternative or a supplement to use zoning. Studies show that communities that employ performance standards, usually in industrial design, and environmental matters, have reached some level of satisfaction with them.[10] Pre-stated performance criteria produce better design and site control in a less confrontational manner than traditional use zoning. If federal and state governments eliminate or decrease environmental controls, one local option to deal with the resultant void will be to increase environmental performance standards.

§ 4.20 Interim and Holding Zones

If a plan for an area is in the process of formation, interim zoning may protect the area pending the adoption of a permanent zone.[1] Interim zoning may also freeze development pending the solution of problems of overburdened public services, such as schools, water, and sewer or to prevent a proliferation of particular uses that a city finds itself unprotected against, such as adult bookstores[2] or fast food restaurants.[3]

Interim zoning is vital in preserving the integrity of the planning and zoning processes.[4] Without a moratorium on development, building activity may occur that will defeat the plan's purposes before it is enacted. The publicity that will necessarily be a part of the planning process may in fact trigger a race by developers to build or at least achieve a vested right to build before new controls, which they fear may be more intrusive than current ones, are recommended for adoption.

Interim zoning may also serve as a growth management tool. There may be areas where zoning has not yet established a desired use or where development pressures are not yet substantial. Or the community may think that development should be postponed while other, closer in areas develop first or until an adequate infrastructure exists to support development. In these situations, a community has two choices. One is the enactment of a growth management system. This will require significant planning and forethought. Alternatively, a wait and see approach may be used where the community simply zones the area for unintensive, low density uses, such as agriculture or large lot single-family residential uses, and requires application for a special permit for

---

10. Porter, Phillips & Lassar, Flexible Zoning: How It Works 82 (1988).

§ 4.20

1. See supra § 3.20 and infra § 9.5.

2. City of Renton v. Playtime Theaters, Inc., 475 U.S. 41, 106 S.Ct. 925, 89 L.Ed.2d 29 (1986).

3. Schafer v. City of New Orleans, 743 F.2d 1086 (5th Cir.1984).

4. See generally Thomas E. Roberts, Interim Development Controls, 3 Zoning and Land Use Controls, Ch. 22 (Patrick Rohan ed. 1989); Robert H. Freilich, Interim Development Controls: Essential Tools for Implementing Flexible Planning and Zoning, 49 J.Urb. Law 65 (1971).

every other kind of use.[5] This kind of zoning is sometimes called hold zoning or underzoning. Though it is practiced, it is not recommended.

Legitimate desires to control future development may prompt the use of the wait and see, hold, or underzoning approach, but these approaches lack the planning that justifies growth controls. The approach is likely used due to a lack of planning expertise or funding in the community, or perhaps due to a fear over whether enabling authority exists for an overt growth management scheme.[6] Ill-conceived, low density designations for large areas of a community make future planning difficult. People will likely build some residences in the areas creating sprawl. This spotty development may also make the area unattractive for alternative uses that may better suit the land in the future.[7] A formal growth management plan, protected during its planning stage by an interim freeze, is the preferred route.

Authority to enact an interim control is often express.[8] If not, courts usually imply it, though some refuse to do so.[9] The control may stringently limit, and sometimes freeze, use, but the relatively short duration of the law mitigates the harm. If it allows a reasonable use over a reasonable time, the ordinances will survive a taking challenge.[10] The longer the duration of the control, the more likely it is to be found a taking.[11]

There are options to the use of interim zoning. Upon learning of proposed development or fearing development, a municipality may hastily pass what purports to be a permanent zoning classification. Such action, not supported by a planing process, is ill advised. The better approach is to adopt a temporary measure pending completion of the planning process.

Another technique is for the city administratively to withhold action on a permit request if the city expects the proposed development to be inconsistent with planned changes in the law. If the permit is delayed long enough to permit passage of the new ordinance, the city can deny the permit based on the new law. Administrative denial is, thus, an informal way to freeze land use. Courts differ over its validity. Some courts uphold the denial where convinced that the city acted to further

---

5. See a description of such a process in Snyder v. Board of County Comm'rs of Brevard County, 595 So.2d 65 (Fla.App. 1991), reversed on other grounds 627 So.2d 469 (Fla.1993).

6. See infra § 9.3.

7. Lane Kendig, Performance Zoning 9 (Planners Press 1988).

8. See, e.g., West's Ann.Cal.Govt.Code § 65858.

9. See, in favor, Collura v. Town of Arlington, 367 Mass. 881, 329 N.E.2d 733 (1975), and against, State ex. rel. Kramer v. Schwartz, 336 Mo. 932, 82 S.W.2d 63 (1935). The issue of authority may turn on

whether the ordinance was enacted as an emergency measure without compliance with standard notice and hearing requirements. See Roberts, supra note 4, § 22.02[3]. See also infra § 9.5.

10. Chioffi v. City of Winooski, 676 A.2d 786 (Vt.1996); Williams v. City of Central, 907 P.2d 701 (Colo.App.1995); Woodbury Place Partners v. City of Woodbury, 492 N.W.2d 258 (Minn.App.1992), cert. denied 508 U.S. 960, 113 S.Ct. 2929, 124 L.Ed.2d 679 (1993). See also infra § 10.8.

11. See infra §§ 9.5 and 10.8.

the general welfare and did not arbitrarily pick on the permit applicant.[12] In other states, they will only uphold the denial if the newly enacted ordinance was pending at the time of the denial.[13] In some jurisdictions, the technique will not work. There may, for example, be a vested right to develop pursuant to the law in effect at the time of the permit application despite a subsequent change in the law.[14]

§ 4.21   Overlay Zoning

An overlay zone places property simultaneously in two zones. Most often this occurs where the use of the property affects two distinct municipal concerns, such as compatibility of use with surrounding lands and the preservation of sensitive lands or protection from problem uses. An overlay zone often implements historic preservation, for example, since historically significant areas near urban centers frequently encompass contiguous commercial and residential areas.[1] In this fashion, the commercial and residential classifications are continued while the overlay imposes historic controls on the portion of the properties within those two zones that comprise the historic area. Another use of overlay zones is to protect environmentally sensitive land. Thus, land zoned for single-family homes may be undevelopable because of an overlay zone showing the land to be on a steep hillside.[2] Other examples include land beneath the flight paths, which may be placed in an airport overlay, and floodplain zoning.[3]

Overlay zones may run afoul of the uniformity clause of the Standard State Zoning Enabling Act.[4] The City of Phoenix created an "inebriate district" as an overlay in a large commercially zoned area. In this bizarrely, but perhaps aptly, named zone, establishments selling alcohol, pawn shops, blood banks, second hand stores, and missions were required to get special permits. Those same uses in the commercial zone, but outside the overlay, were permitted of right. A property owner, whom the city denied a permit to operate a pawn shop in the inebriate zone, challenged the law on uniformity grounds. In Jachimek v. Superior Court In and For County of Maricopa,[5] the court agreed with the property owner, holding that the city could not create an overlay in which use permits were required for certain uses that were not required

---

12. Spector v. Building Inspector of Milton, 250 Mass. 63, 145 N.E. 265 (1924).

13. Smith v. City of Clearwater, 383 So.2d 681 (Fla.App.1980), review dismissed 403 So.2d 407 (Fla.1981); Ben Lomond, Inc. v. City of Idaho Falls, 92 Idaho 595, 448 P.2d 209 (1968).

14. See infra § 5.28 for a discussion of vested rights.

§ 4.21

1. A–S–P Associates v. City of Raleigh, 298 N.C. 207, 258 S.E.2d 444 (1979).

2. See Thurow, Toner & Erley, Performance Controls for Sensitive Lands, ASPO Planning Advisory Service Report Nos. 307 and 308 (1975).

3. See infra § 11.20 (floodplains).

4. See infra § 5.13 for discussion of uniformity.

5. 169 Ariz. 317, 819 P.2d 487 (1991).

for the same uses in the same underlying zone elsewhere within the city.[6]

Not all courts agree with the literal view of *Jachimek*. In A–S–P Associates v. City of Raleigh,[7] the court found an historic overlay that subjected commercial property to restrictions not suffered by other commercially zoned land did not violate the uniformity clause. Giving the enabling act a more relaxed reading than the court in *Jachimek*, the *A-S-P* court acknowledged that the regulations of a particular use district must be uniform, but found that rule not to prohibit overlay districts despite the fact that they imposed additional regulations on some property. After all, said the court, the overlay did "not destroy the uniformity of the regulations applicable to the underlying use-district."[8]

Express statutory authorization may answer concerns over the validity of an overlay. Such legislation existed in the *A-S–P* historic overlay case, but was absent in the *Jachimek* pawn shop case. Perhaps this influenced the courts.

Whether one views an overlay as violating the uniformity clause, it does create a new use district with dual controls. If doubt exists over whether overlays are authorized, a city can achieve the same effect by creating a new zone that contains the controls of the prior underlying zone and the newly desired controls that would otherwise be imposed by overlay.

V. GOVERNMENTAL AND COMMUNITY USES

§ 4.22 Favored Status

Among the vast number of land uses controlled by zoning some are thought to generate special benefits to the public. They include government uses and such community facilities as schools, public utilities, airports, religious uses, and medical facilities. These uses, while perhaps as objectionable to their immediate neighbors as other kinds of uses, are often treated more leniently.

The special treatment afforded to, or sought by, these uses results in a substantial amount of litigation. Government owned or operated uses often claim immunity from the zoning of lower or coequal levels of government. If the government use is immune, uses that are similar to the governmental use, but not allowed by local law, object on uniformity or equal protection grounds to the dissimilar treatment. Regulatory schemes of states and the federal government may authorize or license private uses that conflict with local zoning. Where that occurs, the private licensee will attempt to establish that state law has preempted the local zoning.

---

6. Accord, Boerschinger v. Elkay Enterprises, Inc., 32 Wis.2d 168, 145 N.W.2d 108 (1966).

7. 298 N.C. 207, 258 S.E.2d 444 (1979).

8. 298 N.C. at 230, 258 S.E.2d at 458. See also Franchise Developers, Inc. v. City of Cincinnati, 30 Ohio St.3d 28, 505 N.E.2d 966 (1987)(environmental quality overlay upheld without specific reference to uniformity issue).

Zoning codes may permit public uses in a zone, but ban otherwise identical private uses. They may allow nonprofit private uses that are similar to the permitted public use, but disallow for-profit uses. These distinctions are often unrelated to the land use effects of the various owned and organized uses, but many courts allow them nonetheless.

§ 4.23 Immunity for Governmental Uses

A. General Considerations

The superior sovereign, by virtue of that status, is generally immune from control by subordinate units of government. The supremacy clause of the constitution prevents the application of state or local zoning laws to the federal government.[1] Likewise, local zoning does not bind a state. Courts presume that when the state delegates police power functions to local governments, it does not intend to waive the historical immunity it has as a sovereign. Thus, the delegated power cannot be used against the state.[2]

Immunity is essential for numerous government functions that are unwanted in many locales such as waste disposal,[3] correctional facilities,[4] and group homes for the disabled.[5] While operating a governmental use in noncompliance with local zoning may result in harm to the residents of the city or at least to the immediate neighbors, the carrying out of an essential state function benefits the public at large. If local controls were permitted to exclude these uses, they might have nowhere to go.

Whether immunity attaches depends on the purpose of the land use, not the ownership.[6] This accords with the general rule that zoning regulates use, not ownership.[7] There are decisions to the contrary. In Board of Child Care of the Baltimore Annual Conference of the Method-

---

§ 4.23

1. United States v. Chester, 144 F.2d 415 (3d Cir.1944); Town of Groton v. Laird, 353 F.Supp. 344 (D.Conn.1972). See generally, George R. Wolff, Comment, The Inapplicability of Municipal Zoning Ordinances to Governmental Land Uses, 19 Syracuse L.Rev. 698 (1968).

2. See, e.g., Aviation Services v. Board of Adj. of Hanover Twp., 20 N.J. 275, 119 A.2d 761 (1956). See generally Note, Governmental Immunity from Local Zoning Ordinances, 84 Harv.L.Rev. 869, 878 (1971); Annot., 61 A.L.R.2d 970 (1958).

3. See infra § 10.21.

4. See, e.g., Dearden v. City of Detroit, 403 Mich. 257, 269 N.W.2d 139 (1978); Evans v. Just Open Government, 242 Ga. 834, 251 S.E.2d 546 (1979).

5. See discussion infra § 4.23. The federal Fair Housing Act may bar discrimination against housing for the disabled. See infra § 6.9.

6. Youngstown Cartage Co. v. North Point Peninsula Community Co–Ordinating Council, 24 Md.App. 624, 332 A.2d 718 (1975) (private lessee not entitled to immunity simply because land owned by the state); Tim v. City of Long Branch, 135 N.J.L. 549, 53 A.2d 164 (Err. & App.1947). The private owner of land, as lessor to the government, may not be entitled to invoke the government's immunity where the government is not a party to the action. Montgomery v. Town of Sherburne, 147 Vt. 191, 514 A.2d 702 (1986). But see Thanet Corp. v. Board of Adjustment of Princeton Twp., 108 N.J.Super. 65, 260 A.2d 1 (1969), certification denied 55 N.J. 360, 262 A.2d 207 (1970). See generally, Allan Manley, Annot., Applicability of Zoning Regulation to Nongovernmental Lessee of Government–Owned Property, 84 A.L.R.3d 1187 (1978).

7. See supra § 4.2.

ist Church, Inc. v. Harker,[8] a private operator of a state licensed child care facility sought to be exempt from local zoning law. The court said that preemption depended on ownership by the state and feared that "[w]ere it otherwise, all entities licensed by the state, and providing governmental services, would be entitled to exemption from local land use regulations."[9] The court's fear is misplaced. As numerous decisions attest, private licensees conducting uses on private land will only be exempt if the legislature is found to have so intended.[10]

Privatization of government functions ought not cause a loss of zoning immunity.[11] In City of Louisville v. Gailor,[12] the county contracted with a private corporation to house some of its inmates. The company's chosen site was within the City of Louisville. While the City's Board of Adjustment granted a conditional use permit, the trial court overturned it on appeal. The high court, however, held that the privately operated jail enjoyed the same immunity as a county run jail. The key to zoning and to immunity is use, not ownership, said the court. The question is not who owns the land, but how it is used. Use for a prison, even where delegated to private parties, is still governmental.

Land currently devoted to an immune governmental activity ought to be zoned though the zoning will not be effective while the government use exists.[13] If the land is left unzoned and the immune government function ceases, the local authorities may be left with no way to prevent private land uses at odds with their zoning scheme. The concern is not imaginary since government functions are often the subject of privatization efforts. Still, the case reflects the reluctance of courts to give expansive treatment to immunity claims lest they encourage private-governmental relationships that avoid compliance with local land use laws.[14]

B. Federal

The supremacy clause of the constitution prevents the application of state or local zoning laws to federally operated land uses.[15] Federal

8.   316 Md. 683, 561 A.2d 219 (1989).

9.   316 Md. at 694, 561 A.2d at 225.

10. See, e.g., Board of Supervisors of Crooks Twp. v. ValAdCo, 504 N.W.2d 267 (Minn.App.1993) (hog facilities exempt from local law by state regulation of animal feedlots); Envirotech of America, Inc. v. Dadey, 234 A.D.2d 968, 651 N.Y.S.2d 778, (N.Y.A.D.1996) (medical waste handler licensed by state exempt from local zoning). See generally discussion infra § 4.25.

11. But see Richardson v. McKnight, ___ U.S. ___, 117 S.Ct. 2100, 138 L.Ed.2d 540 (1997), where the Supreme Court held that prison guards who are employees of a private prison are not entitled to qualified immunity for civil rights liability purposes under § 1983. For discussion of § 1983, see infra § 10.23.

12. 920 S.W.2d 887 (Ky.App.1996).

13. Lane County v. Bessett, 46 Or.App. 319, 612 P.2d 297, 301 (1980) (interpreting state law that provided that local zoning may apply to publicly owned property "except property of the United States" as not precluding the adoption of zoning for the land that became effective when federal use terminated). There may be state or local statutes that prevent local zoning of federal uses.

14. See Outerbridge Terminal, Inc. v. City of Perth Amboy, 179 N.J.Super. 400, 432 A.2d 141 (1980).

15. United States v. Chester, 144 F.2d 415 (3d Cir.1944); Town of Groton v. Laird, 353 F.Supp. 344 (D.Conn.1972). See generally Wolff, supra note 1.

regulatory schemes also may preempt local law.[16] The federal government can consent to be governed by local law. Where it recognizes the desirability of some local control, it generally does so by directing federal agencies to consult with local authorities. The agency, though, retains final decisionmaking power. The Federal Urban Land–Use Act of 1968, for example, establishes a general recognition of willingness to cooperate with local authorities by directing that actions taken ''be made to the greatest extent practicable in accordance with planning and development objectives of the local governments and local planning agencies.''[17]

With respect to the federal government it does not matter whether the government owns the property in fee or is the lessee of property. In neither case is its use governed by local regulation. Private lessees of federally owned property may also be exempt if they are carrying out a government function. The Homeless Assistance Act of 1987,[18] for example, requires federal agencies to make surplus or underused federal property available to provide housing to the homeless. Where the army leased twelve single family homes to a local community group, which used the homes to house the homeless violating the town's zoning ordinance, the court held federal law preempted the local zoning ordinance.[19] However, if a court views a use as proprietary, the lessee is subject to local law.[20] Thus, a credit union leasing federally owned property to serve service personnel was held proprietary and subject to local zoning.[21]

C. State and Local Government

A state's immunity extends not only to departments and agencies of the state,[22] but includes local governments when exercising state functions and private licensees operating pursuant to a comprehensive state regulatory programs.[23] Immunity problems also arise between governmental subunits of the state, such as cities, counties, and school districts, where one unit attempts to use land under the zoning control of another unit. Statutes may expressly confirm immunity for a specific use or expressly subject the activity to local control, but legislatures usually fail to deal expressly with immunity, leaving resolution of the issue to the courts. The Standard State Zoning Enabling Act, for example, is silent with respect to regulation of government uses.

16. See, e.g., the limitations on local zoning imposed by federal communications law, infra § 4.25, and the reach of land use agreements under the Endangered Species Act. W.W. Dean & Assocs. v. City of South San Francisco, 190 Cal.App.3d 1368, 236 Cal.Rptr. 11 (1987).

17. 40 U.S.C.A. § 531.

18. 42 U.S.C.A. §§ 11411 et seq.

19. United States v. Village of New Hempstead, 832 F.Supp. 76 (S.D.N.Y.1993).

20. Dupuis v. Submarine Base Credit Union, Inc., 170 Conn. 344, 365 A.2d 1093 (1976).

21. See also Outerbridge Terminal, Inc. v. City of Perth Amboy, 179 N.J.Super. 400, 432 A.2d 141 (1980) (contract between the federal government and a private party for the latter to store jet fuel is not a federal lease entitling the private party to immunity from zoning).

22. Town of Bloomfield v. New Jersey Highway Auth., 18 N.J. 237, 113 A.2d 658 (1955).

23. See infra § 4.24.

The courts have employed several tests to decide whether immunity attaches. The early tests used include the superior sovereign test, the eminent domain test,[24] and the governmental-proprietary test. All have their shortcomings,[25] and are frequently, and derogatorily, referred to as mechanical. The superior sovereign and eminent domain tests embody "might makes right" philosophies and, while having the advantage of simplicity, they ignore the fact that the power or status that confers immunity is unrelated to the purposes of the delegated zoning power.

The governmental-proprietary distinction, likely the most popular early test,[26] is frequently unhelpful because it varies on the context in which courts apply it. A governmental activity for purposes of determining municipal tort liability may not be a governmental activity for purposes of determining immunity from zoning regulations, yet courts are not always careful to avoid mixing precedent. Moreover, no unanimity exists as to what is a governmental function even in the zoning context. For example, in City of Scottsdale v. Municipal Court of City of Tempe,[27] Scottsdale purchased land in Tempe zoned for single family use to build a sewage disposal plant. Scottsdale applied for a permit, which Tempe refused. The court held that Scottsdale could proceed in any event, since sewage disposal was a governmental function, and a state statute had given Scottsdale the power to construct utilities and acquire lands within or without corporate limits. Contrary to *Scottsdale*, in Jefferson County v. Birmingham,[28] the court held a sewage plant to be a proprietary function, so that the city's residential zoning bound the county, precluding it from building a sewage plant.

A growing number of courts, dissatisfied with early cases that they regarded as too permissive in exempting state activities from local zoning,[29] have instituted a balance of interests test.[30] St. Louis County v. City of Manchester[31] evidences this approach where a city sought to put a sewage plant in an area zoned for other uses by the county. The city, pointing to its statutory authority to acquire sewage plants and to place

24. Any governmental unit with such power is automatically immune from zoning restrictions.

25. City of Everett v. Snohomish County, 112 Wash.2d 433, 772 P.2d 992 (1989).

26. Hagfeldt v. City of Bozeman, 231 Mont. 417, 420, 757 P.2d 753, 754 (1988).

27. 90 Ariz. 393, 368 P.2d 637 (1962).

28. 256 Ala. 436, 55 So.2d 196 (1951).

29. Witzel v. Village of Brainard, 208 Neb. 231, 235, 302 N.W.2d 723, 726 (1981) (Hippe, J. dissenting).

30. See City of Crown Point v. Lake County, 510 N.E.2d 684 (Ind.1987); City of Ames v. Story County, 392 N.W.2d 145 (Iowa 1986); Independent School Dist. No. 89 of Oklahoma County v. City of Oklahoma City, 722 P.2d 1212 (Okl.1986); Blackstone Park Improvement Ass'n v.

State Bd. of Standards & Appeals, 448 A.2d 1233 (R.I.1982); City of Temple Terrace v. Hillsborough Ass'n for Retarded Citizens, Inc., 322 So.2d 571 (Fla.App.1975), affirmed 332 So.2d 610 (Fla.1976); Rutgers, State University v. Piluso, 60 N.J. 142, 286 A.2d 697 (1972).

31. 360 S.W.2d 638 (Mo.1962). In Missouri, however, the eminent domain test is first applied. If the governmental authority seeking immunity possesses the power to condemn under the state constitution, and the authority where the land in question finds its power in a statute, the former controls and the use is immune. The balancing test is only used if the two bodies in conflict derive their power from the same source. City of Washington v. Warren County, 899 S.W.2d 863 (Mo.1995).

them outside city boundaries, argued that the county could not regulate its location. The court concluded that requiring the city to submit to reasonable county zoning ordinances could reconcile the statute authorizing county zoning and the statute authorizing extraterritorial sewage plants. Authority to locate plants beyond the city's boundaries did not mean they could be located anywhere.[32]

The balance of interests test places a heavier burden on government to justify its claimed immunity than is the case under the mechanical tests.[33] Even where a use is found immune, the right may not be absolute, as some courts review the use to see that it is operated reasonably.[34] This gives the recipient community some protection that it might not otherwise enjoy. Even the application of a mechanical superior sovereign test may not result in absolute immunity, as the court may subject the state to local laws aimed at public safety.[35]

As with the mechanical approaches, dissatisfaction exists with the balancing approach. Some courts find that it confers too much land use policymaking authority on the courts and lacks predictability. These courts, in turn, have implemented an intent test.[36] Some apply the intent test with a bias in favor of local control and demand a clear expression of an intent to find a use immune.[37] Where statutes do not spell out intent, the intent test shares with the balance of interests test a lack of predictability.

D. Local Government's Self–Exemption

Local governments often exempt their own uses from the operation of their zoning laws. Even where a municipality does not expressly exempt municipal uses, many courts find it is not bound to follow its own ordinances.[38] Some, however, presume that if the code is silent, the city must follow the law.[39] Courts have upheld these exemptions, reasoning that if it is a governmental use, it necessarily promotes the public

---

32. See also Wilkinsburg–Penn Joint Water Authority v. Borough of Churchill, 417 Pa. 93, 207 A.2d 905 (1965).

33. 6 Zoning and Land Use Controls § 40.03[b] (Rohan ed.1990).

34. Blackstone Park Improvement Ass'n v. State Bd. of Standards & Appeals, 448 A.2d 1233, 1239 (R.I.1982); Hagfeldt v. City of Bozeman, 231 Mont. 417, 757 P.2d 753 (1988); Hayward v. Gaston, 542 A.2d 760 (Del.1988).

35. City of Hattiesburg v. Region XII Comm'n on Mental Health & Retardation, 654 So.2d 516 (Miss.1995).

36. City of Everett v. Snohomish County, 112 Wash.2d 433, 772 P.2d 992 (1989); Dearden v. City of Detroit, 403 Mich. 257, 264, 269 N.W.2d 139 (1978); Macon Ass'n for Retarded Citizens v. Macon–Bibb County Planning & Zoning Comm'n, 252 Ga. 484, 314 S.E.2d 218, ap-

peal dismissed 469 U.S. 802, 105 S.Ct. 57, 83 L.Ed.2d 8 (1984); Davidson County v. City of High Point, 85 N.C.App. 26, 354 S.E.2d 280, modified 321 N.C. 252, 362 S.E.2d 553 (1987).

37. Macon Ass'n for Retarded Citizens v. Macon–Bibb County Planning & Zoning Comm'n, 252 Ga. 484, 314 S.E.2d 218, appeal dismissed 469 U.S. 802, 105 S.Ct. 57, 83 L.Ed.2d 8 (1984); Board of Child Care v. Harker, 316 Md. 683, 561 A.2d 219, 224 (1989).

38. Glascock v. Baltimore County, 321 Md. 118, 581 A.2d 822 (1990); Witzel v. Village of Brainard, 208 Neb. 231, 302 N.W.2d 723 (1981); Nehrbas v. Incorporated Village of Lloyd Harbor, 2 N.Y.2d 190, 159 N.Y.S.2d 145, 146, 140 N.E.2d 241, 242 (1957).

39. Clark v. Town of Estes Park, 686 P.2d 777 (Colo.1984).

interest.[40] However, if they follow the governmental/proprietary distinction, the latter activities would not be exempt.[41]

Local government can ultimately get its way since it has the power to amend the law to allow the use it wants for itself.[42] In one case, for example, when its board of adjustment denied a city a permit to put a fire station in a residential zone, the city rezoned the land to permit fire stations. The court held the rezoning valid, finding it to be in the public interest.[43]

Some suggest that since government has the power to amend, it need not bother doing so, but can simply use its land in violation of its own law.[44] This is bad policy. The fact that the power exists does not mean the process is unimportant. Requiring the municipality to go through the amendment process to permit its intended use gives the public a chance to be heard.[45]

§ 4.24   Preemption for Governmental Licensees

Licenses or contracts issued to private persons or entities for uses such as airports, alcohol sales, nuclear facilities, cemeteries, group homes, hospitals, and waste disposal facilities may be exempt from local zoning. While preemption for the licensee is similar to a finding of immunity for a state agency or other governmental body,[1] prevailing on the theory is often more difficult. A governmental use may be immune simply by virtue of the superior sovereign status of the state or by possessing the power of eminent domain,[2] and the question of intent does not enter the picture.[3] With preemption, the issue is intent, and while it can be express, it is often not, so the matter is one of implication. Many courts, loathe to deprive local government of zoning control, demand clear proof of intent to preempt. This is particularly true if the tradition of home rule is strong.[4]

40. Sinn v. Board of Selectmen of Acton, 357 Mass. 606, 259 N.E.2d 557, 559 (1970) ("municipal uses per se are substantially related to the general and specific purposes of zoning").

41. Hunke v. Foote, 84 Idaho 391, 373 P.2d 322 (1962) (electrical substation found proprietary); Nehrbas v. Incorporated Village of Lloyd Harbor, 147 N.Y.S.2d 738, 743 (Sup.Ct.1955); Annot., 61 A.L.R.2d 970 § 7[c] (1958).

42. Dougherty v. Hazleton Zoning Hearing Bd., 20 Pa.Cmwlth. 617, 342 A.2d 768, 771 (1975); Town of Hempstead v. Village of Rockville Centre, 67 Misc.2d 123, 323 N.Y.S.2d 872 (Sup.Ct.1971).

43. City of McAllen v. Morris, 217 S.W.2d 875 (Tex.Civ.App.1948).

44. Id.

45. Witzel v. Village of Brainard, 208 Neb. 231, 302 N.W.2d 723, 726 (1981) (Hippe, J. dissenting).

§ 4.24

1. See supra § 4.23.

2. See discussion supra § 4.23.

3. Edelen v. Nelson County, 723 S.W.2d 887 (Ky.App.1987). With the institution of the intent and balancing of interests tests as trends in governmental immunity cases, immunity is less likely to be granted than is true under the mechanical sovereignty-based test. See discussion supra § 4.23. This toughening up in the immunity area brings those cases more in line with the preemption cases.

4. Board of Child Care v. Harker, 316 Md. 683, 561 A.2d 219, 226 (1989) (noting that the intent to displace local zoning "must be strong indeed"). The state can override home rule if it is clear in doing so. Public Service Company v. Town of Hampton, 120 N.H. 68, 411 A.2d 164 (1980). Preemption is a "fundamental limitation on home rule powers." Albany Area Builders

The infrequency of preemption leaves many land uses subject to multiple permitting processes. Our federal system, and preference for a local role in land use decisions, may justify this, but a cost results. Multiple permitting increases the possibility of a total denial of the requested use. The mere requirement of seeking multiple permits subjects the applicant to the prospect of conflicting conditions. If the conditions imposed by the subordinate government conflict with the higher level or if the former denies a use that the latter allows at a specific location, the subordinate's decision is preempted. But, even if there is no denial and they impose no additional conditions, the process of multi-permitting adds to the cost and the time for development approval.

Preemption may be express, but, as with immunity, legislatures do not often expressly convey their intent regarding preemption. If they do, and do so clearly, the issue resolves itself. A provision that no state license will issue where the activity would be contrary to a local zoning ordinance can eliminate a potential conflict.[5] Conditioning a state or federal permit on compliance with local law indicates an intent not to preempt.[6] Absent statutory guidance, a court must resolve the conflict.

The search for implied preemption looks to whether there is a conflict or inconsistency between state and local law or whether state law so comprehensively occupies a field that intent to preempt must be implied.[7] Courts require clear proof of intent,[8] and recent cases show that numerous uses have fallen short in convincing the courts. This is true with mining,[9] timber harvesting,[10] landfills,[11] and waste management.[12]

Ass'n v. Town of Guilderland, 74 N.Y.2d 372, 377, 547 N.Y.S.2d 627, 629, 546 N.E.2d 920, 922 (1989).

5. See, e.g., West's Ann.Cal.Bus. & Prof.Code § 23790 (alcoholic beverage outlets). Generally, state licensure in California does not preempt local regulation, and most statutes either require the applicant to indicate the zoning is proper or permit the locality to exclude the licensed activity from a particular place.

6. Holiday Point Marina Partners v. Anne Arundel County, 107 Md.App. 160, 666 A.2d 1332, 1335 (1995) (federal and state permits conditioned on compliance with local law supported finding of no preemption), cert. granted 341 Md. 719, 672 A.2d 659 (1996). The condition would not control if it were determined that the permit issuer lacked such authority.

7. Id. See also Appeal of Hoover, 147 Pa.Cmwlth. 475, 608 A.2d 607 (1992).

8. The thoroughness of state review of land use projects also may suggest an intent to preempt. Board of Supervisors of Crooks Twp. v. ValAdCo, 504 N.W.2d 267 (Minn. App.1993). But see Holiday Point Marina Partners v. Anne Arundel County, 107 Md.

App. 160, 666 A.2d 1332, 1335 (1995), cert. granted 341 Md. 719, 672 A.2d 659 (1996) (exhaustive review by Army Corps of Engineers pursuant to federal law did not preempt local law regarding siting of marinas where the process did not address siting and the permit was conditioned on compliance with local law).

9. Gernatt Asphalt Products, Inc. v. Town of Sardinia, 87 N.Y.2d 668, 664 N.E.2d 1226, 642 N.Y.S.2d 164 (1996); San Pedro Mining Corp. v. Board of County Comm'rs of Santa Fe County, 121 N.M. 194, 909 P.2d 754 (1995) (Mining act was ambiguous and did not impliedly preempt county's regulation); Baker v. Snohomish County Dept. of Planning and Community Development, 68 Wash.App. 581, 841 P.2d 1321 (1992) (Surface Mining Act did not preempt local regulation of surface mining), review denied 121 Wash.2d 1027, 854 P.2d 1085 (1993); McClimans v. Board of Supervisors of Shenango Tp., 107 Pa.Cmwlth. 542, 529 A.2d 562 (1987) (ordinance banning strip mining from part of town was not superseded by Pennsylvania Surface Mining Conservation and Reclamation Act); Board of County Comm'rs, La Plata County

A local law that is more restrictive than the state law is not necessarily one that is in conflict. In one case, the zoning law imposed a more stringent distance requirement on the location of marinas from natural oyster beds than did the state water quality law. No preemption was found since there was no language in the state law precluding the adoption of more restrictive controls.[13] In contrast, state regulation of animal feedlots was held to preempt a local law with respect to setbacks. The state determined setbacks on a project specific basis and the zoning law had a fixed setback, so that the feedlot operator could be prosecuted for violating a setback that the state had specifically decided was adequate.[14] In Desert Turf Club v. Board of Supervisors of Riverside County,[15] the court held a local ordinance precluding a state licensed race track invalid where based on the ground that such activity was immoral. The court held that the state's licensing determination had resolved the morals question and that it was not a matter of local option.

Where local law has the effect of totally banning a use that state law allows, implied preemption may be found since the local law may thwart the ability of the state law to achieve its goal.[16] A total ban does not, however, necessarily lead to a finding of preemption. In Gernatt Asphalt

v. Bowen/Edwards Associates, Inc., 830 P.2d 1045 (Colo.1992) (Oil and Gas Conservation Act did not preempt county's authority to enact land-use regulations for oil and gas operations within county). But see Voss v. Lundvall Bros., Inc., 830 P.2d 1061 (Colo. 1992) (Oil and Gas Conservation Act preempted home rule city from enacting land-use ordinance that imposed total ban on drilling).

10. Big Creek Lumber Co., Inc. v. County of San Mateo, 31 Cal.App.4th 418, 37 Cal.Rptr.2d 159 (1995) (Forest Practice Act did not preempt county's zoning ordinance regulating location of commercial timber harvesting).

11. Palermo Land Co., Inc. v. Planning Comm'n of Calcasieu Parish, 561 So.2d 482 (La.1990) (state law did not preempt entire field of regulation of sanitary landfills); Beverly Bank v. Cook County, 157 Ill. App.3d 601, 109 Ill.Dec. 873, 510 N.E.2d 941 (1987) (county and state have concurrent jurisdiction over sanitary landfills), appeal denied 117 Ill.2d 541, 517 N.E.2d 1084 (1987).

12. Waste Resource Technologies v. Department of Public Health of City & County of San Francisco, 23 Cal.App.4th 299, 28 Cal.Rptr.2d 422 (1994) (Integrated Waste Management Act did not preempt city's power to grant exclusive refuse collection permit); IT Corp. v. Solano County Bd. of Supervisors, 1 Cal.4th 81, 820 P.2d 1023, 2 Cal.Rptr.2d 513 (1991) (state laws governing hazardous waste disposal facilities did not expressly or impliedly preempt county's efforts to force removal of wastes unlawfully deposited by facility operator within "buffer" or "setback" zone); Village of Bolingbrook v. Citizens Utilities Co. of Illinois, 158 Ill.2d 133, 198 Ill.Dec. 389, 632 N.E.2d 1000 (1994) (comprehensive regulation of utilities by Public Utilities Act did not preempt village's home rule authority to fine for illegal discharges of untreated sewage); Tri–State Rubbish, Inc. v. Town of New Gloucester, 634 A.2d 1284 (Me.1993) (local ordinance requiring the separation of recyclable materials from nonrecyclable waste was not preempted by state waste management act). But see Talbot County v. Skipper, 329 Md. 481, 620 A.2d 880 (1993) (comprehensive state statutory scheme governing sewage sludge impliedly preempted county regulations).

13. Holiday Point Marina Partners v. Anne Arundel Co., 107 Md.App. 160, 666 A.2d 1332, 1335 (1995), cert. granted 341 Md. 719, 672 A.2d 659 (1996).

14. Board of Supervisors of Crooks Twp. v. ValAdCo, 504 N.W.2d 267 (Minn. App.1993).

15. 141 Cal.App.2d 446, 296 P.2d 882 (1956).

16. Voss v. Lundvall Bros., Inc., 830 P.2d 1061 (Colo.1992) (Oil and Gas Conservation Act preempted home-rule city from enacting land-use ordinance that imposed total ban on drilling).

Products, Inc. v. Town of Sardinia,[17] for example, the mining reclamation act at issue provided that the state law superseded all local laws relating to the mining industry, but the act expressly acknowledged local government power to enact zoning ordinances establishing permissible uses.[18] A mine operator challenged a zoning law that banned mining from the entire town, claiming that a total ban went beyond what the legislature had intended to allow regarding the establishment of use districts. This, the mine operator argued, was buttressed by the stated purpose of the act to foster the mining industry in the state, which could not occur if towns where the minerals were located were allowed to exclude mining. The Court of Appeals disagreed. The legislation allowed local government to determine permissible uses and the court would not by implication narrow the exemption.

Group homes and residential treatment centers for persons in need of close supervision have had mixed results. In some instances the state operates the homes, in which event immunity is likely to be found.[19] If private agencies operate the home, preemption is less likely. However, where a legislative scheme reveals a comprehensive policy to regulate group homes, including their location, preemption is found.[20] State law that defines group homes as single-family use may also supersede zoning.[21] In many instances, however, courts have not been convinced that the legislature intended preemption.[22] Close examination of the statute is

17. 87 N.Y.2d 668, 642 N.Y.S.2d 164, 664 N.E.2d 1226 (1996).

18. Id.

19. Macon–Bibb County Hospital Auth. v. Madison, 204 Ga.App. 741, 420 S.E.2d 586 (1992) (local zoning laws which regulated the hospital authority in the exercise of its governmental functions were preempted by the immunity to zoning regulations traditionally enjoyed by state governments and their agencies). See also Berger v. New Jersey, 71 N.J. 206, 364 A.2d 993 (1976); Town of Southern Pines v. Mohr, 30 N.C.App. 342, 226 S.E.2d 865 (1976).

20. Region 10 Client Management, Inc. v. Town of Hampstead, 120 N.H. 885, 424 A.2d 207 (1980); Abbott House v. Village of Tarrytown, 34 A.D.2d 821, 312 N.Y.S.2d 841 (1970) (boarding home for neglected children was immune to local zoning ordinance because local zoning laws were preempted by an overriding state law and policy favoring the care of neglected and abandoned children); People v. Town of Clarkstown, 160 A.D.2d 17, 559 N.Y.S.2d 736 (1990); Nichols v. Tullahoma Open Door, Inc., 640 S.W.2d 13 (Tenn.App.1982); State ex rel. Thelen v. City of Missoula, 168 Mont. 375, 543 P.2d 173 (1975); City of Los Angeles v. California Dep't of Health, 63 Cal.App.3d 473, 133 Cal.Rptr. 771 (1976); Costley v. Caromin House, Inc., 313 N.W.2d

21 (Minn.1981). See also City of Temple Terrace v. Hillsborough Ass'n for Retarded Citizens, Inc., 322 So.2d 571 (Fla.App. 1975), affirmed, 332 So.2d 610 (Fla.1976), which has been variously cited as standing for and against preemption. It did neither. The court did not decide whether preemption occurred. The court held that a group home was to be treated as a state agency, but remanded the case for the trial court to apply the balancing of interests test to determine whether the state was immune.

21. Missouri ex rel. Ellis v. Liddle, 520 S.W.2d 644 (Mo.App.1975) (the use of a single-family dwelling for up to ten juveniles did not violate the zoning ordinance because state law, and its broad definition of the term "family" superseded the ordinance); Adams County Ass'n for Retarded Citizens, Inc. v. City of Westminster, 196 Colo. 79, 580 P.2d 1246 (1978) (local zoning ordinance was superseded by state law that considered that group homes for the mentally retarded a residential use).

22. Civitans Care, Inc. v. Board of Adj. of City of Huntsville, 437 So.2d 540 (Ala. Civ.App.1983) (state policy of deinstitutionalization did not preempt local zoning regulations which excluded group homes for mentally disabled adults); Board of Child Care v. Harker, 316 Md. 683, 561 A.2d 219 (1989); Macon Ass'n for Retarded Citizens

necessary, and mere use of the word "comprehensive" will not suffice.[23] The type of care facility seeking an exemption also is critical. For example, homes for the mentally retarded may be exempt while treatment centers for substance abusers[24] or emotionally disturbed children may not.[25] Even without state preemption, the federal Fair Housing Act's prohibition against discrimination based on handicap significantly curtails local zoning of group homes and residential treatment centers.[26]

In addition to the Fair Housing Act's preemption, federal legislation preempts local law in numerous other instances. As with state legislation, preemption is sometimes express and frequently partial. The Federal Communications Commission, for example, requires that local law reasonably accommodate radio antennas.[27]

The United States Supreme Court has confronted several controversies involving state land use law and implied preemption. In California Coastal Commission v. Granite Rock Co.,[28] the Court favored state and local government by refusing to find that federal law facially preempted state control of mining on federal lands. Actual conflict would have to be shown, said the Court.[29] Drawing a distinction between land use laws and environmental controls, the Court held that the Federal Land Policy Management Act and the National Forest Management Act might preempt the former, but not the latter.[30] In other cases, the Court found that the Federal Insecticide, Fungicide, and Rodenticide Act (FIFRA) did not preempt local pesticide regulation[31] and that the Clean Water Act allowed state common law nuisance suits against those acting in compliance with federal law.[32]

v. Macon–Bibb County Planning & Zoning Comm'n, 252 Ga. 484, 314 S.E.2d 218, appeal dismissed 469 U.S. 802, 105 S.Ct. 57, 83 L.Ed.2d 8 (1984); Penobscot Area Housing Dev. Corp. v. City of Brewer, 434 A.2d 14 (Me.1981); Township of Washington v. Central Bergen Community Mental Health Center, Inc., 156 N.J.Super. 388, 383 A.2d 1194 (1978). See also City of Kenner v. Normal Life of Louisiana, Inc., 465 So.2d 82 (La.App.1985), affirmed, 483 So.2d 903 (La. 1986) (a local zoning ordinance which limited the number of unrelated people living together as a "single family" was not preempted by a state policy that defined community homes for the mentally retarded as single family units).

23. Incorporated Village of Nyack v. Daytop Village, Inc., 78 N.Y.2d 500, 577 N.Y.S.2d 215, 583 N.E.2d 928 (1991).

24. Incorporated Village of Nyack v. Daytop Village, Inc., 78 N.Y.2d 500, 577 N.Y.S.2d 215, 583 N.E.2d 928 (1991).

25. Hayward v. Gaston, 542 A.2d 760 (Del.1988) (county zoning regulations, enjoining state operation of residential treatment center for emotionally disturbed juveniles, were not preempted by state legislative policy of assisting and caring for emotionally disturbed adolescents committed to its charge).

26. This issue is discussed infra § 6.8.

27. Howard v. City of Burlingame, 937 F.2d 1376 (9th Cir.1991).

28. 480 U.S. 572, 107 S.Ct. 1419, 94 L.Ed.2d 577 (1987).

29. Finding a direct conflict, and hence preemption, see Crystal Bay Marina v. Sweeden, 939 F.Supp. 839 (N.D.Okl.1996).

30. Environmental permitting conditions that regulated, but did not prohibit, mining might be valid but had to be tested in as applied challenges, said the Court.

31. Wisconsin Public Intervenor v. Mortier, 501 U.S. 597, 111 S.Ct. 2476, 115 L.Ed.2d 532 (1991).

32. In International Paper Co. v. Ouellette, 479 U.S. 481, 107 S.Ct. 805, 93 L.Ed.2d 883 (1987), the Court found that the Clean Water Act preempted use of the nuisance law of a state injured by pollution emanating from another state, but found that the nuisance law of a state that is the source of the pollution can be applied.

Even in the absence of federal legislation, a zoning regulation may violate the dormant commerce clause if it constitutes a substantial burden on interstate commerce.[33] In Pike v. Bruce Church, Inc., the Court stated that "[w]here the statute regulates evenhandedly to effectuate a legitimate local public interest, and its effects on interstate commerce are only incidental, it will be upheld unless the burden imposed on such commerce is clearly excessive in relation to the putative local benefits."[34] Most commerce clause violations involve discrimination against interstate commerce, a common pitfall of waste control laws, or actions subjecting interstate business to inconsistent regulation.[35] Land use controls that are not discriminatory or in conflict with other authorities[36] are rarely seen as excessive.[37] Preventing the development of land to preserve agricultural uses and avoid the costs of urban sprawl is not violative of the commerce clause.[38] A zoning law that designates limited zones where manufactured housing is permissible is not an excessive burden on interstate commerce.[39]

§ 4.25 Public Utilities

A. *General Rules*

Public utilities are often exempt from local zoning control. If governmentally owned, they may be immune from local zoning as are other governmental uses.[1] If privately owned, the state law that grants the utility its franchise and regulates its operations may preempt local law. States usually deem exemption from local law necessary to assure that the utility can meet its service obligations, which may be regional, state, or national in character.[2] While local authorities and neighbors may not want an electric substation or oil pipeline in a residential area, the desire

33. See infra § 10.19 for discussion of commerce clause limitations on land use controls.

34. 397 U.S. 137, 142, 90 S.Ct. 844, 847, 25 L.Ed.2d 174 (1970).

35. Panhandle Eastern Pipe Line Co. v. Madison County Drainage Bd., 898 F.Supp. 1302 (S.D.Ind.1995) (county drainage board did not violate interstate commerce by requiring interstate pipeline to relocate lines at its own cost).

36. An inconsistency, not merely a difference, is required. One regulating authority must require conduct that another authority forbids. Panhandle Eastern Pipe Line Co. v. Madison County Drainage Bd., 898 F.Supp. 1302, 1314 n. 5 (S.D.Ind.1995).

37. "A local regulation will satisfy the commerce clause if it 'is rationally related to the social and environmental welfare of the community and does not discriminate against interstate commerce or operate to disrupt its required uniformity.'" Christensen v. Yolo County Bd. of Supervisors, 995 F.2d 161 (9th Cir.1993), citing Construction

Industry Ass'n of Sonoma County v. City of Petaluma, 522 F.2d 897, 909 (9th Cir.1975), cert. denied 424 U.S. 934, 96 S.Ct. 1148, 47 L.Ed.2d 342 (1976). See also Amanda Acquisition Corp. v. Universal Foods Corp., 877 F.2d 496, 505–06 (7th Cir.), cert. denied 493 U.S. 955, 110 S.Ct. 367, 107 L.Ed.2d 353 (1989).

38. Christensen v. Yolo County Bd. of Supervisors, 995 F.2d 161 (9th Cir.1993).

39. Texas Manufactured Housing Association, Inc. v. City of Nederland, 101 F.3d 1095 (5th Cir.1996), cert. denied 117 U.S. 2497, 138 S.Ct.1003 (1997). See also New Hampshire Motor Transportation Ass'n v. Town of Plaistow, 67 F.3d 326 (1st Cir. 1995), cert. denied 517 U.S. 1120, 116 S.Ct. 1352, 134 L.Ed.2d 521 (1996).

§ 4.25

1. See supra § 4.23.

2. See generally Note, Zoning and the Expanding Public Utility, 13 Syracuse L.Rev. 581 (1962).

uniformity

for efficient provision of service may compel insulating the utility from local law. Courts are often bothered by the scenarios they foresee if local law were to apply.[3] As the Florida Supreme Court said in a case involving a local government's attempt to require an electric utility to underground its lines: "If 100 such municipalities each had the right to impose its own requirements with respect to installation of transmission facilities, a hodgepodge of methods of construction could result and costs and resulting capital requirements could mushroom."[4]

State law typically vests authority over public utilities in a state commission and precludes local regulation. Immunity may be automatic or the state commission may be empowered to grant exemptions. In Ohio, for example, the zoning enabling act does "not confer any power on any board of county commissioners or board of zoning appeals in respect to the location, * * * use, or enlargement of any buildings or structures of any public utility."[5] Massachusetts law authorizes a public utility to seek an exemption from local zoning.[6] A state commission may also be authorized to review and reverse local zoning decisions.[7]

Though exempt from local law, a utility probably cannot act with impunity toward local interests. Where a utility must petition the state utility commission for an exemption, the local community has input to assert its interest.[8] This does not guarantee that the local government will have its way, for in considering a request the state commission must weigh all aspects of the public interest and not merely the local interest,[9] but at least it has an opportunity to be heard. State commissions may also attach conditions to utility land uses and activities to protect the local interest.[10]

In some jurisdictions certain utilities are expressly subject to zoning law.[11] Where local authority exists, they frequently permit utilities only

3. See Sager A. Williams, Limiting Local Zoning Regulation of Electric Utilities: A Balanced Approach in the Public Interest, 23 U.Balt.L.Rev. 565 (1994).

4. Florida Power Corp. v. Seminole County, Lake Mary, 579 So.2d 105, 107 (Fla.1991). See similar expression of concern in Chester County v. Philadelphia Electric Co., 420 Pa. 422, 425, 218 A.2d 331, 333 (1966).

5. Ohio Rev.Code Ann. § 303.211.

6. Mass.Gen.Law ch. 40A, § 3 provides that "[l]and or structures used, or to be used by a public service corporation may be exempted in particular respects from the operation of a zoning ordinance or by-law if, upon petition of the corporation, the department of public utilities shall, after notice given pursuant to section eleven and public hearing in the town or city, determine the exemptions required and find that the present or proposed use of the land or structure is reasonably necessary for the convenience or welfare of the public."

If a utility, otherwise required to seek an exemption fails to do so, it has no defense to violating a zoning law. New Jersey v. Jersey Central Power & Light Co., 55 N.J. 363, 262 A.2d 385 (1970).

7. Newport Elec. Corp. v. Town of Portsmouth, 650 A.2d 489 (R.I.1994) (court upheld utility commission reversal of a town's downzoning of utility owned land).

8. See, e.g., Mass.Gen.Law ch. 40A, § 3.

9. Planning Bd. of Braintree v. Dep't of Pub. Utils., 420 Mass. 22, 27, 647 N.E.2d 1186, 1190 (1995).

10. Appeal of Milford Water Works, 126 N.H. 127, 489 A.2d 627 (1985).

11. Ind. Code § 8-1-2-89 (b) (sewage disposal companies are subject to local comprehensive plan, zoning, and subdivision requirements). Ore.Rev.Stat. § 221.420, discussed in Northwest Natural Gas Co. v. City of Portland, 300 Or. 291, 711 P.2d 119 (1985).

—what about Franchise agreements

in commercial and industrial areas. Where authorities allow utilities in residential zones, they handle them as special uses.[12] The special permit technique is useful because it allows a unique use to be conditioned for minimal disruption to the neighborhood.

Where state law is ambiguous or silent, courts must determine whether state law impliedly preempts local law. While generalizations may be imprudent for an issue that turns on non-uniform state regulatory regimes, the cases seem to weigh in favor of implied preemption in the public utility area.[13] This tendency is in contrast to the reluctance to find preemption of local law in many other areas that the state regulates.[14] A concern that the parochial views of multiple localities would destroy effective and low-cost utility service presumably explains this tendency.[15]

B. *What Constitutes a Public Utility*

What constitutes a public utility for the purposes of preemption depends first on the state statutory definition, which may be general or precise, and may itself contain express exemptions.[16] To the extent that a court must construe legislative intent, the fundamental question is whether the efficient and continuous supply of the public service requires that utility not be subject to multiple levels of government control.[17] Where this test is met, courts have shown a willingness to confer immunity on entities that do not precisely fit specific statutory language. Thus, while state law may regulate and exempt "public service corporations," courts are likely to include private corporations that otherwise meet the concept of a public utility.[18] By the same rationale, a public entity that is not, in form, a corporation, such as a municipal electric department, transit authority or water commission, may be treated as a "public service corporation" for the purposes of a preemp-

---

12. See infra §§ 5.24–5.26 (special permits).

13. See, e.g., Howard County v. Potomac Electric Power Co., 319 Md. 511, 573 A.2d 821 (1990) (local government impliedly preempted from regulating transmission lines carrying 69,000 volts in light of broad grant of authority to state utility commission); Algonquin Gas Transmission Co. v. Zoning Bd. of Appeals of City of Meriden, 162 Conn. 50, 291 A.2d 204 (1971); Duquesne Light Co. v. Upper St. Clair Twp., 377 Pa. 323, 105 A.2d 287 (1954) (there must be an express grant of power for a municipality to regulate a utility; it will not be implied). But see Village of Bolingbrook v. Citizens Utilities Co., 158 Ill.2d 133, 198 Ill.Dec. 389, 632 N.E.2d 1000 (1994) (refusing to use implied preemption where village exercises home rule power).

14. See discussion supra §§ 4.23–24.

15. See Florida Power Corp. v. Seminole County, Lake Mary, 579 So.2d 105 (Fla.1991); Newtown Twp. v. Philadelphia Electric Co., 140 Pa.Cmwlth. 635, 594 A.2d 834, 837 (1991) (no power to regulate elec-

tric substation, noting need for uniform treatment). Howard County v. Potomac Electric Power Co., 319 Md. 511, 525, 573 A.2d 821, 828 (1990) (finding that with electric transmission lines the need for a single, uniform law was apparent in the comprehensiveness of the statute).

16. See Ohio and Pennsylvania statutes infra note 29 this section, regarding cellular towers.

17. For varying formulations of this test, see Cellular Telephone Co. v. Rosenberg, 82 N.Y.2d 364, 604 N.Y.S.2d 895, 898, 624 N.E.2d 990, 993 (1993); New Brunswick Cellular Telephone Co. v. Old Bridge Twp. Planning Bd., 270 N.J.Super. 122, 636 A.2d 588, 596 (1993); Commonwealth, Public Utility Commission v. WVCH Communications, 23 Pa.Cmwlth. 292, 351 A.2d 328 (1976).

18. Save The Bay, Inc. v. Department of Public Utilities, 366 Mass. 667, 680, 322 N.E.2d 742 (1975).

tion determination.[19] Many disputed classifications involve radio and other communication facilities, and the case results vary.[20]

Even if an entity is not a public utility under state utility law, it may meet the definition of a public utility for state zoning law purposes and be entitled to preferential treatment. Several states regard public utilities as "inherently beneficial" uses and, as such, they subject them to a more lenient test for the purposes of obtaining a variance.[21] The fact that an entity is not a public utility for state utility law purposes also does not preclude it from meeting the local zoning definition of that use.[22]

C. Cellular Towers and Other Telecommunications Facilities

Cellular telephone towers and other types of telecommunications facilities are a subject of controversy.[23] The public has shown a strong appetite for the communications services that the towers enable, and the number of these towers, which are often three to four hundred feet high, is increasing in response to the demand. Many neighbors, however, deplore them. While they may have health concerns,[24] the dominant objection is that the towers are aesthetically offensive.

Federal and state laws limit local control over cellular towers. The federal Telecommunications Act of 1996 partially preempts zoning of cellular towers by providing that local zoning may not unreasonably discriminate among providers of functionally equivalent services and that zoning cannot have the effect of totally prohibiting such services.[25]

19. Planning Bd. of Braintree v. Dep't of Pub. Utils., 420 Mass. 22, 27, 647 N.E.2d 1186, 1189 (1995).

20. Finding a radio tower to be a public utility, see Marano v. Gibbs, 45 Ohio St.3d 310, 544 N.E.2d 635 (1989). To the contrary, see Mammina v. Zoning Bd. of App. of Town of Cortlandt, 110 Misc.2d 534, 442 N.Y.S.2d 689 (1981).

21. Cellular Telephone Co. v. Rosenberg, 82 N.Y.2d 364, 604 N.Y.S.2d 895, 624 N.E.2d 990 (1993) (applying "more lenient" public utility variance standard to cellular tower). But see Smart SMR of New York, Inc. v. Bor. of Fair Lawn, 152 N.J. 309, 704 A.2d 1271 (1998) (declining to find monopole inherently beneficial).

22. Finding cellular use to be a public utility, see Hawk v. Zoning Hearing Bd. of Butler Twp., 152 Pa.Cmwlth. 48, 618 A.2d 1087, 1090 (1992); Payne v. Taylor, 178 A.D.2d 979, 578 N.Y.S.2d 327 (1991); McCaw Communications v. Marion County, 96 Or.App. 552, 773 P.2d 779 (1989) (cellular use found to be a public utility, but not a necessary one as required by the ordinance). To the contrary, see Bell Atlantic Mobile Systems, Inc. v. Zoning Hearing Bd. of Twp. of O'Hara, 676 A.2d 1255 (Pa.

Cmwlth.1996) (not a public utility where zoning ordinance did not define the term).

23. As to satellite dish antennas, 47 C.F.R. § 25.104 preempts zoning that materially limits transmission or increases costs on users unless the zoning authority can prove it is reasonable. See Christopher Neumann, Note, FCC Preemption of Zoning Ordinances that Restrict Satellite Dish Antenna Placement: Sound Policy or Legislative Overkill? 71 St.John's L.Rev. 635 (1997).

The Telecommunications Act of 1996, 47 U.S.C. § 332, does not expressly preempt local zoning for purposes of regulating digital television facilities, the next wave of progress. The FCC, however, may have implied preemption authority. See, e.g., City of New York v. Federal Communications Commission, 486 U.S. 57, 108 S.Ct. 1637, 100 L.Ed.2d 48 (1988). The wave promises to be of tidal dimensions, as many existing broadcasting towers are loaded to capacity.

24. See Hawk v. Zoning Hearing Bd. of Butler Twp., 152 Pa.Cmwlth. 48, 618 A.2d 1087, 1090 (1992) (upholding finding that tower had no adverse health affects).

25. 47 U.S.C. § 332 (c) (7)(B)(i)(I) and (II).

The Act precludes consideration of the environmental effects of radio frequency emission if the facility complies with federal regulations concerning such emissions. The Act also provides for expedited judicial review of adverse rulings by state or local government bodies. In Bell-South Mobility, Inc. v. Gwinnett County,[26] the county denied a request to build a tower apparently due to neighbors' concerns with safety and visual incompatibility with surrounding lands. Applying the 1996 act, the court held these vague, speculative concerns unpersuasive in light of evidence showing that the departments of public safety and transportation had no objection and a report from an appraiser that these towers had no adverse effect on property values.

In addition to federal limits, the power of local authorities to regulate these uses turns on whether the service provider is exempt under state law as a public utility. The towers may be treated as "inherently beneficial" public utilities since mobile telephone service enhances personal and commercial communications and is valuable for emergency services.[27] In accord with other utility exemption cases discussed above, if a cellular tower is a public utility under state law, it will be exempt as others are exempt.[28] Some states, however, have deprived cellular transmission facilities of the exemption otherwise afforded to public utilities.[29] Immunity may also be issue specific. In New Jersey, for example, a state statute precludes zoning authorities from considering electromagnetic radiation effects.[30]

Even if not public utilities under state utility law, cellular towers may be treated as public utilities for state and local zoning law purposes and be entitled to the preferential treatment they afford to such uses. The New York Court of Appeals, for example, has found the towers to be"inherently beneficial" uses subject to a relaxed variance test.[31] Several courts also have found cellular towers to qualify as public utilities under local law.[32]

D. Undergrounding Utility Lines

Another issue of controversy is whether local government can require utilities to underground their services. Aesthetics generally is the reason undergrounding is desired, though issues of safety may also be alleged. Cost is the problem from the utilities' perspective. In a Missouri

26. 944 F.Supp. 923 (N.D.Ga.1996). See Sprint Spectrum, L.P. v. City of Medina, 924 F.Supp. 1036 (W.D.Wa.1996).

27. See cases cited supra notes 21–22.

28. Oldham County Planning & Zoning Comm'n v. Courier Communications Corp., 722 S.W.2d 904 (Ky.App.1987) (holding that a mobile telephone service seeking to construct a 290 foot tower is a public utility and exempt by state statute).

29. Ohio Rev. Code § 519.211 (B) (specifically conferring power on local government over cellular services); Pa.Cons.Stat. § 102(2)(iv).

30. N. J. Stat. Ann. § 26:2D 1 to 88, discussed in New Brunswick Cellular Telephone Co. v. Old Bridge Twp. Planning Bd., 270 N.J.Super. 122, 636 A.2d 588, 596 (1993).

31. Cellular Telephone Co. v. Rosenberg, 82 N.Y.2d 364, 604 N.Y.S.2d 895, 624 N.E.2d 990 (1993) (applying "more lenient" public utility variance standard to cellular tower). But see Smart SMR of New York, Inc. v. Borough of Fair Lawn Bd. of Adj., 152 N.J. 309, 704 A.2d 1271 (1998) (declining to find monopole inherently beneficial).

32. See supra § 4.25B.

case, the court noted that while the cost of 1.8 miles of overhead lines was roughly $300,000, it soared to $2,000,000 if put underground.[33] In most cases, the courts have invalidated local underground regulations,[34] but there are cases where they have allowed local law to apply.[35] Lacking local control, the state utility commission may be able to require undergrounding.[36]

§ 4.26 Public–Private and Profit–Nonprofit Distinctions

Privately owned facilities and those operated for gain are often denied use rights granted to publicly owned facilities and to nonprofit facilities. To the extent that these distinctions are based on the form of ownership of an operation, they are at odds with the general rule of zoning that ownership is not a legitimate basis for use zoning.[1]

A. *Public v. Private Uses*

Many courts tolerate the public-private distinction without seriously examining the justification.[2] Government may achieve the discriminatory treatment by expressly either allowing its own public use and banning like private uses, or banning all uses and then exempting itself from its

33. Union Electric Co. v. City of Crestwood, 499 S.W.2d 480 (Mo.1973). In a more recent case a utility estimated that undergrounding, if required by all jurisdictions through which the line passed, would cost $2.5 billion. Florida Power Corp. v. Seminole County, Lake Mary, 579 So.2d 105, 106 (Fla.1991).

34. Florida Power Corp. v. Seminole County, Lake Mary, 579 So.2d 105 (Fla. 1991); Union Electric Co. v. City of Crestwood, 499 S.W.2d 480 (Mo.1973); In re Public Service Electric & Gas Co., 35 N.J. 358, 173 A.2d 233 (1961); Cleveland Electric Illuminating Co. v. Village of Mayfield, 53 Ohio App.2d 37, 371 N.E.2d 567 (1977); Vandehei Developers v. Public Service Commission, 790 P.2d 1282 (Wyo.1990); Public Serv. Co. v. Town of Hampton, 120 N.H. 68, 411 A.2d 164 (1980); Duquesne Light Co. v. Upper St. Clair Township, 377 Pa. 323, 105 A.2d 287 (1954) (township had no authority to impose controls on transmission lines, though it is not clear from the opinion whether the township was attempting to require undergrounding).

35. Arizona Public Service Co. v. Town of Paradise Valley, 125 Ariz. 447, 610 P.2d 449 (1980); Benzinger v. Union Light, Heat, & Power Co., 293 Ky. 747, 170 S.W.2d 38 (1943); Kahl v. Consolidated Gas, Elec. Light & Power Co., 191 Md. 249, 60 A.2d 754 (1948), but see Howard County v. Potomac Electric Power Co., 319 Md. 511, 529, 573 A.2d 821, 830 (1990), where the continuing validity of the *Kahl* decision questioned. See also Central Maine Power Co. v. Waterville Urban Renewal Authority, 281

A.2d 233, 240 (Me.1971) (where the court held the power to underground was vested in an urban renewal authority where the city was acting on behalf of the state and expressly limited its ruling to such an authority). In Maun v. United States, 347 F.2d 970 (9th Cir.1965), the court construed the Atomic Energy Act to allow Woodsides, California, to require the undergrounding of power lines to a linear accelerator, which lines passed through the community. After the decision, Congress amended the Atomic Energy Act to restore the AEC to supremacy. 42 U.S.C.A. § 2018. See Pacific Gas and Electric Co. v. State Energy Resources Conservation & Development Commission, 461 U.S. 190, 210, 103 S.Ct. 1713, 1725, 75 L.Ed.2d 752 (1983).

36. Matter of Sleepy Hollow Lake, Inc. v. Public Service Commission, 43 A.D.2d 439, 352 N.Y.S.2d 274 (1974) (commission has authority); Costello v. Department of Public Utilities, 391 Mass. 527, 462 N.E.2d 301 (1984) (commission did not require undergrounding due to cost).

§ 4.26

1. See supra § 4.2 regarding ownership.

2. Cameron v. Zoning Agent of Bellingham, 357 Mass. 757, 260 N.E.2d 143 (1970) (the "public nature" of public housing permitted the discriminatory treatment); Gerzeny v. Richfield Twp., 62 Ohio St.2d 339, 405 N.E.2d 1034 (1980) (100 acre minimum for private park; no minimum for public park).

own ordinance. This is surely a distinction without a difference, but the former has been held valid and the latter invalid by some courts.[3]

The distinction between public and private use has arisen frequently in the context of schools, where it has most often been found wanting.[4] In one case, the court noted that the city offered no reason for prohibiting private schools when it allowed public ones, probably "for the very good reason that none exist[ed]."[5] One case upholding the exclusion of private schools from zones that permitted public schools did so on the ground that private schools do not serve all comers from the community.[6] If schools draw their students from the entire city rather than the neighborhood surrounding the school, the argument of the court is not compelling.

If the reason supporting the classification is that the public facility is for the benefit of the public at large, the validity may turn on whether the private use is open to the public.[7] Where a city allowed public museums, a court struck down an ordinance banning private museums, noting the private museum, like the public one, would be open to serve the public.[8]

Favoring public use over private use, though it lacks a land use justification, may be justified for other reasons. If high density housing is viewed as imposing negative externalities, a city might choose to limit the amount of such housing by permitting only public housing. [9]The same can be said for schools, and most other uses. From a federal equal protection standpoint, a classification based on factors unrelated to the legislative purpose is likely constitutional. In review of mere socioeconomic regulation, not involving a fundamental right or suspect class, the Supreme Court applies a highly deferential, rational basis rule of review that virtually assures the law will be upheld.[10] Limiting negative exter-

3. Jefferson National Bank v. Miami Beach, 267 So.2d 100 (Fla.App.1972), cert. denied 273 So.2d 763 (Fla.1973), as interpreted in City of Kissimmee v. Ellis, 431 So.2d 283 (Fla.App.1983). Such a rule in effect concludes that the governmental versus private distinction, though unrelated to zoning, is not invidiously discriminatory. See infra § 10.14.

4. Catholic Bishop of Chicago v. Kingery, 371 Ill. 257, 20 N.E.2d 583 (1939); City of Miami Beach v. State *ex rel.* Lear, 128 Fla. 750, 175 So. 537, 539 (1937). For a collection of such cases, see Creative Country Day School, Inc. v. Montgomery County Bd. of Appeals, 242 Md. 552, 567, 219 A.2d 789, 796 (1966). See also discussion of schools infra § 4.27.

5. City of Miami Beach v. State ex. rel. Lear, 128 Fla. 750, 175 So. 537, 539 (1937).

6. State ex rel. Wisconsin Lutheran High School Conference v. Sinar, 267 Wis. 91, 65 N.W.2d 43 (1954), appeal dismissed 349 U.S. 913, 75 S.Ct. 604, 99 L.Ed. 1248

(1955). The distinction of *Sinar* was labeled "doubtful" by a later Wisconsin court. State ex rel. Warren v. Reuter, 44 Wis.2d 201, 221, 170 N.W.2d 790, 799 (1969).

7. Golf, Inc. v. District of Columbia, 67 F.2d 575 (App.D.C.1933) (prohibiting private golf driving ranges, though public ones were allowed).

8. City of Kissimmee v. Ellis, 431 So.2d 283 (Fla.App.1983). But see Town of Richmond v. Murdock, 70 Wis.2d 642, 235 N.W.2d 497 (1975) (even if private recreational use serves the public that does not make it a public use).

9. Cameron v. Zoning Agent of Bellingham, 357 Mass. 757, 260 N.E.2d 143 (1970) (the "public nature" of public housing permitted the discriminatory treatment).

10. See discussion infra § 10.14. See also Laurence H. Tribe, American Constitutional Law 1439–1443 (1988).

nalities by excluding private uses does not affect a suspect class or a fundamental right.[11]

Some courts, employing greater scrutiny than is necessary as a matter of federal constitutional law, have invalidated disparate treatment of private land uses. An example is Mahony v. Township of Hampton,[12] where the challenged ordinance allowed gas wells only if operated by the municipality or a privately owned public utility. The owner of a private well challenged the ordinance, and the court found it arbitrary. The town argued that gas wells were serious hazards and attempted to hide behind the presumption of validity that attaches to legislative classifications. Yet, public wells were no less a hazard than private ones, said the court. The town also argued that municipalities and public utilities were more accountable to the public and more fiscally responsible. It was not revealed how those differences related to zoning considerations, but it did not matter since the court did not believe them to be true. The state department of environmental affairs regulated all wells, whatever the ownership, and all were equally accountable. What little evidence there was, disputed the truth of the fiscal argument, but if true, the town could have required a bond of private wells.[13]

B. Profit v. Nonprofit Uses

A distinction similar to the public-private one is the permission given to uses that are nonprofit. As with the private versus public distinction, the profit versus nonprofit distinction is not an invidious one, and will be upheld where a court applies a deferential rule of review. In Town of Huntington v. Park Shore Country Day Camp of Dix Hills, Inc.,[14] the New York Court of Appeals upheld the exclusion of a for-profit tennis club in a district that allowed nonprofit clubs. The court thought it "a point too obvious to belabor that the separation of business from nonbusiness uses"[15] was appropriate. The court's point is problematical, however, since the distinction was not between business and nonbusiness, but between profit and nonprofit. Nonbusiness is not the equal of nonprofit.

Applying a deferential test, the New York court suggested that for-profit uses might be more harmful to an area than nonprofit uses. The former, said the court, were interested in making money and would likely expand, bringing more noise and traffic.[16] The for-gain operation

11. The more sympathetic treatment given to tax supported uses may be perceived like grandfathering non-conforming uses because of their built-up reliance interests, which the Court has upheld. City of New Orleans v. Dukes, 427 U.S. 297, 96 S.Ct. 2513, 49 L.Ed.2d 511 (1976) (no violation of equal protection where pushcart vendors who had operated for eight years were exempted from a newly enacted prohibition). See discussion infra § 4.31 regarding nonconforming uses.

12. 539 Pa. 193, 651 A.2d 525 (1994).

13. It is not clear whether the court was relying on due process or equal protection, or on the state or federal constitution. See also Roselle v. Wright, 37 N.J.Super. 507, 117 A.2d 661 (1955) (private garage would be less harmful in terms of traffic than public one).

14. 47 N.Y.2d 61, 416 N.Y.S.2d 774, 390 N.E.2d 282 (1979).

15. Id. at 66, 390 N.E.2d at 284, 416 N.Y.S.2d at 776.

16. Conditions on size of use, though, could be imposed to limit growth.

was also more likely to become an eyesore in tough times, pumping good money after bad. In contrast, a nonprofit club, the court thought, was more likely to consider the long term benefits to the community than the for-profit group, and the nonprofit would probably have stronger ties to the neighborhood.

If courts apply more rigorous review, the justifications thought up by the New York court in *Huntington* are likely to be insufficient to sustain the distinction. While most courts have agreed with *Huntington* and upheld the profit, nonprofit classification,[17] not all have done so. A Pennsylvania court, for example, invalidated an ordinance that excluded for-profit golf driving ranges and allowed public and nonprofit ones.[18]

Zoning authorities and courts would do well to reexamine the reason for the nonprofit distinction, and to explore what it means to be nonprofit. If it is state corporation law or federal tax law that defines nonprofit status, they should study the relevancy of those statutory regimes to land use considerations. For example, if state corporation law creates a special nonprofit category to establish a different rule of liability or a different process of dissolution, the fact that the reasons supporting these differences have nothing to do with land use should be taken into account.

§ 4.27 Schools

A. *Schools as Neighbors*

Schools, as neighbors, have positive and negative features. Schools, particularly if they serve local residents, provide a sense of community. This is less true today than once was the case, as most schools no longer serve their immediate neighborhood but draw students from the wider community. On the downside, the noise and traffic attendant to school use make nearby residential locations less attractive. Historically, municipalities and courts have often ignored the negatives or presumed that they are outweighed by the positives. Furthermore, the educational atmosphere of schools, particularly elementary schools, is generally considered to benefit from a residential location. Consequently, schools have been granted favored status in zoning.

Nonexistent or lax regulation has allowed virtually unchecked expansion of schools. Universities and colleges, in particular, have taken advantage of this unregulated environment. This expansion, along with increases in the size of schools, their tendency to serve students from outside the neighborhood, and increased use of cars and buses have led to a reexamination of the notion that schools are inherently benign land uses.[1]

17. Other courts have upheld the profit versus nonprofit distinction. See Town of Los Altos Hills v. Adobe Creek Properties, 32 Cal.App.3d 488, 108 Cal.Rptr. 271 (1973); S. Volpe & Co., Inc. v. Board of App. of Wareham, 4 Mass.AppCt.. 357, 348 N.E.2d 807 (1976); Shady Grove v. Parish of Jefferson, 203 So.2d 869 (La.App.1967).

18. Ludwig v. Zoning Hearing Bd. of Earl Twp., 658 A.2d 836 (Pa.Cmwlth.1995).

§ 4.27

1. See the sentiments expressed in

Several school zoning issues arise. First, is whether government can exclude schools from certain zones and, if not, the degree to which it can regulate schools. A second question is whether government can separately classify parochial and private schools and treat them differently than public schools. Finally, is the question of what is a "school" for the purposes of a zoning code.[2]

B. Public Schools

Most ordinances permit public schools to locate as a matter of right in even the most restrictive residential districts.[3] Usually, this occurs because of the philosophy noted above that schools need, and have a positive affect on, residential areas. However, local zoning authorities likely have no choice since public schools, as with other governmental uses,[4] are normally immune from zoning. Immunity may be based on the state constitution or statutory powers granted to schools.[5] Where courts use the traditional immunity tests, particularly the governmental-proprietary test, schools are generally exempt.[6] Most recent cases, however, subject the school immunity question to the balancing of interests test.[7] Immunity is normally conferred, but it may not be absolute, and courts may block school authorities if their actions are found unreasonable.[8] States not permitting exclusion of schools may permit their regulation,[9] though courts have also held the contrary.[10] Though governments do not

Cornell University v. Bagnardi, 68 N.Y.2d 583, 510 N.Y.S.2d 861, 865, 503 N.E.2d 509, 513 (1986) (noting that the controlling factor in permitting a school to locate or expand into residential area is the impact on public welfare and that there is no conclusive presumption that an educational use automatically outweighs its ill effects) and Glenbrook Road Association v. District of Columbia Bd. of Zoning Adj, 605 A.2d 22, 31 (D.C.App.1992). See also Osborne M. Reynolds, Jr., Zoning Private and Parochial Schools-Could Local Governments Restrict Socrates and Aquinas? 24 Urb. Law. 305, 339 (1992).

2. See generally Osborne M. Reynolds, Jr., Zoning Private and Parochial Schools-Could Local Governments Restrict Socrates and Aquinas? 24 Urb. Law. 305 (1992) (reviewing zoning's treatment of public as well as private schools); J. Curry, Public Regulation of the Religious Use of Land 164 (1964); Note, The Immunity of Schools from Zoning, 14 Syracuse L.Rev. 644 (1963); Annot. 11 A.L.R.4th 1084 (1979); Annot., 64 A.L.R.3d 1087 (1973).

3. Public schools are subjected to special permit processes in some communities. Reynolds, supra note 1, at 330, n. 135.

4. See supra § 4.23.

5. Town of Atherton v. Superior Court, 159 Cal.App.2d 417, 324 P.2d 328 (1958) (as a result of *Atherton*, a statute provides for limited regulation by localities over schools

if the locality has provided for school location in a master plan. West's Ann.Cal.Gov't Code §§ 53090–95); Austin Independent School District v. City of Sunset Valley, 502 S.W.2d 670, 672 (Tex.1973); State of Missouri v. Ferriss, 304 S.W.2d 896 (Mo.1957).

6. See Reynolds, supra note 1, at 326.

7. Board of Regents of the Universities and State College of Arizona v. City of Tempe, 88 Ariz. 299, 356 P.2d 399 (1960); Kunimoto v. Kawakami, 56 Haw. 582, 545 P.2d 684 (1976); Rutgers, State University v. Piluso, 60 N.J. 142, 286 A.2d 697 (1972); Independent School District No. 89 of Oklahoma County v. City of Oklahoma City, 722 P.2d 1212 (1986). For a more detailed discussion of the balancing of interests test in the context of immunity, see supra § 4.23.

8. City of Newark v. University of Delaware, 304 A.2d 347, 349 (Del.Ch.1973).

9. See, e.g., Trustees of Union College v. Schenectady City Council, 230 A.D.2d 17, 656 N.Y.S.2d 425 (1997) (total exclusion of educational uses from historic district held unconstitutional; school entitled to a special permit process). See also Edmonds School District No. 15 v. City of Mountlake Terrace, 77 Wash.2d 609, 465 P.2d 177 (1970); School Dist. of Philadelphia v. Zoning Bd. of Adj., 417 Pa. 277, 207 A.2d 864 (1965).

10. State of Missouri v. Ferriss, 304 S.W.2d 896 (Mo.1957); Hall v. Taft, 47 Cal.2d 177, 302 P.2d 574 (1956), superceded by statute.

likely attempt it often, courts have not allowed the exclusion of public schools from an entire municipality.[11]

C. *Private and Parochial Schools*

Where a zoning code permits public schools but excludes private and parochial schools, a question of the legitimacy of the unequal treatment arises. The courts differ over the question, but most require that private schools be permitted if public schools are.[12] This makes sense from a land use perspective as the impact on the community will not differ based on the ownership of the school. The noise and traffic from private students are not greater than from public students.

Differences between private and public schools exist. Whether they justify harsher treatment of private schools is another matter. The leading case upholding the exclusion of private schools from zones where public schools were permitted did so on the ground that private schools do not serve all comers from the community.[13] The court conceded that the surrounding community suffers an equal burden from both classes of schools, but that it benefits from the public school by virtue of the fact that the residents of the area can use the public school. For the "admitted drawbacks"[14] of noise, being entitled to attend the school compensates the community. If, as often happens today, the public schools draw their students from an area broader than the neighborhood surrounding the school, the argument of the court is less compelling than it may have been when made in 1954.

Land use considerations aside, a broad public interest is served by public education, and distinctions favoring them over private schools are not invidious. From a federal equal protection standpoint, such a classification based on factors unrelated to the legislative purpose of zoning is likely constitutional. In review of mere socioeconomic regulation, not involving a fundamental right or suspect class, the Supreme Court applies a highly deferential, rational basis rule of review that virtually assures the law will be upheld.[15] The fact that many courts have invalidated disparate treatment of private schools suggests that these

---

11. Austin Independent School District v. City of Sunset Valley, 502 S.W.2d 670 (Tex.1973).

12. Catholic Bishop of Chicago v. Kingery, 371 Ill. 257, 20 N.E.2d 583 (1939). For a collection of such cases, see Creative Country Day School, Inc. v. Montgomery County Bd. of Appeals, 242 Md. 552, 567, 219 A.2d 789, 796 (1966). See also Reynolds, supra note 1, at 329.

13. State ex rel. Wisconsin Lutheran High School Conference v. Sinar, 267 Wis. 91, 65 N.W.2d 43 (1954), appeal dismissed 349 U.S. 913, 75 S.Ct. 604, 99 L.Ed. 1248 (1955). The distinction of *Sinar* was labelled "doubtful" by a later Wisconsin court. State ex rel. Warren v. Reuter, 44 Wis.2d 201, 221, 170 N.W.2d 790, 799

(1969). See generally J. Curry, Public Regulation of the Religious Use of Land 164 (1964); Annot. 74 A.L.R.3d 14 (1974).

14. *Sinar*, id. at 99, 65 N.W.2d at 47.

15. See generally Laurence H. Tribe, American Constitutional Law 1439–1443 (1988). For such cases exemplifying this rule of almost total deference, see City of New Orleans v. Dukes, 427 U.S. 297, 96 S.Ct. 2513, 49 L.Ed.2d 511 (1976) and Railway Express Agency, Inc. v. New York, 336 U.S. 106, 69 S.Ct. 463, 93 L.Ed. 533 (1949). There are a few aberrant cases. See discussion of City of Cleburne v. Cleburne Living Ctr., 473 U.S. 432, 105 S.Ct. 3249, 87 L.Ed.2d 313 (1985), supra § 4.6 and infra § 10.14.

courts are employing greater scrutiny than is necessary as a matter of federal constitutional law. Since many cases involve parochial schools, it may be that the religious twist triggers this increased judicial review.

While cities generally cannot exclude private schools from zones where they allow public schools, private schools are often subjected to a special permit process that may not be applicable to public schools.[16] This added regulatory burden is one that most courts have upheld, some pointing out that public schools suffer their own regulatory burden by state or local laws on school siting.[17] They will invalidate excessive or unreasonable limitations, however.[18]

Most courts have held that the First Amendment does not insulate parochial schools from zoning controls,[19] but a few courts have held to the contrary.[20] Courts that otherwise might invalidate or closely scrutinize the regulation of religious uses are less likely to favor parochial schools since they are more intensive land uses than most religious uses.[21] Distinguishing between religious use and religious educational use, though, is fraught with difficulty.[22]

Although the First Amendment is usually not found to prohibit the exclusion or regulation of parochial schools, some courts do not indulge in the usual presumption of validity accorded zoning regulations in such cases.[23] Widespread sensitivity to the regulation of religious activities may explain this tendency of the courts. Since most courts find that the enabling act or the equal protection clause requires that private schools be treated like public schools, reaching the First Amendment question is often unnecessary.

Private, non parochial schools, though they have no special First Amendment protection, likely benefit from this more rigorous review since there is no meaningful distinction between parochial and private non parochial schools.[24] At least one court has said that the fact that a

16. Abram v. City of Fayetteville, 281 Ark. 63, 661 S.W.2d 371 (1983); St. John's Roman Catholic Church Corp. v. Town of Darien, 149 Conn. 712, 184 A.2d 42 (1962); City of Las Cruces v. Huerta, 102 N.M. 182, 692 P.2d 1331 (1984). See also Reynolds, supra note 1, at 330.

17. Creative Country Day School, Inc. v. Montgomery County Bd. of Appeals, 242 Md. 552, 219 A.2d 789 (1966).

18. Roman Catholic Welfare Corp. of San Francisco v. City of Piedmont, 45 Cal.2d 325, 289 P.2d 438 (1955) (unreasonable to limit private schools to 1.3% of city, where public schools allowed in 98.7%).

19. Abram v. City of Fayetteville, 281 Ark. 63, 661 S.W.2d 371 (1983); Seward Chapel, Inc. v. City of Seward, 655 P.2d 1293 (Alaska 1982); City of Las Cruces v. Huerta, 102 N.M. 182, 692 P.2d 1331 (1984); Medford Assembly of God v. City of Medford, 72 Or.App. 333, 695 P.2d 1379 (1985).

20. Board of Zoning Appeals v. Decatur, Indiana Co. of Jehovah's Witnesses, 233 Ind. 83, 117 N.E.2d 115 (1954); Jewish Reconstructionist Synagogue of North Shore, Inc. v. Incorporated Village of Roslyn Harbor, 38 N.Y.2d 283, 379 N.Y.S.2d 747, 342 N.E.2d 534 (1975); Diocese of Rochester v. Planning Bd. of Brighton, 1 N.Y.2d 508, 154 N.Y.S.2d 849, 136 N.E.2d 827 (1956).

21. Abram v. City of Fayetteville, 281 Ark. 63, 661 S.W.2d 371 (1983).

22. See discussion of religious uses infra § 4.28.

23. O'Hara's Appeal, 389 Pa. 35, 131 A.2d 587 (1957).

24. State v. Northwestern Preparatory School, Inc., 228 Minn. 363, 37 N.W.2d 370 (1949). See generally Comment, Zoning Out Private Schools Held Invalid, 8 Stan.L.Rev. 712 (1956).

non parochial private school may operate for profit is not a valid basis to distinguish it from a parochial school.[25]

D. Qualifying as a School

Zoning codes may define schools as buildings used for educational or instructional purposes or by reference to whether state or local school officials certify the use as meeting state educational requirements.[26] Where not defined, or where the ordinance is general and must be construed, the courts have little difficulty recognizing certain uses as schools. A school for Jewish children was easily found the equal of other public and private parochial schools that were permitted.[27] In another case, an ordinance that permitted all schools in an apartment district except nursery schools was held invalid. The court found that a nursery school was so similar to other schools that the exclusion was unreasonable.[28]

While some private schools are very much like typical public or parochial schools, others may be called schools by their proprietors only to obtain favorable zoning treatment.[29] The cases range widely. It is not likely that a court would find a ceramics factory and store to have the favorable status of a school merely because the owner conducted classes in ceramics there.[30] A school "for the study of the Holocaust" in a single-family home was found not to be a school under the zoning code because it lacked certification from the state board of regents.[31] Courts denied school status to a "horse riding school,"[32] and a halfway house for recovering alcoholics.[33] However, a court allowed a private dance school in a residential zone under an ordinance that permitted educational or cultural facilities.[34]

25. Creative Country Day School, Inc. v. Montgomery County Bd. of Appeals, 242 Md. 552, 573, 219 A.2d 789, 801 (1966).

26. See, e.g., the zoning ordinance of Miami, Florida, which defines schools as:

Schools, kindergarten. Schools which are preparatory to elementary school and are in compliance with a pupil progression plan approved by the Dade County School Board or a nonpublic school from which the Dade County School Board accepts academic credit.

Schools, private. A building or group of buildings the use of which meets the state requirements for kindergarten, elementary, secondary or high school education and which use does not secure the major part of its funding from any governmental agency.

Schools, secondary. A school licensed by the state and which is authorized to award diplomas for secondary education. Miami Zoning Code § 2502.

27. Brandeis School v. Village of Lawrence, 18 Misc.2d 550, 184 N.Y.S.2d 687 (1959).

28. City of Chicago v. Sachs, 1 Ill.2d 342, 115 N.E.2d 762 (1953).

29. Qualifying as an accessory use to a school is another avenue to gain permission Jay M. Zitter, Annotation, What Constitutes Accessory or Incidental Use of Religious or Educational Property Within Zoning Ordinance, 11 A.L.R.4th 1084 (1979).

30. Annot. 64 A.L.R.3d 1087 (1973). See also City of Chicopee v. Jakubowski, 348 Mass. 230, 202 N.E.2d 913 (1964).

31. Yeshiva & Mesivta v. Rose, 136 A.D.2d 710, 523 N.Y.S.2d 907 (1988).

32. Incorporated Village of Asharoken v. Pitassy, 119 A.D.2d 404, 507 N.Y.S.2d 164 (1986).

33. Conners v. Zoning Hearing Bd. of Chippewa Twp., 88 Pa.Cmwlth. 625, 491 A.2d 304 (1985).

34. Sarti v. City of Lake Oswego, 106 Or.App. 594, 809 P.2d 701 (1991).

The same types of communities disposed to other kinds of snob zoning have given unfavorable treatment to some private schools of great social utility.[35] For example, after being barred from use of their property in two communities, a private institution for the education and residence of handicapped and delinquent boys from New York City was excluded from a residential district of yet another community on the ground that it was not a school. The court held that it was a school and, moreover, that it enjoyed immunity as if it were a state institution carrying out a similar function.[36] In other similar cases, courts found a "home for boys"[37] and a juvenile offenders' learning center[38] to be schools, thus thwarting local efforts to exclude them.

Authorities may treat schools as commercial uses for particular purposes. For example, a classroom and residence hall building project was held to be a commercial use and thus subject to an environmental permitting requirement.[39] Also, a university's construction of a business college was deemed a commercial use for the purposes of assessing an impact fee.[40]

§ 4.28 Religious Uses

Zoning for religious uses[1] is similar in certain respects to zoning for schools.[2] The use of the property for religious purposes is seen as beneficial to a community. Religious buildings may provide a community focal point, giving a neighborhood a sense of identity. In older urban areas, religious institutions provide a base for community rebuilding efforts.[3] Still, religious institutions are not desirable neighbors in all respects. Like schools, they generate noise and traffic and, thus, may depreciate property values in neighboring areas. Their ability to serve as a community resource is also diminished if their congregation is not drawn from the neighborhood. The growth in recent years of the "mega-church," occupying more land, bringing more people from outside the community, and engaging in increasingly diverse activities under a

35. See infra § 6.1.

36. Wiltwyck School for Boys, Inc. v. Hill, 11 N.Y.2d 182, 227 N.Y.S.2d 655, 182 N.E.2d 268 (1962), reargument denied 11 N.Y.2d 1017, 229 N.Y.S.2d 1028, 183 N.E.2d 772 (1962). The court's immunity discussion is vague.

37. Carroll County v. Raymond I. Richardson Foundation, Inc., 71 Md.App. 434, 526 A.2d 81 (Md.Ct.Spec.App.1987). The Fair Housing Act's protection of handicapped may affect this issue. See infra § 6.8.

38. Visionquest National, Ltd. v. Pima County Bd. of Adj., 146 Ariz. 103, 703 P.2d 1252 (1985).

39. In re Spring Brook Farm Foundation, Inc., 164 Vt. 282, 671 A.2d 315 (Vt. 1995).

40. Loyola Marymount University v. Los Angeles Unified School District, 45 Cal. App.4th 1256, 53 Cal.Rptr.2d 424 (1996).

§ 4.28

1. Many zoning codes and cases refer to "church" use reflecting the country's dominant Christian background. Despite such usage, the First Amendment requires that the term be understood to include all religious institutions uses of any faith, whether it be a synagogue, a mosque, a fellowship, or a church.

2. See supra § 4.27.

3. Henry G. Cisneros, Higher Ground: Faith Communities and Community Building, Recent Research Results, HUD USER (Dept. of Housing and Urban Development, April 1996).

religious rubric has led to frequent zoning disputes. While neighbors often have legitimate complaints about large institutional use, in some instances the protests appear levied against non-mainstream religious groups who are feared, disliked, or distrusted because they are different.[4]

Religious use zoning is more suspect than school zoning due to religious freedom guarantees in the federal and state constitutions. The First Amendment and its state counterparts prevent zoning laws from unduly interfering with the free exercise of religion. While constitutional limitations on the zoning power are covered in detail elsewhere in this treatise,[5] concerns over religious freedom and discrimination against some religions cannot be ignored in this discussion. In many cases discussed below that favor religious uses, courts refrain from express determinations that the First Amendment has been violated, but they often admit that their decisions are influenced by the importance of religious freedom in this country.

Three basic approaches are used in dealing with religious uses: (1) allow them in any district as a matter of right, (2) allow them in any residential district only if they obtain a special permit, or (3) exclude them from some residential zones. The first approach dominated early zoning ordinances, but the second has long been the technique employed most often. The third is the least practiced, and is invalid in many states. A fourth possibility is total exclusion from the community. This is likely a rare occurrence. Many courts have suggested in dicta that total exclusion would be invalid and where litigated, that has been the result.[6]

Allowing religious uses in all districts, particularly all residential districts, as a matter of right, is premised on the notion that religious use is inherently beneficial. Several cases reflect this belief and, where true, an attempt to exclude religious uses from residential areas will be held invalid.[7] Typically in these cases, most of which are dated, the courts invalidate the zoning on due process grounds finding that the police power does not extend to the banning of such highly regarded uses. Some courts narrowly interpret the zoning enabling act's provision to zone for "trade, industry, residence, and other purposes" to preclude

---

4. See Kenneth Pearlman, Zoning and the Location of Religious Establishments, 31 Cath. Law. 314 (1988); Terry Rice, Re-evaluating the Balance Between Zoning Regulations and Religious and Educational Uses, 8 Pace L.Rev 1 (1988); Laurie Reynolds, Zoning the Church: The Police Power Versus the First Amendment, 64 B.U.L.Rev. 767 (1984); R. P. Davis, Annotation, Zoning Regulations as Affecting Churches, 74 A.L.R.2d 377 (1960); Curry, Public Regulation of the Religious Use of Land (1964).

5. See infra § 10.18.

6. North Shore Unitarian Soc'y v. Village of Plandome, 200 Misc. 524, 109 N.Y.S.2d 803 (1951). But see Corporation of Presiding Bishop v. Porterville, 90 Cal.

App.2d 656, 203 P.2d 823 (1949), appeal dismissed 338 U.S. 805, 70 S.Ct. 78, 94 L.Ed. 487 (1949), suggesting total exclusion possible.

7. Ellsworth v. Gercke, 62 Ariz. 198, 156 P.2d 242 (1945) (religious uses could not be excluded while schools, golf courses, and swimming pools allowed); Congregation Temple Israel v. Creve Coeur, 320 S.W.2d 451 (Mo.1959); O'Brien v. City of Chicago, 347 Ill.App. 45, 105 N.E.2d 917 (1952); Board of Zoning Appeals of Decatur v. Decatur, Indiana Company of Jehovah's Witnesses, 233 Ind. 83, 117 N.E.2d 115 (1954) (dictum as to exclusion and holding that religious uses subject to reasonable controls).

regulation of religious uses.[8] The growth in size and divergence in use of religious institutions has caused some courts to reexamine whether this routine deference is justified,[9] and one should be wary of relying heavily on older authority that grants or intimates absolute protection.

A common approach is to permit religious uses in some or all residential districts by special permit. Courts that grant religious uses favored status may invalidate ordinances that allow religious use in only some districts. In reviewing administrative decisions that deny a permit to a religious use, some courts refuse to defer to the board's discretion and require the city to justify the denial.[10] This view accords with the favored status view of religious uses. Courts may apply scrutiny to zoning decisions out of concern that there may be a burden on religious freedom or that non-mainstream groups are being discriminated against.[11] Other courts, conceding no special treatment based on the religious nature of the use, put the burden on the applicant to prove that the decision was in error.[12]

When a special permit is required before a religious use is permitted, the courts are watchful that conditions imposed are not unduly onerous or otherwise improper. For example, a special permit could not be denied a religious use in a residential area based on a policy to deny permits where property zoned for business was available to the religious use.[13] The religious use generally must comply with reasonable conditions, such as setback requirements. In a few cases, courts have exempted religious use from other conditions, such as an off-street parking require-

8. See Congregation Temple Israel v. City of Creve Coeur, 320 S.W.2d 451 (Mo. 1959). See also Village Lutheran Church v. City of Ladue, 935 S.W.2d 720 (Mo.App. 1996).

9. Cornell University v. Bagnardi, 68 N.Y.2d 583, 510 N.Y.S.2d 861, 865, 503 N.E.2d 509, 513 (1986). Though the case dealt with a school, the court discussed the problems associated with schools and religious uses. But see Village Lutheran Church v. City of Ladue, 935 S.W.2d 720 (Mo.App.1996).

10. Holy Spirit Ass'n for the Unification of World Christianity v. Rosenfeld, 91 A.D.2d 190, 458 N.Y.S.2d 920 (1983) (for denial of special use permit for a religious use it must be convincingly shown that the proposed use will have a direct and immediate adverse effect upon the community and every effort must be made to accommodate the religious use), but see Cornell University v. Bagnardi, 68 N.Y.2d 583, 510 N.Y.S.2d 861, 865, 503 N.E.2d 509, 513 (1986). See also State ex rel. Synod of Ohio of United Lutheran Church in America v. Joseph, 139 Ohio St. 229, 39 N.E.2d 515 (1942).

11. State ex rel. Lake Drive Baptist Church v. Village of Bayside, 12 Wis.2d 585, 596, 108 N.W.2d 288, 294 (1961).

12. Milwaukie Co. of Jehovah's Witnesses v. Mullen, 214 Ore. 281, 330 P.2d 5 (1958) (no special rule exists exonerating a church from burden of proof necessary to overcome the presumption of regularity of action on the part of an administrative agency); Matthews v. Board of Supervisors, 203 Cal.App.2d 800, 21 Cal.Rptr. 914 (1962); Galfas v. Ailor, 81 Ga.App. 13, 57 S.E.2d 834 (1950); Encuentros Familares, Inc. v. Musgrove, 511 So.2d 645 (Fla.App. 1987); See also East Side Baptist Church of Denver, Inc. v. Klein, 175 Colo. 168, 487 P.2d 549 (1971) (overturning grant of permit to religious use finding board's decision not supported by evidence) and Macedonian Orthodox Church v. Planning Bd. of Twp. of Randolph, 269 N.J.Super. 562, 636 A.2d 96, 100 (1994) . See discussion of judicial review of administrative actions generally, infra § 5.37.

13. Galfas v. Ailor, 81 Ga.App. 13, 57 S.E.2d 834 (1950); State ex rel. Synod of Ohio of United Lutheran Church in America v. Joseph, 139 Ohio St. 229, 39 N.E.2d 515 (1942).

ment, where the number of vehicles was small and the provision of off-street parking would have substantially raised the costs.[14]

In a few states, courts allow the exclusion of religious uses from residential zones.[15] In such cases, a heavy burden may be placed on the zoning authority to prove there are suitable areas zoned for religious uses within the town.[16]

Religious users sometimes purchase improperly zoned land under the assumption that they are exempt from zoning regulations. The purchase may also be motivated by the desire to acquire property zoned for unintensive use because of its lower price. While the officials of the group may express indignant surprise that zoning controls them, under some circumstances sympathizing with their plight is hard. On the other hand, sometimes religious organizations cannot economically compete with business uses for higher priced land in commercial zones. The fact that the only land zoned for religious use lies in zones where land costs are high may invalidate the zoning in some states,[17] but it is not likely to violate the First Amendment.[18]

The determination by zoning administrators and the courts about whether a use qualifies as a religious use or meets the definition of "church"[19] is a delicate one. In our increasingly diverse society religious use takes many forms. Courts may find themselves in a dilemma. They may have historically favored religious uses and be disinclined to define the limits of what is or is not religion. Yet the religious nature of a use may seem highly dubious or so alien that courts may fear a sham to secure favorable zoning. Furthermore and most importantly, religious or not, the use may be harmful to neighbors who deserve protection.

Combined religious-residential use poses problems. Individuals may band together as a "family," in part, for religious purposes. Consider-

14. Board of Zoning Appeals v. Decatur, Indiana Co. of Jehovah's Witnesses, 233 Ind. 83, 117 N.E.2d 115 (1954); Allendale Congregation of Jehovah's Witnesses v. Grosman, 30 N.J. 273, 152 A.2d 569 (1959); Westchester Reform Temple v. Griffin, 22 N.Y.2d 488, 239 N.E.2d 891, 293 N.Y.S.2d 297 (1968).

15. Mumaw v. Glendale, 270 Cal. App.2d 454, 76 Cal.Rptr. 245 (1969); Corporation of Presiding Bishop v. Porterville, 90 Cal.App.2d 656, 203 P.2d 823 (1949), appeal dismissed 338 U.S. 805, 70 S.Ct. 78, 94 L.Ed. 487 (1949); Miami Beach United Lutheran Church v. Miami Beach, 82 So.2d 880 (Fla.1955). In states where special permits are allowed to control religious use location, denials of such permits have the same result.

16. State ex rel. Lake Drive Baptist Church v. Village of Bayside, 12 Wis.2d 585, 600, 108 N.W.2d 288, 296 (1961) (putting burden on state to prove suitable areas exist). See also Jehovah's Witnesses v.

Woolwich Twp., 223 N.J.Super. 55, 537 A.2d 1336 (App.Div.1988) (court must make a thorough exploration and a careful evaluation of the facts bearing on the competing religious and governmental interests).

17. See, e.g., State ex rel. Lake Drive Baptist Church v. Village of Bayside, 12 Wis.2d 585, 108 N.W.2d 288 (1961) (city must prove suitable land is available).

18. See Lakewood, Ohio Congregation of Jehovah's Witnesses, Inc. v. City of Lakewood, Ohio, 699 F.2d 303 (6th Cir.1983).

19. The zoning ordinance of Miami, Florida provides in its definition section as follows:

> Church: A building or structure which by design and construction is primarily intended for the conduct of organized religious services and associated accessory uses. This definition may include meditation gardens.

City of Miami, Florida Zoning Ordinance, § 2502.

ations of religious freedom or rights of privacy may lead courts to protect them from zoning prosecution though their numbers exceed the allowable limits for single-families.[20] The higher the numbers of residents, the more likely it is that nonreligious use will be found,[21] or that the activity will be subjected to residential restrictions regardless of its religious label.

As a general matter, the courts have liberally construed activities to be religious uses or legitimate accessory uses.[22] Without significant inquiry into the assertion that the use was religious, they have approved the following: a day care center,[23] overnight sleeping accommodations,[24] a dwelling house for a rabbi,[25] softball fields,[26] and a recreational center.[27] Homeless shelters, where religious organizations minister to the poor, have been held to be religious uses or valid accessory uses.[28] Some uses that have failed include a radio tower,[29] a storage building,[30] and temporary campsites.[31] A room used for religious worship in a jail was held not to be a "church" so as to invoke a zoning ordinance that barred adult entertainment within 1000 feet of a "church."[32]

The need to define religious use invites a court to interject personal values. In one case a drug center for young people was held to be a religious activity because the court thought "the essential moral alienation of drug abuse seems most directly a religious problem."[33] In

20. See State v. Baker, 81 N.J. 99, 405 A.2d 368 (1979). See discussion supra § 4.5.

21. Marsland v. International Soc'y For Krishna Consciousness, 66 Haw. 119, 657 P.2d 1035 (1983), app. dismissed 464 U.S. 805, 104 S.Ct. 52, 78 L.Ed.2d 72 (1983) (30 persons); People v. Kalayjian, 76 Misc.2d 1097, 352 N.Y.S.2d 115 (1973) (25 persons).

22. See Jeffrey F. Ghent, Annotation, What Constitutes "Church," "Religious Use," or the Like Within Zoning Ordinance, 62 A.L.R.3d 197 (1975); Jay M. Zitter, What Constitutes Accessory or Incidental Use of Religious or Educational Property Within Zoning Ordinance, 11 A.L.R.4th 1084 (1982).

23. Unitarian Universalist Church v. Shorten, 63 Misc.2d 978, 314 N.Y.S.2d 66 (Sup.Ct.1970).

24. Havurah v. Zoning Bd. of Norfolk, 177 Conn. 440, 418 A.2d 82 (1979).

25. Overbrook Farms Club v. Philadelphia Zoning Bd. of Adj., 351 Pa. 77, 40 A.2d 423 (1945).

26. Corporation of Presiding Bishop of Church of Jesus Christ of Latter Day Saints v. Ashton, 92 Idaho 571, 448 P.2d 185 (1968).

27. Keeling v. Board of Zoning Appeals, 117 Ind.App. 314, 69 N.E.2d 613 (Ind.App.1946).

28. The Jesus Center v. Farmington Hills Zoning Bd. of App., 215 Mich.App. 54, 544 N.W.2d 698 (1996); St. John's Evangelical Lutheran Church v. City of Hoboken, 195 N.J.Super. 414, 479 A.2d 935 (1983); Greentree at Murray Hill Condominium v. Good Shepherd Episcopal Church,, 146 Misc.2d 500, 550 N.Y.S.2d 981 (1989).

29. Worcester County Christian Communications, Inc. v. Board of Appeals of Spencer, 22 Mass.App.Ct. 83, 491 N.E.2d 634 (1986). But see Burlington Assembly of God v. Zoning Bd. of Florence, 238 N.J.Super. 634, 570 A.2d 495 (Law Div.1989) (board's refusal to grant variance to permit church to build a radio antenna tower on its property violated church's right to religious freedom and freedom of speech)

30. Grandview Baptist Church v. Zoning Bd. of Davenport, 301 N.W.2d 704 (Iowa 1981).

31. Portage Township v. Full Salvation Union, 318 Mich. 693, 29 N.W.2d 297 (1947), appeal dismissed 333 U.S. 851, 68 S.Ct. 735, 92 L.Ed. 1133 (1948).

32. Hooters, Inc. v. City of Texarkana, 897 F.Supp. 946 (E.D.Tex.1995).

33. Slevin v. Long Island Jewish Medical Center, 66 Misc.2d 312, 316, 319 N.Y.S.2d 937, 944 (Sup.Ct.1971).

another case, a court found a coffeehouse not to be a religious use because it deemed some of its activities nonreligious, such as the showing of antiwar films.[34] As the question intrudes upon sensitive personal beliefs, it is understandable why courts often do not delve deeply into the nature of the purported religious use. Some of these problems can be avoided to the extent that zoning authorities use performance standards[35] treating all institutional uses the same, despite the religious character of the use.[36]

§ 4.29 Airports

Airports, particularly large ones, are land uses with widespread impact on a community. They occupy a great deal of space, and, in many locales, they are expanding in size. They produce an enormous amount of noise, adversely affecting nearby residential uses, and are a safety concern to all. While these issues of land use, noise, and safety are typically ones handled by local government, airports, as vital links in national and international trade and travel, are also regulated by the federal government. This overlapping regulation at times leads to conflict. Takings issues also arise with airport use by the invasion of private airspace and the loss of value of property subject to the noise.[1]

The leading preemption case is City of Burbank v. Lockheed Air Terminal, Inc.,[2] in which the Supreme Court held a municipal ordinance that imposed a curfew on flights between 11 p.m. until 7 a.m. was preempted by federal regulations. The Court implied preemption since it found that federal control of flights would be jeopardized by local regulation. *Burbank's* preemption of local law applies only to controls relating to the noise from aircraft operations.[3] Common law damage remedies for harm from noise and pollution are not preempted.[4] The location of airports can be controlled by zoning.[5] The landing of sea-

34. Synod of the Chesapeake v. City of Newark, 254 A.2d 611, 612 (Del.Ch.1969).

35. These standards deal with such matters as noise, setbacks, parking requirements, and landscaping. See supra § 4.13 and § 4.19.

36. First Amendment problems may still arise. See discussion infra § 10.18.

§ 4.29

1. See generally, Steven H. Magee, Comment, Protecting Land Around Airports: Avoiding Regulatory Taking Claims by Comprehensive Planning and Zoning, 62 J.Air L. & Com. 243 (1996); Pamela B. Stein, Comment, The Price of Success: Mitigation and Litigation in Airport Growth, 57 J. Air L. & Com. 513 (1991); Lee. L. Blackman and Roger P. Freeman, The Environmental Consequences of Municipal Airports: A Subject of Federal Mandate?, 53 J.Air L. & Com. 753 (1987); Leland C. Dol-

ley & Douglas G. Carroll, Airport Noise Pollution Damages: The Case for Local Liability, 15 Urb.Law. 621 (1983).

2. 411 U.S. 624, 93 S.Ct. 1854, 36 L.Ed.2d 547 (1973).

3. See Gustafson v. City of Lake Angelus, 76 F.3d 778 (6th Cir.1996) for an extensive review of authorities. See also State of Minnesota v. Metropolitan Airports Commission, 520 N.W.2d 388 (Minn.1994); Allegheny Airlines, Inc. v. Village of Cedarhurst, 238 F.2d 812 (2d Cir.1956); Pirolo v. City of Clearwater, 711 F.2d 1006 (11th Cir.1983).

4. Bieneman v. City of Chicago, 864 F.2d 463 (7th Cir.1988); Krueger v. Mitchell, 112 Wis.2d 88, 332 N.W.2d 733 (1983).

5. Faux–Burhans v. County Commissioners of Frederick County, 674 F.Supp. 1172 (D.Md.1987), aff'd, 859 F.2d 149 (4th Cir.1988), cert. denied, 488 U.S. 1042, 109 S.Ct. 869, 102 L.Ed.2d 992 (1989); Blue Sky

planes[6] and the location of heliports[7] also have been held proper subjects of local law.

The *Burbank* Court also suggested a proprietor exception.[8] The Court noted that the preemptive limit was placed against the state's use of the police power against a private airport. It then suggested that the result might differ if the airport were publicly owned and the airport imposed the controls in its capacity as an owner.[9] Courts have differed over the importance of proprietorship. Since airport owners bear monetary liability for noise,[10] some courts think that fairness requires that they be able to limit their exposure,[11] and find no preemption.[12] Others apply preemption to all airports.[13]

To stem the tide of local regulation by publicly owned airports, Congress passed the Airport Noise and Capacity Act of 1990 (ANCA).[14] The Act phases out older, noisier Stage II aircraft (i.e. aircraft that meets the noise standards of 1969) by the year 2000 and limits municipal regulation of Stage II aircraft. But ANCA prohibits any local or state government from restricting the operation of Stage III aircraft without FAA approval. Stage III aircraft includes all planes that comply with the more restrictive noise standards set forth by the FAA in 1977–78. Compliance with ANCA is not mandatory, but Congress has incorporated several severe penalties, including the withholding of federal grants if a municipality does not abide by its provisions.[15]

Entertainment, Inc. v. Town of Gardiner, 711 F.Supp. 678, 683 (N.D.N.Y.1989) (parachute jumping could not be regulated, but conceded that land use could); Bethman v. City of Ukiah, 216 Cal.App.3d 1395, 265 Cal.Rptr. 539 (1989); Wright v. County of Winnebago, 73 Ill.App.3d at 344, 73 Ill. App.3d 337, 29 Ill.Dec. 347, 391 N.E.2d 772 (1979). See also San Diego Unified Port Dist. v. Gianturco, 651 F.2d 1306, 1313 (9th Cir.1981).

6. Gustafson v. City of Lake Angelus, 76 F.3d 778 (6th Cir.1996), cert. denied ___ U.S. ___, 117 S.Ct. 81, 136 L.Ed.2d 39 (1996) (ordinance that banned seaplanes from landing on lake was not preempted).

7. Citizens Against Burlington, Inc. v. Busey, 938 F.2d 190, 197 (D.C.Cir.), cert. denied, 502 U.S. 994, 112 S.Ct. 616, 116 L.Ed.2d 638 (1991) (upheld the municipal regulation of a heliport); Garden State Farms, Inc. v. Bay, 77 N.J. 439, 390 A.2d 1177 (1978); Wood v. City of Huntsville, 384 So.2d 1081 (Ala.1980).

8. City of Burbank, 411 U.S. at 635, 93 S.Ct. at 1861, 36 L.Ed.2d at 556, n. 5.

9. Airports may be publicly owned, in which case the effect of zoning raises problems similar to those for other governmental uses or they may be privately owned, in which case they have qualities similar to a

privately owned public utility. See discussions supra at §§ 4.23–25.

10. Griggs v. Allegheny County, 369 U.S. 84, 82 S.Ct. 531, 7 L.Ed.2d 585 (1962).

11. San Diego Unified Port Dist. v. Gianturco, 651 F.2d 1306, 1316 (9th Cir. 1981) (if the government attempting to impose the control is not liable, the proprietor exemption is not available to it). 651 F.2d at 1319.

12. Santa Monica Airport Association v. City of Santa Monica, 659 F.2d 100 (9th Cir.1981); Arrow Air v. Port Authority of New York, 602 F.Supp. 314 (S.D.N.Y.1985); National Aviation v. City of Hayward, 418 F.Supp. 417 (N.D.Cal.1976). New York was allowed to keep out the Concorde due to noise concerns. British Airways v. Port Authority of New York, 558 F.2d 75, aff'd in part, modified in part 564 F.2d 1002 (2d Cir.1977).

13. Harrison v. Schwartz, 319 Md. 360, 572 A.2d 528 (1990).

14. 49 U.S.C. § 2151, repealed by Act of July 5, 1994, Pub. L. No. 103–272, § 7(b), 108 Stat. 1379, subject matter now codified at 49 U.S.C. §§ 47101–47533.

15. See John J. Jenkins, Jr., The Airport Noise and Capacity Act of 1990: Has Congress Finally Solved the Aircraft Noise Problem?, 59 J.Air L. & Com. 1023 (1994).

Where local authorities are not preempted, airport siting is normally handled by special permit rather than made a permitted use. The acreage needed, flight patterns to be followed, and ground traffic access are major concerns of those issuing such permits. The land near airports must also be zoned to be compatible with the airport. Airport zoning limits land use to allow the airport to operate safely and effectively with minimum interference on adjacent uses. Height controls are also used to protect glide paths from obstructions.

Owners of residential properties close to airports frequently try to use trespass, nuisance and inverse condemnation doctrines to secure damages from the noise they must bear. Under the federal constitution, low, repetitious overflights by governmentally owned planes[16] or by planes landing or departing from publicly owned airports[17] that significantly interfere with the use of the land constitute the taking of an easement for which compensation is due. If there are no direct overflights invading the airspace, but the injury is imposed horizontally by proximity to the airport, there is no taking.[18] Numerous state courts, in interpreting their state constitutions, reject the requirement of the federal courts that there be a physical invasion in order for a right of compensation to arise.[19]

Airport zoning which directly limits use or indirectly does so by imposing height controls to create a glide path has been held a taking by several courts, who characterize such zoning as an acquisition of a negative easement.[20] While a regulatory taking requires the showing of a significant diminution in value and, at least in the absence of a total diminution, a balancing of the public benefits secured by the zoning,[21] where an unobstructed glide path is obtained by restrictive zoning, some courts have concluded that the action is an attempt to acquire a resource

16. United States v. Causby, 328 U.S. 256, 66 S.Ct. 1062, 90 L.Ed. 1206 (1946); Annot., 18 A.L.R.4th 542 (1980); Annot. 77 A.L.R.2d 1362 (1974).

17. Griggs v. Allegheny County, 369 U.S. 84, 82 S.Ct. 531, 7 L.Ed.2d 585 (1962).

18. Batten v. United States, 306 F.2d 580 (10th Cir.1962), cert. denied 371 U.S. 955, 83 S.Ct. 506, 9 L.Ed.2d 502 (1963). See infra § 10.3 for further discussion.

19. Jackson v. Metropolitan Knoxville Airport Authority, 922 S.W.2d 860 (Tenn. 1996); Thornburg v. Port of Portland, 233 Ore. 178, 376 P.2d 100 (1962); Martin v. Port of Seattle, 64 Wash.2d 309, 391 P.2d 540, 545 (1964), cert. denied, 379 U.S. 989, 85 S.Ct. 701, 13 L.Ed.2d 610 (1965); Alevizos v. Metropolitan Airports Commission of Minneapolis and St. Paul, 298 Minn. 471, 216 N.W.2d 651 (Minn.1974); Long v. City of Charlotte, 306 N.C. 187, 293 S.E.2d 101 (1982); Henthorn v. Oklahoma City, 453 P.2d 1013 (Okla.1969); Aaron v. City of Los

Angeles, 40 Cal.App.3d 471, 115 Cal.Rptr. 162 (Cal.App.1974), cert. denied, 419 U.S. 1122, 95 S.Ct. 806, 42 L.Ed.2d 822 (1975); City of Philadelphia v. Keyser, 45 Pa. Commw. 271, 407 A.2d 55 (1979). But see Louisville and Jefferson County Air Bd. v. Porter, 397 S.W.2d 146 (Ky.1965) and Fields v. Sarasota–Manatee Airport Authority, 512 So.2d 961 (Fla.App.1987).

20. Indiana Toll Road Commission v. Jankovich, 244 Ind. 574, 193 N.E.2d 237, 241–42 (1963), writ dismissed as improvidently granted, 379 U.S. 487, 85 S.Ct. 493, 13 L.Ed.2d 439 (1965) (case based on independent state ground); Sneed v. County of Riverside, 218 Cal.App.2d 205, 32 Cal.Rptr. 318 (1963); Ackerman v. Port of Seattle, 55 Wn.2d 400, 348 P.2d 664 (1960); Roark v. City of Caldwell, 87 Idaho 557, 394 P.2d 641 (1964).

21. See Penn Central Transportation Co. v. City of New York, 438 U.S. 104, 98 S.Ct. 2646, 57 L.Ed.2d 631 (1978), and discussion infra § 10.6.

for the public. In effect, the action is the acquisition of an on and off ramp in the sky under the guise of the police power.[22] This may be deemed improper since the airport authority, having the power of eminent domain, could have directly acquired the easement. If by design or shortsightedness, it failed to do so, courts may make it pay after the fact.[23] This finding distinguishes such zoning from ordinary zoning, which, when it regulates heights, confers both a benefit and a burden on all within the zone. Thus, while zoning land for agricultural use may not be a taking where the purpose is to preserve agricultural land, where the effect of the zoning is to limit use to agriculture to establish a glide path, a taking may be found.[24]

A number of courts disagree and find that zoning to protect the public from air hazards is a valid police power control and not a taking.[25] Comparing an airport zoning case to the Supreme Court's decision in Penn Central Transportation Co. v. City of New York,[26] the Wyoming Supreme Court rejected the negative easement analogy.[27] It held that a reciprocal benefit to the affected landowner was not required to protect zoning from being declared a taking if the parcel, viewed as a whole, was not significantly affected.[28]

§ 4.30 Hospitals and Medical Facilities

Like other uses described in this chapter, many hospitals and other medical facilities are either publicly owned or are owned by nonprofit groups, and provide necessary social services. Provision of health care comes through a variety of uses, from large medical complexes to group homes for persons in need of supervised care. The zoning treatment of these uses varies.

Particularly in earlier days, hospitals dealing with tuberculosis, mental disorders, handicapped persons, and unwed mothers were frequently separately classified by ordinance, and excluded or confined to less restricted zones. As with other land uses like cemeteries and funeral parlors,[1] hospitals and various treatment centers are reminders of death, disease and other social ills. The Village of Euclid, for example, in the ordinance unsuccessfully challenged in zoning law's leading case, allowed

---

22. Indiana Toll Road Commission v. Jankovich, 244 Ind. 574, 193 N.E.2d 237, 241–42 (1963).

23. Ackerman v. Port of Seattle, 55 Wn.2d 400, 348 P.2d 664, 666 (1960).

24. Roark v. Caldwell, 87 Idaho 557, 394 P.2d 641 (1964). See discussion supra § 3.21 on zoning to lower condemnation costs.

25. Harrell's Candy Kitchen, Inc. v. Sarasota–Manatee Airport Authority, 111 So.2d 439 (Fla.1959); Waring v. Peterson (Fla.App.1962), 137 So.2d 268; Willoughby Hills v. Corrigan, 29 Ohio St.2d 39, 278 N.E.2d 658, cert. denied 409 U.S. 919, 93 S.Ct. 218, 34 L.Ed.2d 181 (1972); Baggett v. City of Montgomery, 276 Ala. 166, 160 So.2d 6 (1963); LaSalle National Bank v. County of Cook, 34 Ill.App.3d 264, 340 N.E.2d 79 (1975).

26. 438 U.S. 104, 98 S.Ct. 2646, 57 L.Ed.2d 631 (1978).

27. Cheyenne Airport Bd. v. Rogers, 707 P.2d 717 (1985). See also Waring v. Peterson, 137 So.2d 268 (Fla.App.1962).

28. See Steven H. Magee, Protecting Land Around Airports: Avoiding Regulatory Taking Claims by Comprehensive Planning and Zoning, 62 J.Air L. & Com. 243 (1996).

§ 4.30

1. See infra § 6.9.

hospitals in the third most restricted residential zone and placed "insane and feeble-minded institutions" in the industrial zone, along with cemeteries, penal institutions, crematories and sewage disposal.[2] To some degree, times have changed.

Health care facilities often resemble commercial uses in nature, but zoning authorities sometimes treat them less restrictively. Though the activity generated by large medical complexes may equal that of major commercial operations, medical facilities are frequently permitted in higher density residential zones subject to a special permit process.[3] Courts will uphold exclusion of hospitals from residential zones,[4] but, viewing hospitals as community assets, a court may require a greater showing of a need to exclude than is true with other uses.[5]

In some instances, state and federal law limit the reach of local zoning. If the operation is governmental, immunity from local control may attach,[6] and even non-governmental health care facilities may be exempt if operating pursuant to state law.[7] The exclusion of small health care facilities for groups such as the mentally retarded may also receive closer scrutiny from the courts under an equal protection analysis.[8] The federal Fair Housing Act also limits zoning of medical facilities for the handicapped.[9]

VI. NONCONFORMING USES

§ 4.31 In General

Nearly all zoning ordinances provide that a use that would be unlawful if established after the passage of an ordinance may continue if it lawfully preexists the adoption of the ordinance. "Nonconforming use" can be a generic term covering all nonconformities, but separating nonconforming situations into four types is useful: (1) nonconforming buildings, (2) conforming uses of nonconforming buildings, (3) nonconforming uses of conforming buildings, and (4) nonconforming uses of land. For example, a building built at the front lot line is a nonconforming building after passage of an ordinance establishing a front yard

2. Village of Euclid v. Ambler Realty Co., 272 U.S. 365, 47 S.Ct. 114, 71 L.Ed. 303 (1926).

3. City of Huntsville v. Morring, 284 Ala. 678, 227 So.2d 578 (1969).

4. Jones v. Los Angeles, 211 Cal. 304, 295 P. 14 (1930).

5. Sisters of Bon Secours Hosp. v. Grosse Pointe, 8 Mich.App. 342, 154 N.W.2d 644 (1967) (exclusion from residential zone not justified where lack of proof that area was one that would suffer a loss of value); Jewish Consumptives' Relief Soc'y v. Town of Woodbury, 230 App.Div. 228, 243 N.Y.S. 686 (1930), affirmed mem. 256 N.Y. 619, 177 N.E. 165 (1931); Urban Farms Inc. v. Franklin Lakes, 179 N.J.Su-

per. 203, 431 A.2d 163 (1981), cert. denied 87 N.J. 428, 434 A.2d 1099 (1981).

6. Macon–Bibb County Hospital Authority v. Madison, 204 Ga.App. 741, 420 S.E.2d 586 (1992). See immunity discussion supra § 4.23.

7. See, e.g., City of Torrance v. Transitional Living Centers, 30 Cal.3d 516, 179 Cal.Rptr. 907, 638 P.2d 1304 (1982) and discussion of licensees supra § 4.24.

8. City of Cleburne v. Cleburne Living Ctr., 473 U.S. 432, 105 S.Ct. 3249, 87 L.Ed.2d 313 (1985) supra § 4.6 and infra § 10.14.

9. See infra § 6.8.

setback requirement. An office building is a nonconforming building in a multi-family zone although it has been abandoned for office use and is occupied by several families. If a single-family house is used for manufacturing furniture in a single-family zone, the building conforms though the use does not. Land may be used for a pig farm, with the land containing no structures rising to the dignity of buildings. If in a single-family use zone, the use would be nonconforming. Certain consequences concerning the continuance and termination of nonconformities may depend on these classifications.

Protection of existing uses was an important goal at zoning's onset.[1] First, zoning was considered a prospective control, whose primary purpose was to control land as it developed and to maintain that control rather than to change existing development. Second, while a true Euclidean zoner was a purist, aiming to divide the landscape into districts having a place for everything and everything in its place, convincing pragmatists that a few nonconforming uses were totally contrary to the public health, safety and welfare was hard. After all, even the purists contemplated cumulative rather than exclusive zones.[2] Thus, while a mom and pop grocery store is a nonconforming use in a single-family zone, the necessity for its termination is not compelling, particularly where single-family uses are permitted in areas zoned for commercial uses. Third, while proponents could convince the body politic of the wisdom of zoning applied prospectively, the political forces against adoption of zoning would have been much stronger if zoning had been applied to require wholesale compliance of existing uses. Fourth, the validity of zoning as a police power measure was in doubt in early years and the risk of unconstitutionality would have been greater if they had not permitted preexisting uses to continue.[3] It, thus, became customary to exempt existing uses to avoid the question.[4]

While the Standard State Zoning Enabling Act makes no provision for the treatment of existing uses, some enabling acts require that nonconforming uses be allowed to continue.[5] Even where not mandated

§ 4.31

1. Eric J. Strauss and Mary M. Giese, Elimination of Nonconformities: The Case for Voluntary Discontinuance, 25 Urb.Law. 159 (1993); Annot., Alteration, Extension, Reconstruction, or Repair of Nonconforming Structure, 63 A.L.R.4th 275 (1989); Annot., Construction of New Building or Structure on Premises Devoted to Nonconforming Use as Violation of Zoning Ordinance , 10 A.L.R.4th 1122 (1979); Strong, Nonconforming Uses: The Black Sheep of Zoning, 7 Inst. on Plan. & Zoning 25 (1968); Young, Regulation and Removal of Nonconforming Uses, 12 Case W.Res.L.Rev. 681 (1961).

2. See supra § 4.3.

3. Earlier cases upholding retroactive applications of zoning-like regulations which terminated preexisting uses dealt with land uses that had nuisance or near-nuisance features. See, e.g., Hadacheck v. Sebastian, 239 U.S. 394, 36 S.Ct. 143, 60 L.Ed. 348 (1915) (brickyard in residential zone); Reinman v. Little Rock, 237 U.S. 171, 35 S.Ct. 511, 59 L.Ed. 900 (1915) (stables in commercial zone).

4. Hansen Brothers Enterprises, Inc. v. Board of Supervisors of Nevada County, 12 Cal.4th 533, 48 Cal.Rptr.2d at 789, 789, 907 P.2d 1324, 1335 (1996).

5. See N.H.Stat.Ann. § 674:16 (zoning ordinance shall not apply to existing structures or to the existing use of any building, but may apply to alterations for different use); N.J.Stat.Ann. § 40:55D–68.; Ore.Rev. Stat. § 215.130 (5).

by state law, most zoning ordinances permit nonconforming uses to continue. Where not so allowed, some courts have held retroactive application invalid as having no substantial relation to the public health, safety and welfare,[6] or as not authorized by enabling acts.[7] Other courts have construed ordinances as permitting preexisting uses to continue to save the ordinance constitutionally,[8] or they have declined to issue an injunction as a discretionary remedy in equity.[9]

§ 4.32 Lawful Existence

In order for nonconforming uses to continue, they must be lawfully established at the time the ordinance making them nonconforming takes effect. The stakes are high, and litigation on the matter is frequent. If the use is not "in existence" at the critical time, expenses incurred in construction will be lost and more expense will be encountered in removing illegal structures that were built. Considerable benefit may also flow from securing legal nonconforming use status due to the monopoly position that it might confer. For example, to be the only flower shop permitted near a cemetery because of nonconforming status is an enviable position for the flower shop owner.

The law of vested rights, discussed elsewhere,[1] controls the establishment of lawful existence to protect a landowner from zoning changes. Difficulties are often encountered when a race ensues between a developer attempting to establish a use and a municipality in the process of enacting a new zoning ordinance that might declare the developer's use illegal. Under the law of vested rights, the one to first cross the finish line does not necessarily prevail. Generally, to acquire immunity from a newly enacted law, a developer must engage in substantial expenditures in good faith reliance on a validly issued building permit. The municipality must also act in good faith, and unreasonable delay in issuing a permit may preclude it from applying a newly enacted law.[2]

A use might be lawful under a zoning ordinance but not be lawful for another reason, in which case it may not be a preexisting lawful use for purposes of the nonconforming use provisions. For example, a building may not qualify as a nonconforming use if it violates a building code.[3] On the other hand, a use has been held lawful for purposes of the nonconforming use doctrine though it violates a restrictive covenant.[4] The two cases are reconcilable, because the violation of the restrictive

6. Jones v. Los Angeles, 211 Cal. 304, 295 P. 14 (1930).

7. Bane v. Township of Pontiac, 343 Mich. 481, 72 N.W.2d 134 (1955).

8. Amereihn v. Kotras, 194 Md. 591, 71 A.2d 865 (1950).

9. City of Toronto v. Hutton (1953), Ont.W.N. 205 (1952), Ontario High Court (injunction issued against nursing home in residential area, but enforcement delayed for 18 months because city reconsidering zoning in area).

§ 4.32

1. See infra § 5.27.

2. See infra § 5.28.

3. State v. Stonybrook, Inc., 149 Conn. 492, 181 A.2d 601 (1962), cert. denied 371 U.S. 185, 83 S.Ct. 265, 9 L.Ed.2d 227 (1962).

4. Gauthier v. Village of Larchmont, 30 A.D.2d 303, 291 N.Y.S.2d 584 (1968), appeal denied 22 N.Y.2d 1028, 295 N.Y.S.2d 1028, 242 N.E.2d 494 (1968).

covenant is of little interest to anyone but private parties. The building code, on the other hand, is a public law and is closely related to zoning.

§ 4.33 Restrictions on Nonconforming Uses

While lawful nonconforming uses are allowed to continue, they are at most tolerated. Unless precluded by state law, municipalities place numerous limitations on nonconforming uses designed to achieve conformance as soon as practicable and reasonable.[1] These include limitations on changes in use,[2] on repairs and alterations,[3] on rebuilding in the event of destruction,[4] and on resuming use after a period of abandonment.[5] Most courts construe rights conferred on nonconforming uses narrowly to promote the goal of early elimination.[6]

§ 4.34 Change in Use

Generally, protected status is lost upon change in use.[1] The rule, however, is hardly absolute. Ordinances may permit some change, reflecting a tension between effectuating the goal of eliminating nonconforming uses at the earliest opportunity and allowing the owner of the nonconforming use some degree of flexibility. Furthermore, a mere change in ownership does not end the nonconforming use.[2]

A. More Intensive Use

In the absence of an ordinance permitting it, a nonconforming use cannot be expanded. Some ordinances flatly provide that no nonconforming use "shall be enlarged or intensified."[3] Others may be less sweeping in their interdiction. For example, an increase in the volume of activity was allowed under an ordinance that provided that "nonconforming uses shall not be enlarged, increased or extended to occupy a greater area of land * * *."[4] Some ordinances allow "limited expansion."[5]

§ 4.33

1. Kaloo v. Zoning Bd. of Appeals for City of Chicago, 274 Ill.App.3d 927, 211 Ill.Dec. 31, 654 N.E.2d 493 (1995); Institute for Evaluation and Planning, Inc. v. Board of Adj. of the Borough of Freehold, 270 N.J.Super. 396, 637 A.2d 235 (1993) (such uses shall be allowed to wither away).

2. See § 4.34.

3. See infra § 4.35.

4. See infra § 4.38.

5. See infra § 4.38.

6. See Rotter v. Coconino County, 169 Ariz. 269, 818 P.2d 704 (1991); Goodwin v. Kansas City, 244 Kan. 28, 766 P.2d 177, 182 (1988); Wyatt v. Board of Adj., 622 P.2d 85, 86 (Colo.App.1980).

§ 4.34

1. Altpa, Inc. v. North Huntington Twp. Zoning Hearing Bd., 67 Pa.Cmwlth. 60, 445 A.2d 1358 (1982); City and County

of Denver, 31 Colo.App. 324, 505 P.2d 44 (1972).

2. Hansen Brothers Enterprises, Inc. v. Board of Supervisors of Nevada County, 12 Cal.4th 533, 48 Cal.Rptr.2d 778, 782, 907 P.2d 1324, 1328 (1996); Matter of Bexson v. Board of Zoning App., 28 A.D.2d 848, 281 N.Y.S.2d 569 (1967). But see Village of Valatie v. Smith, 83 N.Y.2d 396, 632 N.E.2d 1264, 610 N.Y.S.2d 941 (1994) (amortization period terminating nonconforming use on transfer valid).

3. See county ordinance cited in Hansen Brothers Enterprises, Inc. v. Board of Supervisors of Nevada County, 12 Cal.4th 533, 907 P.2d 1324, 1349, 48 Cal.Rptr.2d 778, 803 (1996).

4. Town of Gardiner v. Blue Sky Entertainment Corp. 213 A.D.2d 790, 623 N.Y.S.2d 29 (1995) (overnight camping by skydivers and pilots was part of nonconforming use so that increased camping was permissible). See also Institute for Evalua-

Variations in ordinances make it difficult to fashion a general guide as to what changes will be allowed.[6] However, a sampling of cases gives a flavor of the results courts reach. For example, a nonconforming garage used by a painting contractor for storage purposes was not permitted to be converted to a car repair business where the applicant would park the cars outside and would work on the weekends.[7] A nonconforming private hunting club was found to have unlawfully enlarged its use by allowing nonmembers to use the property.[8] And, a nonconforming ski area could not enlarge the use of its land to include summer recreational activities.[9] However, on the theory that a proposed use need not be identical to the existing use, a public restaurant and bar were permitted to replace a private club.[10]

If only part of a building is used for a nonconforming use, expanding the use to other parts of the building may be improper.[11] On the other hand, if the key to change is the effect on the neighborhood, the code may permit internal expansion.[12]

B. *Similar or Less Intensive Use*

Some ordinances and courts allow a change of use to one of less intensity.[13] For example, the court held the ordinance at issue in Arkam Machine & Tool Co. v. Township of Lyndhurst[14] to permit a nonconforming factory for the manufacture of music boxes employing 80 people to continue as a factory for manufacturing blades and eyeglasses, where only 15 people would be employed.

On first impression permitting changes that move a use in the direction of conformity seems sensible. However, if there is a desire to change, it may be that economics has dictated that the present use should not be continued, making it likely that without permission to

tion and Planning, Inc. v. Board of Adj. of the Borough of Freehold, 270 N.J.Super. 396, 637 A.2d 235 (1993) (mere increase in intensity of use is not fatal to continuation of nonconforming use).

5. See Rotter v. Coconino County, 169 Ariz. 269, 818 P.2d 704 (1991); Watts v. City of Helena, 151 Mont. 138, 439 P.2d 767, 768 (1968).

6. See Amherst v. Cadorette, 113 N.H. 13, 300 A.2d 327 (1973) (extent of a nonconforming use is often carefully defined by local ordinance).

7. Kaloo v. Zoning Bd. of Appeals for City of Chicago, 274 Ill.App.3d 927, 211 Ill.Dec. 31, 654 N.E.2d 493 (1995).

8. State ex rel. Dierberg v. Board of Zoning Adj. of St. Charles County, 869 S.W.2d 865 (Mo.App.1994).

9. Lindstrom v. Zoning Bd. of Appeals of Town of Warwick, 225 A.D.2d 626, 639 N.Y.S.2d 447 (1996).

10. Limley v. Zoning Hearing Bd. of Port Vue Borough, 533 Pa. 340, 625 A.2d 54 (1993).

11. Weber v. Pieretti, 72 N.J.Super. 184, 178 A.2d 92 (Super.Ch.1962), affirmed mem. 77 N.J.Super. 423, 186 A.2d 702 (App.Div.1962), cert. denied 39 N.J. 236, 188 A.2d 177 (1963) (nonconforming bottling plant improperly extended to second floor).

12. Ray's Stateline Market, Inc. v. Town of Pelham, 140 N.H. 139, 665 A.2d 1068 (1995) (convenience store improvements to install doughnut franchise cart operation did not result in impermissible change or extension).

13. Malakoff v. Zoning Bd. of Adj. of City of Pittsburgh, 78 Pa.Cmwlth. 178, 467 A.2d 97(1983) (board of adjustment authorized to allow uses it found to be less detrimental).

14. 73 N.J.Super. 528, 180 A.2d 348 (App.Div.1962).

change it would be abandoned, thus resulting in full conformity.[15] Furthermore, if the city permits a new use that is only in the direction of conformity, the new nonconforming use is likely to prevail for a longer time.

C. Natural Growth: Right of Expansion

A few courts allow what they call "normal" expansion.[16] As one court put it, "[a]n ordinance which would allow the housing of a baby elephant cannot evict the animal when it has grown up, since it is generally known that a baby elephant eventually becomes a big elephant."[17]

In most states where normal expansion is allowed, courts allow a mere increase in the volume of business by natural growth but prohibit changes amounting to a new or different use.[18] In Pennsylvania, the courts go one step further and hold that there is a constitutional right to natural expansion. The right is grounded in the court's view that under the substantive due process guarantee it would be "inequitable to prevent [an owner] from expanding the property as the dictates of business or modernization require."[19]

A right of natural expansion is contrary to the prevailing weight of authority that calls for strict limits on changes.[20] Indicative of this attitude is a recent Arizona decision where the court, obligated by state statute to permit expansion on the original nonconforming parcel, limited the right by prohibiting expansion on an after-acquired parcel.[21]

D. Natural Resources Diminishing Assets Doctrine

The rule prohibiting expansion of a nonconforming use poses particular problems with respect to natural resource extraction where the nature of the use necessarily involves expansion. In quarrying, for example, the operator must either widen or deepen the pit to continue operations.

Many courts apply a diminishing assets doctrine that permits a nonconforming extractive process to expand its mining operation beyond

---

15. See infra § 4.38.

16. People v. Ferris, 18 Ill.App.2d 346, 152 N.E.2d 183 (1958) (expansion of trailer camp proper); Powers v. Building Inspector, 363 Mass. 648, 296 N.E.2d 491 (1973); Redfearn v. Creppel, 455 So.2d 1356 (La.1984). But see Edmonds v. County of Los Angeles, 40 Cal.2d 642, 255 P.2d 772 (1953) (expansion of number of trailer sites need not be allowed).

17. In re Associated Contractors, Inc., 391 Pa. 347, 138 A.2d 99, 102 (1958).

18. Frost v. Lucey, 231 A.2d 441 (Me. 1967); Vermont Brick & Block, Inc. v. Village of Essex Junction, 135 Vt. 481, 380 A.2d 67 (1977); State v. Szymanski, 1 Conn. Cir.Ct. 509, 24 Conn.Supp. 221, 189 A.2d 514 (1962).

19. Silver v. Zoning Bd. of Adj., 435 Pa. 99, 255 A.2d 506 (1969) (owner of a nonconforming apartment building unable to lease multi-bedroom units in a changing market was held to have the right to subdivide some of the apartments).

20. See Rotter v. Coconino County, 169 Ariz. 269, 818 P.2d 704 (1991).

21. Rotter v. Coconino County, 169 Ariz. 269, 818 P.2d 704 (1991), interpreting Ariz.Rev.Stat. § 11–830A which provides that a "nonconforming business use within a district may expand if such expansion does not exceed one hundred per cent of the area of the original business."

the area mined at the time the activity became a nonconforming use.[22] In effect, they define the nonconforming use to include "all that land which contains the particular asset and which constitutes an integral part of the operation, notwithstanding the fact that a particular portion may not yet be under actual excavation."[23]

There are limitations. Generally, a miner must show by objective evidence that it intended to mine the contemplated area at the time the zoning changed. Thus, a New York court held that a nonconforming gravel operation could expand to cover its entire parcel where it was established that the operator had removed gravel from various portions of the entire parcel, had built service roads throughout the parcel, and had built a processing plant in the center of the property.[24] The mere hope to expand, however, is not sufficient; it must be manifested in some fashion. Thus, in an Alaskan case, a miner was limited to expanding to only 13 of 53 acres, where the evidence established that at the time of the zoning change the operation was "so small it was almost unnoticeable."[25]

§ 4.35 Repairs and Alterations

Most ordinances allow repairs to a nonconforming use.[1] If not, courts will typically permit repairs. Such permission makes sense, because there is a general policy, particularly as represented by housing codes, to have buildings in good repair. Generally, the repairs allowed are modest. Ordinances sometimes permit repairs as measured by a percentage of the appraised or assessed value of the building to provide a standard that will permit repairs but eliminate substantial alterations. Assessed values, however, frequently have little relation to market values and values may change over time, both of which can make application of the standard difficult or unfair.

Alterations and structural repairs are usually prohibited on the theory that they will prolong the life of the nonconforming use.[2] Deciding what is a permitted repair and a prohibited alteration is sometimes difficult, but, beyond the specifics of the applicable ordinance, the goal of

---

22. Stephan & Sons v. Municipality of Anchorage, 685 P.2d 98 (Alaska 1984); Hansen Brothers Enterprises, Inc. v. Board of Supervisors of Nevada County, 12 Cal.4th 533, 907 P.2d 1324, 48 Cal.Rptr.2d 778 (1996); County of Du Page v. Elmhurst–Chicago Stone Co., 18 Ill.2d 479, 165 N.E.2d 310 (1960); Flanagan v. Town of Hollis, 112 N.H. 222, 224, 293 A.2d 328 (1972); Moore v. Bridgewater Twp. 69 N.J.Super. 1, 173 A.2d 430 (1961); Smart v. Dane County Board of Adj., 177 Wis.2d 445, 501 N.W.2d 782 (1993); Syracuse Aggregate Corp. v. Weise, 51 N.Y.2d 278, 414 N.E.2d 651, 434 N.Y.S.2d 150 (1980); Gibbons & Reed Company v. North Salt Lake City 19 Utah 2d 329, 431 P.2d 559, 562–563 (1967). But see Teuscher v. Zoning Bd. of App., 154 Conn. 650, 228 A.2d 518 (1967) and Billerica v. Quinn, 320 Mass. 687, 71 N.E.2d 235 (1947).

23. County of DuPage v. Elmhurst–Chicago Stone Co., 18 Ill.2d 479, 165 N.E.2d 310, 313 (1960).

24. Syracuse Aggregate Corp. v. Weise, 51 N.Y.2d 278, 434 N.Y.S.2d 150, 414 N.E.2d 651 (1980).

25. Stephan & Sons v. Municipality of Anchorage, 685 P.2d 98, 101 (Alaska 1984).

§ 4.35

1. Annot., 57 A.L.R.3d 419 (1974).

2. Marris v. City of Cedarburg. 176 Wis.2d 14, 498 N.W.2d 842 (1993).

early elimination determines the issue.[3] Replacing old billboards with new ones, for example, has been disallowed in several cases.[4] Though the new signs might improve the appearance of the nonconforming property, such changes, if allowed, could indefinitely continue a nonconforming use. Meanwhile, of course, the general community, and particularly the immediate neighborhood, has to suffer from older signs or structures that are deteriorating.

Ordinances may allow alterations that are "necessary to assure the safety of the structure"[5] or otherwise required by law. In one case, for example, a court held that a nonconforming nursing home operated in a frame building could be replaced with a new fireproof structure if it did not increase the scale of the nursing home operations.[6] The new structure was necessary for the home to continue to be licensed.

§ 4.36   Conversion to Administrative Permission

Obtaining a variance or special permit can change the status of a legal nonconforming use.[1] Some ordinances require owners of nonconforming uses to apply for a variance or a special permit. Property owners sometimes resist applying because they think nonconforming use status protects them indefinitely, while a special permit or a variance may be considered a matter of discretion, and the continuance of the administrative permission is always open to review. Of course, the assumption that a nonconforming use can continue indefinitely may be erroneous. As the discussion on termination indicates,[2] nonconforming uses do not have the right to continue indefinitely. Thus, in Town of Waterford v. Grabner,[3] the ordinance required an operator of a nonconforming quarry to apply for a renewable four-year permit. He declined to do so and the trial court indicated he need not do so since he had a protected nonconformity. The state supreme court reversed indicating that the real issue was whether the possible termination of the permit after the four years would be unconstitutional as applied to the quarry—if not, the operator could be compelled to apply for the permit.

§ 4.37   Termination of Nonconforming Uses: In General

A nonconforming use is not entitled to continue in perpetuity. Fire, flood, or other cause beyond the owner's control may destroy it involun-

---

3. See, e.g., Mossman v. City of Columbus, 234 Neb. 78, 449 N.W.2d 214 (1989) (replacement of a original mobile home with a new mobile home was prohibited as a structural alteration).

4. Gannett Outdoor Co. of Arizona v. City of Mesa, 159 Ariz. 459, 768 P.2d 191 (1989) (replacement of an existing "multipole" billboard with a new "mono-pole" was not permitted under an ordinance that allowed "reasonable alterations"); Appalachian Poster Advertising Co. v. Zoning Bd. of Adj. of City of Shelby, 52 N.C.App. 266, 278 S.E.2d 321 (1981); Goodrich v. Seligman, 298 Ky. 863, 183 S.W.2d 625 (1944).

5. See ordinance interpreted in Christy v. Harleston, 266 S.C. 439, 223 S.E.2d 861 (1976).

6. In re O'Neal, 243 N.C. 714, 92 S.E.2d 189 (1956). The fact that the ordinance involved did not prohibit structural alterations limits the strength of the case as precedent favoring alterations.

§ 4.36

1. See infra §§ 5.14 and 5.24.

2. See infra § 4.37.

3. 155 Conn. 431, 232 A.2d 481 (1967).

tarily and permission for restoration may not be given. The owner's abandonment may terminate the nonconforming use. The municipality may terminate it through amortization, or a court may find that the nonconformity constitutes a nuisance. We discuss these matters in the following sections of this chapter.

§ 4.38 Destruction and Abandonment

As a general proposition, a destroyed or abandoned nonconforming use cannot be rebuilt.[1] While fairness supports protecting investments in existing uses from newly enacted zoning laws, once the nonconforming use is gone, whether by destruction or abandonment, the investment is lost. At that point, the owner of the land may have to stand on equal footing with the neighbors and comply with current zoning.[2] Nonetheless, in some instances, legislatures and courts permit resumption.

A. *Destruction*

If destruction is involuntary and partial, ordinances often allow rebuilding.[3] Most, however, prohibit rebuilding where destruction, voluntary or involuntary, is substantial.[4] They usually measure substantiality by the percentage of value destroyed.[5] Thus, in Moffatt v. Forrest City[6], an ordinance provided that one could not rebuild a building if it were 60 percent destroyed. The residential part of a building located in a residential zone was totally destroyed although the third of the building used as a meat market was not. The court held the building was more than 60 percent destroyed, so that it could no longer be used for a meat market.

Some courts are sympathetic to owners so as not to compound their calamities. For example, in O'Mara v. City Council of Newark,[7] the authorities assessed a nonconforming duplex in a business zone at $400. After a fire, they assessed the building at $200 and the cost of repairs at $300. The city argued that there was a 75 percent destruction ($300/$400) so that reconstruction was prohibited under the ordinance. The court held that the destruction was $200/$400 or fifty percent and indicated substantial doubt about the constitutionality of the provision, since the market value of the property was $1,800. Since repairs would only cost $300, there was only 17 percent destruction, which did not seem substantial to the court. The court apparently overlooked that the

§ 4.38

1. Red Garter, Inc. v. Cleveland Bd. of Zoning Appeals, 100 Ohio App.3d 177, 652 N.E.2d 260 (1995); Pamlico Marine Co., Inc. v. North Carolina Dept. of Natural Resources and Community Development, 80 N.C.App. 201, 341 S.E.2d 108 (1986).

2. See Matter of Pelham Esplanade v. Board of Trustees, 77 N.Y.2d 66, 565 N.E.2d 508, 510, 563 N.Y.S.2d 759, 761 (1990) ("no absolute entitlement to reestablishment of a nonconforming use"); Hartley v. City of Colorado Springs, 764 P.2d 1216, 1224 (Colo.1988).

3. Manhattan Sepulveda, Ltd. v. City of Manhattan Beach, 22 Cal.App.4th 865, 27 Cal.Rptr.2d 565 (1994).

4. City of Las Cruces v. Neff, 65 N.M. 414, 338 P.2d 731 (1959); Annot. 57 A.L.R.3d 419 (1974).

5. See Manhattan Sepulveda, Ltd. v. City of Manhattan Beach, 22 Cal.App.4th 865, 27 Cal.Rptr.2d 565 (1994) (using fair market value and rejecting city's effort to use replacement cost)

6. 234 Ark. 12, 350 S.W.2d 327 (1961).

7. 238 Cal.App.2d 836, 48 Cal.Rptr. 208 (1965).

expenditure of $300 could perhaps conform the building with little or no loss in market value.

B. Abandonment or Discontinuance

If the owner abandons the use, lawful nonconforming status is lost.[8] Most courts require proof of an overt act and an intention permanently to abandon.[9] For example, in State ex rel. Morehouse v. Hunt[10] a fraternity house was located in an area zoned for single-family residential uses. For 2½ years it was rented as a rooming house and for five years thereafter it was rented to a family who had some servants and rented a room to some students. The zoning board of appeals concluded that the fraternity use was not abandoned, and the court agreed, indicating that the owner did not intend to abandon the use permanently but intended to sell it to a fraternity when the opportunity arose. The court was likely more generous to the landowner than most would be. In another case, where the court held lawful nonconforming status lost, the owner wished to establish a coin-operated laundry where a grocery store use of the premises had ceased some five years earlier.[11] While the ordinance would have permitted a shift from the grocery store to the laundry as a similar or less intensive use, the fact that the premises had been used for noncommercial purposes during the five year interim evidenced intent to abandon.

The burden of proving intent is on the municipality, and it is a difficult one to carry.[12] The job is made easier in some states which presume intent to abandon upon expiration of a specified time period.[13]

A compulsory and temporary cessation does not constitute an abandonment if the stoppage is not due to acts within the owner's control. For example, in City of Fontana v. Atkinson,[14] the county health department ordered the owner of a nonconforming dairy to rebuild corral fences. When they tore down the fences temporarily to permit rebuilding, the city claimed that removal of the fences constituted an abandonment. The court found no abandonment. Similarly, abandonment may

---

8. See County of DuPage v. K–Five Const. Corp., 267 Ill.App.3d 266, 204 Ill. Dec. 702, 642 N.E.2d 164 (1994); Annot., 57 A.L.R.3d 279 (1974).

9. Generally, the intent element is drawn by the courts from use of the word "abandon" in the ordinance. In some cases, it may be express. See Ernst v. Johnson County, 522 N.W.2d 599 (Iowa 1994) (ordinance mandated proof of intent because resumption was prohibited after a "voluntary" interruption). There is a trend dispensing with intent. See City of Glendale v. Aldabbagh, 189 Ariz. 140, 939 P.2d 418 (1997).

10. 235 Wis. 358, 291 N.W. 745 (1940).

11. Attorney General v. Johnson, 355 S.W.2d 305 (Ky.1962). See also Inhabitants of Town of Windham v. Sprague, 219 A.2d 548 (Me.1966).

12. Van Sant v. City of Everett, 69 Wash.App. 641, 849 P.2d 1276 (1993). See also Hon. Patricia A. Hurst , Zoning: The New Presumptions in Favor of Abandonment: It's Time to Burst the Bubble , 45 Rhode Island Bar J. 5 (Nov.1996).

13. County of Isanti v. Peterson, 469 N.W.2d 467 (Minn.App.1991); City of Minot v. Fisher, 212 N.W.2d 837 (N.D.1973); Martin v. Beehan, 689 S.W.2d 29 (Ky.App. 1985); Williams v. Salem Twp., 92 Pa. Cmwlth. 634, 500 A.2d 933 (1985), appeal denied 516 Pa. 615, 531 A.2d 781 (1987).

14. 212 Cal.App.2d 499, 28 Cal.Rptr. 25 (1963). See also Zoning Bd. of Adj. of City of Birmingham v. Davis, 699 So.2d 1264 (Ala.Civ.App.1997); Boles v. City of Chattanooga, 892 S.W.2d 416 (Tenn.App. 1994).

not be found if the use stops due to wartime restrictions, economic depression, and the like—providing the property is devoted to its non-conforming use as soon as reasonably possible.[15] If the owner's miscon-duct is the cause of a restraining order requiring that the use cease for a period of time, nonconforming status may be lost.[16]

Some ordinances provide that if a nonconforming use ceases or is discontinued for a stated period of time, the use may not resume. Periods of six months and one year are common and have been found reason-able.[17] These discontinuance or cessation ordinances should be distin-guished from abandonment ordinances. Under the former, proof of intent may not be required. Traditionally, most courts have treated the word "discontinue" as the equivalent of "abandon," and transported an intent element into discontinuance ordinances.[18] However, a growing number of courts reject this view, relying either on the plain language of the ordinance or the goal of early elimination of nonconforming uses.[19] In some cases, the dispensation of the intent element is broader and applies to "abandonment" language as well.[20]

§ 4.39 Amortization

Amortization provisions require the termination of a nonconforming use after the passage of a period of time from when the use becomes nonconforming or from the time of passage of the amortization ordi-nance.[1] The length of the amortization period varies depending on the

15. In re Associated Contractors, Inc., 391 Pa. 347, 138 A.2d 99 (1958) (office used as residence during housing shortage not an abandonment); Southern Equipment Co., Inc. v. Winstead, 80 N.C.App. 526, 342 S.E.2d 524 (1986) (mere inactivity of ce-ment plant for more than six months due to a slump in business was not an abandon-ment); Hammond v. City of Chicago, 139 Ill.App.3d 98, 93 Ill.Dec. 643, 487 N.E.2d 87 (1985) (discontinuance period suspended during bankruptcy stay).

16. City of Glendale v. Aldabbagh, 189 Ariz. 140, 939 P.2d 418 (1997).

17. City of New Orleans v. Hamilton, 602 So.2d 112 (La.App.1992); Walter v. Harris, 163 A.D.2d 619, 558 N.Y.S.2d 266 (1990); Matter of Sun Oil Co. v. Board of Zoning App. of Town of Harrison, 57 A.D.2d 627, 393 N.Y.S.2d 760 (1977) (ten months found facially reasonable), aff'd 44 N.Y.2d 995, 380 N.E.2d 328, 408 N.Y.S.2d 502 (1978).

18. Boles v. City of Chattanooga, 892 S.W.2d 416 (Tenn.App.1994) (collecting cases on both sides of the issue); In re Associated Contractors, Inc., 391 Pa. 347, 138 A.2d 99 (1958); Dandy Co. v. Civil City, 401 N.E.2d 1380 (Ind.App.1980). See generally Annot., Zoning: Right to Resume Nonconforming Use of Premises After Vol-

untary or Unexplained Break in the Conti-nuity of Nonconforming Use, 57 A.L.R.3d 279 (1974).

19. City of Glendale v. Aldabbagh, 189 Ariz. 140, 939 P.2d 418 (1997) (no proof of intent required; mere nonuse not sufficient and nonuse, to be considered, must be in part attributable to owner); Ka–Hur Enter-prises, Inc. v. Zoning Bd. of City of Prov-incetown, 424 Mass. 404, 676 N.E.2d 838 (Mass.1997); County of Isanti v. Peterson, 469 N.W.2d 467 (Minn.App.1991); Hartley v. City of Colorado Springs, 764 P.2d 1216, 1223 (Colo.1988) (citing cases and exten-sively reviewing the issue); Anderson v. City of Paragould, 16 Ark.App. 10, 695 S.W.2d 851 (1985).

20. Villari v. Zoning Bd. of Adj. of Deptford, 277 N.J.Super. 130, 649 A.2d 98 (1994) (alternative holding).

§ 4.39

1. See generally Jay M. Zitter, Annot., Validity of Provisions for Amortization of Nonconforming Uses 8 A.L.R.5th 391 (1993); Peterson & McCarthy, Amortization of Legal Land Use Nonconformities as Reg-ulatory Takings: An Uncertain Future, 35 Wash.U.J.Urb. & Contemp.L. 37 (1989); Reynolds, The Reasonableness of Amortiza-

significance of the investment and the harmful nature of the use. Nonconforming uses of land, like junkyards, are typically given relatively short periods, since there is no investment in buildings to recoup. Except for uses that consume the land such as mines and quarries,[2] nonconforming uses of land can likely move elsewhere with a minimum of loss. Relatively short periods of amortization also may be appropriate for nonconforming uses of conforming buildings, which can generally be converted to conforming uses without substantial cost.

The periods are typically longest for nonconforming buildings, particularly those that are specialties, such as an oil refinery, which would have a large capital investment and would be difficult to use for any other purpose. The period of amortization may also depend on the type of construction, so that the period would be longer for brick or concrete high-rise buildings and less for temporary, low-rise, inexpensively constructed warehouses. Periods range from thirty days for portable flashing signs,[3] ninety days for adult movie theaters,[4] three years for junkyards,[5] five years for billboards,[6] and 20 to 40 years for nonconforming buildings.[7]

While time periods are the common determinants in amortization ordinances, courts have upheld amortization where the termination date is not ascertainable in advance. For example, in one case transfer of title triggered the end of the nonconforming use.[8] The court upheld the ordinance as a reasonable method of termination nonconforming uses. The court also found that the general rule that a nonconforming use does not end upon transfer of ownership applies only in the absence of amortization legislation.

While amortization was upheld as early as 1929,[9] it did not enjoy substantial use until the 1960s, during which time the technique generated considerable literature.[10] Over the years it has also produced sub-

tion Periods for Nonconforming Uses—Balancing the Private Interest and the Public Welfare, 34 Wash.U.J. Urb. & Contemp. L. 99 (1988); Sussna, Termination of Nonconforming Land Uses, Inst. on Plan. Zoning & Eminent Domain (1989).

2. See supra § 4.34 and infra § 6.9.

3. Art Neon Co. v. City and County of Denver, 488 F.2d 118 (10th Cir.1973).

4. Northend Cinema, Inc. v. City of Seattle, 90 Wash.2d 709, 585 P.2d 1153 (1978), cert.denied, 441 U.S. 946, 99 S.Ct. 2166, 60 L.Ed.2d 1048 (1979) (provision upheld); PA Northwestern Distributors, Inc. v. Zoning Hearing Board, 526 Pa. 186, 584 A.2d 1372 (Pa.1991) (held invalid under state constitution).

5. North Carolina v. Joyner, 286 N.C. 366, 211 S.E.2d 320 (1975).

6. Art Neon Co. v. City and County of Denver, 488 F.2d 118 (10th Cir.1973).

7. See Los Angeles ordinance discussed in City of Los Angeles v. Gage, 127 Cal. App.2d 442, 274 P.2d 34 (1954).

8. Village of Valatie v. Smith, 83 N.Y.2d 396, 632 N.E.2d 1264, 610 N.Y.S.2d 941 (1994). *Valatie* also noted that a prohibition on rebuilding after destruction could serve as a valid amortization period even though the time was unpredictable, citing Matter of Pelham Esplanade v. Board of Trustees, 77 N.Y.2d 66, 563 N.Y.S.2d 759, 565 N.E.2d 508 (1990).

9. State ex rel. Dema Realty Co. v. Jacoby, 168 La. 752, 123 So. 314 (1929).

10. See articles cited supra note. In addition see, Note, Suggested Means of Determining the Proper Amortization Period for Nonconforming Structures, 27 Stan. L.Rev. 1325 (1978); Graham, Legislative Techniques for the Amortization of the Nonconforming Use: A Suggested Formula, 12 Wayne St.L.Rev. 435 (1966); Katarincic,

stantial litigation. Most courts have upheld amortization in principle and have examined the reasonableness of specific applications on a case by case basis.[11]

City of Los Angeles v. Gage[12] is a leading case on amortization of nonconforming uses. Gage owned two lots in Los Angeles and established his use in 1930. One lot was improved with a two-story house with the top floor rented for residential use. The lower floor was Gage's home, with one room used as an office from which he conducted his plumbing supply business. Gage stored plumbing materials on the two lots. In 1946, the city zoned the property for multi-family use and the new ordinance also required the conformance of nonconforming uses within five years.

In upholding the application of the ordinance, the court noted that the noise and traffic caused by Gage's operation was high for a residential neighborhood and that uses such as Gage's impair the goal of the comprehensive plan. The court noted that only a nonconforming use of a conforming building was involved and that the property could immediately be used for a conforming use. This was in marked contrast to a case decided a few years earlier by the same court where it had invalidated the immediate termination of a mental health sanitarium. The latter, said the *Gage* court, involved a significant investment in a nonconforming building. The court further concluded that there is no constitutional difference between an ordinance restricting future uses and one terminating present uses. The test in each case is the public gain compared with the private loss, and amortization provisions are no harsher than ordinances preventing extension, alteration and reuse after abandonment.

The court also suggested that Gage's loss would be small. The business had a large gross revenue; he could buy a suitably zoned lot for about $2,500 more than the value of his present lot; it would only cost him $2,500 to move, and the loss of reestablishing his business was speculative. Moreover, Gage had had time to plan, and had enjoyed a monopoly position for five years.

A few aspects of the case bear comment. First, while in some cases there might be a normal useful life that can be amortized during its

Elimination of Non-conforming Uses, Buildings, and Structures by Amortization—Concept Versus Law, 2 Duq.U.L.Rev. 1 (1963); Moore, The Termination of Nonconforming Uses, 6 Wm. & Mary L.Rev. 1 (1965); Whitnall, Abatement of Nonconforming Uses, 2 Inst. on Plan. & Zoning 131 (1962).

11. See National Advertising Co., v. City of Raleigh, 947 F.2d 1158, 1164, n. 6 (4th Cir.1991)(citing cases); Tahoe Regional Planning Agency v. King, 233 Cal.App.3d 1365, 285 Cal.Rptr. 335 (1991); Lachapelle v. Town of Goffstown, 107 N.H. 485, 225 A.2d 624 (1967); North Carolina v. Joyner,

286 N.C. 366, 211 S.E.2d 320 (1975) (review limited to the reasonableness of specific clauses in as applied challenges); Standard Oil Co. v. Tallahassee, 183 F.2d 410 (5th Cir.1950), cert. denied 340 U.S. 892, 71 S.Ct. 208, 95 L.Ed. 647 (1950) (upholding ten year period for termination of a gasoline station that was located near several governmental buildings). See Zitter, Annot., supra note 1, listing 24 states upholding amortization in general.

12. 127 Cal.App.2d 442, 274 P.2d 34 (1954).

economic life or a period of depreciation,[13] there is in no sense a normal period of amortization for a business such as Gage's. By the time of the opinion, the use had continued for 24 years and would probably have continued indefinitely. While some courts would preclude termination before the end of economic life,[14] the court in *Gage* in effect said that the use can be terminated whenever reasonable, and under the circumstances of this case a five-year termination period was reasonable.

Since the neighborhood had fully developed in residential uses after Gage had established his use, the court perhaps overstated the "rotten apple" effect of the nonconforming use. The trial court, in fact, had found that Gage's use was not harmful to the neighbors. The supreme court chose to ignore this finding, preferring instead to make the blanket assumption that a nonconforming use has a negative effect.

Finally, the suggestion that Gage had a monopoly is arguable. Some nonconforming uses do enjoy monopoly positions because of their location,[15] but it is difficult to understand how Gage's business was any more profitable located where it was.[16] Gage might have had a property tax advantage. Assessors have great difficulty with assessments of land employed in nonconforming uses and they may have assessed the property as residential property.

Harbison v. Buffalo,[17] New York's first case to uphold the general principle of amortization, involved land in a residential zone used to recondition steel drums, a use classified as a junkyard under the ordinance. The ordinance provided that such nonconforming uses were to be terminated in three years. The court remanded the case to determine the reasonableness of the amortization period, directing the trial court to consider such factors as the nature of the business, the improvements involved, the character of the neighborhood and the detriment caused the property owner, such as the cost of relocation and the permissible areas of relocating.

Town of Hempstead v. Romano,[18] decided just a few years after *Harbison*, demonstrates the fact-based nature of amortization challenges. The land in *Romano* had been used as a junkyard since 1926 and in 1930 was zoned residential. Junkyards were to be terminated in three years under the terms of the ordinance. However, each year the junkyard owner had been given a permit to continue and it was not until

---

13. See Grant v. Baltimore, 212 Md. 301, 129 A.2d 363 (1957) (company depreciated signs over a period of five years for tax purposes).

14. National Advertising Co. v. County of Monterey, 211 Cal.App.2d 375, 27 Cal. Rptr. 136 (1962) (court held that a sign had an economic life of 10 years, and that termination prior to the end of that time would be invalid).

15. For example, a nonconforming flower shop near a cemetery which is located in a residential zone.

16. Gage had a wholesale and retail plumbing supply business. Perhaps near neighbors would find it advantageous to buy their plumbing supplies there rather than elsewhere, but it is rather unbelievable that the gains there would not be offset by location in a traffic-generating commercial center.

17. 4 N.Y.2d 553, 176 N.Y.S.2d 598, 152 N.E.2d 42 (1958).

18. 33 Misc.2d 315, 226 N.Y.S.2d 291 (1962).

1961 that the town attempted to terminate the use. The court held the termination provision invalid as applied indicating that a substantial loss would be caused by the termination, partially because junkyards were zoned out of the town, relocation would be expensive, and goodwill would be lost. In counterpoint to the court's analysis, one might ask why 28 years (1961 less 1933) was not treated as an amortization period and why the yearly extensions were not considered illegal, which ordinarily vest no rights.[19]

The validity of amortization, its accounting-sounding lineage aside, does not depend on a precise mathematical analysis. As the *Gage* court noted, the question requires a balance of the private loss against the public gain. In examining the extent of investment, courts may consider the initial capital investment, the investment realization to date, life expectancy, and the existence, and binding nature, of lease obligations. "[A]s the financial investment increases in dimension, the length of the amortization period should correspondingly increase. * * * While an owner need not be given that period of time necessary to recoup his investment entirely the amortization period should not be so short as to result in a substantial loss of his investment."[20]

Courts may question particular techniques. In one case, the court invalidated an amortization schedule that set varying periods from two to five years on signs based on replacement value.[21] The court found sign replacement value irrelevant to the question of the overall loss to the owner's business. Another court invalidated a one year amortization period as applied to signs that had not been fully amortized under federal tax laws.[22]

Another question explored in assessing reasonableness is the justification for eliminating the use. Some nonconforming uses for which short amortization periods are upheld have nuisance-like qualities, such as junkyards and signs. A billboard that is a traffic hazard can be immediately removed, but signs targeted due to their unattractive qualities provide a less compelling reason for immediate termination.[23]

Signs are popular targets of amortization. This is presumably because many cities have intensified their sign regulations in recent years, rendering many signs nonconforming.[24] While traffic hazards and portable signs can be terminated with short or no amortization period, billboards are given a longer time. Most billboards are successfully amortized in three to seven year periods.[25]

19. See infra § 5.28.

20. Modjeska Sign Studios, Inc. v. Berle, 43 N.Y.2d 468, 402 N.Y.S.2d 359, 373 N.E.2d 255, 262 (1977).

21. Art Neon Co. v. City and County of Denver, 488 F.2d 118 (10th Cir.1973).

22. National Advertising Co. v. County of Monterey, 211 Cal.App.2d 375, 27 Cal. Rptr. 136 (1962), disapproved on other grounds, Metromedia, Inc. v. City of San Diego, 23 Cal.3d 762, 154 Cal.Rptr. 212, 592 P.2d 728 (1979).

23. Modjeska Sign Studios, Inc. v. Berle, 43 N.Y.2d 468, 402 N.Y.S.2d 359, 366, 373 N.E.2d 255, 261 (1977).

24. See discussion of signs infra § 10.16 and § 12.2.

25. See cases collected in Zitter, supra note 1.

A few courts hold amortization schemes invalid on their face. In a case that involved a 90 day amortization period for adult book stores, the Pennsylvania court held the ordinance to be a facial taking under the state constitution.[26] The Pennsylvania high court, following its long history of enhanced protection for nonconforming uses, found there was a significant difference between the effect imposed on a nonconforming use by an ordinance restricting future use, and an ordinance that terminated one on a timetable not of the owner's choosing.[27]

§ 4.40 Immediate Termination of Nuisance

When a use is a nuisance, courts can order immediate termination, despite the loss of value sustained. They avoid the taking issue because there is no property right to maintain a nuisance.[1] Courts have also upheld ordinances that provide for immediate termination of uses with nuisance-like qualities without judicial determinations that the uses are common law nuisances.[2]

In two early cases the Supreme Court sustained ordinances that immediately terminated obnoxious uses. In Reinman v. Little Rock[3] it upheld a regulation that prohibited stables as applied to a preexisting stable in a business area. In Hadacheck v. Sebastian,[4] an ordinance prohibited brickyards in an area designated for residential use, and, though the property was reduced in value from $800,000 to $60,000, the Court held it valid as applied to an existing brickyard. "A vested interest," said the Court, "cannot be asserted against [the police power] because of conditions once obtaining."[5]

In the more recent case of Goldblatt v. Town of Hempstead,[6] a restriction on the operation of a quarry rendered its continued operation all but impossible. The Court upheld the regulation, pointing out that where health and safety are involved, a large loss is justified.

In contemporary takings jurisprudence, the fact that none of these cases involved a total economic loss of use is significant since the Court has held that a presumptive taking occurs where a police power control deprives a landowner of all economically viable use.[7] In such a case, the state can only avoid paying compensation under the taking clause if it can show that the ordinance's prohibition duplicates the result it could

26. PA Northwestern Distributors, Inc. v. Zoning Hearing Board, 526 Pa. 186, 584 A.2d 1372 (1991). See also Ailes v. Decatur County Area Planning Comm'n, 448 N.E.2d 1057 (Ind.1983); Hoffmann v. Kinealy, 389 S.W.2d 745 (Mo.1965); and Sun Oil Co. v. City of Upper Arlington, 55 Ohio App.2d 27, 379 N.E.2d 266 (1977).

27. Id., 584 A.2d at 1375.

§ 4.40

1. Lucas v. South Carolina Coastal Council, 505 U.S. 1003, 112 S.Ct. 2886, 120 L.Ed.2d 798 (1992). See infra § 10.6.

2. See, e.g., People v. Miller, 304 N.Y. 105, 106 N.E.2d 34 (1952) (ordinance pre-

cluding keeping of pigeons in residential area valid as applied to preexisting uses).

3. 237 U.S. 171, 35 S.Ct. 511, 59 L.Ed. 900 (1915).

4. 239 U.S. 394, 36 S.Ct. 143, 60 L.Ed. 348 (1915).

5. Id. at 409, 36 S.Ct. at 145.

6. 369 U.S. 590, 82 S.Ct. 987, 8 L.Ed.2d 130 (1962).

7. Lucas v. South Carolina Coastal Council, 505 U.S. 1003, 1026, 112 S.Ct. 2886, 120 L.Ed.2d 798, n. 13 (1992).

obtain in the state courts under the common law of nuisance or other property law principles.[8]

8. Id. See also infra § 10.6.

Chapter 5

ZONING "FORMS OF ACTION": OBTAINING OR RESISTING DEVELOPMENT PERMISSION

Analysis

I.   INTRODUCTION

II.   LEGISLATIVE AND ADMINISTRATIVE ACTION

III.   REZONINGS

165

I. INTRODUCTION

§ 5.1 Zoning "Forms of Action"

After a zoning ordinance implements a comprehensive plan, the process of zoning is normally directed toward the acquisition of development permission for specific tracts. In his seminal work, *The Zoning Game,*[1] Richard Babcock observed that the name of the zoning game is change. The "players" in the game include the property owner/developer, the local government, and the neighbors. Occasionally others may be involved, such as environmental organizations, historic preservation societies, associations of builders, and other governmental units with overlapping authority.

The local government often sets the stage by initially underzoning its territory to place much of the undeveloped land in highly restrictive zones. This means the developer must initiate matters by requesting a change. The neighbors typically play a reactive role, usually resisting the

§ 5.1

1. Richard F. Babcock, The Zoning Game (1966).

change sought by the developer. They may also be proactive. Vigilant current residents who anticipate the possibility of development contrary to their interests, may employ a preemptive strike to have the zoning changed to preclude intensive uses. The government approaches the game with several concerns. It must judge a proposal's consistency with the community's comprehensive plan and determine whether the development will impose costs on the community that exactions or impact fees might mitigate. In some instances, the government may also act as a de facto mediator between other parties.

An owner or developer who wishes to use property in a way that would be improper as presently zoned may have various ways to secure permission. Options include seeking a legislative change through a textual or zoning map amendment, proceeding administratively to seek a variance or special permit, seeking a judicial declaration that the land is improperly or unconstitutionally zoned, or attempting to qualify the property as a nonconforming use. More than one approach may be appropriate and each is peculiar in its requirements and procedure. To highlight the point, Professor Hagman aptly described the options, by analogy to our common law heritage, as the "zoning forms of action."[2]

The primary choice among the forms of action is between legislative, administrative, and judicial relief. Generally, the latter is available, if at all, only after pursuing one or both of the others. As with common law forms of action, choice of form dictates the allegations to be made, decision makers involved, subject matter jurisdiction, evidence to be presented, standing requirements of the parties, kinds of relief allowed and availability of an appeal. Res judicata-like effects may differ, as will opportunities to merge or split "causes of action" or "plead in the alternative." The advocates who customarily appear (for example, lawyers or lay persons) may differ. Depending on the needs of the property owner, one zoning form of action may be preferable to another when alternatives are available.

This chapter considers these forms of action, except the nonconforming use, which is separately considered.[3]

§ 5.2   Coping With the Cost of Land Use Disputes

Whatever the form of action pursued, the costs of the zoning game may be high. Most obvious are the costs to the moving party, typically the developer, who will have acquisition costs for land, financing costs, and planning, architectural and legal fees. Most of these will increase if the permitting process is a prolonged one. There are also financial costs to the neighbors and to the government in responding to the developer's request. The adversarial nature of the process also takes an emotional toll on all concerned. If the game has a loser, as most games do, the loser

2. Donald G. Hagman and Julian Conrad Juergensmeyer, Urban Planning and Land Development Control Law 163 (2d ed.1986).

3. See supra §§ 4.31–.40.

will not be happy. Two opposing tools exist to lessen these costs. First, a developer may bring a so-called SLAPP suit against neighbors. Second, the parties may employ mediation.

A. *SLAPP Suits*

Developers may attempt to recover losses inflicted on them by neighbors' opposition to development.[1] Usually, the effort takes the form of a tort action for defamation or wrongful interference with business relations, and seeks damages suffered as a consequence of the neighbors obstreperousness. Questioning the authenticity of the developers' motives, commentators often denominate such suits "strategic lawsuits against public participation," or SLAPPs. The mere threat of such an action may deter citizen opposition, and, if filed, the suit may quickly deplete citizen resources and thus remove them as obstacles. A SLAPP suit may also be used after the fact to retaliate against those who obstructed the project.

SLAPP suits implicate the First Amendment's right to petition the government for grievances. The Supreme Court has interpreted the First Amendment as giving citizens immunity from liability for damages caused by them while exercising their right to petition. There is, however, no absolute right to defame another or bring unfounded litigation. In the antitrust field, for example, the Supreme Court provides immunity from damages to those urging government to take anticompetitive action under the *Noerr-Pennington* doctrine.[2] A "sham exception" to such immunity provides that liability can attach to petitioning activity that merely hides a direct attempt to interfere with a competitor. While one may sue in tort against the speech or writings of another, the defendant may interpose the First Amendment and thereby elevate the burden on the plaintiff. New York Times v. Sullivan, for example, requires that in libel actions brought by public officials a plaintiff must prove that the defendant published a defamatory statement with actual malice.[3]

Similar rules govern SLAPP suits in the land use context. While the label given these suits, as "lawsuits against public participation," assumes the conclusion that they are motivated to silence or punish the opposition, whether that is the case can only be resolved by litigation.

§ 5.2

1. See John C. Barker, Common–Law and Statutory Solutions to the Problem of SLAPPS, 26 Loy.L.A.L.Rev. 395 (1993); Jennifer E. Sills, Comment, SLAPPS: How Can the Legal System Eliminate Their Appeal, 25 Conn.L.Rev. 547 (1993); Laura J. Ericson–Siegel, Comment, Silencing SLAPPS: An Examination of Proposed Legislative Remedies and a "Solution" for Florida, 20 Fla.St.U.L.Rev. 487 (1992); Marnie Stetson, Note, Reforming SLAPP Reform: New York's Anti–SLAPP Statute, 70 N.Y.U.L.Rev. 1324 (1995); Thomas A. Waldman, Comment, SLAPP Suits: Weaknesses in First Amendment Law and in the Courts' Responses to Frivolous Litigation, 39 U.C.L.A.L.Rev. 979 (1992).

2. Eastern R.R. Presidents Conference v. Noerr Motor Freight, Inc., 365 U.S. 127, 144, 81 S.Ct. 523, 533, 5 L.Ed.2d 464 (1961); United Mine Workers v. Pennington, 381 U.S. 657, 85 S.Ct. 1585, 14 L.Ed.2d 626 (1965); City of Columbia v. Omni Outdoor Advertising, Inc., 499 U.S. 365, 111 S.Ct. 1344, 113 L.Ed.2d 382 (1991) (billboard company not liable under Sherman Act for seeking zoning ordinances restricting competitor).

3. 376 U.S. 254, 84 S.Ct. 710, 11 L.Ed.2d 686 (1964).

The neighbors usually raise the issue as a First Amendment defense. Protect Our Mountain Environment, Inc. v. District Court[4] exemplifies the problem and the process. There, a developer obtained a rezoning of a 500–acre tract for a planned unit development. Several neighbors, organizing themselves as Protect Our Mountain Environment, Inc. (POME), sued, challenging the rezoning on a number of grounds including illegal spot zoning and inconsistency with the county plan. While the spot zoning challenge was pending, the developer sued POME and its attorney contending they had abused the legal process by challenging the rezoning. When POME and its attorney sought dismissal on First Amendment grounds, the trial court, without a hearing and based solely on the pleadings, denied the motion finding POME's motion a sham, not entitled to First Amendment protection. The Colorado Supreme Court reversed the denial of the motion to dismiss, finding that the neighbors' First Amendment rights to petition the government entitled them to greater protection that than afforded by the trial court. The court held that when a defendant raising the First Amendment defense files a motion to dismiss, the plaintiff is then required to prove that the defendant's actions fall outside the scope of protection afforded by the First Amendment.[5]

The increased frequency of SLAPP suits has led several states to pass anti-SLAPP statutes protecting the right of citizens to petition the government without fear of retribution.[6] Generally, the statutes take the form of the procedure authorized in the Colorado *POME* case and put the burden on the plaintiff to show the neighbors' action in resisting the development was in bad faith.[7]

Department of Housing and Urban Development investigations of discrimination under the federal Fair Housing Act raise SLAPP-like concerns. Increased applications to put group homes in residential areas, largely sparked by the 1988 amendment to the Fair Housing Act to

---

4. 677 P.2d 1361 (Colo.1984).

5. Id. at 1369.

6. See, e.g., Cal.Civ.Proc. Code § 425.16; Del. Code Ann. tit. 10, §§ 8136–8138; Mass.Gen.Laws Ann. ch. 231, § 59H; Minn.Stat.Ann. § 554.01–.05; Nev.Rev.Stat. § 41.640–.670; N.Y. Civ. Rights Law §§ 70–a, 76–a and N.Y.Civ.Prac.L. & R. § 3211(g), § 3212(h); R.I.Gen.Laws § 9–33–1 to 9–33–4; Wash.Rev.Code § 4.24.500–.520.

7. Gilman v. MacDonald, 74 Wash.App. 733, 875 P.2d 697, review denied 125 Wash.2d 1010, 889 P.2d 498 (1994). See also Marnie Stetson, Note, Reforming SLAPP Reform: New York's Anti–SLAPP Statute, 70 N.Y.U.L.Rev. 1324 (1995). The Rhode Island statute puts the burden on the moving party:

In any case in which a party asserts that the civil claims * * * against said party are based on said party's lawful exercise of its right of petition or of free speech* * *in connection with a matter of public concern, said party may bring a special motion to dismiss. * * * The court shall grant such special motion if the moving party by the preponderance of the evidence shall demonstrate to the satisfaction of the court (a) that the claim * * * subject to the motion is an action involving petition or free speech * * * and (b) that said moving party did not engage in a course of tortious conduct toward the party against whom such special motion is made. In making its determination, the court shall consider the pleadings and supporting and opposing affidavits stating the facts upon which the liability or defense is based.

Section 9–33–2(a), as interpreted in Hometown Properties, Inc. v. Fleming, 680 A.2d 56 (R.I.1996).

include protection for the handicapped,[8] resulted in increased efforts by neighbors to block the homes by petitioning the government to deny the necessary permits. This neighborhood opposition may be chilled or thwarted by HUD threatening fines and undertaking investigations pursuant to the Fair Housing Act that makes it unlawful to intimidate person in exercise of housing rights. [9]

Fittingly, Berkeley, California, which gave birth to the free speech movement in the 1960s, is the home of one of the most controversial investigations by HUD. When a proposal was made to convert a motel to a home for recovering substance abusers, the neighbors took action. They wrote letters to the local government officials and spoke at public meetings. While the neighbors contended that the home as planned lacked adequate staff for proper operation, the proponents accused them of opposing the home because it was to be occupied by handicapped persons. HUD investigated. It demanded the neighborhood group's membership list, correspondence, meeting minutes and tapes of meetings. It threatened the neighbors with fines of $50,000. After a seven-month investigation, HUD concluded the neighbors had not violated the act.[10]

How one views HUD's efforts may depend on whether, on balance, one sides with the goals of the Fair Housing Act or the First Amendment.[11] While most HUD investigations do not lead to litigation, the chilling effect on speech by the mere threat of investigation and fines may be significant. The dilemma is less difficult where the neighbors conduct is egregious. In United States v. Wagner,[12] for example, the court awarded compensatory and punitive damages against neighbors who violated the Fair Housing Act by filing suit in state court to block a group home. The reckless and callous conduct and discriminatory animus against the handicapped shown by several neighbors justified punitive damages.

B. *Mediation*

Mediation is increasingly used to avoid or defray the high costs of playing the zoning game.[13] The developer and neighbors may use media-

8. See supra § 4.7 and infra § 6.8.

9. 42 U.S.C. § 3617.

10. See Mary Caroline Lee, Note, The Conflict Between "Fair Housing" and Free Speech, 4 Wm. & Mary Bill Rts.J. 1223, 1232 (1996). The Berkeley incident and other investigations around the country generated enough negative publicity that HUD revised its procedures to take greater account of the First Amendment rights at stake. Id. at 1240.

11. See Daniel Barkley, Beyond the Beltway: Fair Housing and the First Amendment, 6 J.Aff. Housing & Community Develop.L. 169 (1997).

12. 930 F.Supp. 1148 (N.D.Tex.1996). See also United States v. Wagner, 940 F.Supp. 972 (N.D.Tex.1996) containing a more thorough statement of facts.

13. See Joseph P. Tomain, Land Use Mediation for Planners, 7 Mediation Q. 163 (1989) (with model ordinance); Edith M. Netter, Using Mediation to Supplement Zoning Hearings, Land Use Law & Zoning Dig. 3, 4 (Oct.1992); Lawrence S. Bacow and Michael Wheeler, Binding Parties to Agreements in Environmental Disputes, 2 Vill.Envtl.L.J. 99 (1991); Gail Bingham and Leah Haygood, Environmental Dispute Resolution: the First Ten Years, 41 Arb. J. 3 (1986); Jeffrey B. Groy and Donald L. Elliott, Land Use Arbitration and Mediation, Ch. 51A, 7 Zoning and Land Use Controls (Rohan ed.Matthew Bender 1992).

tion guided by a planner or, more often, by a trained and neutral third party. If the parties agree on a development plan to settle their differences, it must be presented to the legislative or administrative authority for action. Though not binding, a pact between these generally warring factions carries considerable influence with the decisionmakers. A property owner and the local government may also mediate disputes. Neighbors and other governmental entities may also be parties.

Mediation is useful where zoning authorities have discretion in dealing with land development requests. With the flexible zoning employed today in special use permitting, conditional zoning, and planned unit developments, that discretion often exists. If, however, an all or nothing decision faces the government and there is no room for the parties to suggest a compromise, mediation will not work. If, for example, state law requires that a use variance be based on a finding that the present zoning of the land will not yield a reasonable return and if the board cannot make that finding, no amount of negotiating will matter.

The success of mediation efforts is reportedly high, with settlement arrangements reached in 65 to 70% of the cases.[14] This likely is due to the advantage of having a trained, neutral third party intervene between the adversaries, but it may also be partly attributable to the fact that parties who agree to mediate in the first instance are predisposed to compromise.[15]

Several states expressly provide for mediation in land use disputes. California provides that the court may invite the parties to a land use dispute to consider mediation.[16] In the absence of statutory authorization, developers and neighbors are nonetheless free to mediate a dispute. Without state enabling legislation, mediation of a dispute by a local government could prompt contract zoning concerns.[17]

A settlement reached through either a formal statutory mediation or one conducted privately will not bind the government.[18] If planning or other government officials are involved, state open meetings laws might apply.[19] The California act provides, for example, that its open meetings law and normal hearing procedures do not apply if the mediation involves less than a quorum of the legislative body or a state body.[20]

Under Florida's Land Use and Environmental Dispute Resolution Act[21] a property owner who believes a development order with respect to land use to be unfair or unreasonable can compel the governmental entity issuing the order to mediate the dispute before a special master.[22]

---

14. Edith M. Netter, Using Mediation to Supplement Zoning Hearings, Land Use Law & Zoning Dig. 3, 4 (Oct.1992).

15. Id.

16. West's Ann.Cal.Gov.Code §§ 66030–66034. See also 5 Me.Rev.Stat. Ann. § 3341.

17. See Tomain, supra note 13, at 166.

18. The California act provides that the mediation process authorized does not

preclude the parties from entering mediation outside the act. West's Ann.Cal.Gov. Code § 66031 (d).

19. See Netter, supra note 15, at 6.

20. West's Ann.Cal.Gov.Code § 66032 (b).

21. Fla.Stat.Ann. § 70.51.

22. See David L. Powell, Robert M. Rhodes, and Dan R. Stengle, A Measured

If the parties do not agree, the special master must determine whether the governmental action is unfair or unreasonable, and may recommend alternative solutions to the government.

Arbitration, which differs from mediation in that it results in a binding decision, may also be used in land use matters. In contrast to mediation, where the parties may be inclined to settle, arbitration is more apt to be used between parties who have "a long-standing feud"[23] and cannot negotiate a settlement. Traditionally, its use by government has involved labor disputes, construction contracts, and eminent domain valuation, areas where the government role is akin to a private party. Its use in zoning, which implicates the government's police power, is less common.[24] Several states, though, expressly authorize arbitration in disputes over the siting of hazardous waste facilities.[25]

II. LEGISLATIVE AND ADMINISTRATIVE ACTION

§ 5.3 Delegation to Administrative Body

The Standard State Zoning Enabling Act empowers the legislative body of a locality to zone. In addition to the power to adopt an initial zoning ordinance, the legislative body has the power to amend. While local legislative bodies are not forced to zone, if they do, the Act requires appointment of a zoning commission to make recommendations.[1] The commission can be a planning commission, the legislative body, or a legislative committee. With its role limited to recommendations, the commission has little real power.

The legislative body may also act in an administrative capacity. The action may be overtly administrative, as when the legislative body retains for itself the powers it might otherwise have delegated to a board of adjustment.[2] In addition, the courts may treat some actions that are nominally legislative as quasi-judicial or administrative in character.[3] Several consequences flow from viewing an act as legislative or administrative. Most significantly, the procedures followed differ, as does the scope of judicial review. The characterization of the action also determines whether it can be the subject of a voter initiative or referendum.[4] The immunity of government officials from damage suits may also turn on the kind of action taken.[5]

The Standard State Zoning Enabling Act allows the legislative body to delegate power to an administrative body by establishing a board of adjustment. Section 7 of the Act provides that the board of adjustment

---

Step to Protect Private Property Rights, 23 Fla.St.U.L.Rev. 255, 296 (1995).

23. Groy and Elliott, supra note 13.

24. Id. at § 51A.04[1].

25. R.I.Gen.Laws § 23–19.7–10; Wis. Stat.Ann. § 144.445.

§ 5.3

1. U.S. Dep't of Commerce (rev.ed. 1926).

2. See infra § 5.25.

3. See infra § 5.9.

4. See infra § 5.5.

5. See discussion of immunity from civil rights act liability, infra § 10.26.

[m]ay, in appropriate cases and subject to appropriate conditions and safeguards, make special exceptions to the terms of the ordinance in harmony with its general purpose and intent and in accordance with general or specific rules therein contained.[6]

It further provides that

[t]he board of adjustment shall have the following powers:

    1. To hear and decide appeals where it is alleged there is error in any order, requirement, decision, or determination made by an administrative official in the enforcement of this act or of any ordinance adopted pursuant thereto.

    2. To hear and decide special exceptions to the terms of the ordinance upon which such board is required to pass under such ordinance.

    3. To authorize upon appeal in specific cases such variance from the terms of the ordinance as will not be contrary to the public interest, where, owing to special conditions, a literal enforcement of the provisions of the ordinance will result in unnecessary hardship, and so that the spirit of the ordinance shall be observed and substantial justice done.

Most states have similar provisions in their state enabling acts, though the board may carry a different name, such as a board of appeals.

There is considerable confusion regarding the terminology used in Section 7 to describe the relief that the board of adjustment may grant. A board may grant three kinds of relief: it may reverse or modify the decision of an administrative officer under subsection 1; it may grant what the Standard Act describes as a "special exception" under subsection 2, which practitioners more commonly know as a conditional or special use permit; and it may grant a variance under subsection 3. Unfortunately, the lay public, and some lawyers and courts, use the term "special exception" to refer to all three forms of relief. This confusion stems from the wording of the Standard Act.

The first sentence of Section 7 apparently uses the term special exception in a generic sense to describe all the forms of relief that the board may grant, while subsection 2 uses the term to describe a specific form of relief.[7] The special exception provided for in subsection 2 permits

6. The board is to consist of five members, but no qualifications for members are provided.

7. The term "exception" may also be used to describe one aspect of the authority of an administrative officer which may be reviewed by the board under subsection 1. The use of the word exception in this situation has a specific, accepted meaning. One provision of an ordinance may provide for setbacks in the commercial zones while another provision modifies the setback if the commercial zone is also a transition zone.

An exception in this sense is a provision which modifies (or provides exceptions to) the general provisions of the ordinance for particular circumstances. The matter falls under subsection 1, because whether the exception applies is determined by an administrative officer. Obviously, administrative officials pass on other matters, such as whether a laundromat can be permitted in a zone providing that a laundry is a permitted use. The determination by the administrative official that a laundromat is or is not a laundry may be appealed to the board of

certain uses in a zone if the applicant meets the terms of the ordinance. If so, the board will issue what it might term a special permit, special use permit, conditional use permit or a special exception, all of which are synonymous.[8] Generally, we use the term special permit in this chapter.

Subsection 3 authorizes the issuance of variances. A variance is permitted only by sufferance, that is, the board grants one when because of "special conditions," the property owner suffers "unnecessary hardship."[9]

The variance and the special permit provisions have generated a vast body of law, probably for four major reasons: first, the grant or denial of permission can frequently have substantial economic consequences and is a matter worth fighting over; second, thousands of administrative bodies make decisions; third, these bodies are frequently composed of persons with greater political, economic and practical sense than technical expertise, who frequently overstep the bounds of their quasi-judicial functions; and, fourth, recognizing the inadequacies of the boards, courts are not as willing to defer to boards' judgments as they are to more expert administrative bodies, and this lack of deference invites a judicial rehash of the issues involved.[10]

A board's exercise of these powers leads to problems over the propriety of the delegation of the power by the legislative body.[11] There are two major questions that arise with respect to delegation. One is whether the administrative body or officer acted within the scope provided by the enabling act or the ordinance. A second question is whether the enabling act or the local legislative body provided sufficient standards to guide the discretion of administrative bodies or officials. A municipal governing body may violate its zoning enabling act by delegating excessive authority to its lay bodies,[12] or by imposing no standards to guide lay decisionmaking.[13] The validity of a delegation of power may depend upon the body to whom it transfers that power.[14] While courts

adjustment. See, e.g., Crow v. Board of Adjustment of Iowa City, 227 Iowa 324, 288 N.W. 145 (1939), where building inspector's conclusion that a veterinary hospital was a hospital was reversed by the board.

8. See infra § 5.24.

9. See infra § 5.14.

10. See Green, Are "Special Use" Procedures in Trouble?, 12 Zoning Digest 73 (1960); Notes, Administrative Discretion in Zoning, 82 Harv.L.Rev. 668 (1969).

11. Some codes empower zoning administrators to decide simpler cases within the jurisdiction of a board of zoning appeals, thus raising questions as to the propriety of delegation of power to them. A city may also employ hearing examiners to receive evidence and make recommendations. See 4 K. Young, Anderson's American Law of Zoning § 30.02 (4th ed.1996); Note, Ad-

ministrative Discretion in Zoning, 82 Harv. L.Rev. 668 (1969).

12. Lutz v. Longview, 83 Wash.2d 566, 520 P.2d 1374 (1974) (designating a PUD area a rezoning cannot be delegated to planning commission).

13. People v. Perez, 214 Cal.App.2d Supp. 881, 29 Cal.Rptr. 781 (1963) (with no standards, effect was to grant power to rezone parcel by parcel at discretion of commission).

14. Appeal of Moreland, 497 P.2d 1287 (Okl.1972) (city can empower board of adjustment but not planning commission to approve cluster development plans). A board of adjustment has been held to be an independent agency with powers coming directly from the legislature, which could not be abridged by local government. Township of Dover v. Board of Adjustment of Dover, 158 N.J.Super. 401, 386 A.2d 421 (1978).

vary with respect to these matters, in many states they do not tolerate the very vague standards tolerated in federal administrative law. This may be a reflection of the reality or perception that these local bodies often have little expertise and, unless controlled judicially, are peculiarly apt to make decisions that are arbitrary, based on improper bias, dictated by conflicts of interest, or made because of bribery or other corrupt motives.[15] Most of the work of the board of adjustment deals with special permits and variances, discussed in greater detail below.[16]

§ 5.4   Delegation to Property Owners

Property owners near a proposed development often carry significant political clout in whether a board grants a requested use. Protestors packing the meeting hall may sway legislators who not only are concerned with the effect their action will have on a neighborhood but who also the effect it will have on their chances for reelection.[1] Recognizing the reality of this political power, it may seem a prudent simply to delegate the legal power to decide to the property owners in the vicinity.

The impulse to delegate decisionmaking power to the neighbors is understandable, though not necessarily commendable. It allows those most directly affected to decide the matter. This may be appropriate if the spillover effects of the use are limited to the neighbors who have the delegated power. However, the benefits of granting or denying the proposed use may spread beyond the confines of the neighborhood. Since the legislators have stepped out of the picture to avoid making what might be an unpopular decision, no one may be guarding the public interest. A delegation to neighbors also has the potential of subjecting proponents of change to their neighbors' arbitrary whims, and raises due process concerns.

Several United States Supreme Court cases deal with neighborhood consent ordinances. In a 1912 decision, Eubank v. Richmond,[2] the Court reviewed an ordinance that required the municipality to establish a setback line if two-thirds of the property owners abutting a street requested it. A property owner of a lot who wished to build a house 11 feet from the street was prevented from doing so when his neighbors, by petition, established the setback at 14 feet. The Court held the delegation to violate the due process clause since it contained no standards, allowing the neighbors to act capriciously in their own interests. Three years later, in Thomas Cusack Co. v. Chicago,[3] the Court reviewed an

---

15. For a court expressing some of these suspicions, see Topanga Ass'n for a Scenic Community v. County of Los Angeles, 11 Cal.3d 506, 113 Cal.Rptr. 836, 522 P.2d 12 (1974).

16. See infra §§ 5.14 and 5.24.

§ 5.4

1. The filing of a protest petition by neighbors also imposes a super-majority voting requirement on the decisionmakers.

2. 226 U.S. 137, 33 S.Ct. 76, 57 L.Ed. 156 (1912).

3. 242 U.S. 526, 37 S.Ct. 190, 61 L.Ed. 472 (1917).

ordinance that prohibited signs on public streets where more than half of the buildings were used for residential purposes unless the applicant obtained the consent of a majority of the owners of property on the street. The Court upheld this ordinance. It reasoned that since the ordinance prohibited signs, the owner wishing to put up a sign only stood to gain by being able to seek consent. *Eubank* was distinguished because the restriction was imposed by the property owners. In *Cusack*, they simply waived an existing restriction.[4]

Finally, in State of Washington ex rel. Seattle Title Trust Co. v. Roberge,[5] the ordinance provided that a home for the elderly poor could be built in an area only if neighbors consented. Despite the similarity between the ordinances in *Cusack* and *Roberge*, the *Roberge* Court considered the signs in *Cusack* and the home for the elderly of *Roberge* to be distinguishable. Signs were viewed as nuisances, justifying greater control by property owners. Homes for the elderly, in contrast, had not been determined to be inimical to other uses, and the Court thus invalidated the delegation.

Many courts take these three cases to establish the rule that granting neighbors the power to impose a control violates due process, but granting them the power to waive an existing limitation does not. The cases have, however, "posed a long-standing puzzle to legal theorists,"[6] and many are critical of the rule derived from them.[7] Some courts also find it troubling. As the Supreme Court of Illinois said, the distinction "between 'creating' and 'waiving' a restriction" is too subtle and in any event, each "leave[s] the ultimate determination of * * * the public welfare in the discretion of individuals rather than the city."[8] Despite the critics, the test enjoys support in the case law, and under it, improper delegation is limited to instances where the neighbors can impose the regulation.[9] Where the ordinance prohibits uses unless the

---

4. *Eubank* was also distinguished by Gorieb v. Fox., 274 U.S. 603, 47 S.Ct. 675, 71 L.Ed. 1228 (1927). In *Gorieb*, the ordinance established a setback line for new houses based on the average distance from the street of other houses on the block. The application was automatic, did not depend on consent, and was not an improper delegation. The city merely based its decision on the rational ground that a setback should be established based on de facto setbacks in the area.

5. 278 U.S. 116, 49 S.Ct. 50, 73 L.Ed. 210 (1928).

6. Frank I. Michelman, Political Markets and Community Self–Determination: Competing Judicial Models of Local Government Legitimacy, 53 Ind.L.J. 145, 164 (1977–78).

7. For criticism see Michelman, supra note 6; Note, The Validity of Ordinances Limiting Condominium Conversions, 78 Mich.L.Rev. 124, 137–38 (1979); L. Lynn

Hogue, Eastlake and Arlington Heights: New Hurdles in Regulating Urban Land Use, 28 Case W.Res.L.Rev. 41, 48 (1977). See also David S. Schoenbrod, The Measure of an Injunction: A Principle to Replace Balancing Equities and Tailoring the Remedy, 72 Minn.L.Rev. 627, 658 (1988) (noting the checkered history of the imposition/waiver distinction in other contexts).

8. Drovers Trust & Savings Bank v. City of Chicago, 18 Ill.2d 476, 478–79, 165 N.E.2d 314, 315 (1960).

9. See Howard Twp. Bd. of Trustees v. Waldo, 168 Mich.App. 565, 425 N.W.2d 180 (1988) (approving of the imposition-waiver distinction, but finding an otherwise valid waiver ordinance to be unreasonable in requiring one hundred percent approval); State Theatre Co. v. Smith, 276 N.W.2d 259, 263 (S.D.1979); O'Brien v. City of Saint Paul, 285 Minn. 378, 173 N.W.2d 462 (1969); State v. City of Minneapolis, 255 Minn. 249, 97 N.W.2d 273 (1959). Compare

applicant obtains consent, the ordinance is more likely valid.[10]

An alternative approach is found in Hornstein v. Barry,[11] where a divided District of Columbia Court of Appeals upheld an ordinance that prohibited conversion of rental units to condominiums without the consent of a majority of the renters. The majority viewed the matter as controlled by *Cusack*, the billboard case, to which it gave a broad reading. The court found that *Cusack* was not limited to delegations involving nuisances but applied to any instance where the legislative body specifically found that the use was contrary to the public interest.[12] Then, beginning with the assumption that the city could have banned conversions completely, the court held that the provision allowing conversions to proceed only if consented to by the tenants could only benefit the owners of apartments. The court acknowledged that the tenants might act arbitrarily and in their own self-interest in voting, but that did not matter. In fact, the court assumed that the city passed the ordinance with the idea that the owner would buy out the tenants at attractive prices. This, of course, meant that conversions would occur, defeating the purpose of the law, which was to prevent the loss of rental housing. The court, though, regarded the wisdom of the scheme to be a legislative question, and thought the owner had no basis to complain about the choice confronting him.

The *Hornstein* dissent viewed *Roberge* as controlling and read that case as allowing delegation to a few only where the use was a nuisance. *Roberge*, the court noted, came after *Cusack*, and had distinguished *Cusack* solely with the explanation that it involved a nuisance.[13] Where that is the case, there is no property right. For the dissent, the key concern of *Roberge* and *Eubank*, the cases where the Court invalidated delegations, was that the neighbors controlled the use and could do so arbitrarily. Consequently, the conversion consent requirement should have been set aside.

The approaches of the *Hornstein* majority and dissent are preferable to the deceptively simplistic imposition/waiver analysis. Having the constitutionality of neighborhood consent ordinances turn on a subtle variation in wording between consent and waiver is unfortunate. In both instances a few property owners decide how their neighbor's land will be used. The *Hornstein* arguments focus on two more fundamental propositions. One view is that courts should defer to legislative decisions, and if the city could ban the proposed use outright, no due process injury occurs if neighbors have the power to waive. The other is that judicial intervention is appropriate where the delegation allows arbitrary action, unless the sought-after use is a nuisance.

Curtis v. Board of Supervisors, 7 Cal.3d 942, 104 Cal.Rptr. 297, 501 P.2d 537 (1972).

10. See generally F. Rebecca Sapp, Delegation of Land Use Decisions to Neighboring Groups, 57 U.M.K.C. L.Rev. 101 (1988).

11. 560 A.2d 530 (D.C.1989) (en banc 5 to 4 decision).

12. Id. at 536.

13. Id. at 540.

§ 5.5   Reservation to the People: Initiative and Referendum

In some states the electorate can use initiative and referendum powers to carry out or veto zoning changes.[1] The predominant use of what has become known as ballot box zoning[2] is to prevent growth that the legislative body would otherwise allow. In the typical initiative scenario, a developer announces an intent to develop land presently zoned for an intensive use. Local citizens, realizing their vulnerability to this unwanted development, place an initiative on the ballot to downzone the land before the developer acquires a vested right.[3] The referendum, in contrast, is reactive. Citizens who disagree with an approved upzoning must petition to place the issue on the ballot, hoping to rescind the rezoning at the polls. Usually, the referendum process is permissive, but some communities hold a mandatory referendum on all rezonings.

The use of these powers is controversial, and their validity differs around the country based on state constitutional and statutory provisions. While some applaud ballot box zoning as the essence of direct democracy, others worry that its use may serve to mask illegitimate exclusionary zoning, may render planning efforts superfluous, and may undermine the due process rights of property owners who are subjected to the fancy of the voters.[4]

A majority of states disallow zoning by initiative,[5] but a fairly even split exists with respect to zoning by referendum.[6] Most of those disal-

§ 5.5

1. An initiative is the enactment of legislation by direct vote while a referendum is the rejection or ratification of legislation that has already been enacted.

2. David L. Callies, Nancy C.Neuffer, and Carlito P. Caliboso, Ballot Box Zoning in Hawaii: Initiative, Referendum and the Law, 39 J.Urb.Contemp.L. 53 (1991).

3. See discussion regarding vested rights infra §§ 5.27–5.29.

4. The pros and cons are presented in Robert H. Freilich and Derek B.Guemmer, Removing Artificial Barriers to Public Participation in Land Use Policy: Effective Zoning and Planning by Initiative and Referenda, 21 Urb. Lawyer 511 (1989) (generally taking the favorable view) and David L. Callies, Nancy C.Neuffer, and Carlito P. Caliboso, Ballot Box Zoning in Hawaii: Initiative, Referendum and the Law 39 J.Urb.Contemp.L. 53 (1991) (an unfavorable view). See also David G. Andersen, Comment, Urban Blight Meets Municipal Manifest Destiny: Zoning at the Ballot Box, the Regional Welfare, and Transferable Development Rights, 85 Nw.U.L.Rev. 519 (1991); Cynthia L. Fountaine, Comment, Lousy Lawmaking: Questioning the Desirability and Constitutionality of Legislating By Initiative, 61 S.Cal.L.Rev. 733 (1988).

5. Zoning by initiative disallowed in Transamerica Title Ins. Co. v. City of Tucson, 157 Ariz. 346, 757 P.2d 1055 (1988); Kaiser Hawaii Kai Development Co. v. City of Honolulu, 70 Haw. 480, 777 P.2d 244 (1989); Gumprecht v. City of Coeur D'Alene, 104 Idaho 615, 661 P.2d 1214 (1983); Korash v. City of Livonia, 388 Mich. 737, 202 N.W.2d 803 (1972); State v. Donohue, 368 S.W.2d 432 (Mo.1963) and State ex rel. Childress v. Anderson, 865 S.W.2d 384 (Mo. App.1993); Forman v. Eagle Thrifty Drugs and Markets, Inc., 89 Nev. 533, 516 P.2d 1234 (1973); Smith v. Township of Livingston, 106 N.J.Super. 444, 256 A.2d 85 (1969); San Pedro North, Ltd. v. City of San Antonio, 562 S.W.2d 260 (Tex.Civ.App. 1978); Dewey v. Doxey–Layton Realty Co., 3 Utah 2d 1, 277 P.2d 805 (1954); Lince v. City of Bremerton, 25 Wash.App. 309, 607 P.2d 329 (1980).

Zoning by initiative allowed in Arnel Development Co. v. City of Costa Mesa, 28 Cal.3d 511, 169 Cal.Rptr. 904, 620 P.2d 565 (1980); Florida Land Co. v. City of Winter Springs, 427 So.2d 170 (Fla.1983); League of Women Voters v. Washington County, 56 Or.App. 217, 641 P.2d 608 (Or.App.1982).

lowing voter action find the absence of notice and hearing required by zoning enabling legislation to be fatal.[7] Some courts that allow such action reason that the affected landowner obtains the equivalent of a public hearing through the debate that ensues with the campaign.[8] It is, however, doubtful that there is anything resembling a campaign for the typical initiative or referendum of a specific parcel.[9] If the zoning problem does not involve a community wide issue, it is likely that there will be little debate and that the only ones who will vote will be those living near the parcel in issue.

The concern over notice and hearing explains why courts treat initiatives less favorably than referenda. Arizona, for example, prohibits zoning by initiative because of the absence of notice and a hearing,[10] but allows zoning by referendum on the theory that the zoning process that precedes the referendum provides notice and a hearing.[11] If a state constitutional provision reserves the initiative and the referendum to the people, it will trump a statutory mandate regarding notice and hearing.[12]

Objectors contest whether zoning by the electorate can comply with statutes that call for zoning to be in accord with a comprehensive plan. The New Jersey court thought the use of the initiative and referendum would lead to a piecemeal, non-comprehensive approach to land use control.[13] Besides the question of whether voters possess sufficient exper-

---

6. Zoning by referendum disallowed in Gumprecht v. City of Coeur D'Alene, 104 Idaho 615, 661 P.2d 1214 (1983); West v. City of Portage, 392 Mich. 458, 221 N.W.2d 303 (1974) questioned in Albright v. City of Portage, 188 Mich.App. 342, 470 N.W.2d 657 (1991); Kelley v. John, 162 Neb. 319, 75 N.W.2d 713 (1956) overruled on other grounds, Copple v. City of Lincoln, 210 Neb. 504, 315 N.W.2d 628 (1982); Forman v. Eagle Thrifty Drugs & Markets, Inc., 89 Nev. 533, 516 P.2d 1234 (1973); Township of Sparta v. Spillane, 125 N.J.Super. 519, 312 A.2d 154 (1973); Westgate Families v. County Clerk of Los Alamos, 100 N.M. 146, 667 P.2d 453 (1983); L.A. Ray Realty v. Town Council of Cumberland, 603 A.2d 311 (R.I.1992); San Pedro North Ltd. v. City of San Antonio, 562 S.W.2d 260 (Tex.Civ.App. 1978).

Zoning by referendum allowed in Queen Creek Land & Cattle Corp. v. Yavapai County Bd. of Supervisors, 108 Ariz. 449, 501 P.2d 391 (1972); Yost v. Thomas, 36 Cal.3d 561, 570, 205 Cal.Rptr. 801, 685 P.2d 1152 (1984); City of Fort Collins v. Dooney, 178 Colo. 25, 496 P.2d 316 (1972); City of Winter Springs v. Florida Land Co., 413 So.2d 84 (Fla.App.1982), affd. 427 So.2d 170 (Fla.1983); County of Kauai v. Pacific Standard Life Ins. Co., 65 Haw. 318, 653 P.2d 766 (1982) (dicta), case questioned in Kaiser Hawaii Kai Development Co. v. City of

Honolulu, 70 Haw. 480, 777 P.2d 244 (1989); Greens at Fort Missoula v. City of Missoula, 271 Mont. 398, 897 P.2d 1078 (Mont.1995); R.G. Moore Building Corp. v. Committee for the Repeal of Ord. R(C)–88–13, 239 Va. 484, 391 S.E.2d 587 (1990).

7. See, e.g., Transamerica Title Ins. Co. v. City of Tucson, 157 Ariz. 346, 757 P.2d 1055 (1988).

8. See, e.g., Margolis v. District Ct. In and For Arapahoe County, 638 P.2d 297 (Colo.1981).

9. Callies et al., supra note 2, at n. 35.

10. Transamerica Title Ins. Co. v. City of Tucson, 157 Ariz. 346, 757 P.2d 1055 (1988).

11. Queen Creek Land & Cattle Corp. v. Yavapai County Bd. of Supervisors, 108 Ariz. 449, 501 P.2d 391 (1972).

12. Forman v. Eagle Thrifty Drugs & Markets, Inc., 89 Nev. 533, 516 P.2d 1234 (1973).

13. Township of Sparta v. Spillane, 125 N.J.Super. 519, 312 A.2d 154 (1973). See also Smith v. Township of Livingston, 106 N.J.Super. 444, 256 A.2d 85, 92 (1969); Bird v. Sorenson, 16 Utah 2d 1, 394 P.2d 808 (1964); San Pedro North Ltd. v. City of San Antonio, 562 S.W.2d 260 (1978).

tise to apply planning principles and to consider the ramifications of their decisions, the planning process may also require certain functions that voters cannot perform. In Snohomish County v. Anderson,[14] for example, a state statute directed "the legislative authority" to hold meetings and create procedures for implementing a growth management program. The court, noting that these responsibilities could not be performed by a yes or no vote on a ballot, held that the term "legislative authority" did not include the electorate.[15]

The effect that electoral zoning has on the planning process is not necessarily negative. If the legislative body itself does not live up to the charge that it zone in accord with a comprehensive plan,[16] it may make little difference if the voters also fail in that respect. The voters in fact may be free from the influence of special interest groups, known sometimes to wield significant behind-the-scenes power in city hall. The planning process also can be judicially protected by requiring that the results of a voter enacted or rescinded ordinance meet state planning law.[17] The efficacy of judicial protection of the planning process is undermined, though, if the courts apply a deferential level of review. If they use higher scrutiny, a greater likelihood exists that the voters will be unable to upset the planning process.[18]

A few property owners near the land rezoned or proposed for rezoning might determine the result of an initiative or referendum that does not generate community-wide interest. If they will be the only ones directly affected, they may be the only ones who vote. This makes the action appear like a delegation to neighbors that courts sometimes condemn as a violation of due process.[19]

The Supreme Court dealt with the issue in City of Eastlake v. Forest City Enterprises,[20] where the city charter required that any land use change be approved by 55 percent of the voters in a specially held referendum. A developer sought to put a high rise housing project in an area zoned for light industrial use. The city council approved the rezoning, but a supermajority of voters did not agree. The developer challenged the referendum requirement, basing its claim on those cases holding that standardless delegations of legislative power to property

---

14. 123 Wash.2d 151, 868 P.2d 116 (1994).

15. Id., 868 P.2d at 118. The provision may also be difficult to phrase intelligibly for a ballot. In the *Snohomish* case, the ballot proposition provided:

> Do You approve the Snohomish County planning policies, instituting centralised [sic] control of all urban growth, rural land use and economic development, including comprehensive control over rural services, urban density, and county transportation services with delegation of vital planning functions to private corporations so as to allow no individual appeal?

868 P.2d at 117, n. 4.

16. See supra § 2.11 regarding jurisdictions where the plan is advisory only.

17. Sierra Club v. Kern Cty. Bd. of Super., 126 Cal.App.3d 698, 179 Cal.Rptr. 261 (1981); deBottari v. Norco City Council, 171 Cal.App.3d 1204, 217 Cal.Rptr. 790 (1985).

18. See infra § 5.9 and § 5.37, discussing level of review.

19. See supra § 5.4.

20. 426 U.S. 668, 96 S.Ct. 2358, 49 L.Ed.2d 132 (1976).

owners violated due process.[21] The Court held that since the Ohio constitution expressly reserved the referendum to the people, it was a reservation of power by the people, not a delegation of power to them. This rendered inapposite the line of cases relied on by the developer.

The *Eastlake* majority enthusiastically endorsed the referendum as an important means of direct political participation giving " 'citizens a voice on questions of public policy.' "[22] It is precisely this point that leads to questions as to whether the procedure should be available for parcel-specific rezonings or other acts that do not raise broad questions of community policy. Justice Powell, in his *Eastlake* dissent, noted that the rezoning involved a small parcel and suggested that "[t]he 'spot' referendum technique appears to open disquieting opportunities * * * to bypass normal protective procedures for resolving issues affecting individual rights."[23] Believing that the owner subjected to the referendum has no realistic opportunity to be heard by the electorate, Justice Powell found the process fundamentally unfair.

The initiative and referendum generally are only available to enact or overturn legislative action and not to engage in administrative or adjudicatory decision making.[24] Determining whether an action is legislative for submission to the voters has been troublesome since the differences between these actions are dim.[25] The easier questions involve actions by boards of adjustment and planning commissions, which all agree are administrative or quasi-judicial. As such, variances, subdivision map approvals, and conditional use permits issued by such boards are not subject to direct voter action.[26]

21. See cases discussed supra § 5.4.

22. City of Eastlake v. Forest City Enterprises, 426 U.S. 668, 96 S.Ct. 2358, 49 L.Ed.2d 132 (1976), quoting James v. Valtierra, 402 U.S. 137, 141, 91 S.Ct. 1331, 1333, 28 L.Ed.2d 678 (1971).

23. Id. at 680, 96 S.Ct. at 2365.

24. See W.W. Dean & Associates v. City of South San Francisco, 190 Cal. App.3d 1368, 236 Cal.Rptr. 11 (1987) (application of preestablished standards and conditions to particular land uses is not subject to referendum); Witcher v. Canon City, 716 P.2d 445 (Colo.1986).

25. The term administrative may be used interchangeably with the terms quasi-judicial or adjudicatory. See Carol M. Rose, Planning and Dealing: Piecemeal Land Controls as a Problem of Local Legitimacy, 71 Calif.L.Rev. 837, 866 (1983). The terms, though, focus on different concerns in the context of electoral zoning. Administrative action is not subject to voter action for fear that the business of government would be unduly disrupted if the execution of policy were held up to a vote. Adjudicatory action is not subject to voter action out of concern for the rights of the parties. See Craig N.

Oren, Comment, The Initiative and Referendum's Use in Zoning, 64 Calif.L.Rev. 74, 93–95 (1976). See infra § 5.37 for discussion of the characterization issue in the context of judicial review.

In light of the blurring of the functions, it has been suggested that they all be labeled non-legislative. See Rose at 866, n.122 citing and discussing various views. Citizen's Awareness Now v. Marakis, 873 P.2d 1117 (Utah 1994) (discussing difficulty); Citizens for Quality Growth v. Steamboat Springs, 807 P.2d 1197 (Colo.App.1990) (action of a "city council" can be legislative, executive, quasi-judicial, or administrative). See also David G. Andersen, Comment, Urban Blight Meets Municipal Manifest Destiny: Zoning at the Ballot Box, the Regional Welfare, and Transferable Development Rights, 85 Nw.U.L.Rev. 519, 525 (1991) suggesting the characterization process is uneven, outcome-determinative, and done without adequate exploration of the problems of using the ballot box to zone.

26. Arnel Development Co. v. City of Costa Mesa, 28 Cal.3d 511, 169 Cal.Rptr. 904, 620 P.2d 565 (1980) (variances and subdivision map approvals are adjudica-

The major problem is classifying actions by elected local legislative bodies. Local legislatures engage in a variety of acts, some of which are non-legislative, so that close review of an action is necessary to see whether the legislative label is justified.[27] With respect to rezonings, courts have differed. Some accept the nominal legislative label and others treat them as quasi-judicial.[28] In California, which generally treats rezonings as legislative, the court held a rezoning that was a revision of a zoning boundary pursuant to a previously adopted procedure was administrative action,[29] and in Colorado, a court found a conditional use permit issued by city council was legislative.[30]

The unavailability of the initiative and referendum to review or impose administrative or adjudicatory action may be based on state constitutional or statutory provisions that expressly limit the voter's role to legislation and by implication exclude administrative or adjudicatory action. Some courts cite efficiency concerns, fearing that delay and possible revocation by referendum would adversely affect the successful administration of municipal business.[31] The reasoning of these courts suggests that a state might confer administrative or adjudicatory powers on voters, but if that occurs, a due process issue arises.[32] While notice and hearing to each affected person need not accompany the adoption of a policy applicable to a broad class of persons, those rights do attach when government applies the policy to an individual or a small number of persons.[33] Generally, courts label the former actions adopting policy as

---

tive); Wilson v. Manning, 657 P.2d 251 (Utah 1982).

27. See Forest City Enterprises, Inc. v. City of Eastlake, 41 Ohio St.2d 187, 324 N.E.2d 740 (1975) (no power to referend an administrative act by whatever body it is made); State ex rel. Zonders v. Delaware County Bd. of Elections, 69 Ohio St.3d 5, 630 N.E.2d 313 (1994) (rezoning of specific tract to PUD classification was a legislative act for purposes of referendum).

28. See State ex rel. Zonders v. Delaware County Bd. of Elections, 69 Ohio St.3d 5, 630 N.E.2d 313 (1994) (rezoning is legislative); Arnel Development Co. v. City of Costa Mesa, 28 Cal.3d 511, 169 Cal.Rptr. 904, 620 P.2d 565 (1980) (rezoning by initiative is a legislative act); R.G. Moore Building Corp. v. Committee for the Repeal of Ord. R(C)–88–13, 239 Va. 484, 391 S.E.2d 587 (1990) (rezoning is legislative for purposes of referendum). But see West v. City of Portage, 392 Mich. 458, 221 N.W.2d 303 (1974) (rezoning administrative for purposes of referendum), questioned in Albright v. City of Portage, 188 Mich.App. 342, 470 N.W.2d 657 (1991); Wilson v. Manning, 657 P.2d 251 (Utah 1982).

29. Southwest Diversified, Inc. v. City of Brisbane, 229 Cal.App.3d 1548, 280 Cal. Rptr. 869 (1991) (despite an apparently cat-

egorical rule of the state supreme court treating rezonings as legislative).

30. Citizens for Quality Growth v. Steamboat Springs, 807 P.2d 1197 (Colo. App.1990).

31. Hanson v. City of Granite Falls, 529 N.W.2d 485 (Minn.App.1995); Wennerstrom v. City of Mesa, 169 Ariz. 485, 821 P.2d 146 (1991).

32. Noting that the Montana constitution reserved to the people the right of referendum to "any act of the legislature", not simply "legislative acts," led a concurring judge to conclude that to follow a rule that proscribed referenda for administrative acts was to "perpetuate a fiction that is without [state] constitutional basis." Greens at Fort Missoula v. City of Missoula, 271 Mont. 398, 897 P.2d 1078, 1082 (Mont. 1995) (Justice Nelson, concurring).

33. Bi–Metallic Investment Co. v. State Bd. of Equalization, 239 U.S. 441, 36 S.Ct. 141, 60 L.Ed. 372 (1915). See also John E. Nowak and Ronald D. Rotunda, Constitutional Law § 13.8 at 549 (5th ed.1995). Oddly, the Court in *Eastlake* cited with apparent approval a treatise that stated that the powers of initiative and referendum were available " 'for any matter, legislative or administrative.' " 426 U.S. at 674,

legislative, while they label the latter ones applying policy as adjudicatory or quasi-judicial.[34] When ballot box zoning takes action that falls in the latter categories, it will fail if the process does not provide adequate notice and hearing. State courts have differed over whether zoning by initiative or referendum meet that test.[35]

The initiative and referendum pose questions of process, not substance. As the *Eastlake* Court emphasized, voters cannot, by use of the initiative or referendum power, obtain results otherwise unobtainable by the legislative body. Voters cannot, for example, deny a person the equal protection of the laws or the substantive due process right to be free from arbitrary state action.[36] Thus, the Court in Hunter v. Erickson invalidated a racially discriminatory referendum process on equal protection grounds.[37] Still, it is hard to obtain the proof demanded in equal protection cases,[38] and the test for substantive due process is so lax[39] that it is difficult to prevail on either theory. So, the process used may subvert substantive protection.

III. REZONINGS

§ 5.6 Amendments Generally

The Standard State Zoning Enabling Act provides that "regulations, restrictions, and boundaries may from time to time be amended, supplemented, changed, modified, or repealed."[1] Either the legislative body, a governmental official, or a property owner can initiate amendments. In some states the electorate can also amend through the initiative process. Amendments may be procedural or substantive. Substantive amendments include map amendments that change the zone that applies to a parcel of land and text amendments that change the uses permitted within a zone.

n. 9., 96 S.Ct at 2363. The apparent discrepancy may lie in what is meant by administrative action. The treatise authors who are cited, in a subsequent edition changed their minds, and now say if the act is administrative it is not referable. See E. McQuillen, The Law of Municipal Corporations § 25.246 at 275 (1994 Rev.ed.).

34. See 426 U.S. 668, 681, 96 S.Ct. 2358, 2365, 49 L.Ed.2d 132 (1976) (Stevens, J. dissenting).

35. See discussion, supra this section, at text accompanying notes 5 and 6. The Supreme Court in *Eastlake* dealt only with the delegation of power issue. It did not decide the issue of notice and hearing and did not spell out which actions would be treated as legislative. See Callies, supra note 2, at 72 and Freilich supra note 4, at 513. The majority in *Eastlake* accepted the state court's characterization of the rezoning as legislative, and noted that with re-

spect to administrative relief like zoning variances the Ohio courts had held that the referendum was not available. 426 U.S. at 674, n. 9, 96 S.Ct. at 2363. The dissenters in *Eastlake* would not have allowed Ohio to avoid the impact of due process by characterizing the rezoning as legislative.

36. See City of Eastlake v. Forest City Enterprises, 426 U.S. 668, 96 S.Ct. 2358, 49 L.Ed.2d 132 (1976).

37. 393 U.S. 385, 89 S.Ct. 557, 21 L.Ed.2d 616 (1969), but see limitations in James v. Valtierra, 402 U.S. 137, 91 S.Ct. 1331, 28 L.Ed.2d 678 (1971).

38. See discussion infra § 10.14.

39. See infra § 10.12.

§ 5.6

1. U.S. Dept. of Commerce § 5 (rev.ed. 1926).

Most amendments are site-specific. They are usually sought by way of map amendments, though that avenue of relief may not be the best one. Suppose a property owner wishes to construct a laundromat on land zoned for light commercial use, but the city only permits laundromats in the heavy commercial zone. The property owner generally will apply for a rezoning to a heavy commercial zone. If the legislative body grants the request, the property owner might ultimately be foiled since the rezoning might constitute invalid spot zoning.[2] An alternate avenue for the property owner is to seek a text amendment to change the permitted uses within the zone. Thus, the legislative body may be willing to reconsider whether a laundromat is sufficiently unintensive to include in the list of permitted uses in the light commercial zone.

The notice, if any, provided to citizens will differ according to the type of amendment sought and on who it affects. If the amendment relates to specific land, the owner is generally entitled to personal notice by statute. In any event, if the action is regarded as adjudicatory, due process requires notice.[3] Most state statutes or city ordinances also require that nearby property owners be notified of proposed changes by mail.[4] Failure to abide by individual notice requirements to neighbors will likely invalidate any approval,[5] and may violate the neighbors due process rights.[6] Posting signs on the property that is the subject of the proposal may also be required. If a text amendment is to be made, there are no individuals to be given personal notice since it is legislative in nature.[7] Generally, the only notice given will be newspaper publication as required by the enabling act.[8]

§ 5.7 Neighbor Protests: Extraordinary Majority Requirements

The Standard Zoning Enabling Act provides that if a certain percentage of property owners in or near the area of a proposed change file

2. See infra § 5.10.

3. See Application of Madin, 201 N.J.Super. 105, 492 A.2d 1034 (1985), vacated on other grounds, 103 N.J. 689, 512 A.2d 490 (1986) (issuance of permit by Pinelands Commission without public hearing violates due process); American Oil Corp. v. City of Chicago, 29 Ill.App.3d 988, 331 N.E.2d 67 (1975). See discussion infra § 5.9.

4. Not all require notice, but it may be provided as a courtesy. Wells v. Village of Libertyville, 153 Ill.App.3d 361, 106 Ill.Dec. 193, 505 N.E.2d 740 (1987).

5. See, e.g., Glen Paul Court Neighborhood Ass'n v. Paster, 437 N.W.2d 52 (Minn. 1989) and Schwegmann Bros. Giant Super Markets v. Donelon, 383 So.2d 433 (La.App. 1980), writ denied 385 So.2d 274 (La.1980).

6. See DuLaney v. Oklahoma State Dept. of Health, 868 P.2d 676 (Okl.1993) (due process required) and DeKalb County

v. Pine Hill Civic Club, 254 Ga. 20, 326 S.E.2d 214 (1985), appeal dismissed 474 U.S. 892, 106 S.Ct. 214, 88 L.Ed.2d 214 (1985) (when property is adjacent to county line the failure to publish notice in the paper of the neighboring county does not violate due process or equal protection); Nat'l Boulevard Bank of Chicago v. Will, 112 Ill.App.3d 608, 68 Ill.Dec. 247, 445 N.E.2d 891 (1983) (neighbors have no due process rights to be heard). See also Bogan v. Sandoval Co. Planning and Zoning Commission, 119 N.M. 334, 890 P.2d 395, 407 (N.M.App.1994) (stressing issue is case-specific but not resolving issue).

7. Tillery v. Meadows Const. Co., 284 Ark. 241, 681 S.W.2d 330 (1984). See discussion infra § 5.9 and § 5.37.

8. Standard State Zoning Enabling Act § 4.

a protest, the change can be made only by vote of three-fourths of all the members of the legislative body.[1] The difficulty that a proponent will often encounter in obtaining a supermajority makes the protest petition a significant weapon in the neighbors' arsenal. A drawback is that the filing time for the petition may be short and may have elapsed by the time the neighbors are organized. Though litigation may ensue over the proper construction and interpretation of specific statutory provisions,[2] courts generally hold the process valid. In contrast to direct delegations of the zoning power to property owners, which courts frequently invalidate,[3] they have held protest provisions constitutional when challenged as unlawful delegations of legislative power since elected officials have the final word on whether to change the zoning.[4]

§ 5.8 Grounds for Rezoning

As with the original zoning ordinance, the legislative body must make amendments in "accordance with a comprehensive plan."[1] Under certain circumstances, rezonings should be relatively easy to obtain. If the comprehensive plan for the area designates a use that differs from the existing zoning and if the decision makers are shown that the future contemplated by the plan has arrived, they should rezone the property.[2] If the area is in an interim zone, the fact that a property owner has a definite use in mind might stimulate permanent zoning by the city, though perhaps not the kind the property owner wishes.[3] If there is a considerable amount of vacant property in the area, and property adjacent to the property to be rezoned is zoned for the use desired, changing the boundaries of the adjacent zone to incorporate the owner's property should be relatively easy. Finally, if an area has developed by way of nonconforming uses, special uses and variances, a rezoning that would make the uses permitted uses is appropriate.

§ 5.7

1. U.S. Dep't of Commerce (rev.ed. 1926). The protest petition is applicable only to amendments, not original zoning enactments. See Caspersen v. Town of Lyme, 139 N.H. 637, 661 A.2d 759, 762 (1995), interpreting New Hampshire Rev. Stat.Ann. § 675.5 I (a).

2. See City of Springfield v. Goff, 918 S.W.2d 786 (Mo.1996) (city ordinance requiring a three-fourths majority invalid in light of state law requiring a two-thirds majority); Chicago Title and Trust Co. v. County of Cook, 120 Ill.App.3d 443, 75 Ill. Dec. 767, 457 N.E.2d 1326 (1983) (timing of filing); Webster Assocs. v. Town of Webster, 119 Misc.2d 533, 462 N.Y.S.2d 796 (N.Y.Sup.Ct.1983) (land separated from the tract to be rezoned by a frontage road of an expressway and a grassy median over 200–feet wide is not "directly opposite"). See also Larry D. Scheafer, Annotation, Zoning:

Validity & Construction of Provisions of Zoning Statute or Ordinance Regarding Protest by Neighboring Property Owners, 7 A.L.R.4th 732 (1981).

3. See supra § 5.4.

4. Bredberg v. City of Wheaton, 24 Ill.2d 612, 620, 182 N.E.2d 742, 746 (1962); State Theatre Co. v. Smith, 276 N.W.2d 259, 263 (S.D.1979); Northwood Properties Co. v. Perkins, 325 Mich. 419, 39 N.W.2d 25 (1949).

§ 5.8

1. See Standard Zoning Enabling Act, § 3; Town of Somerset v. County Council, 229 Md. 42, 181 A.2d 671 (1962).

2. See supra §§ 2.11–.13.

3. MacDonald v. Board of Comm'rs for Prince George's County, 238 Md. 549, 210 A.2d 325 (1965) (dissenting opinion).

If none of the above circumstances suggesting the propriety of an amendment exist, the property owner may also argue that conditions have changed since the last zoning and that rezoning would be in the public interest. An argument that rezoning should occur because it will increase the value of the parcel may be persuasive. However, if that is the only argument, and the existing restriction is not unreasonably burdensome, the legislative body should not change the zoning. It should make a change only if it benefits the public health, safety or general welfare.

Many changes of circumstances logically support an argument for a change in zoning. For example, a major highway built through an area zoned for agricultural purposes may justify rezoning to permit more intensive uses. Also, as population increases, some property should be rezoned to permit more intensive uses, but such changes should be based on some rational policy or plan.

Zoning concepts or community needs may change, justifying rezonings even where there has been no physical change in an area. Though the city may have regarded strip commercial zoning as desirable at one time, rezoning areas for shopping centers may better serve the public interest in part because it will help avoid problems associated with on-street parking.[4] Zoning for mixed commercial and residential use may be authorized to relieve transportation burdens associated with long commuter trips. Or, a community originally zoned exclusively for single-family homes may decide, or may be convinced by a developer, that the housing needs of those desirous of living in the town require areas zoned for multi-family use. If these changes are in the public interest, courts will uphold the rezonings over claims of neighbors that they have a right to perpetuation of existing zoning.[5]

Rezoning may also be proper when the existing zoning unreasonably burdens the property and is not necessary to safeguard the public interest. The court in Oka v. Cole[6] upheld a rezoning of property from single-family to multi-family residential when the property was in an area where land costs rendered single-family use economically unattractive and the change did not affect the public interest.

Rezonings are more difficult to justify in a few states that require a showing of a change of physical circumstances,[7] or a mistake in the

4. For an excellent recitation of facts supporting a need for rezoning, see Robinson v. Los Angeles, 146 Cal.App.2d 810, 304 P.2d 814 (1956). See also Roger Arnebergh, Criteria for Rezoning: Valid Reasons, 5 Institute on Planning & Zoning 45 (1964).

5. While there is no right, a court may use reliance as a factor to overturn a rezoning. See Ferris v. City of Alhambra, 189 Cal.App.2d 517, 11 Cal.Rptr. 475 (1961); O'Brien v. St. Paul, 285 Minn. 378, 173 N.W.2d 462, 467 (1969) (court refused to invalidate statute requiring neighborhood consent to a rezoning in part because "numberless homeowners have purchased and improved property relying on the protection of the statute"); Nowicki v. Planning & Zoning Bd. of Town of Milford, 148 Conn. 492, 172 A.2d 386 (1961); Kleidon v. City of Hickory Hills, 120 Ill.App.3d 1043, 76 Ill.Dec. 277, 458 N.E.2d 931 (1983).

6. 145 So.2d 233 (Fla.1962), opinion conformed 145 So.2d 900 (1962).

7. MacDonald v. Board of County Comm'rs for Prince George's County, 238 Md. 549, 210 A.2d 325 (1965). The dissent

original zoning.[8] A significant consequence of using this "change or mistake" rule is that when neighbors challenge a rezoning, the normal presumption of validity does not apply and the burden of proof shifts to the one proposing the zoning change,[9] similar to what occurs when a court treats a rezoning as quasi-judicial.[10] Eggebeen v. Sonnenburg,[11] demonstrates the operation of the rule. There, land zoned for single-family dwellings was rezoned for multi-family use at the request of the property owner. A major reason for the rezoning was that the soils in the area were unstable and the floating foundations required could be economically justified only if they permitted the more intensive use. Had the town known the nature of the soils when it originally zoned the property, it probably would not have zoned the land for single-family dwellings. The original zoning was a mistake, which essentially precluded all development. The court upheld the rezoning, finding it would not adversely affect the public interest.[12]

§ 5.9   Rezoning: Legislative or Quasi–Judicial Action?

Most states treat all zoning changes, whether general or site-specific, as legislative acts and accord them a presumption of validity.[1] Though neighbors can bring a variety of challenges against a site-specific rezoning, such as claims that it is spot zoning, or contract zoning, or not in accord with a comprehensive plan, a court will often allow a rezoning to stand unless the challengers can show that the decision was arbitrary and capricious. According to the Supreme Court "if the validity of the legislative classification for zoning purposes be fairly debatable, the legislative judgment must be allowed to control."[2] The burden is on the

indicates that the requirements of the change or mistake doctrine are judicial gloss not authorized by statute. Compare, on change of circumstances, Harris Trust & Sav. Bank v. Chicago, 107 Ill.App.2d 113, 245 N.E.2d 889 (1969), with LaSalle Nat. Bank v. Village of Skokie, 107 Ill.App.2d 104, 246 N.E.2d 105 (1969). An editorial note, 21 Zoning Digest 162 (1969) states that "[i]t is hard to believe [these cases] * * * were decided by the same court on the same day with opinions written by the same judge. The inconsistencies between the two cases are staggering."

8. City of Virginia Beach v. Virginia Land Investment Ass'n No. 1, 239 Va. 412, 389 S.E.2d 312 (1990); MacDonald v. Board of County Comm'rs for Prince George's County, 238 Md. 549, 210 A.2d 325 (1965), and Offutt v. Board of Zoning Appeals, 204 Md. 551, 105 A.2d 219 (1954). See generally, Barlow Burke, Jr., Change or Mistake Rule in Maryland, 125 Am.U.L.Rev. 631 (1976).

9. Pattey v. Board of County Comm'rs, 271 Md. 352, 317 A.2d 142 (1974); Hughes v. Mayor & Comm'rs of City of Jackson, 296

So.2d 689 (Miss.1974); Roseta v. County of Washington, 254 Or. 161, 458 P.2d 405 (1969).

10. See infra § 5.9.

11. 239 Wis. 213, 1 N.W.2d 84 (1941).

12. Cf. MacDonald v. Board of County Comm'rs for Prince George's County, 238 Md. 549, 210 A.2d 325 (1965) (Barnes, J., dissenting).

§ 5.9

1. Manalapan Realty, L.P. v. Township of Manalapan, 140 N.J. 366, 658 A.2d 1230 (1995) ("The wisdom of a zoning ordinance or an amendment thereto 'is reviewable only at the polls.' "); Wait v. Scottsdale, 127 Ariz. 107, 618 P.2d 601 (1980); Pemberton v. Montgomery County, 275 Md. 363, 340 A.2d 240 (1975). The same is true of a denial of a request to rezone. Hoffman v. City of Town and Country, 831 S.W.2d 223 (Mo.App.1992).

2. Village of Euclid v. Ambler Realty Co., 272 U.S. 365, 388, 47 S.Ct. 114, 71 L.Ed. 303 (1926).

one seeking to overturn the legislative body's action, and the test is difficult to meet.

Over the years, dissatisfaction with the virtually unrestrained power conferred on local governments by this rule of deference has led some courts to review zoning decisions more closely, particularly those involving relatively small parcels.[3] Courts use several routes to do so. Some apply the "change or mistake" rule, which eliminates the deference and reverses the burden of proof.[4] Other courts demand much more proof than historically has been called for in meeting the requirement that zoning be in accord with a comprehensive plan.[5] In some states the presumption of validity has an evanescent quality and vanishes without comment when the courts are suspicious of wrongdoing.[6] The underlying assumption of these efforts, though not always articulated, is that site-specific rezonings are not entitled to deference because they are not truly legislative in character.

A number of courts have expressly rejected the conventional wisdom that all rezonings are legislative and held that rezonings that are quasi-judicial in nature are not entitled to a presumption of validity.[7] Fasano v. Board of County Commissioners[8] is the landmark case. Some seven years after creating a floating zone[9] for mobile home parks to meet local needs for diverse types of housing, the county commissioners rezoned a 32–acre tract from single-family use to mobile home use pursuant to the floating zone. As traditional law would have it, when the neighbors challenged the rezoning, the county and the developer asserted the presumption of validity and argued that the challengers must prove that the rezoning was arbitrary. The court, however, turned the tables on the defendants, requiring them to prove that the rezoning was proper.[10] The rezoning,

---

3. See Daniel R. Mandleker and A. Daniel Tarlock, Shifting the Presumption of Constitutionality in Land–Use Law, 24 Urb. Law 1 (1992); Robert J. Hopperton, The Presumption of Validity in American Land–Use Law: A Substitute for Analysis, A Source of Significant Confusion, 23 B.C.Envtl.Aff.L.Rev. 301 (1996).

4. See supra § 5.8.

5. See supra Ch. 2.

6. See Michael B. Brough, Flexibility Without Arbitrariness in the Zoning System: Observations on North Carolina Special Exception and Zoning Amendment Cases, 53 N.C.L.Rev. 925, 945 (1975). The United States Supreme Court did as much in Nectow v. City of Cambridge, 277 U.S. 183, 48 S.Ct. 447, 72 L.Ed. 842 (1928). Illinois courts act similarly. See Hopperton, supra note 3, at 309–10.

7. Using terminology of administrative law, courts in land use cases may characterize action as administrative or quasi-judicial. Some courts regard them as the same. See Edward M. Bassett, Zoning 131 (1940) and Carol M. Rose, Planning and Dealing:

Piecemeal Land Controls as a Problem of Local Legitimacy, 71 Calif.L.Rev. 837, 859 (1983). The term quasi-judicial or adjudicative, is more appropriate for the question of judicial review discussed in this section because it deals with matters of due process. The term "administrative" is better used in the administrative-legislative distinction made in connection with the delegation issue. See David G. Andersen, Urban Blight Meets Municipal Manifest Destiny: Zoning at the Ballot Box, the Regional Welfare, and Transferable Development Rights, 85 Nw. U.L.R. 519, 525 n.48 (1991). The term administrative may also be contrasted with quasi-judicial, with the former referring to ministerial actions of a zoning administrator, and the latter referring to adjudicatory findings by a board of adjustment. See County of Lancaster v. Mecklenburg County, 334 N.C. 496, 434 S.E.2d 604 (1993).

8. 264 Or. 574, 507 P.2d 23 (1973).

9. See supra § 4.16.

10. In Neuberger v. Portland, 288 Or. 155, 603 P.2d 771 (1979), rehearing denied 288 Or. 585, 607 P.2d 722 (1980), the Ore-

said the court, reflected the application, not the creation, of policy and therefore was not entitled to the presumption of validity reserved for legislative policymaking. The court's main concern was that deferential review inadequately protected the neighbors' interests. Loss of the presumption would make change more difficult, but that was justified due to "the almost irresistible pressures that can be asserted by economic interests on local government."[11]

Similar concerns of fairness arise for the developer or property owner who seeks, but is denied, a rezoning. In Board of County Commissioners v. Snyder,[12] the county denied property owners a rezoning of a one-half acre parcel from single-family use to a classification permitting fifteen units per acre. The commissioners gave no reason when voting against the request. When challenged, the county argued that the deferential "fairly debatable" standard insulated its decision from close review. The Florida supreme court disagreed, and found the denial of the rezoning to be quasi-judicial and subject to strict scrutiny.[13] Thus, the court required the county to prove that its refusal to rezone was not arbitrary.

The *Fasano* doctrine is based on the perceived inapplicability of the separation of powers doctrine to site-specific rezoning requests.[14] The Federalist Papers are its philosophical basis. In Federalist No. 10, James Madison expressed misgivings about the legislative process being captured by factions who act unfairly and without regard to others.[15] For Madison, the large and varied constituency of the national government countered this fear of abuse, for it would provoke coalitions and alliances, and limit small factions from exercising dominant roles. Respect for this process calls for judicial restraint.

Local legislation is different. While federal and state legislatures have large constituencies, local governments often do not.[16] While some commentators argue that courts should treat no acts of local governments as legislative,[17] *Fasano*, in a more limited vein, takes the position

---

gon Supreme Court revised *Fasano*, abandoning the requirement that a challenger show that other properties were not as suitable as his own for the proposed development. Consistency with the comprehensive plan is still required. Id. at 170, 603 P.2d at 779. The other requirements of the test are to show conformity to standards for planning and land-use regulation of the enabling legislation and the showing of public need for the change in question. *Fasano*, 264 Or. at 581–585, 507 P.2d at 27–29.

11. Id. at 588, 507 P.2d at 30.

12. 627 So.2d 469 (Fla.1993). See Thomas G. Pelham, Quasi–Judicial Rezonings: A Commentary on the Snyder Decision and the Consistency Requirement, 9 J. Land Use & Envtl.L. 16 (1994). See also Cooper v. Board of County Commissioners, 101 Idaho 407, 614 P.2d 947 (1980).

13. In Florida, amendments to a comprehensive plan are legislative decisions, subject to the fairly debatable standard of review. Martin County v. Yusem, 690 So.2d 1288 (Fla.1997).

14. 264 Or. 574, 580, 507 P.2d 23, 26 (1973). See Menges v. Board of County Commissioners of Jackson County, 44 Or. App. 603, 606 P.2d 681 (Or.App.1980).

15. The Federalist No.10, at 77 (James Madison) (Clinton Rossiter ed.1961). For a thorough discussion, see Carol M. Rose, Planning and Dealing: Piecemeal Land Controls as a Problem of Local Legitimacy, 71 Calif.L.Rev. 837, 853–857 (1983).

16. Rose, supra note 7, at 855.

17. Rose, supra note 7, at 856, n.70.

that courts should not presume nominally legislative site-specific rezonings valid.

Under the *Fasano* doctrine the character of the action governs the type of review. A zoning ordinance that lays down a general policy reflects widespread community interest or impact. It is legislative in character, and judicial deference is appropriate. In contrast, a rezoning that carries out a previously adopted policy is quasi-judicial. Often, a determination of the use of a specific and relatively small parcel will affect only the parcel owner and the immediate neighbors. When that is the case, limited community interest will mean little or no public debate.[18] This limited interest, in turn, elevates concern over whether the rights of the individuals affected are adequately safeguarded, and deference is inappropriate. The facts in *Fasano* exemplify the rule. The county passed the floating mobile home zone to promote a county wide housing need, and its passage afforded an opportunity for the public and their elected representatives to debate the wisdom of encouraging such housing. On the other hand, the subsequent site-specific rezoning was an application of the policy. Close judicial scrutiny was needed to assure that the rezoning was a proper application of the policy.

Treating rezonings or denials of rezoning requests as quasi-judicial has significant procedural implications beyond shifting the burden of proof and subjecting the action to greater scrutiny. While procedural due process rights do not attach to legislative action,[19] when government adjudicates, due process does apply.[20] The requirements of due process vary[21] and their application to quasi-judicial rezonings is not well developed.[22] The *Fasano* court said there was a right to be heard and to present evidence, the right to an impartial board (one that had no ex parte communications with the parties), and the right to a record with findings of fact.[23] The Florida court in *Snyder* left the procedures to be

18. The mere fact that a site-specific rezoning affects a large number of people does not render the action legislative. See Kahana v. City of Tampa, 683 So.2d 618 (Fla.App.1996) (fact that a large number of persons from a church near a site sought to be rezoned to allow the sale of alcohol would be affected did not make the action legislative).

19. Bi–Metallic Inv. Co. v. State Bd. of Equalization, 239 U.S. 441, 36 S.Ct. 141, 60 L.Ed. 372 (1915). This is precisely the problem with rezonings. As the Idaho Supreme Court noted, "fair dealing and consistent treatment may [be] sacrificed in the procedural informality which accompanies action deemed legislative." Cooper v. Board of County Commissioners, 101 Idaho 407, 410, 614 P.2d 947, 950 (1980).

20. Nasierowski Bros. Inv. Co. v. City of Sterling Heights, 949 F.2d 890 (6th Cir. 1991).

21. See infra § 10.13.

22. Application to traditional administrative bodies like the board of adjustment is more settled, see, e.g , State ex rel. Battershell v. City of Albuquerque, 108 N.M. 658, 777 P.2d 386 (N.M.App.1989), but problems still arise. See discussion infra at § 5.37.

23. Fasano v. Board of County Comm'rs, 264 Or. 574, 507 P.2d 23 (1973). A few years later, the Oregon court backed off from the prohibition against ex parte communications. Neuberger v. City of Portland, 288 Or. 585, 607 P.2d 722 (1980). Regarding impartiality, see Mark W. Cordes, Policing Bias and Conflicts of Interest in Zoning Decisionmaking, 65 N.D.L.Rev. 161 (1989).

followed vague. It did not require findings, but only said there must be substantial evidence to support the ruling.[24]

The *Fasano* doctrine has met with mixed reaction around the country. The American Law Institute's Model Land Development Code adopted it,[25] and numerous states have followed Oregon's lead.[26] Some courts, however, have specifically rejected *Fasano*,[27] generally because the process of classifying acts as legislative or quasi-judicial is too difficult and would consume too much of the courts' time.[28]

§ 5.10   Spot Zoning

Spot zoning is likely the most frequent charge levied against rezonings. To the popular mind, spot zoning means permission to use an "island" of land for a more intensive use than permitted on adjacent properties. In the legal context this definition needs qualification. First, for most courts the term spot zoning is neutral with respect to validity or invalidity and simply describes a certain set of facts.[1] In such jurisdictions, a zone may look like a spot on the zoning map, but it may not be an illegal spot zone.[2] On occasion, however, the spot zoning term is used in a disapproving sense to state a legal conclusion that an act of rezoning is invalid. Second, while spot zoning challenges usually involve an island of more intensive use than surrounding property, some involve instances

---

24. 627 So.2d at 474. See Thomas G. Pelham, Quasi–Judicial Rezonings: A Commentary on the Snyder Decision and the Consistency Requirement, 9 J. Land Use & Envtl.L. 16 (1994).

25. A.L.I. Model Land Development Code, § 2–312(2) and notes (1975).

26. Margolis v. District Ct., 638 P.2d 297 (Colo.1981) (applying *Fasano* only to rezonings but treating rezonings as legislative for purposes of referenda); Tate v. Miles, 503 A.2d 187 (Del.1986); Cooper v. Board of County Comm'rs, 101 Idaho 407, 614 P.2d 947 (1980); Golden v. City of Overland Park, 224 Kan. 591, 584 P.2d 130 (1978); Woodland Hills Conservation Ass'n v. Jackson, 443 So.2d 1173 (Miss.1983); Lowe v. Missoula, 165 Mont. 38, 525 P.2d 551 (1974); Dugger v. City of Santa Fe, 114 N.M. 47, 834 P.2d 424, (N.M.App.), writ quashed, 113 N.M. 744, 832 P.2d 1223 (1992); Forman v. Eagle Thrifty Drugs & Markets, Inc., 89 Nev. 533, 516 P.2d 1234 (1973); Winslow v. Town of Holderness Planning Board, 125 N.H. 262, 480 A.2d 114 (1984); Parkridge v. Seattle, 89 Wash.2d 454, 573 P.2d 359 (1978). See also Kropf v. Sterling Heights, 391 Mich. 139, 215 N.W.2d 179 (1974) (Levin, J., concurring).

27. Wait v. City of Scottsdale, 127 Ariz. 107, 618 P.2d 601 (1980); Arnel Dev. Co. v. Costa Mesa, 28 Cal.3d 511, 169 Cal.Rptr. 904, 620 P.2d 565 (1980); Hall Paving Co. v.

Hall County, 237 Ga. 14, 226 S.E.2d 728 (1976); State, By Rochester Ass'n of Neighborhoods v. City of Rochester, 268 N.W.2d 885 (Minn.1978); Giger v. City of Omaha, 232 Neb. 676, 442 N.W.2d 182 (1989); R. G. Moore Building Corp. v. Committee for the Repeal of Ordinance R(C)–88–13, 239 Va. 484. 391 S.E.2d 587 (1990); Quinn v. Town of Dodgeville, 120 Wis.2d 304, 354 N.W.2d 747 (App.1984), affirmed 122 Wis.2d 570, 364 N.W.2d 149 (1985); McGann v. City Council of the City of Laramie, 581 P.2d 1104 (Wyo.1978).

28. See Arnel Dev. Co. v. Costa Mesa, 28 Cal.3d 511, 169 Cal.Rptr. 904, 620 P.2d 565 (1980).

§ 5.10

1. Bucholz v. City of Omaha, 174 Neb. 862, 120 N.W.2d 270 (1963) (spot zoning is a descriptive, not legal, term).

2. Vella v. Town of Camden, 677 A.2d 1051, 1053 (Me.1996) ("Spot zoning is neutral term encompassing both legal and illegal land use controls."); Bartram v. Zoning Comm'n, 136 Conn. 89, 93, 68 A.2d 308, 310 (1949) (if rezoning of tract serves the public interest it is not spot zoning in "any sense obnoxious to the law"). See generally, Osborne M. Reynolds, Jr., "Spot Zoning"-A Spot That Could Be Removed From the Law, 48 Wash.U.J.Urb. & Contemp.L. 117 (1995).

when the city zones the island parcel for less intensive use than its neighbors. Courts sometimes call this reverse spot zoning.[3] Finally, spot zoning usually refers to a legislative act, such as a rezoning, or to a situation in which the original ordinance creates the island. Courts have not normally applied the term to development permission that comes about by administrative actions like a variance or special permit.[4]

Courts often test accusations of illegal spot zoning with reference to the command of the Standard Zoning Enabling Act that zoning be "in accord with a comprehensive plan."[5] A rezoning that looks like a spot on the zoning map raises a "red flag"[6] of suspicion that the rezoning may have been done to serve private, not public, interests. If the rezoning is shown to be in accord with the plan, that concern is dispelled. Jurisdictions differ over the meaning of the comprehensive plan requirement,[7] and they variously interpret it in spot zoning cases as well. Some courts read the requirement as referring simply to the zoning map. If the map reveals some plan for the area, and if the challenged zoning creates a different zone without any apparent variation in the parcel that justifies the difference, the court may find it invalid.[8] For some courts, zoning in accord with a comprehensive plan may mean only that zoning should be rational.[9] Thus, a court may look beyond a document denominated as a comprehensive plan to find evidence to justify the spot zone.[10]

In many cases, courts skip over specific statutory grounds and ask generally whether the rezoning promotes the public interest. They also frequently invoke the "fairly debatable" test as the standard of review.[11] The use of this constitutional standard is not surprising since the constitutional basis for scrutinizing spot zoning appears to be the equal protection and due process clause guarantees against unreasonably discriminatory or arbitrary action.[12] Yet, review is not likely to be deferential in a jurisdiction that imposes a stringent planning consistency requirement. In such states, a rezoning is tested for its fidelity to a

---

3. City Commission of Miami v. Woodlawn Park Cemetery Co., 553 So.2d 1227 (Fla.App.1989) (denial of request to rezone property from residential to commercial was unlawful as discriminatory reverse spot zoning where parcel was denied the same commercial zoning as that of its surrounding commercial neighbors); Penn Central Transportation Co. v. City of New York, 438 U.S. 104, 132, 98 S.Ct. 2646, 2663, 57 L.Ed.2d 631 (1978) (historic landmark laws upheld against claim that they were discriminatory or "reverse spot" zoning).

4. See Glidden v. Town of Nottingham, 109 N.H. 134, 244 A.2d 430 (1968). But see Enterprise Citizens Action Committee v. Clark County, 112 Nev. 649, 918 P.2d 305, 312 (Nev.1996) (grant of variance found to be spot zoning).

5. U.S. Dept. of Commerce § 3 (rev.ed. 1926).

6. Reynolds, supra note 2, at 120.

7. See supra § 2.11. See also Charles Haar, In Accordance With a Comprehensive Plan, 68 Harv.L.Rev. 1154 (1955); Daniel L.Mandelker, Role of Comprehensive Plan in Land Use Regulation, 74 Mich.L.Rev. 899 (1976); Jan C. Krasnowiecki, Abolish Zoning, 31 Syracuse L.Rev. 719 (1981).

8. See Pumo v. Norristown Borough, 404 Pa. 475, 172 A.2d 828 (1961).

9. Kozesnik v. Township of Montgomery, 24 N.J. 154, 131 A.2d 1 (1957).

10. Watson v. Town of Bernalillo, 111 N.M. 374, 805 P.2d 641 (1991).

11. Kane v. City Council of City of Cedar Rapids, 537 N.W.2d 718 (Iowa 1995); McWaters v. City of Biloxi, 591 So.2d 824 (Miss.1991); Bishop Nursing Home, Inc. v. Zoning Hearing Bd. of Middletown Twp., 162 Pa.Cmwlth. 118, 638 A.2d 383 (1994).

12. See infra §§ 10.12–10.14.

statutorily mandated plan that must precede the zoning ordinance.[13] If the change is consistent with the plan, the rezoning will be valid.[14]

Courts use several factors to determine the reasonableness of a zoning change. These include the uses of surrounding and nearby property, whether conditions in the area have changed, the present use of the property, and the property's suitability for other uses.[15] The overriding question is whether the action bears a substantial relationship to the general welfare of the community.[16] If the different treatment can be justified, a court will not hold that it was improper spot zoning. For example, where a property owner obtained a rezoning from single-family to multi-family to build condominiums on land that contained a vacant and deteriorated building, the court stressed that the proposed use was not significantly different from other nearby uses and found that the entire neighborhood would benefit from the change.[17] In another case, the evidence showed that by rezoning a residentially zoned area containing gravel to permit quarrying, the municipality would receive more taxes and would put the land to its most appropriate use. The court found these factors to overcome a charge of illegal spot zoning.[18]

Courts often define spot zoning as involving a small parcel, presumably because a large area will simply look less like a spot on the map. Still, while size is a factor in spot zoning cases,[19] one ought not emphasize the element too heavily. Size is relative, and for it to be meaningful in a given case, a court must compare the size of the area rezoned with the size of the larger surrounding area with which it differs. In one case, a court found that 635 acres carved out of 7,680 acres and zoned for heavy industry was improper spot zoning.[20] In another case forty acres was large enough not to be stricken.[21] Spot zoning also may be invalid when the authorities have rezoned more than one lot.[22]

Spot zoning cases are not easily reconciled.[23] The courts of some states are more tolerant of it than those in other states, and even within a state, consistency is sometimes difficult to find. It is also at times difficult to identify a court's rationale for holding spot zoning valid or

---

13. See supra § 2.11.

14. Of course, the planning might be invalid as spot planning. See supra § 2.13.

15. Little v. Winborn, 518 N.W.2d 384 (Iowa 1994).

16. Chrobuck v. Snohomish County, 78 Wash.2d 858, 480 P.2d 489 (1971).

17. Boland v. City of Great Falls, 275 Mont. 128, 910 P.2d 890 (Mont.1996).

18. See Kozesnik v. Township of Montgomery, 24 N.J. 154, 131 A.2d 1 (1957) (rezoning held invalid, but for certain technical reasons).

19. Boland v. City of Great Falls, 275 Mont. 128, 910 P.2d 890 (Mont.1996); Cannon v. Murphy, 196 A.D.2d 498, 600 N.Y.S.2d 965 (1993).

20. Chrobuck v. Snohomish County, 78 Wash.2d 858, 480 P.2d 489 (1971). See also Hewitt v. County Comm'rs, 220 Md. 48, 151 A.2d 144 (1959) (a 19-acre tract was not large enough to avoid being found an illegal spot zone).

21. Zopfi v. City of Wilmington, 273 N.C. 430, 160 S.E.2d 325 (1968). See also Watson v. Town of Bernalillo, 111 N.M. 374, 805 P.2d 641, 645 (App.1991) (68 acres deemed large enough to be significant factor in rezoning being upheld).

22. Sullivan v. Town of Acton, 38 Mass.AppCt. 113, 645 N.E.2d 700 (1995).

23. See Watson v. Town of Bernalillo, 111 N.M. 374, 376, 805 P.2d 641, 643 (App. 1991), discussing ad hoc nature of spot zoning jurisprudence.

invalid. Two Connecticut cases decided within a one year period provide an example.

In Bartram v. Zoning Commission of City of Bridgeport,[24] the commission rezoned a lot in a single-family zone to a special business zone to permit the construction of a small shopping center for five retail stores. There were already four stores in the area, which were legal nonconforming uses. The city designed the special business zone to make the use more compatible with residential surroundings by including provisions for setbacks and off-street parking. A number of neighbors opposed the rezoning, and none supported it. During the trial a planning commission member testified that the commission had a policy of relieving traffic congestion by decentralizing business to outlying areas and there was no other shopping area within a mile. That was enough to satisfy the court. With deference to the local zoning authorities, the court found the action was "in accord with a comprehensive plan" and not illegal spot zoning. [25]

One year later, the same court reviewed a similar case, reaching the opposite conclusion. In Kuehne v. Town Council of East Hartford,[26] a town rezoned a small parcel in a residential district for business purposes to allow for a small shopping center of six to eight stores. Two existing business districts were in the area, containing three stores in one, and five in the other. Adjacent owners opposed the change, but other nearby owners signed supportive petitions. The court held the rezoning to be spot zoning concluding that it was not in accordance with any plan and that the land had been singled out for special treatment. While both decisions are vague with respect to what constitutes a plan, in *Bartram* there was a policy articulated, even if oral, and a prior business classification available that appeared to be tailored to bringing business into residential areas. In *Kuehne*, the town had only made a conclusory finding at the time of the rezoning that the general welfare justified the change, but there was no evidence of any prior thought given to the issue and no explanation of how the change benefited the public.

§ 5.11   Contract and Conditional Zoning

Zoning authorities often impose conditions on development permission to mitigate harm to neighbors of the development or to protect the public generally. When this occurs administratively in the special permit or variance process, there is no problem of authority.[1] Particular conditions may be unreasonable, but the Standard Zoning Enabling Act expressly confers the authority to condition use in this administrative process.[2] However, when the imposition of conditions occurs in the

24.   136 Conn. 89, 68 A.2d 308 (1949).

25.   Bartram v. Zoning Comm'n, 136 Conn. 89, 68 A.2d 308 (1949).

26.   136 Conn. 452, 72 A.2d 474 (1950).

§ 5.11

1.   See infra §§ 5.22 and 5.26.

2.   See § 7, Standard State Zoning Enabling Act.

rezoning process, a legislative act, the authority for, and propriety of, the action are often questioned.[3]

A. Tests of Validity

Neighbors often levy the accusation of contract zoning against a conditional rezoning because it may have involved, or appeared to have involved, a bargaining process.[4] The term "contract zoning" is usually pejorative, suggesting that municipalities are not to make deals when making law. Some state courts condemn the practice unless expressly authorized by statute.[5] In many states, however, a rezoning subject to conditions is more favorably received since it provides flexibility to deal with unanticipated problems.[6] As with spot zoning, the basis on which validity hinges lies in whether the court is satisfied that the rezoning serves the public interest. While labels carry the danger of oversimplifying, courts have generally come to call rezonings they find invalid as "contract zoning," and to call rezonings they find legitimate as "conditional zoning."

When courts first confronted conditional rezonings, they balked. The idea that a legislative action would be tailored specifically to a site was contrary to the notion of early Euclidean general use districts where every parcel was subject to the same restrictions.[7] The Standard Act authorized conditions for special permit and variance techniques, but those were limited, administrative solutions for limited problems. Rezonings, however, were legislative and courts thought that the many differences that would result if conditions were attached on an ad hoc, lot by lot, basis would destroy the system.[8] Rezonings were exercises of the regulatory power of government, and contracts, or specific understandings, with individual landowners were thought foreign to that process. Like illegal spot zoning,[9] courts viewed contract zoning as promoting

---

3. Doylestown Twp. v. Teeling, 160 Pa. Cmwlth. 397, 404, 635 A.2d 657, 660 n. 6 (1993).

4. See Judith W. Wegner, Moving Toward the Bargaining Table: Contract Zoning, Development Agreements and the Theoretical Foundations of Government Land Use Deals, 65 N.C.L.Rev. 956 (1987). See also Ronald M. Shapiro, The Case for Conditional Zoning, 41 Temp.L.Q. 267 (1968); Louis W. Doherty, Comment, Chrismon v. Guilford County and Hall v. City of Durham: Redefining Contract Zoning and Approving Conditional Use Zoning in North Carolina, 68 N.C.L.Rev. 177 (1989); Jennifer G. Brown, Note, Concomitant Agreement Zoning: An Economic Analysis, 1985 U.Ill.L.Rev.89; Diehl R. Rettig, Comment, Zoning and Concomitant Agreements, 3 Gonz.L.Rev. 197 (1968); Frank O. Brown, Jr. & Susanne L. Shilling, Conditional Zoning in Virginia, 16 U.Rich.L.Rev. 117 (1981).

5. In Pennsylvania and Maryland, it must be expressly authorized by statute.

Carlino v. Whitpain Investors, 499 Pa. 498, 453 A.2d 1385 (1982); Doylestown Twp. v. Teeling, 160 Pa.Cmwlth. 397, 404, 635 A.2d 657, 660 n. 6 (1993); and Rodriguez v. Prince George's Cty., 79 Md.App. 537, 552, 558 A.2d 742, 749 (1989) (labeling its rule jaundiced). In several states, specific statutory constraints govern conditional zoning. See Iowa Code Ann. § 358A.7; Minn. Stat. Ann. § 462.358, Subd. 2a; Va. Code Ann. § 15.1, analyzed in Wegner, supra note 4, at 992.

6. See discussion supra § 4.15 regarding flexibility in zoning. For cases approving conditional zoning, see infra this section, note 15.

7. Hartnett v. Austin, 93 So.2d 86 (Fla. 1956).

8. Baylis v. Baltimore, 219 Md. 164, 148 A.2d 429 (1959).

9. See supra § 5.10.

private interests and not in accord with the comprehensive plan. Alternatively, some courts held the uniformity requirement of the Standard Act violated where a condition resulted in different rules for different tracts within the same zone.[10]

Over time courts warmed to the idea of conditional zoning, finding that it made sense. A requirement that all land in a zone be treated exactly the same unduly constrained municipal efforts to accommodate conflicts among neighboring land uses. A city that was unable to deal with unique aspects of certain tracts by imposing conditions on use faced the dilemma of having to pick a winner and loser. The city could grant the rezoning and allow unlimited use, thus inflicting harm on the neighbors, or, it could deny the request, precluding a more intensive use to the detriment of the owner, but benefiting the neighbors. The solution to the dilemma was to upzone with conditions protective of the neighbors. If the city could impose conditions, both parties would gain some and lose some, in a sense, enabling the city to mediate the dispute. Nothing improper was being sold or given away, and as one early favorable decision said,

> Since the Town Board could have, presumably, zoned this * * * corner for business without any restrictions, we fail to see how reasonable conditions invalidate the legislation. * * * All legislation 'by contract' is invalid in the sense that a Legislature cannot bargain away or sell its powers. But we deal here with actualities, not phrases.[11]

A few courts differentiate the good from the bad by using a bilateral/unilateral contract distinction. Under this test, valid conditional zoning involves "merely a unilateral promise from the landowner to the local zoning authority as to the landowner's intended use of the land in question, while illegal contract zoning entails a bilateral contract in which the landowner and the zoning authority make reciprocal promises."[12] The test is of dubious value. Often, trying to reconstruct events to see whether there was "merely a unilateral promise from the landowner" will be difficult.[13] More importantly, the test does not answer the central question of whether the action was in the public interest since even a unilateral promise might be improperly induced.[14] Nonetheless, it

---

10. Hartnett v. Austin, 93 So.2d 86 (Fla.1956); V. F. Zahodiakin Eng'g Corp. v. Zoning Bd. of Adjustment, 8 N.J. 386, 86 A.2d 127 (1952); Bartsch v. Planning and Zoning Commission of Town of Trumbull, 6 Conn.App. 686, 506 A.2d 1093 (1986). Objections to the uniformity clause are sometimes met by the response that only reasonable, not identical or absolute, uniformity is required. State ex rel. Zupancic v. Schimenz, 46 Wis.2d 22, 32, 174 N.W.2d 533, 539 (1970); Treme v. St. Louis County, 609 S.W.2d 706, 712 (Mo.App.1980). See discussion of uniformity infra § 5.13.

11. Church v. Town of Islip, 8 N.Y.2d 254, 203 N.Y.S.2d 866, 168 N.E.2d 680 (1960). See also Sylvania Electric Products, Inc. v. City of Newton, 344 Mass. 428, 183 N.E.2d 118 (1962), another early decision upholding conditional zoning.

12. Chrismon v. Guilford County, 322 N.C. 611, 636, 370 S.E.2d 579, 594 (1988).

13. Even contract law questions the usefulness of the differentiation. The distinction was not used in the Second Restatement because of doubts as to its utility. See Restatement of Contracts, 2d, § 1.

14. Wegner, supra note 4, at 979, n. 122.

remains a verbal formula that some courts follow, or at least to which they pay lip service.

Today most courts use a public interest test, similar to that employed in spot zoning cases, to ask whether they should uphold the conditional zoning. Whether by way of the bilateral/unilateral distinction or a test focused on the public interest being served, many courts have upheld zoning with conditions.[15]

Land use law's increased comfort level with conditions or contracts is reflected in the growing number of states that allow municipalities to enter into development agreements.[16] These agreements involve express undertakings of cities to freeze zoning and of developers to provide public services. While development agreements occur in a regulatory setting, accompanied by public hearings, they also embody contractual overtones, and reveal that the law has traveled far from the early objections to contract zoning as bargaining away the police power.

B. Some Examples

A classic use of conditional zoning occurred in Church v. Town of Islip.[17] The owner of a corner lot sought a rezoning from residential to business use. The town granted the rezoning on the condition that the owner execute and record a covenant promising that her building would not occupy more than 25% of the lot, and that she would build a fence six feet high near the border with neighboring residential land, and plant shrubs along the fence, allowing them to grow to six feet in height. The neighbors complained that the zoning was invalid contract zoning, but as the court pointed out, the conditions of which they complained were for their benefit.[18] The real question was whether the upzoning to business use was justified. Noting the lot fronted on one side on a busy thoroughfare and that, due to growth, business zoning was inevitable, the court found the rezoning with the condition was in the public interest.

Similarly, in Chrismon v. Guilford County,[19] a rezoning of agriculturally zoned land to an industrial zone limited use of the property to the sale of chemicals used in agricultural operations. The county im-

---

15. Haas v. City of Mobile, 289 Ala. 16, 265 So.2d 564 (1972); Transamerica Title Insurance Co. v. City of Tucson, 23 Ariz. App. 385, 533 P.2d 693 (1975); J–Marion Co. v. County of Sacramento, 76 Cal.App.3d 517, 142 Cal.Rptr. 723 (1977); King's Mill Homeowners Ass'n v. Westminster, 192 Colo. 305, 557 P.2d 1186 (1976); City of Colorado Springs v. Smartt, 620 P.2d 1060 (Colo.1980); Martin v. Hatfield, 251 Ga. 638, 308 S.E.2d 833 (1983); Goffinet v. Christian County, 65 Ill.2d 40, 2 Ill.Dec. 275, 357 N.E.2d 442 (1976); Chrismon v. Guilford County, 322 N.C. 611, 370 S.E.2d 579 (1988); Sylvania Electric Products, Inc. v. City of Newton, 344 Mass. 428, 183 N.E.2d 118 (1962); Housing & Redevelopment Authority v. Jorgensen, 328 N.W.2d 740 (Minn.1983); Church v. Town of Islip, 8

N.Y.2d 254, 203 N.Y.S.2d 866, 168 N.E.2d 680 (1960); Collard v. Village of Flower Hill, 52 N.Y.2d 594, 421 N.E.2d 818, 439 N.Y.S.2d 326 (1981); Bucholz v. City of Omaha, 174 Neb. 862, 120 N.W.2d 270 (1963); Sweetman v. Town of Cumberland, 117 R.I. 134, 364 A.2d 1277 (1976); City of Redmond v. Kezner, 10 Wash.App. 332, 517 P.2d 625 (1973); Howard v. Elm Grove, 80 Wis.2d 33, 257 N.W.2d 850 (1977).

16. See infra § 5.31.

17. 8 N.Y.2d 254, 203 N.Y.S.2d 866, 168 N.E.2d 680 (1960).

18. Id. at 259, 203 N.Y.S.2d at 869, 168 N.E.2d at 683.

19. 322 N.C. 611, 370 S.E.2d 579 (1988).

posed the condition to avoid the harsh impact of blanket approval for industrial use, which would have allowed several more undesirable uses. When upzoning property, conditional zoning makes sense, said the court, to avoid an "unacceptably drastic change" for the neighbors.[20]

Bilateral contracts, where the municipality promises to rezone land in return for a landowner's promise unrelated to the parcel being rezoned, do take place. In Dacy v. Village of Ruidoso,[21] for example, a village needed some land for a highway but lacked the funds to condemn it. A landowner wanted a rezoning. They arranged a swap. The landowner deeded the desired land to the village and the village deeded a tract that it owned to the landowner. As part of the deal, the village promised that it would rezone the land it deeded to allow multi-family use. The court rightly held the contract to rezone was illegal.[22]

Courts sometimes label situations that involve oral assurances and stipulations made in the rezoning process as contract zoning. In Carlino v. Whitpain Investors,[23] the neighbors objected to an upzoning of land to multi-family use across the street from their home. At the hearing, it was "stipulated" that there would be a 300' buffer and no access to the apartments from the street that divided the properties. Later when the developer was building the apartments, the city insisted that it build an access road to the street. The neighbors sought to enjoin the breach of the stipulation. The court, however, held that the rezoning was not subject to the condition. "[C]ontractually conditioned rezoning,"[24] said the court, had no place in the exercise of the police power.

While the procedure employed in *Carlino* is not a recommended one, it is an overreaction to condemn all conditional zoning based on such cases. An oral representation by a developer that is not memorialized in writing as part of a rezoning may be ill-conceived and, in such event, the condition ought to be unenforceable.[25] Where, however, there is evidence that the city thought through the condition and where it is expressed in writing so that there is no uncertainty, its enforcement may well serve the public interest.[26]

---

20. Id. at 618, 370 S.E.2d at 583.

21. 114 N.M. 699, 845 P.2d 793 (N.M. 1992).

22. Practices that seek to extract concessions that only marginally relate to the proposed development may be improper uses of the regulatory power. In contrast, exactions and impact fees related to the development can be obtained in most jurisdictions without running afoul of the contract zoning prohibition. See infra § 9.8 for discussion of impact fees and exactions.

23. 499 Pa. 498, 453 A.2d 1385 (1982).

24. Id. at 504, n.2, 453 A.2d at 1388.

25. The "stipulation" in *Carlino* appears to have been oral and not well thought out. The court upheld the rezoning.

It did not spend much time on the remedy issue, but it may have been convinced that the stipulation did not induce the rezoning, and that, with or without the stipulation, the rezoning would have taken place. That may make sense, but, as the dissent complains, it seems unfair to the neighbors who were cut short in their opposition. For a similar case, see Mings v. City of Fort Smith, 288 Ark. 42, 701 S.W.2d 705 (Ark. 1986) (developer not estopped from building a parking lot based on assurances given to neighbors at the hearing that there would be no parking lot).

26. See Va.Code § 15.1–491.2:1, which permits a municipality to attach reasonable conditions to rezonings when such conditions are proffered in writing in advance of the public hearing before the governing

C. Conditions Imposed by Private Covenant

Where a city imposes conditions by way of a side agreement that takes the form of a covenant, problems of uncertainty arise. In one case the landowner recorded a restrictive covenant limiting the uses of rezoned land contemporaneously with the rezoning. Years later, after the property had changed hands, a building inspector, unaware of the covenant, issued a permit allowing the new owner to proceed with a use permitted by the relevant business classification.[27] Someone eventually recalled that the city had obtained a covenant, brought it to the inspector's attention, and the inspector revoked the permit. The court invalidated the rezoning in part because of the fact that an examination of the records in the zoning inspector's office did not reveal the zoning restrictions applicable to the tract. This uncertainty properly troubled the court.

Some courts have upheld agreements that take the form of private covenants between a city and landowner,[28] or between neighbors and landowner.[29] Still, unless compelled to resort to such a technique by state law, a city should avoid the practice. While the agreements, if recorded, do provide constructive notice to the public, the land records are not where one expects to find zoning laws. Conditions should be set out in the rezoning amendment. Not only is the chance for confusion or surprise diminished, but the open acknowledgment of conditions eliminates the suspicion that there is something to hide that is aroused by undisclosed, or difficult to find, side deals.

D. Remedies

When an improper rezoning with conditions is found, the remedy may be either to declare the rezoning void, or to allow the rezoning to stand and refuse to enforce the covenant. If a court finds that a rezoning would not have occurred but for the improper introduction of the contract or condition, it holds the rezoning void.[30] In some cases, however, courts have allowed rezonings to stand, apparently on the theory that the rezonings would, or should, have occurred without the condition.[31] Following common law contract principles, if a contract is found illegal, neither party can enforce it. Thus, neither damages nor injunctive relief will generally be available, though restitution may be.[32] On the other hand, if an agreement is found not to constitute an illegal bargaining away of the police power, a court may allow damages for breach of contract against a city.[33]

body by the applicant for the zoning change.

27. Cederberg v. City of Rockford, 8 Ill.App.3d 984, 291 N.E.2d 249 (1972). See also Bartsch v. Planning and Zoning Commission of Town of Trumbull, 6 Conn.App. 686, 506 A.2d 1093 (1986).

28. Sylvania Electric Products, Inc. v. City of Newton, 344 Mass. 428, 183 N.E.2d 118 (1962).

29. State ex rel. Zupancic v. Schimenz, 46 Wis.2d 22, 174 N.W.2d 533 (1970).

30. Cederberg v. City of Rockford, 8 Ill.App.3d 984, 291 N.E.2d 249 (1972).

31. 499 Pa. 498, 453 A.2d 1385 (1982).

32. Dacy v. Village of Ruidoso, 114 N.M. 699, 845 P.2d 793 (N.M.1992).

33. See, e.g., L.J. Stephens v. City of Vista, 994 F.2d 650 (9th Cir.1993) (contract damages allowed to developer for city's breach of settlement agreement).

§ 5.12 Piecemeal or Partial Zoning

"Piecemeal zoning" is an imprecise term used by courts in various ways. Most often "piecemeal" refers to the omission of areas from the coverage of a zoning ordinance. It also may refer to a zoning ordinance that regulates fewer than all the usual elements of height, area, and use, or fewer than all uses. Finally, courts may describe small parcel rezonings as piecemeal zoning. The term appears in the commentary to the Standard State Zoning Enabling Act, which explains that the act's mandate that zoning be in accord with a comprehensive plan "will prevent haphazard or piecemeal zoning * * * and that [n]o zoning should be done without such a comprehensive study."[1] Partial zoning is a term that might be used in place of piecemeal zoning, particularly when referring to geographical reach.[2]

The piecemeal zoning term was first applied to the question of whether the enabling act required municipalities to zone their entire territory when initially embarking on zoning. In his early zoning treatise, Edward M. Bassett points to numerous turn of the century cases invalidating block ordinances, and cautions drafters to zone all the land within their boundaries to avoid this potential pitfall.[3] Bassett, however, did not think it necessarily irrational to omit unpopulated areas from the reach of an ordinance. In fact, Bassett, a principal drafter of the nation's first comprehensive zoning ordinance in New York City, notes that while the city put all of its land in height and area zones, it omitted large portions from the use classifications.[4]

Courts generally do not require that zoning ordinances be all-inclusive in geographical reach,[5] but ordinances that zone a very small

---

§ 5.12

1. Comment to § 3 Standard State Zoning Enabling Act. See also Charles Haar, In Accordance With a Comprehensive Plan, 68 Harv.L.Rev. 1154, 1170 (1955). There are other possible uses of the piecemeal term to focus on aspects of non-comprehensiveness. It could be used temporally to apply to an interim ordinance. Many states authorize interim zoning by statute, thus clarifying this form of noncomprehensive zoning. See supra § 3.20 and infra § 9.5.

An ordinance that regulates fewer than the three usual elements, i.e., height, area, and use, might also be piecemeal . . However, separate ordinances on these matters have historically been sustained. See Welch v. Swasey, 214 U.S. 91, 29 S.Ct. 567, 53 L.Ed. 923 (1909) (upheld height limitations). Other, rather odd, uses of the term appear. An Ohio case labelled as "prohibited piecemeal zoning" an ordinance that banned massage parlors on the basis that prior occupants had engaged in prostitution at the location was invalidated. The courts only explanation preceding the declaration

that the ordinance was piecemeal was that law-abiding citizens were denied a land use solely on the basis of the conduct of others. Oglesby v. Toledo, 92 Ohio App.3d 432, 441, 635 N.E.2d 1319, 1325 (1993).

2. The term "partial zoning" appears in other contexts. See State ex. rel. Casey's General Stores, Inc. v. City Council of Salem, 699 S.W.2d 775 (Mo.App.1985) (ordinance that forbade liquor licenses in stores outside the business district declared invalid "partial zoning"; the defect was one of vagueness in that location of the business district lines was not clear).

3. Edward M. Bassett, Zoning 90, n.1 (1940).

4. Id.

5. Commissioners of Anne Arundel County v. Ward, 186 Md. 330, 46 A.2d 684 (1946); Montgomery County v. Woodward & Lothrop, 280 Md. 686, 376 A.2d 483 (1977), cert. denied 434 U.S. 1067, 98 S.Ct. 1245, 55 L.Ed.2d 769 (1978). But see Fairlawns Cemetery Ass'n v. Zoning Comm'n, 138 Conn. 434, 439, 86 A.2d 74, 77 (1952) (to be

portion of the town's area may fail on the ground that they do not carry out a comprehensive plan. Thus, one court held that zoning less than one-tenth of the town invalid where there was no showing that the ordinance was adopted pursuant to a comprehensive plan.[6] Where a court purports to require that an ordinance apply to the whole town, the rule will not apply to subsequent amendments. In Darlington v. Board of Councilmen,[7] the court held that an ordinance that merely zoned a newly annexed area was valid where the city had in place a comprehensive zoning ordinance.[8] Also, rural portions of a county may be exempted, and in some states, statutes authorize the exclusion of agricultural land.[9]

A few courts use the term piecemeal zoning essentially as a synonym to spot zoning.[10] Like spot zoning,[11] the key to invalidating a rezoning due to its piecemeal nature is its failure to conform to a comprehensive plan. Thus, an upzoning of a six-acre tract from single-family use to multi-family use, which did not meet the court's test of changed conditions and which would have adversely affected neighboring land, was found to be piecemeal and spot zoning.[12] In contrast, a height limit that applied in all historic districts in the town and not simply to complainant's property was comprehensive in nature and thus escaped the more rigorous review applied to piecemeal zonings.[13] In Louisiana, the courts have said that piecemeal or spot zoning is suspect and is subjected to higher scrutiny, but the burden of proof does not change.[14] In reviewing an upzoning of a 432–acre tract from residential to heavy industry to allow a chemical manufacturing plant, a Louisiana court found it was not invalid piecemeal zoning since it extended an adjacent industrial zone and thus was in the public interest.[15] In New Mexico, the courts have said that piecemeal zoning changes, meaning small parcel rezon-

comprehensive plan must cover a substantial geographical part of town).

6. Connell v. Granby, 12 A.D.2d 177, 209 N.Y.S.2d 379 (1961). See also Chapman v. City of Troy, 241 Ala. 637, 4 So.2d 1 (1941) (zoning small portion of city did not meet requirement of zoning in accord with a comprehensive plan).

7. 282 Ky. 778, 140 S.W.2d 392 (1940).

8. Hawkins v. Louisville & Jefferson County Planning and Zoning Commission, 266 S.W.2d 314 (Ky.App.1954). See also Asian Americans for Equality v. Koch, 72 N.Y.2d 121, 527 N.E.2d 265, 531 N.Y.S.2d 782 (1988).

9. See Donald G. Hagman and Julian Conrad Juergensmeyer, Urban Planning and Land Development Control Law § 22.7 at 729 (2d ed.1985).

10. Palermo Land Co., Inc. v. Planning Com'n of Calcasieu Parish, 561 So.2d 482 (La.1990); City of Virginia Beach v. Virginia Land Investment Ass'n No. 1, 239 Va. 412,

389 S.E.2d 312 (1990) (piecemeal downzoning); Amcon Corp. v. City of Eagan, 348 N.W.2d 66 (Minn.1984); Davis v. City of Albuquerque, 98 N.M. 319, 648 P.2d 777 (1982); City of Rusk v. Cox, 665 S.W.2d 233, 235 (Tex.App.1984); Bell v. City of Elkhorn, 122 Wis.2d 558, 364 N.W.2d 144 (Wis.1985).

11. See supra § 5.10.

12. City of Texarkana, 633 S.W.2d 596, 597 (Tex.App.1982).

13. Mandel v. City of Santa Fe, 119 N.M. 685, 894 P.2d 1041 (N.M.App.1995). See also County Council of Prince George's County v. Offen, 334 Md. 499, 639 A.2d 1070 (1994) (comprehensive rezoning of large area not subject to intrusive review to one tract that was downzoned).

14. Palermo Land Co., Inc. v. Planning Com'n of Calcasieu Parish, 561 So.2d 482 (La.1990).

15. Save Our Neighborhoods v. St. John the Baptist Parish, 592 So.2d 908 (La.App.1991).

ings, are only valid if supported by a showing of change conditions or mistake.[16]

§ 5.13 Uniformity and Classification

The Standard State Zoning Enabling Act provides that "regulations shall be uniform for each class or kind of buildings throughout each district, but the regulations in one district may differ from those in other districts."[1] The requirement is essentially a statutory equal protection command that like uses be treated the same.[2] Courts differ over whether the bar to different treatment is absolute. For many courts, more lenient or harsher treatment of one parcel of land will not violate the uniformity clause if there is a reasonable basis for the distinction.[3] Other courts read the provision literally.[4]

Most arguments urging violations of the uniformity clause have dealt with conditional rezonings, and the results are mixed.[5] The lack of uniformity typically relates to uses allowed, with fewer or more uses granted the rezoned parcel. Physical limitations, such as buffering, may also be the basis of complaint. Some courts hold that conditions that do not affect the use of land do not violate the uniformity clause.[6] A California court, taking this view, held that a reversionary clause placed in a rezoning did not violate the uniformity rule since it did not affect use.[7]

Overlay zones also may run afoul of the uniformity clause. In Jachimek v. Superior Court,[8] the Arizona Supreme Court held that a city

16. Miller v. City of Albuquerque, 89 N.M. 503, 554 P.2d 665 (1976) (downzoning of 18–acre tract overturned).

§ 5.13

1. U.S. Dep't of Commerce, § 2 (rev.ed. 1926).

2. Bell v. City Council of Charlottesville, 224 Va. 490, 496, 297 S.E.2d 810, 814 (1982) (clause is "in reality a statutory reaffirmation of the equal protection [clause]").

3. Giger v. City of Omaha, 232 Neb. 676, 691, 442 N.W.2d 182, 194 (1989).

4. Bartsch v. Town of Trumbull, 6 Conn.App. 686, 506 A.2d 1093 (1986).

5. Uniformity argument rejected: Giger v. City of Omaha, 232 Neb. 676, 442 N.W.2d 182 (1989); Oshtemo Charter Twp. v. Central Advertising, 125 Mich.App. 538, 336 N.W.2d 823 (1983); Quinton v. Edison Park Development Corp., 59 N.J. 571, 285 A.2d 5 (1971).

Uniformity clause violated: Boerschinger v. Elkay Enterprises, Inc., 32 Wis.2d 168, 145 N.W.2d 108 (1966); Veseskis v. Bristol Zoning Commission, 168 Conn. 358, 362 A.2d 538 (1975); Bartsch v. Town of Trumbull, 6 Conn.App. 686, 506 A.2d 1093

(1986); Board of County Commissioners v. H. Manny Holtz, Inc., 65 Md.App. 574, 501 A.2d 489 (1985).

See supra § 5.11 regarding conditional zoning.

6. See Board of County Commissioners v. H. Manny Holtz, Inc., 65 Md.App. 574, 586, 501 A.2d 489, 495 (1985) (physical, structural, or architectural limitations are not precluded by uniformity clause) and Montgomery County v. Woodward & Lothrop, Inc. 280 Md. 686, 376 A.2d 483 (1977). The standard act requires that regulations be uniform, not that all land be used in the same fashion. In mixed-use developments, such as PUDs, the fact that there will be various types of single-family and multi-family units has been held not to violate the uniformity clause. Orinda Homeowners Committee v. Board of Supervisors, 11 Cal. App.3d 768, 90 Cal.Rptr. 88 (1970).

7. Scrutton v. County of Sacramento, 275 Cal.App.2d 412, 79 Cal.Rptr. 872 (1969).

8. 169 Ariz. 317, 819 P.2d 487 (1991). But see A–S–P Associates v. City of Raleigh, 298 N.C. 207, 258 S.E.2d 444 (1979), where the court found an historic overlay that

could not create an overlay zone in which it required permits for certain uses in one part of the city but did not require permits for the same uses in the same underlying zone elsewhere within the city.

With flexible zoning techniques such as conditional zoning, cluster zoning, and planned unit developments, uniformity concerns are present because these processes all anticipate some site-specific review and likely involve some negotiation. The results are likely to be non-uniform, and some applicants may get better deals than others.[9] This may be due to differences in the land or due to the skill or influence of the developer doing the negotiating. Some courts note that all who seek rezonings have an equal opportunity to seek out conditions and suggest that this equality of opportunity is all that is needed to satisfy the uniformity requirement.[10]

The major determinants in whether non-uniform zoning will stand are the degree of a court's discomfort with the possibility that differential treatment is unjustified and the willingness of a court to set aside the traditional rule of deferential review. Most courts say that challenges based on lack of uniformity will fail if they deem the difference in treatment justified. Where the burden of proof is placed may spell the difference in outcome. In Giger v. City of Omaha,[11] the city rezoned property and entered into a development agreement by which it gave concessions and obtained exactions from a developer that were unique to this development. The neighbor challenging the ordinance failed to cite any evidence that the conditions were unreasonable, and thus lost his bid. In contrast, in Boerschinger v. Elkay Enterprises, Inc.,[12] the city zoned one parcel within its industrial district to allow rendering plants. While the court acknowledged that it would allow distinctions within a district, it found no such explanation in the record for according the one parcel greater use rights than the others. This lack of evidence led the court to overturn the rezoning.

Courts that narrowly construe the uniformity provision point out that the Standard Act allows for flexibility and non-uniform treatment by authorizing special permits and variances.[13] If a city lists a use as a special use, it may impose conditions on the use under the express language of the standard act.[14] Variances may also be accompanied by conditions.[15]

subjected commercial property to restrictions not suffered by other commercially zoned land did not violate the uniformity clause.

9. See 1 Norman Williams, American Land Planning Law § 31.03 (1988).

10. Chrinko v. South Brunswick Twp., 77 N.J.Super. 594, 187 A.2d 221 (1963). See also Giger v. City of Omaha, 232 Neb. 676, 691, 442 N.W.2d 182, 195 (1989) and A–S–P Associates v. City of Raleigh, 298 N.C. 207, 258 S.E.2d 444 (1979).

11. 232 Neb. 676, 686, 442 N.W.2d 182, 194 (1989).

12. 32 Wis.2d 168, 145 N.W.2d 108 (1966).

13. Board of County Comm'rs v. H. Manny Holtz, Inc., 65 Md.App. 574, 582, 501 A.2d 489, 493 (1985).

14. Bell v. City of Charlottesville, 224 Va. 490, 297 S.E.2d 810 (1982). See supra § 5.26 regarding special uses.

15. See supra § 5.22.

Classification of uses, inevitable in Euclidean zoning, presents problems similar to the uniformity cases.[16] A city may allow restaurants, for example, but prohibit fast food restaurants. A court is likely to uphold such differential treatment if it applies a deferential rule of review.[17] If the difference allows the exclusion or harsher treatment of a religious school[18] or a group home for a protected class,[19] a higher level of judicial scrutiny may apply.

Cases finding classifications valid or invalid are difficult to reconcile. For example, in Kozesnik v. Township of Montgomery,[20] a special permit for a quarry was issued on the condition that it not operate within 400 feet of any existing dwelling. The court held the classification invalid since surrounding undeveloped property also should have had the protection of the condition. In Pierro v. Baxendale,[21] the same court upheld an ordinance permitting boarding houses but excluding hotels and motels on the ground that the latter appealed to transients as distinguished from the boarding houses. The court in Kelly v. Mahoney[22] upheld an ordinance permitting turkey ranches only if the rancher employed dust control methods but permitted chicken ranches without such control. The court did not offer a justification for the classification.

IV. VARIANCES

§ 5.14 Variances: In General

A variance is an administrative authorization to use property in a manner otherwise not allowed by the zoning ordinance. This authorization alleviates the inevitable hardship situations that arise when zoning boundaries drawn across a community do not fit well due to distinctive features of a parcel or area. Under the Standard Act, the power to issue a variance lies with the Board of Adjustment, which the act authorizes to grant

> such variance from the terms of the ordinance as will not be contrary to the public interest, where, owing to special conditions, a literal enforcement of the provisions of the ordinance will result in unnecessary hardship, and so that the spirit of the ordinance shall be observed and substantial justice done.[1]

While many states follow the Standard Act's language, some add the phrase "practical difficulties" as a standard to accompany "unnecessary

---

16. Classification issues are discussed supra §§ 4.2–4.11.

17. See Ben Lomond, Inc. v. City of Idaho Falls, 92 Idaho 595, 448 P.2d 209 (1968); Morris v. Postma, 41 N.J. 354, 196 A.2d 792 (1964).

18. See supra § 4.28.

19. See supra § 4.7 and infra § 6.8.

20. 24 N.J. 154, 131 A.2d 1 (1957), Johnson v. Township of Montville, 109 N.J.Super. 511, 264 A.2d 75 (1970); cf. 801

Avenue C, Inc. v. Bayonne, 127 N.J.Super. 128, 316 A.2d 694 (1974); Tulsa Rock Co. v. Board of County Comm'rs of Rogers County, 531 P.2d 351 (Okl.App.1974).

21. 20 N.J. 17, 118 A.2d 401 (1955).

22. 185 Cal.App.2d 799, 8 Cal.Rptr. 521 (1960).

§ 5.14

1. Standard Zoning Enabling Act § 7.

hardship."[2] Other states have more detailed standards.[3]

Of the various zoning "forms of action"[4] available to obtain development permission, a choice may exist to seek a variance or other relief, such as a rezoning. A variance may be faster and cheaper than a rezoning, and it may require less paperwork and fewer hearings before fewer bodies.[5] A variance is more likely to be overturned on appeal than is a rezoning,[6] and courts may frown on efforts to obtain a variance if the facts clearly do not support the request.[7]

Stringent rules limit grants of variances.[8] Courts frequently assert that variances are to be granted "sparingly,"[9] and they commonly describe the variance as a "safety valve," so that zoning, which would otherwise be unconstitutional as applied, can be made constitutional.[10]

Standing principles also apply, though they are not particularly harsh. To pursue a variance, one must have a legally cognizable interest in the subject property. Courts have held the interests of a lessee,[11] contract purchaser,[12] option holder,[13] purchaser[14] and agent[15] sufficient to

---

2. See, e.g., N.C.Gen.Stat. § 153A–345.

3. See, e.g., Ind. Code Ann. § 36–7–4–918.4 and 918.5.

4. See infra § 5.1.

5. See Enterprise Citizens Action Committee v. Clark County Bd. of Commissioners, 112 Nev. 649, 918 P.2d 305, 312, n. 7 (Nev.1996).

6. The standard of review of administrative actions is traditionally less deferential than with legislative actions. See Kaufman v. Zoning Commission of City of Danbury, 232 Conn. 122, 653 A.2d 798 (1995); West Old Town Neighborhood Ass'n v. City of Albuquerque, 122 N.M. 495, 927 P.2d 529 (App.1996).

7. Enterprise Citizens Action Committee v. Clark County Bd. of Commissioners, 112 Nev. 649, 918 P.2d 305, 312 (Nev.1996) (efforts characterized as "improper attempts to circumvent" a rezoning, the proper avenue).

8. Rigorous criteria may not always be followed. See generally David Newbern, Zoning Flexibility: Bored of Adjustment, 30 Ark.L.Rev. 491 (1976).

9. "The power to authorize such a variance is to be sparingly exercised and only under peculiar and exceptional circumstances, for otherwise there would be little left of the zoning law to protect public rights; prospective purchasers of property would hesitate if confronted by a tribunal which could arbitrarily set aside the zoning provisions designed to establish standards of occupancy in the neighborhood." Application of Devereux Foundation, 351 Pa. 478, 485, 41 A.2d 744, 747 (1945). See also Damaskos v. Board of Appeal of Boston, 359

Mass. 55, 267 N.E.2d 897 (1971); Burbridge v. Governing Body of Mine Hill, 117 N.J. 376, 568 A.2d 527 (1990); Puritan–Greenfield Imp. Ass'n v. Leo, 7 Mich.App. 659, 671, 153 N.W.2d 162, 168 (1967); Kaeser v. Zoning Board of Appeals, 218 Conn. 438, 445, 589 A.2d 1229, 1233 (1991).

10. See Roderick M. Bryden, Zoning: Rigid, Flexible or Fluid? 44 J.Urb.L. 287 (1966); Hon. Joseph Ford, Guidelines for Judicial Review in Zoning Variance Cases, 58 Mass.I.Q. 15 (1973); Richard L. Rosenzweig, From Euclid to Eastlake: Toward a Unified Approach to Zoning Change Requests, 82 Dick.L.Rev. 59 (1977); Ronald M. Shapiro, The Zoning Variance Power: Constructive in Theory, Destructive in Practice, 29 Md.L.Rev. 3 (1969); Thomas Sattler, Comment, Variances and Parcel Rezoning, 60 Neb.L.Rev. 81 (1981).

11. Frank Hardie Advertising, Inc. v. City of Dubuque Zoning Bd. of Adj., 501 N.W.2d 521 (Iowa 1993) (billboard lessee); Ric–Cic Co. v. Bassinder, 252 N.J.Super. 334, 599 A.2d 943 (1991) (commercial tenant); Poster Advertising v. Zoning Bd. of Adjustment, 408 Pa. 248, 182 A.2d 521 (1962). But see Bowen v. Metropolitan Board of Zoning Appeals in Marion County, 161 Ind.App. 522, 526, 317 N.E.2d 193, 197 (1974) (denial of standing to lessee).

12. Sea Island Scenic Parkway Coalition v. Beaufort County Bd. of Adj., 316 S.C. 231, 449 S.E.2d 254 (App.1994), reversed on other grounds, 321 S.C. 548, 471 S.E.2d 142 (1996); Robinson v. City of Huntsville, 622 So.2d 1309 (Ala.Civ.App. 1993).

confer standing.[16]

Despite the judicial admonition for sparing use of variances, in practice applicants may easily obtain variances. If challenged, many variances granted would probably be found invalid for studies show that illegal issuance is a widespread phenomenon.[17] If close judicial supervision of variances occurred, administrative bodies might eventually limit the issuance of variances, but the educational effort involved would be considerable as there are hundreds of boards in most states and the boards are composed of changing members.

Suspicions about abuses of the variance power lead some courts to review the granting of variances closely. Some courts require that the board make findings supporting its decisions.[18] The findings enable the court to determine for itself whether the board obtained the required evidence. The potential for intrusive judicial review calls for a balanced approach. Many courts hesitate to overturn variances too freely for fear of becoming super zoning boards themselves and out of a desire to defer to local community boards. Yet, in some cases, the applicant puts forth little evidence and the board makes little effort to comply with its obligations. In such cases, judicial reversal is necessary to preserve the integrity of the system.[19]

§ 5.15   Area and Use Variances

Variances are generally of two kinds: area variances,[1] which involve modifications for height and building size or placement, and use variances, which allow a use inconsistent with uses permitted of right. The

---

13. Krmpotich v. City of Duluth, 474 N.W.2d 392 (Minn.App.1991), reversed on other grounds, 483 N.W.2d 55 (Minn.1992); Humble Oil & Refining Co. v. Town of Chapel Hill, 284 N.C. 458, 202 S.E.2d 129 (1974) (special permit).

14. N. Pugliese, Inc. v. Palmer Twp. Zoning Hearing Bd., 140 Pa.Cmwlth. 160, 592 A.2d 118 (1991) (right runs with the land, thus it makes no difference whether the application for the variance is sought by the original owner or a successor in title); Cohn v. County Bd. of Supervisors, 135 Cal.App.2d 180, 286 P.2d 836 (1955).

15. Stout v. Jenkins, 268 S.W.2d 643 (Ky.1954).

16. For standing to appeal a variance decision see infra § 5.34.

17. Jesse Dukeminier, Jr. & Clyde L. Stapleton, The Zoning Board of Adjustment: A Case Study in Misrule, 50 Ky.L.J. 273 (1962); Note, Zoning Variances, 74 Harv.L.Rev. 1396 (1961); Note, Administrative Discretion in Zoning, 82 Harv.L.Rev. 668 (1969); W. Christopher Brestel, Jr., Comment, Zoning: Variances Administration in Alameda County, 50 Calif.L.Rev. 101

(1962); Brent Ellis Dickson, Note, The Effect of Statutory Prerequisites on Decisions of Boards of Zoning Appeals, 1 Ind.Legal Forum 398 (1968); Sara Reusch Levitan, Comment, The Legislative–Adjudicative Distinction in California Land Use Regulation: A Suggested Response to Arnel Development Co. v. City of Costa Mesa, 34 Hastings L.J. 425 (1982); Michael D. Donovan, Note, Zoning Variation Administration in Vermont, 8 Vt. L.Rev. 371 (1983).

18. See, e.g. Topanga Ass'n for a Scenic Community v. County of Los Angeles, 11 Cal.3d 506, 113 Cal.Rptr. 836, 522 P.2d 12 (1974); Barnard v. Zoning Bd. of Appeals, 313 A.2d 741 (Me.1974); Fleming v. Tacoma, 81 Wn.2d 292, 502 P.2d 327 (1972) (appearance of fairness requires findings on the record).

19. See, e.g., Enterprise Citizens Action Committee v. Clark County Bd. of Commissioners, 112 Nev. 649, 918 P.2d 305, 312 (Nev.1996).

§ 5.15

1. Sometimes also referred to as bulk or dimensional variances.

typical enabling act does not expressly create these categories, but some courts have read the disjunctive phrasing in their state enabling act that allows variances for "practical difficulties *or* unnecessary hardship," as dictating different standards based on the relief sought. Under such a view, a lesser showing of "practical difficulties" suffices for an area variance based on the assumption that it involves a relatively minor deviation.[2] In contrast, a use variance requires a more stringent showing of "unnecessary hardship." Differentiation between the two makes senses in some cases, but it is hardly universally true that an area variance is minor and a use variance major. A height variance of 10 feet to allow for a taller building might be minor, but a height variance of 200 feet might not. A use variance allowing a factory in a residential zone might have a major impact, but a use variance allowing a part-time home occupation might not.[3]

It is not always easy to decide whether a variance is one of use or area. One can view a density variance, for example, as either. In an area zoned for single-family use on one acre lots, a variance to allow two homes was a use variance in one case (two-family use in single-family zone)[4] and an area variance in another (modification of lot size).[5] Since the effect on the neighbors is the same, the label ought not control, and some courts have criticized the rule.[6]

Use variances pose particular problems. Some statutes and ordinances simply do not allow them.[7] In other states, courts refuse to permit use variances on the theory that they constitute rezonings, and rezonings are a legislative function.[8] The authority of a board of adjustment to issue a use variance turns on whether the court finds that the legislature intended to confer such power and whether such a grant of power is an unconstitutional delegation of legislative authority. Some courts find the discretion granted to the board of adjustment adequately controlled to justify the issuance of a use variance.[9] Even where allowed in theory, use variances are likely to be overturned where the change allowed is significant. This may be true for particularly large parcels[10] or

2. See the leading case of Village of Bronxville v. Francis, 1 A.D.2d 236, 150 N.Y.S.2d 906 (1956), aff'd 1 N.Y.2d 839, 135 N.E.2d 724, 153 N.Y.S.2d 220 (1956). See also City and Borough of Juneau v. Thibodeau, 595 P.2d 626 (Alaska 1979) (reviewing case law around the country).

3. Board of Adj. v. Levinson, 244 S.W.2d 281 (Tex.Civ.App.1951) (variance for a one chair beauty shop in a home found an illegal use variance).

4. Matthew v. Smith, 707 S.W.2d 411 (Mo.1986).

5. Hoffman v. Harris, 17 N.Y.2d 138, 269 N.Y.S.2d 119, 216 N.E.2d 326 (1966).

6. See Bienz v. City of Dayton, 29 Or. App. 761, 566 P.2d 904, 919 (1977).

7. See Cal.Govt.Code § 65906; Kan. Stat.Ann. § 12–715.

8. Cook v. Howard, 134 Ga.App. 721, 215 S.E.2d 690 (1975); Board of Adj. v. Levinson, 244 S.W.2d 281 (Tex.Civ.App. 1951).

9. Compare Livingston v. Peterson, 59 N.D. 104, 228 N.W. 816 (1930), finding an illegal delegation with Matthew v. Smith, 707 S.W.2d 411 (Mo.1986), finding the state code contemplated that the board issue such variances and that the discretion granted was adequately controlled.

10. See Appeal of Catholic Cemeteries Ass'n, 379 Pa. 516, 109 A.2d 537 (1954).

where the use allowed by the variance is not otherwise allowed anywhere in town.[11] In such instances, a legislative rezoning is the proper route.

§ 5.16 Overall Standards and Unnecessary Hardship

The standards that one must meet before the board issues a variance vary among the enabling acts, though most formulations are similar to provisions in the Standard Act. Where there is no statute or ordinance providing more detailed standards, the courts generally have required a four-part showing: (1) that the land in question cannot yield a reasonable return as currently zoned, (2) that the plight of the landowner is due to unique or unusual circumstances and not conditions generally prevailing through the neighborhood, (3) that the variance requested will not alter the essential character of the neighborhood, and (4) that the variance not issue if it would be contrary to the public interest.[1]

Conspicuously absent from the above criteria is the Standard Act's provision that authorizes a variance where the zoning "will result in unnecessary hardship." There is confusion over whether "unnecessary hardship" is a separate standard or whether it is an overall standard established when the applicant meets the above criteria. Courts are not always clear, but support exists for both views. Some courts use the unnecessary hardship language to describe the overall showing of the elements that the applicant must make.[2] For other courts, it specifically embodies the first element noted above and requires a showing that the applicant can make no reasonable return from the property as zoned,[3] a requirement discussed in more detail below.[4]

As with any delegation of legislative authority, standards must be sufficiently clear to guide the administrative decisionmaking and prevent the exercise of uncontrolled discretion. Most courts have found the "unnecessary hardship" standard to meet this test.[5]

---

11. See Bradley v. Zoning Bd. of Appeals, 165 Conn. 389, 334 A.2d 914 (1973) (variance could not permit apartments where zoning code did not allow apartments within the town).

§ 5.16

1. The first three components are usually attributed to Otto v. Steinhilber, 282 N.Y. 71, 24 N.E.2d 851 (1939). The public interest standard is not stated as a separate test in *Otto*, but is subsumed by the other tests. The public interest component is a separate requirement in some jurisdictions. See Arndorfer v. Sauk County Bd. of Adj., 162 Wis.2d 246, 469 N.W.2d 831 (1991); Tyler v. District of Columbia Bd. of Zoning Adj., 606 A.2d 1362 (1992).

2. It was used in this fashion in Otto v. Steinhilber, 282 N.Y. 71, 75, 24 N.E.2d 851, 852 (1939).

3. Maturo v. City of Coral Gables, 619 So.2d 455, 456 (Fla.App.1993) (reviewing Florida law to conclude that a legal hardship means property that is "virtually unusable").

4. See infra § 5.19

5. See Southern Pac. Co. v. City of Los Angeles, 242 Cal.App.2d 38, 51 Cal.Rptr. 197 (1966); Your Home, Inc. v. Town of Windham, 528 A.2d 468 (Me.1987); Tireman–Joy–Chicago Improvement Association v. Chernick, 361 Mich. 211, 105 N.W.2d 57 (1960); Roosevelt Field v. Town of North Hempstead, 277 App.Div. 889, 98 N.Y.S.2d 350 (1950); Consolidated Management, Inc. v. City of Cleveland, 6 Ohio St.3d 238, 452 N.E.2d 1287 (1983); H.A. Steen, Ind., Inc. v. Cavanaugh, 430 Pa. 10, 241 A.2d 771 (1968); Glankler v. City of Memphis, 481 S.W.2d 376 (Tenn.1972).

§ 5.17   Personal or Self–Created Hardship

Administrative bodies sometimes personalize the variance by allowing its propriety to turn on the needs or actions of the owner rather than the nature of the property. Two related situations arise: the personal hardship and the self-created hardship.

Personal hardships may present sympathetic appeal, but they are inappropriate factors in variance proceedings, and where boards grant variances on such grounds, courts uniformly overturn them. Examples include the parents who wanted a variance from setbacks to build a deck in their backyard for their child to play,[1] the owner who sought a variance to enclose a porch for an asthmatic child,[2] and one who had an overcrowded garage and needed more room to store his antique cars.[3]

Self-created hardships occur in two distinct situations. First, there is the owner who builds in violation of the zoning law and then seeks a variance claiming a hardship based on the investment that will be lost if he must remove the illegal structure. The other involves the person who purchases land with knowledge about how the land is zoned, and then seeks a variance based on a hardship in having to comply with the zoning. Boards and courts should treat the two situations separately.

One who builds in violation of the zoning law is not entitled to a variance. To grant a variance in such a situation would reward wrongdoing and encourage others to violate the law. Thus, the owner who built a carport violating setbacks could not obtain a variance to keep the carport after being cited for violating the law;[4] neither could the person who converted a house in a two-family zone to eight rental units.[5] Generally, it does not matter whether the owner had actual knowledge of the law before acting, since the rule of constructive notice applies. Even if an owner makes a good faith mistake, most courts deny a variance.[6] Some support exists for a variance of a minimal nature where good faith is shown.[7] In a jurisdiction applying a lesser, practical difficulties standard for area variances, the courts may not treat the self-created aspect of the hardship as an automatic bar,[8] but this concession invites lawless behavior, and no difference exists in this respect between an area and a use variance.[9]

§ 5.17

1. Larsen v. Zoning Bd. of Adj. of Pittsburgh, 543 Pa. 415, 424, 672 A.2d 286, 290 (1996) (reasoning that "the changing needs of a growing family" are not unnecessary hardships). See *Larsen*, 672 A.2d at 290, n.8, for a long list of such cases in Pennsylvania.

2. In re Kline's Appeal, 395 Pa. 122, 148 A.2d 915 (1959).

3. Allison v. Zoning Bd. of Adj., 97 Pa.Cmwlth. 51, 508 A.2d 639 (1986).

4. Pierce v. Parish of Jefferson, 668 So.2d 1153 (La.App.1996). See also Martin v. Board of Adj., 464 So.2d 123 (Ala.Civ. App.1985).

5. Mills v. City of Manchester, 109 N.H. 293, 249 A.2d 679 (1969). See also Rivera v. City of Phoenix, 186 Ariz. 600, 925 P.2d 741 (Ariz.App.1996).

6. Pollard v. Zoning Bd. of Appeals, 186 Conn. 32, 438 A.2d 1186 (1982).

7. Pyzdrowski v. Board of Adj., 437 Pa. 481, 263 A.2d 426 (1970).

8. See, e.g., DeSena v. Board of Zoning Appeals of Hempstead, 45 N.Y.2d 105, 379 N.E.2d 1144, 408 N.Y.S.2d 14 (1978).

9. See Thomas E. Roberts, Variances, 6 Zoning and Land Use Controls, § 44.02[6][b] (Rohan ed.1987).

When one purchases property and then applies for a variance on the grounds of unnecessary hardship, a difference of opinion exists as to whether the variance should be denied on the ground of self-induced hardship. Most courts consider the transfer of title irrelevant,[10] but some cases contain contrary suggestions.[11] The purchaser knew or should have known of the zoning of the property when purchased. However, since ownership is normally irrelevant to zoning, the transfer of title ought not affect the issue. If the land suffers the requisite hardship, in that the owner can make no reasonable return from its use as zoned, then the board ought to grant a variance. If not, the land becomes permanently zoned in a useless state.

The reasons used to deny a variance to one who violates the law and then seeks relief are not applicable to one who purchases with knowledge. In the former, the owner created the hardship; in the latter, the zoning created the hardship, which pre-existed the purchaser's acquisition of title.[12] The integrity of the law demands that the one who builds in violation of the law not be able to take advantage of it, but it is not an affront to the law to grant relief to one who purchases land where unique circumstances have already zoned the land into a state of uselessness.

One who buys with knowledge of zoning and then obtains a variance arguably reaps a windfall from the increase in value that results from the granting of the variance. This troubles some courts.[13] The purchaser, however, takes the risk that a board will agree that the situation for a variance exists. How that risk is allocated between the seller[14] and the purchaser will vary. A windfall may result, but it is not an unjustifiable one vis-s-vis the public, since the situation assumes that land deserves the variance. It is simply a question of which owner gets the variance, the prior owner or new owner.

10. Myron v. City of Plymouth, 562 N.W.2d 21 (Minn.App.1997), review granted, June 30, 1997; Landmark Universal, Inc. v. Pitkin County Bd. of Adj., 40 Colo. App. 444, 579 P.2d 1184 (1978); Johnny Cake, Inc. v. Board of Appeals, 180 Conn. 296, 429 A.2d 883 (1980); City of Coral Gables v. Geary, 383 So.2d 1127 (Fla.App. 1980); Fail v. LaPorte County, 171 Ind.App. 192, 355 N.E.2d 455 (1976); Chirichello v. Zoning Bd. of Adj., 78 N.J. 544, 397 A.2d 646 (1979); Vacca v. Zoning Hearing Bd., 82 Pa.Cmwlth. 192, 475 A.2d 1329 (1984).

11. Alleghany Enterprises, Inc. v. Board of Zoning Appeals, 217 Va. 64, 225 S.E.2d 383 (1976); Taylor v. District of Columbia Bd. of Zoning Adj., 308 A.2d 230 (1973); Goslin v. Zoning Bd. of Appeals, 40 Ill.App.3d 40, 351 N.E.2d 299 (1976).

New York courts have sometimes been viewed as disallowing a variance to a purchaser. See Clark v. Board of Zoning Appeals, 301 N.Y. 86, 92 N.E.2d 903 (1950),

but *Clark* was not a case where the variance was otherwise justifiable. See Murphy v. Kraemer, 16 Misc.2d 374, 182 N.Y.S.2d 205 (1958). See discussion in Roberts, supra note 9, at § 43.02[6], noting that, in these cases, factors other than purchase with knowledge justify denial of the variance.

12. Murphy v. Kraemer, 16 Misc.2d 374, 375, 182 N.Y.S.2d 205, 206 (1958) ("[S]ince it is not the act of the purchaser which brings the hardship into being, it is incorrect to charge him with having created it.").

13. Sofo v. Egan, 57 A.D.2d 841, 394 N.Y.S.2d 43 (1977); Cowan v. Kern, 41 N.Y.2d 591, 363 N.E.2d 305, 394 N.Y.S.2d 579 (1977) (potential windfall a factor in denial).

14. Who it is assumed would, or might, have received a variance had she sought it.

A different question is presented when one who purchases with knowledge of an existing restriction seeks to recover just compensation on the basis that the zoning restriction effects a taking under the Fifth Amendment. In such a case, courts may treat the personal right to compensation as waived.[15] Thus, a board may grant a variance under state law to permit land to be used according to traditional zoning principles, but if the board denies the variance the courts might not allow an action for compensation.[16] Under variance law, the land is the focus; under constitutional law, the person is.

§ 5.18 Effect on Public

A showing that the public interest not be harmed restates the general rule that all aspects of zoning must be in the public interest. The granting of a variance is no different. Many courts do not list "the public interest" as a separate requirement, but the consideration of it enters into the formula by examining the effect of the proposed variance on the surrounding area. If the requested variance will alter the essential character of the neighborhood, on balance, issuance will not serve the public interest even if the owner suffers from a hardship. Where courts specifically examine the public interest, the burden to show that the variance will not harm the public is on the one seeking it.[1]

An argument that the proposed use would be advantageous to the public, such as the convenience of a shopping center to an area or to meet a need for affordable housing, is not only unnecessary but is usually improper. A board of adjustment lacks the power to decide what the public needs. If the city needs high density, low cost housing, the legislative body should rezone the land or create a new special use category.[2] The board should not decide the issue by way of variance.[3]

Exceptions exist. New Jersey's statute allows for variances for "special reasons."[4] This so-called "d variance" does not require a showing of hardship, but requires a showing that the proposed use will be beneficial to the public.[5] In New York, the courts have crafted a lesser test for public utilities requiring a showing of a public need for service, and not economic hardship to land.[6]

15. See infra § 10.7.

16. See Myron v. City of Plymouth, 562 N.W.2d 21 (Minn.App.1997), review granted, June 30, 1997; Reinking v. Metropolitan Bd. of Zoning Appeals of Marion County, 671 N.E.2d 137 (Ind.App.1996).

§ 5.18

1. State v. Winnebago, 196 Wis.2d 836, 847, 540 N.W.2d 6, 10 (Wis.App.1995).

2. See infra § 5.24.

3. Topanga Ass'n for a Scenic Community v. County of Los Angeles, 11 Cal.3d 506, 113 Cal.Rptr. 836, 522 P.2d 12 (1974).

4. N.J.Stat.Ann. § 40:55D–70d.

5. See Fobe Associates v. Board of Adj., 74 N.J. 519, 379 A.2d 31 (1977) and Kim M. Johannessen, Zoning Variances: Unnecessarily an Evil, Land Use L. & Zon.Dig. 3, 5 (July 1989).

6. Cellular Telephone Co. v. Rosenberg, 82 N.Y.2d 364, 624 N.E.2d 990, 604 N.Y.S.2d 895 (1993); Matter of Consolidated Edison v. Hoffman, 43 N.Y.2d 598, 610, 403 N.Y.S.2d 193, 199, 374 N.E.2d 105, 111 (1978) (requiring showing of public necessity to render safe and adequate service, and that there are compelling reasons, economic or otherwise, which make it more feasible to modify the plant than to use alternative sources of power).

§ 5.19   No Reasonable Return

A widely followed rule is that before the board can issue a variance on the ground of unnecessary hardship, the applicant must show that the land as zoned cannot yield a reasonable return.[1] Where not expressly a part of a statute or ordinance,[2] courts have implied the requirement. The leading case of Otto v. Steinhilber[3] is widely regarded as formulating the rule. The court did so based on meager authority,[4] and offered no reason for the imposition of this strenuous requirement. The *Otto* court's requirement apparently stemmed from its "safety valve" theory,[5] which equated the denial of a variance with the equivalent of a Fifth Amendment taking. Under this theory, a variance is granted only to avoid a taking of property. The requirement limits use of the variance power, and accords with the view that the power should be used sparingly.[6]

In applying the reasonable use rule, the question is not whether an owner will have property that is more valuable if the variance is granted,[7] but whether the land can earn a reasonable return as zoned. As courts have starkly put it, the question is whether the land has been "zoned into inutility"[8] or whether it would be an "economic disaster"[9] if used as currently zoned. As such, the test is essentially the Fifth Amendment taking test.[10] Only if the effect of the zoning is so oppressive that it leaves the owner with no economically viable use is a variance to be granted. It thus becomes a rule of expediency. Granting the variance

Other courts also refer on occasion to the public benefit to be obtained from a proposed use. See, e.g., Williams v. District of Columbia Bd. of Zoning Adj., 535 A.2d 910 (1988) (need to relieve overcrowding of persons in the custody corrections department); National Black Child Development Institute, Inc. v. District of Columbia Board of Zoning Adjustment, 483 A.2d 687, 690 (1984) (fact that petitioner's "work does promote the public welfare" relevant).

§ 5.19

1. See Baker v. Connell, 488 A.2d 1303 (Del.1985); Snyder v. Waukesha County Zoning Bd. of Adj., 74 Wis.2d 468, 247 N.W.2d 98 (1976) (no feasible use); City of Des Moines v. Board of Adj. of City of Des Moines, 448 N.W.2d 696 (Iowa App.1989); Bell v. Cloud, 764 S.W.2d 105 (Mo.App. 1988); Maturo v. City of Coral Gables, 619 So.2d 455 (Fla.App.1993) ("virtually unusable"); Grey Rocks Land Trust v. Town of Hebron, 136 N.H. 239, 614 A.2d 1048 (1992). But see Enterprise Citizens Action Committee v. Clark County Bd. of Commissioners, 112 Nev. 649, 918 P.2d 305, 309 (Nev.1996), noting the various tests of hardship but finding it unnecessary to adopt one.

2. Pa.Stat.Ann. § 10910.2; Me.Rev. Stat.Ann § 4963 (3).

3. 282 N.Y. 71, 24 N.E.2d 851 (1939), reargument denied 282 N.Y. 681, 26 N.E.2d 811 (1940).

4. The *Otto* court cited Edward M. Bassett, Zoning 168–69 (1940), for the proposition. Bassett relied only on comments by a chairman of the New York City Board of Appeals reciting his experience.

5. 282 N.Y. at 75, 24 N.E.2d at 852.

6. See supra § 5.14.

7. Long v. Town of Eliot, 521 A.2d 1190 (Me.1987); City of Des Moines v. Board of Adj. of City of Des Moines, 448 N.W.2d 696, 698–99 (Iowa App.1989) ("a reasonable return," not the "most reasonable return" or "the highest rate of return"). An owner's testimony that the property "was more or less a long-term investment, and without getting a variance, the land isn't worth anything compared to what it would be if we do get the variance," does not meet the test. State v. Winnebago County, 196 Wis.2d 836, 844, 540 N.W.2d 6, 9 (Wis.App.1995).

8. Davis Enterprises v. Karpf, 105 N.J. 476, 481, 523 A.2d 137, 139 (1987).

9. Appeal of Girsh, 437 Pa. 237, 241, 263 A.2d 395, 397, n. 3 (1970).

10. See §§ 10.2–10.6.

is more efficient for the city than waiting to be sued for compensation and running the risk of a large damage award.

Courts require proof of economic loss, not conclusory allegations.[11] It is necessary to show, in what the courts call "dollars and cents proof,"[12] that compliance with the existing ordinance would not be economically feasible. Dollars and cents proof requires evidence of the amount paid for the property, the present value, and costs for maintenance, taxes, and liens. Proof of an inability to sell is probative.[13] If the situation is sufficiently stark, a court may infer that the owner can make no reasonable return.[14] A physical impossibility of use need not be shown. If commercial uses surround a residentially zoned tract, a person can probably live there, but if no market exists for the land for residential use, the owner has likely met the test to obtain a variance.[15]

A plausible argument exists against applying the reasonable use requirement to variances. It is true that a zoning ordinance usually constitutes some hardship because it restricts uses and sometimes reduces property values. Those are necessary hardships that owners must suffer to gain the overall benefit from zoning. However, if an applicant for a variance can show that granting the variance would not adversely affect the public or the neighbors and that the property is unique, perhaps a variance should issue. After all, if no one could be hurt, the present zoning, and therefore the hardship, is unnecessary. Some, though not much, support exists for this view.[16] If courts followed it, legal variances would be much more common.

Jurisdictions lessen the impact of the reasonable use rule if they apply it only to use variances. If a practical difficulties standard is used for area variances, no need arises to show economic uselessness.[17]

§ 5.20 Unique or Unusual Characteristics of Property

Characteristics that are unique or unusual to the property must cause the hardship from which the owner seeks a variance. The premise is that a variance is proper only when the property is different from

11. Matthew v. Smith, 707 S.W.2d 411 (Mo.1986).

12. Id. at 416–17; Crossroads Recreation, Inc. v. Broz, 4 N.Y.2d 39, 149 N.E.2d 65, 172 N.Y.S.2d 129 (1958).

13. Zoning Bd. of Adj. of Hanover Twp. v. Koehler, 2 Pa.Cmwlth. 260, 278 A.2d 375 (1971).

14. Valley View Civic Association v. Zoning Bd. of Adj., 501 Pa. 550, 462 A.2d 637 (1983).

15. See *Valley View*, Id. at 560, 462 A.2d at 642.

16. See, e.g., Levesque v. Hudson, 106 N.H. 470, 214 A.2d 553 (1965), overruled on other grounds by Winslow v. Town of Hold-erness Planning Board, 125 N.H. 262, 480 A.2d 114 (1984). In *Levesque*, the court noted that the owners seeking the variance wanted to use their land for a bank, which would be more profitable than any permitted use. "If they cannot carry out their wish this will constitute hardship. * * * If the granting of a permit would not injuriously affect any public or private rights, then the refusal to grant one would constitute unnecessary hardship * * *." 213 A.2d at 555. In more recent cases, the New Hampshire court has said that unnecessary hardship requires a showing that the property has no reasonable use. Olszak v. Town of New Hampton, 139 N.H. 723, 725, 661 A.2d 768, 771 (1995).

17. See infra § 5.23.

surrounding property. While courts do not require that the owner suffer uniquely in the strict sense of the word, the hardship ought to be unusual. If the problem suffered is widespread, a legislative rezoning is the appropriate vehicle for change.

If the land is physically unique, the classic circumstances for a variance exist. Where setback lines on the sides of a triangular lot limited the useable space of a lot to ten square feet, a variance from the setback requirements was proper.[1] Where a deep ravine crossed a lot, it was similarly considered unusual enough to justify a variance.[2] If the physical characteristics are not limited to the parcel for which the variance is sought, then relief is improper. Topanga Association for a Scenic Community v. County of Los Angeles[3] is illustrative. The administrative body granted a variance to allow a mobile home park on 28 acres that was zoned light agricultural and large lot single family residential. The California supreme court reversed. While the terrain was rugged and contained three stream beds, the developers had not shown that the property was unlike neighboring parcels.[4]

Property in transitional or deteriorating areas may meet the uniqueness requirement.[5] Many such cases involve lots that are either next to more intensive zones or surrounded by more intensive uses. Unique circumstances are more likely to be found in the latter than the former situation. The mere fact that residentially zoned property is next to property zoned for business purposes does not justify a variance.[6] This result is necessary to preserve Euclidean zoning, for if districting is to be used, lines must be drawn somewhere. On the other hand, if a lot is zoned residential, and all, or many, of the surrounding uses are commercial, the lot may meet the test of uniqueness.[7] The question usually turns on how widespread the problem is.

§ 5.20

1. Hoshour v. County of Contra Costa, 203 Cal.App.2d 602, 21 Cal.Rptr. 714 (1962). See also City of Little Rock v. Kaufman, 249 Ark. 530, 460 S.W.2d 88 (1970), Hankin v. Zoning Hearing Bd., 35 Pa. Cmwlth. 164, 384 A.2d 1386 (1978). Cf. City of Coral Gables v. Geary, 383 So.2d 1127 (Fla.App.1980) (triangular lot a classic case for variance but denied because of self-created hardship).

A finding that the characteristics of the property do not qualify for a variance does not necessarily mean that the existing zoning is proper. It may only mean that the zoning should be attacked directly in court as being invalid as applied or that an amendment or a special permit is the proper form of action.

2. Ferry v. Kownacki, 396 Pa. 283, 152 A.2d 456 (1959).

3. 11 Cal.3d 506, 113 Cal.Rptr. 836, 522 P.2d 12 (1974).

4. Id. at 520, 113 Cal.Rptr. at 845, 522 P.2d at 21.

5. Parsons v. Board of Zoning Appeals, 140 Conn. 290, 99 A.2d 149 (1953). However, some courts more properly reverse issuance on the ground that an amendment or a direct attack in court on the constitutionality of the restriction is proper, since the problem is not unique. Reynolds v. Board of Appeal of Springfield, 335 Mass. 464, 140 N.E.2d 491 (1957).

6. Bellamy v. Board of Appeals of City of Rochester, 32 Misc.2d 520, 223 N.Y.S.2d 1017 (1962); Taylor v. District of Columbia Board of Zoning Adj., 308 A.2d 230 (D.C.App.1973).

7. City of Mobile v. Sorrell, 271 Ala. 468, 124 So.2d 463 (1960); Nelson v. Board of Zoning Appeals, 240 Ind. 212, 162 N.E.2d 449 (1959); Valley View Civic Association v. Zoning Bd. of Adj., 501 Pa. 550, 462 A.2d 637 (1983).

The absence of unique or unusual circumstances may not necessarily be fatal. If the property owner establishes that she can earn no reasonable return from the land as zoned, a court may uphold a variance simply out of recognition that, without the variance, a taking may occur. However, where a problem is widespread, then the piecemeal granting of variances to those who step forward will leave the overall zoning problem unfixed. Evidence that other properties share a problem indicates that an amendment covering them all may be the proper "form of action."

§ 5.21 Effect on Neighborhood

A typical ordinance provides that a board should not grant a variance if it would "alter the essential character of the neighborhood."[1] Even if the ordinance does not so provide, most courts require the same. The requirement is presumably tied to the Standard Act's command that the spirit of the ordinance be observed and substantial justice done.[2] It would not likely meet the test if the board permitted a commercial use in a residential zone that was actually committed to residential uses for the change would alter the character of the neighborhood.[3] If, however, a residential zone contains commercial uses established by nonconforming uses or previously granted variances or special use permits, a variance for commercial use will not alter the character of the area.[4] It also may not meet the test if the variance would generate an increase in traffic,[5] or would otherwise result in depreciation of property values in a neighborhood.[6]

Since local governments employ the variance to relieve hardship, any relief granted by a variance should be the minimum necessary to achieve that purpose. The variance should not confer benefits not enjoyed by neighboring property. For example, an undersized lot zoned for large lot single-family use is not entitled to a variance for multi-family use but only to a variance for single-family use, that being the zoning in the area.[7] A minimum variance rule is often a part of the state statute[8] or ordinance; if not, a court may imply it.[9]

Though the number of protestors and the intensity of the objections should not dictate the result, as a matter of practical administration,

§ 5.21

1. Anon v. Coral Gables, 336 So.2d 420 (Fla.App.1976).

2. Consolidated Management, Inc. v. City of Cleveland, 6 Ohio St.3d 238, 452 N.E.2d 1287 (1983).

3. Wilson v. Borough of Mountainside, 42 N.J. 426, 201 A.2d 540 (1964); Dubin v. Wich, 120 N.J.L. 469, 200 A. 751 (Sup.Ct. 1938); Otto v. Steinhilber, 282 N.Y. 71, 24 N.E.2d 851 (1939), reargument denied 282 N.Y. 681, 26 N.E.2d 811 (1940); Bellamy v. Board of Appeals of City of Rochester, 32 Misc.2d 520, 223 N.Y.S.2d 1017 (1962).

4. Guadagnolo v. Mamaroneck Bd. of Appeals, 52 A.D.2d 902, 383 N.Y.S.2d 377 (1976); Nelson v. Board of Zoning Appeals, 240 Ind. 212, 162 N.E.2d 449 (1959).

5. Corbett v. Zoning Board of Appeals, 283 App.Div. 282, 128 N.Y.S.2d 12 (1954).

6. Greenwich Gas Co. v. Tuthill, 113 Conn. 684, 155 A. 850 (1931).

7. Hamer v. Town of Ross, 59 Cal.2d 776, 31 Cal.Rptr. 335, 382 P.2d 375 (1963).

8. See,   e.g.,   Fla.Stat.Ann. § 163.225(3)(a)(5).

9. Duncan v. Village of Middlefield, 23 Ohio St.3d 83, 491 N.E.2d 692, 696 (1986).

boards seldom issue variances when neighbors appear and vigorously oppose the request.[10] The absence of objections from neighbors may also be evidence that there will be no adverse effect on surrounding areas.[11]

§ 5.22   Conditions

Under the express terms of the Standard Act a board can grant a variance with conditions attached to prevent or mitigate adverse effects on the public or the neighborhood.[1] This is in contrast to a general rezoning where the legislative body may be forced either to grant or deny the application, and may not limit the rezoning by contract or impose conditions.[2] Even where the statute and ordinance do not confer such authority, a court may imply the power to condition variances.[3]

Conditions must relate to the property rather than the applicant.[4] The conditions that boards normally impose, as with conditional rezonings and special permits, are designed to reduce the adverse impact of the variance and protect neighbors. These may include landscape buffers or screening,[5] height or lighting limits,[6] or off-street parking.[7] A variance issued on the condition that a restaurant in a residential zone be closed during certain evening hours has been held valid.[8] A condition also may be imposed to force use of the variance in a timely manner.[9] A variance also may be limited to a term of years, and then be subject to review.[10]

Issuing a variance on the condition that the property remain under the applicant's ownership is improper. Variances run with the land and conditions attached to variances run as well.[11] A limitation on the

---

10. See Luger v. City of Burnsville, 295 N.W.2d 609 (Minn.1980); Minney v. Azusa, 164 Cal.App.2d 12, 330 P.2d 255 (1958), appeal dismissed 359 U.S. 436, 79 S.Ct. 941, 3 L.Ed.2d 932 (1959).

11. See U–Haul Co. of New Hampshire, Inc. v. City of Concord, 122 N.H. 910, 451 A.2d 1315 (1982).

§ 5.22

1. A board "may * * * subject to appropriate conditions and safeguards, make special exceptions to the terms of the ordinance in harmony with its general purpose and intent * * *." Standard Act § 7. The term special exception in this portion of the Standard Act is a generic term that includes a variance.

2. See supra § 5.11.

3. Vlahos Realty Co., Inc. v. Little Boar's Head District, 101 N.H. 460, 146 A.2d 257 (1958); Warren v. Frost, 111 R.I. 217, 301 A.2d 572 (1973).

4. See Walter M. Strine, Jr., The Use of Conditions in Land–Use Control, 67 Dick.L.Rev. 109 (1963); Robert F. Wood, Note, Zoning Amendments and Variances Subject to Conditions, 12 Syracuse L.Rev. 230 (1960).

5. Everson v. Zoning Bd. of Adj., 395 Pa. 168, 149 A.2d 63 (1959).

6. Miller Pump Service, Inc. v. Worcester Twp., 59 Pa.Cmwlth. 21, 428 A.2d 779 (1981).

7. Woodbury v. Zoning Bd. of Review of City of Warwick, 78 R.I. 319, 82 A.2d 164 (1951).

8. Montgomery County v. Mossburg, 228 Md. 555, 180 A.2d 851 (1962); Annot., 99 A.L.R.2d 227 (1965). A condition of operating hours on a liquor store held ultra vires where another state agency regulated such stores. Bora v. Zoning Bd. of Appeals, 161 Conn. 297, 288 A.2d 89 (1972).

9. Ambrosio v. Zoning Bd. of Appeals, 196 Misc. 1005, 96 N.Y.S.2d 380 (Sup.Ct. 1949) (variance not used to terminate in six months).

10. Guenther v. Zoning Bd. of Review of City of Warwick, 85 R.I. 37, 125 A.2d 214 (1956).

11. National Black Child Development Institute, Inc. v. District of Columbia Board of Zoning Adjustment, 483 A.2d 687, 690 (D.C.App.1984); Huntington v. Zoning Bd. of App., 12 Mass.AppCt. 710, 428 N.E.2d

number of employees might be valid if related to land use problems such as traffic and parking,[12] but to condition a laundromat by requiring the constant presence of an attendant has been held invalid on the ground that such a regulation is not a zoning matter.[13] The power cannot be used to exact land for public use if no nexus exists between the burden the community must bear from the use allowed by the variance and the land exacted.[14]

Where a court holds a condition invalid, it must decide whether to revoke the variance or allow it to stand unconditioned. If the court deems the variance irrevocably tainted by the condition in that the board would not have issued it without the illegal condition, it will order revocation.[15] If, however, the board should have issued the variance without the condition, it should remain in force. Such may be the case where a variance is limited to the owner who obtained it.[16]

§ 5.23　Practical Difficulties

Many enabling acts and ordinances provide for the issuance of a variance if practical difficulties exist as well as unnecessary hardship. The phrase is important because, as discussed above,[1] it sometimes leads to the creation of a separate, less stringent test for area variances. For many courts the terms are interchangeable and there is but one test.[2] Where the statute uses the conjunctive "and," some courts require the applicant to satisfy both requirements. Where the disjunctive "or" is used, separate tests are more likely to be applied.[3]

The elements of a separate "practical difficulties" test are not well defined, except that the test is less rigorous than for the unnecessary hardship standard. Courts usually toss several factors together in a balancing test between the property owner and the community. They include whether, or to what degree, the owner can pursue the permitted use without a variance, what the financial hardship is, the degree of variation sought, the harm to the neighbors, whether alternatives exist, whether the hardship is self-imposed, and whether the interests of

826 (1981); Cohn v. County Bd. of Supervisors, 135 Cal.App.2d 180, 286 P.2d 836 (1955).

12. National Black Child Development Institute, Inc. v. District of Columbia Board of Zoning Adjustment, 483 A.2d 687, 690 (D.C.App.1984).

13. DeVille Homes, Inc. v. Michaelis, 201 N.Y.S.2d 129 (1960).

14. Gordon v. Zoning Bd. of App., 126 Misc.2d 75, 481 N.Y.S.2d 275 (1984). See the discussion of the constitutional nexus requirement infra § 10.5.

15. Bora v. Zoning Bd. of Appeals, 161 Conn. 297, 288 A.2d 89 (1972).

16. National Black Child Development Institute, Inc. v. District of Columbia Board of Zoning Adjustment, 483 A.2d 687, 690 (D.C.App.1984). But see St. Onge v. Donovan, 127 A.D.2d 880, 511 N.Y.S.2d 700 (1987).

§ 5.23

1. See supra § 5.15.

2. 165 Augusta Street, Inc. v. Collins, 9 N.J. 259, 87 A.2d 889 (1952); Abel v. Zoning Bd. of Appeals, 172 Conn. 286, 374 A.2d 227 (1977); Marchi v. Town of Scarborough, 511 A.2d 1071 (Me.1986).; Bienz v. City of Dayton, 29 Or.App. 761, 566 P.2d 904 (1977).

3. See City and Borough of Juneau v. Thibodeau, 595 P.2d 626 (Alaska 1979) (collecting the cases on this point).

justice will be served.[4] The New York legislature recently adopted a statutory test for area variances that closely approximates these factors and authorizes a balancing test.[5] The statute, however, does not use the "practical difficulties" language, and the state high court has held that an applicant no longer needs to show practical difficulties as a separate element for an area variance.[6]

Some financial hardship must exist, though how much is not clear. Courts take the position that the mere showing that land could be used more profitably does not suffice.[7] Tests of "significant economic injury"[8] and loss beyond "mere inconvenience"[9] have been used. Significantly, however, they do not apply the onerous requirement of showing economic inutility used for use variances under the unnecessary hardship test.

V.   SPECIAL PERMITS

§ 5.24   Special Permits

A. *In General*

Section 7 of the Standard State Zoning Enabling Act provides that the Board of Adjustment shall have the power to "hear and decide special exceptions to the terms of the ordinance upon which such board is required to pass under such ordinance."[1] Before the board can exercise the power, the legislative body must list the uses to be treated as special. The board may issue a permit for only those uses listed and only if the conditions set forth in the ordinance are met.[2] The label applied to this permit varies. Court, commentators, and ordinances may follow the enabling act's language and refer to it as a special exception, or they may term it a special use permit, a conditional use permit, or simply a special permit. The terms are used interchangeably.[3] The term special permit is used here.

The special permit process is designed to deal with uses that by their nature are difficult to fit within any use zone where they can operate by right. These uses may be especially sensitive and need special protection or they may pose unusual harm to neighboring land. The administrative

---

4. See, e.g., Duncan v. Village of Middlefield, 23 Ohio St.3d 83, 491 N.E.2d 692 (1986); Wachsberger v. Michalis, 19 Misc.2d 909, 191 N.Y.S.2d 621 (1959).

5. McKinney's N.Y. Town Law § 267–b, adopted in 1992.

6. Sasso v. Osgood, 86 N.Y.2d 374, 657 N.E.2d 254, 633 N.Y.S.2d 259 (1995).

7. Metropolitan Bd. of Zoning Appeals v. McDonald's Corp., 481 N.E.2d 141 (Ind. App.1985).

8. Fulling v. Palumbo, 21 N.Y.2d 30, 233 N.E.2d 272, 286 N.Y.S.2d 249 (1967).

9. Gara Realty, Inc. v. Zoning Bd. of Review, 523 A.2d 855 (R.I.1987).

§ 5.24

1. U.S. Dept. of Commerce (rev.ed. 1926).

2. Piscioneri v. Zoning Hearing Bd. of Borough of Munhall, 523 Pa. 597, 568 A.2d 610 (1990).

3. By ordinance, there may different names given to permits based on the issuing body. See, e.g., City of Pittsburgh Code § 993.01, described in Klein v. City of Pittsburgh, 164 Pa.Cmwlth. 521, 540, 643 A.2d 1107, 1116 (1994) (Council-issued permits are labeled conditional uses and board issued permits are called special exceptions).

process deals with these uses on a case by case basis to take these concerns into account. The term "special" relates to the type of use rather than the uniqueness of the property as with a variance.[4] A more descriptive term might be "unusual uses," a term some courts use.[5] For example, an airport has such unusual characteristics that many ordinances do not list it as an absolutely permitted use in any zone but allow it only under particular circumstances. Other uses customarily subject to special permits include religious uses,[6] recreational facilities,[7] schools,[8] hospitals, drug treatment centers, child care facilities, gas stations, landfills, gun clubs, and dog kennels.

Special permit requirements may be found invalid if they operate in a discriminatory or oppressive manner. While the equal protection guarantee applies to all uses, some invoke greater judicial scrutiny than others. Where fundamental or important rights or suspect or quasi-suspect classes are involved, courts may review special permit requirements closely.[9] In Cleburne v. Cleburne Living Center, Inc.,[10] the Supreme Court faced an ordinance that subjected group homes for the mentally-retarded to a special permit process, but allowed such uses as fraternities, multi-family use, hospitals, sanitariums, and nursing homes to operate by right. Finding no rational basis to treat group homes more harshly than these similar permitted uses, the Court invalidated the ordinance on equal protection grounds. Despite the *Cleburne* Court's insistence that it was not treating the mentally retarded as a quasi-suspect class, the case uses a more demanding test than usually applied to socioeconomic legislation.[11] Courts may also invalidate special permit requirements as applied to persons protected by the Fair Housing Act.[12]

B. *Distinguishing Features*

Like a variance, a special permit normally involves an administrative process.[13] The two are fundamentally different, however. A variance is permission to engage in an otherwise prohibited act because of hardship.[14] In contrast, a special permit allows a use specifically autho-

4. Mayflower Prop. v. Fort Lauderdale, 137 So.2d 849 (Fla.App.1962); City of St. Petersburg v. Schweitzer, 297 So.2d 74 (Fla.App.1974), cert. denied 308 So.2d 114 (Fla.1975).

5. Metropolitan Dade County v. Fuller, 515 So.2d 1312 (Fla.App.1987).

6. See, e.g., State ex rel. Synod of Ohio of United Lutheran Church in America v. Joseph, 139 Ohio St. 229, 39 N.E.2d 515 (1942).

7. Kotrich v. County of Du Page, 19 Ill.2d 181, 166 N.E.2d 601 (1960), appeal dismissed 364 U.S. 475, 81 S.Ct. 243, 5 L.Ed.2d 221 (1960), rehearing denied 365 U.S. 805, 81 S.Ct. 466, 5 L.Ed.2d 463 (1961).

8. O'Hara's Appeal, 389 Pa. 35, 131 A.2d 587 (1957). Cf. L'Hote v. New Orleans,

177 U.S. 587, 20 S.Ct. 788, 44 L.Ed. 899 (1900).

9. See   discussion   § 10.12   and §§ 10.14–.15.

10. 473 U.S. 432, 105 S.Ct. 3249, 87 L.Ed.2d 313 (1985). See also Macdonald Advertising Co. v. City of Pontiac, 916 F.Supp. 644 (E.D.Mich.1995).

11. See infra § 10.14.

12. See supra § 4.7 and infra § 6.8.

13. The power to issue the permit may be retained by the legislative body. See § 5.3. But see Depue v. City of Clinton, 160 N.W.2d 860 (Iowa 1968) (legislative body may not retain power where state statute mandates the creation of a board of adjustment).

14. See supra § 5.14

rized by the legislative body. A showing that prestated standards are met is required, but a hardship showing is not necessary.

The special permit also differs from a rezoning. A rezoning is a legislative change in use classification. Issuance of a special permit does not change the underlying zone. It is an administrative act issued for a particular use. For example, a special permit may allow a supermarket of a certain size with required parking and screening in a high density residential zone, but the land retains its residential zoning classification. However, with a general rezoning of the property from residential to commercial, the new zoning to permit a supermarket would also permit use of the property for any other commercial use allowed in that zone. The greater the effect that a development will have on a community the more likely the community will handle it by way of amendment, rather than the special permit process.[15]

The legislative-administrative difference becomes clouded where the legislative body retains the power to issue special permits. Floating zones, which are legislative acts, also closely resemble special permits.[16] In both instances, certain uses deemed sufficiently important or unusual for the community so that those interested in pursuing them are subjected to an ad hoc approval process. Courts vary over whether they should treat these nominally legislative actions as legislative or quasi-judicial for purposes of judicial review.[17]

C. Growth in Use

From the inception of zoning, the use of the special permit has grown. Its increased and widespread use is part of the transition from rigidity to flexibility, or, some might say, the evolution of zoning to nonzoning. When an ordinance provides for numerous special permits, cities make decisions on an ad hoc discretionary basis, and districting becomes less evident and less important.[18] This practice resembles the British approach to land use, which historically has not been a districting system. Instead, in a system somewhat like our special permit process,[19] the British have not allowed development generally of right,

---

15. See Neighborhood Bd. No. 24 v. State Land Use Commission, 64 Haw. 265, 639 P.2d 1097 (1982) (theme park covering 103 acres of agricultural land which included rides, restaurants, fast food shops, retail stores, exhibits, theaters, amphitheater, bank, nurseries, 12 acres of parking, sewage treatment plant and other related support services, designed to attract approximately 1.5 million people annually, did not qualify for a special permit under a state law that allotted such permits for "unusual and reasonable uses.")

16. See supra § 4.16.

17. See discussion infra § 5.37.

18. See generally Daniel L. Mandelker, Delegation of Power and Function in Zon-

ing Administration, 1963 Wash.U.L.Q. 60; Joseph P. Stevens, Note, The Use and Abuse of the Special Permit in Zoning Law, 35 Brooklyn L. Review 258 (1969); H. Louis Nichols, Powers and Duties of the Zoning Board of Adjustment, 1975 Plan. Zoning & Eminent Domain Inst. 121; Sara Reusch Levitan, Comment, The Legislative–Adjudicative Distinction in California Land Use Regulation: A Suggested Response to Arnel Development Co. v. City of Costa Mesa, 34 Hastings L.J. 425 (1982); Michael D. Donovan, Note, Zoning Variation Administration in Vermont, 8 Vt.L.Rev. 371 (1983).

19. Donald G. Hagman, Urban Planning and Land Development Control Law 613 (1975). See also Malcolm Grant, Urban Planning Law 197–226 (1987).

and property owners must obtain permission to use land for most purposes.[20]

A court will likely invalidate an ordinance that handles all uses by special permit. The court in Rockhill v. Township of Chesterfield[21] faced a situation that almost went that far. The authorities zoned the entire township for agricultural and residential uses, and no other use was possible without issuance of a special permit. The court found the ordinance beyond the scope of the enabling statute since the zoning was neither uniform nor comprehensive. It placed too many uses subject to "local discretion without regard to districts, ruled by vague and elusive criteria, [and was] ... the antithesis of zoning."[22] The *Rockhill* court's objection may be overstated. If the standards are adequate and written into the ordinance, there is no reason to require control of land use by districting rather than a case by case regulatory scheme.

§ 5.25 Standards

The most frequent objection to the issuance of special permits is that the legislature failed to provide adequate standards for guiding administrative discretion.[1] Typically, an ordinance listing potential special uses requires that the board find that the applicant meets specific predetermined conditions. For example, an ordinance may permit airports only if a tract of 200 acres is available, the flight path is not over any areas zoned for multi-family use, there are no schools under the flight path, and there is a heavy industrial buffer zone around the airport. The ordinance may also contain more general standards requiring the board to find that the use will not materially endanger the public health and safety, that it will not substantially impair the value of adjoining property, and that the use will be in harmony with the surrounding area. It is with these generalized standards that problems of vagueness or improper delegation may occur.[2]

Standards "may not be so general or tautological as to allow unchecked discretion"[3] by the administrative body. However, universal agreement is lacking on how general the standards may be to meet this test. If an ordinance simply provides that the board of adjustment shall find that the granting of the special permit "will not adversely affect the

---

20. See David L. Callies and Malcolm Grant, Paying for Growth and Planning Gain:An Anglo–American Comparison of Development Conditions, Impact Fees, and Development Agreements, 23 Urb.Law. 221, 226 (1991).

21. 23 N.J. 117, 128 A.2d 473 (1957).

22. Id. at 127, 128 A.2d at 479. Even the tolerant California courts have held such broad use of special permits invalid. People v. Perez, 214 Cal.App.2d Supp. 881, 29 Cal.Rptr. 781 (1963). See also Board of Supervisors v. Southland Corp., 224 Va. 514, 297 S.E.2d 718 (1982).

§ 5.25

1. See Orlando E. Delogu and Susan E. Spokes, The Long–Standing Requirement That Delegations of Land Use Control Power Contain "Meaningful" Standards to Restrain and Guide Decision–Makers *Should Not* Be Weakened, 48 Me.L.Rev. 49 (1996).

2. See also discussion of delegation problem with respect to variances, supra § 5.16.

3. Tandem Holding Corp. v. Board of Zoning Appeals of the Town of Hempstead, 43 N.Y.2d 801, 802, 373 N.E.2d 282, 284, 402 N.Y.S.2d 388, 389 (1977).

public interest," a court may invalidate the grant as an unlawful delegation of legislative power to an administrative body.[4] Under such a standard, a court may see the legislative body as abdicating to an administrative body the ultimate question of public interest that the legislature is to decide for itself. An ordinance that requires the board to find that the use "will not adversely affect the value of adjacent property" is more likely to be upheld.[5] The specific focus on value of the adjacent area is narrower and less subjective than a broad charge to "determine the public interest."

For many courts the standards can be vague. In Kotrich v. County of Du Page,[6] the ordinance provided for a limited number of special uses including public outdoor recreation centers in single-family zones. The county allowed special permits "for the location of special classes of uses which are deemed desirable for the public welfare within a given district or districts, but which are potentially incompatible with typical uses herein permitted within them * * * ."[7] The court held that language sufficient to permit a nonprofit club which included a clubhouse, swimming pool, tennis courts and parking area.[8]

Courts are inclined to uphold generalized standards.[9] To do otherwise might demand the impossible. The mere fact that the legislative body does not employ precise standards does not necessarily mean that it is simply avoiding the hard thinking necessary to establish standards which anticipate many situations. Predicting all types of problems that may arise is difficult, if not impossible. Furthermore, an ordinance reduces discretion and curbs flexibility to the extent that it sets detailed standards.

While some flexibility is a good thing, there are limits. To the extent discretion is uncontrolled, the potential for arbitrariness increases, and due process concerns arise.[10] Washington guards against this concern by upholding general standards but putting the burden on the decisionmaking authority to justify its decision when challenged.[11]

---

4. See, e.g., Jackson v. Guilford County Board of Adjustment, 275 N.C. 155, 166 S.E.2d 78 (1969) and State ex rel. Humble Oil and Refining Co. v. Wahner, 25 Wis.2d 1, 130 N.W.2d 304 (1964), but see Town of Richmond v. Murdock, 70 Wis.2d 642, 235 N.W.2d 497 (1975).

5. See Gorham v. Town of Cape Elizabeth, 625 A.2d 898 (Me.1993).

6. 19 Ill.2d 181, 166 N.E.2d 601 (1960), appeal dismissed 364 U.S. 475, 81 S.Ct. 243, 5 L.Ed.2d 221 (1960), rehearing denied 365 U.S. 805, 81 S.Ct. 466, 5 L.Ed.2d 463 (1961), but questioned in Geneva Residential Ass'n v. City of Geneva, 77 Ill.App.3d 744, 34 Ill.Dec. 177, 397 N.E.2d 849 (1979). See also Hawkins v. County of Marin, 54 Cal.App.3d 586, 126 Cal.Rptr. 754 (1976) for a lenient view.

7. Id. at 187, 166 N.E.2d at 604.

8. See also, Tullo v. Township of Millburn, 54 N.J.Super. 483, 149 A.2d 620 (App. Div.1959); Mandelker, Delegation of Power and Function in Zoning Administration, 1963 Wash.U.L.Q. 60.

9. See Edward Kraemer & Sons, Inc. v. Sauk County Bd. of Adj., 183 Wis.2d 1, 515 N.W.2d 256, 261, n. 5 (1994) and cases cited therein.

10. For some courts, there is no property right if there is discretion. See infra § 10.12.

11. Sunderland Family Treatment Services v. City of Pasco, 127 Wash.2d 782, 903 P.2d 986, 993 (1995).

In some jurisdictions, the legislative body may issue special permits.[12] Legislative bodies often establish a dual system where they keep authority to issue special permits for uses that will have a large impact on the city, and delegate to the administrative board those special uses with lesser impact.[13] When a legislative body retains the power to issue the special permit, as in *Kotrich*, a court may review such actions with greater deference than it would accord administrative findings.[14] This is based on the recognition that since the legislative body may amend the ordinance if it likes, it makes no sense to require it to adhere to standards. Thus, guidelines in an ordinance that provided for issuance of special permits by the legislative body as long as the use met "minimum requirements adopted to promote the health, safety, morals, comfort, prosperity and general welfare of the town * * *" were held sufficient to overcome a vagueness challenge.[15]

The practice of legislative bodies deciding whether to grant special permits troubles some.[16] As Justice Klingbiel of the Illinois Supreme Court argued "it is not part of the legislative function to grant permits * * * or decide particular cases. Such activities are * * * judicial in character [and] to place them in the hands of legislative bodies * * * is to open the door completely to arbitrary government."[17] Consequently, many courts treat special permit decisions as administrative for the purposes of the standard of review regardless of the body that hears the matter.[18]

In determining whether to issue a special permit, a board is not to substitute its judgment for the legislative judgment and is not to impose

---

12. But see Depue v. City of Clinton, 160 N.W.2d 860 (Iowa 1968) (legislative body may not retain power where state statute mandates the creation of a board of adjustment).

13. See, e.g., City of Pittsburgh Code § 993.01, described in Klein v. City of Pittsburgh, 164 Pa.Cmwlth. 521, 539, 643 A.2d 1107, 1116 (1994). Council-issued permits were labeled conditional uses and included atomic reactors, schools, and government uses. Board-issued permits were called special exceptions.

14. See Byrum v. Board of Supervisors, 217 Va. 37, 225 S.E.2d 369 (1976), but see Cole v. City Council of City of Waynesboro, 218 Va. 827, 241 S.E.2d 765 (1978); Zylka v. City of Crystal, 283 Minn. 192, 167 N.W.2d 45 (1969) (where authority to issue permit is retained by legislative body, the ordinance need not specify standards, but denial cannot be arbitrary denial). But see, Zebulon Enterprises, Inc. v. DuPage County, 146 Ill.App.3d 515, 100 Ill.Dec. 191, 496 N.E.2d 1256 (1986) (where first amendment freedoms are at issue, the review is more stringent).

15. Town of Richmond v. Murdock, 70 Wis.2d 642, 235 N.W.2d 497 (1975); City of Miami Beach v. Mr. Samuel's, Inc., 351 So.2d 719 (Fla.1977). But First Amendment considerations may lead to a requirement of more specific standards. See, e.g., MacDonald Advertising Co. v. City of Pontiac, 916 F.Supp. 644 (E.D.Mich.1995).

16. See also discussion supra § 5.9 regarding the treatment of site-specific rezonings as quasi-judicial.

17. Ward v. Village of Skokie, 26 Ill.2d 415, 186 N.E.2d 529, 533 (1962) (concurring opinion).

18. Lund v. City of Tumwater, 2 Wash. App. 750, 472 P.2d 550 (1970); State ex rel. Manchester Improvement Co. v. City of Winchester, 400 S.W.2d 47 (Mo.1966); Powers v. City of Danbury, 154 Conn. 156, 222 A.2d 337 (1966); Clements' Appeal, 2 Ohio App.2d 201, 207 N.E.2d 573 (1965); Essick v. City of Los Angeles, 34 Cal.2d 614, 213 P.2d 492 (1950); Matter of Rothstein v. County Operating Corp., 6 N.Y.2d 728, 185 N.Y.S.2d 813, 158 N.E.2d 507 (1959).

unlisted criteria.[19] If the legislative body determines that a particular use is a permissible special use, the board cannot use the inherent attributes of the use to deny a permit. In O'Hara's Appeal,[20] for example, while the ordinance listed schools as special uses, the board denied a permit due to an anticipated increase in traffic and because a school would disrupt the quiet of the residential neighborhood. The court found the reasons for the denial improper. Every special use, especially schools, would increase traffic and would disrupt, to some degree, the residential character of the area. By listing schools as special uses, the legislative body had determined that schools could locate in residential areas despite these effects. The board's denial of the permit on these grounds was inconsistent with the legislation authorization and, thus, impermissible.[21] Similarly, a court held it improper for a board to deny a permit in State ex rel. Synod of Ohio of United Lutheran Church in America v. Joseph[22] due to a "policy" of the board not to allow churches in residential zones if property in a business zone was available for such purposes. The court held that the ordinance provided for churches as a special use in residential zones, and that the permit should issue since the church met the listed standards.

As a general proposition, courts will not overturn an administrative finding unless there is a manifest abuse of discretion.[23] If a legislative body hears the permit request, a court may show even more deference.[24] Yet, where an owner is challenging a permit denial, some courts impose greater scrutiny than when a neighbor is challenging the grant of a permit. This depends on whether the court views the process as a privilege or a right. The traditional view is that there is no absolute right to a special permit.[25] The Standard State Zoning Enabling Act provides that a board "may" grant a special exception and, for some courts, this language confers significant discretion on the administrative body. A different view is that by listing a use under the special use process, the legislative body creates a presumption that the board should grant a permit unless there is strong reason to deny it.[26]

19. See West Texas Water Refiners, Inc. v. S & B Beverage Co., Inc., 915 S.W.2d 623 (Tex.App.1996).

20. 389 Pa. 35, 131 A.2d 587 (1957). See also City of Naples v. Central Plaza of Naples, 303 So.2d 423 (Fla.App.1974) (standards must be specified or they can not be applied). But see Gorham v. Town of Cape Elizabeth, 625 A.2d 898 (Me.1993).

21. But see Gorham v. Town of Cape Elizabeth, 625 A.2d 898 (Me.1993).

22. 139 Ohio St. 229, 39 N.E.2d 515 (1942).

23. See infra § 5.37.

24. Id.

25. L & M Realty v. Village of Millbrook Planning Bd., 207 A.D.2d 346, 615 N.Y.S.2d 434 (1994); Tandem Holding Corp. v. Board of Zoning Appeals of the Town of Hempstead, 43 N.Y.2d 801, 373 N.E.2d 282, 402 N.Y.S.2d 388 (1977); Gulf Oil Corp. v. Board of Appeals of Town of Framingham, 355 Mass. 275, 244 N.E.2d 311 (1969).

26. Keiger v. Winston–Salem Bd. of Adjustment, 278 N.C. 17, 178 S.E.2d 616 (1971); Archdiocese of Portland v. County of Washington, 254 Or. 77, 458 P.2d 682 (1969); Harts Book Stores, Inc. v. City of Raleigh, 53 N.C.App. 753, 281 S.E.2d 761 (1981).

§ 5.26 Conditions

As with variances, boards can condition special permits. The ordinance may list specific conditions, but it may expressly confer the authority to impose additional conditions under more general language. Alternatively, a court may imply the authority from the nature of the special permit.[1] The Standard Zoning Enabling Act provides for "appropriate conditions and safeguards."[2]

In Montgomery County v. Mossburg,[3] the ordinance allowed special permits if the use was compatible with the general development plan for the neighborhood, would not adversely affect the health and safety of residents in the area and would not be detrimental to development of adjacent properties or the general neighborhood. The court held such language sufficient to justify a condition imposing early closing hours on a special permit to expand a nonconforming restaurant. In Whittaker & Gooding Co. v. Scio Township,[4] the court upheld a five-year time limit on the operation of gravel removal operation on the grounds that the community had a right to limit the activity to a definite period. Other common conditions include off-street parking, minimum acreage, access, and landscaping.

Conditions must relate to the use allowed by the permit.[5] Thus, a condition requiring the recipient of a special permit to dedicate land for a public road and pay to build the road was held invalid where the special permittee's use of the land did not generate the traffic problem to be addressed by the condition.[6] If courts see issuance of a permit as a privilege rather than a right, they allow greater discretion. As a result, even if the validity of conditions is doubtful, the courts may estop an owner who accepts the special permit with conditions from a later attack on the conditions.[7]

An ordinance may require a board to impose conditions. For example, in Chambers v. Zoning Board of Adjustment,[8] the property owner applied for a permit to construct a housing project. The ordinance authorized a permit if no on-site garage or other satisfactory automobile storage space was provided. The board waived the condition on the

---

§ 5.26

1. Pearson v. Shoemaker, 25 Misc.2d 591, 202 N.Y.S.2d 779 (1960).

2. Section 7, Standard State Zoning Enabling Act (1926).

3. 228 Md. 555, 180 A.2d 851 (1962).

4. 122 Mich.App. 538, 332 N.W.2d 527 (1983), but see Room & Board Homes and Family Care Homes v. Gribbs, 67 Mich.App. 381, 241 N.W.2d 216 (1976) (five year limit on group home held invalid).

5. See Steuben County v. National Serv–All, Inc., 556 N.E.2d 1354 (Ind.App. 1990) (condition attached to landfill that permit would be revoked if county ordinance regulating the disposal of solid waste were violated was held to be a valid zoning

condition, and not an improper effort of the zoning board to control the waste disposal business). At a minimum, the condition must relate to the police power. See Cupp v. Board of Supervisors of Fairfax County, 227 Va. 580, 318 S.E.2d 407 (1984).

6. Cupp v. Board of Supervisors of Fairfax County, 227 Va. 580, 318 S.E.2d 407 (1984).

7. Convent of Sisters of St. Joseph v. Winston–Salem, 243 N.C. 316, 90 S.E.2d 879 (1956); River Birch Assoc. v. City of Raleigh, 326 N.C. 100, 388 S.E.2d 538 (1990).

8. 250 N.C. 194, 108 S.E.2d 211 (1959).

ground that street parking was adequate, but the court held the waiver improper since the ordinance gave the board no discretion to waive the condition.

VI. VESTED RIGHTS AND DEVELOPMENT AGREEMENTS

§ 5.27 The Vesting Issue

When land use controls change, they may adversely affect development proposals in the permit processing mill if the municipality applies the new law to them. When challenges arise about what development rights exist, the traditional rule is that a court applies the law that exists at the time of its decision.[1] This, of course, will be the new law, which the municipality will have enacted by the time the challenge reaches the court. Knowing this, developers, fearing potentially more restrictive laws or hearing of such municipal plans, may seek permits and build quickly pursuant to existing law. If successful, the doctrine of nonconforming uses will protect them.[2]

This scenario sets off a "race of diligence"[3] between the municipality seeking to change the law and the developer seeking to build. Despite the traditional rule, courts may refuse application of a new law based on considerations of fairness or equity. Thus, even short of establishing a nonconforming use by completing a project, at some point it will be too late for the government to change the rules of the game. Determining the point in time when a project is far enough along to acquire immunity from changing laws is the subject of the law of vested rights and estoppel.[4]

The vested rights doctrine is a common law rule developed from, or explainable by reference to, the due process clause of the Fourteenth

§ 5.27

1. People ex rel. Eitel v. Lindheimer, 371 Ill. 367, 21 N.E.2d 318 (1939); Sunny Slope Water Co. v. City of Pasadena, 1 Cal.2d 87, 33 P.2d 672, 674 (1934); Town of Longboat Key v. Lands End, Ltd., 433 So.2d 574 (Fla.App.1983); Alscot Investing Corp. v. Incorporated Village of Rockville Centre, 64 N.Y.2d 921, 488 N.Y.S.2d 629, 477 N.E.2d 1083 (1985). See also County of Kauai v. Pacific Standard Life Ins. Co., 65 Haw. 318, 653 P.2d 766 (1982), noting the traditional rule that permits can be revoked pursuant to newly passed ordinances.

2. Zoning changes do not apply to uses lawfully in existence at the time a change becomes effective. See supra § 4.31.

3. Downham v. City Council of Alexandria, 58 F.2d 784, 788 (E.D.Va.1932).

4. See generally Grayson P. Hanes, On Vested Rights to Land Use and Development, 46 Wash. & Lee L.Rev. 373 (1989);

Morgan R. Bentley, Note, Effects of Equitable Estoppel and Substantial Deviations to Vested Rights in DRI Projects: A New Approach, 43 Fla.L.Rev. 767 (1991); David G. Heeter, Zoning Estoppel: Application of the Principles of Equitable Estoppel and Vested Rights to Zoning Disputes, 1971 Urban L.Ann. 63; Charles Siemon, Wendy Larsen, and Douglas R. Porter, Vested Rights: Balancing Public and Private Development Expectations 31 (1982); David L. Callies, Nukolii and Vested Rights, 36 Land Use L. & Zoning Dig. 14 (1983); Benjamin Kudo, Nukolii: Private Development Rights and the Public Interest, 16 Urb. Law. 279 (1984); Donald G. Hagman, Estoppel and Vesting in the Age of Multi–Land Use Permits, 11 SW.U.L.Rev. 545, 571–575 (1979); Thomas E. Roberts, Interim Development Controls, 3 Zoning and Land Use Controls, Ch. 22 (Rohan ed.1989).

Amendment.[5] Government cannot divest property rights arbitrarily, and at some point in the development process a developer's right to proceed achieves constitutional protection. The main focus of vested rights is on the actions of the developer.[6] Under the majority rule to acquire a vested right, and therefore immunity from a newly enacted law, a developer must (1) engage in substantial expenditures (2) in good faith reliance (3) on a validly issued building permit.[7]

The doctrine of estoppel, drawn from equity, focuses on instances when, due to the nature of the government conduct, applying a newly enacted law to a developer would be inequitable. A common statement of the rule is that courts will estop government from applying a new law when a developer (1) makes a substantial change of position or engages in substantial expenditures (2) in good faith reliance (3) upon some act or omission of the government (4) so that applying a new law would be highly inequitable.[8]

While the lineage and focus of vested rights and estoppel doctrines differ, a comparison of the elements listed above shows them to be quite similar. The labels are, in fact, often used interchangeably[9] so that efforts to keep the doctrines separate may be futile. It is also typically unnecessary to distinguish between them since fairness is the premise of both and since the results of the tests are most always the same.[10] In some instances, estoppel may provide relief that vested rights would not since estoppel does not necessarily require a permit.[11] In the material that follows, we treat cases involving reliance on permits under the vested rights label (though courts in some of the cases use estoppel terminology along with or instead of vested rights). In a separate section entitled estoppel we cover cases that turn on conduct not based on a permit.

§ 5.28 Vesting Under Building Permits

In most states, a building permit standing alone does not vest a right to continue if the law changes. Under the majority rule to acquire a vested right a developer must (1) show substantial expenditures, obligations, or harm (2) incurred in good faith reliance (3) on a validly issued building permit.[1] If the authorities have issued a permit, they may

---

5. Town of Paradise Valley v. Gulf Leisure Corp., 27 Ariz.App. 600, 557 P.2d 532 (1976).

6. To the extent that the issue is treated as one of due process, the strength of the public interest must be considered. See infra § 10.12.

7. Avco Community Developers, Inc. v. South Coast Regional Comm'n, 17 Cal.3d 785, 553 P.2d 546, 132 Cal.Rptr. 386 (1976).

8. Florida Companies v. Orange County, 411 So.2d 1008, 1010 (Fla.App.1982).

9. See, e.g., County of Kauai v. Pacific Standard Life Ins. Co., 65 Haw. 318, 653 P.2d 766 (1982); Miller v. Board of Adj., 521 A.2d 642 (Del.Super.1986).

10. Heeter, supra note 4, at 64–65.

11. State ex rel. Humble Oil v. Wahner 25 Wis.2d 1, 130 N.W.2d 304 (1964).

§ 5.28

1. See Avco Community Developers, Inc. v. South Coast Regional Comm'n, 17 Cal.3d 785, 132 Cal.Rptr. 386, 553 P.2d 546 (1976).

revoke it if the zoning classification changes before the developer incurs substantial obligations under the permit.

A. Substantial Reliance

Developers must show substantial reliance on a permit. In considering expenses or harm, most courts do not consider the purchase price of the land since its use to vest rights would allow the developer to freeze zoning.[2] Where courts use the purchase price, it is only one factor.[3] While some courts require that actual construction commence,[4] many courts consider other reliance as well, such as contract obligations.[5] The harm that would follow if compliance with the new law is required must be a "serious loss, rendering the improvements essentially valueless."[6] Rodee v. Lee[7] illustrates the basic rule and its rationale. In that case, while applications for building permits were pending, the city changed the ordinance to require 100 rather than 50 foot widths for lots in the area. Because of the shape of the property involved, the developer could develop only four rather than eleven house sites. However, the property owner showed no hardship greater than anyone else in having his plans disrupted by the new ordinance, and the court held him bound by it.

People ex rel. National Bank of Austin v. County of Cook[8] illustrates the kind of expenditures that are necessary. The developer obtained permission to construct multi-family dwellings. A tight money market delayed construction. Because of local opposition, the county rezoned the property to single family use. The evidence showed that employees of the developer, an architectural designer and supervisor, spent considerable time thinking about the development of the apartment complex and making preliminary sketches. The wages paid to these employees for the time spent on the project amounted to $1600. The court held that such evidence did not show the expenditure of substantial sums or the incurring of substantial obligations and did not show reliance on the permits.[9]

Courts measure substantial reliance in various ways. Many courts hold that a landowner must have invested a certain amount of money in

---

2. See William C. Haas, Inc. v. City of San Francisco, 605 F.2d 1117 (9th Cir. 1979); Gackler Land Co., Inc. v. Yankee Springs Twp., 427 Mich. 562, 398 N.W.2d 393, n. 4 (1986).

3. Tremarco Corp. v. Garzio, 32 N.J. 448, 161 A.2d 241 (1960).

4. Sykesville v. West Shore Communications, Inc., 110 Md.App. 300, 677 A.2d 102 (1996) (construction must be substantial and visible); Thompson v. Department of Envtl. Conservation, 130 Misc.2d 123, 495 N.Y.S.2d 107 (Sup.Ct.1985).

5. Hussey v. Town of Barrington, 135 N.H. 227, 604 A.2d 82 (1992); Town of Hillsborough v. Smith, 276 N.C. 48, 170 S.E.2d 904 (1969); Whitehead Oil v. City of Lincoln, 245 Neb. 660, 515 N.W.2d 390

(1994); State ex rel. Schroedel v. Pagels, 257 Wis. 376, 43 N.W.2d 349 (1950); Largo v. Imperial Homes Corp. 309 So.2d 571 (Fla.App.1975).

6. Town of Orangetown v. Magee, 88 N.Y.2d 41, 665 N.E.2d 1061, 643 N.Y.S.2d 21, 25 (1996).

7. 14 N.J.Super. 188, 81 A.2d 517 (1951).

8. 56 Ill.App.2d 436, 206 N.E.2d 441 (1965). See also O'Hare Internat'l Bank v. Zoning Bd., 37 Ill.App.3d 1037, 347 N.E.2d 440 (1976).

9. Cf. Town of Hillsborough v. Smith, 276 N.C. 48, 170 S.E.2d 904 (1969); Application of Campsites Unlimited, 287 N.C. 493, 215 S.E.2d 73 (1975).

the project. To avoid difficulty in setting an arbitrary amount, some courts adopt a ratio approach, and require that expenditures already made be substantial compared with the total project cost. In Clackamas County v. Holmes,[10] however, the court stated that though a developer must have incurred substantial costs toward completion of the job, vesting of rights should not be based solely on the ratio of expenditures to total project cost. The defendants had taken actions to ready the property for chicken farming, but the county rezoned the property to residential use before they could secure a building permit. The court found that the type of preparations made by a property owner should be considered. It concluded that a right to proceed had vested since the defendants had acted in good faith and since the expenses incurred were substantial and directly related to its intended uses.

B. Good Faith

Developers must make expenditures in good faith.[11] Engaging in expenditures or incurring obligations when aware of the fact that an ordinance that would prohibit the use is pending and that adoption is imminent is in bad faith.[12] While acts made in "unseemly haste" just before the effective date of an ordinance have been found in bad faith,[13] mere knowledge that the municipality might make a change has been held insufficient.[14] If it is shown that the developer misled the government or acted in reliance on a permit known to be invalid, no rights will vest.[15]

If the city or the neighbors take an appeal alleging invalidity of the permit or the underlying law on which it is based, expenses incurred during appeal will not be in good faith.[16] Waiting for the appeal time to run its course may place a serious strain on the economic viability of a project, but a developer who proceeds during appeal does so at risk.[17] One court suggests that neighbors protesting a permit who plan to appeal take steps to assure notice such as filing of lis pendens, quick

---

10. 265 Or. 193, 508 P.2d 190 (1973). Cf. Webber v. County of Clackamas, 42 Or.App. 151, 600 P.2d 448 (1979).

11. Sakolsky v. Coral Gables, 151 So.2d 433 (Fla.1963). See also Hollywood Beach Hotel Co. v. Hollywood, 329 So.2d 10 (Fla.1976).

12. Town of Hillsborough v. Smith, 276 N.C. 48, 170 S.E.2d 904 (1969); Von Bokel v. City of Breese, 100 Ill.App.3d 956, 56 Ill.Dec. 242, 427 N.E.2d 322 (1981); Boron Oil Co. v. Kimple, 445 Pa. 327, 284 A.2d 744 (1971).

13. Billings v. California Coastal Comm'n, 103 Cal.App.3d 729, 163 Cal.Rptr. 288 (1980).

14. Application of Campsites Unlimited, 287 N.C. 493, 215 S.E.2d 73 (1975); Miller v. Dassler, 155 N.Y.S.2d 975, 979 (Sup.Ct.1956).

15. See City of Coral Gables v. Puiggros, 376 So.2d 281 (Fla.App.1979); Kirk v. Village of Hillcrest, 15 Ill.App.3d 415, 304 N.E.2d 452 (1973). See also discussion of illegal permits infra this section.

16. Godrey v. Zoning Board of Adj., 317 N.C. 51, 344 S.E.2d 272 (1986) (developer had knowledge of suit); Torello v. Board of Zoning App. of New Haven, 127 Conn. 307, 16 A.2d 591 (1940) (developer bound despite lack of notice). See also Smith v. Building Comm'r, 367 Mass. 765, 328 N.E.2d 866, 870 (1975), noting that amendment adopted during litigation over a permit will apply if the permit is determined to be invalid. But see Crow v. Board of Adj., 227 Iowa 324, 288 N.W. 145 (1939), discussed infra this section.

17. See Charles Siemon, Wendy Larsen, and Douglas R. Porter, Vested Rights: Balancing Public and Private Development Expectations 31 (1982).

service of process, and injunctive relief.[18] The stalled developer might attempt to protect itself by seeking to have the neighbors post a bond.

A similar problem may arise if voters seek a referendum to amend the law on which a permit is based before the developer incurs substantial expenses. In County of Kauai v. Pacific Standard Life Insurance Co.,[19] the court said that a referendum process initiated after final discretionary action by the government would not alter a vested right, but that permits issued after the referendum process is started are not safe to rely on. When voters get into the act, the referendum vote becomes the final discretionary act. This is apparently true even if the election is a year or two away. Concerns over long-term delay and the court's use of the final discretionary action rule,[20] have prompted criticism of the Hawaii decision, widely known as the *Nukolii* case.[21]

C. Permit Requirement

Avco Community Developers, Inc. v. South Coast Regional Commission,[22] illustrates the permit requirement. Developer Avco owned some 8000 acres upon which it planned to construct a planned community. Developing in phases, Avco obtained permits from the county to subdivide and grade 74 acres. As Avco was in the process of installing storm drains, streets, and other utilities, and had spent or incurred liabilities of $2.7 million, the state's coastal act became effective, requiring that it obtain a permit from the coastal commission. Seeking to avoid this new regulatory hoop, Avco claimed a vested right to proceed. The court held against the developer since it had not obtained a final building permit from the county by the date the new permit requirement became effective. The court conceded that there might be instances when something less than a final building permit would vest rights, but here the county had not yet approved even a detailed building project.

Some courts have relaxed the demand for a final building permit by vesting rights upon the happening of the final discretionary act.[23] In that event, the label no longer controls. In several cases the issuance of a special permit has been found to vest rights although the city had not yet issued a building permit.[24] Approval of a site plan, seen by some as

---

18. Petty v. Barrentine, 594 S.W.2d 903, 905 (Ky.App.1980), discussed Siemon, Larsen, and Porter, supra note 17.

19. 65 Haw. 318, 653 P.2d 766 (1982).

20. See discussion of final discretionary action rule infra at subsection C.

21. For criticism of the case, see David L. Callies, Nukolii and Vested Rights, 36 Land Use L. & Zoning Dig. 14 (1983); Benjamin Kudo, Nukolii: Private Development Rights and the Public Interest, 16 Urb.Law. 279 (1984).

22. 17 Cal.3d 785, 132 Cal.Rptr. 386, 553 P.2d 546 (1976), cert. denied 429 U.S. 1083, 97 S.Ct. 1089, 51 L.Ed.2d 529 (1977); Carty v. Ojai, 77 Cal.App.3d 329, 143 Cal. Rptr. 506 (1978); Colonial Inv. Co. v. Lea-

wood, 7 Kan.App.2d 660, 646 P.2d 1149 (1982). See generally Donald G. Hagman, The Vesting Issue: Rights of Fetal Development vis-a-vis Abortions of Public Whimsey, 7 Envt'l.L. 519 (1977).

23. County of Kauai v. Pacific Standard Life Ins. Co., 65 Haw. 318, 653 P.2d 766 (1982); Milcrest Corp. v. Clackamas County, 59 Or.App. 177, 650 P.2d 963 (1982).

24. Town of Stephens City v. Russell, 241 Va. 160, 399 S.E.2d 814 (1991); Town of Paradise Valley v. Gulf Leisure Corp., 27 Ariz.App. 600, 557 P.2d 532 (1976).

having "virtually replaced the building permit as the most vital document in the development process,"[25] also has been found sufficient.

D. *Right to Obtain Permit Based on Existing Zoning*

There is no right to a development permit based on the zoning that existed when the developer acquired the land.[26] If a developer purchases land to build an industrial plant and the city rezones the land for residential use on the day following purchase, the developer has no right to a permit to build an industrial plant. The result is the same even if the developer applies for a permit before the zoning change occurs. If the city denies the permit because of a post-application change in zoning, the courts will not order issuance of the permit unless the zoning change was invalid.[27] Such actions will not only frustrate the development plans, but the property may be worth much less than the purchase price if the buyer paid a price based on the assumption that it could develop according to existing zoning. Thus, acquisition costs and pre-application spending must take into account the risk that development permission might not be obtained due to a future downzoning.

In some jurisdictions rights vest under the law in existence at the time of application. In such states, if the city changes the zoning after the developer applies for a permit, it cannot validly deny the permit on the basis that the application does not comply with current zoning.[28] If the authorities hold an application to permit a change in zoning, and the permit denied once the change is made, some courts will overturn the denial.[29] Other courts use a balancing test providing that an applicant is entitled to a permit based on the law in effect at the time of application unless there are countervailing compelling public interests.[30] These rules apparently do not require a showing of expenditures in reliance on a permit.[31]

E. *Municipal Good Faith*

Municipalities, like developers, must act in good faith. Some courts that otherwise follow the late-vesting majority rule make an exception if a municipality changes its law primarily to thwart a particular development.[32] Most instances of governmental bad faith are encountered where authorities drag their feet and mislead or otherwise hinder an applicant in the permitting process. If a permit is willfully withheld by deceptive

---

25. Board of Supervisors v. Medical Structures, Inc., 213 Va. 355, 192 S.E.2d 799, 801 (1972).

26. Town of Stephens City v. Russell, 241 Va. 160, 399 S.E.2d 814 (1991); Western Land Equities, Inc. v. City of Logan, 617 P.2d 388, 391 (Utah 1980) (a landowner has no vested right in existing or anticipated zoning).

27. See, e.g., Smith v. Winhall Planning Comm'n, 140 Vt. 178, 436 A.2d 760 (1981).

28. West Main Assocs. v. City of Bellevue, 106 Wash.2d 47, 720 P.2d 782 (1986).

29. Gibson v. Oberlin, 171 Ohio St. 1, 167 N.E.2d 651 (1960); State ex rel. Mumma v. Stansberry, 5 Ohio App.2d 191, 214 N.E.2d 684 (1964); Dade County v. Jason, 278 So.2d 311 (Fla.App.1973).

30. Western Land Equities, Inc. v. Logan, 617 P.2d 388 (Utah 1980).

31. See Zaremba Dev. Co. v. City of Fairview Park, 84 Ohio App.3d 174, 616 N.E.2d 569 (1992).

32. See, e.g., Smith v. Winhall Planning Comm'n, 140 Vt. 178, 436 A.2d 760 (1981).

conduct, a new intervening law will not apply.[33] Courts do not, however, universally treat action taken in response to a particular development proposal as bad faith. If a court finds that protection of the general welfare motivated a new law, the court will apply the law even where permit issuance triggered its passage.[34]

F. Pending Ordinance Rule

Under the pending ordinance rule, if a change in the law is pending at the time of application, no rights may vest.[35] This is clearly true in a majority rule state since time of application is not a vesting event. Nevertheless, even in jurisdictions inclined to vest rights earlier, a number uphold denial of a permit based on a later-adopted ordinance that was pending at the time the developer filed the application.[36] If the government has announced an intent to consider a change, courts following the rule recognize that no sound justification exists to confer benefits on a property owner who has not yet incurred obligations based on existing law, particularly where the government set in motion changes in the law before the developer's appearance on the scene. If coupled with the power to divest rights due to serious public health or safety concerns, the pending ordinance rule is a compromise between fairness to developers and the need to protect the public interest.[37]

G. Moratoria to Protect Planning Process

In a jurisdiction with an early vesting rule, the proper course for government contemplating a change but fearing that uses will vest before its change becomes effective is to pass an interim ordinance freezing development.[38] Protection of the planning process requires this for without it developers could defeat the plan before it begins by inconsistent vested uses. In some jurisdictions, however, authority to impose a freeze or moratorium on development may be questionable.[39]

33. Figgie Int'l v. Town of Huntington, 203 A.D.2d 416, 610 N.Y.S.2d 563 (1994); Pokoik v. Silsdorf, 40 N.Y.2d 769, 358 N.E.2d 874, 390 N.Y.S.2d 49 (1976); Dubow v. Ross, 254 App.Div. 706, 3 N.Y.S.2d 862 (1938).

34. Manalapan Realty v. Township Comm., 140 N.J. 366, 658 A.2d 1230 (1995); Spector v. Building Inspector, 250 Mass. 63, 145 N.E. 265, 268 (1924) (no evidence of "unworthy motives" by the city); Franchise Realty Interstate Corp. v. City of Detroit, 368 Mich. 276, 118 N.W.2d 258 (1962); Almquist v. Town of Marshan, 308 Minn. 52, 245 N.W.2d 819 (1976).

35. A. Copeland Enterprises, Inc. v. City of New Orleans, 372 So.2d 764 (La. App.1979); Crittenden v. Hasser, 41 Colo. App. 235, 585 P.2d 928 (1978).

36. See Sherman v. Reavis, 273 S.C. 542, 257 S.E.2d 735 (1979); A. J. Aberman, Inc. v. City of New Kensington, 377 Pa. 520, 105 A.2d 586 (1954) (applicant has constructive notice of pending change);

Smith v. City of Clearwater, 383 So.2d 681 (Fla.App.1980), cert. denied, 403 So.2d 407 (Fla.1981); Ben Lomond, Inc. v. City of Idaho Falls, 92 Idaho 595, 448 P.2d 209 (1968); Chicago Title & Trust Co. v. Village of Palatine, 22 Ill.App.2d 264, 160 N.E.2d 697 (1959).

37. See Donald G. Hagman, Estoppel and Vesting in the Age of Multi–Land Use Permits, 11 SW.U.L.Rev. 545, 571–575 (1979).

38. See Williams v. Griffin, 91 Nev. 743, 542 P.2d 732 (Nev.1975); State ex rel. SCA Chem. Waste Serv. v. Konigsberg, 636 S.W.2d 430 (Tenn.1982).

39. See discussion infra § 9.5. See also Thomas E. Roberts, Interim Development Controls, 3 Zoning and Land Use Controls, Ch. 22 at §§ 22.02 and 22.04 (Rohan ed.1989) on the relationship of vested rights and interim controls.

Even if unable formally to impose a freeze, administrative action by a municipality to delay approval, while new studies are completed and the new law enacted, is likely to prevent vesting in most states if the action is not deceptive.[40]

H. Illegally Issued Permit

As a general proposition, no rights will vest pursuant to an illegally issued permit.[41] However, the rule is not ironclad. While courts are reluctant to let the public interest suffer, as it presumably will if actions conceded to be illegal are allowed to persist, the strength of the public interest may matter. For example, a court is not likely to prevent a city from enforcing a flood plain ordinance where concerns with public safety are at issue, but enforcement of an aesthetics-based ordinance may not be as compelling.[42] Further, though exceptional circumstances must exist, there are numerous cases where rights in illegal permits have been found to have vested or municipalities have been estopped.[43] The length of time that the city permits the illegal action to continue[44] and the clarity of the illegality may make a difference.

Where the development is clearly illegal, the courts are not inclined to favor the violator. For example, in City of Raleigh v. Fisher,[45] the city had allowed the defendant to conduct a bakery business in a house in a residential zone for several years. The building inspector had issued several permits for additions and improvements with knowledge that the use violated the zoning ordinance. The city had also collected a privilege license tax for eight years. When the city decided to enforce its ordinance, the court upheld the city. If the result were otherwise, an employee of the city could deliberately misconstrue the law, frustrating public policy.

An applicant for a permit cannot blindly rely on the statements or actions of government officials that authorize a use. Everyone is presumed to know the extent of power of local officials,[46] and courts impose an obligation on an applicant to exercise reasonable diligence to find out whether an authorized action is legal.[47] In Parkview Associates v. City of New York,[48] a city official issued a permit allowing a 31–story building

---

40. See Roberts, Id. at § 22.04[2][b].

41. Garnick v. Zoning Hearing Bd., 58 Pa.Cmwlth. 92, 427 A.2d 310, 312 (1981); Miller v. Board of Adj., 521 A.2d 642 (Del.Super.1986).

42. See Hansel v. City of Keene, 138 N.H. 99, 634 A.2d 1351, 1354 (1993).

43. Cases dealing with illegal permits often speak of estoppel, as opposed to vested rights, as the basis for examining whether to allow revocation. The result, regardless of label, is the same.

44. See cases discussing estoppel infra § 5.29.

45. 232 N.C. 629, 61 S.E.2d 897 (1950). See also Winston–Salem v. Hoots Concrete

Co., 47 N.C.App. 405, 267 S.E.2d 569 (1980), review denied 301 N.C. 234, 283 S.E.2d 131 (1980); Board of County Comm'rs v. Echternacht, 194 Colo. 311, 572 P.2d 143 (1977); Harrell v. Lewiston, 95 Idaho 243, 506 P.2d 470 (1973).

46. Miller v. Board of Adj., 521 A.2d 642 (Del.Super.1986).

47. See Lehman v. City of Louisville, 967 F.2d 1474 (10th Cir.1992). Cf. Jones v. City of Aurora, 772 P.2d 645 (Colo.App. 1988).

48. Parkview Assocs. v. City of New York, 71 N.Y.2d 274, 519 N.E.2d 1372, 525 N.Y.S.2d 176 (1988).

based on an incorrect reading of the zoning map, and the building was constructed. The proper height control, however, limited the building to nineteen stories. Noting that only the "rarest cases"[49] justify estoppel against a city, the court held that an applicant cannot assume the city officials know or are properly following the law. If "reasonable diligence by a good-faith inquirer would have disclosed the facts and the bureaucratic error,"[50] no defense exists.[51] The court sustained a demolition order and the builder removed the top twelve stories.[52]

Some courts use a doctrine of "honest error" to preclude permit revocation in situations involving a good faith mistake by an official, made within the apparent scope of authority.[53] Such cases emphasize that a property owner seeking a permit is entitled to rely on an official's decisions that are incorrect but fairly debatable.[54]

If the "illegality" of the permit was ambiguous when granted and the applicant proceeded in good faith, some courts have refused to allow a city to revoke the permit. In Crow v. Board of Adjustment of Iowa City,[55] for example, after receiving a supporting opinion from the city attorney, the building inspector issued a permit to a property owner to build a veterinary hospital in a district that permitted hospitals. The property owner purchased a lot, demolished a house on it, began excavating, purchased materials and entered into contracts. Objecting citizens appealed the issuance of the permit to the board of adjustment, which ruled that hospitals did not include veterinary hospitals. The court held that the ordinance was ambiguous and that in such a case the issuance of the permit conferred a vested right where the permittee had materially changed his position.[56]

49. 525 N.Y.S.2d at 176.

50. 525 N.Y.S.2d at 176.

51. Turco v. Town of Barnstead, 136 N.H. 256, 615 A.2d 1237 (1992) (Concurring with rule of *Parkview*, but reasonably diligent inquiry would not have disclosed critical facts); Healey v. Town of New Durham, 140 N.H. 232, 665 A.2d 360 (1995) (inquiry would have revealed lack of authority of official to make representations).

52. See Cutting a Building Down to Size, Very Carefully, N.Y. Times, Oct. 1, 1992, p. 3B.

53. City of Berea v. Wren, 818 S.W.2d 274 (Ky.App.1991) (court refused to allow revocation where map and ordinance conflicted leading to wrongful permit issuance). See also Rosbar Co. v. Board of Appeals, 67 A.D.2d 709, 412 N.Y.S.2d 641 (1979); Jantausch v. Borough of Verona, 41 N.J.Super. 89, 124 A.2d 14 (1956); Town of Highland Park v. Marshall, 235 S.W.2d 658 (Tex.Civ. App.1950); Commonwealth, Department of

Envtl. Resources v. Flynn, 21 Pa.Cmwlth. 264, 344 A.2d 720 (1975); Permanent Fin. Corp. v. Montgomery County, 308 Md. 239, 518 A.2d 123 (1986).

54. Jantausch v. Borough of Verona, 41 N.J.Super. 89, 124 A.2d 14 (1956) (though one cannot rely "where no semblance of compliance").

55. 227 Iowa 324, 288 N.W. 145 (1939).

56. Similarly in Township of Pittsfield v. Malcolm, 375 Mich. 135, 134 N.W.2d 166 (1965), a permit was issued for a dog kennel on the ground that it was a use similar in character to other uses permitted in the zone, and the ordinance provided that uses similar in character could be permitted. The court held that a dog kennel was clearly not similar to other uses permitted by the ordinance, but $45,000 had been spent building the kennel. See also Grand Haven Township v. Brummel, 87 Mich.App. 442, 274 N.W.2d 814 (1978). Cf. Harrell v. Lewiston, 95 Idaho 243, 506 P.2d 470 (1973).

I. Municipal Liability for Wrongfully Issued Permits

While a property owner may fail to establish a vested right in an improperly issued permit, all is not necessarily lost for a property owner may have a damage action in tort for the loss sustained because of the wrongfully issued permit. Municipalities are generally immune for liability in tort for governmental or discretionary actions, but exceptions exist. In L.A. Ray Realty v. Town of Cumberland,[57] for example, the court held that the town's adoption and enforcement of an illegal ordinance constituted intentional interference with a developer's contractual relations. The town lost its governmental immunity because the court found that its actions were egregious. However, since the actions were nonetheless found governmental, liability was capped at $100,000 under the state tort liability act. Government may also be liable for mere negligence where its actions are ministerial.[58]

J. Zoning Change Invalid

An alternative argument in dealing with a vested rights issue is to focus on the validity of the later-enacted downzoning. A court may preserve the rights of the permittee by holding the rezoning invalid as applied.[59]

§ 5.29 Estoppel

Courts generally say that estoppel requires that a landowner or developer (1) make a substantial change of position or engage in substantial expenditures (2) in good faith reliance (3) upon some act or omission of the government (4) so that applying a new law would be highly inequitable.[1] When the public health, safety and welfare are at stake, successfully asserting such a claim is difficult. Courts are reluctant to leave the public unprotected due to an error by a governmental body or official.[2] Consequently, courts usually apply the elements of estoppel from a government-protective perspective.

As noted above,[3] some confusion exits as to whether estoppel differs from vested rights, and if so how. In several cases discussed in the prior section on vested rights, the courts referred to estoppel as the, or a, basis for decision. Those cases, however, involved complaints of reliance on permits. The cases discussed in this section deal with instances where government conduct other than a valid permit was the focus of concern. Here estoppel is the only argument available.

In Town of Largo v. Imperial Homes Corp.,[4] the developer bought two parcels of property relying on assurances that the town would zone

---

57. 698 A.2d 202 (R.I.1997). See also Alger v. City of Mukilteo, 107 Wash.2d 541, 730 P.2d 1333 (1987) (city held liable for $1.4 million for maliciously revoking permit); Prince George's County v. Blumberg, 44 Md.App. 79, 407 A.2d 1151 (1979).

58. Snyder v. City of Minneapolis, 441 N.W.2d 781 (Minn.1989).

59. Gruber v. Township of Raritan, 39 N.J. 1, 186 A.2d 489 (1962).

§ 5.29

1. Florida Companies v. Orange County, 411 So.2d 1008, 1010 (Fla.App.1982).

2. Healey v. Town of New Durham, 140 N.H. 232, 665 A.2d 360, 367 (1995).

3. See supra § 5.27.

4. 309 So.2d 571 (Fla.App.1975), Jones v. U.S. Steel Credit Corp., 382 So.2d 48 (Fla.App.1979), cert. denied 389 So.2d 1111 (1980). Cf. Pasco County v. Tampa Dev.

to allow construction of multi-family dwellings. Of two tracts purchased on such assurances, one tract was zoned for multi-family use, and the other left unzoned, permitting any use. Municipal review of the developer's master plan evoked no objections, and a planner hired by the town to study its ordinance for comprehensive amendment recommended high-density zoning for the developer's land. The town tentatively approved this proposed zoning, but because of resident objections, it ultimately zoned the parcels for the most restrictive single family use. When challenged, the town argued that the developer had not obtained a building permit thus no rights had vested. The court said a permit was not needed to estop the town, and held that the builders had a right to rely on actions of the governing body taken over a four-year period.

Some cases involve both a vested rights argument relating to permit reliance and an estoppel argument relating to other conduct.[5] Avco Community Developers, Inc. v. South Coast Regional Commission,[6] discussed above,[7] is an example. The developer lost its argument that it had a vested right to complete development pursuant to certain preliminary permit approvals since the court said it needed a final building permit. The developer then turned to estoppel. Conceding it lacked a final building permit, the developer argued that an agreement it had reached with the county called for it to sell some land to the county at below market price in return for county approval of the project. Noting that the state had approved the agreement, the developer argued that the court should estop the state from enforcing the new law. While the court read the arrangement differently, it held that the agreement as construed by the developer was unenforceable as a contracting away of the police power. It would not estop the government from enforcing the new act based on an agreement that was contrary to public policy.

Governmental tolerance of an illegal use over a long term forms the basis for many estoppel cases. A long time lapse alone, however, even when coupled with governmental notice of the illegal activity, normally will not give rise to estoppel. A developer must show some municipal action, typically the erroneous issuance of a permit. Where property was used for business purposes in a residential zone for twenty years, no estoppel arose because, while the city knew of the violation, no "active acquiescence" by the municipality existed.[8] However, where forty-four years passed without enforcement and where the city had erroneously issued a building permit twenty-seven years earlier, the city was es-

Corp., 364 So.2d 850 (Fla.App.1978); Town of West Hartford v. Rechel, 190 Conn. 114, 459 A.2d 1015 (1983).

5. See, e.g., Healey v. Town of New Durham, 140 N.H. 232, 665 A.2d 360 (1995).

6. 17 Cal.3d 785, 132 Cal.Rptr. 386, 553 P.2d 546 (1976), appeal dismissed, cert. denied 429 U.S. 1083, 97 S.Ct. 1089, 51 L.Ed.2d 529 (1977); Carty v. Ojai, 77 Cal.

App.3d 329, 143 Cal.Rptr. 506 (1978); Colonial Inv. Co. v. Leawood, 7 Kan.App.2d 660, 646 P.2d 1149 (1982). See generally Donald G. Hagman, The Vesting Issue: Rights of Fetal Development vis-a-vis Abortions of Public Whimsey, 7 Envt'l.L. 519 (1977).

7. See supra § 5.28.

8. In re Appeal of Crawford, 110 Pa. Cmwlth. 51, 531 A.2d 865 (1987).

topped.[9] Even two years of inaction, coupled with express permission, was sufficient for estoppel in one case.[10] Generally, the statute of limitations is not available as a defense since the illegal use is a "continuing crime."[11]

§ 5.30 Statutory Solutions to Uncertainty

The case-by-case, equitable determinations of vested rights and estoppel are difficult to reconcile and result in great uncertainty, particularly for the development community. Large-scale development that takes a long time to get underway and complete has not fared well under the common law vesting rule. Unfortunately, municipal planning is often inadequate or out of date, and the ill-advised nature of the present controls only comes to the attention of governmental decision makers when someone applies for developmental permission. The late-vesting common law rule affords government a chance to correct its mistakes by changing the rules and then denying the developmental permission.

Some see the common law rule as anti-development and have called for change. Professor Hagman, in proposing legislation on the subject, complained that the rule is "excessively protective of the right of government to change its mind,"[1] that this "luxury of irresponsibility"[2] chilled desirable development, and that the government ought to "learn to play fair."[3] As noted,[4] some courts have changed the common law rule to be more developer protective. Legislatures also increasingly have stepped into the fray to pass statutes that enhance developer rights.

The scope of protective statutes varies. Under a Pennsylvania statute, "no subsequent change or amendment in the zoning, subdivision, or other governing ordinance" can be applied to adversely affect the right of one with an approved plan for five years.[5] In one case when a municipality increased water and sewer connection fees, a developer sought exemption based on the statute. The court agreed, finding the utility charges were "other governing ordinances" that the city could not apply against the developers.[6]

Massachusetts law provides that if a developer submits a subdivision plan to a planning board for approval, and gives written notice of the submission to the town clerk before the effective date of a new ordi-

---

9. Knake v. Zoning Hearing Bd., 74 Pa.Cmwlth. 265, 459 A.2d 1331 (1983). See also Boise City v. Wilkinson, 16 Idaho 150, 102 P. 148 (1909) (40 years inaction).

10. Caporali v. Ward, 89 Pa.Cmwlth. 621, 493 A.2d 791 (1985).

11. See, e.g., People v. Fletcher Gravel Co., 82 Misc.2d 22, 368 N.Y.S.2d 392 (1975). But see City of New Orleans v. Coles, 646 So.2d 475 (La.App.1994) (two year statute of limitations applied to prevent suit by city where state statute expressly applied to zoning enforcement).

§ 5.30

1. Donald G. Hagman, Estoppel and Vesting in the Age of Multi–Land Use Permits, 11 S.W.U.L.Rev. 545 (1979).

2. Donald G. Hagman, The Vesting Issue: Rights of Fetal Development vis-a-vis Abortions of Public Whimsey, 7 Envt'l.L. 519, 539 (1977).

3. Id.

4. See supra § 5.27 D.

5. Pa.Stat.Ann. tit. 53, § 10508(4)(ii).

6. Board of Comm'rs v. Toll Bros., Inc., 147 Pa.Cmwlth. 298, 607 A.2d 824 (1992).

nance, the law in effect at the time the plan was submitted governs the plan. If the board approves the plan, the same law will apply for eight years from the date of approval.[7]

Massachusetts also provides that the holder of a building permit may complete construction if the permit was granted before notice of a hearing on a subsequent zoning change was made, construction commenced within six months of issuance of the permit, and construction proceeded in good faith, continuously to completion.[8] Under the statute, the permit issued must be valid. If found invalid on appeal, the permit is void ab initio and a new zoning law applies.[9]

Colorado's Vested Property Rights Act creates a vested right in a site specific development plan. Once approved the plan is immune for three years from new zoning or initiatives that would impair the approved plan. The right, however, is subject to several exceptions. The landowner may consent to new laws, or may be compelled to do so if the government discovers natural or man-made hazards, or if the owner receives compensation for all costs and liabilities incurred after approval.[10] In Villa at Greeley, Inc. v. Hopper,[11] after the town approved a project for a pre-parole facility, the voters of the county amended the city charter to require voter approval of the location and siting of any such facility. The developer sought refuge in the act, but the court said that while the developer had a vested right, the charter amendment had divested it. All was not lost, however, since the only basis for divestment was the compensation provision, which the court found to have been impliedly used. The court remanded the case for compensation to be determined.

If a vested right statute confers immunity on one with "a building permit," a court may need to determine what "permits" qualify. A permit denominated a "zoning permit" properly issued allowing a quarry operation in a residential zone was held not to be a "building permit" in one case.[12] The statute in that case defined a building permit as one that contained a finding of compliance with the state building code, which the quarry permit lacked. Thus, the statute did not protect the holder of the quarry permit from the effect of an amendment to the code banning quarry use enacted after the permit was issued.

Generally, statutory vested rights laws do not abrogate the common law rule, which remains an alternative argument for one who does not gain protection from the statute.[13] In the above case, for example, the

7. Mass.Gen.Laws Ann. c. 40A, § 6.

8. Mass.Gen.Laws Ann. c. 40A, § 6.

9. Smith v. Building Comm'r, 367 Mass. 765, 328 N.E.2d 866, 870 (1975) (permit defect was remediable on remand and the statutory immunity continued after remediation).

10. West's Colo.Rev.Stat.Ann. § 24–68–105 (1).

11. 917 P.2d 350 (Colo.App.1996).

12. Simpson v. City of Charlotte, 115 N.C.App. 51, 443 S.E.2d 772, 775 (1994).

13. See Villa at Greeley v. Hopper, 917 P.2d 350 (Colo.App.1996) A statutory abrogation would be unconstitutional if it purported to limit rights beyond what the courts had deemed constitutionally required.

court said that the quarry permit holder was entitled to try to establish a common law right by showing good faith substantial reliance on the permit.[14]

The immunity that exists may be limited to new laws directed specifically at the development in question. Under the Colorado statute, a vested right remains subject to new laws "which are general in nature and are applicable to all property."[15] Under North Carolina's statute, an approved plan is not immune from new "overlay zoning which imposes additional requirements but does affect the allowable type or intensity of use."[16]

§ 5.31 Development Agreements

One solution to the vagaries of vested rights is the use of development agreements, which fix the rights of developers and municipalities as of a certain date and limit the power of government to apply new ordinances to approved projects.[1] Development agreements not only bring greater certainty for the developer who obtains a promise by the municipality to freeze the regulations on the site for a period of time, but they also may enhance the ability of municipalities to impose exactions and conditions.[2] Several states have passed statutes specifically enabling development agreements.[3] At least one court implied the authority.[4]

The California act provides that government may enter into an agreement with a property owner that deals with permitted uses, density or intensity of use, height and size of buildings, and the reservation or dedication of land for public purposes.[5] The agreement may specify a

14. Simpson v. City of Charlotte, 115 N.C.App. 51, 443 S.E.2d 772, 776 (1994).

15. West's Colo.Rev.Stat.Ann. § 24–68–105 (2).

16. N.C.Gen.Stat. § 160A–385.1(e)(2).

§ 5.31

1. See generally Daniel J. Curtin, Jr. & Scott A. Edelstein, Development Agreement Practice In California and Other States, 22 Stetson Law Review 761 (1993); Judith W. Wegner, Moving Toward the Bargaining Table: Contract Zoning, Development Agreements, and the Theoretical Foundations of Government Land Use Deals, 65 N.C.L.Rev. 957 (1987); David L. Callies, Developers' Agreements and Planning Gain, 17 Urb.Law. 599 (1985); Crew, Development Agreements After Nollan v. California Coastal Commission, 22 Urb.Law. 23 (1990); Delaney, Development Agreements: The Road from Prohibition to "Let's Make a Deal!" 25 Urb.Law. 49 (1993); Porter, Whither Development Agreements? Urb. Land 34 (Sept.1987).

2. Development agreements got their start in California, where the development

community and legislature reacted to Avco Community Dev., Inc. v. South Coast Regional Comm'n, 17 Cal.3d 785, 132 Cal. Rptr. 386, 553 P.2d 546 (1976), a decision seen as exemplifying the harsh nature of common law vesting, discussed above at § 5.28. See Curtin and Edelstein, supra note 1; William G. Holliman, Jr., Development Agreements and Vested Rights in California, 13 Urb.Law. 44 (1981).

3. Ariz.Rev.Stat.Ann. § 9–500.05; Cal. Govt.Code §§ 65864–65899; Colo.Rev.Stat. Ann. § 24–68–101 to 106; Fla.Stat. §§ 163.3220–.3243; Haw.Rev.Stat. §§ 46–121 to 46–132; Nev.Rev.Stat.Ann § 278.0201; N.J.Stat.Ann. § 40:55D–45.2; Md.Code Ann. Art. 28, §§ 7–116(c) and 7–121; Wash.Rev.Stat. §§ 36.70B.170–.210.

4. Giger v. City of Omaha, 232 Neb. 676, 442 N.W.2d 182 (1989). See also Sprenger, Grubb & Assoc. v. City of Hailey, 127 Idaho 576, 903 P.2d 741 (Idaho 1995) (court finds development agreement not breached by city, stating it need not decide whether an agreement freezing regulations could be enforced after many years).

5. Cal.Govt.Code § 65865.2.

duration of apparently any length, but it is subject to annual review to determine developer compliance. The law that exists at the time of the execution of the agreement applies to the project during the agreement's duration. The government cannot apply newly enacted laws to the project that are inconsistent with the agreement.[6]

The idea of a "development agreement ordinance" is oxymoronic under the view of early decisions that condemned contract zoning.[7] Yet times have changed, and, as with the trend to accept conditional zoning,[8] legislatures and courts increasingly accept development agreements as legitimate planning tools. The development agreement idea, however, is not entirely new. In some jurisdictions, annexation agreements have been used to achieve planning objectives.[9] The development agreement also finds support in the vested rights statutes that confer immunity from zoning changes for a fixed period.[10] While those statutes may not refer to an "agreement" being made, the legislatures that passed them likely understood that a city would engage in some form of bargaining or negotiation before it approved a plan that it knew would freeze development rights on the parcel.

The development agreement is not a contract in the common law sense, or at least, not simply a contract. California's statute declares a development agreement to be a legislative act, while Hawaii's declares it an administrative act.[11] If legislative, the land is in effect rezoned to permit a specific use pursuant to the terms of the agreement/ordinance. If administrative, the action is similar to the issuance of a special permit. Questions of validity may hinge on whether the focus is on the agreement's contractual or regulatory aspects.

When a dispute arises, a court may view it as presenting a straightforward contract issue. For example, in Sprenger, Grubb & Associates, Inc. v. City of Hailey,[12] a development agreement reached in 1973 as part of an annexation contained a promise by the city that it would "take all other action as may be required [by the developer] to develop the annexed real property in * * * substantial compliance with [the developer's master plan]."[13] In 1993, the city downzoned some of the land from general business to limited business. In refusing to find a breach by the city, the court examined the uses allowed in the new business classification, and found they were in "substantial compliance" with the master plan that envisioned comparatively small commercial centers, not major retail operations.[14]

6. Cal.Govt.Code § 65866.

7. See supra § 5.11.

8. Id.

9. See Wegner, supra note 1, at 995. See also Ill.Stat.Ann. §§ 11.15.1 to 11.15.5 and Meegan v. Village of Tinley Park, 52 Ill.2d 354, 288 N.E.2d 423 (1972); Morrison Homes Corp. v. City of Pleasanton, 58 Cal. App.3d 724, 130 Cal.Rptr. 196 (1976).

10. See supra § 5.30.

11. Cal.Govt.Code § 65867.5 and Haw. Rev.Stat. §§ 46–121 to 46–132.

12. 127 Idaho 576, 903 P.2d 741 (Idaho 1995).

13. Id. at 745.

14. Finding no breach, the court was able to avoid the question of whether an agreement freezing zoning for twenty years would be valid.

Even if statutorily authorized, a development agreement can be seen as an illegal "bargaining away of the police power" violative of the reserved powers doctrine[15] or, as a species of spot zoning not in the public interest and violative of due process.[16] A governmental promise not to change the zoning of a tract, perhaps in an agreement in which the developer promises to dedicate land, may trouble some courts.[17] Such a practice, however, is not revolutionary, and differs from conditional zoning only in degree and in terminology. The idea of a freeze may be justified by the need to meet due process rights of property owners as identified in some of the vested rights and estoppel cases.[18] The question of whether the public interest, on balance, is served can be tested in the courts where resolution should follow the principles used in cases dealing with contract and conditional zoning.[19]

The validity of a freeze may also depend on the agreement's duration. Somewhat surprisingly, the California and Hawaii statutes set no time limit. In contrast, the Florida act sets ten years as the maximum length.[20] If the agreement has no cut off date, it is likely to cause problems when the parties attempt to enforce it decades after they executed it.[21]

To overcome the argument that it has made an improper bargain, a legislative body may aid its case by identifying broad public benefits beyond the more obvious benefits to developers. The preamble of the California act, for example, notes the need for certainty to avoid the waste of resources, the discouragement of investment, and the increase in the cost of housing that occurs when local government halts development in mid-course. Florida law emphasizes as well the need to assure the provision of adequate public facilities

A second question that may arise is whether government termination, on grounds other than developer noncompliance, constitutes a taking under the Fifth Amendment, or, in contract terms, whether it is a breach justifying an award of damages. If the reason for termination involves public health or safety, there is likely no breach since most statutes authorize termination or modification for such reasons of health or safety.[22] If no reservation of power is incorporated into the contract by the statute and if not otherwise express in the contract, a court might imply such a power to protect vital public interests without requiring the payment of compensation or damages. If, however, the agreement is terminated on grounds that would not meet the statutory grounds of

---

15. See Wegner, supra note 1, at 966–968, discussing Stone v. Mississippi, 101 U.S. (11 Otto) 814, 25 L.Ed. 1079 (1880) and Callies & Grant, note 1, at 242.

16. See supra § 5.10 regarding spot zoning.

17. *Avco*, supra note 2, suggests this.

18. See supra §§ 5.28–.29.

19. See Giger v. City of Omaha, 232 Neb. 676, 442 N.W.2d 182 (1989).

20. Fla.Stat. §§ 163.3229.

21. This occurred in *Sprenger*, where the Idaho court faced an agreement entered into in 1973 and allegedly breached by the city in 1993. While the court found the agreement was not breached by a downzoning, it suggested a freeze might not be enforceable "many years later." 903 P.2d at 746.

22. Cal.Govt.Code § 65865.3(b) (health or safety).

health and safety, a regulatory taking might be found. The developer could point to specific expectations based on the contract, an important factor in takings cases.[23] Whether the loss sustained would be great enough would be fact-specific, requiring an examination of whether a reasonable use remained.[24]

A third constitutional problem may arise with conditions or exactions that are a part of the agreement. If the agreement contains a provision that a developer will agree to deed land to the government or pay impact fees to support infrastructure needs, it is not clear whether the constitutional nexus test applies.[25] If the agreement is viewed purely as a police power measure, the test should apply, but it should not apply if the contractual aspects control. If the nexus test does not apply, and the government can bargain well, the government may obtain exactions it could not constitutionally impose by regulation. In enforcing settlement agreements, there is support for using contract theory. In Leroy Land Development v. Tahoe Regional Planning Agency,[26] for example, the court held that the nexus test did not apply to a negotiated settlement agreement.[27]

These questions regarding development agreements have not been the subject of much reported litigation. Since studies show the agreements are being used,[28] the lack of case law may mean the parties are generally satisfied with the results, a conclusion that endorses the idea of expressly validating government-developer negotiations. Another explanation is that the cost of litigation is too great, though significant amounts of other land use litigation suggests that is not the reason. The statutes are also relatively new, most being products of the 1980s, and more time is needed to judge their validity and their effectiveness.

VII. JUDICIAL REVIEW

§ 5.32 Introduction[1]

Provisions for judicial review of land use controls vary from state to state depending not only on the type of action being challenged but also

23. See infra §§ 10.2–.11.

24. See Wegner, supra note 1, at 1031.

25. See infra § 10.5.

26. 939 F.2d 696 (9th Cir.1991).

27. See also Stephens v. City of Vista, 994 F.2d 650 (9th Cir.1993), where damages were awarded to a landowner for city's breach of a promise in a settlement agreement that guaranteed density. See Wegner, supra note 1 at 1000, n.250; Daniel J. Curtin, Jr., Protecting Developers' Permits to Build: Development Agreement Practice in California and Other States, 18 Zoning and Plan.L.Rep. 85, 91 (Dec.1995), suggesting the nexus test ought not apply based on the rationale of Leroy.

28. See David L. Callies & Malcolm Grant, Paying for Growth and Planning Gain: An Anglo–American Comparison of Development Conditions, Impact Fees, and Development Agreements, 23 Urb.Law. 221, 241 (1991) citing a study of California use by Cowart, Kresmodel & Stewart, Development Agreements: Widespread Use Exceeds Expectations, 1986 Quarterly Report, Center for Real Estate and Urban Economics, Univ. Calif. at Berkeley. But, at the end of 1995, it was reported that no development agreements had been approved in Hawaii, some ten years after passage. See Curtin, supra note 1, Zoning & Plan.L.Rep. at 90.

§ 5.32

1. Sections 5.32 through 5.36 and 5.38 through 5.40 are edited, modified and updated versions of Chapter 23 of Donald G. Hagman and Julian Conrad Juergensmeyer,

on general state statutes relating to judicial review, specific zoning enabling act requirements, administrative review acts, and on local ordinance provisions.[2] A key determinant in the nature of judicial review is whether the challenged action is legislative or administrative.

The Standard State Zoning Enabling Act has no provision for review of legislative decisions or procedures for attacking the constitutionality of zoning ordinances. Only a few states provide special procedures to review local legislative decisions.[3] In the absence of special statutory provisions, parties usually obtain review of such decisions through a *de novo* action for injunctive relief or a declaratory judgment.

Many states authorize an appeal from a local zoning board or planning commission under the same procedures available for appeals from state administrative agencies. If courts treat rezonings as administrative decisions, similar appeals may be available. The Standard Act provides for review of decisions of the board of adjustment.[4] Appeal from the board is by petition to a court of record alleging why the board decision is illegal.

§ 5.33   Types of Actions

A.   *Certiorari*

In those states that have the Standard Act, review of an administrative body's decision is by writ of certiorari. Since the writ is designed to review decisions of lower judicial bodies, it is appropriately applied to boards of adjustment, which are administrative or quasi-judicial.[1]

Under some ordinances, the board of adjustment does not make the final decision, but its decision may be appealed to a higher body, typically the legislative body. When the legislative body decides a matter ordinarily entrusted to a zoning board, it is exercising an administrative function rather than a legislative function, so a writ of certiorari to it is appropriate. For example, in North Carolina if a local city council issues special permits, the statute provides for review by writ of certiorari.[2]

Urban Planning and Land Development Control Law (2d ed.1986). Chapter 23 was written by Fred Bosselman and Clif Weaver and we thank them for their permission to use these sections, as modified, here. Any errors occurring in the editing process are ours.

2. See, e.g., Louis Levy, Judicial Review of Zoning Cases—New Rules? 6 Tulsa L.J. 1 (1969); Comment, The State of Zoning Administration in Illinois: Procedural Requirements of Judicial Intervention, 62 Nw.U.L.R. 462 (1967). As to federal review, see Robert J. Hopperton, Standards of Judicial Review in Supreme Court Land Use Opinions: A Taxonomy, An Analytical

Framework, and a Synthesis, 5 Wash. U.J.Urb. & Contemp.L. 1 (1997).

3. N.C.Gen.Stat. § 160A–364.1.

4. Standard Zoning Enabling Act § 7, U.S. Dep't Commerce (rev.ed.1926).

§ 5.33

1. Jackson v. Spalding County, 265 Ga. 792, 462 S.E.2d 361 (1995).

2. N.C.Gen.Stat. § 160A–381. See also Sun Ray Homes, Inc. v. Dade County, 166 So.2d 827 (Fla.App.1964). When a rezoning is treated as a quasi-judicial or administrative decision under the law of a particular state, the appropriate method of review

The writ of certiorari is not generally available to review decisions of legislative bodies where they are acting in a legislative capacity.[3] Review of such decisions is usually by injunction or declaratory judgment.

B. Appeal

The term appeal is applied to a provision for court review created by statute. Statutes differ from state to state, but usually, as with writs of certiorari, the term applies to administrative bodies when exercising quasi-judicial functions.[4]

Zoning and planning boards may or may not be included within the state administrative acts' provisions for judicial review of administrative decisions.[5] Both certiorari and appeal procedures involve review based on the record made before the local board, as opposed to those types of review that involve a *de novo* trial before the court.

C. Mandamus

A writ of mandamus is usually available to review administrative decisions that are ministerial, not discretionary. Parties frequently employ it to seek an order directing the issuance of a building permit which the city denied them on the assumption their request was not authorized. Mandamus may also be used to order restoration of a revoked permit. If the government abuses its discretion, the writ is also sometimes available. Usually, such matters as issuance of a variance or special permit are discretionary, so the writ may not be an appropriate mechanism for judicial review.[6] However, if the ordinance clearly spells out the standards for a special permit and the applicant definitely meets the standards, a writ of mandamus may be proper.[7]

Mandamus is usually not available with respect to legislative action or inaction. However, when statutorily provided, a party may bring mandamus to require the local legislative body to hold hearings and issue a decision for curative amendments.[8] Mandamus also may be appropriate to test the validity of an ordinance.[9] For example, a writ of mandamus may be brought against an officer to issue a building permit alleging that the denial of the permit is invalid on a number of grounds:

may be by writ of certiorari. Higby v. Board of County Comm'rs of El Paso County, 689 P.2d 635 (Colo.App.1984).

3. Gregory v. Board of County Comm'rs of Rogers County, 514 P.2d 667 (Okl.1973); Application of Frank, 183 Neb. 722, 164 N.W.2d 215 (1969). But See Westminster Presbyterian Church v. Jackson, 253 Miss. 495, 176 So.2d 267 (1965).

4. V.S.H. Realty, Inc. v. Rochester, 118 N.H. 778, 394 A.2d 317 (1978).

5. See, e.g., 60 ILCS 1/110–50, providing for application of act to zoning boards of appeal.

6. State ex rel. Killeen Realty Co. v. East Cleveland, 169 Ohio St. 375, 160 N.E.2d 1 (1959); Casino Motor Co. v. Needham, 151 Me. 333, 118 A.2d 781 (1955).

7. City and County of San Francisco v. Superior Court of San Francisco, 53 Cal.2d 236, 1 Cal.Rptr. 158, 347 P.2d 294 (1959). Courts differ on whether the approval of a subdivision map is ministerial. Compare Kelly v. Bethany, 588 P.2d 567 (Okl.1978) with Simac Design, Inc. v. Alciati, 92 Cal. App.3d 146, 154 Cal.Rptr. 676 (1979).

8. Board of Supervisors of East Norriton Township v. Gill Quarries, Inc., 53 Pa. Cmwlth. 194, 417 A.2d 277 (1980).

9. Garrison v. Fairmont, 150 W.Va. 498, 147 S.E.2d 397 (1966); Clairmont Development Co. v. Morgan, 222 Ga. 255, 149 S.E.2d 489 (1966).

that the statute does not authorize the ordinance, that the ordinance is unconstitutional or unconstitutionally applied, that the city adopted it without following appropriate procedures, that the city's actions have estopped it from applying the ordinance, or that the city has misconstrued the ordinance.

In California, mandamus is the remedy authorized by statute for testing the adequacy of a local government's general plan. The statute establishes detailed procedures for this purpose.[10]

D. Injunction

The injunction action is also a means of obtaining judicial review of an ordinance. If a person is violating an ordinance or threatening to violate the ordinance, an injunction may be an appropriate mechanism for review.[11] The injunction may also be used where enforcement of the ordinance will result in irreparable damage, such as the threat of being jailed or fined. The injunction can also be used to challenge the constitutionality of the ordinance as applied, to establish that the ordinance was adopted improperly, or that the statute did not authorize the zoning.[12]

Injunctions have been used to prevent a city from interfering with a nonconforming use,[13] to test the validity of conditions attached to a permit,[14] and to test a zoning officer's construction of the ordinance.[15] While the injunction might be used to enjoin enforcement, it is usually not available to require or prevent the adoption of an ordinance.[16]

E. Declaratory Judgment

In many states, a declaratory judgment is the typical method of seeking judicial review of land use controls.[17] There must be an actual controversy—advisory opinions are not rendered in declaratory judgment actions. In a few states the actual controversy requirement is strictly construed.[18] In most states, a landowner who has been denied a permit or who has been threatened by enforcement of a zoning ordinance is involved in a controversy and can bring a declaratory judgment action. The constitutionality of the ordinance, either in general, or as applied, is

---

10. West's Ann.Cal.Gov't. Code §§ 65750 ff. See Resource Defense Fund v. Santa Cruz County, 133 Cal.App.3d 800, 184 Cal.Rptr. 371 (1982).

11. Ramaker v. Cities Serv. Oil Co., 27 Wis.2d 143, 133 N.W.2d 789 (1965).

12. Lacey v. Warren, 7 Mich.App. 105, 151 N.W.2d 245 (1967); Pyramid Corp. v. DeSoto County Bd. of Supervisors, 366 F.Supp. 1299 (N.D.Miss.1973); Thompson v. Miami, 167 So.2d 841 (Fla.1964), on remand 169 So.2d 838 (1964), cert. denied 176 So.2d 511 (1965).

13. London v. Detroit, 354 Mich. 571, 93 N.W.2d 262 (1958).

14. Naper Aero Club v. DuPage County, 30 Ill.2d 447, 197 N.E.2d 1 (1964).

15. Carp v. Board of County Comm'rs, 190 Kan. 177, 373 P.2d 153 (1962).

16. State ex rel. Michigan City Plan Comm'n v. Laporte Superior Court No. 1, 260 Ind. 587, 297 N.E.2d 814 (1973); Citizens for Orderly Dev. & Env't v. Phoenix, 112 Ariz. 258, 540 P.2d 1239 (1975).

17. Since an appeal or certiorari is often available for review of administrative decisions, a declaratory judgment might not be available to review administrative decisions. Triangle Ranch, Inc. v. Union Oil Co., 135 Cal.App.2d 428, 287 P.2d 537 (1955).

18. See Woods v. Newton, 349 Mass. 373, 208 N.E.2d 508 (1965).

a proper matter for a declaratory judgment action.[19] An action for declaratory judgment is frequently combined with an action for an injunction.

F. Alternative Remedies

Mandamus, injunction and declaratory judgment actions may be barred if an alternative remedy is available, such as appeal or certiorari. For example, a Texas statute precludes attacks on most zoning board decisions except by certiorari.[20] Similarly, a California statute requires that no plain, speedy, and adequate remedy exist in the ordinary course before a writ of mandamus can issue.[21]

A similar division of opinion exists about whether an injunction is available if an adequate legal remedy is available.[22] An injunction may be available to test the constitutionality of an ordinance even though certiorari would also be a possible route.[23] The fact that the ordinance may be enforced by a criminal proceeding does not bar an injunction action, since the injunction affects property rights that the criminal remedy does not affect.[24] Similar problems of availability of an alternative remedy may apply with respect to declaratory judgment actions.

§ 5.34 Standing

A. In General

To bring an action, one must have standing, and the rules of standing may differ among the different kinds of action for review.[1] The standing rules discussed here for state courts are distinct from Article III standing for federal courts,[2] and they are notably less complex.

As for decisions of the zoning board, the Standard Act provides that "[a]ny person * * * aggrieved by any decision of the board of adjustment or any taxpayer" may petition the court.[3] Some states have dropped the phrase "or any taxpayer," so courts may more narrowly construe standing in those states as to taxpayer actions. The Standard Act also gives

19. Fulton Cama, Inc. v. Trustees of Farmingdale, 72 A.D.2d 813, 421 N.Y.S.2d 907 (1979).

20. City of San Angelo v. Boehme Bakery, 144 Tex. 281, 190 S.W.2d 67 (1945).

21. West's Cal.Code of Civil Procedure § 1086. Some states allow more liberal collateral attack. See, e.g., State ex rel. Union Limestone, Inc. v. Bumgarner, 110 Ohio App. 173, 168 N.E.2d 901 (1959).

22. See Dade County v. National Bulk Carriers, Inc., 450 So.2d 213 (Fla.1984); Kula v. Prososki, 219 Neb. 626, 365 N.W.2d 441 (1985).

23. Telegraph–Lone Pine Venture Co. v. Bloomfield, 85 Mich.App. 560, 272 N.W.2d 136 (1978). But see Ragano v. Rigot, 25 Pa.Cmwlth. 428, 360 A.2d 779 (1976).

24. State ex rel. Jacobson v. New Orleans, Dep't of Safety & Permits, 166 So.2d 520 (La.App.1964).

§ 5.34

1. John D. Ayer, The Primitive Law of Standing in Land Use Disputes: Some Notes From a Dark Continent, 55 Iowa L.Rev. 344, 346 (1969).

2. See discussion of Article III standing limitation on exclusionary zoning claims based on the equal protection clause, infra at § 6.10.

3. Standard State Zoning Enabling Act § 7. See Mark Bobrowski, The Zoning Act's "Person Aggieved" Standard: From Barvenik to Marshlian, 1996 W.N.Eng.L.Rev. 385 (focusing on law of Massachusetts).

"proper local authorities of the municipality" standing to "institute any appropriate action or proceedings,"[4] though the conferral of such standing by the statutes does not mean that others could not bring an action or proceeding.[5]

The courts have evolved essentially consistent rules on the standing issue for several different classes of litigants: those with an interest in the property that is the subject of the dispute, neighbors, taxpayers, competitors, citizens' associations, local governments, and extraterritorial litigants.

B. *Property Interest*

The Standard Act requires that persons be aggrieved.[6] The owner of the property that is the subject of the dispute is an aggrieved person and owners include co-owners and contract vendors.[7] Mortgagees and tenants also are ordinarily aggrieved, though it may be necessary for these plaintiffs to assert they are agents for the owner, that the owner has joined in the action, or that they have suffered special damages different from the main owner. A conditional vendee may not be able to bring a mandamus action because he may not be able to assert a clear and present right to force the concerned official to act as the vendee would have it.[8] In an action for injunctive relief, it is likely that most of the above described persons could meet the test of establishing special damages peculiar to them.

C. *Neighbors*

Where persons have interests in property that adjoins property directly affected by a zoning decision, they are likely to be specially and beneficially interested in the zoning decision and hence will have standing.[9] Where the neighbor asserting standing does not have property adjoining the parcel directly affected, the chances that a court will recognize that the neighbor has standing diminish, as a practical matter, in proportion to the distance of the property from the parcel directly affected. Persons likely to be granted standing include those: in the same subdivision as the parcel whose use is in issue, or within the distance specified in some ordinances for invoking an extraordinary majority vote of the board or legislative body, or persons to whom notice must be given under an ordinance, or persons owning parcels that must be shown on the site plan accompanying a petition for a zoning change or administrative permission. Courts may grant other persons nearby standing,[10] but

4. Standard State Zoning Enabling Act § 8.

5. Blankenship v. Michalski, 155 Cal. App.2d 672, 318 P.2d 727 (1957).

6. Standard State Zoning Enabling Act § 7.

7. Appeal of R. & A. Miller, Inc., 18 Pa.Cmwlth. 360, 336 A.2d 433 (1975) (contract vendor).

8. Forbes v. Hubbard, 348 Ill. 166, 180 N.E. 767 (1932); Metroweb Corp. v. Lake County, 130 Ill.App.3d 934, 85 Ill.Dec. 940,

474 N.E.2d 900 (1985); Yusuf v. Villa Park, 120 Ill.App.3d 533, 76 Ill.Dec. 175, 458 N.E.2d 575 (1983). See also Community Treatment Centers, Inc. v. City of Westland, 970 F.Supp. 1197 (E.D.Mich.1997) (contingent expectation sufficient).

9. Robinson v. Indianola Mun. Separate Sch. Dist., 467 So.2d 911 (Miss.1985).

10. Summit Township Taxpayers Ass'n v. Summit Township Bd., 49 Pa.Cmwlth. 459, 411 A.2d 1263 (1980). See generally Allison Dunham, Private Enforcement of

at some point they will deny standing, such as to an owner of land 7½ miles from the parcel affected by the rezoning.[11] As to injunctions, it would be difficult for persons with property far removed to prove special damages.

D. Taxpayers

If the statute gives taxpayers standing without the necessity of being specially aggrieved, as Section 7 of the Standard Act provides, taxpayers may bring a variety of judicial actions. Even absent such an express provision, some courts have held that all citizens or taxpayers have sufficient interest in proper zoning to bring an action.[12] Sometimes a statute provides for taxpayer action only if a certain number join in the petition or after the taxpayers have first requested municipal officials to take action.[13]

E. Competitors

Generally, a competitor as competitor does not have standing, though the matter may be confused with the merits of the case, since zoning to regulate competition is generally considered invalid.[14] While the competition may damage the competitor, it is not the kind of damage entitling one to enjoin the activity.[15] Drafting the petition to qualify the competitor in another noncompetitive class may avoid the problem by removing the taint.

F. Citizen Associations

Some courts confer standing on an association on the theory that if its members own property or reside in the area, the association, acting as their agent, is a proper party to sue.[16] In some states, such as Oregon, statewide citizens' organizations are frequent plaintiffs in land use litigation. In California, they frequently form groups with euphonious acronyms to fight particular projects. Where courts deny standing on the ground that an association is not a property owner and therefore is not an aggrieved person,[17] suing in the name of an association member who

City Planning, 20 Law & Contemp. Prob. 463, 477 (1955).

11. City of Greenbelt v. Jaeger, 237 Md. 456, 206 A.2d 694 (1965). See Renard v. Dade County, 261 So.2d 832 (Fla.1972).

12. See, e.g., Brady v. Board of Appeals of Westport, 348 Mass. 515, 204 N.E.2d 513 (1965).

13. Monsey Mfg. Co. v. Ocko, 14 A.D.2d 925, 222 N.Y.S.2d 29 (1961).

14. See supra § 3.17.

15. Ratner v. Richmond, 136 Ind.App. 578, 201 N.E.2d 49 (1964); City of Eureka v. Litz, 658 S.W.2d 519 (Mo.App.1983); Universal Life Church, Inc. v. State, 158 Cal. App.3d 533, 205 Cal.Rptr. 11 (1984). Contra, Metro. Dade County v. Reineng Corp., 399 So.2d 379 (Fla.App.1981).

16. Society Created To Reduce Urban Blight (SCRUB) v. Zoning Bd. of Adj. of the City and County of Philadelphia, 682 A.2d 1 (Pa.Cmwlth.1996); Save a Valuable Environment (SAVE) v. City of Bothell, 89 Wash.2d 862, 576 P.2d 401 (1978); B.E.M. Homeowners Ass'n v. Fort Worth, 372 S.W.2d 364 (Tex.Civ.App.1963); East Camelback Homeowners Ass'n v. Arizona Found. for Neurology & Psychiatry, 19 Ariz.App. 118, 505 P.2d 286 (1973).

17. Stocksdale v. Barnard, 239 Md. 541, 212 A.2d 282 (1965); Concerned Olympia Residents for the Env't v. Olympia, 33 Wash.App. 677, 657 P.2d 790 (1983); Citizens Growth Management Coalition of West Palm Beach, Inc. v. West Palm Beach, 450 So.2d 204 (Fla.1984).

is also a property owner who falls within the class of aggrieved persons will avoid the problem.

G. Local Governments

The local government may be aggrieved entitling it to appeal a decision from its own board of adjustment, as may officers of the local government charged with supervision of the ordinance who believe the government has made an error.[18] An administrative body may not have authority to appeal a judicial reversal of its own decision to a higher court because of the general rule that subordinate courts have no standing to appeal a reversal of their own decisions.[19]

The Standard Act allows proper local authorities to institute any appropriate proceedings or actions, and an injunction has often been used for such purposes.[20] In some states a local government may institute an appeal from a final decision of its own zoning board.[21]

H. Extraterritorial Litigants

Earlier cases denied standing to extraterritorial litigants. As recently as 1968, a New York court held that the Town of Huntington was not an aggrieved party that had standing to challenge the issuance of a special permit by the Town of Oyster Bay to build a shopping center on the border of Huntington.[22] This narrow view of standing is understandable given the strong localized origins of zoning.[23] Courts also usually denied individual property owners in other municipalities standing.[24]

A 1968 federal case, however, Township of River Vale v. Orangetown,[25] recognized extraterritorial rights, allowing River Vale to intervene to show that a decision of Orangetown would reduce property tax revenues and increase municipal expenditures. In another case of that era, a court granted standing to a property owner of an adjacent tract across a town boundary to challenge a rezoning.[26]

The trend is to allow a challenge to zoning decisions both by neighboring governments[27] and by property owners in neighboring juris-

---

18. Ex parte City of Huntsville, 684 So.2d 123 (Ala.1996). The town's ordinances or actions must be in issue. Rossetti v. Chittenden County,674 A.2d 1284 (Vt. 1996).

19. Lansdowne Borough Bd. of Adjustment's Appeal, 313 Pa. 523, 170 A. 867 (1934).

20. Standard State Zoning Enabling Act § 8.

21. Kline v. Board of Township Trustees of Chester Township, 13 Ohio St.2d 5, 233 N.E.2d 515 (1968). But See City of Hammond v. Board of Zoning Appeals, 152 Ind.App. 480, 284 N.E.2d 119 (1972).

22. Town of Huntington v. Town Bd. of Oyster Bay, 57 Misc.2d 821, 293 N.Y.S.2d 558 (1968).

23. See Village of Mount Prospect v. Cook County, 113 Ill.App.2d 336, 252 N.E.2d 106 (1969).

24. Wood v. Freeman, 43 Misc.2d 616, 251 N.Y.S.2d 996 (1964), affirmed mem. 24 A.D.2d 704, 262 N.Y.S.2d 431 (1965); Cablevision Division of Sammons Communications, Inc. v. Zoning Hearing Bd. of City of Easton, 13 Pa.Cmwlth. 232, 320 A.2d 388 (1974).

25. 403 F.2d 684 (2d Cir.1968).

26. Braghirol v. Town of Chester, 70 Misc.2d 812, 334 N.Y.S.2d 944 (Sup.Ct. 1972).

27. Village of Northbrook v. Cook County, 126 Ill.App.3d 145, 81 Ill.Dec. 413, 466 N.E.2d 1215 (1984); Board of County Commissioners v. City of Thorton, 629 P.2d

dictions.[28] This trend is consistent with the growing recognition of the regional impact of individual zoning decisions.

Standing in exclusionary zoning cases presents special considerations.[29] Several states grant nonresidents standing to maintain general exclusionary zoning challenges.[30] Unlike federal law, they need not show site-specific injury. In nonresidential exclusionary zoning, excluded groups may also have standing. In Halfway House, Inc. v. City of Portland,[31] for example, the court held that an operator of houses for prerelease prisoners and parolees had standing based on economic injury to challenge an ordinance that totally excluded such facilities from the municipality.[32]

§ 5.35   Conditions Precedent

A.   Ripeness

Some courts refuse to entertain a challenge to a zoning ordinance unless the property owner has put forth a specific development proposal.[1] Other states by statute have made the presentation of specific development plans a prerequisite to judicial review.[2] The United States Supreme Court requires that a property owner present a well-defined development proposal and obtain a final decision on its acceptability in order to bring a challenge under the taking clause or due process clause.[3] Federal ripeness rules are considered elsewhere.[4]

B.   Equities

Although "unclean hands" is properly a defense to an equitable action rather than a condition precedent to its filing, some courts have required conditions that cannot easily be categorized but by their similarity to this ancient concept. Thus, a Massachusetts court denied the owner of a nonconforming use standing to litigate the validity of a

605 (Colo.1981); Village of Franklin v. City of Southfield, 101 Mich.App. 554, 300 N.W.2d 634 (1980).

28. Scott v. Indian Wells, 6 Cal.3d 541, 99 Cal.Rptr. 745, 492 P.2d 1137 (1972); Allen v. Coffel, 488 S.W.2d 671 (Mo.App. 1972).

29. See infra § 6.10.

30. Southern Burlington County N.A.A.C.P. v. Township of Mt. Laurel, 67 N.J. 151, 336 A.2d 713 (1975) (Mt. Laurel I), appeal dismissed, cert. denied 423 U.S. 808, 96 S.Ct. 18, 46 L.Ed.2d 28 (1975); Urban League of Essex County v. Mahwah Twp., 147 N.J.Super. 28, 370 A.2d 521 (1977); Suffolk Housing Serv. v. Town of Brookhaven, 91 Misc.2d 80, 397 N.Y.S.2d 302 (1977) mod. 63 A.D.2d 731, 405 N.Y.S.2d 302 (1978); Stocks v. City of Irvine, 114 Cal.App.3d 520, 170 Cal.Rptr. 724 (1981).

31. 670 A.2d 1377 (Me.1996).

32. See also Bossier City Medical Suite, Inc. v. City of Bossier City, 483 F.Supp. 633 (W.D.La.1980) (woman seeking abortion and medical clinic providing abortion service each had standing to challenge restrictive zoning ordinance).

§ 5.35

1. Norwood Builders v. Des Plaines, 128 Ill.App.3d 908, 84 Ill.Dec. 105, 471 N.E.2d 634 (1984). But see Porpoise Point Partnership v. St. Johns County, 470 So.2d 850 (Fla.App.1985).

2. Appeal of Miller, 87 Pa.Cmwlth. 254, 487 A.2d 448 (1985); Winston Corp. v. Board of Supervisors of Patton Township, 88 Pa.Cmwlth. 208, 489 A.2d 303 (1985).

3. Williamson County Regional Planning Commission v. Hamilton Bank, 473 U.S. 172, 105 S.Ct. 3108, 87 L.Ed.2d 126 (1985), on remand 779 F.2d 50 (6th Cir. 1985).

4. See infra § 10.10.

change of a neighboring nonconforming use.[5] The Florida supreme court held that a person who knowingly put up a billboard without a permit had no standing to challenge the destruction of the billboard.[6]

§ 5.36 Defenses

A. *Exhaustion of Remedies*

The doctrine of exhaustion of remedies is concerned with whether parties have pursued *administrative* remedies. For example, under the Standard Act, appeals alleging an error in any order by an administrative official go to the board of adjustment.[1] It is generally improper to go directly to court after the order by the administrative official.[2]

While the Standard Act provides for a writ of certiorari from a decision by the board of adjustment, some statutes or ordinances provide for an appeal from the board to the legislative body, which then sits as a super administrative body. If the statute or ordinance so provides, going to court after the board of adjustment decision may not be proper because one has not exhausted administrative remedies.[3] In states where an appeal to a state administrative agency is available, litigants must exhaust this remedy before they commence judicial review.[4]

The general rule with respect to mandamus, injunction and declaratory judgment actions is the same—one must first exhaust administrative remedies. Exceptions, however, tend to swallow the rule. If the attack is on the validity of the zoning ordinance as a whole, e.g., adoption under improper procedures or unconstitutionality, most states allow a direct proceeding in court.[5] The rationale is that an administrative body does not have authority to question the validity of the ordinance it is applying. On the other hand, if the issue is that the zoning is invalid as applied, applying for a special permit or a variance and pursuing statutory appeals to higher administrative bodies and statutory routes of appeal may be necessary.[6] Seeking an amendment may also be necessary. The exhaustion doctrine applies because issuance of the permit or variance or rezoning may relieve the invalid or unconstitutional application of the ordinance to the property.[7]

5. Sherrill House, Inc. v. Board of Appeal, 19 Mass.App.Ct. 274, 473 N.E.2d 716 (1985), review denied 394 Mass. 1103, 477 N.E.2d 595 (1985).

6. Department of Transp. v. Durden, 471 So.2d 1271 (Fla.1985).

§ 5.36

1. Standard State Zoning Enabling Act § 7 U.S. Dept. Commerce (rev.ed.1926).

2. Kunz & Co. v. State of Utah, 913 P.2d 765 (Utah App.1996); Elizabeth City v. LFM Enterprises, Inc., 48 N.C.App. 408, 269 S.E.2d 260 (1980); Caulwal Const. Co. v. Burwell, 136 Misc. 259, 240 N.Y.S. 456 (1930).

3. Contris v. Richmond County, 238 Ga. 731, 235 S.E.2d 19 (1977).

4. General Electric Credit Corp. v. Metropolitan Dade County, 346 So.2d 1049 (Fla.App.1977).

5. City of Amarillo v. Stapf, 129 Tex. 81, 101 S.W.2d 229 (1937); Village of Bourbonnais v. Herbert, 86 Ill.App.2d 367, 229 N.E.2d 574 (1967).

6. Florentine v. Darien, 142 Conn. 415, 115 A.2d 328 (1955).

7. Bird Road Baptist Church, Inc. v. Stevens, 155 So.2d 420 (Fla.App.1963); Indiana Toll Rd. Comm'n v. Jankovich, 244 Ind. 574, 193 N.E.2d 237 (1963), cert.

Courts may also not require exhaustion where only an issue of law is presented[8] or where one brings mandamus to compel the performance of purely ministerial duties.[9] A statute may permit an action without exhaustion of remedies under certain specified circumstances.[10] If a zoning body fails to follow the spirit of a previous court decision, and zones again in a way that denies the property owner the previous relief, a court is not likely to require the property owner to begin again and exhaust administrative remedies.[11] Administrative remedies are not considered adequate in such a case.

If the plaintiff challenges the jurisdiction of the local agency, exhausting remedies may not be necessary.[12] Where exhaustion would be futile, a party need not attempt it, but no consensus exists in defining futility.[13]

Because of a general belief that parties should resolve land use disputes at the local government level whenever possible, several states require persons to attempt to resolve their dispute at the local level before bringing suit. A statute may require a person who plans to challenge the validity of a land use regulation or decision to notify a local government of the claim of invalidity during the appropriate administrative proceedings. Some states require the filing of a written notice of claim with the local government far enough in advance of litigation so that the government can correct the alleged error.[14] In other states, a neighbor who wishes to challenge the validity of a local decision approving a development proposal must have filed an appearance during the local proceedings and raised all claims at that time.[15]

Even if no statutory rule is in effect, litigants would be well advised to avoid creating the appearance of "sandbagging." An issue raised for the first time in court may suggest to the judge that the parties might have avoided the litigation if they had raised the issue earlier. Even in a *de novo* proceeding, where the failure to have raised the issue below may not cause the exclusion of evidence relating to the issue, the court may

granted 377 U.S. 942, 84 S.Ct. 1352, 12 L.Ed.2d 305 (1964), petition for cert. dismissed 379 U.S. 487, 85 S.Ct. 493, 13 L.Ed.2d 439 (1965).

8. Bourgeois v. Bedford, 120 N.H. 145, 412 A.2d 1021 (1980) (whether a commission could attach conditions to subdivision approval).

9. Dato v. Vernon Hills, 91 Ill.App.2d 111, 233 N.E.2d 48 (1968) (conditions); State ex rel. Great Lakes Pipe Line Co. v. Hendrickson, 393 S.W.2d 481 (Mo.1965) (ministerial duties).

10. Jelinski v. Eggers, 34 Wis.2d 85, 148 N.W.2d 750 (1967) (injunction permitted without appealing denial of variance).

11. Hillsborough County v. Twin Lakes Mobile Home Village, 166 So.2d 191 (Fla.App.1964).

12. Social Spirits, Inc. v. Colonie, 74 A.D.2d 933, 426 N.Y.S.2d 148 (1980); Board

of Adjustment v. Levinson, 244 S.W.2d 281 (Tex.Civ.App.1951).

13. Compare Call v. Feher, 93 Cal. App.3d 434, 155 Cal.Rptr. 387 (1979) (issuance of adverse agency staff opinion does not make appeal to agency futile) with Orion Corp. v. State, 103 Wash.2d 441, 693 P.2d 1369 (1985) (where grant of relief would be inconsistent with purpose of statute it need not be sought).

14. DeKalb County v. Bembry, 252 Ga. 510, 314 S.E.2d 900 (1984).

15. Schatz v. Zoning Hearing Bd. of Upper Dublin Township, 21 Pa.Cmwlth. 112, 343 A.2d 90 (1975); La Costa Beach Homeowner's Ass'n v. Wayne, 89 Cal. App.3d 327, 152 Cal.Rptr. 355 (1979). See also West's Cal.Gov't. Code § 65009(b)(1).

view such evidence with little sympathy if the parties are raising it for the first time. Similarly, the local government attorney who attempts at trial to devise a creative rationale for the local legislative body's action by ascribing to it a purpose that was not immediately apparent on the face of the proceedings, may find that the court views such a rationale with skepticism.[16]

States also require opponents of a development permit to exhaust remedies. If an appeal is available, they must file an appeal before seeking judicial review.[17] Courts differ as to whether parties affected by a government-initiated rezoning of property must seek a variance before bringing judicial proceedings.[18]

When the local government brings a civil proceeding to enforce its ordinance, it need not have exhausted all administrative remedies before commencement of the action.[19] Courts differ on whether the defendant in an enforcement action may raise defenses without having exhausted administrative remedies appropriate to those defenses. Thus, one court held that the right to claim a nonconforming use was lost because the defendant failed to register such use pursuant to the local ordinance.[20] The defendant may, however, assert the invalidity of the ordinance being enforced without exhausting administrative remedies.[21]

B. *Limitations Periods*

The time within which one must seek judicial review of a land use decision may vary from ten days to infinity. By statute, some administrative decisions become binding unless appealed within periods as short as ten days.[22] On the other hand, if government makes a land use decision without giving the notice required by due process, a person who is entitled to receive such notice may have an infinite time within which to challenge the decision.[23]

Policy considerations suggest that short statutes of limitations are appropriate for decisions that mark the final stages of a development process and involve the technical approval of detailed plans and drawings. Actual construction usually commences shortly after these decisions are made; consequently, developers may expend large sums of money in reliance on these decisions within a relatively short period. Unless the binding effect of these decisions takes place soon, the court may face the difficult prospect of ordering that a completed structure be

---

16. Warren v. Lane County, 297 Or. 290, 686 P.2d 316 (1984).

17. Williams v. Kirkwood, 537 S.W.2d 571 (Mo.App.1976). But see Laws v. Lee, 471 N.E.2d 1229 (Ind.App.1984).

18. Compare O'Rourke v. Tulsa, 457 P.2d 782 (Okl.1969) with Florentine v. Darien, 142 Conn. 415, 115 A.2d 328 (1955).

19. City of Hattiesburg v. L. & A. Contracting Co., 248 Miss. 346, 159 So.2d 74 (1963); Bradley v. South Londonderry, 64 Pa.Cmwlth. 395, 440 A.2d 665 (1982).

20. City of Scranton v. Baiderman, 74 Pa.Cmwlth. 367, 460 A.2d 1199 (1983).

21. Johnson's Island, Inc. v. Board of Township Trustees, 69 Ohio St.2d 241, 431 N.E.2d 672 (1982).

22. Vernon's   Ann.Tex.Civ.Stat. § 231.021.

23. See, e.g., Ludwick v. Yamhill County, 72 Or.App. 224, 696 P.2d 536 (1985), review denied 299 Or. 443, 702 P.2d 1112 (1985).

dismantled. Consequently, statutes often impose time limits of thirty to sixty days for the judicial review of decisions such as building permits and final subdivision plat approval.[24]

Much land use litigation involves the validity of regulations on their face or as applied to specific land. Statutes of limitations applicable to such suits vary widely, but generally, the time on a facial claim runs from the date of enactment and the time on an as-applied claim runs from the date of the final administrative decision as to use.[25] Some require that an action be brought within thirty days[26] or two months,[27] and bar state law and federal constitutional challenges not filed within the period.[28] Other courts, finding a claim of invalidity to constitute a continuing wrong, hold there is no time bar to bring a declaratory judgment action.[29]

C. Laches

Courts apply the equitable defense of laches in situations to which no statute of limitations is applicable. If a party has delayed prosecuting a claim while the other party has proceeded in good faith to construct a building or continue an existing business, laches may bar judicial review. Laches is most frequently employed as a defense by the developer against a suit by neighbors who unduly delayed bringing a challenge to the permit by which the developer obtained the right to build.[30] In such cases the question of when the neighbors obtained legally effective notice is frequently at issue.[31]

In exceptional circumstances laches may bar a local government from enforcement of a zoning ordinance because of a long history of failure to enforce the ordinance.[32] Similarly, laches may bar a developer from claiming the validity of a permit when he took no action in reliance on it for a substantial time.[33]

24. Wegman v. Iowa City, 279 N.W.2d 261 (Iowa 1979); Nantucket Land Council, Inc. v. Planning Bd., 5 Mass.App.Ct. 206, 361 N.E.2d 937 (1977).

25. See Hensler v. City of Glendale, 8 Cal.4th 1, 876 P.2d 1043, 23 Cal.Rptr. 244 (1994), cert. den. 513 U.S. 1184, 115 S.Ct. 1176, 130 L.Ed.2d 1129 (1995). See also Ranch 57 v. City of Yuma, 152 Ariz. 218, 731 P.2d 113 (1986) (four years).

26. Bolser v. Zoning Bd. for Aubry Twp., 228 Kan. 6, 612 P.2d 563 (1980).

27. N.C.Gen.Stat. § 1–54.1. (action accrues upon adoption of ordinance; see N.C.Gen.Stat. § 160A–364.1). See also West's Cal.Gov't. Code § 65009 (90 days to challenge adequacy of general plan).

28. See Pinehurst Area Realty, Inc. v. Village of Pinehurst, 100 N.C.App. 77, 394 S.E.2d 251 (1990), cert. denied 501 U.S. 1251, 111 S.Ct. 2890, 115 L.Ed.2d 1055 (1991).

29. Amerada Hess Corp. v. Acampora, 109 A.D.2d 719, 486 N.Y.S.2d 38 (1985).

Rejecting the continuing wrong theory, see Robinson v. City of Seattle, 119 Wash.2d 34, 830 P.2d 318 (1992).

30. Conley v. Warne, 236 N.W.2d 682 (Iowa 1975); Drain v. Clackamas County, 36 Or.App. 799, 585 P.2d 746 (1978).

31. Gagne v. Cianbro Corp., 431 A.2d 1313 (Me.1981).

32. Hancock v. Hueter, 118 Mich.App. 811, 325 N.W.2d 591 (1982); Wieck v. District of Columbia Bd. of Zoning Adjustment, 383 A.2d 7 (D.C.App.1978) (city's failure to enforce ordinance despite threats may create bar of laches). But see Lane County v. Oregon Builders, Inc., 44 Or.App. 591, 606 P.2d 676 (1980); Ferris v. Las Vegas, 96 Nev. 912, 620 P.2d 864 (1980); Cohalan v. Lechtrecker, 56 N.Y.2d 861, 453 N.Y.S.2d 427, 438 N.E.2d 1142 (1982).

33. York–Green Associates v. Board of Supervisors, 87 Pa.Cmwlth. 93, 486 A.2d 561 (1985) (five years); Robert L. Rieke Bldg. Co., Inc. v. Olathe, 10 Kan.App.2d

D. Indispensable Parties

The failure to join an indispensable party can be a valid defense. This situation sometimes arises when a complex regulatory structure confuses plaintiffs who then choose the wrong agency as the defendant.[34]

Local governments most commonly employ this defense when neighbors seeking to invalidate a rezoning or variance sue them. In some states, the property owner who obtained the rezoning or variance must be joined as a defendant in such an action and the failure to do so gives the local government a valid defense.[35]

E. Estoppel

Situations in which courts estop local government from changing a zoning ordinance because of a property owner's reliance on an existing permit are discussed elsewhere.[36] In addition, an estoppel may arise if an agent of the local government acting within the scope of her powers induced an action later found in violation of the ordinance.[37]

§ 5.37 Standard of Review

Courts have struggled to develop standards of review for land use decisions that balance the need to protect both property owners and the public from abuses of power, on the one hand, with the desire not unduly to interfere with the legislative process, on the other.[1] Courts in zoning's early years often tipped the scales in favor of the latter concern to avoid entangling themselves in the affairs of zoning. In many states that has changed. As courts have grown jaded due to the practice of zoning authorities to both over and under-regulate,[2] they have increased the intensity of their review.[3] They have accompanied, and justified, that

239, 697 P.2d 72 (1985) (builder used lower density than maximum allowed).

34. South Hollywood Hills Citizens Ass'n v. King County, 101 Wash.2d 68, 677 P.2d 114 (1984).

35. Thompson v. Town Council of Town of Westerly, 487 A.2d 498 (1985); Riverhill Community Ass'n v. Cobb County Bd., 236 Ga. 856, 226 S.E.2d 54 (1976); Westlund v. Carter, 193 Colo. 129, 565 P.2d 920 (1977).

36. See supra §§ 5.28 and 5.29.

37. Town of West Hartford v. Rechel, 190 Conn. 114, 459 A.2d 1015 (1983) (city may be estopped to enforce ordinance when agent induced violation).

§ 5.37

1. See generally Robert J. Hopperton, Standards of Judicial Review in Supreme Court Land Use Opinions: A Taxonomy, An Analytical Framework, and a Synthesis, 5 Wash.U.J.Urb. & Contemp.L. 1 (1997); Daniel R. Mandelker and A. Dan Tarlock, Shifting the Presumption of Constitutional-

ity in Land–Use Law, 24 Urb.Law.1 (1992); Carol M. Rose, Planning and Dealing: Piecemeal Land Controls as a Problem of Local Legitimacy, 71 Calif.L.Rev. 837 (1983); Robert J. Hopperton, The Presumption of Validity in American Land–Use Law: A Substitute for Analysis, A Source of Significant Confusion, 23 B.C.Envtl.Aff.L.Rev. 301 (1996).

2. Professors Mandelker and Tarlock refer to over-regulation as resulting in individual losses and causing group exclusionary effects, and under-regulation as resulting in environmental degradation. See Mandelker and Tarlock, supra note 1.

3. See Melinda Westbrook, Connecticut's New Affordable Housing Appeals Procedure: Assaulting the Presumptive Validity of Land Use Decisions, 66 Conn.B.J. 169, 176 (1992), noting tendency of distinction between legislative and administrative actions to fade and result in increased review of so-called legislative matters. See also developments described in Chapter 6 on exclusionary zoning, on rezoning review in Chap-

increase by a growing unease with the appropriateness of treating the actions of zoning authorities as the equivalent of Acts of Congress and acts of state legislatures, and deferring to them under separation of powers doctrine.

A. *Legislative Acts*

Traditionally, courts accord legislative actions of local authorities a presumption of validity. Using the fairly debatable standard of review enunciated in Village of Euclid v. Ambler Realty Co.,[4] the burden placed on the challenger is onerous. Often denominated the rational basis test, in its more deferential application, a better name is the conceivable basis test.[5] While the standards are enunciated in similar language, application varies from state to state.

In recent decades, numerous courts have expressed dissatisfaction with granting such deference to local legislation.[6] In some instances courts have concluded that the quasi-judicial nature of site-specific rezonings disqualified them from the deferential review to which true legislation was entitled.[7] Despite enactment by local legislative body, such rezonings in some states are subjected to strict scrutiny.[8]

In other instances the presumption of validity has been reversed and higher scrutiny applied because the actions taken have affected fundamental rights or suspect classes. This has occurred frequently in challenges to exclusionary zoning practices,[9] where special standards for review may be used. A classic example is the complex system for review of exclusionary zoning in New Jersey.[10] Also, in Pennsylvania, a local government that seeks to exclude completely any particular type of land use bears the burden of showing that such use is noxious in character.[11] Similarly, in some Fifth Amendment takings litigation and First Amendment speech and religion cases, deferential review may not be used.[12]

B. *Administrative Acts*

In many states a presumption of validity attaches to administrative

ter 5, on plan consistency in Chapter 2, and on constitutional issues of the Fifth and First Amendments in Chapter 10.

4. 272 U.S. 365, 47 S.Ct. 114, 71 L.Ed. 303 (1926).

5. The Tennessee Supreme Court refers to it as the "any possible reason" standard and notes that it "is hard to imagine a more difficult undertaking" than having to overcome it. McCallen v. City of Memphis, 786 S.W.2d 633, 641 (Tenn.1990).

6. See Mandelker and Tarlock, supra note 1, at 5–7.

7. The leading case of Fasano v. Board of County Comm'rs, 264 Or. 574, 507 P.2d 23 (1973)discussed supra § 5.9.

8. Board of County Comm'rs v. Snyder, 627 So.2d 469 (Fla.1993).

9. See infra Ch. 6.

10. See Southern Burlington County NAACP v. Mount Laurel, 92 N.J. 158, 456 A.2d 390 (1983), on remand 207 N.J.Super. 169, 504 A.2d 66 (1984), and the subsequent legislative establishment of the Council on Affordable Housing. See Hills Dev. Co. v. Township of Bernards, 103 N.J. 1, 510 A.2d 621, 644 (1986).

11. McKee v. Montgomery, 26 Pa. Cmwlth. 487, 364 A.2d 775 (1976). In California the local government has the burden of proof in justifying the need for any direct limitation on the number of dwelling units. West's Ann.Cal.Evid.Code § 669.5.

12. See infra §§ 10.6 and 10.15.

zoning actions, which courts review with some degree of deference.[13] The justification for deferring to administrative zoning board decisions lies in the judgment that the board members are experts in whom courts ought to place some trust[14] or that they have a familiarity with local conditions that the courts lack.[15] The expertise argument loses some force where, as often happens, there are no specific qualifications for membership on a board. Ruling on relatively vague standards like "unnecessary hardship," the common variance standard, also does not require expertise.[16] Familiarity with local conditions also cuts both ways, as some courts worry that the familiarity breeds influence peddling and results in lack of objectivity.[17]

There is potential for confusion with respect to the deference accorded administrative acts since legislative acts also enjoy a presumption of validity and deferential review, but there are important differences. In language that resembles the fairly debatable standard for legislation, courts say that they will not overturn an administrative ruling unless it is arbitrary or capricious,[18] but their review is less deferential than that accorded legislation.[19] Furthermore, statutory requirements and due process protections not applicable to legislation often accompany the administrative decision-making process. Generally by statute, substantial evidence must support an administrative action.[20] The burden may remain on the challenger, but in many states, the board must make findings so that the court can assure itself that the board has acted properly.[21] In contrast, evidence need not accompany legislative action to

13. Hills Dev. Co. v. Township of Bernards, 103 N.J. 1, 510 A.2d 621, 644 (1986); Roy v. Kurtz, 357 So.2d 1354 (La.App. 1978); Louisville & Jefferson County Planning & Zoning Comm. v. Ogden, 307 Ky. 362, 210 S.W.2d 771 (1948). But see Jennings v. Dade County, 589 So.2d 1337, 1343, n. 3 (Fla.App.1991), describing review as non-deferential.

14. Gordon Paving Co. v. Blaine County, 98 Idaho 730, 572 P.2d 164, 164 (1977).

15. Connecticut Resources Recovery Auth. v. Planning and Zoning Comm'n, 225 Conn. 731, 626 A.2d 705, 716 (1993); Cowan v. Kern, 41 N.Y.2d 591, 363 N.E.2d 305, 394 N.Y.S.2d 579 (1977).

16. Rose, supra note 1, at 860.

17. See supra § 5.14.

18. Matter of Fulling v. Palumbo, 21 N.Y.2d 30, 286 N.Y.S.2d 249, 250, 233 N.E.2d 272, 273 (1967).

19. West Old Town Neighborhood Ass'n v. City of Albuquerque, 122 N.M. 495, 927 P.2d 529 (1996); Sunderland Family Treatment Servs. v. City of Pasco, 127 Wash.2d 782, 903 P.2d 986 (1995); Protect Hamden/North Haven from Excessive Traffic & Pollution, Inc. v. Planning & Zoning

Comm., 220 Conn. 527, 600 A.2d 757 (1991). But see McCallen v. City of Memphis, 786 S.W.2d 633 (Tenn.1990), where the court finds no meaningful difference between legislative and administrative or quasi-judicial actions and vests all with a highly deferential conceivable basis standard of review.

20. See, e.g.,West's Rev. Code Ann. § 7.16.120(4)-(5) and Sunderland Family Treatment Servs. v. City of Pasco, 127 Wash.2d 782, 903 P.2d 986 (1995); Appeal of Chatelain, 164 Vt. 597, 664 A.2d 269 (1995); Matthew v. Smith, 707 S.W.2d 411, 417 (Mo.1986). But see Roy v. Kurtz, 357 So.2d 1354, 1355 (La.App.1978) ("rather sketchy" evidence sufficed).

21. County Council of Prince George's County v. Brandywine Enter., Inc., 109 Md. App. 599, 675 A.2d 585, 595 (1996); Fields v. Kodiak City Council, 628 P.2d 927 (Alaska 1981); Packer v. Hornsby, 221 Va. 117, 267 S.E.2d 140, 141 (1980); Topanga Assn. for a Scenic Community v. County of Los Angeles, 11 Cal.3d 506, 522 P.2d 12, 113 Cal.Rptr. 836 (1974); Alcorn v. Rochester Zoning Bd. of Adjustment, 114 N.H. 491, 322 A.2d 608, 610 (1974); Fleming v. Tacoma, 81 Wash.2d 292, 502 P.2d 327 (1972).

sustain its legitimacy[22] and courts following the deferential rule will look for any conceivable reason to uphold a legislative act.

Where the administrative body is engaged in adjudicating rights of individuals, as is usually the case with zoning boards, courts require procedural due process.[23] While the demands of due process vary, this likely means that those affected have a right to be heard and present evidence, a right to cross examination, and a right to a record with findings of fact.[24] Still, courts are fond of noting that " 'procedural informality is the hallmark of administrative hearings.' "[25] Thus, it has been held not violative of due process to take evidence from a witness who is not under oath.[26] But, a court held due process violated when, at a second hearing on a permit application, a board received testimony adverse to the property owner after advising the owner's attorney that he need not attend the hearing since no additional evidence would be heard.[27] If action is legislative, rather than adjudicative, procedural due process rights do not apply.[28]

The deal making nature of local zoning, whether labeled legislative or administrative, coupled with enhanced concern of bias and conflict of interest that exists by virtue of the fact that it is a localized process, suggests a need for judicial oversight.[29]

§ 5.38 Nature of Relief to Be Granted

A. Administrative Proceedings

When a court reviews an administrative proceeding, such as the decision of a zoning board granting or denying a variance, principles of state administrative law usually govern the nature of the relief to be granted by the court. If the court does not affirm the decision below, it will typically remand the case to the administrative board,[1] although in

22. Jennings v. Dade County, 589 So.2d 1337, 1343, n. 3 (Fla.App.1991); Bar Harbour Shopping Center, Inc. v. Andrews, 23 Misc.2d 894, 196 N.Y.S.2d 856, 867 (Sup. Ct.1959).

23. Jackson v. Spalding County, 265 Ga. 792, 462 S.E.2d 361 (1995); County of Lancaster v. Mecklenburg, 334 N.C. 496, 434 S.E.2d 604 (1993). See also infra § 10.13.

24. Compare Coral Reef Nurseries, Inc. v. Babcock Co., 410 So.2d 648, 652–53 (Fla. App.1982), and Kaelin v. City of Louisville, 643 S.W.2d 590 (Ky.1982), recognizing a right to cross-examination with Barton Contracting Co. v. City of Afton, 268 N.W.2d 712, 716 (Minn.1978) and Zimarino v. Zoning Bd. of Review of Providence, 95 R.I. 383, 187 A.2d 259 (1963), finding no such right.

25. See Mohilef v. Janovici, 51 Cal. App.4th 267, 58 Cal.Rptr.2d 721, 734 (1996) and cases cited therein.

26. Id. See also Monte Vista Prof. Bldg., Inc. v. City of Monte Vista, 35 Colo. App. 235, 531 P.2d 400 (1975); Messer v. Snohomish Co. Bd. of Adjustment, 19 Wash. App. 780, 578 P.2d 50 (1978) (no right to de novo hearing).

27. Sclavenitis v. City of Cherry Hills Village Bd. of Adjustment, 751 P.2d 661 (Colo.App.1988).

28. Bi–Metallic Inv. Co. v. State Bd. of Equalization, 239 U.S. 441, 36 S.Ct. 141, 60 L.Ed. 372 (1915). See supra § 5.9.

29. See Mark W. Cordes, Policing Bias and Conflicts of Interest in Zoning Decisionmaking, 65 N.D.L.Rev. 161 (1989).

§ 5.38

1. Duggan v. Cook, 60 Ill.2d 107, 324 N.E.2d 406 (1975).

so doing it will sometimes establish principles of law that give the board little choice in deciding the case.[2] On other occasions the court will find that the record at the initial hearing was inadequate to decide the matter and will remand to the board for new hearings to develop an appropriate record.[3]

If the court concludes that no possible set of facts would support the board's decision, it may reverse the board without remanding for a new hearing.[4] Such a disposition would be appropriate, for example, if the court found that the board lacked jurisdiction to issue the decision. Most land use decisions are fact-sensitive, however, and the most common disposition is a remand to the board so that both sides may further develop the facts in a manner consistent with the court's statement of the law.

B. *Legislative Proceedings*

The nature of the relief to be granted by a court in reviewing a local legislative decision is far more perplexing than with administrative decisions. Courts regularly review a wide range of administrative and quasi-judicial decisions and the principles of law governing the appropriate judicial procedures are familiar. However, when local legislative bodies make decisions involving the use of individual parcels of land they are playing a role so unlike typical "legislative" activity that some courts have felt compelled to treat such decisions as if they were quasi-judicial decisions.[5]

In those states in which local land use decisions are considered legislative, the courts have faced a dilemma in determining what type of relief to award when the legislative decision is found to have been in violation of law. If a *state* legislative decision is found unconstitutional, a court will ordinarily enjoin the operation of the legislation but will not tell the legislature what alternative laws it needs to pass. However, use of such an approach may allow the local government to avoid any meaningful judicial review by continually enacting new laws that frustrate the landowner's desires in a different fashion each time.

The courts of the different states have used a wide range of principles in establishing the appropriate relief for a landowner who succeeds in proving his zoning invalid. In some cases the courts have simply left the parcel unzoned,[6] or reinstated the plaintiff's original zoning.[7]

---

2. Framingham Clinic v. Zoning Bd. of Appeals, 382 Mass. 283, 415 N.E.2d 840 (1981).

3. McCarron v. Zoning Hearing Bd., 37 Pa.Cmwlth. 309, 389 A.2d 1227 (1978).

4. Speedway Bd. of Zoning Appeals v. Popcheff, 179 Ind.App. 399, 385 N.E.2d 1179 (1979) (denial of variance reversed without remand); Tucker v. Zoning Bd. of Adjustment, 62 Pa.Cmwlth. 615, 437 A.2d 499 (1981) (grant of variance reversed without remand).

5. Fasano v. Board of County Comm'rs, 264 Or. 574, 507 P.2d 23 (1973).

6. Board of Supervisors v. Rowe, 216 Va. 128, 216 S.E.2d 199 (1975).

7. H. Dev. Corp. v. Yonkers, 64 A.D.2d 690, 407 N.Y.S.2d 573 (1978).

From the developer's standpoint, the preferred remedy is an order directing the local government to allow the developer's proposed use. Pennsylvania has by statute made this remedy available.[8] The Illinois courts reach the same result without specific statutory authority.[9]

A court may give the local government a specific time to develop new zoning for the property.[10] The trial court in Michigan retains jurisdiction to review and approve an amended ordinance.[11] In Virginia courts require the local government to allow the plaintiff's proposed use but permit it to impose reasonable conditions.[12] Whatever relief is made available the court should not permanently enjoin the local government from changing its zoning because conditions may change in the future.[13]

C. *Consent Decrees*

When parties settle a land use case, they often embody the settlement in a consent agreement approved by the court. Careful drafting of such decrees is essential.[14] A decision of the California Supreme Court interpreted a consent decree awarding the developer a vested right to proceed with the development of all its property substantially in accordance with an attached master plan. The court held that this decree did not prevent the local government from subjecting the developer to a subsequently enacted growth control ordinance severely limiting the number of building permits to be issued each year.[15] In another such case, the Georgia Supreme Court found that a consent decree between a kennel operator and the local government did not prevent more extensive relief against the kennel operator in a separate suit brought by a homeowners' association.[16]

D. *Monetary Liability*

Money damages may be available to a property owner or developer on a number of grounds. The Fifth Amendment taking clause requires that just compensation be provided when property is taken, and in some instance excessive regulations can be deemed to be takings.[17] Monetary

---

8. 53 Penn.Stat. § 11006–A(1).

9. Sinclair Pipe Line Co. v. Richton Park, 19 Ill.2d 370, 167 N.E.2d 406 (1960); Norwood Builders v. Des Plaines, 128 Ill. App.3d 908, 84 Ill.Dec. 105, 471 N.E.2d 634 (1984).

10. City of Atlanta v. McLennan, 237 Ga. 25, 226 S.E.2d 732 (1976), appeal after remand 240 Ga. 407, 240 S.E.2d 881 (1977).

11. Ed Zaagman, Inc. v. Kentwood, 406 Mich. 137, 277 N.W.2d 475 (Mich.1979). See also Sultanik v. Board of Supervisors, 88 Pa.Cmwlth. 214, 488 A.2d 1197 (1985); City of Miami Beach v. Weiss, 217 So.2d 836 (Fla.1969), opinion conformed 219 So.2d 127 (1969).

12. City of Richmond v. Randall, 215 Va. 506, 211 S.E.2d 56 (1975).

13. May Dep't Stores v. St. Louis, 607 S.W.2d 857 (Mo.App.1980); Town of Longboat Key v. Kirstein, 352 So.2d 924 (Fla. App.1977), cert. denied 364 So.2d 887 (1978).

14. See David L. Callies, The Use of Consent Decrees in Settling Land Use and Environmental Disputes, 21 Stet.L.Rev. 871 (1992).

15. Pardee Constr. Co. v. Camarillo, 37 Cal.3d 465, 208 Cal.Rptr. 228, 690 P.2d 701 (1984).

16. Life for God's Stray Animals, Inc. v. New North Rockdale County Homeowners Ass'n, 253 Ga. 551, 322 S.E.2d 239 (1984).

17. See infra §§ 10.2–.11.

liability for other constitutional and federal statutory rights is also available under Section 1983, the federal civil rights law.[18]

State tort law may also be the basis for suit for actions deemed ministerial or for governmental actions that are egregious in nature.[19]

§ 5.39　Relief Under Federal Law

Many land use regulations pose issues arising under various clauses of the federal constitution. Increasingly, parties also allege that land use controls conflict with federal statutes, such as the Fair Housing Act.[1]

A detailed analysis of the rules of federal jurisdiction and procedure is beyond the scope of this book. The tactical advantages of the federal versus the state courts to plaintiffs or defendants will vary from district to district. In any claim, however, consideration should be given to the question of whether to bring the case in federal court or state court.

A.　*Standing*

The federal courts have their own complex and confusing rules of standing that have frequently tripped up unwary plaintiffs. Attempts to use the federal courts to challenge exclusionary zoning have often been defeated by the absence of a plaintiff who can demonstrate injury within the meaning of the federal requirements.[2]

On the other hand, the federal courts have been very receptive to First Amendment claims,[3] frequently using an "overbreadth" analysis that allows the plaintiff to challenge vague and overly broad regulations without showing that the particular defect will harm the plaintiff.[4]

B.　*Removal*

If the plaintiff brings a land use case in the state courts, but raises federal constitutional or statutory claims in the complaint, the defendant is entitled to remove the case to the federal courts even though there is no diversity of citizenship between the parties.[5] The federal court may not remand the case to the state court if the defendant has completed the steps necessary for a valid removal.[6]

Local government attorneys are often unaware of the potential advantages of removal. Whenever a plaintiff files a case in the state

---

18. See infra § 10.23. See also discussion of the federal fair housing action supra § 4.7 and infra § 6.8.

19. See discussion supra § 5.28 I.

§ 5.39

1. See discussion supra § 4.7 and infra § 6.8.

2. Warth v. Seldin, 422 U.S. 490, 95 S.Ct. 2197, 45 L.Ed.2d 343 (1975). See discussion infra § 10.14.

3. See, e.g., Schad v. Borough of Mt. Ephraim, 452 U.S. 61, 101 S.Ct. 2176, 68 L.Ed.2d 671 (1981).

4. NAACP v. Alabama, 377 U.S. 288, 84 S.Ct. 1302, 12 L.Ed.2d 325 (1964), on remand 277 Ala. 89, 167 So.2d 171 (1964). See, e.g., Solomon v. City of Gainesville, 763 F.2d 1212 (11th Cir.1985); 754 Orange Ave., Inc. v. West Haven, 761 F.2d 105 (2d Cir.1985).

5. 28 U.S.C.A. § 1441(b).

6. Thermtron Prod., Inc. v. Hermansdorfer, 423 U.S. 336, 96 S.Ct. 584, 46 L.Ed.2d 542 (1976).

court raising a federal constitutional or statutory issue, the astute defendant's attorney will compare the records of the local state and federal courts in regard to that particular constitutional issue and will use that comparison as part of the tactical decision to remain in state court or remove the case to federal court.

C. Civil Rights Statutes

The federal civil rights statute, Section 1983, forms the basis for many land use cases. We discuss it in detail elsewhere in the book.[7] State courts have concurrent jurisdiction over § 1983 claims and many states have civil rights laws similar to Section 1983 that may provide similar relief.[8] Moreover, some state courts may be more willing to award substantial damages in land use cases than most federal courts.[9]

D. Bankruptcy

Land use disputes occasionally arise bankruptcy proceedings. The developer who seeks the protection of the federal bankruptcy court obtains a powerful ally. The court's power to absolve the developer of his debts includes debts owed by the developer to a local government. Creative bankruptcy lawyers have occasionally characterized a developer's obligation to comply with land use controls as a "debt." Usually, such an obligation would be a debt only if reduced to a money judgment in favor of the local government.[10] A bankruptcy court lacks authority to waive lawful police power regulations.

E. Eleventh Amendment

The Eleventh Amendment limits the jurisdiction of the federal courts involving suits against a state. Plaintiffs may commence such suits in the federal courts only if the state has expressly waived sovereign immunity.[11]

Under most circumstances, local governments are not entitled to claim the benefit of the Eleventh Amendment because courts have not treated them as agents of the state for that purpose.[12] However, under those land use control programs having a significant element of state supervision, the local government might be able to claim that it was acting as an agent of the state for Eleventh Amendment purposes.[13]

---

7. See infra § 10.23.

8. Bell v. Mazza, 394 Mass. 176, 474 N.E.2d 1111 (1985).

9. Dickerson v. Young, 332 N.W.2d 93 (Iowa 1983).

10. Ohio v. Kovacs, 469 U.S. 274, 105 S.Ct. 705, 83 L.Ed.2d 649 (1985).

11. Pennhurst State Sch. v. Halderman, 465 U.S. 89, 104 S.Ct. 900, 79 L.Ed.2d 67 (1984); Edelman v. Jordan, 415 U.S. 651, 94 S.Ct. 1347, 39 L.Ed.2d 662 (1974), rehearing denied 416 U.S. 1000, 94 S.Ct. 2414, 40 L.Ed.2d 777 (1974); Atascadero State Hosp. v. Scanlon, 473 U.S. 234, 105 S.Ct. 3142, 87 L.Ed.2d 171 (1985), rehear-ing denied 473 U.S. 926, 106 S.Ct. 18, 87 L.Ed.2d 696 (1985); Cannon v. Univ. of Health Sciences, 710 F.2d 351 (7th Cir. 1983).

12. Mt. Healthy City Sch. Dist. Bd. of Educ. v. Doyle, 429 U.S. 274, 97 S.Ct. 568, 50 L.Ed.2d 471 (1977), appeal after remand 670 F.2d 59 (6th Cir.1982).

13. See Lake Country Estates, Inc. v. Tahoe Regional Planning Agency, 440 U.S. 391, 99 S.Ct. 1171, 59 L.Ed.2d 401 (1979); Bosselman & Bonder, Potential Immunity of Land Use Control Systems from Civil Rights and Antitrust Liability, 8 Hastings Const.L.Q. 453 (1981).

F. Preemption

If a federal regulatory system preempts local regulation, the federal courts may grant injunctive relief against inconsistent local regulations. Preemption may be express or implied from statutory language, from the pervasiveness of the federal regulatory system, or from conflict between federal law and local regulation.[14] A finding of preemption requires clear intent, and is not presumed from broad purpose clauses or similar statutory language.[15]

§ 5.40 Enforcement

A. Historical Inadequacies

Despite the theoretical breadth of the powers of enforcement, the enforcement programs of many local governments have historically been so lax that the chance that inspectors will discover many violations is remote.

B. Public Enforcement Actions

While criminal proceedings are not statistically numerous, and while people do not often think of zoning ordinance violations as criminal acts, many zoning ordinances provide for criminal penalties. For example, a Detroit ordinance provides that:

> Any person, persons, firm or corporation or anyone acting in behalf of said person * * * violating any of the provisions of this Ordinance shall upon conviction thereof be subject to a fine of not more than * * * ($500.00) * * * or to imprisonment in the Detroit House of Correction for a period of not more than ninety (90) days, or to both.
> * * *
>
> Each day that a violation of this Ordinance is continued or permitted to exist without compliance shall constitute a separate offense punishable upon conviction in the manner prescribed in this Section.[1]

As in other criminal cases, proof must be beyond a reasonable doubt,[2] and the burden is on the state. In several states and ordinances, the provisions are in the nature of a civil action to recover a penalty.[3]

Some ordinances declare that a violation of the ordinance constitutes a nuisance. Ordinance provisions of this kind are more frequent in

---

14. Capital Cities Cable, Inc. v. Crisp, 467 U.S. 691, 104 S.Ct. 2694, 81 L.Ed.2d 580 (1984). Preemption is discussed supra § 4.24.

15. Guschke v. Oklahoma City, 763 F.2d 379 (10th Cir.1985).

§ 5.40

1. Detroit, Mich., Official Zoning Ordinance Sec. 24 (1963).

2. State v. McNulty 111 Ohio App.3d 828, 677 N.E.2d 405 (1996); State v. Laurel Crest Academy, 2 Conn.Cir. 294, 198 A.2d 229 (1963); State v. Seich, 98 N.J.Super. 466, 237 A.2d 648 (1967); State v. Loux, 76 N.J.Super. 409, 184 A.2d 755 (1962).

3. City of Palos Heights v. Pakel, 121 Ill.App.2d 63, 258 N.E.2d 121 (1970) (action to recover fine for violation of zoning ordinance while quasi-criminal in nature, is civil in form and is tried and reviewed as a civil proceeding); City of Philadelphia v. Kenny, 28 Pa.Cmwlth. 531, 369 A.2d 1343 (1977).

states such as California that permit local governments to define uses considered nuisances.[4] Thus, the City of Torrance, California provides:

> Any building or structure * * * or any use of property * * * contrary to the provisions of this Article, shall be and the same is hereby declared to be, unlawful, and a public nuisance.[5]

While the Standard Act does not specifically authorize the use of injunctions, the language is broad and general enough to allow them and injunctions are widely used to enforce zoning ordinances. Some statutes specifically authorize injunctive relief.[6] Rather than a criminal sanction, it is the remedy violators would expect to be applied. Typically, the injunction is used to order compliance with the ordinance.[7] A major advantage of the injunction over a criminal proceeding is that the public can take an appeal with respect to the former. That likely will not be possible with respect to criminal proceedings.

C. *Private Enforcement Actions*

Perhaps most zoning violations come to the attention of public officials because of complaints of private parties. In a sense then, the private party is the initiator of machinery to enforce the ordinance. The private party may also be the relator in a mandamus proceeding, forcing the public official to take action. Finally, a private person may be able to enforce the ordinance directly.

If a clear violation of the zoning ordinance occurs and the officer empowered to enforce the ordinance has no discretion in the matter, a private party can seek to compel enforcement through mandamus. As with other types of proceedings, there are problems of standing. While the petitioner of a writ must be beneficially interested,[8] enforcement is a matter of public interest that might entitle any citizen to bring the writ.[9] If there is some question as to whether there is a violation, mandamus may not lie. For example, where a city attorney concluded the ordinance had not been violated, the court held a private party unable to compel the attorney to institute a lawsuit.[10] Sometimes mandamus will not lie because the private party can sue directly to seek enforcement.[11] Since legislative bodies usually perform discretionary rather than administrative acts, mandamus does not typically lie against a legislative body.

Perhaps most typically, a private person seeks to enforce a zoning ordinance by bringing an injunction action. The major problem is that of standing. Some ordinances specially provide for standing. For example, a District of Columbia regulation provides that:

---

4. West's Ann.Cal.Gov.Code § 38771.

5. Torrance, Cal., Mun.Code § 92.23.2.

6. Minn.Stat.Ann. § 462.362.

7. See, e.g., Adams v. Cowart, 224 Ga. 210, 160 S.E.2d 805 (1968) enjoining continuation of trailer park that violated ordinance. Note, The Injunction—A Method of Zoning Enforcement, 15 Syracuse L.Rev. 546 (1964).

8. See West's Ann.Cal.Code Civ.Proc. § 1086.

9. Blankenship v. Michalski, 155 Cal. App.2d 672, 318 P.2d 727 (1957).

10. Id.

11. Pansa v. Sitrin, 27 A.D.2d 636, 275 N.Y.S.2d 689 (1966).

any neighboring property owner or occupant who would be specially damaged by any * * * violation may, in addition to all other remedies provided by laws, institute [sic] injunction, or other appropriate action or proceeding to prevent such unlawful erection * * * or use, or to correct or abate such violation or to prevent the occupancy of such *building, structure,* or land.[12]

The ordinance appears to set two tests, neighboring and specially damaged. While ordinarily both tests must be met, courts may allow recovery when some vaguer test of "interest" is met.[13] Special damage could be shown without being a neighbor. For example, residents at the beginning of a long road might object to the development of a large quarry at the end of the road that would generate heavy traffic. Note that the quoted ordinance permits occupants to bring an action, which could include specially damaged tenants.[14]

Taxpayers can bring injunction actions in some states. Notice to city officials demanding they take action and their refusal to do so may be a prerequisite to the taxpayer suit.

A private individual can bring an action on a nuisance theory alleging violation of the ordinance. An action for damages can be brought in connection with an injunction action even though there is no attempt to enjoin the activity.[15] The plaintiff must show some special damage in order to recover.

There may be some greater likelihood that owners would obey zoning ordinances if violation of them would lead to greater civil liability. For example, in Hutchinson v. Cotton,[16] the defendant was using his garage to manufacture a product with a power planer. The use was in violation of the zoning ordinance. A child sustained injuries when he fell into the planer and claimed in a subsequent law suit that violation of the zoning ordinance was negligence per se.[17] While the court denied recovery on that theory, if

> the injured party be within the class of persons for whose benefit and protection the ordinance was enacted, * * * there was a violation of that ordinance * * * and * * * an injury proximately resulted * * * [civil recovery for violations of an ordinance may be proper.][18]

A person specially injured can generally bring an action without a prior request to authorities to enforce the ordinance and without seeking

---

12. District of Columbia, Zoning Regulations § 8105.2 (1963) (Italics in original).

13. Boyd v. Donelon, 193 So.2d 291 (La.App.1966) affirmed 250 La. 366, 195 So.2d 643 (1967).

14. Daub v. Popkin, 5 A.D.2d 283, 171 N.Y.S.2d 513 (1958), affirmed mem., 4 N.Y.2d 1024, 177 N.Y.S.2d 528, 152 N.E.2d 544 (1958).

15. McIvor v. Mercer–Fraser Co., 76 Cal.App.2d 247, 172 P.2d 758 (1946).

16. 236 Minn. 366, 53 N.W.2d 27 (1952).

17. See also Neuber v. Royal Realty Co., 86 Cal.App.2d 596, 195 P.2d 501 (1948).

18. Comment, Zoning Law as Evidence of Negligence, 47 Neb.L.Rev. 732, 737 (1968).

a writ of mandate to compel them to do so.[19] If there is a statutory remedy providing private party a judicial route to seek enforcement of the ordinance, or some administrative route, they should pursue that route generally. Frequently, however, a statutory route is not available. In private enforcement actions, there has usually been no administrative or legislative decision that can be made the basis for appeal, and the statutory provisions often are based on such a decision. Mandamus may not be a proper remedy where the plaintiff can proceed directly against a violator of an ordinance.[20]

19. Fitzgerald v. Merard Holding Co., 106 Conn. 475, 138 A. 483 (1927).

N.Y.S.2d 689 (1966).

20. Pansa v. Sitrin, 27 A.D.2d 636, 275

Chapter 6

EXCLUSIONARY ZONING

---

§ 6.1   Introduction: The Evils of Exclusionary Zoning

A shallow, Pollyannish view of zoning is that it is a system with everything in its place and a place for everything. Indeed, early proponents of zoning analogized it to simple practices of good housekeeping: the piano in the parlor, not the bedroom; the stove in the kitchen, not the pantry.[1] In practice, however, zoning provides no place for some uses, for along with the basic separation of uses that is the essence of Euclidean zoning comes the total exclusion of uses that the community has no room for or does not wish to accommodate.

A zoning ordinance may exclude a few specific undesired uses, such as heavy industry or adult entertainment, or exclude general categories, such as all industrial or high density residential uses. The total or near-total exclusion of such uses by very small or truly rural communities is not surprising and generally not controversial. However, when larger cities and towns in the path of development engage in exclusionary

§ 6.1
1. See James Metzenbaum, 1 The Law of Zoning 9 (2d ed.1955). Metzenbaum represented Euclid in Village of Euclid v. Ambler Realty Co., 272 U.S. 365, 47 S.Ct. 114, 71 L.Ed. 303 (1926).

practices, misgivings and questions arise as to whether this is a proper use of the zoning power. It is particularly troubling when they intend the exclusion to discriminate, or when zoning has the effect of discriminating, against persons because of wealth or race. That state enabling acts and local government processes have been and are being used to further racial discrimination is especially disheartening. We should expect more from government.

Varying motives lie behind exclusionary zoning. Some are fiscal in nature as governments try to encourage development of land uses that will produce high tax revenue and to discourage or prevent land uses that will cost government more than the tax revenue they produce. Business and industry typically are positive tax ratables, while high density, lower cost housing is negative. Education is the key cost component a community faces with housing. Generally, the more bedrooms, the more school age children. Thus, lower cost single-family homes with four bedrooms are a poor tax deal. High rise luxury apartments with few bedrooms are a good tax deal.[2]

Non-fiscal motivations also exist. High cost zoning requirements may be designed to achieve aesthetic benefits and open space. They may also be used to "preserve property values" and protect the "character" of the community. Often, these are loaded terms that mask class and race discrimination.

The practice of exclusionary zoning, or snob zoning as it is sometimes called, strikes at the core of the police power that local governments exercise. The Supreme Court upheld the separation of uses as a constitutional exercise of a state's police power in Village of Euclid v. Ambler Realty Co.[3] There, the Court specifically approved the use of zoning to effect economic segregation in housing when it upheld the exclusion of apartments from single-family districts with the unflattering declaration that apartments in districts of "private houses" were "mere parasites."[4] The *Euclid* Court, however, warned that there were limits to the parochial use of this delegated power. There might be, said the Court, instances "where the general public interest would so far outweigh the interest of the municipality that the municipality would not be allowed to stand in the way."[5]

As the popularity of zoning grew, local governments and courts ignored the regional welfare implications raised by the *Euclid* Court. Courts, in fact, turned regional welfare on its head courts by allowing suburban areas to justify exclusion based on the availability of land elsewhere in the region to serve the excluded use.[6] As Professor Briffault has observed, this concept is paradoxical because if the proper focus of planning is regional, then local government ought not have the power to

---

2. See generally George Sternlieb, Housing Development and Municipal Costs (1973).

3. 272 U.S. 365, 47 S.Ct. 114, 71 L.Ed. 303 (1926).

4. 272 U.S. at 394, 47 S.Ct. at 120.

5. 272 U.S. at 390, 47 S.Ct. at 119.

6. Duffcon Concrete Products v. Borough of Cresskill, 1 N.J. 509, 64 A.2d 347 (1949), discussed infra § 6.9.

zone in the first instance.[7] In the ensuing half-century after the 1926 *Euclid* decision, the practice of exclusionary zoning flourished, and the Supreme Court did not restrain it. Indeed, in 1977, well after the practice was deeply entrenched, the Court gave its blessing to parochial zoning practices in Village of Arlington Heights v. Metropolitan Housing Development Corp.[8]

While nonresidential uses may be wrongly excluded,[9] the exclusion of high density, lower cost housing is far and away the major problem with exclusionary zoning. The increase in the cost of housing that results from the use of exclusionary controls is well documented.[10] The problem, though, goes beyond high cost housing in the suburbs. Exclusionary zoning promotes sprawl and raises the cost of providing municipal services.[11] Furthermore, those left behind find themselves alone in the urban core. Their tax base is diminished by the exodus of middle and upper income persons who have abandoned the city to these sprawl developments on the outskirts. Many businesses move out as well, and inner-city residents who wish to work at the fleeing businesses, are left with long and difficult commutes to work.

Communities use various methods to exclude low and moderate cost housing. They include regulations mandating a minimum lot size and minimum house size, large lot-frontage requirements, and limitations or bans on multi-family housing and manufactured housing. Zoning and subdivision controls are the standard vehicles used, but building codes requiring the use of expensive materials may also be employed. These practices, as they involve economic discrimination and affect the provision of affordable housing, are the primary focus of this chapter. Racially discriminatory zoning is covered elsewhere in this treatise.[12]

The gravity of these problems continues to produce proposals for change.[13] The increasing severity of housing shortages due in part[14] to exclusionary zoning has led to the use in some states of the reverse technique of inclusionary zoning.[15]

7. Richard Briffault, Our Localism: Part II—Localism and Legal Theory, 90 Colum.L.Rev. 346, 369 (1990).

8. 429 U.S. 252, 97 S.Ct. 555, 50 L.Ed.2d 450 (1977), discussed infra § 10.14.

9. See infra §§ 6.2–.6.

10. See Not in My Back Yard: Removing Barriers to Affordable Housing (Report of Advisory Commission on Regulatory Barriers to Affordable Housing 1991).

11. See infra Ch. 9 on growth management.

12. Equal protection implications are covered infra § 10.14 and use of the federal Fair Housing Act is covered supra § 4.7 and infra § 15.11. See also Richard Thompson Ford, The Boundaries of Race: Political Geography in Legal Analysis, 107 Harv.L.Rev. 1841 (1994).

13. See Jerry Frug, The Geography of Community, 48 Stan.L.Rev. 1047 (1996); Richard Briffault, The Local Government Boundary Problem in Metropolitan Areas, 48 Stan.L.Rev. 1115 (1996); Quintin Johnstone, Government Control of Urban Land Use: A Comparative Major Program Analysis, 39 N.Y.L.Sch.L.Rev. 373 (1994).

14. Local government and its exercise of zoning power should not be used as a scapegoat to shoulder all blame for the housing problems we face. See Patricia Salkin, Barriers to Affordable Housing: Are Land–Use Controls the Scapegoat, Land Use L. & Zoning Dig., April, 1993, at 3.

15. See infra § 6.7.

§ 6.2 Minimum Lot Size

The requirement of large minimum lot sizes is a popular device used by suburban communities.[1] Minimum lot sizes of 5,000 square feet,[2] 20,000 square feet,[3] 40,000 square feet,[4] three acres[5] and five acres[6] are common and have been upheld often. Courts sustaining these minimums generally do so on the ground that the ordinances carry out the standard zoning or subdivision enabling acts' goals of avoiding congestion in the streets, securing safety from fire, preventing overcrowding, and obtaining adequate light and air.[7] Upholding a one acre minimum lot size used by a Boston suburb, the court in Simon v. Town of Needham[8] noted that the larger the lot, the greater the freedom from noise, the better the opportunity for rest, and the lesser the danger from fire. The court recognized that a town ought not use limitations that would exclude "thrifty and respectable citizens,"[9] but it found one acre to be reasonable based in part on its finding that twelve nearby suburbs of Boston had similar restrictions.

Health and safety justifications, however, are generally make-weights. Communities enact minimum lot controls to preserve the character and tax base of a community. After all, it is called snob zoning for a reason. Still, in the absence of some form of heightened scrutiny, courts sustain minimum lot size requirements. That is certainly the case under federal constitutional law, where, so long as the complaints involve only wealth discrimination and an assertion of a right to adequate housing, courts apply a highly deferential standard of review.[10]

The courts of several states have come to recognize that the principle of "the larger the lot the better" does not promote the public interest. For example, twenty two years after deciding the *Simon* case, the same Massachusetts court invalidated a 100,000 square foot minimum lot size, noting that as lot size requirements increase, "the law of diminishing returns will set in at some point."[11] Other courts have invalidated minimum lot sizes of one-half acre,[12] 2–acres,[13] and 2½ acres.[14]

§ 6.2

1. Susan Ellenberg, Note, Judicial Acquiescence in Large Lot Zoning: Is it Time to Rethink the Trend?, 16 Colum.J.Envtl.L. 183 (1991).

2. Clemons v. City of Los Angeles, 36 Cal.2d 95, 222 P.2d 439 (1950).

3. Padover v. Township of Farmington, 374 Mich. 622, 132 N.W.2d 687 (1965).

4. Josephs v. Town Bd. of Clarkstown, 24 Misc.2d 366, 198 N.Y.S.2d 695 (1960).

5. Johnson v. Town of Edgartown, 425 Mass. 117, 680 N.E.2d 37 (1997).

6. Honeck v. Cook County, 12 Ill.2d 257, 146 N.E.2d 35 (1957); Fischer v. Bedminster Twp., 11 N.J. 194, 93 A.2d 378 (1952); See Town of Sun Prairie v. Storms, 110 Wis.2d 58, 327 N.W.2d 642 (1983).

7. See generally Gavin L. Phillips, Annot., Validity of Zoning Laws Setting Minimum Lot Size Requirements, 1 A.L.R.5th 622 (1992).

8. 311 Mass. 560, 42 N.E.2d 516 (1942).

9. 311 Mass. at 566, 42 N.E.2d at 519.

10. Ybarra v. Town of Los Altos Hills, 503 F.2d 250 (9th Cir.1974). See also Village of Arlington Heights v. Metropolitan Housing Development Corp., 429 U.S. 252, 97 S.Ct. 555, 50 L.Ed.2d 450 (1977), discussed infra § 10.14.

11. Aronson v. Town of Sharon, 346 Mass. 598, 604, 195 N.E.2d 341, 345 (1964).

12. Christine Bldg. Co. v. City of Troy, 367 Mich. 508, 116 N.W.2d 816 (1962). See also Morris v. City of Los Angeles, 116

In a significant opinion striking down a four-acre minimum lot size, National Land & Investment Co. v. Kohn,[15] the Pennsylvania Supreme Court persuasively articulated the case against large lot zoning. Applying a form of heightened scrutiny, the court found the town's justifications wanting. Health factors, said the town, would require on-site sewage disposal. That concern, said the court, was to be dealt with by the town's sanitary board. The roads were alleged to be inadequate, but the evidence showed they would not reach their capacity for another seven years. The town wanted to preserve a greenbelt. Cluster zoning might do the job, said the court, but an area dotted with houses every four acres would not be a true greenbelt. There was a historic site to protect, but the court noted that it was placed in a two-acre zone. The town's interest in preserving its semi-rural character was viewed as a matter of private, not public, interest. Large landowners, desirous of keeping out higher density housing, can enter into private controls to achieve their goals.

The town wanted to keep out "those pressing for admittance" and the question was whether the town could "stand in the way of the natural forces which send our growing population into hitherto undeveloped areas in search of a comfortable place to live."[16] The court concluded that its effort to do so did not promote the public interest and invalidated the ordinance on substantive due process grounds. While the ordinance implicated the third party rights of those living in cities, it violated the due process right of the landowner-developer.

Large minimum lot sizes are most likely valid in bonafide rural areas where they are a form of agricultural preservation.[17] In that context, courts have upheld minimum lot sizes of 50,[18] 80[19] and 160[20] acres. So used, they have characterized them as "reverse exclusionary zoning," indicative of efforts by rural communities to prevent developers who cater to middle and upper income buyers from engaging in leapfrog development.[21]

Cal.App.2d 856, 254 P.2d 935 (1953) holding a 5,000 square foot minimum invalid as applied to a lot where other houses in the area were on smaller lots.

13. Board of County Supervisors of Fairfax County v. Carper, 200 Va. 653, 107 S.E.2d 390 (1959).

14. County of Du Page v. Halkier, 1 Ill.2d 491, 115 N.E.2d 635 (1953).

15. 419 Pa. 504, 215 A.2d 597 (1965). See also Appeal of Kit–Mar Builders, Inc., 439 Pa. 466, 268 A.2d 765 (1970) (invalidating two acre minimum).

16. 419 Pa. at 532, 215 A.2d at 612.

17. See infra § 13.10. See also Johnson v. Town of Edgartown, 425 Mass. 117, 680

N.E.2d 37 (1997) upholding a three acre minimum for ecological reasons.

18. Codorus Twp. v. Rodgers, 89 Pa. Cmwlth. 79, 492 A.2d 73 (1985).

19. Ada County v. Henry, 105 Idaho 263, 668 P.2d 994 (1983).

20. Wilson v. County of McHenry, 92 Ill.App.3d 997, 48 Ill.Dec. 395, 416 N.E.2d 426 (1981). But see Hopewell Twp. Bd. of Supervisors v. Golla, 499 Pa. 246, 452 A.2d 1337 (1982) (requirement allowing only five houses on a 140 acre tract was invalidated).

21. Patrick J. Skelley, Note, Defending the Frontier (Again): Rural Communities, Leap–Frog Development, and Reverse Exclusionary Zoning, 16 Va.Envtl.L.J. 273 (1997).

§ 6.3   Minimum Floor Space

Exclusionary zoning is also achieved through minimum floor space requirements. Lionshead Lake, Inc. v. Township of Wayne[1] is the most famous, or perhaps infamous, case sustaining the validity of minimum floor space requirements.[2] Wayne Township, New Jersey, required a minimum of 768 square feet for single story houses, 1000 square feet for two story houses with an attached garage, and 1200 square feet for two story houses without an attached garage. A builder of houses containing 484 square feet challenged the ordinance. The court noted that small houses might create health problems, but more broadly found that ordinance preserved property values by precluding the construction of what it called "shanties" that could adversely affect the aesthetics and character of the community.

As with minimum lot size, minimum house size ordinances are generally based on makeweight arguments of health and aesthetics. Wayne township, for example, sought to justify its ordinance in part based on a study showing that minimum house sizes were related to health. Overcrowding is a legitimate health concern, but an ordinance that places no limit on the number of occupants per square feet does nothing to limit overcrowding. Furthermore, a sliding scale, like Wayne Township's, based on the number of stories and the existence of an attached garage, makes a health argument nonsensical.[3]

An aesthetics goal is closer to the mark, but still unconvincing. The size of a house does not determine its beauty. A large house is not necessarily pleasing to view, nor is a small one necessarily offensive. The relationship of house size to lot size is a legitimate aesthetic concern, but ordinances such as Wayne Township's do not control that.[4] Size, however, does say something about cost and the larger the house size required, the more affluent the buyers must be.

The New Jersey Supreme Court implicitly overruled *Lionshead Lake* in Home Builders League of South Jersey v. Township of Berlin.[5] *Berlin* held that an ordinance prescribing minimum floor areas for residences was invalid because it appeared to be directed toward economic segregation, rather than the public health or safety or the preservation of the character of neighborhoods. Other courts also have disagreed with *Lionshead Lake*. The Connecticut Supreme Court, for example, found a 1300 square foot minimum invalid, noting that the 1026 square foot house

§ 6.3

1. 10 N.J. 165, 89 A.2d 693 (1952), appeal dismissed 344 U.S. 919, 73 S.Ct. 386, 97 L.Ed. 708 (1953).

2. See Haar, Wayne Township: Zoning for Whom?—In Brief Reply, 67 Harv.L.Rev. 986 (1954); Haar, Zoning for Minimum Standards: The Wayne Township Case, 66 Harv.L.Rev. 1051 (1953); Nolan & Horack, How Small a House?—Zoning for Minimum Space Requirements, 67 Harv.L.Rev. 967 (1954). See also Williams & Wacks, Segregation of Residential Areas Along Economic Lines: Lionshead Lake Revisited, 1969 Wis. L.Rev. 827.

3. See Appeal of Medinger, 377 Pa. 217, 104 A.2d 118 (1954).

4. Home Builders League of South Jersey, Inc. v. Township of Berlin, 81 N.J. 127, 145, 405 A.2d 381, 391 (1979).

5. 81 N.J. 127, 405 A.2d 381 (1979).

that the plaintiff had intended to build at a cost of $59,000 would cost an additional $10,000 if he were forced to comply with the 1300 square foot requirement.[6]

§ 6.4 Multi-family Housing

Multi-family housing occupies a special niche in zoning history. In one of the most callous comments in zoning case law, the Supreme Court declared that apartments in districts of "private houses" were "mere parasites."[1] Perhaps the parasite reference was directed solely toward the monolithic, block tenements common in the early years of the twentieth century, but the implication that the occupants of those parasitical buildings were undesirable was unescapable. In fact, the federal district court judge in *Euclid* had held the ordinance unconstitutional in part because he found it classified "the population and segregate[d] them according to their income or situation in life."[2]

Apartment zones historically have served as buffer zones to protect the residents of the single-family home from the noise and traffic of commercial and industrial areas. This practice, of course, means that more people live close to intensive land use activities to protect the few. And, it means that the more numerous children in the apartments serve as buffers for the safety of the fewer children living in single-family homes. If further evidence of the class motive behind the different types of residential districts is needed, consider that the state not only permits people to live in multi-family housing, but the state builds much of it. At the same time, the state holds the power to exclude apartment dwellers from areas occupied by single-family houses on the theory that such exclusion promotes the public, health, safety and welfare. The matter needs reexamination.[3]

Multi-family, high density housing is not simply set apart from single-family detached homes, but is often provided limited land in many cities. It may also be excluded totally. The degree to which such exclusion is permitted generally tracks the permissibility of large lot zoning and minimum house size ordinances. In Appeal of Girsh,[4] a developer of luxury high rise apartments challenged an ordinance that totally excluded apartments. Following its *National Land* decision,[5] the Supreme Court of Pennsylvania invalidated the ordinance, and rejected as irrelevant the argument that apartments would burden the town financially. The jobs, said the court, had moved to the suburbs and the people were

6. Builders Service Corp., Inc. v. Planning & Zoning Comm'n of Town of East Hampton, 208 Conn. 267, 545 A.2d 530 (1988). See also Appeal of Medinger, 377 Pa. 217, 104 A.2d 118 (1954); Frischkorn Constr. Co. v. Lambert, 315 Mich. 556, 24 N.W.2d 209 (1946).

§ 6.4

1. Village of Euclid v. Ambler Realty Co., 272 U.S. 365, 394, 47 S.Ct. 114, 120, 71 L.Ed. 303 (1926). For an almost equally

unflattering view, see Lewis v. Gollner, 129 N.Y. 227, 29 N.E. 81 (1891).

2. 297 Fed. 307, 316 (N.D.Ohio 1924).

3. See, e.g., Edward Ziegler, Jr., The Twilight of Single–Family Zoning, 3 U.C.L.A.J.Envtl.L. & Policy 161 (1983).

4. 437 Pa. 237, 263 A.2d 395 (1970).

5. 419 Pa. 504, 215 A.2d 597 (1965), discussed supra § 6.2.

entitled to move there as well. Small communities that demonstrate credible and legitimate reasons can probably ban multi-family use.[6] The total exclusion, or unduly limited provision, of land for high density housing may clash with the fair share housing requirements imposed in some states.[7]

The moderate or lower income multi-family housing developer faces an uphill struggle. In the rezoning game, a developer hopes to acquire property zoned for some unintensive use and obtain its upzoning to high density residential use. Once developed, the property generates an income stream that returns a profit on the developer's original investment. If the developer had developed land initially zoned for high density residential use, its profit might be nil or even negative because land so zoned is usually expensive. Therefore, the only profit comes from the public action of rezoning. This rezoning technique is one of the few ways moderate and lower income housing can be built, yet it typically will not work as envisioned since legislative bodies that routinely rezone for others, infrequently rezone for developers of lower income housing. When the legislative body does rezone, the voters often show their displeasure by petitioning for a referendum and then disapproving the rezoning.

§ 6.5   Manufactured Housing

Manufactured housing, which represents an increasing percentage of the country's housing stock, plays an important role in state and municipal planning efforts to ease the affordable housing crisis.[1] Off-site built houses are not inexpensive, but, at a cost that is on the average one-half that of site-built houses, they are clearly more affordable.[2] Also, they do not require government subsidies.

Despite the benefits of manufactured housing, negative attitudes, like those exhibited toward multi-family housing, have resulted in the placement of legal obstacles to limit the use of manufactured housing or mobile homes. While apartments were seen as parasites in single-family neighborhoods, mobile homes were viewed as "slums on wheels" occupied by "[t]railer folk [who] for the most part are nomads at heart."[3] In the past, communities often banned manufactured housing entirely,[4] or found other ways to keep mobile homes out, such as allowing them for only temporary use, or subjecting them to building codes designed for

6. See Countrywalk Condominiums, Inc. v. City of Orchard Lake Village, 221 Mich.App. 19, 561 N.W.2d 405 (1997) (traffic safety).

7. See infra § 6.6.

§ 6.5

1. S. Mark White, State and Federal Planning Legislation and Manufactured Housing: New Opportunities for Affordable, Single–Family Shelter, 28 Urb.Law. 263 (1996).

2. Id. at 264.

3. Streyle v. Board of Property Assessment, 173 Pa.Super. 324, 98 A.2d 410 (1953).

4. Vickers v. Township Committee of Gloucester Twp., 37 N.J. 232, 181 A.2d 129 (1962), appeal dismissed, cert. denied 371 U.S. 233, 83 S.Ct. 326, 9 L.Ed.2d 495 (1963), overruled by Southern Burlington County NAACP v. Mount Laurel Twp., 92 N.J. 158, 456 A.2d 390 (1983).

houses built on-site, which they could not meet.[5] Where not totally excluded, mobile homes were confined to such unattractive land that a de facto ban resulted. [6]

The traditional bases of exclusion, that mobile homes and trailer camps are unattractive, unsafe, detrimental to property values and likely to retard city growth along desired lines, are less compelling today.[7] The perception that the occupants of manufactured housing are transients and undesirable neighbors may persist in some areas, but the reality is otherwise.[8] The industry has changed dramatically. The image of short tubular trailers being towed around the country by people who could find no housing in the immediate post-World War II era is passé. Trailers have changed to mobile homes, which have changed to manufactured housing.

More than the language has changed.[9] First, mobile homes are no longer mobile.[10] Once in place, only one in one hundred is ever moved.[11] They are also safer and more attractive. In 1975, Congress passed the National Manufactured Housing Construction and Safety Standards Act to reduce the personal and property damage suffered due to poorly constructed homes and to improve their quality.[12] As a consequence, safety has greatly increased.[13] The exterior design of manufactured homes is more like conventional houses in appearance. Municipal concerns that children from the mobile homes will overrun them, resulting in burdensome education costs, are imaginary. Most buyers of manufactured homes today have no children living with them.

Following the safety and appearance improvements in manufactured housing, state laws have changed over the past twenty years. Some twenty states have legislation that deprives local government of the free

---

5. Federal law now preempts state or local laws regarding safety standards for manufactured housing. 42 U.S.C.A. § 5401 et seq.

6. This still occurs. See English v. Augusta Twp., 204 Mich.App. 33, 514 N.W.2d 172 (1994).

7. Id. See generally Molly A. Sellman, Equal Treatment of Housing: A Proposed Model State Code for Manufactured Housing, 20 Urb.Law. 73 (1988); Susan N. Chernoff, Note, Behind the Smokescreen: Exclusionary Zoning of Mobile Homes, 25 Wash. U.J.Urb. & Contemp.L. 235 (1983); Bartke & Gage, Mobile Homes: Zoning and Taxation, 55 Cornell L.Rev. 491 (1970).

8. Don Oldenburg, Moving Mobile Homes: They Have a New, Improved Image and Are Up, Washington Post, Jan. 16, 1992, at C5.

9. The meanings of these terms vary. Under New Hampshire law, a manufactured home is a "structure, transportable in one or more sections, which, in the traveling mode, is 8 body feet or more in width and 40 body feet or more in length, or when

erected on site, is 320 square feet or more, and which is built on a permanent chassis and designed to be used as a dwelling with or without a permanent foundation when connected to required utilities, which include plumbing, heating and electrical heating systems contained therein." N.H.Stat. Ann. § 674:31.

10. See James Milton Brown and Molly A. Sellman, Manufactured Housing: The Invalidity of the "Mobility Standard," 19 Urb. Law. 367 (1987).

11. Yee v. City of Escondido, 503 U.S. 519, 523, 112 S.Ct. 1522, 1526, 118 L.Ed.2d 153 (1992).

12. 42 U.S.C.A. § 5401 et seq.

13. While studies after Hurricane Andrew showed that manufactured homes did not survive as well as site-built homes, they are safer than site-built homes in earthquakes. See Keyes & Winter, The Manufactured Home: Design and Construction, Urban Land 27, 29 (Jan.1996).

wheeling ability of the past to discriminate against manufactured housing.[14] These statutes vary in approach. Vermont sweepingly prohibits any zoning regulation that excludes manufactured homes, "except upon the same terms and conditions as conventional housing is excluded."[15] Others allow specific, but limited, differential treatment of manufactured housing.[16]

In some states, legislation simply prohibits total exclusion.[17] Under such statutes, an acceptable and common method of zoning is to limit manufactured homes to parks that are away from residential areas for site-built homes. However, municipal compliance with these statutes does not immunize the ordinance from review on constitutional grounds. New Hampshire's statute, for example, prohibits total exclusion but gives wide discretion to municipalities as to where manufactured housing can be located. Attempting to take advantage of this discretion, a town limited manufactured homes to lots along unpaved roads or, if along a paved road, set back at least 500 feet. The court held the ordinance unconstitutional, finding that its discriminatory treatment did not fairly advance the alleged goal of preserving the "Currier and Ives" charm of the town.[18]

Courts in some states have held that cities cannot sequester manufactured housing in parks. A leading case is Robinson Township v. Knoll,[19] where the court held that a zoning ordinance that limited mobile homes to mobile home parks was an invalid exercise of the police power. Rejecting as outdated the view that mobile homes were necessarily unsafe and unattractive, the court said that off-site built housing could not be subjected to a per se exclusion from other residential areas. Safety and appearance controls, however, were allowable to assure the compatibility of any manufactured home with the site-built homes in the area.

A number of courts, unconvinced that manufactured housing has changed from its darker "trailer" days or preferring to defer to the judgment of the legislative body, uphold limitations on the placement of manufactured homes.[20] In jurisdictions that allow such exclusionary

---

14. See S. Mark White, State and Federal Planning Legislation and Manufactured Housing: New Opportunities for Affordable, Single–Family Shelter, 28 Urb. Law 263, 266, n.17 (1996).

15. Vt.Stat.Ann., Tit. 24, § 4406(4)(A). See Appeal of Lunde, 688 A.2d 1312 (Vt. 1997).

16. West's Fla.Stat.Ann. § 320.8285 (5) (only roofing and siding materials).

17. See, e.g., N.H.Rev.Stat.Ann. § 674.32; N.C.Gen.Stat. § 160A–383.1.

18. Town of Chesterfield v. Brooks, 126 N.H. 64, 69, 489 A.2d 600, 604 (1985).

19. 410 Mich. 293, 302 N.W.2d 146 (1981). See also Petition of Carpenter v. City of Petal, 699 So.2d 928 (Miss.1997)

(per se restriction of mobile homes to parks invalid); Cannon v. Coweta County, 260 Ga. 56, 389 S.E.2d 329 (1990); Bourgeois v. Parish of St. Tammany, 628 F.Supp. 159 (E.D.La.1986); Luczynski v. Temple, 203 N.J.Super. 377, 497 A.2d 211 (1985); Geiger v. Zoning Hearing Bd. of North Whitehall Twp., 510 Pa. 231, 507 A.2d 361 (1986).

20. See City of Lewiston v. Knieriem, 107 Idaho 80, 685 P.2d 821 (1984); Mack T. Anderson Insurance Agency, Inc. v. City of Belgrade, 246 Mont. 112, 803 P.2d 648 (1990); City of Brookside Village v. Comeau, 633 S.W.2d 790 (Tex.), cert. denied 459 U.S. 1087, 103 S.Ct. 570, 74 L.Ed.2d 932 (1982); Sweitzer v. City of O'Fallon, 135 Ill.App.3d 1, 89 Ill.Dec. 886, 481 N.E.2d 729 (1985) (structures have not changed significantly); Warren v. Municipal Officers of Town of

practices, municipalities interested in excluding off-site built homes from areas of site-built single-family homes still must take care to exclude them specifically. If not specifically prohibited, a mobile home might be found a "single-family dwelling" allowable in a residential zone.[21] That, after all, is a normal reading of the term, and courts often construe zoning ordinances to allow the broadest use of land.[22]

Federal law also limits exclusionary practices. The National Manufactured Housing Construction and Safety Standards Act expressly prohibits states from enacting safety standards that differ from federal ones.[23] Zoning ordinances that determine the permissibility of siting by reference to state or local building or safety codes that differ from the federal standards are preempted.[24] The act, however, does not preempt ordinances that exclude manufactured housing on the basis that they may diminish property values.[25] Courts have also held that a special charge for utility hookups of residential dwellings not meeting local energy efficiency standards was not preempted by federal law since the charge was not a construction standard, but a method to recover additional costs of servicing inefficient dwellings.[26]

A significant problem for those who own mobile homes is having to move when a park closes, and closings are on the rise. Parks, once relegated to fringe areas of town, may now be in the path of development. The consequent high land value induces the park owner to sell, leaving the homeowner the choice of moving the "mobile" home or abandoning it. Since relocation costs are high, and have risen dramatically in recent years, the choice may be illusory. In response, some municipalities require the park owner and park purchaser to assist the evicted homeowners by paying a portion of their relocation costs.

Park owners challenged a relocation assistance ordinance of Bloomington, Minnesota, claiming it was a taking. In Arcadia Development Corp. v. City of Bloomington,[27] the court rejected the claims. The crux of the takings claim was that the park owners were being forced to solve housing problems that were not of their making. The court disagreed,

Gorham, 431 A.2d 624 (Me.1981); Mobile Home City of Chattanooga v. Hamilton County, 552 S.W.2d 86 (Tenn.App.1976), cert. denied 431 U.S. 956, 97 S.Ct. 2678, 53 L.Ed.2d 273 (1977); Town of Stonewood v. Bell, 165 W.Va. 653, 270 S.E.2d 787 (1980); Duckworth v. City of Bonney Lake, 91 Wash.2d 19, 586 P.2d 860 (1978).

21. Ciavarella v. Zoning Bd. of Adj. of Hazle Twp., 86 Pa.Cmwlth. 193, 484 A.2d 420 (1984) (mobile home once affixed to concrete slab deemed a single-family dwelling); Hansman v. Oneida County, 123 Wis.2d 511, 366 N.W.2d 901 (modular home not a mobile home), review denied 125 Wis.2d 583, 375 N.W.2d 215 (1985).

22. Upper Salford Twp. v. Collins, 542 Pa. 608, 669 A.2d 335, 336 (1995).

23. 42 U.S.C.A. § 5403(d).

24. Scurlock v. City of Lynn Haven, 858 F.2d 1521 (11th Cir.1988); Colorado Manufactured Housing Ass'n v. Board of County Com'rs of County of Pueblo, 946 F.Supp. 1539 (D.Colo.1996).

25. Texas Manufactured Housing Ass'n, Inc. v. City of Nederland, 101 F.3d 1095 (5th Cir.1996), cert. denied 117 S.Ct. 2497, 138 L.Ed.2d 1003 (1997); City of Brookside Village v. Comeau, 633 S.W.2d 790 (Tex.), cert. denied 459 U.S. 1087, 103 S.Ct. 570, 74 L.Ed.2d 932 (1982); Gackler Land Co., Inc. v. Yankee Springs Twp., 427 Mich. 562, 398 N.W.2d 393 (1986).

26. Washington Manufactured Housing Ass'n v. Public Utility Dist. No. 3 of Mason County, 124 Wash.2d 381, 878 P.2d 1213 (1994).

27. 552 N.W.2d 281 (Minn.App.1996).

finding that park owners had reaped a benefit of charging rents for homes based in part on the immobility of the mobile homes.[28] The Washington Supreme Court reached the opposite result under a different rubric. It held the state's relocation act not to effect a taking, but found it did violate substantive due process because it unfairly singled out park owners to bear a social problem not of their making and was unduly oppressive.[29]

§ 6.6   Fair Share Requirements

The crux of the problem with exclusionary zoning is the lack of recognition of regional responsibilities for local government. The traditional supposition that zoning is a local matter conflicts with the fact that in metropolitan areas local governments are not "islands unto themselves" but are part of a larger socioeconomic region. In 1975, the state supreme courts of New Jersey, Pennsylvania, and New York imposed regional responsibilities on local governments to open their land for the provision of affordable housing.

The landmark case of Southern Burlington County NAACP v. Township of Mt. Laurel[1] was the first to require that a municipality's land use regulations provide a realistic opportunity for low and moderate income housing. In the early 1970s, Mt. Laurel Township, which lies seven miles from Camden and ten miles from Philadelphia,[2] presented the classic picture of a community practicing exclusionary zoning. The township was zoned for low density single-family housing (70%), industrial use (29%) and commercial use (1%). Sixty-five percent of the land was vacant. No land was zoned to permit multi-family housing or mobile homes. The New Jersey Supreme Court invalidated the ordinance, finding it to be violative of the due process and equal protection guarantees of the state constitution. Local zoning, the court said, cannot foreclose the opportunity for low and moderate income families to obtain housing, and regulations must affirmatively provide a realistic opportunity for such housing, at least to the extent of the municipality's fair share of the region's needs.[3]

In the same year that *Mt. Laurel* was decided, the high courts of Pennsylvania and New York Supreme Courts adopted similar positions. In Willistown Township v. Chesterdale Farms, Inc.,[4] the Pennsylvania court held that communities in the path of population growth are obligated to zone land where housing can be built that is affordable to all

---

28. Id. at 286. The court also rejected due process and equal protection claims.

29. Guimont v. Clarke, 121 Wash.2d 586, 854 P.2d 1 (1993), cert. denied 510 U.S. 1176, 114 S.Ct. 1216, 127 L.Ed.2d 563 (1994). Washington has a unique interpretation of the takings clause and substantive due process. See Richard L. Settle, Regulatory Taking Doctrine in Washington: Now You See It, Now You Don't, 12 U. Puget Sound L.Rev. 339 (1989).

§ 6.6

1. 67 N.J. 151, 336 A.2d 713 (1975) (Mt. Laurel I), appeal dismissed, cert. denied 423 U.S. 808, 96 S.Ct. 18, 46 L.Ed.2d 28 (1975).

2. 67 N.J. at 161, 336 A.2d at 718.

3. 67 N.J. at 174, 336 A.2d at 724.

4. 462 Pa. 445, 341 A.2d 466 (1975).

who wish to live there. In Berenson v. Town of New Castle,[5] the New York court held that zoning must provide a balanced and cohesive community, which includes provision of land for middle and lower income persons. A few other state courts have followed these leads.[6]

Implementation of these judicially mandated fair share requirements has been modest.[7] The Pennsylvania and New York courts have not followed an activist approach to insure compliance.[8] Only the New Jersey court has done so. When the *Mt. Laurel* case returned to the New Jersey high court eight years after the court's fair share mandate,[9] the court found the township's ordinance remained "blatantly exclusionary," that there was "widespread noncompliance with the constitutional mandate," and it decided "to put some steel into" the original doctrine.[10] In *Mt. Laurel II*, the court enumerated criteria by which communities might determine their fair share. All areas of the state designated as growth areas by the State Development Land Guide were subjected to the *Mt. Laurel* obligation. This replaced the vague label of "developing municipalities." Besides the removal of restrictive barriers, inclusionary devices such as density bonuses and mandatory set asides were to be used. Mobile homes could not be prohibited. Builders' remedies were to be used to reward a successful challenger and provide specific relief that would lead to actual housing being built. All fair share litigation was to be assigned to a specific corps of three judges, and there were special procedures for review of residential exclusionary zoning cases. Once the obligation was met, other zoning measures to maintain high cost areas or to protect environmentally sensitive lands would be permitted.

Mt. Laurel II provoked angry reaction in New Jersey because, in contrast to the toothless *Mt. Laurel I* opinion, it worked.[11] Some praised it. Professor Haar, for example, lauds what he calls the "audacious activism" of the New Jersey court.[12] It also prompted the state legislature to act. In 1985, the state passed its Fair Housing Act, which established the Council on Affordable Housing (COAH) to oversee implementation of the *Mt. Laurel* obligation.[13] The supposed advantage of the act is that it establishes an administrative mechanism that can more efficiently mediate disputes than can the courts through protracted and costly litigation. COAH has the power to define housing regions and

---

5. 38 N.Y.2d 102, 378 N.Y.S.2d 672, 341 N.E.2d 236 (1975).

6. Associated Home Builders of Greater Eastbay, Inc. v. City of Livermore, 18 Cal.3d 582, 557 P.2d 473, 135 Cal.Rptr. 41 (1976) (dicta); Britton v. Town of Chester, 134 N.H. 434, 595 A.2d 492 (1991).

7. John M. Payne, Rethinking Fair Share: The Judicial Enforcement of Affordable Housing Policies, 16 Real Est.L.J. 20, 22 (1987).

8. See John M. Payne, Doctrine & Politics in Exclusionary Zoning Litigation, 12 Real Est.L.J. 359 (1984).

9. 92 N.J. 158, 456 A.2d 390 (1983) (*Mt. Laurel II*).

10. 92 NJ. at 199, 456 A.2d at 410.

11. Id.

12. Charles M. Haar, Suburbs Under Siege: Race, Space, and Audacious Judges (1996). See also Book Note, Public Choice Theory: A Unifying Framework for Judicial Activism, 110 Harv.L.Rev. 1161 (1997), reviewing Haar's book.

13. N.J.Stat.Ann. §§ 52:27D–301 to 52:27D–329. The court upheld the act in Hills Development Co. v. Bernards Twp., 103 N.J. 1, 510 A.2d 621 (1986).

establish criteria by which fair share allotments are determined. Municipalities may apply to COAH for approval of their housing plans. While use of COAH is not mandatory, municipalities are encouraged to participate because a certification of approval by COAH creates a presumption of validity in favor the local zoning scheme should it be challenged in court.

Legislative fair share mandates and enforcement mechanisms are used in some states as well. An early entry was Massachusetts, which in 1969 created a state agency with power to override local zoning decisions.[14] The act, commonly known as the anti-snob zoning act, provides developers of low and moderate cost housing with a special permitting process before local zoning boards. If a permit is denied, a direct appeal to the state Housing Appeals Committee lies.

Several states require that municipalities address housing needs in their comprehensive planning legislation. In California, local governments must prepare a general plan that includes a housing element that provides for the government's share of regional housing needs.[15] The legislation imposes specific limitations on the power of localities to disapprove affordable housing projects.[16] Florida also requires that local governments adopt a housing element as a part of their comprehensive plan.[17] Connecticut[18] and Rhode Island[19] have started programs that share and mix the attributes of the Massachusetts and California approaches.

Local governments tend to resist fair share mandates. There is widespread noncompliance reported in California, for example, despite the fact that the courts have the power to suspend a city's land use powers if noncompliance is shown.[20] The lack of compliance is attributed to the high cost of bringing suit and the lack of organized representation of the people in the need of housing.[21]

In New Jersey, the judicial and legislative *Mt. Laurel* processes were estimated in 1996 to have produced some 13,000 units of affordable housing.[22] In Massachusetts, some 21,000 units have been built.[23] Whether these numbers indicate success or failure is subject to argument.

14. Mass.Gen.Laws Ann. c. 40B, §§ 20–23. See Paul K. Stockman, Note, Anti–Snob Zoning in Massachusetts: Assessing One Attempt at Opening the Suburbs to Affordable Housing, 78 Va.L.Rev. 535 (1992).

15. West's Ann.Cal.Govt.Code § 65584(a). See also Ariz.Rev.Stat.Ann. § 9–461.05(D); Oregon Rev.Stat.Ann. § 197.307.

16. West's Ann.Cal.Govt.Code § 65589.5.

17. West's Fla.Stat.Ann. § 163.3177 and § 163.3184. See Connerly & Smith, Developing a Fair Share Housing Policy for Florida, 12 J.Land Use & Envtl.L. 63, 78 (1996).

18. See Conn.Gen.Stat § 8–30g and Town Close Assoc. v. Planning and Zoning Comm'n of Town of New Canaan, 42 Conn. App. 94, 679 A.2d 378 (1996).

19. R.I.Gen.Laws § 45–53.

20. West's Ann.Cal.Govt.Code § 65755, discussed in Ben Field, Why Our Fair Share Housing Laws Fail, 34 Santa Clara L.Rev. 35, 49 (1993).

21. Field, supra note 20, at 49.

22. See John M. Payne, Norman Williams, Exclusionary Zoning, and the Mount Laurel Doctrine: Making the Theory Fit the Facts, 20 Vt.L.Rev. 665, 674 (1996).

23. See Connerly & Smith, supra note 17, at 86.

Those terms after all are relative.[24] Amazingly, it was not until 1997 that a low and moderate cost housing development was approved by the Township of Mt. Laurel.[25]

A fair share requirement translates into negative and affirmative steps. In the negative sense, a community must not overuse the common high cost zoning techniques of large minimum lot size and house size. These standards must be relaxed for parts of town by rezoning land to permit high density housing. The removal of prohibitions on mobile homes may be necessary. These are essentially passive in that government is not to stand in the way to impede construction of low and moderate cost housing. But, active steps may also be necessary. This may include the adoption of a streamlined permitting process for such housing, and the use of inclusionary zoning through mandatory set-asides or density bonuses.

§ 6.7 Inclusionary Housing Techniques

Inclusionary housing programs are designed to achieve the actual construction of low and moderate cost housing.[1] They may be used to fulfill a fair share requirement imposed on local government by the state legislature or judiciary or they may be enacted voluntarily. A carrot or stick approach may be used. A density bonus may be given to a developer who promises to commit part of a development to low or moderate cost housing. Or, the permitting authority may require that an approved development set aside part of the development for low and moderate cost housing or pay a "linkage fee"[2] for government construction of such housing.

A. Mechanics of the Set–Aside

As a condition of development permission, a developer may be required to set aside a percentage of the units for sale to persons of low or moderate income. Set-asides, which generally range from 5 percent to 35 percent and average 15 percent, may be on-site integrated units, or off-site. An on-site requirement works as follows. Assuming a 20 percent set-aside and a 100 unit development, the developer must set aside 20 units. The 20 inclusionary units must be sold below market price, say 60 percent. Since the inclusionary units are dispersed among the non-inclusionary units, they must be of comparable quality. Sales are limited to persons meeting maximum income guidelines, often set at earning no more than 80 percent of the area's median income. Since a buyer is paying a below market price of $60,000, covenants in the deeds must

---

24. Payne, supra note 22, at 674.

25. Ronald Smothers, Ending Battle, Suburb Allows Homes for Poor, New York Times, April 12, 1997, p.5, describing the ugly struggle to secure approval of 140 townhouses on 63 acres in Mt. Laurel.

§ 6.7

1. See generally Laura M. Padilla, Reflections on Inclusionary Housing and a Re-

newed Look at its Viability, 23 Hofstra L.Rev. 539 (1995); Jennifer M. Morgan, Comment, Zoning For All: Using Inclusionary Zoning Techniques to Promote Affordable Housing, 44 Emory L.J. 359 (1995); Thomas E. Roberts, Inclusionary Zoning, 1 Zoning and Land Use Controls, Ch.3A (Rohan ed.1994).

2. See infra § 9.8C.

impose resale controls to assure continued use by persons meeting the income guidelines.

The off-site or segregated set-aside allows the developer to build the 20 inclusionary units apart from the other units. This may be on a part of the same tract as the balance of the project. In one hillside project, for example, the developer put the standard units at the top of the hill and the inclusionary units at the bottom.[3] Alternatively, the developer may be able to build the housing elsewhere in town. Off-site or segregated units need not be of a quality equal to the non-inclusionary units, and thus need not be sold below the market price. In the same hillside project referred to above, the units at the bottom of the hill were fairly small (567 to 997 sq. ft.), and, while they had an exterior appearance like the units at the top of the hill, they lacked certain amenities, such as custom cabinets and fireplaces. The developer offered these "no frills" units for sale at $35,000 to $60,000, while it marketed the units at the top of the hill from $150,000 to $200,000.[4]

A density bonus may be used to induce a developer to set aside some housing that is affordable to low or moderate income persons, or it may be used in combination with a mandatory set-aside to mitigate any economic loss the developer might incur. In the 100–unit project with a 20 percent set-aside, a 20 percent density bonus would allow a total of 120 units with 24 inclusionary units.

Inclusionary set-asides are not widely used outside New Jersey and California. A recent survey found fifty-two inclusionary ordinances in California.[5] There are pockets of use elsewhere. Montgomery County, Maryland has used inclusionary zoning since 1973. A 12.5 percent set aside is imposed and a 20 percent density bonus given.[6] The modest use nationwide is likely attributable to the political disinclination to employ what some regard as "Robin Hood" schemes. There are also questions of legality.

A fee may be charged instead of a set-aside. Usually called a linkage fee, the money is earmarked for housing trust funds used to construct low cost housing. The fee is particularly appropriate when applied to developers of nonresidential property.

B. Legality

Authority to enact an inclusionary zoning ordinance may be questioned. The Standard Zoning Enabling Act contains little language to

---

3. N.Y. Times, Feb. 29, 1984 at 15, col.5.

4. Id. Depending in large part on the elasticity of supply, the costs of inclusionary zoning may be absorbed by the developer, passed on to the purchasers of the market rate units, or passed back to the owners of undeveloped land in lower sales prices. For differing views on the economic effects, see Robert C. Ellickson, The Irony of "Inclusionary" Zoning, 54 S.Cal.L.Rev. 1167

(1981) and Andrew G. Dietderich, An Egalitarian's Market: The Economics of Inclusionary Zoning Reclaimed, 24 Fordham Urb.L.J. 23 (1996).

5. Marc T. Smith, Charles J. Delaney, and Thomas Liou, Inclusionary Housing Programs: Issues and Outcomes, 25 Real Est.L.J. 155, 165 (1996). Forty-five were mandatory. The average set-aside was 15%.

6. Id. at 169.

support the implication of such power other than the general recitation of promotion of the general welfare. The authority to enact inclusionary programs is likely to be more easily implied in a "fair share" jurisdiction where local governments are under an obligation to broaden housing opportunities.[7]

In Board of Supervisors of Fairfax County v. DeGroff Enterprises, Inc.,[8] the Virginia Supreme Court held that the state's enabling act only permitted zoning directed toward the physical characteristics of land.[9] Just as the court had invalidated large lot zoning that excluded persons for socioeconomic reasons, so too zoning to include persons for such reasons was invalid. The court in Southern Burlington County NAACP v. Township of Mt. Laurel[10] rejected the *DeGroff* physical limitation view. All physical zoning limitations have socioeconomic effects, said the court, and it would be incongruous to suggest that inclusionary zoning was invalid when the need to use such a device had arisen by the employment of exclusionary techniques.

When linkage fees are used, specific enabling legislation may also be needed.[11] Courts may also regard fees as revenue, rather than regulatory, measures. If so, they must meet state law regarding the levying of taxes, and most will fail that test.[12]

Developers may claim that inclusionary zoning is an uncompensated taking under the Fifth Amendment. While having to meet a set-aside obligation may diminish the profitability of a development, the economic impact will not be so severe as to amount to a taking in most cases.[13] The more difficult question is whether, despite the amount of the loss, the shortage of affordable housing is a burden that is justifiably put on owners of undeveloped land and developers. This raises the nexus issue dealt with by the Supreme Court in the context of land exactions in Nollan v. California Coastal Commission.[14]

The question to be answered is whether the development upon which the set-aside or fee is imposed generates a need for low and moderate cost housing or otherwise aggravates the affordable housing problem the community faces to a substantial degree.[15] The strongest case in favor of constitutionality can be made for the charging of fees to nonresidential development. Commercial development creates a wide

---

7. See discussion supra § 6.6.

8. 214 Va. 235, 198 S.E.2d 600 (1973).

9. The court was not persuaded that the Virginia enabling act's authorization of zoning to create a "harmonious community" allowed inclusionary set-asides.

10. 92 N.J. 158, 456 A.2d 390 (1983).

11. See Merrill & Lincoln, Linkage Fees and Fair Share Regulations: Law and Method, 25 Urb.Law. 223 (1993). See infra § 9.8C.

12. See Wash.Rev.Code Ann. § 82.02.200; Sintra, Inc. v. City of Seattle,

119 Wash.2d 1, 829 P.2d 765, cert. denied 506 U.S. 1028, 113 S.Ct. 676, 121 L.Ed.2d 598 (1992); R/L Associates, Inc. v. City of Seattle, 113 Wash.2d 402, 780 P.2d 838 (1989); San Telmo Assocs. v. City of Seattle, 108 Wash.2d 20, 735 P.2d 673 (1987) (housing preservation ordinance was an invalid tax).

13. See discussion infra § 10.6.

14. 483 U.S. 825, 107 S.Ct. 3141, 97 L.Ed.2d 677 (1987); see discussion infra § 10.5.

15. See discussion of the "substantially advances" test infra § 10.5.

spectrum of housing needs beyond that of the highly paid executive. In Commercial Builders of Northern California v. City of Sacramento,[16] the court found no taking under a program that levied a fee against nonresidential development to be paid into a housing trust fund for the construction of low and moderate cost housing. The city produced "a careful study [that] revealed the amount of low-income housing that would likely become necessary as a direct result of the influx of new workers [from] the nonresidential development."[17]

For residential development the nexus is met if on-site integrated inclusionary units are required to meet a goal of promoting socioeconomic integration. In such a case, the community has determined that non-integrated housing projects are harmful to the public welfare. Any project that does not contain a socioeconomic mix would exacerbate existing segregation. The case is less clear for set-aside ordinances that do not require a socioeconomic mix of inclusionary and non-inclusionary units, but have the sole aim of providing needed housing. There is disagreement whether that need is created by high cost residential development.[18] Resolution of a takings challenge will probably turn on how much scrutiny a court applies in examining the sufficiency of the nexus.[19]

Inclusionary zoning should not have difficulty meeting substantive due process or equal protection challenges, particularly if a low level rational basis test is used.[20] The goals of increasing the supply of affordable housing and promoting socioeconomic integration are legitimate.[21] Charging those who contribute to the problem is likely a rational means to carry out those goals. Particular ordinances, of course, may be excessive and thus invalid under a substantive due process challenge. In one case, for example, a 50 percent mandatory set-aside on mobile home parks was invalidated on due process and equal protection grounds because the renters of the non-inclusionary units would have faced significant rent increases.[22]

---

16. 941 F.2d 872 (9th Cir.1991), cert. denied 504 U.S. 931, 112 S.Ct. 1997, 118 L.Ed.2d 593 (1992).

17. 941 F.2d at 873. See also Terminal Plaza Corp. v. City & County of San Francisco, 177 Cal.App.3d 892, 223 Cal.Rptr. 379 (Cal.Ct.App.1986) (upholding fees charged against conversion of single room occupancy hotels).

18. Holmdel Builders Ass'n v. Township of Holmdel, 121 N.J. 550, 583 A.2d 277 (1990) (construction of high cost housing leaves less land for lower cost housing). But see Lawrence Berger, Inclusionary Zoning Devices as Takings: The Legacy of the Mount Laurel Cases, 70 Neb.L.Rev. 186, 218 (1991) (new high cost housing will create lower cost housing by filtering down effect).

19. See discussion infra § 9.8 and § 10.5 regarding exactions.

20. See discussion infra §§ 10.12 and 10.14.

21. See, e.g., California Housing Finance Agency v. Elliott, 17 Cal.3d 575, 131 Cal.Rptr. 361, 551 P.2d 1193 (1976) (mix of lower and higher income groups a valid goal of state housing finance laws); Southern Burlington County NAACP v. Township of Mt. Laurel, 92 N.J. 158, 456 A.2d 390 (1983); Infants v. Virginia Housing Development Auth., 221 Va. 659, 272 S.E.2d 649 (1980).

22. Van Dalen v. Washington Twp., 205 N.J.Super. 308, 500 A.2d 776 (1984).

§ 6.8   The Fair Housing Act

Under the federal Fair Housing Act it is unlawful to make housing unavailable "because of race, color, religion, sex, familial status, * * * national origin [or handicap]."[1] The act applies to discrimination by private[2] and public parties, and over the years it has been increasingly used to challenge exclusionary zoning practices.[3] The bulk of the FHA zoning cases involve racial and handicap discrimination. In addition, a few FHA zoning cases have dealt with discrimination on the basis of religion,[4] sex[5] and familial status.[6]

A.   *Racial Discrimination*

It is widely held that a violation of the FHA can be based on a showing of discriminatory intent or discriminatory effect.[7] Recognition of a discriminatory effect test under the FHA is particularly vital in race discrimination cases since the alternative of relying on the equal protection clause is typically not feasible.[8] This is due to the Supreme Court's holding that a violation of the equal protection clause based on racial discrimination requires proof of intent.[9] Even then, the government can escape liability if it can show that it would have made the same decision without using race as a factor.[10]

---

§ 6.8

1. 42 U.S.C.A. § 3604. When passed in 1968 the act covered race, color, religion, and national origin. Sex was added in 1974; familial status and handicap protection were added in 1988.

2. See discussion infra § 15.11 regarding private discrimination.

3. See generally James A. Kushner, Combating Housing Discrimination in the 1980's (1983).

4. Le Blanc–Sternberg v. Fletcher, 67 F.3d 412 (2d Cir.1995) (zoning ordinance limiting use of rabbi's home for prayer services), cert. denied ___ U.S. ___, 116 S.Ct. 2546, 135 L.Ed.2d 1067 (1996).

5. Doe v. City of Butler, 892 F.2d 315 (3d Cir.1989) (zoning limitation on number of women who could occupy group homes for abused women does not alone establish discriminatory effect, because the resident limitation would have a comparable effect on males if a group home for recovering male alcoholics were established).

6. Doe v. City of Butler, 892 F.2d 315 (3d Cir.1989) (allegation that restriction on the number of residents who could occupy home for abused women operated to limit, or exclude, women with children in violation of the familial status provision of Title VIII remanded for further proof). See Michael P. Seng, Discrimination Against Fam-

ilies With Children and Handicapped Persons Under the 1988 Amendments to the Fair Housing Act, 22 John Marshall L.Rev. 541 (1989); Edward Allen, Six Years After Passage of the Fair Housing Amendments Act: Discrimination Against Families With Children, 9 Admin.L.J.Am.U. 297 (1995).

7. See Metropolitan Housing Dev. Corp. v. Village of Arlington Heights, 558 F.2d 1283 (7th Cir.1977) (decision on remand), cert. denied 434 U.S. 1025, 98 S.Ct. 752, 54 L.Ed.2d 772 (1978); United States v. City of Black Jack, 508 F.2d 1179 (8th Cir.1974), cert. denied 422 U.S. 1042, 95 S.Ct. 2656, 45 L.Ed.2d 694 (1975). See also John E. Theuman, Annot., Evidence of Discriminatory Effect Alone As Sufficient To Prove, or To Establish Prima Facie Case of Violation of Fair Housing Act, 100 A.L.R.Fed. 97 (1990).

8. See generally Reginald Leamon Robinson, The Racial Limits of the Fair Housing Act: The Intersection of Dominant White Images, the Violence of Neighborhood Purity, and the Master Narrative of Black Inferiority, 37 Wm. & Mary L.Rev. 69 (1995) for a critique of the act.

9. Village of Arlington Heights v. Metropolitan Housing Dev. Corp., 429 U.S. 252, 97 S.Ct. 555, 50 L.Ed.2d 450 (1977).

10. Id. See discussion infra § 10.14. The "same decision" test is also used by some courts in FHA cases. See Smith & Lee

While plaintiffs have shown discriminatory intent in some FHA racial zoning cases,[11] the bulk of the cases rely on an effects or disparate impact test. While a narrow reading of the "because of" language in the FHA could be interpreted to require a showing of motivation, most courts have held that proof of discriminatory effect establishes a prima facie violation of the act. The reasoning of the courts is that since most acts of racial discrimination today are not overt, a requirement that a person prove intent would frequently be insurmountable and would eviscerate the congressional goal to promote fair housing.[12] Though the Supreme Court has not clearly endorsed an effects test under the FHA,[13] it has held that similar language in Title VII employment discrimination legislation does not require proof of intent, and lower courts have followed that lead in interpreting the FHA.[14]

Huntington Branch NAACP v. Town of Huntington[15] illustrates the operation of the disparate impact test. There, the plaintiff challenged a town's refusal to rezone a 14.4 acre parcel from single-family to multi-family to permit construction of a subsidized housing project that would be largely minority in occupancy. Using a disparate impact test, the court found the refusal violated the FHA. The town's population was 95% white and 3.35% black. Seventy percent of the black population lived in two neighborhoods. The town had a shortage of affordable housing, and while 7% of its overall population needed subsidized housing, 24% of its black population needed such housing. There was, however, little land zoned for multi-family housing and the little that was available was in the predominantly minority urban renewal area.

The Second Circuit found the town's rejection of the request imposed disproportionate harm on blacks as a group and had a segregative impact on the community as whole. The town was unable to rebut the prima facie case. To do so, the court said the town must present legitimate, bona fide justifications for its action, and show that less discriminatory alternatives were not available. Seven reasons were offered justifying the refusal to rezone; all were found wanting. Two justifications, that the rezoning was inconsistent with the town's zoning ordinance and contrary to the town's housing plan, both of which relegated the type of housing sought to the urban renewal area, begged the question. Three justifications could be resolved by design modifica-

Assocs., Inc. v. City of Taylor, 102 F.3d 781, 794 (6th Cir.1996).

11. See, e.g., Resident Advisory Bd. v. Rizzo, 564 F.2d 126 (3d Cir.1977), cert. denied 435 U.S. 908, 98 S.Ct. 1458, 55 L.Ed.2d 499 (1978) (city's actions delaying and frustrating the construction in white neighborhood of a low-income housing project likely to be predominantly minority in occupancy were done with discriminatory intent).

12. See Griggs v. Duke Power Co., 401 U.S. 424, 91 S.Ct. 849, 28 L.Ed.2d 158 (1971), where the Court held that under Title VII of the Civil Rights Act of 1964 an employment practice that produced a racially discriminatory effect was actionable.

13. Metropolitan Housing Dev. Corp. v. Village of Arlington Heights, 558 F.2d 1283 (7th Cir.1977), cert. denied 434 U.S. 1025, 98 S.Ct. 752, 54 L.Ed.2d 772 (1978).

14. See Griggs v. Duke Power Co., 401 U.S. 424, 91 S.Ct. 849, 28 L.Ed.2d 158 (1971), where the Court held that under Title VII of the Civil Rights Act of 1964 an employment practice that produced a racially discriminatory effect was actionable.

15. 844 F.2d 926 (2d Cir.1988), aff'd 488 U.S. 15, 109 S.Ct. 276, 102 L.Ed.2d 180 (1988) (per curiam).

tions. They included parking problems, inadequate recreation areas, and undersized units. Traffic was asserted to be a problem but there was no proof. Finally, health concerns were raised based on the proximity to a railway substation and sewage capacity. There was, however, no proof that the substation posed a health threat, and the sewage problem was not advanced until trial. The court ordered the land rezoned.

B. Discrimination Against the Handicapped

Congress added protection for the handicapped in the Fair Housing Amendments Act of 1988 (FHAA). In contrast to the other classes of persons protected by the FHA, the provisions covering the handicapped classification are fairly extensive. Discrimination against the handicapped is expressly defined to include a refusal to make reasonable accommodations in rules necessary to afford handicapped persons an equal opportunity to use a dwelling.[16] The act defines a handicap broadly to include "a physical or mental impairment which substantially limits one or more of such person's major life activities."[17] This includes, for example, the mentally ill, recovering addicts, and persons infected with AIDS.[18] But, not all group homes for persons in need of supervision qualify as "handicapped" under the act.[19] Also, the act does not protect anyone who is a direct threat to the health or safety of others. A significant amount of litigation involving both private and public defendants has ensued interpreting these provisions.[20]

Group homes of unrelated persons seeking to locate in single-family areas often run afoul of zoning codes that limit use by a "family" defined as any number of related persons or unrelated persons up to a certain number.[21] The successful exclusion of group homes by way of such a definition depends on the exemption in the FHAA of "any reasonable * * * restrictions regarding the maximum number of occupants permitted to occupy a dwelling."[22]

In City of Edmonds v. Oxford House, Inc.,[23] the Supreme Court narrowly construed this exemption. The City of Edmonds' zoning ordinance defined a family as any number of persons related by blood, marriage, or adoption, but it allowed only a maximum of five unrelated persons to qualify as a family. Without seeking a variance from this provision, Oxford House opened a home for 12 persons recovering from

---

16. 42 U.S.C.A. § 3604(f)(3)(B).

17. 42 U.S.C.A. § 3602(h)(1).

18. Support Ministries For Persons With AIDS, Inc. v. Village of Waterford, 808 F.Supp. 120 (N.D.N.Y.1992).

19. See, e.g., Sunderland Family Treatment Services v. City of Pasco, 127 Wash.2d 782, 903 P.2d 986 (1995) (abused and neglected children not "handicapped" under state law, which used the federal act's definition).

20. See Daniel R. Mandelker, Zoning Discrimination Against Group Homes Under the Fair Housing Act, Land Use Law 3 (Nov.1994); Matthew J. Cholewa and

Dwight H. Merriam, Federal Zoning Regulation: The Fair Housing Amendments Act and Its Override of Local Control, 18 Zoning and Planning Report, No. 2 (Feb.1995); Laurie C. Malkin, Comment, Troubles at the Doorstep: The Fair Housing Act of 1988 and Group Homes for Recovering Substance Abusers, 144 U.Pa.L.Rev. 759 (1995).

21. See supra § 4.5.

22. 42 U.S.C.A. § 3607(b)(1).

23. 514 U.S. 725, 115 S.Ct. 1776, 131 L.Ed.2d 801 (1995).

alcohol and drug abuse in an area zoned for single-family use. The city charged Oxford House with violating its ordinance, and Oxford House claimed the city's ordinance, as applied to it, violated the Fair Housing Act. The city then sought refuge in the statutory exemption that permits occupancy restrictions.

The Court held that the limitation of five unrelated persons was not an occupancy limit within the meaning of the act. Distinguishing between land use restrictions, designed to foster a family environment, and maximum occupancy restrictions, designed to protect health and safety, the Court held that only the latter come with the FHAA's exemption. Since the code provision limiting occupancy to five unrelated persons also allowed an unlimited number of related persons to live together, the Court concluded that its goal was preservation of family character, not health and safety. The dissent thought the plain language of the statute, exempting "any" restriction, precluded the Court from only exempting absolute occupancy restrictions.

Though *Edmonds* is important in that it deprived cities of a significant exemption from the handicap coverage of the FHAA insofar as single-family zoning is concerned, the case did not decide whether a facially neutral code provision that precludes group homes of unrelated handicapped persons from living in single-family areas is unlawful or whether allowance of such homes in other zones is a reasonable accommodation under the FHAA.[24]

Developing case law in the lower courts is mixed and in flux, but it seems headed in the direction of holding that municipalities must make reasonable accommodations to allow the handicapped to live in single-family neighborhoods. One court rejected the argument that the allowance of nursing homes in the area zoned for hospitals was a reasonable accommodation.[25] Blanket exclusions of group homes, said the court, were "precisely the sort of isolation that the FHAA was enacted to forbid,"[26] and there was no proof in the case before the court to justify the exclusion. In another case, a court required a city to raise the limit on the number of persons who could live in group homes from six persons to nine, since nine was needed to make the home profitable. The court, however, rejected a plea that twelve-person homes should be allowed out of concern that homes of such numbers might fundamentally alter the nature of single-family neighborhoods.[27]

Courts disagree on how strenuous the burden is on the city to show that its proposed accommodation is reasonable. In Oxford House–C v. City of St. Louis,[28] the single-family classification generally allowed up to

---

24. 514 U.S. at 737, 115 S.Ct. at 1783.

25. Hovsons, Inc. v. Township of Brick, 89 F.3d 1096 (3d Cir.1996).

26. Id. at 1103.

27. Smith & Lee Assocs., Inc. v. City of Taylor, 102 F.3d 781 (6th Cir.1996). The court reasoned that since the average family size in the city was 2.84 persons, a rule requiring the city to allow twelve residents in areas zoned for single-family use might substantially alter the nature of the neighborhoods. This concern was compounded since the city was prohibited from dispersing homes.

28. 77 F.3d 249 (8th Cir.), cert. denied ___ U.S. ___, 117 S.Ct. 65, 136 L.Ed.2d 27 (1996).

three unrelated persons, but raised the limit to eight for group homes for the handicapped. This was still too limiting for the plaintiff who claimed that the eight person limit would destroy the financial viability of the home. Using the deferential rational basis test borrowed from equal protection jurisprudence, the court concluded the limit of eight was justified by the city's interest in maintaining the quiet of a residential area.[29]

Other courts have rejected equal protection analysis as inappropriate in an FHAA case. In Bangerter v. Orem City Corporation,[30] the court noted that rational basis review is the standard applied with respect to the mentally retarded under equal protection since they are not regarded as a suspect or quasi-suspect class. In contrast, the court said the fact that the handicapped are an expressly protected class under the statute compels a heavier burden on the government. The statute, said the court, only allows discrimination based on direct threats to health and safety. Additionally, the court held that requirements that benefit rather than harm the handicapped may be justified.[31]

Many ordinances subject group homes to a special or conditional use permitting process. If the process applies only to the handicapped it violates the FHAA,[32] and likely the equal protection clause as well.[33] Conditions deemed unjustified include a requirement that a group reapply for a permit every year[34] and a 24–hour supervision requirement.[35] Even a special permitting process that is facially neutral and applies to similar uses may be invalid. Proponents of group homes argue that the permitting process itself is stigmatizing, and some lower courts have agreed.[36] The Seventh Circuit, however, found that towns have a legitimate interest in conducting nondiscriminatory, public hearings.[37]

Some ordinances require spacing between group homes to promote the deinstitutionalization process and prevent the re-isolation of the handicapped in new group home ghettoes.[38] For that reason, the Eighth

---

29. 77 F.3d at 252. See also Familystyle of St. Paul, Inc. v. City of St. Paul, 923 F.2d 91 (8th Cir.1991). The Eighth Circuit uses the compelling interest test in FHA race-based cases. See United States v. City of Black Jack, 508 F.2d 1179 (8th Cir.1974), cert. denied 422 U.S. 1042, 95 S.Ct. 2656, 45 L.Ed.2d 694 (1975).

30. 46 F.3d 1491 (10th Cir.1995).

31. In *Bangerter*, the court remanded the issue of whether the city's 24–hour supervision requirement on group homes for the mentally handicapped met the test. See also Larkin v. Michigan Dept. of Social Services, 89 F.3d 285 (6th Cir.1996), following the 10th Circuit.

32. Bangerter v. Orem City Corp., 46 F.3d 1491 (10th Cir.1995).

33. See City of Cleburne v. Cleburne Living Center, 473 U.S. 432, 105 S.Ct. 3249, 87 L.Ed.2d 313 (1985) discussed supra § 4.6.

34. Bangerter v. Orem City Corp., 46 F.3d 1491 (10th Cir.1995).

35. Turning Point, Inc. v. City of Caldwell, 74 F.3d 941 (9th Cir.1996).

36. Stewart B. McKinney Foundation, Inc. v. Town Plan & Zoning Comm'n of Town of Fairfield, 790 F.Supp. 1197, 1219–20 (D.Conn.1992).

37. United States v. Village of Palatine, 37 F.3d 1230 (7th Cir.1994). See also Oxford House-C v. City of St. Louis, 77 F.3d 249 (8th Cir.1996), cert. denied ___ U.S. ___, 117 S.Ct. 65, 136 L.Ed.2d 27 (1996); Turning Point, Inc. v. City of Caldwell, 74 F.3d 941 (9th Cir.1996) (implicitly approving special use process in general, but finding a specific condition invalid).

38. See Kevin J. Zanner, Comment, Dispersion Requirements for the Siting of Group Homes: Reconciling New York's Padavan Law with the Fair Housing Amend-

Circuit found that a state mandated dispersal requirement of one quarter mile between group homes did not violate the FHAA.[39] In contrast, the Sixth Circuit found such a statute violated the FHAA.[40] The latter court read an intervening Supreme Court decision in the employment context to reject the idea that the benign desire to help the handicapped was not intentional discrimination. The court further found that the state did not carry its burden of proving the necessity of dispersal.

The degree to which the Fair Housing Amendments Act will spell the end of the single-family zone that lies at the heart of Euclidean zoning remains to be seen. The Court labeled such a fear "exaggerated" in *Edmonds*.[41] The clear trend in the lower courts, though, is against municipalities and in favor of empowering the handicapped to live wherever they wish in group homes with reasonable limitations on numbers. Economics play a part, and it is likely that higher density areas of low and moderate income housing will accept the vast bulk of group homes. High land values in the more exclusive single-family areas will make them economically unfeasible as sites for such homes even if federal law allows them to locate there.

§ 6.9 Exclusion of Non–Residential Uses: LULUs

While almost every use of land is a legitimate use somewhere, many cities entirely exclude or severely limit particular kinds of uses. Bans may be broad, covering all industrial and most commercial uses, or they may be specific, targeting uses known popularly as LULUs (locally unwanted land uses). They include such uses as hazardous waste dumps, sewage treatment facilities, landfills, hog farms, mining operations, junkyards, billboards, cemeteries, funeral parlors, correctional facilities, and adult entertainment.

While some might describe lower cost housing and group homes as locally unwanted land uses, we have chosen to treat those uses separately. As discussed above,[1] exclusion of residential uses is a matter of particular concern and specific action in a number of states. Residential use is also protected by the federal Fair Housing Act.

In contrast, in most states the exclusion of nonresidential uses is presumed valid[2] and not subject to fair share requirements that apply to

ments Act of 1988, 44 Buff.L.Rev. 249 (1996).

39. Familystyle of St. Paul, Inc. v. City of St. Paul, 923 F.2d 91 (8th Cir.1991). But see Horizon House Developmental Services, Inc. v. Township of Upper Southampton, 804 F.Supp. 683 (E.D.Pa.1992).

40. Larkin v. Michigan Dept. of Social Services, 89 F.3d 285 (6th Cir.1996).

41. 514 U.S. 725, 737, 115 S.Ct. 1776, 1783, 131 L.Ed.2d 801 (1995). See also Stephan C. Hall, Comment, City of Edmonds v. Oxford House, Inc.: A Comment on the Continuing Vitality of Single–Family Zon-

ing Restrictions, 71 Notre Dame L.Rev. 829 (1996).

§ 6.9

1. See supra §§ 6.2–6.5.

2. Marshfield Family Skateland, Inc. v. Town of Marshfield, 389 Mass. 436, 450 N.E.2d 605, appeal dismissed 464 U.S. 987, 104 S.Ct. 475, 78 L.Ed.2d 675 (1983); Lambros, Inc. v. Town of Ocean Ridge, 392 So.2d 993 (Fla.App.1981); but see Beaver Gasoline Co. v. Zoning Hearing Board of Borough of Osborne, 445 Pa. 571, 285 A.2d 501 (1971) (challenger shows that ordi-

housing.[3] However, if fundamental rights are adversely affected by exclusion, the presumption of validity disappears, and strict judicial scrutiny will follow.

In an early, leading case, Duffcon Concrete Products v. Borough of Cresskill,[4] the New Jersey Supreme Court upheld the total exclusion of heavy industrial uses. The court found that it was not arbitrary for a small town to exclude such uses to preserve its residential character where industrially zoned land was available in the region. Many other courts have followed suit, allowing the exclusion of a variety of uses, many more innocuous than the LULUs listed above.[5]

Single-use zoning, allowing only residential uses, has been held reasonable for the "bedroom community" that lies on the fringe of a larger, metropolitan area where needed services are readily available nearby.[6] While some courts have narrowly interpreted the standard enabling act's directive that "the local legislative body may divide the municipality into districts"[7] as precluding a single zone,[8] that language is generally seen as permissive.[9]

The regional view cuts two ways. Under *Duffcon*,[10] the municipality was allowed to avoid providing for heavy industry because land was available elsewhere in the region for that purpose. However, if all towns in a region, acting in their parochial self-interest entirely exclude a use, the general welfare may be harmed.[11] Thus, in some instances, a municipality may have to accommodate a use to benefit the larger geographical region.[12] Nonetheless, the obligation to take into account the regional

---

nance totally prohibits a legitimate use of land burden of proof shifts to the municipality to show its constitutionality).

3. Gernatt Asphalt Products, Inc. v. Town of Sardinia, 87 N.Y.2d 668, 642 N.Y.S.2d 164, 664 N.E.2d 1226 (1996) (fair share rule applied to housing does not apply to the exclusion of industrial uses); Town of Los Altos Hills v. Adobe Creek Properties, Inc., 32 Cal.App.3d 488, 108 Cal.Rptr. 271 (1973) (no particular solicitude for commercial recreational use).

4. 1 N.J. 509, 64 A.2d 347 (1949).

5. Gernatt Asphalt Products, Inc. v. Town of Sardinia, 87 N.Y.2d 668, 642 N.Y.S.2d 164, 664 N.E.2d 1226 (1996) (mining); Marshfield Family Skateland, Inc. v. Town of Marshfield, 389 Mass. 436, 450 N.E.2d 605, appeal dismissed 464 U.S. 987, 104 S.Ct. 475, 78 L.Ed.2d 675 (1983) (video arcade); Appeal of Green & White Copter, Inc., 25 Pa.Cmwlth. 445, 360 A.2d 283 (1976) (heliports); Town of Los Altos Hills v. Adobe Creek Properties, Inc., 32 Cal. App.3d 488, 108 Cal.Rptr. 271 (1973) (commercial recreational use).

6. See Valley View Village v. Proffett, 221 F.2d 412 (6th Cir.1955); Bartolomeo v.

Town of Paradise Valley, 129 Ariz. 409, 631 P.2d 564 (1981); Town of Los Altos Hills v. Adobe Creek Properties, Inc., 32 Cal.App.3d 488, 108 Cal.Rptr. 271 (1973); Town of Lebanon v. Woods, 153 Conn. 182, 215 A.2d 112 (1965); McDermott v. Village of Calverton Park, 454 S.W.2d 577 (Mo.1970).

7. Standard Zoning Enabling Act, § 2.

8. Gundersen v. Village of Bingham Farms, 372 Mich. 352, 126 N.W.2d 715 (1964); Matthews v. Board of Zoning Appeals of Greene County, 218 Va. 270, 237 S.E.2d 128 (1977) (dicta).

9. Valley View Village v. Proffett, 221 F.2d 412 (6th Cir.1955); Town of Lebanon v. Woods, 153 Conn. 182, 215 A.2d 112 (1965); McDermott v. Village of Calverton Park, 454 S.W.2d 577 (Mo.1970). But see Trail Mining, Inc. v. Village of Sun, 619 So.2d 118 (La.App.1993) (ordinance that banned mining held invalid as a "single industry restriction" that was not in accord with a comprehensive plan).

10. See supra note 4.

11. See discussion supra § 6.1.

12. Exton Quarries, Inc. v. Zoning Bd. of Adj. of West Whiteland, 425 Pa. 43, 228 A.2d 169 (1967).

welfare that is applied to limit the exclusion of residential uses may not apply to nonresidential uses.[13]

Courts may find a total exclusion of a nonresidential use arbitrary under particular circumstances. A total prohibition of outdoor theaters within a town village was found unreasonable where more than 57% of the land in the town was vacant, there was ample land for residential and industrial development, and the land surrounding the tract on which the challenger wished to build a theater was either unimproved or devoted to heavy industrial uses.[14] A de facto total ban on fast food restaurants, engineered by creating a zone for such restaurants but not zoning any land for them, was also invalidated.[15] The court found traffic considerations might justify denial of such zoning for the challenger's site, but nothing explained the total exclusion.[16] The legitimacy of total bans may also turn on whether sufficient differences exist between uses allowed and uses barred to pass muster under an equal protection analysis.[17]

A. Exclusion Infringing Fundamental Rights

Excluding certain uses, even for small communities, is less justifiable if the exclusion infringes on a suspect class or a fundamental or important right. This may include signs,[18] religious practices, abortion clinics,[19] adult entertainment,[20] and other uses that implicate First Amendment speech or religion rights or Fourteenth Amendment substantive due process rights.[21] In such cases, the burden is likely to be put on the municipality to justify the restriction. These issues are discussed elsewhere.[22]

B. State Preemption of Local Exclusion

Governmentally owned, operated, or licensed facilities may be immune from local zoning under the doctrine of preemption. Such activities

13. Gernatt Asphalt Products, Inc. v. Town of Sardinia, 87 N.Y.2d 668, 642 N.Y.S.2d 164, 664 N.E.2d 1226 (1996) (total exclusion of mining valid).

14. People ex rel. Trust Co. of Chicago v. Village of Skokie, 408 Ill. 397, 97 N.E.2d 310 (1951).

15. Wenco Management Co. v. Town of Carrboro, 53 N.C.App. 480, 281 S.E.2d 74 (1981).

16. In Pennsylvania, which deprives any totally exclusionary ordinance of the presumption of validity, courts are more likely to find ordinances invalid. See, e.g., Beaver Gasoline Co. v. Zoning Hearing Bd. of Borough of Osborne, 445 Pa. 571, 285 A.2d 501 (1971) (gas stations); Crown Wrecking Co., Inc. v. Zoning Hearing Bd. of Ross Twp., 71 Pa.Cmwlth. 310, 454 A.2d 683 (1983) (landfill).

17. Pierro v. Baxendale, 20 N.J. 17, 118 A.2d 401 (1955) (excluding motels while allowing boarding houses valid); Katobimar Realty Co. v. Webster, 20 N.J. 114, 118 A.2d 824 (1955) (excluding shopping center while allowing light industry invalid). See discussion supra § 4.2 regarding use classifications.

18. See infra § 10.16 and § 12.3.

19. See discussion infra § 10.15.

20. While non obscene sexually oriented speech is protected by the First Amendment, the protection is minimal. See infra § 10.17.

21. See discussion infra § 10.12. Exclusion based on race or disability and, in some states, high density residential exclusion may also trigger strict review. See discussion supra § 6.6.

22. See infra Ch. 10.

as municipal landfills, correctional facilities, and group homes often fall into this category.[23] These issues are discussed elsewhere.[24]

C. Environmental Justice Concerns

Unwanted land uses must go somewhere. When a town is successful in excluding a specific type of use or relegating it to some part of town, those in power have kept it out of their backyards and put it in someone else's. In recent years, attention has focused on whether LULUs, primarily hazardous waste facilities and landfills, are disproportionately sited in minority or low-income neighborhoods.[25] This environmental racism or environmental justice movement has sought to prove the charge and to rectify the siting process to equitably distribute LULUs among the broader population.

Studies produce conflicting conclusions as to whether minority and low-income neighborhoods are disproportionately burdened by LULUs, and, if so, whether it is the siting process that causes this result.[26] Professor Vicki Been, who has extensively studied the issue,[27] observes that market forces, rather than the siting process, may be responsible for lowering land values near LULUs. Thus, it may be that some LULUs have been sited in or near affluent white communities, and, those then living there, in possession of the financial wherewithal to do so, move away, leaving low-cost housing behind for racial minorities and the poor. Furthermore, she notes that if the siting process is to blame in whole or in part, and the "solution" is development of an equitable siting process, market forces may destroy its effectiveness if affluent whites vacate an area that is chosen as a new LULU site.[28]

Legal remedies for siting facilities in minority or low-income communities have been difficult to come by.[29] At first blush, equal protection seems an obvious choice. But, if racial discrimination is the basis for the suit, discriminatory intent must be shown, and that is difficult to do.[30]

23. Preemption in the context of governmental uses is discussed supra § 4.24.

24. See supra § 4.23–.30.

25. See Robert W. Collin, Review of the Legal Literature on Environmental Racism, Environmental Equity, and Environmental Justice, 9 J.Envtl.L. & Litig. 121 (1994); Rudolph C. Hasl, Symposium Environmental Justice: The Merging of Civil Rights and Environmental Activism, 9 St. John's J. Legal Comment 437 (1994).

26. See Daniel Kevin, "Environmental Racism" and Locally Undesirable Land Uses: A Critique of Environmental Justice Theories and Remedies, 8 Vill.Envtl.L.J. 121 (1997); Lawrence J. Straw, Jr., Environmental Justice: Racial Gerrymandering for Environmental Siting Decisions, 14 Va. Envtl.L.J. 665 (1995).

27. Vicki Been and Francis Gupta, Coming to the Nuisance or Going to the Barrios?, A Longitudinal Analysis of Environmental Justice Claims, 24 Ecology L.Q. 1 (1997); Vicki Been, Analyzing Evidence of Environmental Justice, 11 J.Land Use & Envtl.L 1 (1995); Vicki Been, Locally Undesirable Land Uses in Minority Neighborhoods: Disproportionate Siting or Market Dynamics?, 103 Yale L.J. 1383 (1994).

28. See Been, supra note 27, 103 Yale L.J. at 1392.

29. See Luke W. Cole, Environmental Justice Litigation: Another Stone in David's Sling, 21 Fordham Urb.L.J. 523 (1994), detailing litigation strategies.

30. Id. at 539–41. See also discussion supra § 6.8 and infra § 10.14. Hawkins v. Town of Shaw, 437 F.2d 1286 (5th Cir. 1971) found racial discrimination in the provision of municipal services based on impact. *Hawkins* was disapproved by the Court in Washington v. Davis, 426 U.S. 229, 244 n. 12, 96 S.Ct. 2040, 48 L.Ed.2d 597 (1976).

Poverty-based claims are even less likely to succeed since no suspect class is involved.

Efforts to use various federal civil rights statutes show some promise of success. Title VI of the Civil Rights Act of 1964, for example, prohibits racial discrimination in programs that receive federal assistance.[31] In one case, a court ordered that a city provide minorities with services equal to those provided whites pursuant to Title VI.[32] The Fair Housing Act, Title VIII, may also be used, though linking the siting of a LULU to the provision of services in connection housing is problematical.[33]

Various legislative proposals have been made to require the collection of data on LULU locations, to assure public participation in the siting process, to give "preference" in siting to those areas that at present have no LULUs, and to remove sites from minority communities.[34] An Executive Order issued by President Clinton requires federal agencies to identify and address disproportionately high adverse health effects of LULUs in minority and low-income communities.[35]

To the extent that racial discrimination in the sale and rental of housing or in lending practices makes it difficult for minorities to move out of LULU-affected neighborhoods, strengthening fair housing act enforcement will help. The negative effect of LULUs, wherever located, also may be mitigated by strengthening environmental laws that regulate them and by enforcing those laws that exist. Finally, to the extent that government decisionmaking is at fault in excessively burdening a small portion of the population with the adverse effects of LULUs, measures to assure equitable distribution of LULUs can be developed. In the end, though, the unyielding effects of market forces likely will still leave the poor worse off than the rich.

D. Natural Resource Extraction

Natural resource extraction poses a distinct regulatory problem since it not only uses land, but consumes it, and if the consumption is to occur, it must occur where the resource is located.[36] The land has special value for resource extraction, and zoning which precludes the use destroys that value. Moreover, those deposits close to urbanized areas are likely to be most valuable since transportation costs will be lower.

---

31. 42 U.S.C.A. § 2000d. The Third Circuit has held that a private right of action exists under Title VI based on a showing of discriminatory effect. Chester Residents Concerned For Quality Living v. Seif, 132 F.3d 925 (3d Cir.1997).

32. Johnson v. City of Arcadia, 450 F.Supp. 1363 (M.D.Fla.1978). Intent to discriminate must be shown under the statute, but regulations implementing the act use an effects test. See Cole, supra note 29, at 530 n. 29.

33. See Cole, supra note 29, at 536.

34. See a description of these proposals in Kevin, supra note 26, at 130.

35. Exec. Order No. 12,898, 59 Fed. Reg. 7,629 (1994).

36. See Bruce M. Kramer, Local Land Use Regulation of Extractive Industries: Evolving Judicial and Regulatory Approaches, 14 UCLA J.Envtl.L. & Policy 41 (1996) for a detailed examination of the topic.

The use of lands for oil and gas production, mining, quarrying, topsoil removal and sand and gravel operations is as difficult to reconcile with other uses of lands as any.[37] Exploitation of natural resources produces odors, dust, use of heavy equipment, large amounts of truck traffic, noise—and, in the case of oil and gas production—danger of fire and explosion. Moreover, few uses are as unaesthetic as natural resource extraction sites. Therefore, there are a number of grounds on which such activities can be precluded or regulated under the police power. For example, ordinances often only allow resource extraction in agricultural and heavy industrial zones and such uses are frequently handled on a special permit basis even in such zones.[38]

Earlier cases tended to favor extractive industry and used various reasons to allow the extraction. Courts have held prohibitory ordinances invalid where extraction was permitted in more densely populated areas,[39] where the surrounding area was occupied by other intensive uses,[40] where the area involved was not densely populated[41] and where denial of rights to drill to one would confer a monopoly on others.[42] Prohibitory ordinances have also been held invalid where, for example, a quarry preexisted neighboring development,[43] where the value of the property is substantially reduced[44] or on the ground that the operation was temporary and that neighbors could be temporarily inconvenienced in order to permit exploitation of the mineral value of the land.[45] Zoning of a site having natural resources for quarry operations is also not as likely to be held invalid as spot zoning.[46]

More recent cases have concluded that there is no special right to zoning that permits extraction, and the total exclusion of mining has been upheld as a valid exercise of the police power.[47] As stated by the California Supreme Court in Consolidated Rock Products Co. v. City of Los Angeles:

> Too many cases have been decided upholding the constitutionality of comprehensive zoning ordinances prohibiting the removal of natural products from lands in certain zones for us now to accept at full

37. See generally Fred P. Bosselman, The Control of Surface Mining: An Exercise in Creative Federalism, 9 Nat.Resources J. 137 (1969).

38. See Callies & Quay, Zoning for Gravel Pits: Simultaneous Rehabilitation According to Plan, 4 Land–Use Controls Q. 43 (1970).

39. Pacific Palisades Ass'n v. City of Huntington Beach, 196 Cal. 211, 237 P. 538 (1925).

40. City of North Muskegon v. Miller, 249 Mich. 52, 227 N.W. 743 (1929).

41. Clouser v. City of Norman, 393 P.2d 827 (Okl.1964).

42. Braly v. Board of Fire Comm'rs of City of Los Angeles, 157 Cal.App.2d 608, 321 P.2d 504 (1958).

43. Herman v. Village of Hillside, 15 Ill.2d 396, 155 N.E.2d 47 (1958).

44. East Fairfield Coal Co. v. Booth, 166 Ohio St. 379, 143 N.E.2d 309 (1957) (where prohibition of strip coal mining would reduce value from $1,000,000 to $17,-000).

45. Village of Terrace Park v. Errett, 12 F.2d 240 (6th Cir.), cert. denied 273 U.S. 710, 47 S.Ct. 100, 71 L.Ed. 852 (1926).

46. Kozesnik v. Montgomery Twp., 24 N.J. 154, 131 A.2d 1 (1957).

47. Gernatt Asphalt Products, Inc. v. Town of Sardinia, 87 N.Y.2d 668, 642 N.Y.S.2d 164, 664 N.E.2d 1226 (1996).

value the suggestion that there is such an inherent difference in natural products of the property that in a case where reasonable minds may differ as to the necessity of such prohibition the same power to prohibit the extraction of natural products does not inhere in the legislative body as it has to prohibit uses of other sorts.[48]

It is true that resources must be extracted where they are located, if extracted anywhere, but place has value in other situations too. For example, it is because a downtown area zoned for commercial high rises is there rather than elsewhere, that it has high value. Zoning the site for single-family residential use may take as much value as prohibiting the drilling of oil from the site. A good corner for a filling station may result in unique values that are as substantially impaired by residential zoning as they would be if an ordinance prohibited the removal of sand and gravel which happened to be the makeup of the soil on the corner.

While many ordinances banning mining exempt existing uses under the doctrine of nonconforming uses,[49] the nuisance-like aspects of such operations may justify immediate termination of existing uses. In Hadacheck v. Sebastian,[50] the Court upheld an ordinance requiring the immediate termination of an operating brickyard. The brickyard preexisted other development in the area and the economic effect of the closure was to reduce the value of the land from $800,000 to $60,000.[51] Still, the Court found that the negative effects of the brickyard on expanding residential uses in the area justified its termination.

A takings challenge of an act prohibiting mining of a natural resource turns on whether the effect of the act as applied to the land deprives it of all economically viable use, and if so, whether the mining operation can nonetheless be banned as a nuisance.[52] In many instances the initial showing cannot be made since there will be some economic value left for purposes other than mining.[53] If the economic loss is partial, the strength of the public interest must be balanced against the loss sustained.[54]

E. The Death Industry: Cemeteries and Funeral Parlors

48. 57 Cal.2d 515, 529, 20 Cal.Rptr. 638, 648, 370 P.2d 342, 351 (1962), appeal dismissed 371 U.S. 36, 83 S.Ct. 145, 9 L.Ed.2d 112 (1962).

49. See supra § 4.34.

50. 239 U.S. 394, 36 S.Ct. 143, 60 L.Ed. 348 (1915).

51. See also Goldblatt v. Town of Hempstead, 369 U.S. 590, 82 S.Ct. 987, 8 L.Ed.2d 130 (1962); West Brothers Brick Co. v. City of Alexandria, 169 Va. 271, 192 S.E. 881, appeal dismissed 302 U.S. 658, 58 S.Ct. 369, 82 L.Ed. 508 (1937).

52. See Keystone Bituminous Coal Ass'n v. DeBenedictis, 480 U.S. 470, 107 S.Ct. 1232, 94 L.Ed.2d 472 (1987) (prohibi-

tion of coal mining that causes surface subsidence not a taking); Florida Rock Industries v. United States, 18 F.3d 1560 (Fed. Cir.1994), cert. denied 513 U.S. 1109, 115 S.Ct. 898, 130 L.Ed.2d 783 (1995). See generally infra §§ 10.6 and 10.8.

53. See Hadacheck v. Sebastian, 239 U.S. 394, 36 S.Ct. 143, 60 L.Ed. 348 (1915); Goldblatt v. Town of Hempstead, 369 U.S. 590, 82 S.Ct. 987 8 L.Ed.2d 130 (1962); Keystone Bituminous Coal Ass'n v. DeBenedictis, 480 U.S. 470, 107 S.Ct. 1232, 94 L.Ed.2d 472 (1987).

54. See Florida Rock Industries, Inc. v. United States, 18 F.3d 1560 (Fed.Cir.1994), cert. denied 513 U.S. 1109, 115 S.Ct. 898, 130 L.Ed.2d 783 (1995).

Cemeteries may be permitted in residential, commercial or agricultural districts. As reminders of death, however, they may not always be welcome by neighbors.[55] The drop in property values due to the psychological depression of adjacent or nearby residential users may be recognized as a basis to limit cemetery location or operation.[56] Were it not for this reminder of death, the open space and park-like aspect of cemeteries would make them desirable neighbors.

Local governments are as free to limit cemetery location as with any commercial use. In an early case, the Supreme Court upheld an ordinance that totally precluded burials in a city.[57] Cemeteries are often regulated by the state,[58] and this may lead to the preemption of local law.[59] Though cemetery lands are subdivided and sold, they are not usually subject to ordinary subdivision ordinances.[60]

Like most land uses, devoting land to cemetery use is not necessarily a permanent decision. As development pressures grow, so too will the pressure to move non-productive uses, such as cemeteries. Those located in areas where property values have risen may be targets for reuse. Highway or other public improvements may also compel their removal. State statutes may regulate the process.[61] There may be religious objections from family members to the disturbance of grave sites, but these have not fared well.[62]

Like cemeteries, funeral homes are often not welcome in residential neighborhoods, and the body of nuisance and zoning law on funeral homes is substantial.[63] Some courts conclude that funeral parlors are nuisances per se or can be nuisances in residential areas,[64] so it is not surprising that funeral parlors are not often a permitted use in residential areas. Some ordinances may attempt to exclude them in commercial zones.[65] Despite the fact that they may be nicely landscaped, funeral

---

55. See Martin M. Moore, Improving the Image and Legal Status of the Burial Services Industry, 24 Akron L.Rev. 565 (1991); Joel E. Smith, Annot.,Zoning Regulations in Relation to Cemeteries, 96 A.L.R.3d 921 (1980).

56. See, e.g., International Funeral Services, Inc. v. DeKalb County, 244 Ga. 707, 261 S.E.2d 625 (1979) (setback variance denied to a cemetery due in part to "psychological needs" of neighbors), overruled on other grounds, Jackson v. Spalding County, 265 Ga. 792, 462 S.E.2d 361 (1995).

57. Laurel Hill Cemetery v. City & County of San Francisco, 216 U.S. 358, 30 S.Ct. 301, 54 L.Ed. 515 (1910).

58. See, e.g., West's Ann.Cal.Bus. & Prof.Code §§ 9600–770.

59. See discussion of preemption supra § 4.24.

60. Sometimes special state statutes apply to cemetery subdivisions. See, e.g., Vernon's Ann.Mo.Stat. § 214.040.

61. See Hughes v. Cobb County, 264 Ga. 128, 441 S.E.2d 406 (1994).

62. See Lyng v. Northwest Indian Cemetery Protective Ass'n, 485 U.S. 439, 108 S.Ct. 1319, 99 L.Ed.2d 534 (1988) (Indian objection to road building on government land for traditional Indian religious practices cannot prevail against government use of its own land); City of Kansas City v. United States, 192 F.Supp. 179 (D.Kan. 1960). See generally Margaret B. Bowman, The Reburial of Native American Skeletal Remains: Approaches to the Resolution of a Conflict, 13 Harv.Envtl.L.Rev. 147 (1989).

63. Joel E. Smith, Annot., Construction and Application of Zoning Regulations in Connection With Funeral Homes, 92 A.L.R.3d 328 (1980).

64. See infra Ch. 14.

65. Sweet v. Campbell, 282 N.Y. 146, 25 N.E.2d 963 (1940).

parlors do generate traffic and may generate feelings of disquietude leading to depression of neighborhood property values. As a result, they are often handled on a special permit basis. Under such handling, the movement of bodies and traffic can appropriately be controlled through the use of screening and off-street parking.

§ 6.10 Standing to Challenge Exclusionary Zoning

Various persons seek standing to challenge the exclusionary effects of a town's zoning ordinance on general or site-specific bases.[1] These include property owners subject to the restriction, residents of the town who have limited housing choices due to the restriction, and nonresidents who cannot acquire property in the town due to the ordinance. These nonresidents may be individuals seeking housing, or developers interested in acquiring property for housing or other uses. Standing rules differ between federal and state courts.

Standing in federal court to attack exclusionary land use ordinances on equal protection grounds is limited.[2] In Warth v. Seldin[3] four categories of plaintiffs challenged the Penfield, New York ordinance as exclusionary. The groups included nonresidents unable to find housing in the town; taxpayers in nearby Rochester bearing a disproportionate share of low income costs; Penfield residents denied benefits of living in an integrated community; and associations representing contractors unable to construct low-income housing in Penfield. The Court denied standing to all of them because none could show how they were personally injured by the ordinances. The Court held that two showings must be made. First, there must be but-for causation, that is there must be "specific, concrete facts" proving harm to plaintiffs. Second, the plaintiffs must show a possibility of redress to them by the Court's intervention. With respect to the nonresidents who could find no affordable housing in the area, the Court noted that there was inadequate proof that elimination of exclusionary zoning practices would lead to the construction of affordable housing.

Standing was found in Arlington Heights v. Metropolitan Housing Development Corp.[4] where construction of housing on a specific site was in issue. A developer of federally subsidized housing was granted standing on the basis of its preliminary expenditures on the project and its interest in providing low cost housing in areas where it was scarce. Additionally, a black employee of a nearby plant alleged that he was unable to find affordable housing near his place of work. Because his claim was based on a particular project, he proved an injury in fact. In

---

§ 6.10

1. General issues of standing in zoning cases are discussed supra § 5.34.

2. Standing rules under the Fair Housing Act or under the Americans with Disabilities Act may differ. See Oak Ridge Care Center, Inc. v. Racine County, 896 F.Supp. 867 (E.D.Wis.1995).

3. 422 U.S. 490, 95 S.Ct. 2197, 45 L.Ed.2d 343 (1975).

4. 429 U.S. 252, 97 S.Ct. 555, 50 L.Ed.2d 450 (1977).

most exclusionary zoning cases, there will be no specific project, and under the rule of *Warth*, standing in federal courts will be lacking.

Several state courts, which are not restricted by Article III as are the federal courts, have rejected *Warth* and developed more liberal standing rules.[5] In New Jersey nonresidents are granted standing to maintain general exclusionary zoning challenges.[6] They need not show site-specific injury. Similar rules are followed in California[7] and New York.[8]

Those who own property wishing to develop it for low or moderate cost housing have standing to sue on the basis of injury to their property rights.[9] Mere ownership of property[10] or mere status as a taxpayer,[11] coupled with a general interest in a diverse community, has been held insufficient to confer standing. The general rule, that one cannot litigate the rights of third parties, prevails.[12]

In nonresidential exclusionary zoning, similar standing problems arise. In Halfway House, Inc. v. City of Portland,[13] for example, an operator of houses for pre-release prisoners and parolees was held to have standing based on economic injury to challenge an ordinance that totally excluded such facilities from the municipality.[14]

Standing to sue under the federal Fair Housing Act is liberally construed. The Supreme Court has removed prudential limitations on suits brought under the act, leaving only Article III restraints.[15] Courts, thus, generally require only a showing of an injury in fact and the likelihood that the court can redress the injury.[16] In challenging exclusionary zoning practices, there is no requirement that the city has applied the offending ordinance so long as it is likely that it will be applied.[17]

5. See David C. Keating, Exclusionary Zoning: In Whose Interests Should the Police Power Be Exercised?, 23 Real Est.L.J. 304 (1995).

6. Southern Burlington County NAACP v. Mt. Laurel Twp., 67 N.J. 151, 336 A.2d 713 (1975) (Mt. Laurel I), appeal dismissed, cert. denied 423 U.S. 808, 96 S.Ct. 18, 46 L.Ed.2d 28 (1975); Urban League of Essex County v. Mahwah Twp., 147 N.J.Super. 28, 370 A.2d 521, cert. denied 74 N.J. 278, 377 A.2d 682 (1977).

7. Stocks v. City of Irvine, 114 Cal. App.3d 520, 170 Cal.Rptr. 724 (1981).

8. Suffolk Housing Services v. Town of Brookhaven, 91 Misc.2d 80, 397 N.Y.S.2d 302 (1977), modified 63 A.D.2d 731, 405 N.Y.S.2d 302 (1978).

9. Cannon v. Coweta County, 260 Ga. 56, 389 S.E.2d 329 (1990).

10. Caspersen v. Town of Lyme, 139 N.H. 637, 661 A.2d 759 (1995).

11. Suffolk Housing Services v. Town of Brookhaven, 91 Misc.2d 80, 397 N.Y.S.2d

302 (1977), modified 63 A.D.2d 731, 405 N.Y.S.2d 302 (1978).

12. Precision Equities, Inc. v. Franklin Park Borough Zoning Hearing Bd., 166 Pa. Cmwlth. 607, 646 A.2d 756 (1994), appeal denied 540 Pa. 588, 655 A.2d 518 (1995).

13. 670 A.2d 1377 (Me.1996).

14. See also Bossier City Medical Suite, Inc. v. City of Bossier City, 483 F.Supp. 633 (W.D.La.1980) (woman seeking abortion and medical clinic providing abortion service each had standing to challenge restrictive zoning ordinance).

15. Gladstone, Realtors v. Village of Bellwood, 441 U.S. 91, 99 S.Ct. 1601, 60 L.Ed.2d 66 (1979); See generally Michael E. Rosman, Standing Alone: Standing Under the Fair Housing Act, 60 Mo. L. Rev. 547 (1995).

16. 441 U.S. at 103, 99 S.Ct. at 1609.

17. LeBlanc–Sternberg v. Fletcher, 67 F.3d 412, 424 (2d Cir.1995). See also Bryant Woods Inn Inc., v. Howard County, 124 F.3d 597 (4th Cir.1997).

Standing issues also arise with respect to persons outside a municipality who are adversely affected by land use decisions within the municipality. These issues are discussed elsewhere.[18]

18. See supra § 5.34.

Chapter 7

SUBDIVISION CONTROL LAW

Analysis

I. INTRODUCTION

II. SUBDIVISION REGULATIONS

III. MAPPING FOR FUTURE STREETS AND OTHER PUBLIC IMPROVEMENTS

IV. PLANNED UNIT DEVELOPMENTS

I. INTRODUCTION

§ 7.1 Types of Subdivision Controls: In General

With the exception of zoning which regulates the use of land, and building and housing codes which regulate construction, the land development control law system at the local level consists of regulatory techniques that focus primarily on residential development. Subdivision regulations, maps for future streets and public improvements, planned unit development and subdivided land sales regulations are examples of these residential regulatory techniques.

Subdivision regulation generally refers to controls implemented during the land subdividing stage of the development process and includes such measures as platting procedures and controls, design regulation, improvement requirements, dedication requirements, in-lieu fees, performance bonds and the like. Official mapping is another kind of land use control which implements planning by giving precise locations of future streets, parks and sites for other public facilities within a local jurisdiction. Planned unit developments are residential developments that include multifamily and single-family housing and that may also include commercial development. Subdivided land sales regulations, although often implemented through state and federal statutes, are designed to regulate local and interstate real estate sales, particularly the sale of subdivided lands or lots.

In developing an understanding of the land development regulatory techniques discussed in this chapter, it is important to keep their primary residential focus in perspective. While primarily directed toward residential development, they are often cross-matched with complimentary techniques and integrated into the overall land development control law system. For example, although subdivision regulations are generally independent of zoning regulations, planned unit developments, which often include commercial uses, are often found within zoning regulations but are increasingly found in subdivision regulation ordinances.

II. SUBDIVISION REGULATIONS

§ 7.2 Introduction and History

Subdivision regulation is a land use control based on the police power and is second in importance only to zoning as a land use control device. As with zoning, a local government may need specific state statutory or constitutional authorization to enact subdivision regulations based on whether the jurisdiction follows a home rule power or Dillon's rule view of local government authority.[1] Unlike zoning, which controls the use of land and remains important before, during and after development, subdivision regulation generally refers to controls implemented during the development process. Once land is subdivided, subdivision regulations have little or no application until redevelopment, at which time re-subdivision may or may not be necessary. Although the subdivision of land occurs early in the development process, its impact on the community is lasting because "[t]he pattern of a subdivision becomes the pattern of a community, which in turn may influence the character of an entire city."[2]

Modern subdivision regulations include such measures as platting procedures and controls; design regulations including such items as layout of streets, street width, street grading and surfacing, drainage, sidewalks, sewers, water mains, lot size and screen plantings; improvement, reservation and dedication requirements; in-lieu fees; performance bonds and the like.

Prior to the 1920's the primary purpose of subdivision regulations was to provide a more efficient method for selling and conveying subdivided land. Early subdivision statutes, or "Maps and Plats Acts" as they were usually called, required that maps or "plats" of the subdivision be recorded in the local land records office. The plat was required to show roads, parks, lots and blocks and the surveyed dimensions of these features.[3] Once recorded, land within the subdivision could be conveyed by reference to the lot number and subdivision name and the page and volumes numbers of the plat records books at which the plat in question was recorded. This avoided the expense and possible confusion inherent in using a metes and bounds plus government survey description of each individual lot every time it was conveyed.[4] Even though subdivision regulation has moved into another dimension today, most states still have platting statutes which are now often separate from the statutes authorizing subdivision control.[5]

The second period of subdivision regulation evolved from a recognition that subdivision regulations could be expanded to accomplish the substantive objective of controlling urban development.[6] As a result of

§ 7.2

1. See Lemm Development Corp. v. Bartlett, 133 N.H. 618, 580 A.2d 1082 (N.H. 1990); New Jersey Shore Builders Ass'n v. Township of Marlboro, 248 N.J.Super. 508, 591 A.2d 950 (N.J.Super.1991). For a discussion of the need for zoning power authorization, see supra § 3.5.

2. R. Freilich and M. Schultz, Model Subdivision Regulations Planning and Law 1 (American Planning Association 1995).

3. See, e.g., Law of Mar. 31, 1885, SB 125 (1885) Colo.Laws; Colo.Rev.Stat. § 6603–21 (1908).

4. It also made deeds a lot shorter!

5. For references to and capsule analyses of the subdivision and platting statutes of each of the 50 states see E. Yokley, The Law of Subdivisions, Ch. 14 (2d ed. 1981).

6. For a thorough discussion of the four historical periods of subdivision regulation see R. Freilich and M. Schultz, Model

land speculation in the 1920's, millions of vacant platted lots of such unusable sizes as 20 by 80 feet existed. Lots in these subdivisions were often undeveloped and had different owners. The diverse ownership and partial development prevented effective re-platting though many of the lots were tax delinquent and hence in public ownership. New suburban development "jumped" these unusable, close-in subdivisions and left "slums" of vacant lands. Some of these "slums" could be removed only by condemnation and urban renewal.[7] Some of this platted land was also improved with streets and utilities. Through the 1920's, local governments often provided these improvements from public funds or by special assessment. During the 1930's many of these special assessment bonds were in default.

In response to the problems created by land speculation and premature development, the Department of Commerce published the Standard City Planning Enabling Act in 1928 which contained provisions on subdivision control.[8] This act[9] shifted the emphasis of subdivision regulations from a device for selling and conveying land to one of providing a means to implement community comprehensive planning. In addition to recognizing the need for a method to transfer lots by reference to a plat, the act also emphasized the need for a method to require internal improvements within the subdivision. The model statute included provisions concerning the "arrangement of streets in relation to other existing or planned streets and to the master plan, for adequate and convenient open spaces of traffic, utilities, access of fire fighting apparatus, recreation, light and air, and for avoidance of congestion of population, including minimum width and area of lots."[10] Following the adoption of state enabling acts patterned after the model statutes, state courts upheld local government use of subdivision regulations as a land use control device to shape the growth of the entire community.[11]

The third period of subdivision regulation began in the late 40's when the pent up demand for housing generated the postwar building boom that became known as "urban sprawl."[12] This period was marked by an increasing awareness of the demands that rapidly expanding

Subdivision Regulations, supra note 2, at 1–8.

7. See, e.g., People ex rel. Gutknecht v. Chicago, 414 Ill. 600, 111 N.E.2d 626 (1953) (state urban renewal legislation could be used to condemn and reassemble vacant "slum" lands).

8. Standard City Planning Enabling Act, U.S. Dep't of Commerce (1928) (hereinafter referred to as "SPEA"). Title II of SPEA, Subdivision Control, is reprinted in the American Law Institute, a Model Land Development Code, Tentative Draft No. 1, 224, 244–253 (1968).

9. In addition to the SPEA, many states base modern subdivision enabling legislation on two other model acts: the Municipal Planning Enabling Act and the Municipal Subdivision Regulation Act. The latter two acts are reprinted in E. Bassett, F. Williams, A. Bettman and R. Whitten, Model Laws for Planning Cities, Counties and States (1935).

10. SPEA § 14 (1928).

11. See, e.g., Mansfield & Swett, Inc. v. Town of West Orange, 120 N.J.L. 145, 198 A. 225 (1938).

12. For a major governmental report focusing on the need to control urban sprawl as the number one priority in land-use planning see National Commission on Urban Problems (Douglas Commission), Alternatives to Urban Sprawl, Research Report No. 15 (1968).

suburban areas placed on local government facilities and services. Concern was focused on the needs of the new subdivision residents for parks, recreation facilities and adequate roads. Many local governments experienced great economic pressure to provide these facilities and services to the new development. At the same time local officials remembered the financial difficulties that were created in the 30's by excessive reliance on special assessments to fund various subdivision improvements.[13] Subdivision regulations were amended to include provisions which required developers to dedicate park and school sites,[14] on-site roads,[15] widen off-site streets,[16] and contribute funds where the need for such facilities was in areas other than the subdivision but within the general vicinity.[17] In response to the demand for control of urban sprawl, subdivision regulations have been modified to incorporate new techniques which go far beyond the needs of residents within the subdivision. Subdivision regulations are more frequently being used to delay or deny development where it can be shown that the subdivision will cause serious off-site drainage problems and flooding, reduce environmental quality, or contribute to existing problems of inadequate local government facilities.[18]

The fourth and most recent period of subdivision regulation emphasizes the relationship of the individual subdivision to its external community environment through the local government comprehensive planning process. Current emphasis is being placed on the rate of subdivision development activity. This period of the history of subdivision regulation is marked by attempts to integrate regulations into a comprehensive growth management and planning program[19] with the objective of phasing in new development in coordination with the orderly provision of adequate public facilities.[20]

---

13. In the 1930's many local governments faced bankruptcy when the economy collapsed and revenues which secured special assessment bonds disappeared. Most local governments assumed that increased property taxes resulting from new development would generate sufficient revenue for maintaining public facilities. The collapse of the development market in the late 1920's demonstrated the uncertainty of the assumption.

14. See, e.g., Rosen v. Village of Downers Grove, 19 Ill.2d 448, 167 N.E.2d 230 (1960) (dedication of public school site).

15. See, e.g., Brous v. Smith, 304 N.Y. 164, 106 N.E.2d 503 (1952) (dedication of roads internal to subdivision).

16. See, e.g., Ayres v. City of Los Angeles, 34 Cal.2d 31, 207 P.2d 1 (1949) (dedication of perimeter streets bordering subdivision).

17. See, e.g., Jenad, Inc. v. Village of Scarsdale, 18 N.Y.2d 78, 271 N.Y.S.2d 955, 218 N.E.2d 673 (1966) (in lieu fee for recreational purposes upheld); Associated Home

Builders v. Walnut Creek, Inc., 4 Cal.3d 633, 94 Cal.Rptr. 630, 484 P.2d 606 (1971), appeal dismissed 404 U.S. 878, 92 S.Ct. 202, 30 L.Ed.2d 159 (1971) (in lieu fee for recreation and open space upheld).

18. See, e.g., Eschete v. New Orleans, 258 La. 133, 245 So.2d 383 (1971) (drainage); Pearson Kent Corp. v. Bear, 28 N.Y.2d 396, 322 N.Y.S.2d 235, 271 N.E.2d 218 (1971) (inadequate off-site roads); Salamar Builders Corp. v. Tuttle, 29 N.Y.2d 221, 325 N.Y.S.2d 933, 275 N.E.2d 585 (1971) (environmental protection of off-site water resources).

19. See ch. 9 infra.

20. See, e.g., Golden v. Planning Board of Town of Ramapo, 30 N.Y.2d 359, 334 N.Y.S.2d 138, 285 N.E.2d 291 (1972), appeal dismissed 409 U.S. 1003, 93 S.Ct. 440, 34 L.Ed.2d 294 (1972) (constitutionality of subdivision development timing ordinance upheld); see Freilich, Golden v. Town of Ramapo, Establishing a New Dimension in American Planning Law, 4 Urb.Law ix (Summer 1972); cf. Bosselman, Can the

§ 7.3 Relation to Planning

As with zoning, subdivision regulation is a land use control that implements comprehensive planning.[1] The relationship between planning and subdivision control, however, has historically been viewed as closer than in zoning.[2] This close relationship between subdivision regulation and planning stems at least in part from the combination of those two concepts in the Standard City Planning Enabling Act, and the total omission of subdivision regulation and one terse reference to a "comprehensive plan" in the Standard Zoning Enabling Act.[3] More specifically, in the zoning process the legislative body and the board of zoning adjustment (or Board of Zoning Appeals) often have major roles to play while the planning commission acts only in an advisory capacity. In the subdivision control process, the planning commission is usually given the a major role in the formulation and implementation of subdivision regulations. The planning commission is also usually given a major role in the drafting and implementation of comprehensive plans.

Furthermore, although in those states which have not yet embraced comprehensive planning and the consistency requirement for all land use regulations, there is no necessary relation between either zoning or subdivision controls and comprehensive plans,[4] the statutes of many of these states require a comprehensive plan or at least a plan having a major street element before local governments can regulate subdivisions.[5] In other states an official map is required as a prerequisite to subdivision regulation. In some jurisdictions the statutes specifically require that the subdivision review process include findings as to the compatibility of the subdivision plat with the plan or map.[6] In imposing these planning requirements, the statutes generally follow the guidance of one or more of the model or standard acts. At least one court has held that a planning board could rely on a comprehensive plan to disapprove a subdivision plat even though the master plan had not been formally adopted.[7]

While necessary conformity between planning and subdivision control has traditionally been greater than the conformity between planning

Town of Ramapo Pass a Law to Bind the Rights of the Whole World?, 1 Fla.St. U.L.Rev. 234 (1973).

§ 7.3

1. See Cunningham, Land–Use Control—The State and Local Programs, 50 Iowa L.Rev. 367, 435 (1965) ("Ideally, both zoning and subdivision controls are tools for effectuating comprehensive land-use plans.").

2. Id. at 417.

3. See supra § 2.8.

4. Model Subdivision Regulations, supra § 7.2 n. 2, at 2 ("Just as the zoning requirement contained in the Standard Zoning Enabling Act ... that zoning 'be in accordance with a comprehensive plan' has never been interpreted to require that a master plan precede adoption of a zoning ordinance ... a master plan generally has been held not to be required in order to adopt valid subdivision regulations ...").

5. See, e.g., Colo.Rev.Stat. §§ 31–23– 213; Utah Code Ann. 1953, 10–9–25.

6. See, e.g., Ill.—S.H.A. Ch. 24 ¶ 11– 12–8 ("the municipality shall determine whether a proposed plat of subdivision or re-subdivision complies with the official map.").

7. Neiderhofer v. Gustafson, 45 A.D.2d 812, 357 N.Y.S.2d 196 (3d Dep't 1974); cf. Lordship Park Ass'n v. Board of Zoning Appeals, 137 Conn. 84, 75 A.2d 379 (1950).

and zoning, the matter is relative. Much subdivision regulation still takes place without reference to a comprehensive plan.[8] In many jurisdictions, the plan is only a general guide, it is often not legislatively adopted, and property owners may not be afforded a hearing on the plan. In such circumstances subdivision denial based on non-compliance with the plan may be beyond the authority of the plat reviewing agency.[9] The trend for the future would seem to be that established by those states which require zoning and subdivision regulation to be consistent with a comprehensive plan.[10]

§ 7.4 Relation to Zoning

It is usually necessary for a developer to comply with both zoning and subdivision regulations.[1] Although the two types of controls are intended to complement each other within the development process, they are often administered by different agencies. They are also often subject to separate enabling statutes each with its own particular requirements. As a consequence, subdivision regulations and zoning are often administered so as to appear to be working at cross-purposes. Some jurisdictions have integrated the two types of controls into a local development code which provides a consolidated procedure for considering both the zoning change and the subdivision proposal.

While the authority to approve subdivisions and the power to zone are usually authorized by separate statutes,[2] some subdivision control legislation requires that a plat conform to zoning regulations.[3] Courts have also held that local government authority to require conformance may be inferred from the general purposes to be served by subdivision control regulation.[4] Where the enabling legislation is silent on the relationship between the two types of controls, the local regulations often require that plats comply with local zoning.

Courts have also held that subdivision proposals may be rejected where they do not conform to zoning regulations.[5] Some courts have held that subdivision review may not be used so as to amend zoning because the exercise of such a power would effectively amount to a usurpation of

---

8. See Nelson, The Master Plan and Subdivision Control, 16 Me.L.Rev. 107 (1964).

9. Lordship Park Ass'n v. Board of Zoning Appeals, 137 Conn. 84, 75 A.2d 379 (1950). But see Krieger v. Planning Comm'n of Howard County, 224 Md. 320, 167 A.2d 885 (1961).

10. See, e.g., West's Ann.Cal.Gov't Code § 66474(a); West's Fla.Stat.Ann. § 163.3202; Ill.—S.H.A. Ch. 24, ¶ 11–12–8; Board of County Comm'rs v. Gaster, 285 Md. 233, 401 A.2d 666 (1979).

§ 7.4

1. Oakland Court v. York Twp., 128 Mich.App. 199, 339 N.W.2d 873 (Mich.App. 1983).

2. For a discussion of zoning enabling acts see supra ch. 3.

3. See, e.g., N.J.Stat.Ann. § 40:55D–38.

4. See, e.g., Benny v. Alameda, 105 Cal. App.3d 1006, 164 Cal.Rptr. 776 (1980).

5. See, e.g., People v. Park Ridge, 25 Ill.App.2d 424, 166 N.E.2d 635 (1960); Durland v. Maresco, 53 A.D.2d 643, 384 N.Y.S.2d 503 (1976). Krawski v. Planning & Zoning Comm'n, 21 Conn.App. 667, 575 A.2d 1036 (Conn.App.1990).

the authority of the local zoning board.[6] Where the subdivision control ordinance imposes additional requirements, however, courts have held that mere compliance with the zoning ordinance is not sufficient.[7]

If an approved subdivision exists and a zoning ordinance is subsequently passed which would prevent the lots from being used as subdivided, the subdivider has no vested right to develop the subdivision.[8] Similarly, where the owner of unsold lots requests a variance, an old subdivision can be forced to comply with new subdivision regulations.[9] On the other hand, vested rights in nonconforming lots are sometimes recognized, particularly where houses have been built on some lots or sewers and water lines installed.[10] Some statutes and ordinances provide that once a subdivision is approved, the municipality is precluded from exercising its powers inconsistent with the approval for a period of time.[11] These statutes have been interpreted, however, to apply to changes in local but not state land use regulations.[12]

§ 7.5 Definition of Subdivision

The Standard City Planning Enabling Act did not define the term "subdivision." As a result, the definition of subdivision in statutes and ordinances varies and is unclear in many states. Most broadly it is the division of one parcel of land into more than one parcel.[1] Many state statutes, however, define the term as a division of land into a minimum number of parcels.[2] Where a definition is omitted from the statute, courts have generally construed the statute to authorize each local government to define the term.[3] Local ordinances, however, may not

6. See, e.g., Shapiro v. Town of Oyster Bay, 27 Misc.2d 844, 211 N.Y.S.2d 414 (1961), affirmed 20 A.D.2d 850, 249 N.Y.S.2d 663 (1964); Goodman v. Board of Comm'rs, 49 Pa.Cmwlth. 35, 411 A.2d 838 (1980); Snyder v. Zoning Bd., 98 R.I. 139, 200 A.2d 222 (1964).

7. See e.g., Shoptaugh v. Board of County Comm'rs, 37 Colo.App. 39, 543 P.2d 524 (1975); Popular Refreshments, Inc. v. Fuller's Milk Bar & Recreation Center, Inc., 85 N.J.Super. 528, 205 A.2d 445 (App.Div. 1964), certification denied 44 N.J. 409, 209 A.2d 143 (1965).

8. See, e.g., Lake Intervale Homes, Inc. v. Parsippany–Troy Hills Township, 28 N.J. 423, 147 A.2d 28 (1958); York Township Zoning Bd. of Adjustment v. Brown, 407 Pa. 649, 182 A.2d 706 (1962); Kappadahl v. Alcan Pacific Co., 222 Cal.App.2d 626, 35 Cal.Rptr. 354 (1963). Smith v. Winhall Planning Comm'n, 140 Vt. 178, 436 A.2d 760 (1981).

9. See, e.g., Blevens v. Manchester, 103 N.H. 284, 170 A.2d 121 (1961).

10. Gruber v. Mayor and Township Comm. of Raritan Township, 39 N.J. 1, 186 A.2d 489 (1962); Wood v. North Salt Lake,

15 Utah 2d 245, 390 P.2d 858 (1964); Western Land Equities, Inc. v. Logan, 617 P.2d 388 (Utah 1980); Smith v. Winhall Planning Comm'n, 140 Vt. 178, 436 A.2d 760 (1981).

11. See, e.g., Pa.Stat.Ann.Tit. 53, § 10508(4) (5 years); N.J.Stat.Ann. § 40.55D–49 (3 Years).

12. Island Properties, Inc. v. Martha's Vineyard Comm'n, 372 Mass. 216, 361 N.E.2d 385 (1977); Ocean Acres v. State, 168 N.J.Super. 597, 403 A.2d 967 (App.Div. 1979), certification denied 81 N.J. 352, 407 A.2d 1226 (1979).

§ 7.5

1. See, e.g., Mass.Gen.Laws c. 41, § 81L (two or more).

2. See, e.g., Conn.Gen.Stat.Ann. § 8–18 (three or more); West's Rev.Code Wash. Ann. 58.17.020 (five or more).

3. See, e.g., Delaware Midland Corp. v. Westhampton Beach, 79 Misc.2d 438, 359 N.Y.S.2d 944, 946 (1974), affirmed 39 N.Y.2d 1029, 387 N.Y.S.2d 248, 355 N.E.2d 302 (1976).

generally expand the statutory definition.[4]

In general, the term subdivision is defined so as to require that the division be for the purpose of sale, lease or building development.[5] Division for other purposes may not constitute a subdivision.[6] Condominium development has been held not to be a subdivision.[7] In some statutes the number of divisions may be given a time horizon, so that property is not considered subdivided if not more than 3 lots are created within any five year period. Some statutes also expressly exempt subdivisions which do not involve creation of new streets[8] or the extension of existing streets,[9] which divide land among family members,[10] or which are the result of partition actions or testamentary divisions of real property.[11]

In many states there are loopholes, and subdividers engage in elaborate schemes to divide in a way which is not a "subdivision."[12] They thereby avoid the required approval and thus may avoid the imposition of subdivision exactions.[13] Avoidance is more common where there are no statutes or ordinances that are designed to cover less significant subdivisions. For example, in Pratt v. Adams[14] the court voided a scheme where one parcel was conveyed to several persons in joint tenancy and the persons then "suffered" the creation of 12 parcels through a partition action, the referee setting up an elaborate scheme for roads, easements, buildings restrictions etc. as part of the partition order.

§ 7.6 The Subdivision Approval Process

The imposition of subdivision improvement requirements occurs during the subdivision approval process. Although many variations exist in the subdivision approval process from state to state, generalizations about the process can be made. The essential requirement of subdivision control is that a subdivider cannot convey subdivided lands without a recorded subdivision plat.[1] The subdivider is prohibited from recording

---

4. See, e.g., Peninsula Corp. v. Planning and Zoning Comm'n, 151 Conn. 450, 199 A.2d 1 (1964); Dearborn v. Town of Milford, 120 N.H. 82, 411 A.2d 1132 (1980); Martorano v. Board of Comm'rs, 51 Pa. Cmwlth. 202, 414 A.2d 411 (1980).

5. See, e.g., Pa.Stat. Title 53, § 10201(21).

6. See, e.g., Pa.Stat. Title 53, § 10201(21) (subdivision for agricultural purposes exempted); N.J.Stat.Ann. 40:55D–7 (subdivision over five acres for agricultural use); Conn.Gen.Stat.Ann. § 8–18 (subdivision for municipal, conservation or agricultural purposes exempted).

7. See, e.g., Gerber v. Town of Clarkstown, 78 Misc.2d 221, 356 N.Y.S.2d 926 (1974); but see N.H.Rev.Stat.Ann. § 672.14 (condominium development included); Colo. Rev.Stat. § 12–61–401.

8. See, e.g., Stoker v. Irvington, 71 N.J.Super. 370, 177 A.2d 61 (1961); Donovan v. New Brunswick, 50 N.J.Super. 102, 141 A.2d 134 (1958); Urban v. Planning Bd.

of Manasquan, 124 N.J. 651, 592 A.2d 240 (N.J. 1991).

9. See, e.g., Dube v. Senter, 107 N.H. 191, 219 A.2d 456 (1966).

10. See, e.g., Kiska v. Skrensky, 145 Conn. 28, 138 A.2d 523 (1958).

11. See, e.g., N.J.Stat.Ann. 40:55D–7; Metzdorf v. Rumson, 67 N.J.Super. 121, 170 A.2d 249 (1961).

12. See Gerard v. San Juan County, 43 Wash.App. 54, 715 P.2d 149 (Wash.App. 1986) (sequence of conveyances used to get short plat exemptions to create 18 parcel subdivision struck down).

13. See § 7.8 infra.

14. 229 Cal.App.2d 602, 40 Cal.Rptr. 505 (1964).

§ 7.6

1. One court has held, however, that such a mandatory recordation requirement results in an unconstitutional restraint on

the plat until the approval of the local subdivision approval agency has been obtained.[2]

While most state enabling acts provide for a two-step approval process,[3] some local governments include an additional preliminary step referred to as a preapplication conference. At the conference the local agency or its staff will familiarize the applicant with the subdivision regulations and answer general questions. At the same time the applicant will provide the agency with the basic idea of the proposal.

The submission of a "preliminary plat" follows and constitutes the first formal step in the subdivision approval process. The regulations usually require that the applicant submit a detailed drawing of the proposed subdivision. Included on the drawing are the necessary improvements and indications of which improvements will be dedicated to public use. The local agency may then approve, disapprove, or conditionally approve the preliminary plat, usually after a properly noticed hearing.[4] In some states the right to subdivide may vest following approval of the preliminary plat.[5] Reasons for disapproval are usually required to be made in writing and the final decision is subject to judicial review.[6] Preliminary plat approval usually authorizes the subdivider to begin construction of the improvements provided a surety bond for their completion is posted.[7]

After preliminary plat approval, the subdivider usually has one year within which to submit a final plat for approval.[8] Before the final plat is approved the subdivider must demonstrate substantial conformance to the preliminary plat and any conditions that the local agency has imposed. Some statutes require approval of the final plat if all requirements imposed on approval of the preliminary plat are satisfied.[9] Courts often construe such provisions so as to make approval of the final plat a ministerial as opposed to a discretionary act.[10] Once the final plat is approved, the subdivider may record the plat and legally convey lots within the subdivision.

Many states set time limits within which the local agency must act on either preliminary or final plats.[11] If the agency takes no action within

alienation. Kass v. Lewin, 104 So.2d 572 (Fla.1958). Although the case has never been specifically overruled, it has been distinguished to death and now superseded by Florida's growth management regulations. See J. Juergensmeyer and J. Wadley, Florida Land Use and Growth Management Law § 5.04 (1997).

2. See 4 R. Anderson, Anderson's American Law of Zoning § 25.05 (3d ed.1986) (updated 1996) (supplemented).

3. Id. at § 23.11.

4. Id. at § 23.12.

5. See, e.g., Western Land Equities v. Logan, 617 P.2d 388 (Utah 1980).

6. See, e.g., West's Rev.Code Wash. Ann. 58.17.180.

7. See SPEA, § 14.

8. See, e.g., Nev.Rev.Stat. 278.360(1) (permitting, however, a one year extension).

9. See, e.g., West's Ann.Cal.Gov't Code § 66458; Pa.Stat. Tit. 53, § 10508(4). Also see, Golden State Homebuilding Assocs. v. City of Modesto, 26 Cal.App.4th 601, 31 Cal.Rptr.2d 572 (Cal.App. 1994).

10. See, e.g., Youngblood v. Board of Supervisors, 22 Cal.3d 644, 150 Cal.Rptr. 242, 586 P.2d 556 (1978); Hakim v. Board of Comm'rs, 27 Pa.Cmwlth. 405, 366 A.2d 1306 (1976).

11. See, e.g., Ill.—S.H.A. ch. 24, ¶ 11–12–8; N.J.Stat.Ann.§ 40:55D–1 et seq.

this period, the plat is deemed approved.[12] Approval of the preliminary or final plat, however, does not constitute acceptance by the local government of the dedicated improvements. Such acceptance, and the responsibility for maintaining the improvements, occurs when the local government makes a formal decision to accept.

The subdivision control process may also include devices designed to achieve sufficient flexibility for the modification of subdivision control requirements.[13] Enabling statutes often authorize administrative relief in the form of variances where a strict application of the regulations would cause unusual and unnecessary hardship on the subdivider.[14] However, unlike zoning variances which are usually granted by the board of adjustment upon appeal from the decision of an administrative official, variance relief from subdivision regulations is usually granted by the same agency which originally reviewed the subdivision proposal. Absent a provision authorizing the zoning board of adjustment to grant variances from subdivision regulations, such board has been held without power to do so.[15] When a local agency has authority to vary the strict application of a subdivision ordinance, courts have held it can only do so by making findings of fact supported by evidence.[16]

§ 7.7 Enforcement Methods, Sanctions and Required Improvement Guarantees

The effectiveness of subdivision regulations, like all land use control devices, depends upon the presence of fair and efficient enforcement methods, sanctions and required improvement guarantees.[1] One of the model enabling statutes provides:

> Whoever ... sells ... any land by reference to or exhibition of or by other use of a plat of a subdivision, before such plat has been approved ... and recorded ... shall ... pay a penalty of $100 for each lot.... The municipal corporation may enjoin such transfer ... or may recover the said penalty.[2]

---

12. Id. It has been suggested, however, that it is doubtful that a court will permit a subdivision project to proceed if it will seriously jeopardize public health and safety. See Schultz & Kelley, Subdivision Improvement Requirements and Guarantees: A Primer, 28 Wash.U.J.Urb. & Contemp.L. 3, n. 183 at 38 (1985).

13. See, e.g., Canter v. Planning Bd., 7 Mass.App.Ct. 805, 390 N.E.2d 1128 (1979); Blevens v. Manchester, 103 N.H. 284, 170 A.2d 121, 124 (1961).

14. See, e.g., N.J.Stat.Ann. § 40:55D–51(a).

15. See Noonan v. Zoning Bd. of Review, 90 R.I. 466, 159 A.2d 606 (1960).

16. See, e.g., Smith v. Township Comm. of Twp. of Morris, 101 N.J.Super. 271, 244 A.2d 145 (1968).

§ 7.7

1. For a detailed discussion of enforcement methods and improvement guarantees see R. Freilich & M. Schultz, Model Subdivision Regulations: Text and Commentary 117–159 (Amer. Planning Association, 1995); B. Royal, Subdivision Improvement Guarantees (Am.Soc'y of Planning Officials, Planning Advisory Serv. Report No. 298, January 1974); Schultz & Kelley, Subdivision Improvement Requirements and Guarantees: A Primer, 28 Wash.U.J.Urb. & Contemp.L. 1 at 38–106 (1985).

2. Dep't of Commerce, Standard City Planning Enabling Act § 16 (1928).

In addition to the sanction of civil fine and injunction,[3] statutes in various states provide other sanctions. Sometimes the sale of a lot in an unapproved subdivision is made a criminal act resulting in the imposition of a fine or imprisonment.[4] A local government or purchaser may set aside the conveyance under some statutes.[5] Generally, the option of using a metes and bounds provision is not available if the land involved is covered by the subdivision statute because the statute makes a circumventing conveyance by such a description illegal. As a result, if land is sold that is within the definition of a required subdivision, the statute has been violated.[6] The statute may also preclude the issuance of building permits in lands that should be but have not been submitted for subdivision approval.[7] This sanction is the most controversial because it places the penalty not upon the subdivider but upon the buyer of a lot in an unapproved subdivision. Some courts have refused to uphold this type of sanction.[8]

In addition to enforcement methods and sanctions, local governments also utilize performance bonds which protect both the governmental entity and the public against uncompleted improvements required by subdivision regulations. This is appropriate because although subdivision regulations are utilized to implement local planning and as a means of placing the burden of public improvements on the subdivider, local governments are also interested in the livability of the subdivision for prospective buyers who have often been left remediless. For example, in Hocking v. Title Ins. & Trust Co.,[9] the buyer sought damages from a title insurance company insuring her lot on the ground that the lot had no access because streets required by ordinance were not built and this constituted a defect in title. Under the ordinance, the city was to have obtained a bond from the subdivider to insure the improvement of streets, but failed to do so. Despite its neglect the city would not issue a building permit. The court concluded that the problem was not one of title. A properly required performance bond, however, would have provided funds to build the street.

The performance bond mechanism also allows the subdivider to obtain building permits and begin the construction and sale of lots so as to develop an income stream that enables him to pay for improvements. Once the reviewing local government has approved the plat, however, such performance bonding requirements may not be imposed.[10] Alterna-

3. See Lake County v. Truett, 758 S.W.2d 529 (Tenn.App.1988) (Developer prohibited by injunction from other sales); Johnson v. Hinds County, 524 So.2d 947 (Miss.1988) (injunction against developer of illegal subdivision).

4. See, e.g., N.M.Stat.Ann. 1978, § 3–26–14; Wyo.Stat. 1977, § 15–1–511.

5. See, e.g., West's Ann.Cal.Gov't Code § 66499.32; Gen.L.R.I.1956, § 45–23–13; Wis.Stat.Ann. 236.31(3).

6. See § 7.5 supra.

7. See, e.g., West's Rev.Code Wash. Ann. 58.17.210.

8. See, e.g., Keizer v. Adams, 2 Cal.3d 976, 88 Cal.Rptr. 183, 471 P.2d 983 (1970); State ex rel. Craven v. Tacoma, 63 Wn.2d 23, 385 P.2d 372 (1963).

9. 37 Cal.2d 644, 234 P.2d 625 (1951).

10. See, e.g., McKenzie v. Arthur T. McIntosh Co., 50 Ill.App.2d 370, 200 N.E.2d 138 (1964).

tively, if the final plat is not approved by the local government, a subdivider who has posted a performance bond or deposited money to insure the completion of plat improvements, may recover the bond or deposit.[11] Since performance bonds generally name the local government as obligee, only such local government may initiate an action to enforce the bond.[12] Neither purchasers of land in the subdivision who are seeking to have the improvements installed nor contractors seeking monies due for construction work rendered in the proposed subdivision may bring such enforcement actions.[13]

§ 7.8   Exactions on Subdivision Approval

As a result of the rapid suburbanization of the United States, there has been a growing acceptance of the use of land use regulations to both accommodate suburban growth and maintain the quality of governmental services. The influx of new residents into suburban areas has forced local governments to provide new streets, water and sewer lines, recreational and educational facilities, police and fire buildings and open space. The increased demand for these local government services in turn raises the difficult question of how a community should finance such services and programs without overburdening either the already strained property tax base or existing local residents who have already contributed to the financing of existing improvements.

Many local governments have chosen to cope with growth-induced financial difficulties by employing a variety of means, including subdivision exactions, to shift the cost of providing capital improvements to the new residents who create the need for them. A subdivision exaction has been defined as "one form of subdivision control, which requires that developers provide certain public improvements at their own expense."[1] No aspect of subdivision control law has interested the casebook authors and the law review article writers more than the question of what kinds of conditions, required dedications, payment of fees and improvements can be imposed for subdivision approval.[2] This emphasis reflects the fact

---

11. See, e.g., Cammarano v. Borough Allendale, 65 N.J.Super. 240, 167 A.2d 431 (1961).

12. See, e.g., Town of Stoneham v. Savelo, 341 Mass. 456, 170 N.E.2d 417 (1960); Pacific County v. Sherwood Pacific, Inc., 17 Wash.App. 790, 567 P.2d 642 (1977).

13. See, e.g., Gordon v. Robinson Homes, Inc., 342 Mass. 529, 174 N.E.2d 381 (1961) (purchasers); City of University City ex rel. Mackey v. Frank Miceli & Sons Realty & Bldg. Co., 347 S.W.2d 131 (Mo. 1961) (adjoining property owners); Weber v. Pacific Indemnity Co., 204 Cal.App.2d 334, 22 Cal.Rptr. 366 (1962) (unpaid contractor).

§ 7.8

1. Pavelko, Subdivision Exactions: A Review of Judicial Standards, Wash. U.J.Urb. & Contemp.L. 269, 270 (1983).

2. A partial list of "classic" law review materials includes: Adelstein & Edelson, Subdivision Exactions and Congestion Externalities, 5 J.Legal Stud. 174 (1976); Burchell, Edelstein & Listokin, Fiscal Impact Analysis as a Tool for Land Use Regulation, 7 Real Est.L.J. 132 (1978); Ellickson, Suburban Growth Controls: An Economic and Legal Analysis, 86 Yale L.J. 385 (1977); Ferguson & Rasnic, Judicial Limitations on Mandatory Subdivision Dedications, 13 Real Est.L.J. 250 (1985); Hanna, Subdivisions: Conditions Imposed by Local Government, 6 Santa Clara Lawyer 172 (1966); Heyman and Gilhool, The Constitutionality of Imposing Increased Community Costs on New Subdivision Residents Through Subdivision Exactions, 73 Yale L.J. 1119 (1964); Johnston, Constitutionality of Subdivision Control Exactions: The Quest for a Rationale,

that most subdivision litigation these days concerns exactions. Since subdivision exactions are part of the larger issue of developer funding of infrastructure which is one of the key tenets of growth management law, a brief review of the origins of developer funding requirements as part of the subdivision process and their current legal status will be made at this point but the reader is referred to Chapter 9 on growth management for a broader and more in depth analysis.[3]

A. *Historical Perspective on Subdivision Exactions*

Required dedications as a prerequisite for subdivision plat approval were the first land use regulations developed to shift the capital expense burden from local governments to the developer and new residents. Dedication involves a conveyance of an interest in land to the government for a public purpose.[4] Dedications required under subdivision regulations should be distinguished from common law dedications. Common law dedication involves an offer to dedicate and a corresponding acceptance by a local government. Under common law dedication a developer is estopped from later questioning the acceptance. In subdivision regulation dedication, however, questions of legislative authority and constitutionality arise.[5]

Early subdivision enabling statutes authorized local governments to adopt subdivision regulations that required developers to provide and dedicate improvements such as streets.[6] These early statutes were designed to eliminate the confusion of disconnected street systems resulting from earlier voluntary dedications and to avoid future public debt like that incurred as a result of subdivisions made defunct by the real estate crash of the 1920's.[7] Courts often upheld these early mandatory dedications on the "privilege" theory that:

> The owner of a subdivision voluntarily dedicates sufficient land for streets in return for the advantage and privilege of having his plat

52 Cornell L.Q. 871 (1967); Pavelko, Subdivision Exactions: A Review of Judicial Standards, supra note 1; Reps & Smith, Control of Urban Land Subdivision, 14 Syracuse L.Rev. 405 (1963); Trichelo, Subdivision Exactions: Virginia Constitutional Problems, 11 U.Rich.L.Rev. 21 (1976); Yearwood, Subdivision Law: Timing and Location Control, 44 J.Urban L. 585 (1967); Note, Municipalities: Validity of Subdivision Fees for Schools and Parks, 66 Colum.L.Rev. 974 (1966); Note, Subdivision Exactions: Where is the Limit? 42 Notre Dame Law 400 (1967); Note, Subdivision Land Dedication: Objectives and Objections, 27 Stan.L.Rev. 419 (1975); Note, Money Payment Requirements as Conditions to the Approval of Subdivision Maps: Analysis and Prognosis, 9 Vill.L.R. 294 (1964);

3. See specifically, § 9.8.

4. P. Rohan, Zoning and Land Use Controls § 45.04[2] (1982). The dedicated interest may be an easement or a fee entitlement. See Generally 23 Am.Jur.2d Dedications (1965).

5. See Pavelko, supra note 1, n. 9 at 270; 4 R. Anderson, American Law of Zoning § 23.26 (2d ed. 1976).

6. See Melli, Subdivision Control in Wisconsin, 1953 Wis.L.Rev. 389, 455; R. Freilich and P. Levi, Model Subdivision Regulations: Text and Commentary 3 (Amer.Soc'y of Planning Officials, 1975); R. Freilich and M. Schultz, Model Subdivision Regulations Planning and Law, p. 1 (American Planning Association) (1995)

7. See Note, Money Payment Requirements as Conditions to the Approval of Subdivision Maps: Analysis and Prognosis, supra note 2, at 296; see generally § 7.2 supra.

recorded.[8]

During the post-World War II land development boom, many local governments began experiencing severe political and economic pressure from the need to provide facilities and services to new development. Increasingly, subdivision regulations were amended to impose new requirements that developers dedicate park and school sites, widen off-site streets, or contribute funds for a wide variety of purposes.[9] During this period the "in lieu" fee developed as a refinement of required dedications.[10] For example, to require each subdivision to dedicate land to educational purposes would not solve the problem of providing school facilities for developing suburban areas because the sites would often be inadequate in size and imperfectly located.[11] The in-lieu fee solves this problem by substituting a money payment for dedication when the local government determines the latter is not feasible.

Also during the 1950's, the "privilege" theory of granting governmental benefits and permits came under intense criticism.[12] In response to this criticism the Supreme Court began to enlarge the concept of "property" to include the reasonable expectation of government grants, permits and benefits.[13] Therefore, at the very time that local governments were expanding their use of exactions the privilege theory rationale for mandatory dedication appeared destined for obsolescence as the subdivision of property began to seem more like a right than a privilege.[14]

As a result of increased demands by local governments for more contributions, and increased reluctance to characterize governmental permits as privileges, courts began to draw back from the approval previously given to principles of mandatory dedication.[15] Based on this retrenchment, some commentators suggested that exactions should be permissible only for facilities that are of exclusive benefit to the new

---

8. Ridgefield Land Co. v. Detroit, 241 Mich. 468, 217 N.W. 58 (1928). See also Brous v. Smith, 304 N.Y. 164, 106 N.E.2d 503 (1952); Ayres v. City Council of Los Angeles, 34 Cal.2d 31, 207 P.2d 1 (1949); Garvin v. Baker, 59 So.2d 360 (Fla.1952); Pavelko, supra note 1, at 283.

9. See, e.g., Blevens v. Manchester, 103 N.H. 284, 170 A.2d 121 (1961); City of Buena Park v. Boyar, 186 Cal.App.2d 61, 8 Cal.Rptr. 674 (1960); R.M. Yearwood, The Law and Administration of Subdivision Regulation: A Study in Land Use Control 40, 152–62 (1966).

10. J. Juergensmeyer and R. Blake, Impact Fees: An Answer to Local Governments' Capital Funding Dilemma, 9 Fla.St. Univ.L.Rev. 415, 418 (1981); J. Nicholas, A. Nelson, and J. Juergensmeyer, A Practitioner's Guide to Development Impact Fees, Ch.4 (1991).

11. R. Anderson, supra note 5, at § 19.42.

12. See Reich, The New Property, 73 Yale L.J. 733 (1964).

13. See, e.g., Speiser v. Randall, 357 U.S. 513, 78 S.Ct. 1332, 2 L.Ed.2d 1460 (1958); Flemming v. Nestor, 363 U.S. 603, 80 S.Ct. 1367, 4 L.Ed.2d 1435 (1960), rehearing denied 364 U.S. 854, 81 S.Ct. 29, 5 L.Ed.2d 77 (1960); Sherbert v. Verner, 374 U.S. 398, 83 S.Ct. 1790, 10 L.Ed.2d 965 (1963); Shapiro v. Thompson, 394 U.S. 618, 89 S.Ct. 1322, 22 L.Ed.2d 600 (1969); Goldberg v. Kelly, 397 U.S. 254, 90 S.Ct. 1011, 25 L.Ed.2d 287 (1970); Bell v. Burson, 402 U.S. 535, 91 S.Ct. 1586, 29 L.Ed.2d 90 (1971), conformed 124 Ga.App. 220, 183 S.E.2d 416 (1971).

14. See Bosselman & Stroud, Pariah to Paragon: Developer Exactions in Florida 1975–85, 14 Stetson L.Rev. 527, 529 (1985).

15. Id.

subdivision, such as internal subdivision streets, sewers and neighborhood parks.[16] They concluded that facilities whose benefit extends beyond a subdivision, such as arterial roads and regional parks, were not appropriate subjects for exactions even if the facilities were of substantial benefit to the residents of the subdivision as well.[17]

In contrast to the exclusive benefit theory, in 1964, cost-accounting was advocated as a method for evaluating cost-shifting devices in an article published in the Yale Law Journal by Ira Michael Heyman and Thomas K. Gilhool.[18] This article proposed a new way of evaluating the validity of subdivision exactions. "Given a proper cost-accounting approach," said the authors, "it is possible to determine the costs generated by new residents and thus to avoid charging the newcomers more than a proportionate share." The fact that the general public would also benefit from the exaction is immaterial "so long as there is a rational nexus between the exaction and the costs generated by the creation of the subdivision."[19]

The great appeal of this theory lay in its common sense approach. The transaction between developer and municipality was to be evaluated from an accounting standpoint in the same manner as any other business transaction. If it appeared that the costs were fairly apportioned between the affected parties the transaction should survive judicial scrutiny. Such a theory liberated the developers from the fiction that they were obtaining some sort of privilege, but it also provided local government with a flexible theory that could justify demands for payment of money as easily as for dedication of land. Because the theory was not tied to the financing of any particular type of government facility or service, it could be broadly applied across the whole range of government provision of infrastructure.

B. *Current Judicial View of the Legality of Exactions*

The validity of exactions is generally subject to a two-tiered constitutional attack. The preliminary and sometimes dispositive objection to required payments by developers for capital expenses is that they are not authorized by state statute or constitution[20] and therefore are void as ultra vires.[21] If constitutional, statutory, or general home rule authority

---

16. See Reps & Smith, supra note 2, at 405.

17. Id. Cases consistent with the "exclusive benefit" or "special benefit" test include State ex rel. Noland v. St. Louis County, 478 S.W.2d 363 (Mo.1972); McKain v. Toledo City Plan Commission, 26 Ohio App.2d 171, 270 N.E.2d 370 (1971); Pioneer Trust & Savings Bank v. Village of Mount Prospect, 22 Ill.2d 375, 176 N.E.2d 799 (1961).

18. See Heyman & Gilhool, supra note 2, at 1119.

19. Id. at 1137.

20. See, e.g., City of Montgomery v. Crossroads Land Co., 355 So.2d 363 (Ala.

1978) (in lieu fees for recreational purposes not authorized by state statute); Admiral Dev. Corp. v. Maitland, 267 So.2d 860 (Fla. App.1972) (dedication and in lieu fees for park and recreational purposes not authorized by city charter). See also Heyman & Gilhool, supra note 2, at 1134, n. 66 (citing cases where issue of statutory authority was dispositive).

21. The power of a local government to exercise various subdivision controls, including impact fees, is derived from general state statutes, private acts, and municipal charters. E. Yokley, The Law of Subdivisions 7 (1963).

is found, the local ordinance is alternatively challenged as a disguised tax which violates various state constitutional strictures,[22] an unreasonable exercise of the police power in violation of the rational nexus test,[23] or as a taking.[24]

Despite earlier negative reaction to such payment requirements, based on the exclusive benefit theory, state courts currently tend to validate them as a proper and reasonable exercise of police power.[25] In fact, as discussed elsewhere, recent decisions have extended judicial approval of required dedications to include impact fees and linkage programs.[26]

The current positive judicial attitude did not develop over night. Two early landmark decisions regarding subdivision exactions placed an almost insurmountable burden on local governments seeking money payments for extradevelopment capital spending from developers whose activities necessitated such expenditures. In Pioneer Trust & Savings Bank v. Village of Mount Prospect,[27] a developer challenged the validity of an ordinance requiring subdividers to dedicate one acre per sixty residential lots for schools, parks, and other public purposes. In determining whether required dedications or money payments for recreational or educational purposes represented a valid exercise of the police power, the Illinois Supreme Court propounded the "specifically and uniquely attributable" test. The court focused on the origin of the need for the

22. See, e.g., Call v. West Jordan, 606 P.2d 217 (Utah 1979), on rehearing 614 P.2d 1257 (1980) (in lieu fees for flood control, park, and recreational purposes attacked as ultra vires, an unreasonable regulation, and as an unconstitutional tax); Jordan v. Village of Menomonee Falls, 28 Wis.2d 608, 137 N.W.2d 442 (1965), appeal dismissed 385 U.S. 4, 87 S.Ct. 36, 17 L.Ed.2d 3 (1966) (in lieu fees for school, park, and recreational purposes attacked as ultra vires, an unreasonable regulation and as an unconstitutional tax), cert. dismissed, 385 U.S. 4, 87 S.Ct. 36, 17 L.Ed.2d 3 (1966). See generally Heyman & Gilhool, supra note 2, at 1122, 1146.

23. J. Nicholas, A. Nelson, and J. Juergensmeyer, A Practitioner's Guide to Development Impact Fees, Ch.4 (1991).

24. J. Nicholas, A. Nelson, and J. Juergensmeyer, A Practitioner's Guide to Development Impact Fees, Ch.4 (1991).

25. See, e.g., Associated Home Builders, Inc. v. Walnut Creek, 4 Cal.3d 633, 94 Cal.Rptr. 630, 484 P.2d 606 (1971) (subdivision fees for recreation purposes approved), cert. dismissed 404 U.S. 878, 92 S.Ct. 202, 30 L.Ed.2d 159 (1971), Billings Properties, Inc. v. Yellowstone County, 144 Mont. 25, 394 P.2d 182 (1964) (required dedication for recreational purposes upheld); Jenad, Inc. v. Village of Scarsdale, 18 N.Y.2d 78, 271

N.Y.S.2d 955, 218 N.E.2d 673 (1966) (in lieu fees for recreational purposes upheld); Call v. West Jordan, 606 P.2d 217 (Utah 1979), on rehearing 614 P.2d 1257 (1980) (in lieu fee for flood control, park, and recreational purposes upheld); Jordan v. Village of Menomonee Falls, 28 Wis.2d 608, 137 N.W.2d 442 (1965), appeal dismissed 385 U.S. 4, 87 S.Ct. 36, 17 L.Ed.2d 3 (in lieu fee for school, park, and recreational purposes upheld). See also Georgia–Pacific Corp. v. California Coastal Com., 132 Cal. App.3d 678, 183 Cal.Rptr. 395 (1982); Grupe v. California Coastal Com., 166 Cal. App.3d 148, 212 Cal.Rptr. 578 (1 Dist.1985).

26. Bosselman and Stroud, Mandatory Tithes: The Legality of Land Development Linkage, 9 Nova L.J. 381 (1985).

27. 22 Ill.2d 375, 176 N.E.2d 799 (1961). Ironically, a recent Illinois decision interprets the *Pioneer Trust* standard to be consistent with the proportionate share impact fee concept which developed on the basis of the dual rational nexus cases designed to provide an alternative to the *Pioneer Trust* test. Northern Ill. Home Bldrs. Ass'n v. County of Du Page, 165 Ill.2d 25, 208 Ill.Dec. 328, 649 N.E.2d 384 (Ill.1995). See discussion of *Du Page* case at J. Juergensmeyer and J. Wadley, Florida Land Use and Growth Management Law § 17.05 (1997).

new facilities and held that unless the village could prove that the demand for additional facilities was "specifically and uniquely attributable" to the particular subdivision, such requirements were an unreasonable regulation not authorized by the police power. Thus, where schools had become overcrowded because of the "total development of the community" the subdivider could not be compelled to help fund new facilities which his activity would necessitate.

A related and equally restrictive test was delineated by the New York court in Gulest Associates, Inc. v. Town of Newburgh.[28] In that case developers attacked an ordinance which charged in lieu fees for recreational purposes. The amounts collected were to be used by the town for "neighborhood park, playground or recreation purposes including the acquisition of property."[29] The court held that the fee was an unreasonable regulation tantamount to an unconstitutional taking because the funds collected were not used solely for the benefit of the residents of the particular subdivision charged, but rather could be used in any section of town for any recreational purposes. In essence, the *Gulest* "direct benefit" test required that funds collected from required payments for capital expenditures be specifically tied to a benefit directly conferred on the homeowners in the subdivision which was charged. If recreational fees were used to purchase a park outside the subdivision, the direct benefit test was not met and the ordinance was invalid.

Perhaps the reason behind this initial restrictive approach was an underlying judicial suspicion that payment requirements for extradevelopment capital expenditures were in reality a tax. Unlike zoning, payment requirements did not fit neatly into traditional conceptions of police power regulations. By applying the restrictive *Pioneer Trust* and *Gulest* tests, courts imposed the substantial requirements of a special assessment on such payment requirements. This was consistent with perceiving them as a tax. Unfortunately, it effectively precluded their use for most extradevelopment capital funding purposes. Despite this early trend, the *Pioneer Trust* and *Gulest* tests became difficult to reconcile with the planning and funding problems imposed on local governments by the constant acceleration of suburban growth. This restrictiveness also became difficult to rationalize with the judicial view of zoning ordinances as presumptively valid. Consequently, courts were not convinced of the practical or legal necessity of such stringent standards for the validation of required payments for extradevelopment capital funding.

The turning point in judicial acceptance of exactions came in a decision by the Wisconsin Supreme Court in Jordan v. Village of Menomonee Falls,[30] which is widely recognized as having established the dual

---

28. 25 Misc.2d 1004, 209 N.Y.S.2d 729 (1960), affirmed 15 A.D.2d 815, 225 N.Y.S.2d 538 (1962). The Gulest decision was overruled in Jenad, Inc. v. Village of Scarsdale, 18 N.Y.2d 78, 271 N.Y.S.2d 955, 957, 218 N.E.2d 673 (1966).

29. 209 N.Y.S.2d at 732.

30. 28 Wis.2d 608, 137 N.W.2d 442 (1965), appeal dismissed 385 U.S. 4, 87 S.Ct. 36, 17 L.Ed.2d 3 (1966).

rational nexus test. In response to a developer's attack upon an ordinance requiring developers to pay in lieu fees for educational and recreational purposes as both unauthorized by statute and as an unconstitutional taking without just compensation, the court first concluded that the fee payments were statutorily authorized and then focused first on the *Pioneer Trust* "specifically and uniquely attributable" test.

The Wisconsin Supreme Court expressed concern that it was virtually impossible for a local government to prove that money payment or land dedication requirements were assessed to meet a need *solely* generated by a particular subdivision. Suggesting a substitute test, the court held that money payment and dedication requirements for educational and recreational purposes were a valid exercise of the police power if there was a "reasonable connection" between the need for additional facilities and the growth generated by the subdivision. This first "rational nexus" was sufficiently established if the local government could demonstrate that a series of subdivisions had generated the need to provide educational and recreational facilities for the benefit of this stream of new residents. In the absence of contrary evidence, such proof showed that the need for the facilities was sufficiently attributable to the activity of the particular developer to permit the collection of fees for financing required improvements.[31]

The *Jordan* court also rejected the *Gulest* direct benefit requirement, declining to treat the fees as a special assessment. Therefore, it imposed no requirement that the ordinance restrict the funds to the purchase of school and park facilities that would directly benefit the assessed subdivision. Instead, the court concluded that the relationship between the expenditure of funds and the benefits accruing to the subdivision providing the funds was a fact issue pertinent to the reasonableness of the payment requirement under the police power. The *Jordan* court did not expressly define the "reasonableness" required in the expenditure of extradevelopment capital funds; however, a second "rational nexus" was impliedly required between the expenditure of the funds and benefits accruing to the subdivision. The court concluded that this second "rational nexus" was met where the fees were to be used exclusively for site acquisition and the amount spent by the local government in constructing additional school facilities was greater than the amounts collected from the developments creating the need for additional facilities.

This second "rational nexus" requirement inferred from *Jordan*, therefore, is met if a local government can demonstrate that its actual or projected extradevelopment capital expenditures earmarked for the substantial benefit of a series of developments are greater than the capital payments required of those developments. Such proof establishes a sufficient benefit to a particular subdivision in the stream of residential growth such that the extradevelopment payment requirements may be deemed to be reasonable under the police power.

31. Id.

While the dual rational nexus quickly became the standard view of state courts, the United States Supreme Court evaluated the federal constitutional standards which must be met by exaction programs in two cases, Nollan v. California Coastal Commission,[32] and Dolan v. City of Tigard.[33] In spite of much sound and fury, the emphasis in *Nollan* on "essential nexus" and the emphasis in *Dolan* on "rough proportionality" have essentially left the dual rational nexus standard intact or, according to some, have suggested that the federal standard is less demanding.[34] We discuss these cases in detail in Chapter 9[35] and Chapter 10.[36]

III. MAPPING FOR FUTURE STREETS AND OTHER PUBLIC IMPROVEMENTS

§ 7.9 In General[1]

Official mapping provisions are another kind of land use control that implements planning. An official map gives precise locations of future streets within and sometimes without a municipality and sometimes also includes sites for parks and other public improvements.[2] The basis for the regulation is that there is hardly any determinant of future land development as important as the location of future streets. If buildings are placed that interfere with the logical extension of streets, the public authorities are put in the unenviable position of placing major streets around scattered existing development or acquiring improvements at great cost.

The Standard City Planning Enabling Act[3] provided that a plat of an area could be adopted showing streets for future acquisition. Adoption of the plat was a reservation of the indicated streets but was neither the opening of a street nor the taking of land. The Standard Act provision was not widely adopted. The means were too expensive, since compensa-

---

32. 483 U.S. 825, 107 S.Ct. 3141, 97 L.Ed.2d 677 (1987).

33. 512 U.S. 374, 114 S.Ct. 2309, 2317–20, 129 L.Ed.2d 304 (1994).

34. See § 9.8B.infra.

35. See infra § 9.8 B.

36. See infra § 10.5.

§ 7.9

1. For a comprehensive discussion of official maps see 4 R. Anderson, American Law of Zoning §§ 26.01–26.16 (3d ed. (1986)); see also Rohan, Zoning and Land Use Controls §§ 46.01–.04 (1984); Brown, Reservation of Highway and Street Rights-of-Way by Official Maps, 66 W.Va.L.Rev. 73 (1964); Waite, The Official Map and the Constitution in Maine, 15 Maine L.Rev. 3 (1963); Note, Problems of Advance Land Acquisition, 52 Minn.L.Rev. 1175 (1968); Note, Municipal Street Control v. Private

Property Rights, 14 Syracuse L.Rev. 70 (1963).

2. Professor Beuscher gave a classic explanation: "In essence the official map is a simple device. It is one way, but not the only way, to fix building lines. The official map may plat future as well as existing streets. Where future streets are mapped, subdividers must conform to the mapped street lay-out, unless they can prevail upon the proper officials to amend the map. Public sewer and water will be installed only in the bed of the mapped streets. Even more important, a landowner who builds in the bed of the mapped street may be refused compensation for his building when the street is ultimately opened and the mapped land taken." Kucirek and Beuscher, Wisconsin's Official Map Law, 1957 Wis.L.Rev. 176, 177.

3. U.S. Dep't of Commerce, § 21 (1928).

tion was paid for the reservation for whatever period of time land was reserved. When the street itself was opened, the Act provided that additional compensation would be paid, except for buildings erected in contravention of the easement.

In addition to adoption of a major street plat, streets could also be approved under the Standard Act if shown on the master plan, if on an approved subdivision plat or if specially approved. Unless approved in one of these ways, Section 18 of the Act provided the municipality could not accept, lay out, open, improve, grade, pave, curb or light any street, or lay or authorize water mains or sewers. In addition, buildings could not be erected nor building permits issued unless the street giving access to the building had been approved in one of the four ways.

The competitor to the street plat of the Standard Act became known as the official map because the device was so denominated in Section 4 of the Municipal Planning Enabling Act suggested by Bassett and Williams.[4] The Bassett and Williams Act relied on the police power and formed the basis for legislation in many states. Local governments under the Act could adopt an official map showing existing and future streets and parks. No permit for building in the mapped areas could be issued, unless the land affected would not yield a fair return, in which case a permit in the nature of a variance[5] could be issued to relieve the hardship[6] up to the point of permitting a fair return. Provisions were included similar to those in the Standard Act for preventing utilities in streets and for prohibiting the issuance of building permits where access streets to proposed buildings were not shown on the official map. A requirement that access streets be approved and improved as a condition for issuance of a building permit is valid.[7] The theory is that building permits can be conditioned on reasonable requirements for streets meeting minimum planning and construction standards.

The Municipal Mapped Streets Act also served as another model.[8] Amendments to the model act's official map were automatic when streets were shown on an approved subdivision plat. Buildings could be authorized by variance for two reasons: lack of reasonable return or where the interest of the owner in the use of his property outweighed that of the municipality in preserving the integrity of the official map. As with the other models, utilities could not be placed except on approved streets and building permits could not be issued for proposed buildings which did not have access to approved streets. As with the Municipal Planning Enabling Act, the Municipal Mapped Streets Act contemplated that compensation would be paid only if land was actually taken for a street; no compensation was paid upon adoption of the map or for buildings taken that were not permitted by variance. As a practical

4. Reprinted in E. Bassett, F. Williams, A. Bettman & R. Whitten, Model Laws for Planning Cities, Counties, and States 40 (1935).

5. See supra § 5.14.

6. See supra § 5.16.

7. Brous v. Smith, 304 N.Y. 164, 106 N.E.2d 503 (1952).

8. Reprinted in Model Laws, supra note 4, at 89.

matter, compensation is never paid, particularly for minor streets, since they are usually obtained by dedication required as a condition for subdivision approval.[9]

A few states have statutes which, rather than authorize variances, seek to keep the restriction within the scope of the police power by limiting the period of time that it can apply. For example, under the statute in Miller v. Beaver Falls,[10] parks could be designated on a map and once designated no compensation would be paid for buildings if the site was acquired. However, the reservation was void if the site was not acquired by the local government within three years. The court held this provision invalid as beyond the scope of the police power and constituting a taking for which compensation should be paid. The court distinguished between street reservations and park reservations, admitting that the reservation would be valid as to streets because they are narrow, well-defined and absolutely necessary.

Statutes often make official map provisions available to state highway departments. Some states also have special statutes authorizing highway reservations.[11]

§ 7.10   Relation to Master Plan and Planning

As with zoning, official maps or something like them preceded master planning, as a historical matter. In some colonial towns there was one proprietor who owned the land and the town was laid out by map showing dedicated public places. The law of dedication then applied.[1] Where many owners were involved, as in the case of L'Enfant's plan for Washington, D.C., commissioners were given authority to plat the town, owners conveyed property in trust, and a plan was adopted with dedicated areas shown. Regulations similar to modern-day official maps protected future streets in New York City as early as 1806. Modern official map acts sometimes require some master planning as a prerequisite to official mapping. Acts based on the Standard Act and the Municipal Mapped Streets Act require at least a major street plan, though statutes strictly based on the Bassett and Williams model would not require any kind of plan as a prerequisite.[2] The difference between the major street plan and the official map is that the former only gives general locations, whereas the latter specifies locations and widths to survey accuracy and has the legal effects noted in the previous section.

§ 7.11   Relation to Zoning Setbacks

An official map, like zoning, restricts improvements. Unlike zoning it does not restrict uses requiring no improvements. Since official maps

---

9. See § 7.8 supra.

10. 368 Pa. 189, 82 A.2d 34 (1951).

11. See Brown, Reservation of Highway and Street Rights-of-Way by Official Maps, 66 W.Va.L.Rev. 73 (1964); Mandelker, Planning the Freeway: Interim Controls in Highway Programs, 1964 Duke L.J. 439.

§ 7.10

1. See § 7.8 supra.

2. See § 7.9 supra for descriptions of these model and standard acts.

can be used to designate future street widths as well as new streets, the official map device bears some resemblance to front yard requirements in zoning.[1] A front yard requirement under zoning is theoretically used to secure air and light, improve appearance, prevent overcrowding, mitigate problems of traffic safety on intersections and the like. Practically, the front yard requirement can be used as an official map for the purpose of reducing costs of acquisition when streets are widened. Improvements are in fact kept from the front yard. The official map is also related to zoning in that front yards are often measured from the edge of the officially mapped street rather than the actual street.

Setback provisions,[2] which may be part of the zoning, or subdivision ordinance, or a separate ordinance, are also used to keep improvements from beds of existing but to-be-widened streets.[3]

Setback and front yard requirements under private restrictions have some of the effects of official maps, even if not motivated by a desire to ease the financial burden of acquiring street sites.

§ 7.12 Relation to Subdivision Control

Streets are typically shown on subdivision plats and are often approved in conjunction with the subdivision plat approval. As with official maps, subdivision controls provide that unless a street is approved in some way, streets cannot be opened or improved or utilities placed. Likewise, as with official maps, buildings cannot be built in the streets shown on the subdivision plat and building permits cannot be issued.

Subdivisions and official maps are related in another way under statutes following the Bassett and Williams model.[1] It provides the planning commission with authority to approve subdivision plats showing new streets, highways, or freeways, or the widening thereof only after adoption of the official map. Under other statutes, a subdivision can be rejected if it does not comply with an official map.[2] If no official map has been adopted, a major or master street plan[3] does not have that effect, and the subdivision cannot be rejected, although streets are placed differently than on the master plan.[4]

§ 7.13 Constitutionality

Most of the cases on official maps discussed by the treatise writers and included in the casebooks deal with constitutional problems. This

§ 7.11

1. See § 7.9, note 4.

2. See § 4.13 supra.

3. See generally, R. Black, Building Lines and Reservations for Future Streets (1935), which is a classic study.

§ 7.12

1. See § 7.9 note 4 supra.

2. See Nigro v. Planning Bd. of Saddle River, 122 N.J. 270, 584 A.2d 1350 (N.J. 1991).

3. See § 7.10 supra.

4. Lordship Park Ass'n v. Board of Zoning Appeals, 137 Conn. 84, 75 A.2d 379 (1950). But see Krieger v. Planning Comm'n of Howard County, 224 Md. 320, 167 A.2d 885 (1961).

recognizes that property owners whose land is affected by mapped reservation often complain that the prohibition against development constitutes a taking. Landowners also argue that the use of official mapping statutes constitutes an improper attempt to depress the value of mapped land until the power of eminent domain can be exercised.

Actually, official map type provisions were more constitutionally secure at an earlier period than in the nearer past. In the very early days, landowners were so delighted to have roads on their property that land could be had by the public for the asking and compensation was seldom heard of. In that tradition, In re Furman St.[1] held that the owner of a building subsequently erected in the bed of an officially mapped street in 1819 was not entitled to any compensation for the building when the street was actually opened, even though the statute did not address the question of compensation for buildings built in mapped streets. The court stated that the mapping and orderly development of the area had in effect already compensated property owners in the area due to increased values.

Forster v. Scott,[2] however, led to some doubts about the constitutionality of the official map statute. In that case an entire lot was covered by a street reservation and there was no provision for variance. It was not surprising that the court held the provision invalid, as it would today if a land use restriction makes an entire separately owned parcel virtually unusable.[3] However, the case led many to assume that official mapping was constitutionally risky without payment of compensation.

In Gorieb v. Fox[4] the U.S. Supreme Court upheld the fixing of a setback line along streets. Therefore it was not a major step in Headley v. Rochester[5] for the New York court to approve an official map provision which reserved 25 feet from a large lot for a widened street. The court technically reached this result because the landowner did not apply for the variance to relieve hardship authorized by the statute, but the case is read more broadly than that because courts often do not apply an exhaustion of remedies doctrine when a constitutional issue is raised.[6] Similarly, in State ex rel. Miller v. Manders,[7] even though a substantial portion of a lot was reserved for a street, and the owner was denied a building permit, the court refused to hold the statute unconstitutional where no variance was first sought.[8]

§ 7.13

1. 17 Wend. 649 (N.Y.Sup.Ct. of Judicature 1936).

2. 136 N.Y. 577, 32 N.E. 976 (1893).

3. But see Consolidated Rock Products Co. v. Los Angeles, 57 Cal.2d 515, 20 Cal. Rptr. 638, 370 P.2d 342 (1962), appeal dismissed 371 U.S. 36, 83 S.Ct. 145, 9 L.Ed.2d 112 (1962).

4. 274 U.S. 603, 47 S.Ct. 675, 71 L.Ed. 1228 (1927).

5. 272 N.Y. 197, 5 N.E.2d 198 (1936).

6. Compare Jensen v. New York, 42 N.Y.2d 1079, 399 N.Y.S.2d 645, 369 N.E.2d 1179 (1977) (not required to seek permit) with 59 Front St. Realty Corp. v. Klaess, 6 Misc.2d 774, 160 N.Y.S.2d 265 (1957) (variance required).

7. 2 Wis.2d 365, 86 N.W.2d 469 (1957).

8. See generally Waite, The Official Map and the Constitution in Maine, 15 Me.L.Rev. 3 (1963).

While compensation is clearly due where a municipality permanently acquires a street, park or other public site, the official map statutes state they intend no taking, and a temporary reservation does not appear to be an undue burden under the police power. Support for the constitutionality of official map statutes and reservations as interim development restrictions can be found in the interim zoning cases.[9] However, courts have held official mapping statutes unconstitutional where the statute authorizes a reservation for a specific number of years.[10] Where the official map statutes operate more like zoning, imposing a restriction against improvements for an indefinite rather than a fixed time, with variances to relieve hardship, the courts are more disposed to approve.[11] The latter kind of statute may actually be a greater burden on the property than the fixed period reservations—the time period may be longer, the landowner has to prove hardship and even if proved he is not entitled to do what he wants, he can only do what must be allowed to reduce the hardship.

Recent litigation and legislative changes in Florida highlight the current issues in regard to the constitutionality of statutory provisions authorizing official maps. The controversy began with Joint Ventures, Inc. v. Department of Transportation.[12] The Florida Department of Transportation (DOT) recorded a "map of reservation" pursuant to the relevant Florida statutory provision which precluded the issuance of development permits or construction of improvements for a five year period which could be extended for another five years.[13] A landowner filed suit claiming that the effect of the statutory provision for maps of reservation was to take property without compensation. Although the lower courts dismissed the suit they certified the issue to the Supreme Court of Florida which held in a 4 to 3 decision that the statutory provision was facially unconstitutional because it illegally froze property sales in an attempt to depress property values in anticipation of the exercise of eminent domain and that the map therefore effected a "taking."

Four years later the Supreme Court of Florida decided another mapping case and this time found the use of the map to be a valid exercise of the police power. In Palm Beach County v. Wright,[14] the question certified to the court was:

9. See § 3.20 supra.

10. Miller v. Beaver Falls, 368 Pa. 189, 82 A.2d 34 (1951) (3 year reservation for parks); Urbanizadora Versalles, Inc. v. Rivera Rios, 701 F.2d 993 (1st Cir.1983) (14 year reservation for highway); Lomarch Corp. v. Mayor & Common Council, 51 N.J. 108, 237 A.2d 881 (1968) (1 year reservation for parks); Joint Ventures, Inc. v. Department of Trans., 519 So.2d 1069 (Fla. 1st DCA 1988), Aff'd 563 So.2d 622 (Fla. 1990) (5 years for roads).

11. Palm Beach County v. Wright, 612 So.2d 709 (Fla.App.1993) (Thoroughfare map authorized by comprehensive plan held constitutional).

12. 519 So.2d 1069 (Fla.App.1988), aff'd, 563 So.2d 622 (Fla.1990).

13. Fla. Stat.Ann. § 337.241(1).

14. 641 So.2d 50 (Fla.1994). See R. Freilich and D. Bushek, Integrating Land-Use and Transportation: The Case of Palm Beach County v. Wright 18 #2 ABA State and Local Law News 1 (Winter 1995).

Is a county thoroughfare map designating corridors for future road-ways, and which forbids land use activity that would impede future construction of a roadway, adopted incident to a comprehensive county land use plan enacted under the local government compre-hensive planning development regulation act, facially unconstitu-tional under *Joint Ventures* . . . ?

The Supreme Court of Florida answered in the negative and stressed that the map in *Wright* was designed to implement the Palm Beach County comprehensive Plan. The court explained that its decision in *Joint Ventures* was based on the unconstitutionality of the "map of reservation" statute, which violated due process and not because it was a taking per se. The court further reasoned that the fact that the thor-oughfare map is not recorded and can be amended twice a year meant that it limited development only to the extent necessary to ensure compatibility with the land use plan. The key distinction to the court was that the purpose of Palm Beach County's map was to serve as a valuable long range planning tool while the statutory map reservation used by DOT in *Joint Ventures* was designed to freeze and depress property values.

Before *Wright* was decided, the Florida Legislature responded to *Joint Ventures* in 1990 by enacting a provision on "Roadway Corridor Official Maps," which it amended in 1995.[15] Under this new provision if a local government designates a "transportation corridor" in its compre-hensive plan then before it can grant any zoning change or building permit for land located within the map corridor it must give DOT notice after which DOT must inform the land owner whether it intends to acquire the land in question.

The Florida experience suggests that mapping which is part of comprehensive plan implementation will be looked on favorably by the courts but that state transportation mapping is suspect if there is no purchase plan to back it up.

§ 7.14 Effect of Official Map on Marketability of Title

Generally, a zoning ordinance is not an encumbrance on title that makes property unmarketable, except where property is improved with an illegal nonconforming building. Perhaps because the official map usually designates roads and in some respects is like an easement for roads, the general rule is different in the case of official maps. A widening line has been construed to be an encumbrance as has a future mapped street over part or all of the property (despite the likely unconstitutionality of the official map provision if enforced in the latter case). The official map is an encumbrance as to buildings illegally built in the mapped area.[1] Even where a building preexisted the mapping of

---

15. Fla. Stat. § 337.243(1996). In 1992, the Florida Legislature repealed the map reservation provision disapproved of in *Joint Ventures*, Laws of 1992, c 92–152 § 108.

§ 7.14

1. Bibber v. Weber, 199 Misc. 906, 102 N.Y.S.2d 945 (1951), affirmed mem. 278 App.Div. 973, 105 N.Y.S.2d 758 (1951). But see Lansburgh v. Market St. Ry. Co., 98

the street, the mapping provision was found to be an encumbrance.[2] The difference in the cases may be that the official map provisions appear to be more like easements to the court or that buyers generally would not be on guard for such provisions, as they would or should be in the case of zoning.

IV. PLANNED UNIT DEVELOPMENTS

§ 7.15 Definition and History

The planned unit development (PUD) is a recent and innovative approach to land use development. Its parentage is a union of cluster zoning[1] and subdivision platting. The definition of a PUD which is most frequently encountered is:

> 'Planned unit development' means an area of land, controlled by a landowner, to be developed as a single entity for a number of dwelling units, and commercial and industrial uses, if any, the plan for which does not correspond in lot size, bulk, or type of dwelling or commercial or industrial use, density, lot coverage and required open space to the regulations established in any one or more districts created, from time to time, under the provisions of a municipal zoning ordinance enacted pursuant to the conventional zoning enabling act of the state.'[2]

A PUD which contains only residential uses may be called a planned unit residential development (PURD) and a purely commercial uses planned unit development may be called a planned unit commercial development (PUCD). We use the acronym PUD here to refer to both. A PUD is primarily an alternative to traditional zoning since it provides a mixing of uses. The location and identification of the permitted uses are provided on the PUD map or plat, which closely resembles a subdivision plat. Development approval is generally granted for the PUD at one time rather than on a lot by lot basis and in that way closely tracks the subdivision approval process.

The planned unit development concept is sometimes traced to a provision contained in Section 12 of Bassett's Model Planning Enabling Act of 1925.[3] Under that section:

Cal.App.2d 426, 220 P.2d 423 (1950) distinguishing New York cases.

2. See generally Kucirek & Beuscher, Wisconsin's Official Map Law, 1957 Wis. L.Rev. 176, 201–11.

§ 7.15

1. See 5 Zoning and Land Use Controls § 32.05[1][b] (P. Rohan & E. Kelly 1997) (discussing advantages of clustering).

2. U.S. Advisory Commission on Intergovernmental Relations, ACIR State Legislative Program, 1970 Cumulative Supp. 31–36–00 at 5 (1969).

3. Basset, Laws of Planning Unbuilt Areas, in Neighborhood and Community Planning, Regional Survey Vol. VII, 272–73 (1929). Model legislation for PUDs was proposed in 1965. Babcock, Krasnowiecki and McBride, The Model State Statute, 114 U.Pa.L.Rev. 140 (1965). See D. Mandelker, Land Use Law § 9.29 (3rd ed. 1993).

the legislative body [could] authorize the planning board to make * * * changes upon approving subdivision plats, when the owner [submitted] a plan designating the lots on which apartment houses and local shops are to be built and indicating the maximum density of population and the minimum yard requirements per lot. Section 12 also limited the average population density and the total land area covered by buildings in the entire subdivision to that permitted in the original zoning district * * *. Upon the approval of the planning board following a public hearing with proper notice, the changes were to become part of the municipality's zoning regulations.[4]

Although available since the 1920's, planned unit development provisions were not widely utilized until the 1960's. The new-found popularity of planned unit developments coincides with large scale development in the post second world war era. By the early sixties the incompatibility of traditional zoning and larger residential developments was recognized, and the push for the adoption of planned unit development ordinances began.[5] Today, large mixed use developments are the rule rather than the exception, and planned unit development (PUD) regulations represent one attempt to avoid the problems of large scale development under conventional zoning notions.

Planned unit developments are basically designed to permit the development of entire neighborhoods, or in some cases even towns, based on an approved plan. The completed development usually includes a variety of residential types, common open space for recreation, parks, and in some cases, commercial or even industrial areas. Since the entire project is preplanned the completed development can be based upon a logical and coherent mixture of uses.

The PUD principle is that a land area under unified control can be designed and developed in a single operation, usually by a series of prescheduled phases, and according to an officially approved "plan." The plan does not necessarily have to correspond to the property and use regulations of the zoning district in which the development is located. As can be seen from the definition, the planned unit development concept abandons the lot by lot approach to development, and is primarily an alternative to zoning.

The Supreme Court of Oregon in Frankland v. City of Lake Oswego,[6] listed to following objectives of planned unit developments:

(1) to achieve flexibility;

---

4. Krasnowiecki, Planned Unit Development: A Challenge to Established Theory and Practice of Land Use Control, 114 U.Pa.L.Rev. 47, 48 (1965).

5. See, e.g., Goldston and Scheuer, Zoning of Planned Residential Developments, 73 Harv.L.Rev. 241 (1959); Symposium: Planned Unit Development, 114 U.Pa. L.Rev. 1–170 (1965).

6. 267 Or. 452, 517 P.2d 1042 (Or. 1973).

(2) to provide a more desirable living environment than would be possible through the strict application of zoning ordinance requirements;

(3) to encourage developers to use a more creative approach in their development of land;

(4) to encourage a more efficient and more desirable use of open land; and

(5) to encourage variety in the physical development pattern of the city.[7]

Cluster development and planned unit development are sometimes viewed as the same thing. It is more accurate to define cluster development as a device for grouping dwellings to increase dwelling densities on some portions of the development area in order to have other portions free of buildings.[8] Many planned unit developments use cluster development as a technique but the notion of planned unit development concept typically encompasses more.[9]

§ 7.16 Relationship to Zoning

Under typical zoning, there is no close relation to a plan[1] and the landscape is divided "into districts ... [and] [a]ll ... regulations shall be uniform ... throughout each district...."[2] In planned unit developments, the area is not districted. A commercial use may be next to a residential use and different types of residential uses may be mixed with no intention of placing them in districts. Special conditions and controls may apply without uniformity to some commercial uses and not to others, so as to better integrate the commercial and residential development. Spot zoning[3] (in a descriptive sense of a small parcel of property controlled differently than adjacent parcels) is or may be the rule in a PUD, rather than something to be avoided.

The PUD technique may not be compatible with a typical zoning enabling act, thus leading to difficulties in the implementation of a planned unit development.[4] There may be no territorial districts and uniformity of use within a district under PUDs.[5] Zoning without district-

7. Id. at 1047.

8. Chrinko v. South Brunswick Township Planning Bd., 77 N.J.Super. 594, 187 A.2d 221 (Law Div.1963) is a leading case explaining and upholding cluster zoning.

9. See generally, Dyckman, Book Review 12 UCLA L.Rev. 991 (1965); Urban Land Institute, New Approaches to Residential Land Development, Tech.Bull. No. 40 chs. 1–2 (1961).

§ 7.16

1. The plan to which zoning is to accord is usually read to mean the scheme of zoning itself. See ch. 2 supra.

2. U.S. Dept of Commerce, A Standard State Zoning Enabling Act § 2 (rev. ed 1926). See § 4.1 supra.

3. See § 5.10 supra.

4. See Krasnowiecki, Planned Unit Development: A Challenge to Established Theory and Practice of Land Use Control, 114 Un.Pa.L.Rev. 47 (1965).

5. See generally, Turner and Morgan, Planned Development Zoning: A Texas Perspective, Ch. 5, Inst. Planning, Zoning and Eminent Domain (1992).

ing and without uniformity within districts may be held invalid as it was in Rockhill v. Chesterfield Township.[6] The whole town was in effect, a single district in which residential and agricultural uses were permitted, but all other uses were permitted only by special permit under a standard of benefit to the general development of the township.[7] Similarly, floating zones have been held invalid because they are not preapplied to a particular area so as to show on a zoning map.[8] A PUD may not involve a precise zoning map. A PUD is often treated as a floating zone under local ordinances.[9] When conditions have been imposed on zoning, giving rise to so-called contract zoning, the courts have sometimes held the zoning invalid. In a PUD, conditions are imposed that may vary from parcel to parcel, and contract zoning issues may also arise.[10]

Therefore, to avoid adverse judicial decisions, to avoid the impairing effects of non-unitary development controls, and to devise schemes permitting more flexibility, PUD developers have sought routes around conventional zoning. In some cases the special use permit is used under the legal fiction that a PUD could be viewed as a single development having such special characteristics as to be appropriate for special permit treatment. The special permit[11] is a device which allows a special use to be established subject to conditions. But more than a few courts did not see anything special about large-scale development.[12] Variances[13] have sometimes also been misused to permit planned unit developments.[14] Other PUD developers sought to accomplish PUDs under subdivision enabling acts.[15] Those Acts generally had the advantage of providing more administrative than legislative control and of allowing the use of conditions. But stretching the subdivision enabling acts to cover PUDs was fraught with danger when millions of dollars were to be invested in a PUD. Therefore, pressures began to develop for special enabling legislation for PUDs.[16]

The zoning-like provisions for the PUD are described in the model acts. For example, one of the model PUD enabling acts provides:

    (a) Permitted Uses. An ordinance adopted pursuant to this Act shall set forth the uses permitted....

    (b) ... (1) An ordinance adopted pursuant to this Act shall establish standards governing the density, or intensity of land use....

---

6. 23 N.J. 117, 128 A.2d 473 (1957).

7. See generally §§ 5.24–.26 supra.

8. Eves v. Zoning Bd. of Adjustment, 401 Pa. 211, 164 A.2d 7 (1960). City of Waukesha v. Town Bd., 198 Wis.2d 592, 543 N.W.2d 515 (Wis.App.1995). See generally supra § 4.16.

9. A "sinking zone" may also be used. See Craig, Planned Unit Development as Seen from City Hall, 114 U.Pa.L.Rev. 127, 130 (1965); § 4.16 supra.

10. See § 4.17 and § 5.11 supra.

11. See §§ 5.24–.26 supra.

12. See Rockhill v. Chesterfield Township, supra note 6.

13. See §§ 5.14–.23 supra.

14. See Goldston & Scheuer, Zoning of Planned Residential Developments, 73 Harv.L.Rev. 241, 250 (1959).

15. See § 7.2 supra.

16. See § 7.15 supra.

(2) Said standards shall take into account that the density, or intensity of land use, otherwise allowable on the site under the provisions of a zoning ordinance previously enacted pursuant to [the general zoning enabling act] may not be appropriate for a Planned Unit ... Development.... [17]

As the commentary on the Act indicates, intensity of land use includes such density concepts as number of dwelling units per acre or minimum square footage of lot area per dwelling unit. But the Act uses intensity of land use more broadly to include a balancing of bulk, height, open space and dwelling units to reach a permitted concentration.

The Act also provides for other zoning-like controls:

(f) ... An ordinance adopted pursuant to this Act shall set forth the standards and criteria by which the design, bulk and location of buildings shall be evaluated.... [18]

The intensity of use is often carried out by a scheme entitled land-use intensity (LUI). Even if the local ordinance does not expressly provide for LUI, a developer may want to conform to LUI in order to qualify the development for FHA insured loans.

The FHA has devised standards for PUD and it determines the appropriate LUI and assigns a number. The LUI number is based on a planning analysis and a real estate judgment regarding the proposed site, its community, and the market. For example, if the FHA should determine that the area measured in square feet can be developed at an LUI of a designated number, the developer can easily determine from charts available from FHA the proper or required:

(1) Total floor area of all buildings (floor area ratio);[19]

(2) Total open space (open space ratio);

(3) Open space not used for cars (livability space);

(4) Open space planned for active and passive recreation (recreation space);

(5) Total parking spaces for the number of planned dwelling units, some of which may be on the streets (total car ratio); and

(6) Total offstreet parking spaces (occupant car ratio).[20]

§ 7.17 Legal Status of PUDs

PUD ordinances have been upheld even where not specially authorized by enabling legislation. The first clear-cut and still leading case upholding PUD is Cheney v. Village 2 at New Hope, Inc.[1] An Ordinance

17. Babcock, Krasnowiecki, McBride, The Model State Statute, 114 U.Pa.L.Rev. 140, 144–145 (1965).

18. Id. at 152.

19. See § 4.14 supra.

20. Further descriptions of the FHA–LUI are in Henke, Planned Unit Development and Land Use Intensity, 114 U.Pa.

L.Rev. 15 (1965); Bair, How to Regulate Planned Unit Developments for Housing—Summary of a Regulatory Approach, 17 Zoning Digest 185 (1985).

§ 7.17

1. 429 Pa. 626, 241 A.2d 81 (1968). See, Frankland v. City of Lake Oswego, 267 Or. 452, 517 P.2d 1042 (1973); Zuker &

had created a PUD district and another ordinance[2] rezoned an area PUD that had previously been zoned single family. The PUD zone permitted a wide variety of residential uses as well as professional, public, recreational and commercial uses. The ordinance provided that the buildable land could be developed up to 80 percent residential and 20 percent commercial. A minimum of 20 percent of the land had to be devoted to open space. The residential density could not exceed 10 units per acre, no building could exceed 12 units and no residence could include more than two bedrooms. There were no traditional setback and side-yard requirements, though a distance of 24 feet was required between buildings. The court rejected arguments that the PUD did not accord with a previously adopted comprehensive plan by indicating that a plan can be changed by adoption of the PUD ordinance if done deliberately and thoughtfully.[3] The court also rejected the allegations that the PUD ordinances constituted spot zoning and that there was an improper delegation of legislative authority because the planning commission had to decide exactly where, within a particular PUD district, specific types of buildings should be placed.[4]

The court reviewed in detail whether the planning commission, the legislative body or the board of adjustment could most appropriately handle the details of the development and concluded that the planning commission was appropriate. The legislative body would otherwise involve itself in too much detail. The board of adjustment functions were to hear appeals, to grant variances and to issue special permits. The court did not believe that any of those powers were as appropriate to implementation of PUD details as were the powers conferred on a planning commission. The court regarded final PUD detailed review as not materially different from subdivision approval, a traditional planning commission function.[5]

Cheney might not have been decided favorably to PUDs,[6] since the Pennsylvania court hardly had the reputation of approving novel approaches to land use controls. However, the *Cheney* decision might not be followed in all states. For example, the California court which would have been expected to uphold PUDs,[7] departed from its earlier tradition of authorizing virtually standardless delegation of authority to adminis-

Wolffe, Supreme Court Legalizes PUD: New Hope from New Hope, 2 Land Use Controls No. 2, at 32 (1968). But see Lutz v. Longview, 83 Wash.2d 566, 520 P.2d 1374 (1974).

2. See § 4.16 supra on floating zones.

3. See § 5.8 supra.

4. See § 5.10 supra.

5. Something much like a PUD was approved in Bigenho v. Montgomery County Council, 248 Md. 386, 237 A.2d 53 (1968), though the legislative body rezoned particular parts of a large tract, some for local

community use, some for commercial office uses, some for industrial uses and some for multiple family uses.

6. Among other cases, Eves v. Zoning Bd. of Adjustment, supra § 7.16, note 8, was precedent for holding the PUD invalid, see 2 Zoning Digest 178 (1968).

7. The California courts generally are more disposed to approve whatever a municipality does including approval of novel land use controls, than the courts of any other state. See e.g., §§ 4.16–4.19 supra.

trative agencies, and in Millbrae Association for Residential Survival v. Millbrae[8] established some important limitations on PUDs.

In California, as in many states, a rezoning can be accomplished only by the local legislature after notice and hearing. In order to comply with that requirement, the City of Millbrae enacted an ordinance which provided a two-step approval of PUDs. In the first step, property was rezoned as a planned development by the legislature after notice and hearing. However, this rezoning was only in the nature of a generalized plan for development. The rezoning provided for only the general size, location and use of proposed buildings and structures, the location and dimensions of streets, parking areas, open areas and other public and private facilities and uses. After the rezoning, the two-step ordinance required the developer to submit a precise plan, which was in the nature of the detailed development plan. The precise plan could be approved by the planning commission alone. But in the precise plan, which was approved by the planning commission without legislative actions, the developer departed from the approved generalized plan and added seven additional apartments to the high-rise buildings, reduced the size of a golf course, increased the number of parking spaces and relocated two high-rise buildings. The plaintiffs alleged that such changes constituted a rezoning which had to be accomplished legislatively. The developer argued that the changes were details that could be authorized by an administrative body as in the case of special permits or variances. The court held:

> while the change in the number of apartments in each of the high-rise buildings would properly be the subject of the precise plan under the ordinance so long as it did not increase the "general size" of the buildings as delineated in the general plan, the other changes amount to a substantial alteration of the general plan since they materially and fundamentally change the location of two of the high-rise buildings and the size of the parking areas and the open areas.[9]

In short, the court upheld the PUD technique in general, but did not permit substantial changes in the planned development plan without legislative action. The California court was thus unwilling to allow delegation to the planning commission to the extent permitted by the Pennsylvania court. The case is notice to developers that some courts will superintend what is "substantial" and not uphold whatever changes the planning commission approves. Since to be safe the developer must go to the legislative body for any "substantial" change between the generalized and the detailed plan (and presumably for any changes of the generalized plan by amendments to the detailed plan), considerable flexibility is lost.

8. 262 Cal.App.2d 222, 69 Cal.Rptr. 251 (1968). Compare Peachtree Dev. Co. v. Paul, 67 Ohio St.2d 345, 423 N.E.2d 1087 (1981); Mullin v. Planning Bd., 17 Mass. App.Ct. 139, 456 N.E.2d 780 (1983).

9. 262 Cal.App.2d at 245, 69 Cal.Rptr. at 267.

As previously indicated,[10] when courts proved indisposed to allow PUD development under typical zoning enabling legislation, PUD developers began to look for other alternatives. A few states had adopted Bassett's model provisions[11] which appeared to authorize PUDs under subdivision-like authority. But in Hiscox v. Levine[12] the court held approval of a development by a planning commission under authority of a statute based on the Bassett model to be invalid. The developer had submitted a plan for a 100–acre subdivision which involved cluster zoning.[13] It showed one house to the half acre rather than one to the acre as called for by the zoning. However, the balance of the 100 acres was dedicated for a park. The court held that the action of the administrative board in allowing lot size reductions for such a large tract was an encroachment on legislative authority. In reviewing the history and language of the Bassett Act, Krasnowiecki concludes that the Hiscox case was improperly decided.[14]

Krasnowiecki also points to language in the subdivision sections of the Standard City Planning Enabling Act which would appear to enable planning commissions to approve PUDs in the several states that adopted the provisions. The act provides that the planning board:

> shall have the power to agree with the applicant upon use, height, area or bulk requirements or restrictions governing buildings and premises within the subdivision, provided such requirements or restrictions do not authorize the violation of the then effective zoning ordinance of the municipality.[15]

The Act also provided:

> regulations may provide for the proper arrangement of streets ... , for adequate and convenient open spaces for traffic, utilities, access of fire-fighting apparatus, recreation, light and air, and for the avoidance of congestion of population, including minimum width and areas of lots.[16]

The trial court in Mann v. Fort Thomas[17] upheld the constitutionality of a PUD ordinance based on the above sections of the Standard Act and sustained a planning commission's denial of an application for a PUD.[18]

Whether PUDs can be authorized under conventional subdivision enabling acts or not, special enabling legislation for PUDs clarifies the matter, and the suggested model acts contain subdivision-like provisions.

10. Supra § 7.16.

11. See § 7.15 supra.

12. 31 Misc.2d 151, 216 N.Y.S.2d 801 (1961).

13. Id.

14. Krasnowiecki, Planned Unit Development: A Challenge to Established Theory and Practice of Land Use Control, 114 U.Pa.L.Rev. 47, 80–83 (1965).

15. Standard Act § 15. Violation of the zoning ordinance could be avoided through use of a sinking zone. See Craig, Planned Unit Development as Seen from City Hall, 114 U.Pa.L.Rev. 127, 130 (1965).

16. Standard Act § 14. See § 4.8 on lot size as a zoning or as a subdivision matter.

17. 437 S.W.2d 209 (Ky.1969).

18. On appeal, the court did not reach the merits of the issue due to the developer's lack of standing.

For example, the model act suggested by the ACIR defines the plan to include "a plat of subdivision ... private streets, ways and parking facilities, common open space and public facilities ...,"[19] all of which matters are part of typical subdivision controls. In other sections the Act calls for the development of standards on "the amount, location and proposed use of common open space,"[20] provisions for municipal acceptance of "the dedication of land or any interest therein for public use and maintenance"[21] and that

> the authority granted to a municipality to establish standards for the location, width, course and surfacing of public streets and highways, alleys, ways for public service facilities, curbs, gutters, sidewalks, street lights, parks, playgrounds, school grounds, storm water drainage, water supply and distribution, sanitary sewers and sewage collection and treatment, shall be vested in [the body designated to administer the ordinance enacted to implement the Act].[22]

§ 7.18 Planned Unit Development Approval Process

Planned unit development ordinances generally provide a comprehensive review procedure that requires the developer to submit detailed information on the project, including a concept or master plan; and also allow the municipality to condition approval on changes made in the project. Because of the flexibility of the procedure and the opportunity for negotiation between local government and prospective developers PUD ordinances have been criticized for institutionalizing the bargaining process of land development.[1] However, the flexibility of planned unit development ordinances does allow local government to have input in the development process. Furthermore, by structuring a PUD ordinance to encourage beneficial uses a municipality can develop the future to fit its image.

Most planned unit development ordinances provide for a detailed review procedure. Planned unit development ordinances generally provide for a two-step process in the approval or disapproval of a large scale development. The first step is the establishment of an overlay district or master plan.[2] Planned development districts must be developed in accordance with the officially approved plan.[3]

The application process generally begins with conferences between the developer and the local government planning department and other

19. U.S. Advisory Commission on Intergovernmental Relations, An Act Authorizing Municipalities to Provide for Planned Unit Development, § 3(4) in 1970 Cumulative ACIR State Legislative Program 31–36–00 at 5 (1969). See Sternlieb, Burchell, Hughes & Listokin, Planned Unit Development Legislation: A Summary of Necessary Considerations, 7 Urb.L.Ann. 71 (1974).

20. Id. § 4(b)(1) at 6.

21. Id. § 34(c)(1) at 7.

22. Id. § 4(e) at 8.

§ 7.18

1. N. Williams, American Land Planning Law, § 48.02 (1st ed. 1987).

2. See Baers, Zoning Code Revisions to Permit Mixed Use Development, 7 Zoning and Planning L.Rep., 81, 85 (1984).

3. A concept plan is a professionally prepared overall concept of the project. See Aloi, Implementation of a Planned Unit Development, 2 Real Est.L.J. 523, 525 (1974).

agencies involved in the approval process. The general purpose of the preapplication conferences is for the developer and the local government officials to assess the relationship of the proposed project to the existing community. If all goes well, the petitioners for the PUD zoning submit their application along with any required materials.

The developer will then conduct prehearing conferences with the local planning and zoning commission to iron out problem areas and negotiate acceptable compromises. The planning and zoning commission generally can make written proposals for changes in either the petition or the concept plan. After appropriate public notice is given, a public hearing is held before the planning and zoning commission. The planning and zoning commission then makes its official findings and recommends either approval, conditional approval or disapproval.[4]

The final step in the initial application process is approval by the local government legislative body. Upon receiving the planning and zoning commission's recommendation, the legislative body holds a public hearing on the application, and may either grant the proposed rezoning to PUD; deny it; or grant the rezoning with conditions or modifications. If the legislative body approves the proposed application for rezoning, the concept plan of development is adopted as an amendment to the zoning code.

After a concept plan has been approved it establishes a master plan of usages. Any area development within the planned community district is a planned unit development. The second step of the large scale development is approval of the individual planned unit developments. Planned unit developments can be rezoned by resolution, after the master development plan has been adopted, since they are now in accordance with the amended zoning code.

The planned unit development procedure offers a number of benefits. First, the local government's polestar in evaluating a project is whether it is in accordance with the planning and development objectives of the jurisdiction. Second, by providing a detailed application procedure and requiring a concept plan, the local government is in a better position to evaluate the project. Third, the multistep process affords many opportunities for input from the local government's various planning, zoning and architectural commissions, thus allowing the municipality to structure future developments to conform with its growth plans.

Planned unit development regulations contain substantive standards to ensure that a project will be developed in accordance with the long range development plans. These standards can solve a number of problems. For instance, what assurance does a local government have that the developer will complete the project as it proposed in the plan?

---

4. By keeping the planning board in an advisory capacity and deferring the decision to the city council a local government may avoid a delegation of authority challenge. See Aloi, Implementation of a Planned Unit Development, 2 Real Est.L.J. 523, 532 (1974); see also Hiscox v. Levine, supra § 7.17, note 12 and accompanying text.

Fortunately, most PUD regulations contemplate that most projects will be staged developments. Most PUD ordinances provide safeguards to guarantee the different stages of the project will be completed. First, since the local government's legislative body still must approve individual PUDs by resolution, it retains some leverage over the developer. Second, most regulations establish timing controls as to when certain facilities must be built, thereby insuring the entire community will be completed. For example, a regulation may require a park to be built before high density, high profit housing can be developed. Finally, the local government may require an annual report from the developer appraising the project's progress.[5]

Many PUD regulations have substantive provisions which can encourage creative and beneficial developments. Generally, the entire project cannot exceed a certain density level. However, individual planned unit developments may have much higher densities. Also, restrictions may allow the developer to transfer excess PUD densities from one parcel to another as long as the density for the whole project must remain the same.

Most PUD ordinances require a computed amount of common open space. Since open space reduces the total lot count, it is seldom utilized under traditional zoning regulations. Ordinances may provide the PUD developer with a number of ways to satisfy the open space computation. For example, the computation may prefer areas left in or restored to their natural habitat, than areas such as golf courses. Accordingly, the percentage of space which would count as open space would be greater for natural habitat than that for golf courses. This type of incentive zoning allows a city to encourage beneficial uses in the ordinance and preserve those areas for the future.

§ 7.19 Private Restrictions

PUDs typically utilize commonly owned facilities and space to a much greater extent than the conventional development. As a result, complicated restrictions and covenants are necessary. The restrictions and covenants are private matters, though the public has an interest in them. Therefore, as with conventional subdivisions, the restrictions and covenants utilized in PUDs are subject to review under some subdivided land sales acts.[1]

The model acts for PUDs[2] also have provisions to protect the public interest in private restrictions. One model act[3] provides that the common

---

5. In Frankland v. City of Lake Oswego, 267 Or. 452, 517 P.2d 1042 (Or.1973), the Supreme Court of Oregon stressed that although a key aspects of PUDs is flexibility of design and use, "these objectives can be secured only if the planning authority retains its control by, at a minimum, overseeing and approving general development plans of a developer" and that discretion is properly in the hands of the planning authority and not the developer. Id at 1047.

§ 7.19

1. See §§ 7.20–7.22 infra.

2. See text § 7.17 at notes 19–22 supra, and accompanying text.

3. See Babcock, Krasnowiecki & McBride, The Model State Statute, 114 U.Pa.L.Rev. 140, 146–150 (1965).

open space need not be dedicated to the public but that the local government is authorized to require establishment of an organization to own and maintain the common open space. If the open space is not properly maintained, the Act authorizes the local government to maintain the space and to assess the lot owners.[4]

The elaborate negative and affirmative restrictions, covenants, conditions and easements are typically so extensive that an association or a corporation must be established as the organization to administer the provisions. The powers of the organization may include many of the functions typically performed by the government, so that the organizations created, typically a homes association, have been called private government.[5]

Suggested Legal Documents for Planned–Unit Development[6] a HUD publication, contains recommended forms for a declaration of covenants, conditions and restrictions and articles of incorporation and by-laws for a homes association. The declaration provides that the easements, restrictions, covenants, and conditions run with the land described in the declaration and bind and benefit the owner of each parcel of property. The declaration deals with annexation of additional properties; confers membership in the association to the owner of property subject to assessment by the association; provides for voting rights in the association with suggestions for division of power between the developer and the lot owners; states the rights of the association and the lot owners to use property; provides for maintenance assessments; states the rules applying to party walls (which may be present because of cluster zoning and condominium development); establishes standards; provides that the association will maintain and repair the privately owned buildings and trees, shrubs, grass and the like; states the use restrictions; provides easements and contains general provisions dealing with enforcement, severability and amendment.

As with conventional subdivisions, the complicated covenants and restrictions in PUDs are the source of litigation. For example, in Mountain Springs Association of New Jersey Inc. v. Wilson[7] the covenants provided that land could be sold only with consent of the association or to a member of the association. The defendant's grantor sold without complying with provision. The defendant grantee was willing to join the association but was not willing to pay dues for water and garbage collection. The association sued to compel the defendant to pay full dues or to reconvey the land. The court held the covenant was unenforceable

4. See § 15.13 infra.

5. See § 15.1 infra. On private control and management; see also U.S. Dep't Housing and Urban Development, FHA, Planned–Unit Development with a Homes Association, Land Planning Bull. No. 6 Jan. (1970); Urban Land Institute, The Homes Association Handbook, Art.: Art.

711.050725 No. 50, Technical Bull. No. 50 at 304–361 (1964).

6. U.S. Dep't of Housing and Urban Development, Federal Housing Administration and Veterans Administration, FHA Form 1400, VA 26–8200 (Rev.1973).

7. 81 N.J.Super. 564, 196 A.2d 270 (Ch.Div.1963).

as restricting free alienation and conferring unconscionable power to the association over prospective purchasers.

The lengthy articles of incorporation and by-laws that are contained in the suggested form establish the institution for accomplishing the matters controlled by the declaration and provide for directors, officers, committees, finances and the like.

The amount of powers and responsibility given to the private government, of course, varies from new town to new town and from PUD to PUD. For example, the association may not have the responsibility to maintain and repair individually owned properties. That may be the responsibility of the individual owner. Moreover, public government may exercise some of the functions, such as architectural control under a zoning or PUD ordinance. Special districts or special assessment districts may be used as an alternative to provision of water and sewage services by the association.[8]

V. SUBDIVIDED LAND SALES

§ 7.20 In General

The real estate boom of the last three decades caused property development to flourish all over the United States. Unfortunately, this period also saw the rise of fraudulent developers who sold worthless property, as well as well-intentioned developers who lacked sufficient capital or managerial skills to complete development projects and deliver the developed land as promised.[1] As a result, innocent purchasers were spending large sums of money to purchase real estate that was either worthless or that would never be developed as planned.[2] In response to these abuses, federal and state regulation was enacted to regulate the land sales industry.[3] The purpose of federal and state regulations is to protect purchasers by placing them in an equal bargaining position with developers through registration, disclosure and anti-fraud requirements.[4]

Local subdivision regulations which require platting, recordation, dedication and the like are to be distinguished from state and federal acts which are designed to regulate real estate sales, particularly the sale of subdivided lands. These acts police the practice of sales of lots or parcels within large scale developments to minimize possible fraud on potential purchasers or lessees, either through misrepresentation or non-representation of the terms and conditions of sale, the financing arrange-

---

8. For an example of a special district created to maintain open space see West's Ann.Cal. Gov't Code §§ 50575–50628. See also Volpert, Creation and Maintenance of Open Spaces in Subdivisions: Another Approach, 12 U.C.L.A.L.Rev. 830 (1965).

§ 7.20

1. James R. Pomeranz, The State of Caveat Emptor in Alaska as it Applies to

Real Property, 13 Alaska L.Rev. 237, 250 (1996).

2. Id.

3. Id. at 251.

4. Id.

ments, the condition of the property, or restrictions on use. At least 17 states have enacted new laws or revised existing laws since 1953 to impose varying degrees of control over the sale of subdivided lands.[5] A Uniform Land Sales Practice Act has been promulgated by the National Conference of Commissioners on Uniform State Laws.[6] And the federal government has enacted an Interstate Land Sales Full Disclosure Act.[7]

§ 7.21 State Regulation

State regulation has basically taken two forms. A number of states have enacted subdivided land acts, authorizing a special agency to supervise the sale of subdivided lands.[1] In other states, the agency which polices the sale of securities has been given jurisdiction over some real estate sales. In both cases, jurisdiction over land sales may be restricted in some way, for example, to sales of out-of-state lands,[2] to all sales of subdivided in-state land,[3] or to the installment sales of both out-of-state and in-state subdivided lands.[4]

A. Subdivided Lands Acts

California continues to have among the broadest of the state subdivided land statutes. It applies to improved as well as unimproved land, to land divided for financing as well as for lease or sale, and whenever 5 or more lots are involved unless the lots are larger than 160 acres.[5] Offerings in planned unit developments, condominiums, cooperative apartments, and time-share estates as well as subdivisions are covered.[6]

Before subdivided land may be offered for sale or lease by any person, such person shall notify the Department of Real Estate of their intention to sell or lease and shall file with the department an application for public report including: a statement of the condition of the title to the land; a statement of all terms and conditions upon which it is intended to dispose of the land together with copies of any contracts intended to be used; a statement of the provisions which have been made for public utilities; a statement of the use or uses for which the subdivision will be offered; a statement of any provisions which limit the use or occupancy of the parcels in the subdivision; a statement of the

5. See G. Lefcoe, Land Development Law 426 n. 58 (1966).

6. Model Land Sales Practice Act, 7A U.L.A. 669 (1969). Ten jurisdictions have adopted the Model Act: Alaska Stat. 34.55.004–34.55.046; Conn.Gen.Stat.Ann. §§ 20–329a to 20–329m; West's Fla.Stat. Ann. §§ 498.001–498.063; Hawaii Rev.Stat. §§ 484–1 to 484–22; Idaho Code §§ 55–1801 to 55–1823; Kan.Stat.Ann. 58–3301 to 58–3323; Minn.Stat.Ann. §§ 83.20–83.42; Mont.Code Ann. 76–4–1201 to 76–4–1251; S.C.Code 1976, §§ 27–29–10 to 27–29–210; Utah Code Ann.1953, 57–11–1 to 57–11–21.

7. See § 7.22 infra.

§ 7.21

1. A parallel set of law exists in many of these states regulating the sale of real estate securities, e.g., McKinney's N.Y.— Gen.Bus.Law §§ 352e–352j. See generally G. Lefcoe, Land Finance Law 1121–45 (1969).

2. Ohio Rev.Code § 1707.01(B).

3. N.Y.—McKinney's Real Prop.Law § 337(1).

4. West's Fla.Stat.Ann. §§ 498.001–498.063.

5. West's Ann.Cal.Bus. & Prof.Code § 11000.

6. Id. § 11004.5.

amount of indebtedness which is a lien upon the subdivision and which is incurred to pay for the construction of any onsite or offsite improvement, or any community or recreational facility including the amount of indebtedness to be incurred by any special district, entity, taxing area or assessment district within the boundaries of which the subdivision is located.[7]

After receiving all the required information, the Real Estate Commissioner is to make an examination of the subdivision, and unless there are grounds for denial, issue a public report authorizing the sale or lease of lots in the subdivision.[8] The report is to contain the data furnished the Commissioner and which the Commissioner determines is necessary to implement the purposes of the Act.[9] A copy of the public report must be given to every prospective purchaser by the owner, subdivider or agent prior to the execution of a binding contract or agreement for the sale or lease of any lot in the subdivision.[10]

Grounds for denying a public report include: failure to provide in the contract or other writing the use or uses for which the parcels are offered together with any covenants or conditions relative thereto; that sale or lease would constitute misrepresentation to or deceit or fraud of the purchasers or lessees; inability to deliver title or other interest contracted for; inability to demonstrate that adequate financial arrangements have been made for all offsite improvements or any community, recreational or other facilities included in the offering; failure to make a showing that the parcels can be used for the purpose for which they are offered; inadequacy of agreements or bylaws to provide for management or other services pertaining to common facilities; and failure to demonstrate adequate financial arrangements have been made for any guarantee or warranty included in the offering.[11]

The California scheme goes farther than most subdivided lands acts by, for example, requiring the real estate commissioner to find that reasonable arrangements have been made to assure completion of the subdivision and all offsite improvements included in the offering.[12] Most subdivided lands acts merely require full disclosure of the basic data of interest to a prospective purchaser. Some states reach only misstatements and not omissions by merely requiring, for example, that the advertising to be used by the subdivider be furnished to a state agency for a review of its accuracy.

B. Application of Basic Securities Law

A number of states have expanded their basic securities regulation laws to specifically cover real estate sales.[13] As with subdivided land sales laws, these statutes generally apply to the sale of subdivided lands; isolated sales are generally exempt transactions. The application of blue

7. Id. § 11010.

8. Id. § 11018.

9. Id.

10. Id. § 11018.1

11. Id. § 11018; see also Id. § 11018.5.

12. Id. § 11018.5(a)(1).

13. See, e.g., Me.Rev.Stat.Ann. tit. 32, § 751.

sky laws to land sales is usually designed to do no more than insure full disclosure, like most subdivided lands acts. However, at least one state requires that the proposed sale be found "not on grossly unfair terms."[14]

Whether the general corporate securities law can be used when it does not by its terms encompass real estate sales depends on the statute itself, how broadly the corporation commissioner construes his authority, and whether the court will uphold a broad interpretation of "security."[15]

For example, in State v. Silberberg[16] before sales of real estate were specifically covered by the corporate security law, occupiers of a cooperative housing corporation purchased shares in the corporation and occupied a unit of the building. Upon payment of the full purchase price, the occupier received a deed for the space he occupied. The court ruled that the transaction constituted a sale of real estate which was not a security within the meaning of the Ohio Securities Act. On the other hand, before jurisdiction over such transactions was transferred to the real estate commission, several persons in California attempted to form a country club and sold memberships. The court considered the memberships to be within the statutory definition of security which included "any beneficial interest in title to property" and within the regulatory purpose of the corporate securities act, even though memberships were purchased for use and enjoyment rather than as an investment on which a return of capital was expected.[17]

In California, before authority over the sale of subdivided lands was transferred to the real estate commissioner, the sale of subdivided lands was frequently considered to be the sale of a security because of the broad statutory definition of "security" and because the corporation commissioner was aggressive in so classifying interests in title to property. Under the corporate securities law, the corporation commissioner applied a "fair, just and equitable" test before permitting the sale. Thus, application of the general corporate securities law in California to the sale of subdivided lands resulted in more rigorous scrutiny than the subdivided land act now requires. However, as stated above, some of the real estate commissioner's required findings approach a "fair, just and equitable" test.

Besides protecting purchasers, state land sales regulations in some situations protect developers.[18] In Stepanov v. Gavrilovich, the defendants, who were developers, purchased forty-four acres of unimproved land which they subdivided into one hundred and fifty residential lots.[19] The defendants hired Alaska Geological Consultants to test the soil to

---

14. Ohio Rev.Code § 1707.33(G).

15. Ordinarily, if there is no tangible title or interest to realty conveyed but only a right to share in profits or distribution of assets, the interest is considered a security. 1 CCH Blue Sky L.Rep. 1641 (1954).

16. 166 Ohio St. 101, 139 N.E.2d 342 (1956).

17. Silver Hills Country Club v. Sobieski, 55 Cal.2d 811, 13 Cal.Rptr. 186, 361 P.2d 906 (1961).

18. Pomeranz at 253, supra § 7.20, note 1.

19. Stepanov v. Gavrilovich, 594 P.2d 30, 32 (Alaska 1979).

determine whether the land was suitable for building.[20] The tests did not detect permafrost, which if present can hinder the safety of structures build on the land.[21] The defendants then sold various lots in the tract to several contractors who built single-family homes upon them.[22] A short time after construction the houses began to subside because of the presence of permafrost in the land.[23] Due to the heat generated by the new houses, the permafrost under them melted, causing them to settle.[24] The contractors who purchased the lots sued the defendants, claiming breach of an implied warranty of fitness and strict liability.[25]

The court held that in enacting the Uniform Land Sales Practices Act for Alaska, the legislature clearly intended to impose a system of controls on the activities of large-scale subdividers such as the defendants.[26] One of the controls that the legislature intended to impose is civil liability when subdividers fail to disclose to a purchaser a physical characteristic of the subdivided land, such as permafrost, which adversely affects the usefulness of the land.[27] But, when the condition is unknown to the subdivider, he is liable only if it is one that he or she could have learned of through the exercise of reasonable care.[28] Therefore, while the purpose of the act is to impose a system of controls on the activity of large scale subdividers, the act also shields subdividers from liability for defects that cannot be detected with reasonable care.[29]

§ 7.22 Federal Regulation

On the federal level, beginning in 1962, the Federal Trade Commission attempted to exert some control over interstate land sales under its authority to prevent unfair or deceptive acts or practices in commerce. The FTC program was abated in deference to the Post Office department which exercised jurisdiction under authority to prosecute for the use of the mails to execute a fraudulent scheme. Federal legislation specifically dealing with the problem of land sales was originally proposed to place the matter under SEC jurisdiction, but the U.S. Department of Housing and Urban Development (HUD) was eventually given jurisdiction. The federal provisions are contained in the Interstate Land Sales Full Disclosure Act (ILSFDA), enacted in 1968.[1]

---

20. Id.

21. Id. at 32–33.

22. Id.

23. Id.

24. Id.

25. Id. at 33.

26. Id. at 35.

27. Id.

28. Id.

29. Pomeranz at 254, § 7.20, supra note 1.

§ 7.22

1. 15 U.S.C.A. §§ 1700–1720. The following lists the major scholarly analysis of the ILSFDA: Coffey & Welch, Federal Regulation of Land Sales: Full Disclosure Comes Down to Earth, 21 Case W.Res. 5 (1969), Feferman, Interstate Land Sales Full Disclosure Act, 33 Tex.B.J. 625 (1970); Freidman, Regulation of Interstate Land Sales: Is Full Disclosure Sufficient? 20 Urb.L.Ann. 137 (1980); Gandal, General Outline of the Interstate Land Sales Full Disclosure Act, 3 Real Est.L.J. 3 (1974); Gose, Interstate Land Sales, 9 Real Prop.Prob. & Tr.J. 7 (1974); Krechter, LS–MFD: Land Sales Mean Full Disclosure, 4 Real Prop.Prob. & Tr.J. 1 (1969); Krechter, Federal Regulation of Interstate Land Sales, 4 Real Prop.Prob. & Tr.J. 327 (1969); Malloy, The Interstate Land Sales Full Disclosure Act: Its Require-

The purpose of the ILSFDA is to "deter or prohibit the sale of land by use of the mails or other channels of interstate commerce through misrepresentation of material facts relating to the property."[2] As originally adopted, the ILSFDA emphasized disclosure and registration of real estate development proposals and purchase conditions. The act was designed to protect the purchasers and leasees of property by requiring the preparation of a "Property Report" in order to disclose important information about the property and proposed improvements.[3] Through disclosure and registration requirements, purchasers were allegedly less likely to be influenced by "get rich quick promoters" because of the availability of better information.[4] The ILSFDA was amended, however, in 1979 to shift its emphasis away from the extensive paperwork and registration requirements. The amended act emphasizes anti-fraud protection, consumer rights, and enforcement against serious sales abuses by unscrupulous developers.[5]

The ILSFDA's disclosure and anti-fraud provisions are patterned after similar provisions of the Securities Act of 1933 and the Security Exchange Act of 1934.[6] The 1979 amendments added provisions for

ments, Consequences, and Implications for Persons Participating in Real Estate Development, 24 B.C.L.Rev. 1187 (1983); Morris, The Interstate Land Sales Full Disclosure Act: Analysis and Evaluation, 24 S.C.L.Rev. 331 (1972); Peretz, Rescission under the Interstate Land Sales Full Disclosure Act, 58 Fla.B.J. 297 (1984); Pridgen, The Interstate Land Sales Full Disclosure Act: The Practitioner's Problems and Suggestions for Improvement, 4 Real Est.L.J. 127 (1975); Walsh, Consumer Protection in Land Development Sales, 42 Pa.B.A.Q. 38 (1970); Walsh, The Role of the Federal Government in Land Development Sales, 47 Notre Dame Law. 267 (1971); Whitney, Standing and Remedies Available to the Department of Housing and Urban Development Under the Interstate Land Sales Full Disclosure Act, 6 GMU.L.Rev. 171 (1983); Young, Land Sales and Development: Some Legal and Conceptual Considerations, 3 Real Est.L.J. 44 (1974); Comment, A Handbook to the Interstate Land Sales Full Disclosure Act, 27 Ark.L.Rev. 65 (1973); Comment, The Interstate Land Sales Full Disclosure Act: An Analysis of Administrative Policies Implemented in the Years 1968–75, 26 Cath. U.L.Rev. 348 (1977); Note Regulating the Subdivided Land Market, 81 Harv.L.Rev. 1528 (1968); Note, "Rainbow City"—The Need for Federal Control in the Sale of Undeveloped Land, 46 Notre Dame Law. 733 (1971); Comment, Applying the Interstate Land Sales Full Disclosure Act, 51 Or.L.Rev. 381 (1972); Note, Exemptions from the Registration Requirements in the Interstate Land Sales Full Disclosure Act,

15 Real Prop.Prob. & Tr.J. 334 (1980); Note, Consumer Protection and the Interstate Land Sales Full Disclosure Act, 48 St. John's L.Rev. 947 (1974); Note, Regulation of Interstate Land Sales, 25 Sta.L.Rev. 605 (1973); Note, Interstate Land Sales Regulation, 1974 Wash.U.L.Q. 123; Comment, Protecting the Buyer: New Regulations Under the Interstate Land Sales Full Disclosure Act, 1974 Wis.L.Rev. 558.

2. Conf.Rep. No. 1785, 90th Cong., 2d Sess. 161 (1968), reprinted in 1968 U.S.Code Cong. & Ad.News 3053, 3066.

3. 15 U.S.C.A. § 1703(a), (b); see also Flint Ridge Development Co. v. Scenic Rivers Ass'n of Oklahoma, 426 U.S. 776, 778, 96 S.Ct. 2430, 2433, 49 L.Ed.2d 205 (1976), rehearing denied 429 U.S. 875, 97 S.Ct. 198, 50 L.Ed.2d 159 (1976) (recognizing that the purpose of the ILSFDA is to prevent false and deceptive practices in the sale of land by requiring developers to disclose information needed by potential purchasers).

4. See Cumberland Capital Corp. v. Harris, 621 F.2d 246, 250 (6th Cir.1980).

5. See generally, Dept. of Housing and Urban Development, Office of Interstate Land Sales Registration Biennial Rep. To Congress, 3–4 (March 1981). For a thorough discussion of the amended act see Malloy, supra note 1.

6. Flint Ridge Development Co. v. Scenic Rivers Ass'n of Oklahoma, 426 U.S. 776, 778, 96 S.Ct. 2430, 2433, 49 L.Ed.2d 205 (1976), rehearing denied 429 U.S. 875, 97 S.Ct. 198, 50 L.Ed.2d 159 (1976).

increased damages and enforcement.[7] The amendments also established contractual rights for private enforcement[8] and reduced the threshold for application of the anti-fraud provisions to subdivisions with 25 or more lots from the previous threshold of 100 or more lots.[9] Finally, the amendments were designed to reduce paperwork and compliance costs to developers by providing for state certification procedures that eliminate the need for duplicate registrations with state agencies as well as with the department.[10] The act now permits states requiring substantially similar standards for land sales and development to implement state registration requirements that also satisfy federal registration requirements.[11] At least two states with major land sales and development industries, California and Florida, have been certified under the ILSF-DA's provisions.[12] While the state certification provisions eliminate wasteful duplication, registration under a certified state plan does not exempt a person from the other provisions of the ILSFDA.

7. 15 U.S.C.A. §§ 1702, 1709. See generally, Biennial Rep. To Congress, supra note 5, at 4.

8. Pub.L. No. 96–153, title IV, §§ 403, 405, 93 Stat. 1127, 1130 (1979) (now codified at 15 U.S.C.A. § 1703(d)). For a discussion of the act's recission remedy see Peretz, supra note 1.

9. Pub.L. No. 96–153, title IV, § 402, 93 Stat. 1123 (1979) (now codified at 15 U.S.C.A. § 1702(a)(1)).

10. See Biennial Rep. to Congress, supra note 5, at 25.

11. 15 U.S.C.A. § 1708.

12. Biennial Rep. to Congress, supra note 5, at 21.

Chapter 8

BUILDING AND HOUSING CODES

Analysis

---

§ 8.1 In General

Building and housing codes have existed for centuries but most of the evolution of the codes has occurred in recent years.[1] Their modern history in the U.S. began with the adoption of the Tenement House Act for the City of New York in 1901.[2] Traditionally they were not generally treated as land use control devices because land use controls are focused on land, and the relationship between buildings and land.[3] Building and housing codes, on the other hand, deal with matters of construction and maintenance, that is, with matters inward from the outside skin of a building. Currently, however, the building permit and certificate of occupancy stages of development have become the focal points for many

§ 8.1

1. Eric Damian Kelly, Fair Housing, Good Housing or Expensive Housing? Are Building Codes Part of the Problem or Part of the Solution?, 29 J. Marshall L. Rev. 349, 350 (1996).

2. The Act was held constitutional in Tenement House Dept. of New York v. Moeschen, 179 N.Y. 325, 72 N.E. 231 (1904), aff'd without opinion, 203 U.S. 583, 27 S.Ct. 781, 51 L.Ed. 328 (1906). See Judith A. Gilbert, Tenements and Takings: Tenement House Department of New York v. Moeschen As A Counterpoint to Lochner v. New York, 18 Fordham Urb.L.J. 437 (1991).

For an historical treatment of the development of housing code standards in the United States, see Public Health Service, U.S. Dep't of Health, Education & Welfare, Basic Housing Inspection 1–3 (1976); The National Commission on Urban Problems, Housing Code Standards: Three Critical Studies 6–12 (1969).

3. See infra § 8.3. See generally Proceedings of the 1969 Conference on Code Enforcement, Bureau of Government Research, Rutgers University; Bosselman, The Legal Framework of Building and Housing Ordinances, (pts. 1 & 2) II, The Mun. Att'y 39, 67 (1970).

growth management and infrastructure funding regulations thereby bringing at least that aspect of building codes into the mainstream of land use regulation.[4]

The basic goal of building and housing codes is to ensure that buildings are safe, sanitary, and increasingly, convenient and efficient.[5] Building codes are primarily derived from structural safety standards and are generally enforced against new construction. Attention to existing properties is usually given only to those which have been severely damaged or have such serious deficiencies as to render them dangerous. Most codes also require existing structures that are being remodeled to include certain improvements.[6] Housing Codes were originally authorized by environmental health laws, and deal primarily with conditions which must be maintained in existing residential buildings to protect the public health, safety and welfare and the well-being of their occupants.[7] Post-construction maintenance of commercial and state-owned buildings is governed by several supplemental codes such as electrical codes, fire codes, mechanical codes, plumbing codes and others.[8]

Building code standards are classified as belonging to one of two types: (1) specification or (2) performance. Most codes rely heavily on standards of the specification or prescriptive type. That is, the code will require the use of a specific type or grade of material to achieve the desired result. Architects are generally opposed to this sort of code, because they believe it stifles innovation and can be counterproductive in some situations.[9] These codes are usually compiled from specifications developed by various building industry trade associations. Performance standards, on the other hand, permit the use of any material that is able to meet a performance standard. Development of performance standards was required as part of the Energy Conservation Standards for New Building Act of 1976.[10] Though performance standards are favored by architects, they are sometimes impractical to use, expensive to administer and tend to centralize the related administrative functions.[11]

4. See § 8.8 infra.

5. Kelly, supra note 1, at 349.

6. Id. at 354.

7. Jane McGrew and John Bates, Code Enforcement: The Federal Role, 14 Urb. Law. 1, 2 (1982). A statutory definition of housing codes reads as follows: "any code or rule intending postconstruction regulation of structures which would include but not be limited to standards of maintenance, condition of facilities, condition of systems and components, living conditions, occupancy, use and room sizes." Fla.Stat.Ann. § 553.71(5).

8. See, e.g., Fla.Stat.Ann. § 553.19, § 553.06, § 663.557, § 553.06, "Thermal Efficiency Code," § 553.900.

9. See, e.g., Energy Building Regulations: The Effect of the Federal Performance Standards on Building Code Administration and Conservation of Energy in New Buildings, 13 U.C.D.L.Rev. 330, 336–7 nn. 32–35 (1980) [hereinafter cited as Energy Building Regulations].

10. Pub.L. No. 94–385, 90 Stat. 1144, 42 U.S.C.A. §§ 6831–40.

11. Conservation and Efficient Use of Energy: Hearings Before a Subcomm. of the House Comm. on Government Operations, 93rd Cong., 1st Sess. 33–35 (1973). Performance standards are also regularly used in the U.S. National Conf. of States on Building Costs & Standards, Inc., Survey on Utilization of Systems Analysis Designs in State Energy Conservation Codes (1979).

Building codes frequently have land use control consequences even though that is not their primary purpose.[12] The relation of buildings to one another is an important aspect of urban land use control and many key tenets of urban design regulation such as setback provisions were first found in building codes.[13] Height limits were also originally imposed in building codes rather than in zoning codes.[14]

Another land use control aspect of building codes is the requirement frequently contained in them for building permits and certificates of occupancy. The issuance of a building permit is usually the last point at which the local government can exercise leverage regarding the type of development that will be permitted on the land, and the certificate of occupancy is the last permission needed to use the new improvements. Consequently, land use control authorities use these permits to check compliance with various land use controls.[15] Local governments can also use the issuance of these permits as the point at which to assess and collect payments for capital facilities required to service the new development.[16]

Housing codes also have an indirect impact on land use to the extent that the degree of code enforcement in areas of deteriorating housing may effect the degree of abandonment of residential use. The courts have held that overenthusiastic enforcement of building and housing codes, motivated by a desire to encourage abandonment can result in a taking without just compensation.[17]

§ 8.2 Model Codes

After passage of the Housing Act of 1954, local governments were expected to develop and implement both housing and building codes to qualify for federal urban renewal and public housing programs. Qualification for these programs required that the city submit a "workable program" to the administrator. As a result, between 1955 and 1968, housing code adoption increased 100%, nationally.[1]

12. An interesting example of these "consequences" is reflected in Florida's recent strengthening of its coastal construction building standards. See Fla.Stat.Ann. §§ 161.54–161.56. These provisions establish minimum state building codes for coastal construction, require local implementation, and also establish state overview and sanctions.

13. See, e.g., Klinger v. Bicket, 117 Pa. 326, 11 A. 555 (1887) (upholding prohibition of wood building in fire zone).

14. See Welch v. Swasey, 214 U.S. 91, 29 S.Ct. 567, 53 L.Ed. 923 (1909) (allowing regulation of building height).

15. See Avco Community Developers, Inc. v. South Coast Regional Comm., 17 Cal.3d 785, 132 Cal.Rptr. 386, 553 P.2d 546 (1976), appeal dismissed, cert. denied 429 U.S. 1083, 97 S.Ct. 1089, 51 L.Ed.2d 529

(1977); City of Boynton Beach v. V.S.H. Realty, Inc., 443 So.2d 452 (Fla.App.1984); Friends of Mammoth v. Board of Supervisors, 8 Cal.3d 247, 104 Cal.Rptr. 761, 502 P.2d 1049 (1972); Polygon Corp. v. Seattle, 90 Wash.2d 59, 578 P.2d 1309 (1978); City of Houston v. Walker, 615 S.W.2d 831 (Tex. Civ.App.1981), error refused n.r.e. See also infra § 8.6.

16. See infra § 9.8.

17. Amen v. Dearborn, 718 F.2d 789 (6th Cir.1983), cert. denied 465 U.S. 1101, 104 S.Ct. 1596, 80 L.Ed.2d 127 (1984).

§ 8.2

1. U.S. Nat'l Comm'n on Urban Problems, Building the American City 227 (1968). The workable program requirement was repealed in 1974 with passage of the

A number of model building codes have been developed. They include the National Building Code of the American Insurance Association, the Uniform Building Code of the International Conference of Building Officials, the Southern Standard Building Code of the Southern Building Code Conference and the Basic Building Code of the Building Officials Conference of America. Additionally, there are widely used supplemental codes that include: the National Electric Code, prepared by the National Fire Protection Association; the ASHRAE documents for heating, ventilating and air conditioning, named for its sponsor, the American Society of Heating, Refrigeration and Air Conditioning Engineers; and the National Plumbing Code, developed by the American Society of Mechanical Engineers.[2]

The Uniform Building Code, the Southern Standard Building Code, and the Basic Building Code are regional in effect, though to delineate those boundaries one would need to refer to individual state and local laws. The Southern Standard Building Code is generally used in Florida, Georgia, Alabama, South Carolina, North Carolina, Virginia, Tennessee, Mississippi, and Texas, and the Uniform Building Code sponsored by the International Conference of Building Officials is used in California, for example.

Due to the complexity of building regulation, only the largest jurisdictions attempt to develop their own building codes.[3] Therefore, state and local building codes are increasingly based on one of the four nationally recognized codes, since most jurisdictions can not afford to write and keep up-to-date their own codes. Three of these model code organizations are comprised of state and local building officials,[4] and the fourth is an insurance trade association.

Model codes generally reflect the state of the art of building rather than scientific engineering data and are therefore easily amended by localities with differing views. The organizations which promulgate the model codes for the most part lack funds to support all their provisions with sound engineering data, and in some cases even urge local deviations. Additionally, the update processes for the model codes are independent of one another.[5] Thus, approval of a new technology or design under one of the national codes does not ensure its approval by the other code groups[6]. Often, instead of accepting these model codes intact, local governments make revisions, additions, deletions, and amendments, which in an overwhelming majority of cases are more restrictive in nature.[7] This has resulted in considerable variety in codes from one locale to another.

Housing and Community Development Act of 1974, 42 U.S.C.A. §§ 5301–5308.

2. Eric Damian Kelly, Fair Housing, Good Housing or Expensive Housing? Are Building Codes Part of the Problem or Part of the Solution? 29 J. Marshall L. Rev. 349, 351 (1996).

3. Id.

4. The three groups are the Building Officials and Code Administrators (BOCA), International Conference of Building Officials (ICBO), and the Southern Building Code Congress International (SBCCI).

5. Kelly, supra note 2, at 351.

6. Id.

7. U.S. Dep't of Housing & Urban Dev., Final Report of the Task Force on Housing Costs 35 (May 1978).

For example, an ordinance providing that a house trailer used for living or sleeping for more than 30 days in one year was subject to the local building code had been upheld.[8] Now, however, localities in some states are preempted from exercising such power.[9] As a result of local variations, Congress enacted the National Mobile Home Construction and Safety Standards Act of 1974.[10] This set national standards so that industrialized home building became much more feasible.[11]

Not only do the model building codes vary in terms of general construction requirements, but they vary in scope, so that they may or may not include provisions for setbacks from other buildings and streets, multiple dwelling laws (which apply to apartment houses and boarding houses), health codes that deal with plumbing, sewerage, drainage, light and ventilation, house trailer codes and fire codes. If these kinds of provisions are not in the basic building code they are usually covered by separate local ordinances. In addition, there are sometimes separate boiler codes, electrical codes, elevator codes, heating codes and mechanical codes. These codes may be either promulgated by the state or drawn from specifications and standards set by the respective trade or professional associations.

The model codes are comprehensive and very detailed, and include sections on administration of the code, permitting, fees, inspection, fire district restrictions, classification of buildings by construction, fire protection within the building itself, and minimum safety requirements or characteristics for materials used in construction. Reference is also made in the codes to standards adopted by the individual industrial trade associations for their particular product.[12]

Although most promulgation and enforcement of building and housing codes has been done at the local level, state and federal governments, through legislation and responsible administrative bodies, have played a role in causing the marked increase in the number of building and housing codes enacted by city governments.[13]

---

8. Lower Merion Township v. Gallup, 158 Pa.Super. 572, 46 A.2d 35 (1946), appeal dismissed 329 U.S. 669, 67 S.Ct. 92, 91 L.Ed. 591 (1946); Duckworth v. Bonney Lake, 91 Wash.2d 19, 586 P.2d 860 (1978); Duggins v. Town of Walnut Cove, 63 N.C.App. 684, 306 S.E.2d 186 (1983), review denied 309 N.C. 819, 310 S.E.2d 348 (1983), appeal dismissed 466 U.S. 946, 104 S.Ct. 2145, 80 L.Ed.2d 532 (1984), but see Derry Borough v. Shomo, 5 Pa.Cmwlth. 216, 289 A.2d 513 (1972).

9. E.g., West's Ann.Cal. Health & Safety Code §§ 18000–18124.5. See also California Factory–Built Housing Law, West's Ann.Cal. Health & Safety Code §§ 19960–19997.

10. 42 U.S.C.A. § 5401–26, and a portion of the Housing and Community Development Act of 1980, 94 Stat. 1640, 42 U.S.C.A. §§ 5401, 5402.

11. See infra § 8.5 for discussion of preemption.

12. See, e.g., Southern Standard Building Code (1979).

13. See Code Enforcement: The Federal Role, 14 Urb.Law. 1, 2 (1982). See also West's Fla.Stat.Ann. §§ 161.54–161.56 (establishing minimum state building codes for coastal construction to be implemented locally).

§ 8.3 Relation to Zoning

Some provisions of the building and housing codes and related laws were incorporated into modern zoning ordinances, though it is common to find similar provisions either in building codes or zoning codes or both. For example, fire prevention ordinances which prohibited wooden buildings in certain areas of the city were a kind of precursor to zoning which excludes buildings used for certain purposes, such as commercial or industrial, from parts of a city for reasons of public health, safety or welfare. The yard requirements of modern zoning ordinances are similar to the setback requirements under some fire and building codes. Heights of buildings are controlled under zoning though at an earlier time and sometimes even today, they are controlled under building codes, including "zoned" building codes that provide for different heights in different areas of the city.[1] Zoning bulk regulations dealing with portion of yard covered and density of population overlap housing code matters. A building permit frequently can be issued only after compliance with building and zoning ordinances and other ordinances as well.

It is often important to distinguish between building code ordinances and zoning ordinances. In Florida, for example, a zoning ordinance is invalid if notice requirements are not complied with, whereas building regulations are not held to such strict notice prerequisites to be valid. The court, in Fountain v. Jacksonville,[2] held an ordinance which required structural modifications on buildings located near air installations to reduce internal noise invalid, because procedural requirements in promulgating the ordinance were not followed. The city's argument that the standard was more akin to a building code than a zoning amendment met with little success.[3] In another case, because the court construed an off-street parking requirement to be a building rather than a zoning ordinance matter,[4] the court upheld a variance that did not otherwise meet the criteria for a zoning variance.

§ 8.4 Unauthorized and Unconstitutional Applications of Codes

As with other regulations, the two major routes for attacking the application of a building or housing code are to allege that the regulation is not authorized by a statute or home rule power or that it is unconstitutional. For example in Safer v. Jacksonville,[1] a Florida district court of appeal held that enabling legislation behind the housing code was valid, but that the specific code provisions (one requiring each dwelling unit to

§ 8.3

1. Brougher v. Board of Pub. Works, 107 Cal.App. 15, 290 P. 140 (1930).

2. Fountain v. Jacksonville, 447 So.2d 353 (Fla.App.1984).

3. Id. at 354.

4. Siller v. Board of Supervisors, 58 Cal.2d 479, 25 Cal.Rptr. 73, 375 P.2d 41

(1962); cf. Off Shore Rest. Corp. v. Linden, 30 N.Y.2d 160, 331 N.Y.S.2d 397, 282 N.E.2d 299 (1972).

§ 8.4

1. 237 So.2d 8 (Fla.App.1970). See also Early Estates, Inc. v. Housing Bd. of Review, 93 R.I. 227, 174 A.2d 117 (1961).

contain a sink, lavatory, tub or shower connected with potable hot water, and another code provision requiring at least two conveniently located electrical outlets per habitable room) were not demonstrably related to the health or safety of tenants, generally. The court concluded that the provisions were not authorized by the statute. Challenges to the position taken by the court in *Safer*, both in Florida and other jurisdictions, generally have failed and the requirement that specific provisions be demonstrably related to health and safety remains intact.[2]

Regulations can also be challenged as unreasonable and therefore unconstitutional. The issue has most often been raised when the codes are applied to older buildings. The property owner often loses these battles as in Queenside Hills Realty Co. v. Saxl,[3] a leading case. While the lodging house involved in the case met the standards of the codes when it was built, it did not have the wet pipe sprinkling system required by a new code. The court upheld the application of the new code requirements to the building and indicated that the legislature may decide the level of protection required for safety from fire and that if a building is unsafe per a legislatively established standard, it must be made safe, whatever the cost, or closed, despite loss of value. The building's owners raised an equal protection issue, since the sprinkling system was only applied to pre–1944 lodging houses, the Court held that the legislature could properly draw such lines because the risk in older buildings is greater.

While the courts often compare the cost of compliance with the value of the building, a more relevant consideration might be the cost of compliance as compared to the value of the building after compliance. For example, if a sprinkling system cost $25,000 in a building worth $30,000 and after compliance the building would still be worth only $30,000, the requirement might be viewed as too onerous on the owner. On the other hand, public interest in safety might nonetheless justify the requirement. If the building is worth $50,000 after compliance, a court might be much more disposed to uphold the regulation.

Courts often hold zoning ordinances that operate retroactively on nonconforming buildings unconstitutional and typically come to a contrary conclusion on housing codes. There are several possible reasons for the difference. Zoning was primarily adopted to control prospective development and nonconformities were typically protected under early zoning ordinances because of a fear that zoning would be held unconstitutional if applied retroactively. Courts began to believe that themselves, and some still do.[4] Housing codes, on the other hand, regulate the minimum conditions for occupancy, not development, and are applied

2. E.g., Stallings v. Jacksonville, 333 So.2d 70 (Fla.App.1976); City of St. Louis v. Brune, 515 S.W.2d 471 (Mo.1974).

3. 328 U.S. 80, 66 S.Ct. 850, 90 L.Ed. 1096 (1946). See also McCallin v. Walsh, 64 A.D.2d 46, 407 N.Y.S.2d 852 (1978), order affirmed 46 N.Y.2d 808, 413 N.Y.S.2d 922, 386 N.E.2d 833 (1978).

4. See supra §§ 4.31–4.40 (nonconforming uses).

retroactively to rid buildings of nonconformities caused by deterioration, obsolescence or changes in minimum housing requirements.

Moreover, most housing code standards are directly related to the public health and safety. Suppose the Court in *Queenside Hills Realty* had held the statute violated the due process clause as applied, and subsequently a fire occurred which could have been prevented by elimination of the nonconformity. The courts are reluctant to risk such results. Many zoning standards are less directly grounded on health and safety concerns. Substantial personal injury is unlikely if a building were built two feet closer than a newly imposed setback line permitted. The property owner often loses an attack on the housing code provisions,[5] unless the requirements deal with peripheral matters rather than matters basic to health and safety.[6]

If building and housing codes were "zoned," so that one code did not apply to all housing in the jurisdiction, problems of unreasonable application to older housing might be reduced. Opponents of uniform codes argue that one set of minimum standards in a normally diverse community ignores legitimate differences between neighborhoods resulting from age, structure type and socio-economic factors. Some localities are developing separate codes for historic buildings and districts.[7] Though different standards may lessen the impact of enforcing codes in the more deteriorated neighborhoods, they may be difficult to support. Zoned codes might be judicially accepted if they are based on substantial distinctions, reasonably related to the goal sought to be achieved and evenly applied.[8] Differential enforcement may be a feasible way to deal with differences in a community's housing. If it is utilized it should be acceptable as long as enforcement is uniform in the selected areas.[9] On the other hand, if enforcement of code provisions is not uniform, not based on substantial distinctions nor related to acceptable goals, a violation of equal protection may be found.[10] In Dowdell v. Apopka,[11] disparate provision of municipal services, such as paved roads, running water and sewer systems, between black and white neighborhoods led to

5. Kaukas v. Chicago, 27 Ill.2d 197, 188 N.E.2d 700 (1963), appeal dismissed 375 U.S. 8, 84 S.Ct. 67, 11 L.Ed.2d 40 (1963); City of Chicago v. Sheridan, 40 Ill. App.3d 886, 353 N.E.2d 270 (1976); Adamec v. Post, 273 N.Y. 250, 7 N.E.2d 120 (1937); Miller v. Foster, 244 Wis. 99, 11 N.W.2d 674 (1943).

6. City of Columbus v. Stubbs, 223 Ga. 765, 158 S.E.2d 392 (1967); Barrett v. Hamby, 235 Ga. 262, 219 S.E.2d 399 (1975).

7. See also Aesthetic Regulation and Historic Preservation, infra ch. 12.

8. See Brennan v. Milwaukee, 265 Wis. 52, 60 N.W.2d 704 (1953) and Abbott, Housing Policy, Housing Codes and Tenant Remedies: An Integration, 56 B.U.L.Rev. 1, 105 (1976) for enumerated conditions.

9. Polaka, Housing Codes and Preservation of Urban Blight—Administrative and Enforcement Problems and Proposals, 17 Vill.L.Rev. 490, 519 (1972).

10. See Mlikotin v. Los Angeles, 643 F.2d 652 (9th Cir.1981); Village of Riverwoods v. Untermyer, 54 Ill.App.3d 816, 12 Ill.Dec. 371, 369 N.E.2d 1385 (1977). Cf. Dowdell v. Apopka, 698 F.2d 1181 (11th Cir.1983); Fairfax Countywide Citizens Association v. County of Fairfax, Va., 571 F.2d 1299 (4th Cir.1978), cert. denied 439 U.S. 1047, 99 S.Ct. 722, 58 L.Ed.2d 706 (1978); Hawkins v. Town of Shaw, 437 F.2d 1286 affirmed in banc, 461 F.2d 1171 (5th Cir. 1972); Amen v. Dearborn, 718 F.2d 789 (6th Cir.1983), cert. denied 465 U.S. 1101, 104 S.Ct. 1596, 80 L.Ed.2d 127 (1984).

11. 698 F.2d 1181 (11th Cir.1983).

a finding of intentional discrimination based on race. Typically, however, building and housing codes are not zoned. It has been argued that they could be, with very low jurisdiction-wide requirements, which could be variably increased on a neighborhood basis.[12]

The question whether temporary eviction can be a taking of property within the meaning of the Fifth Amendment thus entitling a tenant to compensation has also posed problems for courts. There had been some disagreement concerning regulatory takings and compensation in some jurisdictions, but the Seventh Circuit Court of Appeals, in Devines v. Maier[13] (*Devines II*) likely put the issue to rest. In *Devines I*,[14] the court held that a constitutional taking had occurred when the city ordered tenants to temporarily vacate their uninhabitable dwelling to permit repairs, pursuant to the housing code. The Seventh Circuit remanded the case to the district court to determine the amount of compensation due plaintiffs.

When the district court determined the amount of compensation due, the city appealed in light of intervening Supreme Court cases.[15] In *Devines II*[16], the Seventh Circuit reversed the district court's award of compensation and overturned its holding in *Devines I*. The court reasoned that when the state creates a property right in the form of a possessory leasehold, and conditions possession on the continued habitability of the premises for the term of the lease, if the state later temporarily evicts a tenant because the premises are unfit for human habitation there is no taking. Housing codes are a valid exercise of the police power, and it is reasonable for a city to take measures to assure that its housing stock remains habitable. The property right is constitutionally protectible but retention of the right is subject to a reasonable condition such as continued habitability.

§ 8.5   State and Federal Preemption

Over half of the states have adopted statewide building codes drafted by one of the three major building code organizations, most of which are mandatory.[1] In Oregon v. Troutdale,[2] the court held that the provision of the state building code permitting "single-wall" construction, did not preempt a city ordinance which required "double-wall" construction in new buildings within the city. The court determined that because the construction standards regulated builders rather than municipal government, the city could adopt building code requirements in addition to or

---

12. Babcock & Bosselman, Citizen Participation: A Suburban Suggestion for the Central City, 32 Law & Contemp. Prob. 221 (1967).

13. 728 F.2d 876 (7th Cir.1984), cert. denied 469 U.S. 836, 105 S.Ct. 130, 83 L.Ed.2d 71 (1984).

14. Devines v. Maier, 665 F.2d 138 (7th Cir.1981).

15. Texaco, Inc. v. Short, 454 U.S. 516, 102 S.Ct. 781, 70 L.Ed.2d 738 (1982), and

Loretto v. Teleprompter Manhattan CATV Corp., 458 U.S. 419, 102 S.Ct. 3164, 73 L.Ed.2d 868 (1982).

16. Devines v. Maier, 728 F.2d 876, 883–4 (7th Cir.1984), cert. denied 469 U.S. 836, 105 S.Ct. 130, 83 L.Ed.2d 71 (1984).

§ 8.5

1. 5 Housing & Dev.Rep. 754 (1977).

2. 281 Or. 203, 576 P.2d 1238 (1978).

more stringent than the statewide code, but not incompatible with its provisions. State regulations were to establish basic uniform standards which would reasonably safeguard health, safety, welfare and comfort. In an appropriate case, however, the need for uniformity of the law may be a sufficient basis for legislative preemption at state level.

In California, the administrative code allowed a city or county to determine changes or modifications in the state's building requirements where appropriate because of local conditions.[3] "Local conditions" had been construed rather loosely, until 1977, when the California attorney general defined local conditions as those which could be broadly labeled as geographical or topographical, excluding local political, economic or social concerns as destructive of any attempt to achieve statewide uniformity. Code uniformity reduces housing costs, increases the efficiency of the private housing construction industry and helps meet housing needs of the state.[4] Uniform codes are generally based on professional expertise, research and testing not routinely available to local agencies.[5] Evidence of the desirability of uniformity can be seen in the development of model codes and their subsequent adoption as law by state legislatures.

Federal mobile home construction and safety standards were established by the Secretary of HUD pursuant to the National Mobile Home Construction and Safety Standards Act of 1974.[6] Whenever a federal mobile home construction and safety standard is in effect, no state or political subdivision shall have authority to enact or maintain any standard which is not identical to the federal standard.[7]

Federal preemption is much less a potential problem now than before enactment of the 1974 Housing and Community Development Act.[8] Congress was dissatisfied with code enforcement under the "workable program," and the new act entitled individual communities to decide for themselves the most appropriate building and housing standards. HUD now encourages development of more effective standards through the National Institute of Building Sciences,[9] a private organization chartered by the statute.

More recently, the federal government established the Building Energy Performance Standards (BEPS).[10] Existing building codes do not take climatic variations or energy use into account, but only regulate design and construction of buildings, principally for protecting the public

3. West's Ann.Cal. Health & Safety Code, § 17958.5.

4. But see Eric Damian Kelly, Fair Housing, Good Housing or Expensive Housing? Are Building Codes Part of the Problem or Part of the Solution?, 29 J. Marshall L. Rev. 349 (1996).

5. 60 Op.Att'y Gen. 234 (Cal.1977).

6. 42 U.S.C.A. § 5403(a). See § 8.2 at n. 10.

7. 42 U.S.C.A. § 5403(d). See also Title VI. Other provisions include enforcement, correction of defects, state role, prohibited acts.

8. 42 U.S.C.A. §§ 5301–5308.

9. H.R.Rep. No. 93–1279, 93rd Cong., 2d Sess. 134 (1974).

10. Building Energy Standards Act of 1976, as amended, 42 U.S.C.A. §§ 6801–6873. In 1981, these standards were made voluntary. Id.

health and welfare.[11] Congress chose to effect energy conservation in buildings through existing codes,[12] based on the presumption that it would be more efficient and economical to use building code officials to enforce the standards rather than to develop an alternative mechanism. The department of energy was responsible for promulgating energy conservation standards for new buildings while HUD was required to formulate cost-effective "weatherization" standards for existing housing rehabilitated with federal funds.

Most states had already adopted building energy conservation standards recommended in the Energy Policy and Conservation Act of 1975[13] which made funds available to each state for development of a conservation plan meeting certain enumerated requirements.[14]

§ 8.6   Methods of Enforcement

A.   *Building Codes*[1]

Municipal or state building codes are enforced by the commissioner of buildings or similar official under powers delegated by the city's charter or state constitution or statutes.[2]

The building code usually requires submission of plans for the project for approval by the building official. Forms are provided, and the application must include a description of the work and its location. For new construction or major alterations, the application must include a lot diagram showing compliance with local zoning, foundation plans, floor and roof plans, detailed architectural, structural and mechanical drawings. The code officials examine the plans submitted for compliance with the code, and other applicable laws and regulations. If plans comply, then they are approved in writing and notice is given to the applicant. When plans fail to comply, the application and plans will be rejected in writing with reasons clearly stated. Rejected applications may be revised and resubmitted until standards are met. Minor alterations (not affecting health, fire or structural safety of the building) and ordinary repairs (replacement or renewal of existing work during ordinary maintenance) usually do not require plan approval. Application for plan approval and the work permits are often separate processes, but may be applied for all at once.

---

11. See, e.g., Southern Standard Building Code (1997), or Uniform Building Code (1997).

12. 42 U.S.C.A. § 6831 et seq., but conservation measures may be implemented in other ways. Energy efficient buildings may be encouraged by tax credits, e.g., 26 U.S.C.A. § 23.

13. 89 Stat. 871, 42 U.S.C.A. § 6201.

14. These standards were based on ASHRAE guidelines—prescriptive standards which were much more easily en-

forced than BEPS could be. Aderman, Energy Standards for New Buildings, 11 Nat.J. 1084 (1979).

§ 8.6

1. See generally, W. Correale, A Building Code Primer, xiii–xv, 1–13 (1979).

2. A look at the Florida code provides a common example of the mechanics of operation. See West's Fla.Stat.Ann. § 553.70-.895.

To insure that health and safety requirements are met during the building process, the building official is authorized to enter and inspect any premises or building to check for compliance with code and other applicable laws. Necessary tests are conducted at the direction of the building official, and the expense is borne by the owner or lessee of the property.

Final inspection is made upon completion of the work by a building official, and the architect, engineer or other supervisor of the work may be present also. The owner must be notified of any failures of the work to comply with code provisions. A certificate of occupancy will be issued when a building is found to substantially conform to applicable laws and regulations, and to the approved plans and code provisions. A temporary certificate of occupancy can be issued for 60–90 days if occupancy of the building (or relevant portion) will not endanger public safety during that period.

B. *Housing Codes*

A violation of the housing code usually comes to the attention of local government officials when a tenant files a complaint or as the result of a survey of an area by the administrative agency of the local government. If by complaint, building officials conduct an inspection and make a report, the matter is thereafter treated as if discovered by survey, namely, the landlord is served with notice of a hearing and there is a finding that the violation exists. The administrative or judicial body having jurisdiction then typically orders repairs, a period for compliance is set, followed by a reinspection. If the repairs have not been made the compliance period is usually extended. If the repairs have still not been made (or the building is beyond repair in the first instance) the landlord can be ordered to vacate the building or to demolish it, or can be fined or imprisoned.[3] A city would be overstepping its police power, however, to require a building to be demolished without paying the owner compensation, if repairs could be made to the building to meet the code requirements.[4]

In some jurisdictions there are other available remedies. For example, under the New York Receivership Law[5] if a serious defect is found, the Commissioner of Real Estate can be appointed by the court as a receiver to collect rent and make repairs out of the rents.[6] The tenant is

3. See, e.g., Ill.—S.H.A. ch. 38, ¶ 12–5.1. Alternatively, the list of violations and compliance date may be served first, leaving the landlord to request a hearing. See also City of Bakersfield v. Miller, 64 Cal.2d 93, 48 Cal.Rptr. 889, 410 P.2d 393 (1966), cert. denied 384 U.S. 988, 86 S.Ct. 1890, 16 L.Ed.2d 1005 (1966). Defendant was given five years to comply with city building code. When he refused, the city filed suit compelling him to comply with the code. After six years of litigation, the court finally held that the city had the power to set, define and apply standards.

4. Horton v. Gulledge, 277 N.C. 353, 177 S.E.2d 885 (1970). But see State v. Jones, 305 N.C. 520, 290 S.E.2d 675 (1982). Cf. Dickerson v. Young, 332 N.W.2d 93 (Iowa 1983).

5. N.Y.—McKinney's Mult.Dwell.Law § 309(5)(c)(1).

6. And under the Spiegel Law, also in New York, where tenant rent is paid by welfare agencies, the payments may be withheld so long as the housing code is violated. N.Y.—McKinney's Soc.Services Law § 143–b.

also given protection against eviction so long as violations of the housing code exist.[7] Rent strikes, a method by which tenants can petition courts to collect rent and stay eviction proceedings pending repairs, have been more symbolic than successful.[8]

In other states, statutes provide that a tenant can notify the landlord of a defect, and if it is not repaired, the tenant can repair the defect himself and deduct the expenses from the monthly rent.[9] Statutes in other states allow tenants to sue for damages if injured as a result of an injury caused by violation of the housing code.[10]

Tenants have also sought housing code compliance by arguing that rent is not due where there are housing code violations on the theory that the violation constitutes a breach of an implied warranty of habitability, which is an implied promise by the landlord that the premises are fit for human occupation and will remain so throughout the lease term.[11] This theory underlies an increasing amount of code violation cases. Javins v. First Nat'l Realty Corp.[12] presented an innovative approach to the issue. The landlord sued for possession for non-payment of rent, and the tenants countered with housing code violations as a defense. The court applied traditional contract principles to this residential rental situation and found an implied warranty of habitability measured by the housing code requirements.

Code violations may not be sufficient to render the premises unsafe or unsanitary and make the lease contract illegal and unenforceable, but nonetheless give rise to remedies for contract breach including damages and specific performance. Violations also can be a defense to actions for possession for nonpayment of rent even if, through no fault of the tenant, they arise after the lease is signed. Statutes may vary from state to state. In Florida, for example, the applicable statute requires a tenant to deposit rent with the court when he or she sues a landlord for housing code violations.[13] The tenant is not entitled to remain on the premises during pendency of the litigation, but the statute does protect the cause of action after vacation of the leasehold.[14]

7. See Comment, Rent Receivership: An Evaluation of Its Effectiveness as a Housing Code Enforcement Tool in Connecticut Cities, 2 Conn.L.Rev. 687 (1970).

8. N.Y.—McKinney's Real Prop.Acts. Law § 769 et seq. See Lipsky, Protest in City Politics: Rent Strikes, Housing and the Power of the Poor, ch. 6 & 7 (1970).

9. West's Ann.Cal.Civ. Code §§ 1941–1942; Mont.Codes Ann. 42–201 & 42–202. See Reste Realty v. Cooper, 53 N.J. 444, 251 A.2d 268 (1969) (tenant constructively evicted because of code violations).

10. La.—L.S.A.–Civ. Code arts. 2232, 2693–2695.

11. Rent abatement is a remedy frequently granted in cases based on this theory, see, e.g., Hinson v. Delis, 26 Cal.App.3d 62, 102 Cal.Rptr. 661 (1972); Timber Ridge Town House, Inc. v. Dietz, 133 N.J.Super. 577, 338 A.2d 21 (1975). Compare Pines v. Perssion, 14 Wis.2d 590, 111 N.W.2d 409 (1961).

12. 428 F.2d 1071 (D.C.Cir.1970), cert. denied 400 U.S. 925, 91 S.Ct. 186, 27 L.Ed.2d 185 (1970). See also, Vanlandingham v. Ivanow, 246 Ill.App.3d 348, 186 Ill.Dec. 304, 615 N.E.2d 1361 (1993); Hilder v. St. Peter, 144 Vt. 150, 478 A.2d 202 (Vt.1984).

13. West's Fla.Stat.Ann. § 83.60(2).

14. K.D. Lewis Enterprises Corp., Inc. v. Smith, 445 So.2d 1032 (Fla.App.1984).

Owners or landlords may also be liable for injuries to tenants caused by defects in the premises, though this is usually limited to situations in which the landlord knew of the defect at the time of leasing or took no action to repair after reasonable notice.[15] A landlord cannot contract out of his liability for negligence since such contracts violate public policy.[16]

There are also several legislatively established auxiliary programs such as rental assistance[17] for lower income tenants. This enables qualifying tenants to afford decent housing in the private market. Landlords can provide code-related improvements and at the same time maintain a reasonable return on their investment without creating a greater rent burden on tenants.[18]

Outright grants and loans are available to both eligible homeowners and landlords for bringing their properties into compliance with code standards. These programs can go a long way toward preventing abandonment. With the Housing and Community Development Act of 1974,[19] the federal government permitted money derived from the community development block grant program to support elimination of detrimental housing conditions through code enforcement in deteriorating or deteriorated areas, in which such enforcement may be expected to arrest the decline.[20] Technical assistance and information are available to local officials, as are funds for innovative projects dealing with both housing and building codes.[21] Creation of other economic incentives, such as property tax abatements or downward assessments of rehabilitated properties and urban homesteading, in addition to federal tax credits, may help make such properties more attractive investments.

§ 8.7 Problems With Enforcement

Camara v. Municipal Court[1] and See v. Seattle[2] held that building inspectors must have either consent or a search warrant to look for violations of a housing code having criminal penalties. These cases only inconvenience administration and present no impossible barriers to

15. Avon–Avalon, Inc. v. Collins, 643 So.2d 570 (Ala.1994); Reitmeyer v. Sprecher, 431 Pa. 284, 243 A.2d 395 (1968) (limited by the holding in Presley v. Acme Markets, Inc., 213 Pa.Super. 265, 247 A.2d 478 (1968)).

16. Boyd v. Smith, 372 Pa. 306, 94 A.2d 44 (1953). It has been proposed that mere ownership or maintenance of a slum building should be a tort. Sax & Hiestand, "Slumlordism" as a Tort, 65 Mich.L.Rev. 869 (1967). See also Blum & Dunham, "Slumlordism" as a Tort—A Dissenting View, 66 Mich.L.Rev. 451 (1968). But see Matthews v. Mountain Lodge Apartments, Inc., 388 So.2d 935 (Ala.1980).

17. 42 U.S.C.A. § 1473(f)(g), i.e., § 8 of the 1937 Housing Act was amended to create a rent subsidy program.

18. See, e.g., City of St. Louis v. Brune, 515 S.W.2d 471 (Mo.1974); 42 U.S.C.A. § 1473(g) and 24 C.F.R. § 882 et seq.

19. 42 U.S.C.A. §§ 5301–18.

20. Id. §§ 5301(c)(2), 5305(a)(3).

21. See, e.g., U.S. Dep't of Hous. & Urban Dev., Rehabilitation Guidelines 1980; U.S. Dep't of Hous. & Urban Dev., Designing Rehab Programs: A Local Government Guidebook (1979); Bldg. Officials & Code Adm'rs Int'l, Inc., Code Enforcement Guidelines for Residential Rehabilitation (1975).

§ 8.7

1. 387 U.S. 523, 87 S.Ct. 1727, 18 L.Ed.2d 930 (1967).

2. 387 U.S. 541, 87 S.Ct. 1737, 18 L.Ed.2d 943 (1967).

enforcement. Marshall v. Barlow's, Inc.,[3] although it involved an inspection by an OSHA agent of business premises, upheld the warrant requirement as established in Camara and See.

As stated above, housing code inspections are most often triggered by complaints though there are other techniques such as systematic inspection schedules or area wide inspections. Selected area inspections are more important, primarily in communities with community development, urban renewal or other targeted areas of preservation and rehabilitation.

Where building and housing code enforcement is primarily triggered by complaints, buildings can deteriorate rapidly if no complaints are made. Complaints may not be filed with public authorities due to the threat of retaliatory eviction. The retaliatory nature of an eviction may itself be a defense to eviction,[4] although retaliatory motive may be difficult to prove.[5] Municipal ordinances can regulate entry of inspectors, and can require inspections prior to sale or reletting, but cannot impose criminal sanctions for refusal to comply with warrantless searches.[6]

Despite a generally favorable judicial response to upholding the constitutionality of housing codes and their enforcement, enforcement problems remain. In many cities a multiplicity of agencies deal with the problem: different agencies for different parts of the code, different agencies for new buildings, for old buildings, for administration, for compliance. Inspectors are inadequate in number and frequently are not well trained.[7] Inspections, re-inspections, orders, extension of time to comply with orders, partial compliance being equated with good faith and the hope that compliance may be obtained short of court proceedings all delay the time prior to imposition of judicial sanctions. Once in court, problems may become moot if tenants move. Since criminal sanctions are

3. 436 U.S. 307, 98 S.Ct. 1816, 56 L.Ed.2d 305 (1978).

4. Edwards v. Habib, 397 F.2d 687 (D.C.Cir.1968), cert. denied 393 U.S. 1016, 89 S.Ct. 618, 21 L.Ed.2d 560 (1969); Clore v. Fredman, 59 Ill.2d 20, 319 N.E.2d 18 (1974); S.P. Growers Ass'n. v. Rodriguez, 17 Cal.3d 719, 131 Cal.Rptr. 761, 552 P.2d 721 (1976); Voyager Village, Ltd. v. Williams, 3 Ohio App.3d 288, 444 N.E.2d 1337 (1982); Sims v. Century Kiest Apts., 567 S.W.2d 526 (Tex.Civ.App.1978); Wright v. Brady, 126 Idaho 671, 889 P.2d 105 (Idaho App. 1995). But see Hurricane v. Kanover, Ltd., 651 P.2d 1218 (Colo.1982, en banc). See also C.G.S.A. § 52–540a; Ill.—S.H.A. ch. 80, ¶ 71.

5. Retaliatory eviction can only be used as a defense for eviction if the eviction was in retaliation for reporting violations of laws or regulations which directly affect the leasehold. For example, reporting lessor's violations of antitrust laws did not support

lessee's defense of retaliatory eviction in subsequent action. Mobil Oil Corp. v. Rubenfeld, 48 A.D.2d 428, 370 N.Y.S.2d 943 (1975), order affirmed 40 N.Y.2d 936, 390 N.Y.S.2d 57, 358 N.E.2d 882 (1976), reargument denied 41 N.Y.2d 1009, 395 N.Y.S.2d 1027, 363 N.E.2d 1194 (1977).

6. See, e.g., Currier v. Pasadena City, 48 Cal.App.3d 810, 121 Cal.Rptr. 913 (1975), cert. denied 423 U.S. 1000, 96 S.Ct. 432, 46 L.Ed.2d 375 (1975); Cincinnati Bd. of Realtors, Inc. v. Cincinnati, 47 Ohio App.2d 267, 353 N.E.2d 898, 1 O.O.3d 341 (1975), judgment affirmed 46 Ohio St.2d 138, 346 N.E.2d 666 (1976); Wilson v. Cincinnati, 46 Ohio St.2d 138, 346 N.E.2d 666 (1976).

7. Howe, Code Enforcement in Three Cities: An Organizational Analysis, 13 Urb. Law. 65, 74 (1981). See also Comptroller General of the U.S., Enforcement of Housing Codes: How It Can Help Achieve the Nation's Housing Goal (1972).

involved, process may be difficult to serve, procedures are slow and the burden of proof difficult.

The courts have shown great reluctance to impose criminal sanctions for failure to comply with repair orders. Such penalties are neither effective nor do they create an economic incentive for the landowner to comply with the codes. As a result judicial proceedings are often suspended when the defendant shows some last minute efforts at compliance, sentences are suspended or fines when imposed, are small. Failure of the judiciary to impose jail sentences and the tendency to avoid stiff sanctions result in a system in which landowners include numerous petty fines in calculating their costs of doing business.[8]

While the courts are willing to broadly uphold the constitutionality of housing codes, they are not as willing to uphold convictions for violations. Courts are generally unwilling to force owners of housing to subsidize it or face criminal sanctions as the alternative.[9]

Municipalities are more frequently being held liable for negligent inspections of both new construction and existing housing, due to the erosion of sovereign immunity and the public duty doctrine.[10] In Manors of Inverrary XII Condominium Association v. Atreco–Florida, Inc.,[11] a Florida district court of appeal held that a building inspector's approval of a building permit and on-site inspections prior to issuance of a certificate of occupancy were operational, thus the sovereign immunity doctrine did not protect the municipality from liability for the negligence of the inspector in approving the plans, specifications, and construction, none of which met the requirements of the applicable building code.[12] The Wisconsin Supreme Court held a city liable for damages caused by fire because the inspector should have foreseen that his negligent inspection might result in harm.[13] After an inspection and recommendation for demolition of a building had been made but no action taken by the city or owner, when the building collapsed and two children were killed, a city in New York was found liable for failure to carry out its statutory duty.[14] The United States Supreme Court, in Block v. Neal[15] held Farmers Home Administration liable under the Tort Claims Act, for

---

8. See, e.g., Grad, New Sanctions and Remedies in Housing Code Enforcement, 3 Urb.Law. 577 (1971); Love, Landlord's Liability for Defective Premises, Caveat Lessee, Negligence or Strict Liability?, 49 Wis. L.Rev. 38 (1975).

9. See, e.g., People v. Rowen, 9 N.Y.2d 732, 214 N.Y.S.2d 347, 174 N.E.2d 331 (1961); Gribez & Grad, Housing Code Enforcement: Sanctions and Remedies, 66 Colum.L.Rev. 1254, 1271–72 (1966).

10. Stone & Rinker, Governmental Liability for Negligent Inspections, 57 Tul. L.Rev. 328 (1982). See Note, Municipal Liability for Negligent Building Inspection, 65 Iowa L.Rev. 1416 (1980).

11. 438 So.2d 490 (Fla.App.1983), petition for review dismissed 450 So.2d 485 (Fla.1984).

12. Id. at 494.

13. Coffey v. Milwaukee, 74 Wis.2d 526, 247 N.W.2d 132 (1976).

14. Runkel v. New York, 282 App.Div. 173, 123 N.Y.S.2d 485 (1953). See also Gannon Personnel Agency, Inc. v. New York, 57 A.D.2d 538, 394 N.Y.S.2d 5 (1977); Campbell v. Bellevue, 85 Wash.2d 1, 530 P.2d 234 (1975); compare Quinn v. Nadler Bros., Inc., 92 A.D.2d 1013, 461 N.Y.S.2d 455 (1983), order affirmed 59 N.Y.2d 914, 466 N.Y.S.2d 292, 453 N.E.2d 521 (1983).

15. 460 U.S. 289, 103 S.Ct. 1089, 75 L.Ed.2d 67 (1983).

failure to properly inspect a house during construction. Defects found in the house were attributable to the negligent inspection and did not fall within the misrepresentation exception to the Act. Government can be protected from the danger of excessive damages by enacting statutes which put a ceiling on the amount of damages recoverable against it.[16] The government can also be exempted from liability for failure to inspect or negligent inspection if the property is not owned by the government.[17]

Vacation and demolition orders are also sanctions. Vacation orders inconvenience tenants, and both vacation and demolition orders can lead to a reduction of the available housing stock. Though most housing codes have provisions allowing municipalities to put teeth into enforcement through vacate orders, receivership, municipal repair, demolition or denial of tax depreciation allowances, local governments are reluctant to use these mechanisms extensively.[18] Alternatively, there are some instances in which enforcement of housing codes is undertaken in a discriminatory manner.[19] Municipalities rarely collect enough money in fines to offset enforcement costs, and because expenses for code administration and enforcement come from general revenues there is seldom enough in public coffers to support public repair of housing code violations.

§ 8.8   Issuance of Building Permits and Certificates of Occupancy

Until recently, the issuance of building and certificate of occupancy permits was considered a non-discretionary or ministerial act.[1] The applicant was entitled to them as long as she had complied with applicable building codes and construction procedures.[2] Today, issuance is frequently made dependent upon compliance by the applicant with

---

16. See, e.g., West's Fla.Stat.Ann. § 768.28(5); Ill.—S.H.A. ch. 85, ¶ 2–102; Mont.Code Ann. §§ 2–9–101 to 2–9–105; Or.Rev.Stat. § 30.270; Utah Code Ann., §§ 63–30–22 & 63–30–34; Wis.Stat.Ann. § 893.80(3).

17. West's Ann.Cal. Gov't Code § 818.6; Ill.—S.H.A. ch. 85, ¶¶ 2–105 & 2–207; West's Ann.Ind. Code § 34–4–16.5–3(11); Nev.Rev.Stat. § 41.033; N.J.Stat. Ann. § 59:2–6; Utah Code Ann.1953, § 63–30–10(4).

18. J. Hartman, Housing and Social Policy 67 (1975). But see Devines v. Maier, 728 F.2d 876 (7th Cir.1984), cert. denied 469 U.S. 836, 105 S.Ct. 130, 83 L.Ed.2d 71 (1984).

19. See, e.g., Espanola Way Corp. v. Meyerson, 690 F.2d 827 (11th Cir.1982), cert. denied 460 U.S. 1039, 103 S.Ct. 1431, 75 L.Ed.2d 791 (1983); Amen v. Dearborn, 718 F.2d 789 (6th Cir.1983), cert. denied 465 U.S. 1101, 104 S.Ct. 1596, 80 L.Ed.2d 127 (1984).

§ 8.8

1. Prentiss v. City of South Pasadena, 15 Cal.App.4th 85, 18 Cal.Rptr.2d 641 (1993) (California Environmental Quality Act did not apply as issuance of building permit free of historical architectural conditions was a "ministerial project"); Incorporated Village of Atlantic Beach v. Gavalas, 81 N.Y.2d 322, 615 N.E.2d 608, 599 N.Y.S.2d 218 (1993) (building permit issuance was not an agency action for which an Environmental Impact Statement was required under State Environmental Quality Review Act since underlying ordinance did not entrust municipal building inspector with type of discretion which would allow grant or denial to be based on environmental concerns).

2. Daniel J. Curtin, Jr., California Land Use and Planning Law 194 (17th ed.1997).

numerous other requirements—especially those requiring the payment of infrastructure finance regulatory payments such as impact and linkage fees. The issuance of these permits has thus become a focal point of the enforcement and implementation of various growth management programs.[3]

3. See § 9.8 infra.

Chapter 9

GROWTH MANAGEMENT

Analysis

---

§ 9.1 The Growth Management Concept

The traditional land use control devices—zoning and subdivision control—have always had at least a potential effect on the growth rate and patterns of those local governmental entities which employ them. For example, zoning codes which include density allocations for the permitted use zones set a theoretical maximum population figure for the jurisdiction. Subdivision control ordinances likewise affect allowable population limits and the speed at which development occurs by setting minimum lot sizes and requiring construction of capital facilities before plat approval can be obtained or before building permits will be issued. Nonetheless, controlling the maximum population of a community and the rate at which growth will occur is at best a minor goal of traditional zoning and subdivision control ordinances.[1]

---

§ 9.1

1. The Douglas Commission recognized the limitations of traditional zoning techniques in 1968. See The National Commission on Urban Problems, Building the American City (1968); The National Com-

The growth management plans which came in vogue in the 1970's and 1980's utilized many traditional land use control techniques but for the primary purpose of regulating the pace and extent of growth.[2] Thus, the issues of how much growth should occur and *when* it should occur became as important as the traditional height, bulk and use aspects of Euclidean zoning's preoccupation with *where* development will be permitted.

The decision of various communities to manage growth has been prompted by a variety of interrelated factors—many laudable and some suspect. Key factors include concern for the effects of growth on environmentally sensitive areas and scarce environmental resources,[3] crowding of public facilities, the economic and social effects of the energy crisis of the 1970's and the steady decrease of non-renewable energy stores, the decrease of federal money allocations to local and state governments for a wide variety of land use and public facilities programs, the high unemployment rate in the late 1970's and early 1980's, and an acceleration of the rate of growth in the so-called "sunbelt" states. However one evaluates these factors, the growth management movement of recent years has had the effect of making land use planning and control law a more popular and controversial topic at the grass roots level than it has ever been before. "Manage Growth", "Stop Growth", "Make Growth Pay For Itself", and "Support the Population Cap" have become familiar bumper sticker slogans. There is little if any doubt that exclusionary motives including even racial and economic discrimination lurk behind some of the proposals[4] but at the very least the controversies which envelope nearly all growth control proposals have brought much needed public interest and attention to the land use planning and control process. In fact, it seems quite possible that growth management provides the primary theme and coherence for land use regulation and environmental protection as we enter the twenty-first century.[5]

mission on Urban Problems, Alternatives to Urban Sprawl (Res. Report No. 15, 1968).

2. An extensive overview and analysis of these programs and their legal implications are found in the Urban Land Institute's Management and Control of Growth Series, to wit: Urban Land Institute, Management and Control of Growth Vol. I (1975), Vol. II (1975), Vol. III (1975), Vol. IV (1978); Urban Land Institute, The Permit Explosion: Coordination of the Proliferation (1976); Urban Land Institute, Growth and Change in Rural America (1979).

3. See Freilich and Davis, Saving the Land: The Utilization of Modern Techniques of Growth Management to Preserve Rural and Agricultural America, 13 Urb. Law. 27 (1981).

4. The "wolf of exclusionary zoning hides under the environmental sheepskin worn by the stop-growth movement." Bosselman, Can the Town of Ramapo Pass a Law to Bind the Rights of the Whole World?, 1 Fla.St.U.L.Rev. 234, 249 (1973). See D. Godschalk, D. Brower, L. McBennett, B. Vestal & D. Herr, Constitutional Issues of Growth Management, ch. 6 (1979); Cutler, Legal and Illegal Means for Controlling Community Growth on the Urban Fringe, 1961 Wis. L. Rev. 370; Fischel, Exclusionary Zoning and Growth Controls: A Comment on the APA's Endorsement of the Mount Laurel Southern Burlington County NAACP v. Township of Mount Laurel Doctrine, 40 Wash U.J.Urb. & Contemp.L. 65 (1991); Galowitz, Interstate Metro–Regional Responses to Exclusionary Zoning, 27 Real Prop. Prob. & T.J. 49 (1992); Meck and Tucker, A Response to William F. Fischel, 40 Wash. U.J.Urb. & Contemp.Law 75 (1991).

5. See § 1.3 supra.

In looking ahead, it should be noted that three interrelated concepts are becoming intertwined with the concept of growth management: carrying capacity, impact analysis and sustainable development. The origin of all of these sometimes overlapping concepts is environmental law.

"Carrying capacity" is used to determine environmental criteria upon which to ground land use decisions and refers to the extent to which land in its natural or current state can be developed without destruction of the ecosystem.[6]

"Impact analysis" in its current usage is no doubt a transfer of the concepts involved in environmental impact studies conducted pursuant to environmental protection statutes.[7] Generally today, carrying capacity is just one way of evaluating the impact of development.

The seminal conceptual examination of impact analysis was done by Fred Bosselman, who defined impact analysis as "the process of examining a particular land development proposal and analyzing the impact it will have on a community."[8] Bosselman suggests that the acceptance of impact analysis techniques reflects two trends in government policy toward land use regulation:[9]

(1) Regulation should respond to specific development proposals: The policy that the formulation of land use controls should be delayed until the developer's intentions are known has been reflected in the weakening of legal support for the principle that a developer should be entitled to develop if his proposal is consistent with pre-established regulations adopted pursuant to a comprehensive plan.

(2) Development standards should be predictable: The policy that a greater degree of predictability ought to be found in the local process of responding to development proposals, has been reflected in the increasing uneasiness of courts toward local regulations that lack a "scientific" basis.

---

6. The term "carrying capacity" is also sometimes used to refer to the ability of the infrastructure in a given area to support new development: for example the excess or unused sewage treatment or water treatment capacity of the existing private and/or governmental facilities. See Juergensmeyer and Wadley, Florida Land Use and Growth Management Law, Ch. 22.

For a discussion of Monroe County's (Florida) use of carrying capacity in its comprehensive plan, see Grosso, Florida's Growth Management Act: How Far We Have Come, and How Far We Have Yet to Go, 20 Nova L. Rev. 589 (1996); see also Rothrock, Oregon's Goal Five: Is Ecologically Sustainable Development Reflected, 31 Williamette L. Rev. 449 (1995); Tarlock, Local Government Protection for Biodiver-

sity: What is Its Niche?, 60 Chi. L. Rev. 555 (1993).

7. See §§ 11.2–.5 infra. See also, Schaenman & Muller, Land Development: Measuring the Impacts, Urban Land Institute, Management and Control of Growth, Vol. II 494 (1975); Gruen, Gruen & Associates, The Impacts of Growth: An Analytical Framework and Fiscal Example, Id. at 512; Fiscal Impact: Methods and Issues, Id. at 534; Ashley Economic Services, The Fiscal Impact of Urban Growth, Id. at 543; Real Estate Research Corp., The Costs of Sprawl: Detailed Cost Analysis, Id. at 577.

8. Bosselman, Linkage, Mitigation and Transfer: Will Impact Analysis Become the Universal Antidote to Land Use Complaints? (1985).

9. Id. at 2.

The use of impact analysis in regard to infrastructure funding is discussed below.[10] Three even newer ways of translating the impact analysis concept into land use regulation are "linkage," "mitigation," and "transfer." Again, Fred Bosselman has provided the definitions and examples:

linkage is a system by which a developer who wants to build one thing is required to also build something else; e.g., an office developer is required to build housing

mitigation is a system by which a developer who will cause some adverse environmental impact is required to counterbalance that impact by creating an equivalent benefit; e.g., a project that will destroy wetlands is required to create equivalent wetlands elsewhere

transfer is a system by which a certain type or degree of development is made conditional on the extinguishment of an equivalent right to undertake such development elsewhere; e.g., a height increase is made contingent on acquisition of air rights over a historic structure somewhere else.

Although the future course of growth management is far from certain, concentration on the impact of development would seem to be an essential ingredient of any growth management program.[11]

"Sustainable development," in its broadest context, is a concept of social change in which the population and intended functions of a community can be maintained into the indefinite future without degrading community institutions, the means of production, systems of infrastructure, the resource base, and natural and man-made environments. Sustainable development embraces the environment as a mainstream scientific and economic factor in all policy, planning, and decision-making. The concept has been applied in a variety of contexts and to denote a wide range of issues, including urban sprawl, new economic development, inner-city and "brownfield" redevelopment, local small business, a strong local economy, environmental justice, ecosystem management, resource recycling, agriculture, biodiversity, lifestyles, "green" buildings, energy conservation, and pollution prevention.[12]

While the terms "sustainable" and "development" each have a variety of meanings alone, together they are apt to suggest many varying ideas to the people who employ them. Thus, the implementation of sustainable development initiatives is problematic. Nonetheless, the concept is increasingly a subject of intense discussion among policy-makers and community groups, and is likely to remain an issue in land use planning in the twenty-first century, and thus to become an additional concern for land use planning and control law, particularly in the area of growth management.[13]

10. See § 9.7 infra.

11. Bosselman, supra note 8, at 3.

12. See generally, Symposium on Sustainable Development, 31 Willamette L.Rev., 261, Issue #2 (1995).

13. See Rothrock and Tarlock articles,

§ 9.2 Growth Management Programs

Land use control planners and attorneys are still searching for effective and permissible ways of formulating and implementing growth management programs. Several signals have emerged.[1] The most important of these is that "timed" or "phased" growth control measures are more palatable for courts and the electorate than population caps. One early commentator identified and discussed five primary motivations for regulating the timing of urban development: (1) to economize on the costs of municipal facilities and services; (2) to retain municipal control over the eventual character of development; (3) to maintain a desirable degree of balance among various uses of land; (4) to achieve greater detail and specificity in development regulations; and (5) to maintain a high quality of community services and facilities.[2]

The first major victory before the courts for pro-growth management forces occurred in litigation contesting the phased growth plan developed by Ramapo, New York. This plan used a residential development timing technique for the avowed purpose of eliminating premature subdivision, urban sprawl, and development without adequate municipal facilities and services. The plan did not rezone or reclassify any land into different residential or use districts but provided that any person engaged in residential development must obtain a special permit.

> The standards for the issuance of special permits are framed in terms of the availability to the proposed subdivision plat of five essential facilities or services, specifically: (1) public sanitary sewers or approved substitutes; (2) drainage facilities; (3) improved public parks or recreation facilities, including public schools; (4) State, county, or town roads—major, secondary, or collector; and (5) firehouses. No special permit shall issue unless the proposed residential development has accumulated 15 development points, to be computed on a sliding scale of values assigned to the specified improvements under the statute.[3]

supra, note 6.

§ 9.2

1. See generally DeGrove, Balanced Growth: A Planning Guide for Local Government (1991); Kelly, Managing Growth: Policies, Techniques, and Impacts (1993); Bollens, State Growth Management: Intergovernmental Frameworks and Policy Objectives, 58 J. Am. Planning Ass'n 454 (1992) (examining state growth programs in 13 states).

2. Fagin, Regulating the Timing of Urban Development, 20 Law & Contemp. Prob. 298 (1955). See also, Freilich and White, Transportation Congestion and Growth Management: Comprehensive Approaches to Resolving America's Major Quality of Life Crisis, 24 Loy. L.A.L. Rev. 915 (1991).

3. Golden v. Planning Board of Town of Ramapo, 30 N.Y.2d 359, 368, 334 N.Y.S.2d 138, 285 N.E.2d 291 (1972), appeal dismissed 409 U.S. 1003, 93 S.Ct. 436, 34 L.Ed.2d 294 (1972). See Bosselman, Can the Town of Ramapo Pass a Law to Bind the Rights of the Whole World?, 1 Fla.St. U.L.Rev. 234 (1973).

For commentary on the Ramapo plan and its techniques, see 2 Management and Control of Growth (Scott ed., 1975). In addition to the Bosselman article, this volume includes The Ramapo Case: Five Commentaries, Id. at 32; Silverman, A Return to the Walled Cities: Ramapo As an Imperium in Imperio, Id. at 52; and Franklin, Controlling Urban Growth: But for Whom? Id. at 78. See also Rohan, 1 Zoning and Land Use Controls § 4.05 (1984); Elliot and Marcus, From Euclid to Ramapo: New Directions in

A developer, by agreeing to provide those improvements that would bring the proposed plat within the number of development points needed could advance the date of subdivision approval. Also applications to the "Development Easement Acquisition Commission" for a reduction in assessed valuation were authorized.

In essence the "timed" or "phased" growth programs, like Ramapo's, generally limit the number of residential and/or commercial units which can be built in a specified period of time. Along with the Ramapo, New York, plan, other prototypes for this approach were developed in Florida,[4] and Colorado.[5] These programs are generally tied to the availability of public services and capital improvements. Sometimes a point system is established according to which a developer or the parcel of land sought to be developed must have a certain number of points before development is allowed. Points are earned or awarded on the basis of availability of public services and/or design criteria.[6]

A second type of growth management program is the "population cap."[7] Under the population cap approach the local government entity sets the maximum number of dwelling units which will be allowed to be built in the jurisdiction. Perhaps the most famous of these is the Boca Raton plan in Florida.[8] Equally famous, though somewhat different, is the Petaluma plan in California,[9] which set a cap on the number of dwelling units that could be built within a five-year period.

Land Development Controls, 1 Hofstra L. Rev. 56 (1973); Emanuel, Ramapo's Managed Growth Program: After Five Years Experience in 3 Management and Control of Growth 302 (Scott ed., 1975); Urbanczyk, Note, Phased Zoning: Regulation of the Tempo and Sequence of Land Development, 26 Stan. L. Rev. 585 (1974); Note, A Zoning Program for Phased Growth: Ramapo Township's Time Controls on Residential Development, 47 N.Y.U.L. Rev. 723 (1972).

4. See Juergensmeyer and Wadley, Florida Land Use and Growth Management Law, Ch. 19 (Looseleaf); D. Godschalk, D. Brower, L. McBennett, B. Vestal & D. Herr, Constitutional Issues of Growth Management, ch. 20 (Sanibel, FL) (1979).

5. See, Godschalk et al, supra note 4, ch. 18 (Boulder, CO). See Robinson v. Boulder, 190 Colo. 357, 547 P.2d 228 (1976).

6. The refinement of the "point system" is usually attributed to attorney Kirk Wickersham, Jr. See Wickersham, The Permit System of Managing Land Use and Growth, Urban Land Institute, Management and Control of Growth, Vol. IV (1978).

In 1983, the Town of Ramapo eliminated the point system due to slow growth rates in the New York Metropolitan area. See Geneslaw and Raymond, Planning (June 1983) at 8.

7. See § 9.3 infra note 2. See also Lamm and Davison, Legal Control of Population Growth and Distribution in a Quality Environment: The Land Use Alternative, 49 Denver L.J. 1 (1972).

8. See City of Boca Raton v. Boca Villas, 371 So.2d 154 (Fla.App.1979), cert. denied 381 So.2d 765 (Fla.1980). Juergensmeyer and Wadley, supra note 4, § 19.09; Godschalk et al., supra note 4, ch. 19 (Boca Raton, FL).

9. See Construction Industry Association of Sonoma County v. Petaluma, 375 F.Supp. 574 (N.D.Cal.1974), reversed 522 F.2d 897 (9th Cir.1975), cert. denied 424 U.S. 934, 96 S.Ct. 1148, 47 L.Ed.2d 342 (1976); Godschalk et al., supra note 4, ch. 17 (Petaluma, CA).

Representative "anti" and "pro" Petaluma articles are collected in 2 Management and Control of Growth (Scott ed., 1975). They include Hart, The Petaluma Case, Id. at 127; Gray, The City of Petaluma: Residential Development Control, Id. at 149; Gruen, The Economics of Petaluma: Unconstitutional Regional Socio–Economic Impacts, Id. at 173; Misuraca, Petaluma v. The T.J. Hooper: Must the Suburbs be Seaworthy?, Id. at 187.

A third form of growth control delineates the area or areas for staged future urban growth, outside of which urban development is restricted, deferred, or prohibited.[10] The provision of municipal services usually occurs only within the boundaries of the growth areas. The state planning programs of Oregon[11] and Minnesota[12] provide for such urban growth boundaries.[13]

A fourth approach to growth control is to forego the establishment of ultimate or periodic numbers but to avoid, deter, or overcome many problems associated with growth by conditioning the issuance of building permits or plat approval on the existence of public improvements and capital facilities or requiring that developers pay fees which will be used by the proper governmental authority to provide the roads, schools, parks, sewer and water facilities, and/or police protection which will be needed because of the new development.[14] This approach is often referred to as a "Concurrency Requirement,"[15] or an adequate public facilities (often referred to as APF) requirement.[16]

Developing along with these various approaches to growth management are the increased usage of the so-called "temporary" growth control measures such as development moratoria and withheld municipal services.[17]

Of the four approaches, programs employing concurrency or adequate public facilities requirements have been identified by one commentator as "the most basic, most useful and most easily defensible."[18] It is important, however, that any determinations of adequacy or inadequacy of the public facilities be rational, preferably having some quantifiable

---

10. See generally Easley, American Planning Ass'n, Planning Advisory Service Rep. No. 440, Staying Inside the Lines: Urban Growth Boundaries (1992); Epstein, Where Yards are Wide: Have Land Use Planning and Law Gone Astray?, 21 Wm & Mary Envtl. L. & Pol'y Rev. 345 (1997).

11. See Or.Rev.Stat. § 199.410; see also Knapp and Nelson, The Regulated Landscape: Lessons on State Land Use Planning from Oregon, Ch. 2 (1992).

12. See Minn.Stat.Ann. § 473.861 (requiring a regional urban growth area for a five county area around metropolitan Minneapolis and St. Paul).

13. Washington requires designation of areas within which urban growth will not be permitted. See Wash.Rev. Code Ann. § 36.70A.110(1).

14. See §§ 9.5, 9.6, 9.7 infra.

15. Florida imposes "concurrency" requirements as part of its mandatory state planning law: "public facilities and services needed to support development shall be concurrent with the impacts of such development...." Fla. Stat. Ann. § 163.3177(10)(h). See Boggs and Apgar,

Concurrency and Growth Management: A Lawyer's Primer, 7 J. Land Use & Envtl.L. 1 (1991); Pelham, Adequate Facilities Requirements: Reflections on Florida's Concurrency System for Managing Growth, 19 Fla.St.U.L.Rev. 973 (1992). See generally Robertson, Concurrency and its Relation to Growth Management, 20 Nova L.Rev. 891 (1996).

16. In 1990, Washington began requiring local governments to link development approval and provision of facilities. Wash. Rev. Code Ann., ch. 36.70A. See Smith, Planning for Growth, Washington Style, in State and Regional Comprehensive Planning: Implementing New Models for Growth Management (Buchsbaum and Smith eds., 1993); Walsh and Pearce, The Concurrency Requirement of the Washington State Growth Management Act, U. Puget Sound L. Rev. 1025 (1993).

17. See §§ 9.5 and 9.6 infra; Layman, Concurrency and Moratoria, 71 Fla. B.J. 49 (Jan. 1997).

18. Kelly, Zoning and Land Use Controls, § 4.01[2] (1996); See also Pelham supra note 15.

basis upon which the determinations are made,[19] to insure that the program is well designed, that deficiencies are accurately identified, and that new development will in fact be served by the provision of the required facilities.[20] This approach allows local governments to establish a direct causal link to fundamental health, safety and welfare issues related to essential public facilities. In addition, it allows the developer to assess the feasibility of curing the inadequacies if necessary for development to proceed.

Negotiation between regulatory agencies and developers is one of the hallmarks of growth management programs—especially those based on the fourth approach. Also, it is one of the characteristics which distinguishes growth management from traditional zoning oriented land use regulation.[21] In many jurisdictions negotiation is based on practice or on the nature of the infrastructure finance requirements or point systems approaches that form a part of the jurisdiction's growth management program. A few jurisdictions, however, have provided statutory framework for negotiation through the enactment of Development Agreements Acts.[22]

A "Development Agreement"[23] is a voluntary, bargained for, agreement entered into between a developer and a land use control authority—usually a local government. Conceptually, it combines contract and police power based regulatory principles. The primary purpose of the agreement from the developer's perspective is to vest her rights to develop in exchange for promises made to the local government in regard to infrastructure finance, clustering, maintenance of open space, environmental mitigation, design, or other obligations. The local government agrees to "freeze" its regulations for an extended period of time in order to get the developer committed on one or more of the points just mentioned. Development agreements are discussed in detail in § 5.31, above.

Practically all of the land use regulation and control concepts discussed in this Hornbook can be of service to the diversity of approaches to growth management.[24] Moratoria, withheld or delayed gov-

---

19. For helpful practitioners' references see generally Brevard, Capital Facilities Planning (1993); Kelly, Managing Community Growth: Policies, Techniques and Impacts (1993). See also DeChiara and Koppelman, Manual of Housing/Planning and Design Criteria (facility needs for housing); Transportation Research Board, The Highway Capacity Manual (1985) (road capacities); National Recreation and Park Ass'n, Recreation, Park and Open Space Standards and Guidelines (Lancaster, ed., 1983).

20. See Pelham, supra note 15, at 1016–20; see also Durden, Layman, and Ansbacher, Waiting for the Go: Concurrency, Takings, and the Property Rights Act, 20 Nova L.Rev. 661 (1996).

21. Consider, for example, the traditional prohibition of contract zoning. See § 5.11, supra.

22. Citations to the statutes may be found supra at § 5.31, note 31.

23. See Development Agreements: Practice, Policy and Prospects, (Porter and Marsh, eds.,1989); Johnson and Ziegler, Development Agreements: Analysis, Colorado Case Studies, Commentary, Rocky Mountain Land Use Institute (1993); Curtin, Development Agreement Practice in California and Other States, 22 Stetson L.Rev. 761 (1993); Juergensmeyer & Wadley, Florida Land Use and Growth Management Law Ch.8 (1997).

24. See 1 Management and Control of Growth 24–31 (Scott ed., 1975) for an extensive list of regulatory concepts.

ernmental services, infrastructure financing, impact fees, transferable development rights, carrying capacity, impact analysis, and sustainable development will be highlighted in this chapter. Nonetheless, other concepts such as farmland preservation, building codes, building permits, comprehensive planning, conditional zoning, transferable development rights, easements, eminent domain, environmental controls, height restrictions, historic districts, holding zones, planned unit developments, subdivision control, and zoning may be employed to manage urban growth. As consulting the index will indicate, these other concepts are explored at greater length throughout this Hornbook.

§ 9.3   Power of Local Government to Establish Growth Management Programs

To the extent that a unit of local government uses traditional land use control measures such as zoning or subdivision control or minor variations thereof, the "power" issue is no different nor more difficult than that encountered by local governments in other land use planning and control activities. The police power automatically possessed by the local government on home rule power theories or specifically delegated to it pursuant to zoning enabling acts suffices.[1]

Many growth management programs and devices, however, involve often controversial approaches and tools, relatively new to land development control. The small number of decisions emanating from the courts of last resort in most jurisdictions coupled with scant guidance on some of the most basic federal constitutional issues from the United States Supreme Court leave planners and attorneys with inadequate guidance.[2]

The lack of clear judicial precedent has led many local governments to seek special legislative delegation or approval from their state legislatures. Still another approach employed by units of local government to buttress the legal status of their growth management activities is to submit their growth management plans or policies to the referendum by the electorate.[3]

The use of a referendum in this area seems to stem from the decision of the Supreme Court of the United States in James v. Valtierra.[4] In this 1971 decision, the Supreme Court reversed a three-judge panel's holding that article 34 of the California Constitution which required voter approval of proposed low rent housing projects violated equal protection principles. The Court refused to impose the compelling state interest criteria because it found that article 34 made no distinc-

---

§ 9.3

1. See generally, ch. 3 supra; Juergensmeyer and Gragg, Limiting Population Growth in Florida and the Nation: The Constitutional Issues, 26 U.Fla.L.Rev. 758 (1974).

2. See D. Godschalk, D. Brower, L. McBennett, B. Vestal & D. Herr, Constitutional Issues of Growth Management (1979); Bosselman, Growth Management and Constitutional Rights—Part I: The Blessing of Quiet Seclusion, 8 Urb. L. Ann. 3 (1974).

3. See Juergensmeyer and Gragg, supra note 1.

4. 402 U.S. 137, 91 S.Ct. 1331, 28 L.Ed.2d 678 (1971).

tion based on race, and declined to extend the compelling state interest test to classifications based on wealth. The Court placed great stress on the referendum as a procedure for democratic decision-making, saying, "[R]eferendums demonstrate devotion to democracy, not to bias, discrimination, or prejudice."[5]

Taking the lead from this statement, the idea developed that submission of a growth management program to referendum and voter approval helps insulate such programs from equal protection, "exclusionary", discriminatory and related attacks. The Petaluma, Sanibel and Boca Raton plans were submitted to referendum and approved by the electorate. The first two have survived attack in the courts and the third has not.[6]

Another source of power for local governments to practice growth management stems from state legislative and constitutional environmental protection provisions. Florida, Illinois, Massachusetts, Michigan, Montana, New Mexico, New York, North Carolina, Pennsylvania, Rhode Island and Virginia have provisions in their state constitution guaranteeing their citizens a healthful environment.[7] Arguably a local government is required by such constitutional provisions or the state statutes implementing them to exercise their land use control powers in such a way as to protect environmentally sensitive land or endangered resources. This "duty" might be used as a justification of at least some elements of a growth management program. The court decisions at this point are sparse and indecisive.

A final justification for growth management by a unit of local government may be founded on mandated local government planning. As discussed elsewhere,[8] Florida's local governments are required to engage in comprehensive planning and to exercise their land use control powers consistently with those plans. The elements required to be included in the comprehensive plans inevitably raise growth management issues. A Florida court has held that the Local Government Comprehensive Planning Act which mandates the comprehensive planning also constitutes a source of power for local governments since all of their actions must be consistent with their plans.[9]

§ 9.4 Limitations on the Power of Local Governments to Establish Growth Management Programs

The leading publication dealing with constitutional issues and growth control lists the following federal constitutional challenges to

5. Id. at 143; see also City of Eastlake v. Forest City Enterprises, 426 U.S. 668, 96 S.Ct. 2358, 49 L.Ed.2d 132 (1976), on remand 48 Ohio St.2d 47, 356 N.E.2d 499 (1976).

6. See § 9.2 supra. On the subject of referenda in land use control, see § 3.10 and § 5.5 supra.

7. See generally Godschalk, supra note 2, ch. 8.

8. See supra §§ 2.12–2.13.

9. Home Builders and Contractors Association v. Board of County Commissioners of Palm Beach County, 446 So.2d 140 (Fla. App.1983), cert. denied 451 So.2d 848 (Fla. 1984).

growth management programs: (1) the general due process challenge, (2) the taking challenge, (3) the regional welfare challenge, (4) the equal protection challenge, and (5) the right to travel challenges.[1]

Growth management programs are land use planning and control activities and are therefore exercises of the police power just as much as is zoning or subdivision control. The general limitations which apply to all exercises of the police power apply to growth management. There is an especially close parallel between the limitations placed upon exclusionary zoning activities and the potential limitations placed on growth management programs. These general and specific limitations are discussed elsewhere.[2]

Several constitutional hurdles that growth management programs must survive that manifest themselves a bit differently in a growth control controversy than in a regular zoning dispute include the arguments that growth control measures constitute takings or are denials of substantive due process or equal protection. They are discussed elsewhere.[3]

A constitutional claim worth attention here is the constitutional right to travel, which is sometimes raised as an objection to growth controls. When local government limits growth, the argument goes, fewer houses are built and some people are excluded from settling in the town.[4] Professor Siegan, for example, believes that "[e]recting barriers to travel and occupancy interferes with a free society's ideals of mobility and opportunity * * *."[5] Absent a vital and pressing need, which he finds generally lacking, growth controls should not be allowed.[6]

The courts, however, have not found that growth controls improperly impinge on a right to travel, or more specifically, a right to migrate to

§ 9.4

1. See D. Godschalk, D. Brower, L. McBennett, B. Vestal & D. Herr, Constitutional Issues of Growth Management (1979). The following, slightly more comprehensive list which also includes potential state constitutional issues is found in Juergensmeyer and Wadley, Florida Land Use and Growth Management Law § 19.01:

1. Violation of constitutional home rule power.

2. Violation of substantive due process under the federal constitution.

3. Violation of police power as a taking of property.

4. Violation of equal protection.

5. Violation of right to travel.

2. See supra § 6.6.

3. See Ch. 10 infra (§ 10.8B regarding growth control moratoria; § 10.12, substantive due process, and § 10.14, equal protection). See generally, Juergensmeyer and Gragg, Limiting Population Growth in Flor-

ida and the Nation: The Constitutional Issues, 26 U.Fla.L.Rev. 758 (1974); see also Bosselman, Growth Management and Constitutional Rights—Part I: The Blessing of Quiet Seclusion, 8 Urb. L. Ann. 3 (1974); Lamm and Davison, Legal Control of Population Growth and Distribution in a Quality Environment: The Land Use Alternative, 49 Denver L.J. 1 (1972); Denny, Note, That Old Due Process Magic: Growth Control and the Federal Constitution, 88 Mich. L. Rev. 1245 (1990); Stone and Seymour, Regulating the Timing of Development: Takings Clause and Substantive Due Process Challenges to Growth Control Regulations, 24 Loy.L.A.L.Rev. 1205 (1991).

4. See also Denny, Note, That Old Due Process Magic: Growth Control and the Federal Constitution, 88 Mich.L.Rev.1245, 1275 (1990)(arguing for right of unburdened interstate travel).

5. Siegan, Conserving and Developing the Land, 27 San Diego L.Rev. 279, 284 (1990).

6. Id.

another state, or to a particular community within a state. The Supreme Court of California rejected a right to travel objection to an ordinance that prohibited the issuance of building permits until the city met its infrastructure needs.[7] The court reasoned that since "[m]ost zoning and land use ordinances affect population growth and density, to insist that such zoning laws are invalid unless the interests supporting the exclusion are compelling in character * * * would result in wholesale invalidation of land use controls and endanger the validity of city and regional planning."[8]

The right to travel is one of those "doctrinal messes" in constitutional law.[9] The parameters of the right are unclear. The Supreme Court has used it to strike down residency requirements that affect one's ability to vote and obtain welfare benefits,[10] but refused to find that it bars residency requirements for divorce.[11] Its source in the constitution is disputed. It may be the equal protection clause, the privileges and immunities clause, the commerce clause, or possibly the substantive protection afforded by the due process clause.[12] The level of scrutiny applied is not settled. Those who assert the right often characterize it as a fundamental right, seeking strict scrutiny, but in some cases lower scrutiny has been used. Finally, courts differ over whether the right is applicable only to interstate travel, or also reaches intrastate travel.[13]

It is doubtful that the Supreme Court would find a growth control to violate the constitution.[14] In the first place, showing the requisite standing to raise a right to travel argument under the Court's restrictive standing rules applicable to zoning challenges would be difficult.[15] Secondly, and on the merits, the Court has upheld other types of zoning

---

7. Associated Home Builders of Greater Eastbay, Inc. v. City of Livermore, 18 Cal.3d 582, 557 P.2d 473, 135 Cal.Rptr. 41 (1976). See also In re Township of Warren, 247 N.J.Super. 146, 588 A.2d 1227 (1991) (occupancy preference to residents for lower income housing units did not infringe upon constitutional right to travel); Texas Manufactured Housing Ass'n, Inc. v. City of Nederland, 905 F.Supp. 371, 380 (E.D.Tex. 1995), aff'd 101 F.3d 1095 (5th Cir.1996); cert denied ___ U.S. ___, 117 S.Ct. 2497, 138 L.Ed.2d 1003 (1997); CEEED v. California Coastal Zone Conservation Commission, 43 Cal.App.3d 306, 118 Cal.Rptr. 315 (1974).

8. Id., *Livermore,* 18 Cal.3d 582, 557 P.2d 473, 485, 135 Cal.Rptr. 41, 53.

9. See generally Zubler, The Right to Migrate and Welfare Reform: Time for Shapiro v. Thompson to Take a Hike, 31 Val. Univ.L.Rev. 893 (1997).

10. Dunn v. Blumstein, 405 U.S. 330, 336, 92 S.Ct. 995, 999, 31 L.Ed.2d 274 (1972) (right to vote in state elections on equal basis with other citizens); Shapiro v.

Thompson, 394 U.S. 618, 89 S.Ct. 1322, 22 L.Ed.2d 600 (1969) (welfare benefits).

11. Sosna v. Iowa, 419 U.S. 393, 95 S.Ct. 553, 42 L.Ed.2d 532 (1975).

12. Shapiro v. Thompson, 394 U.S. 618, 89 S.Ct. 1322, 22 L.Ed.2d 600 (1969) (equal protection); Edwards v. California, 314 U.S. 160, 62 S.Ct. 164, 86 L.Ed. 119 (1941) (invalidated state law against bringing nonresident indigents into state under commerce clause); Lutz v. City of York, 899 F.2d 255 (3d Cir.1990) (substantive due process). See also Note, That Old Due Process Magic: Growth Control and the Federal Constitution, 88 Mich.L.Rev.1245 (1990) (arguing the privileges and immunities and commerce clause be used).

13. Lutz v. City of York, 899 F.2d 255 (3d Cir.1990) (recognizing right to intrastate travel but holding anti-crusing ordinance valid under intermediate scrutiny).

14. See Denny, supra note 3, at 1276 (agreeing that it is unlikely that Court would apply strict scrutiny to such a challenge).

15. See infra § 10.14D.

ordinances that have similar potential exclusionary effects. In Village of Belle Terre v. Boraas,[16] the Court rejected the argument that a village's narrow definition of "single-family" for zoning purposes violated the right to travel of a group of unrelated college students from living together. In Village of Arlington Heights v. Metropolitan Housing Development Corp.,[17] the Court implicitly endorsed economic exclusionary zoning when it upheld the exclusion of multi-family housing from a suburb of Chicago. While *Arlington Heights* specifically addressed, and found wanting, the claim that the application of the ordinance violated the equal protection clause due to its racially discriminatory effect, the Court ignored the possibility that the ordinance affected other rights.

One short-lived success for the right to travel argument came when the district court in the *Petaluma* case found that city's quota on housing violated the right to travel.[18] The Ninth Circuit, however, overturned the decision on appeal, finding the plaintiff builder's association lacked standing to raise the rights of unknown third parties.[19] State courts interpreting state constitutions may differ. Though it has not styled it as a right to travel, the Pennsylvania Supreme Court's decision in National Land & Investment Co. v. Kohn[20] limits local zoning that affects the ability of persons living in the region to move to a community.

§ 9.5 Growth Management Techniques: Moratoria and Interim Controls.

Moratoria are legally authorized periods for the delay or abeyance of some activity. The adoption of a building permit or development approval moratorium is an increasingly frequently used approach by local governments to halt or slow growth until new growth management programs, new comprehensive plans and/or new zoning ordinances can be adopted and implemented. At times, an interim zoning ordinance is also adopted.[1]

The "power" of local governments to adopt moratoria or interim regulations is far from settled. Some cases focus on the precise delega-

---

16. 416 U.S. 1, 7, 94 S.Ct. 1536, 39 L.Ed.2d 797 (1974).

17. 429 U.S. 252, 263, 97 S.Ct. 555, 562, 50 L.Ed.2d 450 (1977).

18. See discussion of *Petaluma*, supra § 9.2.

19. Construction Industry Ass'n of Sonoma County v. City of Petaluma, 375 F.Supp. 574 (N.D.Cal.1974), rev'd, 522 F.2d 897 (9th Cir.1975), cert. denied 424 U.S. 934, 96 S.Ct. 1148, 47 L.Ed.2d 342 (1976). See also Northern Illinois Home Builders Ass'n, Inc. v. County of Du Page, 165 Ill.2d 25, 208 Ill.Dec. 328, 649 N.E.2d 384, 397 (1995) (developer lacked standing).

20. 419 Pa. 504, 215 A.2d 597 (1965), discussed in more detail supra § 6.2.

§ 9.5

1. See supra § 3.20A and § 5.28G. See generally, Freilich, Interim Development Controls: Essential Tools for Implementing Flexible Planning and Zoning, 49 J.Urb.Law 65 (1971); Freilich, Development Timing, Moratoria, and Controlling Growth in 2 Management and Control of Growth 361 (Scott ed., 1975); Heeter, Interim Zoning Controls: Some Thoughts on Their Abuses, Id. at 409; Juergensmeyer and Wadley, Florida Land Use and Growth Management Law, Ch. 20; Urbanczyk, Note, Phased Zoning: Regulation of the Tempo and Sequence of Land Development, 26 Stanford L. Rev. 585 (1974).

tion of zoning power to the local government and the related issue of whether a moratorium must be enacted in the same manner (procedure, notice, hearings, etc.) as zoning ordinances. Other cases approach the validity and power issues from the exercise of the police power point of view.[2]

In spite of much recent litigation, the best summary of the requirements for a valid moratorium can be found in the 1976 decision of the Supreme Court of Minnesota in Almquist v. Town of Marshan.[3] That court opined that a moratorium on building permits is valid if:

(1) It is adopted by the local government in good faith

(2) It is not discriminatory

(3) It is of limited duration

(4) It is for the purpose of the development of a comprehensive zoning plan, and

2. See § 9.3 supra; Rathkopf, The Law of Zoning & Planning § 11.03[1]. The leading cases discussing the governmental power issue include Collura v. Arlington, 367 Mass. 881, 329 N.E.2d 733 (1975); City of Sanibel v. Buntrock, 409 So.2d 1073 (Fla. App.1981), review denied, 417 So.2d 328 (Fla.1982); Schrader v. Guilford Planning and Zoning Comm., 36 Conn.Supp. 281, 418 A.2d 93 (1980); Fletcher v. Porter, 203 Cal. App.2d 313, 21 Cal.Rptr. 452 (1962); Board of Supervisors v. Horne, 216 Va. 113, 215 S.E.2d 453 (1975); Matthews v. Board of Zoning Appeals, 218 Va. 270, 237 S.E.2d 128 (1977); Jason v. Dade County, 37 Fla. Supp. 190 (Cir.Ct. Dade County 1972); Metropolitan Dade County v. Rosell Construction Corp., 297 So.2d 46 (Fla.App.1974); Alexander v. City of Minneapolis, 267 Minn. 155, 125 N.W.2d 583 (1963); Bittinger v. Corporation of Bolivar, 183 W.Va. 310, 395 S.E.2d 554 (1990).

3. 308 Minn. 52, 245 N.W.2d 819 (1976). Leading cases discussing each of the requirements are as follows:

(1) *Good faith*: Condor Corp. v. City of St. Paul, 912 F.2d 215 (8th Cir.1990); Williams v. City of Central, 907 P.2d 701 (Colo.App.1995); Lake Illyria Corp. v. Gardiner, 43 A.D.2d 386, 352 N.Y.S.2d 54 (1974); Campana v. Clark, 82 N.J.Super. 392, 197 A.2d 711 (1964); Mayer Built Homes, Inc. v. Steilacoom, 17 Wn. App. 558, 564 P.2d 1170 (1977);

(2) *Not discriminatory*: Ogo Associates v. Torrance, 37 Cal.App.3d 830, 112 Cal. Rptr. 761 (1974); Stubblefield Constr. Co. v. City of San Bernardino, 32 Cal. App.4th 687, 38 Cal.Rptr.2d 413 (1995); Almquist v. Marshan, 308 Minn. 52, 245 N.W.2d 819 (1976); Morales v. Haines,

349 F.Supp. 684 (N.D.Ill.1972), judgment affirmed in part, vacated in part 486 F.2d 880 (7th Cir.1973);

(3) *Limited duration*: First English Evangelical Lutheran Church of Glendale v. County of Los Angeles (First English II), 210 Cal.App.3d 1353, 258 Cal.Rptr. 893 (1989), cert. denied 493 U.S. 1056, 110 S.Ct. 866, 107 L.Ed.2d 950 (1990); Marin Mun. Water Dist. v. K.G. Land Calif. Corp., 235 Cal.App.3d 1652, 1 Cal.Rptr.2d 767 (1991); Williams supra this note; Almquist supra this note; Lake Illyria supra this note; Campana, supra this note; Deal Gardens, Inc. v. Board of Trustees of the Village of Loch Arbour, 48 N.J. 492, 226 A.2d 607 (1967); Schiavone Constr. Co. v. Hackensack Meadowlands Dev. Comm'n, 98 N.J. 258, 486 A.2d 330 (1985);

(4) and (5) *Development of Comprehensive Plan and its Prompt Adoption*: Almquist, supra; Alexander v. City of Minneapolis, 267 Minn. 155, 125 N.W.2d 583 (1963); Ogo, supra; Campana, supra; Meadowland Regional Dev. Agency v. Hackensack Meadowlands Dev. Comm., 119 N.J.Super. 572, 293 A.2d 192 (1972), cert. denied 62 N.J. 72, 299 A.2d 69 (1972); Simpkins v. Gaffney, 315 S.C. 26, 431 S.E.2d 592 (1993); Pennington County v. Moore, 525 N.W.2d 257 (S.D. 1994); Walworth Co. v. Elkhorn, 27 Wis.2d 30, 133 N.W.2d 257 (1965). See also Layman, Concurrency and Moratoria, 71 Fla. B.J. 49 (Jan. 1997); Annotation, Validity and Effect of "Interim" Zoning Ordinance, 30 A.L.R.3d 1196 (1970).

(5) The local government acts promptly to adopt such a plan.

Based on the Supreme Court's opinion in First English Evangelical Lutheran Church v. County of Los Angeles,[4] some have argued that the temporary denial of all use effected by a moratorium is a taking of the present right to use property requiring just compensation under the Fifth Amendment. As we discuss elsewhere,[5] such an argument misreads *First English*. The general rule is that one is guaranteed a reasonable use over a reasonable period of time, and that the mere loss of the present right to use land is not a taking.[6] Takings can occur, however, if there is unreasonable delay.

Moratoria and interim controls play an important role in protecting the planning process by limiting the ability of developers to acquire vested rights to pursue development that may conflict with planning goals.[7] A community contemplating a change in its land use law may wish to freeze development by interim ordinance until the changes are in place.[8] If unable to formally impose a moratorium, administrative delay approval of permit requests until the new law is enacted will prevent vesting in most states so long as the action is not deceptive.[9]

§ 9.6 Growth Management Techniques: Capital Improvement Programming[1]

As discussed earlier,[2] a potentially effective growth management approach is the use of the timing and location of public facilities to guide

---

4. 482 U.S. 304, 318, 107 S.Ct. 2378, 2388, 96 L.Ed.2d 250 (1987).

5. See infra § 10.9 C.

6. See Williams v. City of Central, 907 P.2d 701 (Colo.App.1995); Woodbury Place Partners v. City of Woodbury, 492 N.W.2d 258 (Minn.App.1992); McCutchan Estates Corp. v. Evansville–Vanderburgh County Airport Auth. Dist., 580 N.E.2d 339 (Ind. App.1991); Dufau v. United States, 22 Cl. Ct. 156 (1990) aff'd without opinion, 940 F.2d 677 (Fed.Cir.1991); Guinnane v. City & County of San Francisco, 197 Cal.App.3d 862, 241 Cal.Rptr. 787 (1987), cert. denied 488 U.S. 823, 109 S.Ct. 70, 102 L.Ed.2d 47 (1988).

7. See supra § 5.28 G.

8. See Williams v. Griffin, 91 Nev. 743, 542 P.2d 732 (Nev.1975); State ex rel. SCA Chem. Waste Serv. v. Konigsberg, 636 S.W.2d 430 (Tenn.1982).

9. See Thomas E. Roberts, Interim Development Controls, 3 Zoning and Land Use Controls, § 22.04[2][b] (Rohan ed.1989).

§ 9.6

1. Much of the text of §§ 9.6 & 9.7 is based on T. Roberts, Funding Public Capital Facilities: How Community Planning Can Help, ch. 1 of The Changing Structure of Infrastructure Finance (J. Nicholas ed.1985). Excerpted with permission of Thomas H. Roberts.

2. See § 9.2, supra. Leading cases analyzing the withholding or delaying of governmental services as a growth management approach include Associated Home Builders v. Livermore, 18 Cal.3d 582, 135 Cal.Rptr. 41, 557 P.2d 473 (1976); Dateline Builders, Inc. v. City of Santa Rosa, 146 Cal.App.3d 520, 194 Cal.Rptr. 258 (Cal.Ct. App.1983); Smoke Rise, Inc. v. Washington Suburban Sanitary Comm., 400 F.Supp. 1369 (D.Md.1975); Robinson v. Boulder, 190 Colo. 357, 547 P.2d 228 (1976).

See also Biggs, No Drip, No Flush, No Growth: How Cities Can Control Growth Beyond Their Boundaries by Refusing to Extend Utility Services, 22 The Urb. Law. 285 (1990); Deutsch, Capital Improvement Controls as Land Use Devices, 9 Envtl. Law 61 (1978); Harris, Environmental Regulations, Zonings and Withheld Municipal Services: Takings of Property as Multi-government Actions, 25 U.Fla.L.Rev. 635 (1973); Ramsay, Control of the Timing and Location of Government Utility Extensions, 26 Stan.L.Rev. 945 (1974); Forestell, and Seeger, Water Facilities and Growth Planning in 2 Management and Control of Growth 457

and shape a community's development. By deciding where to put water lines, sewers, roads, and other public facilities, and by deciding when to put them there, a community is not only making public investment decisions but, more important, is setting a pattern and establishing a framework for the much larger amount of private development that will be influenced by these public decisions. By consciously locating and timing such investments not only in response to present needs but also as a catalyst for future growth and change, a community can exercise a great deal of leverage on its development pattern. Planners generally refer to this approach as Capital Improvement Programming.

A Capital Improvement Program (CIP) is an annually compiled schedule of public construction activity covering the next five or six years, stating what public improvements will be built, where they will be built, and when, along with costs, sources of funding, and other pertinent information. It is an organized way for a community to discuss what it wants to do, what it can afford to do, what its priorities are, and how the projects will be coordinated.

The idea of capital improvements programming has been around for a long time. In fact, it evolved at about the same time in the history of American urban planning as land use regulation. In older cities such as Baltimore, Philadelphia, Pittsburgh, and Cleveland, the capital improvements program became the centerpiece of the planning program. In most places, however, communities moved more readily into the regulatory side of planning than they did into orderly fiscal planning, budgeting, and public investment programming. Urban planning in the United States today would certainly be much stronger if both the public regulatory and public investment sides of the coin had evolved together. In recent years, with the stress that has been placed first on growth management and now on managing scarce fiscal resources, the time has become ripe for public capital investment planning to blossom.

Hence, even though capital improvements planning is an old idea, its widespread and institutionalized use as part of the comprehensive planning process would really be a long overdue innovation in most cities and counties. Moreover, the imaginative combination of regulatory and investment concepts, such as through the imposition of impact fees as a form of development regulation, is an even more innovative aspect of community planning.

The current year of the multi-year capital improvements program can become the basis for that year's annual operating budget. Also each year the capital improvements program is recompiled, dropping the first year and adding a new fifth (or sixth) year. Hence, a capital improvements program can serve as a policy implementation link between a long-range plan such as the comprehensive plan or one of the functional

(Scott ed., 1975); Hirst and Hirst, Capital Facilities Planning as a Growth Control Tool, Id. at 461; Rivkin, Sewer Moratoria as a Growth Control Technique, Id. at 473; Herman, Note, Sometimes There's Nothing More to Give: The Justification for Denying Water Service to New Consumers to Control Growth, 44 Stan.L.Rev. 429 (1992).

components thereof, and the actual line-item budgeting of funds for carrying out the plan.

Included among the many benefits of capital improvements programming are the following:

1. It can insure that plans for needed community facilities will actually be carried out by translating them into "bite-sized" chunks.

2. It allows various capital improvement proposals to be tested against sets of policies. Certain proposed projects may be someone's pet ideas but may not survive the tests of relevance, feasibility, or need.

3. It permits the multiyear scheduling of capital improvements that require more than one year to construct.

4. It provides an opportunity to acquire future public sites and rights-of-way before the costs go up.

5. It provides an opportunity for long-range financial planning and management.

6. It stabilizes tax rates through debt management.

7. It avoids costly and embarrassing instances of poor timing and noncoordination, such as paving a street and then tearing it up to install a sewer, or completing a school building before the water line reaches it.

8. It provides an opportunity for citizen participation and the involvement of specific interest groups in public matters that affect them.

9. It fosters better overall management of city or county affairs.

In a broader sense, capital improvements programming can also help a community establish the maximum amount of debt that it wishes to incur. It can focus on the various types of financing devices that can or should be resorted to, including traditional ones such as revenue bonds and special assessments, or some of the newer, innovative ones such as tax increment financing or impact fees.

Capital improvements programming can help determine the availability and applicability of state and federal financial participation. And perhaps most important, at least from a community planning point of view, capital improvements programming can enable a community to focus on, and select among, community objectives such as economic development in general, industrial development in particular, tourism, downtown redevelopment, neighborhood revitalization, and environmental protection.

Capital improvement programming is also an invaluable growth management tool. It can help determine whether, where, and how various parts of the community will develop. It can set priorities—for example, between the extension of public services into the urban fringe and the filling in and strengthening of services within substantially developed areas.

The planning agency should play a major role in developing its community's capital improvements program. If possible, the planning staff (and possibly the planning commission) should be designated the official body in charge of annually compiling and analyzing the various departmental needs, estimating the amount of funds available over the period of time involved, relating the departmental needs to the community's plans and to the amount of funds available, negotiating the priorities and differences among the various parties, and recommending a final program for public hearings and adoption by the governing body. The planner's actual role will depend upon the laws, customs, and structure of its particular local government and the extent to which these can be changed. In some cases the finance or budget officer or an interdepartmental committee may play a central role. At a minimum, however, the planning agency should be given ample opportunity to participate in the early stages and not simply react toward the end of the process.

§ 9.7 Growth Management Techniques: Infrastructure Finance.[1]

Traditionally the responsibility to provide so-called "infrastructure" has fallen to local government. Potable water, waste water collection and treatment, solid waste collection and disposal, streets, parks, and public schools generally fall into the category of "infrastructure." These services are required for the community to function in a manner that the public health, safety and welfare are protected. There is no doubt that growing communities require expanded water and waste water facilities, new schools additional fire stations and the like. The issue which has arisen is how are these services to be paid for?

It might seem that when a community experiences population growth, it would be a financial boon to all concerned—more people, more jobs, more trade, and more dollars being imported into the county and recirculated within the county. This, then, should lead to a larger tax base, more tax revenues, and more opportunity for local government to provide and pay for the public facilities that people want and need, possibly even more efficiently and at a higher level of quality than before.

Unfortunately, it doesn't usually happen that way. It is true that new outside money comes in, in the form of payroll, investments, and purchases. It is also true that the level of county government activity increases: there is more development to regulate, more public facilities to build, more community services to provide, and more taxes to collect. But generally the public revenues don't come in fast enough or in the

§ 9.7

1. See generally Roberts, Funding Public Capital Facilities: How Community Planning Can Help, ch. 1 of The Changing Structure of Infrastructure Finance (J. Nicholas ed.1985).

right way to cover growing public costs. So things get out of joint: public costs go up, the availability and quality of public services go down, and the burden of additional costs is unfairly distributed, or at least that is how it is perceived by the citizenry.

Typically, there are four kinds of money shortage problems that arise in a local government experiencing growth, particularly rapid growth:

1.   Not enough increased revenue to cover increased expenses.

2.   Not enough revenues early enough to cover front-end costs of new public facilities (negative cash flow).

3.   Not enough revenue available in the right places or for the right purposes.

4.   Inequitable distribution of the cost burden.

Problem 1, not enough increased revenue to cover increased expenses, can be caused by (1) inelastic revenue sources, (2) undependability of grant sources, or (3) the voters' refusal to countenance higher taxes.

An inelastic revenue source is one that does not grow fast enough to compensate for the offsetting effects of increased service demands or inflation. A sales tax, for example, is a fairly elastic response to the effects of inflation, because it grows in direct proportion to sales receipts, which in turn grow in direct proportion to inflation. In contrast per-gallon fuel taxes are a good example of inelastic taxes, because the revenue they produce does not increase as the cost of fuel increases, nor does it increase as fuel efficiency (that is, mileage per gallon) increases. Typical local governmental revenues, such as the ad valorem real property tax or business licenses and fees, may or may not be elastic, depending upon how careful local government officials are to see that property assessments and other components of revenue are periodically updated. Inasmuch as various types of development (such as residential, commercial, and industrial development) rarely produce real estate tax revenues in direct proportion to the services they consume, it is also important that local government constantly keep a close watch on the relative amounts of the various types of development it is experiencing (or permitting or encouraging) and also on the total mixture of revenues (that is, general property taxes, special assessments, user charges, business licenses, and other fees) that each type of development is producing.

Undependability of grant sources can be a serious cause of revenue shortages in local government. Federal and state funding policies can change quickly; and although federal aid can be a useful source of funding, it can also lead a local government to overcommit itself, only to find that the grants it anticipated are not forthcoming because of a change in the political or fiscal climate, leading to a change in the law or in authorization or appropriation levels. If the grants are forthcoming, they may not come when they were supposed to, or the amount may be computed conservatively or inequitably.

A third typical cause of revenue shortages in growing localities is voters' opposition to higher taxes. "Taxpayer revolts" can be caused by general economic conditions or by specific dissatisfaction with the effects of growth, and they can result in the defeat of bond issues, pressure on public officials to keep taxes low, or replacement of officials at the polls with new ones who say they will keep taxes down. In any case, the result is less revenue to meet mounting expenses.

Problem 2, cash flow problems—that is, not having money in hand early enough to cover front-end costs—are the bane of any growing community, and particularly local governments confronted with rapid growth and development. Although new real estate development adds value to the tax roll, which will eventually produce more tax revenue for the city or county, these funds are not available ahead of time when they are needed to provide new public facilities. The traditional answer to this timing problem is to borrow the money by issuing bonds and paying them off over the life of a facility, usually several decades. There are limitations on this procedure, including legal debt limits, refusal by the voters or the elected officials to incur the debt, lack of identifiable or predictable future revenues to pledge (as in the case of revenue bonds), and a reluctance to charge all taxpayers for growth costs inflicted by new growth (as in the case of general obligation bonds). In addition, the currently high level of interest rates makes public borrowing more expensive than ever.

Problem 3, not enough revenue available in the right places or for the right purposes, is another funding problem typically experienced by a locality faced with new growth. In this case the amount of available funds grows, but not in such a way as to make funds available for specific purposes. One example is the revenue produced by user charges within a special taxing district or public service district, which cannot be drained off and used for some other purpose—nor should it be, however meritorious the other purpose.

Other examples include various federal and state assistance programs which make funding available only for certain projects or categories. Not only are such limitations unresponsive to local needs and priorities, but they can also tempt local governments into compounding their financial problems, for example by accepting a grant to construct a capital facility, without paying adequate attention to the true life-cycle cost of the facility, including long-term operating and maintenance costs.

Problem 4 is the inequitable distribution of the cost burden. It is common for taxpayers to feel that they are being unfairly treated in one way or another, and this feeling is almost always exacerbated in a growing area, where residents may feel that they are being made to pay not only for their own services but for the expense of accommodating newcomers as well. Sometimes this situation is brought on by the high front-end cost of new development, discussed as problem 2 above. Sometimes it is caused by the fact that the new residents demand and receive a higher level or quality of services than was provided before, such as more libraries or better garbage collection, and the higher costs of these improved services are shared by all. Sometimes taxes rise simply because of an increase in per capita costs brought on by higher densities or a larger or more complex population, as in the case of police protection costs.

Inequitable tax burdens can also occur in a growing area when one unit of government provides services to another unit of government or to the citizens of another unit. An example is the provision of sewer or water service by a municipality to the surrounding area. There is always a strong risk that the providing government may charge too much or too little for the service, creating an inequity in either case. The most common situation is for the providing government to charge enough to cover the direct costs of the service but not enough to cover the full range of indirect costs of urban impacts that go along with it. Conflicting interpretations of these complex fiscal interrelationships can easily lead to public disagreements about who is subsidizing whom.

Whenever citywide or county-wide revenue sources are used to pay for the impact of new development, such as by paying off general obligation bonds or by covering increased annual operating costs, the original residents often feel that their taxes are being raised to pay for the costs of new development; and sometimes they are. (It is also often true, however, that much of the original residential development is subsidized by commercial and industrial property tax to begin with.) Although these same residents may often benefit financially from the new growth as a result of increased economic activity in the area (new jobs, more trade, new markets for services), these benefits are not proportionally distributed. Thus a retiree or a farmer, for example, may benefit less than a merchant or insurance agent, but his taxes go up nevertheless.

As often as not, these four types of revenue shortage problems occur in combined and overlapping fashion or with additional complications. For instance, the demand for a particular public service may grow evenly in proportion to the growth rate, whereas the provision of the service may have to grow in periodic increments. Fire protection is a common example: once a fire station is constructed, equipped, and manned, it can service a certain number of additional residences that are built within its service radius without a corresponding increase in cost. However, at some point a second station or additional equipment must be provided to handle additional demand beyond the capacity or reach of the original station. Hence, while the growth may occur evenly, the public cost of servicing that growth occurs in periodic jumps, making it more difficult to allocate costs and raise revenues in a manner that is viewed as equitable by all concerned. In short, new development often brings surprises in the form of unanticipated public costs.

New development produces additional capital costs, and it also produces increased operating and maintenance costs. This discussion deals with capital costs because they constitute the large, conspicuous, early expenditures that are most directly associated with new development, whereas operating and maintenance costs tend to be absorbed into government-wide operations and funded by the locality-at-large for the benefit of the locality-at-large. However, as discussed above, new development can also increase public service costs for current and new residents alike, and this should not be overlooked in an examination of the total effects of new development.

Two distinct types of capital facility impact costs resulting from new development can be identified, as well as a third, somewhat vaguer "in-between" category. The two types are on-site (or intradevelopment) costs and off-site (or extradevelopment) costs.

On-site costs are the regular capital costs that occur within a development or that are intimately and directly related to a development. In the typical case of a residential subdivision these include, at a minimum, local streets and drainage. As the density or size of a subdivision increases, sanitary sewers, water lines, more substantial drainage facilities and related rights-of-way, and neighborhood park and playground facilities become customary on-site improvements. In addition, street lights and sidewalks may be viewed as normal improvement costs, depending upon conditions. In short, whatever it takes to convert raw land into fully groomed, finished building sites, according to whatever standards the local government seeks to attain for its people, should be viewed as on-site costs and should be funded as such. Off-site costs are those that affect the community at large with no direct connection to new development.

§ 9.8 Growth Management Techniques: Developer Funding of Infrastructure

A common concern of most growth management programs is the availability and financing of public facilities. In the past, general revenues, special assessments and service districts, and ad hoc negotiations with developers have been the usual methods of finance. An ever increasing number of local governments—even those without full scale growth management programs—have adopted policies and programs designed to make new development and not existing residents bear the cost of new capital improvements such as schools, roads, parks, and sewer and water treatment facilities necessitated by the new development.[1] Three major

---

§ 9.8

1. Infrastructure finance in general is discussed in § 9.7 supra.

Impact fees and infrastructure finance have become increasingly popular topics for books and law review articles. The major publications relied upon in the preparation of this section include Juergensmeyer and Blake, Impact Fees: An Answer to Local Governments Capital Funding Dilemma, 9 Fla.St.U.L.Rev. 415 (1981); Juergensmeyer, Drafting Impact Fees to Alleviate Florida's Pre–Platted Lands Dilemma, 7 Fla.Envt'l and Urb.Issues 7 (Apr.1980). Juergensmeyer, Funding Infrastructure: Paying the Costs of Growth Through Impact Fees and other Land Regulation Charges, Ch. 2 of The Changing Structure of Infrastructure Finance (J. Nicholas ed. 1985); Juergensmeyer and Wadley, Florida Land Use and Growth Management Law Ch. 17 (looseleaf); James C. Nicholas, Arthur C. Nelson and Julian C. Juergensmeyer, A practitioner's Guide to Development Impact Fees

categories of developer funding requirements can be identified: (1) Required Dedications, (2) Impact Fees, and (3) Linkage and Mitigation Fees.

A. *Required Dedications*

Required dedications or payments in lieu thereof were the original approach to developer funding of infrastructure and developed in connection with subdivision regulations. Their history and current usage are discussed in detail above in Chapter 7 on Subdivision Regulation. A brief summary of required dedications and in-lieu fees will be given at this point to facilitate the discussion of impact fees and linkage and mitigation programs. The reader is referred to Chapter 7's more detailed discussion[2] but reminded that required dedications are becoming more and more entwined with impact fees which are discussed below.

The first land use regulation developed to shift the capital expense burden to the developer and new residents was the required dedication. Local governments conditioned their approval of a subdivision plat upon the developer's agreement to provide and dedicate such improvements as streets and drainage ways. Required dedications for these intradevelopment capital improvements are now a well accepted part of subdivision regulation and are generally approved by the courts.[3]

The "in lieu" fee developed as a refinement of required dedications. For example, to require each subdivision to dedicate land to educational purposes would not solve the problem of providing school facilities for

(1991) [Hereinafter cited as Practitioner's Guide]; J. Juergensmeyer, The Development of Regulatory Impact Fees: The Legal Issues, Ch. 8 of Development Impact Fees (Nelson ed. 1988); Nicholas, The Calculation of Proportionate Share Impact Fees, 408 A.P.A.Plan Advisory Ser. Rep. (1988); Frank and Rhodes, Development Exactions (1987); Development Impact Fees: Policy Rationale, Practice, Theory, and Issues (Nelson ed. 1988); Nelson, Paying for Growth's Impacts: A Guide to Impact Fees (1992); Bauman and Ethier, Development Exactions and Impact Fees: A Survey of American Practices, 50 Law & Contemp. Prob. 51 (1987); Dana, Land Use Regulation in an Age of Heightened Scrutiny, 75 N.C.L.Rev. 1243 (1997); Delaney, et al., The Needs–Nexus Analysis: A Unified Test for Validating Subdivision Exactions, User Impact Fees, and Linkage, 50 Law & Contemp. Prob. 139 (1987); Holloway and Guy, Development Impact Fees and the Essential Nexus: Substantially Related or Reasonably Related to Legitimate State Interests, 20 Proc. of the Mid–Atlantic Acad. of Legal Stud. in Bus. 102 (1994); Holloway and Guy, Land Dedication conditions and Beyond the Essential Nexus: Determining "Reasonably Related" Impacts of Real Es-

tate Development Under the Takings Clause, 27 Tex.Tech L.Rev. 73 (1996); Huffman, et al., Who Bears the Burden of Development Impact Fees, Am. Planning Ass'n J., Winter 1988; Keenan and Buchsbaum, Report on the Subcommittee on Exactions and Impact Fees, 23 Urb. Law. 627 (1991); Lee, Sudden Impact: The Effect of Dolan v. City of Tigard on Impact Fees in Washington, 71 Wash.L.Rev. 205; Mudge, Impact Fees for the Conversion of Agricultural Land: A Resource–Based Development Policy for California's Cities and Counties, 19 Ecology L.Q. 63 (1992); Nelson, Development Impact Fees: The Next Generation, 26 Urb. Law. 541 (1994); Siemon and Zimet, Who Should Pay for Free Public Schools in an Expensive Society?, 20 Stetson L.Rev. 725 (1991); Stroud and Trevarthen, Defensible Exactions After Nollan v. California Coastal Commission and Dolan v. City of Tigard, 25 Stetson L.Rev. 719 (1996); Taub, Development Exactions and Impact Fees, C872 ALI–ABA 269 (1993); White, Development Fees and Exemptions for Affordable Housing: Tailoring Regulations to Achieve Multiple Public Objectives, 6 J. Land Use & Envtl.L. 25 (1990).

2. See § 7.8A, supra.

3. See § 7.8B, supra.

developing suburban areas, because the sites would often be inadequate in size and inappropriately located. The in lieu fee solves this problem by substituting a money payment for dedication when the local government determines the latter is not feasible.

B. Impact Fees

Impact fees are charges levied by local governments against new development in order to generate revenue for capital funding necessitated by the new development. These fees play an increasing role in the efforts of local governments to cope with the economic burdens of population growth such as the need for new parks, roads, schools, jails, public buildings and sewer and water treatment facilities.

Although the impact fee owes its origin to the impact analysis concepts of environmental law, it is functionally similar to the in lieu fee, discussed above, in that both are required payments for capital facilities. In fact, the terms are sometimes used interchangeably. The impact fee concept, however, is a much more flexible cost shifting tool. Because in lieu fees are predicated on dedication requirements, they can only be used where required dedications can be appropriately utilized. In the case of sewer and water facilities, public safety facilities, and similar capital outlays, required dedications are not always an appropriate device to shift a portion of the capital costs to the development, because one facility (and parcel of land) can service a very wide area and there is little need for additional land in extending these services.

The distinction between in lieu fees and impact fees results in several decided advantages for impact fees. First, impact fees can be used to fund types of facilities and capital expenses which are not normally the subject of dedication requirements and in lieu fees, and can more easily be applied to facilities to be constructed outside the development (extradevelopment or nonsite related) as well as those inside the development (intradevelopment or site related). Second, impact fees can be applied to developments platted before the advent of required dedications or in lieu fees and thus impose on incoming residents their fair share of these capital costs. A third advantage is that impact fees can be applied to condominium, apartment, and commercial developments which create the need for extradevelopment capital expenditures, but generally escape dedication or in lieu fee requirements because of the small land area involved or the inapplicability of subdivision regulations. Finally, impact fees can be collected at the time building permits or certificates of occupancy are issued and when growth creating a need for new services occurs, rather than at the time of platting.[4]

---

4. Thus, the so-called pre-platted lands problem can be avoided. The "pre-platted lands" problem refers to the situation, especially prevalent in various sunbelt states, in which thousands and thousands of acres of land were platted during the land booms in the earlier part of the twentieth century before required dedications and exactions were standard. Those lands can frequently be sold and developed without the local government having any way of obtaining the dedications exactions or in lieu fees that would be obtained if the land were being platted today. See Juergensmeyer, Drafting Impact Fees to Alleviate Florida's Pre-platted Lands Dilemma, 7 Fla.Envt'l and Urban

1. Economic Analysis[5]

In the early days of impact fees, the 1960's and 1970's, there was extensive debate over whether the economic underpinnings of impact fees are applicable to government activities other than utility type services. Those who argued for restricting the concept to utility type services based their reasoning on the existence of a physical connection between the benefitted unit and the facilities to be constructed with the fees collected. Moreover, they argued that utility type services are "closed ended" in that only those who pay the fee and receive the service benefit from the capital expansion as distinct from non-payers receiving a benefit. An "open ended" system, such as a road or park, is different, they argued. In such "open ended" systems it is either impossible or impractical to exclude non-payers from benefiting from the capital improvement.

The reasoning on the other side was that local governments face a host of capital expansion costs which may be reasonably anticipated because of new development. (1) If the present system of roads or parks has to be expanded to meet the needs of new development, (2) if the fees imposed were no more than what the local government unit would incur in accommodating the new users of the road or park system, and (3) if the fees are expressly earmarked and spent for road and park expansion, then the same economic logic applies as it does to utility type services.

These two positions are often characterized as the "exclusiveness of benefit" analysis and the "but not for" analysis. Those who adhere to the exclusiveness of benefit position argue that only those facilities which can be provided for the exclusive benefit of the individual paying the cost are fit candidates for impact fees. The premise of their argument is that if there is a public benefit from the expansion of a public facility, i.e., some individuals who do not pay for the expansion may use the facility, then individual payments would have to be classified as a tax rather than a fee. Such payments being taxes follows from the premise that there may be benefits flowing to individuals who have not paid for the facility. Thus, according to this position, only those public facilities which possess the capability to exclude non-payers (or free-riders) are fit candidates for impact fees.

Issues 7 (April 1980); Schnidman and Baker, Planning for Platted Lands: Land Use Remedies for Lot Sale Subdivisions, 11 Fla. State Univ.L.Rev. 505 (1983).

Impact fees are also collected at one or more of the following stages of development: (1) rezoning, (2) platting, (3) development order issuance, (4) building permit issuance, and (5) certificate of occupancy issuance. Collecting them late in the development process is best for the developer since he has no (or low) finance charges to pay on the impact fee amount. Local governments prefer collecting the fee as early

as possible in the development process so that funds will be available to start construction in time to provide infrastructure when the development is completed.

5. The economic analysis given below based on Chapters 5, 9, 10, 11 of Practitioners's Guide. See also, Nicholas, Florida's Experience With Impact Fees, ch. 3 of The Changing Structure of Infrastructure Finance (J. Nicholas ed. 1985); James C. Nicholas, Impact Exactions: Economic Theory, Practice, and Incidence, 50 Law & Contemp. Prob. 85 (1987).

The argument is based, in part, on the economic theory of externalities. An externality is an effect of an action by one individual upon another. Externalities can be either positive or negative. If an externality is positive it is seen as a social benefit, and if it is negative it is seen as a social cost. The majority of regulations promulgated under the police power are attempts by government to stop the creation of negative externalities, i.e., to stop individuals from creating social costs. An example of such an exercise would be prohibition of excessive noise. Such a prohibition is not to benefit those who would have to suffer the noise but rather to stop others (noise makers) from causing harm. The opposite is where an individual is required to create a social benefit. An example would be a municipal concert hall. The requiring of individuals to provide, in whole or in part, a concert hall is not for the prevention of harm to the public. Rather, it is to benefit the public.

While there is no question that government is empowered to undertake such actions, requirements for individual financial participation in the creation of social benefits are exercises of the taxation powers of government rather than regulations under the police power. Given that a public park is not for the exclusive benefit of those who paid for it, it would follow, based upon the exclusiveness of benefit principle, that any requirement for individuals to financially contribute to a public park would be an act of taxation rather than of regulation. Returning to the theory of externalities; requirements to prohibit negative externalities (social costs) are considered to be regulatory under the police power to protect the public while requirements to create social benefits are seen as taxation to benefit the public. In this way the right and/or ability to exclude non-payers is very important to whether an assessment to expand a public facility will be seen as a regulatory fee or a tax.

Those who subscribe to the "but not for" argument take a different tack. Their premise is that if the facilities would not have to expand but for new development, then new development should be required to pay for that expansion. Use and benefit are seen differently in this position. It is not, herein, a matter of who uses or receives benefit from the particular facility but rather what (or who) caused the need for the facility. This line of reasoning views the theory of externalities differently. Take the example of a public park. If new development results in population growth that overcrowds the public parks, a social cost will have been created. This social cost is the loss of public use of the public park. A regulation to prevent the imposition of such public costs would have to be seen, therefore, as an exercise of the police power. While both sides of this argument would agree that requirements to create a public benefit would be an exercise of the taxation powers, the divergence comes in what constitutes a public cost.

The conservative position, characterized herein as the exclusive benefit argument, holds that public costs are only those direct impositions of harm such as excessive noise. The "but not for" position sees the loss of an existing public benefit as being a social cost. Thus, one side would argue that requiring impact fees for facilities such as parks would be taxation because the entire public, rather than only those who pay, will receive the benefit (use). The counter argument is that failure of park expansion will impose a public cost. Inasmuch as new development is the source of this public cost then regulations to prohibit such a cost would be exercises of the police power and a fee. These two positions can be argued ad infinitum but fortunately for the development of impact fees most courts have accepted the "but not for" approach.

The Florida courts addressed this issue early in the development of impact fees in that state. In Hollywood, Inc. v. Broward County,[6] the court wrote:

> . . . benefit accruing to the community generally does not adversely affect the validity of a development regulation ordinance as long as the fee does not exceed the cost of the improvements required by the new development and the improvements adequately benefit the development which is the source of the fee.

The Wisconsin and Utah courts have also addressed this matter. In Jordan v. Village of Menomonee Falls,[7] the court wrote:

> In most instances it would be impossible for the municipality to prove that the land required to be dedicated for a park or school site is to meet a need solely attributable to the anticipated influx of people in the community to occupy this particular subdivision. On the other hand, the municipality might well be able to establish that a group of subdivisions approved over a period of several years had been responsible for bringing into the community a considerable number of people making it necessary that the land dedications required of the subdividers be utilized for school, park and recreational purposes for the benefit of such influx. In the absence of contravening evidence this would establish a reasonable basis for finding that the need for the acquisition was occasioned by the activity of the subdivider.

The Utah court looked at the same issue in Call v. West Jordan.[8] In *Call* the court dealt directly with the issue of exclusiveness of benefit as a criterion to separate regulatory fees from taxes. The court wrote:

> We agree that the dedication should have some reasonable relationship to the needs created by the subdivision. . . . But it is so plain as to hardly require expression that if the purpose of the ordinance is properly carried out, it will redound to the benefit of the subdivision as well as the general welfare of the whole community. The fact that it does so, rather than solely benefiting the individual subdivision, does not impair the validity of the ordinance.[9]

In these various cases the courts are saying that the fact the entire community may use or enjoy the facilities is not the important point.

6. 431 So.2d 606, 612–613 (Fla.App. 1983).

7. 28 Wis.2d 608, 617, 137 N.W.2d 442, 447 (1965).

8. 606 P.2d 217, 219 (Utah 1979), on rehearing 614 P.2d 1257 (1980).

9. Id. at 220.

Rather, what is important is that the need for the facility is occasioned by new development and that new development itself benefits. But, it is clear that the new development need not be the exclusive recipient of the benefits. Thus, the courts are aligned with the "but not for" position. The message here is clear—exactions can benefit the entire community as long as the need for the exaction is reasonably related to the needs of new development and as long as new development itself benefits from that exaction.

Thus, the two main economic analysis principles of impact fee assessment may be stated as (1) the cost imposed through the fee must flow reasonably from those costs to be borne by local government which are reasonably attributable to new development and (2) new development must benefit from the expenditure of the fees collected.

2. Impact Fees and Comprehensive Planning

The increased emphasis being placed on the need and even requirement for consistency between comprehensive plans and land use regulatory activities of local governments makes necessary, or at least wise, the inclusion of language in comprehensive plans which will authorize and support impact fees. The following language is suggested as the embodiment of the planning principles inherent in impact fees:

I. Land development shall not be permitted unless adequate capital facilities exist or are assured.

II. Land development shall bear a proportionate cost of the provision of the new or expanded capital facilities required by such development.

III. The imposition of impact fees and dedication requirements are the preferred methods of regulating land development in order to assure that it bears a proportionate share of the cost of capital facilities necessary to accommodate that development and to promote and protect the health, safety, and general welfare.[10]

Principle III ties directly to the capital improvement program (CIP) element of comprehensive plans.[11] Without such an element or planning process and the levels of service for infrastructure items which they should establish, it is difficult if not impossible to determine the proportionate share of new development.[12] Impact fees programs established without a CIP to underpin them are particularly vulnerable to attack under the rational nexus requirements discussed below.

The intergovernmental co-ordination elements of comprehensive plans are also increasingly important in regard to impact fee programs. Considerable controversy has arisen in Florida over whether municipali-

10. The impact fee "Magna Carta" language was drafted by Julian C. Juergensmeyer, James C. Nicholas, Thomas H. Roberts and is published in The Changing Structure of Infrastructure Finance 15 (J. Nicholas, ed. 1985).

11. See § 9.6, supra.

12. See Practitioner's Guide Ch 12. See also City of Fayetteville v. IBI, Inc., 280 Ark. 484, 659 S.W.2d 505 (Ark.1983) (requiring "reasonably definite" plan for expenditure of impact fees).

ties are subject to the impact fee programs enacted by their counties.[13] Although the constitutional framework in a given state for its local governments may determine the outcome of the conflict, intergovernmental coordination can also play a key role.

3. Legal Evolution and Current Legal Status of Impact Fees

In the early stages of impact fee development, they were subjected to two principal attacks: (1) First, impact fees were challenged as unreasonable regulations which were not acceptable exercises of the police power which made them "disguised" and unauthorized taxes. (2) Second they were attacked on the theory that they were not authorized by state statute or constitutional provision and therefore were void as *ultra vires* acts of the governmental entities which had enacted them.[14]

The characterization of impact fees as land use regulations or taxes presents a complex problem which has already been analyzed above in the economic analysis discussion in this section. Because impact fees are functionally similar to dedications and to other land use planning and growth management tools, the regulation tag appears appropriate but their revenue raising nature and purpose also makes them look very much like taxes to some commentators.

The choice a court makes in "tagging" the impact fee "regulatory fee" or "tax" will often be determinative of its validity.[15] If the tax label is adopted, the impact fee will be invalidated unless express and specific statutory authorization for the tax exists. Even if statutory authorization is present, constitutional limitations on taxation may still invalidate the statute. Alternatively, if the impact fee is construed as a police power regulation, very broad legislative delegation will suffice. Once past this statutory hurdle, the clear trend among state courts is to validate such extradevelopment capital funding payment requirements as a valid exercise of the police power. Not surprisingly, therefore, most state courts have summarily labeled extradevelopment impact fees as either a tax or

13. See City of Ormond Beach v. Volusia County, 535 So.2d 302 (Fla.App.1988); Seminole County v. City of Casselberry, 541 So.2d 666 (Fla.App.1989).

14. Compare McCarthy v. City of Leawood, 257 Kan. 566, 894 P.2d 836 (1995) with Home Builders Ass'n of Cent. N.Y. v. County of Onondaga, 151 Misc.2d 886, 573 N.Y.S.2d 863 (1991).

15. See Heyman and Gilhool, The Constitutionality of Imposing Increased Community Costs on New Subdivision Residents Through Subdivision Exactions, 73 Yale L.J. 1119, 1146–55 (1964). Compare the following cases: Montgomery v. Crossroads Land Co., 355 So.2d 363 (Ala.1978) (in lieu fee a tax); Venditti–Siravo, Inc. v. Hollywood, 39 Fla.Supp. 121 (17th Cir.Ct.1973) (impact fee an invalid property tax); Haugen v. Gleason, 226 Or. 99, 103, 359 P.2d 108, 110 (1961) (in lieu fee borders on tax);

Montgomery v. Crossroads Land Co., 355 So.2d 363 (Ala.1978) (in lieu fee a tax); Contractors and Builders Ass'n of Pinellas County v. Dunedin, 329 So.2d 314 (Fla. 1976), on remand 330 So.2d 744 (Fla.App. 1976) (impact fee properly earmarked not a tax); Western Heights Land Corp. v. City of Fort Collins, 146 Colo. 464, 362 P.2d 155 (1961) (not a tax because not intended to defray general municipal expenses); Home Builders Ass'n of Greater Salt Lake v. Provo City, 28 Utah 2d 402, 503 P.2d 451 (1972) (charge for services not a general revenue measure); Jenad, Inc. v. Scarsdale, 18 N.Y.2d 78, 271 N.Y.S.2d 955, 218 N.E.2d 673 (1966) (not a tax but a reasonable form of planning); Call v. West Jordan, 606 P.2d 217 (Utah 1979), on rehearing 614 P.2d 1257 (in-lieu fee not a tax but a form of planning).

regulation in a result-oriented fashion that avoids an adequate theoretical or policy-directed explanation.[16]

There are two rationales either implicit or expressly cited in those decisions which apply the tax label to impact fees. The first is a simplistic observation that impact fees are a positive exaction of funds and are therefore a tax. This criterion is an untenable basis for distinction because it exalts form over function. It ignores similar police power regulations which mandate that the developer expend great amounts of funds for streets, sewers, and other capital improvements within the development. Any distinction between impact fees and similar police power regulations made on the basis that impact fees are imposed prior to the issuance of building permits rather than after the approval of plats is a distinction without a difference.[17]

The second rationale used to label impact fees as taxes is the theory that funds for education, recreation, and public safety purposes cannot be raised under the police power. This assertion is based on the conviction that such facilities should be financed solely from general revenues provided by the community as a whole and is discussed above.

The second, and often dispositive objection to impact fees has been that they were not authorized by state statute or constitutional provision and therefore were void as *ultra vires* acts of the governmental entities which had enacted them. The authority or ultra vires issue has been resolved in many states today by the enactment of impact fee enabling acts.[18] The key issue in states with such authorization acts is whether they are general in nature or only authorize specific types of impact fees such as road impact fees.[19] Some states follow the practice of the state legislature authorizing impact fees for specified counties or other units of local government.[20]

Of those states without authorization or enabling statutes which have considered the issue, most have found authority in home rule power, planning and consistency requirements, or on the theory that

---

16. The tax versus regulation dichotomy is not a key issue in California because the taxing power of local governments greatly exceeds that of local governments in most other states. Impact "fees" are consequently frequently labeled "taxes" even if they could satisfy the requirements for a "fee" in other jurisdictions. See Associated Homebuilders of Greater East Bay, Inc. v. Livermore, 56 Cal.2d 847, 17 Cal.Rptr. 5, 366 P.2d 448 (1961), vacating 11 Cal.Rptr. 485 (Ct.App.1961); English Manor Corp. v. Vallejo Sanitation and Flood Control Dist., 42 Cal.App.3d 996, 117 Cal.Rptr. 315 (1974).

17. See § 7.8 supra.

18. These states include Arizona, California, Georgia, Maine, Nevada, Oregon, Texas and Vermont. See Practitioners

Guide, supra note 5 at Ch. 4. A model impact fee authorization act can be found in Ch. 15 of the Practitioner's Guide. Id. See also, J. Nicholas and D.Davidson, Impact Fees in Hawaii: Implementing the State Law (1992); Morgan, Recent Developments in the Law of Impact Fees with Special Attention to Legislation, 1990 Institute on Planning, Zoning, and Eminent Domain, § 4; Morgan, State Impact Fee Legislation: Guidelines for Analysis, Land Use L. & Zoning Dig. (Mar. 1990 & April 1990); Leitner & Schoettle, A Survey of State Impact Fee Enabling Legislation, 25 Urb.Law. 491 (1993).

19. Road impact fee authorization statutes are found in New Jersey, Illinois, Virginia, Washington and West Virginia. Id.

20. Id.

impact fees are land use regulations and that a local government with general land use regulatory authority may enact them as part of that power.

The main authority problem which remains is that of whether the power of a local government to enact impact fees extends to all types of infrastructure or is limited to certain infrastructure items. Jurisdictions with impact fee authorization statutes generally have no problem with this issue since their statutes usually contain a list of permissible impact fees. In those states without such a list or without any statutory provisions on impact fees, educational facilities have been the most troublesome to courts.[21]

In Florida, a jurisdiction without an impact fee authorization statute, the battle over whether local governments can enact school impact fees based on their general land use regulatory powers has been particularly intense. It was finally resolved in favor of school impact fees by the Supreme Court of Florida's 1991 decision in St. John's County v. Northeast Fla. Builders Ass'n.[22] The court found no preemption or prohibition in the Florida Constitution or statutes relating to educational funding. The court also rejected the argument that a school impact fee violates the "free" or "uniform" provisions of the Florida Constitution relevant to public education.

A recent decision by the Supreme Court of Colorado, Board of Cty. Com'rs, Douglas County v. Bainbridge, Inc.,[23] runs counter to the current judicial trend. Although the Colorado court found, as did the Florida court , that the state's legislature had not pre-empted school finance, it held the school impact fees invalid on the theory that the provision in the Colorado statutes permitting counties to collect in lieu fees at the subdivision platting stage of development controls the maximum school related fees that can be collected and that counties have no implied powers to require additional infrastructure funding for schools at the time of building permit or certificate of occupancy issuance.[24]

4. *Reasonable Exercises of the Police Power*

As has been indicated, most state courts have recognized impact fees as permissible exercises of the police power. Once a jurisdiction's courts or legislative enactments have established this principle, the focus of controversy shifts to the standard of reasonableness which must be met since all exercises of the police power must be "reasonable."

In the early development stage of impact fees, two landmark decisions placed an almost insurmountable burden on local governments in

---

21. See Siemon and Zimet, Who Should Pay for Free Public Schools in an Expensive Society?, 20 Stetson L.Rev 725 (1991).

22. 583 So.2d 635 (Fla.1991). The case is discussed at length in Juergensmeyer and Wadley, Florida Land Use and Growth Management Law Ch. 17 (1997).

23. 929 P.2d 691 (Colo.1996).

24. The Colorado school finance statute was amended prior to the decision in the case to prohibit future school impact fees. Id.

this regard. In Pioneer Trust & Savings Bank v. Mount Prospect,[25] a developer challenged the validity of an ordinance requiring subdividers to dedicate one acre per sixty residential lots for schools, parks, and other public purposes. In determining whether required dedications or money payments for recreational or educational purposes represented a reasonable exercise of the police power, the Illinois Supreme Court propounded the "specifically and uniquely attributable" test. The court focused on the origin of the need for the new facilities and held that unless the village could prove that the demand for additional facilities was "specifically and uniquely attributable" to the particular subdivision, such requirements were an unreasonable regulation not authorized by the police power. Thus, where schools had become overcrowded because of the "total development of the community" the subdivider could not be compelled to help fund new facilities which his activity would necessitate.

A related and equally restrictive test was delineated by the New York court in the short-lived decision of Gulest Associates, Inc. v. Newburgh.[26] In that case developers attacked an ordinance which charged in lieu fees for recreational purposes. The amounts collected were to be used by the town for " 'neighborhood park, playground or recreational purposes including the acquisition of property.' "[27] The court held that the fee was an unreasonable regulation tantamount to an unconstitutional taking because the funds collected were not used solely for the benefit of the residents of the particular subdivision charged, but rather could be used in any section of town for any recreational purposes. In essence, the *Gulest* "direct benefit" test required that funds collected from required payments for capital expenditures be specifically tied to a benefit directly conferred on the homeowners in the subdivision which was charged. If recreational fees were used to purchase a park outside the subdivision, the direct benefit test was not met and the ordinance was invalid.

Despite this early trend, the *Pioneer Trust* and *Gulest* tests became difficult to reconcile with the planning and funding problems imposed on local governments by the constant acceleration of suburban growth. This restrictiveness also became difficult to rationalize with the judicial view of zoning ordinance as presumptively valid. Consequently, courts were not convinced of the practical or legal necessity of such stringent standards for the validation of required payments for extradevelopment capital funding.

At first, in turning away from the restrictive standards of *Gulest* and *Pioneer Trust*, state courts developed divergent and conflicting police power criteria for assessing the validity of extradevelopment capital

25. 22 Ill.2d 375, 176 N.E.2d 799 (1961).

26. 25 Misc.2d 1004, 209 N.Y.S.2d 729 (Sup.Ct.1960), affirmed 15 A.D.2d 815, 225 N.Y.S.2d 538 (1962). The *Gulest* decision was overruled in Jenad, Inc. v. Scarsdale., 18 N.Y.2d 78, 271 N.Y.S.2d 955, 218 N.E.2d 673 (1966).

27. Id. at 730.

funding fees.[28] The test which quickly became the standard view of state courts was suggested by the Wisconsin Supreme Court in Jordan v. Village of Menomonee Falls.[29] A two part "rational nexus" test of reasonableness for judging the validity of impact fees can be discerned in the decision. In response to a developer's attack upon the ordinance as both unauthorized by state statute and as an unconstitutional taking without just compensation, the Jordan court addressed the constitutionality of in lieu fees for educational and recreational purposes. After concluding that the fee payments were statutorily authorized, the court focused first on the *Pioneer Trust* "specifically and uniquely attributable" test.

The Wisconsin Supreme Court expressed concern that it was virtually impossible for a municipality to prove that money payment or land dedication requirements were assessed to meet a need solely generated by a particular subdivision. Suggesting a substitute test, the court held that money payment and dedication requirements for educational and recreational purposes were a valid exercise of the police power if there was a "reasonable connection" between the need for additional facilities and the growth generated by the subdivision. This first "rational nexus" was sufficiently established if the local government could demonstrate that a series of subdivisions had generated the need to provide educational and recreational facilities for the benefit of this stream of new residents. In the absence of contrary evidence, such proof showed that the need for the facilities was sufficiently attributable to the activity of the particular developer to permit the collection of fees for financing required improvements.[30]

The *Jordan* court also rejected the *Gulest* direct benefit requirement, declining to treat the fees as a special assessment. Therefore, it imposed no requirement that the ordinance restrict the funds to the purchase of school and park facilities that would directly benefit the assessed subdivision. Instead, the court concluded that the relationship between the expenditure of funds and the benefits accruing to the subdivision providing the funds was a fact issue pertinent to the reasonableness of the payment requirement under the police power.

The *Jordan* court did not expressly define the "reasonableness" required in the expenditure of extradevelopment capital funds; however, a second "rational nexus" was impliedly required between the expenditure of the funds and benefits accruing to the subdivision. The court concluded that this second "rational nexus" was met where the fees were to be used exclusively for site acquisition and the amount spent by the village in constructing additional school facilities was greater than

---

28. See, Jordan v. Menomonee Falls, 28 Wis.2d 608, 137 N.W.2d 442 (1965); Call v. West Jordan, 606 P.2d 217 (Utah 1979), on rehearing 614 P.2d 1257 (1980).

29. 28 Wis.2d 608, 137 N.W.2d 442 (1965).

30. Id. at 447. It is somewhat ironic that the Illinois court has now interpreted the *Pioneer Trust* test to be met by impact fee programs which meet the rational nexus test. See Northern Ill. Home Builders v. County of Du Page, 165 Ill.2d 25, 208 Ill. Dec. 328, 649 N.E.2d 384 (Ill.1995).

the amounts collected from the developments creating the need for additional facilities.

This second "rational nexus" requirement inferred from *Jordan*, therefore, is met if a local government can demonstrate that its actual or projected extradevelopment capital expenditures earmarked for the substantial benefit of a series of developments are greater than the capital payments required of those developments. Such proof establishes a sufficient benefit to a particular subdivision in the stream of residential growth such that the extradevelopment payment requirements may be deemed to be reasonable under the police power. The concept of benefits received is clearly distinct from the concept of needs attributable. As the *Jordan* court recognized, the benefit accruing to the new development, although it need not be direct, is a necessary factor in analyzing the reasonableness of impact fee payment requirements.[31]

With the adoption by most state courts of the dual rational nexus test, the focus of impact fee controversies shifted to the calculation of impact fees so as to meet the first prong of the test. Since the test provides that a developer can be charged no more than her proportionate share of the cost of new infrastructure, the calculation process must take into account not only the cost of the new infrastructure that the new development requires but credits for payments that have been or will be made by the developer outside the impact fee program. Furthermore, the developer can not be required to pay for the unmet infrastructure costs of previously permitted development.

The Supreme Court of Utah in Banberry Dev. Corp. v. South Jordan City,[32] addressed these issues in the following language that has become widely accepted throughout the country for its specificity and clarity in giving the rules to follow in order to meet the first prong of the dual rational nexus test:

> [To] comply with the standard of reasonableness, a municipal fee ... must not require newly developed properties to bear more than their equitable share of the capital costs in relation to benefits conferred.

> To determine the equitable share of the capital costs to be borne by newly developed properties, a municipality should determine the relative burdens previously borne and yet to be borne by those properties in comparison with the other properties in the municipality as a whole; the fee in question should not exceed the amount sufficient to equalize the relative burdens of newly developed and other properties.

> Among the most important factors the municipality should consider in determining the relative burden already borne and yet to be borne by newly developed properties and other properties are the

---

31. Id. at 448.

32. 631 P.2d 899 (Utah 1981). See also Lafferty v. Payson City, 642 P.2d 376 (Utah 1982).

following, suggested by the well-reasoned authorities cited below: (1) the cost of existing capital facilities; (2) the manner of financing existing capital facilities (such as user charges, special assessments, bonded indebtedness, general taxes, or federal grants); (3) the relative extent to which the newly developed properties and the other properties in the municipality have already contributed to the cost of existing facilities (by means such as user charges, special assessments, or payments from proceeds of general taxes); (4) the relative extent to which the newly developed and the other properties in the municipality will contribute to the cost of existing capital facilities in the future; (5) the extent to which the newly developed properties are entitled to a credit.[33]

Once the development of impact fee law had become clarified and relatively uniform in the state courts, the Supreme Court of the United States decided two cases which evaluated the federal constitutional standards which must be met by programs requiring developer funding of infrastructure: Nollan v. California Coastal Commission[34] and Dolan v. City of Tigard.[35] A look at *Dolan* will provide the opportunity to consider the effect of both cases on the rational nexus standards for impact fees.[36]

In Dolan v. City of Tigard,[37] the Supreme Court of Oregon used the "reasonable relationship" test to uphold the validity of the city's requirement that a landowner dedicate land for improvement of a storm drainage system and for a bicycle/pedestrian pathway. The Oregon court considered its usage of the "reasonable relationship" test consistent with the "essential nexus" language contained in *Nollan*. In a 5–4 decision, the Supreme Court of the United States reversed the Oregon decision. Chief Justice Rehnquist, writing for the majority, first explained that the Court granted certiorari to resolve a question left open by *Nollan* "of what is the required degree of connection between the exactions imposed by the city and the projected impacts of the proposed development."[38]

The Chief Justice went on to characterize the attack by the landowner Dolan on the constitutional validity of the city's actions as being grounded in the contention that the Supreme Court in *Nollan* "had abandoned the 'reasonable relationship' test in favor of a stricter 'essential nexus' test"[39] and further commented that the Supreme Court of Oregon had read *Nollan* "to mean that an exaction is reasonably related to an impact if the exaction serves the same purpose that a denial of the permit would serve."[40]

---

33.   631 P.2d at 903–04.

34.   483 U.S. 825, 107 S.Ct. 3141, 97 L.Ed.2d 677 (1987). The case is also discussed infra at § 10.5.

35.   512 U.S. 374, 114 S.Ct. 2309, 129 L.Ed.2d 304 (1994). The case is also discussed at § 10.5, infra.

36.   The discussion which follows of the Supreme Court's invasion of the dual rational nexus test parallels that found in J.

Juergensmeyer and J. Wadley, Florida Land Use and Growth Management Law § 17.05 (1977).

37.   317 Or. 110, 854 P.2d 437 (1993).

38.   512 U.S. 377, 114 S.Ct. 2309, 2312, 129 L.Ed.2d 304 (1994).

39.   Id. at 2315.

40.   Id.

The majority had no problem, as it had in *Nollan*, finding an essential nexus between governmental action and the governmental interest and the permit condition and therefore reached the second issue, i.e., "whether the degree of the exactions demanded by the city's permit conditions bear the required relationship to the projected impact of petitioners proposed development."[41]

In answering this question, the majority opinion first turned to state court decisions because, as Chief Justice Rehnquist phrased it, "they have been dealing with this question a good deal longer than we have...." The examination of state court decisions began with Billings Properties, Inc. v. Yellowstone County and Jenad, Inc. v. Scarsdale.[42] Without any discussion of what the standard used was in those cases or why it was deficient, the majority opinion rejected the standard used as "too lax to adequately protect petitioner's right to just compensation if her property is taken for a public purpose."[43]

The opinion next turned to a case previously discussed in this section, Pioneer Trust & Savings Bank v. Mount Prospect,[44] and, in a comment of considerable potential importance to local governments which enact impact fee programs, concluded that the Federal Constitution does *not* require such exacting scrutiny as the *Pioneer Trust* court's *specific and uniquely attributable test* requires.

The Chief Justice then turned to state court decisions of which he approved. One of these is Jordan v. Menomonee Falls,[45] the important Wisconsin decision that established the dual rational nexus test and is discussed at length earlier in this section. Surprisingly, the Chief Justice did not refer to the *Jordan* test by its usual name but instead referred to it as a "form" of the reasonable relationship test. This part of the decision seems to leave us with the specific and uniquely attributable test being stricter than the Constitution requires, the "generalized statements as to the necessary connection between the required dedication and the proposed development" required by a few state courts being *too lax*, and the form of the reasonable relationship test adopted by a majority of state courts as the constitutionally acceptable standard.

Instead of calling the "acceptable test" the "dual rational nexus test" the court comes up with a new label, to wit:

> We think the "reasonable relationship" test adopted by a majority of the state courts is closer to the federal constitutional norm than either of those previously discussed. But we do not adopt it as such, partly because the term "reasonable relationship" seems confusingly similar to the term "rational basis" which describes the minimal level of scrutiny under the Equal Protection Clause of the Four-

---

41. Id at 2318.

42. Discussed above at footnote 25.

43. Id. at 2319.

44. See text at footnote 25 and note that the case has been re-interpreted by the Illinois courts in Northern Ill. Home Build-

ers v. County of Du Page, 165 Ill.2d 25, 208 Ill.Dec. 328, 649 N.E.2d 384 (1995).

45. 28 Wis.2d 608, 137 N.W.2d 442 (1965). See discussion in text at footnote 29, above.

teenth Amendment. We think a term such as "rough proportionality" best encapsulates what we hold to be the requirement of the Fifth Amendment. No precise mathematical calculation is required, but the city must make some sort of individualized determination that the required dedication is related both in nature and extent to the impact of the proposed development.[46]

It would seem that the majority may have actually liberalized the standard required of local governments in most states since the Chief Justice concludes that "No precise mathematical calculation is required, but the city must make some effort to quantify its findings in support of ... [its] dedication requirement."[47] As discussed throughout this section, most state courts and statutes require local governments enacting impact fee and other exaction programs to have precise mathematical calculations and to make considerable efforts to quantify their findings.

Arizona, California, and a few other courts[48] cases have considered the meaning of *Dolan* for developer funding fees.[49] The Arizona and California cases intertwine. The Arizona Court of Appeals in Home Builders Ass'n of Central Arizona v. City of Scottsdale,[50] deduced that the United States Supreme Court's remand of Ehrlich v. Culver City[51] (a case in which the city required a developer to pay an impact type fee for recreational facilities when it sought approval to build apartments to replace a private tennis club) for reconsideration in light of the *Dolan* decision implied that the *Dolan* tests can apply to impact fee cases. However, the court of appeals proceeded to distinguish *Dolan* and determined that a *Dolan* analysis was not appropriate in the *Scottsdale* case:

> Unlike Tigard's ordinance, Scottsdale's (ordinance) allows its staff no discretion in setting the fees which are based upon a standardized schedule. The fees are tailored to the type of development involved and are uniform within each class of development. Because the fees are standardized and uniform, and because the ordinance permits no discretion in its application, a prospective developer may know precisely the fee that will be charged. The Scottsdale ordinance, therefore, does not permit a Dolan-like ad hoc, adjudicative determination.[52]

46. 512 U.S. 374, 391, 114 S.Ct. 2309, 2319–20, 129 L.Ed.2d 304 (1994).

47. Id.

48. See McCarthy v. City of Leawood, 257 Kan. 566, 894 P.2d 836, 845 (1995) and Clajon Production Corp. v. Petera, 70 F.3d 1566 (10th Cir.1995), both finding *Dolan* inapplicable to non-physical conditions. See Commercial Builders v. City of Sacramento, 941 F.2d 872 (9th Cir.1991), cert. denied 504 U.S. 931, 112 S.Ct. 1997, 118 L.Ed.2d 593 (1992) (*Nollan* inapplicable to fees). See also Sparks v. Douglas County, 127 Wash.2d 901, 904 P.2d 738 (Wash.1995) ("Under Dolan, a land use regulation does not effect a taking if the local government shows by individualized determination that its exaction is 'roughly proportional' to the impact of the development.")

49. See also infra § 10.5C.

50. 183 Ariz. 243, 902 P.2d 1347 (Ariz. App.1995), aff'd, 187 Ariz. 479, 930 P.2d 993 (1997), cert. denied ___ U.S. ___, 117 S.Ct. 2512, 138 L.Ed.2d 1015 (1997).

51. 512 U.S. 1231, 114 S.Ct. 2731, 129 L.Ed.2d 854 (1994).

52. 183 Ariz. 243, 902 P.2d 1347, 1352 (1995).

Although, the Supreme Court of Arizona unanimously affirmed the court of appeals decision,[53] the court saw the *Dolan* issue somewhat differently, It agreed with the language just quoted but added:

> We note, however, that there may be good reason to distinguish the Dolan adjudicative decision from the Scottsdale legislative one. Ehrlich v. City of Culver City* * * dramatically illustrates the differences between the two exactions.* * * On remand from the United States Supreme Court for reconsideration in light of Dolan, the California Supreme Court held the record insufficient to show that the fee was roughly proportional to the public burden of replacing recreational facilities that would be lost as a result of rezoning Ehrlich's property. The California court suggested that the Dolan analysis applied to cases of regulatory leveraging that occur when the landowner must bargain for approval of a particular use of its land.... The risk of that sort of leveraging does not exist when the exaction is embodied in a generally applicable legislative decision.
>
> Dolan may also be distinguished from our case on another ground. There, the city demanded that Mrs. Dolan cede a part of her property to the city, a particularly invasive form of land regulation that the court believed justified increased judicial protection for the landowner. Here, Scottsdale seeks to impose a fee, a considerably more benign form of regulation.[54]

As indicated in the quoted language from the *Scottsdale* case above, following remand of its decision in *Ehrlich* by the Supreme Court of the United States, the California Court of Appeal, in a divided and unpublished decision, reaffirmed its earlier ruling in favor of Culver City. In a long, rambling decision made especially confusing by the "concurring in part—dissenting in part" statements of several justices, the Supreme Court of California reversed and remanded.[55]

The holding starts out with a direct statement responsive to the speculation over the impact of *Dolan*, to wit:

> We conclude that the tests formulated by the high court in its Dolan and Nollan opinions for determining whether a compensable regulatory taking has occurred under the takings clause of the Fifth Amendment to the federal Constitution apply under the circumstances of this case, to the monetary exaction imposed by Culver City as a condition of approving plaintiffs request that the real property in suit be rezoned to permit the construction of a multi-unit residential condominium. We thus reject the city's contention that the heightened takings clause standard formulated by the court in Nollan and Dolan applies only to cases in which the local land use

53. 187 Ariz. 479, 930 P.2d 993 (1997), cert. denied ___ U.S. ___, 117 S.Ct. 2512, 138 L.Ed.2d 1015 (1997).

54. Id. at 1000.

55. 12 Cal.4th 854, 50 Cal.Rptr.2d 242, 911 P.2d 429 (1996), cert. denied ___ U.S. ___, 117 S.Ct. 299, 136 L.Ed.2d 218 (1996).

authority requires the developer to dedicate real property to public use as a condition of permit approval.[56]

Unfortunately for those seeking a clear answer to the speculation over the meaning of *Dolan*, the California court ties its above-quoted conclusion to its interpretation of the California Mitigation Fee Act.[57]

In spite of much sound and fury, it seems that the emphasis in *Nollan* on "essential nexus" and the emphasis in *Dolan* on"rough proportionality," have not changed things very much. While the Supreme Court has not decided whether to expand *Nollan* and *Dolan* beyond physical exactions, and while state courts have split on that question, it may not matter in most states since those cases have essentially left the dual rational nexus standard intact and perhaps suggested that the federal standard is less demanding.

Now that the authority and tax v. regulations issues have been largely resolved in most jurisdictions—or at least the battle lines clearly drawn—other legal attacks are taking the spotlight. These include (a) the credits issue, (2) the capital versus non-capital expenditures problem, (3) equal protection issues, and (4) exclusionary considerations.

The credits issue, discussed above in connection with the *Banberry* case and the problem of calculating impact fees so as to comply with the first prong of the dual rational nexus test, is of particular concern to the development industry. In a certain sense it not only a logical extension of the problem of applying the rational nexus test but it re-raises the issue of how to reconcile taxes which can be or was used for building infrastructure and which were or are being paid on the same development that is charged impact fees.[58]

The capital expenditures versus non capital expenditures problem is not new but its previous resolution is being questioned. From the very beginning, commentators have limited the expenditure of impact fees to capital infrastructure items. To spend them on operation and maintenance or for items with a very short "life" has been considered improper and most impact fee ordinances and authorization statutes are very

---

56. Id. at 433.

57. "We arrive at this conclusion not by reference to the constitutional takings clause alone, but within the statutory framework presented by the Mitigation Fee Act. (Gov. Code, section 66000 et seq.).... We thus interpret the Act's 'reasonable relationship' standard, as applied to the development fee at issue in this case, as embodying the standard of review formulated by the high court in its Nollan and Dolan opinions.... Applying this standard in this case, we conclude, first, that the city has met its burden of demonstrating the required connection or nexus between the rezoning ...and the imposition of a monetary exaction to be expended in support of recreational purposes as a means of mitigat-

ing that loss. We conclude, however, that the record before us is insufficient to sustain the city's determination that plaintiff pay a so-called mitigation fee of $280,000 as a condition for approval of his request that the property be rezoned to permit the construction of a condominium project. Because the city may be able to justify the imposition of some fee under the recently minted standard of Dolan, we follow the Oregon Supreme Court's disposition in that case and direct that the cause be remanded to the city for additional proceedings in accordance with this opinion." Id.

58. See Nicholas, The Calculation of Proportionate Share Impact Fees, 408 A.P.A.Plan advisory Serv.Rep (1998).

careful and precise in their definition of "capital."[59] A few jurisdictions are beginning to question whether or not the restrictions to "capital" expenditures might not be relaxed. Often it is difficult for local governments to spend impact fee moneys if they can only be used for capital and the local government has no source of revenue to repair and maintain the infrastructure items once they are constructed. The development industry some times would prefer to see maintenance and repair included in the impact fee expenditures list rather than not have the infrastructure item preserved.

The equal protection issue arises because different types of development are charged different fees and developments permitted prior to the enactment of an impact fee program pay no such fees. Neither of these occurrences has found much sympathy from the courts thus far[60] but if discriminatory intent rather than impact analysis based differences can be shown a court might be more sympathetic.

The existence of discriminatory intent would not only raise the equal protection issue but would fit in with concerns over the exclusionary effect of impact fees and other developer funding of infrastructure devices. A comment in this regard by the New Jersey Supreme Court in New Jersey Builders Ass'n v. Bernards Township,[61] focuses the issue:

> The variety of governmental devices used to impose public facility costs on new development reflect a policy choice that higher taxes for existing residents are less desirable than higher development costs for builders, and higher acquisition costs for new residents. An obvious concern is that the disproportionate or excessive use of development exactions could discourage new development or inflate housing prices to an extent that excludes large segments of the population from the available market.[62]

The debate over this aspect of impact fees is just beginning.[63] Many jurisdictions are trying to mitigate the exclusionary impact by exempting low and moderate income housing and other socially desirable developments from impact fees.[64] The development of certain linkage programs, discussed below, are designed to use impact fees to provide funding for such socially desirable uses as low and moderate income housing.

---

59. See Practitioner's Guide, Ch. 16, Model Development Impact Fee Ordinances.

60. Northern Ill. Home Builders Ass'n v. County of Du Page, 251 Ill.App.3d 494, 190 Ill.Dec. 559, 621 N.E.2d 1012 (Ill.App. 1993) (concluding no equal protection violation from differing fees), aff'd, 165 Ill.2d 25, 208 Ill.Dec. 328, 649 N.E.2d 384 (Ill.1995); Ivy Steel & Wire Co. v. City of Jacksonville, 401 F.Supp. 701 (M.D.Fla.1975).

61. 108 N.J. 223, 528 A.2d 555 (N.J. 1987).

62. Id. at 560.

63. See Been, Exit as a Constraint on Land Use Exactions: Rethinking the Unconstitutional Conditions Doctrines, 91 Colum.L.Rev.4 473 (1991) and Sterk, Competition Among Municipalities As A Constraint on Land Use Exactions, 45 Vand.L.Rev. 831 (1992).

64. See White, Development Fees and Exemptions for Affordable Housing: Tailoring Regulations to Achieve Multiple Public Objectives, 6 J.Land Use Envtl.Law 25 (1990). A problem with providing exemptions is that the impact fee program will not have adequate funds to build the needed infrastructure. See Practitioners Guide., Ch.10.

C. *Linkage and Mitigation Fees*

The success of impact fees in raising funds for infrastructure items such as roads, parks, schools, jails, public buildings, and other "hard" or traditional infrastructure items has led many local governments to explore the possibility of using them for "so-called 'soft' or 'social' " infrastructure such as child care facilities, low income housing,[65] art in public places, and environmental mitigation programs.[66]

Developer funding requirements designed to raise capital funds for the "soft" or "social" infrastructure items are usually referred to as "linkage fees" and are viewed as the latest form of exaction.[67] Linkage fees charge commercial developers a fee to provide for expanded services that are incurred by the community because of the new development.

> Underlying every linkage program is the fundamental concept that new downtown development is directly "linked" to a specific social need. The rationale is fairly simple: Not only does the actual construction of the commercial buildings create new construction jobs, but the increased office space attracts new businesses and workers to fill new jobs. The new workers need places to live, transit systems, day care facilities, and the like. From the perspective of linkage proponents, the new commercial development is directly linked both to new employment opportunities and to increased demand for improved municipal facilities and services.[68]

The judicial attitude toward linkage programs has been somewhat mixed with the greatest enthusiasm coming from the California and New Jersey courts. One of the earliest "linkage" programs was San Francisco transit fee imposed on downtown commercial development.[69] It was upheld in Russ Building Partnership v. City and County of San Francisco.[70] In Commercial Builders v. City of Sacramento,[71] the court upheld a

---

65. For discussion of inclusionary zoning for low and moderate cost housing, see supra § 6.7.

66. See Thomas W. Ledman, Local Government Environmental Mitigation Fees: Development Exactions, The Next Generation, 45 Fla.L.Rev.835 (1993); Fred P. Bosselman and Nancy E. Stroud, Mandatory Tithes: The Legality of Land Development Linkage, 9 Nova L.J. 381 (1985); Anne E. Mudge, Impact Fees for Conversion of Agricultural Land: A Resource-Based Development Policy for California's Cities and Counties, 19 Ecology L.Q. 63 (1992); Alterman, Evaluating Linkage and Beyond: Letting the Windfall Genie Out of the Exactions Bottle, 34 Wash.U.J.Urb. & Contemp.L. 3 (1988); Merrill and Lincoln, Linkage Fees and Fair Share Regulations: Law and Method, 25 Urb.Law. 223 (1993).

67. "[L]inkage refers to a variety of programs that require developers to contribute toward new affordable housing, employment opportunities, child care facilities,

transit systems and the like, in return for the city's permission to build new commercial developments." C. Andrew and D. Merriam, Defensible Linkage, Ch.19, Development Impact Fees (Nelson, ed. 1988).

68. Id. at 228. See also, Kayden & Pollard, Linkage Ordinances and the Traditional Exactions Analysis: The Connection Between Office Development and Housing, 50 Law and Contemp. Probs. 127 (1987).

69. Terminal Plaza Corp. v. City & County of San Francisco, 177 Cal.App.3d 892, 223 Cal.Rptr. 379 (Cal.App.1986) (upholding fees charged against conversion of single room occupancy hotels) was decided earlier but received considerably less attention.

70. 199 Cal.App.3d 1496, 246 Cal.Rptr. 21 (1987).

71. 941 F.2d 872 (9th Cir.1991), cert. denied 504 U.S. 931, 112 S.Ct. 1997, 118 L.Ed.2d 593 (1992).

city ordinance which conditioned nonresidential building permits upon the payment of a fee for housing to offset expenses associated with the influx of low-income workers for the new project. The developers argued that the ordinance was a taking because it placed the burden of paying for the housing upon the new development without a sufficient showing that nonresidential development contributed to the need for new low-income housing in proportion to that burden. The court found no taking, however, as the fee was enacted only after a study revealed that the need for low-income housing would rise as a direct result of demand from workers on the new development. The court found that "[t]he burden assessed against the developers thus bears a rational relationship to a public cost closely associated with such development."[72] The court seemingly broadened its holding beyond the imposition of a fee for low-income housing when it stated that "[a] purely financial exaction, then, will not constitute a taking if it is made for the purpose of paying a social cost that is reasonably related to the activity against which the fee is assessed."[73]

Perhaps the most famous linkage case thus far decided is the New Jersey case, Holmdel Builders Ass'n v. Township of Holmdel,[74] which upheld the imposition of fees on commercial and non-inclusionary residential developments for the construction of low income housing per the local government's responsibilities under the *Mt. Laurel* doctrine.[75]

Not all linkage fee programs have fared as well as those just discussed. In San Telmo Assoc. v. City of Seattle,[76] the Supreme Court of Washington had before it a Seattle housing preservation ordinance which provided that property owners who wished to demolish low income housing units had to replace a specified percentage of the housing to be demolished with other suitable housing or contribute to the city's low income housing replacement fund. The court found the requirement to constitute an unauthorized tax.

The list of issues raised in regard to the validity of linkage fees is almost identical to the list of issues regarding to validity of impact fees.[77] These include authority of the local government to enact linkage programs,[78] illegal tax rather than land use regulation,[79] violation of due

---

72. Id. at 874.

73. Id. at 876. The *Commercial Builders* court also rejected the developers' contention that *Nollan* requires a more stringent taking standard, holding that "*Nollan* does not stand for the proposition that an exaction ordinance will be upheld only where it can be shown that the development is directly responsible for the social ill in question. Rather, *Nollan* holds that where there is no evidence of a nexus between the development and that problem that the exaction seeks to address, the exaction cannot be upheld." Id.

74. 121 N.J. 550, 583 A.2d 277 (1990).

75. See supra § 6.6 for a discussion of *Mt. Laurel* I and *Mt. Laurel* II, and § 6.7 for discussion of inclusionary zoning.

76. 108 Wash.2d 20, 735 P.2d 673 (1987). See also Sintra, Inc. v. City of Seattle, 119 Wash.2d 1, 829 P.2d 765 (1992) (ordinance was found to be an illegal tax, and when the city persisted in applying the ordinance to other property, court found behavior which led to § 1983 damages).

77. See § 9.8B supra.

78. See Holmdel, note 74; Bonan v. City of Boston, 398 Mass. 315, 496 N.E.2d 640 (1986) (court did not reach issue of authority which was raised by lower court).

process, equal protections or takings provisions of U.S. and state constitutions,[80] and the standard to be applied to govern the reasonableness of the exercise of the police power.

In this last regard, *Holmdel* is of particular interest since it held that linkage programs for low income housing need not meet the rational nexus test:

> We conclude that the rational-nexus test is not apposite in determining the validity of inclusionary zoning devices generally or of affordable housing development fees in particular. * * * Inclusionary zoning through the imposition of development fees is permissible because such fees are conducive to the creation of realistic opportunities for the development of affordable housing; development fees are the functional equivalent of mandatory set-asides; and it is fair and reasonable to impose such fee requirements on private developers when they possess, enjoy, and consume land, which constitutes the primary resource for housing.[81]

Whether linkage programs will develop on a parallel course to impact fees and become a reflection of them as far as the legal issues and standards are concerned is one of the current but unresolved issues of growth management law. A similar issue exists in regard to environmental mitigation fees which are assessments made by local governments against new development to reimburse the community for the new development's proportionate negative impact on the community's environment.[82] Whether these fees will parallel impact fees, and or linkage programs, and become another legally authorized and acceptable aspect of developer funding to offset the impact of development is also an issue of current and considerable importance.

§ 9.9 Growth Management Techniques: Transferable Development Rights Programs

A. *General Theory: Mitigating Potential Wipeouts*

Euclidean zoning and related land use regulations necessarily create uneven impacts on landowners. Landowners in areas where higher intensity development is encouraged economically benefit, while landowners in areas where land is protected from development are hurt.[1] A

---

79. San Telmo Assoc. v. City of Seattle, note 76.

80. For a full discussion of due process, equal protection, and taking challenges, see Merrill and Lincoln, Linkage Fees and Fair Share Regulations: Law and Method, 25 Urb.Law. 223 (1993).

81. 121 N.J. 550, 583 A.2d 277, 288.

82. See Thomas W. Ledman, Local Government Environmental Mitigation Fees: Development Exactions, The Next Generation, 45 Fla.L.Rev.835 (1993).

§ 9.9

1. A TDR program is a growth management tool in which the development potential from sensitive lands is transferred to non-sensitive lands through private market transactions. They have been the subject of numerous articles. See, e.g., John M. Armentano, Preserving Environmentally Sensitive Land, 25 Real Est.L.J. 197 (1996); Herbert M. Balia, The Long Island Pine Barrens Protection Act—A Model of Compromise Between Home Rule and State Intervention in Land Use Control, 66–Oct. N.Y.St.B.J. 42 (1994); Antonio Herman

fairer system would allow all landowners to benefit from an area's development, and require all benefitted landowners to pay the costs associated with the preservation and protection of sensitive land in the area.[2] Transferable Development Right (TDR) programs are frequently incorporated into growth management programs because they offer that alternative by separating the need to preserve a particular parcel of land and the right of the landowner to develop that land. The advantage of the TDR is that it provides a means to economically benefit owners of sensitive land by a means other than development of that land or the payment of public funds and thereby to mitigate the adverse economic effect of many land use regulations.

There are economic benefits which arise from protecting environmental quality. By requiring landowners of non-sensitive land to buy development rights from the owners of sensitive land, the government is forcing developers to "internalize" the costs associated with land development.[3] The traditional zoning oriented approach to development regulation permits private landowners that are benefitted from environmental amenities not to consider the social costs of destroying environmental or similar benefits enjoyed by a community. If places are made for bald eagles, the community is better for it. If those places are lost, the community as well as the bald eagles are worse for it. TDRs create a greater social efficiency by forcing the developers that benefit from land preservation to recognize the costs associated with such preservation.

Benjamin & Charles Weiss, Jr., Economic and Market Innovations as Instruments of Environmental Policy in Brazil and the United States, 32 Tex Int'l L.J. 67 (1997); Madelyn Glickfield, Update on Transfer of Development Rights, c431 ALI–ABA 1375 (1989); Terrence D. Moore, New Jersey's Special Place: The Pinelands National Reserve, 168–APR N.J.Law. 25 (1995); Richard J Roddewig & Cheryl A. Inghram, Transferable Development Rights Programs: TDRs and the Real Estate Marketplace, 401 Planning Advisory Service Rep. 1 (1987); Philip J. Tierney, Bold Promises but Baby steps: Maryland's Growth Policy to the Year 2020, 23 U.Balt.L. Rev. 461 (1994); James T.B. Tripp & Daniel J. Dudek, Institutional Guidelines for Designing Successful Transferable Rights Programs, 6 Yale J.Reg. 369 (1989); Jennifer L. Bradshaw, Comment, The Slippery Slope of Modern Takings Jurisprudence in New Jersey, 7 Seton Hall Const.L.J. 433 (1997); Sean F. Nolan Cozata Solloway, Note and Comment, Preserving Our Heritage: Tools to Cultivate Agricultural Preservation in New York State, 17 Pace L.Rev. 591 (1997); Joseph D. Stinson, Note and Comment, Transferring Development Rights: Purpose, Problems, and Prospects in New York, 17 Pace L.Rev. 319 (1996); John Stokes, Keys to a Successful TDR Program, Presentation to a National to Roundtable on TDR, New York, October 21, 1997.

For discussions of the severing and acquisition of development rights under British law, see Cullingworth, Town and Country Planning on Britain (10th ed.1988); Grant, Urban Planning Law, Chs 1 & 4 (1987).

2. See supra § 3.24 for discussion of more far reaching programs of windfall recapture and mitigation wipeout.

3. Thus TDR programs deal with the failure of the market to equate social benefits and costs with private costs and benefits. Under Euclidean zoning, significant costs are created by development that generally are not borne by the development. At the same time, owners of environmentally sensitive land are forced to provide a significant benefit to society without getting compensated. This creates a failure in the market in which the development is being priced too low (because it is not internalizing the costs it creates) and the owners of sensitive lands are not getting the values they deserve. See Frederick Goddard, Economic Theory for Analysis of Natural Resources and the Environment 23 (1993).

Under Euclidean zoning, local governments must either buy sensitive land or regulate it heavily and risk a takings challenge.[4] To prevent takings challenges that drain the public fisc, local governments often grant some development on each parcel through some type of a variance or similar procedure. This results in urban sprawl, environmental resource depletion, and public safety problems. The constitutional and budgetary limitations of zoning thus limit the effectiveness of land protection programs. By separating the development potential of the parcel from the land itself, and creating a market in which that development potential can be separately purchased, TDR programs provide value to the owners of preserved properties and avoid takings challenges without threatening the effectiveness of the preservation plan.[5]

B. How TDRs Work

TDR programs separate the development potential of a parcel from the land itself, and create a market where that development potential can be sold. Planning agencies then identify areas they wish to protect and other areas which are suitable for development.[6] An effective TDR program will have delineated sending and receiving zones.[7] Since the need to protect sensitive land is often the impetus for TDR arrangements, identifying the land from which development potential will be sent, the sending zones, is relatively simple.[8] Local governments quite often have a difficult time, politically and practically, identifying receiving zones that will then have more dense development than would otherwise be allowed.[9]

Sending zones, as the name suggests, are simply zones or areas that will export development potential. The sending areas should be identified as areas for limited development within the context of a comprehensive plan.[10] The plan could designate an area for limited development for any number of reasons: habitat preservation,[11] wetland protection, erosion control,[12] protection of historic resources,[13] and agricultural land retention.[14]

4.　Regulatory takings are considered in Ch. 10.

5.　It would follow that if TDRs are not considered in the takings calculus, development regulating entities would lose a significant incentive to use a program which is more fair and efficient than current, regulation-based land use control. This is the dilemma posed by the *Suitum* case discussed below.

6.　See Stinson, supra note 1, at 328–29.

7.　See Tripp and Dudek, supra note 1, at 376.

8.　See James C. Nicholas, Hackensack Meadowlands Development Commission's Program of Transferable Development Rights 10–11 (Oct. 1997) [hereinafter Hackensack proposal].

9.　See Tierney, supra note 1, at 496. See also Hackensack proposal, supra note 8, at 10–11.

10.　Solloway, supra note 1, at 626–27.

11.　See Glisson v. Alachua County, 558 So.2d 1030 (Fla.App.1990) (considering a TDR scheme designed, in part, to protect wildlife habitat).

12.　See Suitum v. Tahoe Regional Planning Agency, ___ U.S. ___, 117 S.Ct. 1659, 137 L.Ed.2d 980 (1997).

13.　See *Suitum*, Amicus brief of City of New York, 1997 WL 10278.

14.　See Tierney, supra note 1, at 496.

Generally sending area property owners are required to record a covenant running with the land permanently removing certain development rights. Once a landowner in a sending zone has received her TDRs, she no longer has the right to develop the land in the manner or manners restricted by the general regulations and the restrictions contained in the covenant.[15] However, the regulating agency prepares, or at least should prepare, a list of residual uses of the land after the TDRs have been sold. This accomplishes two things: 1) it helps protect against a takings claim if TDRs are not considered relevant to the takings analysis;[16] and 2) it helps determine the "non-development" value of the land. Non-development uses might include agriculture, beekeeping, bird watching, primitive camping and other recreational use. A recently discovered popular residual use of wetlands near metropolitan areas is as "antenna farms." The land can also be used in a "mitigation bank" system.[17]

In order to achieve fairness, the TDRs must have a meaningful economic value. To make sure a market is created, there must be a balance between sending and receiving zones.[18] If there are too many TDRs on the market, the price falls and the fairness of the TDR scheme is questionable. Additionally, if receiving area property owners need not acquire TDRs in order to attain their desired level of intensity, then there will be no demand for those rights and their economic value will be zero. Ideally, each owner of restricted land would get enough TDRs to mitigate the development value loss and the value of the use of those TDRs in the receiving area will deliver that value to the sending area property owners.

Receiving zones are regions set aside by the regulating jurisdiction to accept development potential from restricted land elsewhere in the jurisdiction.[19] To maintain a market for the TDRs from the sending zone, receiving zones must be growing areas with a market demand for increased density.[20] In a free market, the value of the TDRs will be set near the marginal value of that increased density.[21] However, if landowners in receiving zones can increase density through variances or rezoning, those administrative procedures are, in effect, competing with TDRs. If it costs less to go through the administrative process for a rezoning, the TDR market will flounder. Local governments instituting TDR programs should be careful not to cannibalize the TDR program by providing administrative alternatives to the market. Additionally, if receiving areas are already "over-zoned," marginal increases in land development intensity will have no economic value and so also will TDRs have no economic value.

15. See Stinson, supra note 1, at 329.

16. See Lucas v. South Carolina Coastal Council, 505 U.S. 1003, 112 S.Ct. 2886, 120 L.Ed.2d 798 (1992). For a discussion of takings generally, see infra §§ 10.2–11.

17. See § 9.8C, supra.

18. See Stinson, supra note 1, at 341–42.

19. See Tierney, supra note 1, at 496–97.

20. See Stinson, supra note 1, at 347–348.

21. See Tripp & Dudek, supra note 1, at 376.

Chapter 10

CONSTITUTIONAL LIMITATIONS ON LAND USE CONTROLS

Analysis

I. INTRODUCTION

II. THE TAKING ISSUE

I. INTRODUCTION

§ 10.1 Introduction

A. *The Property Conflict in American Society*

Alexis de Tocqueville noted that "the love of property" is "keener" in the United States than it is anywhere else, and that Americans "display less inclination toward doctrines that in any way threaten the way property is owned."[1] In the context of property in land, de Tocqueville's observation reflects what Fred Bosselman calls the land ethic of opportunity, the view of land as things, parcels and interests, used to create wealth.[2] However, as Bosselman notes, other land ethics influence Americans' views of property. In tension with the ethic of opportunity is the land ethic of responsibility, which views parcels of property as interdependent parts of an ecological and social whole.[3] These conflicting land ethics result in intense conflict over the extent to which government may affect private property rights for the greater good of society. The battle ground for this jurisprudential issue is the constitutional law of land use, not only the Fifth Amendment takings clause, but also protections of due process, equal protection, free speech, and religious freedoms.[4]

Given that property is the oldest branch of the common law,[5] the legal fundamentals of property ownership are surprisingly vague. Any law student would feel much more comfortable defining crime, tort, or contract than property, possession, or ownership.[6] Precise meanings for these property concepts do not in fact exist,[7] and this complicates the

---

§ 10.1

1. Alexis de Tocqueville, Democracy in America 614 (J. Mayer & M. Lerner, eds. 1966).

2. See Fred Bosselman, Four Land Ethics: Order, Reform, Responsibility, Opportunity, 24 Envtl.Law 1429 (1994).

3. See John A. Humbach, Law and a New Land Ethic, 74 Minn.L.Rev 339 (1989).

4. See infra §§ 10.12–18.

5. Common law property dates directly to William the Conqueror, the Norman victor of the Battle of Hastings in 1066. Corne-

lius J. Moynihan, Introduction to the Law of Real Property 1–8 (2d.ed.1988).

6. See generally Carol M. Rose, Possession as the Origin of Property, 52 U.Chi. L.Rev. 73 (1985) (discussing the elusive nature of the concepts of ownership and property).

7. See Ruckleshaus v. Monsanto Corp., 467 U.S. 986, 104 S.Ct. 2862, 2872–74, 81 L.Ed.2d 815 (1984) (discussing the difficulty of defining "property"); U.S.A. v. Dollfus Mieget Co. S.A., [1952] 1 All E.R. 572, 581 (H.L.) (stating that "the English law has never worked out a completely logical and

resolution of land use conflicts between individual property rights and the social interest. The absence of consistent standards has made the constitutional protection of property susceptible to change, as different social and judicial outlooks have gained power over time. Justice Holmes' statement that "[e]very opinion tends to become a law"[8] has proved especially true concerning constitutional land use issues.

Broadly, the endpoints on the line of opposing views in this area are a "proacquisitive position," which favors individual wealth, and a "prosocial position," which argues for supremacy of the common good.[9] The proacquisitive position sees the value of land in what it can produce for the individual. Adherents sometimes describe this right as "inherent in human nature" or part of the "natural law." Differences exist among these adherents. Richard Epstein espouses a libertarian position arguing that the eminent domain clause should protect against all government efforts of redistribution of personal or real property.[10] Justice Scalia rejects the libertarian view, favoring a utilitarian approach, and gives enhanced protection only to land.[11]

The prosocial position is a manifestation of the social function theory of ownership first popularized as a jurisprudential theory of ownership by the great Leon Duguit.[12] Under the social function theory, the ownership of property is not absolute or immutable but a changing concept, constantly redefined to permit ownership of property to fill whatever role society assigns it at a given time.[13] The individual has an obligation not to use property in violation of the public right.[14] Economic losses may result, but the value of a parcel of land "has no economic value in the absence of the society around it."[15] As Justice Jackson put

exhaustive definition of 'possession' "). See also James W. Ely, Jr., The Guardian of Every Other Right: A Constitutional History of Property Rights 6 (1992) ("property is a dynamic concept") and Rose, supra note 6 (discussing the elusive nature of these concepts).

8. Lochner v. New York, 198 U.S. 45, 76, 25 S.Ct. 539, 547, 49 L.Ed. 937 (1905) (Holmes, J., dissenting).

9. For a range of views see Carol M. Rose, Property as the Keystone Right? 71 Notre Dame L. Rev. 329 (1996); Robert C. Ellickson, Property in Land, 102 Yale L.J. 1315, 1390–91 (1993); Gregory S. Alexander, Takings and the Post–Modern Dialectic of Property, 9 Const.Commentary 259 (1992); Bernard H. Siegan, Constitutional Protection of Property and Economic Rights, 29 San Diego L.Rev. 161 (1992).

10. Richard A. Epstein, Takings: Private Property and the Power of Eminent Domain (1985); Richard A. Epstein, Lucas v. South Carolina Coastal Council: A Tangled Web of Expectations, 45 Stan.L.Rev. 1411 (1993).

11. See Bosselman, supra note 2 at 1501, regarding Justice Scalia's views, and

Richard A. Epstein, Lucas v. South Carolina Coastal Council: A Tangled Web of Expectations, 45 Stan.L.Rev. 1411 (1993) comparing his views with those of Justice Scalia.

12. Lectures of Prof. M.E. Kadam of the Un. of Geneva prepared for the Faculte Internationel Pour L'Enseignement du Droit Compare entitled La Notion et les Limites de la Propriete Privee en Droit Compare. See also Julian Conrad .Juergensmeyer & James Wadley, The Common Lands Concept: A "Commons" Solution to a Common Environmental Problem, 14 Nat.Res.J. 361, at 380 (1974).

13. See Eric T. Freyfogle, Context and Accommodation in Modern Property Law, 41 Stan.L.Rev. 1529 (1989).

14. See Myrl L. Duncan, Property As a Public Conversation, Not a Lockean Soliloquy: A Role for Intellectual and Legal History in Taking Analysis, 26 Envtl.L. 1095, 1142–1144 (1996).

15. Penn Central Transp.Co. v. City of New York, 42 N.Y.2d 324, 397 N.Y.S.2d 914, 918, 366 N.E.2d 1271 (1977).

it, "not all economic interests are 'property rights'; only those economic advantages are 'rights' which have the law back of them."[16] Property, in other words, has no fixed meaning.

The independence and interdependence of land parcels are other lenses through which to view the conflict over property. Some theorists begin with land as independent from society. They divide land into parcels for people to use. Others see land in an ecologically and socially interdependent context. For them, the artificial parceling of land creates secondary rights. As Eric Freyfogle observes, if one views land as a commodity, then property is not the land or "the thing itself, but the owner's power over the thing."[17] So viewed, property "lose[s] its tethers with any particular spot on the landscape [and becomes] an imaginary ideal [where] an owner's legal rights transen[d] the details of place."[18]

Commentators have described these independent and interdependent positions, respectively, as those of a "transformative economy" and an "economy of nature."[19] They contrast anthropocentrism with biocentrism, and natural law with the law of nature. The division can be seen on the Court as well. Justice Scalia endorsed the former view in Lucas v. South Carolina Coastal Council quoting with approval Lord Coke, who said "For what is land but the profits thereof?"[20] Justice Blackmun endorsed the latter view in Sierra Club v. Morton, by quoting John Donne: "No man is an Iland, intire of itselfe; every man is a piece of the Continent * * *."[21]

Expectations play an important role in defining property rights, but how expectations are shaped and how they are affected by new learning and changed circumstances is not clear. The history of property law is important in determining expectations of rights in land, but differences of opinion exist over what history shows.[22] Some say that history supports freedom to use land without legislative interference.[23] Under this view, landowners may do as they wish with their property limited only by the common law nuisance requirement that they do no harm to others.[24] Others say that legislative restrictions on land use that went

16. United States v. Willow River Power Co. 324 U.S. 499, 502, 65 S.Ct. 761, 764, 89 L.Ed. 1101 (1945).

17. Eric T. Freyfogle, The Owning and Taking of Sensitive Lands, 43 U.C.L.A.L.Rev. 77, 97 (1995).

18. Id.

19. These terms are used by Joseph Sax in Property Rights and the Economy of Nature: Understanding Lucas v. South Carolina Coastal Council, 45 Stan.L.Rev. 1433, 1442 (1993).

20. Lucas v. South Carolina Coastal Council, 505 U.S. 1003, 1017, 112 S.Ct. 2886, 2894, 120 L.Ed.2d 798 (1992).

21. 405 U.S. 727, 760, n. 2, 92 S.Ct. 1361, 1378, 31 L.Ed.2d 636 (1972) (Blackmun, dissenting).

22. See generally James W. Ely, Jr., The Enigmatic Place of Property Rights in Modern Constitutional Thought in Bill of Rights in Modern America After 200 Years at 93 (David J. Bodenhamer and James W. Ely, Jr.eds.1993).

23. See Roger Pilon, Property Rights, Takings, and a Free Society, 6 Harv. J.L.Pub. Policy 165 (1983); Roger J. Marzulla, The Constitution, Regulatory Takings and Property Rights, Statement in Hearings Before House Committee on the Judiciary, 104th Cong., 1st Sess. (1995), available on Lexis, Legis. Library CNGTST File.

24. See Douglas W. Kmiec, The Original Understanding of the Taking Clause is Neither Weak Nor Obtuse, 88 Colum.L.Rev. 1630, 1637 (1988).

well beyond the common law of nuisance were found with some frequency in colonial and the early post-Revolutionary times.[25] To them, this suggests that an expectation of free land use, limited only by nuisance law, is unwarranted.

Whether one view among these will dominate remains to be seen. Also, whether one view ought to dominate is a question that proponents of each view should ask themselves. Minimizing public rights may impair our cultural and historical resources and may devastate our natural resources, upsetting critical ecological balances. Minimizing private rights may mean destabilizing investment in land.[26] Perhaps, "in a democratic society the existence of multiple ethics must be accepted."[27]

B. Overview of the Constitutional Issues

The most vital constitutional provision regarding this conflict over property is the taking clause of the Fifth Amendment, which provides that private property shall not be "taken for public use without just compensation."[28] This provision is the basis of "the taking issue,"[29] which deals with the degree to which land can be regulated to protect the public interest. The question, as we will see, often becomes one of line drawing under the reasoning of Justice Holmes that "if regulation goes too far it will be recognized as a taking."[30]

Many constitutional land use concerns, however, do not squarely fall on Holmes' Fifth Amendment scale, but implicate the Fourteenth Amendment. For example, substantive due process looks to the benefits that a regulation confers on society to decide whether the regulation is within the scope of government authority and examines whether its goal is accomplished in a rational manner.[31] Procedural due process oversees the methods of adjudicating rights of landowners, requiring that an opportunity be given to challenge deprivations of property before an impartial decisionmaker.[32] Further, the guarantee of equal protection limits government regulation from irrational classifications, and has the most force when ordinances affect the land use rights of suspect classes or the exercise of fundamental rights of some in ways different from others.[33]

---

25. See John F. Hart, Colonial Land Use Law and Its Significance for Modern Takings Doctrine, 109 Harv.L.Rev. 1252 (1996); William Michael Treanor, The Original Understanding of the Takings Clause and the Political Process, 95 Colum.L.Rev. 782 (1995); David L. Callies, Robert H. Freilich, and Thomas E. Roberts, Cases and Materials on Land Use 1–3 (2d ed.1994).

26. See Carol M. Rose, A Dozen Propositions on Private Property, Public Rights, and the New Takings Legislation, 53 Wash. & Lee L.Rev. 265, 297 (1996).

27. Bosselman, supra note 2, at 1511. See also Robert C. Ellickson, Liberty, Prop-

erty, and Environmental Ethics, 21 Eco. L.Q. 397 (1994) urging accommodation.

28. U.S. Const. Amend. 5. The takings guarantee applies to the states through the Fourteenth Amendment's due process requirement. Chicago, B. & Q. R.R. Co. v. Chicago, 166 U.S. 226, 235–41, 17 S.Ct. 581, 584–86, 41 L.Ed. 979 (1897).

29. See infra § 10.2.

30. Pennsylvania Coal v. Mahon, 260 U.S. 393, 415, 43 S.Ct. 158, 160, 67 L.Ed. 322 (1922).

31. See infra § 10.12.

32. See infra § 10.13.

33. See infra § 10.14

First Amendment protections of free speech and religion also curtail the power of government to regulate land use. The First Amendment is especially relevant concerning ordinances that regulate signs, sex-oriented businesses, and religious uses.[34]

II. THE TAKING ISSUE

✳ § 10.2 Framing the Taking Issue

A. *Its Constitutional Home*

The provision in the Fifth Amendment that prohibits government from taking property for a public use without just compensation is the centerpiece of constitutional land use law.[1] The Supreme Court's opinions dealing with the question of when land use regulations constitute takings have not set a clear course, and no doubt some would consider that description to be overly kind. Yet, since the taking issue deals with one of the most contentious matters in American society,[2] it is not surprising that the Supreme Court has struggled to establish precise guidelines. Perhaps the problem is that the Court has spent too much energy trying to define a taking, and too little defining property.[3]

The complexity of the issue has drawn the attention of many writers and an enormous amount of literature exists addressing what is, or what ought to be, the law.[4] This part of Chapter 10 focuses on the taking issue by tracing its path through the major Supreme Court decisions, and then dealing with salient problem areas, such as the meaning of investment-backed expectations, the definition of property for purposes of a taking claim, the remedy available, and rules of ripeness. We treat the related topics of eminent domain, public use, and just compensation elsewhere.[5]

---

34. See infra §§ 10.15–18.

§ 10.2

1. The Fifth Amendment, which obligates the federal government to pay compensation, was applied to the states through the Fourteenth Amendment in Chicago, B. & Q. R.R. v. Chicago, 166 U.S. 226, 235–41, 17 S.Ct. 581, 584–86, 41 L.Ed. 979 (1897).

2. See supra § 10.1.

3. United States v. Willow River Power Co., 324 U.S. 499, 502, 65 S.Ct. 761, 764, 89 L.Ed. 1101 (1945). See also supra § 10.1.

4. A short list is provided here. Other works are cited throughout the chapter dealing with specific issues. Setting the stage is The Taking Issue, a 1973 book by Fred Bosselman, David L. Callies, and John Banta. Two early, influential articles are Frank Michelman, Property, Utility, and Fairness: Comments on the Ethical Foundations of "Just Compensation," 80 Harv. L.Rev. 1165 (1967) and Joseph L. Sax, Takings and the Police Power, 74 Harv.L.Rev. 36 (1964). Two collections of recent articles

from a variety of perspectives are Institute of Bill of Rights Symposium: Defining Takings: Private Property and the Future of Government Regulation, 38 Wm. & Mary L.Rev. 749 (1997) and Takings: Land Development Conditions and Regulatory Takings after Dolan and Lucas (David L. Callies ed.1996). Other articles include Carol M. Rose, Property Rights, Regulatory Regimes, and the New Takings Jurisprudence: An Evolutionary Approach, 57 Tenn.L.Rev. 577 (1990); Douglas W. Kmiec, The Original Understanding of the Taking Clause Is Neither Weak nor Obtuse, 88 Colum.L.Rev. 1630 (1988); Andrea L. Peterson, The Takings Clause: In Search of Underlying Principles (pt. 1), 77 Cal.L.Rev. 1301 (1989); Frank Michelman, Takings, 1987, 88 Colum.L.Rev. 1600 (1988); Carol M. Rose, Mahon Reconstructed: Why the Takings Issue Is Still a Muddle, 57 S.Cal.L.Rev. 561 (1984).

5. See infra Chapter 16.

The taking issue is concerned with whether, and if so when, the Fifth Amendment requirement that just compensation be paid when the government "takes" property should be applied when the government "regulates" property. The physical connotation of the word "take" argues against applying the clause to regulatory impacts. It also seems to be agreed that the founders intended to require compensation only for physical expropriations of property.[6] Yet, the Court has "not * * * read [the taking clause] literally,"[7] but, over the years, has interpreted the word "take" to include the effect of regulations in some instances. This has given rise to the doctrine of regulatory takings, or, in terms perhaps more familiar to the legal ear, the doctrine of constructive takings.[8] The reach of the takings clause is expanded even further by the Court's reading of the "public use" phrase to encompass any conceivable public purpose.[9] Hence, regulations for public purposes may become Fifth Amendment takings.

The Court frequently says that the Fifth Amendment is designed to prevent the government "from forcing some people to alone bear public burdens which, in all fairness and justice, should be borne by the public as a whole."[10] To effectuate that goal, the courts must determine when a regulation that is otherwise a valid exercise of the police power should be converted into an exercise of the power of eminent domain due to its excessive effect or unwarranted nature. Since the Constitution does not prohibit the taking of property, crossing the line from the police power to the eminent domain power does not invalidate the regulation. It means that compensation is due.

The United States appears to stand alone in providing constitutionally compelled compensation for the effects of land regulations on development value.[11] Generally, under English,[12] Australian,[13] Canadian,[14]

---

6. See Lucas v. South Carolina Coastal Council, 505 U.S. 1003, 1015, n. 15, 112 S.Ct. 2886, 2893, 120 L.Ed.2d 798 (1992) and William M. Treanor, The Origins and Original Significance of the Just Compensation Clause of the Fifth Amendment, 94 Yale L.J. 694 (1985).

7. Penn Central Transportation Co. v. New York City, 438 U.S. 104, 142, 98 S.Ct. 2646, 2668, 57 L.Ed.2d 631 (1978) (Rehnquist, J., dissenting), rehearing denied 439 U.S. 883, 99 S.Ct. 226, 58 L.Ed.2d 198 (1978).

8. See, e.g., Harris v. Town of Lincoln, 668 A.2d 321 (R.I.1995) (using "constructive taking" term).

9. See Jed Rubenfeld, Usings, 102 Yale L.J. 1077 (1993), discussing the disappearance of "for public use" from the compensation clause. See infra § 16.4.

10. Armstrong v. United States, 364 U.S. 40, 49, 80 S.Ct. 1563, 1569, 4 L.Ed.2d 1554 (1960).

11. See J. Peter Byrne, Ten Arguments for the Abolition of the Regulatory Takings Doctrine, 22 Ecol.L.Q. 89, 106 (1995), asserting that "no other country in the world provides constitutional or general protection for the 'development value' of land."

12. Malcolm Grant, Urban Planning Law (1982); Malcolm Grant, If Tigard Were an English City: Exactions Law in England Following the Tesco Case, Ch. 17 in Takings: Land Development Conditions and Regulatory Takings After Dolan and Lucas (David L.Callies ed.1996).

13. Byrne, supra note 11, at 108–109.

14. R.J. Bauman, Exotic Expropriations: Government Action and Compensation, 52 The Advocate 561 (1994); Eric C.E. Todd, The Law of Expropriation and Compensation in Canada (2d ed.1992); Donald G. Hagman and Dean Misczynski, Compensable Regulation, Ch. 11 at 280 in Windfalls for Wipeouts: Land Value Capture and Compensation (Donald G. Hagman and Dean Misczynski eds.1978).

and German[15] law restrictions on rights to develop land can be imposed without compensating landowners, though statutory requirements of payment are applicable in some instances.

B. Inverse Condemnation

Aptly named, the action in inverse condemnation is the procedural context in which the taking issue arises.[16] Direct appropriations under the power of eminent domain occur by condemnation proceedings brought by the state against a property owner.[17] These direct condemnation proceedings establish that the taking is for a public use or purpose and assess just compensation to be paid to the owner. In contrast, the taking issue explored here arises from the consequences of government action with respect to property, unaccompanied by an offer of compensation or an action to condemn. When a government dams a river, flooding upstream property, or zones land for open space so that no economically viable use can be made of it, no offer of compensation precedes the act. An owner who thinks the action has effected a taking and that compensation ought to be paid has the burden to initiate suit against the government.

§ 10.3   Physical Invasions as Takings

A. The Loretto Per Se Test

Governmentally induced physical invasions trigger special concern since the Court treats the right to exclude as the paramount property right.[1] The fact that land was invaded has been critical in numerous cases where takings have been found, such as where a government dam caused flooding of upstream property,[2] where military planes engaged in frequent, low-level flights over land wreaking havoc with the chicken farm below,[3] and where the government required the owner of a pond, which had been made navigable by dredging, to allow entry to the boating public.[4] While the vast majority of cases relevant to land use law involve non-invasive regulations, the physical taking doctrine is impor-

---

15. Thomas Lundmark, "Takings" and Environmental Law in Germany, in North European Environmental Law 309 (ed. E. Hollo and K. Marttinen); Carl–Heinz David, Compensation Aspects of the "Takings Issue" in German and American Law: A Comparative View, Ch. 16 in Takings:Land Development Conditions and Regulatory Takings After Dolan and Lucas (David L.Callies ed.1996); Katharina Richter, Compensable Regulation in the Federal Republic of Germany, 5 Ariz.J.Int'l & Comp.L. 34 (1988).

16. See United States v. Clarke, 445 U.S. 253, 100 S.Ct. 1127, 63 L.Ed.2d 373 (1980).

17. See infra Chapter 16 discussing the power of eminent domain.

§ 10.3

1. See Kaiser Aetna v. United States, 444 U.S. 164, 176, 100 S.Ct. 383, 391, 62 L.Ed.2d 332 (1979). See generally Richard A. Epstein, Takings, Exclusivity and Speech: The Legacy of Pruneyard v. Robins, 64 U.Chi.L.Rev. 21 (1997) and Frank Michelman, The Common Law Baseline and Restitution of the Lost Commons: A Reply to Professor Epstein, 64 U.Chi.L.Rev. 57 (1997).

2. Pumpelly v. Green Bay & Mississippi Canal Co., 80 U.S. (13 Wall.) 166, 20 L.Ed. 557 (1871).

3. United States v. Causby, 328 U.S. 256, 66 S.Ct. 1062, 90 L.Ed. 1206 (1946).

4. Kaiser Aetna v. United States, 444 U.S. 164, 176, 100 S.Ct. 383, 391, 62 L.Ed.2d 332 (1979).

tant to a full understanding of the regulatory taking doctrine. Also, while regulatory measures usually have only economic impacts, they sometimes result in physical invasions. Subdivision approvals, for example, that call for developers to provide land to be used for streets, parks, sidewalks, and schools may implicate the physical taking doctrine.

In Loretto v. Teleprompter Manhattan CATV Corp.,[5] the Court established a per se taking test for physical invasions. The City of New York required lessors of residential property to permit the installation of cable television facilities on their buildings. When a cable company installed a metal box on the roof of Loretto's apartment building and ran cable wires down its side, Loretto alleged a taking had occurred. The intrusion was minor. The boxes were small, the wires thin, and neither interfered with Loretto's use of her property.[6] Nonetheless, the Court held that a permanent physical occupation of property by a third party pursuant to state authority is a taking, regardless of the scope or economic impact of the intrusion. Noting that the right to exclude is "one of the most treasured strands in an owner's bundle of property rights,"[7] the Court held that the fact that a permanent invasion has occurred is determinative. The strength of the public interest and the overall impact on the property's value are not relevant.

Labeling its ruling "narrow,"[8] the Loretto Court exempted temporary physical invasions from its per se test, using two cases decided shortly before Loretto as examples where the per se test was not applicable. In Kaiser Aetna v. United States,[9] the government imposed a navigational servitude on a once non-navigable pond made navigable with government permission. The servitude allowed public use of the pond. Noting the physical character of the invasion, albeit temporary, and the property owner's expectations of private use, on balance the Court found a taking. In PruneYard Shopping Center v. Robins,[10] no taking was found where state law required shopping center owners to allow third parties to exercise speech and petitioning rights. The Court found the invasion was temporary and limited in nature and that it did not seriously interfere with the owner's expectations.[11]

In Nollan v. California Coastal Commission,[12] the Court modified the definition of permanent for purposes of the per se Loretto rule. In Nollan, the state coastal commission required the Nollans to deed an easement allowing the public to walk along the beachfront side of their ocean lot in return for permission to build a larger house. At first blush, Loretto appeared inapplicable since the invasion was not a permanent

5. 458 U.S. 419, 102 S.Ct. 3164, 73 L.Ed.2d 868 (1982).

6. While the majority characterized the boxes as "large," the dissent said they measured 4' x 4' x 4.' 458 U.S. at 443, 102 S.Ct. at 3180 (Blackmun, J., dissenting).

7. Id., quoting from Kaiser Aetna, 444 U.S. at 179–180, 100 S.Ct. at 393.

8. 458 U.S. at 441, 102 S.Ct. at 3179.

9. 444 U.S. 164, 100 S.Ct. 383, 62 L.Ed.2d 332 (1979).

10. 447 U.S. 74, 100 S.Ct. 2035, 64 L.Ed.2d 741 (1980).

11. If an invasion is not permanent, the Penn Central multi-factor balancing test controls. See discussion infra § 10.6.

12. 483 U.S. 825, 107 S.Ct. 3141, 97 L.Ed.2d 677 (1987).

occupation. The Court, nonetheless, found *Loretto* applied. While it acknowledged that the easement did not allow people permanently to station themselves on the land, it said a classic right of way easement to pass back and forth is permanent for purposes of the rule of *Loretto*.[13]

A second aspect of *Nollan* acknowledged an exception to *Loretto* of great significance to land use regulations. Interpreted literally, *Loretto* raised the specter that conditions imposed in the permitting process that resulted in physical occupations, such as subdivision exactions of land for schools or roads, were per se takings.[14] A straightforward application of the *Loretto* per se rule would have meant that a taking had occurred in *Nollan* without further inquiry,[15] but the Court said that requiring the easement as a condition for issuing a land use permit would avoid that conclusion if the state could show that a nexus existed between the effects of the landowner's proposed development and the land that was being exacted for easement use.[16] The nexus was found wanting in *Nollan*, but the principle rescued many land use controls.[17]

The narrow nature of the *Loretto* per se test was confirmed by the Court in Yee v. City of Escondido.[18] There, the combination of state landlord-tenant law and a local rent control ordinance gave mobile home tenants the right to continue to occupy the land on which their homes sat at below market rents for so long as the terms of their leases were met and the landlord continued to use the land for rental purposes. Some lower courts had held these types of controls to be physical takings, but in *Yee* the Supreme Court disagreed and refused to give *Loretto* an expansive reading. "[R]equired acquiescence" of an owner was necessary to invoke the per se test and that was not present in *Yee* where the lessors had voluntarily opened their land to the lessees.

13. 483 U.S. 825, 831, 107 S.Ct. 3141, 3145, 97 L.Ed.2d 677.

14. The *Loretto* Court rejected the argument that the cable installations were valid as conditions for residentially leased property. 458 U.S. at 439 n.17, 102 S.Ct at 3178. The concern over *Loretto's* impact on exactions was voiced by several. See John J. Costonis, Presumptive and Per Se Takings: A Decisional Model For The Taking Issue, 58 N.Y.U. L. Rev. 465, 495 (1983); Andrea L. Peterson, The Taking Clause in Search of Underlying Principles (Part I)—A Critique of Current Takings Clause Doctrine, 77 Calif.L.Rev. 1299, 1338 (1989).

15. The Nollans and amici in the *Nollan* case argued that *Loretto* controlled, rendering the condition a per se taking. The Court rejected this. See Gilbert L. Finnell, Jr., Public Access To Coastal Public Property: Judicial Theories and the Taking Issue, 67 N.C.L.Rev. 627, 665, n.293 (1989).

16. See further discussion of the nexus test infra § 10.5.

17. Sparks v. Douglas County, 72 Wash.App. 55, 863 P.2d 142, 144 (1993)

(invasions of property, such as required dedications, usually are takings under *Loretto*, but permission to develop land may be conditioned on the owner's agreement to dedicate a portion of his property to public use if the regulatory exaction reasonably prevents or compensates for adverse public impacts of the proposed development). *Nollan's* discussion of the nexus justification for physical invasions assumed the power of the state to forbid construction. In Dolan v. City of Tigard, 512 U.S. 374, 114 S.Ct. 2309, 2317–20, 129 L.Ed.2d 304 (1994), the Court did not limit the nexus justification to such instances.

18. 503 U.S. 519, 112 S.Ct. 1522, 118 L.Ed.2d 153 (1992). See also Moerman v. California, 17 Cal.App.4th 452, 21 Cal. Rptr.2d 329 (1993) and Christy v. Hodel, 857 F.2d 1324 (9th Cir.1988), rejecting physical taking argument where state-relocated or state-protected species injured private property since the state did not control wild animals.

Furthermore, the lessors were not required to rent in perpetuity. They could terminate the leases by changing the use.[19]

B. Non-trespassory invasions

Harm from a government operation that is nuisance-like, but does not result in a physical invasion, generally is not found to be a taking. For example, in cases where airplane overflights cause harm to the use of the land below from noise, a critical fact for the courts has been that the noise invaded the land from above. The Court found a taking in such a case in United States v. Causby.[20] Though the *Causby* opinion used nuisance language to describe the harm suffered, lower courts have seized on the fact that *Causby* involved overflights to deny compensation in cases where the noise came from adjacent land.[21]

Non-trespassory harm may be a taking if the harm is peculiar to the land, and not community wide in nature. In Richards v. Washington Terminal Co.,[22] a landowner complained of injury from smoke, dust, cinders, and gases emitted from an adjoining railroad. The Court found no taking because the loss did not stem from a direct invasion. The burden suffered was one shared in common with the community and not compensable. However, a taking was found with respect to harm suffered from a tunnel built by the railroad next to plaintiff's property, which used a fanning system that forced the gases and dust collected in the tunnel directly onto plaintiff's land.[23]

Some state courts, relying on state constitutions, find takings in a wider range of instances involving non-trespassory invasions than is true under the federal constitution. In large part this is based on provisions contained in nearly one-half of the states' constitutions that require compensation where land is "taken or damaged."[24] In Thornburg v. Port of Portland, for example, the court found a taking where airport noise came from adjacent land rather than from above.[25]

§ 10.4 Regulatory Impacts As Takings

A. The Early Cases: Mugler and Pennsylvania Coal

In the 1887 decision of Mugler v. Kansas,[1] the Court rejected the idea that an improper or excessive use of the police power became a

---

19. See Seawall Associates v. City of New York, 74 N.Y.2d 92, 542 N.E.2d 1059, 544 N.Y.S.2d 542 (1989), where owners were required to lease property, not simply continue existing leases, and the state court found a physical taking.

20. 328 U.S. 256, 66 S.Ct. 1062, 90 L.Ed. 1206 (1946).

21. Batten v. United States, 306 F.2d 580 (10th Cir.1962); Branning v. United States, 654 F.2d 88 (Ct.Cl.1981).

22. 233 U.S. 546, 34 S.Ct. 654, 58 L.Ed. 1088 (1914).

23. Id. at 557, 34 S.Ct. at 658. See generally William B. Stoebuck, Nontrespassory Takings in Eminent Domain (1977); William B. Stoebuck, Condemnation by Nuisance: The Airport Cases in Retrospect

and Prospect, 71 Dick.L.Rev. 207 (1967) and Joseph L. Sax, Takings, Private Property and Public Rights, 81 Yale L.J. 149, 164 (1971).

24. See Felts v. Harris County, 39 Tex. Sup.J. 218, 915 S.W.2d 482, 484, n. 4 (1996) (listing 22 states in addition to Texas with such damage language).

25. 244 Or. 69, 415 P.2d 750 (1966). But see Felts v. Harris County, 39 Tex. Sup.J. 218, 915 S.W.2d 482 (1996), where the court held that the reduction in value due to traffic noise from a new highway was not compensable, since the burden was viewed as one similar to that suffered by others in the area.

taking. In *Mugler,* a state alcohol prohibition law rendered a brewery almost worthless. When the brewery owner argued that his property had been taken and that he should receive compensation, the Court labeled the argument an "inadmissible"[2] interpretation of the constitution. The view of the *Mugler* Court was that regulations under the police power were not burdened by a requirement of compensation.[3] Exercises of the police power were to be reviewed solely under the substantive due process standard that required the Court to uphold a law if it promoted a legitimate public end in a rational way. If the test was met, that was the end of the matter.

The Court's expansion of the taking clause to include regulations is generally viewed as having arisen in the 1922 decision, Pennsylvania Coal v. Mahon.[4] A Pennsylvania statute prohibited mining beneath residential areas in such a way as to cause mine subsidence. Subsidence or cave-ins from mining were common throughout the Pennsylvania anthracite coal region, and had led to numerous deaths and widespread property damage.[5] When a coal company announced its intention to mine under the Mahons' house, they sought an injunction. The coal company claimed that the statute was an unconstitutional taking of mineral rights since the statute effectively prohibited it from excavating the coal that the company had expressly reserved to itself in conveying the land to the Mahons' predecessor in title.

The Court agreed with the coal company. The majority opinion, written by Justice Holmes, showed the strong influence of its author's pragmatic view of private contract law: that contracts, and by extension the mineral rights that the coal company had reserved, are legal duties inextricably bound up with "the consequences of its breach."[6] To Holmes, contracts were legal relationships in which a party had simply but inextricably agreed either to perform or "suffer in this way or that by judgment of the court."[7] With this outlook, the Fifth Amendment

§ 10.4

1. 123 U.S. 623, 8 S.Ct. 273, 31 L.Ed. 205 (1887).

2. Id. at 664, 8 S.Ct. at 298.

3. Fred Bosselman, David L. Callies, and John Banta, The Taking Issue 120 (1973).

4. 260 U.S. 393, 43 S.Ct. 158, 67 L.Ed. 322 (1922). The birthdate of the regulatory taking doctrine is debated. Perhaps it was earlier. Professor Ely notes that the Court had intimated that regulations could become takings before 1922. See James W. Ely, Jr., The Fuller Court and Takings Jurisprudence, 1996 J. Sup.Ct. History, vol. II at 120. Then again, perhaps it was later. Professor Brauneis notes problems with viewing *Pennsylvania Coal* itself as a taking case. See Robert Brauneis, The Foundation of Our "Regulatory Takings" Jurisprudence: The Myth and Meaning of Justice Holmes's Opinion in Pennsylvania Coal v. Mahon, 106 Yale L.J. 613 (1996).

5. The *Pennsylvania Coal* decision gives only sparse information on the facts of the case. For this background, see F. Bosselman, et al., supra note 3, at ch. 8; Carol M. Rose, Mahon Reconstructed: Why the Takings Issue is Still a Muddle, 57 S.Cal. L.Rev. 561 (1984); Charles Siemon, Of Regulatory Takings and Other Myths, 1 J. Land Use & Envtl. L. 105 (1985).

6. Holmes, The Path of the Law, 10 Harv.L.Rev. 457, 458 (1897).

7. Id. See generally *Pennsylvania Coal,* 260 U.S. at 414–15, 43 S.Ct. at 159–60.

taking issue resolved itself. Holmes considered the issue a "question of degree,"[8] and warned that "[w]e are in danger of forgetting that a strong public desire to improve the public condition is not enough to warrant achieving the desire by a shorter cut than the constitutional way of paying for the change."[9] The famous, or perhaps infamous, test he established was that "while property may be regulated to a certain extent, if regulation goes too far it will be recognized as a taking."[10] In this case the statute went too far since it made it commercially impracticable to mine certain coal that had been expressly reserved to advance a purpose that Holmes regarded as predominantly private in nature.

Pennsylvania Coal was a monumental decision, and though it remains a vital element in contemporary takings law, it left numerous problems in its wake.[11] The generality of the "too far" test was one. Diminution in value, Holmes said, was one factor to be used to determine how far a regulation could go. However, it was not clear what the diminution was in *Pennsylvania Coal*.[12] The Court also did not say what factors other than diminution in value are relevant. Holmes also did not cite, much less discuss, *Mugler*, leaving its validity unclear, and likely extending its life. In dissent, Justice Brandeis made it clear that he regarded *Mugler* as inconsistent with the Court's holding,[13] and *Mugler* has appeared frequently in subsequent court opinions.

Some authors have suggested that *Pennsylvania Coal* was simply wrongly decided.[14] Others have argued that the decision does not rest on the taking clause but on substantive due process grounds, and that it only uses its taking language metaphorically.[15] Lending support to the argument that *Pennsylvania Coal* was a due process case is the fact that compensation, the mandated remedy of the Fifth Amendment, was neither sought nor awarded, and with good reason: the state was not a party to the case. Since both litigants were private, the entire discussion of the Fifth Amendment taking clause, some suggest, may be regarded as dictum.[16] Even treating the case as a taking, the issue of the appropriate remedy for a regulatory taking was left hanging for decades.[17]

8. *Pennsylvania Coal*, 260 U.S. at 415, 43 S.Ct. at 160.

9. Id. at 416, 43 S.Ct. at 160.

10. Id. at 416, 43 S.Ct. at 160.

11. Virtually all taking articles deal with *Pennsylvania Coal*, but some that concentrate on the case include Robert Brauneis, The Foundation of Our "Regulatory Takings" Jurisprudence: The Myth and Meaning of Justice Holmes's Opinion in Pennsylvania Coal v. Mahon, 106 Yale L.J. 613 (1996); J. Peter Byrne, Ten Arguments for the Abolition of the Regulatory Takings Doctrine, 22 Ecol.L.Q. 89 (1995); Carol M. Rose, Mahon Reconstructed: Why the Takings Issue is Still a Muddle, 57 S.Cal.L.Rev. 561 (1984); E.F.Roberts, Mining with Mr. Justice Holmes, 30 Vand.L.Rev. 287 (1986); Bosselman, et al. supra note 3.

12. See discussion in Byrne supra note 11, at 97 and the dissent of Justice Brandeis, 260 U.S. 393, 419, 43 S.Ct. 158, 161, 67 L.Ed. 322 (1922).

13. 260 U.S. at 418, 43 S.Ct at 161.

14. See Byrne, supra note 11, and Bosselman, et al., supra note 3, at ch. 8.

15. See Siemon, supra note 5; Norman Williams, Jr., R. Marlin Smith, Charles Siemon, Daniel R. Mandelker & Richard F. Babcock, The White River Junctions Manifesto, 9 Vt.L.Rev. 193, 208–14 (1984).

16. Williams, et al., supra note 15, at 209–10.

17. See infra § 10.9.

These uncertainties over *Pennsylvania Coal* explain the references to "so-called regulatory takings" prevalent in opinions and articles. The confusion stems in large part from the striking similarity of the tests used to determine violations of substantive due process and takings.[18] While the due process test applied in *Mugler* did not consider the degree of loss suffered by the property owner to be relevant, that factor worked its way into the Court's later statements of the rule. In the 1894 decision of Lawton v. Steele, for example, the Court said the validity of a police power regulation depends on whether the measure promotes the public interest by a means reasonably necessary to accomplish the purpose, which "is not unduly oppressive upon individuals."[19] The subsequent *Pennsylvania Coal* decision restated the *Lawton* substantive due process test in taking's language. The result has been a confusion of tongues and minds.[20] Determining whether courts have used, or ought to use, substantive due process or the taking clause to adjudicate disputes over allegedly excessive land use controls is a topic of long-standing debate.[21]

The view of the 1920s Court with respect to the questions surrounding the regulatory takings doctrine of *Pennsylvania Coal* is difficult to judge since, in the years shortly after the case, the Court ignored it in several important decisions, preferring to deal with alleged regulatory excesses as substantive due process matters. A few years after *Pennsylvania Coal* the Court decided the landmark case of Village of Euclid v. Ambler Realty Co.,[22] holding that zoning on its face did not violate the substantive due process guarantee to be free from arbitrary state action. Though the opinion echoed Holmes' idea that the validity of police power measures involve questions of degree, saying that "[t]he line which in this field separates the legitimate from the illegitimate assumption of power is not capable of precise delimitation,"[23] it cited neither the taking clause nor *Pennsylvania Coal*.[24]

Two years after *Euclid* the Court decided another land use case, again failing to cite *Pennsylvania Coal*. In Nectow v. City of Cambridge,[25] the Court looked at zoning as applied to a particular tract, and found it

18. This issue is dealt with also infra § 10.12.

19. 152 U.S. 133, 137, 14 S.Ct. 499, 501, 38 L.Ed. 385 (1894).

20. See Eide v. Sarasota County, 908 F.2d 716, 720 (11th Cir.1990); Pearson v. City of Grand Blanc, 961 F.2d 1211 (6th Cir.1992).

21. See discussions in William B. Stoebuck, Police Power, Takings and Due Process, 37 Wash. & Lee L. Rev. 1057 (1980) and John J. Costonis, Presumptive And Per Se Takings: A Decisional Model For The Taking Issue, 58 N.Y.U. L. Rev. 465, 551 (1983).

22. 272 U.S. 365, 47 S.Ct. 114, 71 L.Ed. 303 (1926).

23. Id. at 387, 47 S.Ct. at 118.

24. The Court's failure hardly seems like oversight since the district court in *Euclid* did speak to the taking issue. 297 Fed. 307, 310–12 (N.D.Ohio 1924).

25. 277 U.S. 183, 48 S.Ct. 447, 72 L.Ed. 842 (1928). Concluding that the case is a substantive due process case, see Daniel R. Mandelker, Land Use Law § 2.12 (3d ed.1993); Lawrence Berger, Public Use, Substantive Due Process and Takings—An Integration, 74 Neb.L.Rev. 843, 864 (1995); Charles L. Siemon and Julie P. Kendig, Judicial Review of Local Government Decisions: "Midnight in the Garden of Good and Evil", 20 Nova L.Rev. 707, 719 (1996); Edward J. Sullivan, Substantive Due Process Resurrected Through the Takings Clause: Nollan, Dolan, and Ehrlich, 25 Envtl.L. 155, 159 (1995).

invalid on due process grounds. The Court held that the zoning of the tract for residential use did not, under the circumstances, promote the public interest.[26] Despite the lack of reference to the Fifth Amendment in the *Euclid* and *Nectow* opinions, on occasion in recent years, the Court has loosely referred to them as takings cases, further confusing the line between substantive due process and takings.[27]

B. *The Modern Era*

The next important regulatory taking decision, Penn Central Transportation Co. v. New York City,[28] came in 1978, more than fifty years after *Pennsylvania Coal.* New York City declared Grand Central Station a historic landmark, requiring the owner to seek municipal permission to make changes in the structure. After the designation, Penn Central leased the airspace above the station to a developer who planned to build a 55–story office complex. When the railroad and its lessees sought a certificate of appropriateness from the city's landmark commission, permission was denied with the uncharitable characterization that the proposed tower was an "aesthetic joke."[29] The railroad claimed its inability to build in the airspace was a taking.

The Court admitted that the taking issue was "a problem of considerable difficulty,"[30] and that there was no " 'set formula' for determining when 'justice and fairness' require that economic injuries caused by public action be compensated by the government, rather than remain

26. Id. at 188, 48 S.Ct. at 448. The Court did not give the owner's dollar loss. The owner did lose a contract to sell a part of the land due to the ordinance, but no evidence was presented as to the diminution in value of the tract. The Court made no reference to this except to say the effect of the ordinance was "serious and highly injurious." Id. See infra § 10.12.

In the same year as *Nectow,* the Court decided Miller v. Schoene, 276 U.S. 272, 48 S.Ct. 246, 72 L.Ed. 568 (1928). There, a disease carried and spread by cedar trees was killing Virginia's apple trees. Litigation arose when the state required the affected cedars be destroyed to protect the apple industry. The *Miller* Court said the legislature had a choice: failure to act would protect cedars as much as legislation would protect apple trees. The choice was therefore directly within the state's police power, and the act was found reasonable based on *Mugler* and *Euclid.* 276 U.S. at 279, 48 S.Ct. at 247.

27. The Court has referred to the 75% diminution in value in *Euclid* as evidence of how far a regulation can go without being a taking. Concrete Pipe and Products of California, Inc. v. Construction Laborers Pension Trust for Southern California, 508 U.S. 602, 646, 113 S.Ct. 2264, 2291, 124 L.Ed.2d

539(1993); Lucas v. South Carolina Coastal Council, 505 U.S. 1003, 1073, 112 S.Ct. 2886, 2923, 120 L.Ed.2d 798 (Stevens, J. dissenting) (1992); Penn Central Transp. Co. v. City of New York, 438 U.S. 104, 131, 98 S.Ct. 2646, 2662, 57 L.Ed.2d 631 (1978). Justice Stevens speaks of *Euclid* as fusing due process and takings in Moore v. City of East Cleveland, 431 U.S. 494, 97 S.Ct. 1932, 52 L.Ed.2d 531 (1977). See also Maureen S. Kordesh, "I Will Build My House With Sticks": The Splintering of Property Interests Under the Fifth Amendment May Be Hazardous to Private Property, 20 Harv. Envtl.L.Rev. 397, 407(1996); Jan G. Laitos, The Public Use Paradox and the Takings Clause, 13 J. Energy Nat. Resources & Envtl. L. 9, 50. Professor Mandelker speaks to this issue, but also concludes that *Euclid* is best treated as a substantive due process cases. See Daniel R. Mandelker, Land Use Law § 2.33–34 (3d ed.1993).

28. 438 U.S. 104, 98 S.Ct. 2646, 57 L.Ed.2d 631 (1978). The Court did decide an important public use case, Berman v. Parker, which is discussed infra Ch. 16.

29. Id. at 118, 98 S.Ct. at 2656. The station was built to accommodate a 20–story tower as part of its original design. 438 U.S. at 115, 98 S.Ct. at 2654.

30. Id. at 123, 98 S.Ct. at 2659.

disproportionately concentrated on a few persons."[31] While the Court admitted the test involved "essentially ad hoc, factual inquiries,"[32] it attempted to be more concrete in its analysis than Holmes had been in *Pennsylvania Coal*. It listed three factors for consideration: (1) the economic impact on the claimant, (2) the extent to which the regulation interfered with investment-backed expectations, and (3) the character or extent of the government action.[33]

In weighing these factors, the Court held that the historic preservation ordinance was not a taking because it left the station exactly as it had been, it did not amount to a physical invasion of the property, and it did not violate the original investment-backed expectations of the owners. The railroad argued a total loss of use had occurred by focusing on the airspace alone. The Court, however, said the relevant measure was the whole parcel, and with respect to it, the record showed that the railroad was able to earn a reasonable return under its present use. The Court also said there was no proof of loss of all airspace. A smaller tower might be approved, and the transferable development rights available to the station owner mitigated the loss.[34]

While *Penn Central's* ad hoc test can be faulted for lack of precision and predictability, the Court unnecessarily made matters worse in Agins v. Tiburon,[35] where it held that an ordinance designed to preserve open space did not constitute a facial taking of five acres of unimproved land by limiting the owner to building from one to five houses. The difficulty with *Agins* is not its result, which is easy to understand since the owners, not having submitted a plan for approval, made no showing that they suffered any significant loss. The problem with *Agins* is that in its general statement of takings principles, it used the substantive due process test of *Nectow* and *Euclid* to say that "[t]he application of a general zoning law to particular property effects a taking if the ordinance does not substantially advance legitimate state interests [citing *Nectow*], or denies an owner economically viable use of his land [citing *Penn Central*]"[36] The Court furthered explained that "[a]lthough no precise rule determines when property has been taken * * *, the question necessarily requires a weighing of private and public interests."[37]

The first prong of *Agins,* the ordinance does not substantially advance legitimate state interests, is an awkward fit in the Fifth Amendment taking inquiry since it is designed to judge the validity of a law. It is unlikely that the *Agins* Court meant to say that the *Nectow* rule would be applied to find a law that promotes an illegitimate end is a taking. If a law fails to promote a legitimate end, as was true in *Nectow*, it is invalid

31.   Id. at 124, 98 S.Ct. at 2659.

32.   Id. at 124, 98 S.Ct. at 2659.

33.   Id.

34.   Id. at 137, 98 S.Ct. at 2666. Transferable development rights are discussed supra § 9.9.

35.   447 U.S. 255, 100 S.Ct. 2138, 65 L.Ed.2d 106 (1980).

36.   Id. at 260, 100 S.Ct. at 2141. The seeds for this use of *Nectow* were sown in *Penn Central*. 438 U.S. at 127, 98 S.Ct. at 2660–2661.

37.   447 U.S. 255, 260, 100 S.Ct. 2138, 2141, 65 L.Ed.2d 106 (1980).

and it makes no sense to proceed to discuss whether compensation is due under the Fifth Amendment.[38] Further, and focusing on the means rather than the ends, it is also unlikely that the *Agins* Court meant that the mere conclusion that a law substantially advances an admittedly valid public interest would save it from being a taking, even if an economically viable use remained.[39] In more recent cases, the Court has taken steps to refine the *Agins* test. In doing so, it has clarified some matters, left others hanging, and created new issues as well.

§ 10.5 Refining the Substantially Advances Test: the Essential Nexus

A. *Nollan v. California Coastal Commission*

In Nollan v. California Coastal Commission,[1] the Court applied the "substantially advances" test of *Agins*.[2] When the owners of a beachfront lot sought permission to build a larger house, the state coastal commission conditioned the permit on the granting of an easement to allow the public to walk along the beachfront side of the lot. The state-asserted interest was to protect the public's ability to see the beach from the street, to prevent congestion on the beach, and to overcome psychological barriers to the use of the beach resulting from increased shoreline development. The Court had no quarrel with the legitimacy of the state's goals, but disagreed that the lateral access easement along the beach front would promote them. Stressing the word "substantially" in the *Agins* formula, the Court employed heightened scrutiny and found the interests asserted by the state would not have been substantially advanced by the easement sought. Thus, *Nollan* uses the "substantially advancing" language of *Agins* and *Nectow* to direct the initial focus of a taking challenge to the justification for singling out a property owner to contribute land for public use.

The *Nollan* "substantially advancing" test insists that when the state conditions development permission on the owner dedicating property to public use it may only do so without paying compensation if the dedicated land is "reasonably necessary"[3] to prevent or counteract

---

38. See Estate and Heirs of Sanchez v. County of Bernalillo, 120 N.M. 395, 398, 902 P.2d 550, 553 (1995), interpreting the state constitution to avoid a literal reading of its version of the *Agins* test. It held that a taking is not established by simply showing a regulation is not reasonably related to a proper purpose. If the case involves no appropriation, it does not implicate the Fifth Amendment unless its significantly affects beneficial use. Such a regulation may be invalid, but it is not a taking. 902 P.2d at 552. See also Jarold S. Kayden, Land Use Regulations, Rationality, and Judicial Review: The RSVP in the Nollan Invitation (Part I), 23 Urb.Law. 301, 314 (1991) and Norman Williams, White River Junc-

tion Manifesto, 9 Vt.L.Rev. 193, 213 (1984), discussing the *Agins* and *Nectow* mixture.

39. See Del Oro Hills v. City of Oceanside, 31 Cal.App.4th 1060, 37 Cal.Rptr.2d 677, 686 (1995), cert. denied 516 U.S. 823, 116 S.Ct. 86, 133 L.Ed.2d 43 (1995).

§ 10.5

1. 483 U.S. 825, 107 S.Ct. 3141, 97 L.Ed.2d 677 (1987).

2. See discussion supra § 10.4.

3. *Nollan*, 483 U.S. at 834, 107 S.Ct. at 3147, refers to the restriction being "reasonably necessary" and is quoted with approval by Dolan v. City of Tigard, 512 U.S. 374, 388, 114 S.Ct. 2309, 2318, 129 L.Ed.2d 304 (1994).

anticipated adverse public effects of the proposed development. The word "substantially" is given emphasis by the Court to make it clear that low-level, rational basis scrutiny is insufficient to test the strength of the nexus.[4]

B. *Dolan v. City of Tigard*

Even if a causal connection between the adverse impact of the development project and the condition is established, it still must be shown that the amount exacted is proportional to the harm. That issue was dealt with in Dolan v. City of Tigard.[5] In *Dolan*, the owner of a plumbing and electric supply store sought a permit to double the store's size and pave the parking lot. For flood control and traffic management reasons, the city required the owner to convey to it affirmative easements on the portion of her lot lying within the 100–year floodplain adjacent to a creek and on an additional 15–foot strip of land. The latter was for a pedestrian and bicycle path. The two requirements amounted to approximately 10% of Dolan's property.

The *Dolan* Court held that once the *Nollan* nexus test is met, the state must show that the extent of the exaction is proportional. The *Dolan* Court agreed that the paving of the parking lot would increase stormwater runoff and exacerbate flooding problems, justifying the city in requiring some mitigation response by the owner. However, it was not clear to the Court why the city asked for an easement permitting the public to use Dolan's floodplain land. Physical access did not seem necessary to effect the flood control purpose. The Court also agreed that the store's expansion would lead to more traffic, so that asking the owner to help the city cope with traffic problems made sense. Yet, the city had only found that the pedestrian/bicycle pathway could offset this increased demand. That was not good enough for the Court. The city needed to quantify the traffic increase, at least in some general way, to show that the pathway would offset some of the traffic.

Dolan adopts what it calls a rule of "rough proportionality"[6] to set "outer limits" as to how a city may achieve what the Court called the "commendable task of land use planning."[7] While the burden is on the government to show a degree of connection, the Court does not demand a "precise mathematical calculation, but [rather] some sort of individualized determination that the required dedication is related both in nature and extent to the impact of the proposed development."[8] Though *Dolan's* phrasing of "rough proportionality" is new,[9] the Court acknowledges

---

4. This test of *Nollan* was not novel. State courts across the country used similar tests for years to judge the validity of land exactions, primarily in subdivision cases, and the Court in *Nollan* said its approach was consistent with all states except California.

5. 512 U.S. 374, 114 S.Ct. 2309, 129 L.Ed.2d 304.

6. Id. at 391, 114 S.Ct. at 2319–20.

7. Id. at 395, 114 S.Ct. at 2322.

8. Id. at 395, 114 S.Ct. at 2322.

9. Though the term was new to the Court, Fred P. Bosselman and Nancy Stroud first used the term in "Legal Aspects of Development Exactions," in Development Exactions 70, 103 (James E. Frank and Robert M. Rhodes, eds., 1987), where they wrote: "On balance, the trend of the law seems to offer wide support for the use

that its test is the same as the dedication test followed by the vast majority of state courts.[10]

C. Applications of Nollan and Dolan

The *Nollan* and *Dolan* cases raise several questions. These include whether their tests are to be used for legislatively imposed conditions as well as for adjudicatory ones, whether they apply to regulations that do not cause a physical invasion, and, when they apply, what degree of judicial scrutiny is to be used.

The legislative-adjudicatory question arises because exactions are imposed on development in two distinct settings that may call for different levels of review. As Chief Justice Rehnquist said in *Dolan*, the burden is on a challenger to prove the invalidity of a generally applicable law, but where an adjudicative decision is made, the burden must switch to the government.[11] Where a dedication requirement is a part of legislation generally applicable to all development, courts are reluctant to review the condition with demanding scrutiny. If, for example, all residential development must convey an easement of five feet for sidewalk use or if all commercial property must pay a set transportation fee per square foot of development, the public can debate the propriety of the charge and the legislative process is designed to protect persons from unfairness.

Lower courts have used the Court's emphasis on the ad hoc or discretionary nature of an exaction process to find the *Nollan* and *Dolan* rules inapplicable to broad-based legislative conditions.[12] Where property owners must bargain on a case by case basis, in what is essentially an adjudicatory setting, the safeguards of the open legislative process are lost, and concern arises that the individual may be compelled to give more than a fair share. The issue is analogous to state court treatment of site-specific rezoning as quasi-judicial rather than legislative. The former involves greater scrutiny, which is justified out of fear that the due process rights of the property owner require added protection.[13]

of development exactions for an almost unlimited range of purposes as long as the purpose reflects a problem created to some degree by the particular development, the amount of the exaction bears some rough proportionality to the share of the problem caused by the development, and the exaction will be used to alleviate the particular problem created."

10. The Court cites Montana and New York decisions as too relaxed and Illinois, New Hampshire, New Jersey, Ohio, and Rhode Island cases as too strict. 512 U.S. at 390, 114 S.Ct. at 2319 n.7.

11. *Dolan*, 512 U.S. at 391, 114 S.Ct. at 2320 n.8.

12. Home Builders Ass'n of Central Arizona v. City of Scottsdale, 187 Ariz. 479, 930 P.2d 993 (1997), cert. denied ___ U.S. ___, 117 S.Ct. 2512, 138 L.Ed.2d 1015 (1997) (finding *Dolan* not applicable to a uniform legislative fee); Ehrlich v. City of Culver City, 12 Cal.4th 854, 867, 50 Cal. Rptr.2d 242, 911 P.2d 429, 438 (1996), cert. denied ___ U.S. ___, 117 S.Ct. 299, 136 L.Ed.2d 218 (1996); Parking Association of Georgia, Inc. v. City of Atlanta, 264 Ga. 764, 450 S.E.2d 200, 202, n. 3 (1994), cert. denied 515 U.S. 1116, 115 S.Ct. 2268, 132 L.Ed.2d 273 (1995) (all parking lots to have 10% of paved area devoted to landscaping not a taking and, since legislative, not subject to *Dolan*); Commercial Builders v. City of Sacramento, 941 F.2d 872 (9th Cir.1991), cert. denied 504 U.S. 931, 112 S.Ct. 1997, 118 L.Ed.2d 593 (1992); Arcadia Development v. City of Bloomington, 552 N.W.2d 281 (Minn.App.1996).

13. See discussion of the *Fasano* doctrine, supra § 5.9. The tie between *Dolan* and *Fasano* is suggested in Robert H. Freilich and David W. Bushek, Thou Shalt Not

In cases such as *Dolan*, where the property owner is asked to convey easements to the government as part of a discretionary, ad hoc permitting process, there is concern that the government is attempting to leverage its police power to gain land for which it would otherwise have to pay. The labeling of the practice as " 'out-and-out extortion' "[14] by Justice Scalia in *Nollan* reveals the intensity of the Court's concern. Adequate protection for the property owner, by way of more demanding judicial review, prevents the use of the permitting process as a vehicle to acquire property for a public purpose unrelated to the activity for which the permit is sought.

Whether the heightened scrutiny of *Nollan* and *Dolan* rises to the level of "intermediate scrutiny" in the traditional three tiers of constitutional review standards, or falls somewhere below that standard, is disputed.[15] What is not disputed is that the Court rejected the lowest level rational basis scrutiny in these cases.[16] Whatever the appropriate level of higher scrutiny, it applies to the means, and not the ends. Both *Nollan* and *Dolan* showed traditional deference to the states' goals, but that deference disappeared when it came to the means.

Opinions differ over whether the heightened scrutiny of *Nollan* and *Dolan* applies to non-physical conditions, such as impact fees. The Court, historically and in recent years, has shown great solicitude for property owners who suffer a loss of the right to exclude.[17] In both *Nollan* and *Dolan*, the Court attributed importance to the fact that the application of the regulations resulted in physical invasions. In *Nollan*, as a justification for imposing non-deferential review, the Court said it was inclined to be "particularly careful"[18] where an actual conveyance of property was required, implying that in only such cases would higher scrutiny be used.[19] In *Dolan*, the Court's difficulty with the floodplain easement arose from the owner's loss of the right to exclude.[20]

Lower courts have reacted differently to the question of extending *Nollan* and *Dolan* to fee requirements. Some courts, stressing the Court's historical concern with physical invasions, observe that both *Nollan* and *Dolan* implicated that interest and find nothing in the

Take Title Without Adequate Planning: The Takings Equation After Dolan v. City of Tigard, 27 Urb.Law. 187, 196, n.42 (1995).

14. 483 U.S. at 837, 107 S.Ct. at 3149.

15. See Daniel A. Crane, Comment, A Poor Relation? Regulatory Takings After Dolan v. City of Tigard, 63 U.Chi.L.Rev. 199, 238, n. 68 (1996).

16. The Court did raise some doubts by saying the condition did not meet "the most untailored standards" and that it "utterly fail[ed] to further the end advanced as the justification * * *." 483 U.S. at 837–38, 107 S.Ct. at 3149. But the overall thrust of the opinion, see especially note 3, leaves little doubt that higher scrutiny was used.

17. See discussion of *Loretto*, supra § 10.3.

18. 483 U.S. at 841, 107 S.Ct. at 3151.

19. The Court's statement describes its reading of the word "substantial," and it is this word that lies at the heart of the debate over whether *Nollan* broke with prior law. See Jarold S. Kayden, Land Use Regulations, Rationality, and Judicial Review: The RSVP in the Nollan Invitation (Part I), 23 Urb.Law. 301, 314 (1991); Douglas W. Kmiec, The Original Understanding of the Taking Clause Is Neither Weak nor Obtuse, 88 Colum.L.Rev. 1630 (1988).

20. 483 U.S. at 841, 107 S.Ct. at 3150–51.

opinions to justify an extension to fee cases.[21] Yet, another court finding the cases applicable to fees, noted the similarity of fees to exactions in the permitting process, and found that in both instances, the government may improperly leverage the police power control to seek a benefit unrelated to the development's projected impact.[22]

The extension of *Nollan* and *Dolan's* heightened scrutiny to regulations that are not physically invasive reintroduces the dilemma of distinguishing due process issues from taking issues.[23] If the challenged action does not result in a permanent physical invasion or cause a loss of economically viable use, it is difficult to see what is taken that must be compensated for. Rather, the issue becomes one of potential arbitrary state action, which is the essence of substantive due process. The more widely higher scrutiny applies, the more the Court returns to a type of *Lochner*-era review,[24] this time under the label of the Fifth Amendment rather than the Fourteenth Amendment.[25]

§ 10.6 Refining the Economic Impact Test: Total and Partial Deprivations

In Pennsylvania Coal v. Mahon[1] and Penn Central Transportation Co. v. City of New York,[2] the Court treated the economic impact of a regulation as an important, if not the primary, factor in determining whether a taking had occurred. Those cases, however, provided little guidance as to how much of an impact was tolerable, and they left unanswered the question as to whether the nuisance-like character of a use justified a total deprivation of economic use.

The issues were dealt with, but not resolved, in 1987 in Keystone Bituminous Coal Association v. DeBenedictis,[3] where the Court upheld a Pennsylvania anti-subsidence statute that was strikingly similar to the legislation invalidated in *Pennsylvania Coal*. The Court held the law did not effect a taking because it promoted a legitimate public interest in preventing the nuisance-like effects of mining and did not deny the coal owner all economically viable use. While the *Keystone* majority and dissent both recognized that activities that are nuisance-like in character

---

21. Home Builders Ass'n of Central Arizona v. City of Scottsdale, 187 Ariz. 479, 930 P.2d 993 (1997), cert. denied, ___ U.S. ___, 117 S.Ct. 2512, 138 L.Ed.2d 1015 (1997); McCarthy v. City of Leawood, 257 Kan. 566, 894 P.2d 836, 845 (1995); Commercial Builders v. City of Sacramento, 941 F.2d 872 (9th Cir.1991), cert. denied, 504 U.S. 931, 112 S.Ct. 1997, 118 L.Ed.2d 593 (1992); Clajon Production Corp. v. Petera, 70 F.3d 1566 (10th Cir.1995).

22. Ehrlich v. City of Culver City, 12 Cal.4th 854, 867, 50 Cal.Rptr.2d 242, 911 P.2d 429, 438 (1996), cert. denied, ___ U.S. ___, 117 S.Ct. 299, 136 L.Ed.2d 218 (1996).

23. See supra § 10.4 and infra § 10.12.

24. Lochner v. New York, 198 U.S. 45, 25 S.Ct. 539, 49 L.Ed. 937 (1905). See Rich-ard E. Levy, Escaping Lochner's Shadow: Toward a Coherent Jurisprudence of Economic Rights, 73 N.C.L.Rev. 329 (1995).

25. See Note, Taking A Step Back: A Reconsideration of the Takings Test of Nollan v. California Coastal Commission, 102 Harv.L.Rev. 448, 452 (1988).

§ 10.6

1. 260 U.S. 393, 415, 43 S.Ct. 158, 160, 67 L.Ed. 322 (1922), discussed supra § 10.4.

2. 438 U.S. 104, 98 S.Ct. 2646, 57 L.Ed.2d 631 (1978), discussed supra § 10.4.

3. 480 U.S. 470, 107 S.Ct. 1232, 94 L.Ed.2d 472 (1987).

are subject to stringent state regulation, the members of the Court did not agree that a nuisance-like exception justified a denial by the state of all value.[4] In examining this issue, a distinction is drawn between common law nuisances and legislative regulation of activities that are nuisance-like.

A. Total Deprivations

In 1992, the Court established what it called a categorical taking rule in Lucas v. South Carolina Coastal Council.[5] The owner of two beachfront lots was unable to build due to the application of a setback rule adopted to deter sand dune loss and beach erosion. Accepting the state trial court's finding that the lots subject to the regulation were valueless, the Court held that where a regulation deprives a property owner of all economically viable use a taking occurs unless the state can prove that the regulation does no more to restrict use than what the state courts could do under background principles of property law or the law of private or public nuisance.[6] The Court remanded the case to the state court to see whether the state could carry its burden of proof.[7]

The *Lucas* Court's categorical rule is not a rule of absolute liability, but, as is true with the categorical *Loretto* rule regarding permanent physical occupations, it is a burden switching tool. It means that where a law denies all economically beneficial use, no "case-specific inquiry into the public interest advanced in support of the restraint [occurs]."[8] When the property owner makes the showing of a total deprivation of all economically beneficial use, the burden switches to the government, which must show that property or nuisance law justify the restriction to avoid paying compensation.

Where a total deprivation of economically beneficial use occurs, the state can insulate itself from paying compensation only if the prohibition "inhere[s] in the title itself, in the restrictions that background principles that the State's law of property and [private or public] nuisance already place upon land ownership."[9] The holding means that legislatures cannot impose new limitations that effect total economic deprivations unless the state courts could impose the same limit under the common law. The test is not limited to a backward look at what the state courts have held in specific cases pursuant to the common law. The

---

4. In the same term that *Keystone* was decided, Chief Justice Rehnquist, author of the Court's *Keystone* dissent, said in dicta that an activity that might otherwise constitute a taking might be "insulated [from that determination] as a part of the State's authority to enact safety regulations." First English Evangelical Lutheran Church of Glendale v. County of Los Angeles, 482 U.S. 304, 107 S.Ct. 2378, 96 L.Ed.2d 250 (1987).

5. 505 U.S. 1003, 112 S.Ct. 2886, 120 L.Ed.2d 798 (1992).

6. 505 U.S. at 1027, 112 S.Ct. at 2899.

7. The state court, on remand, found no justification in property or nuisance law

for prohibiting building close to the dune line, and ordered that the trial court determine the amount of compensation to be paid. Lucas v. South Carolina Coastal Council, 309 S.C. 424, 424 S.E.2d 484, 486 (1992).

8. *Lucas,* 505 U.S. at 1015, 112 S.Ct. at 2893. In *Nollan,* the Court makes it clear that *Loretto* is not absolute and that a permanent physical occupation can avoid the finding of a taking if it meets the nexus test. See discussion supra § 10.3.

9. 505 U.S. at 1029, 112 S.Ct. at 2900.

principles, not holdings, of state law control, and the power of the courts under the common law is not fixed. Thus, the Court acknowledges that new prohibitions may be imposed if deemed necessary by virtue of changed circumstances or new knowledge.[10]

State common law likely will vary with respect to what the background principles of property are. Yet, the latitude that states will have to shape this defense is unclear since the *Lucas* Court warns that state courts can only engage in "objectively reasonable application[s] of relevant precedents."[11]. In the highly influential pre-*Lucas* decision of Just v. Marinette County,[12] the Wisconsin Supreme Court held that a prohibition against filling wetlands did not effect a taking, reasoning that under state property law "an owner of land has no absolute and unlimited right to change the essential natural character of his land so as to use it for a purpose for which it was unsuited in its natural state."[13] Presumably, Wisconsin is free to continue to apply such a principle to taking challenges. In one post-*Lucas* case, the Oregon Supreme Court held that the doctrine of custom justified a public right of access on private beach property, precluding the conclusion that a taking had occurred.[14] The Supreme Court allowed that decision to stand.[15] In another decision, the Colorado Supreme Court held that its doctrine of nuisance law could preclude the spread of radioactive contamination.[16] An intermediate appellate court in Michigan, however, found that filling a wetland was not a nuisance.[17]

B. Partial Deprivations

If a regulation's economic effect is less than total, the *Penn Central–Agins* multi-factor balancing test is used,[18] and the burden of proof is on the property owner.[19] In balancing the state interest against the private

---

10. 505 U.S. at 1030–31, 112 S.Ct. at 2901 (citing Restatement Second of Torts).

11. *Lucas*, 505 U.S. at 1032, n.18, 112 S.Ct at 2902.

12. Just v. Marinette County, 56 Wis.2d 7, 201 N.W.2d 761 (1972).

13. Id. at 768. See also Rowe v. Town of North Hampton, 131 N.H. 424, 553 A.2d 1331 (1989). See generally Dowling, General Propositions and Concrete Cases: The Search for a Standard in the Conflict between Individual Property Rights and the Social Interest, 1 Fla.St.U.J. Land Use & Env'tl. Law 353 (1985).

14. Stevens v. City of Cannon Beach, 317 Or. 131, 854 P.2d 449 (1993), cert. denied, 510 U.S. 1207, 114 S.Ct. 1332, 127 L.Ed.2d 679 (1994). See David J. Bederman, The Curious Resurrection of Custom: Beach Access and Judicial Takings, 96 Colum.L.Rev. 1375 (1996).

15. Though not without dissent. See Stevens v. City of Cannon Beach, 317 Or. 131, 854 P.2d 449 (1993), cert. denied, 510 U.S. 1207, 114 S.Ct. 1332, 127 L.Ed.2d 679 (1994).

16. State v. The Mill, 887 P.2d 993 (Colo.1994). See also Public Access Shoreline Hawaii v. Hawai'i County Planning Comm'n, 79 Hawai'i 425, 903 P.2d 1246 (1995), cert. denied 517 U.S. 1163, 116 S.Ct. 1559, 134 L.Ed.2d 660 (1996) (gathering rights of native Hawaiians on undeveloped land need not accord with western concepts of property).

17. K & K Const., Inc., v. Department of Natural Resources, 217 Mich.App. 56, 551 N.W.2d 413 (1996) (state constitutional declaration regarding conservation of natural resources not a principle of property law). Reversed on other grounds, 1998 WL 130936 (Mich.1998). See generally Fred P. Bosselman, Limitations Inherent in the Title to Wetlands at Common Law, 15 Stan. Envtl.L.J. 247, 303 (1996).

18. *Lucas*, 505 U.S. at 1015, 112 S.Ct. at 2893.

19. Florida Rock Ind., Inc. v. United States, 18 F.3d 1560 (Fed.Cir.1994).

loss, partial deprivation cases differ from the categorical taking rules of *Loretto* and *Lucas*, where the inquiry into the public interest advanced only arises by way of defense.[20] These categorical rules protect property in the extreme cases of permanent physical occupation and total wipeouts of economic use. With partial deprivation cases, the inquiry into the public interest occurs as part of the case in chief.

Penn Central listed the character of the government action as one of three factors to examine.[21] In *Agins*, the Court explained that "[a]lthough no precise rule determines when property has been taken * * *, the question necessarily requires a weighing of private and public interests."[22] The governmental action factor requires an assessment of the "purpose and importance of the public interest,"[23] which then must be weighed against the loss.[24]

Measuring the strength of the public interest takes into account the fact that "not all police power values are equal."[25] A health and safety concern should carry more weight than an aesthetic-based control. In *Keystone*, the Court found a state prohibition against mining that caused subsidence dealt with a "significant threat to the common welfare,"[26] including public safety and the protection of drinking water supplies. More generalized purposes, unrelated to health or safety, also have been given weight. In *Penn Central*, the Court found an historic landmark preservation program that protected the city's economic base in tourism and preserved the city's overall quality of life was important in assessing a taking challenge.

The propriety of balancing is questioned by some.[27] The statement of the Court in *Pennsylvania Coal* that "a strong public desire to improve the public condition is not enough to warrant achieving it by a shorter cut than the constitutional way of paying for the change"[28] suggests that

20. *Loretto*, 458 U.S. at 440, 102 S.Ct. at 3179 (noting the "multifactor inquiry generally applicable to nonpossessory governmental activity" is not affected by its decision).

21. *Penn Central*, 438 U.S. at 124, 98 S.Ct. at 2659. The other two were the economic impact on the claimant and the extent to which the regulation interfered with investment-backed expectations. See Kavanau v. Santa Monica Rent Control Bd., 16 Cal.4th 761, 941 P.2d 851, 860, 66 Cal. Rptr.2d 672, 681 (1997) (listing ten factors).

22. 447 U.S. at 260, 100 S.Ct. at 2141.

23. Loveladies Harbor, Inc. v. United States, 28 F.3d 1171, 1176 (Fed.Cir.1994). If a physical invasion occurs, a taking is more likely to be found. See discussion of physical invasions supra § 10.3.

24. Bernardsville Quarry, Inc. v. Borough of Bernardsville, 129 N.J. 221, 608 A.2d 1377 (1992) ("whether a regulatory measure effectuates the taking of property requires a multifactor balancing test that serves to weigh the public interest in enacting the regulation against private property interests affected by it").

25. John J. Costonis, Presumptive And Per Se Takings: A Decisional Model For The Taking Issue, 58 N.Y.U. 465, 499 (1983).

26. Keystone Bituminous Coal v. DeBenedictis, 480 U.S. 470, 107 S.Ct. 1232, 94 L.Ed.2d 472 (1987).

27. William B. Stoebuck, Police Power, Takings, and Due Process, 37 Wash. & Lee L.Rev. 1057, 1065 (1980). Professor Stoebuck considers balancing dangerous because it would allow government to appropriate land and destroy "property rights completely." Id. His article, of course, preceded *Loretto* and *Lucas*, which establish that complete destruction will not entail balancing. See Costonis, supra note 25 at 497 n. 126.

28. 260 U.S. 393, 416, 43 S.Ct. 158, 160, 67 L.Ed. 322 (1922).

no balancing is to occur. In Holmes view, however, *Pennsylvania Coal* involved a case of total diminution in value,[29] and it also involved what the Court later characterized as "a physical restriction"[30] of land. Both factors are consistent with *Loretto* and *Lucas*, which preclude balancing only in such categorical takings.

The matter of balancing has proven confusing. In one case, for example, the Federal Circuit acknowledged that a partial economic loss taking case requires a "classic exercise of judicial balancing of competing values,"[31] but then rejected the proposition that "when Government acts in pursuit of an important public purpose, its actions are excused from liability."[32] As Professor Brownstein notes, a test that ignores public purpose and focuses solely on the impact to the owner is not a balancing test.[33] He also observes that if no balancing occurs, property rights gain greater protection than personal liberties such as free speech, which depend in part on the strength of the public interest.

The balancing conundrum stems from the awkward transition that courts face in moving from the police power to the eminent domain power in regulatory or constructive taking cases. Treating regulatory takings like physical takings for all purposes is an ill-considered approach for the issues are not necessarily the same. In a physical taking, the question is the property owner's loss, not the taker's gain, but in a physical taking case, the property owner is passive. In a regulatory taking case that may or may not be true. In a *Nollan*-type case, where a nexus is missing, property is exacted in the regulatory process because of where the land is and not because of something the landowner has done. Therefore, the strength of the public interest is not relevant. In an economic partial deprivation case, however, the nexus is met, and the state is regulating active uses by the property owner that affect public interests. Balancing takes into account the fact that property values, like police power values, are relative.[34] At bottom, the issue of balancing returns to a blend of substantive due process and regulatory takings ideas.[35] Acceptance of the idea that an excessive regulation can become a taking does not demand that the goals of the regulation be ignored.

§ 10.7 Investment–Backed Expectations

Distinct investment-backed expectations are a factor in both *Lucas-*

---

29. See also Hudson County Water Co. v. McCarter, 209 U.S. 349, 353, 28 S.Ct. 529, 530, 52 L.Ed. 828 (1908), where Holmes' concern with protecting property from excesses extended to those police power exercises that rendered property "wholly useless."

30. Andrus v. Allard, 444 U.S. 51, 67, 100 S.Ct. 318, 327, n. 22, 62 L.Ed.2d 210 (1979). While the restriction in *Pennsylvania Coal* affected the right to possess, use restrictions allow the owner the right of possession. See Costonis, supra note 25 at 537, n.291.

31. Florida Rock Industries, Inc. v. United States, 18 F.3d 1560, 1571 (Fed.Cir. 1994).

32. Id. The public interest factor is thus reduced to the necessary prerequisite that any regulation promote a valid state interest.

33. See Alan E. Brownstein, Constitutional Wish Granting and the Property Rights Genie, 13 Const.Commentary 7, 26–29 (1996). See also Costonis, supra note 25, at 499–500.

34. Costonis, supra note 25, at 499.

35. See discussion supra § 10.4.

type total deprivation cases and *Penn Central*-type partial deprivations.[1] The concept lacks precision, but it is no stranger to the courts who, as part of the common law tradition, are accustomed to expectations playing a role in defining property rights. While the expectations' factor is a general part of the takings formula, it is particularly important in determining the effect of purchasing property with notice of existing restrictions and in defining the proper unit of property used to measure the economic impact of a regulation.[2]

The Court first expressly used the "distinct investment-backed expectations" term in *Penn Central*.[3] It traced the concept to *Pennsylvania Coal*, where the state's anti-subsidence statute abrogated an express contractual reservation of the right to remove coal free from liability for damage to the surface.[4] The fact that *Pennsylvania Coal* was a private dispute where the surface owner bought the land with notice of the prior severance of the mineral rights suggests a high degree of expectation on both sides to the contract that the coal could be removed without liability for surface damage.[5]

In *Penn Central*, the Court found that the railroad's belief that it could use the airspace did not qualify as a reasonable or distinct investment-backed expectation. It was sufficient for taking purposes, held the Court, that the railroad's primary expectation of using Grand Central Station as a railroad terminal and office building, established by sixty-five years of use, was unaffected by the landmark designation.[6]

A. *Purchase Price as Basis of Expectation*

Courts have generally refrained from allowing the purchase price of land to qualify as an investment-backed expectation, which would permit an owner to claim a taking based on a downzoning of the property after purchase.[7] An example is the case of Haas & Co. v. City of San Francisco,[8] where a developer acquired land in the prestigious Russian Hill neighborhood of San Francisco and proposed to erect two apartment buildings, one of twenty-five stories, the other of thirty-one. The land was zoned to allow high-rises and sat amid low-rise buildings. Perhaps foreseeably, neighbors' objections sparked a "battle for Russian Hill,"[9]

---

§ 10.7

1. See supra § 10.6.

2. See generally Daniel R. Mandelker, Investment–Backed Expectations in Takings Law, 27 Urb.Law. 215 (1995); Robert M. Washburn, Reasonable Investment–Backed Expectations As a Factor in Defining Property Interests, 49 Wash.U. J.Urb. & Contemp.L. 63 (1996); John J. Delaney and Emily J. Vaias, Recognizing Vested Development Rights as Protected Property in Fifth Amendment Due Process and Taking Claims, 49 Wash.U. J.Urb. & Contemp.L. 27 (1996).

3. 438 U.S. at 124–25, 98 S.Ct. at 2659.

4. Id. at 129, 98 S.Ct. at 2661 (citing *Pennsylvania Coal*, 260 U.S. 393, 414, 43 S.Ct. 158, 159–60, 67 L.Ed. 322 (1922)).

5. Frank Michelman, Property, Utility, and Fairness: Comments on the Ethical Foundations of "Just Compensation" Law, 80 Harv.L.Rev. 1165, 1212 (1967).

6. 438 U.S. at 135–37, 98 S.Ct. at 2665–66.

7. See, e.g., New Port Largo v. Monroe County, 95 F.3d 1084 (11th Cir.1996) (purchase price does not create a property right immunizing the landowner from future land use changes).

8. 605 F.2d 1117 (9th Cir.1979).

9. See Robert C. Ellickson and A. Dan Tarlock, Land–Use Controls, Cases and Ma-

and the land ultimately was downzoned to a forty-foot height limit, consistent with neighboring uses. The land had been purchased for $1.6 million, was worth $2.0 million zoned for high-rises, and valued at $100,000 when zoned with the forty-foot limit. These "disappointed expectations" based on what was paid for the land did not create a taking.[10] In effect, the deal was what it seemed, "too good to be true." As the *Lucas* Court said, one buys property with the understanding that it is subject to the police power of the state and "necessarily expects the use of his property to be restricted, from time to time, by various newly enacted measures."[11]

A similar issue arises with states' vested rights laws where at some point a developer's reliance through expenditures on a building permit may confer an immunity from a newly enacted ordinance.[12] Such a vested right may form the basis for finding a distinct investment-baked expectation to use in the takings test.[13] But, the finding of such an expectation in a given development project does not necessarily equal a taking, particularly where the owner is left with an economically viable use.[14]

B. Purchase with Notice

A number of courts hold that one cannot complain of a taking based on restrictions to which the land was subject at the time of purchase.[15] The hardship is considered self-imposed.[16] In *Lucas v. South Carolina Coastal Council*,[17] the Court said that the state need not pay an owner compensation if the "proscribed use interests were not part of [the owner's] title to begin with,"[18] and that owners' understandings of the state's power over land are shaped by the " 'bundle of rights' they acquire when they obtain title to property."[19] These statements have

terials 334–338 (1981) for a description of the struggle.

10. *Haas*, 605 F.2d at 1121.

11. *Lucas*, 505 U.S. at 1027, 112 S.Ct. at 2886.

12. See discussion supra §§ 5.27–28.

13. See Daniel R. Mandelker, Investment–Backed Expectations in Takings Law, 27 Urb.Law. 215, 238, n.92 (1995); John J. Delaney and Emily J. Vaias, Recognizing Vested Development Rights as Protected Property in Fifth Amendment Due Process and Taking Claims, 49 Wash.U. J.Urb. & Contemp.L. 27 (1996) (listing 30 states that treat a vested right as a property interest).

14. Corn v. City of Lauderdale Lakes, 95 F.3d 1066 (11th Cir.1996).

15. City of Virginia Beach v. Bell, 1998 WL 120262 (Va.1998); Gazza v. New York State Dept. of Environmental Conservation, 89 N.Y.2d 603, 679 N.E.2d 1035, 657 N.Y.S.2d 555, cert. denied 118 S.Ct. 58, 139 L.Ed.2d 22 (1997); M & J Coal Co. v. United States, 47 F.3d 1148, 1153 (Fed.Cir.

1995); Grant v. South Carolina Coastal Council, 319 S.C. 348, 461 S.E.2d 388 (S.C. 1995); Hunziker v. State of Iowa, 519 N.W.2d 367 (Iowa 1994), cert. denied, 514 U.S. 1003, 115 S.Ct. 1313, 131 L.Ed.2d 195 (1995); Ward v. Harding, 860 S.W.2d 280 (Ky.1993), cert. denied, 510 U.S. 1177, 114 S.Ct. 1218, 127 L.Ed.2d 564 (1994); Kudloff v. City of Billings, 260 Mont. 371, 860 P.2d 140 (Mont.1993). But see Vatalaro v. Dept. of Envtl. Regulation, 601 So.2d 1223 (Fla. App.1992), review denied, 613 So.2d 3 (Fla. 1992). (In Applegate v. United States, 35 Fed.Cl. 406 (1996), the court said that the rule of *Lucas* that a buyer assumes ownership subject to regulatory scheme in effect at time of purchase applies only to regulatory takings, not physical takings).

16. Wheeler v. City of Wayzata, 533 N.W.2d 405 (Minn.1995).

17. 505 U.S. 1003, 112 S.Ct. 2886, 120 L.Ed.2d 798 (1992).

18. 505 U.S. at 1027, 112 S.Ct. at 2899.

19. Id.

been read to endorse the rule that purchase with notice of restrictions in existence at the time of acquisition bars a taking claim.[20]

Whether that is what the *Lucas* Court meant and whether the Court will sustain that interpretation, remains to be seen.[21] *Lucas'* holding was that a law that denies all economically beneficial use requires that the state pay compensation unless the law duplicates the result that a court could have reached under the state's background principles of property or nuisance law. Arguably, this establishes a test independent from the self-created hardship rule[22] under which a court must look solely to principles predating the adoption of the legislative restriction and ignore events like purchase after the restriction.[23] Thus, while the *Lucas* Court acknowledged that property rights are subject to the police power, and that an owner expects "to be restricted, from time to time, by various measures newly enacted by the State," it qualified this expectation by saying that title to land is not subject to a police power measure that "*subsequently* eliminate[s] all economically viable use."[24] So viewed, a landowner may have a claim for compensation when the legislative restraint totally deprives the land of economic value regardless of when adopted, but the landowner may not claim compensation from those legislative restrictions adopted before purchase that partially deprive the land of economic value. The issue remains unclarified.

The propriety of the zoning of the land must be separated from the owner's action for compensation for a taking. While fairness does not require compensation to an individual to cover an economic loss that should have been expected, the zoning of the land, if invalid, ought to be corrected to maintain a rational land use plan. Thus, while purchase

---

20. M & J Coal Co. v. United States, 47 F.3d 1148, 1153 (Fed.Cir.1995); Grant v. South Carolina Coastal Council, 319 S.C. 348, 461 S.E.2d 388, (1995); Hunziker v. State of Iowa, 519 N.W.2d 367 (Iowa 1994), cert. denied, 514 U.S. 1003, 115 S.Ct. 1313,131 L.Ed.2d 195 (1995); Ward v. Harding, 860 S.W.2d 280 (Ky.1993), cert. denied, 510 U.S. 1177, 114 S.Ct. 1218, 127 L.Ed.2d 564 (1994); Kudloff v. City of Billings, 260 Mont. 371, 860 P.2d 140 (1993). But see Vatalaro v. Dept. of Envtl. Regulation, 601 So.2d 1223 (Fla.App.1992), review denied, 613 So.2d 3 (Fla.1992).

21. A footnote in Nollan v. California Coastal Commission raises some question about this rule. In the *Nollan* footnote, Justice Scalia said that the Nollans' rights were not altered simply because they purchased the land after the coastal commission's easement policy was in force. If the commission could not have compelled the prior owners to convey an easement without compensating them, the Justice wrote, they "must be understood to have transferred their full property rights" to the Nollans. 483 U.S. 825, 833, 107 S.Ct. 3141, 3147, 97 L.Ed.2d 677 (1987). This is at odds

with the general idea that the reasonableness of an expectation matters. Professor Mandelker suggests that one can read *Nollan* to mean that purchase with notice is not an absolute bar to a taking claim. Mandelker, supra note 13, at 221 and 244. Another view is that purchase with knowledge is a not a bar in physical taking claims, and *Nollan* did involve a physical invasion. See Applegate v. United States, 35 Fed.Cl. 406 (1996).

22. Unless that rule itself is a background rule of property law.

23. See K & K Construction, Inc. v. Department of Natural Resources, 217 Mich.App. 56, 551 N.W.2d 413, 417 (1996), (transfer of title that follows the adoption of a regulation does not deprive the new owner of a right to compensation where the regulation totally deprives the land of economic viability and is not based on background principles of state property law), reversed on other grounds, 1998 WL 130936 (Mich.1998).

24. 505 U.S. at 1027–28, 112 S.Ct. at 2899–2900 (emphasis added).

subject to an existing restraint may disallow an action for compensation, it will not necessarily prevent an action to challenge the validity of the restriction under state land use law.[25]

§ 10.8 Defining the Unit of Property: Segmentation

The extent of economic impact of a regulation is dependent on the unit of property used by a court to measure the loss. The choice of a broad or narrow approach will often be determinative. Choosing only the portion of land affected by a regulation increases the prospects of a total diminution in value. That, in turn, invokes the *Lucas* categorical taking rule. The concept of property as a bundle of rights does not necessarily translate into a requirement that each strand in the bundle be regarded as separate for the purposes of the Fifth Amendment. Defining the relevant unit of property is a process bound up with the overall test of when "fairness and justice" require that compensation be paid, and is particularly tied to assessing the reasonable investment backed expectations of an owner.[1] In this setting, a rigid rule does not fit.[2] Adopting a categorical severance approach would encourage strategic efforts of the owner to subdivide, and strip the law of its concern for protecting reasonable expectations.[3] The Court has generally rejected that approach.

In *Pennsylvania Coal*, the Court did not overtly discuss the segmentation issue. The majority, however, appeared to treat the coal that had to be left in place to comply with the statute as the relevant measure for its "too far" test. Focusing on the affected coal may be deemed fair since the case arose in the context of a private dispute where the surface owner bought the land with notice of the prior severance. This suggests a high degree of expectation on both sides to the contract that the coal could be removed. It is also a factor that will not exist in most taking cases. In the later *Keystone* case, the Court viewed *Pennsylvania Coal* as having used a broader approach to defining property. Thus, *Keystone* read the statement of Justice Holmes that the statute had made it "commercially impracticable to mine certain coal" to reflect a finding that the company's mining operations as a whole could not be conducted profitably if the coal affected by the Kohler Act had to be left in place.[4]

A. *The Whole Parcel Rule*

In the modern takings era, the Court has used a broad definition for regulatory taking cases involving economic impact.[5] In *Penn Central*, the

25. See Lopes v. City of Peabody, 417 Mass. 299, 629 N.E.2d 1312 (1994).

§ 10.8

1. Lucas v. South Carolina Coastal Council, 505 U.S. 1003, 1016, n. 7, 112 S.Ct. 2886, 2894, 120 L.Ed.2d 798 (1992).

2. See generally, Maureen Straub Kordesh, "I Will Build My House with Sticks": The Splintering of Property Interests Under the Fifth Amendment May be Hazard-

ous to Private Property, 20 Harv. Envtl.L.Rev. 397 (1996).

3. See Justice Stevens' dissent in *Lucas*, 505 U.S. at 1064–66, 112 S.Ct. at 2919–2920.

4. Keystone Coal v. DeBenedictis, 480 U.S. 470, 107 S.Ct. 1232, 94 L.Ed.2d 472 (1987).

5. A narrow view is used for physical invasions like *Loretto* that involve a loss of the right to exclude.

railroad claimed a total economic loss of its airspace above Grand Central Station by application of the landmark designation. The railroad, however, was wrong to limit the focus to the airspace above the terminal, for, as the Court said, " '[t]aking' jurisprudence does not divide a single parcel into discrete segments, [but] focuses on the nature and extent of the interference in the parcel as a whole."[6] Viewing the whole parcel, the loss of the airspace still left the railroad with a reasonable use.

Since *Penn Central*, the Court has fairly consistently used a broad or whole parcel approach,[7] though not without dissent.[8] In *Keystone*, for example, where the Court faced a statute virtually identical to the one invalidated in *Pennsylvania Coal*, it rejected the coal companies' plea to use the coal that had to be left in place (the "support estate") as the measuring unit. The Court thought it unreasonable to allow the coal companies to claim a total loss where only 2% of their coal was required to be left in place. Looking at the entire mining operations of the various companies or even at specific mines, no evidence existed to show that mining would be unprofitable. The support estate, though in one sense a separate property right under state law, had no value apart from ownership of the surface or mineral estate, and thus the Court refused to look at it alone.

While the Court has rejected the narrow segmented approach in these cases, it also has disavowed what it styled an "extreme" approach at the opposite end of the spectrum. In dicta, the *Lucas* Court voiced disapproval of the method used by the New York Court of Appeals' in the *Penn Central* case. There the state court looked to all the land owned by the railroad in the vicinity of Grand Central Station as relevant.[9]

In recent years property owners have paid increased attention to the segmentation issue, hoping to take advantage of the categorical *Lucas* rule and avoid the balancing test of *Agins* and *Penn Central*. Thus, they have asked courts to adopt the position that the relevant parcel is solely the land for which the permit is sought. The courts, however, have refused to do so.[10] Instead, in most cases, the courts have examined the reasonable expectations of the owner by reference to the whole parcel.[11]

---

6. 438 U.S. at 130–31, 98 S.Ct. at 2662.

7. Andrus v. Allard, 444 U.S. 51, 100 S.Ct. 318, 62 L.Ed.2d 210 (1979); Keystone Bituminous Coal Ass'n v. De Benedictis, 480 U.S. 470, 107 S.Ct. 1232, 94 L.Ed.2d 472 (1987); Concrete Pipe and Products of California, Inc. v. Construction Laborers Pension Trust, 508 U.S. 602, 113 S.Ct. 2264, 124 L.Ed.2d 539 (1993).

8. See the dissenting opinions in *Penn Central* and *Keystone*.

9. *Lucas*, 505 U.S. at 1016, n.7, 112 S.Ct. at 2894.

10. Loveladies Harbor, Inc. v. United States, 28 F.3d 1171, 1182 (Fed.Cir.1994).

11. Corn v. City of Lauderdale Lakes, 95 F.3d 1066 (11th Cir.1996); Zealy v. City of Waukesha, 201 Wis.2d 365, 548 N.W.2d 528 (1996); Quirk v. Town of New Boston, 140 N.H. 124, 663 A.2d 1328, 1332 (1995) (agreeing with *Loveladies* that affected portion may at times be used, but generally whole tract is to be the focus); Clajon Production Corp. v. Petera, 70 F.3d 1566 (10th Cir.1995); Presbytery of Seattle v. King County, 114 Wash.2d 320, 787 P.2d 907, cert. denied, 498 U.S. 911, 111 S.Ct. 284, 112 L.Ed.2d 238 (1990); Cheyenne Airport Bd. v. Rogers, 707 P.2d 717 (Wyo.1985); Broadwater Farms Joint Venture v. United States, 35 Fed.Cl. 232 (1996) (loss of 12 of 27 lots as result of regulatory action not compensable taking); K & K Construction, Inc. v. Department of Natural Resources, 1998 WL 130936 (Mich.1998).

The segmentation question generally involves a fact-specific inquiry into the history of the land's ownership and use.[12] In Loveladies Harbor, Inc. v. United States,[13] 199 acres of a 250–acre parcel had been developed before the imposition of wetlands controls. Later, when the owner sought permission to develop the 51–acre remainder, the state allowed it to develop 12.5 acres but required dedication of the development rights for the other 38.5 acres to the state.[14] When a federal permit was sought, the United States Army Corps of Engineers, at the rather ungracious urging of the state, denied the owner a permit to develop the 12.5 acre parcel. In the taking claim that followed, the Federal Circuit held that in these circumstances, the trial court had not clearly erred in finding the relevant parcel to be the 12.5 acres for which a permit was sought.[15]

B. Temporal Segmentation: Moratoria

Interim development controls that may temporarily freeze land use activities raise the segmentation issue in the temporal context. The general rule is that one is guaranteed a reasonable use over a reasonable period of time, and that the mere loss of the present right to use land is not a taking.[16] Under a segmented view, some have argued that a temporary denial of all use is a taking of the present right to use property. This notion was generated in part by a statement of the Court in First English Evangelical Church v. County of Los Angeles[17] to the effect that temporary takings that deny all use are like permanent takings. But, the Court was addressing the general issue of a compensation remedy in that case, not the issue of segmentation.

To the extent that *First English* addressed the issue, it, in fact, rejected the idea of totally severing present and future use rights and adopted a middle of the road approach. In its basic holding that compensation must be paid for the period of time that a regulation effects a taking, the Court refused to accept a broad temporal view that present and future use rights could be joined to deny compensation.[18] At the

12. See a list of factors in East Cape May Assoc. v. New Jersey, 300 N.J.Super. 325, 693 A.2d 114 (1997).

13. 28 F.3d 1171 (Fed.Cir.1994).

14. Id.

15. The trial court had determined that it would be unfair to include the 199 acres developed before the regulatory schemes had been adopted and that since the developer had been forced to dedicate development rights for 38.5 acres of the remainder to the state, that acreage should not be counted. 28 F.3d at 1181. See also Twain Harte Associates, Ltd. v. County of Tuolumne, 217 Cal.App.3d 71, 265 Cal. Rptr. 737 (1990) (whether contiguous parcels to be treated as one a question of fact on remand).

16. See Williams v. City of Central, 907 P.2d 701 (Colo.App.1995); Woodbury Place Partners v. City of Woodbury, 492 N.W.2d

258 (Minn.App.1992); McCutchan Estates Corp. v. Evansville–Vanderburgh County Airport Auth. Dist., 580 N.E.2d 339 (Ind. App.1991), 488 U.S. 823, 109 S.Ct. 70, 102 L.Ed.2d 47 (1988); Dufau v. United States, 22 Cl.Ct. 156 (1990) aff'd without opinion, 940 F.2d 677 (Fed.Cir.1991); Guinnane v. City & County of San Francisco, 197 Cal. App.3d 862, 241 Cal.Rptr. 787 (1987), cert. denied.

17. 482 U.S. 304, 318, 107 S.Ct. 2378, 2388, 96 L.Ed.2d 250 (1987).

18. *First English* generated some confusion by saying that temporary takings that deny all use were like permanent takings. However, when the Court made that analogy, it was not addressing the segmentation issue, but the remedy issue. Unfortunately, the Court's language has led some to contend that *First English* stands for the notion of temporal severance. See John E.

other end of the time line, the Court suggested that property owners must tolerate normal delays in the land use permitting process without compensation.[19] Thus, the total loss of a right to use the land during the period of normal delay is not compensable. Since *First English*, most courts have rejected the narrow severance argument in dealing with moratoria as takings.[20]

§ 10.9   The Compensation Remedy

A. *The Invalidation or Compensation Debate*

In First English Evangelical Lutheran Church v. County of Los Angeles,[1] the Court held that the remedy for a regulatory taking, as with a physical taking, is compensation. In so holding, the Court put to rest the long debated issue of whether *Pennsylvania Coal* was a Fifth Amendment taking case, or a Fourteenth Amendment substantive due process case for which invalidation was an adequate remedy. Several state courts and many commentators had viewed the police power and the eminent domain powers as different in kind, not simply in degree. Under this view, an overreaching exercise of the police power was invalid on substantive due process grounds but was not, by its overreaching, converted into an exercise of eminent domain.[2] This view was consistent with *Pennsylvania Coal,* which was a case between private parties where the remedy was to deny injunctive relief, not to order that compensation be paid. Thus, the "taking" language of the *Pennsylvania Coal* was considered "metaphorical."[3]

The remedy issue had been ducked by the Court in several cases in the 1980s. The first discussion of the issue came in 1981 when Justice Brennan in dissent in San Diego Gas & Electric Co. v. City of San Diego,[4] argued that regulatory takings were true Fifth Amendment takings, and

Fee, Comments, Unearthing the Denominator in Regulatory Taking Claims, 61 U.Chic.L.Rev. 1535, 1543 (1994), but it does not. See cases cited supra note 11.

19. See Frank Michelman, Takings, 1987, 88 Colum.L.Rev. 1600, 1621 (1988) and Thomas E. Roberts, Zoning Moratoria as Regulatory Takings, in Recent Developments in Environmental Preservation and the Rights of Property Owners, 20 Urb. Law. 969, 1012, 1017 (Eds. Bozung and Alessi). See also Margaret J. Radin, The Liberal Conception of Property: Cross Currents in the Jurisprudence of Takings, 88 Col.L.Rev. 1667, 1675–76 (1988), questioning whether *First English* endorses the severance of the period of time when use is lost by an interim ordinance.

20. See cases cited in note 11 and discussion infra § 10.10.

§ 10.9

1. 482 U.S. 304, 107 S.Ct. 2378, 96 L.Ed.2d 250 (1987).

2. See generally, Robert H. Freilich, Solving the Taking Equation: Making the Whole Equal the Sum of its Parts, 15 Urb. Law. 447 (1983); Daniel R. Mandelker, Land Use Takings: The Compensation Issue, 8 Hast.Const.L.Q. 491 (1981); Norman Williams, Jr., R. Marlin Smith, Charles Siemon, Daniel R. Mandelker & Richard F. Babcock, The White River Junction Manifesto, 9 Vt.L.Rev. 193 (1984) (discussing the *Mugler* decision).

3. See discussion of the metaphor theory in Williamson County Regional Planning Commission v. Hamilton Bank, 473 U.S. 172, 197, 105 S.Ct. 3108, 3122, 87 L.Ed.2d 126 (1985) .

4. 450 U.S. 621, 101 S.Ct. 1287, 67 L.Ed.2d 551 (1981).

that compensation should be the mandatory remedy. Still, the Court decided that case on other grounds and avoided the issue in several other cases as well. Though the 1987 *First English* case decided the issue, the opinion did not delve into the relationship between the police power and the eminent domain power or explain its view of *Pennsylvania Coal*. The Court simply assumed that an excessive regulation depriving a person of all use implicated the Fifth Amendment, and from that, a compensation remedy ineluctably followed.[5]

B. Permanent or Temporary Taking: The State's Choice

The *First English* view of the Fifth Amendment is that compensation is the sole remedy for a taking. A court cannot use the Fifth Amendment to invalidate a law that takes property so long as it promotes a public purpose, since the Constitution does not proscribe the taking of property.[6] A court can only award compensation. Even then, the state, not the court, decides whether the compensation should be paid on the basis of a permanent taking or a temporary taking. The state has the option of keeping the regulation in place and paying compensation for a permanent taking, or rescinding the excessive regulation and paying only for the period of the take.

Compensation is due for the period of time that the taking endured, and the beginning point in calculating compensation depends on whether the challenge is facial or as-applied.[7] With a facial challenge, the date of enactment starts the compensation meter running since by definition it is the mere enactment of the law that effects the taking. In contrast, in an as-applied challenge, the taking does not commence until the law is definitely applied to a landowner. The date the act generally becomes effective is not determinative because the landowner suffers no harm from that occurrence and has no cause of action. The beginning date generally will be when the action is ripe and the statute of limitations begins to run.[8] In order for a taking claim to be ripe, an owner must obtain a final decision as to what uses will be allowed by following the local permitting processes.[9] The time that passes in obtaining a final decision is not compensable since subjecting a landowner to a permitting process does not effect a taking.[10] If the state elects to rescind the regulation when the court finds that it has gone "too far," the date of

---

5. The Court repeatedly referred to a denial of "all use", rather than merely economically viable use, but did not intend to alter the test for when a taking occurs. It apparently used the "all use" language because the assumption in the case was that all use had been denied, and the Court's holding did not deal with substance but with the remedy.

6. Hawaii Housing Auth. v. Midkiff, 467 U.S. 229, 104 S.Ct. 2321, 81 L.Ed.2d 186 (1984).

7. See generally Gregory M. Stein, Pinpointing the Beginning and Ending of a Temporary Regulatory Taking, 70 Wash. L.Rev. 953 (1995).

8. Stein, supra note 7, at 960.

9. Williamson County Regional Planning Comm'n v. Hamilton Bank, 473 U.S. 172, 105 S.Ct. 3108, 87 L.Ed.2d 126 (1985). See infra § 10.10.

10. United States v. Riverside Bayview Homes, Inc. 474 U.S. 121, 127, 106 S.Ct. 455, 458, 88 L.Ed.2d 419 (1985). Also, in *First English* the Court suggests that a property owner must suffer, without compensation, losses of use attributable to the normal delays of the permitting process.

rescission is the taking's ending point. If the state elects to keep the law in place, the question is moot since the taking becomes permanent.

C. *Moratoria as Temporary Takings*

First English generated confusion about whether moratoria or interim controls that freeze use are per se compensable takings because the opinion said that " 'temporary takings' which, as here, deny a landowner all use * * * are not different in kind than permanent takings * * *."[11] Taken out of context, the apparent reach of this statement is to treat temporary freezes as takings. The temptation to read the case as applying to interim controls is furthered by two other factors. First, there is the failure to recognize that *First English* was not decided on the merits. It was a remedy case. Second is the fact that *First English* itself involved a moratorium. The Court, however, was not speaking to the substantive issue of when a taking should be found, and, in fact, it did not decide that the moratorium in the case was a taking, but remanded the matter to the state courts.[12] Though the Court's language is a bit loose in retrospect, there is no real doubt that it simply used the temporary taking phrase to describe the lesser of the two remedies available to the state once a taking is found. The courts in post-*First English* cases have read the high court's opinion as merely remedial and have held interim development controls that deny all use are not takings if reasonable in duration.[13]

Where the state elects to rescind the regulation and pay compensation for only a temporary taking, various measures of damages have been used. Rental return is probably the most frequently used. It requires the calculation of the rent the parties would have negotiated for the period of the taking.[14] Other methods include use of the option price, where compensation that equals the market value of an option to buy the land during the take is awarded,[15] and before and after valuation.[16] Lost profits are not recoverable.[17]

It is often assumed that the compensation required by the Fifth Amendment means money, but the Court has not held that to be the

---

11. 482 U.S. 304, 318, 107 S.Ct. 2378, 2388, 96 L.Ed.2d 250 (1987).

12. On remand the state court found that neither the interim or the permanent control were takings. 210 Cal.App.3d 1353, 258 Cal.Rptr. 893 (1989).

13. See Williams v. City of Central, 907 P.2d 701 (Colo.App.1995); Woodbury Place Partners v. City of Woodbury, 492 N.W.2d 258 (Minn.App.1992); McCutchan Estates Corp. v. Evansville–Vanderburgh County Airport Auth. Dist., 580 N.E.2d 339 (Ind. App.1991); Dufau v. United States, 22 Cl. Ct. 156 (1990) aff'd without opinion, 940 F.2d 677 (Fed.Cir.1991); Guinnane v. City & County of San Francisco, 197 Cal.App.3d 862, 241 Cal.Rptr. 787 (1987) cert. denied 488 U.S. 823, 109 S.Ct. 70, 102 L.Ed.2d 47 (1988).

14. See Yuba Natural Resources, Inc. v. United States, 904 F.2d 1577 (Fed.Cir. 1990); City of Austin v. Teague, 570 S.W.2d 389 (Tex.1978).

15. See Lomarch Corp. v. Mayor of Englewood, 51 N.J. 108, 237 A.2d 881 (N.J. 1968).

16. Wheeler v. City of Pleasant Grove, 896 F.2d 1347 (11th Cir.1990). Barnes, Comment, Just Compensation or Just Damages: The Measure of Damages for Temporary Regulatory Takings in Wheeler v. City of Pleasant Grove, 74 Iowa L.Rev. 1243 (1989).

17. PDR Development Corp. v. City of Santa Fe, 120 N.M. 224, 900 P.2d 973 (1995). See infra §§ 16.10–17.

case.[18] In dealing with non-traditional, constructive takings, non-monetary compensation might be adequate in some cases. The granting of transferable development rights, for example, may in some cases qualify as a constitutional form of compensation. The issue was discussed though not decided in *Penn Central*[19] and in Suitum v. Tahoe Regional Planning Agency.[20]

§ 10.10 Ripeness and Forum Selection in Taking Claims

A. *The Leading Cases: Hamilton Bank and MacDonald*

Williamson County Regional Planning Commission v. Hamilton Bank of Johnson City[1] and MacDonald, Sommer & Frates v. Yolo County[2] impose ripeness and forum selection requirements on Fifth Amendment taking claims.[3] In *Hamilton Bank*, a developer received preliminary plat approval in 1973 for a cluster home development from the planning commission. The developer then conveyed open space easements to the county and began putting in roads and utility lines. Over the next few years, the commission reapproved the preliminary plans on several occasions. In 1977, the county changed the density provisions of its zoning ordinance and in 1979 it advised the developer that its project was subject to the 1977 ordinance. The commission rejected revised plats submitted in 1980 and 1981 for numerous reasons, some based on the new law and some based on the old law. The developer then brought suit in federal court.

The Court found the action unripe, noting that a taking claim is premature until the "government entity charged with implementing the regulation has reached a final decision."[4] This had not occurred since the developer had not "sought variances that would have allowed it to develop the property according to its proposed plat."[5] While the developer contended that it had done everything possible to resolve the matter, the Court was not convinced that a final decision had been obtained. The

---

18. See Douglas T. Kendall and James E. Ryan, "Paying" for Change: Using Eminent Domain to Secure Exactions and Side-step *Nollan* and *Dolan*, 81 Va.L.Rev. 1801, 1837 (1995).

19. *Penn Central*, 438 U.S. at 135–38, 98 S.Ct. at 2665–66. The dissent in *Penn Central* did not rule out the idea that transferable development rights might be a proper form of compensation. See Kendall and Ryan, supra note 18, at 1838. See supra § 9.9.

20. ___ U.S. ___, 117 S.Ct. 1659, 137 L.Ed.2d 980 (1997). In *Suitum*, a ripeness decision, see discussion infra § 10.10 B, the concurring opinion of Justice Scalia takes the position that TDRs are not a use of land for the purposes of determining whether property has been taken, but are relevant only as to compensation.

§ 10.10

1. 473 U.S. 172, 105 S.Ct. 3108, 87 L.Ed.2d 126 (1985).

2. 477 U.S. 340, 106 S.Ct. 2561, 91 L.Ed.2d 285 (1986).

3. Suits brought under the due process and equal protection clauses are generally subject to the final decision rule described below, but not the compensation rule. See infra § 10.10F and Thomas E. Roberts, Ripeness and Forum Selection in Fifth Amendment Takings Litigation, 11 J. Land Use & Envtl.L. 37, 68 (1995); Jeffrey Lyman, Finality Ripeness in Federal Land Use Cases from *Hamilton Bank* to *Lucas*, 9 J. Land Use & Envtl. L. 101, 127 (1993).

4. 473 U.S. 172, 186, 105 S.Ct. 3108, 3116, 87 L.Ed.2d 126 (1985).

5. Id. at 188, 105 S.Ct. at 3117.

Court noted that the Board of Zoning Appeals had the authority to grant variances dealing with five of the eight objections, and that the commission itself had the power to grant variances to solve the other objections.

A second problem was that the landowner had not used the inverse condemnation process available in state court. Even assuming the restrictions were so severe that they constituted a taking, the Constitution is not violated unless compensation is not paid, and the Court held the action premature on that basis as well.

A year later, the Court decided the *MacDonald* case. There, the developer submitted a preliminary plan to subdivide its residentially zoned land into 159 lots for single family and multi-family housing. After the planning commission rejected the plan due to inadequacies in access, police protection, water and sewer services, the developer filed suit asserting that its property was being condemned to open space.

The Court found the action was not ripe since the developer had not obtained a final decision as to what kind of development would be allowed. The developer failed to convince the Court that it had, with its one application, done enough. "Unfair procedures, [or] futile [ones]" need not be pursued, said the Court, but the "rejection of exceedingly grandiose development plans does not logically imply that less ambitious plans will receive similarly unfavorable reviews."[6]

B. *Seeking a Final Decision*

Hamilton Bank and *MacDonald* require that a challenger obtain a final decision on a meaningful application for development to make an as-applied taking action ripe. Physical taking claims are not subject to the final decision requirement since the physical invasion itself establishes what has been taken.[7] Likewise, a property owner making a facial taking claim is not subject to the final decision rule since, by definition, the mere enactment of the law, and not its application, takes the property.[8]

The final decision requirement is theoretically distinct from the requirement of exhaustion of administrative remedies, but in practice the distinction blurs. The former addresses whether one must seek some confirmation by the initial decisionmaker that a denial is final, and the latter addresses whether one is obligated to climb the administrative ladder to seek review of that final decision. For ripeness purposes, resort to a board of adjustment, for example, is required if the board possesses the power to waive or grant a variance from a regulation, but is not required if the board has only the power to review the application of the regulation. *Hamilton Bank* provides an example. The Court said the

---

6. MacDonald, Sommer & Frates v. Yolo County, 477 U.S. 340, 351 nn. 8, 9, 106 S.Ct. 2561, 2568, 91 L.Ed.2d 285 (1986).

7. Sinaloa Lake Owners Ass'n v. City of Simi Valley, 882 F.2d 1398, 1402 (9th Cir.1989) cert. denied, 494 U.S. 1016, 110 S.Ct. 1317, 108 L.Ed.2d 493 L.Ed.2e 493 (1990). But see Harris v. City of Wichita,

862 F.Supp. 287, 291 (D.Kan.1994) (stating in dicta that law is unclear).

8. Yee v. City of Escondido, 503 U.S. 519, 112 S.Ct. 1522, 118 L.Ed.2d 153 (1992). See also Galbraith v. City of Anderson, 627 N.E.2d 850 (Ind.App.1994).

property owner had to seek permission of both the board of adjustment and the planning commission for variances because both bodies had the power to relieve the property owner of the alleged hardships.[9] But, the Court said the developer would not be required to appeal the planning commission's rejection of the plat to the board of adjustment since the board had the power only to review, not participate in, that decision.[10]

Identifying the initial decisionmaker is troublesome, and case law instructs that it is a mistake to view the term "initial decisionmaker" narrowly. The driving force behind the rule is to give the governing body a "realistic opportunity and reasonable time within which to review its zoning legislation vis-a-vis the particular property."[11] Resort to the legislative body may be necessary, in addition to seeking a variance, where the current zoning classification is dated.[12] In seeking a final decision, if a variance or other procedure exists that might permit the project to proceed, it must be used unless applying would be futile.

When the *MacDonald* Court suggested that the denial of "exceedingly grandiose" plans did not mean that "less ambitious plans" would also be rejected, it created an obligation of reapplication in situations where the initial application is not a realistic one. Determining when that obligation arises is a guessing game with but few clues, only some of which are helpful. The Court, for example, referred to the *MacDonald* project as an "intense type of residential development," and intimated that the " 'five Victorian mansions' " sought in Agins v. City of Tiburon and the nuclear power plant in San Diego Gas & Electric Co. v. City of San Diego were of the grandiose variety.[13] The proposed fifty-five story office tower atop Grand Central Station in the *Penn Central* case was also likely "grandiose" in the ripeness sense, since the Court noted that the landmark commission might approve a smaller tower.

A reapplication process creates a dilemma. Using *Penn Central* as an example, if one were pursuing the Grand Central project, one might apply for a forty-story tower after failing to get approval for the fifty-five story proposal. If the forty-story proposal is rejected, one then might seek twenty-five stories. At some point the downsizing will render the project economically unattractive, but if the developer gains approval of a lesser request, it presumably waives any objection to losses based on the prior denials.

---

9.   473 U.S. at 188, 105 S.Ct. at 3117.

10.   Id. at 193, 105 S.Ct. at 3120. But see Acierno v. Mitchell, 6 F.3d 970 (3d Cir.1993) (repeated denials of a building permit by the building inspector did not constitute final action where appeal to a board of adjustment available).

11.   Hernandez v. City of Lafayette, 643 F.2d 1188, 1200 (5th Cir.1981).

12.   Hernandez v. City of Lafayette, 643 F.2d 1188, 1200 (5th Cir.1981); Celen-

tano v. City of West Haven, 815 F.Supp. 561 (D.Conn.1993). Where development permission is denied and the land then immediately downzoned, a request for rezoning may not be required since the recent nature of the downzoning may show finality and futility. Hoehne v. County of San Benito, 870 F.2d 529, 535 (9th Cir.1989). But see Southern Pacific Transp. Co. v. City of Los Angeles, 922 F.2d 498 (9th Cir.1990).

13.   *MacDonald*, 477 U.S. at 353, n.9, 106 S.Ct. at 2568.

The requirement of repeated downsizing requests, drawn from *Mac-Donald*, goes beyond the *Hamilton Bank* Court's concern for a final decision based on the proposed development to become a de facto rule that dictates negotiation and compromise by the developer. The goal changes from ripeness to litigation avoidance. If the parties can agree, there will be no suit. This lightens the courts' dockets, but it also deprives the developer of the ability to challenge perceived overreaching by the government in the initial denial. Clarification is needed.

In the absence of clarification from the Court, statutory solutions are possible. Florida, for example, forces a final decision by compelling a municipality to issue a ripeness determination after a property owner files notice of intent to sue under the state's statutory "takings" remedy. If a determination is not issued within 180 days, the government's prior action is treated as the final decision.[14]

In Suitum v. Tahoe Regional Planning Agency,[15] the Court addressed final decision ripeness in the context of transferable development rights. In *Suitum*, the landowner had received a final decision from the land use authority that she could not build on her parcel, but she had not applied for transferable development rights that were available. The Court held that she did not need to do so. Leaving open the question of whether TDRs might be taken into account in determining whether a taking had occurred, their existence did not relate to the allowable uses of the land of the claimant.[16] Once that use was established, the Court held the final decision ripeness requirement met.[17]

C. *Seeking Compensation from the State Courts*

All taking claims, physical and regulatory, facial and as-applied, are subject to the requirement that the property owner seek compensation from the state by way of an action in inverse condemnation.[18] The reason lies in the inherent nature of the Fifth Amendment. It does not proscribe the taking of property, but only mandates a taking without compensation. This mandate is satisfied by post-taking compensation.[19]

---

14. West's Fla.Stat.Ann. § 70.001 (4). This procedure relates only to Florida's statutory "takings" cause of action, and not to Fifth Amendment taking claims. A state might use such an approach in Fifth Amendment litigation as well. See Patrick W. Maraist, A Statutory Beacon in the Land Use Ripeness Maze: The Florida Private Property Rights Protection Act, 47 Fla. L. Rev. 411 (1995).

15. ___ U.S. ___, 117 S.Ct. 1659, 137 L.Ed.2d 980 (1997).

16. See supra § 9.9 for a discussion of transferable development rights.

17. 117 S.Ct. at 1667.

18. See Southern Pacific Transportation Co. v. City of Los Angeles, 922 F.2d 498, 505 (9th Cir.1990). There is some dispute. See, e.g., Christensen v. Yolo County, 995 F.2d 161 (9th Cir.1993) (court assumes, without discussion, that facial claim is ripe). In Adamson Companies v. City of Malibu, 854 F.Supp. 1476 (C.D.Cal.1994), the court found a facial takings claim ripe in federal court without prong two having been met but did so by mistakenly relying on Yee v. City of Escondido, 503 U.S. 519, 112 S.Ct. 1522, 118 L.Ed.2d 153 (1992). In *Yee*, the Court heard a facial takings claim and noted that it was not subject to prong one finality. The Court did not address prong two, which in fact had been met.

19. *Hamilton Bank*, 473 U.S. at 194, 105 S.Ct. at 3120. See Thomas E. Roberts, Fifth Amendment Taking Claims in Federal Court: The State Compensation Requirement and Principles of Res Judicata, 24 Urb.Law. 479 (1992).

The 1985 *Hamilton Bank* ruling requires taking claimants to seek compensation from the state courts "if the state provides an adequate procedure for seeking just compensation." The initial impact of this requirement was limited, since, at that time, there were several states that did not have a compensation remedy. In 1987, however, the Court held in First English Evangelical Lutheran Church v. County of Los Angeles[20] that the self-executing nature of the Fifth Amendment required a compensation remedy. Since *First English*, a state is constitutionally obligated to have a compensation remedy,[21] and the only question is whether the remedy is adequate. In almost all cases it is.

The burden on the property owner to establish inadequacy of the state's compensation remedy is difficult to carry. Uncertainty and perceived hostility do not equal inadequacy.[22] The procedure need not be statutorily authorized.[23] It is sufficient that the courts of the state will hear the claim even if the contours of the action are unclear. In rare instances, futility can be established by proving that the state courts have rejected taking claims that are on all fours with the challenger's case. Since takings claims are usually highly ad hoc affairs, this will not often occur, but it does happen.[24]

Once a property owner has pursued the compensation remedy, the law of res judicata and issue preclusion will usually preclude a Fifth Amendment claim from being maintained in federal court. Adjudication of the claim in state court bars a subsequent suit in federal court under the full faith and credit statute.[25] Collateral attack of the state court judgment is not available in federal district court. A property owner who is dissatisfied with the results obtained from the state court is limited to appealing directly to the United States Supreme Court. While there is disagreement over whether the action pursued in state court is a federal or state-based claim, under even the latter view, once litigated, rules of issue preclusion likely will bar a suit in federal court on the federal claim since the issues being tried in state court would be the same.[26]

---

20. 482 U.S. 304, 107 S.Ct. 2378, 96 L.Ed.2d 250 (1987). Prior to *First English*, some state courts, notably Florida, New York, and California, rejected money damages as possible relief for regulatory takings. See supra § 10.9.

21. See Carson Harbor Village v. City of Carson, 37 F.3d 468, 474 (9th Cir.1994); Tari v. Collier County, 846 F.Supp. 973, 976 (M.D.Fla.1994).

22. Austin v. City and County of Honolulu, 840 F.2d 678, 680 (9th Cir.1988), cert. denied, 488 U.S. 852, 109 S.Ct. 136, 102 L.Ed.2d 109 (1988); Crooked Lake Dev., Inc.v. Emmet County, 763 F.Supp. 1398 (W.D.Mich.1991); Aiello v. Browning–Ferris, Inc., 1993 WL 463701 (N.D.Cal.1993).

23. Southview Associates v. Bongartz, 980 F.2d 84 (2d Cir.1992); J. B. Ranch, Inc. v. Grand County, 958 F.2d 306, 308–309

(10th Cir.1992); Lerman v. City of Portland, 675 F.Supp. 11, 16 (D.Me.1987); Drake v. Town of Sanford, 643 A.2d 367 (Me.1994). But see Kruse v. Village of Chagrin Falls, 74 F.3d 694 (6th Cir.1996) (holding that in a physical taking case uncertain state remedy need not be used).

24. See Naegele Outdoor Advertising, Inc. v. City of Durham, 803 F.Supp. 1068 (M.D.N.C.1992); Schnuck v. City of Santa Monica, 935 F.2d 171 (9th Cir.1991).

25. 28 U.S.C. § 1738.

26. See Roberts, supra note 3, at 60. See also Dodd v. Hood River County, 59 F.3d 852 (9th Cir.1995); Guetersloh v. Texas, 930 S.W.2d 284 (Tex.App.1996).

Mixing ripeness, full faith and credit, and res judicata principles has paradoxical consequences. Viewing the matter through the lens of ripeness, one expects a suit to lie in federal court after doing what is required in state court. Yet, engaging in the process necessary to give rise to the claim also terminates it. The ripeness label is misleading and its continued use by courts is unfortunate.

Still, the rules are justifiable if one thinks that one lawsuit is enough. Furthermore, it is unclear that harm results. A federal forum is denied, but that does not violate the constitution. Our dual system presumes state court competency. Furthermore, state courts have greater experience in land use matters than federal courts. If the matter is thought to be in need of change, the Court has two solutions: rewrite the law of res judicata and full faith and credit or rewrite the law of the Fifth Amendment.[27]

§ 10.11 Takings Legislation

In recent years, many states have considered, and a few have adopted, legislation commonly labeled "takings legislation."[1] The legislative efforts do not define constitutional takings, which is a job for the judicial branch, but rather impose procedural steps to be followed in the adoption and application of land use regulations and establish new causes of action for landowners. The takings bills introduced in recent years generally have been reactions against the takings law developed in the courts, which from the viewpoint of the proponents is perceived as underprotective of the property rights of landowners. Two distinct types of bills have been considered: takings impact or assessment bills and compensation bills.

A. Impact or Assessment Laws

Takings impact legislation requires specified state agencies or local governmental entities to assess the likely economic effect of any proposed law that might affect land values. The inspiration for takings impact laws was Executive Order 12630 issued in 1988 by President Reagan, which uses a process roughly analogous to the environmental impact statement required for federal action under the National Environmental Policy Act (NEPA).[2]

The federal executive order directs federal agencies to prepare a takings implication assessment (TIA) to determine whether proposed actions are likely to effect a taking, to estimate the cost to the agency of

---

27. See Roberts, supra note 3, at 72–73. Congress may try its hand. In 1997, the House of Representatives passed a bill defining final decision ripeness and eliminating the need to sue in state court. 105th Congress, 1st Sess., H.R. 1534. Congress, however, may not have the power to define when a cause of action arises under the Fifth Amendment.

§ 10.11

1. See generally Mark W. Cordes, Leapfrogging the Constitution: The Rise of State Takings Legislation, 25 Eco.L.Q. 187 (1997).

2. See discussion at § 11.2 regarding NEPA.

paying compensation, and to consider less intrusive alternatives.[3] A TIA must be prepared at each step of the rule making process, and be submitted to the Office of Management and Budget for review. While the order uses Fifth Amendment takings terminology, it directs agencies to use a definition of a taking that does not restate existing case law. Instead, the order uses a definition characterized by its principal drafter as a " 'conservative view' of takings law * * * resolving * * * uncertainty in favor of the affected individual rights."[4] The TIA is designated as an internal management tool, and is not subject to judicial review.[5]

A dozen or so states have takings impact laws.[6] These laws require state agencies, and in some instances local governments,[7] to conduct a study of all proposed rules to determine their potential impact on property values, but they vary widely in specifics. Unlike the federal executive order, state statutes normally do not direct the use of legislative taking standards, but direct agencies to refer to existing case law.[8]

It is questionable whether the benefits of these risk assessment laws will outweigh the high costs of compliance.[9] The people, paper, and time that it will take to comply may significantly slow government action. If the requirements are sufficiently onerous, the regulators simply may not take action. That, of course, may be the result that proponents desire. The government may also realize some savings by not having to pay compensation awards for precipitous, ill-considered regulations. Individuals who are left unregulated will benefit, but their neighbors and the public generally will be harmed if the process induces excess timidity in regulators.

---

3. Executive Order 12360, 53 Fed.Reg. 8859 (March 15, 1988).

4. Mark L. Pollot, The Effect of the Federal Takings Executive Order, Land Use Law & Zoning Dig. 3, 5 (May 1989) (author was principal draftsman of executive order). See also James M. McElfish, Jr., The Takings Executive Order: Constitutional Jurisprudence or Political Philosophy? 18 Envtl. L.Rep. 10474 (Nov.1988).

5. McKinley v. United States, 828 F.Supp. 888, 892 (D.N.M.1993). Reportedly, the order has gone mostly unused. See Nancie G. Marzulla, State Private Property Rights Initiatives as a Response to "Environmental Takings," 46 S.C.L.Rev. 613, 630 n.109 (1995).

6. See, e.g., Del. Code Ann., tit. 29, § 605; Idaho Code § 67–8003; Ind. Code § 4–22–2–32; Miss. Code Ann. §§ 17–1–3 and 95–3–29; Mo. Code Ann. §§ 536.017 and 536.018; Tenn. Code § 12–1–201 et seq.; Utah Code §§ 63–90a–1 through 63–90a–4 and § 78–34a–1 through 78–34a–4; West Va. Code Ann. §§ 22–1A–1 to 6; Wyo. Stat. § 9–5–301–305. See listing in David

Coursen, Property Rights Legislation: A Survey of Federal and State Assessment and Compensation Measures, 26 Envtl. L.Rep. 10239, 10249 (May 1996).

7. Utah, for example, imposes a lesser obligation on political subdivision of the state than it does on state agencies. The former need only develop guidelines to address physical takings or exactions. Utah Stat.Ann. § 63–90a–3.

8. See, e.g., Wyo.Stat. § 9–5–302 and 305 (constitutional implications determined by current case law and it is not the purpose of the act to expand or reduce private property protections). See also Mo.Stat. Ann. § 536.017 and Del.Code Ann. tit. 29, § 605 (c). But see Utah Stat.Ann. § 63–90–4(2).

9. Professor Rose thinks that "[a]t best, such overblown procedural requirements are simply wasteful and redundant, and at worst they are a kind of harassment of regulators." Carol M. Rose, A Dozen Propositions on Private Property, Public Rights, and the New Takings Legislation, 53 Wash. & Lee L.Rev. 265, 288 (1996).

The most significant defect of the impact acts is the "mission impossible"[10] they create by requiring a determination of whether a proposed action is a taking on its face. The test for a facial taking is that a challenger must show that the mere enactment of a law effects the taking, and one must decide that there is no set of circumstances under which the law can constitutionally be applied.[11] That is a tall order. Whether the case involves a nexus issue, examining whether the means of governmental action will substantially advance the intended ends, or an economic impact issue, facts must usually be adduced in an as-applied setting. It is theoretically possible to establish that a regulation is a taking on its face, but as the Court said in *Keystone*, it is an "uphill battle."[12] Numerous facial taking claims have failed,[13] and it is unlikely that the impact acts will produce many findings of facial takings.

B. Compensation Laws

Compensation bills have been introduced in many states, but have passed in only a few.[14] These bills generally require that compensation be paid when property owners suffer a specific percentage of diminished value as a result of government regulation.[15] In two states, Arizona[16] and Washington,[17] voters rescinded compensation laws passed by the legislatures.[18] Florida and Texas have comprehensive compensation laws and Louisiana and Mississippi have compensation laws of limited scope.

In 1995, Florida enacted the Bert J. Harris Private Property Rights Protection Act, which creates a new cause of action for governmental regulations that inordinately burden real property.[19] Florida's use of the "inordinate burden" standard, rather than a set percentage of lost value, is a major difference from other states' compensation laws.[20] The ques-

---

10. Robert H. Freilich and RoxAnne Doyle, Taking Legislation: Misguided and Dangerous, Land Use L. & Zoning Dig. 3, 4 (Oct.1994).

11. See generally Michael C. Dorf, Facial Challenges to State and Federal Statutes, 46 Stan.L.Rev. 235 (1994).

12. Keystone Bituminous Coal Ass'n v. DeBenedictis, 480 U.S. 470, 495, 107 S.Ct. 1232, 1247, 94 L.Ed.2d 472 (1987).

13. Keystone Bituminous Coal Ass'n v. DeBenedictis, 480 U.S. 470, 107 S.Ct. 1232, 94 L.Ed.2d 472 (1987); Agins v. City of Tiburon, 447 U.S. 255, 100 S.Ct. 2138, 65 L.Ed.2d 106 (1980); Hodel v. Virginia Surface Min. and Reclamation Ass'n, Inc., 452 U.S. 264, 101 S.Ct. 2389, 69 L.Ed.2d 1 (1981); Penn Central Transp. Co. v. City of New York, 438 U.S. 104, 98 S.Ct. 2646, 57 L.Ed.2d 631 (1978).

14. See Coursen, supra note 6 and Richard S. Wright, Comment, A Half-Hearted Attempt at Regulatory Taking Reform in the Land Use Context: The Proposed North Carolina Property Rights Act, 31 Wake For.L.Rev. 809 (1996). Congress

has also considered several takings bills. See, e.g., Private Property Protection Act of 1995, H.R. 925, 104th Cong., 1st Sess.

15. For a summary see Recent Legislation, Land–Use Regulation-Compensation Statutes—Florida Creates Cause of Action for Compensation of Property Owners When Regulation Imposes "Inordinate Burden," 109 Harv.L.Rev. 542 (1995).

16. Sections §§ 37–220, 221, 222 of the Arizona Code were rescinded in a statewide referendum.

17. Protection of Private Property Act, Wash.Rev.Code § 36.70A.370, rescinded by voters in November, 1995.

18. See " 'Takings' Crowd Rebuffed," San Francisco Examiner, November 19, 1995, p. E–5.

19. Fla.Stat.Ann. § 70.001 (2).

20. The act has already generated significant comment. Articles that tend to be critical include Julian Conrad Juergensmeyer, Florida's Private Property Rights Protection Act: Does It Inordinately Burden

tion of when the burden reaches the point of being inordinate is judicial. The Florida act is significantly different procedurally from traditional inverse condemnation claims. Under the Florida act, if an application for development permission is rejected, a property owner can file a notice of claim. The government must then advise the property owner of the permissible land uses by issuing a so-called ripeness decision. If the government fails to issue such a determination within six months, the matter is deemed ripe.[21] A property owner can also submit an offer to settle, which obligates the government to negotiate and develop its own settlement offer.[22]

In contrast to Florida's inordinate burden standard, other states use fixed percentage reductions. The Texas statute defines a statutory taking as a market value reduction of 25% of the portion of land affected permanently or temporarily by governmental action.[23] The act applies to most state agency actions, but only covers municipalities when they are acting extraterritorially.[24] The government has the choice between an invalidation and compensation remedy.[25] Louisiana provides a cause of action for governmental actions that result in a diminution in value of 20% or more of agricultural[26] or forestry[27] property. The Mississippi statute sets 40% as the triggering loss in value and it applies only to forest land.[28]

Bills that have either been rejected, tabled, or passed but rescinded by voters, have tended to be more extreme than those of the above states. Washington's experience is one example. The legislature passed a compensation law that defined as a statutory taking a regulation having the effect of diminishing the value of any part of real property to any degree for a public benefit.[29] The act's "any diminution" standard applied to segmented portions of land, heightening the effect of the act. Arguably the "public benefit" language meant that if a law were found to promote health or safety, and not simply a vague public benefit, compensation would not be required despite a diminution in value.[30] No

the Public Interest? 48 U.Fla.L.Rev. 695 (1996); Roy Hunt, 48 U.Fla.L.Rev. 709 (1996); and, Sylvia R. Lazos Vargas, Florida's Property Rights Act: A Political Quick Fix Results in a Mixed Bag of Tricks, 23 Fla.St.Univ.L.Rev. 315 (1995). For complimentary article, see David L. Powell, Robert M. Rhodes, and Dan R. Stengle, A Measured Step to Protect Private Property Rights, 23 Fla.St.U.L.Rev. 255, 296 (1995). (authors were drafters of the bill).

21. Fla.Stat.Ann. § 70.001 (5)(a).

22. Fla.Stat.Ann. § 70.001(4). Mediation is another device the property owner can invoke.

23. Vernon's Tex.Stat.Ann. § 2007.002 (5). See George E. Grimes, Jr., Comment, Texas Private Real Property Rights Preservation Act: A Political Solution to the Regulatory Takings Problem, 27 St.Mary's L.J. 557 (1996).

24. Vernon's Tex.Code.Ann., Government Code § 2007.003 (4)(b).

25. Vernon's Tex.Stat.Ann. § 2007.023. The invalidation remedy is established as the presumptive remedy but the state can ask to pay damages and keep the law in place. The act is unclear as to damages for loss of use from the time the taking started until the judicial decree of invalidity.

26. La.Stat. § 3:3602 (11) and § 3:3610.

27. La.Stat. § 3:3622.

28. Miss. Code Ann. §§ 49–33–1 to 49–33–17.

29. Initiative 164.

30. See Richard L. Settle, J. Tayloe Washburn, and Charles R. Wolfe, Washington State Regulatory Reform: Jekyll and

judicial clarification will be forthcoming, however, since voters rejected the law by referendum.

The future of compensation laws is uncertain, and their one-sided nature disheartening. Whether more states pass such acts and whether the ones passed prove to confer greater, or too much, protection on landowners remains to be seen. If a defect of judicially-developed taking law is that it underprotects the developer, the defect of the assessment and compensation laws is that they underprotect the neighbors and the public. The central difficulty with these efforts to treat property owners more fairly is the notable omission of any effort to recapture for the public the windfall gains conferred on landowners by virtue of public improvements and government regulation. We have discussed the windfalls and wipeouts dilemma of land use regulation earlier and commend it to you at this point.[31]

III. DUE PROCESS AND EQUAL PROTECTION

§ 10.12 Substantive Due Process

Substantive due process oversees the exercise of the police power by requiring that a land use regulation promote the health, safety, morals, or general welfare by a rational means.[1] It protects against arbitrary or capricious actions,[2] which " 'may not take place no matter what procedural protections accompany them' * * *."[3] Substantive due process grew out of natural law theories of the seventeenth and eighteenth centuries where all men were thought to be possessed of certain fundamental rights that no government should infringe,[4] but the doctrine's legitimacy as a federal constitutional right law has long been contested.

The use of substantive due process to overturn legislative action has waxed and waned over the course of our constitutional history. The doctrine was a high hurdle for governmental regulations to clear during the first part of the twentieth century when the Court, often viewed as acting as a kind of superlegislature, gave little deference to the other branches of government.[5] Starting in 1934 with Nebbia v. New York,[6]

Hyde '95, Land Use L. & Zoning Dig. 3 (Sept.1995).

31. See supra § 3.24.

§ 10.12

1. Sometimes the Court adds that the measure also cannot be unduly oppressive upon the affected class. See Lawton v. Steele, 152 U.S. 133, 14 S.Ct. 499, 38 L.Ed. 385 (1894), discussed in text infra § 10.12 C, for problems this creates in distinguishing taking claims. For a general discussion of substantive due process, see John E. Nowak & Ronald D. Rotunda, Constitutional Law, Ch.11 (5th ed.1995).

2. Nectow v. City of Cambridge, 277 U.S. 183, 48 S.Ct. 447, 72 L.Ed. 842 (1928);

PruneYard Shopping Center v. Robins, 447 U.S. 74, 84–85, 100 S.Ct. 2035, 2042, 64 L.Ed.2d 741 (1980); Village of Arlington Heights v. Metropolitan Housing Development Corp., 429 U.S. 252, 263, 97 S.Ct. 555, 562, 50 L.Ed.2d 450 (1977) (a landowner has a right to be free from arbitrary or irrational zoning actions).

3. Harris v. City of Akron, 20 F.3d 1396, 1405 (6th Cir.1994).

4. Nowak & Rotunda, supra note 1, 364 (5th ed.1995).

5. See Nowak & Rotunda, supra note 1, at 374.

6. 291 U.S. 502, 54 S.Ct. 505, 78 L.Ed. 940 (1934).

however, the Court turned away from using substantive due process as a device to frustrate the legislative will. The high court and other courts today may articulate substantive due process as a theoretical constraint on government action, but, by according great deference to the legislative branch, most courts do not use it to strike down legislation unless fundamental rights are affected. Usually unsuccessful and still controversial,[7] substantive due process continues to be a basis of complaint in many land use cases, and appears to have emerged of late dressed in the garb of takings claims.[8]

A. Major Supreme Court Cases: The 1920s and 1970s

In 1926, the Supreme Court upheld a comprehensive zoning ordinance against a substantive due process challenge in Village of Euclid v. Ambler Realty Co.[9] The Court's general endorsement of zoning opened the doors to everything land use control law is today. Prior to *Euclid*, state courts that had addressed the constitutionality of zoning were divided. While most had upheld zoning, some had found zoning's interference with free market forces to be an arbitrary invasion of property rights.[10] Thus, *Euclid* was a critical confrontation between unrestricted development rights and the ability of cities to plan and manage growth.

Euclid's zoning ordinance divided the village into six use districts and zoned Ambler Realty's land into several residential and industrial classifications. The realty company challenged the ordinance on its face claiming that the mere existence of the ordinance greatly reduced the value of its land and thus deprived it of its rights under the Fourteenth Amendment. The Court disagreed, finding the zoning ordinance was a legitimate police power regulation due to the public interest in segregating incompatible land uses. *Euclid* set a deferential tone: "If the validity of the legislative classification for zoning purposes be fairly debatable, the legislative judgment must be allowed to control."[11] The Court attributed no significance to the 75 percent diminution in the landowner's property value as a result of the adoption of the ordinance.[12] The *Euclid* Court, however, did issue a warning that when zoning came to be challenged in an as-applied rather than facial context, it might be found arbitrary.

---

7. Justice Scalia calls it an oxymoron. United States v. Carlton, 512 U.S. 26, 39, 114 S.Ct. 2018, 2025, 129 L.Ed.2d 22 (1994). Judge Posner notes it is "a tenacious but embattled concept." Coniston Corp. v. Village of Hoffman Estates, 844 F.2d 461, 465 (7th Cir.1988).

8. See discussion supra § 10.5.

9. 272 U.S. 365, 47 S.Ct. 114, 71 L.Ed. 303 (1926). The Court had upheld limited controls against substantive due process attacks in Hadacheck v. Sebastian, 239 U.S. 394, 36 S.Ct. 143, 60 L.Ed. 348 (1915) and Reinman v. City of Little Rock, 237 U.S. 171, 35 S.Ct. 511, 59 L.Ed. 900 (1915).

10. Compare Goldman v. Crowther, 147 Md. 282, 128 A. 50 (Md.1925) (zoning unconstitutional) and Lincoln Trust Co. v. Williams Building Corp., 229 N.Y. 313, 128 N.E. 209 (1920) (zoning valid).

11. 272 U.S. at 388, 47 S.Ct. at 118.

12. See Hadacheck v. Sebastian, 239 U.S. 394, 36 S.Ct. 143, 60 L.Ed. 348 (1915), where a land use provision precluding brickyards in residential areas, causing a 92.5% diminution in value, was sustained by the Court in a substantive due process challenge.

Two years later the Court fulfilled its *Euclid* warning, finding a zoning ordinance invalid on substantive due process grounds. In Nectow v. City of Cambridge,[13] a landowner lost a contract to sell a large parcel of land because the city had zoned a small strip of the property for residential use. While a master appointed by the lower state court had found no justification for placing the boundary through Nectow's land, rather than down the middle of the street, the state supreme court was unwilling to second guess where the zoning boundary had been set and upheld the zoning. The Supreme Court, however, followed the master's findings and held that the zoning of the tract for residential use was arbitrary and did not promote the public interest.[14]

It is tempting to think that, in the 1920s, *Nectow's scrutiny* was the norm and *Euclid's deference* the anomaly, but, at least in the land use arena that was not the case. In three other cases in the late 1920s, the Court used *Euclid's* deferential test to sustain land use controls in as-applied, substantive due process challenges.[15] After the *Euclid* Court set the stage for relaxed due process review of land use controls, it left the development of constitutional land use law to the state courts during the next half-century. With but few exceptions, it was not until the 1970s that the Supreme Court reentered the land use field.[16]

In 1974, the Court declined an opportunity to reinvigorate substantive due process in Village of Belle Terre v. Boraas.[17] An ordinance allowed only "families," defined as related persons or not more than two unrelated adults, to live in a single family homes. The effect, and likely

13. 277 U.S. 183, 48 S.Ct. 447, 72 L.Ed. 842 (1928). Concluding that the case is a substantive due process case, see Daniel R. Mandelker, Land Use Law § 2.12 (3d ed.1993); Lawrence Berger, Public Use, Substantive Due Process and Takings—An Integration, 74 Neb.L.Rev. 843, 864 (1995); Charles L. Siemon and Julie P. Kendig, Judicial Review of Local Government Decisions: "Midnight in the Garden of Good and Evil", 20 Nova L.Rev. 707, 719 (1996); Edward J. Sullivan, Substantive Due Process Resurrected Through the Takings Clause: Nollan, Dolan, and Ehrlich, 25 Envtl.L. 155, 159 (1995).

14. Id. at 188, 48 S.Ct. at 448. The owner did lose a contract to sell a part of the land due to the ordinance, but no evidence was presented as to the diminution in value of the tract. The Court made no reference to this except to say the effect of the ordinance was "serious and highly injurious." Id.

15. Zahn v. Bd. of Public Works, 274 U.S. 325, 47 S.Ct. 594, 71 L.Ed. 1074 (1927) (upholding exclusion of business from residential zone despite fact that the area was in path of commercial development and value of land would be greatly enhanced if

used for business); Gorieb v. Fox, 274 U.S. 603, 47 S.Ct. 675, 71 L.Ed. 1228 (1927) (setback ordinance upheld), and Miller v. Schoene, 276 U.S. 272, 48 S.Ct. 246, 72 L.Ed. 568 (1928) (police power justified killing infected cedar trees to protect the apple industry).

16. In 1962, in Goldblatt v. Town of Hempstead, 369 U.S. 590, 82 S.Ct. 987, 8 L.Ed.2d 130 (1962), a quarry operator sued when the Town of Hempstead amended its land use ordinances in such a way as to shut down plaintiff's operation. The Court upheld the ordinance, emphasizing the presumption of validity such legislative actions have in our tripartite system of government. Had less restrictive measures been available to the town, the plaintiff might have won his case. None existed and plaintiff's whole business had to be written off as a casualty of the town's legitimate police power regulation.

Berman v. Parker, 348 U.S. 26, 75 S.Ct. 98, 99 L.Ed. 27 (1954), an eminent domain case discussed infra Ch. 16, has also played an important role in land use regulation. See discussion infra on aesthetics, Ch. 12.

17. 416 U.S. 1, 94 S.Ct. 1536, 39 L.Ed.2d 797 (1974).

purpose, of the ordinance was to prevent groups of students from a nearby university from living together in the small village. A landowner who rented his house to six unrelated students brought suit on several grounds, urging the Court to find "that social homogeneity is not a legitimate interest of government."[18] The ordinance would have failed had any type of exacting scrutiny been applied,[19] but it survived because the Court used the deferential rational basis test. The Court was not troubled since it saw the ordinance as merely regulating social and economic affairs, and not implicating any fundamental rights or affecting any suspect class. While the Court dealt with the challenge on equal protection grounds,[20] several state courts, refusing to accept the *Belle Terre* Court's deferential posture, have invalidated ordinances with restrictive family definitions relying on state constitutional provisions of substantive due process or privacy.[21]

Three years later, substantive due process rose phoenix-like in *Moore v. City of East Cleveland*.[22] *Moore*, like *Belle Terre*, involved a regulation aimed at allowing only "single families" in single homes. The ordinance had a complex definition of family which precluded the plaintiff from living with her son and two grandsons (who were also first cousins). Well aware of the quagmire it was stepping into, the plurality entered the "treacherous field" of substantive due process to strike down the ordinance only because the special sanctity of the family was at stake. The Court found the ordinance to be an "intrusive regulation of the family," distinguishing it from the *Belle Terre* ordinance, which affected only unrelated persons. Under strict scrutiny review, the city could establish no justification for "slicing deeply into the family" in order to reduce congestion or crime.

The *Moore* case is a limited revival of substantive due process. At most, the Court is likely to use the strict scrutiny of *Moore* only when related persons are affected by a land use control.[23] The difficulty of enticing the Court to use substantive due process is reflected in the fact that only five justices voted in *Moore* to overturn a state court conviction of a grandmother for allowing a second grandchild to live with her upon the death of his mother.[24]

B. Relationship to Fourteenth Amendment Equal Protection and Procedural Due Process Guarantees

18. Id. at 3, 94 S.Ct. at 1538.

19. See dissent of Justice Marshall, 416 U.S. at 12–20, 94 S.Ct. at 1542–46.

20. The deferential test employed for equal protection is the same as that used for substantive due process. See Nowak & Rotunda, supra note 1, at 362. For a discussion of equal protection problems in land use law, see infra § 10.14.

21. City of Santa Barbara v. Adamson, 27 Cal.3d 123, 164 Cal.Rptr. 539, 610 P.2d 436 (1980); New Jersey v. Baker, 81 N.J.

99, 405 A.2d 368 (1979); Charter Twp. of Delta v. Dinolfo, 419 Mich. 253, 351 N.W.2d 831 (1984).

22. 431 U.S. 494, 97 S.Ct. 1932, 52 L.Ed.2d 531 (1977).

23. See Armendariz v. Penman, 75 F.3d 1311, 1318 (9th Cir.1996).

24. In recent cases, some members of the Court have criticized the case. See United States v. Carlton, 512 U.S. 26, 39, 114 S.Ct. 2018, 2025, 129 L.Ed.2d 22 (1994) (Scalia, J., concurring in judgment).

Perhaps due to its amorphous nature, substantive due process tends to be confused with other constitutional guarantees such as equal protection, procedural due process, the First Amendment, and, most particularly, the taking clause. While the test for equal protection challenges and substantive due process challenges is the same,[25] the two guarantees differ. Equal protection examines the rationality of governmental classifications of people and property while substantive due process concerns the rationality of the restraints. Procedural due process is concerned with whether the method of application of a law is fair, and substantive due process deals with whether the result is fair.[26] While distinct in theory, they sometimes merge in judicial analysis.[27] Conduct that is challenged as arbitrary, such as the denial of a permit in retaliation against a developer for seeking judicial review of a city's zoning laws, might also be viewed as a violation of free speech rights.[28]

C. Relationship to Fifth Amendment Regulatory Taking Doctrine

Confusion between substantive due process and the regulatory taking doctrine is a most troubling area for constitutional land use law. This is understandable since the formulations of the two constraints, except for remedy, is sometimes identical. While substantive due process is most often expressed as imposing a requirement that a law promote a legitimate public end in a rational manner,[29] the Court has said on occasion that substantive due process also means that laws ought not be unduly oppressive upon the affected class.[30] This "unduly onerous" prong of substantive due process, created in 1894,[31] created no doctrinal problem until Pennsylvania Coal v. Mahon[32] when the Court used the same idea to suggest that excessive regulations, those that went "too far," were Fifth Amendment takings.[33] The two tests are virtually indistinguish-

25. Nowak & Rotunda, supra note 1, at 362. For a discussion of equal protection problems in land use law, see infra § 10.14.

26. See discussion of procedural due process, infra § 10.13.

27. Town of Orangetown v. Magee, 88 N.Y.2d 41, 665 N.E.2d 1061, 1066, 643 N.Y.S.2d 21, 26 (1996); Coniston Corp. v. Village of Hoffman Estates, 844 F.2d 461 (7th Cir.1988).

28. Nestor Colon Medina & Sucesores, Inc. v. Custodio, 964 F.2d 32 (1st Cir.1992) (retaliation possibly First Amendment violation, but not a violation of substantive due process). But see Carr v. Town of Dewey, 730 F.Supp. 591 (D.Del.1990) (substantive due process used).

29. See Honeywell, Inc. v. Minnesota Life and Health Ins. Guaranty Ass'n, 86 F.3d 766, 773 (8th Cir.1996).

30. Nollan v. California Coastal Commission, 483 U.S. 825, 845, 107 S.Ct. 3141,

3153, 97 L.Ed.2d 677 (1987) (dissenting opinion); Goldblatt v. Town of Hempstead, 369 U.S. 590, 595, 82 S.Ct. 987, 990, 8 L.Ed.2d 130 (1962); Lawton v. Steele, 152 U.S. 133, 137, 14 S.Ct. 499, 501, 38 L.Ed. 385 (1894). See also Bethlehem Evangelical Lutheran Church v. City of Lakewood, 626 P.2d 668, 674 (Colo.1981); Presbytery of Seattle v. King County, 114 Wash.2d 320, 787 P.2d 907 (1990). But see Arcadia Development Corp. v. City of Bloomington, 552 N.W.2d 281 (Minn.App.1996) refusing to add this third prong.

31. Lawton v. Steele, 152 U.S. 133, 137, 14 S.Ct. 499, 501, 38 L.Ed. 385 (1894).

32. 260 U.S. 393, 43 S.Ct. 158, 67 L.Ed. 322 (1922).

33. *Pennsylvania Coal* was regarded by many as a substantive due process case for years. See discussion supra § 10.4.

able, and, over the years, the Court has incorporated its substantive due process case law into its takings formula.[34]

Faced with a regulation alleged to be excessive in its impact on an individual, a court might find that the regulation is unduly onerous and thus void under substantive due process or that it goes ''too far'' and becomes a taking under *Pennsylvania Coal,* requiring the payment of compensation. Differences in the remedy allowed or mandated and in the standard of review used make the choice critical.[35] Under the due process clause, the remedy may be injunctive relief and/or damages, while just compensation is the sole, but mandatory, remedy under the taking clause. Low level scrutiny is applied to substantive due process challenges, but, increasingly, higher scrutiny is applied to taking claims.

The apparent choice to sue under the Fifth Amendment or the Fourteenth Amendment may be illusory. The Court has held in other areas that where there is an explicit textual source in the constitution it must be used to determine liability rather than generalized notions of substantive due process.[36] If the Fifth Amendment taking clause qualifies as sufficiently explicit under this theory, the unduly onerous substantive due process test should be subsumed by it.[37] Given the Court's recognition of the regulatory taking doctrine, there is no justification for a duplicative test under substantive due process.

Substantive due process claims premised on arbitrary state action,[38] which allege that an act is an invalid police power control, are not duplicative of taking claims and must be distinguished from claims that an action has an unduly onerous economic impact. Though the latter, duplicative claim should fade into obscurity, the former should not since it is independent from a taking claim. For example, a property owner's complaint that a regulation was adopted solely in response to neighbor prejudices,[39] or as retaliation against a developer for seeking judicial

34. See discussion of *Agins*, supra § 10.6. See also Lawrence Berger, Public Use, Substantive Due Process, and Takings: An Integration, 74 Neb.L.Rev. 843 (1995).

35. Eide v. Sarasota County, 908 F.2d 716 (11th Cir.1990).

36. Whitley v. Albers, 475 U.S. 312, 106 S.Ct. 1078, 89 L.Ed.2d 251 (1986); Graham v. Connor, 490 U.S. 386, 109 S.Ct. 1865, 104 L.Ed.2d 443 (1989).

37. See Armendariz v. Penman, 75 F.3d 1311 (9th Cir.1996) (issue of a taking for a private purpose must be brought under the Fifth Amendment, not substantive due process). Several other cases discuss the issue in land use matters, without clear resolution. Bickerstaff Clay Products Co., Inc. v. Harris County, 89 F.3d 1481 (11th Cir.1996) (finding due process claim with respect to public use subsumed by the Fifth

Amendment); Miller v. Campbell County 945 F.2d 348 (10th Cir.1991); Pearson v. City of Grand Blanc, 961 F.2d 1211 (6th Cir.1992). See generally Thomas E. Roberts and Thomas C. Shearer, Land–Use Litigation: Takings and Due Process Claims, 24 Urb.Law. 833, 836 (1992).

38. See, e.g., Village of Euclid v. Ambler Realty Co., 272 U.S. 365, 47 S.Ct. 114, 71 L.Ed. 303 (1926); Nectow v. Cambridge, 277 U.S. 183, 48 S.Ct. 447, 72 L.Ed. 842 (1928); Village of Belle Terre v. Boraas, 416 U.S. 1, 94 S.Ct. 1536, 39 L.Ed.2d 797 (1974); and Moore v. City of East Cleveland, 431 U.S. 494, 97 S.Ct. 1932, 52 L.Ed.2d 531 (1977).

39. Marks v. City of Chesapeake, 883 F.2d 308 (4th Cir.1989). But see Church of Jesus Christ of Latter-Day Saints v. Jefferson County, 721 F.Supp. 1212 (N.D.Ala. 1989).

review of a city's actions[40] might be held to violate substantive due process due to its arbitrary nature. Lacking a legitimate public purpose, such state action would not be characterized as a taking and thus sustainable with the payment of just compensation. Rather, the action would be invalidated.

D. *Substantive Due Process Today: A Tool of Limited Use*

The degree of deference a court affords the government is critical to the outcome of a claim of substantive due process. The Supreme Court recognizes a "right to be free from arbitrary or irrational zoning actions,"[41] but, in the absence of a fundamental right, the review is deferential.[42] Several lower federal courts articulate a test that makes the challenger's job even more difficult. Thus, the action must shock the conscience,[43] be "egregiously unacceptable,"[44] or be "truly horrendous."[45] These tests reflect the lack of judicial appetite in the federal courts to use substantive due process in the land use area to revive *Lochner* type review.[46] In some courts, pursuit of a substantive due process claim in the absence of a fundamental right may prove embarrassing to the lawyer who asserts it. The Seventh Circuit, for example, responded to a developer's claim by saying that " '[s]ubstantive due process' has the distinct disadvantage, from plaintiffs' perspective, of having been abolished in the late 1930s when the Supreme Court threw over Lochner."[47] Some federal courts will on occasion find violations of substantive due process.[48] State courts vary, but some are quite active in overseeing land use law through due process.[49] Courts that do intervene are more likely to find delaying and deceptive conduct by the government as arbitrary[50]

40. Carr v. Town of Dewey, 730 F.Supp. 591 (D.Del.1990). But see Nestor Colon Medina & Sucesores, Inc. v. Custodio, 964 F.2d 32 (1st Cir.1992) (retaliation possibly First Amendment violation, but not a violation of substantive due process).

41. Village of Arlington Heights v. Metropolitan Housing Development Corp., 429 U.S. 252, 263, 97 S.Ct. 555, 562, 50 L.Ed.2d 450 (1977).

42. National Paint & Coatings Assn. v. City of Chicago, 45 F.3d 1124, 1129 (7th Cir.1995) (if substantive due process exists it is limited to fundamental rights, which exclude property). See Ronald J. Krotoszynski, Jr., Fundamental Property Rights, 85 Geo.L.J. 555 (1997) (arguing that current liberty-based substantive due process be extended to property rights).

43. Harris v. City of , 20 F.3d 1396, 1401 (6th Cir.1994).

44. Licari v. Ferruzzi, 22 F.3d 344, 347 (1st Cir.1994).

45. Nestor Colon Medina & Sucesores, Inc. v. Custodio 964 F.2d 32, 45 (1st Cir. 1992).

46. See Richard E. Levy, Escaping Lochner's Shadow: Toward a Coherent Jurisprudence of Economic Rights, 73 N.C. L. Rev. 329 (1995).

47. Gosnell v. City of Troy, 59 F.3d 654, 658 (7th Cir.1995).

48. Some are colored by political or religious discrimination. See cases supra notes 39 and 40. Others involve solely economic harm. See Elsmere Park Club Ltd. Partnership v. Town of Elsmere, 771 F.Supp. 646 (D.Del.1991). See Kenneth Bley, Substantive Due Process and Land Use: The Alternative to a Takings Claim in Takings: Land Development Conditions and Regulatory Takings after Dolan and Lucas, Ch. 14 (David L. Callies ed.1996).

49. See, e.g., Orangetown v. Magee, 88 N.Y.2d 41, 643 N.Y.S.2d 21, 665 N.E.2d 1061 (1996).

50. Blanche Road Corp. v. Bensalem Twp., 57 F.3d 253, 267 (3d Cir.1995).

than to second guess the wisdom of zoning land for a particular purpose.[51]

The degree of review may also depend on whether the challenged action is legislative or administrative. The difference is important since a court may hypothesize a rational basis for a legislative action but insist on actual proof for administrative action.[52] While all courts agree that review of economic claims is deferential, some treat all zoning actions, including variances, as legislative for the purposes of reviewing the substance of an action.[53] Other courts divide acts along more traditional lines and confer less deference to administrative acts.[54] Even then, the review is described as "extremely narrow."[55]

E. *The Property Interest Required*

In addition to varying degrees of receptivity to the merits of arbitrary and capricious substantive due process claims, a conflict exists among the courts as to the property interest sufficient to invoke such a claim.[56] While ownership of an interest in land is sufficient for some courts,[57] others require a property owner to establish a right or entitlement in a permit.[58] The showing is difficult to make since an entitlement exists only if there is a strong likelihood or virtual assurance that the permit will be issued. If the regime vests the decisionmaker with discretion, there is no entitlement. Since land use permitting processes generally do confer discretion on the authorities, a developer who seeks, or needs, to establish a property right in a permit loses its case at the outset.[59] If one has no right to a permit, there is no need to determine whether the action denying it was arbitrary.

Property rights in permits sometimes are found.[60] A vested right acquired under the state's zoning law may also be regarded as a property interest.[61] Even then, the owner must still show an arbitrary denial to

---

51. New Port Largo, Inc. v. Monroe County, 95 F.3d 1084 (11th Cir.1996) (wisdom of zoning land for airport was was for legislature to decide).

52. Id. at 479.

53. Shelton v. City of College Station, 780 F.2d 475 (5th Cir.1986).

54. See listing and discussion of cases in Pearson v. City of Grand Blanc, 961 F.2d 1211, 1220 (6th Cir.1992).

55. Id.

56. See listing and discussion in Pearson v. City of Grand Blanc, 961 F.2d 1211, 1220 (6th Cir.1992), characterizing the lack of uniformity as remarkable.

57. DeBlasio v. Zoning Bd. of Adjustment, 53 F.3d 592 (3d. Cir.1995), cert. denied, 516 U.S. 937, 116 S.Ct. 352, 133 L.Ed.2d 247 (1995); Polenz v. Parrott, 883 F.2d 551, 555 (7th Cir.1989); Sundheim v. Board of County Commissioners, 904 P.2d 1337 (Colo.App.1995).

58. Triomphe Investors v. City of Northwood, 49 F.3d 198 (6th Cir.1995),

cert. denied, 516 U.S. 816, 116 S.Ct. 70, 133 L.Ed.2d 31 (1995); Gardner v. City of Baltimore, 969 F.2d 63 (4th Cir.1992); RRI Realty Corp. v. Incorporated Village of Southampton, 870 F.2d 911 (2d Cir.1989); Cedarwood Land Planning v. Town of Schodack, 954 F.Supp. 513 (N.D.N.Y.1997).

59. Kelley Property Development, Inc. v. Town of Lebanon, 226 Conn. 314, 627 A.2d 909 (Conn.1993) (one must show that the local law so narrowly circumscribes discretion that there is "a virtual assurance of approval").

60. Reserve, Ltd. v. Longboat Key, 17 F.3d 1374 (11th Cir.1994) (a property interest in a permit after significant expenditures in reliance on governmental actions); Town of Orangetown v. Magee, 88 N.Y.2d 41, 665 N.E.2d 1061, 1068, 643 N.Y.S.2d 21, 28 (1996).

61. See John J. Delaney and Emily J. Vaias, Recognizing Vested Development Rights as Protected Property in Fifth Amendment Due Process and Taking

prevail. If the state has a rational reason for its action, it will not violate due process. Courts applying a deferential standard of review are not likely to find a violation of due process.[62] Some courts, using more scrutiny, have held that the denial of a permit to which an applicant was entitled is a violation of substantive due process.[63]

The entitlement test for property stems from the Supreme Court's "new property" cases that deal with procedural due process rights in government benefits.[64] Oddly, this theory of "new property" is used in the land use area to shrink property rights for substantive due process purposes despite the fact that the right to use land has not historically been thought of as a government benefit.[65] The problem with the entitlement test comes when it is used as the sole source of property rights. If that is the law, the government can insulate its land use regulations from judicial review simply by adopting discretionary processes. As the Seventh Circuit observed, "a single local ordinance providing that 'we may put your land in any zone we want, for any reason we feel like' would abolish all property rights in land overnight."[66]

F. *Finality and Ripeness*

Finality and ripeness issues with respect to substantive due process are similar to those discussed previously with regard to Fifth Amendment taking claims.[67] The Court in *Hamilton Bank* applied the final decision rule not only to Fifth Amendment taking claims but also those substantive due process claims that allege, in a manner identical to the Fifth Amendment, that a regulation has gone too far (the so-called due process takings claim). While the *Hamilton Bank* opinion did not refer expressly to the just compensation prong in its due process discussion, other courts have held that consistency with the rationale of *Hamilton Bank* regarding the Fifth Amendment claim requires that a party asserting a "due process taking" must seek compensation from the state.[68] The point ought not matter since it is unlikely that such a cause

Claims, 49 Wash.U. J.Urb. & Contemp.L. 27 (1996) (listing 30 states that treat a vested right as a property interest).

62. Decarion v. Monroe County, 853 F.Supp. 1415 (S.D.Fla.1994).

63. See, e.g., Walz v. Town of Smithtown, 46 F.3d 162 (2d Cir.1995); Bateson v. Geisse, 857 F.2d 1300 (9th Cir.1988); Bello v. Walker, 840 F.2d 1124 (3d Cir.), cert. denied, 488 U.S. 868, 109 S.Ct. 176, 102 L.Ed.2d 145 (1988); Sullivan v. Town of Salem, 805 F.2d 81 (2d Cir.1986); Scott v. Greenville County, 716 F.2d 1409 (4th Cir. 1983).

64. Goldberg v. Kelly, 397 U.S. 254, 90 S.Ct. 1011, 25 L.Ed.2d 287 (1970) (welfare payments constitute a property right); Perry v. Sindermann, 408 U.S. 593, 92 S.Ct. 2694, 33 L.Ed.2d 570 (1972) (tenured teaching position constitutes a property right); Bd. of Regents v. Roth, 408 U.S. 564, 92 S.Ct. 2701, 33 L.Ed.2d 548 (1972) (unten-

ured teacher had no right to a hearing when his contract of employment was not renewed).

65. As the Court said in Nollan v. California Coastal Commission: "[T]he right to build on one's own property—even though its exercise can be subjected to legitimate permitting requirements—cannot remotely be described as a 'governmental benefit.'" 483 U.S. 825, 833 n. 2, 107 S.Ct. 3141, 3146, 97 L.Ed.2d 677 (1987). See Thomas E. Roberts, Karen Milner and Robert McMurray, Land Use Litigation: Doctrinal Confusion Under the Fifth and Fourteenth Amendments, 28 Urb.Law. 765 (1996).

66. River Park, Inc. v. City of Highland Park, 23 F.3d 164, 166 (7th Cir.1994).

67. See discussion supra § 10.10.

68. See Southview Associates, Ltd. v. Bongartz, 980 F.2d 84, 98 (2d Cir.1992); Rocky Mountain Materials & Asphalt, Inc.

of action will continue to be recognized.[69]

Most courts have held that the final decision requirement applies also to as-applied arbitrary and capricious substantive due process claims.[70] As is the case with the Fifth Amendment, the rule is not applicable to facial claims.[71] While the requirement that compensation be sought has been held not to apply to substantive due process arbitrary and capricious claims,[72] some courts take the position that a cause of action for any due process claim, substantive or procedural, is not complete until state post-deprivation remedies have been used.[73] In Zinermon v. Burch,[74] a five-member majority of the Court, in dicta, said that a substantive due process action is actionable regardless of potentially adequate state remedies.[75] Numerous courts have followed this statement,[76] but some lower courts have concluded that one must show that state remedies are inadequate in order to state a substantive due process claim.[77] It has also been held that no violation of substantive due process can occur where the victim of the deprivation has in fact received

v. Bd. of County Comm'rs, 972 F.2d 309 (10th Cir.1992); Baranowski v. Borough of Palmyra, 868 F.Supp. 86 (M.D.Pa.1994). See also Rockler v. Minneapolis Community Development Agency, 866 F.Supp. 415, 418 (D.Minn.1994) (held procedural and substantive due process claims that "fall squarely within the federal takings claim" unripe until compensation sought in state court). But see Sinaloa Lake Owners Association v. City of Simi Valley, 882 F.2d 1398, 1404 (9th Cir.1989).

69. See Armendariz v. Penman, 75 F.3d 1311 (9th Cir.1996); Macri v. King County, 126 F.3d 1125, 1129 (9th Cir.1997) (substantive due process is not a "loophole" to avoid suing in state court). See also Roberts and Shearer, supra note 37, at 836.

70. Christopher Lake Development Co. v. St. Louis County, 35 F.3d 1269 (8th Cir.1994); Southview Associates v. Bongartz, 980 F.2d 84 (2d Cir.1992), cert. denied, 507 U.S. 987, 113 S.Ct. 1586, 123 L.Ed.2d 153 (1993); Eide v. Sarasota County, 908 F.2d 716 (11th Cir.1990), cert. denied, 498 U.S. 1120, 111 S.Ct. 1073, 112 L.Ed.2d 1179 (1991); Rivervale Realty Co., Inc. v. Town of Orangetown, 816 F.Supp. 937, 942 (S.D.N.Y.1993). See also Anderson v. Alpine City, 804 F.Supp. 269 (D.Utah 1992), where the court explores the Tenth Circuit's view as to ripeness for due process claims.

71. Kawaoka v. City of Arroyo Grande, 17 F.3d 1227, 1231 (9th Cir.1994).

72. Southview Associates v. Bongartz, 980 F.2d 84, 96 (2d Cir.1992), cert. denied 507 U.S. 987, 113 S.Ct. 1586, 123 L.Ed.2d 153 (1993); Greenbriar, Ltd. v. City of Ala-

baster, 881 F.2d, 1570, 1574 n. 8 (11th Cir.1989); Rivervale Realty Co., Inc. v. Town of Orangetown, 816 F.Supp. 937, 942 (S.D.N.Y.1993); Patrick Media Group, Inc. v. City of Clearwater, 836 F.Supp. 833 (M.D.Fla.1993); Cox v. City of Lynnwood, 72 Wash.App. 1, 863 P.2d 578, 582 (Wash. App.1993).

73. See discussion infra § 10.13 regarding *Parratt* doctrine.

74. 494 U.S. 113, 125, 110 S.Ct. 975, 983, 108 L.Ed.2d 100 (1990).

75. See discussion in Larry Alexander, Constitutional Torts, the Supreme Court, and the Law of Noncontradiction: An Essay on Zinermon v. Burch, 87 Nw.U.L.Rev. 576 (1993) and Craig W. Hillwig, Comment, Giving Property All the Process That's Due: A "Fundamental" Misunderstanding About Due Process, 41 Cath.U.L.Rev. 703 (1992).

76. McKinney v. Pate, 20 F.3d 1550 (11th Cir.1994); Southview Associates, Ltd. v. Bongartz, 980 F.2d 84 (2d Cir.1992), cert. denied, 507 U.S. 987, 113 S.Ct. 1586, 123 L.Ed.2d 153 (1993); Southern Pacific Transp. Co. v. City of Los Angeles, 922 F.2d 498 (9th Cir.1990), cert. denied, 502 U.S. 943, 112 S.Ct. 382, 116 L.Ed.2d 333 (1991); Lanmar Corp. v. Rendine, 811 F.Supp. 47 (D.R.I. 1993). See cases cited in Kenneth B. Bley, Use of the Civil Rights Acts to Recover Damages in Land Use Cases, Land Use Institute: Planning, Regulation, Litigation, Eminent Domain and Compensation (ALI-ABA 1995).

77. New Burnham Prairie Homes, Inc. v. Village of Burnham, 910 F.2d 1474, 1481 (7th Cir.1990).

an adequate post-deprivation hearing.[78]

§ 10.13 Procedural Due Process

The Fifth and Fourteenth Amendments prohibit government from depriving "any person of life, liberty or property without due process of law."[1] Judicial refinement of what process is "due" for what degree of deprivation and for what personal interest has been going on for decades.[2] The guarantee offers both substantive and procedural protection. In contrast to substantive due process, which looks primarily at why a deprivation occurred,[3] procedural due process asks how the deprivation came to be.

Procedural due process rights do not attach to legislation of general applicability.[4] If a rezoning is deemed legislative, the due process clause does not require that affected persons be given notice or a hearing.[5] State law may provide for some type of notice and hearing, but the constitution does not demand it. Thus, a critical question is whether to characterize a given land use decision as legislative or quasi-judicial.[6] The same question, with possibly different results, may also be asked for the purposes of deciding which acts can be put to a referendum vote,[7] and whether personal immunity from liability exists.[8] Also, an act may be regarded as legislative for the purposes of substantive due process, yet quasi-judicial for procedural due process questions.[9]

For procedural due process to attach there must be administrative or quasi-judicial decisionmaking. In land use, the decisions of the various zoning boards and commissions typically are viewed as administrative or

78. Archuleta v. Colorado Department of Institutions, 936 F.2d 483 (10th Cir. 1991).

§ 10.13

1. For a general discussion of procedural due process, see John E. Nowak and Ronald D. Rotunda, Constitutional Law, Ch. 13 (5th ed.1995).

2. See generally William W. Van Alstyne, Cracks In "The New Property": Adjudicative Due Process in the Administrative State, 62 Cornell L.Rev. 445 (1977).

3. See discussion supra § 10.12.

4. Bi–Metallic Inv. Co. v. State Bd. of Equalization, 239 U.S. 441, 36 S.Ct. 141, 60 L.Ed. 372 (1915). This is not always true under state law, as various "sunshine" laws illustrate. See, e.g., West's Fla.Stat.Ann. § 286.011, which prohibits the "meeting" of any "board or commission of any state agency" at which "official acts are to be taken" behind closed doors of any sort. Such meetings are "declared to be public meetings open to the public at all times." These laws were designed to prevent the

abuse sometimes present where legislative zoning decisions were made, where ex parte contacts and alleged "deal making" behind closed doors often occur. As examples of state efforts to cure those abuses, see Fasano v. Board of County Comm'rs, 264 Or. 574, 507 P.2d 23 (1973); Roseta v. County of Washington, 254 Or. 161, 458 P.2d 405 (1969).

5. Pro–Eco, Inc. v. Bd. of Commissioners of Jay County, 57 F.3d 505. 512 (7th Cir.1995); Jacobs, Visconsi, & Jacobs v. City of Lawrence, 927 F.2d 1111 (10th Cir.1991).

6. Pearson v. City of Grand Blanc, 961 F.2d 1211, 1220 (6th Cir.1992).

7. See supra § 5.5.

8. See infra § 10.26.

9. Shelton v. City of College Station, 780 F.2d 475, 482 (5th Cir.1986) (while variance was treated as legislative for purposes of substantive due process deferential review, court suggested that a procedural due process issue in a variance proceeding might demand actual evidence of a rational basis).

quasi-judicial.[10] Actions by legislative bodies pose problems. Site specific rezonings present the major difficulty since they often constitute applications of previously adopted policies to particular parcels. For that reason many courts treat these nominally legislative acts as quasi-judicial.[11] However, the mere fact that a generally applicable law is provoked by a specific development proposal does not render it quasi-judicial.[12]

To state a procedural due process claim one must show a legitimate entitlement under state law to that which is sought.[13] This poses a major hurdle in land use disputes since courts require a showing that the granting of a permit is a virtual certainty. If, as is often the case, the zoning authorities have discretion in deciding whether to grant a permit, no protectable property interest exists.[14]

Where a property right exists and the action taken is quasi-judicial in nature, the process that is due varies.[15] The essence of procedural due process requires notice and an opportunity to be heard before an impartial decisionmaker,[16] but the specifics are determined according to the particular situation.[17] The fact that an act violates state law does not constitute a per se violation of due process.[18] Cross-examination may or may not be required.[19] There is no right to pre-trial discovery.[20]

Rights can be waived and if one has actual notice of a hearing, the mere fact that personal notice was not given cannot be the basis of a due process objection.[21] However, if the notice is misleading, it may violate due process. In one case, for example, a city council published notice of

10. Id.

11. See discussion supra § 5.9.

12. Pro–Eco, Inc. v. Bd. of Commissioners of Jay County, 57 F.3d 505, 512 (7th Cir.1995).

13. Goldberg v. Kelly, 397 U.S. 254, 90 S.Ct. 1011, 25 L.Ed.2d 287 (1970) (welfare payments constitute a property right); Perry v. Sindermann, 408 U.S. 593, 92 S.Ct. 2694, 33 L.Ed.2d 570 (1972) (tenured teaching position constitutes a property right). Board of Regents v. Roth, 408 U.S. 564, 92 S.Ct. 2701, 33 L.Ed.2d 548 (1972) (untenured teacher had no right to a hearing when his contract of employment was not renewed). But see River Park, Inc. v. City of Highland Park, 23 F.3d 164 (7th Cir.1994), where the Seventh Circuit held that ownership of land was sufficient to assert a procedural due process claim.

14. Triomphe Investors v. City of Northwood, 49 F.3d 198 (6th Cir.1995), cert. denied, 516 U.S. 816, 116 S.Ct. 70, 133 L.Ed.2d 31 (1995); Gardner v. City of Baltimore, 969 F.2d 63 (4th Cir.1992); RRI Realty Corp. v. Incorporated Village of Southampton, 870 F.2d 911 (2d Cir.1989).

15. Mathews v. Eldridge, 424 U.S. 319, 96 S.Ct. 893, 47 L.Ed.2d 18 (1976) (mandating use of a balancing test to determine

what process is due). See Nowak and Rotunda, supra note 1, at 554–555.

16. See, e.g., Hartland Sportsman's Club v. Town of Delafield, 35 F.3d 1198 (7th Cir.1994) (notice held sufficient); Harris v. County of Riverside, 904 F.2d 497 (9th Cir.1990).

17. Mathews v. Eldridge, 424 U.S. 319, 96 S.Ct. 893, 47 L.Ed.2d 18 (1976); Rogin v. Bensalem Twp., 616 F.2d 680 (3d Cir.1980).

18. First Assembly of God of Naples v. Collier County, 20 F.3d 419 (11th Cir.1994), cert. denied 513 U.S. 1080, 115 S.Ct. 730, 130 L.Ed.2d 634 (1995) (failure to codify laws as required by state law not a violation of due process); Hartland Sportsman's Club v. Town of Delafield, 35 F.3d 1198 (7th Cir.1994) (that town exceeded authority under state law in granting permit did not violate substantive due process).

19. Coral Reef Nurseries, Inc. v. Babcock Co., 410 So.2d 648, 652–53 (Fla.App. 1982) (required); Mohilef v. Janovici, 51 Cal.App.4th 267, 58 Cal.Rptr.2d 721 (1996) (not required). See supra § 5.37.

20. Mohilef v. Janovici, 51 Cal.App.4th 267, 58 Cal.Rptr.2d 721 (1996).

21. Hroch v. City of Omaha, 4 F.3d 693 (8th Cir.1993).

its intent to consider the rezoning a specific tract. An affected landowner, aware of the meeting and that the proposed rezoning suited his plans, did not attend. At the hearing, the council adjourned to executive session and rezoned the land in a manner different from its proposal to the detriment of the landowner. The court found a violation of due process.[22]

The process that may be required does not always have to be given prior to the deprivation. Post-deprivation remedies available in state court suffice to meet the constitutional requirement where the deprivation occurs as the result of random or unpredictable actions.[23] If, for example, an applicant has met all requirements to obtain a building permit but city officials refuse to issue the permit, no federal cause of action for a violation of procedural due process exists if the state law allows the applicant to seek a writ of mandamus from the state courts.[24] On the other hand, where established state procedure authorizes a deprivation without due process, such as an ordinance that allows a property interest to be divested without a hearing,[25] state remedies do not need to be pursued. In one case, state law required that a committee making recommendations on landfill permit requests include representatives of the solid waste industry. An unsuccessful applicant for a landfill permit complained that the composition of the hearing panel to include the applicant's competitors created a bias that violated due process. The challenger was not required to pursue state remedies since it was the established procedure that was being questioned.[26]

Generally, procedural due process claims have been exempted from the final decision ripeness requirement that is applied to taking claims.[27] Courts have differed over whether the compensation requirement applies to procedural due process.[28] However, if the deprivation occurs as the result of random or unpredictable actions and if a post-deprivation

22. Nasierowski Bros. Inv. Co. v. City of Sterling Heights, 949 F.2d 890, 892 (6th Cir.1991). See also Resolution Trust Corp. v. Town of Highland Beach, 18 F.3d 1536 (11th Cir.1994) (no notice of hearing given).

23. Parratt v. Taylor, 451 U.S. 527, 101 S.Ct. 1908, 68 L.Ed.2d 420 (1981), overruled on other grounds, 474 U.S. 327, 106 S.Ct. 662, 88 L.Ed.2d 662 (1986). *Parratt* is inapplicable where deprivation is caused by conduct pursuant to established procedure. Zinermon v. Burch, 494 U.S. 113, 110 S.Ct. 975, 108 L.Ed.2d 100 (1990).

24. New Burnham Prairie Homes, Inc. v. Village of Burnham, 910 F.2d 1474, 1479 (7th Cir.1990).

25. Porter v. DiBlasio, 93 F.3d 301 (7th Cir.1996).

26. Macene v. MJW, Inc., 951 F.2d 700, 705 (6th Cir.1991) (while a due process claim was stated, the court found no due process violation since the committee only made recommendations).

27. Nasierowski Bros. Inv. Co. v. City of Sterling Heights, 949 F.2d 890, 895 (6th Cir.1991); Harris v. County of Riverside, 904 F.2d 497 (9th Cir.1990); Landmark Land Co. v. Buchanan, 874 F.2d 717 (10th Cir.1989). But see Baldini West, Inc. v. New Castle County, 852 F.Supp. 251 (D.Del. 1994); Unity Ventures v. Lake County, 841 F.2d 770 (7th Cir.1988); Taylor Investment Ltd. v. Upper Darby Twp., 983 F.2d 1285 (3d Cir.1993).

28. Yes: Rivervale Realty Co., Inc. v. Town of Orangetown, 816 F.Supp. 937, 942 (S.D.N.Y.1993); Rockler v. Minneapolis Community Development Agency, 866 F.Supp. 415, 418 (D.Minn.1994) (held procedural and substantive due process claims that "fall squarely within the federal takings claim" to be unripe until compensation sought in state court). No: Picard v. Bay Area Regional Transit District, 823 F.Supp. 1519, 1523 (N.D.Cal.1993).

remedy is available in state court, then the *Parratt* doctrine requires that the state process be used.[29]

§ 10.14 Equal Protection

The Fourteenth Amendment's guarantee of equal protection requires that classifications promote a legitimate government end in a rational way.[1] The guarantee is often implicated in land use law since the essence of many controls, particularly Euclidean zoning, is to classify land and people. In cases dealing with zoning's effect on economic interests, the restraint is more theoretical than real since such ordinances are reviewed under a highly deferential standard. Distinctions between commercial and residential use or types of commercial use, or between single-family and multi-family use are not likely to be invalidated. Only where controls affect suspect or quasi-suspect classes or fundamental or important rights is the equal protection clause a meaningful limit. Thus, distinctions based on race will fail, and special limitations on the mentally retarded, religious uses, or clinics that perform abortions are likely to be reviewed closely.

A. *Deferential Review: Belle Terre*

The rational basis test used by the Supreme Court to test social and economic legislation under the equal protection clause approximates a rule of non-review. As Justice Thomas recently said for a unanimous Court:

> [E]qual protection is not a license for courts to judge the wisdom, fairness, or logic of legislative choices. In areas of social and economic policy, a statutory classification that neither proceeds along suspect lines nor infringes fundamental constitutional rights must be upheld against equal protection challenge if there is any reasonably conceivable state of facts that could provide a rational basis for the classification. * * * Where there are "plausible reasons" for Congress' action, "our inquiry is at an end." * * * [A] legislative choice is not subject to courtroom fact-finding and may be based on rational speculation unsupported by evidence or empirical data.[2]

This rational or conceivable basis test is not applicable if a zoning ordinance categorizes uses on the basis of a suspect class (race, national origin, and, to a lesser extent, alienage) or a fundamental interest (such

29. Parratt v. Taylor, 451 U.S. 527, 101 S.Ct. 1908, 68 L.Ed.2d 420 (1981), overruled on other grounds, 474 U.S. 327, 106 S.Ct. 662, 88 L.Ed.2d 662 (1986). *Parratt* is inapplicable where deprivation is caused by conduct pursuant to established procedure. Zinermon v. Burch, 494 U.S. 113, 110 S.Ct. 975, 108 L.Ed.2d 100 (1990).

§ 10.14

1. For a general discussion of equal protection, see John E. Nowak and Ronald

D. Rotunda, Constitutional Law 595–956 (5th ed.1995). For the similarity to, and differences from, substantive due process, see id. at 362.

2. F.C.C. v. Beach Communications, Inc., 508 U.S. 307, 313–16, 113 S.Ct. 2096, 2101–2102, 124 L.Ed.2d 211 (1993).

as religion, speech, privacy, right to travel, right to vote).[3] In that event, strict scrutiny applies, which requires a compelling governmental interest to justify the law. When strict scrutiny is applied courts almost always strike down the law in question. A middle ground of intermediate scrutiny looks for a purpose substantially related to an important governmental interest. This intermediate standard appears most often in gender and legitimacy-based classifications.[4]

A prime example of federal deference to a zoning ordinance attacked on equal protection grounds is Village of Belle Terre v. Boraas.[5] The challenged ordinance differentiated between related and unrelated persons. It allowed only "families" to live in single-family homes and defined "family" as including only related persons or not more than two unrelated adults. The effect, and likely purpose, of the ordinance was to prevent groups of students from a nearby university from living together in single-family houses in the small village. A landowner who rented his house to six unrelated students brought suit on several grounds, urging the Court to find "that social homogeneity is not a legitimate interest of government."[6] The Court was not troubled by the law since it saw the ordinance as merely regulating social and economic affairs, and not implicating any fundamental rights or affecting any suspect class. In an opinion by Justice Douglas, the Court cast aside any constitutional objection, stating:

> The regimes of boarding houses, fraternity houses and the like present urban problems. More people occupy a given space; more cars rather continuously pass by; more cars are parked; noise travels with crowds.

> A quiet place where yards are wide, people few, and motor vehicles restricted are legitimate guidelines in a land use project addressed to family needs * * *. The police power is not confined to elimination of filth, stench, and unhealthy places. It is ample to lay out zones where family values, youth values, and the blessings of quiet seclusion, and clean air make the area a sanctuary for people.[7]

Seeking the application of strict scrutiny, the *Belle Terre* plaintiffs claimed that the village's ordinance infringed their right to travel, but the Court dismissed the claim with a curt statement that the law was not aimed at transients. The right to travel argument has also been raised in challenges to growth management programs, but without success.[8]

Plaintiffs' argument found a sympathetic ear with Justice Marshall, who in dissent viewed the ordinance as affecting fundamental rights of association and privacy, which required strict scrutiny. Had strict scruti-

---

3. Nowak and Rotunda, note 1, at 600–606.

4. See, e.g., Craig v. Boren, 429 U.S. 190, 197, 97 S.Ct. 451, 457, 50 L.Ed.2d 397 (1976), rehearing denied 429 U.S. 1124, 97 S.Ct. 1161, 51 L.Ed.2d 574 (1977); Nowak and Rotunda, supra note 1, at 600–607.

5. 416 U.S. 1, 94 S.Ct. 1536, 39 L.Ed.2d 797 (1974). See also § 10.12.

6. Id. at 3, 94 S.Ct. at 1538.

7. Id. at 5, 94 S.Ct. at 1539.

8. See discussion supra § 9.4.

ny been applied, the ordinance would have failed. As Justice Marshall observed, an ordinance designed to protect the quiet of a neighborhood should focus on the source of the noise, such as automobiles, rather than the legal or biological relationship of the persons occupying the houses in the neighborhood. Several state courts have refused to accept the *Belle Terre* Court's deferential posture in the context of zoning excluding unrelated persons. Applying greater scrutiny, they have invalidated such ordinances relying on state constitutional provisions of equal protection,[9] substantive due process and privacy rights.[10]

B. More Exacting Scrutiny: Cleburne

While the Court normally adheres to a deferential standard of review in equal protection challenges to land use regulations,[11] the Court broke from its usual posture in City of Cleburne v. Cleburne Living Center, Inc.[12] There the Court found a violation of the equal protection clause where a city zoning ordinance excluded group homes for the mentally retarded from a zone where apartment houses, fraternity and sorority houses, hospitals, and nursing homes for the aged were permitted. The Court was urged to classify the mentally retarded as a "quasi-suspect" class so as to trigger intermediate scrutiny, but it refused to do so. Nonetheless, the Court proceeded to find the ordinance invalid by examining, and refuting, the reasons the city offered for handling housing for the mentally retarded under a special classification. The Court said it was using the rational basis test, but it was not the "traditional" test of *Belle Terre*.[13]

The *Cleburne* opinion sparked numerous attempts by developers and others to obtain some form of heightened scrutiny. Most have been unsuccessful. Developers, asserting economic interests, have been unable to convince courts to apply *Cleburne*-like scrutiny to permit denials.[14] A shelter for battered women and a day care center were also refused such scrutiny.[15] Courts have differed over whether halfway homes for prison-

9. Kirsch v. Prince George's County, 331 Md. 89, 626 A.2d 372 (1993) (using both federal and state constitutions to find ordinance imposing more stringent regulations on occupancy of rental units by university students to violate equal protection); College Area Renters and Landlord Ass'n. v. City of San Diego, 43 Cal.App.4th 677, 50 Cal.Rptr.2d 515 (1996).

10. City of Santa Barbara v. Adamson, 27 Cal.3d 123, 164 Cal.Rptr. 539, 610 P.2d 436 (1980); New Jersey v. Baker, 81 N.J. 99, 405 A.2d 368 (1979); Charter Twp. of Delta v. Dinolfo, 419 Mich. 253, 351 N.W.2d 831 (1984).

11. See Village of Arlington Heights v. Metropolitan Housing Development Corp., 429 U.S. 252, 97 S.Ct. 555, 50 L.Ed.2d 450 (1977) (upholding exclusion of multi-family housing); Hodel v. Indiana, 452 U.S. 314, 101 S.Ct. 2376, 69 L.Ed.2d 40 (1981) (up-

holding the Surface Mining and Reclamation Act limiting coal mining in prime farmland areas).

12. 473 U.S. 432, 105 S.Ct. 3249, 87 L.Ed.2d 313 (1985).

13. See comments of Marshall, J. concurring in *Cleburne*, 473 U.S. at 455, 105 S.Ct. at 3262.

14. Jacobs, Visconsi & Jacobs Co. v. City of Lawrence, 927 F.2d 1111 (10th Cir. 1991) (shopping center); Pontarelli Limousine, Inc. v. City of Chicago, 929 F.2d 339 (7th Cir.1991) (airport livery services). But see Armendariz v. Penman, 75 F.3d 1311, 1326 (9th Cir.1996).

15. Doe v. City of Butler, 892 F.2d 315 (3d.Cir.1989) (shelter case based on substantive due process but test the same); Howard v. City of Garland, 917 F.2d 898 (5th Cir.1990) (day care).

ers deserve more exacting scrutiny.[16] *Cleburne* scrutiny has been used to find a substantive due process violation where a palm reader was denied a permit based on the religious objections of neighbors.[17] In short, it is likely that one must be a member of a vulnerable or politically unpopular group, which is subjected to irrational fear or prejudice, in order to avail oneself of this enhanced judicial review.

Developers' contentions that permit denials violate equal protection are tested under the rational basis standard, and they are almost always rejected. This is true in both state[18] and federal courts.[19] In case of invidious discrimination, such as granting or denying a permit based on personal or political reasons, a court may find a violation of equal protection.[20] Such cases, however, are rare, and, the unimaginative trial judge who cannot find a conceivable basis for the governmental action is likely to be reversed on appeal.[21] To label the test as "highly deferential" overstates its influence.[22]

In examining the willingness of courts to strike zoning classifications, state courts' use of the doctrine of spot zoning should be considered since the doctrine is built on equal protection considerations of

16. Bannum v. City of St. Charles, 2 F.3d 267 (8th Cir.1993) (no); Freedom Ranch, Inc. v. Board of Adjustment, 878 P.2d 380 (Okl.App.1994) (no); Bannum v. City of Louisville, 958 F.2d 1354 (6th Cir. 1992) (yes).

17. Marks v. City of Chesapeake, 883 F.2d 308 (4th Cir.1989). See also Love Church v. City of Evanston, 671 F.Supp. 515 (N.D.Ill.1987) (alternative holding that treatment of religious uses did not pass deferential review).

18. Security Management Corp. v. Baltimore County, 104 Md.App. 234, 655 A.2d 1326 (1995) (that nearby land rezoned while challenger's was not does not violate equal protection); Boulder City v. Cinnamon Hills Assoc., 110 Nev. 238, 871 P.2d 320 (1994) (no violation of equal protection because one elderly housing project approved and challenger's project denied because of citizen opposition and a glut of such housing). See also Stubblefield Construction Co. v. City of San Bernardino, 32 Cal.App.4th 687, 38 Cal.Rptr.2d 413 (1995); Mayhew v. Town of Sunnyvale, 41 Tex.Sup. Ct.J. 517, ___ S.W.2d ___ (Tex.1998), 1998 WL 107927.

19. Crowley v. Courville, 76 F.3d 47 (2d.Cir.1996) (allegation of selective enforcement requires proof that maliciously singled out); Strickland v. Alderman, 74 F.3d 260 (11th Cir.1996) (alleged selective enforcement unproven); Rubinovitz v. Rogato, 60 F.3d 906 (1st Cir.1995) (standards establishing malice or bad faith must be scrupulously met); Haves v. City of Miami, 52 F.3d 918 (11th Cir.1995) (banning resi-

dential occupancy of houseboats but grandfathering of existing houseboats in one area did not violate equal protection); Cohen v. City of Des Plaines, 8 F.3d 484 (7th Cir. 1993) (ordinance that allowed churches to operate non-profit day care centers in single-family districts, but required other operators of day care centers to obtain special use permits did not violate equal protection clause, since it was rationally related to legitimate government purpose of avoiding interference with religion).

20. See, e.g., Cordeco Development Corp. v. Santiago Vasquez, 539 F.2d 256 (1st Cir.1976), cert. denied, 429 U.S. 978, 97 S.Ct. 488, 50 L.Ed.2d 586 (1976) where a delay in issuing permit, coupled with limitations on the permit when issued that made land worthless was found to be a violation of equal protection where the city issued a permit to members of a politically influential family that owned neighboring land. But see Nestor Colon Medina & Sucesores, Inc. v. Custodio, 964 F.2d 32, 41 (1st Cir. 1992), expressing concern over use of equal protection in such cases.

21. Front Royal and Warren County Ind. Park Corp. v. Town of Front Royal, 922 F.Supp. 1131, 1152, n. 30 (W.D.Va. 1996) (equal protection violated where trial court could not conceive of a valid reason for city's denial of sewer service), reversed, 135 F.3d 275 (4th Cir.1998).

22. See quotation from F.C.C. v. Beach Communications, Inc., 508 U.S. 307, 313–16, 113 S.Ct. 2096, 2101–2102, 124 L.Ed.2d 211 (1993), supra note 2.

unjustified and dissimilar treatment between parcels.[23] The same is true for cases based on the uniformity provision of the Standard State Zoning Enabling Act.[24]

C. Discrimination on Race or Poverty Grounds

Discrimination against persons on the basis of race and economic status through land use controls has a long history in this country and it continues to be pervasive.[25] Techniques have ranged from the overt to the subtle.

Municipalities adopted ordinances restricting where people could live on the basis of race at the beginning of the twentieth century when blacks began migrating to cities from the rural south.[26] In Buchanan v. Warley,[27] the Court found that an ordinance that established zones on racial lines violated the due process property right of "a white man to dispose of his property to a person of color if he saw fit * * *."[28] Racially restrictive zoning, however, persisted for decades in defiance of *Buchanan*.[29] Racial segregation was also promoted by federal housing practices. In the 1930s, when the federal government began loan guarantees to save the housing industry, it required that racially restrictive covenants be put in deeds for transactions to qualify.[30]

One is not likely to find an overt racial classification in a zoning ordinance today. The same is not true, however, with ordinances which restrict on the basis of wealth.[31] Because racial minorities are disproportionately represented among lower income groups, communities can practice racial exclusion simply by zoning out housing projects which cater to those of modest means. In such cases claims of disproportionate racial impact may be made.

In the 1977 decision of Village of Arlington Heights v. Metropolitan Housing Development Corporation,[32] the ability to attack zoning ordi-

23. See, e.g., Kinzli v. City of Santa Cruz, 539 F.Supp. 887, 894 (N.D.Cal.1982); Green v. County Council of Sussex County, 508 A.2d 882, 889 (Del.Ch.1986).

24. See discussion supra § 5.13.

25. See generally Douglas S. Massey and Nancy A. Denton, American Apartheid: Segregation and the Making of the Underclass (1993); Jon C. Dubin, From Junkyards to Gentrification: Explicating a Right to Protective Zoning in Low–Income Communities, 77 Minn.L.Rev. 739 (1993); Daniel R. Mandelker, Racial Discrimination and Exclusionary Zoning: A Perspective on Arlington Heights, 55 Tex.L.Rev.1217 (1977).

26. For a history of racially exclusionary practices, see Dubin, supra note 25; Kushner, Apartheid in America: An Historical and Legal Analysis of Contemporary Racial Residential Segregation in the United States, 22 How.L.J. 547 (1979).

27. 245 U.S. 60, 38 S.Ct. 16, 62 L.Ed. 149 (1917).

28. Id. at 80, 38 S.Ct. at 20.

29. Such laws were kept "on the books" for years (until 1969 in Texas and 1975 in Florida) and even adopted as late as 1945 in Miami. Dubin, supra note 24, at 749–751.

30. See Drinan, Untying the White Noose, 94 Yale L.J. 435, 437 (1984).

31. See James v. Valtierra, 402 U.S. 137, 91 S.Ct. 1331, 28 L.Ed.2d 678 (1971). There the Court upheld a California constitutional provision requiring local referenda on low income public housing projects. The Court dismissed plaintiff's challenge to the provision, calling the poor one "of the diverse and shifting groups that make up the American people."

32. 429 U.S. 252, 97 S.Ct. 555, 50 L.Ed.2d 450 (1977), on remand 558 F.2d 1283 (7th Cir.1977), cert. denied 434 U.S. 1025, 98 S.Ct. 752, 54 L.Ed.2d 772 (1978), on remand 469 F.Supp. 836 (D.Ill.1979), affirmed 616 F.2d 1006 (7th Cir.1980).

nances restricting multifamily developments as racially discriminatory was dealt a major blow by the Supreme Court. There, a developer wished to build a federally subsidized public housing project on land zoned for single family use. Arlington Heights refused to rezone the land, invoking a buffer policy which allowed multifamily zoning only when it could serve as a buffer between single family use and industrial use. The developer, whose site did not meet that criterion, brought an equal protection attack.

The Court upheld Arlington Heights' refusal to rezone, holding that the equal protection clause requires proof of discriminatory intent rather than effect in the zoning context. Intent is much harder to prove than effect. Even though the failure of Arlington Heights to rezone would have a disproportionate impact on racial minorities, the Court held that this could only be used as evidence of intent. Discriminatory intent could be proved by showing a "clear pattern" of discriminatory effect even if the ordinance is neutral on its face. The usefulness of that approach must be questioned, however, since the Court seemingly ignored the "clear pattern" of Arlington Heights' lily-white complexion.

A second way to prove discriminatory intent under the *Arlington Heights* test is to show substantive departures from established zoning policy.[33] Because Arlington Heights had always been zoned in a highly exclusionary manner and had applied its buffer policy in a substantially uniform manner, plaintiffs could not challenge the failure to rezone on that ground. If a city, upon learning that a racially integrated housing project is being considered for a tract that is zoned for high density housing, quickly downzones the land to low density use, the requisite intent to discriminate may be shown.[34] But, the lesson of *Arlington Heights* is that the many communities that zone little or no land for high density housing by right are immunized from liability.

Discrimination on the basis of wealth is practiced by zoning for single-family use only (thus excluding multifamily use), precluding manufactured housing, and requiring large lots or houses so as to exclude all but the upper economic strata. These practices, which generally fall under the rubric of exclusionary zoning, are dealt with in depth in Chapter 6. At this point we limit our discussion to their equal protection implications.

Economic segregation was approved by the Court in *Euclid*, where it upheld the exclusion of apartment houses from single-family districts with the unflattering view that apartments in such districts of "private houses" were "mere parasites" stealing light and open space and were "near to being nuisances" endangering children.[35] Fifty years later, *Arlington Heights* reinforced this holding by implicitly finding that the village's exclusion of multi-family use did not violate equal protection.

33. The Court cited Kennedy Park Homes Ass'n v. Lackawanna, 436 F.2d 108 (2d Cir.1970), cert. denied 401 U.S. 1010, 91 S.Ct. 1256, 28 L.Ed.2d 546 (1971).

34. See. e.g., Scott v. Greenville County, 716 F.2d 1409 (4th Cir.1983).

35. 272 U.S. at 394, 47 S.Ct. at 120.

The Court, noting that it had previously held that housing was not a fundamental right[36] and poverty not a suspect classification,[37] observed that the developer did not base its complaint on the "generous *Euclid* test."[38] That was a certain loser, and the only reason the developer got anywhere in *Arlington Heights* was due to the allegation of racial discrimination.

In sum, land use claims based on racial and economic discrimination under the federal constitution's equal protection clause generally will fail. Economic discrimination claims will fail because they will not trigger strict scrutiny. Racial discrimination claims will trigger strict scrutiny, but intent must be shown to establish such a claim and that is difficult to do. Such conclusions, however, by no means end the matter. Economic discrimination effected through exclusionary zoning practices is actionable under the statutory or constitutional law of a number of states.[39] Racial discrimination in zoning can be challenged without proof of intent under the federal Fair Housing Act, where a showing of effect is sufficient to raise a prima facie case.[40]

D. Standing

Federal standing law is a further limit on the availability of equal protection attacks on exclusionary land use ordinances.[41] The most important standing decisions are Warth v. Seldin[42] and Arlington Heights v. Metropolitan Housing Development Corp.[43]

Warth involved a challenge to the exclusionary nature of the zoning ordinance of Penfield, a suburban town adjacent to Rochester, New York. There were four categories of plaintiffs: low income nonresidents unable to find housing in Penfield; taxpayers in Rochester bearing a disproportionate share of low income costs; Penfield residents denied benefits of living in an integrated community; and associations representing contractors unable to construct low-income housing in Penfield.

---

36. Village of Arlington Heights v. Metropolitan Housing Development Corp., 429 U.S. 252, 260 n. 5, 97 S.Ct. 555, 560, 50 L.Ed.2d 450 (1977) (citing Lindsey v. Normet, 405 U.S. 56, 92 S.Ct. 862, 31 L.Ed.2d 36 (1972)).

37. Id. at 260 n.5, 97 S.Ct. at 560 (citing San Antonio Indep. School District v. Rodriguez, 411 U.S. 1, 93 S.Ct. 1278, 36 L.Ed.2d 16 (1973)).

38. 429 U.S. at 263, 97 S.Ct. at 562.

39. The state approach to discriminatory zoning is best seen in the two Mt. Laurel decisions. Southern Burlington County NAACP v. Township of Mt. Laurel (Mt. Laurel I), 67 N.J. 151, 336 A.2d 713 (1975), appeal dismissed and cert. denied 423 U.S. 808, 96 S.Ct. 18, 46 L.Ed.2d 28 (1975); Southern Burlington County NAACP v. Township of Mt. Laurel (Mt. Laurel II), 92 N.J. 158, 456 A.2d 390 (1983). These cases are discussed supra § 6.6.

40. Huntington Branch NAACP v. Town of Huntington, 844 F.2d 926 (2d Cir. 1988). See discussion of Fair Housing Act supra § 6.8.

41. Regarding the standing doctrine generally, see William A. Fletcher, The Structure of Standing, 98 Yale L.J. 221 (1988); Stephen L. Winter, The Metaphor of Standing and the Problem of Self–Governance, 40 Stan. L. Rev. 1371 (1988); Gene R. Nichol, Jr. Rethinking Standing, 74 Calif.L.Rev. 68 (1984).

42. 422 U.S. 490, 95 S.Ct. 2197, 45 L.Ed.2d 343 (1975).

43. 429 U.S. 252, 97 S.Ct. 555, 50 L.Ed.2d 450 (1977), on remand 558 F.2d 1283 (7th Cir.1977), cert. denied 434 U.S. 1025, 98 S.Ct. 752, 54 L.Ed.2d 772 (1978), on remand 469 F.Supp. 836 (D.Ill.1979), affirmed 616 F.2d 1006 (7th Cir.1980).

The Court denied standing to all of them because none could show how they were personally injured by the ordinances. For example, with respect to the nonresidents who could find no affordable housing in the area, the Court noted that there was inadequate proof that the injury they suffered would be remedied by judicial intervention. Elimination of exclusionary zoning practices would not necessarily lead to the construction of affordable housing. The Court said two showings were necessary. First, there must be but-for causation, that is there must be "specific, concrete facts" proving harm to plaintiffs. Second, the plaintiffs must show a possibility of redress to them by the Court's intervention. The *Warth* test is hard to meet, for as the dissent noted, the opinion "tosses out of court almost every conceivable kind of plaintiff" in an exclusionary zoning case.[44]

Standing was found in *Arlington Heights* due to rare circumstances. A religious order had sold land at a below market price to a developer of federally subsidized housing. The developer was granted standing on the basis of its preliminary expenditures on the project and its interest in providing low cost housing in areas where it was scarce. Additionally, a black employee of a nearby plant alleged that he was unable to find affordable housing near his place of work. Because his claim was based on a particular project and not speculation as to possible future projects (as in *Warth*), the black plaintiff proved an injury in fact. In most exclusionary zoning cases, there will be no specific project, and under the rule of *Warth*, standing in federal courts will be lacking. State courts, which need not apply Article III standing rules, may grant standing in such cases.[45]

IV. FIRST AMENDMENT

§ 10.15 First Amendment Issues

Land use controls implicate rights protected by the First Amendment most frequently in the regulation of billboards and other signs, sexually oriented adult businesses, and religious uses.[1] The extent, even existence, of such protection has not always been clear. When a lower court confronting a zoning regulation that banned live entertainment opined that " 'First Amendment guarantees were not involved [since the

---

44. Id. at 520, 95 S.Ct. at 2216. A plaintiff may be able to take advantage of broader state court standing rules since state courts are not obligated to follow *Warth*. See Stocks v. City of Irvine, 114 Cal.App.3d 520, 170 Cal.Rptr. 724 (1981) (standing granted to non-resident low-income persons to challenge the City of Irvine's land use ordinance and *Warth* held not applicable in California state courts). See also Home Builders League, Inc. v. Township of Berlin, 81 N.J. 127, 405 A.2d 381 (N.J.1979).

45. See, e.g. Home Builders League, Inc. v. Township of Berlin, 81 N.J. 127, 405 A.2d 381 (1979); Stocks v. City of Irvine, 114 Cal.App.3d 520, 170 Cal.Rptr. 724 (1981).

§ 10.15

1. For a general discussion of First Amendment issues, see John E. Nowak and Ronald D. Rotunda, Constitutional Law 986 (5th ed.1995).

case dealt] solely with a zoning ordinance,' '"[2] and based its opinion on Supreme Court precedent,[3] the Supreme Court said the court had misread the law. The zoning power, said the Court, is not "infinite and unchallengeable,'"[4] and it is the nature of the right affected, not the power being exercised, that dictates the level of judicial review.[5] While strict scrutiny tests the validity of controls that impinge fundamental rights, not all First Amendment rights rise to that level. This is particularly true of adult zoning that affects non-obscene sexually oriented speech and sign controls that affect commercial speech. Courts are likely to review more closely regulations that affect noncommercial speech and religious uses.

§ 10.16 Sign Controls

The regulation of signs for reasons of traffic safety and aesthetics has a long history in this country.[1] Though commonplace, sign regulation is perilous for it must tread a narrow path between regulating too much speech or too little speech to avoid running afoul of the First Amendment.[2] The more expansive the control and the more speech that it affects, the more likely it will be found to deny avenues of protected communication and violate the First Amendment. The obvious answer to regulating too much speech is to fine-tune the regulation to minimize its impact on speech by banning fewer types of signs. However, this choice is problematical since the narrower the control, the more likely it will be found improperly to favor one type of speech over another.[3]

A. *Billboards and Other Commercial Signs*

Constitutional litigation over sign regulations is of recent origin since it was not until 1976 that the Supreme Court held that the First Amendment protected commercial speech. Even then, the protection conferred was limited. Commercial speech, said the Court, was not "wholly outside" the First Amendment.[4] Despite this unenthusiastic welcome, the door was opened to the outdoor advertising industry, and a barrage of billboard litigation followed. Though cases have swamped

---

2. Schad v. Borough of Mount Ephraim, 452 U.S. 61, 64, 101 S.Ct. 2176, 2180, 68 L.Ed.2d 671 (1981).

3. Young v. American Mini Theatres, Inc., 427 U.S. 50, 96 S.Ct. 2440, 49 L.Ed.2d 310 (1976).

4. *Schad*, 452 U.S. at 64, 101 S.Ct. at 2180.

5. Id. at 68, 101 S.Ct. at 2182.

§ 10.16

1. See discussion of aesthetics infra § 12.2.

2. See generally Mark Cordes, Sign Regulation After Ladue: Examining the Evolving Limits of First Amendment Protection, 74 Neb.L.Rev. 36 (1995); Symposium on the Regulation of Free Expression in the Public Forum, 14 St. Louis U.Pub.

L.Rev. 439 (1995); Katherine Dunn Parsons, Comment, Billboard Regulation After Metromedia and Lucas, 31 Houston L.Rev. 1555 (1995); Alan C. Weinstein, Sign Regulation After City of Ladue v. Gilleo: Still No Answer to the Problem of Content–Based Regulations, 17 Zoning & Plan.L.Rep. 65, 70 (1994); R. Douglas Bond, Note, Making Sense of Billboard Law: Justifying Prohibitions and Exemptions, 88 Mich.L.Rev. 2482 (1990).

3. City of Ladue v. Gilleo, 512 U.S. 43, 114 S.Ct. 2038, 129 L.Ed.2d 36 (1994).

4. Virginia State Bd. of Pharmacy v. Virginia Citizens Consumer Council, 425 U.S. 748, 761, 96 S.Ct. 1817, 1825, 48 L.Ed.2d 346 (1976).

lower courts, the only billboard case to reach the Supreme Court is Metromedia, Inc. v. City of San Diego.[5]

The San Diego ordinance at issue in *Metromedia* banned all commercial billboards with two categories of exceptions. First, there were twelve exemptions for such matters as informational and governmental messages, commemorative historical plaques, religious symbols, time and temperature signs, and temporary political campaign signs.[6] Second, on-site commercial signs were exempt. In effect, the ordinance banned all off-site commercial billboards, the lifeline of the outdoor advertising industry. The Court upheld the restrictions on commercial speech but invalidated the restrictions on noncommercial speech. In doing so, the Court produced five separate opinions, making it a difficult case from which to draw guidance.[7]

Justice White's plurality opinion upheld the restriction on commercial speech under the four-part test of Central Hudson Gas & Electric Corp. v. Public Service Commission.[8] To be valid, a restriction on commercial speech must (1) concern a lawful activity and not be misleading; (2) the asserted governmental interest must be substantial; if (1) and (2) are yes, (3) the regulation must directly advance the governmental interest asserted; and (4) the regulation cannot be more extensive than is necessary to serve that interest. The plurality found all four parts satisfied.[9] The two goals furthered by the ordinance, traffic safety and aesthetics, were considered substantial. Acknowledging that the ordinance was underinclusive in that the permitted on-site commercial billboards were "equally distracting and unattractive," the Court held the classification constitutional. The city "may [have] believe[d]", said the Court, that off-site billboards posed "a more acute problem" than on-site signs, and since the speech affected was commercial, favoring one kind of commercial speech over another was permissible.[10]

The noncommercial speech aspects of San Diego's zoning law received greater scrutiny and did not fare as well. The ordinance allowed only on-site *commercial* advertising.[11] Because it failed to provide also for on-site *noncommercial* advertising (which would be no more distracting or unattractive than commercial billboards), that portion of the law was found facially unconstitutional. This was considered impermissible content-based regulation and not a reasonable time, place, or manner

5. 453 U.S. 490, 101 S.Ct. 2882, 69 L.Ed.2d 800 (1981), on remand 32 Cal.3d 180, 185 Cal.Rptr. 260, 649 P.2d 902 (1982).

6. Id. at 495, 101 S.Ct. at 2886.

7. They ranged from a concurrence that thought the entire ordinance unconstitutional because neither traffic nor aesthetic concerns were sufficiently serious to justify the free speech infringement, to three separate dissents who thought the aesthetic purposes of the ordinance alone to be sufficient, who would have upheld a law banning all billboards, and who believed the plurality botched the issue of noncommercial signs and thought adequate alternatives were available.

8. 447 U.S. 557, 100 S.Ct. 2343, 65 L.Ed.2d 341 (1980).

9. 453 U.S. at 507, 101 S.Ct. at 2892.

10. Id. at 511–12, 101 S.Ct. at 2894–95.

11. An on-site sign may be defined as one identifying the use occurring on the premises where it is located. See Outdoor Systems, Inc. v. City of Mesa, 997 F.2d 604 (9th Cir.1993).

restriction. "Insofar as the city tolerates billboards at all," said the Court, "it cannot choose to limit their content to commercial messages."[12]

Despite varying analytical approaches, all the Justices in *Metromedia* agreed that aesthetics is a legitimate and substantial governmental interest in the evaluation of restraints on First Amendment speech rights. They reaffirmed that view in Members of the City Council of the City of Los Angeles v. Taxpayers for Vincent,[13] where they held that the city could ban political posters from public property to further its interest in traffic safety and aesthetics so long as the ordinance did not discriminate between types of speech. While aesthetic concerns support restraints on both commercial and noncommercial speech, a municipality runs the risk of undermining its assertion of aesthetics as a goal to the extent that it grants exemptions.[14]

While the Court remains split on the value to assign to commercial speech, the 1993 decision in City of Cincinnati v. Discovery Network, Inc.[15] shows that the gap between commercial and noncommercial speech has narrowed since *Metromedia*. In *Discovery*, the Court invalidated a ban on commercial newsracks, and in so doing, applied its commercial speech test with more force than had previously been the case. In 1989, Cincinnati gave permission to publishers of newspapers that contained almost exclusive commercial content to place their newsracks on public property. Experiencing a quick change of mind, in 1990 the city, concerned for safety and aesthetics, began enforcing an "outdated" ordinance against "commercial handbills."[16]

The *Discovery* Court put the burden on the city to show a reasonable fit between its concededly legitimate safety and aesthetic goals and its means. It was incumbent on the city to show that its regulation of speech was no more extensive than necessary. Under the intermediate scrutiny test of *Central Hudson*,[17] the city failed to carry the burden. The "outdated" handbill ordinance was designed to prevent litter not newsracks, and the city had made no recent effort to assess the gains in safety and aesthetics from the ordinance against the restraint on speech. Finally, the effort enabled the city to eliminate only sixty-two of some two thousand newsracks. The *Discovery* opinion did not leave cities without means of regulating newsracks and other forms of commercial speech, but it required them to do their homework and refine their methods.

---

12. 453 U.S. at 513, 101 S.Ct. at 2895. A number of courts have stricken ordinances favoring commercial billboards over noncommercial ones. See Bond, Making Sense of Billboard Law: Justifying Prohibitions and Exemptions, 88 Mich.L.Rev. 2482 (1990).

13. 466 U.S. 789, 104 S.Ct. 2118, 80 L.Ed.2d 772 (1984).

14. See City of Ladue v. Gilleo, 512 U.S. 43, 114 S.Ct. 2038, 129 L.Ed.2d 36 (1994); City of Cincinnati v. Discovery Network, Inc., 507 U.S. 410, 113 S.Ct. 1505, 123 L.Ed.2d 99 (1993).

15. 507 U.S. 410, 113 S.Ct. 1505, 123 L.Ed.2d 99 (1993).

16. Id. at 416, 113 S.Ct. at 1510.

17. Id. at 415–30, 113 S.Ct. at 1509–17.

The application of intermediate scrutiny in *Discovery* demonstrated increased, but reserved, support for commercial speech. The majority declined to go along with Justice Blackmun who, in concurring, urged the Court to treat truthful, commercial speech on par with noncommercial speech. The majority also characterized its holding as narrow, emphasizing that the city's distinction between commercial and noncommercial speech had "absolutely no bearing on the interests it asserted."[18] *Discovery's* intermediate scrutiny also was limited to ordinances that distinguish between commercial and noncommercial speech, suggesting that the more stringent regulation of off-site commercial billboards is not to be subjected to higher scrutiny.

Bans on off-site commercial billboards, as approved in *Metromedia*, appear to have survived *Discovery's* increased protection of commercial speech. In *Discovery*, Cincinnati relied principally on the *Metromedia* plurality's relaxed treatment of commercial speech to justify its law. Just as San Diego did not have to prove that off-site commercial billboards were more harmful than on-site billboards, Cincinnati suggested that the Court ought not require it to show that the newsracks it banned were more harmful than those permitted. This argument, said the Court, "seriously underestimate[d] the value of commercial speech."[19] When reminded of the lack of concern for commercial speech shown in *Metromedia*, the Court distinguished Cincinnati's and San Diego's ordinances. Cincinnati drew distinctions between commercial and noncommercial speech, which are subject intermediate scrutiny.[20] The portion of San Diego's ordinance that was approved distinguished between types of commercial speech, which apparently must only satisfy a lower level of scrutiny.[21]

B. *Yard Signs*

Yard signs scattered through residential neighborhoods tell neighbors and passers by a number of things: for whom the posting resident thinks they should vote, what the position of the resident is on various issues, which houses are for sale and which ones have sold, and who is painting or remodeling houses in the neighborhood. They also may identify who lives in a home and advertise the pursuit of a home occupation. Though less intrusive than the traditional billboard, yard signs nonetheless are targets of regulations based on traffic safety and visual clutter concerns. As with billboards, First Amendment problems arise when local government regulates them.

---

18. Id. at 428, 113 S.Ct. at 1516.

19. Id. at 418, 113 S.Ct. at 1510.

20. "Unlike rational basis review, the *Central Hudson* [intermediate scrutiny] standard does not permit us to supplant the precise interests put forward by the State with other suppositions." Florida Bar v. Went for It, Inc., 515 U.S. 618, 115 S.Ct. 2371, 132 L.Ed.2d 541 (1995).

21. 507 U.S. at 424 n.20, 113 S.Ct. at 1514. The level of review can be gleaned from the *Discovery* Court's affirmation of *Metromedia's* speculation that the city may have thought off-site commercial billboards posed a "more acute problem," and from the *Discovery* Court's willingness to supply its own speculation that the reason for San Diego's favoring of on-site commercial signs was to guide visitors to their intended destinations. See also Outdoor Systems, Inc. v. City of Mesa, 997 F.2d 604 (9th Cir.1993).

When a New Jersey town enacted a zoning ordinance prohibiting posting "for sale" signs to limit panic selling or "white flight," the Supreme Court wasted no time in striking down the control as a free speech violation in Linmark Assoc., Inc. v. Township of Willingboro.[22] The ordinance was not a mere restriction of time, place, and manner because reasonable alternatives for landowners wishing to sell were not available, and it was not content-neutral. Though the speech regulated was commercial, the "for sale" messages were vital community information.[23]

In City of Ladue v. Gilleo,[24] a residential suburb of St. Louis banned virtually all signs except "for sale" signs and few others.[25] Margaret Gilleo's 8.5 inch by 11 inch window sign proclaiming that she was "For Peace in the Gulf" was not among the exceptions, and she sued to enjoin enforcement of the act against her. Describing the case as "in some respects * * * the mirror image"[26] of *Linmark*, the Court held that the city banned "too much" speech. The Court, noting the nation's historic respect for "liberty in the home,"[27] viewed noncommercial sign posting from one's home as an important, unique, and "venerable means of communication." For the Court the regulation was essentially a total ban on this "distinct medium of expression," and left persons with no reasonable options to communicate quickly, directly, and cheaply with their neighbors. Just as the Court did in *Discovery*, the Court in *Ladue* did not deprive cities of all power to regulate noncommercial signs on residential property. While cities cannot likely ban such signs, reasonable regulations that deal with location, size, number and color should pass muster.[28]

By choosing to deal with the Ladue ordinance as an instance of regulating "too much" speech, the Court left hanging the validity of regulations that choose among types of speech, and thus may regulate "too little" speech.[29] The question is significant since most sign control ordinances fall into this category. While case law is mixed, a critical factor in the validity of a selective law is the degree to which the subject of an exempted sign relates to the activities on or near the land on which it is located. The more direct the relationship, the higher the likelihood that courts will uphold it.[30] For example, highway directional signs must

---

22. 431 U.S. 85, 97 S.Ct. 1614, 52 L.Ed.2d 155 (1977).

23. See also Daugherty v. East Point, 447 F.Supp. 290 (N.D.Ga.1978). Where panic selling is proved, courts may uphold the ordinance. See, e.g., Barrick Realty, Inc. v. Gary, 491 F.2d 161 (7th Cir.1974).

24. 512 U.S. 43, 114 S.Ct. 2038, 129 L.Ed.2d 36 (1994).

25. There were ten exempt categories, including in addition to "for sale" signs, signs for religious institutions, schools, nonprofit organizations, and residence identification.

26. 512 U.S. at 48, 114 S.Ct. at 2042.

27. Id. at 58, 114 S.Ct. at 2047.

28. 114 S.Ct. at 2047, n.17. See also South–Suburban Housing Center v. Greater South Suburban Bd. of Realtors, 935 F.2d 868 (7th Cir.1991) (aesthetic-based regulations on placement and number of "for sale" signs upheld).

29. See Cordes, supra note 2.

30. See Rappa v. New Castle County, 18 F.3d 1043 (3d Cir.1994). See generally Alan C. Weinstein, Sign Regulation After City of Ladue v. Gilleo: Still No Answer to the Problem of Content–Based Regulations, 17 Zoning & Plan.L.Rep. 65, 70 (1994).

appear at intersections and warning signs at dangerous curves. Even if a city bans all other signs, a compelling interest in traffic safety exists in allowing the highway signs.[31] Both *Metromedia* and *Ladue* support the idea that signs identifying activities on-site find favor over off-site signs.[32] The on-site commercial billboard in *Metromedia* held an attraction for the Court that the off-site board lacked. *Ladue* also recognized the home as a place where noncommercial signs have greater justification than commercial ones. Unlike Gilleo's personal antiwar message, commercial signs have less claim to be located in residential areas, and ought to be subject to greater regulation.[33]

§ 10.17   Regulating the Sex–Business: Erogenous Zoning

Regulation of sexually oriented businesses (known among regulators as SOBs) is a distinct area of land use planning because they are thought to cause unique problems.[1] Regulators say that adult uses, such as bookstores, movie theaters, nude dancing, and massage parlors, "attract an undesirable quantity and quality of transients"[2] resulting in an increase in crime, especially prostitution. As a consequence, property values drop, and those neighbors who are able to do so move elsewhere.[3] Erogenous zoning is usually done through either a "scattering" or "concentrating" method. The scattering method spaces adult uses sufficiently far apart to disperse the negative effects that accompany them. The concentration method lumps all such businesses in one area, sometimes called a "combat zone."[4] That zone may deteriorate, but the rest of the city is spared. Singling out adult uses for special treatment raises free speech concerns. While courts accord no First Amendment protection to obscene speech, they protect non-obscene, sexually oriented speech, at least to a degree.

The scattering or dispersal method came under review in Young v. American Mini Theatres,[5] where a Detroit ordinance prohibited the location of an adult movie theater within 1,000 feet of another such theater or 10 other establishments thought to produce similar effects.

---

31. Ackerley Communications of Mass. v. City of Cambridge, 88 F.3d 33, n. 9 (1st Cir.1996) (allowing speed limit and directional signs where other signs, including noncommercial signs were banned, could likely survive strict scrutiny).

32. Defining on-site versus off-site can pose problems. See Cordes, supra note 2.

33. Id.

§ 10.17

1. See generally J. Gerard, Local Regulation of Adult Businesses (1992); F. Strom, Zoning Control of Sex Businesses: The Zoning Approach to Controlling Adult Entertainment (1977); Alan C. Weinstein, The Renton Decision: A New Standard for Adult Business Regulation, 32 Wash.J.Urb. & Contemp.L. 91 (1987); Alan C. Weinstein,

Courts Take a Close Look at Adult Regs, 46 Land Use L. & Zoning Dig. 3 (May 1994); J. Gerard, New Developments in the Effective Preclusion of Adult Businesses by Zoning, 17 Zoning & Plan.L.Rep. 26 (1994).

2. Young v. American Mini Theatres, Inc., 427 U.S. 50, 55, 96 S.Ct. 2440, 2445, 49 L.Ed.2d 310 (1976), rehearing denied 429 U.S. 873, 97 S.Ct. 191, 50 L.Ed.2d 155 (1976).

3. See Rachel Simon, Note, New York City's Restrictive Zoning of Adult Businesses: A Constitutional Analysis, 23 Fordham Urb.L.J. 187 (1996).

4. See Northend Cinema, Inc. v. City of Seattle, 90 Wash.2d 709, 585 P.2d 1153 (1978).

5. 427 U.S. 50, 96 S.Ct. 2440, 49 L.Ed.2d 310 (1976).

Justice Stevens upheld the ordinance in a plurality opinion. The Court found the ordinance a valid exercise of the city's zoning power and not an impermissible prior restraint on free speech. The city did not aim the regulation at suppressing ideas. Rather, the ordinance had the permissible purpose of maintaining neighborhood character and documented studies of the effects of the regulated uses supported the law. It also did not significantly foreclose opportunities for the regulated uses because the market, the Court said, was "essentially unrestrained."[6] In language that reflects the Court's ambiguous feelings toward the zoning of SOBs, Justice Stevens declared that

> [e]ven though we recognize that the First Amendment will not tolerate the total suppression of erotic materials * * * few of us would march our sons and daughters off to war to preserve the citizen's right to see "specified sexual activities" exhibited in the theaters of our choice. Even though the First Amendment protects communication in this area from total suppression, we hold that the state may legitimately use the content of these materials as the basis for placing them in a different classification from other motion pictures.[7]

The Court upheld the concentration technique in City of Renton v. Playtime Theatres,[8] and, in doing so, expanded local control over adult uses beyond that allowed in *Young*. Renton, a Seattle suburb, banned adult theaters from locating within 1000 feet of any residential zone, single or multi-family dwelling, park, school, or church. While the city did not expressly create a combat zone, the effect of the distance limitations was to limit adult theaters to an area of 520 acres, 5 percent of the city. The regulation was undeniably content-based in that one determined affected theaters by asking what kind of movies they played. Nonetheless, the Court treated the ordinance as content-neutral because it found that the predominant intent was directed at the secondary effects of the message, not the message itself. As a content-neutral ordinance, it would pass constitutional muster if it served a substantial governmental interest and did not unreasonably foreclose other avenues of communication. Renton's ordinance met the test.

Overturning the court of appeals decision, which had relied on *Young*, the Court held that first-hand studies are unnecessary to uphold a city's regulation of adult uses. Unlike Detroit in the *Young* case, Renton had done no studies on the effects of adult theaters and in fact had no such theaters in town. Instead, the city relied on studies of nearby Seattle, whose experiences with adult uses it was trying to avoid. This was sufficient said the Court. A city meets its First Amendment

6. Id. at 62, 96 S.Ct. at 2448.

7. Id. at 70, 96 S.Ct. at 2452. The dissent found this notion "wholly alien" to the First Amendment. Id. at 86, 96 S.Ct. at 2460.

8. 475 U.S. 41, 106 S.Ct. 925, 89 L.Ed.2d 29 (1986).

burden if it relies on evidence that it reasonably believes relevant to the problem against which it is legislating.

Renton confirmed the long-standing rule that if the goal of legislation is suppression of the subject matter the law will presumptively violate the First Amendment as content-based. How pure a city's efforts must be to be treated as content-neutral is unclear. The City of Renton avoided being found to harbor an intent to suppress because the Court accepted the lower court's finding that the city's "predominate intent" was to deal with secondary effects and this, said the Court, "was more than adequate to establish that the city's [goal] was unrelated to suppression * * * ."[9] This suggests that the Court might regard a mixed motive as content-neutral.[10]

Reasonable alternative avenues of communication must be left open. In *Renton,* the Court found that 520 acres equaling 5 percent of the city "easily" met the test.[11] Unlike Detroit, where the market opportunities were essentially unrestrained, the court of appeals found that none of the 520 acres was commercially viable as theater sites. That, said the *Renton* Court, was not relevant. While "practically none" of the land was for sale or lease, the theater operators had "to fend for themselves in the real estate market * * * ."[12]

While *Renton's* relaxed application of the reasonable alternative requirement allows local government to limit adult uses to unattractive land in small sections of town, total exclusion is highly suspect. An ordinance that prohibited any form of "live entertainment," including but not limited to nude dancing, was struck down by the Court in Schad v. Borough of Mount Ephraim.[13] The Court found Mount Ephraim's ordinance an impermissibly overbroad exclusion of entertainment of all sorts. While the Court is likely to judge a total ban closely, *Schad* and *Renton* do not hold that such a restriction could never survive. Mount Ephraim had offered possible justifications such as parking, trash pick-up and police protection problems. The Court summarily rejected these since no evidence had been presented supporting them. The mere allegation that live entertainment was available outside Mount Ephraim's city limits also was not sufficient to justify the restriction.[14] In sum, the requirement is reasonableness, and that calls for a fact-based determination of a city's justification. While Mount Ephraim failed, a small community with land regionally available for adult uses might meet the test.

9. Id. at 48, 106 S.Ct. at 929.

10. Showing predominate intent may not be difficult. A recitation of reliance on "secondary effects" may suffice since legislative findings may not be necessary. See Lakeland Lounge of Jackson, Inc. v. City of Jackson, 973 F.2d 1255, 1258, n. 1 (5th Cir.1992). See generally, Elena Kagan, Private Speech, Public Purpose: the Role of Governmental Motive in First Amendment Doctrine, 63 U.Chi.L.Rev. 413 (1996) .

11. 475 U.S. 41, 54, 106 S.Ct. 925, 932, 89 L.Ed.2d 29 (1986).

12. Id.

13. 452 U.S. 61, 101 S.Ct. 2176, 68 L.Ed.2d 671 (1981).

14. The Court intimated that total exclusion of a use might be valid if sufficient evidence were presented to justify it and it was not discriminatory. Id. at 75, n. 18, 101 S.Ct. at 2186.

§ 10.18 Religious Uses

A. *Do Religious Uses Make Good Neighbors? Does It Matter?*

The view of religious uses as neighbors has changed over the years. In zoning's early years most zoning authorities and courts saw religious uses as "inherently beneficial" to residential areas and treated them as preferred uses, virtually exempt from zoning.[1] Generally, the buildings were small and served persons living close by.[2] The presence of a religious organization, typically a church or synagogue, provided a moral tone for a neighborhood, and its building was a center for community activity. Minimal friction existed with the First Amendment. Most communities treated religious uses with favor, and the courts did not regard the favoritism as a violation of the establishment clause.[3] When cities tried to exclude religious uses from residential areas, some courts found such exclusions arbitrary.[4]

Concern over the negative effects of institutional religious uses has grown over time, causing local governments to reconsider the propriety of preferential treatment. The so-called "mega-church" trend leads to land use projects of sizeable dimensions with frequent and varied activities, whose intrusiveness in a neighborhood cannot be ignored.[5] When activities expand beyond traditional worship (itself a loaded term) to include housing for elderly members, day-care centers, radio and television broadcasting, combined residential-worship use, and homeless shelters, the prospects of neighborhood conflict increase.

Neighbors also may doubt the benefits of a place of worship in a neighborhood if the congregation has no ties to the neighborhood. In our ever more mobile society, this increasingly is the case. Intolerance of diverse faiths may also play a role in community acceptance when the new neighbor is not the traditional church or synagogue, but a mosque, temple, or fellowship. Some or all of these factors have led communities to regulate religious uses more stringently than in the past. Usually this means treating religious uses on a par with other institutional uses since, as with much land development, they produce secular problems of

§ 10.18

1. See Cornell University v. Bagnardi, 68 N.Y.2d 583, 510 N.Y.S.2d 861, 865, 503 N.E.2d 509, 513 (1986). Though the case dealt with a school, the court discussed changing attitudes with respect to schools and religious uses. An early critic of "judicial favoritism" to churches was the Oregon Supreme Court. Milwaukie Co. Jehovah's Witnesses v. Mullen, 214 Or. 281, 330 P.2d 5 (1958). Some courts still treat religious use as "inherently beneficial." Kali Bari Temple v. Board of Adj. of Twp. of Reading-ton, 271 N.J.Super. 241, 638 A.2d 839 (1994).

2. See "Not All Rejoice When a Church Opens Next Door," Chicago Tribune, 1 (Oct. 6, 1996, 1996 WL 2714373).

3. See generally Ira C. Lupu, Reconstructing the Establishment Clause: The Case Against Discretionary Accommodation of Religion, 140 U.Pa.L.Rev. 555 (1991).

4. See State ex rel. Lake Drive Baptist Church v. Village of Bayside Bd. of Trustees, 12 Wis.2d 585, 108 N.W.2d 288, 300 (1961). See also discussion of state court treatment of religious uses in § 4.27.

5. See" 'Mega' Church Raises Thorny Issues," Atlanta Jour. and Const., C 3 (Feb.3,1993), 1993 WL 3337533.

noise, traffic, parking, storm runoff, and erosion. As a result, First Amendment challenges are increasingly common.[6]

B. Free Exercise Clause

How far land use controls must go in accommodating religious practices under the First Amendment is not clear. While the free exercise clause absolutely protects religious beliefs, government can regulate religious conduct.[7] As for the regulation of conduct, the Court held in Sherbert v. Verner[8] that government cannot substantially burden the free exercise of religion unless it has a compelling interest and uses the least restrictive means to advance this interest. Lower courts have characterized the Supreme Court's case law applying this test as "fluid precedent," in an area " 'dotted with unanswered questions.' " [9]

Three federal courts of appeals decisions in the 1980s exemplify the most common religious-use zoning disputes. In each case the ordinance was found not to constitute a substantial burden on the exercise of religion. In Messiah Baptist Church v. County of Jefferson,[10] the county denied a special permit to construct a church in a district zoned for agricultural uses for reasons dealing with access, erosion, and the lack of fire protection. The Tenth Circuit held that the construction of a house of worship on the particular tract of land was not integrally related to the church's beliefs. The church made no showing that alternative sites were unavailable, and while exclusion from the agricultural district where land values were lower may have made the practice of religion more expensive, that incidental burden did not violate the free exercise clause. In a similar case, where a city excluded religious uses from low density residential zones, the Sixth Circuit in Lakewood, Ohio Congregation of Jehovah's Witnesses v. City of Lakewood,[11] held that the First Amendment did not "require the City to make all land or even the cheapest or most beautiful land available to churches."[12] And in Grosz v. City of Miami Beach,[13] the city prevented a rabbi from conducting organized religious services in his home. Other places conducive to worship, which would not infringe on the quiet of the neighborhood, were available in town.

---

6. Kenneth Pearlman, Zoning and the Location of Religious Establishments, 31 Cath.Law. 314 (1988); Terry Rice, Re-evaluating the Balance Between Zoning Regulations and Religious and Educational Uses, 8 Pace L.Rev. 1 (1988); Laurie Reynolds, Zoning the Church: The Police Power Versus the First Amendment, 64 B.U.L.Rev. 767 (1984); Scott D. Godshall, Land Use Regulation and the Free Exercise Clause, 84 Colum.L.Rev. 1562 (1984).

7. Church of the Lukumi Babalu Aye, Inc. v. City of Hialeah, 508 U.S. 520, 113 S.Ct. 2217, 2227, 124 L.Ed.2d 472 (1993). For a general discussion of freedom of religion, see John E. Nowak and Ronald D. Rotunda, Constitutional Law 986 (5th ed.1995).

8. 374 U.S. 398, 83 S.Ct. 1790, 10 L.Ed.2d 965 (1963).

9. Messiah Baptist Church v. County of Jefferson, 859 F.2d 820, 823 (10th Cir. 1988). See also LeBlanc–Sternberg v. Fletcher, 67 F.3d 412 (2d Cir.1995).

10. 859 F.2d 820 (10th Cir.1988).

11. 699 F.2d 303 (6th Cir.1983).

12. Id. at 307. See also Marsland v. International Society for Krishna Consciousness, 66 Haw. 119, 657 P.2d 1035 (Haw.1983), appeal dismissed, 464 U.S. 805, 104 S.Ct. 52, 78 L.Ed.2d 72 (1983); Seward Chapel, Inc. v. City of Seward, 655 P.2d 1293 (Alaska 1982).

13. 721 F.2d 729 (11th Cir.1983).

Constitutional violations are likely if discrimination occurs in the administration of an otherwise valid ordinance. In Islamic Center v. City of Starkville,[14] where the city denied a special permit to a Muslim mosque, a First Amendment violation was found. The record revealed that the city had granted nine Christian churches permits, and the mosque's application was the only one ever rejected.

Even if a substantial burden is found, the compelling interest test does not apply to claims challenging neutral laws of general applicability under the Court's 1990 decision in Employment Division v. Smith.[15] Following *Smith*, several courts, treating zoning ordinances as laws of general applicability, refused to apply strict scrutiny and upheld the exclusion of a church from a commercial district[16] and the designation of a church as an historic landmark.[17] Under *Smith*, an ordinance that is neutral on its face will be subjected to strict scrutiny only if shown to have been motivated by religious animus. In Church of Lukumi Babalu Aye, Inc. v. City of Hialeah,[18] the Court found that a city adopted zoning, health, and animal cruelty ordinances prohibiting the ritual slaughter of animals specifically to target one church's religious conduct. Applying the compelling interest test, the Court found that the ordinances were not narrowly tailored to achieve the city's interests.

The decision in Employment Division v. Smith[19] provoked outcry from some, fearing the end of religious freedom.[20] Lower court decisions that had used *Smith* to deny free exercise claims in the zoning context were cited as examples of a need for greater protection.[21] In response, Congress enacted the Religious Freedom Restoration Act of 1993 (RFRA).[22] The act purported to restore the compelling interest test of *Sherbert*, but the Court invalidated the act. In City of Boerne v. Flores ,[23] the Court found RFRA an unconstitutional exercise of Congress' remedial powers under Section Five of the Fourteenth Amendment.

C. *Problem Uses: Homeless Shelters, Home Worship, and Historic Landmarks*

The exclusion of homeless shelters, soup kitchens, and home worship groups from residential areas and the designation of religious structures as historic landmarks pose claims of particular difficulty.

---

14. 840 F.2d 293 (5th Cir.1988).

15. 494 U.S. 872, 110 S.Ct. 1595, 108 L.Ed.2d 876 (1990).

16. Cornerstone Bible Church v. City of Hastings, 948 F.2d 464 (8th Cir.1991) (dismissing free exercise claim, but remanding hybrid speech-religion claim).

17. St. Bartholomew's Church v. City of New York, 914 F.2d 348 (2d Cir.1990), cert. denied, 499 U.S. 905, 111 S.Ct. 1103, 113 L.Ed.2d 214 (1991).

18. 508 U.S. 520, 533–35, 113 S.Ct. 2217, 2227, 124 L.Ed.2d 472 (1993).

19. 494 U.S. 872, 110 S.Ct. 1595, 108 L.Ed.2d 876 (1990).

20. The fear was exaggerated. See Christopher L. Eisgruber & Lawrence G. Sager, The Vulnerability of Conscience: The Constitutional Basis for Protecting Religious Conduct, 61 U. Chi.L.Rev. 1245 (1994).

21. See Douglas Laycock and Oliver S. Thomas, Interpreting the Religious Freedom Restoration Act, 73 Tex L.Rev. 209, 234 (1994).

22. 42 U.S.C.A. § 2000bb et seq.

23. ___ U.S. ___, 117 S.Ct. 2157, 138 L.Ed.2d 624 (1997).

When religious organizations open their doors to house the homeless or feed the hungry, neighbors object. While disparate elements in many communities concede the need for shelters, they contest their location. Neighbors fear that shelter guests will harass them on the streets and sidewalks, that guests will trespass on nearby private property, that some guests will be substance abusers, and that organizers will bus the guests from other parts of town or other communities. Overall, they fear that the safety and reputation of their neighborhood are at risk if they allow the shelter.[24] Some see such exclusionary efforts as representing a system of "socio-economic apartheid"[25] and others endorse the concerns as legitimate.[26]

Courts have held zoning exclusions of shelters from religious operations not to violate the free exercise clause.[27] Shelters fared better under the short-lived RFRA.[28] Some courts found the activity to be religious in nature, noting that charity toward the needy is an important aspect of many religions, or refused to engage in such an inquiry, deeming the determination of whether particular conduct is religious to be a matter within the exclusive province of the group asserting the right.[29] Some courts held that under RFRA, zoning could not prohibit existing religious operations from opening shelters, reasoning that it is a substantial burden to move the religious operation to fulfill the religious mission to the poor.[30] Once authorities gave permission for a religious use to locate at a specific location, they could not choose the types of allowable religious activities.[31] Such decisions based on RFRA now lack precedential value. With the Court's decision in City of Boerne v. Flores ,[32] finding RFRA unconstitutional, religious uses, including shelters, are again subject to neutral laws of general applicability, such as zoning.

24. Jesus Center v. Farmington Hills Zoning Bd. of App., 215 Mich.App. 54, 544 N.W.2d 698, 700 (1996).

25. Douglas Laycock and Oliver S. Thomas, Interpreting the Religious Freedom Restoration Act, 73 Tex L.Rev. 209, 222 (1994).

26. Western Presbyterian Church v. Board of Zoning Adj. of Dist. of Columbia, 862 F.Supp. 538, 546 (D.D.C.1994).

27. First Assembly of God of Naples v. Collier County, 20 F.3d 419 (11th Cir.), opin. modified, 27 F.3d 526 (11th Cir.1994), cert. denied, 513 U.S. 1080, 115 S.Ct. 730, 130 L.Ed.2d 634 (1995) (exclusion of homeless shelter in church did not violate free exercise clause).

28. See Marc–Olivier Langlois, Note, The Substantial Burden of Municipal Zoning: The Religious Freedom Restoration Act as a Means to Consistent Protection for Church–Sponsored Homeless Shelters and Soup Kitchens, 4 Wm. & Mary Bill Rts.J. 1259 (1996); Simon J. Santiago, Comment, Zoning and Religion: Will The Religious Freedom Restoration Act of 1993 Shift the

Line Toward Religious Liberty?, 45 Am. U.L.Rev. 199 (1995).

29. Jesus Center v. Farmington Hills Zoning Bd. of App., 215 Mich.App. 54, 544 N.W.2d 698, 703 (1996).

30. Jesus Center v. Farmington Hills Zoning Bd. of App., 215 Mich.App. 54, 544 N.W.2d 698, 704, n. 11 (1996); Western Presbyterian Church v. Board of Zoning Adj. of Dist. of Columbia, 862 F.Supp. 538, 545 (D.D.C.1994).

31. Id. See also Alpine Christian Fellowship v. County Commissioners of Pitkin County, 870 F.Supp. 991 (D.Col.1994), where a similar rationale was used to prevent the exclusion of a school from a church. However, where the religious organization is seeking an initial location in a community, forcing it to use land in an area zoned for shelters has been held not to constitute a substantial burden. Daytona Rescue Mission, Inc. v. City of Daytona Beach, 885 F.Supp. 1554 (M.D.Fl.1995).

32. ___ U.S. ___, 117 S.Ct. 2157, 138 L.Ed.2d 624 (1997).

Home worship is a sensitive area to regulate since no norm exists for where, when, or how often religious services take place. While a city could not ban private prayer at home, and while no city is likely to attempt to do so, problems arise when a person opens a home to regular worship services.[33] Where zoning ordinances prohibit small groups from gathering in homes for religious services, courts have found free exercise violations.[34] The larger the group and the more frequent the meetings, the less likely that courts will protect the activity.[35]

The designation of religious buildings as historic landmarks is common. So are disputes over the propriety of such designations under both the First Amendment's religion and speech clauses and the Fifth Amendment's takings clause.[36] Many communities, particularly downtown areas, contain architecturally significant churches, synagogues, and other religious buildings with exterior features that give the city character and beauty. Their preservation is important. Yet, the buildings may be aging and expensive to maintain, and the congregation that must spend its funds on maintenance may be unable to carry out its desired religious mission. A leading case involves New York City's landmark designations of St. Bartholomew's Church and its adjacent community building.[37] In search of funds to support its religious mission, the church planned to gain rental income by tearing down its community building and erecting a fifty-nine story office tower. The Landmarks Commission denied the request to raze the building. The Second Circuit found no infringement of the church's free exercise right since it regarded the law as a neutral law of general applicability under the rule of *Smith*. The city restricted numerous religious and nonreligious buildings for neutral aesthetic reasons, and no intent to discriminate against religious beliefs existed. Keeler v. Mayor & City Council of Cumberland reached the opposite conclusion.[38]

D. *Establishment Clause*

The desire to avoid treading on free exercise rights puts government in a Catch 22 situation: if zoning authorities exempt religious uses, an

33. See Ann L. Wehener, Comment, When a House is Not a Home But a Church: A Proposal for Protection of Home Worship from Zoning Ordinances, 22 Cap. U.L.Rev. 491 (1993).

34. State v. Cameron, 100 N.J. 586, 606, 498 A.2d 1217, 1227 (1985); Kali Bari Temple v. Board of Adj. of Twp. of Reading-ton, 271 N.J.Super. 241, 638 A.2d 839 (1994); Farhi v. Commissioners of Borough of Deal, 204 N.J.Super. 575, 499 A.2d 559 (1985).

35. See Grosz v. City of Miami Beach, 721 F.2d 729 (11th Cir.1983); Christian Gospel Church, Inc. v. City and County of San Francisco, 896 F.2d 1221 (9th Cir. 1990).

36. Richard F. Babcock and David A. Theriaque, Landmarks Preservation Ordinances: Are the Religion Clauses Violated

by Their Application to Religious Properties, 7 J. Land Use & Envtl.L. 165 (1992); Ted L. Wills, Note, Religious Landmarks, Guidelines for Analysis: Free Exercise, Takings, and Least Restrictive Means, 53 Ohio State L.J. 211 (1992).

37. St. Bartholomew's Church v. City of New York, 914 F.2d 348 (2d Cir.1990), cert. denied, 499 U.S. 905, 111 S.Ct. 1103, 113 L.Ed.2d 214 (1991).

38. 940 F.Supp. 879 (D.Md.1996). In First Covenant Church v. City of Seattle, 120 Wash.2d 203, 840 P.2d 174 (1992), the Washington Supreme Court found *Smith* inapplicable since landmark law was not neutral. Massachusetts found the designation of the interior of a church violative of its state constitution. Society of Jesus of New England v. Boston Landmarks Commission, 409 Mass. 38, 564 N.E.2d 571 (1990).

establishment clause problem may arise. Under Lemon v. Kurtzman,[39] to survive an establishment clause challenge, an ordinance must have a secular purpose, must not have as its primary effect the advancement of religion, and must not foster an excessive entanglement with religion. In Larkin v. Grendel's Den,[40] the Court invalidated an ordinance that gave a "church" a veto power over an application for a liquor license for an establishment within 500 feet of the church. The ordinance had a valid secular purpose of insulating religious uses from the disruptive activities that accompany the use of alcohol, but the Court held that by vesting veto authority in the religious organization, the ordinance both advanced religion and resulted in an excessive church-state entanglement.

Cohen v. City of Des Plaines,[41] involved a more common example of zoning favoritism, the simple exemption of religious uses from obligations that others must obey. There, an ordinance allowed religious organizations to operate day care centers as a matter of right, but required all others to obtain a special permit. A nonreligious applicant whom the city denied a permit challenged the favoritism shown to religious uses as a violation of the establishment clause. The court held the favoritism justified. Construing the ordinance to exempt only nonprofit religious day care centers, the court found its primary purpose was to minimize governmental interference with religious uses, which it regarded as a secular purpose.

The courts have not yet deeply explored the parameters of zoning exemptions and the establishment clause. That the issue remains of concern to land use regulators is evidenced by the concurrence of Justice Stevens in City of Boerne v. Flores.[42] In that case, a Catholic church claimed to be exempt from a city's historic landmark laws based on the Religious Freedom Restoration Act. While the Court held the act unconstitutional on other grounds, Stevens thought the grant of an exemption from the neutral landmark law reflected an unconstitutional preference for religion.

V. COMMERCE CLAUSE

§ 10.19 Commerce Clause-based Limitations

The commerce clause is both a source of power for federal land use controls and a negative restraint on state and local land use laws. Such federal laws as the Surface Mining Control and Reclamation Act, the Clean Water Act, particularly the Section 404 wetlands controls, and the

39. 403 U.S. 602, 91 S.Ct. 2105, 29 L.Ed.2d 745 (1971).

40. 459 U.S. 116, 103 S.Ct. 505, 74 L.Ed.2d 297 (1982). See also Farris v. Minit Mart Foods, Inc. No. 37, 684 S.W.2d 845 (Ky.1984).

41. 8 F.3d 484 (7th Cir.1993).

42. ___ U.S. ___, 117 S.Ct. 2157, 138 L.Ed.2d 624 (1997).

Endangered Species Act are direct regulations of private land use activities and are based on the commerce clause. These acts are considered elsewhere.[1] Commerce clause-based acts promoting communications functions, such as satellite dishes and cellular telephones, indirectly control land use in that they preempt local zoning.[2]

Our concern at this point is with limitations on the freedom of local government to regulate land use that may arise from federal antitrust laws based on the commerce clause and with limitations on state and local laws that affect the interstate shipment of waste that arise from the negative or dormant commerce clause.

§ 10.20 Antitrust

A. *State Action Immunity for Local Government*

Land use regulations frequently have anticompetitive effects that raise possible federal antitrust liability concerns. The facts of City of Columbia v. Omni Outdoor Advertising, Inc.[1] illustrate the problem. When a new outdoor advertising company tried to break into the local market of Columbia, South Carolina, it ran into significant opposition. Much of the opposition allegedly came from a local company that controlled 95% of the billboard business in town. Eventually, the city enacted a restrictive billboard measure that had the effect of banning most new billboards and allowing most existing ones to continue in place. The law clearly favored the hometown business and disadvantaged the outsider. The outside company brought suit against the city and the competitor alleging their conduct constituted a conspiracy in restraint of trade under the Sherman Act.[2]

In a broad ruling favoring municipalities,[3] the Court held that the city was immune from liability under the state action doctrine of Parker v. Brown.[4] In *Parker*, the Court had held that sovereign immunity shielded a state from liability for anticompetitive action. Subsequently, the Court held that municipalities acquired derivative immunity only when they were carrying out clearly articulated state policies.[5] The

---

§ 10.19

1. For coverage of wetlands, see infra §§ 11.9–.12 and of endangered species, see infra § 11.16. For a more in depth coverage, see William H. Rodgers, Jr., Environmental Law (2d ed.1994). For coverage of the Surface Mining Control and Reclamation Act, see Barlow Burke, Jr., Robert E. Beck, and Cyril A. Fox, Jr., Cases and Materials on Mineral Law (1994).

2. See discussion supra § 4.25.

§ 10.20

1. 499 U.S. 365, 111 S.Ct. 1344, 113 L.Ed.2d 382 (1991). See Korn, Note, Municipal Antitrust Liability: A Question of Immunity, 42 Wash.U.J.Urb. & Contemp.L. 413 (1992) (favoring outcome) and Note,

The Supreme Court: 1990 Term, Antitrust Immunity: City of Columbia v. Omni Outdoor Advertising, Inc., 105 Harv.L.Rev. 77, 360 (1991) (criticizing opinion).

2. § 15 U.S.C. § 1.

3. *Omni* followed two other cases that had also conferred significant protection to municipalities. See Town of Hallie v. City of Eau Claire, 471 U.S. 34, 105 S.Ct. 1713, 85 L.Ed.2d 24 (1985) and Fisher v. City of Berkeley, 475 U.S. 260, 106 S.Ct. 1045, 89 L.Ed.2d 206 (1986).

4. 317 U.S. 341, 63 S.Ct. 307, 87 L.Ed. 315 (1943).

5. City of Lafayette v. Louisiana Power & Light Co., 435 U.S. 389, 98 S.Ct. 1123, 55 L.Ed.2d 364 (1978).

antitrust immunity doctrine requires a delegation that authorizes the suppression of competition, and in *Omni*, the Court found the state's delegation of zoning power to the city "amply met" the test. The billboard regulations were enacted pursuant to state law modeled after the Standard State Zoning Enabling Act that allowed the city to regulate the location of uses. "The very purpose of zoning regulation," the Court said, "is to displace unfettered business freedom."[6]

Omni went on to hold that the immunity existed even if the local action exceeded the delegated authority. Under the law of most states, while it is recognized that zoning may affect competition, zoning for the purpose of controlling competition is illegal.[7] For antitrust purposes, however, the delegated authority is interpreted more broadly so as to minimize federal interference with state law. Thus, even if the City of Columbia had enacted the billboard law with the intent of suppressing competition in violation of state law, it would not have mattered. Procedural or substantive defects are irrelevant.

While the *Parker* doctrine protected the city from liability, the *Noerr-Pennington* doctrine saved the hometown competitor.[8] *Noerr-Pennington* prevents persons from being penalized for exercising their First Amendment right to petition the government. Private parties can urge the government to enact anticompetitive laws, which are to their economic benefit, without fear of antitrust liability. There is, however, a sham exception. If the anticompetitive tool is the government process itself, and not the outcome, liability may ensue. Filing a frivolous lawsuit or objection in a pending action with no expectation of winning, but simply to harass and delay a competitor, is not protected by the First Amendment. In *Omni*, the alleged anticompetitive action was not the lobbying effort but the result, and, thus, the private party was immune.[9]

Before *Omni* there had been some question as to whether there were conspiracy exceptions to *Parker* and *Noerr-Pennington* immunity. As a final blow to disgruntled competitors, the *Omni* Court said "no" to both. The Court was unwilling to allow even a narrow conspiracy exception for corruption. If bribery of local officials is involved, other federal and state laws will apply.

B. Antitrust Remedies and the Local Government Antitrust Act of 1984

In addition to injunctive and declaratory relief, treble damages are available against private parties for antitrust violations under the Clayton Act.[10] Local governments, however, are immune from monetary

---

6. City of Columbia v. Omni Outdoor Advertising, Inc., 499 U.S. 365, 372, 111 S.Ct. 1344, 1350, 113 L.Ed.2d 382 (1991).

7. Ensign Bickford Realty Corp. v. City of Livermore, 68 Cal.App.3d 467, 137 Cal. Rptr. 304 (1977).

8. Eastern R.R. Presidents Conference v. Noerr Motor Freight, Inc., 365 U.S. 127, 81 S.Ct. 523, 5 L.Ed.2d 464 (1961) and

United Mine Workers v. Pennington, 381 U.S. 657, 85 S.Ct. 1585, 14 L.Ed.2d 626 (1965).

9. See also Village Supermarket, Inc. v. Mayfair Supermarkets, Inc., 269 N.J.Super. 224, 634 A.2d 1381 (1993).

10. 15 U.S.C.A. §§ 12–26.

liability. Shortly after a 28.5 million dollar treble damage verdict against a Chicago suburb, Congress enacted the Local Government Antitrust Act of 1984.[11] It forbids antitrust damage claims against local governments and their officials: "no damages, interest on damages, costs or attorney's fees may be recovered under Section 4, 4A, or 4C of the Clayton Act * * * from any local government, or official or employee thereof acting in an official capacity."[12] Both the plain language of the Section and the legislative history of the Act make clear that a local government is absolutely immune from antitrust damage claims even though the local government may have acted beyond its authority or in bad faith.

In summary, private parties lobbying for land use measures are potentially liable for antitrust treble damage claims, unless they can bring themselves within the *Noerr-Pennington* doctrine. Local governments exercising land use authority will generally be protected by the *Parker* doctrine. In the rare case where they are not, they are still immune from damage claims, as are their public officials when acting in their official capacity. Local governments remain subject to injunctive relief, and compliance with injunctions may in some cases be expensive. Still, with *Omni*, this threat is not great. As Professor Wolf has observed, "local land use regulators who engag[e] in arguably anticompetitive activities [are] no longer pursuing a high-risk activity."[13]

§ 10.21 State and Local Efforts to Control Waste Disposal

The siting of waste disposal facilities virtually assures controversy. Potential neighbors who do not want them in their "backyards" will likely protest zoning and siting decisions on various state law grounds.[1] The regulated user may also object to restrictive local laws. Generally, however, subjecting facilities to special permitting processes and imposing distance controls, two common features of local law, are valid.[2] Constitutional difficulties arise when state or local government choose the parochial options of excluding waste facilities, discouraging the importation of waste by charging higher fees, or in the reverse, hoarding waste for the benefit of local business. When government opts for one of these paths, the disadvantaged businesses have a potent ally in the dormant commerce clause.

A state cannot isolate itself from interstate trade. State or local laws that unduly burden or discriminate against interstate commerce violate

---

11. 15 U.S.C.A. §§ 34–36. The case of Unity Ventures v. County of Lake, 631 F.Supp. 181 (N.D.Ill.1986) was "the straw that broke the camel's back." David L. Callies, Robert H. Freilich and Thomas E. Roberts, Cases and Materials on Land Use 366 (1994).

12. 15 U.S.C.A. § 35(a).

13. Michael Allan Wolf, *Euclid* at Threescore Years and Ten: Is This the Twi-

light of Environmental and Land–Use Regulation? 30 U.Rich.L.Rev. 961, 981 (1996).

§ 10.21

1. See § 6.9 regarding LULUs.

2. See Shortlidge and White, The Use of Zoning and Other Local Controls for Siting Solid and Hazardous Waste Facilities, 7 Nat.Res. & Envt. 3 (1993).

the dormant commerce clause.[3] Though waste may have no value, the fact that one must pay to get rid of waste converts it into an article of commerce.[4] And, with the mountains of waste that we produce, the business of transporting and processing waste is a big business.

The Supreme Court has invalidated numerous state and local efforts to exclude waste from out of state. When New Jersey, finding itself running short of landfill space, banned the import of waste from out of state, the Court held the discriminatory treatment unconstitutional.[5] When Alabama imposed a higher fee on waste generated out of state, the Court found it also to be unconstitutionally discriminatory.[6] When Michigan delegated to its counties the power to exclude waste generated outside the county, the Court invalidated a county ordinance that took up the state's invitation.[7] The Court reasoned that local governmental units can no more discriminate than the state itself. The fact the ordinance banned in-state waste along with out-of-state waste did not save it.

Some states and communities ban the export of waste.[8] Those efforts too have failed. Keeping waste at home is important to maintain a supply for local disposal sites. Recently, Clarkstown, New York, needed a new transfer station to sort waste, but apparently could not afford to build it. A local developer agreed to build and operate the facility, in return for the town's promise to provide a minimum waste flow and allow the charging of a high tipping fee. To assure a flow of waste, the town adopted an ordinance that required all waste generated in town or brought to town to be taken to the private facility. The Court held the ordinance invalid.[9] Hoarding waste for the benefit of one local private operator was classic protectionism that the commerce clause was designed to prevent. The Court's message is fairly clear. If a state or local government uses its regulatory powers to control waste, it may not favor local businesses. Only if the government itself enters the business itself as a "market participant" and not a regulator is it exempt from the commerce clause.[10]

In recent years Congress has considered a number of bills seeking to overcome the Court's interpretation of the commerce clause. Most of the bills authorize bans against out of state waste or allow the charging of

3. C & A Carbone, Inc. v. Town of Clarkstown, 511 U.S. 383, 114 S.Ct. 1677, 128 L.Ed.2d 399 (1994).

4. Id. at 389, 114 S.Ct. at 1682.

5. City of Philadelphia v. New Jersey, 437 U.S. 617, 98 S.Ct. 2531, 57 L.Ed.2d 475 (1978).

6. Chemical Waste Management, Inc. v. Hunt, 504 U.S. 334, 112 S.Ct. 2009, 119 L.Ed.2d 121 (1992).

7. Fort Gratiot Sanitary Landfill, Inc. v. Michigan Dept. of Natural Resources, 504 U.S. 353, 112 S.Ct. 2019, 119 L.Ed.2d 139 (1992).

8. See John Turner, The Flow Control of Solid Waste and the Commerce Clause: Carbone and its Progeny, 7 Vill.Envtl.L.J. 203 (1996).

9. C & A Carbone, Inc. v. Town of Clarkstown, 511 U.S. 383, 114 S.Ct. 1677, 128 L.Ed.2d 399 (1994).

10. See Swin Resource Systems v. Lycoming County, 883 F.2d 245 (3d.Cir.1989), cert. denied, 493 U.S. 1077, 110 S.Ct. 1127, 107 L.Ed.2d 1033 (1990) (lower tipping fee charged by county operated facility held valid).

higher fees.[11] If passed, such legislation would dispense with the commerce clause problem, but there would remain a potential equal protection challenge.[12]

VI. LITIGATION ISSUES AND SECTION 1983

§ 10.22 Choice of Forum: Some General Considerations

Constitutional land use claims, particularly those involving the Fifth and Fourteenth Amendments, have not received a particularly warm welcome in the federal courts. The Court of Appeals for the First Circuit, for example, has repeatedly emphasized that "federal courts do not sit as a super zoning board or a zoning board of appeals."[1] In one noteworthy example, a landowner sought damages for deprivation of civil rights because the city refused to grant the landowner a gravel removal permit.[2] Despite claims that the city had attempted to give a competitor an advantage over the landowner, the court held that the local zoning board had properly addressed and disposed of the landowner's permit application.[3] In chastising the landowner for bringing the "frivolous" civil rights action, the court stated that "[i]f all that were required to secure federal jurisdiction were loose claims of conspiracy and corruption, virtually any case of this type could be brought into the federal court."[4] The court then taxed the landowner with double costs.

Other federal courts also have expressed reluctance. The Seventh Circuit has used strong language to advise its district courts against becoming arbiters of local land use disputes. In one case, a developer complained that a permit denial was arbitrary because the decision had been made in a private session with no reasons given and there were no criteria to guide the decision, all in violation of state law. The court said in response: "[i]f the plaintiffs can get us to review the [decision], we cannot imagine what zoning dispute could not be shoehorned into federal court * * *, there to displace or postpone consideration of some worthier object of federal judicial solicitude."[5] It was simply a "garden-variety zoning dispute dressed up in the trappings of constitutional law."[6] With apparent jealousy, the Sixth Circuit has observed that "the Federal Circuit is fortunate in not having to deal with zoning cases."[7]

---

11. See Philip Weinberg, Congress, the Courts, and Solid Waste Transport: Good Fences Don't Always Make Good Neighbors, 25 Envtl.L. 57 (1995).

12. Id.

§ 10.22

1. Raskiewicz v. New Boston, 754 F.2d 38, 44 (1st Cir.1985), cert. denied 474 U.S. 845, 106 S.Ct. 135, 88 L.Ed.2d 111 (1985); Chiplin Enterprises v. Lebanon, 712 F.2d 1524 (1st Cir.1983). See also Hynes v. Pasco County, 801 F.2d 1269 (11th Cir.1986).

2. Raskiewicz v. New Boston, 754 F.2d 38 (1st Cir.1985).

3. Id.

4. Id. at 44.

5. Coniston Corp. v. Village of Hoffman Estates, 844 F.2d 461, 467 (7th Cir. 1988).

6. Id.

7. Pearson v. City of Grand Blanc, 961 F.2d 1211, 1219 (6th Cir.1992).

The antipathy of these federal courts toward land use claims perhaps explains in part their enthusiastic application of several rules that permit them to reduce their role. Several of these rules have been discussed in preceding sections, such as the adoption of a narrow view of what constitutes a protectable property interest,[8] a strict application of the ripeness doctrine in takings,[9] due process and equal protection claims,[10] and an expansive reading of the *Parratt* post-deprivation remedy doctrine regarding due process claims.[11] Federal courts have also demonstrated a willingness to abstain in land use cases.[12]

This attitude is important to keep in mind in the choice of a forum. As a general matter, federal and state courts have concurrent jurisdiction over land use claims raising constitutional or other federal law claims. Whether a particular state court is more or less hospitable to land use claims than the local federal court, however, is a moot question in many cases since the state court will be the only forum available.

§ 10.23   The Federal Civil Rights Act: § 1983

A. *Procedural, not Substantive, Protection*

The statute used to assert constitutional claims in most land use cases is Section 1983 of the Civil Rights Act of 1871, which states:

> Every person who, under color of any statute, ordinance, regulation, custom, or usage, of any state or territory, subjects or causes to be subjected, any citizen of the United States or other person within the jurisdiction thereof to the deprivation of any rights, privileges, or immunities secured by the Constitution and laws, shall be liable to the party injured in an action at law, suit in equity, or other proper proceeding for redress.[1]

Enacted as implementing legislation under section five of the Fourteenth Amendment, § 1983 was designed to protect the civil rights of the newly freed slaves. Moving far beyond its original purpose, § 1983 has practically become a federal tort law, and a large body of case law has developed surrounding the use of this statutory avenue for the protection of federal rights.[2]

Section 1983 creates no substantive rights. It is an enabling statute, providing a procedural vehicle for a person to secure damages or injunctive relief for the violation of federal constitutional or statutory rights.

---

8. See § 10.12.
9. See § 10.10.
10. See §§ 10.12–14.
11. See §§ 10.12–13.
12. See infra § 10.27.

§ 10.23

1. 42 U.S.C.A. § 1983.

2. For a general discussion of the Civil Rights Acts, see Sword and Shield Revisited: A Practical Approach to Section 1983 (Mary Massaron Ross ed.1998); Sheldon H. Nahmod, Civil Rights and Liberties: The Law of Section 1983 (3d.ed.1991); Kenneth B. Bley, Use of the Civil Rights Acts to Recover Damages in Land Use Cases, Land Use Institute: Planning, Regulation, Litigation, Eminent Domain and Compensation (ALI–ABA 1995); Rockwell, Constitutional Violations in Zoning: The Emerging Section 1983 Damage Remedy, 33 U.Fla.L.Rev. 168 (1981).

One must establish the deprivation of a right secured by the constitution or laws of the United States. In land use, generally this will involve the Fifth Amendment's requirement of compensation for the taking of property, free speech or religious rights under the First Amendment, or due process or equal protection violations under the Fourteenth Amendment. The substantive law of those provisions, not § 1983, determines when an action lies.

The § 1983 cause of action is particularly important since the option of bringing suit directly on the constitutional provision in question may not exist or, if it does, may be less attractive. While the Fifth Amendment's taking clause is self-executing, and an action in inverse condemnation lies to permit the recovery of just compensation,[3] whether direct actions are available for other rights is not clear. The Court has held that direct suits are available against the federal government for conduct violative of the Fourth Amendment[4] and the due process clause of the Fifth Amendment.[5] Direct actions against state or local governments based on the Fourteenth Amendment may or may not be implied.[6] The availability of a suit based on § 1983 usually obviates the question.[7]

Developers first became interested in § 1983 when the Supreme Court in 1972 extended the statute's protection from personal constitutional rights to include property interests.[8] Two other developments in the 1970s enhanced the interest. In 1976 Congress passed the Civil Rights Attorney's Fees Award Act,[9] providing attorney's fees to prevailing parties in § 1983 litigation. The Court then held in 1978 that municipalities were "persons" subject to § 1983 liability.[10] The presence of a defendant with the financial resources to pay off a judgment, with attorney's fees available to boot, made the statutory cause of action even more attractive. These openings have led to a barrage of § 1983 lawsuits by property owners and developers.

B. The Basic § 1983 Cause of Action

There are two "essential elements" of a § 1983 cause of action: the complained of conduct (1) must have resulted in (a) the deprivation of (b) a right, privilege or immunity secured by the constitution or laws of

---

3. First English Evangelical Lutheran Church v. County of Los Angeles, 482 U.S. 304, n. 9, 107 S.Ct. 2378, 96 L.Ed.2d 250 (1987).

4. Bivens v. Six Unknown Agents, 403 U.S. 388, 91 S.Ct. 1999, 29 L.Ed.2d 619 (1971).

5. Davis v. Passman, 442 U.S. 228, 99 S.Ct. 2264, 60 L.Ed.2d 846 (1979).

6. See Rogin v. Bensalem Twp., 616 F.2d 680 (3d Cir.1980).

7. Some courts have held that the existence of § 1983 precludes a direct action. See Azul-Pacifico, Inc. v. City of Los Angeles, 973 F.2d 704 (9th Cir.1992), cert. denied 506 U.S. 1081, 113 S.Ct. 1049, 122

L.Ed.2d 357 (1993); Thomas v. Shipka, 818 F.2d 496 (6th Cir.1987).

8. Lynch v. Household Fin. Corp., 405 U.S. 538, 92 S.Ct. 1113, 31 L.Ed.2d 424 (1972).

9. 42 U.S.C.A. § 1988.

10. Monell v. Dept. of Social Services, 436 U.S. 658, 98 S.Ct. 2018, 56 L.Ed.2d 611 (1978). In a footnote, the Court limited its holding to local government units that are not part of the state for Eleventh Amendment purposes. Notwithstanding this limiting footnote, counties have been held subject to § 1983 liability. VanOoteghem v. Gray, 628 F.2d 488 (5th Cir.1980), cert. denied 451 U.S. 935, 101 S.Ct. 2031, 68 L.Ed.2d 334 (1981).

the United States and (2) must have been committed by a person acting "under color of state law."[11] Both intentional and negligent deprivations may be actionable, but no single standard of care applies in all § 1983 cases; rather, the standard of care demanded depends on the specific constitutional or statutory right under consideration.[12] With respect to violations of due process, for example, the Court in Daniels v. Williams[13] noted that to prevail in a § 1983 claim a plaintiff must prove a violation of an underlying constitutional right. Mere negligence is not sufficient conduct upon which to base a Fourteenth Amendment due process claim.[14]

C. *Deprivation*

To state a claim, plaintiff must prove that the defendant *deprived* the plaintiff of a "right, privilege or immunity secured by the constitution or laws of the United States * * * ."[15] The deprivation element is usually expressed in terms of a violation of an express right created by the constitution.[16] The claim must assert that a specific right was infringed. In cases under the Bill of Rights, the question of deprivation is usually self-evident. A violation of the Fourth Amendment is complete when an illegal search occurs and by such a search the government deprives the individual of a protected right. However, as the Supreme Court pointed out in Parratt v. Taylor,[17] alleged violations of the due process clause require a different analysis.[18] Under that clause, the deprivation of a property right, is not per se a deprivation of a constitutional right. It is only when the deprivation of the property right is accomplished without due process, that it becomes a deprivation of a constitutional right.[19] Because due process can, depending on the circumstances, be provided either before or after the deprivation of property, simple proof of a deprivation of property will not suffice to show a constitutional deprivation.[20] Rather, in order to sustain a claim, it is necessary to show that state law fails to afford adequate pre-or post-deprivation remedies.[21]

D. *Under Color of State Law*

Individual government officials' actions are "under color of state law" when the government official acts within the scope of his or her duties.[22] An official's actions are also actionable if taken "while clothed

---

11. Parratt v. Taylor, 451 U.S. 527, 535, 101 S.Ct. 1908, 1913, 68 L.Ed.2d 420 (1981).

12. Id.

13. 474 U.S. 327, 106 S.Ct. 662, 88 L.Ed.2d 662 (1986).

14. Id.

15. 14 U.S.C.A. § 1983.

16. See, e.g., Monroe v. Pape, 365 U.S. 167, 81 S.Ct. 473, 5 L.Ed.2d 492 (1961) (claimed deprivation of Fourth Amendment rights); Estelle v. Gamble, 429 U.S. 97, 97 S.Ct. 285, 50 L.Ed.2d 251 (1976), rehearing denied 429 U.S. 1066, 97 S.Ct. 798, 50 L.Ed.2d 785 (1977) (claimed deprivation of Eighth Amendment rights).

17. 451 U.S. 527, 101 S.Ct. 1908, 68 L.Ed.2d 420 (1981).

18. Id. at 537, 101 S.Ct. at 1914.

19. Id. at 541, 101 S.Ct. at 1916.

20. Id. at 540–41, 101 S.Ct. at 1915–16.

21. Id. at 540–41, 101 S.Ct. at 1915–16.

22. Monroe, 365 U.S. at 167, 81 S.Ct. at 473.

with the authority of state law."[23] As stated by the Supreme Court, "[m]isuse of power, possessed by virtue of state law and made possible because the wrongdoer is clothed with the authority of state law, is action taken 'under color of' state law."[24] In addition, activities pursued under a municipal ordinance are sufficient to meet the "under color of state law" requirements.[25] Thus, state or local officials act "under color of state law" when they either act within the scope of their duties or misuse power granted to them by the state.

Plaintiffs have frequently sought to make the government entity itself answer for the actions of its offending officials and employees. One method tested by plaintiffs is the doctrine of *respondeat superior*. At common law, "[a] master is subject to liability for the torts that servants commit while acting in the scope of their employment."[26] Plaintiffs, however, have enjoyed little success in applying this doctrine to civil rights claims, and most courts hold that the doctrine has no place in the civil rights field.[27] The result is that, in order to recover against the government entity, the plaintiff must show that the "conduct" was conduct of the entity itself. However, since the entity can act only through its officials and employees, the line between direct liability for its own acts and no *respondeat superior* liability for the acts of its agents is not always easy to draw.

Municipal corporations and other political subdivisions act under color of state law, and are directly liable, if an alleged injury or deprivation is the "natural consequence of [an official] policy or custom."[28] There is no precise definition of "policy,"[29] but a single action by a city official may suffice. In Pembaur v. City of Cincinnati,[30] the Court held that a municipality is liable "where—and only where—a deliberate choice to follow a course of action is made from among various alternatives by the official or officials responsible for establishing final policy with respect to the subject matter in question."[31]

In land use cases, a municipality may be liable not only through the adoption of a zoning ordinance,[32] but also by taking other official action, such as where a city council denies a building permit.[33] The action of a

23. Id. at 184, 81 S.Ct. at 482.

24. United States v. Classic, 313 U.S. 299, 326, 61 S.Ct. 1031, 1043, 85 L.Ed. 1368 (1941), rehearing denied 314 U.S. 707, 62 S.Ct. 51, 86 L.Ed. 565 (1941).

25. Home Telephone & Telegraph Co. v. Los Angeles, 211 U.S. 265, 29 S.Ct. 50, 53 L.Ed. 176 (1908).

26. Restatement of the Law of Agency, Second, § 219.

27. Williams v. Vincent, 508 F.2d 541 (2d Cir.1974); Johnson v. Glick, 481 F.2d 1028 (2d Cir.1973), cert. denied 414 U.S. 1033, 94 S.Ct. 462, 38 L.Ed.2d 324 (1973); Fleenor v. Adams, 390 F.Supp. 258 (E.D.Tenn.1974).

28. Smith v. Ambrogio, 456 F.Supp. 1130, 1135 (D.Conn.1978).

29. See Steven Stein Cushman, Municipal Liability under S 1983: Toward a New Definition of Municipal Policymaker, 34 B.C.L.Rev. 693 (1993); Michael T. Burke and Patricia A. Burton, Defining the Contours of Municipal Liability Under Title 42 U.S.C. § 1983: Monell Through City of Canton v. Harris, 18 Stet.L.Rev. 511 (1989).

30. 475 U.S. 469, 106 S.Ct. 1292, 89 L.Ed.2d 452 (1986).

31. Id. at 483, 106 S.Ct. at 1300.

32. Id. at 480, 106 S.Ct. at 1298.

33. Bateson v. Geisse, 857 F.2d 1300 (9th Cir.1988). See also WAM Properties, Inc. v. Desoto County, Florida, 758 F.Supp. 1468 (M.D.Fla.1991) (council authorization of a lawsuit for code violations constituted an act of official governmental policy).

building inspector taken pursuant to authority from the board of adjustment has been held to be official policy.[34] The powers granted to a planning director and to a planning commission also have been held sufficient to cause their actions in issuing permits to be official policy for § 1983 liability purposes.[35] Where a mayor vetoed a zoning ordinance in an attempt to bribe a developer, it was held not to be official policy of the city.[36] The mayor was not a policymaker in zoning matters, and the city council overrode the veto.

§ 10.24   Exhaustion of Remedies

Generally, a plaintiff need not exhaust state judicial or administrative remedies before seeking redress in federal court under § 1983. The section provides a remedy that is supplementary to any state remedies,[1] and the Court has held that requiring exhaustion would thwart the purpose of the statute.[2] There are, however, significant qualifications to this rule. A cause of action must exist and must be ripe, and in certain instances this requires pursuit of state administrative and judicial remedies.

Resort to state court is necessary for Fifth Amendment taking claims in most cases. Since the Fifth Amendment is satisfied by post-taking compensation, the Court has held that a property owner must use available state procedures.[3] Characterizing the case as a § 1983 case does not avoid this requirement.[4] While the Court has phrased the requirement of seeking compensation from the state in terms of ripeness, the preclusive effects accorded to a state court judgment generally will bar a subsequent suit in federal court.[5]

A similar requirement exists for procedural due process claims. As with the Fifth Amendment, a post-deprivation remedy by way of a cause of action in state court may cure a potential due process violation. Under Parratt v. Taylor[6] and Hudson v. Palmer,[7] a damage action for random, unauthorized acts of state officials must be pursued in state court.[8] Again, once a state court adjudicates an issue, the federal courts must

34. Video Intern. Production, Inc. v. Warner–Amex Cable Communications, Inc., 858 F.2d 1075 (5th Cir.1988), cert. denied 491 U.S. 906, 109 S.Ct. 3189, 105 L.Ed.2d 697 (1989). See also Rodrigues v. Village of Larchmont, 608 F.Supp. 467 (S.D.N.Y.1985) (board of zoning appeals decisions are official policy).

35. Hutchison v. City of Huntington, 198 W.Va. 139, 479 S.E.2d 649 (W.Va.1996).

36. Manor Healthcare Corp. v. Lomelo, 929 F.2d 633 (11th Cir.1991).

§ 10.24

1. Monroe v. Pape, 365 U.S. 167, 173–74, 183, 81 S.Ct. 473, 476–77, 481–82, 5 L.Ed.2d 492 (1961).

2. Patsy v. Board of Regents, 457 U.S. 496, 102 S.Ct. 2557, 73 L.Ed.2d 172 (1982).

3. Williamson County Regional Planning Comm'n v. Hamilton Bank, 473 U.S. 172, 105 S.Ct. 3108, 87 L.Ed.2d 126 (1985).

4. Id.

5. See discussion supra § 10.10.

6. 451 U.S. 527, 101 S.Ct. 1908, 68 L.Ed.2d 420 (1981).

7. 468 U.S. 517, 104 S.Ct. 3194, 82 L.Ed.2d 393 (1984).

8. See Schwartz, The Post-deprivation Remedy Doctrine of Parratt v. Taylor and Its Application to Cases of Land Use Regulation, 21 Ga.L.Rev. 601 (1987).

give it full faith and credit.[9] The Supreme Court has suggested that the *Parratt-Hudson* rule applies only to procedural due process, but some courts have applied it to substantive due process as well.[10]

Another qualification to the non-exhaustion rule deals with finality. While exhaustion of administrative remedies is not required, finality of decision is.[11] Exhaustion of remedies refers to use of procedures to provide redress to an injured party. Finality asks whether the government has reached a definitive position that inflicts injury. While "conceptually distinct,"[12] as the Court says, the distinction blurs in practice. Under the final decision rule, multiple applications for development may need to be made and a variance sought to render a case ripe.[13] Confusion between finality and exhaustion has lead to numerous unripe cases being filed in federal court.[14] This final decision ripeness requirement applies not only to as-applied taking claims, but also to arbitrary and capricious substantive due process claims and equal protection claims.[15]

§ 10.25 Relief Available Under § 1983

Section 1983 provides that the offending person is liable "in an action at law, suit in equity, or other proper proceeding for redress."[1] The choice of remedy lies within the discretion of the court, and depends on the circumstances of the case.[2]

A. *Actual Damages*

9. 28 U.S.C. § 1738.

10. Most courts reject the application of *Parratt* to substantive due process. See Wood v. Ostrander, 879 F.2d 583 (9th Cir. 1989), cert. denied 498 U.S. 938, 111 S.Ct. 341, 112 L.Ed.2d 305 (1990); Morello v. James, 810 F.2d 344 (2d Cir.1987); Gilmere v. City of Atlanta, 774 F.2d 1495 (11th Cir.1985), cert. denied 476 U.S. 1115, 106 S.Ct. 1970, 90 L.Ed.2d 654 (1986). But see Weimer v. Amen, 870 F.2d 1400 (8th Cir. 1989) (finding *Parratt* applicable); New Burnham Prairie Homes, Inc. v. Village of Burnham, 910 F.2d 1474, 1481 (7th Cir. 1990).

See discussion supra § 10.12. See also Larry Alexander, Constitutional Torts, the Supreme Court, and the Law of Noncontradiction: an Essay on Zinermon V. Burch, 87 NW.U.L.Rev. 576 (1993); Craig W. Hillwig, Comment, Giving Property All the Process That's Due: a "Fundamental" Misunderstanding about Due Process, 41 Cath. U.L.Rev. 703 (1992); John Mixon, Compensation Claims Against Local Governments for Excessive Land–Use Regulations: A Proposal for More Efficient State Level Adjudication, 20 Urb.Law. 675, 715 (1988); Martin A. Schwartz, Section 1983 Litigation, 11 Touro L.Rev. 299, 307–308 (1995) (arguing that *Parratt* should only apply to procedural

due process); Frederic S. Schwartz, The Postdeprivation Remedy Doctrine of Parratt v. Taylor and Its Application to Cases of Land Use Regulation, 21 Ga.L.Rev. 601 (1987) (arguing against use of *Parratt* in substantive due process cases); Rodney M. Confer, Constitutional Law in the Eighth Circuit: Postdeprivation Remedy Defeats a Substantive Due Process Claim, 26 Creighton L.Rev. 697 (1993) (*Parratt* applies to both types of due process claims).

11. Williamson County Regional Planning Comm'n v. Hamilton Bank, 473 U.S. 172, 105 S.Ct. 3108, 87 L.Ed.2d 126 (1985).

12. Id. at 192, 105 S.Ct. at 3119.

13. See discussion § 10.10.

14. See Thomas E. Roberts, Ripeness and Forum Selection in Fifth Amendment Takings Litigation, 11 J.Land Use & Envtl.L. 37 (1995).

15. Id. at 68. See also discussion supra § 10.12.

§ 10.25

1. 42 U.S.C.A. § 1983.

2. Adickes v. S.H. Kress & Co., 398 U.S. 144, 232, 90 S.Ct. 1598, 1642, 26 L.Ed.2d 142 (1970).

Actual damages are recoverable under § 1983, but they must be proven. They will not be presumed.[3] Where mitigation is possible, the plaintiff must take reasonable, affirmative steps to reduce damages.[4] When a plaintiff is unable to prove actual damages, nominal damages are available.[5]

B. *Punitive Damages*

Punitive damages may be allowed under § 1983.[6] Because federal standards apply, punitive damages may be awarded in states that do not allow them.[7] They are available against individual defendants,[8] but are not available against municipalities.[9] However, municipal immunity to punitive damages may be waived and, where a statute so provides, a municipality may be liable to indemnify its employees against punitive damage awards.[10] Actual damages need not be shown in order to sustain a punitive damage award,[11] but the defendant's conduct must have been willful or in gross disregard of the plaintiff's rights.[12] Some courts, however, require a showing of malice or bad faith.[13]

C. *Equitable Relief*

Where otherwise proper, injunctions and other equitable relief are generally available under § 1983. Preliminary injunctions are also available where they are necessary to preserve the status quo and to prevent irreparable harm.[14]

D. *Attorney's Fees*

The Civil Rights Attorney's Fees Awards Act of 1976 enables courts to award attorney's fees to prevailing parties in § 1983 actions.[15] The amount of an award is within the discretion of the trial court.[16] Furthermore, the Supreme Court has held that the Eleventh Amendment is not a bar to awarding attorney's fees against states and political subdivisions of states.[17] Nor is legislative[18] or judicial immunity a bar to such awards.[19]

---

3. Carey v. Piphus, 435 U.S. 247, 98 S.Ct. 1042, 55 L.Ed.2d 252 (1978).

4. Meyers v. City of Cincinnati, 14 F.3d 1115 (6th Cir.1994); Atcherson v. Siebenmann, 458 F.Supp. 526 (S.D.Iowa 1978), reversed in part and remanded 605 F.2d 1058 (8th Cir.1979).

5. Tatum v. Houser, 642 F.2d 253 (8th Cir.1981).

6. Merritt v. De Los Santos, 721 F.2d 598 (7th Cir.1983).

7. Garrick v. Denver, 652 F.2d 969 (10th Cir.1981).

8. Smith v. Wade, 461 U.S. 30, 103 S.Ct. 1625, 75 L.Ed.2d 632 (1983).

9. City of Newport v. Fact Concerts, Inc., 453 U.S. 247, 101 S.Ct. 2748, 69 L.Ed.2d 616 (1981).

10. Kolar v. Sangamon, 756 F.2d 564 (7th Cir.1985); Bell v. Milwaukee, 746 F.2d 1205, 1270 (7th Cir.1984).

11. Ryland v. Shapiro, 708 F.2d 967 (5th Cir.1983), on remand 586 F.Supp. 1495 (D.La.1984).

12. Bunn v. Central Realty of Louisiana, 592 F.2d 891 (5th Cir.1979).

13. De La Cruz v. Pruitt, 590 F.Supp. 1296 (D.Ind.1984).

14. Wright v. Chief of Transit Police, 527 F.2d 1262 (2d Cir.1976), appeal after remand 558 F.2d 67 (2d Cir.1977).

15. 42 U.S.C.A. § 1988.

16. Reel v. Arkansas Dept. of Correction, 672 F.2d 693 (8th Cir.1982); Gautreaux v. Chicago Housing Authority, 690 F.2d 601 (7th Cir.1982), cert. denied 461 U.S. 961, 103 S.Ct. 2438, 77 L.Ed.2d 1322 (1983).

17. Hutto v. Finney, 437 U.S. 678, 98 S.Ct. 2565, 57 L.Ed.2d 522 (1978), rehearing denied 439 U.S. 1122, 99 S.Ct. 1035, 59 L.Ed.2d 83 (1979).

The federal government and its agencies, however, are immune to such awards.[20] Some courts have allowed recovery of expert witness fees.[21]

Because the purpose of the Civil Rights Attorney's Fees Awards Act is to open the judicial system to persons with civil rights grievances, "prevailing plaintiffs" are entitled to attorney's fees.[22] In determining whether a plaintiff is a "prevailing party," the question is whether the plaintiff has been successful on a central issue; the plaintiff need not prevail on all issues.[23] However, a prevailing party is only potentially eligible for attorney's fees and the court must consider the extent of the recovery obtained. If a party seeks substantial damages and recovers only nominal damages, no attorney's fee is available.[24] A final judgment is not necessary for an award of attorney's fees. Both favorable settlements[25] and consent decrees[26] are outcomes upon which attorney's fees may be based.

The court decides the question of whether one is a "prevailing party,"[27] and defendants, including municipal employers, have in some instances been held to be prevailing parties and entitled to attorney's fees.[28] Defendants are considered prevailing parties only when they can prove that the plaintiff's underlying claim is "frivolous, unreasonable, or groundless."[29]

§ 10.26 Immunities

If a court finds that a deprivation of a constitutional right has occurred, money damage actions may nonetheless be barred by immunities. Immunity rules differ for governmental entities and individuals.

---

18. Gates v. Collier, 616 F.2d 1268 (5th Cir.1980), rehearing granted 636 F.2d 942 (5th Cir.1981), rehearing denied 641 F.2d 403 (5th Cir.1981).

19. Rheuark v. Shaw, 477 F.Supp. 897 (N.D.Tex.1979), judg. aff'd in part, reversed in part 628 F.2d 297 (5th Cir.1980), cert. denied 450 U.S. 931, 101 S.Ct. 1392, 67 L.Ed.2d 365 (1981). But see Supreme Court of Virginia v. Consumers Union, 446 U.S. 719, 100 S.Ct. 1967, 64 L.Ed.2d 641 (1980), on remand 505 F.Supp. 822 (D.Va.1981), appeal dismissed 451 U.S. 1012, 101 S.Ct. 2998, 69 L.Ed.2d 384 (1981).

20. Smith v. Puett, 506 F.Supp. 134 (D.Tenn.1980).

21. Ramos v. Lamm, 713 F.2d 546 (10th Cir.1983). But cf. Liberles v. Daniel, 619 F.Supp. 1016, 1019 (N.D.Ill.1985) (criticism of *Ramos*).

22. Hensley v. Eckerhart, 461 U.S. 424, 103 S.Ct. 1933, 76 L.Ed.2d 40 (1983).

23. Best v. Boswell, 696 F.2d 1282 (11th Cir.1983), rehearing denied 703 F.2d 582 (11th Cir.1983), cert. denied Best v.

Eagerton, 464 U.S. 828, 104 S.Ct. 103, 78 L.Ed.2d 107 (1983).

24. Farrar v. Hobby, 506 U.S. 103, 113 S.Ct. 566, 121 L.Ed.2d 494 (1992).

25. Maher v. Gagne, 448 U.S. 122, 100 S.Ct. 2570, 65 L.Ed.2d 653 (1980).

26. Charles v. Coleman, 689 F.2d 774 (8th Cir.1982).

27. See Russo v. New York, 672 F.2d 1014 (2d Cir.1982), modified 721 F.2d 410 (2d cir.1983); Hanrahan v. Hampton, 446 U.S. 754, 100 S.Ct. 1987, 64 L.Ed.2d 670 (1980), rehearing denied 448 U.S. 913, 101 S.Ct. 33, 65 L.Ed.2d 1176 (1980).

28. See Campbell v. Cook, 706 F.2d 1084 (10th Cir.1983), where the plaintiff's action was "frivolous or groundless." See also Burr v. Town of Rangeley, 549 A.2d 733 (Me.1988); Carter v. Rollins, 634 F.Supp. 944 (D.Mass.1986).

29. Hensley v. Eckerhart, 461 U.S. 424, 103 S.Ct. 1933, 76 L.Ed.2d 40 (1983); Roadway Express, Inc. v. Piper, 447 U.S. 752, 100 S.Ct. 2455, 65 L.Ed.2d 488 (1980).

There are also distinctions between absolute immunity and qualified immunity.[1]

Immunities are a consideration under § 1983 even though the statute nowhere provides for them. The Supreme Court got around that statutory void by finding that immunity from damages under § 1983 will be implied if such immunity existed at common law at the time § 1983 was adopted and if implying such an immunity would be consistent with the purposes of § 1983. The Court reasoned that a tradition of some immunity was so deeply rooted in our law that "congress would have specifically so provided had it wished to abolish the doctrine."[2]

A. Governmental Immunities

Local governments have no immunity from money damage awards. In 1978 the Court held in Monell v. New York City Dept. of Social Services[3] that local governments were "persons" subject to § 1983, but it did not decide whether they might nevertheless in some instances be immune from money damages for their violations of the statute. In 1980 in Owen v. City of Independence,[4] the Court held that because no qualified immunity existed at common law at the time § 1983 was enacted, no qualified immunity could be implied. The Court has also held that state sovereign immunity rules cannot be applied to protect local government from liability in suits brought in state court.[5] Punitive damages are an exception. Municipalities are absolutely immune from such awards.[6] While some have questioned whether *Monnell* and *Owens* preclude governmental immunity for legislative actions, it seems established that no immunity exists.[7]

The state, in contrast to municipalities, is absolutely immune from suit in federal court for money damages under the Eleventh Amendment.[8]

B. Individual Immunities: Absolute and Qualified

§ 10.26

1. See generally Alan K. Shin, The Ultimate Standard: Qualified Immunity in the Age of Constitutional Balancing, 81 Iowa L.Rev. 261 (1995).

2. Pierson v. Ray, 386 U.S. 547, 554, 87 S.Ct. 1213, 1218, 18 L.Ed.2d 288 (1967).

3. 436 U.S. 658, 98 S.Ct. 2018, 56 L.Ed.2d 611 (1978).

4. 445 U.S. 622, 100 S.Ct. 1398, 63 L.Ed.2d 673 (1980).

5. Howlett v. Rose, 496 U.S. 356, 110 S.Ct. 2430, 110 L.Ed.2d 332 (1990).

6. City of Newport v. Fact Concerts, Inc., 453 U.S. 247, 101 S.Ct. 2748, 69 L.Ed.2d 616 (1981).

7. See Goldberg v. Town of Rocky Hill, 973 F.2d 70 (2d Cir.1992); Aitchison v. Raffiani, 708 F.2d 96, 98–100 (3d Cir.1983);

Bruce v. Riddle, 631 F.2d 272, 279 (4th Cir.1980); Hernandez v. City of Lafayette, 643 F.2d 1188, 1193–94 (5th Cir. Unit A 1981), cert. denied, 455 U.S. 907, 102 S.Ct. 1251, 71 L.Ed.2d 444 (1982); Haskell v. Washington Township, 864 F.2d 1266, 1277 (6th Cir.1988); Reed v. Village of Shorewood, 704 F.2d 943, 952–53 (7th Cir.1983); Gorman Towers, Inc. v. Bogoslavsky, 626 F.2d 607, 613–14 (8th Cir.1980); Kuzinich v. County of Santa Clara, 689 F.2d 1345, 1349–50 (9th Cir.1982); Espanola Way Corp. v. Meyerson, 690 F.2d 827 (11th Cir. 1982), cert. denied 460 U.S. 1039, 103 S.Ct. 1431, 75 L.Ed.2d 791 (1983). See also Sheldon H. Nahmod, Civil Rights and Liberties: The Law of Section 1983 § 6.20 (3d.ed.1991).

8. Lake Country Estates, Inc. v. Tahoe Regional Planning Agency, 440 U.S. 391, 99 S.Ct. 1171, 59 L.Ed.2d 401 (1979).

Public officials who are sued in their individual capacities may be able to assert absolute or qualified immunity. Judges, legislators, and prosecutors (when initiating and presenting the state's case) all have absolute immunity.[9] In the land use context, absolute immunity arises typically with respect to those claiming to have acted in a legislative capacity. Courts use a functional test to determine whether an action is legislative for the purposes of conferring absolute immunity.[10]

While many zoning ordinances, including rezonings, will qualify as legislative,[11] site-specific actions raise the most question. The Third Circuit breaks the question into two parts of substance and procedure. The substantive component requires that the action taken makes general policy or involves the community at large. Decisions that involve the application of pre-existing policy or apply to only a small number of persons will normally be viewed as non-legislative.[12] The procedural component requires that the action be taken through established legislative procedures.[13] In applying this test in Acierno v. Cloutier, the Third Circuit held that an ordinance that revoked a previously approved development plan of a single landowner pursuant to the town's sunset provisions was administrative, not legislative.[14] The court found, though, that the rezoning of the same tract from planned unit development to single-family residential was legislative even though it was directed at only one parcel.[15]

Absolute immunity has also been extended to regional legislators[16] and to mayors acting legislatively.[17] While city officials who possess

9. Id. (granting immunity to members of board of regional authority formed by interstate compact). Conferring absolute immunity on local government officials, see Aitchison v. Raffiani, 708 F.2d 96, 98–100 (3d Cir.1983); Reed v. Village of Shorewood, 704 F.2d 943, 952–53 (7th Cir.1983); Espanola Way Corp. v. Meyerson, 690 F.2d 827, 829 (11th Cir.1982), cert. denied 460 U.S. 1039, 103 S.Ct. 1431, 75 L.Ed.2d 791 (1983); Kuzinich v. County of Santa Clara, 689 F.2d 1345, 1349–50 (9th Cir.1982).

10. See Orange Lake Assoc., Inc. v. Kirkpatrick, 21 F.3d 1214 (2d Cir.1994); Acierno v. Cloutier, 40 F.3d 597 (3d Cir. 1994).

11. Brown v. Crawford County, 960 F.2d 1002 (11th Cir.1992) (moratorium on mobile homes pending plan revision was legislative).

12. Acierno v. Cloutier, 40 F.3d 597 (3d Cir.1994); Bartlett v. Cinemark, Inc., 908 S.W.2d 229 (Tex.App.1995). See discussion supra regarding legislative and quasi-judicial characterization for purposes of level of judicial review, §§ 5.9 and 5.37, and for purposes of availability of referendum, supra § 5.5.

13. See Key West Harbour Development Corp. v. City of Key West, 738

F.Supp. 1390 (S.D.Fla.1990) (commission's action that otherwise would be regarded as legislative denied that status due to failure to follow commission's own rules). A mere technical violation will not defeat an act from being characterized as legislative. Acierno v. Cloutier, 40 F.3d 597, 613 (3d Cir.1994)

14. 40 F.3d 597 (3d Cir.1994). But see Key West Harbour Development Corp. v. City of Key West, 738 F.Supp. 1390 (S.D.Fla.1990).

15. See also the extension of absolute liability to municipal councils or similar bodies acting in a legislative capacity in Aitchison v. Raffiani, 708 F.2d 96, 98 (3d Cir.1983); Kuzinich v. County of Santa Clara, 689 F.2d 1345 (9th Cir.1982); Hernandez v. City of Lafayette, 643 F.2d at 1193; Gorman Towers, Inc. v. Bogoslavsky, 626 F.2d 607 (8th Cir.1980); Bruce v. Riddle, 631 F.2d 272 (4th Cir.1980).

16. Lake Country Estates, Inc. v. Tahoe Regional Planning Agency, 440 U.S. 391, 99 S.Ct. 1171, 59 L.Ed.2d 401 (1979).

17. Aitchison v. Raffiani, 708 F.2d 96 (3d Cir.1983); Hernandez v. City of Lafayette, 643 F.2d 1188 (5th Cir.1981), cert.

legislative power will lose absolute immunity if they are found to have acted administratively, they may still be entitled to qualified immunity.[18]

The test for qualified immunity is set out in Harlow v. Fitzgerald:[19]

[G]overnment officials performing discretionary functions generally are shielded from liability for civil damages insofar as their conduct does not violate clearly established statutory or constitutional rights of which a reasonable person would have known.[20]

The qualified immunity of *Harlow* may be used by various executive officials, including local school board members, prison officials, police officers, and building and zoning officers.

Harlow created an objective standard, and dispensed the requirement of prior case law that had required a showing that the official had acted with a good faith belief of legality. This revision of the test for qualified immunity is especially valuable to local officials because it may encourage early dismissal of § 1983 cases, before the officials are subjected to the burdens and costs of lengthy litigation.[21]

This qualified immunity can be defeated by showing malice, ill will or wanton conduct on the part of the official charged. An example is Walz v. Town of Smithtown,[22] where the town's highway superintendent told landowners that he would issue them a permit for excavation of a highway to enable them to connect to the public water supply if they would convey a 15–foot strip of their property to the town. This action was held to violate substantive due process, and no qualified immunity existed. The highway official, said the court, could not have reasonably believed that he had the discretion to deny permits "as a means of extorting land."[23]

§ 10.27 Abstention

The possibility of abstention may frustrate one who seeks to challenge local land use decisions in federal court.[1] While the Supreme Court says that "[a]bstention from the exercise of federal jurisdiction is the exception, not the rule,"[2] and that abstention is an "extraordinary and narrow exception to the duty of a district court to adjudicate a controver-

denied, 455 U.S. 907, 102 S.Ct. 1251, 71 L.Ed.2d 444 (1982); Searington Corporation v. Incorporated Village of North Hills, 575 F.Supp. 1296 (E.D.N.Y.1981).

18. Scott v. Greenville County, 716 F.2d 1409 (4th Cir.1983).

19. 457 U.S. 800, 102 S.Ct. 2727, 73 L.Ed.2d 396 (1982).

20. Id. at 818, 102 S.Ct. at 2738.

21. Harlow v. Fitzgerald, 457 U.S. 800, 102 S.Ct. 2727, 73 L.Ed.2d 396 (1982); Mitchell v. Forsyth, 472 U.S. 511, 105 S.Ct. 2806, 86 L.Ed.2d 411 (1985).

22. 46 F.3d 162 (2d Cir.1995).

23. Id. at 169.

§ 10.27

1. See Brian Blaesser, Closing the Federal Courthouse Door on Property Owners: the Ripeness and Abstention Doctrine in Section 1983 Land Use Cases, 2 Hofstra Prop.L.J. 73 (1988). See generally James C. Rehnquist, Taking Comity Seriously: How to Neutralize the Abstention Doctrine, 46 Stan. L. Rev. 1049 (1994) .

2. Colorado River Water Conserv. Dist. v. United States, 424 U.S. 800, 814, 96 S.Ct. 1236, 1244, 47 L.Ed.2d 483 (1976).

sy properly before it,"[3] lower federal courts have used the *Pullman,
Burford, Younger* and *Colorado River* doctrines to abstain from adjudicating § 1983 claims in the land use area fairly often.

Under the *Pullman* abstention doctrine,[4] a federal district court may refrain from deciding constitutional questions that hinge on difficult state law issues, if a constitutional ruling would be avoided by resolution in state court of those state issues.[5] When a federal court invokes the *Pullman* abstention doctrine, the federal action is not dismissed. Rather, it is stayed pending decision in the state court of the uncertain state law issues.[6]

A number of courts relying on the *Pullman* abstention doctrine have held that adjudication of state law issues in land use cases would alleviate the necessity of addressing federal constitutional questions.[7] In Stallworth v. Monroeville,[8] for example, the plaintiffs petitioned the city to rezone their property from residential to commercial use, and the city denied the application. The plaintiffs then initiated suit in state court, but the action was dismissed. Plaintiffs again sought a rezoning from the city, which was again denied. Plaintiffs then filed suit in federal court alleging violations of their Fifth and Fourteenth Amendment rights. The federal court, however, refused to hear the case, invoking the abstention doctrine. The court noted that zoning questions are "uniquely of local import" and that state courts are familiar with local law and factual nuances.[9] The court further said that the interpretation of state statutes is a matter of state law and that the state courts had not yet fully addressed the statutes in question.[10] Where it is clear that no state law interpretation would eliminate the need to address the federal constitutional questions, *Pullman* abstention is inappropriate.[11]

Under *Burford* abstention, a federal court may decline to hear a case where a federal decision of the case would risk interfering with complex state regulatory schemes concerning important state policies for which expeditious and adequate judicial review is afforded in state courts.[12] Under *Burford*, plaintiffs are not able to preserve their right to return to federal court once a decision has been rendered at the state level.

3. County of Allegheny v. Frank Mashuda Co., 360 U.S. 185, 188–189, 79 S.Ct. 1060, 1063, 3 L.Ed.2d 1163 (1959).

4. Railroad Commission of Texas v. Pullman Co., 312 U.S. 496, 61 S.Ct. 643, 85 L.Ed. 971 (1941).

5. Id.

6. England v. Louisiana State Board of Medical Examiners, 375 U.S. 411–422, 84 S.Ct. 461, 468, 11 L.Ed.2d 440 (1964).

7. See, e.g., Edwards v. Arkansas Power & Light Co., 683 F.2d 1149 (8th Cir. 1982); Lapham v. California Energy Resources Conservation and Development Comm'n, 705 F.2d 358 (9th Cir.1983); C–Y Development Co. v. Redlands, 703 F.2d 375

(9th Cir.1983); Sederquist v. Tiburon, 590 F.2d 278 (9th Cir.1978); Fountain v. Metropolitan Atlanta Rapid Transit Authority, 678 F.2d 1038 (11th Cir.1982); Ahrensfeld v. Stephens, 528 F.2d 193 (7th Cir.1975).

8. 426 F.Supp. 236 (S.D.Ala.1976).

9. Id. at 239.

10. Id. at 240.

11. See e.g., Neufeld v. City of Baltimore, 964 F.2d 347 (4th Cir.1992); Gwynedd Properties, Inc. v. Lower Gwynedd Township, 970 F.2d 1195 (3d Cir.1992); Blodgett v. Santa Cruz County, 502 F.Supp. 204 (N.D.Cal.1980).

12. Burford v. Sun Oil Co., 319 U.S. 315, 63 S.Ct. 1098, 87 L.Ed. 1424 (1943).

Rather, the federal action is dismissed.[13] Although the Supreme Court has only applied Burford once and has refused to apply it in two other cases,[14] lower courts find it attractive.[15]

Courts differ over what comprises a complex regulatory scheme in land use cases for the purposes of *Burford* abstention. The Eleventh Circuit holds that zoning decisions must be vested in a "single forum" to qualify.[16] The fact that an enabling act provides that a city "may" appoint a board of adjustment, as the standard act does, has also been held to reveal a lack of state interest in uniformity.[17] In contrast, the Fourth Circuit says that abstention is proper if the state has a comprehensive regulatory scheme and that there is no requirement that a specialized state agency exist to resolve zoning disputes.[18] Courts that are reluctant to use the *Burford* doctrine standing alone in land use cases may apply it in combination with the *Pullman* doctrine.[19]

A third abstention doctrine comes from Younger v. Harris.[20] Under the *Younger* doctrine, if a parallel proceeding in a state court is pending and that proceeding involves largely the same issues as the federal proceeding, the federal court should dismiss the case.[21] *Younger's* goal is to avoid friction between state and federal courts. As with *Burford* abstention, the proceeding in the federal court is dismissed, and the plaintiff does not retain the right to return to federal court once the state court has issued a decision.[22]

The *Younger* abstention doctrine is applied in land use cases where a pending state court proceeding involves the same issues as the federal proceeding. In Community Treatment Centers, Inc. v. City of Westland,[23] the court, applying *Younger,* noted that it was "well-established that for abstention purposes, the enforcement and application of zoning ordinances and land-use regulations is an important state and local interest."[24] In that case, an organization sought a special use permit to

---

13. Stallworth v. Monroeville, 426 F.Supp. 236 (S.D.Ala.1976).

14. Colorado River Water Conservation District v. United States, 424 U.S. 800, 96 S.Ct. 1236, 47 L.Ed.2d 483 (1976) and New Orleans Public Service, Inc. v. Council of City of New Orleans 491 U.S. 350, 109 S.Ct. 2506, 105 L.Ed.2d 298 (1989).

15. See James C. Rehnquist, Taking Comity Seriously: How to Neutralize the Abstention Doctrine, 46 Stan. L. Rev. 1049, 1079 (1994) .

16. Nasser v. City of Homewood, 671 F.2d 432, 440 (11th Cir.1982). See also International Broth. of Elec. Workers, Local Union No. 1245 v. Public Service Commission of Nevada, 614 F.2d 206 (9th Cir. 1980); Heritage Farms, Inc. v. Solebury Township, 671 F.2d 743, 746 (3d Cir.1982) (*Burford* abstention inappropriate where state policy on local land use regulation not based on uniformity concerns).

17. Id.

18. Browning–Ferris, Inc. v. Baltimore County, 774 F.2d 77, 80 (4th Cir.1985).

19. See, e.g., C–Y Development Company v. Redlands, 703 F.2d 375 (9th Cir.1983).

20. 401 U.S. 37, 91 S.Ct. 746, 27 L.Ed.2d 669 (1971).

21. *Younger,* 401 U.S. at 40–41, 91 S.Ct. at 748. While *Younger* involved a criminal proceeding, the doctrine has been extended to civil proceedings. Ohio Civil Rights Com'n v. Dayton Christian Schools, Inc., 477 U.S. 619, 106 S.Ct. 2718, 91 L.Ed.2d 512 (1986).

22. Colorado River Water Conservation District v. United States, 424 U.S. 800, 816, 96 S.Ct. 1236, 1245–46, 47 L.Ed.2d 483 (1976).

23. 970 F.Supp. 1197 (E.D.Mich.1997).

24. Id. at 1223.

operate prerelease center for federal prisoners. When the city denied the permit, the organization sued in state court, and while that action was pending, it sued in federal court. By the time the district court ruled on the defendant's motion to dismiss, the case had been appealed to the state intermediate appellate court. Federal interference with the state proceedings was deemed inappropriate.[25]

Younger abstention has been rejected when it appears that irreparable harm will ensue. For example, one court refused to apply *Younger* abstention when an action was pending in state court since it found that the residents of a group home for recovering alcoholics would suffer irreparable harm if they lost their home through the state court proceeding before the federal court could act on their constitutional claim.[26]

A final doctrine that deserves mention stems from Colorado River Water Conservation District v. United States,[27] where the Court held that a federal court should decline to exercise jurisdiction in limited circumstances where state proceedings are pending so as to avoid duplicative litigation. In contrast to the above three abstention doctrines, which are concerned with comity and federalism, the rule of *Colorado River* is based on considerations of judicial economy.[28] The discretion to dismiss is to be exercised sparingly, and in most land use cases where a *Colorado River* dismissal has been sought, the courts have refused the request.[29]

25. See also Central Avenue News, Inc. v. Minot, 651 F.2d 565 (8th Cir.1981).

26. Sullivan v. City of Pittsburgh, 811 F.2d 171 (3d Cir.1987), cert. denied 484 U.S. 849, 108 S.Ct. 148, 98 L.Ed.2d 104 (1987) (alternative holding).

27. 424 U.S. 800, 96 S.Ct. 1236, 47 L.Ed.2d 483 (1976).

28. Michael T. Gibson, Private Concurrent Litigation in Light of Younger, Pennzoil, and Colorado River, 4 Okla.City U.L.Rev. 185, 259 (1989).

29. See Baskin v. Bath Township Board of Zoning Appeals, 15 F.3d 569 (6th Cir.1994) (strict identity of issues between state and federal proceedings required); Lake Lucerne Civic Ass'n, Inc. v. Dolphin Stadium Corp., 878 F.2d 1360 (11th Cir. 1989); Khal Charidim Kiryas Joel v. Village of Kiryas Joel, 935 F.Supp. 450 (S.D.N.Y. 1996); Warner Cable Communications Inc. v. Borough of Schuylkill Haven, 784 F.Supp. 203 (E.D.Pa.1992). But see Marcus v. Twp. of Abington, 1993 WL 534279 (E.D.Pa.1993); Redner v. City of Tampa, 723 F.Supp. 1448 (M.D.Fla.1989).

Chapter 11

ENVIRONMENTAL ASPECTS OF
LAND USE CONTROLS

Analysis

I. INTRODUCTION

II. NATIONAL ENVIRONMENTAL POLICY ACT (NEPA)

III. LAND USE AND POLLUTION CONTROL LAWS—CLEAN AIR

IV. LAND USE AND POLLUTION CONTROL LAWS—CLEAN WATER

I. INTRODUCTION

§ 11.1 Introduction

Scarcely a concern before the 1960's, environmental aspects of land use control have become a primary consideration of land use planners. Even during the environmental renaissance of the 1960's, land use planning and control did not receive the attention focused on air and water pollution. Air and water were viewed as public trusts to be shared by all. Land was considered a matter of private property generally out of governmental reach. That attitude has changed markedly in the last two decades. Nowhere has that attitude changed more dramatically than in regard to environmentally related land use regulations.[1]

It would be a mistake to attribute the new land use concern with environmental matters to a mere extension of traditional land use controls because environmental regulations are often based on subjective value judgments giving priority to ecological quality.[2] Another unique aspect of environmental land use is the major role played by federal and state governments. Although not true national planning measures, the National Environmental Policy Act (NEPA) and its state progeny provide for explicit environmental weighting in agency decision making.

While NEPA's goals and the accompanying Clean Air and Clean Water Acts' implementing measures are primarily concerned with pollution abatement through emission and effluent standards, land use policies are factored in to a significant degree. At the very minimum, land use planners will have to consider carefully those federal acts when siting a development with possible pollution problems.

A second branch of environmental land use involves environmentally sensitive lands. Lands may be environmentally sensitive for many reasons, but the most common examples of sensitive lands are (1) wetlands, (2) coastal zones, (3) floodplains, and (4) habitat areas for endangered species. Regulations concerning these locales are closer to traditional land use controls because they deal with land as such. As with restrictive zoning, environmental land use controls are often attacked as "takings" of property prohibited by the Fifth and Fourteenth amendments. When such attacks will be successful is an increasingly complex issue which is discussed in depth in Chapter 10.

§ 11.1

1. See Natural Resources Defense Council, Land Use Controls in the United States 1 (1977); Juergensmeyer, The American Legal System and Environmental Pollution, 33 U.Fla.L.Rev. 439 (1971). Environmental land use encompasses the effects of and impact on land use planning imposed by environmental protection measures emanating from state and federal constitutions, statutes and regulations, as well as from common law and statutory decisions. For general information on environmental law, see Rodgers, Environmental Law (2d.ed 1994).

2. D. Mandelker, Environment and Equity; A Regulatory Challenge XI (1981) (Professor Mandelker attributes this thought to Professor A. Dan Tarlock).

The basic problem in all environmental land use decisions is that land is a finite resource. There must be room not only for houses, shopping malls, and paper mills, but for wetlands, beaches, barrier islands and snail darters. Industrial and economic growth are considered desirable, but so are clean air and water. Somewhere a balance must be struck.

Development on environmentally sensitive land must be cautiously done. Both future and present needs have to be considered. While a residential subdivision in a prime aquifer recharging wetland may expand a local government's tax base, the bargain may prove faustian when drinking wells dry up.

The laws and regulations now governing that balance are the subject of this chapter. This chapter deals primarily with federal controls, but it should be noted that state and local environmental controls also play a major role in land use planning. Furthermore, local governments are working themselves back into the forefront of land use planning of all types including environmental and sensitive lands regulation. This trend is boosted by sympathetic federal and state regulations requesting local implementation. The end result may be, and to a large extent already is, a comprehensive multi-tiered system of interlocking federal, state, and local controls in environmental land use.

The overlap in this layered regulatory interlock can lead to complicated jurisdictional problems. Of even greater concern may be the complications arising from policy conflict. Zoning development away from one environmentally sensitive area may add development pressure to another. These jurisdictional and policy conflicts are part and parcel of the approach governments at all levels have taken to the problem of environmental land use. Whether such a complicated approach really works is still, even after more than two decades of focused analysis, uncertain.

II. NATIONAL ENVIRONMENTAL POLICY ACT (NEPA)

§ 11.2 Introduction to the Statute

Through the National Environmental Policy Act (NEPA),[1] Congress hoped to insure that federal agencies would consider the environmental effects of their actions. Thus NEPA requires that agencies develop procedures for doing so and requires them to prepare environmental impact statements (EISs) on major federal actions that may have a significant impact on the environment. Many states have adopted legislation patterned on NEPA, and state courts often use NEPA cases to

---

§ 11.2

1. Pub.L. No. 91–190, 83 Stat. 852, codified at 42 U.S.C.A. §§ 4321–4361 (1995). For a general review of this statute which, remarkably, has remained virtually amend-ment-free since its enactment in 1969, see Rodgers, NEPA at Twenty: Mimickry and Recruitment in Environmental Law, 20 Envt'l Law 485 (1990); Rodgers, Environmental Law, Ch. 9 (2d ed. 1994).

interpret their own state acts.[2] NEPA and its state copies are a powerful force affecting land use planning and control.[3]

Title I of NEPA has five sections. Section 101(a) of NEPA provides "that it is the continuing policy of the Federal Government, in cooperation with State and local governments, and other concerned public and private organizations, to use all practicable means and measures, including financial and technical assistance, in a manner calculated to foster and promote the general welfare, to create and maintain conditions under which man and nature can exist in productive harmony, and fulfill the social, economic, and other requirements of present and future generations of Americans."[4] Section 102, the heart of NEPA, gives a statement of purpose and a declaration of policy expressing a federal commitment to preserve and enhance the environment.[5] That section indicates that to the fullest extent possible all federal policies, regulations and laws will be interpreted in accordance with NEPA policies. All agencies of the Federal Government are also directed to utilize systematic, interdisciplinary decision-making and to develop means of giving appropriate weight to environmental amenities and values. Subsection 102(c), worth quoting in full, is the core of NEPA. Federal agencies must:

> include in every recommendation or report on proposals for legislation and other major Federal actions significantly affecting the quality of the human environment, a detailed statement by the responsible official on—
>
> > (i) the environmental impact of the proposed action,
> >
> > (ii) any adverse environmental effects which cannot be avoided should the proposal be implemented,
> >
> > (iii) alternatives to the proposed action,
> >
> > (iv) the relationship between local short-term uses of man's environment and the maintenance and enhancement of long-term productivity, and
> >
> > (v) any irreversible and irretrievable commitments of resources which would be involved in the proposed action should it be implemented.[6]

Subsection (c) continues with imposition of a duty to consult with and obtain comments from other specialized federal agencies having competency about a matter before making the detailed statement. The statements and the comments, including comments of state and local agencies are to be made available to the President, to the Council on

---

2. Nicholas A. Robinson, SEQRA's Siblings: Precedents From Little NEPAS in the Sister States, 46 Albany L.Rev. 1155 (1982).

3. See Alaska Wilderness Recreation & Tourism Assoc. v. Morrison, 67 F.3d 723 (9th Cir.1995) (finding that it was unreasonable not to reconsider land use alternatives in an EIS); Smith v. U.S. Forest Serv., 33 F.3d 1072 (9th Cir.1994) (finding that an agency inadequately reviewed the effects to a 5,000 acre piece of land under NEPA).

4. 42 U.S.C.A. § 4331.

5. 42 U.S.C.A. § 4332.

6. 42 U.S.C.A. § 4332.

Environmental Quality (CEQ) and to the public and are to accompany the proposal through the agency review process.

All agencies are also to review their statutory authority, regulations, policies and procedures to permit compliance with NEPA policy and are to recommend changes where necessary.[7] NEPA does not affect any duty to comply with other environmental quality requirements, nor to consult or coordinate in other non-environmental matters with any Federal or State agencies.[8] Finally, NEPA policies and goals supplement those set forth in other authorizations of federal agencies.[9]

§ 11.3 Council on Environmental Quality

A. *Annual Report and Guidelines*

Title II of NEPA establishes the Council on Environmental Quality (CEQ).[1] The CEQ provides assistance to the President, who is required to prepare the annual Environmental Quality Report.[2] This report is like an environmental state of the union review. CEQ gathers information and conducts research on environmental issues, suggests new policies, and checks governmental actions to see if they conform with environmental goals.[3] Besides advising the President and collecting and reporting data on conditions and trends in the environment, the CEQ also oversees agency compliance with NEPA;[4] the CEQ's primary function is to watchdog the environmental review process in the agencies of the federal government.[5] To achieve this goal the CEQ publishes guidelines to help agencies implement NEPA, consults with each agency on acceptable methodologies, and reviews the EISs prepared by the various agencies.

Although CEQ's Guidelines[6] were originally regarded as advisory only, they have nonetheless proven to be persuasive authority in court interpretations of NEPA. The absence of formal agency regulatory status was cured by a 1977 Executive Order[7] authorizing the CEQ to issue binding EIS regulations. Although the new regulations are not treated as controlling, they are accorded considerable weight.[8]

CEQ requires that each federal agency prepare its own guidelines.[9] Agency guidelines are to list those types of agency actions which are

---

7. 42 U.S.C.A. § 4333.

8. 42 U.S.C.A. § 4334.

9. 42 U.S.C.A. § 4335.

§ 11.3

1. 42 U.S.C.A. § 4341–4347.

2. Called "Environmental Quality," the report is published annually in the fall.

3. 42 U.S.C.A. § 4342.

4. Rodgers, Environmental Law § 9.1 (2d ed.1994).

5. But see Rodgers at § 9.2, supra note 4, (arguing that the role of the Council on Environmental Quality is being diminished).

6. 43 Fed.Reg. 55,990 (1978); 40 C.F.R. Pt. 1500 (1996).

7. Exec. Order No. 11,991; 42 Fed. Reg. 26,967 (1977).

8. Andrus v. Sierra Club, 442 U.S. 347, 99 S.Ct. 2335, 60 L.Ed.2d 943 (1979). But see Sierra Club v. Sigler, 695 F.2d 957 (5th Cir.1983), rehearing denied 704 F.2d 1251 (5th Cir.1983) (holding that the 1978 CEQ regulations are controlling). See generally Mandelker, NEPA Law & Litigation §§ 2:10–13 (2d ed.1993).

9. For agency guidelines, see, e.g. Environmental Protection Agency, 40 C.F.R. § 6.100 et seq. (1996); Post Office, 39 C.F.R. Pt. 775 et seq. (1996).

likely to have a significant impact on the environment and which would therefore require an EIS.[10] The guidelines must identify the agency officials responsible for preparing EISs and establish procedures for consulting with other agencies for providing public information on environmentally significant projects.[11]

The CEQ Guidelines offer no further elaboration on what a major action or what a significant effect is. Each agency is to decide what types of projects are major or significant. An agency may prepare an Environmental Assessment (EA).[12] An EA provides evidence and analysis for the determination of whether to prepare an EIS or a finding of no significant impact.[13]

When the agency has decided that a proposed action is major and will have a significant impact on the environment, the CEQ Guidelines recommend that the agency prepare a draft EIS for circulation to other agencies and to the public for comment.[14] The agency's effort must be its best, as if its product were a final EIS, but the agency is required to consider outside comments and incorporate them into the final EIS whenever appropriate.

B. The EIS Requirement

The CEQ guidelines provide that the EIS is to be written in plain language with appropriate graphics.[15] Simple, clear prose is stressed, and the final result should be readily comprehensible by the public.[16]

Strict requirements on format, page limits, and style are established.[17] To reduce paperwork, CEQ provides that the EIS is to be analytic rather than encyclopedic.[18] Length of discussion should be in direct correlation to importance. Only if the potential environmental problems are great or the proposed project is of an unusually large size should there be a need for an EIS of more than one hundred and fifty pages in length.[19]

The probable impact of the proposed project should be described in reference to direct and indirect effects, as well as possible conflicts with land use policies, plans, and controls of all levels of government having jurisdiction over the project site.[20]

Alternatives are an essential part of the EIS.[21] All reasonable alternatives are to be described and analyzed for their environmental impacts.[22] Alternatives include abandonment of the project and delay for further study. Even those alternatives which are not within the preparing agency's powers are to be discussed.

---

10. 40 C.F.R. § 1502.4.

11. Id. § 1502.17

12. Id. § 1508.4

13. Id. § 1508.9

14. Id. § 1502.19

15. Id. § 1502.2

16. Id.

17. Id. § 1502.7, § 1502.8.

18. Id. § 1502.2(a).

19. Id. § 1502.7.

20. Id. § 1502.14–16.

21. Id. § 1502.14.

22. Id. § 1502.14–16.

The EIS is to describe environmental effects which cannot be avoided and actions that could mitigate adverse environmental effects.[23] A study of the relationship between short term use of man's environment and the maintenance and enhancement of long term productivity should include a discussion of environmental trade-offs. These include the extent to which the action would foreclose future options, or cause an irreversible and irretrievable commitment of resources.

If the agency has prepared a cost-benefit analysis for the project, it should be submitted with the EIS.[24] If it is determined that a cost benefit analysis is not necessary for the proposed action, the agency should still submit a discussion of relevant non-environmental considerations of a project.

Properly utilized, the EIS process achieves two goals. First, it forces agencies to consider the environmental effect of their decisions. Second, it provides a disclosure statement showing both the environmental consequences of the proposed action and the agency's decision making process.

Environmental groups use the EIS process as a legal handle to challenge agency action. The legal issues involved depend on whether or not an EIS was prepared. If not, the plaintiff will argue the need for an EIS. Using NEPA standards, the reviewing court will examine the facts surrounding the case to see if the action has *federal* involvement, if the action is *major,* and if the action *significantly affects* the environment.[25] If so, the court will order an EIS prepared.

If an EIS was prepared, but the agency decides to proceed with its action despite adverse environmental consequences, the issue becomes whether the reviewing court will overturn the administrative decision. The plaintiff here has a heavy burden. An enormous amount of litigation has occurred regarding this last point, and the decisions are anything but uniform.[26]

III. LAND USE AND POLLUTION LAWS—CLEAN AIR

§ 11.4 Basic Scheme of the Clean Air Act

The regulation and direction of new development is at the heart of land use controls. The Clean Air Act[1] makes these controls serve a clean air master. Land use planners and controllers theoretically had always been concerned with planning and controlling land uses in a way to

---

23. Id. § 1502.16.

24. Id. § 1502.23.

25. See Shea, The Judicial Standard for Review of Environmental Impact Statement Threshold Decisions, 9 Envtl.Aff. 63 (1980); Rodgers, Environmental Law § 9.5 (2d ed.1994).

26. See Mandelker, NEPA Law & Litigation (2d ed.1993).

§ 11.4

1. 42 U.S.C.A. § 7401 et seq. The Clean Air Act was substantially modified in 1977 and 1990. All references reflect those amendments.

minimize air pollution, but the levels of pollution in many major metropolitan areas were a clear indication that theory had not been translated into practice.

The Clean Air Act targets both stationary sources (e.g., industrial smokestacks, dust from grain loading docks, etc.) and mobile sources (e.g., auto and truck exhaust) of air pollution.[2] Mobile sources are generally not of primary concern to land use planners and will not be covered here.[3] Stationary sources are another matter. For instance, the siting of a major coal burning power plant could be subject to state and local land use regulation as well as EPA jurisdiction under the Clean Air Act.[4]

While the states are delegated the authority to design plans to reduce air pollution directly, the basic framework of the Clean Air Act consists of federal authority over five broad statutory areas. They are (1) creation of national ambient air quality standards, (2) creation of air quality control regions, (3) approval of State Implementation Plans, (4) emission standards for specified new sources of air pollution, and (5) emission standards for hazardous air pollutants. Each area will be discussed in turn.

A. *National Ambient Air Quality Standards (NAAQS)*

The Clean Air Act requires the Environmental Protection Agency (EPA) to establish primary and secondary national ambient air quality standards (NAAQS).[5] Primary standards are those necessary to protect public health.[6] The public whose health is to be protected includes particularly sensitive citizens such as bronchial asthmatics and emphysematics who in the normal course of daily activity are exposed to the ambient environment.[7] EPA has decided that health is impaired if, for example, there is more than 0.03 parts per million (p.p.m.) sulfur dioxide in the air on an average in a region or if there is more than 0.14 p.p.m. sulfur dioxide in the air more than once a year.[8] Similar standards are set for other pollutants.

Secondary standards are those necessary to protect public welfare.[9] The public welfare "includes, but is not limited to, effects on soils, water, crops, vegetation, manmade materials, animals, wildlife, weather, visibility, and climate, damage to and deterioration of property, and hazards to

---

2. 42 U.S.C.A. § 7408(a)(1)(B).

3. For a discussion of mobile sources, see J. Rose, Legal Foundations of Environmental Planning 259 (1983). Land use planners do address traffic and roadway concerns in the transportation element of most comprehensive plans.

4. Existing stationary sources are controlled by the states with federal review only in regard to the state implementation plan. New construction of certain specified sources of air pollution are directly controlled by the federal government and are the topic of the following sections.

5. 42 U.S.C.A. § 7408(a)(1), § 7409. See, e.g., NRDC v. Train, 545 F.2d 320 (2d Cir.1976); Friends of the Earth v. Potomac Electric Power, 419 F.Supp. 528 (D.D.C. 1976).

6. 42 U.S.C.A. § 7409(b)(1).

7. Rodgers, Environmental Law § 3.3 (2d ed.1994).

8. 40 C.F.R. § 50.4. See id. §§ 50.6–.12 for standards for other pollutants.

9. 42 U.S.C.A. § 7409(b)(2).

transportation, as well as effects on economic values and on personal comfort."[10] According to EPA, for example, the public welfare is affected by sulfur dioxide if there is more than 0.5 p.p.m. as a "maximum concentration" exceeded more than once per year. NAAQS are to be reviewed and revised as appropriate every five years.[11]

States are required to submit to EPA an implementation plan designed to maintain NAAQS inside their borders within three years after NAAQS promulgation.[12] If the state implementation plan (SIP) meets EPA standards it will be approved. Once approved, the SIP is enforceable by either federal or state authorities.[13] If a state fails to promulgate an adequate SIP, the EPA Administrator will issue sufficient regulations to bring the recalcitrant state into line.[14]

B. *Air Quality Control Regions*

Air quality control regions are areas characterized by similar air pollution problems. Individual states are responsible for setting up these regions within their borders. However, the EPA itself must establish the precise pollution limitations in the air quality control regions themselves.

Regions are classified as either attainment or non-attainment areas. Attainment areas[15] are those geographic areas with air considered clean under the Act. The key to these areas is the Prevention of Significant Deterioration in Air Quality (PSD) provisions of the Clean Air Act.[16] PSD areas have air quality better than NAAQS requires. They are divided into two subclasses. Large national parks and wilderness areas are Class I, where almost no air quality degradation is allowed. All other areas are Class II, which allows moderate air pollution increases, provided they do not exceed NAAQS. State governors may reclassify Class II areas as either Class I or Class III, which allows a tradeoff of more pollution for greater industrial expansion. Again, no NAAQS may be violated.

For a "major" new source to be built in a PSD area, a permit is required. The applicant must show that no NAAQS will be violated, and that "best available control technology" (BACT) will be used for *all* pollutants.

Non-attainment areas are those localities not meeting primary and secondary NAAQS.[17] The 1990 Amendments added classifications within

10. 42 U.S.C.A. § 7602(h). See Rodgers, supra note 7.

11. 42 U.S.C.A.§ 7409(d).

12. 42 U.S.C.A. § 7410(a)(1).

13. Id. § 7413.

14. Id. § 7410(c)(1).

15. See, e.g., Alabama Power Co. v. Costle, 606 F.2d 1068 (D.C.Cir.1979), opinion superseded, on reconsideration 636 F.2d 323 (D.C.Cir.1979); Sierra Club v. EPA, 540 F.2d 1114 (D.C.Cir.1976), cert. denied 430 U.S. 959, 97 S.Ct. 1610, 51 L.Ed.2d 811

(1977), judgment vacated and remanded 434 U.S. 809, 98 S.Ct. 42, 54 L.Ed.2d 66 (1977). See 42 U.S.C.A. § 7407(d)(1)(A)(ii).

16. 42 U.S.C.A. § 7470(4) et seq.

17. See, e.g., PPG Industries, Inc. v. Costle, 630 F.2d 462 (6th Cir.1980); Republic Steel Corp. v. Costle, 621 F.2d 797 (6th Cir.1980); New England Legal Found. v. Costle, 475 F.Supp. 425 (D.Conn.1979), affirmed in part, jurisdiction reserved in part 632 F.2d 936 (2d Cir.1980) affirmed 666 F.2d 30 (2d Cir.1981). See also State of N.J., Dept. of Environ. Protect. v. United

non-attainment areas and assigned different deadlines for the various classifications, they include: marginal, moderate, serious, severe, and extreme. Development in non-attainment areas is very difficult. To get a permit, an applicant must comply with the "lowest achievable emission rate" (LAER) and show that "offset" requirements are met.[18] "Offset" means that for any new pollutant source, emissions from existing sources within the air quality control region must be reduced such that a net improvement in air quality occurs.[19] "The strategy of the offset approach is to encourage the states 'to develop plans which allow construction of new pollution sources where accompanied by a corresponding reduction in an existing pollution source.' In effect, a new emitting facility can be built 'if an existing pollution source decreases its emissions or ceases operations as long as a positive net air quality benefit occurs.' "[20] LAER is defined as "the most stringent emission limitation ... contained in the implementation plan of any state."[21] Thus any proposed industrial development can only be made at great cost, since not only must the best pollution control devices be used, but the plant owners must either significantly reduce pollution at some other owned source or pay for a similar reduction at another firm's plant.

C. *State Implementation Plans*

Each state is required to develop state implementation plans (SIPs) sufficient to meet all national primary and secondary air quality standards.[22] SIP's are not comprehensive plans for controlling all pollutants from all sources within a state.[23] Rather, they are plans that provide "for implementation maintenance and enforcement"[24] of national primary and secondary ambient air quality standards within each air quality region (or portions of an air quality region) in a given state.[25] If a sufficient SIP is not received by EPA, the EPA will impose one until the

---

States E.P.A., 626 F.2d 1038 (D.C.Cir.1980). Also see 42 U.S.C.A. § 7407(d)(1)(A)(i).

18. See 42 U.S.C.A. § 7501 (defining LAER) and § 7503 (establishing permit requirements and offsets program).

19. The use of offsets within the same source is called "bubbling." Recognizing the need to address economic considerations, the EPA in 1979 adopted rules authorizing use of the bubble concept. Under the program, the EPA interpreted the NSPS definition of source to allow netting the effects of multiple emission points within a single family. Thus, the plant wide approach treats a facility as if it were covered by a bubble, applying emissions limitations to it as a single source. This interpretation was upheld in Chevron U.S.A., Inc. v. Natural Resources Defense Council, Inc., 467 U.S. 837, 104 S.Ct. 2778, 81 L.Ed.2d 694 (1984), rehearing denied 468 U.S. 1227, 105 S.Ct. 28, 82 L.Ed.2d 921 (1985) (where congressional intent cannot be determined, review is limited to whether agency's con-

struction is reasonable; bubbling interpretation valid). Also see 42 U.S.C.A. § 7503(c).

20. Rodgers, Environmental Law § 3.7 (2d ed.1994) quoting Citizens Against the Refinery's Effects, Inc. v. United States E.P.A., 643 F.2d 183–85 (4th Cir.1981).

21. 42 U.S.C.A. § 7501(3)(a).

22. Id. § 7410(a)(1). Rules governing SIPs are listed at 40 C.F.R. Pt. 51 et seq. See also Union Electric Co. v. EPA, 427 U.S. 246, 96 S.Ct. 2518, 49 L.Ed.2d 474 (1976), rehearing denied, 429 U.S. 873, 97 S.Ct. 189, 50 L.Ed.2d 154 (1976); Train v. NRDC, 421 U.S. 60, 95 S.Ct. 1470, 43 L.Ed.2d 731 (1975), vacated in part 516 F.2d 488 (5th Cir.1975), opinion supplemented 539 F.2d 1068 (5th Cir.1976); Bunker Hill Co. v. EPA, 572 F.2d 1286 (9th Cir.1977).

23. Rodgers, Environmental Law § 3.6 (2d ed.1994).

24. 42 U.S.C.A. § 7410(a).

25. Rodgers, supra note 23.

state comes through.[26] Each SIP must contain categories showing: (1) attaining the standards within the time prescribed; (2) inclusion of emission limitations and other controls to maintain compliance; (3) monitoring; (4) pre-construction review of new sources; (5) interstate pollution; (6) administrative requirements for state authority; (7) inspection and testing of motor vehicles; (8) a revision authority; (9) a construction ban for non-attainment areas; (10) no significant deterioration; and (11) the collection of fees to cover the costs of permit programs.[27]

The above categories are the federal standards all states must meet. Otherwise, the joint federal/state cooperation at the heart of the Clean Air Act controls, and the individual states are pretty much left to their own in determining the exact "hows" of NAAQS attainment with a federal carrot and stick. An approved SIP is the carrot. The stick is two pronged: a federally imposed plan and the possible withholding of federal funds for highway, sewer, and other projects deemed pollution causing.

D. New Source Performance Standards (NSPS)

Section III of the Clean Air Act requires the EPA Administrator to promulgate "standards of performance" for all stationary sources not in existence as of the date of applicable regulations and to facilities that are reconstructed or modified after the date of application of the regulation.[28] This is in direct contrast to the congressional mandate directing individual state action concerning existing sources. Apparently, Congress was concerned that some states would succumb to the mentality of equating dirty air with more jobs.

To counter that tendency, Section III new source standards require emission controls which

> [reflect] the degree of emission limitation achievable through the application of the best system of emission reduction which (taking into account the cost of achieving such reduction and any nonair quality health and environmental impact and energy requirements) the Administrator determines has been adequately demonstrated.[29]

What exact standard will be used depends on whether the proposed site is a non-attainment area or an attainment (PSD) area.[30]

EPA has been lethargic in implementing new source performance standards.[31] In part, the reason for the alleged foot dragging is the difficulty in setting a NSPS that industry can achieve without—so they

---

26. 42 U.S.C.A. § 7410(c)(1)(A).

27. Rodgers, Environmental Law Air and Water, vol. 1, section 3.11, 264–265.

28. 42 U.S.C.A. § 7411.

29. Id. § 7411(a)(1).

30. See supra note 15 and accompanying text.

31. The following cases give a good overview of the problems NSPS implementation has caused. National Lime Association v. EPA, 627 F.2d 416 (D.C.Cir.1980);

ASARCO, Inc. v. EPA, 578 F.2d 319 (D.C.Cir.1978); Portland Cement Association v. Ruckelshaus, 486 F.2d 375 (D.C.Cir. 1973), cert. denied 417 U.S. 921, 94 S.Ct. 2628, 41 L.Ed.2d 226 (1974), appeal after remand 513 F.2d 506 (D.C.Cir.1975), cert. denied 423 U.S. 1025, 96 S.Ct. 469, 46 L.Ed.2d 399 (1975), rehearing denied 423 U.S. 1092, 96 S.Ct. 889, 47 L.Ed.2d 104 (1976).

say—going broke. Intense industrial lobbying resulted not only in the slow NSPS implementation, but the 1977 Amendments themselves.[32]

There is one interesting land use consequence of the stationary new source provisions. Because the emission limits are the same throughout the nation, industry cannot "shop around" for a jurisdiction that will treat them benignly by allowing more pollution than somewhere else. Therefore, as to new stationary sources, the regulations do not determine location.

E. Hazardous Pollutants

Section 112 of the Clean Air Act covers "hazardous air pollutants." The 1990 Amendments changed the classification of hazardous materials from a definitional classification to a discreet list. The list includes nearly 200 hazardous pollutants.[33] The list shall be periodically reviewed by the administrator, and when necessary shall be revised, adding pollutants which may be adverse to human health or the environment.[34] For each listed source category, the EPA will issue standards that will be applied to both new and existing sources and that will require the maximum degree of emission reduction achievable.[35]

IV.   LAND USE AND POLLUTION CONTROL LAWS—CLEAN WATER

§ 11.5   The Clean Water Act as a Land Use Control Measure

The Federal Water Pollution Control Act[1] is the primary national statute for preventing water pollution. Substantially amended in 1972, 1977 (when it was denominated the Clean Water Act), and 1987, the Clean Water Act along with NEPA and the Clean Air Act completes a trilogy of federal environmental juggernauts which provide considerable federal control over some forms of land use.

The Clean Water Act is largely administered by the Environmental Protection Agency (EPA).[2] The section most pertinent to land use controls is the dredge and fill program under section 404. However, Section 404 is an exception in that the United States Army Corps of Engineers has primary jurisdiction, with EPA playing a reviewing and a possible veto role. Congress in 1972 created a separate permit program

---

32. One result of this successful lobbying effort is the inclusion of § 317 in the 1977 amendments (codified at 42 U.S.C.A. § 7617). It provides that before publishing notice of any proposed rulemaking under § 111 (NSPS), the Administrator must prepare "an economic impact assessment respecting such standard or regulation." 42 U.S.C.A. § 7617(b). Even though limited by a subsequent section preventing any change in the "basis on which a standard or regulation is promulgated," id. § 7617(e), this

provision gives polluting industries a good legal handle.

33. Id. § 7412(b)(1).

34. Id. § 7412 (b)(2).

35. Rodgers, Environmental Law § 3.8 (2d ed.1994).

§ 11.5

1. 33 U.S.C.A. § 1251 et seq.

2. Id. § 1251(d).

under Section 404 for the discharge of dredge and fill material.[3] Those who qualify for a Section 404 permit are exempt from the National Pollutant Discharge Elimination System (NPDES) permit system.[4] Section 404 is discussed at length in this chapter in part VI.

The Clean Water Act directs the EPA to establish research programs and provides for grants for research and development and for pollution control programs.[5] The amounts provided for such grants, however, are modest compared with the massive funds for construction of publicly owned treatment works, for which the EPA makes larger grants.[6] Conditions are imposed on eligibility for these grants, including the requirement that a facility be in accord with any applicable areawide waste treatment management plan.[7] As with the Clean Air Act, two standards for clean water must be met, emission or effluent[8] standards and ambient standards.[9] The ambient standards are set by the states and can and do vary. Often water pollution does not come out of the end of a pipe, but results from water runoff, and the Act addresses these non-point sources.[10] Anything that does come out of a pipe is a point source, and the Act provides control by requiring that a permit be obtained from EPA for the discharge of any pollutant.[11] As with the Clean Air Act, much of the federal power is willingly delegated to any state which is able to administer a program to the federal requirements.

A. *Grants*

As with the Clean Air Act, the Clean Water Act can encourage land use control as dictated by water quality needs through conditions on grants. Thus, in order to obtain a grant for pollution control programs,[12] recipient states and other eligible governmental agencies can be required to establish land use controls. Grants for treatment works[13] are also available only if consistent with any existing areawide waste treatment management plan,[14] and with an applicable continuing planning process and only if the treatment work constitutes a priority need.[15] However powerful the grant inducements, they do not constitute direct control.

B. *Areawide Waste Treatment Management Plans*

Areawide Waste Treatment Management Plans[16] are required to be prepared according to EPA guidelines for areas where urban-industrial concentrations have produced substantial water quality control problems, but there are no sanctions if they are not prepared; and EPA has no power to impose them as is also the case under the Clean Air Act. If prepared, permits to discharge pollutants and grants for treatment

---

3. Rodgers, Environmental Law § 4.6 (2d ed.1994). 33 U.S.C.A. § 1344.

4. Rodgers, supra note 3. 33 U.S.C.A. § 1342(a)(1).

5. 33 U.S.C.A. §§ 1254–1266.

6. Id. §§ 1281–1287.

7. Id. § 1288(d).

8. Id. §§ 1311, 1316.

9. Id. § 1313.

10. Id. § 1314(f).

11. Id. §§ 1341–1345. See also id. § 1362(14).

12. Id. § 1256.

13. Id. § 1281(g).

14. Id. § 1288(d).

15. Id. § 1284.

16. Id. § 1288.

works must be consistent with the plans. The plans constitute a land use control because they cover such things as indicating where future treatment works are to be located and establishment of construction priorities for treatment works. More pervasively, the areawide plans are to "regulate the location, modification, and construction of any facilities within such area which may result in any discharge in such area. . . . "[17] This could include regulations over any private or publicly owned sewage treatment plant as well as any other point source of water pollution, such as a paper mill. Additionally, "methods" (including land use requirements) are to be included "to control" non-point source pollution from agriculture and mining operations[18] and to control pollution from construction sites.[19] These provisions, in short, require control over many land uses of an industrial, agricultural, mining, or construction nature.

C. Standards and Deadlines

Section 101 still contains the unachieved goal of attaining "fishable and swimmable" waters by 1983 and the complete elimination of pollution discharge by 1985.[20] Recognizing that these goals would not be met when the 1977 Clean Water Act Amendments were introduced, Congress established a three-step process setting forth new standards and deadlines. Separate standards and deadlines were set for pollution from various sources and types.

Conventional pollutants, defined in general to include sewage and sewage-related waste, must meet effluent standards based on the "best conventional pollutant control technology" (BCT).[21] BCT is a medium strict standard allowing economic considerations. The deadline was March 31, 1989, and no waivers are provided for.[22] Toxic pollutants, listed by the EPA (some 129–different substances were initially listed) as deserving special concern, must meet effluent standards based on the "best available technology economically achievable" (BAT).[23] BAT is the most stringent standard and is based on the best performer in any industrial class. The deadline established by the 1987 amendments was July 1, 1984, with no allowance for waiver or economic consideration, but was extended to March 31, 1989.[24] Nonconventional pollutants, defined as neither conventional nor toxic, must also be controlled by BAT standards.[25] However, the deadline was also March 31, 1989. These (and the prior 1972) standards and deadlines[26] are responsible for a great

17. Id. § 1288(b)(2)(C)(ii).

18. Id. § 1288(b)(2)(F).

19. Id. § 1288(b)(2)(H).

20. Id. § 1251.

21. Id. § 1311(b)(2)(E).

22. Id.

23. Id. § 1317(a)(2). See also Hercules, Inc. v. EPA, 598 F.2d 91 (D.C.Cir.1978); T. Schoenbaum, Environmental Policy Law 724–26 (1982).

24. 33 U.S.C.A. § 1311(b)(2)(C). For a case illustrating judicial leniency, see Chemical Mfrs. Ass'n. v. Natural Resources Defense Council, Inc., 470 U.S. 116, 105 S.Ct. 1102, 84 L.Ed.2d 90 (1985).

25. Id. § 1311(b)(2)(A).

26. For a chart explaining these rather confusing deadlines, see Percival, et al, Environmental Regulation: Law, Science and Policy 889 (1996)

bulk of the total litigation involving the Clean Water Act.[27]

D. Variable Emission Limitations

While the effluent limitation standards are the same nationally, special effluent limitations or other control strategies can be applied by EPA to point sources discharging into particular waters.[28] These special limitations which vary by location could mean, for example, that water pollution considerations would "force" a paper mill from one location to another with all the direct and indirect land use consequences such locational decisions imply.

E. Continuing Planning Process

Once the standards are established, each state must identify those waters which cannot be made clean to the standard by effluent limitations alone. Maximum daily pollutant loads must be assigned such waters. Each state must have a continuing planning process, roughly the equivalent of implementation plans under the Clean Air Act, and therefore not surprisingly often referred to as the implementation plan. The implementation plan can be approved by EPA only if it provides at least for EPA set effluent limitations, incorporates areawide waste management plans, provides for maximum daily pollutant loads, includes procedures for revision of water quality standards and indicates there is available authority for intergovernmental cooperation and power to implement effluent and water quality limitations and standards.[29]

F. Nonpoint Sources

A nonpoint source is undefined but is often used in the Act.[30] It is best understood in contrast to a point source, which is defined as "any discernible, confined and discrete conveyance, including but not limited to any pipe, ditch, channel, tunnel, conduit, well, discrete fissure, container, rolling stock, concentrated animal feeding operation, or vessel or other floating craft, from which pollutants are or may be discharged."[31] Thus, a nonpoint source is any source of water pollution or pollutants not associated with a "discrete conveyance."[32] Nonpoint source pollution includes runoff from fields, forest lands, and construction activity.[33] The most common nonpoint sources facing land use planning are agricultural and urban runoff. Other nonpoint pollution sources result from silviculture and mining operations. Nonpoint sources produce a wide variety of

---

27. See generally EPA v. National Crushed Stone Association, 449 U.S. 64, 101 S.Ct. 295, 66 L.Ed.2d 268 (1980), on remand 643 F.2d 163 (4th Cir.1981); E.I. du Pont de Nemours & Co. v. Train, 430 U.S. 112, 97 S.Ct. 965, 51 L.Ed.2d 204 (1977); Appalachian Power Co. v. United States EPA, 671 F.2d 801 (4th Cir.1982); California & Hawaiian Sugar Co. v. EPA, 553 F.2d 280 (2d Cir.1977); American Frozen Food Institute v. Train, 539 F.2d 107 (D.C.Cir. 1976); American Meat Institute v. EPA, 526 F.2d 442 (7th Cir.1975).

28. 33 U.S.C.A. § 1312.

29. Id. § 1313(e)(3).

30. Rodgers, Environmental Law § 4.5 (2d ed.1994).

31. Id. § 1362(14).

32. Rodgers, supra note 30. Umatilla Waterquality Protective Association, Inc. v. Smith Frozen Foods, Inc., 962 F.Supp. 1312 (1997), Trustees For Alaska v. EPA, 749 F.2d 549 (9th Cir.1984), National Wildlife Federation v. Gorsuch, 693 F.2d 156, 166 & n. 28 (D.C.Cir.1982).

33. Rodgers, supra note 30 at § 4.4.

pollutants, such as: sediments, minerals, nutrients, pesticides, organic wastes, waste oils and thermal pollution.[34]

The nonpoint source[35] problem is particularly susceptible to regulation by land use control. While municipal and industrial waste discharges require expensive treatment facilities, nonpoint sources can be controlled through changes in land use policies. The only other options are to provide a collection point so that the runoff becomes a point source or ban enough point sources from the area so that water quality standards are met.

Agricultural nonpoint source pollution results from irrigation, erosion, animal waste, fertilizer and pesticide runoff. Additionally, poor irrigation and tillage practices result in soil erosion, which depletes soil fertility as it pollutes. To control agricultural runoff, techniques such as conservation tillage, terracing, contouring, strip cropping, and drainage construction projects are used.[36]

The Clean Water Act combats agricultural runoff through section 319 management programs, with implementation left to state and local governments.[37] The nonpoint source program is expected to proceed with the states first gathering information on the various categories of nonpoint sources and processes to achieve suitable controls. Second, it can be expected that states will develop management programs to control the sources of pollution identified.[38] The Act also dictates that "best management practices and measures" must be employed to reduce pollutants.[39]

Urban runoff contributes to nonpoint pollution problems by funneling oil, heavy metals, and sediment into streams and groundwater supplies. The key villain in urban runoff is construction; rainwater that used to slowly filter through earth is now met by concrete and asphalt.

G. Governmental Facilities

Governmental facilities are often bad neighbors from a land use point of view but are often exempt from traditional land use controls. However, not even federal government facilities are exempt under the Clean Water Act unless specifically exempted by the President, and not even the President can exempt projects from the national effluent limitations. Such facilities must comply as if owned by any other person and must comply not only with federal but with state, interstate and local requirements respecting control and abatement of pollution.[40]

H. Clean Lakes

While no sanction for noncompliance is indicated, each state is required to identify publicly owned fresh water lakes and to establish "methods (including land use requirements), to control sources of pollution of such lakes."[41] If the above mentioned information is submitted to

---

34. Id.

35. 33 U.S.C.A. § 1314(f).

36. National Conference of State Legislatures, Land Management: Sustaining Resources Values 163 (Oct. 1983) [hereinafter cited as National Conference]. See also J. Juergensmeyer & J. Wadley, Agricultural Law § 23.4 (1982).

37. 33 U.S.C.A. § 1329.

38. See Rodgers, Environmental Law: Air and Water, vol. II, section 4.2A, 9.

39. 33 U.S.C.A. § 1329 (b)(2)(A).

40. 33 U.S.C.A. § 1323(a).

41. Id. § 1324(a).

the EPA, then grants are available to "carry out methods and procedures" approved by EPA.[42]

I. *Permit System*

Despite the previously described powerful inducements, one might quibble over whether they represent direct land use control. The permit system established by the Federal Water Pollution Control Act (FWPCA), however, clearly involves direct control. The National Pollutant Discharge Elimination System (NPDES) requires an EPA permit to discharge any pollutant from a point source into any waters of the United States. The permit can be issued only if the discharger complies with all standards in the FWPCA. The Administrator, after opportunity for a public hearing, is authorized to issue a permit for the discharge of any pollutant upon condition that the discharger meet the applicable "best technology" effluent requirement.[43] The Administrator is also authorized to write conditions into the permits, "including conditions on data and information collection, reporting, and such other requirements as he deems appropriate."[44] States can administer permits only if EPA has approved a state permit program that meets EPA standards and if a continuing planning process is in existence.[45] No permit can be issued which conflicts with any areawide waste treatment plan.[46]

Publicly owned waste treatment plants are required to have permits. These permits can be conditioned to assure standards are met. If the conditions are violated, EPA has power to seek a court order prohibiting any further use of the treatment plant by a new source of pollution.[47] Popularly called the "sewer ban" provision, it could make new development impossible unless other alternative means of disposal were found which, of course, would also have to comply with the Water Act. Private sources of pollution must also comply and permits are denied where water quality standards or effluent limitations cannot be met.[48]

V. LAND USE AND POLLUTION CONTROL LAWS—SAFE DRINKING WATER, HAZARDOUS WASTES AND QUIETUDE

§ 11.6 The Safe Drinking Water Act

The Safe Drinking Water Act (SDWA)[1] has a land use control effect in that it seeks to ensure that public water supply systems do not endanger the public health. A public water system is defined as:

42. Id. § 1324(b), § 1324(c). Also for "model" acts which provide examples of methods that might be used, see, e.g., Washington Shoreline Management Act of 1971, West's Rev.Code Wash.Ann. ch. 90.58; Wisconsin Shoreland Zoning Law, Wis.Stat.Ann. 59.971, 144.26; Tahoe Regional Planning Compact, P.L. 91–158, 83 Stat. 360, Dec. 18, 1969.

43. Id. § 1342(a)(1), Rodgers, Environmental Law § 4.8 (2d ed.1994).

44. Id. § 1342(a)(2). Rodgers, supra note 43.

45. 40 C.F.R. Pt. 123.

46. 33 U.S.C.A. § 1342(a).

47. Id. § 1342(h).

48. Ipsen & Rasch, Enforcement Under the Federal Water Pollution Control Act Amendments of 1972, 9 Land & Water L.Rev. 369 (1974).

§ 11.6

1. 42 U.S.C.A. § 300f et seq. See also Environmental Defense Fund, Inc. v. Costle, 578 F.2d 337 (D.C.Cir.1978).

a system for the provision to the public of water for human consumption through pipes or other constructed conveyances, if such system has at least fifteen service connections or regularly serves at least twenty-five individuals. Such term includes (i) any collection, treatment, storage, and distribution facilities under control of the operator of such system and used primarily in connection with such system, and (ii) any collection or pretreatment storage facilities not under such control which are used primarily in connection with such system.[2]

The EPA sets standards to identify maximum contaminant levels (MCL) that may cause adverse health effects.[3] If a contaminant is found, a maximum contaminant level goal (MCLG) is set. A MCLG must be "set at the level at which no known or anticipated adverse effects on the health of persons occur and which allows an adequate margin of safety."[4]

Once a MCLG is established, EPA must require a MCL that is feasible.[5] Feasible means the use of the best technology, treatment techniques and other means that EPA finds are available.[6] A MCL is not feasible if it is not economically or technologically feasible to ascertain the level of contaminant.[7] If the MCL is not feasible, then EPA will still require a treatment technique that would prevent known or anticipated adverse effects to the extent possible.[8]

A state or EPA may issue variances to public water systems that cannot meet a MCL because of raw water sources which are available to the system.[9] Variances will only be issued after the application of best technology[10] and if the issuance of the variance does not result in an unreasonable risk to health. EPA will also consider costs in the determination for a variance.[11]

If a system is unable to meet the MCL for reasons other than its raw water sources, it may be granted an exemption.[12] As with a variance, an exemption will only be granted if it will not result in the unreasonable risk to health.[13]

As with most environmental statutes, the chief land use effect of the SDWA lies in enforcement. The states have primary authority for enforcing the national primary regulations provided they meet federal

2. 42 U.S.C.A. § 300f(4) (1997).

3. Id. § 300g–1(b)(1)(A)(i).

4. Id. § 300g–1(b)(4)(A).

5. Id. § 300g–1(b)(4)(B).

6. Id. § 300g–1(b)(4)(D).

7. Id.

8. Id. § 300g–1(b)(7)(A).

9. Id. § 300g–4(a)(1)(A).

10. Id.

11. Id.

12. See generally, Id. § 300g–5.

13. Id. § 300g–5(a)(3).

standards.[14] EPA will provide enforcement authority if a state either fails or chooses not to meet federal standards. However, EPA's enforcement authority under the SDWA is quite limited in comparison to the Clean Water Act. First, EPA has discretion in whether to bring an enforcement action or not. Second, EPA can only file a civil suit for a SDWA violation, it cannot issue administrative compliance orders.[15] Although the enforcement provisions were strengthened in the 1986 Amendments,[16] the SDWA remains quite weak and generally an unenforced regulation.[17] The SDWA's teeth are short, and the only likelihood of their being lengthened in the near future is if a large metropolitan area's water becomes too poisonous to drink.

§ 11.7 Deadly Garbage—The Resource Conservation and Recovery Act (RCRA) and the Comprehensive Environmental Response, Compensation, and Liability Act of 1980 (CERCLA/"Superfund")

Spawned by tragedies such as Love Canal, public and political interest in hazardous waste disposal remains high despite recent assaults on environmental regulation—perhaps because the issue strikes so close to home since a primary risk of improper waste disposal is the poisoning of drinking water supplies.

Concern over safe disposal of hazardous materials fits easily into the land use planners' bag of worries. From decades of experience in siting private and municipal garbage dumps, land use planners can be expected to pay close attention to regulations concerning the proper disposal of the deadly garbage our technological-based society produces. Through years of neglect, federal, state and local officials have allowed the creation of some 50,000 hazardous waste dumps. More than a thousand are considered real and immediate hazards. These figures reveal the national nightmare hazardous wastes have become.

Enacted in 1976, the Resource Conservation and Recovery Act (RCRA)[1] is the nation's first line of defense against the hazardous waste nightmare. RCRA is based on a "cradle to grave" system of regulation. Separate standards cover the production, transportation, and disposal of hazardous wastes.[2] RCRA generally applies to currently active facilities that generate and manage hazardous wastes. Hazardous wastes are identified by "taking into account toxicity, persistence, and degradability

---

14. Id. § 300g–2(a).

15. Id. § 300g–3(a)(1)(B). See also J. Rose, Legal Foundations of Environmental Planning 405 (1983). See generally Douglas, Safe Drinking Water Act of 1974—History and Critique, 5 Envtl.Aff. 501 (1976).

16. See generally, Id. § 300g–3.

17. For an interesting perspective, see A. Dan Tarlock, Safe Drinking Water: A Federalism Perspective, 21 Wm. & Mary Envt'l.L & Pol'y Rev. 223 (1997) (discussing 1986 amendments).

§ 11.7

1. 42 U.S.C.A. § 6901 et seq. For an excellent analysis of the enormously complicated RCRA program, see J. Quarles, Federal Regulation of Hazardous Waste: A Guide to RCRA, (Env'l Law Inst. 1982). See generally, Rodgers, Environmental Law: Hazardous Wastes & Substances, Vol. 4 (1992).

2. Id. §§ 6922, 6923, 6924, 6925.

in nature, potential for accumulation in tissue, and other related factors such as flammability, corrosiveness, and other hazardous characteristics."[3]

Disposal is allowed only upon obtaining a permit.[4] Permits are issued only if the waste is covered by a manifest[5]—the ubiquitous document responsible for keeping track of the waste from production to disposal. Unlike the feeble SDWA, RCRA's fangs include civil and criminal penalties for either permit violations or document falsification.[6] Injunctive relief is also available upon a finding of an "imminent and substantial endangerment to health or the environment."[7]

Perhaps the best known of the hazardous waste statutes is the Comprehensive Environmental Response, Compensation, and Liability Act of 1980 (CERCLA).[8] Nicknamed "superfund," CERCLA establishes a pool of money collected as a tax on toxic chemical manufacture.[9] This money is to be used for expenses entailed in the presidentially implemented "national contingency plan."[10] This plan is the basis for hazardous waste site cleanup. If federal standards are met, this responsibility can be delegated to the states.[11] Where RCRA looks primarily to current and future problems, CERCLA is a backward-looking regulation; it regulates abandoned and inactive hazardous waste sites.

Certainly the most litigated, aspect of CERCLA is the provision requiring hazardous waste generators to pay for cleanup costs and natural resource destruction (if the resources are owned by a governmental entity).[12] Even though it is a perfect example of pollution laws paying for themselves, recovery of cleanup costs has been extremely slow.

Both CERCLA and RCRA create liability for landowners. Under CERCLA, liability is far reaching and at times seemingly inequitable. As might be expected, CERCLA imposes liability on the party responsible for the actual contamination. This may include the owners or operators of the facility, persons or entities who arranged for the treatment or disposal of the hazardous wastes at the facility and persons that transported the hazardous substances to the facility. Any parties falling within one of these categories is liable for the cleanup costs regardless of whether they were actually responsible for the contamination.

Perhaps the most controversial aspect of CERCLA is the liability of the current owner. CERCLA imposes strict liability on the current owner. An owner may be held liable for the cleanup costs for his property even if he was not responsible for the contamination.[13]

3. Id. § 6921(a).

4. Id. § 6925.

5. Id. § 6922(a)(5).

6. Id. § 6928.

7. Id. § 6973(a). See also United States v. Price, 688 F.2d 204 (3d Cir.1982).

8. 42 U.S.C.A. § 9601 et seq.

9. Id. § 9611.

10. Id. §§ 9604(a), 9605.

11. Id. § 9604(c), (d).

12. Id. § 9607.

13. For example see United States v. Tyson, 25 Env't Rep. Cas. (BNA) 1897 (E.D.Pa.1986).

CERCLA does provide three statutory defenses to the owner's strict liability. They are: an act of god; an act of war; or an act or omission of a third party.[14] Obviously, the first two defenses are not very helpful. The third defense, an act or omission of a third party seems to offer some hope. This defense requires the satisfaction of three elements: no direct or indirect relationship, contractual or otherwise; the defendant need have exercised due care with respect to the hazardous substance; and the defendant took precautions against foreseeable acts and omissions of third parties and the consequences that could foreseeably result from such acts or omission.[15]

In 1986, CERCLA was amended by the Superfund Amendments and Reauthorization Act (SARA). SARA defines "contractual relationship" to include "land contracts, deeds, or other instruments transferring title or possession" unless certain conditions were met.[16] The third party defense in § 9607(b) together with the conditions set forth in SARA make up the "innocent purchaser" defense.

Under the innocent purchaser defense, a land owner must first prove that he acquired the property after the disposal or placement of hazardous substances on the property. He must also prove by preponderance of the evidence that either: he did not know or had reason to know that any hazardous substance was on the property; or that he is a governmental entity which acquired the property by escheat, the exercise of eminent domain, or any other involuntary transfer; or the defendant acquired the facility by inheritance.[17]

Most often, defendants choose to prove they did not know or have reason to know of the contamination. The Act requires that a defendant "have undertaken, at the time of acquisition, all appropriate inquiry into the previous ownership and uses of the property."[18] This seems to indicate that a prudent purchaser should order at least a Phase I environmental audit before closing a transaction.

As mentioned previously, RCRA was enacted as a forward-looking regulation. RCRA imposes liability for civil penalties, criminal penalties and imposes liability for the actual cleanup or financing for the cleanup of hazardous substances. Its main purpose was to regulate active management of hazardous substances.[19] However the Solid Waste Amendments of 1984 added the requirement for the cleanup of former hazardous waste sites to RCRA. Case law suggests that owners should conduct a reasonable investigation of the property before purchasing, much like they should to minimize liability under CERCLA.[20]

---

14. Id. § 9607(b).

15. Id. § 9607(b)(3).

16. Id. § 9601(35)(A).

17. Id. § 9601(35)(A).

18. Id. § 9601(35)(B).

19. See Rodgers, supra note 1.

20. See United States v. Price, 523 F.Supp. 1055 (D.N.J.1981), 688 F.2d 204 (3d Cir.1982); United States v. Waste Industries, 734 F.2d 159 (4th Cir.1984).

§ 11.8 Noise Control Act of 1972

The basic thrust of the Noise Control Act[1] is that EPA is required to set noise emission limits for new products that produce considerable noise. Examples are transportation vehicles, construction equipment, and other kinds of motors and engines.[2] As true with the Clean Air and Clean Water Acts, emission limitations that apply nationwide do not have many land use implications.

To be sure, if trucks are made to run more quietly, areas now inundated by noise from trucks will become more pleasant places. But that land use result hardly involves direct EPA control of land use.

EPA is also required to publish noise standards necessary to protect the public health and welfare, and to publish information on techniques for control of noise.[3] While that authority might be broad enough to permit EPA to suggest how industrial noise can be controlled, which in turn might involve such land use techniques as buffer zones or performance standards, states are not required to apply such techniques.[4]

Airport location may be affected by the EPA under the Noise Act, for it was directed to study such matters.[5] It is also to recommend regulations for control and abatement of noise to the Federal Aviation Agency, which then will promulgate appropriate regulations,[6] including those necessary to protect the public health and welfare. Under such regulations, the FAA might consider such land use matters as locations of airports, requiring large sites, airport zoning and limitations on uses around airports to include only those that are noise insensitive or are easy to insulate from noise. But as of this writing, the FAA has shown no inclination to flex any direct land use control muscle.

The EPA can also promulgate noise standards for railroad equipment and motor carriers engaged in interstate commerce.[7] But these provisions are probably not broad enough to authorize the EPA to, for example, restrict locations of railroad or truck yards or rail lines or highways.

As with the Clean Water Act, if states and localities come up with noise control programs, the federal government must play by state and local rules. Federal agencies and activities "shall comply with Federal, State, interstate, and local requirements respecting control and abatement of environmental noise to the same extent that any person is subject to such requirements. The President may exempt ...[activities

§ 11.8

1. 42 U.S.C.A. § 4901 et seq. See also Comment, Toward the Comprehensive Abatement of Noise Pollution: Recent Federal and New York City Noise Control Legislation, 4 Ecology L.Q. 109 (1974).

2. 42 U.S.C.A. § 4905(a)(1)(C).

3. Id. § 4904.

4. Some zoning ordinances already apply sophisticated performance standards, including noise emission standards, for determining whether a particular industrial use is allowable in a zone. See supra §§ 4.11, 4.19.

5. 42 U.S.C.A. § 4906.

6. 49 U.S.C.A. § 1431(c).

7. 42 U.S.C.A. §§ 4916, 4917.

or facilities] in the paramount interest of the United States [except in several specified situations].... "[8]

VI.   LAND USE AND ENVIRONMENTALLY SENSITIVE LANDS: WETLANDS

§ 11.9   Definition and Importance of Wetlands

To many people the idea of "wetlands" conjures up images of dismal, dank, mosquito-ridden, snake-infested, miasmic swamps to either be avoided or paved over. Indeed, this notion has been so prevalent in our nation's collective subconscious that we have destroyed over fifty percent of our wetland resources.[1] They were lost beneath the crunching blow of drag lines and dredges making way for subdivisions, trailer parks, agribusiness and dumps. For those with the above delusion this turn of events may seem just fine; the best swamp is a drained swamp. Yet as a nation, we are just now beginning to realize that wetlands may be the most important (economically, as well as ecologically) of all environmentally sensitive lands.

Saltwater marshes are the most biologically productive lands on earth, producing more than twice the biomass of our most fertile hayfields.[2] Such estuarine areas also serve an essential role as nurseries for seven of the ten most commercially valuable fish and shellfish consumed in this country.[3] Fresh water wetlands play an important (critical, in some areas) role in aquifer recharge, pollution control (through a remarkably efficient system of capture and filtration), flood control, prevention of soil erosion and as wildlife habitat.[4] Absent adequate wetlands protection, there will occur a dramatic drop in fish, shellfish, wildlife, and timber production nationwide with a corresponding rise in flood damage, soil loss, fresh water depletion (accompanied by salt water intrusion in coastal areas) and general environmental degradation as pollutants concentrate.

With wetlands' value identified and need for protection recognized, the first hurdle toward sensible management is definitional. There is simply no standard, all inclusive definition of a wetland that meets all needs.[5] Marshes, swamps, bogs, some types of hardwood forested areas,

---

8.   Id. § 4903(b).

§ 11.9

1.   U.S. Fish and Wildlife Service, Wetlands Status and Trends (1991). It seems that our common law stretching back to the Middle Ages has recognized the importance and unique character of wetlands much more than our legal system has in the recent past. See F. Bosselman, Limitations Inherent in the Title to Wetlands at Common Law, 15 Stan.Envtl.L.J. 247 (1996).

2.   See E. Horwitz, Our Nation's Wetlands 1, 21 (1978) (Interagency Task Force Report coordinated by the Council on Environmental Quality).

3.   McHugh, Management of Estuarine Fisheries, A Symposium on Estuarine Fisheries, 3 Am. Fisheries Soc'y Special Publication (1966). The top ten species are shrimp, salmon, tuna, oysters, menhaden, crabs, lobsters, flounders, clams and haddock. The three exceptions to the estuarine dependent rule are tuna, lobsters, and haddock.

4.   U.S. Fish and Wildlife Service, Wetlands Status and Trends (1991).

5.   For definitional examples, see, e.g., National Academy of Sciences Report, Wetlands: Characteristics and Boundaries, 1995; U.S. Army Corps of Engineers, Wetland definition, 33 C.F.R. § 328.3(b) (1994);

sloughs, wet meadows, natural ponds, potholes and river overflow areas have all been described as wetlands. Basically, the term "wetlands" is generic and refers to areas supporting vegetation capable of withstanding wet conditions. This occurs where land levels are low and ground water levels are high.

§ 11.10 The Federal Presence

As with other types of environmental land use control, wetlands protection is characterized by a strong federal and state regulatory presence. From a "do as you damn well please" attitude, wetlands development has become dominated by a bewildering array of state and federal regulations and permit requirements. In addition, many states with substantial wetlands acreage have local regulations tied in with the broader federal and state programs.[6]

Because permits at all levels must be obtained before any form of development may occur in a wetland area it is important to understand the regulatory interplay in the permitting process and the federal, state, and local jurisdictions involved.

A. The Rivers and Harbors Act of 1899

The granddaddy of all wetland regulations was not designed to conserve wetlands at all. When President McKinley signed the Rivers and Harbors Act of 1899, his intent was to protect navigable waters to the extent they were safe for shipping.[1] Thus jurisdiction was provided over "navigable waters" alone. Nevertheless, by prohibiting the obstruction or alteration of "navigable waters" of the United States without recommendation by the Chief of Engineers and authorization by the Secretary of the Army,[2] section 10 of the Rivers and Harbors Act has become of considerable importance in wetlands regulation and conservation.

The Army Corps of Engineers defines "navigable waters" as "those waters that are subject to the ebb and flow of the tide and/or are presently used, or have been used in the past, or may be susceptible for use to transport interstate or foreign commerce."[3] Whether a waterbody comes under the above definition is a regulatory decision made by the

---

HR 961, Clean Water Act Amendments, Title VII, Section 804, Amending 33 U.S.C. § 1162(28) (Adding new definition). See also, E. Goodman, Defining Wetlands for Regulatory Purposes: A Case Study in the Role of Science in Policymaking, 2 Buff. Envtl.L.J. 135 (1994); W. Rodgers, Environmental Law § 4.6 (2nd ed.1994).

§ 11.10

6. "Wetlands are currently the scene of hard fought legal and political battles about the proper scope of governmental regulation of land." F. Bosselman, Limitations Inherent in the Title to Wetlands at Com-

mon Law, 15 Stan.Envtl.L.J. 247, 248 (1996). Professor Bosselman suggests that two long-running cases should be watched for how the takings issue will be applied to wetlands: Florida Rock, Indus. v. United States, 18 F.3d 1560 (Fed.Cir.1994) cert. denied. 513 U.S. 1109, 115 S.Ct. 898, 130 L.Ed.2d 783 (1995) and Loveladies Harbor, Inc. v. United States, 28 F.3d 1171 (Fed.Cir. 1994).

1. 33 U.S.C.A. §§ 401–418.

2. Id. § 403. See W. Rodgers, Environmental Law § 4.1 (2nd ed.1994).

3. 33 C.F.R. § 329.4.

division engineer based upon a report prepared at the district level.[4] The decision, as it would be considering the above definition, is based upon the past, present, or potential presence of interstate or foreign commerce and the physical capabilities of the waterbody for use by such commerce.[5]

While many environmentally sensitive wetlands are not covered by this definition, some larger areas are. Section 10's applicability to wetlands regulation was verified by the Fifth Circuit Court of Appeals in Zabel v. Tabb.[6] There, two developers applied for a permit to dredge and fill in the navigable waters of Boca Ciega Bay, near St. Petersburg, Florida, in order to build a trailer park. The project was denied the necessary permits by the Corps of Engineers. Under normal circumstances (at that time) the matter would probably have ended there. However, the permit denial was issued solely on the basis of environmental concerns-the project would neither interfere with navigation nor flood control. The developers cried foul in that they believed the Corps had no authority to deny a dredge and fill permit on purely environmental grounds,[7] and the district court agreed with them.[8] In a sweeping opinion, Judge John R. Brown reversed the district court and held that the Corps had indeed such power, and could base its permitting decisions either partially or wholly on ecological reasons.[9]

B. Section 10 Jurisdiction

Federal jurisdiction under section 10 is complicated by water level changes. Jurisdiction over tidal water extends to the mean high water line.[10] The mean high water line is calculated by using tidal cycle data.

4. Id., § 329.14.

5. Id., § 329.6.

6. 430 F.2d 199 (5th Cir.1970), cert. denied 401 U.S. 910, 91 S.Ct. 873, 27 L.Ed.2d 808 (1971).

7. Actually, the Corps had broadened its jurisdiction through regulation in 1968. The regulations allowed the Corps to consider public interest and environmental factors. 33 C.F.R. § 209.120 (superseded by 42 Fed.Reg. 37, 133 (1977)).

8. 430 F.2d at 201.

9. Judge Brown's decision was prefaced by an extraordinary preface which is well worth quoting in its entirety:

It is the destiny of the Fifth Circuit to be in the middle of great, oftentimes explosive issues of spectacular public importance. So it is here as we enter in depth the contemporary interest in the preservation of our environment. By an injunction requiring the issuance of a permit to fill in eleven acres of tidelands in the beautiful Boca Ciega Bay in the St. Petersburg–Tampa, Florida area for use as a commercial mobile trailer park, the District Judge held that the Secretary of the Army and his functionary,

the Chief of Engineers, had no power to consider anything except interference with navigation. There being no such obstruction to navigation, they were ordered to issue a permit even though the permittees acknowledge that "there was evidence before the Corps of Engineers sufficient to justify an administrative agency finding that [the] fill would do damage to the ecology or marine life on the bottom." We hold that nothing in the statutory structure compels the Secretary to close his eyes to all that others see or think they see. The establishment was entitled, if not required, to consider ecological factors and, being persuaded by them, to deny that which might have been granted routinely five, ten, or fifteen years ago before man's explosive increase made all, including Congress, aware of civilization's potential destruction from breathing its own polluted air and drinking its own infected water and the immeasurable loss from a silent-spring-like disturbance of nature's economy. We reverse.

Id. at 200–01.

10. 33 C.F.R. § 329.12(a)(2).

The ordinary high water mark, which defines federal jurisdiction in nontidal water is not so easily determined. As defined by regulation,

> [t]he "ordinary high water mark" on non-tidal rivers is the line on the shore established by the fluctuations of water and indicated by physical characteristics such as a clear, natural line impressed on the bank; shelving; changes in the character of soil; destruction of terrestrial vegetation; the presence of litter and debris; or other appropriate means that consider the characteristics of the surrounding areas.[11]

Because of the definitional complexity of section 10, setting jurisdiction in nontidal lakes and rivers (whose shore areas are often classified as wetlands) is accomplished by using eyewitness accounts, photographs, and surveys of biological and physical data.[12]

One important land use aspect of section 10 jurisdiction concerns artificial canals. Real estate developers have used these canals for more than a decade to attract buyers looking for "waterfront" property with lake or ocean access. These canals often run into section 10 problems when constructed within tidal areas.[13] Greater jurisdictional uncertainties occur when canals are constructed in inland waters not subject to tidal flow.[14]

A favorite tactic of developers to escape section 10 jurisdiction is to build a series of unconnected canals.[15] Unconnected canals are not "navigable" and are thus not regulated by section 10. These canals invariably become connected, allowing ocean or lake access, through somewhat mysterious activities, usually undertaken late at night with the aid of bulldozers and draglines. Indeed, these canals are occasionally opened up by environmental officials worried about the adverse ecological effects resulting from stagnant water.

While this activity still occurs,[16] a section 10 violation was found in the washing out of an earthen plug (during a heavy storm) that separat-

---

11. Id., § 329.11(a)(1). Nontidal waters are subject to fluctuation based on rain fall, topography, and other factors in a complex fashion. Calculations of water levels in a tidally dominated system, on the other hand, are by no means simple but are at least related to the mathematically predictable nature of tidal waves.

12. See, e.g, United States v. Cameron, 466 F.Supp. 1099, 1111 (M.D.Fla.1978). In examining the admissibility of extensive survey data introduced by the government, the court recognized that

> the ordinary high water line is not readily susceptible to a uniform and precise definition which will provide guidance for each and every case. Rather, the term is best regarded as a concept which denotes the point at which the bed of a lake or river ceases and the shore or fast lands begins, a point which may be capa-

ble of proof by a variety of methods depending upon the facts and circumstances of the particular case.

Among the available methods the court noted are the use of a clear natural line of changing physical characteristics, biological changes, or upon reliable water elevation data. Id.

13. See United States v. Sexton Cove Estates, 526 F.2d 1293 (5th Cir.1976).

14. See National Wildlife Federation v. Alexander, 613 F.2d 1054, 1066 (D.C.Cir. 1979), appeal after remand 665 F.2d 390 (D.C.Cir.1981) (§ 10 held not to apply).

15. United States v. Sexton Cove Estates, 526 F.2d 1293 (5th Cir.1976) (§ 10 jurisdiction does not include unconnected canals).

16. United States v. Hanna, 19 Env't Rep.Cas. (BNA) 1068 (D.S.C.1983).

ed the developer's canal from a navigable water. Because the violation occurred when the plug washed out, not in the building the canal,[17] the case may not be very persuasive precedent in light of the millions of dollars to be made in selling waterfront property. It seems that to find a section 10 violation in this kind of ditch digging, it will take a court willing to find a violation based on the developer's intent. While certainly possible, intent is not an easy thing to prove.

§ 11.11   Section 404 of the Clean Water Act

A. *Corps of Engineers' 404 Jurisdiction*

While section 10 of the Rivers and Harbors Act gave some limited protection to certain wetlands under the "navigable waters" rubric,[1] it was not until the passage of section 404 of the Federal Water Pollution Control Act[2] in 1972 that wetlands were protected as valuable entities unto themselves.[3] The Corps of Engineers jurisdiction under section 404 over dredge and fill activities is extended to "waters of the United States."[4] The legislative history of the Act indicates congressional intent that the term be given the broadest constitutional interpretation unencumbered by agency determinations which would have been made or may be made for administrative purposes. The following summarizes the Corps' definition of "waters of the United States:"

1) all waters which are currently used, or were used in the past, or may be susceptible to use in interstate commerce including waters subject to the ebb and flow of the tide;

2) all interstate wetlands;

3) all other waters such as intrastate lakes, rivers, streams mudflats, sandflats, wetlands, sloughs, prairie potholes, wet mead-

---

17. Id. at 1077.

§ 11.11

1. The Rivers and Harbors Act of 1899 is discussed supra § 11.10. With the advent of § 404 of the Clean Water Act (discussed infra), jurisdiction under § 10 of the Rivers and Harbors Act is exercised less frequently. This is because § 404 has a much broader geographic reach. However, § 10 is still useful in situations where, for instance, a § 404 exemption applies and § 10 is the only protection left. See, e.g., Save Our Sound Fisheries Association v. Callaway, 387 F.Supp. 292, 305 (D.R.I.1974).

2. Pub.L.No. 92–500, § 404, 86 Stat. 816 (1972) (codified at 33 U.S.C.A. § 1344). Since the 1977 amendments to the FWPCA, Clean Water Act of 1977, Pub.L.No. 95–217, § 67, 91 Stat. 1566 (amending 33 U.S.C.A. § 1344), the Act has been known as the Clean Water Act. Further discussion of the

Clean Water Act's impact on land use planning is discussed in § 11.5 of this chapter. See generally, W. Rodgers, Environmental Law § 4.6 (2nd ed.1994).

3. One study indicates that § 404 reduced the annual destruction of wetlands by half-from 660,000 acres per year to 330,-000 acres per year in 1981. Supposedly, this reduction was accomplished without unreasonable moratoria on development. Comment, Corps Recasts § 404 Permit Program, Braces for Political, Legal Skirmishes, 13 Envtl.L.Rep. 10129 (May 1983).

4. 33 U.S.C.A. § 1144 provides the authority for the Secretary of the Army to issue permits after notice and hearing for the discharge of dredged or fill material into the "navigable waters" at specified disposal sites. However, 33 U.S.C.A. § 1162(7) defines "navigable waters" to mean "the waters of the United States including the territorial seas."

ows, playa lakes, or natural ponds, the use, degradation or destruction of which could affect interstate or foreign commerce;

4) all impoundments of waters otherwise defined as waters of the United States under the definition;

5) tributaries of waters in paragraphs (1) and (4);

6) the territorial seas;

7) wetlands adjacent to waters identified in paragraphs (1) through (6);

8) waters of the United States do not include prior converted cropland.

Number 3 above is particularly important. It states that section 404 covers not only those water bodies suitable for navigation under section 10 of the Rivers and Harbors Act, but almost any wetland area in the nation if injury to it could "affect interstate commerce."

In the seminal case of United States v. Holland,[5] a federal court found section 404's broad definition of federally controlled waters to be within commerce clause authority. The court stated:

> Congress and the courts have become aware of the lethal effect pollution has on all organisms. Weakening of any of the life support systems bodes disaster for the rest of the interrelated life forms. To recognize this and yet hold that pollution does not affect interstate commerce unless committed in navigable waters below the mean high water line would be contrary to reason. Congress is not limited by the "navigable waters" test in its authority to control pollution under the commerce clause.[6]

To ensure enforcement of section 404's congressional mandate, the federal courts have forced the Corps of Engineers to accept and police their jurisdictional authority. The Corps had first avoided this responsibility by promulgating regulations giving it authority only over navigable waters below the mean high water line. These regulations were struck down in Natural Resources Defense Council, Inc. v. Callaway,[7] where the court found the Corps' self-limitation an unlawful act in derogation of their responsibilities under section 404. Thus, the above eight categories of "waters of the United States" is a judicially imposed interpretation of congressional intent factored through the Corps' rulemaking process.[8]

---

5. 373 F.Supp. 665 (M.D.Fla.1974).

6. Id. at 673.

7. 392 F.Supp. 685 (D.D.C.1975).

8. The expansive jurisdiction of the Corps under § 404 is under broad attack by special interests. They claim the present jurisdiction goes beyond congressional intent and that it usurps state authority. Additionally, even though states are authorized to assume § 404 authority, 33 U.S.C.A. § 1144(g), only Michigan and New Jersey have been delegated Section 404 permitting authority. In part, the reason for this lack of state enthusiasm is the difficulty in meeting the statutory criteria and the lack of incentive to do so; no funding is authorized. See American Bar Ass'n, Concerning the Use of Water Related Lands: Flood Hazard Areas, Mudflows and Wetlands, at J–3 (1982). Attempts were made in the 97th Congress to limit § 404 jurisdiction, but were not successful. See S. 773, H.R. 383, H.R. 393, and H.R. 3962, 97th Cong., 1st Sess. (1981).

Once implemented, these definitions were found to cover up to sixty percent of all U.S. wetlands.[9]

Upon assuming such inclusive jurisdiction, the Corps was faced with the common problem of defining wetlands. The eventually-agreed-on definition is:

> [T]hose areas that are inundated or saturated by surface or ground water at a frequency and duration sufficient to support, and that under normal circumstances do support, a prevalence of vegetation typically adapted for life in saturated soil conditions. Wetlands generally include swamps, marshes, bogs, and similar areas.[10]

B. Discharge of Dredged Materials

Through Section 404, the Corps regulates the discharge of dredged or fill materials. The Corps defines the "discharge of dredged material as ... any addition of dredged material into, including any redeposit of dredged material within, the waters of the United States."[11] Dredged material is defined as any material that is excavated or dredged from waters of the United States.[12] Fill material is defined as any material used to replace an aquatic area with dry land.[13]

Activities that do not involve discharges covered by Section 404 are not regulated by the Corps even if they have negative effects on wetlands.[14] However, the Corps' definition of discharge has been expanded. Its definition includes landclearing activities that result in an incidental redeposit of wetland material.[15] However, landclearing that does not use mechanized equipment or involves the cutting of vegetation without disturbing the root system is not subject to regulation.[16]

C. Statutory Exemptions from Section 404

Section 404 applies to the discharge of dredge or fill material and dredging and draining. It does not cover any wastewater or pollutant discharged for waste disposal purposes.[17] Certain dredge or fill activities are specifically exempted by statute. Those include the discharge of dredged or fill material from "normal" farming, silviculture, ranching

---

9. See Note, The Wetlands Controversy: A Coastal Concern Washes Inland, 52 Notre Dame Law Rev. 1015, 1017 (1977).

10. 33 C.F.R. § 328.3(b). Also see 40 C.F.R. § 230.3(T). Under present practice, both the U.S. Fish and Wildlife Service and the Corps will inspect low-lying areas to determine if contemplated activities would be sufficient to trigger § 404 permitting. For cases examining Corps wetland jurisdiction under this definition, see United States v. DeFelice, 641 F.2d 1169 (5th Cir.1981), cert. denied 454 U.S. 940, 102 S.Ct. 474, 70 L.Ed.2d 247 (1981); Bayou Des Familles Development Corp. v. United States Corps of Engineers, 541 F.Supp. 1025 (E.D.La. 1982); Bayou St. John Improvement Association v. Sands, 13 ELR 20011, 1982 WL 17499 (E.D.La.1982); Avoyelles Sportsmen's

League, Inc. v. Marsh, 715 F.2d 897 (5th Cir.1983).

11. 33 C.F.R. § 323.2(d)(1).

12. Id. § 323.2(c).

13. Id. § 323.2(e). Also see 33 C.F.R. § 323.2(f).

14. See United States v. Pozsgai, 999 F.2d 719 (3d Cir.1993), cert. denied 510 U.S. 1110, 114 S.Ct. 1052, 127 L.Ed.2d 373 (1994).

15. 33 C.F.R. § 323.2(d)(1)(iii).

16. Id. § 323.2(d)(2)(ii).

17. Id. § 323.2(d)(2)(i). Pollutant discharge is covered by § 402(a) of the Clean Water Act, discussed supra at § 11.5.

and other specified activities, usually of a temporary or emergency nature.[18] However, if land has not been farmed for so long that drainage is necessary, then the exemption does not apply.[19]

These exceptions do not apply if the activity results in changing navigable waters to a new use or if circulation of the affected waters is changed or reduced. In Avoyelles Sportsmen's League, Inc. v. Alexander (Avoyelles I),[20] these exemptions were construed narrowly in a challenge brought under section 404 concerning an operation converting wetland forest to agricultural use. The court reasoned the exemption for farming applied only to ongoing activity and not the type of clearing operation (hardwood wetland to soybean fields) in dispute. The court concluded that the "normal farming" exemption from section 404 does not extend to projects that convert wetlands to dry lands.[21]

D. *Mitigation*

Although a developer may be delighted when a dredge and fill permit is granted, the process many times is not over. The national goal endorsed by the Corps is for a "no net loss of wetlands."[22] Therefore the Corps may require changes to the plans of a project and will usually require some kind of mitigation to offset or reduce the adverse impacts to wetlands.

The Corps will consider three methods of mitigation. They include: avoidance, minimization, and compensation. In evaluating the appropriate form of mitigation, the Corps will first determine if avoiding negative adverse impacts to wetlands is altogether possible.[23] If all out avoidance is not possible, then the Corps will determine if the adverse impacts can be minimized. This may require alterations of the development plans.

The last resort, and perhaps the most controversial is the use of compensatory mitigation. Compensatory mitigation involves the creation of new wetlands, rehabilitation of degraded wetlands, or the conservation of existing functional wetlands. Generally, compensatory mitigation must take place within the watershed where the adverse impacts were caused. The amount of mitigation depends upon the nature of the mitigation. Generally, one to one ratios are the minimum. For example, for each acre of wetlands destroyed, another acre of wetlands must be created, rehabilitated or preserved. The ratios differ according to the

18. 33 U.S.C.A. § 1144(f).

19. 33 C.F.R. § 323.4(a)(1)(ii).

20. 473 F.Supp. 525 (W.D.La.1979). Also see 33 U.S.C. § 1144(f)(1)(b).

21. Id. at 534–35. Any type of fill or dredge material discharge, even those de minimis in nature, are subject to § 404. See id. at 532. See also Minnehaha Creek Watershed District v. Hoffman, 597 F.2d 617 (8th Cir.1979); United States v. Carter, 12 ELR 20682, 1982 WL 17509 (S.D.Fla.1982); J. Juergensmeyer & J. Wadley, Agricultural Law § 23.3 (1982).

22. See Memorandum of Agreement Between EPA and Dept. of Army Concerning the Determination of Mitigation Under the Clean Water Action Section 404(b)(1), Guidelines, 55 Fed. Reg. 9210, 9211 (March 12, 1990).

23. 40 C.F.R. § 230.10(a) & (d). Also see Memorandum of Agreement Between EPA and Dept. of Army Concerning the Determination of Mitigation Under the Clean Water Action Section 404(b)(1), Guidelines, 55 Fed. Reg. 9210, 9211 (March 12, 1990).

type of mitigation used. In cases where wetlands are created, it may be required that two or three acres be created for every acre destroyed.

Mitigation banking is another approach to mitigating adverse impacts to wetlands. Under this system, third parties either create, restore, or acquire functional wetlands. The third party then sells mitigation credits to developers who need them to compensate for adversely affecting wetlands caused by their development. Generally, as in compensatory mitigation, the mitigation bank must be located within the watershed where the adverse impacts occur. The advantage to this form of mitigation is that the third party is usually more knowledgeable about wetland creation and preservation than most developers and this leads to more successful mitigation projects.

E. General Permits

One potential way around the individual permit system is the use of a general permit.[24] General permits may be issued by the Corps of Engineers under section 404 for activities with minimal adverse environmental effects, both separately and cumulatively.[25] These permits may be issued on a state, regional, or nationwide basis and activities so permitted generally do not require individual permits.[26] Whether general permits actually relax the paperwork requirement for wetlands development is problematic.[27] It is known that the permit requirements are very expensive due to the quantity of scientific data needed. Because of that expense, outside of large corporate interests, more developers will only estimate the effect of their activities on the wetlands environment. They often only discover that effect when sued by the Corps for a section 404 violation.[28]

F. Individual Permits

Individual permits are required when discharges are not exempt or are not permitted by a general permit. The individual permitting process itself is currently based on statutory and regulatory guidelines covering and promulgated by both the Corps of Engineers and the Environmental Protection Agency.[29] When the Corps receives an application, the proposed activity is initially reviewed to see if it is in "the public interest."[30] Factors considered include conservation, economics, aesthetics, fish and wildlife values and general environmental concerns, among others.[31] A wetlands review is then conducted by the Corps.[32] The regulatory pre-

---

24. See generally 33 C.F.R. § 330.

25. 33 U.S.C.A. § 1144(e)(1).

26. Nationwide permits may be for specific discharges in any location or for discharges in a certain area. The permits may also be subject to various conditions imposed by the Corps of Engineers.

27. For an opinion that general permits are now the "Jekyll and Hyde" feature of § 404, creating more confusion and uncertainty than under the strictly individual permit system, see Parish & Morgan, Histo-

ry, Practice and Emerging Problems of Wetlands Regulation: Reconsidering Section 404 of the Clean Water Act, 27 Land & Water Rev. 43, 57–60 (1982).

28. Id. at 59–60.

29. For Corps regulations, see generally 33 C.F.R. § 325.

30. 33 C.F.R. § 320.4(a)(1).

31. Id. § 320.4(a)(2).

32. Id. § 320.4(j).

sumption is that wetlands are vital areas that constitute a productive and valuable public resource, the unnecessary alteration or destruction of which should be discouraged as contrary to the public interest.[33] If an activity is determined by the Corps not to be in the "public interest," a permit will not be issued.[34]

Even if an activity is found not to be against the "public interest," the Corps must still follow certain permitting guidelines[35] set out by the Environmental Protection Agency as authorized by section 404(b).[36] If proposed activity would cause or contribute to "significant degradation" of waters of the United States no permit may be issued. Effects leading to a finding of significant degradation include:

(1) Significantly adverse effects of the discharge of pollutants on human health or welfare, including but not limited to effects on municipal water supplies, plankton, fish, shellfish, wildlife, and special aquatic sites.

(2) Significant adverse effects of the discharge of pollutants on life stages of aquatic life and other wildlife dependent on aquatic ecosystems. . . .

(3) Significantly adverse effects of the discharge of pollutants on aquatic ecosystem diversity, productivity, and stability. . . .

(4) Significantly adverse effects of discharge of pollutants on recreational, aesthetic, and economic values.[37]

Section 404(b)(1) dictates that the filling of wetlands cannot occur if there is a practicable alternative available with less adverse impacts.[38] An

---

33. Id. § 320.4(b)(1). Wetlands considered to perform functions important to public interest include:

(i) Wetlands which serve significant natural biological functions, including food chain production, general habitat and nesting, spawning, rearing and resting sites for aquatic or land species;

(ii) Wetlands set aside for study of the aquatic environment or as sanctuaries or refuges;

(iii) Wetlands the destruction or alteration of which would affect detrimentally natural drainage characteristics, sedimentation patterns, salinity distribution, flushing characteristics, current patterns, or other environmental characteristics;

(iv) Wetlands which are significant in shielding other areas from wave action, erosion, or storm damage. Such wetlands are often associated with barrier beaches, islands, reefs and bars;

(v) Wetlands which serve as valuable storage areas for storm and flood waters;

(vi) Wetlands which are ground water discharge areas that maintain minimum baseflows important to aquatic resources and those which are prime natural recharge areas;

(vii) Wetlands which serve significant water purification functions; and

(viii) Wetlands which are unique in nature or scarce in quantity to the region or local area. Id.

34. The Eleventh Circuit has ruled that neither § 404 of the Clean Water Act nor the due process clause requires the Corps to give an applicant a trial-type hearing before denying a dredge and fill permit. Buttrey v. United States, 690 F.2d 1170, 13 ELR 20085 (C.A. 5 1982).

35. The general purpose of the EPA's guidelines is to "restore and maintain the chemical, physical, and biological integrity of waters of the United States through the control of discharges or dredged or fill material." 40 C.F.R. § 230.1(a).

36. Id. § 230.10(b), (c).

37. Id. § 230.10(c).

38. 40 C.F.R. § 230.10(a).

applicant has the burden to show that there were no practicable alternatives.[39] In evaluating practicable alternatives, availability, cost, logistics, and technology are considered. Therefore practicable alternatives must be both feasible and available.

Section 404(b)(1) also distinguishes water dependent activities from those that are not. Non-water dependent activities are those activities that do not have to be located on or around water, such as housing or office facilities. For non-water dependent activities there is a presumption of alternatives.[40]

Furthermore, no permit may be issued where the discharge of dredged or fill material violates any state water quality standard, toxic effluent standard, jeopardizes a threatened or endangered species, or harms a marine sanctuary.[41] When reviewing a permit application possibly affecting a threatened or endangered species, the Corps will consult interested state wildlife agencies as well as the United States Fish and Wildlife Service.[42] If no exemption exists, a finding by the Secretary of the Interior concerning the discharge's impact on the species or their habitat will be considered final by the Corps.[43]

Both state and federal fish and wildlife services can be of considerable importance in dredge and fill permit applications. The Corps must give "great weight" to these agencies' determinations when wildlife may be affected by development in a wetland area.[44] While the Corps may ignore state or federal wildlife agency recommendations, the Environmental Protection Agency may block any permit authorization by the Corps.[45]

As can easily be seen, the regulatory roadblocks to wetlands alteration are formidable indeed.[46] However, only a third of the process has been completed. State and local permits must also be acquired. Individual states and localities may have stricter guidelines than those followed by the Corps. They may also be more lenient, but since one has to gather all permits, state and federal, that supposed leniency will not matter if the Corps says no.

39. Section 404(b)(1). Also see Bersani v. U.S.A. EPA, 489 U.S. 1089, 109 S.Ct. 1556, 103 L.Ed.2d 859 (1989).

40. 40 C.F.R. § 230.10(a)(3).

41. Id. § 230.10(b).

42. Id. § 230.10(b)(3).

43. Id. § 230.30(c).

44. 33 C.F.R. § 230.4(c). The Fish and Wildlife Coordination Act also requires the Corps to give these agencies' reports "full consideration." 16 U.S.C.A. § 662(b).

45. 33 U.S.C.A. § 1144(c). EPA Regional Administrators may deny, restrict the use of, or withdraw particular sites if they have reason to believe that an alteration is likely to result in significant loss or damage to fisheries, shellfish, wildlife habitat or recreation areas. Id.

46. For a complete analysis of the federal permitting process under § 404, see Parish & Morgan, supra note 27, at 68–73. Section 404 roadblocks may, in addition to the withdrawn 1982 amendments, be further lessened by the new memoranda of agreements (MOAs) the Corps has with the Departments of Interior, Agriculture, Commerce, Transportation and the EPA. Environmental groups and some politicians see these MOAs as removing environmental groups' input into the decisionmaking process. See Comment, supra note 3, at 10134.

§ 11.12   Wetlands Protection: An Uncertain Future

Even after two decades of progress in controlling wetlands destruction, the future of federal and state regulatory programs is unclear. Section 404 is under attack from both private development interests and the federal government itself.[1] While state programs are becoming more numerous,[2] federal funding cutbacks and various Proposition 13–type state revenue restrictions are making it more difficult to develop and implement state wetlands regulations.

Coastal wetlands programs have generally been more successful than inland ones.[3] Once public awareness of inland wetland values catches up with the known worth of saltwater marshes, the protection offered may balance out. Coupled with that perception problem, however, is the need to convince state and national legislatures and courts that wetlands regulation does not prevent development in the broad sense.[4] The aggravations of paperwork are certainly there, but only a minute percentage of development permits nationally are denied due to wetlands considerations.[5] Yet until public perceptions concerning wetlands change to reflect the modern knowledge of wetlands value-and it is changing-true wetlands protection, necessarily coordinated at federal, state, and local levels, will not occur.

VII.   LAND USE AND ENVIRONMENTALLY SENSITIVE LANDS—COASTAL ZONES

§ 11.13   Coastal Zone Values

The intense population pressures exerted upon coastal areas combined with their inherent fragility make them a microcosm of land use practice and theory. In recent years, the tides of coastal regulation have dramatically changed. Unfettered construction in the coastal zone has been greatly curtailed due to issues ranging from protection of sea turtles to prevention of erosion. Nonetheless, the battle will inevitably continue since it has been estimated that by the year 2010, 53.6 percent of the nation's population will reside within fifty miles of the coast, with some individual state population percentages, such as Florida's, rising to

---

§ 11.12

1. See Comment, Corps Recasts § 404 Permit Program, Braces for Political, Legal Skirmishes, 13 Envtl.L.Rep. 10129 (May 1983); M. Blumm, The End of Environmental Law? Libertarian Property, Natural Law, and the Just Compensation Clause in the Federal Circuit, 25 Envtl.L. 171 (1995); R. Ausness, Regulatory Takings and Wetland Protection in the Post–Lucas Era, 30 Land & Water L.Rev. 349 (1995).

2. See National Conference of State Legislatures, Land Management: Sustaining Resource Values 198 (Oct.1983).

3. Dawson, Wetlands Regulation, 6 Zoning & Planning L.Rep. 164 (1983).

4. Id.

5. Id. Environmental interest groups contend that § 404 itself is neither unreasonably burdensome nor time consuming. In fact, the Corps' own study tends to show that wetlands regulation delays cost only 0.7% of the total price of even controversial projects. See Comment, supra note 1, at 10133. See generally, The Conservation Foundation, Protecting America's Wetlands: AN Action Agenda, The Final Report of the National Wetlands Policy Forum (1988).

over 99 percent.[1]

Coastal zones are actually comprised of two separate types of environmentally sensitive lands. Wetlands, in the form of estuarine areas, form a substantial percentage of the coastal zone. While wetlands protection in general has already been discussed, it should be noted that many states distinguish between inland wetlands and coastal wetlands.[2] Virtually all coastal states protect estuarine wetlands through coastal zone management programs or comprehensive plans.[3] Only a few protect inland wetlands as such.[4]

The other environmentally sensitive aspect of coastal zones is the substance most often identified with the coast—sand. Sand bars and dunes play an important role in protecting inland areas from flooding and coastal areas from severe storm damage and erosion.[5] That role, however, can only be played when sufficient vegetation is present to secure the sand from undue erosion.[6] Coastal construction tends to hasten the natural erosion rate.

It has been estimated that 90 percent of the nation's beaches are eroding.[7] The Atlantic coast has receded an average of two to three feet per year, while the Gulf coast has receded an average of four to five feet annually.[8] To further exacerbate the problems of erosion, global warming will result in an accelerated sea level rise. The sea level could rise by up to a foot in the next century.[9]

Erosion has disastrous effects on coastal property. The combined effects of erosion and sea level rise will result in many coastal communities being subject to "inundation, increased frequency and severity of

§ 11.13

1. Steven A. Edwards, "Estimates of Future Demographic Changes in the Coastal Zone" 17 Coastal Management 229, 236–37 (1989). Although the 451 coastal counties in the United States account for only 20 percent of the nation's total land area, from 1960 to 1970 the populations in these areas increased by 13 million, contrasted with 11 million in the rest of the country. Perrin Q. Dargan III, "Staking Out New Territory: CZMA Reathorization Amendments" 9 Natural Resources & Envt. 32 (1995).

2. See, e.g., Burrows v. Keene, 121 N.H. 590, 432 A.2d 15 (1981) (distinguishes between "unique" value of saltwater marshes and all other inland wetlands). See also supra § 11.9.

3. For instance, Florida requires that all local governments in coastal areas integrate a coastal element into every local governments comprehensive plan. Fla. Stat. Ann. § 163.3177(6)(g). Florida also has a specific statute pertaining to coastal management and comprehensive planning. Fla. Stat.Ann. § 163.3178.

4. See supra § 11.12. In part, the greater protection given coastal wetlands

may be due to the fact that the commercial value of estuaries has long been recognized—the great majority of commercially valuable fish and shellfish spend part of their lives in estuarine areas. Maloney & O'Donnell, Drawing the Line at the Ocean Front: The Role of Construction Setback Lines in Regulating Development of the Coastal Zone, 30 U.Fla.L.Rev. 383, 389 (1978).

5. See, e.g., McNulty v. Town of Indialantic, 727 F.Supp. 604 (M.D.Fla.1989).

6. National Conference of State Legislatures, Land Management; Sustaining Resource Values 66 (Oct. 1983).

7. Dennis J. Hwang, Shoreline setback Regulations and the Takings Analysis, 13 U. Haw.L.Rev. 1, 2 (1991).

8. Id.

9. Hwang, supra note 7 at 2. "A one foot rise in sea level could result in an estimated shoreline retreat of 75 feet in parts of New Jersey, 200 feet along the coast of South Carolina and 1,000 feet along some parts of the Florida coast." Id.

storms and wave surge, increased rates of shoreline erosion, wetlands inundation and recession, modification of dynamic coastal physical properties, and damage to or reduction of shoreline protective structures and facilities."[10]

Thus, the concern of coastal zone management is that development not unduly interfere with natural coastal processes. Where needed, moratoria are placed on building permits. More commonly, coastal setback lines, density restrictions and construction standards are established. Just how and through what authority coastal zone regulation is accomplished is the subject of the following section.

§ 11.14 Legislative Responses to Coastal Management Needs

A. Coastal Zone Management Act

The National Coastal Zone Management Act of 1972 (CZMA)[1] was the nation's first attempt to develop a comprehensive coastal zone protection plan. Shoreline regulation was historically a local concern until coastal resources (such as offshore oil and gas) became economically and politically important. Such resources led to a federal/state conflict over jurisdiction and revenue collection. The CZMA was a congressional attempt to defuse the growing polarization between the federal government and the states over these resource management issues. As such, the Coastal Act relies on joint federal/state cooperation and funding.

The CZMA's genesis came from a two-year presidential commission study of maritime resources published in 1969. Commonly called the Stratton Commission, the report of the Commission on marine science, engineering and resources[2] highlighted the importance of shoreline areas. It noted that while less than ten percent of the country's land area could be considered coastal, over forty percent of the nation's population lived near the coast (at that time) with the trend toward ever greater growth. The Commission recommended a federally supported, state administered Coastal Management Act. The resulting CZMA was enacted after four years of Congressional attention on October 27, 1972.

The CZMA proceeds under a two-tiered process whereby states obtain federal financial assistance for coastal zone protection by

> 1) developing a comprehensive, long-range coastal management plan meeting federal statutory criteria; and

> 2) getting approval for that plan followed by state implementation.[3]

---

10. Paul Klain and Marc Hershman, Response of Coastal Zone Management Programs to Sea Level Rise in The United States, 18 Coastal Management 143, 143 (1990).

§ 11.14

1. 16 U.S.C.A. § 1451 et seq.

2. Report of the Comm'n on Marine Science, Engineering & Resources (Jan. 1969).

3. Natural Resources Defense Council, Land Use Controls in the United States 100 (Moss ed. 1977). Chapter 6, beginning on page 98, is a comprehensive and readable

To meet the CZMA's requirements for matching funds, the state program must comply with the act's statutory coastal management program in the judgment of the Secretary of Commerce.[4] The pieces of the federal pie each coastal state seeks are the CZMA's grants covering development and implementation of state coastal programs. The program development grants (which help states devise their plans) are known as section 305 grants, and the state implementation grants (which help put the plans into practice) are called section 306 grants. By 1990, most of the thirty-five coastal states and territories had passed statutory measures to protect coastal areas and twenty-nine had programs approved under CZMA.[5] These states and territories comprise over ninety percent of the nation's coastline, including the Great Lakes.[6]

The structure and scope of coastal zone management programs vary widely from state to state. Congress intended this diversity as a means of reflecting individual state concerns. Each state plan must, however, include the following:

1) an identification of the boundaries of the coastal zone subject to the management program;

2) a definition of what shall constitute permissible land and water uses within the coastal zone which have a direct and significant impact on the coastal waters;

3) an inventory and designation of areas of particular concern within the coastal zone;

4) an identification of the means by which the state proposes to exert control over the land and water uses referred to in paragraph 2) including a listing of relevant constitutional provisions, legislative enactments, regulations and judicial decisions;

5) broad guidelines on priority of uses in particular areas, including specifically those uses of lowest priority;

6) a description of the organizational structure proposed to implement the management program, including the responsibility and interrelationships of local, areawide, state, regional, and interstate agencies in the management process;

7) a definition of the term "beach" and a planning process for the protection of, and access to, public beaches and other public coastal areas of environmental, recreational, historical, aesthetic, ecological, or cultural value;

discussion of the history and policies of the Coastal Zone Management Act.

4. The U.S. Secretary of Commerce is assigned the responsibility of administering the Act's provisions. That responsibility has been delegated to the National Oceanic and Atmosphere Administration (NOAA), one of the agencies of the Commerce Department. An office of Coastal Zone Management has

been created within NOAA to implement the Act.

5. Perrin Q. Dargan III, Staking Out New Territory: CZMA Reauthorization Amendments, 9 Natural Resources & Envt. 32 (1995).

6. Nat'l Conference of State Legislatures, Land Management; Sustaining Resource Values 203 (Oct.1983).

8) a planning process for energy facilities likely to be located in, or which may significantly affect, the coastal zone, including, but not limited to, a process for anticipating and managing the impacts from such facilities;

9) a planning process for (A) assessing the effects of shoreline erosion (however caused), and (B) studying and evaluating ways to control, or lessen the impact of, such erosion, and to restore areas adversely affected by such erosion.[7]

Importantly, state programs must have viable coordinating mechanisms with local governments and designate a specific state agency to administer the program.[8] States with approved programs are given "federal consistency" authority which assures that federal actions are consistent with state coastal management programs.[9]

Section 307 of the CZMA provides for federal/state consistency. The section requires that activities affecting the coastal zone supported or conducted by federal agencies must be consistent with approved state programs to the "maximum extent practicable." Of more importance to the private developer is the subsection providing that private activities significantly affecting land and water uses in the coastal zone and which require federal licenses and permits must be consistent with the state's approved program.[10] The state must approve the applicant's certification of consistency for the federal license or permit to be granted. However, a state's determination of inconsistency may be overturned by the Secretary of Commerce if he establishes that consistency does in fact exist.[11] Finally, federal agencies may not approve state or local applications for federal assistance for activities significantly affecting the coastal zone if they are inconsistent with the state's approved coastal management program.[12]

The entire CZMA was reviewed by Congress in 1980 to determine whether it should be reauthorized. The result was a series of amend-

---

7. 16 U.S.C.A. § 1455(d)(2). It is worth noting that the definition of a coastal management plan in the CZMA tracks the definition of a plan in model planning legislation adopted by the American Law Institute. See D. Mandelker, Environment and Equity 138 (1981).

8. See H.R.Rep.No. 97–628, 97th Cong., 2d Sess. 24 (1982) (report of Congressman Jones of North Carolina of the Committee on Merchant Marine and Fisheries concerning the Ocean and Coastal Resources Management and Development Block Grant Act).

9. 16 U.S.C.A. § 1456(c). By 1990, twenty-nine of the thirty-five coastal states had federally approved coastal zone management programs. See Dargan, supra note 5.

10. 16 U.S.C.A. § 1456(c)(3). In American Petroleum Institute v. Knecht, 609 F.2d 1306 (9th Cir.1979), the court considered the question of just how specific state land use control policies in state coastal management programs must be. The court rejected petitioner's position that state programs must be sufficiently specific to inform those desiring to develop in coastal areas of the rules and conditions they must comply with. The court held that the CZMA does not require "detailed criteria" that private developers can rely on without "interaction between the relevant state agencies and the user." Id. at 1312. The court quoted with approval language of the district court suggesting that the CZMA did not require a "zoning map" committing the state before it received the exact proposal of a private developer. Id.

11. 16 U.S.C.A. § 1456(v)(3).

12. Id. at § 1456(d).

ments referred to as the Coastal Management Improvement Act of 1980.[13] Greater clarity in the policy behind the CZMA was made through additions in the statement of congressional findings (found in section 302). These policies again reflect a strong desire to manage and protect coastal resources through joint federal/state cooperation. The resources themselves, from fisheries to defense installation sitings, are spelled out in considerable detail.[14] The section 306 implementation grant process was revised so that each complying state must use a greater proportion of the grant money (up to thirty percent) to implement these policies spelled out by Congress in section 302. The entire program was also reauthorized for five years.[15]

The 1980 amendments included a new section of activities entitled the "Coastal Resource Improvement Program."[16] This may be the most important change made by the 1980 legislation.[17] This section assumed the states were ready to move the CZMA from planning into implementation and management. It provides states with incentives to implement their management programs in view of specific objectives and results. In general, the section gives federal assistance to states in "meeting low-cost construction, land acquisition, and shoreline stabilization costs associated with the designation of areas of preservation and restoration, the revitalization of urban waterfronts and parks, and public access to coastal acres."[18]

Section 306A(b)(1), the preservation subsection, is based on an assumption that through low-cost construction, environmentally sensitive areas could be protected and increased public access established. Such objectives could be reached by building paths through dunes (environmentally sensitive areas in themselves) to channel public access to beach areas. These paths or trails could be accompanied by signs, exhibits, and other "small scale construction programs" complementing a state's coastal zone management program.[19]

In locales already developed, section 306A(a) provides assistance in urban waterfront and port development. The program stresses public access to port areas, rehabilitation of piers, bulkhead restoration and piling removal or replacement to the extent such activities comport with the policies behind the CZMA. Grants under this section could be used to devise urban waterfront redevelopment programs not eligible for any other federal funding.

In 1990, the CZMA was amended again by the Coastal Zone Act

---

13. These amendments are listed in their entirety in Id. § 1451 et seq.

14. Id. § 1452(2).

15. See H.R.Rep.No. 97–628, supra note 8, at 26.

16. 16 U.S.C.A. § 1455a.

17. See H.R.Rep.No. 97–628, supra note 8, at 26.

18. Id.

19. Id. This subsection stresses the "acquisition of fee simple and other interests in land" in order to meet the listed objectives in environmentally sensitive lands.

Reauthorization Amendments (CZARA).[20] The amendments dealt primarily with two issues. The consistency provision was amended to read that "[e]ach Federal agency activity within or outside the coastal zone . . . shall be carried out in a manner which is consistent to the maximum extent practicable with the enforceable policies of approved state management programs."[21] With this amendment, Congress overturned the United States Supreme Court's ruling in Secretary of the Interior v. California.[22] This amendment ensures that all federal activities that affect the coastal zone, whether they take place in or out of the zone, are covered under the consistency provisions.[23]

The other section of the CZARA, Section 6217, addresses the problem of coastal nonpoint source pollution.[24] Each state that has an approved coastal management program is required "to develop and implement management measures for nonpoint source pollution to restore and protect coastal waters, working in close conjunction with other State and local authorities."[25] Each State Coastal Nonpoint Pollution Control Program must contain the following:

1) Identification of land uses which individually or cumulatively may cause or contribute significantly to a degradation of coastal waters;

2) Identification of critical coastal areas adjacent to coastal waters within which any new land uses or substantial expansion of existing land uses shall be subject to management measures;

3) Management measures to implement and to continue revision of additional management measures to maintain water quality standards and to protect designated uses;

4) Provisions for technical and other assistance to local governments and the public for implementing management measures;

5) Opportunities for public participation in all aspects of the program;

6) Mechanisms to improve coordination among State agencies and between State and local officials responsible for land use and environmental programs;

20. See Pub. L. No. 101–508 §§ 6203, 6208(a), 104 Stat. 1388 (1990).

21. 16 U.S.C. § 1456(c)(1)(A) (emphasis added).

22. 464 U.S. 312, 104 S.Ct. 656, 78 L.Ed.2d 496 (1984), on remand 729 F.2d 614 (9th Cir.1984). There, the Department of the Interior rejected California's contentions that federal sale of oil and gas leases in certain OCS tracts off California required a consistency review under § 307(c)(1) of the CZMA. The district court entered summary judgment and the court of appeals affirmed. By a 5–4 vote the Supreme Court held Interior's sale of OCS oil and gas leas-es do not constitute activity "directly affecting" California's coastal zone within § 307(c)(1)'s meaning. Consistency review was thus not required. Justice Stevens delivered a stinging dissent which quite clearly showed that OCS leasing was very much within the consistency domain of the CZMA.

23. Dargan, supra note 5, at 33.

24. Pub. L. No. 101–508, Tit. VI; § 6217, 104 Stat. 1388–314 to 1388–319 (1990).

25. 16 U.S.C. § 1455b(a)(1).

7) A proposal to modify the boundaries of the State Coastal Zone in response to evaluation of whether the State's coastal boundary extends inland to the extent necessary to control the land and water uses that have a significant impact on coastal waters of the state.[26]

The requirement for modification of the coastal boundary under number seven above may result in land use controls reaching further inland than prior to CZARA. The guidelines focus on five specific causes of nonpoint source pollution: 1) agricultural runoff; 2) silvicultural or forestry runoff; 3) urban runoff, including developed and developing areas; 4) marinas and recreational boating; and 5) hydromodification, including channelization, dams, and erosion of streambanks and shorelines.[27]

B. *The Coastal Barrier Resources Act*

The passage of the Coastal Barrier Resources Act (CBRA)[28] in 1982 gives additional protection to coastal zones. Coastal barriers are islands or spits consisting chiefly of sand which have the effect of protecting landward areas from direct wave action.[29] A typical example is Cape Hatterras, North Carolina. Because they consist of unstable sediments and serve as "natural storm protection buffers," coastal barriers are particularly ill suited for development.[30] Yet, by providing financial assistance in the form of subsidies and flood insurance, the federal government actively encouraged coastal barrier development for years.[31] It is the purpose of the Coastal Barrier Resources Act to restrict development through the termination of federal assistance in undeveloped coastal barriers.[32]

The Act is quite simple in its approach. It first sets up a "Coastal Barrier Resources System" consisting of all undeveloped coastal barriers located on the Atlantic and Gulf Coasts.[33] This system is carefully mapped and the boundaries set.[34] With some exceptions,[35] "no new expenditures or new financial assistance may be made available under authority of any federal law for any purpose within the [Coastal Barrier Resource] System."[36] Thus, any state permitted development will have to pay its own way.

In Bostic v. U.S., the Fourth Circuit affirmed the legality of CBRA's denial of federal subsidies.[37] In *Bostic*, plaintiffs challenged the designa-

---

26. 16 U.S.C § 1455b(b).

27. See NOAA & EPA, Coastal Nonpoint Pollution Control Program: Program and Approval Guidance 3 (1993).

28. 16 U.S.C.A. § 3501 et seq.

29. Id. § 3502(1)(A). For purposes of the Act, adjacent wetlands are included in the statutory coverage. Id. § 3502(1)(B).

30. Id. § 3501(a)(3).

31. Id. § 3501(a)(4).

32. See Dawson, Wetlands Regulation, 6 Zoning & Planning L.Rep. 154 (1983).

33. 16 U.S.C.A. § 3503.

34. Id. Boundary modification is made through § 3503(c).

35. These exceptions include energy exploration and exploitation, maintenance of existing channels and roads and necessary military activities. Id. § 3505.

36. Id. § 3504(a).

37. 753 F.2d 1292 (4th Cir.1985).

tion of their property as part of an undeveloped coastal barrier. They claimed that this designation disqualified certain construction on the property for federal flood insurance and denied them substantive due process. The court held that clear statutory language and history suggested that property designated on a map as "an undeveloped coastal barrier" illustrates a clear intent to include that property as such. The court also ruled that the designation bore a rational relation to the Act's objectives since withdrawing federal flood insurance from certain development on less developed portions of particular islands "prevents wasteful subsidies for construction that would not be feasible if developers had recourse only to the private insurance market."[38]

In 1990, the Coastal Barrier Improvement Act (CBIA) amended the Coastal Barrier Resources Act.[39] CBIA added nearly 820,000 new acres, which tripled the acreage under the initial system.[40] Most of these lands were aquatic habitat associated with the original coastal barriers.[41] CBIA also requires the heads of the federal agencies to report and certify compliance directly with the Interior Department and Congressional Committees.[42]

It has been noted that CBRA has several advantages, including: 1) combining environmental protection and federal deficit reduction capabilities; 2) provision of alternatives to property acquisition when funds are limited; 3) avoiding takings claims since denial of subsidies takes away only a privilege and not a right; 4) promotion of State and local land use programs since these entities retain their authority to make decisions about what takes place on CBRA land.[43]

C. Coastal Zone Regulation: An Uncertain Future

Coastal zone protection of environmentally sensitive lands is, as illustrated by the preceding discussions, a complicated process. Federal, state, and local plans, acts, policies, and laws must all be consulted before development may take place in coastal areas. Whether such a mish-mash of competing jurisdictions can reach the desired goal of comprehensive, cohesive, and consistent management has not yet been demonstrated.

With recent federal budget cutbacks and regulatory changes, future coastal management and protection will be more and more a state and local activity. That trend has the possibility of destroying more than a decade of progress in protecting sensitive coastal lands, unless, of course, state and local governments respond to the challenge and provide the funding and expertise needed. Of even greater importance, however, is a fundamental change in attitude. Economic development through an

---

38. Id. at 1294.

39. Pub. L. No. 101–591, 104 Stat. 2931 (1990).

40. Elise Jones, "The Coastal Barrier Resources Act: A Common Cents Approach To Coastal Protection" 21 Envtl.L. 1015, 1048 (1991).

41. Id.

42. 16 U.S.C. § 3506(b). CBIA requires federal agencies to promulgate regulations to assure compliance with CBRA by November 16, 1991.

43. Jones, supra note 40 at 1062–63.

enlarged tax base must be seen as the chimera it really is in environmentally sensitive coastal areas.

VIII. LAND USE AND ENVIRONMENTALLY SENSITIVE LANDS—FLOOD PLAINS

§ 11.15 Flood Plain Use and Abuse

Flood plains are areas adjacent to rivers, streams, or other waterbodies subject to periodic flooding of some degree.[1] They form an important component of a particular geographic area's watershed. A watershed is the land's natural drainage system.[2] Over geologic time, floods are as natural as the river channel itself.[3] The river channel and flood plain combine to form the drainage pathway for each watershed.[4]

Flood plains are of three basic types. The most common are those associated with major rivers whose flooding is characterized by slow water movement over low land gradients, such as the Mississippi and Nile.[5] Because the land is flat, a large amount of flood prone development occurs in this type of flood plain. The other flood plain types are those located in mountain valleys and coastal areas.[6]

While not all flood plain areas are environmentally sensitive, a substantial proportion (usually wetlands and coastal zones) are. Even those areas not normally noted for their environmental value have a sensitivity all their own—if you live on them without precautions they can kill you. Furthermore, every structure built on a flood plain has the effect of increasing the intensity of any given flood, often making flood damage even greater to those areas downstream. Thus, flood plain regulation is a close relative (incestuous, in the case of wetlands and coastal zones) to land use regulations in other, nonhazardous, environmentally sensitive lands.

A. Flood Plain Values

Flood plains serve much the same purposes as wetlands.[7] In fact, many wetlands are part of flood plains. Historically, the most important human flood plain benefit is agricultural.[8] Flood-water deposition of silt and nutrients allowed the Nile and Tigris and Euphrates Rivers to serve as "cradles of civilization."[9] Agricultural practices were designed to

§ 11.15

1. National Science Foundation, A Report on Flood Hazard Mitigation, 250 (Sept. 1980).

2. Kusler & Platt, Physical Characteristics of Flood Plains and Wetlands, Conference on Local Options for Flood Plain and Wetlands Management, at I–32 (Sept.1982). Watersheds are drainage basins formed by geologic and gravitational forces. They form the route for water flowing downhill and can be as narrow as a mountain valley or as wide as a prairie. Id. at I–31.

3. Id. at I–32.

4. Id.

5. Nat'l Conference of State Legislatures, Land Management; Sustaining Resource Values, 63 (Oct. 1983) [hereinafter cited as Nat'l Conference].

6. Id.

7. See supra § 11.9.

8. Kasler & Platt, supra note 2, at I–49.

9. Id. at I–50.

match the rise and fall in floodwaters. When the waters were in normal floodstage, crops were not endangered because they were not yet planted. People were not endangered because they were not so dumb as to build on land subject to yearly flooding. Today, in an unfortunate commentary on our intelligence, there are almost six and one-half million homes built on flood hazard areas in this country.[10]

B. Development in Flood Plains

In contrast to the practices of years gone by, today's society has moved from an agricultural orientation to one divorced from the cycles of the seasons. Residential, commercial, and agricultural development is now widespread in flood plain areas. This development is often due to ignorance or nonchalance concerning flood hazards.[11] Draining, dredging, filling, diking and impoundment building are all used to create habitable land in flood plains. If done with foresight (i.e., building houses on stilts or earth embankments) and away from the most hazardous areas, some development can successfully occur in flood plains. If not, situations as ironic as that found in the Everglades region of South Florida can happen. There, a fifty-mile sheet flow of floodplain water was reduced by development to a twelve-foot wide spillway.[12] Because the Everglades' extremities are bordered with levees and canals to protect residential and agricultural development, the water forced through this spillway is too much for the natural absorption processes of the reduced surface area of the Everglades to accept.[13] Thus, the water management control districts involved must make the choice between destroying Everglades habitat as the water rises or opening up the levees and flooding the developed land.[14]

C. Flood Plain Regulation

Although closely related, flood plain protection is more readily acceptable to most courts than is wetlands regulation.[15] This is probably true because the public hazard of flooding is better understood than the detriment accruing to the public through wetlands destruction.[16] Another reason is that flood plain regulations are the oldest and most extensive of all sensitive land programs.[17]

Flood plain mapping must occur before land use regulations can properly control development there. Once mapped, specific zoning laws can be applied by the appropriate local or state authorities.[18] Mapping reveals to these authorities, among other things, two flood plain areas of note for land use purposes; floodways and flood fringes. Floodways are

10. Id.

11. Id.

12. Nat'l Conference, supra note 5, at 64.

13. Id.

14. Id.

15. Dawson, Wetlands Regulation, 6 Zoning & Planning, L.Rep. (pt. II) 162 (Nov.1983).

16. Id. This is true even though wetlands serve as one of nature's best flood protection devices.

17. J. Kusler, Regulating Sensitive Lands 22 (1980). At least twenty-four states and seventeen thousand local governments have flood plain programs, usually adopted in order to qualify for federal flood insurance. Id.

18. Id. at 23.

the unobstructed stream channel and overbank areas where flooding is most common. Structural development of any sort is generally prohibited there.[19] Flood fringes are adjacent to floodways and are subject to less flooding and less damage (or potential damage) when floods do occur. A variety of land uses are permitted in flood fringe areas provided precautions such as elevation are taken.[20]

The National Flood Insurance Program[21] is a key component in flood plain development.[22] Local governments must have a comprehensive flood plain regulatory plan in order for buildings in the flood plain to get federal flood insurance.[23] Without such insurance, lending institutions and mortgage companies will usually not finance development or support resale of property in flood prone areas.[24]

D. Judicial Reaction to Flood Plain Regulation

Because flood protection is a legitimate police power objective, courts have been very favorable in their reactions to flood plain land use ordinances.[25] For instance, in Turnpike Realty Co. v. Town of Dedham,[26] the court upheld a flood plain ordinance so severely restricting development that the restricted land was reduced in value from $431,000 to $53,000. In Usdin v. State,[27] a New Jersey court upheld a restrictive flood plain ordinance on ecological grounds. In examining the taking issue, the court stated that ecological principles must be balanced with the landowners' rights, and that a proper police power function of the state is to prevent serious ecological harm.[28]

Some cases, while not critical of flood plain regulations in general, have found problems with certain implementations of those regulations. If no real flood danger is proved up at the trial level, a court may be very sympathetic to a landowners' taking plea.[29] Likewise, if *all* pecuniary value of a landowners' property is lost due to flood plain regulations, courts will frequently find a taking.[30] Even if all economic value is

---

19. Id.

20. Id.

21. 42 U.S.C.A. § 4001 et seq.

22. The National Flood Insurance Program has many critics who contend that in practice it has made matters worse. In the 1990s, a number of reforms have been considered by Congress. See Charles T. Griffith, The National Flood Insurance Program: Unattained Purposes, Liability in Contract, and Takings, 35 Wm. & Mary L.Rev. 727 (1994).

23. Nat'l Conference, supra note 5, at 202.

24. Id.

25. See, e.g., Turner v. County of Del Norte, 24 Cal.App.3d 311, 101 Cal.Rptr. 93 (1972); Vartelas v. Water Resources Commission, 146 Conn. 650, 153 A.2d 822 (1959); Iowa Natural Resources Council v. Van Zee, 261 Iowa 1287, 158 N.W.2d 111

(1968); First English Evangelical Lutheran Church of Glendale v. County of Los Angeles, 210 Cal.App.3d 1353, 258 Cal.Rptr. 893 (Cal.App.1989).

26. 362 Mass. 221, 284 N.E.2d 891 (1972), cert. denied 409 U.S. 1108, 93 S.Ct. 908, 34 L.Ed.2d 689 (1973).

27. 173 N.J.Super. 311, 414 A.2d 280 (1980), affirmed 179 N.J.Super. 113, 430 A.2d 949 (1981).

28. Id. at 319, 414 A.2d at 288. See also Saul Jay Singer, Flooding the Fifth Amendment: The National Flood Insurance Program and the "Takings" Clause, 17 B.C. Envtl. Aff. L. Rev. 323, 370 (1990).

29. Sturdy Homes, Inc. v. Township of Redford, 30 Mich.App. 53, 186 N.W.2d 43 (1971).

30. See, e.g., Dooley v. Town Plan & Zoning Commission, 151 Conn. 304, 197 A.2d 770 (1964); Baker v. Planning Board,

destroyed, the state may be able to avoid paying compensation if it can show that it would be a nuisance to build in the flood plain or otherwise be contrary to background principles of state property law.[31]

IX. LAND USE AND ENVIRONMENTALLY SENSITIVE LANDS—THE ENDANGERED SPECIES ACT

§ 11.16 The Endangered Species Act as a Land Use Control

A. ESA Overview

The Endangered Species act (ESA)[1] has proved to be a useful land use control tool in environmentally sensitive areas. The United States Supreme Court described the Act as "the most comprehensive legislation for the preservation of Endangered Species ever enacted by any Nation."[2] Its secret for success lies in its ability to alter or even halt development that threatens a plant or wildlife species listed by the Secretary of the Interior as threatened or endangered.[3] This ties in with the Act's stated purpose "to provide a means whereby the ecosystems upon which endangered species and threatened species depend may be conserved." [4]

The land use element in the Endangered Species Act is Section 4. This Section reflects ecological reality; there is no use in protecting a plant or wildlife species if that species has no place to live. Section 4 authorized the Secretary of Interior to designate areas of "critical habitat" for specified species.[5] Section 3 of the ESA defines critical habitat for a threatened or endangered species as the "specific areas within the geographical area occupied by the species, at the time it is listed."[6] If the designation of the critical habitat is not determinable at the time the species is listed, the Secretary may do so up to one year after the species is listed.[7] Even areas outside the geographical area can be determined as critical habitat if the Secretary determines such areas as essential for the species' conservation.[8]

A critical habitat is limited, however, and "shall not include the

353 Mass. 141, 228 N.E.2d 831 (1967); Morris County Land Imp. Co. v. Parsippany-Troy Hills Township, 40 N.J. 539, 193 A.2d 232 (1963).

31. Lucas v. South Carolina Coastal Council, 505 U.S. 1003, 112 S.Ct. 2886, 120 L.Ed.2d 798 (1992); Just v. Marinette County, 56 Wis.2d 7, 201 N.W.2d 761 (Wis. 1972). See also supra § 10.6.

§ 11.16

1. 16 U.S.C.A. §§ 1531–1543.

2. Tennessee Valley Authority v. Hill, 437 U.S. 153, 180, 98 S.Ct. 2279, 57 L.Ed.2d 117 (1978).

3. The process to be followed by the Secretary in adding or subtracting a species from the act's domain is found at 16 U.S.C.A. § 1533(a), (b).

4. Id. § 1531(b).

5. Id. § 1533(a)(3)(A).

6. Id. § 1532(5)(A)(i).

7. Id. § 1533(b)(6)(C)(ii).

8. Id. § 1532(5)(A)(ii).

entire geographical area which can be occupied"[9] by the species. Furthermore, the Secretary may, with the so called "God Squad" provision, determine that a critical habitat may be excluded if exclusion outweighs the benefits.[10] His power is limited, however, if the species will become extinct as a result of the failure to designate such area as critical habitat.[11]

Section 4 authorizes the Secretary to list species of plants, fish, and wildlife as threatened or endangered.[12] Currently there are over 1,500 species listed as either threatened or endangered.[13] Section 3 of the ESA defines "endangered species" as species that are "in danger of extinction throughout all or a significant portion of its range."[14] The Act exempts insects that present an overwhelming risk to man.[15] Threatened species are defined in Section 3 as any species "which is likely to become an endangered species within the foreseeable future throughout all or a significant portion of its range."[16] Whether a particular species falls within one of these categories is determined on "the basis of the best scientific and commercial data available."[17]

B. Section 9 "Takes"

Section 9 acts as the triggering mechanism of the ESA. Section 9 prohibits the taking of any protected species by both federal and private parties.[18] Section 3 of the Act defines "take" as "to harass, harm, pursue, hunt, shoot, wound, kill, trap, capture, or collect, or attempt to engage in any such conduct."[19] The Secretary defines "harm" as "an act which actually kills or injures wildlife. Such act may include significant habitat modification or degradation where it actually kills or injures wildlife by significantly impairing essential behavioral patterns, including breeding, feeding, or sheltering."[20] The United States Supreme Court upheld the Secretary's definition of "harm," but limited its application to circumstances where there is substantial evidence linking the habitat modification and the actual death or injury to the protected species.[21] The Secretary also defines "harass" broadly as "an intentional or negligent act or omission which creates the likelihood of injury to wildlife by annoying it to such an extent as to significantly disrupt normal behavioral patterns."[22]

C. Incidental Takings

Although there appears to be no flexibility in the "take" definition, this is not completely true. Sections 7(b)(4) and 10(a) allow for "incidental takings" of protected species. An incidental taking is defined as "a

9. Id. § 1532(5)(C).

10. Id. § 1536(e)-(h).

11. Id.

12. Id. § 1533(a)(1).

13. 50 C.F.R. 17.12.

14. 16 U.S.C.A. § 1532(6).

15. Id.

16. § 1532(20).

17. § 1533(b)(1)(A).

18. § 1538(a)(1).

19. § 1532(19).

20. 50 C.F.R. 17.3.

21. Babbitt v. Sweet Home Chapter of Communities for a Great Oregon, 515 U.S. 687, 115 S.Ct. 2407, 132 L.Ed.2d 597 (1995).

22. 50 C.F.R. 17.3.

taking [that is] otherwise prohibited, if such taking is incidental to, and not the purpose of, carrying out of an otherwise lawful activity."[23] The process of attaining an incidental taking permit differs slightly between a taking involving a federal action and involving a private action.

In the application for an incidental taking permit, a federal action, such as the review for a Section 404 Dredge and Fill Permit, will trigger Section 7 of the Act. The federal agency, such as the Corps of Engineers, must first consult with the U.S. Fish and Wildlife Service (FWS) or the National Marine Fisheries Service (NMFS) to determine whether any protected species may be present in the area of the proposed development.[24] If there are protected species present and it has not been established that the development will not likely jeopardize the continued existence of the protected species or injure its critical habitat, then the FWS or NMFS will issue a Biological Assessment Report.[25] The report contains the agency's opinion on what the impacts of the federal agency's action will be and suggestions for conservation measures. Most importantly, the Biological Assessment may allow incidental takings.

If there is no federal action involved, then Section 10 of the Act applies. Section 10 requires a conservation plan first be prepared and submitted to the Secretary before an incidental taking permit is granted.[26] The conservation plan must show the expected impacts, the steps that will be taken to minimize and mitigate any takings, show that the taking will not appreciably reduce the likelihood of the survival of the species, and what alternative actions were considered and why they were not utilized.[27] The Secretary must also be assured that there will be adequate funding for the conservation plan.[28] The permit may be issued subject to terms and conditions that the Secretary deems necessary.[29] Furthermore, the Secretary may revoke a permit if the permittee is not complying with the terms and conditions of the permit.[30]

D. *Constitutionality As Applied to Development on Private Land*

The property clause of Article IV of the constitution confers power on Congress to regulate activity on the public lands,[31] and the commerce clause provides the basis for regulating activity on other land. National Association of Home Builders of the United States v. Babbit[32] illustrates the ESA's application to development on private land. That case involved the Delhi Sands flower-loving fly (the Fly), which has its home and last remaining habitat in San Bernardino County, California. The day before the county was to begin construction of a hospital, the Fly was listed as endangered. The listing suspended construction, which was to occur on

---

23. Id. See also Friends of Endangered Species, Inc. v. Jantzen, 760 F.2d 976 (9th Cir.1985).

    24. 16 U.S.C.A. § 1536(c)(1).

    25. Id.

    26. Id. § 1539(a)(2)(A).

    27. Id.

    28. Id. § 1539(a)(2)(B)(iii).

    29. Id. § 1539(a)(2)(B).

    30. Id. § 1539(a)(2)(C).

    31. See Kleppe v. New Mexico, 426 U.S. 529, 96 S.Ct. 2285, 49 L.Ed.2d 34 (1976).

    32. 949 F.Supp. 1 (D.D.C.1996).

Fly habitat. Eventually, the hospital was built 250 feet north of the original site. The Fish and Wildlife Service then held up a highway realignment necessitated by the new siting of the hospital, contending that it would encroach on the corridor the Fly needs to travel between colonies. At that point, the County, along with the home builders association, challenged the power of Congress to dictate land use on the basis of the Fly's connection to interstate commerce.

The challenge was a broad one. The plaintiffs did not seek to show that the regulations implementing the ESA imposed an economic burden on them. Their attack was simply that whether the Fly became extinct was none of the federal government's business. The district court would have nothing of it. Intrastate activity could be controlled if it had an interstate impact, said the court. That was the case with the ESA. Congress enacted the ESA because of fears over the unknown effects that the extinction of species would have on the existence of mankind. Mankind included the nation; hence, interstate commerce.

Wildlife, including the Fly, was an article of commerce, said the court. Furthermore, the government was able to show that insects, including the Fly, moved in commerce. Prior to being listed, insect collectors had traded the Fly both within and outside California. While the trade had stopped due to the listing, that did not result in a loss of the Fly's connection to interstate commerce, as the plaintiffs argued. To accept this argument would "turn the Act on its head," said the court.[33]

A property owner can make other constitutional challenges, such as Fifth Amendment takings claims, to actions taken under the ESA. Constitutional issues are covered in Chapter 10.

33. Id. The court found its holding supported by Palila v. Hawaii Department of Land and Natural Resources, 471 F.Supp. 985 (D.Haw.1979), aff'd 639 F.2d 495 (9th Cir.1981), where the ESA was held to constitutionally apply to a bird found only in Hawaii. The Fly case was affirmed at 130 F.3d 1041 (D.C.Cir.1997), pet. for cert. pending, March 5, 1998.

Chapter 12

AESTHETIC REGULATION AND HISTORIC PRESERVATION

Analysis

I. Aesthetic Regulation and Architectural Control
II. Historic Preservation

I. AESTHETIC REGULATION AND ARCHITECTURAL CONTROL

II. HISTORIC PRESERVATION

I. AESTHETIC REGULATION AND ARCHITECTURAL CONTROL

§ 12.1 Introduction

What is beauty? Our individual preferences are conditioned by educational, social and environmental factors. What is pleasing to the eye depends upon to whom the eye belongs. As David Hume, a Scottish philosopher, has said, beauty in things exists in the mind that contemplates them. Thus, as a basis for regulation of land uses, statutes and ordinances grounded *solely* on furthering of aesthetic purposes have been, at least until recently, difficult to justify.[1]

In land use control lore, an aesthetic control attempts to preserve or improve the beauty of an area. All zoning is to a certain extent based on the desire for beauty. Some of this country's first planning efforts arose from what was called the "city beautiful" movement.[2] In one of the earliest zoning decisions, the Supreme Court of the United States in Village of Euclid v. Ambler Realty Co.,[3] validated zoning as a reasonable exercise of the police power, taking the view that law must respond to the changing demands and needs of urban areas. After *Euclid* and until 1954, however, aesthetics alone was not considered a valid purpose for land use measures. Courts required that such measures be coupled with more traditional grounds to be sustained.[4]

In 1954, Justice Douglas noted in Berman v. Parker[5] that public safety, health, morality, peace and quiet, law and order—which are some of the more conspicuous examples of the traditional application of the police power—merely illustrate the scope of the power and do not limit it. He further observed that the concept of public welfare includes values which are "spiritual as well as physical, aesthetic as well as monetary. It is within the power of the legislature to determine that the community should be beautiful as well as healthy."[6] Subsequently, in People v. Stover,[7] the New York Court of Appeals determined that aesthetic purposes would support a restriction on the use of land. More recent cases extend legal support for the validity and necessity of aesthetic considerations in natural resource allocation and land use planning.[8]

Consideration of aesthetics in the promulgation of federal regulations was essentially guaranteed in 1969, with passage of the National Environmental Policy Act.[9] NEPA made consideration of aesthetic objec-

§ 12.1

1. See John J. Costonis, Icons and Aliens: Law, Aesthetics, and Environmental Change (1989); Shawn Rice, Zoning Law: Architectural Appearance Ordinances & the First Amendment, 76 Marq.L.Rev. 439 (1993); Norman Williams, Scenic Protection as a Legitimate Goal of Public Regulation, 38 Wash.U.J.Urb. & Contemp. L. 3 (1990); Michael Pace, Note, Aesthetic Regulation: A New General Rule, 90 W.Va.L.Rev. 581 (1987); Russell P. Schropp, Note, The Reasonableness of Aesthetic Zoning in Florida: A Look Beyond the Police Power, 10 Fla.St. U.L.Rev. 441 (1982); Bufford, Beyond the Eye of the Beholder: A New Majority of Jurisdictions Authorize Aesthetic Regulation, 48 UMKC L. Rev. 125 (1980).

2. See § 2.4.

3. 272 U.S. 365, 47 S.Ct. 114, 71 L.Ed. 303 (1926).

4. See, e.g., Board of Supervisors v. Rowe, 216 Va. 128, 216 S.E.2d 199 (1975) (protecting property values); Cochran v. Preston, 108 Md. 220, 70 A. 113 (1908) (height restrictions in Washington Monu-

ment vicinity upheld on safety and aesthetic grounds).

5. 348 U.S. 26, 75 S.Ct. 98, 99 L.Ed. 27 (1954).

6. Id. at 29, 75 S.Ct. at 100.

7. 12 N.Y.2d 462, 240 N.Y.S.2d 734, 191 N.E.2d 272 (1963) appeal dismissed 375 U.S. 42, 84 S.Ct. 147, 11 L.Ed.2d 107 (1963) (regulation requiring removal of clothesline from front yard).

8. See, e.g., Members of City Council v. Taxpayers for Vincent, 466 U.S. 789, 805, 104 S.Ct. 2118, 2129, 80 L.Ed.2d 772 (1984) (holding that "[i]t is well settled that the state may legitimately exercise its police powers to advance [a]esthetic values"); Metromedia, Inc. v. City of San Diego, 453 U.S. 490, 507–08, 101 S.Ct. 2882, 2892–93, 69 L.Ed.2d 800 (1981) (plurality opinion) (concluding that the appearance of the city constitutes a substantial governmental goal).

9. National Environmental Policy Act of 1969, 42 U.S.C.A. §§ 4321–4370. See § 11.2 supra.

tives a fundamental part of national policy by requiring an assessment of a project's impact on the built environment. Congress intended that creation and maintenance of a productive harmony between man and the environment be a national goal, to the end that the nation may be assured safe, healthy, productive, and aesthetically and culturally pleasing surroundings.[10] Enforcement of NEPA by courts has led to enactment of similar statutes in several states.[11]

In spite of the jurisprudential support given aesthetic control as a valid regulatory goal in recent years, problems still exist. Courts are repeatedly forced to determine whether a particular aesthetic regulation is a proper use of the police power.[12] Questions also arise when the adequacy of due process, in either the creation or application of the aesthetic control, is called into question.[13] Measures based on visual compatibility principles, analogous to zoning rationale, are fairly easy to sustain, but if the compatibility requirements are vague, overbroad or ambiguous, serious due process and First Amendment problems may be indicated.[14] Sign control ordinances are particularly susceptible to First Amendment attacks.[15] Another charge frequently leveled at an aesthetics-based regulation is that the affected property has been taken.[16]

On the whole, the courts' shift in favor of aesthetic-based regulation recognizes that pleasing surroundings are protectable as part of the public welfare. Commentators have suggested that zoning ordinances enacted primarily for aesthetic objectives should be recognized as a legitimate means of implementing community values.[17] This would enable courts to discontinue upholding ordinances prohibiting uses that are aesthetically offensive, such as billboards, under the fiction that they constitute public health and safety hazards.[18]

This first part of this chapter explores regulation of aesthetic values in two specific areas, sign control and architectural regulation. In each of these areas, aesthetic considerations loom large and particular attention must be given to the ways in which aesthetics relate to the public health, safety and welfare.

---

10. Id. § 4331.

11. E.g., West's Ann.Cal.Pub.Res.Code § 21000(b); Minn.Stat.Ann. § 116B.02; N.Y.—McKinney's Envir.Conserv.Law § 8–0101–0117. This sort of cause and effect situation is mirrored to some extent by the experience with the National Historic Preservation Act, and subsequently enacted similar state laws. See § 12.8, infra.

12. See Jeffrey F. Ghent, Annotation, Zoning Regulation of Architectural Style, 41 ALR 3d 1392, 1401–03 (1971 & Supp. 1993).

13. Id.

14. Rice, supra note 1, at 448–51; Costonis, Law and Aesthetics: A Critique and A Reformulation of the Dilemmas, 80 Mich.

L.Rev. 355, 360–361 (1981). See supra §§ 10.2, 10.3.

15. See, e.g., 44 Liquormart, Inc. v. Rhode Island, 517 U.S. 484, 116 S.Ct. 1495, 134 L.Ed.2d 711 (1996); Whitton v. City of Gladstone, 832 F.Supp. 1329 (W.D.Mo. 1993), aff'd in part, rev'd in part 54 F.3d 1400 (8th Cir.1995); Providence Journal Co. v. City of Newport, 665 F.Supp. 107 (D.R.I. 1987).

16. See § 10.2.

17. John J. Costonis, Law & Aesthetics: A Critique and a Reformulation of the Dilemmas, 80 Mich. L. Rev. 355 (1981).

18. See Pace, supra note 1, at 592–93. See also Dukeminier, Zoning for Aesthetic Objectives: A Reappraisal, 20 Law & Contemp.Probs. 281 (1955).

§ 12.2 The Trend Toward Sign Control

Billboard and sign regulation is not a new phenomenon. People have long protested the unsightliness of billboards, and legislatures have attempted to appease them from time to time. Courts, however, in the early part of the twentieth century, were not receptive to these moves. In the 1905 case of City of Passaic v. Paterson Bill Posting, Advertising & Sign Painting Co., the court invalidated an ordinance which imposed setback and height restrictions, reasoning that aesthetic considerations were matters of luxury, and necessity alone justified exercise of the police power.[1] Some later opinions were not quite so rigidly set, and courts allowed regulation of signs for traffic safety and health purposes or to preserve the scenery obliterated by the erection of signs.[2]

More recently, courts have recognized aesthetic concerns as being a valid justification for use of the police power.[3] An early opinion sustaining aesthetic values as sufficient grounds for a community to ban all off-premise signs was Cromwell v. Ferrier.[4] The New York Court of Appeals reasoned that exercise of the police power should extend to those aesthetic considerations which bear substantially on the economic, social, and cultural patterns of a community or district.[5] "Advertising signs and billboards ... often are egregious examples of ugliness ... just as much subject to reasonable controls ... as enterprises which emit offensive noises, odors or debris."[6] But elsewhere, an ordinance which attempted to require property owners to provide for "beauty, attractiveness, aesthetics and symmetry in commercial signs ..." was invalidated.[7] The court distinguished between ordinances with a primary goal of furthering aesthetics, and those with other immediate goals, only secondarily considering aesthetics.[8] The latter were a valid use of the police power, while the former were not.[9] It seems that a majority of states now hold that a

§ 12.2

1. 72 N.J.L. 285, 62 A. 267, 268 (N.J.Err. & App.1905). See also Commonwealth v. Boston Advertising Co., 188 Mass. 348, 74 N.E. 601 (1905); People v. Green, 85 App.Div. 400, 83 N.Y.S. 460 (1903); Bryan v. Chester, 212 Pa. 259, 61 A. 894 (1905).

2. St. Louis Gunning Advertisement Co. v. St. Louis, 235 Mo. 99, 137 S.W. 929 (1911). Cf. General Outdoor Advertising Co. v. Indianapolis, Dep't of Pub. Parks, 202 Ind. 85, 172 N.E. 309 (1930).

3. This has been the case since Berman v. Parker, 348 U.S. 26, 75 S.Ct. 98, 99 L.Ed. 27 (1954). Undoubtedly, Dukeminier, Zoning for Aesthetic Objectives: A Reappraisal, 20 L. & Contemp.Probs. 281 (1955) and John J. Costonis, Law & Aesthetics: A Critique and A Reformulation of the Dilemmas, 80 Mich. L. Rev. 355 (1981) have been influential as well.

4. 19 N.Y.2d 263, 279 N.Y.S.2d 22, 225 N.E.2d 749 (1967), reargument denied 19 N.Y.2d 862, 280 N.Y.S.2d 1025, 227 N.E.2d 408 (1967). See also Oregon City v. Hartke, 240 Or. 35, 400 P.2d 255 (1965) (junkyard).

5. Id. at 272.

6. Id.

7. Mayor & City Council v. Mano Swartz, Inc., 268 Md. 79, 299 A.2d 828 (1973).

8. Id.

9. Id. See also Donnelly Advertising Corp. v. Mayor & City Council, 279 Md. 660, 370 A.2d 1127 (1977) (ordinance upheld-aesthetics a secondary goal). Cf. Berberian v. Housing Auth., 112 R.I. 771, 315 A.2d 747 (1974). As recently as 1991, the court in Coscan Washington, Inc. v. Maryland–National Capital Park & Planning Comm'n, 87 Md.App. 602, 590 A.2d 1080 (Md.App. 1991) upheld an ordinance prohibiting the use of vinyl siding because the ordinance was not based solely on aesthetics.

regulation based solely upon aesthetic considerations is legitimate.[10]

There are many ways to impose restrictions on signs, ranging from total exclusion from a given area, to limitation of location, size, height, and setback from the street. Distinctions are made between on-and off-premise signs, between those located in urban or residential areas, and between commercial and noncommercial signs. The First Amendment protection afforded speech often comes into play when a statute or ordinance is not carefully drafted and infringes on the protected right.[11] If similarly situated signs are categorized or treated differently by the ordinance, an equal protection problem may exist.

§ 12.3   Sign Regulation

Outdoor advertising and signs are not always controlled by zoning alone. Some municipalities attempt to regulate signs separately through a comprehensive ordinance. Statutes authorizing state sign control and enabling municipal regulation predate zoning, though courts have not always found them valid.[1] Private nuisance actions have also been used as a means of ridding certain locale of unsightly billboards.[2] The power to regulate and restrict outdoor advertising may even be found in state constitutional provisions, as was the case in General Outdoor Advertising Co. v. Department of Public Works.[3] The court found that this power could be delegated to municipalities, and its use could be justified to reduce traffic obstructions, to promote traffic safety and to avoid nuisances.[4]

Similar regulations prohibiting signs near major highways and public places are traditionally considered valid.[5] Such regulations were upheld by the Sixth Circuit in Wheeler v. Commissioner of Highways.[6] The court found that the regulations furthered the purposes of providing maximum visibility, preventing unreasonable distraction to drivers and

---

10.   Sarah L. Goss, Nat'l Park Serv. & Nat'l Ctr. for Preservation Law, Propriety of Using the Police Power for Aesthetic Regulation: A Comprehensive State-by-State Analysis (1992); Michael Pace, Note, Aesthetic Regulation: A New General Rule, 90 W.Va.L.Rev. 581, 592–93 (1987) ("While a majority of jurisdictions now seem to approve of aesthetic regulation. the specific instances where it might support such regulation appear to vary significantly"). See also Shawn Rice, Zoning Law: Architectural Appearance Ordinances & the First Amendment, 76 Marq.L.Rev. 439, 445 (1993) (citing Bufford, Beyond the Eye of the Beholder: A New Majority of Jurisdictions Authorize Aesthetic Regulation, 48 UMKC L.Rev. 125 (1980)).

11.   See supra § 10.16.

§ 12.3

1.   St. Louis Gunning Advertisement Co. v. St. Louis, 235 Mo. 99, 137 S.W. 929 (1911); City of Passaic v. Paterson Bill Post-ing, Advertising & Sign Painting Co., 72 N.J.L. 285, 62 A. 267 (1905); People v. Green, 85 App.Div. 400, 83 N.Y.S. 460 (1903). The use of zoning, of course, came later in 1926, with the decision in Village of Euclid v. Ambler, 272 U.S. 365, 47 S.Ct. 114, 71 L.Ed. 303 (1926).

2.   See infra § 14.4, for discussion of private nuisance.

3.   289 Mass. 149, 193 N.E. 799 (1935).

4.   193 N.E. at 805.

5.   See, e.g., Illinois Highway Advertising Control Act of 1971, 225 Ill.Comp.Stat. 440/1 (1996) (discussed in Scadron v. City of Des Plaines), 989 F.2d 502 (7th Cir. 1993).

6.   822 F.2d 586 (6th Cir.1987).

interference with traffic regulation, preserving the natural scenic beauty, and promoting maximum safety and welfare of thruway users.[7] The issue of compensation under the takings clause for the application of these ordinances to existing billboards appears unsettled.[8] One court suggested that the government had the power to apply regulations to existing signs, for it was the presence of the highway in the first place which gave the signs their value, inferring that no compensation was necessary.[9]

Attempts to regulate sign usage have traditionally led to taking challenges. One early theory upon which taking claims were based was that the sign erected on landowner's property became a fixture of the property, and therefore was realty, if that was the landowner's intent.[10] Such signs were treated differently if placed by the owner on property of another pursuant to an advertising lease. The current view is that fixtures attached to real estate under a lease are to be treated as real estate for valuation purposes, and when severed, the value attributed to the sign is treated as personalty and credited to the tenant.[11]

Some states found that the existence of a right of removal is a proper basis for denial of compensation to the lessee for the value of his sign.[12] A few states have determined that advertising signs are personalty rather than realty;[13] thus, the state can require the lessee to remove the sign at his own expense.

Under the Highway Beautification Act of 1965,[14] which prohibits signs within 660 feet of the right of way along interstate and primary highway systems, unless an area is zoned for commercial or industrial uses, compensation must be paid for the removal of signs predating the law. The act provided the stimulus for many states to control signs along highways or risk loss of federal funds. Funding for compensation has lagged, and at its current level it is doubtful that targeted billboards will be removed in the near future. Because the act only took aim at signs

7. Id. at 587 (citing Ky.Rev.Stat.Ann. § 177.850).

8. See Kelbro Inc. v. Myrick, 113 Vt. 64, 30 A.2d 527 (Vt.1943) (sidestepping the issue of the takings claim). See also § 10.16, supra. Two leading cases indicating that billboard removal laws are not Fifth Amendments takings are Art Neon Co. v. City and County of Denver, 488 F.2d 118 (10th Cir.1973) and Naegele Outdoor Advertising, Inc. v. City of Durham, 803 F.Supp. 1068 (M.D.N.C.1992).

9. New York State Thruway Auth. v. Ashley Motor Court, Inc., 10 N.Y.2d 151, 156, 176 N.E.2d 566, 569, 218 N.Y.S.2d 640, 643 (1961).

10. Teaff v. Hewitt, 1 Ohio St. 511 (1853). The Supreme Court of Mississippi, in 1996, found a billboard to be a "trade fixture" and subsequently awarded compensation for its removal. Lamar Corp. v. State Highway Comm'n of Miss., 684 So.2d 601 (Miss.1996).

11. 2 P. Nichols, Eminent Domain § 5.81(2) (rev.3d ed.1970). See City of Buffalo v. Michael, 16 N.Y.2d 88, 262 N.Y.S.2d 441, 209 N.E.2d 776 (1965); Rochester Poster Advertising Co. v. State, 27 Misc.2d 99, 213 N.Y.S.2d 812 (1961), affirmed mem. 11 N.Y.2d 1036, 230 N.Y.S.2d 30, 183 N.E.2d 911 (1962); Uniform Relocation Assistance & Real Property Acquisition Policies Act of 1970, 42 U.S.C.A. § 4655(1).

12. E.g., City of Doraville v. Turner Communications, 236 Ga. 385, 223 S.E.2d 798, 800–01 (1976); Mayor of Baltimore v. Gamse & Bro., 132 Md. 290, 104 A. 429 (1918).

13. E.g., City of Scottsdale v. Eller Outdoor Advertising Co. of Arizona, Inc., 119 Ariz. 86, 579 P.2d 590, 596 (Ariz.App. 1978); Aquafine Corp. v. Fendig Outdoor Advertising Co., 155 Ga.App. 661, 272 S.E.2d 526, 527 (1980).

14. 23 U.S.C.A. § 131.

within 660 feet of federally aided highways, the proscription stimulated a proliferation of large billboards in rural areas set just beyond that line.

Justifications given for regulating signs through the police power have shifted from one emphasis to another. As with similar non-zoning regulations, zoning ordinances controlling signs along highways have been upheld to protect travelers. Other rationales[15] were stated to avoid the allegation that the regulation was being upheld solely on aesthetic grounds. Realistically, however, grounds for sustaining the regulation were based on either aesthetics[16] or the preservation of property, particularly in areas where signs would mar the historic or naturally scenic character of the area and interfere with the tourist industry.[17]

Some courts view preservation of property concerns as separate from aesthetic purposes. Aesthetic regulations have long been sustained when coupled with another legitimate police power purpose,[18] but aesthetics standing alone is now recognized as a valid exercise of the police power in many jurisdictions.[19]

Total exclusion of all types of signs from a municipality has not been allowed, for it may be unreasonable and violative of First Amendment considerations.[20] Exclusion of off-premise signs or billboards from residential areas has been held a reasonable application in light of compatibility and preservation of property value theories.[21] The Supreme Court

15. See, e.g., South–Suburban Hous. Ctr. v. Greater South Suburban Bd. of Realtors, 713 F.Supp. 1068 (N.D.Ill.1988) aff'd in part, reversed in part 935 F.2d 868 (7th Cir.1991) (proliferation of "for sale" signs would undermine stability of racially integrated neighborhood); Murphy, Inc. v. Town of Westport, 131 Conn. 292, 40 A.2d 177 (1944) (endangering public health by emphasis on advertisements for liquor, tobacco); St. Louis Gunning Advertisement Co. v. St. Louis, 235 Mo. 99, 137 S.W. 929 (1911) (immoral acts might be performed behind signs, trash might accumulate).

16. See Dukeminier, Zoning for Aesthetic Objectives: A Reappraisal, 20 Law & Contemp.Probs. 218 (1955).

17. See, e.g., Globe Newspaper Co. v. Beacon Hill Architectural Comm'n, 421 Mass. 570, 659 N.E.2d 710 (1996); Intervine Outdoor Advertising, Inc. v. City of Gloucester City Zoning Bd. of Adjustment, 290 N.J.Super. 78, 674 A.2d 1027 (1996).

18. Little Pep Delmonico Restaurant, Inc. v. Charlotte, 252 N.C. 324, 113 S.E.2d 422 (1960), overruled State v. Jones, 305 N.C. 520, 290 S.E.2d 675 (1982) (aesthetics alone is sufficient); United Advertising Corp. v. Borough of Metuchen, 42 N.J. 1, 198 A.2d 447 (1964).

19. See U.S. West Communications, Inc. v. City of Longmont, 924 P.2d 1071

(Colo.App.1995), aff'd 948 P.2d 509 (1997); Sprenger, Grubb & Assocs., Inc. v. City of Hailey, 127 Idaho 576, 903 P.2d 741 (Idaho 1995); General Food Vending Inc. v. Town of Westfield, 288 N.J.Super. 442, 672 A.2d 760 (1995). See also Bufford, Beyond the Eye of the Beholder: A New Majority of Jurisdictions Authorize Aesthetic Regulation, 48 UMKC L.Rev. 125 (1980).

20. See City of Ladue v. Gilleo, 512 U.S. 43, 114 S.Ct. 2038, 129 L.Ed.2d 36 (1994) (holding that an ordinance that banned all residential signs unless they were included in one of ten exceptions violated the residents' right to free speech).

21. E.g., Metromedia, Inc. v. City of San Diego, 453 U.S. 490, 101 S.Ct. 2882, 69 L.Ed.2d 800 (1981); Elco v. R.C. Maxwell Co., 292 N.J.Super. 118, 678 A.2d 323 (1996); Lamar Advertising v. State Dep't of Transportation, 694 So.2d 1256 (Ala.1996); John Donnelly & Sons, Inc. v. Outdoor Advertising Bd., 369 Mass. 206, 339 N.E.2d 709 (1975); Naegele Outdoor Advertising Co. v. Village of Minnetonka, 281 Minn. 492, 162 N.W.2d 206 (1968). But see People v. Goodman, 31 N.Y.2d 262, 338 N.Y.S.2d 97, 290 N.E.2d 139 (1972), reargument denied 32 N.Y.2d 705, 343 N.Y.S.2d 1026, 296 N.E.2d 459 (1973) (off-premise signs totally excluded from resort island).

has also upheld an ordinance that banned signs on public property.[22] Courts have generally given their imprimatur to the regulatory purposes served by exclusion. In John Donnelly & Sons v. Campbell, the United States Supreme Court affirmed a decision by the First Circuit, which upheld the constitutionality of a state statute which was intended to abolish billboards completely.[23] Although the Court rejected traffic safety as a substantial state interest, it found that the statute did advance the state's interest in aesthetics and tourism.[24] Another ordinance excluding off-premise signs throughout a township was upheld in Suffolk Outdoor Adv. Co. v. Hulse,[25] where the sign owners were given a three year amortization period within which to remove the signs.

Many of the sign cases involve the propriety of a classification which prohibits some signs and permits others. The off-site versus on-site classification is commonly upheld.[26] The equal protection argument stresses that the aesthetic impact of a sign does not vary with its location. The Supreme Court, however, has tolerated the distinction, finding that a city may believe that off-site billboards pose "a more acute problem" than on-site billboards. If the ordinance simply favors one kind of commercial speech over another, it is permissible.[27] Billboards have been treated separately and distinguished from other signs on the ground that the former are more likely to be unattractive, to restrict normal development, and be deliberately conspicuous.[28]

There is little case law concerning dimensional controls as a means of regulating signs. Laws controlling the size of signs have been upheld for such divergent reasons as public safety[29] and pure aesthetics.[30] Height

22. City Council of Los Angeles v. Taxpayers for Vincent, 466 U.S. 789, 104 S.Ct. 2118, 80 L.Ed.2d 772 (1984).

23. 639 F.2d 6,7 (1st Cir.1980), aff'd 453 U.S. 916, 101 S.Ct. 3151, 69 L.Ed.2d 999 (1981).

24. Id. at 12.

25. 43 N.Y.2d 483, 402 N.Y.S.2d 368, 373 N.E.2d 263 (1977), reargument denied 43 N.Y.2d 951, 403 N.Y.S.2d 1029, 374 N.E.2d 1251 (1978), appeal dismissed 439 U.S. 808, 99 S.Ct. 66, 58 L.Ed.2d 101 (1978). But see Ackerley Communications v. City of Cambridge, 88 F.3d 33 (1st Cir. 1996) (holding that an ordinance violated the First Amendment by discriminating between on-site and off-site signs, because signs with on-site messages were protected by a grandfather clause of the state law).

26. See § 10.16, supra.

27. 453 U.S. 490, 511–12, 101 S.Ct. 2882, 2894–95, 69 L.Ed.2d 800 (1981).

28. Ackerley Communications v. R.F. Krochalis, 108 F.3d 1095 (9th Cir.1997) ("[P]roliferation and location of billboards in the City can contribute to visual blight, traffic hazards and a reduction of property values."); John Donnelly & Sons v. Campbell, 639 F.2d 6, 12 (1st Cir.1980), aff'd 453 U.S. 916, 101 S.Ct. 3151, 69 L.Ed.2d 999 (1981) ("Far better justifications for the [billboard restriction] are the preservation of the state's natural beauty for all its inhabitants, and the consequent enhancement of one of its great economic resources, the tourist industry."); National Advertising Co. v. County of Monterey, 211 Cal. App.2d 375, 27 Cal.Rptr. 136 (1962).

29. Board of Adjustment v. Osage Oil & Transp. Inc., 258 Ark. 91, 522 S.W.2d 836 (1975), appeal dismissed, cert. denied 423 U.S. 941, 96 S.Ct. 350, 46 L.Ed.2d 273 (1975) (to keep signs from falling on passersby); National Advertising Co. v. City of Raleigh, 947 F.2d 1158 (4th Cir.1991) (to reduce traffic hazards).

30. Outdoor Communications, Inc. v. City of Murfreesboro, 59 F.3d 171 (6th Cir. 1995) (elimination of confusing advertising and promotion of aesthetics); People v. Goodman, 31 N.Y.2d 262, 338 N.Y.S.2d 97, 290 N.E.2d 139 (1972), reargument denied 32 N.Y.2d 705, 343 N.Y.S.2d 1026, 296 N.E.2d 459 (1973) (compatibility with natural beauty of Fire Island, N.Y.).

restrictions have been sustained on similar grounds.[31] Many ordinances which prohibit new signs also seek to require removal of existing ones as soon as possible. Already existing signs which do not comply with the ordinance are treated as nonconforming signs, and have been given the same protection as other nonconforming uses. Courts allow amortization schedules which provide for removal after a reasonable period.[32]

Compensation requirements under the Highway Beautification Act are generally strictly applied,[33] and federal funding will be withheld if signs are removed and owners are not compensated.[34] However, the compensation provisions do not offer billboard owners a private right of action for compensation.[35]

In some jurisdictions, signs have been removed immediately and without compensation. In Markham Advertising Co. v. State,[36] the petitioners challenged a Washington state statute which prohibited billboards under certain circumstances, and declared it unlawful to maintain them after a certain date. The petitioner's signs had been lawfully erected prior to the enactment of the statute but became unlawful before the effective date of the Federal Highway Act which required compensation for forced removal; thus, the signs were removed and no compensation was paid. The court found that Congress had not intended to preempt state regulation of highway advertising but rather had intended to encourage state control by offering financial incentives. Therefore, language in the federal statute mandating payment of compensation was found inapplicable.[37]

31. Sun Oil Co. v. Madison Heights, 41 Mich.App. 47, 199 N.W.2d 525 (1972) (ordinance limiting high rise signs to 20 feet valid).

32. For a good discussion of the amortization concept in connection with nonconforming uses, see, e.g., Harbison v. Buffalo, 4 N.Y.2d 553, 152 N.E.2d 42, 176 N.Y.S.2d 598 (1958). See also Outdoor Graphics, Inc. v. City of Burlington, 103 F.3d 690 (8th Cir.1996); Georgia Outdoor Advertising, Inc. v. City of Waynesville, 900 F.2d 783 (4th Cir.1990).

33. See, e.g., Root Outdoor Advertising, Inc. v. City of Fort Collins, 759 P.2d 59 (Colo.App.1988), modified 788 P.2d 149 (Colo.1990).

34. 42 Op. Att'y Gen. 331 (1966). See also State v. Adams, 506 F.Supp. 60 (D.S.D.), affirmed 635 F.2d 698 (8th Cir. 1980), cert. denied 451 U.S. 984, 101 S.Ct. 2316, 68 L.Ed.2d 841 (1981). But see Ackerley Comm. Inc. v. Seattle, 92 Wn.2d 905, 602 P.2d 1177 (1979) (statute applies only to signs within scope of its definition), cert. denied 449 U.S. 804, 101 S.Ct. 49, 66 L.Ed.2d 7 (1981).

35. National Advertising Co. v. City of Ashland, 678 F.2d 106 (9th Cir.1982) (hold-

ing that compensation provisions of the Highway Beautification Act do not create rights enforceable by billboard owners). See also Newman Signs, Inc. v. Sinner, 796 F.2d 247 (8th Cir.1986).

36. 73 Wash.2d 405, 439 P.2d 248 (1968), appeal dismissed 393 U.S. 316, 89 S.Ct. 553, 21 L.Ed.2d 512 (1969), rehearing denied 393 U.S. 1112, 89 S.Ct. 854, 21 L.Ed.2d 813 (1969). See also City of Whitewater v. Vivid Inc., 140 Wis.2d 612, 412 N.W.2d 519 (Wis.App.1987), rev. denied (holding that compensation not necessary when city is not acting pursuant to its police power, but rather as a landowner); Suffolk v. Town of Southampton, 60 N.Y.2d 70, 455 N.E.2d 1245, 468 N.Y.S.2d 450 (1983) (power to remove without compensation is not preempted if reasonable amortization period is allowed); La Pointe Outdoor Advertising v. Florida Dep't of Transp., 398 So.2d 1370 (Fla.1981) (statute is unambiguous, no compensation for nonconforming illegally-erected billboards).

37. 73 Wash.2d 405, 439 P.2d 248 (1968), appeal dismissed 393 U.S. 316, 89 S.Ct. 553, 21 L.Ed.2d 512 (1969).

§ 12.4 Sign Control and First Amendment Conflicts

Sign controls often raise First Amendment issues because messages on signs are to a greater or lesser extent protected speech. Generally, signs which convey noncommercial messages are accorded full protection under the amendment while commercial speech is given only limited protection.[1]

Noncommercial speech may not be regulated strictly on the basis of its content, but reasonable time, place and manner restrictions may be imposed. Whether time, place and manner restrictions are reasonable is weighed against the alternative means for communication still available to the speaker. In City of Ladue v. Gilleo, the United States Supreme Court invalidated an ordinance that prohibited all residential signs except those falling within one of ten specific exemptions.[2] The Court found that residential signs were an important medium of expression and that adequate substitutes were not available.[3]

Protection was granted to commercial speech contained in signs by the Court in Linmark Assoc. Inc. v. Township of Willingboro.[4] Because the township determined that the high rate of home sales was due to panic selling by white residents, it enacted an ordinance banning "for sale" signs. The purpose was to forestall "white flight," because the governing body felt the absence of signs would diminish the fear that the change in racial composition of the community would reduce property values. Even though the "for sale" signs were considered commercial speech, the Court invalidated the ordinance, holding that the ban restricted the content of the expression and was not solely a time, place and manner restriction. Though alternative means of communication were available, they were neither as effective nor as economically feasible as the prohibited signs. Finally, the Township failed to establish that the actual effect of the ordinance supported its purpose.

Commercial billboard regulation, although it raises free speech issues, has generally been upheld because of a state's interest in protecting the health, safety and general welfare of the community. Usually, time, place and manner restrictions are found to be reasonable.[5] But an ordinance enacted by the City of San Diego did not fare so well. Off-site billboards were completely banned throughout the city. On-site signs

§ 12.4

1. For a discussion of commercial and noncommercial speech, see § 10.16 supra.

2. 512 U.S. 43, 114 S.Ct. 2038, 129 L.Ed.2d 36 (1994).

3. Id. at 2046.

4. 431 U.S. 85, 97 S.Ct. 1614, 52 L.Ed.2d 155 (1977); see also South–Suburban Housing Ctr. v. Greater South Suburban Bd. of Realtors, 713 F.Supp. 1068 (N.D.Ill.1988) aff'd in part, reversed in part 935 F.2d 868 (7th Cir.1991).

5. See Rzadkowolski v. Village of Lake Orion, 845 F.2d 653 (6th Cir.1988); Resort Development Int'l, Inc. v. City of Panama City Beach, 636 F.Supp. 1078 (N.D.Fla. 1986); John Donnelly & Sons, Inc. v. Outdoor Advertising Bd., 369 Mass. 206, 339 N.E.2d 709 (1975); Suffolk Outdoor Advertising Co. v. Hulse, 43 N.Y.2d 483, 402 N.Y.S.2d 368, 373 N.E.2d 263 (1977), affirmed per curiam 439 U.S. 808, 99 S.Ct. 66, 58 L.Ed.2d 101 (1978). See also Anheuser–Busch, Inc. v. Schmoke, 101 F.3d 325 (4th Cir.1996) (upholding constitutionality of ban on billboard advertising of alcoholic beverages).

were allowed if they fell within the statutory definition, or within certain exceptions that were included to allow government signs, historical plaques, and time and temperature signs, for example. In other words, the ordinance generally permitted on-site commercial signs to be displayed, but prohibited those with no commercial content.

The U.S. Supreme Court, in Metromedia, Inc. v. San Diego,[6] found the ordinance to be unconstitutional on its face. Continuing to observe the distinction drawn between commercial and noncommercial speech and indicating that the former is more easily regulated than the latter, the Court invalidated the ordinance insofar as it applied to noncommercial speech.[7] Using the four part test enunciated in Central Hudson Gas and Electric Corp. v. Public Service Commission,[8] the Court questioned whether the ordinance directly advanced the governmental interests in traffic safety and visual appearance of the city. Following the general rule, the Court did not disagree with the "accumulated, common sense judgments of local lawmakers and of the many reviewing courts" that billboards were a hazard to traffic safety.[9] Further, the Court noted that aesthetic judgments such as those made by the City were subjective and would be carefully scrutinized only if they were a public rationalization of an impermissible purpose.[10]

But the Court found the ordinance afforded greater protection to commercial speech than to noncommercial speech, and that the City did not adequately explain this disparate treatment. Insofar as San Diego chose to tolerate billboards, it could not limit their content to commercial messages only, choosing to value that form of communication over noncommercial communication.[11] Further the City could not limit noncommercial speech to selected topics; e.g., those exceptions allowed in the ordinance. The Court reasoned that because some noncommercial messages could be conveyed on billboards throughout commercial and industrial zones, other messages had to be allowed as well. To do otherwise would be to regulate content impermissibly. The Court rejected the City's suggestion that the ordinance was a reasonable time, place and manner restriction, because noncommercial speech alternatives were insufficient, inappropriate and prohibitively expensive.

Because the plurality determined a total prohibition of outdoor advertising was not before the court, it chose not to address the ques-

6. 453 U.S. 490, 101 S.Ct. 2882, 69 L.Ed.2d 800 (1981), on remand 32 Cal.3d 180, 185 Cal.Rptr. 260, 649 P.2d 902 (1982).

7. The *Metromedia* plurality suggested that content-based distinctions within the category of commercial speech were permissible. Id. at 514.

8. 447 U.S. 557, 100 S.Ct. 2343, 65 L.Ed.2d 341 (1980). The test is: (1) First Amendment protects commercial speech only if it concerns lawful activity and is not misleading, (2) a restriction on commercial speech is valid only if it seeks to implement a substantial governmental interest, (3) di-

rectly advances that interest, and (4) reaches no further than necessary to accomplish the given objective.

9. Metromedia, Inc. v. San Diego, 453 U.S. 490, 509, 101 S.Ct. 2882, 2893, 69 L.Ed.2d 800 (1981), on remand 32 Cal.3d 180, 185 Cal.Rptr. 260, 649 P.2d 902 (1982).

10. Id. at 510, 101 S.Ct. at 2893.

11. See also John Donnelly & Sons v. Campbell, 639 F.2d 6 (1st Cir.1980), judgment affirmed 453 U.S. 916, 101 S.Ct. 3151, 69 L.Ed.2d 999 (1981).

tion. Justice Brennan disagreed, however, and wrote separately to emphasize that the practical effect of the statute was to eliminate billboards as an effective medium of communication for any speaker desiring to express political or other noncommercial information.[12] He found that neither traffic safety nor aesthetic objectives, the avowed purposes of the ordinance, were sufficient to save it. If a community could show it had a sufficiently substantial governmental interest which was directly furthered and that a more narrowly drawn restriction would not promote that goal, Justice Brennan would be willing to concede that a municipality might justify a total billboard ban.[13]

An ordinance regulating sign usage on public property successfully withstood a constitutional challenge. At stake in Members of Los Angeles City Council v. Taxpayers for Vincent[14] was an ordinance prohibiting the erection of any type of sign on public property. Vincent, a candidate for local office, had placed campaign signs on the crossbars of power poles. The city promptly removed them. Vincent filed suit claiming the ordinance unconstitutionally abridged his political speech, protected by the First Amendment.

The United States Supreme Court analogized appellant's posted signs to billboards, reaffirmed its conclusion in *Metromedia* that a city has a sufficiently substantial interest in justifying content-neutral prohibition of billboards for aesthetic reasons,[15] and held that the ordinance was not invalid. Public property not by tradition or designation a forum for public communication may be reserved by the state for its intended purposes, communicative or otherwise, as long as the regulation of speech is reasonable and not an attempt to suppress expression merely because public officials oppose the speaker's view.[16] The ordinance curtailed no more speech than necessary to accomplish its purpose because it attacked the medium (posted signs on government property) rather than the message.

A recent subject of litigation has been the constitutionality of ordinances that ban newsracks on city sidewalks. In City of Cincinnati v. Discovery Network, the Supreme Court invalidated an ordinance that banned newsracks that distributed commercial handbills.[17] The Court found that the ordinance was an impermissible content-based restriction because it did not ban newsracks that contained newspapers.[18] The First Circuit recently considered the constitutionality of a complete ban on newsracks in Boston's Beacon Hill Historic District.[19] The court upheld

---

12. 453 U.S. at 525, 101 S.Ct. at 2901.

13. Id. at 528, 101 S.Ct. at 2903.

14. 466 U.S. 789, 104 S.Ct. 2118, 80 L.Ed.2d 772 (1984), on remand 738 F.2d 353 (9th Cir.1984).

15. 104 S.Ct. at 2130.

16. Id. at 2134. For further discussion of the constitutional issues, see supra § 10.16.

17. 507 U.S. 410, 113 S.Ct. 1505, 123 L.Ed.2d 99 (1993).

18. Id. at 430.

19. Globe Newspaper Co. v. Beacon Hill Architectural Comm'n, 100 F.3d 175 (1st Cir.1996).

the ban, finding that it was a content-neutral time, place and manner restriction.[20]

§ 12.5   Architectural Control

Ordinances that provide for architectural design review are increasingly being enacted to control the appearance of structures.[1] Architectural design review is one example of zoning based on aesthetics.[2] Like sign regulation, the standards or criteria to be applied may be included in the zoning scheme or may be enacted separately. Typically, a board is established to review designs in accordance with enumerated criteria including compatibility with surrounding area, the effect of allowing the design on neighboring property values and certain common stylistic features. Some boards also attempt to prevent monotony by requiring that the designs not be too similar while other boards may require conformity or harmony with the community's existing or even desired architecture.[3] These boards consider all proposed buildings in a district and hold the authority to disapprove a design and deny a building permit if the requirements of the ordinance are not met.[4]

In 1954, dictum by the Supreme Court in Berman v. Parker[5] introduced an expanded conception of the public welfare that included aesthetics.[6] Before the *Berman* decision most courts held that architectural design review regulations could not be based solely on aesthetics.[7] Many courts invalidated land use regulations based purely on aesthetics because they objected to the subjective nature of aesthetics.[8] Courts also worried that majorities could use aesthetic regulation to impose their tastes on minorities.[9] Additionally, judges were concerned that the use of the police power to promote aesthetics infringed on private property rights.[10] In spite of these concerns, Justice Douglas in *Berman* opined that "[i]t is within the power of the legislature to determine that the community should be beautiful as well as healthy, spacious as well as clean, well-balanced as well as carefully patrolled."[11] Today, a majority of states allow architectural design review regulations based solely on aesthetic considerations.[12] The remaining states are either undecided or

20. Id. at 189.

§ 12.5

1. Kenneth Regan, You Can't Build That Here: The Constitutionality of Aesthetic Zoning and Architectural Review, 58 Fordham L. Rev. 1013, 1019 (1990).

2. Id. at 1015.

3. Shawn G. Rice, Zoning Law: Architectural Appearance Ordinances and the First Amendment, 76 Marq.L.Rev. 439, 446 (1993).

4. Id.

5. Berman v. Parker, 348 U.S. 26, 75 S.Ct. 98, 99 L.Ed. 27 (1954).

6. Stephanie L. Bunting, Unsightly Politics: Aesthetics, Sign Ordinances, and Homeowners Speech in City of Ladue v. Gilleo, 20 Harv.Envtl.L.Rev. 473, 479 (1996).

7. Id. at 477.

8. Id.

9. Id. at 478.

10. Id.

11. Berman v. Parker, 348 U.S. 26, 33, 75 S.Ct. 98, 102–03, 99 L.Ed. 27 (1954).

12. Rice at 445, supra note 3.

require more than a pure aesthetic basis in order to justify architectural design review ordinances.[13]

An early case upholding architectural design review is State ex rel. Saveland Park Holding Corp. v. Wieland.[14] The ordinance under scrutiny provided that a building permit would not be issued if the building were so at variance with existing structures that it would cause substantial depreciation in property values. Although the express purpose of the ordinance was to protect property values, the court characterized it as being based on aesthetics, and upheld it on both grounds.[15]

A more recent case sustaining an architectural review board decision is Reid v. Architectural Bd. of Review.[16] The board had disapproved a permit for a single-story, ten-foot high house built of glass and concrete in a rough U-shape, which rambled through a grove of trees on a lot surrounded by a ten-foot fence. While the house otherwise complied with zoning requirements, it was to be built in an area of stately, older, two-and-a-half story houses. The architectural review board concluded that it should not be built, for it did not comply with the ordinance which required that the buildings maintain the high character of community development and protect real estate from impairment or destruction of value. The court held that maintenance of a high character of community appearance was within the scope of the general welfare, and while aesthetics alone would not be sufficient to sustain the ordinance, it was not enacted solely for that purpose.

Not surprisingly, these cases also involved the issue of whether the standards were adequate to guide administrative decisions. The purported standards in both ordinances were vague, but the courts did not find them so vague as to be an improper delegation of authority.[17]

A third major case in this milieu is State ex rel. Stoyanoff v. Berkeley.[18] The court upheld a denial of a building permit by an architectural review board on grounds that the proposed building would not fit the architectural character of the neighborhood, and would reduce the property values of neighboring homes. The proposed residence was to be a pyramid-like structure with a flat top, and triangular windows or doors at the corners. This was found to have an adverse aesthetic impact in a community of conventional residences of rather substantial value.

13. Id.

14. 269 Wis. 262, 69 N.W.2d 217 (1955), cert. denied 350 U.S. 841, 76 S.Ct. 81, 100 L.Ed. 750 (1955). Cf. Hankins v. Rockleigh, 55 N.J.Super. 132, 150 A.2d 63 (1959) (ordinance invalid as applied).

15. See supra § 3.14 regarding preservation of values.

16. 119 Ohio App. 67, 192 N.E.2d 74 (1963).

17. See also Nadelson v. Township of Millburn, 297 N.J.Super. 549, 688 A.2d 672

(1996) (holding that an ordinance that required alterations to residences in historic district to avoid incongruity with Colonial Revival style of district was not unconstitutionally vague); Park Home v. City of Williamsport, 545 Pa. 94, 680 A.2d 835 (1996). Cf. Morristown Road Associates v. Mayor & Common Council, 163 N.J.Super. 58, 394 A.2d 157 (1978) (standards too vague, ordinance stricken).

18. 458 S.W.2d 305 (Mo.1970).

An interesting complement to these three cases is LaSalle National Bank v. Evanston.[19] The city refused to change a zoning designation and allow building of high-rise apartments near Lake Michigan, partly on the grounds that the building would disrupt the city's attempt to effect a gradual tapering of building heights toward the open lakefront and park area, which was used for recreational purposes. The court found that aesthetic qualities were properly cognizable, and when coupled with reasonable restrictions on population density, the refusal to rezone was valid.[20]

Although it is possible that the legitimacy of aesthetic regulation may vary with the kind of aesthetic control at issue, the courts have not made distinctions on these grounds. Statutes and ordinances perceived to be based exclusively or primarily upon aesthetic considerations have been either sustained or struck, according to the perception of validity of such regulation in a given jurisdiction. Decisions upholding ordinances based solely on aesthetics continued to grow in number, and in 1984, the Supreme Court affirmed aesthetics as a proper basis for the exercise of the state police power for the general welfare in City Council of City of Los Angeles v. Taxpayers for Vincent.[21] Nonetheless, some courts still persist in requiring that additional grounds, such as protection of property values, density control, promotion of tourism, and protection of the public health and safety, be present.[22]

In addition to the general considerations affecting the validity of architectural controls, two constitutional issues frequently appear. Ordinances establishing procedures for architectural design review must set forth standards which are not unduly vague. The creation of standards that are not unduly vague can be a challenging task for legislatures given the subjective nature of aesthetics.[23] Such measures must also be narrowly drawn and must further a sufficiently substantial governmental purpose to avoid running afoul of First Amendment considerations.

The vagueness-due process challenge was raised in both *Saveland Park* and *Reid*, but each court held that the standards involved were adequate to support the factual determinations made in those cases.[24] Other courts have held architectural design ordinances to be unconstitutionally vague when the standards were not adequate to control the

19. 57 Ill.2d 415, 312 N.E.2d 625 (1974).

20. See also Landmark Land Co. v. City and County of Denver, 728 P.2d 1281 (1986) (upholding height limit to preserve mountain view from several city parks).

21. 466 U.S. 789, 805, 104 S.Ct. 2118, 2129, 80 L.Ed.2d 772 (1984) ("It is well settled that the state may legitimately exercise its police powers to advance aesthetic values.").

22. See, e.g., Village of Hudson v. Albrecht, Inc., 9 Ohio St.3d 69, 458 N.E.2d 852, 857 (1984), appeal dismissed 467 U.S. 1237, 104 S.Ct. 3503, 82 L.Ed.2d 814 (1984); Rice at 444, supra note 3.

23. Regan at 1025, supra note 1.

24. See Reid v. Architectural Bd. of Review, 119 Ohio App. 67, 192 N.E.2d 74 (1963); State ex rel. Saveland Park Holding Corp. v. Wieland, 269 Wis. 262, 69 N.W.2d 217 (1955), cert. denied 350 U.S. 841, 76 S.Ct. 81, 100 L.Ed. 750 (1955). Compare Historic Green Springs, Inc. v. Bergland, 497 F.Supp. 839 (E.D.Va.1980).

exercise of the reviewing board's discretion.[25] Proper standards are necessary for reasonable implementation of aesthetic zoning because they help avoid the abuse of discretion inherent in decisions based on aesthetics.[26] When standards incorporated into an ordinance are sufficiently certain that they can be understood by the regulated group, implemented by the administering agency, and applied by the reviewing court, the chances that the ordinance will survive judicial scrutiny are greatly increased.[27] Standards may be found in the consistency or patterns of community preference.[28] For example, communities may favor billboard controls[29] or preservation of historic-architectural "ensembles" such as New Orleans' Vieux Carre.[30] Thus, the presence of expressly articulated standards is exceedingly important. When combined with separation of powers considerations and the judiciary's inability to determine community aesthetic values, such standards will often warrant granting a legislative presumption of validity to an architectural control.[31]

Aesthetic regulation based on the offensiveness of the expression or architectural design can amount to censorship, and thus raise freedom of expression concerns. While the Supreme Court has not addressed the question of whether architecture is speech, many support the idea that it is a form of protected expression.[32] Permit denials, such as those in *Reid*, *Stoyanoff* and *Saveland Park*, are in a sense content-based restrictions on expression rather than simply time, place and manner regulations. A connection between the offensive expression and a threat to a substantial governmental interest may be sufficient to rebut a First Amendment challenge. The question becomes one of how to define a community's burden of proving that failure to regulate "design as expression" would threaten a substantial governmental interest. In *Penn Central*,[33] the court found that the interest in preserving landmarks was sufficiently substantial to withstand a taking claim. Whether the rationale would

25. R.S.T. Builders, Inc. v. Village of Bolingbrook, 141 Ill.App.3d 41, 95 Ill.Dec. 423, 489 N.E.2d 1151 (1986); De Sena v. Board of Zoning Appeals, Village of Hempstead, 45 N.Y.2d 105, 379 N.E.2d 1144, 408 N.Y.S.2d 14 (1978); Anderson v. of Issaquah, 70 Wash.App. 64, 851 P.2d 744 (1993).

26. Regan at 1022–23, supra note 1.

27. See, e.g., Morristown Road Assoc. v. Mayor & Common Council, 163 N.J.Super. 58, 394 A.2d 157 (1978).

28. See generally Costonis, Law and Aesthetics: A Critique and Reformulation of the Dilemmas, 80 Mich.L.Rev. 355 (1982).

29. United Advertising Corp. v. Borough of Metuchen, 42 N.J. 1, 198 A.2d 447 (1964); People v. Goodman, 31 N.Y.2d 262, 338 N.Y.S.2d 97, 290 N.E.2d 139 (1972), reargument denied 32 N.Y.2d 705, 343 N.Y.S.2d 1026, 296 N.E.2d 459 (1973).

30. Maher v. New Orleans, 516 F.2d 1051 (5th Cir.1975), cert. denied 426 U.S. 905, 96 S.Ct. 2225, 48 L.Ed.2d 830 (1976).

31. See Metromedia, Inc. v. San Diego, 453 U.S. 490, 101 S.Ct. 2882, 69 L.Ed.2d 800 (1981) (Rehnquist, J., dissenting), on remand 32 Cal.3d 180, 185 Cal.Rptr. 260, 649 P.2d 902 (1982).

32. Rice at 450, supra note 3. See also John Nivala, Constitutional Architecture: The First Amendment and the Single Family House, 33 San Diego L.Rev. 291, 316 (1996). But see Thomas Pak, Free Exercise, Free Expression, and Landmarks Preservation, 91 Colum.L.Rev. 1813 (1991) (arguing that not all structures should be entitled to First Amendment protection).

33. Penn Cent. Transp., Co. v. New York, 438 U.S. 104, 98 S.Ct. 2646, 57 L.Ed.2d 631 (1978), rehearing denied 439 U.S. 883, 99 S.Ct. 226, 58 L.Ed.2d 198 (1978).

stand in the face of a First Amendment challenge is yet an unresolved issue.[34]

Restrictive covenants are alternatives to the public regulation of aesthetics. Restrictive covenants are land use controls that deprive from private agreement to restrict the use of land.[35] The general absence of state action reduces, but does not eliminate, First Amendment considerations.[36] Currently, many states allow aesthetic control through restrictive covenants.[37] Many states approve these covenants if they are exercised reasonably and in good faith.[38] Additionally, courts have been less stringent in scrutinizing aesthetic standards in covenants, thus providing a flexible, yet private answer to aesthetic regulation.[39]

II.   HISTORIC PRESERVATION

§ 12.6   Introduction

In opening the analysis of aesthetics and architectural regulation, our first concern was with a definition of beauty or aesthetically pleasing.[1] Now we must pose an equally difficult question, what is *historic*? Does it mean "old" or "significant in history" or both? Whatever definition is formulated, the most essential aspect of the concept is *why* should we preserve, protect or restore "historic" resources.

Professor Robert Stipe's list of reasons for preserving historic resources deserves to be and has become a classic.

> First, we seek to preserve because our historic resources are all that physically link us to our past. Some portion of that patrimony must be preserved if we are to recognize who we are, how we became so and, most important, how we differ from others of our species. * * *

> Second, we strive to save our historic and architectural heritage simply because we have lived with it and it has become part of us. The presence of our physical past creates expectations and anticipations that are important parts of our daily lives. We tend to replace them only when they no longer have meaning, when other needs are more pressing, and do so with caution, knowing how our environment creates us and how we create our environment.

> Third, we save our physical heritage partly because we live in an age of frightening communication and other technological abilities, as well as in an era of increasing cultural homogeneity. In such a

---

34. See John Nivala, Constitutional Architecture: The First Amendment and the Single Family House, 33 San Diego L.Rev. 291 (1996) (arguing that the exterior design of a private home is constitutionally-protected expression of the inhabitants). See also Pak at 1816, supra note 32; Regan, supra note 1; Rice, supra note 3.

35. Regan, supra note 1, at 1030. See infra §§ 15.4–.9 regarding private controls.

36. Regan at 1029–30, supra note 1. See infra § 15.10, regarding constitutional issues.

37. Id.

38. Id.

39. Id.

§ 12.6

1. See § 12.1 supra.

situation we subconsciously reach out for any opportunity to maintain difference and uniqueness.

Fourth, we preserve historic sites and structures because of their relation to past events, eras, movements and persons that we feel are important to honor and understand. * * * Nostalgia and patriotism are important human emotions for preservation, and important human emotions must be served. But the important point is that the historic associations inherent in preserved structures and sites should encourage much more than mere nostalgia and patriotism. They are potential sources of imagination and creativity in our attempts to understand and appreciate the past—a past distant from us, but a time that can still offer much to guide us.

Fifth, we seek to preserve the architecture and landscapes of the past simply because of their intrinsic value as art. * * *

Sixth, we seek to preserve our past because we believe in the right of our cities and countryside to be beautiful. Here, with much regret, we must reorganize the essential tawdriness of much contemporary design and construction. Much of it is junk; it assaults our senses. We seek to preserve the past, not only because it is unique, exceptional, architecturally significant or historically important, but also because in most cases what replaces it will be inhuman and grotesque. Potentially, of course, many old buildings could be demolished and replaced with contemporary structures of equal functional or aesthetic value. Yet, recent experience has shown that this is not likely, and until it is we shall preserve our past in order to preserve what is left of our pleasing and humane urban and rural landscape.

Finally, and most important of all, we seek to preserve because we have discovered—all too belatedly—that preservation can serve an important human and social purpose in our society. Ancestor worship and aesthetic motivations are no longer enough: our traditional concern with great events, great people and great architects will not serve society in any full measure. The problem now is to acknowledge that historic conservation is but one aspect of the larger problem, basically an environmental one, of enhancing, or perhaps providing for the first time, a quality of human life.[2]

§ 12.7 History of Historic Preservation in the United States

Historic preservation[1] in the United States began in the mid 1800's with a private attempt to rescue Mt. Vernon from an uncertain fate. At

2. Robert Stipe, Why Preserve Historic Resources?, Legal Techniques in Historic Preservation (1972). See also 36 Law & Contemp.Probs. (Summer 1971) to which the just cited publication is a companion volume.

§ 12.7

1. In the preface to the well-respected work, A Handbook on Historic Preservation Law, the editor, Christopher Duerksen, addresses what is meant by preservation law:

Just what is "preservation law"? It is a collage, cutting across and drawing from

the time the only means for protecting a landmark of historical significance was private purchase by preservationists. The focus was generally local, and aimed at preventing destruction of a single building.[2]

Congress injected itself into the preservation field some time later when it began purchasing Civil War battlefield sites. This action resulted in United States v. Gettysburg Electric Railway Co.,[3] which involved condemnation of private property for the creation of a national battleground memorial. The Court rejected the narrow view that the condemnation was not for a valid public purpose, and held that preservation of an important monument to the country's past was a proper purpose. Thus, the tool of eminent domain was established as a valid method for protecting our historical heritage.

A more complicated and less well settled question was that of whether government regulatory powers could be similarly employed to limit uses or structures not inherently noxious, particularly without payment of compensation to the owner. Although regulation is now a well-recognized preservation technique, early decisions were not as broad minded about the application of the police power for such purposes. One of the first steps toward a more expansive use of regulatory power came in Welch v. Swasey,[4] where the United States Supreme Court upheld a Boston ordinance limiting building heights under the state police power, notably for fire prevention. Seventeen years later, the Court, in Village of Euclid v. Ambler Realty,[5] validated a zoning regulation which reduced the plaintiff's property value by almost 90%. The Court found that the burden was imposed in a nondiscriminatory manner, and the benefits accrued to all property owners as well; thus the regulation was reason-

several other established areas of law: land use and zoning, real property, taxation, local government, constitutional, and administrative. In many ways preservation law, particularly at the local level, is closest to land use and zoning; the rules are very similar. For example, the standards that dictate governmental behavior in enacting and administering zoning ordinances are virtually identical to those applicable to local landmark and historic district laws, and the constitutional doctrines governing regulation of private property are similar.

But preservation law has outgrown its local law origins and now has its own distinctive provisions—pertinent state and federal administrative procedures, an indigenous regulatory scheme, and special tax laws to name only a few. As a result, the days when preservationists had only to know how to run the local historical museum are gone. Today they must know local zoning and land-use law, how the federal income tax code works, what the state enabling law pro-

vides, and what the U.S. Supreme Court thinks about preservation ordinances and private property. Id. at xxii.

For discussions of the development of historic preservation law in the United States and abroad, see generally J. Sax, "Is Anyone Minding Stonehenge? The Origins of Cultural Property Protection in England," 78 Calif.L.Rev 1543 (1990); J. Sax, "Heritage Preservation As A Public Duty: Abbe Gregoire and the Origins of an Idea," 88 Mich.L.Rev 1142 (1990); Rose, Preservation and Community: New Directions in the Law of Historic Preservation, 33 Stan. L.Rev. 473 (1981).

2. See C. Hosmer, Presence of the Past (1965).

3. 160 U.S. 668, 16 S.Ct. 427, 40 L.Ed. 576 (1896). See also Roe v. Kansas ex rel. Smith, 278 U.S. 191, 49 S.Ct. 160, 73 L.Ed. 259 (1929).

4. 214 U.S. 91, 29 S.Ct. 567, 53 L.Ed. 923 (1909).

5. 272 U.S. 365, 47 S.Ct. 114, 71 L.Ed. 303 (1926).

able. With this expansive view of the police power, these cases laid the groundwork that allowed preservation programs to grow.

About the same time, the use of the historic district as a preservation tool was gaining considerable support not just for economic but for architectural reasons. In 1931, Charleston, South Carolina, enacted the first law that was effective to protect an historic area, the city's pre-civil war district. The Vieux Carre, in New Orleans, was established pursuant to a Louisiana Constitutional amendment in 1936,[6] and in 1939, San Antonio passed a preservation law. By 1956, still only a handful of cities had enacted such laws. They were very controversial, but despite owner opposition, nearly all challenges to historic district ordinances were rejected.[7]

§ 12.8 Preservation at the Federal Level

Federal legislation has also played an important role in the advancement of preservation. In 1906, Congress passed the Antiquities Act,[1] allowing the President to designate national monuments, primarily from federally-owned sites. Ten years later, the National Park Service was created, and it soon became the primary focus for federal preservation efforts. In 1935, Congress enacted the Historic Sites Act,[2] which for the first time conceived of historic preservation as national policy. In addition, the Act extended the Department of Interior's authority beyond federally owned properties to identify and survey historic sites throughout the country. This program later became the framework for the National Register of Historic Places. Not much later came the National Trust for Historic Preservation Act,[3] which facilitated private participation in preservation by creating a non-profit congressionally chartered corporation. Finally, in 1966, Congress passed the National Historic Preservation Act (NHPA),[4] which has become the basis for most of the administrative and protective devices, as well as the financial incentives, through which national preservation policy is now implemented.

The National Historic Preservation Act (NHPA)[5] provides the authority for a number of activities which implement the federal historic preservation program:[6] i) the National Register of Historic places, identi-

---

6. See Louisiana—L.S.A.–Constitution Art. 14, § 22A (creating the Vieux Carre Commission to preserve such buildings in the district as it deems to have archaeological and historical significance).

7. City of New Orleans v. Impastato, 198 La. 206, 3 So.2d 559 (1941) (upholding Vieux Carre Ordinance); Opinion of the Justices, 333 Mass. 773, 128 N.E.2d 557 (1955) (upholding creation of historic district commissions in Boston and Nantucket).

§ 12.8

1. 16 U.S.C.A. § 431 et seq.

2. Id. § 461 et seq.

3. Id. § 468.

4. Id. § 470 et seq.

5. Pub.L. No. 89–655, 80 Stat. 915, codified at 16 U.S.C.A. § 470 et seq.

6. See generally, C. Duerksen ed, A Handbook on Historic Preservation 214 (1983); Julia H. Miller, A Survey of Federal, State, and Local Laws Governing Historic Resource Protection, Preservation Information 1 (1997).

fying and listing historic and cultural resources;[7] ii) an expanded national register to include sites of state and local significance, establishing standards for evaluating historic significance;[8] iii) the matching grants-in-aid program, encouraging preservation activities at the state and local levels;[9] iv) the Advisory Council on Historic Preservation, providing information on historic properties to the executive and other federal agencies;[10] and v) the "section 106" review process, for protection of federal resources.

Under the act, "historic resources of federal interest" are broadly defined, so that not only nationally significant properties, but those important at local and state levels as well, are eligible for designation.[11] Listing on the National Register qualifies a property for participation in most of the federal incentive and protective programs.[12] Most properties find their way onto the Register through local initiative, followed by a process of state review and nomination in accordance with federal criteria.[13]

The National Historic Preservation Fund[14] provides matching grants to the states to carry out the purposes of the NHPA. The monies are used to conduct statewide surveys, prepare nominations to the National Register, and develop state preservation plans. In addition, the funds are used to support the necessary administrative structure of state programs, and financially assist the restoration of Register properties within the state.[15] This portion of the act has been a great impetus in establish-

---

7. 16 U.S.C.A. § 470a. An important aspect of the National Register is the National Historic Landmarks Program. Operated under the auspices of the National Park Service, the program provides for designation and protection of national landmarks. Once designated, a national landmark receives even greater protection from the impact of federal projects than even the § 106 review process provides. See 16 U.S.C.A. § 470a(a)(1)(B). See also Duerksen, supra note 6, at 228.

8. Id. § 470a(a)(2); see infra note 7. The criteria are found at 36 C.F.R. § 60.4.

9. 16 U.S.C.A. § 470a(c).

10. Id. § 470i–470j.

11. 36 C.F.R. § 60.4. The National Register criteria for evaluation are:

The quality of significance in American history, architecture, archeology, engineering, and culture is present in districts, sites, buildings, structures, and objects that possess integrity of location, design, setting, materials, workmanship, feeling, and association and

(a) that are associated with events that have made a significant contribution to the broad patterns of our history; or

(b) that are associated with the lives of persons significant in our past; or

(c) that embody the distinctive characteristics of a type, period, or method of construction, or that represent the work of a master, or that possess high artistic values, or that represent a significant and distinguishable entity whose components may lack individual distinction; or

(d) that have yielded, or may be likely to yield, information important in prehistory or history. Id.

12. 16 U.S.C.A. § 470f .

13. Properties may become eligible for inclusion on the register when nominated by: 1) a State Historic Preservation Officer, qualified local government, or individual, 2) the head of a federal agency, 3) the Secretary of the Interior, by designating the property as a National Landmark, or 4) by Congress. See Duerksen, supra note 6, at 197.

14. 16 U.S.C.A. § 470h. See also Id. § 470a(d).

15. Due to recent cutbacks in funding, most federal money is now being spent on surveying and documentation of historic sites and structures, and little money is available for the less critical programs.

ing historic preservation at the state level, and its requirements for participation in the grants program have led to greater administrative uniformity among state activities.

The Advisory Council on Historic Preservation (ACHP) is a cabinet level body which advises the president and Congress on preservation matters. It also comments on federal projects which may impact on historic properties, and aids in coordinating activities of federal agencies affecting preservation.[16] Its principal role, however, is the review and comment responsibility under section 106 of the Act.[17]

Section 106[18] brings together all elements of the federal preservation program to provide the basic federal legal protection for historic properties. Federal agencies must seek the council's comments for any action they wish to pursue which may affect a property either on or eligible for inclusion on the National Register of Historic Places. Like NEPA,[19] the provision mandates that an evaluation and analysis process be followed prior to approval of federal projects affecting historic properties. However, the ACHP's recommendations are not binding, and a proposed action may proceed once the review process is completed, regardless of a disfavorable recommendation. This does not mean section 106 review is entirely without teeth. Even a determination of whether it is necessary to comply can take several years to complete. It is important to note that the Section 106 review process is applicable only to federal agencies and agencies proceeding with federally funded projects. Thus, state or local regulation is necessary to impose any sort of review process on projects affecting historic properties that are proposed by state or local governments, or by private individuals.

Two other federal statutes are important in establishing the federal structure for national historic preservation: the National Environmental Policy Act (NEPA) and the Department of Transportation Act (DTA). NEPA requires consideration of impact on cultural environment as part of the environmental impact statement process.[20] Section 4(f) of the Department of Transportation Act contains some of the strongest language of all federal acts relevant to historic preservation because it *prohibits* federal approval or funding of transportation projects that require the use, direct or indirect, of historic sites unless there is no feasible or prudent alternative and the project includes all possible planning to minimize harm to the site.[21]

In addition to the NHPA, NEPA, and DTA, several other federal statutes provide a number of other tools and incentives to preservation-

---

16. 16 U.S.C.A. § 470j.

17. Id. § 470f.

18. Id.

19. 42 U.S.C.A. §§ 4321–70d .

20. 42 U.S.C. § 4321 (it is the continuing responsibility of the Federal Government to use all practical means ... to ...

preserve important historic, cultural, and natural aspects of our national heritage). Also see supra §§ 11.2, 11.3.

21. 49 U.S.C. § 303. See Julia Miller, A Survey of Federal, State, and Local Laws Governing Historic Resource Protection 7 (1997).

ists. They include the Coastal Zone Management Act,[22] the Surface Mining Control and Reclamation Act,[23] and the Archeological Resources Protection Act.[24] Several statutes provide federal aid for preservation through loans, grants and use of surplus government buildings.[25] The Public Buildings Cooperative Use Act[26] directs the General Services Administration to give preference to use of historic buildings for federal offices.

The Tax Reform Act of 1976 and the Economic Recovery Tax Act of 1981 created federal tax incentives, reflecting a shift in the policy of the Internal Revenue Code from penalizing to encouraging property owners to invest in preservation.[27] To qualify for a rehabilitation investment credit, a taxpayer must incur qualified expenses for rehabilitation of a certified historic structure. This eligibility determination relies heavily on the State Historic Preservation Officer's (SHPO) review of a lengthy application and recommendation to the regional office of the Secretary of the Interior. Any property or district on the National Register is automatically certified historic, and property within a registered district may also be certified if the enabling ordinance and the ordinance creating the district qualify under National Register Criteria. Once the structure is certified, the proposed rehabilitation work itself must also be reviewed and certified. In making the review, the SHPO follows the Department of Interior's "Standards for Rehabilitation and Guidelines for Rehabilitating Historic Buildings," to determine whether the work is consistent with the historic character of the building.[28] Finally, to qualify for the tax benefits, the building must have been "substantially rehabilitated."[29] In the 1986 tax reform act, Congress limited the availability and amount of the credit.[30]

The legal role of the federal government, in spite of all of the federal acts discussed above, is largely confined to regulating its own activities with respect to historic properties. Despite their limitations, the federal legislation has had a marked catalytic effect on programs at state and

22. See e.g., The National Coastal Zone Management Act, 16 U.S.C.A. §§ 1451–65. For an insightful analysis of the CZMA as applied to Preservation objectives, see generally Schmitz, The Coastal Zone Management Act's Role in Historic Preservation, Vol. 4 No. 6 Preserv'n L.Rptr. (Dec.1985). See also §§ 11.14, supra.

23. 30 U.S.C. § 1201 ("no surface mining operations . . . shall be permitted which will adversely affect any . . . places included in the National Register of Historic Sites unless approved jointly by the regulatory authority and the Federal, State, or local agency with jurisdiction over the . . . historic site."). See Julia Miller, A Survey of Federal, State, and Local Laws Governing Historic Resource Protection 7 (1997).

24. 16 U.S.C. § 470. See Julia Miller, A Survey of Federal, State, and Local Laws

Governing Historic Resource Protection 13 (1997).

25. E.g., 42 U.S.C.A. §§ 5304(h), 5318 (Block Grants and Urban Development Action Grants).

26. 40 U.S.C.A. § 611(c) (1997).

27. Tax Reform Act of 1976, 26 U.S.C.A. §§ 167, 168 (permitting accelerated depreciation); Economic Recovery Tax Act of 1981, 26 U.S.C.A. §§ 44, 48(g) (allowing investment tax credits).

28. See 36 C.F.R. § 67.7.

29. 26 U.S.C.A. § 47(c)(1)(A)(i).

30. See White and Keating, Historic Preservation and Architectural Control Law, 24 Urb.Law. 865 (1992); Cheverine and Hayes, Rehabilitation Tax Credit: Does is Still Provide Incentive? 10 Va. Tax Rev. 167 (1990).

local levels. All states and territories have enacted historic preservation laws, and at least 832 historic districts or landmark commissions had been created as of 1981.[31]

§ 12.9 State Historic Preservation Law

The 1980 amendments to the National Historic Preservation Act (NHPA) greatly increased the states' role under the federal preservation scheme. The diminished federal involvement, while reducing funding, has given states the opportunity to assume greater responsibility for preservation and to better respond to the individual needs of the state. Various types of laws have been utilized: grants of power to local governments to preserve historic resources through zoning, establishment of historic districts and commissions, creation of state agencies with preservation powers, state registers of historic places, environmental policy acts which consider the adverse effects of government actions on historic resources, and even inclusion of historic preservation policy in a few state constitutions.[1]

States can delegate regulatory authority in several ways. Most provide localities with power to enact historic district zoning, and some allow for landmark designation.[2] The standard zoning power generally can be used to protect historic areas and to require special standards and review procedures for actions proposed within them. Regulations which designate landmarks or establish historic districts have generally been upheld by courts as a valid use of local authority to promote the general welfare.[3]

Most states authorize local preservation bodies to acquire historic properties.[4] These may be acquired not only in fee simple but in less-

---

31. Directory of American Preservation Commissions III (S. Dennis ed. 1981); Beckwith, Appendix of State & Territorial Historic Preservation Statutes and Session Laws, 11 N.C.Cent.L.J. 308 (1980).

§ 12.9

1. E.g., La.—LSA–Const.art. 6, § 17; Cal.Const.art. 13, § 8; Md.Const.art. 51; Mo.Const.art. 3, § 48; N.Y.Const.art. 14, § 4.

2. Leonard A. Zax, Protection of the Built Environment: A Washington D.C. Case Study in Historic Preservation, 19 B.C. Envtl.Aff.L.Rev. 651 (1992). See e.g., West's Ann.Cal.Gov't Code §§ 50280–50290; Colo.Rev.Stat. 24–80–1201 to 24–80–1202; D.C.Code Encycl. §§ 5.801 to 5.805; West's Fla.Stat.Ann. §§ 380.501–380.515; Hawaii Rev.Stat. §§ 46–4.5, 246–34; N.Y.—McKinney's Gen.Munic.Law § 96–a.

3. See, e.g., Estate of Tippett v. City of Miami, 645 So.2d 533 (Fla.App.1994)

(where landowner claimed that creation of historic district that included her property was an unconstitutional taking); Figarsky v. Historic Dist. Comm'n, 171 Conn. 198, 368 A.2d 163 (1976) (denial of demolition permit by historic commission upheld where local preservation ordinance incorporated by reference state enabling statute); A–S–P Assoc. v. Raleigh, 298 N.C. 207, 258 S.E.2d 444 (1979) (approving legislative grant of authority to locality for creation of historic district); City of Santa Fe v. Gamble–Skogmo, Inc., 73 N.M. 410, 389 P.2d 13 (1964) (city had sufficient authority to impose criminal sanctions for violations of preservation ordinance). See, generally, D. Cavarello, "From Penn Central to United Artists' I + II: The Rise to Immunity of Historic Preservation Designation From Successful Takings Challenges," 22 B.C. Envt'l.Aff.L.Rev. 593 (1998).

4. Beckwith, Developments in the Law of Historic Preservation and a Reflection on Liberty, 12 Wake Forest L.Rev. 93 (1976).

than-fee interests, such as facade or conservation easements.[5] Acquisition power also includes that of eminent domain which results in condemnation for a public purpose and payment of just compensation. Localities also have the responsibility of raising funds to foster preservation and maintain the properties under their dominion.[6]

Acquisition of full ownership of property is expensive and often has the effect of removing property from the local tax base. These drawbacks have limited its use as a preservation tool. On the other hand, enabling local governments or other bodies to accept preservation easements, or enter into and enforce partial acquisition contracts and covenants, results in less cost but offers many of the same protective benefits.[7]

Another technique enjoying some recent success is the use of a revolving funds program to purchase, or to acquire options on historic properties. Once purchased, a structure is sold to a new owner who covenants to maintain the building's historic character. The money realized from this sale is then reused to purchase and protect other historic structures.

Some states have enacted tax laws to aid and promote historic preservation. Among the available methods are granting localities specific power to reduce tax burdens on historic properties[8] and giving tax credits for restoration of buildings in historic districts.[9] The state may in some cases provide financing to the locality to the extent revenues are reduced. Under such a scheme, if a structure is subsequently destroyed or put to incompatible use, the owner repays taxes saved.[10] One of the greatest barriers to use of this device by state and local government is the fear of lost revenue.[11]

5. United States v. Albrecht, 496 F.2d 906 (8th Cir.1974). See generally John J. Hollingshead, Conservation Easements: A Flexible Tool for Land Preservation, 3 Envtl.L. 319 (1997); George M. Covington, Conservation Easements: A Win/Win for Preservationists and Real Estate Owners, 84 Ill.B.J. 628 (1996). A preservation easement may be created by purchase or donation. Put simply, it is an agreement between a landowner and a locality or charitable organization giving the latter the right to monitor and protect the architectural and historic integrity of the property. The concept represents a statutory departure from the common law's hostility toward easements in gross. See § 13.12, infra and § 15.3, infra.

6. See, e.g., West's Fla.Stat.Ann. § 704.06; Mich.Comp.Laws Ann. § 5.3395; N.Y.—McKinney's Gen.Mun.Law § 119–aa to 119–dd.

7. The advantages are primarily financial. Because the cost of a typical facade easement is around 10% of the structure's value, the amount of money normally required to purchase just one

historic structure can now be used to protect 10 structures (assuming similar value) through acquisition of only a preservation easement. An added benefit is that the cost of maintenance and repairs is borne by the owner, further lessening the locality's financial commitment. Finally, federal tax incentives in the form of charitable deductions for donation of easements make this preservation technique especially popular with property owners. See generally, Lord, The Advantages of Facade Easements, Legal Techniques in Historic Preservation, National Trust for Historic Preservation in the U.S., 35 (1971).

8. Or.Rev.Stat. 358.475–358.565.

9. Ala. Code § 11–68–5(11) (1996). For discussion of federal tax law, see supra § 12.8.

10. Wilson & Winkler, Response of State Legislation to Historic Preservation, 36 Law & Contemp.Probs. 329 (1971).

11. Carolyn Ells Cheverine & Charlotte Mariah Hayes, Rehabilitation Tax Credit: Does it Still Provide Incentives, 10

There are also laws or programs in several states within state environmental policy acts (SEPA), which require extensive review of planned activities. These acts essentially mirror the policy and provisions of NEPA.[12] In nearly every SEPA, historic properties are included within the definition of the environment, and a permit to demolish a registered property would probably come under review. This is an important supplement to preservation at the state level because activities which would be generally outside the scope of other laws may be covered by a SEPA.[13]

Although most states, with or without a SEPA, have adopted their own version of § 106 of the NHPA, there are some exceptions which make it essential to check the exact language of the relevant state statute. Florida, for example, has modeled its statute after the stronger § 4f of the DTA.[14]

§ 12.10 Historic Preservation at the Local Level

The most important preservation work occurs at the local level, and it is here that the major issues are encountered and resolved. It was from a local regulation which allowed designation of landmarks in New York City that Penn Central Transportation Co. v. New York[1] arose. There, the Supreme Court of the United States affirmed community power to adopt ordinances which control what owners of historic buildings can do with their properties.

It is no accident that local regulation plays such an important role in our preservation scheme. As noted above,[2] the NHPA provides protection from only the potentially intrusive projects of federal government agencies. Thus, even if a locality is listed on the National Register of Historic Places, additional protection is needed to prevent alteration or demolition of historic properties by private individuals or state and local governments. This protection usually comes in the form of a local preservation ordinance.

Generally, local regulatory schemes are fairly simple and are usually considered to be just another type of zoning control. A preservation program is typically initiated by a locality through appropriate enabling legislation, which establishes a preservation overlay zone, sets forth criteria for inclusion in the district, and creates some sort of a preservation review board. Under the scheme, owners of designated historic

Va. Tax Rev. 167 (1990); Miriam Joels Silver, Note, Federal Tax Incentives for Historic Preservation: A Strategy for Conservation and Investment, 10 Hofstra L. Rev. 887 (1982); Powers, Tax Incentives for Historic Preservation, 12 Urb.Law. 103 (1980).

12. Stephen M. Johnson, NEPA and SEPA's in the Quest for Environmental Justice, 30 Loy.L.A.L.Rev. 565 (1997).

13. NEPA and NHPA, again, only regulate federal use of its own property or major federal actions with significant effect on the environment. A SEPA would catch state activities which otherwise would fall through the cracks in federal law.

14. Fla.Stat.Ann. § 267.061.

§ 12.10

1. 438 U.S. 104, 98 S.Ct. 2646, 57 L.Ed. 631 (1978), rehearing denied 439 U.S. 883, 99 S.Ct. 226, 58 L.Ed.2d 198 (1978).

2. See supra, § 12.8.

properties must seek board approval prior to proceeding with any proposed alterations to the property. The amount of authority vested in a review board varies and may extend to cover demolition and new construction or may be limited to regulating exterior alterations.

As might be expected legal challenges, including the taking challenge, are frequently raised and litigated at this stage.[3] Owners of designated property, dissatisfied with the review board's denial of a certificate of appropriateness,[4] often question the sufficiency of due process in both the creation[5] and application of the preservation ordinance. Many localities have successfully anticipated the problem and have thwarted such attacks through careful ordinance drafting. Seeking to avoid vagueness challenges, localities often incorporate NHPA review standards, for which a considerable body of interpretive case law already exists.[6] Safety valves, allowing for exception to the regulatory scheme where economic hardship would occur, are another means of dealing with a potential taking challenge.[7]

A good preservation or landmarks control program commonly contains three elements: 1) a survey, to establish the basis for designation and regulation; 2) a means of providing technical and economic assistance, to aid historic property owners, and 3) some sort of synchronization with the jurisdiction's comprehensive plan, zoning ordinances or other regulatory programs.[8]

The 1980 amendments to the NHPA emphasized surveys and inventories. Under the amended act, states must maintain surveys to be eligible for National Register nomination and federal funding programs.[9] Surveys are also useful in providing direction to a preservation program. Using a well-documented survey as a guide, a community can carefully and rationally select those areas or structures it deems most worth protecting.[10] An added benefit is that such documentation provides a

---

3. See, e.g., *Penn Central*, supra note 1.

4. A certificate of appropriateness is a fundamental requirement of any preservation ordinance. It is essentially a requirement that proposed changes to an historic structure within a designated district be reviewed by a preservation commission to ensure that the changes are in harmony with the character, significant features, and atmosphere of the structure or area. See generally, Recommended Model Provisions for a Preservation Ordinance, National Trust for Historic Preservation (1983), reprinted as Appendix A in a Handbook on Historic Preservation Law, infra note 6.

5. Metropolitan Dade County v. P.J. Birds, Inc., 654 So.2d 170 (Fla.App.1995) (upholding designation of portion of tourist attraction as historic site); Caspersen v. Town of Lyme, 139 N.H. 637, 661 A.2d 759 (N.H.1995) (holding that zoning ordinance was properly enacted).

6. A Handbook on Historic Preservation Law 83 (C. Duerksen, ed. 1983).

7. Id. at 87.

8. Id. at 37.

9. Pub.L. No. 96–515, §§ 201(a), 202 (1980), codified at 16 U.S.C.A. § 470a (requiring the states to maintain a statewide inventory and permitting the Secretary of the Interior to make 70% grants for state and local surveys).

10. South of Second Assoc. v. Georgetown, 196 Colo. 89, 580 P.2d 807 (1978), appeal after remand 199 Colo. 394, 609 P.2d 125 (1980). The ordinance here designated the whole town an historic district. The Colorado Supreme Court struck the law because the local commission treated areas within the district differently, indicating district boundaries should have been more precise.

record of the designation decision, useful in the event of a court challenge.[11]

While most historic preservation plans tend to focus on what a property owner may do with his designated property, another successful approach used in addition to a regulatory scheme is to provide landmark owners technical and economic assistance. The idea is to defuse economic concerns weighing against preservation and make participation easier on historic property owners. In *Penn Central*,[12] New York City used a transferable development rights (TDR)[13] system to mitigate the financial effects of building permit denial. Other measures include financial assistance through reduction of property taxes, direct grant or revolving fund programs, and donation of facade easements qualifying for federal tax deductions, as well as educational programs, providing technical assistance through publications and workshops.[14]

Coordination of a preservation program is important legally, since a growing number of states require local governments to have comprehensive plans which include a preservation element.[15] This is especially important when a preservation ordinance comes under attack in court. If a local government can demonstrate that preservation is part of its overall plan to promote general community welfare, the local preservation ordinance stands a much better chance of surviving judicial scrutiny.

Commentators have suggested that, in order to avoid invalidating early zoning ordinances, courts often held that the existence of comprehensive plans could be implied from the combined effect of zoning ordinances, regulations and maps.[16] Although none really existed, the finding of a comprehensive landmarks program was important to the success of New York's Landmarks Program in *Penn Central*.[17] By looking at the local landmarks law and the properties designated under it, the Supreme Court was able to satisfy the requirement, albeit by legal fiction, that zoning be "in accordance with a comprehensive plan."[18]

In addition to the legal benefits it provides, a coordinated preservation program has some practical advantages as well. A well-ordered preservation plan will make acquisition of federal funding easier for local governments.[19] Synchronization of building, fire, and housing codes with

---

11. Bohannan v. San Diego, 30 Cal. App.3d 416, 106 Cal.Rptr. 333 (1973); Manhattan Club v. New York City Landmarks Preservation Comm'n, 51 Misc.2d 556, 273 N.Y.S.2d 848 (1966). See also Duerksen, supra note 6.

12. See supra, note 1.

13. See § 9.9 supra.

14. See Duerksen, supra note 6 at 42, 43.

15. See, e.g., West's Fla.Stat.Ann. § 163.3177(6)(f)(1)(e) which includes preservation as a mandatory element of a local comprehensive plan.

16. .Haar, In Accordance With a Comprehensive Plan, 68 Harv.L.Rev. 1154 (1955).

17. See Duerksen, supra note 6 at 35.

18. 438 U.S. at 132, 133, 98 S.Ct. at 2663. See also § 2.13.

19. E.g., NEPA requires an environmental impact statement which includes consideration of the project's effect on aesthetics and the built environment. Citizens to Preserve Overton Park v. Volpe, 401 U.S. 402, 91 S.Ct. 814, 28 L.Ed.2d 136 (1971), on remand 335 F.Supp. 873 (D.Tenn.1972), on remand 357 F.Supp. 846

preservation policies can do much for the success of a local program, since building officials usually consider safety of the building first, and only secondarily look to its special aesthetic or historic qualities.[20]

Because most preservation ordinances are implemented through overlay zoning, it is especially important that the plan be consistent with the applicable zoning. Problems arise when a preservation ordinance forbids alteration or demolition of a certain landmark but the zoning classification provides an incentive to tear it down by permitting a more lucrative use. Downzoning may work to ease this sort of development pressure.[21] To be truly effective, historic preservation must go beyond mere design and move broadly into the zoning realm by considering, in addition, such matters as density of development and permitted uses.[22] This integration will help satisfy concerns expressed by courts, notably the Supreme Court in *Penn Central*, about comprehensiveness, and further strengthen the legal status of preservation in general.

A final issue that merits discussion in regard to local preservation programs and the ordinances which establish them is that of owner consent or owner objection.[23] The issue has become increasingly important since an owner objection provision was added to the National Historic Preservation Act by the 1980 amendments. Pursuant to that provision, owners must be given an opportunity to object to the listing of their property in the National Register and if they do object, the property may not be listed.[24] There is no requirement that state and local programs must include such provisions but landowner opposition is particularly difficult to overcome at the local level.

§ 12.11 Proper Use of the Police Power: Warding Off Takings Claims and Other Constitutional Challenges

When a local government adopts a preservation ordinance, typically three issues arise: whether the new ordinance treats property owners fairly, how it affects the interrelationships among the local government's departments and its other programs, and the cost to the local government. A well thought out and carefully drafted ordinance can go a long way toward solving the second concern. Cities are increasingly providing

(D.Tenn.1973); W.A.T.C.H. v. Harris, 603 F.2d 310 (2d Cir.1979), cert. denied 444 U.S. 995, 100 S.Ct. 530, 62 L.Ed.2d 426 (1979).

20. Some progress was made in this vein when the National Trust for Historic Preservation, the American Institute of Architects and the Building Officials and Code Administrators got together and amended the Basic Building Code to provide specifically for restoration of landmarks. See B.O.C.A., Basic Building Code § 576.1 (1981).

21. Acierno v. Cloutier, 40 F.3d 597 (3d Cir.1994); Amdur v. Chicago, 638 F.2d 37 (7th Cir.1980), cert. denied 452 U.S. 905, 101 S.Ct. 3031, 69 L.Ed.2d 406 (1981).

22. C. Weaver & R. Babcock, City Zoning: The Once and Future Frontier, 120, 121 (1979).

23. See generally, E.L.Hunt, J. McPherson and C. Brinson, Historic Preservation in Florida Ch. 5 (1988).

24. 16 U.S.C.A. § 470 et seq. See 36 CFR 60.6.

for wider use of historic districts in their plans for the future.[1] It is possible, through revitalization of downtown areas, to increase the property tax base and to acquire federal funding through block grants.[2] Often, landmarks can be a tremendous asset in renewal of a city if building owners and local governments are willing to collaborate and adapt the building to new uses.[3]

The cry of the unwilling property owner whose parcel is designated as a landmark is usually that of "taking." Prior to the Supreme Court decision in *Penn Central*, courts found their way around the issue using several rationales. The Fifth Circuit upheld the New Orleans Vieux Carre ordinance which called for preserving the "tout ensemble" of the historic French Quarter.[4] It reasoned that the ordinance sought a legal constitutional end using permissible means, since the operation of the Vieux Carre commission satisfied due process standards by providing reasonable legislative and practical guidance to, and control over, administrative decision making. In Rebman v. Springfield,[5] a zoning ordinance which placed the plaintiff's property in an historic district around Abraham Lincoln's home did not result in a taking but was a valid exercise of police power for zoning purposes. Thus, denial of the building permit for proposed construction not in keeping with the character of the historical area surrounding Lincoln's home was appropriate under the ordinance. In a New York case, designation of a building as a landmark was held not confiscatory when the owner was guaranteed a reasonable return on his investment with an option to demolish if no scheme to provide reasonable return could be devised.[6]

Whether historic regulation is a taking of the owner's property or a permissible exercise of the police power and thus not compensable is a question not completely answered by *Penn Central*. Pressure from real estate lobbyists concerned about the extent to which courts allowed regulation to reduce property values led to the 1980 amendments to the NHPA. The act now allows a property owner to object to having his building automatically placed on the National Register.[7]

§ 12.11

1. One way to do this may be to pattern the ordinance somewhat after the Federal Public Buildings Cooperative Use Act, 40 U.S.C.A. § 601a. Cities can designate properties and use the space for offices. Designated properties owned by government can be sold to private entities for similar utilization with the proviso that the historic integrity of the building be maintained. For an example of inner conflict see Heritage Hill Ass'n v. City of Grand Rapids, 48 Mich.App. 765, 211 N.W.2d 77 (1973) where a variance was granted by one of the local government's departments for demolition of a building in a historic preservation district designated by another of the local government's departments.

2. 42 U.S.C.A. § 5303.

3. For example, in Boston, Faneuil Hall; in Baltimore, Inner Harbor; and in Washington, D.C., Old Post Office. See Trustees of Sailors' Snug Harbor v. Platt, 29 A.D.2d 376, 288 N.Y.S.2d 314 (1968) (retained group of Greek revival buildings and adapted to new use).

4. Maher v. New Orleans, 516 F.2d 1051 (5th Cir.1975), cert. denied 426 U.S. 905, 96 S.Ct. 2225, 48 L.Ed.2d 830 (1976).

5. 111 Ill.App.2d 430, 250 N.E.2d 282 (1969).

6. Manhattan Club v. New York City Landmarks Preservation Comm'n, 51 Misc.2d 556, 273 N.Y.S.2d 848 (1966).

7. See 16 U.S.C.A. § 470a(a)(6), accord 36 C.F.R. § 60. Note that while this measure may appear to make National Register

Local ordinances frequently authorize preservation commissions to require affirmative duties of landowners through anti-neglect or minimum maintenance measures to prevent demolition by neglect.[8] In a typical scenario, the local historic district commission is empowered to identify buildings needing repair and notify owners. If work is not commenced within a certain time, a hearing is held. After the hearing, repairs may be undertaken at city expense and a lien placed on the property. May a preservation ordinance do this without effectuating an unconstitutional taking?[9] Restrictions on private property rights have been long in existence. Some of these, based on general societal considerations such as easements by necessity, regulation of water rights, and zoning, recognize a state's right to limit or control the use of private property.[10]

Inclusion of the taking clause in the Bill of Rights represented a compromise between absolute individual property rights and the government's right to take property,[11] but determination of what constitutes a taking is "a question of degree ... and therefore cannot be disposed of by general propositions."[12] Several approaches have been used by the courts to make this determination, including physical invasion,[13] noxious use,[14] balancing of interests[15] and diminution in value tests. The latter adapts well to cases which do not involve physical invasion or noxious use problems. In *Penn Central*, however, the Court determined that diminution of value alone was not enough and that one must focus on

listing more difficult, it is in reality a pro-preservation compromise. As originally introduced, the bill containing the 1980 NHPA Amendments required the affirmative support of a majority of residents of the proposed district. As enacted, the amendment instead requires that a majority of owners oppose the proposed listing. As a practical matter therefore the amendment does not substantially interfere with National Register listing. See generally, Cavarello, "From Penn Central to United Artists' I + II: The Rise to Immunity of Historic Preservation Designation from Successful Takings Challenges, 22 B. C. Envt'l Aff. L.Rev 593 (1995).

8. Note, Affirmative Maintenance Provisions in Historic Preservation: A Taking of Property?, 34 S.C.L.Rev. 713 (1983).

9. More complete discussions of the taking issue are found at §§ 10.2–10.11.

10. See, e.g., Charleston, S.C., Code §§ 54–23 to 54–35 (1977); Coral Gables, Fla., Code § 9.4 (1981); New Orleans, La., Code (Vieux Carre) art. III, §§ 65–35 to 65–40 (1978).

11. Loren A. Smith, Life, Liberty & Whose Property? An Essay on Property Rights, 30 U.Rich.L.Rev. 1055 (1996); See, e.g., Frazier, The Green Alternative to Clas-

sical Liberal Property Theory, 20 Vt.L.Rev. 299 (1995); Byrne, Ten Arguments for the Abolition of the Regulatory Takings Doctrine, 22 Ecology L.Q. 89 (1995); Walker & Avitabile, Regulatory Takings, Historic Preservation and Property Rights Since Penn Central: The Move Toward Greater Protection, 6 Fordham Envtl.L.J. 819 (1995); Kayden, Historic Preservation and the New Takings Cases: Landmarks Preserved, 6 Fordham Env'tl L.J. 779 (1995); Powell, Relationship Between Property Rights and Civil Rights, 15 Hastings L.J. 135 (1963); Note, Property, Philosophy & Regulation: The Case Against a Natural Law Theory of Property Rights, 17 Willamette L.Rev. 527 (1981).

12. Pennsylvania Coal Co. v. Mahon, 260 U.S. 393, 416, 43 S.Ct. 158, 160, 67 L.Ed. 322 (1922).

13. E.g., Northern Transportation Co. v. Chicago, 99 U.S. (9 Otto) 635, 25 L.Ed. 336 (1878).

14. E.g., Hadacheck v. Sebastian, 239 U.S. 394, 36 S.Ct. 143, 60 L.Ed. 348 (1915); Mugler v. Kansas, 123 U.S. 623, 8 S.Ct. 273, 31 L.Ed. 205 (1887).

15. E.g., Pennsylvania Coal v. Mahon, 260 U.S. 393, 43 S.Ct. 158, 67 L.Ed. 322 (1922).

the uses that the regulation allowed as well.[16] The taking issue is discussed in detail in Chapter 10 of this treatise, but a few specific comments regarding its handling in historic preservation cases is warranted.

While the existence of an historic district, as a comprehensive scheme which includes both landmark sites and historic districts, will generally withstand judicial scrutiny,[17] taking problems are potentially greater with respect to designation of an isolated landmark.[18] Ordinances usually require a certificate of appropriateness before any exterior changes to the landmark can be made, and may also make affirmative maintenance demands. To avoid a claim of taking, the ordinance may provide for exceptions to certain restrictions on the property if the landowner cannot get a reasonable return on his investment, or for other economic assistance.[19] If the cost of maintenance is prohibitive to the landowner, the likelihood that it will be deemed a taking increases. For example, an owner unable to restore from an economic standpoint must establish that it is impractical to sell or lease the property, or that there is no market for it at a reasonable price.[20]

Application of a landmarks law to noncommercial landowners can be problematic. If maintenance of the landmark either physically or financially prevents or seriously interferes with carrying out a charitable purpose, the regulation may be considered invalid. While the test enunciated by the New York court in Trustees of Sailors' Snug Harbor v. Platt[21] has proven workable for charitable organizations it may not meet the rigid proscriptions of the First Amendment when applied to religious organizations.[22]

Courts have tended to sidestep this issue, although it is often raised. This may be due to the complexity of the question and difficulty of drawing a bright line, but the crux of a case generally involves the taking

16. Penn Cent. Transp. Co. v. New York, 438 U.S. 104, 136, 98 S.Ct. 2646, 2665, 57 L.Ed.2d 631 (1978), rehearing denied 439 U.S. 883, 99 S.Ct. 226, 58 L.Ed.2d 198 (1978).

17. Id. at 130, 98 S.Ct. at 2662.

18. Compare, e.g., Maher v. New Orleans, 516 F.2d 1051 (5th Cir.1975), rehearing denied 521 F.2d 815 (5th Cir.1975), cert. denied 426 U.S. 905, 96 S.Ct. 2225, 48 L.Ed.2d 830 (1976) with Penn Central Transportation Co. v. City of New York, 438 U.S. 104, 136, 98 S.Ct. 2646, 2665, 57 L.Ed.2d 631 (1978), rehearing denied 439 U.S. 883, 99 S.Ct. 226, 58 L.Ed.2d 198 (1978). See generally, Pinkerton, Aesthetics and the Single Building Landmark, 15 Tulsa L.J. 610 (1980).

19. Manhattan Club v. New York City Landmarks Preservation Comm'n, 51 Misc.2d 556, 273 N.Y.S.2d 848 (1966).

Transferrable development rights may be an alternate means to compensate an owner. See Penn Central, 438 U.S. at 137, for a discussion of TDR's. See also Costonis, Development Rights Transfer: An Exploratory Essay, 83 Yale L.J. 75 (1973).

20. Lafayette Park Baptist Church v. Board of Adjustment, 599 S.W.2d 61 (Mo. App.1980).

21. 29 A.D.2d 376, 288 N.Y.S.2d 314 (1968).

22. Churches also challenged landmark designations under the Religious Freedom Restoration Act (RFRA), but the act was held unconstitutional in City of Boerne v. Flores, 117 S.Ct. 2157, 138 L.Ed.2d 624 (1997). See supra § 10.18C. Hamilton, The Religious Freedom Restoration Act: Letting the Fox into the Henhouse under Cover of Section 5 of the Fourteenth Amendment, 16 Cardozo L.Rev. 357 (1994).

issue, and resolution of the First Amendment problem may be unnecessary.

In Lutheran Church in America v. New York,[23] the church protested the designation as a landmark of the former Morgan Mansion, which it had been using for offices. The church, which had planned to demolish the mansion and construct a building more suitable for its administrative offices, argued that the designation interfered with its ability to pursue charitable goals and was therefore a taking. Rather than considering whether the church could put the building to any use, the court determined that since the designation effectively prevented the church from continuing to use the building as it had been used, the application of the landmark ordinance was void.[24] This decision has been strongly criticized,[25] and its rationale directly conflicts with language in *Penn Central* and earlier zoning cases.[26]

In contrast, when the First Presbyterian Church of York[27] protested the designation of a Victorian house which it wanted to demolish to make room for church parking, the court did not find a taking. It held the ordinance valid under a reasonable use test, where, as in this case, the property was located within an historic district. In Vestry of St. Bartholomew's Church v. City of New York, a church challenged the application of the city's Landmarks Preservation law to the church's attempt to replace a church-owned building with an office tower.[28] Although the church was not in an historic district, the Second Circuit upheld the ordinance because an ordinance will only be invalidated if it prevents a church from carrying out its religious and charitable missions in its current buildings.[29]

Churches have also challenged landmark designations under the Religious Freedom Restoration Act (RFRA). The zoning authorities of Boerne, Texas, denied the Catholic Archbishop a building permit to enlarge a church on the basis of the City's historic presentation ordinance. The Archbishop brought suit challenging the application of the

23. 35 N.Y.2d 121, 316 N.E.2d 305, 359 N.Y.S.2d 7 (1974).

24. Id. at 129, 359 N.Y.S.2d at 15, 316 N.E.2d at 310. Other cases which have invalidated landmark designations as applied to churches include: St. James Methodist Church v. Kingston, (No. 76–1239, Ulster county Sup.Ct., N.Y., May 6, 1977) (notice requirement of ordinance not met). But in Lafayette Park Baptist Church v. Scott, 553 S.W.2d 856 (Mo.App.1977), the court stated that demolition must be permitted only if economics of restoration are such that no other use would be feasible. But here, the church had constructive notice of property's location in historic district, and the designation remained.

25. See Note, Use of Zoning Restrictions to Restrain Property Owners from Altering or Destroying Historic Landmarks,

1975 Duke L.J. 999, 1013; Note, Environmental Control—Land Use—Historical Preservation, 1975 Wis.L.Rev. 260, 276.

26. 438 U.S. 104, 125, 98 S.Ct. 2646, 2659, 57 L.Ed.2d 631 (1978), rehearing denied 439 U.S. 883, 99 S.Ct. 226, 58 L.Ed.2d 198 (1978). See also Goldblatt v. Town of Hempstead, 369 U.S. 590, 82 S.Ct. 987, 8 L.Ed.2d 130 (1962); Hadacheck v. Sebastian, 239 U.S. 394, 36 S.Ct. 143, 60 L.Ed. 348 (1915).

27. First Presbyterian Church v. City Council, 25 Pa.Cmwlth. 154, 360 A.2d 257 (1976). See also Society for Ethical Culture v. Spatt, 51 N.Y.2d 449, 434 N.Y.S.2d 932, 415 N.E.2d 922 (1980), reargument dismissed 52 N.Y.2d 1073, 438 N.Y.S.2d 1029, 420 N.E.2d 413 (1981).

28. 914 F.2d 348, 350 (2d Cir.1990).

29. Id. at 351.

ordinance to the church as a violation of RFRA. The district court entered judgment for the city holding RFRA unconstitutional on the theory in passing the Act, Congress exceeded its authority under Section 5 of the Fourteenth Amendment to the U.S. Constitution.[30] The Fifth Circuit reversed[31] and the Supreme Court granted certiorari. The Supreme Court reversed the Fifth Circuit and agreed with the District Court that Congress exceeded its authority in enacting RFRA.[32]

The designation of the interior of a church presents a particularly sensitive religious freedom issue to the courts. In Society of Jesus of New England v. Boston Landmarks Commission,[33] the court struck down the designation of the interior of a church saying that the "configuration of the church interior is so freighted with religious meaning that it must be considered part and parcel of the Jesuits' religious worship."[34]

Ultimately, the most troublesome aspect of applying landmark laws to religious buildings is the imposition of financial burdens. Maintenance requirements can be fiscally oppressive, especially if the structure has outlived its usefulness to the congregation and cannot be sold. Another problem arises when funds earmarked for charitable purposes are required to be diverted to cover maintenance and repair costs. Tax relief or exemptions granted by federal, state or local schemes are meaningless to churches and synagogues because they already enjoy tax-exempt status.[35] On the other hand, it can be argued that the tax exemption given to religious/charitable institutions gives them a responsibility to help maintain the commonly-held values of our society. They are presumably nonprofit institutions, devoted to goals above and beyond the mercenary and should be in a less favorable position to claim that they need to make a profit on their property.

30. Flores v. Boerne, 877 F.Supp. 355 (1995) aff'd and remanded 119 F.3d 341 (5th Cir.1996).

31. 73 F.3d 1352 (5th Cir.1996).

32. City of Boerne v. Flores, ___ U.S. ___, 117 S.Ct. 2157, 138 L.Ed.2d 624 (1997). See also, Keeler v. City Council of Cumberland, 940 F.Supp. 879 (D.Md.1996); Hamilton, The Religious Freedom Restoration Act: Letting the Fox into the Henhouse under Cover of Section 5 of the Fourteenth Amendment, 16 Cardozo L.Rev. 357 (1994).

33. 409 Mass. 38, 564 N.E.2d 571 (1990). See Costonis, Icons and Aliens: Law,

Aesthetics and Environmental Change (1989); Murtagh, Keeping Time: The History and Theory of Preservation in America (1988).

34. Id. at 573.

35. See Comm. of Religious Leaders of the City of N.Y., Final Report of the Interfaith Commission to Study Landmarking of Religious Property 7–22 (1982); Note, First Amendment Challenges to Landmarks Designation Statutes, 11 Fordham Urb.L.J. 115 (1983).

Chapter 13

AGRICULTURAL LAND PROTECTION AND PRESERVATION*

Analysis

§ 13.1 Agricultural Land and Urban Planning and Land Development Control Law

Planners and land use attorneys for many years gave very little attention to farmland or agricultural uses. Although many if not most zoning ordinances included an agricultural land use category, farmland was generally viewed from the urban perspective as a temporary use or holding category. As the urban area expanded, farmland was to "give way" to residential, commercial or industrial uses. For planners, agricultural lands were those left blank or white on the land use map unless

* The authors appreciate the assistance of Professor James Wadley and Professor Arthur C. Nelson in the preparation of this Chapter.

593

they were already surrounded by development in which case the holding category concept was applied.[1]

Today, both planners and attorneys increasingly recognize the importance and even necessity for including agricultural lands as a permanent land use category in plans and land development control codes. In fact, there is growing recognition of the need to extend special preservation and protection concepts to farmland for many of the same reasons that historic[2] and environmentally sensitive areas[3] are accorded special treatment and protection.[4]

By according special treatment to agricultural lands, societal needs to preserve food and fibre production are fulfilled and urban needs for open space and buffer zones are also met. The accomplishment of these goals is usually sought through use of the same planning and land use control tools encountered in other subject areas such as zoning, subdivision control, districting, clustering, transferable development rights, and private mechanisms. Special modifications of the usual approaches and concepts are frequently required and are analyzed in the sections which follow.

§ 13.2 The *Historic* Need to Protect Farmland

Until relatively recently, interest in protecting farmland near urban areas was grounded largely in concerns about food and fibre production capability. That is, there was a substantial fear that if too much agricultural land was converted to non-farm uses, the nation's capacity to produce adequate supplies of food would be jeopardized and food costs would rise.

These fears were based on two facts. First, major amounts of farmland were being converted to non-farm uses. Second, the characteristics of ideal agricultural land and of ideal development land are almost identical-i.e., level, relatively free from vegetation, good drainage, accessible to transportation, and in large parcels. Consequently, a severe threat to farmland was considered to exist particularly on the urban fringe due to the competition between developers and farmers for use of the same land.[1] Normal economic conditions place a much higher value

§ 13.1

1. E. Roberts, Getting Ready for the Ag Revolution, 49 Planning 4 (June 1983).

2. See supra Chapter 12.

3. See supra Chapter 11.

4. See James E. Holloway & Donald C. Guy, Emerging Regulatory Emphasis on Coordinating Land Use, Soil Management and Environmental Policies to Promote Farmland Preservation, Soil Conservation and Water Quality, 13 Zoning & Plan. L. Rep. 49 (1990). See also Agricultural Land: A Forgotten Natural Resource: A Symposium, 20 Gonz.L.Rev. 627 (1984-85); Myrl L. Duncan, Agriculture as a Resource: State-wide Land Use Programs for the Preservation of Farmland, 14 Ecology L. Q. 401 (1987).

§ 13.2

1. The most valuable agricultural land is cropland of which there were 382 million acres in 1992. Statistical Abstract, Table 365 (1995). About 50 million acres of this land is within 50 miles of the 100 largest urbanized areas. O. Furuseth and J. Pierce, Agricultural Land in Urban Society (1982). Most of the cropland is found within the suburban and exurban counties of metropolitan areas. Arthur C. Nelson, The Analytic Basis for an Effective Prime Farmland

on land used for development than on land used for agricultural production thus predetermining the victory of development interests over agricultural interests if only economic factors determine the outcome of the conflict.[2] On the theory that large scale conversion of agricultural lands to urban uses threatened the future of the national or local agricultural sector, land use control authorities became interested in imposing restrictions or providing incentives to prevent or deter conversion of agricultural lands to non-agricultural uses. The need for and justification of such farmland protection programs was therefore especially grounded on the perceived high rate of conversion.[3]

Data regarding trends in the aggregate agricultural land base have supported the concern that much farm land was being lost from agricultural production. For example, it is estimated that 35,000 acres are lost every week to developments.[4] In 1978, the United States Department of Agriculture's Soil Conservation Service (now the Natural Resources Conservation Service) research indicated that roughly 5 million acres of rural land are lost yearly through urban development, through isolation as a result of urban development, and through destruction for the benefit of new water supply projects.[5]

Landscape Preservation Scheme in the U.S.A., 6 Jr. of Rural Studies 337 (1991).

2. Traditional economic theory suggests that as agricultural land supply is reduced through conversion to urban uses, its value will rise until land at the urban fringe is actually more valuable for agricultural uses than for urban uses. Urban sprawl would stop. Richard F. Muth, Economic Change and Rural–Urban Land Conversions, 29 Econometrica 1 (1961). This assumes that market forces apply equally to land used for agriculture and urban activities. They do not for four reasons: (1) overvaluation of land for urban development because of economic subsidies; (2) low density land use regulation; (3) conflicts between urban and agricultural land uses; and (4) the impermanence syndrome. Arthur C. Nelson, Preserving Prime Farmland in the Face or Urbanization, 58 J.Am.Plan. Ass'n 467 (1992). See infra § 13.3, note 4, for definition of the impermanence syndrome.

3. The need for farmland preservation is controversial and the statistics differ considerably depending on which "side" is using them. The exaggeration of these statistics has been alleged by the Urban Land Institute which "believes that pressures for farmland preservation are based on inaccurate and incomplete information and on assertions and distortions rather than on rational analysis." Urban Land Institute, Has the "Farmland Crisis" Been Overstated?: Recommendations for Balancing Urban and Agricultural Land Needs, 1983

Zoning and Planning Law Handbook 235, 266 (Strom, ed.1983) [hereinafter cited as Urban Land Institute].

See also William E. Church, Symposium: Stewardship of Land and Natural Resources, Farmland Conversion: The View From 1986, 1986 U. Ill. L. Rev. 521, 533 (observing that the NALS underestimated the U.S. cropland base because it relied on the figures of the 1977 National Resources Inventory of the Soil Conservation Service, which were considerably lower than the figures announced by the 1982 NRI); Fischel, The Urbanization of Agricultural Land: A Review of the National Agricultural Lands Study, 58 Land Economics 236 (1982) (NALS overstated farmland conversion rate by a factor of 2 or even higher); Raup, An Agricultural Critique of the National Agricultural Lands Study, 58 Land Economics 260 (1982); E. Roberts, The Law and the Preservation of Agricultural Land (1982). The NALS Report and criticisms of the report are analyzed in Malone, Environmental Regulation and Land Use, § 6.03 (1992).

4. H.R.Rep. No. 1400, 95th Cong., 2d Sess. 7 (1978). It seems that very little empirical work on farmland inventories has been done since the late 1970's.

5. Id. at 8. This figure varies greatly depending on the source. See, e.g., Merriam, Making TDR Work, 56 N.C.L.Rev. 77 (1978) (1.4 million acres); Roe, Innovative Techniques to Preserve Rural Land Resources, 5 Envtl.Aff. 419 (1976) (1 million

Rural lands are being urbanized at rates that exceed the population growth rate. The loss of farmland is more severe in some areas of the country than others. Between 1950 and 1972, 17 states lost 20% of their taxable farmland, 9 states more than 30%, 4 states more than 40%, and the states of New Hampshire and Rhode Island lost more than 50%. The overall result of continued suburban migration has been the loss of 119 million acres of farmland between 1954 and 1974. This is equal to an area three times the size of New England.[6]

Recent studies confirm that much of the nation's best farmland has been lost to farming.[7] The U.S.D.A. Agricultural Fact Book reported that between 1989 and 1994, the number of acres of land in farming dropped from 991.2 million to 794.8 million.[8] This computes into an average loss of 3.3 million acres per year.[9]

§ 13.3   The *Changing* Need to Protect Farmland

Although the interest in farmland preservation historically originated from concerns about the impact of the high rate of conversion of farmland to other uses upon food production capability, there seems to be little evidence that the nation is suffering to the degree anticipated. While uncertainties remain,[1] growing evidence suggests that increases in productivity and new technologies have actually increased food production capacity and that the nation as a whole has more such capacity now than it did ten or twenty years ago when far more land was in agriculture.[2] Nevertheless, there remains a high level of interest in

acres); National Agricultural Lands Study, Final Report (1981) (3 million acres) [hereinafter cited as Final Report].

6. Bonner & Sidor, Issues in Land Use, 1975 Land Resources Today 4 (January 1975). Particularly noteworthy is the conversion of agricultural lands in Florida. In 1980 it was forecast that, at the then current rate of conversion, Florida would lose all its prime agricultural land in less than 20 years. M. Cutter, N.Y. Times, July 7, 1980 at Al9, col 1. Recent studies report that south Florida alone lost 610,000 acres of farmland to development between 1983 and 1993. The Orlando Sentinel, July 15, 1993 at B1. See also, Schnidman, Smiley, and Woodbury, Retention of Land for Agriculture: Policy, Practice and Potential in New England (1990); The Vanishing Farmland Crisis (Baden, ed. 1984); Vining, The Future of American Agriculture, 48 J. Am. Plan. Ass'n 112 (1982); Freilich and Davis, Saving the Land: The Utilization of Modern Techniques in Growth Management to Preserve Rural and Agricultural America, 13 Urb. Law. 27 (1981).

7. Farmland Lost in Urban Sprawl, Chicago Tribune, Oct. 26, 1996 (p. 11) (based on data from Northern Illinois University.)

8. USDA Fact Book 16 (1996).

9. Between 1982 and 1992, more than 41 million acres of agricultural land was converted to urban or low density nonrural uses (such as hobby farms and ranchettes). (Compare Statistical Abstract of the United States 1995 reporting the 1992 Census of Agriculture with Statistical Abstract of the United States 1985 reporting the 1982 Census of Agriculture.) This equates to nearly two acres of land lost for each new resident added. Given the historical rate of farmland conversion, by the middle of the 21st Century the United States could move from being an exporter of food to an importer. American Farmland Trust, Farming on the Fringe (1997). As the best farmland is lost, marginally productive land is brought into resource uses through heavy applications of chemicals but with potentially adverse environmental consequences. Rutherford H. Platt, The Farmland Conversion Debate, 37 Professional Geographer 433 (1982).

§ 13.3

1. See supra § 13.2, notes 4 and 9.

2. See, e.g., B. Delworth Gardiner, Plowing Ground in Washington: The Political Economy of U.S. Agriculture (Pacific

farmland preservation throughout the nation. This can be explained in part by uncertainties that persist over the consequences of converting farmland and by the fact that farming marginal lands may be environmentally harmful.[3] It is also difficult to gauge world wide demand for American agricultural commodities. A major reason for continued interest, however, is a shift in focus from fears over losing food production capability toward a fear of losing the advantages which come from having cities surrounded with open, less developed areas.

In this shifting paradigm, three different emerging concerns tend to dominate decision-making regarding farmland preservation. These are: 1) that the demographics of farming are changing so that small farms on the urban fringe are particularly vulnerable to urban pressures and therefore need to be protected in order to preserve the attractiveness and amenities of rural lifestyles;[4] 2) that farmers within the urban fringe are increasingly the targets of nuisance actions generated by changing conditions in the vicinity;[5] and 3) that urban residents are discovering the need for open space as an element of psychological well-being and quality of life and therefore benefit from less developed areas surrounding urban areas. Of these three, the last is probably the least well articulated but probably has the most significant influence on contemporary decisions to develop farmland preservation programs.

Farm demographics have significantly changed from the mid-part of this century. There are far fewer farms, farmers on the whole are much older, there is great disparity in production between large and small farms and there appears to be a significant move in the direction of corporate agriculture. This has caused concerns that agriculture may be

Research Institute for Public Policy, San Francisco 1995).

3. See supra § 13.2, note 9.

4. This is sometimes referred to as the "Impermanence Syndrome." When farmers see urban families moving into agricultural areas, they begin calculating their exit strategy from farming. It usually takes the form of making no further investments in capital such as barns, irrigation systems, and reproducing livestock. The effect is that because of the perceived threat of invasion by urban sprawl, many more farmers than would actually be put out of business from conversion decide to reduce production. David Berry, Ernest Leonardo, and Kenneth Bieri, The Farmer's Response to Urbanization, Regional Science Research Institute Discussion Paper Series No. 92 (Regional Science Research Institute, University of Massachusetts, Amherst, MA. 1976; Thomas Plaut, The Effects of Urbanization of the Loss of Farmland at the Rural–Urban Fringe: A National and Regional Perspective, Regional Science Research Institute Discussion Paper) Series No. 94 (Regional Science Re-

search Institute, University of Massachusetts, Amherst, MA, 1976). Ultimately, the critical mass of farming production needed to sustain key components of the local farming economy—such as chemists, implement dealers and mechanics, and laborers—collapses. Thomas L. Daniels and Arthur C. Nelson, "Is Oregon's Farmland Preservation Program Working?" 6 Jr. of Rural Studies 114 (1990); Arthur C. Nelson, Preserving Prime Farmland in the Face of Urbanization, 58 J.Am.Plan.Ass'n 467 (1992).

5. Consider a family that buys a two acre tract of land in a farming region. They may believe they have purchased peace and quiet in a pastoral setting with exclusive views of open space. They do not realize that active farming produces smells, glare from nighttime lights, noise during the day and at night, aerial spraying of fertilizers, pesticides, and herbicides that drift into nearby yards, and slow moving vehicles on local roads often during peak commuting hours. David Berry and Thomas Plaut, Retaining Agricultural Activities Under Urban Pressures: A Review of Land Use Conflicts and Policies, 9 Policy Sciences 153 (1978).

moving from a popular base to an industrial base which, in turn, has fueled fears that food production capability will become so concentrated in the hands of relatively few producers that food monopolies will likely result.[6] For example, it has been predicted that within the next several years traditional seed companies will disappear. There will be only four grain consortiums and two vegetable consortiums. These entities will supply the inputs and control marketing, processing, and distribution of crops.[7] Already only 20 percent of the farms produce over 85 percent of the nation's agricultural output.[8] Further, there is a sense that the change in farming from family dominated farms to corporate agriculture is destroying the attractive values of rural America. As a result, there is much interest in trying to preserve the small farm structure of farming.[9] One key to keeping small farm agriculture strong is the ability of small farms to compete successfully with larger, often corporate, entities.

These demographic concerns have prompted a number of jurisdictions to adopt restrictions on the types of businesses which are allowed to own farmland or engage in farming.[10] Typically, these statutes permit only non-corporate entities to engage in agriculture. For corporations to own farmland or operate farms, they typically must be family-farm or small-farm corporations. The rationale behind these statutes is that the smaller farms need protection against not only the direct pressures of large scale agriculture but also against indirect pressures on farmland. The goal of these statutes seems to be to preserve the small farms which are, in many if not most cases, the ones which are also the most vulnerable to the economic pressures of the urban fringe. Thus, it is thought that by keeping the small farms intact a popular-based agriculture can be maintained. While these approaches are not directly targeted toward preserving farmland within the urban fringe, they are designed to keep small farms in farming and to better resist the conversion pressures that result from the inability to compete with larger operations. In many areas, as a matter of state policy, these programs are coupled with efforts to help small farms find production alternatives,

6.   See generally, N. Hamilton, Tending the Seeds: The Emergence of a New Agriculture in The United States, 1 Drake J. of Agricultural Law 7 (1996); N. Hamilton, Plowing New Ground: Emerging Policy Issues in a Changing Agriculture, 2 Drake J. of Agricultural Law 181 (1997); J. Wadley, Small Farms: The USDA, Rural Communities and Urban Pressures, 21 Washburn L. J. 478 (1982).

7.   Doan's Agricultural Report, Sept. 12, 1997.

8.   B. Gardner, Plowing Ground in Washington: The Political Economy of U.S. Agriculture, 119 (Pacific Research Institute for Public Policy, San Francisco) (1995).

9.   See Future Directions in Rural Development Policy: Findings and Recommen-

dations of the National Commission on Agriculture and Rural Development Policy (December 1990). This Commission was mandated by the Food Security Act of 1985 and its report was presented to the President in 1989.

10.   See e.g. Kansas Stat.Ann. § 17–5901 et. seq. Similar restrictions are found in North Dakota, South Dakota, Nebraska, Iowa Michigan, Missouri, Oklahoma, Wisconsin and Minnesota. See B. Slayton, A Legislative Experiment in Rural Culture: The Anti–Corporate Farming Statutes, 59 UMKC L. Rev. 679 (1991); Smart and Hoberg, Corporate Farming in the Anti–Corporate Farming States, Nat'l Center for Agric. Res. & Info. (1989); J. Wadley, Agriculture and Farm Law, § 47.10p in Thompson on Real Property (Thomas ed.) (1994).

such as organic gardening or specialty crops, which thrive well only in close proximity to urban areas.

Concerns regarding the vulnerability of farms to nuisance-type problems resulting from the influx of urban residents into formerly rural or agricultural areas have triggered two different kinds of responses which bear on the question of farmland preservation. First, virtually every state now has what are popularly called "right-to-farm" laws. These laws, in one way or another, seek to shield farmers from nuisance claims that might result from normal farming operations.[11] These laws are typically enacted on a jurisdiction-wide basis and tend to codify the "coming to the nuisance defense." Second, some jurisdictions have sought to minimize the extent to which urban immigrants into rural areas can pressure farming operations to conform to the newly emerging notions of what the area should be like by enacting exemptions from zoning authority in favor of farms.[12] In these states, farms that are established in an area are considered as a matter of law not to be nuisances provided they were there before the arrival of the complainant or are being conducted in accordance with established agricultural practices.[13]

Typical of the statutory language of these approaches is that found in the Georgia Statute:[14]

> No agricultural or farming operation, place, establishment, or facility, or any of its appurtenances, or the operation thereof, shall be or shall become a nuisance, either private or public, as a result of changed conditions in or around the locality of such agricultural or farming operation, place, establishment, or facility if such agricultural or farming operation, place, establishment, or facility has been in operation for one year or more.

The extent to which these statutes are seen as being designed to encourage farmers to keep their land in farming is illustrated by the case of Finlay v. Finlay.[15] In this case, one farmer complained that another farmer was maintaining a nuisance upon his land. The farmer against whom the complaint was brought argued that the operation was shielded by the "Protection of Farmland and Agricultural Activities Act" of the jurisdiction. The court held that the provisions of the statute protecting the farmer from nuisance claims could only be invoked against non-farmers and had no effect on claims brought by one farmer against another.

11. See J. Hand, Right-to Farm Laws: Breaking New Ground in the Preservation of Farmland, 45 U.Pitt.L.R. 289 (1984); Dana Ann Bradbury, "Suburban Sprawl and the Right to Farm," 22 Washburn Univ. L. Rev. 448 (1986); Mark B. Lapping and Nels R. Leutwiler, Agriculture in Conflict: Right-to-Farm Laws and the Pari–Urban Milieu for Farming, Sustaining Agriculture In Cities (W. Lockeretz ed, 1987); Jerome B. Rose, Farmland Preservation Policy and Programs, 24 Nat. Res. Jr. 591 (1984). See also infra § 14.6.

12. See. e.g., Kansas Stat.Ann. § 12–715b; 19–2921.

13. See, e.g., Kansas Stat.Ann. § 2–3201 et seq.

14. Ga. Code Ann. § 41–1–7.

15. 18 Kan.App.2d 479, 856 P.2d 183 (1993).

Other jurisdictions have sought to shield farms from these kinds of pressure in other ways. Where the pressures seem likely to be exacerbated by changing neighborhoods, a number of jurisdictions have sought to protect the small farms through zoning exceptions. Typical of this approach is the Kansas statute:[16]

> No zoning regulation shall apply to the use of land for agricultural purposes nor for the erection and maintenance of agricultural buildings so long as such agricultural buildings are used for agricultural purposes and no other. Dwellings, garages and other similar accessory buildings shall not be considered as agricultural buildings. All buildings, including agricultural buildings may be regulated as to set-back requirements from public roads so as to protect the future use and improvement of such roads.

The rationale of these zoning exemption approaches appears to be that if the land can be shielded from the pressures to conform to the land use patterns that arise when non-agricultural development occurs in areas that were formerly dominantly agricultural in nature, the farm operations will be more likely to remain in those areas. Otherwise, the costs associated with making the structures conform to the zoning codes or the risks attendant upon becoming a non-conforming use under the code might well persuade a farmer to convert the use of the land to a non-agricultural use.

In these jurisdictions, the question usually will be whether the operation is truly an agricultural one or not. This question arises from the propensity of zoning codes to treat intensive agricultural operations as commercial rather than agricultural. It was held, for example, that a piggery was not a farming operation in Town of Mt. Pleasant v. Van Tassell.[17] Thus small farms may be given the benefit of the exception whereas the larger, more commercial oriented ones, may not.

In two recent cases in Iowa, the zoning exemption was invoked to protect large, commercial hog operations. In Racine Police & Fire Commission v. Budish[18] and Kuehl v. Cass County,[19] the Iowa Supreme Court considered facilities which would accommodate between 2,000 and 5,000 hogs as excluded from the zoning. In doing so, the court overturned a long-standing precedent, Farmegg Products, Inc. v. Humboldt County.[20] It specifically rejected the argument that to be exempt as an agricultural use, the facility must be used in conjunction with a traditional agricultural use otherwise in existence. That view had been the basis for excluding "commercial" agricultural uses since they were not considered "traditional" in nature. Under the new view, not only will small farms near urban areas benefit from the exception, larger ones will as well. This may pose problems for jurisdictions that are interested in farmland

16.   Kansas Stat.Ann. § 19–1960.

17.   166 N.Y.S.2d 458 (N.Y. 1957). But see Fields v. Anderson Cattle Co., 193 Kan. 558, 396 P.2d 276 (Kan. 1964) where two feedlots for cattle and sheep within 700 feet of the city limits were not considered to be commercial but were agricultural uses.

18.   359 N.W.2d 181 (Iowa 1995).

19.   555 N.W.2d 686 (Iowa 1996).

20.   190 N.W.2d 454 (Iowa 1971).

preservation primarily because of the connection between small farms and "open space." Jurisdictions of this type might find that "commercial" or "industrial" agriculture threatens their views of desirable "open space." Other jurisdictions, that are interested in farmland preservation because of the connection between farming and food production, may have difficulty as well with the idea of protecting non-traditional, large scale commercial farms as part of their preservation strategy even though they are the primary contributors to food production, simply because their size and scale suggests that they may not need the same degree or level of protection as do smaller farms. As such, they may be forced to rethink whether they are going to hold on to traditional views of agriculture or protect agriculture regardless of its format.

One of the most recent concerns that seems to be motivating an interest in keeping land in agricultural use is that availability of open space is closely aligned to psychological well-being. As such, the proximity to open space becomes an important component in the quality of one's life. Thus, regardless of any fears regarding food supplies or cost, the fact that an area surrounding or within an urban area is undeveloped or open warrants efforts to keep that area in that condition.[21] In this sense, farms function as public open space[22] which is to be tenaciously protected. When farmland is protected under this guise, the benefit seems to work both ways—to the urban resident now living in or near the countryside, quality of life is improved because of the psychological effects of open space. The farmer who is thereby allowed to continue to farm also benefits because there is some evidence that the ability to control how one's land is used is particularly important to farmers and is therefore one measure of their quality of life.[23]

§ 13.4   Farmland Preservation in Farm States

It might appear to many that some states, such as those located in the nation's heartland, would not have much interest in farmland preservation since there may be less pressure there to convert the land to non-farm uses. The reality is that farmland is pressured even in areas that are apparently dominated by agricultural uses. First, land is lost in those areas to other causes: water and power development, wildlife and resources preservation or protection, highway construction and its attendant ability to attract growth and development, particularly at interchanges[1] or in the towns and cities served by major highways.[2] It is

21. See T. Hiss, The Experience of Place (1991); P. Langdon, A Better Place to Live: Reshaping the American Suburb (1994).

22. Hiss, supra note 21 at 146.

23. J. Wadley and P. Falk, Lucas and Environmental Land Use Control in Rural Areas: Whose Land Is It Anyway, 19 Wm. Mitchell L. R. 331, 359 (1993): "Modern theorists have suggested various reasons why psychological well-being may be jeopar-

dized due to excessive government intrusion into property use and enjoyment. . . . "

§ 13.4

1. See generally S. Shirmer and T. Wilson, Milestones: A History of the Kansas Highway Commission and the Department of Transportation (1986); J. Erickson, The Effects of Highways on Agricultural and Public Land (unpublished manuscript, Washburn University School of Law, Topeka, Ks. (1993)).

estimated, for example, that every mile of highway costs 40 acres of prime farmland.[3] Second, even states that appear to be dominated by farms are actually quite urban. In Kansas, for example, the only major source of income, by industry, that brings in less money to the state than agriculture is mining. Agriculture in Kansas generates only 3.7 percent of the state's income.[4] As a general rule throughout rural America, the non-farm rural population tends to exceed the farm population by an 8–to-1 margin.[5] Thus, even in rural areas, there are growing urban pressures. Finally, states where farmland abounds appear to be places to which farmers relocate when they are displaced by urban development elsewhere. These newcomers appear to have had the impact of bidding farmland prices up (even for farm-type uses) which makes it more difficult for farmers in those areas to stay in business where expansion of the farmland is seen as necessary but is now cost-prohibitive and consequently easier for that land to be converted to other uses.

Even in rural areas, there is an interest in keeping land in farming. These efforts tend to protect existing farmers against conversion pressures that emanate both within and without the agricultural sector. In addition, there is a widespread interest in rural areas of preserving open spaces, aesthetically pleasing environments, recreation sites, and cheap food supplies geographically proximate to urban consumption centers.[6] In contrast to urban interests, however, these areas tend to be more interested in programs which offer "specific economic incentives to individual farmers to remain in farming ... because they contribute to the delicate balance required for a viable farm industry and agribusiness support industry."[7]

These areas also tend to be concerned with protecting agriculture in the aggregate as opposed to protecting particular kinds of agricultural land. Hence these areas tend to adopt state-or area-wide strategies (e.g differential taxation) which are almost always ineffective in specific locations—such as where it is no longer economical to farm, where the "farmers" are not dependent on farming for their incomes and where the urban use value greatly exceeds the farm use value. Indeed, to give tax breaks in such areas often appears in rural areas to engender feelings of inequity or that the public is improperly subsidizing particular farmers or that the tax breaks accomplish virtually nothing in terms

---

2. "Each change in the country's transportation system has changed the nature of its construction booms, by changing people's ideas of where it was convenient to have their workplaces (which must be convenient to transportation), where they live (two or three hours, at the most, from work), and where they could go to get away from it all (something like a five-or six-hour radius from home)—time constraints that have themselves stayed more or less constant. The 1980's post-interstate boom suddenly, and for the first time, brought heavy development pressure on all sorts of settings simultaneously—center-city business and residential districts, older suburbs,

shore areas, farmlands, resort communities, faraway deep woods ...." T. Hiss, The Experience of Place 129 (1991).

3. Shirmer and Wilson, supra, note 1.

4. Kansas Earnings by Industry, Wichita State University Center for Economic Development and Business Research (1993).

5. J. Wadley, Small Farms: The USDA, Rural Communities and Urban Pressures, 21 Washburn U.L.J. 478, 484–487 (1982).

6. Id. at 493.

7. Id.

of keeping the land in farming. Finally in farming areas, the goals of farmland preservation are often pitted directly against the goals of rural development so that there may be a greater interest in encouraging the kind of "economic growth" that can compete with **farm loss pressures** (e.g. bringing in corporate hog farms) rather than in farmland preservation per se which as often as not simply replaces concerns over the loss of farmland with nuisance or environmental concerns.

Planners and land use regulators in these states need to be particularly sensitive to the reality of the farming situation within the state, with the conflicts between farmland preservation and open area preservation, and with the problems associated with trying to keep land in farming as opposed to trying to pursue environmental objectives that are largely irrelevant to the goal of keeping land in farming. To fail to do so is likely to rapidly alienate farmers or to fail for lack of popular support.

§ 13.5 Making Farmland Preservation Work

Farmland protection programs, if they are to be successful, must respond to the factors which determine the conversion of farmland to non-agricultural uses.[1] Many forces and factors are involved.

A primary factor contributing to the loss of prime agricultural land is increasing land values.[2] The farmer on the urban fringe is placed in an especially uncomfortable position. Although possessing a different understanding of the land, of the relationship of people to the land, and of the problems and costs of land ownership, the farmer may not hold such an affection for the soil that he will hold out in the face of massive profits. The temptation to sell is undoubtedly connected to the proximity of the farmland to the urban fringe. Since average suburban land values are dramatically higher when utilized for building purposes than for cultivation or grazing, the farmer is likely to take his profits and leave farming altogether.[3]

Another factor that must be considered in evaluating preservation alternatives is the changing nature of farmland ownership. Urbanites, investors, syndicates, retirees, and corporations have entered the agricultural land market in increasing numbers. In 1976 alone, 35 percent of farmland purchases were made by local non-farmers, non-county residents, and others.[4] Investors, both foreign and domestic, appear to view land acquisition as a hedge against inflation. Urbanites and retirees, on the other hand, purchase suburban and rural land to escape the pace of urban life. Developers purchase rural land because it provides large,

§ 13.5

1. See Julian Conrad Juergensmeyer, Implementing Agricultural Preservation Programs: A Time to Consider Some Radical Approaches?, 20 Gonz. L. Rev. 701 (1984–85).

2. In a five year period the average per-acre price for all farmland increased approximately 65 percent. R. Gloudemans, Use Value Farmland Assessments: Theory, Practice and Impact 4 (1974).

3. Healy & Short, New Forces in the Market for Rural Land, 46 Appraisal J. 190 (1978) (suburban land values average 1,800% more when utilized for building purposes than agricultural uses).

4. Id.

contiguous, relatively inexpensive parcels of land for commercial, industrial, recreational, and housing developments. Finally, farmers and agricultural corporations purchase additional acreage to take advantage of economies of scale. On the other side of rural land demand is the slowly disappearing family farm. The family farmer is confronted with factors such as an inability to compete against the large agricultural corporations coupled with pressure to sell at a profit.[5]

As the foregoing discussion suggests, whether or not a farmer will sell his land to buyers for non-agricultural use is determined by the interrelationship of complex socio-economic factors. These include: (1) demographic factors, such as the farmer's age and state of health and whether or not he has children who want to be farmers; (2) economic factors, including not only the fair market value of the land but also the profit that can be made from the land if it is farmed (these two factors are determined by such considerations as income tax, estate tax, transportation costs, energy costs, and the like); (3) transitional factors, such as the landowner's interest in pursuing a non-farm occupation or moving to another climate; and (4) so called secondary factors, such as nuisance complaints by non-farm neighbors about farm odors and pesticides, decrease in the availability of farm labor, supplies, and services, and increase in government regulation of farming activities.[6]

The quest for farmland preservation must be balanced against the needs and demands of the non-farm public and against the direct and indirect social costs that any viable program will involve. A multitude of land use planning concepts are currently in vogue as potential "solutions" to the problem. They include zoning, cluster zoning, compensable regulation plans, negative easements and purchase of development rights, land banking, large lot zoning, open space zoning, planned unit developments, purchase and leaseback programs, agricultural service districts, transferable development rights, differential taxation, eminent domain, public rights of first refusal, and public and private land trusts.[7]

Planners who see the goal of farmland preservation to be the protection of open space rather than the protection of the farm production base may not see that there is still a significant farm interest in farmland preservation. They may therefore seriously discount the extent to which farmers may see their own need to change their economic base as more important to them than farmland preservation may be to those who simply desire to preserve open space. As a result, farmers may be very interested in engaging in the very things the preservation efforts are designed to eliminate. There is a common assumption among plan-

---

5. Farm Unit Size: Preservation of the Family Farm, J. Juergensmeyer & J. Wadley, Agricultural Law § 4.1 (1982).

6. See Keene, Agricultural Land Preservation: Legal and Constitutional Issues, 15 Gonz.L.Rev. 621 (1980); J. Juergensmeyer, The Future of Government Regulation of Agriculture, 3 No.Ill.L.Rev. 253 (1984).

7. An increasingly popular concept, which has important land use regulation consequences but is primarily a fortification of the "coming to the nuisance" defense, is the so-called "right to farm" laws. See § 13.3 supra.

ners and the public at large that farmland preservation programs will inherently appeal to farmers. It often comes as a great surprise when farmers are among the first to withdraw or withhold their support from the programs. It is also probably assumed that if the land can be kept in farming, farmers will be interested in farming it. This ignores the extent to which farmers resent any transfers of control over land use decision-making to a non-farm dominated body. The unfortunate reality is that some of the most effective preservation efforts are the most intrusive into those decisions and are therefore the most resisted by the farmers themselves.[8]

For virtually any farmland preservation programs to succeed, some consideration must be given to a much neglected aspect of farm economics. If it is desired that land in a particular area remain in farming, it is important that the farming activity be economically feasible. In a very vital sense, the farm must have access to the inputs needed to make the venture successful as well as have a market for the produce. Two things tend to jeopardize this. First, when planners pursue an agenda that is grounded on a concern not directly related to farming (such as open space preservation), there seems to be a tendency to link the program to other environmental interests such as habitat protection or tree preservation? This engenders a much different perspective relative to the agricultural land and seems to make the program restrictive of any practice that is seen as having the capacity of "destroying" the natural condition of the area. This is often interpreted in the farming sector as an effort to "rescue the area before it is too late" as if no legitimate activity is or can occur in the area. In this setting, even many agricultural practices that may be considered vital to the economic success of the farming operation are no longer tolerable. Under such circumstances, the farm may be literally "open-spaced" to death.

The other factor which jeopardizes farmer support for farmland preservation programs is the impact of general development in the area. This is an aspect of farm economics that is not always recognized in the development of farmland preservation plans and is what farm economists would call "critical mass." In order for a single farm to survive, there have to be enough other farms in the area to warrant the presence of vital support services. To have access to seed suppliers, fertilizer dealers, farm implement dealers and service areas, produce distributors and so forth, it is vital to have enough farms that those industries will remain in the area. If they leave, the farmer will need to go further afield to find the inputs or the marketing outlets that are needed. This may greatly increase the costs to the farmer and make the enterprise less viable. In this sense, there is an observable domino effect. If some farms leave, others will leave. If too many leave, the support structure leaves as well. If the support structure leaves, other farmers may be forced to leave farming no matter how well conceived the preservation

---

8. J. Wadley, Agriculture and Farm Law, §§ 47.07 in Thompson on Real Prop- erty (Thomas ed.) (1994).

program is. The economic reality is that it may no longer be feasible to continue farming in that area. For years, the data has suggested that for every five farms to leave farming, one support industry leaves.[9] Most planning approaches do not consider the relationship between farms and the vast support structure that farming needs as part of the agricultural area to be preserved.

It should also be remembered that farmland preservation viewed from a societal land use planning perspective involves complex competing needs and values. Land preserved for farmland is not available for urban expansion and consequently may have serious consequences in regard to the cost and availability of housing, commercial centers and industrial sites.[10]

§ 13.6 Farmland Defined

An obvious prerequisite to the structuring of farmland protection programs is the identification of the land and uses deemed to merit protection. If the protective legislation or enactment defines agricultural real estate generally in terms of rural or open space lands, the protective blanket may be so broad as to include lands that have no real value for cultivation and grazing. If, alternatively, agricultural land is defined narrowly, buffer lands that effectively separate farmland from the urban fringe may not be protected. The importance of seeking a definition of agricultural lands does not lie in developing a hard and fast meaning for the term or in developing any hierarchy of definitional preference. The true value of such an inquiry is found in the realization that the definition of agricultural land is only one variable of many that must be assessed in any given land preservation and use plan.[1]

The definition of "agricultural land" used in the National Agricultural Lands Study follows:

> "Agricultural lands" are lands currently used to produce agricultural commodities, including forest products, or lands that have the potential for such production. These lands have a favorable combination of soil quality, growing season, moisture supply, size and accessibility. This definition includes about 590 million acres of land that has no potential for cultivated crop use but is now in agricultural uses including range, pasture, or forestland. There were 1.361 billion acres of agricultural land in 1977.[2]

Another typical definition of "farmland" is "a piece of land consisting of a fixed number of acres which is used primarily to raise or produce

9. J. Wadley, The Future of Government Regulation: Biting the Hand that Feeds Us? 3 No.Ill.L.R. 299 (1983).

10. R. Alterman, The Challenge of Farmland Preservation: Lessons from a Six–Nation Comparison, 63 J.Am.Plan. Ass'n 220, 224 (Spring 1997).

§ 13.6

1. For a more detailed discussion of "agriculture", "farming", "farmers" and "farmland," see J. Wadley, Agriculture and Farm Law, §§ 47.05 in Thompson on Real Property (Thomas ed.) (1994).

2. National Agricultural Lands Study, Final Report xx (1981).

agricultural products, and the customary buildings which accompany such activities."[3] The U.S. Department of Commerce in its 1969 census indicated that "farmland as defined in that census included all land contained within the physical boundaries of a farm including cropland, woodland, and pasture."[4]

Since many farmland preservation efforts concentrate on the protection of "prime farmland," that concept also merits definition. The U.S. Department of Agriculture's Natural Resources Conservation Service (NRCS) defines "prime farmland" as:

> land that has the best combination of physical and chemical characteristics for producing food, feed, forage, fiber, and oilseed crops, and is also available for these uses (the land could be cropland, pastureland, rangeland, forest land, or other land, but not urban built-up land or water). It has the soil quality, growing season, and moisture supply needed to economically produce sustained high yields of crops.... In general, prime farmlands have an adequate and dependable water supply from precipitation or irrigation, a favorable temperature and growing season ... and few or no rocks.... Prime farmlands are not excessively erodible or saturated with water for a long period of time, and they either do not flood frequently or are protected from flooding.[5]

A popular land use oriented definitional approach is to define "farmland" as "a parcel of land used for agricultural activities" and to then define "agriculture" as:

> The production, keeping or maintenance for sale, lease or personal use of plants and animals useful to man, including but not limited to: forages and sod crops; grains and seed crops, dairy animals and dairy products; poultry and poultry products; livestock, including beef cattle, sheep, swine, horses, ponies, mules, or goats, or any mutations or hybrids thereof, including the breeding and grazing of any or all of such animals; bees and apiary products; fur animals; trees and forest products; fruits of all kinds, including grapes, nuts and berries; vegetables; nursery, floral, ornamental and greenhouse products; or lands devoted to a soil conservation or forestry management program.[6]

Although farmland and farming are generally defined in terms of the uses to which the land is put, it is not inappropriate to consider also the nature of the individual or the entity who engages in farming as well as the level or intensity of the use.[7] The value of such a consideration is to avoid the possibility that land may be "kept in farming" even though it is occupied and used by individuals who have no significant economic

---

3. Rohan, Agricultural Zoning, 3 Zoning & Land Use Controls 17 (1978).

4. Comment, Preservation of Florida's Agricultural Resources Through Land Use Planning, 27 U.Fla.L.Rev. 130 (1974).

5. 7 C.F.R. § 657.5(a) (1997).

6. H. Moskowitz & C. Lindbloom, The Illustrated Book of Development Definitions 23–24 (1981).

7. J. Wadley, Agriculture and Farm Law, §§ 47.07 in Thompson on Real Property (Thomas ed.) (1994).

interest in the farming activity. This would be the case, for example, with those who own "country ranch estates" of approximately 10 acres in size who claim all of the tax benefits of differential assessment yet cannot engage in any significant agricultural activity on a tract that size other than perhaps the maintenance of hobby animals such as horses. If the definition of farmland is simply a soil-based definition or requires the keeping of animals that are useful to man, the land may well qualify for agricultural treatment even though it may be the intention of the jurisdiction to exclude it.

Similarly, if there is no consideration of the intensity of the use, activities which probably should be treated as commercial activities might well fall within the scope of farming. Many land use ordinances such as zoning codes appear to take the position that if the "farming" activity is sufficiently "commercial" in nature, it should not be treated the same as more traditional and therefore less intense uses. In these situations, agricultural activity is perceived to be a low to moderate density use by nature whereas more intense activities should be considered commercial in nature. If that is the case in other aspects of the land use regulatory scheme in the jurisdiction, the definitions used for farmland preservation programs should operate in the same paradigm. Otherwise, the different programs may work at cross purposes.

§ 13.7 Land Use Planning and Farmland Protection

The increased usage and importance of comprehensive land use planning at all levels of government are discussed elsewhere in this Hornbook. True comprehensive land use planning is recent in origin. Even more recent is the inclusion in the scope of planning activities of farmland preservation and protection considerations. This phenomenon is occurring at all governmental levels-federal, state, regional and local.[1]

A. Federal

The concern of federal agencies with the agricultural lands preservation and protection problem represents a relatively recent and significant change of position. In 1974, a U.S. Department of Agriculture (USDA) study concluded that "Although thousands of acres of farmland are converted annually to other uses * * * we are in no danger of running out of farmland."[2]

A shift in USDA policy began the next year. By 1976, the Secretary of Agriculture announced a new USDA policy aimed at discouraging federal government activities that would convert prime agricultural land

§ 13.7

1. See generally Anita P. Miller & John B. Wright, Report of the Subcommittee on Innovative Growth Management Measures: Preservation of Agricultural Land and Open Space, 23 Urb. Law. 821 (1991); Frank Schnidman, The Evolving Federal Role in Agricultural Land Preservation, 18 Urb. Law. 423 (1986).

2. U.S. Dep't of Agriculture, Econ.Res. Sem., Our Land and Water Resources: Current and Prospective Supplies and Uses, Misc.Publ. No. 1,290 (Wash.D.C. U.S.G.P.O. 1974). See F. Schnidman, Agricultural Land Preservation: The Evolving Federal Role, ALI–ABA, Land Use Regulation and Litigation 100 (1984).

to other uses and at encouraging state and local authorities to advocate the protection of such land.[3] In 1978, USDA issued a revised and considerably stronger policy directed toward committing USDA agencies to intercede with all other federal government agencies when conversion of prime farmland is threatened.[4]

The second most significant federal government policy revision in regard to farmland preservation, was the action taken in 1976 by the Council on Environmental Quality (CEQ) directing all federal agencies to consider the loss of prime farmland when preparing the environmental impact statements (EIS) required by the National Environmental Policy Act of 1969.[5] Compliance was purely voluntary under the 1976 action but in 1980 CEQ made the requirement mandatory.[6]

In spite of the changes in federal agency policies, federal government programs were still considered the cause of the loss of thousands of acres of prime agricultural land annually. Continuing concern over such government activities led to the establishment in June 1979 of the National Agricultural Lands Study (NALS) to assess and propose remedies for the problem.[7] The recommendations contained in the final report of the NALS are broad and extensive and directed toward five objectives: (1) information sharing by state and local governments concerning successful agricultural lands preservation programs; (2) articulation of a national policy on agricultural lands preservation and its implementation; (3) federal support of state and local government programs; (4) financial assistance for protection programs; and (5) clarification of land information base statistics and data.

To help accomplish these five goals, the study makes five categories of recommendations. The first category concerns the characteristics of successful agricultural lands preservation programs and how they can serve as guidelines for development of new programs. The suggestions are: (a) that agricultural lands preservation programs should be combined with a comprehensive growth management system; (b) that state governments should assume an active role in the programs; (c) that protection programs should be adopted before development patterns foreclose some or many options; (d) that accurate information should be used in developing the programs; (e) that able political leadership should be sought as a key element of success; (f) that agricultural land protection programs should support the economic viability of agriculture in the area; and (g) that considerable attention should be given to assuring that protection programs are legally defensible.

The second category of recommendations relates to "national policy and federal agency initiatives." Most of these recommendations are

3. Report to the Congress by the Comptroller General, Preserving America's Farmland–A Goal the Federal Government Should Support, (CED–79–109) 7 (1979) [hereinafter cited as Report to the Congress by the Comptroller General].

4. Id.

5. Id. at 35.

6. CEQ, Memoranda for Heads of Agencies of August 11, 1980.

7. Report to the Congress by the Comptroller General, at 49–52.

vague and general. The three remaining categories of recommendations are technical assistance and education, financial assistance, and information and research needs.

At least partially in response to the NALS recommendations, Congress enacted the Farmland Protection Policy Act (FPPA)[8] as part of the Food and Agriculture Act of 1981. This Act requires USDA to develop criteria for identifying the effects of federal programs on farmland conversion and requires all divisions and units of the federal government to use the criteria to identify and take into account the adverse effects of federal actions on preservation of farmland and how to avoid such adverse effects. The Act contains a specific prohibition of any legal challenges to federal programs or activities based on the Act.[9] Although no action was taken on the Farmland Protection Policy Amendments of 1983,[10] and several other proposed bills,[11] proposals to repeal and strengthen the Act still occur.[12]

The Secretary of Agriculture's rule for implementation of the FPPA establishes criteria for identifying the effects of federal programs on conversion of agricultural lands to non-agricultural uses.[13] Five "land evaluation criteria" are established pursuant to which parcels will be evaluated and assigned a score from 0 to 100 representing the value of the land as farmland in comparison to other land in the area. This "scoring" is to be performed by the NRCS. The federal agency whose action might lead to conversion of the agricultural land must assess the suitability of the tract in question for protection by using twelve "site assessment criteria."[14]

In addition to attempting to change federal agency policies regarding farmland conversions, the federal government has sought to implement devices which encourage farmers to keep their land in farming by reducing the economic or tax burdens on the property.[15] The most

---

8. Pub.L. No. 97–98 (Dec. 22, 1981), 7 U.S.C.A. §§ 4201–4209.

9. 7 U.S.C.A. § 4209 provides: "This chapter shall not be deemed to provide a basis for any action, either legal or equitable, by any person or class of persons challenging a Federal project, program, or other activity that may affect farmland."

10. See § 2004, the Farmland Protection Policy Act Amendments of 1983, 99th Cong., 1st Sess. § 2 (1983).

11. H.R. 5316, 100th Cong. (1988) (proposing to revise the Act with respect to the conversion of farmland to nonagricultural uses); S. 2548, 99th Cong. (1986) (proposing that the Act require the Secretary of Agriculture to provide technical assistance and farmland easements).

12. H.R. 5987, 102nd Cong. (1992) (proposing to extend the protections of the Act to farmland zoned for residential or

commercial development). See generally Johnson and Fogleman, The Farmland Protection Policy Act: Stillbirth of a Policy?, 1986 U. of Ill.L.Rev. 563. The "Farms for the Future Act of 1990," 7 U.S.C.A. § 4201, authorizes the Secretary of Agriculture to make federal loan guarantees and interest rate assistance available to lending institution in states with state operated preservation funds. 7 U.S.C.A. § 1465. Vermont qualifies. See Campbell–Mohn, Breen and Futrell, Environmental Law: From Resources to Recovery 323 (1993).

13. 7 C.F.R. § 658 (1997).

14. 7 C.F.R. § 658.5 (1997).

15. Other examples include Chapter 12 of the Bankruptcy Code, 11 U.S.C. §§ 1201–3 and the 1990 Farm Bill, Food, Agriculture, Conservation and Trade Act of 1990, Pub. L. No, 101–624, 104 Stat. 3359 (codified as amended in scattered sections of 7 U.S.C. and 16 U.S.C.).

prominent of these changes occurred with the adoption, in 1976, of Section 2032A of the Internal Revenue Code.[16] As a general rule, a decedent's property is taxed at its fair market value at the time of death.[17] As a result, heirs were often forced to sell family farms because the farms could not produce sufficient income to pay the estate taxes because the location of the lands often made them more valuable for non-farm purposes.[18] Congress adopted Section 2032A as an exception to that general rule in order to encourage farmers, particularly in urban fringe areas, to keep the land in farming.[19] By using actual use value for agricultural purposes rather than fair market value, the size of the taxable estate will be reduced which, in turn, reduces the estate tax liability at decedent's death. This, it is hoped, will increase the profits from the farm sufficient to allow for the payment of any tax liability without a sale of any part of the farm. In this sense, Section 2032A operates much the same way as state differential taxation programs. In practice, the impact of the statute is to typically reduce the value of the estate by between 40 and 60 percent. By statute, the reduction in value may not exceed $750,000.[20] In addition, if the land is not kept in farming for a specified period after the decedent's death, there is a recapture of the tax savings.

To be eligible for the special use valuation, the land must "qualify." To do so, the farm assets must constitute a substantial portion of the decedent's estate. Specifically, the real and personal property of the farm business must constitute at least 50 per cent of the adjusted value of the gross estate and the real estate must equal at least 25 percent of the adjusted value. The business must be a qualified business which not only includes farming but also may include small closely held businesses of a non-farm nature.[21] The property must be used in that business for qualified purposes (including farming) for five of the eight years prior to decedent's death by the decedent or a member of the decedent's family who qualify as having materially participated in the operation of the business. Upon death, the land must pass to a qualified heir, who likewise must generally continue to put the land to a qualified use for the next 10 years.

The ability to value the farm at its actual use, as opposed to fair market, value is an election that must affirmatively be made. An election agreement signed by all of the heirs must be executed and filed with the election or, at the latest, at the time of the filing of the return.[22] This

16. I.R.C. §§ 2032A(a)-(i).

17. I.R.C. § 2031.

18. H.R. Rep. No. 1380, 94th Cong., 2d Sess. 22 (1976).

19. See, generally, Note, Taxation: Valuation of Farmland for Estate Tax Purposes, Qualifying for I.R.C. § 2032A Special Use Valuation, 23 Washburn L.J. 638 (1984); Comment, Valuation of Farmland for Estate Tax Purposes, A consideration of Section 2032A and the New Treasury Regulations, 27 Loy.L.Rev. 140 (1981).

20. § 2032A(a)(2).

21. See Bruce W. Bringardner, Planning to Qualify Non–Farm Business Real Estate for Special Use Valuation, 64 J. Tax. 130 (March, 1986).

22. See McDonald v. Commissioner (1987), 89 T.C. 293, aff'd in part, reversed in part 853 F.2d 1494 (8th Cir.1988).

election document binds the heirs to the agreement to keep the land in farming for the 10 year period and consents to the recovery, by the United States, of any tax savings. An automatic lien arises in favor of the Federal Government that can be enforced if the land ceases to be used for the qualified purpose within the specified post-death period.

One of the most important aspects of the qualification requirements is the concept of material participation. The test is satisfied if, during the eight year period preceding the earliest of either the date of decedent's death, the date decedent became disabled, or the date that the decedent retired, there must be periods aggregating five years or more during which there was material participation by the qualified heir or a member of the decedent's family in the operation of the farm.[23] This requirement may be satisfied in various ways, most of which are designed to insure that the farming operation is an active one and that the participants are at risk regarding the success of the venture. Assuming financial responsibility for the operation, providing the labor required, participating in the daily management decisions of the farm, and regularly inspecting the operation all generally qualify. Leasing the land is a bit problematic. Crop-share leases tend to be acceptable; cash leases are almost invariably fatal to the ability to elect special use valuation since the participants tend to be less at risk.[24]

This aspect of the statute reinforces other farmland preservation devices and strategies because it insures that the farming operation will be an active one. On the other hand, farmers may resent some farmland approaches which make the likelihood of their economic success less certain because this election assumes the viability of the farming operation for at least 10 years beyond the life of the farmer. Thus, where farmers in the area consider the farmland preservation strategies too intrusive into their ability to control their farming operations, sufficient farmers may abandon farming so that the success of the remaining farmers may become uncertain. This may cause farmers to fear that their ability to realize an estate tax savings may be jeopardized and, as a result, they too may oppose the preservation approaches.

The legislative history of Section 2032A and commentary since its adoption suggest that it was primarily designed to encourage farmers to keep their land in farming from one generation to the next.[25]

A final activity at the federal level that evidences a more active role for the federal government in the area of farmland preservation is the adoption, in 1990, of the Farms for the Future Act.[26] Under the provisions of this act, which was funded only for a project in Vermont and which "sunset" (that is, expired by its own terms) on Sept. 30, 1996, federal assistance was to be made available to state trust funds to help

---

23. J. Juergensmeyer & J. Wadley, Agricultural Law § 36.2 (1982).

24. Id.

25. See, e.g., R. Campfield, M. Dickinson, and Wm. Turnier, Taxation of Estates, Gifts and Trusts (1991).

26. Uncodified. Noted after 7 U.S.C. § 4201.

purchase development rights, conservation easements and other interests, including the fee to the land. This act was, in part, the impetus for a subsequent provision in the 1996 farm bill which was designed to fund approximately 20 local programs in 18 states. This program has been somewhat narrow in scope and only authorizes the purchase of conservation easements on 55,000 acres of farmland.[27]

B. State and Regional

Not all states have state comprehensive plans[28] but Oregon and Florida are notable examples of those who do. Farmland and agricultural land use policies are given considerable attention in the plans of both states.

In fact, preservation of agricultural land is said to have been the primary motivation behind the adoption of the Oregon comprehensive planning statute.[29] The goals and guidelines for Oregon's agricultural lands are now formulated as follows:[30]

Goal 3: Agricultural Lands

To preserve and maintain agricultural lands.

Agricultural lands shall be preserved and maintained for farm use, consistent with existing and future needs for agricultural products, forest and open space and with the state's agricultural land use policy expressed in ORS 215.243 and 215.700.

27. Sec. 338 of the Federal Agricultural Improvement and Reform Act of 1996, § 7 U.S.C. 7201 et. seq. See Programs in 19 states offered federal assistance, 7 Farmland Pres. Rept. 1 (Oct. 1996); Federal Farmland Protection Funds Released, American Farmland 10 (Fall 1996).

28. See Orlando E. Delogu, A Comprehensive State and Local Government Land Use Control Strategy to Preserve the Nation's Farmland is Unnecessary and Unwise, 34 U.Kan.L.Rev. 519 (1986). See also Myrl L. Duncan, Agriculture as a Resource: Statewide Land Use Programs for the Preservation of Farmland, 14 Ecology L.Q. 401 (1987); Teri E. Popp, A Survey of Agricultural Zoning: State Responses to the Farmland Crisis, 24 Real Prop.Prob. & Tr.J. 371 (1989). But see Sam Sheronick, Note, The Accretion of Cement and Steel onto Prime Iowa Farmland: A Proposal for a Comprehensive State Agricultural Zoning Plan, 76 Iowa L.Rev. 583 (1991); Gladys B. Green, Comment, Preservation of Kentucky's Diminishing Farmland: A Statutory Analysis, 5 J.Min.L. & Pol'y 305 (1989–90).

29. Or.Admin.R. 660–15–000(3) (1997); T. Pelham, State Land Use Planning and Regulation 158 (1979). See also Juergensmeyer, Introduction: State and Local Land Use Planning and Control in the Agricultural Context, 25 S.D.L.Rev. 463 (1980).

30. Or Admin.R. 660–15–000(3) (1997). The Oregon Land Use Information Center is on line at http://darkwing.uoregon.edu/p̄ppm/landuse/land-use.html. Goal 3 is at http://darkwing.uoregon.edu/p̄ppm/landuse/goal3.html. Goal 3 was first adopted December 1974 and amended subsequently December 1983, February 1988, August 1992, and February 1994. The implementation of Oregon's agricultural lands preservation goal is discussed in Rochette, Prevention of Urban Sprawl: The Oregon Method, 3 Zoning & Planning L.Rep. 25 (1980). See also Averil Rothrock, Oregon's Goal 5: Is Ecologically Sustainable Development Reflected?, 31 Williamette L.Rev. 449 (1995). Key Oregon cases on point are Lane County v. Land Conservation & Dev. Comm'n, 138 Or.App. 635, 910 P.2d 414 (1996); Department of Land Conservation & Dev. v. Curry County, 132 Or. App. 393, 888 P.2d 592 (1995); Department of Land Conservation & Dev. v. Coos County, Bussmann 117 Or.App. 400, 844 P.2d 907 (1992). See generally Coughlin, Oregon's Program of State Standards and Local Planning Regulations, in Coughlin & J. Keene eds. The Protection of Farmland: A Reference Guidebook for State and Local Government, 239 (1981).

Uses

> Counties may authorize farm uses and those non-farm uses defined by commission rule that will not have significant adverse effects on accepted farm or forest practices.

Implementation

> Zoning applied to agricultural land shall limit uses which can have significant adverse effects on agricultural and forest land, farm and forest uses or accepted farming or forest practices.

Counties shall establish minimum sizes for new lots or parcels in each agricultural land designation. The minimum parcel size established for farm uses in farmland zones shall be consistent with applicable statutes. If a county proposes a minimum lot or parcel size less than 80 acres, or 160 acres for rangeland, the minimum shall be appropriate to maintain the existing commercial agricultural enterprise within the area and meet the requirements of ORS 215.243.

Counties authorized by ORS 215.316 may designate agricultural land as marginal land and allow those uses and land divisions on the designated marginal land as allowed by law.

LCDC shall review and approve plan designations and revisions to land use regulations in the manner provided by ORS Chapter 197.

Definitions

Agricultural Land—in western Oregon is land of predominantly Class I, II, III and IV soils and in eastern Oregon is land of predominantly Class I, II, III, IV, V and VI soils as identified in the Soil Capability Classification System of the United States Soil Conservation Service, and other lands which are suitable for farm use taking into consideration soil fertility, suitability for grazing, climatic conditions, existing and future availability of water for farm irrigation purposes, existing land-use patterns, technological and energy inputs required, or accepted farming practices. Lands in other classes which are necessary to permit farm practices to be undertaken on adjacent or nearby lands, shall be included as agricultural land in any event.

More detailed soil data to define agricultural land may be utilized by local governments if such data permits achievement of this goal.

Agricultural land does not include land within acknowledged urban growth boundaries or land within acknowledged exceptions to Goals 3 or 4.

    * * *

Guidelines

A. Planning

1. Urban growth should be separated from agricultural lands by buffer or transitional areas of open space.

2. Plans providing for the preservation and maintenance of farm land for farm use should consider as a major determinant the carrying capacity of the air, land and water resources of the planning area. The land conservation and development actions provided for by such plans should not exceed the carrying capacity of such resources.

B. Implementation

1. Non-farm uses permitted within farm use zones under ORS 215.213(2) and (3) and 215.283(2) and (3) should be minimized to allow for maximum agricultural productivity.

2. Extension of services, such as sewer and water supplies into rural areas should be appropriate for the needs of agriculture, farm use and non-farm uses established under ORS 215.213 and 215.283.

3. Services that need to pass through agricultural lands should not be connected with any use that is not allowed under ORS 215.203, 215.213, and 215.283, should not be assessed as part of the farm unit and should be limited in capacity to serve specific service areas and identified needs.

4. Forest and open space uses should be permitted on agricultural land that is being preserved for future agricultural growth. The interchange of such lands should not be subject to tax penalties.

Florida's first state comprehensive plan had little legal significance within the state of Florida because it was adopted only as a *guideline* for state activities.[31] It was important, nationally, however, in that it illustrated an alternate approach to planning for agricultural issues. It took a broader approach than the Oregon plan and treated farmland protection as just one of many concerns faced by the state's agricultural sector. Finally, the act placed equal emphasis upon Florida agriculture's water, land, government regulation, energy, marketing, and farm labor problems.[32]

Florida's present state comprehensive plan[33] is now "intended to be a direction-setting document."[34] Its goals and policies "shall be reasonably applied where they are economically and environmentally feasible," not contrary to the public interest, and consistent with the protection of private property rights.[35] While Florida's first state comprehensive plan

31. Fla.Stat.Ann. § 23.0114(1). See J. Juergensmeyer & J. Wadley, Florida Land Use and Growth Management Law § 4.02 (1997). A new state comprehensive plan was adopted by the Florida legislature in 1985. Fla.Stat.Ann. § 187.201.

32. Division of State Planning, Fla. Dep't of Admin. The Florida State Comprehensive Plan.

33. Fla.Stat.Ann. Ch. 187.

34. Fla.Stat.Ann. § 187.101(2).

35. Id. § 187.101(3).

included a specific "Preservation of Agricultural Land" objective,[36] the plan is now statutory and reviewed biennially by the state legislature.[37] The current plan includes a broader "Agriculture" provision, as follows:[38]

(23) Agriculture.—

(a) Goal.—Florida shall maintain and strive to expand its food, agriculture, ornamental horticulture, aquaculture, forestry, and related industries in order to be a healthy and competitive force in the national and international marketplace.

(b) Policies.—

1. Ensure that goals and policies contained in state and regional plans are not interpreted to permanently restrict the conversion of agricultural lands to other uses.

2. Encourage diversification within the agriculture industry, especially to reduce the vulnerability of communities that are largely reliant upon agriculture for either income or employment.

3. Promote and increase international agricultural marketing opportunities for all Florida agricultural producers.

4. Stimulate research, development, and application of agricultural technology to promote and enhance the conservation, production, and marketing techniques available to the agriculture industry.

5. Encourage conservation, wastewater recycling, and other appropriate measures to assure adequate water resources to meet agricultural and other beneficial needs.

6. Promote entrepreneurship in the agricultural sector by providing technical and informational services.

7. Stimulate continued productivity through investment in education and research.

8. Encourage development of biological pest controls to further the reduction in reliance on chemical controls.

9. Conserve soil resources to maintain the economic value of land for agricultural pursuits and to prevent sedimentation in state waters.

10. Promote the vitality of Florida's agricultural industry through continued funding of basic research, extension, inspection, and analysis services and of programs providing for marketing and technical assistance and the control and eradication of diseases and infestations.

11. Continue to promote the use of lands for agricultural purposes by maintaining preferential property tax treatment through the greenbelt law.

36. The Florida State Comprehensive Plan, supra note 32.

37. Fla.Stat.Ann. § 187.101(1).

38. Id. § 187.201(23).

12. Ensure that coordinated state planning of road, rail, and waterborne transportation systems provides adequate facilities for the economical transport of agricultural products and supplies between producing areas and markets.

13. Eliminate the discharge of inadequately treated wastewater and stormwater runoff into waters of the state.

Oregon and Florida also offer examples of regional planning. Florida's adoption of portions of Article 7 of the American Law Institute's Model Land Development Code[39] results in the institution of two distinct but interrelated regional land use planning and control concepts: (1) Areas of critical state concern and (2) Developments of Regional Impact. The idea behind "areas of critical state concern" is that certain areas of the state because of the nature of the land area, for example, prime agricultural land or environmentally sensitive land, are of such importance to the entire state that matters concerning their use or protection should be decided with state or regional government participation and not just by local governments. The development of regional impact concept is that certain types of development wherever they are located impact so significantly on the entire state or major portions thereof, that such developments should be undertaken only after state and regional considerations have been invoked.

C. Local

Another recent development in the land use control area is the requirement via state legislation that all units of local government formulate and adopt comprehensive plans that meet state specified standards. The important enforcement mechanism in such statutes is the so-called consistency requirement,[40] whereby the state statute requires all subsequent land use regulations by local governments to be consistent with the state comprehensive plan.

A specifically required element of such a plan normally includes planning for agricultural lands and related activities. Thus, the Florida act provides for a "future land use plan element designating proposed future general distribution, location, and extent of"[41] agricultural uses as well as the requirement that each local government comprehensive plan contain an "open space element."[42]

Perhaps the greatest role local government comprehensive plans can play is pulling it all together. Professor Arthur C. Nelson has observed that agricultural land preservation works best, and may work only, if the best elements of all techniques are choreographed. A local comprehensive plan must state the public interest in preserving such land, which is accomplished usually by citing the economic contributions and taking

---

39. Fla.Stat.Ann. ch. 380 (The Environmental Land and Water Management Act of 1972). See J. Juergensmeyer & J. Wadley, Florida Land Use and Growth Management Law ch. 23 (1997); Finnel, American Law Institute Model Land Development Code: A Critique, (pt. 11) 29 Land Use L. & Zoning Dig. 4 (1977).

40. See supra § 2.13.

41. Fla.Stat. § 163.3177(6)(a).

42. Id. § 163.3177(6)(e).

notice that because urban and agricultural land uses are fundamentally incompatible they must be clearly separated. Zoning is used to provide for the market demand for rural lifestyles but in locations and in a manner that does not interfere with agricultural activities that are expected of the remaining agricultural area. Property taxation based only on agricultural productivity and not urban uses is applied to those areas that are subject to exclusive agricultural zoning; the logic would be sensible since these lands would be for most practical purposes removed from the urban land market and speculation for conversion would be reduced if not eliminated. Right-to-farm laws would supplement these efforts. While no single technique is effective by itself (and can be counterproductive), the combination of techniques allows them to be mutually reinforcing.[43]

§ 13.8 Zoning of Farmland

In spite of recent changes and innovations in the land use control area, zoning remains the most frequently used and potentially the most effective land use control device to protect and preserve agricultural lands.[1] Nonetheless, serious limitations exist on the effectiveness of zoning, in its traditional format, as a solution to the preservation problem.[2]

43. See Arthur C. Nelson and James B. Duncan, Growth Management Principles and Practices (1995). Professor Nelson further suggests that a direct test of this assertion is possible, if one compares Washington County, Oregon, and Clark County, Washington. Both are within the Portland–Vancouver–Salem Consolidated Metropolitan Statistical Area which has a 1995 population of about two million. Both counties have the same climate, land area, land features, soils, and access to markets. The only differences are that they are separated by the Columbia River and are in different states. Except for zoning, both use the same agricultural land preservation techniques. Washington County directs rural residential development into clearly designated areas away from agriculture and then applies exclusive agricultural use zoning to the rest. Clark County applies a five acre minimum lot size throughout the agricultural area. Between 1977 and 1992, Washington County grew 62.2 percent (from 204,700 to 338,-200) while Clark County grew a comparable 59.3 percent (from 163,600 to 260,000). Land in farms in Washington County fell by 8,000 acres or 0.09 acres per new resident but in Clark County it fell by 19,000 acres or 0.20 acres per new resident, or twice the rate. Whereas agricultural sales *rose* in Washington County by 6.4 percent in real terms (about $10 million), they *fell* by 29.0 percent in Clark County (about $17 million). (All figures based on City and County

Data Book for 1983 and 1992, and the U.S. Census of Agriculture for 1977 and 1992.)

§ 13.8

1. See generally Teri E. Popp, A Survey of Agricultural Zoning: State Responses to the Farmland Crisis, 24 Real Prop. Prob. & Tr. J. 371 (1989); Teri E. Popp, A Survey of Governmental Response to the Farmland Crisis: States' Application of Agricultural Zoning, 11 U. Ark. Little Rock L.J. 515 (1988–89).

2. As Professor Arthur C. Nelson has commented, nonexclusive agricultural zoning as applied in most places around the United States is a false panacea for preserving agricultural land. Suppose, for example, that a county has 100,000 acres of agricultural land extending across an area measuring 12.5 miles by 12.5 miles. Suppose the market demand for rural residential homesites is 1,000 homes. If those homes are distributed randomly throughout the agricultural area it would be easy to see that farmers everywhere would be impacted by low density urban households. One solution that is all too often ignored is directing the legitimate market demand for rural residences to specific areas where their location and natural features minimizes impacts on farmers. Arthur C. Nelson and James B. Duncan, Growth Management Principles and Practices (1995). All too often, however, it is the owners of the rest of the agricultur-

The key characteristic of use categories under traditional or Euclidean zoning is that all use zones are "cumulative," meaning that all higher, i.e., more preferred, uses are permitted in "lower" categories. Since the urban planners who traditionally drafted zoning ordinances were development oriented, "agricultural use" was ranked at or near the bottom, meaning that uses ranked "higher" were frequently permitted in agricultural zones no matter how inconsistent or competing they were with agricultural activities. Even those traditional zoning ordinances that allow only agricultural and specified other uses in agricultural zones proceed to permit so many inappropriate uses that the result is the same.[3]

Modern zoning ordinances are increasingly noncumulative in nature: all or specified use zones are to be devoted exclusively to the designated use, and even so-called "higher" uses are excluded. Given the failures of cumulative zoning to protect agricultural lands as discussed above, it is not surprising to find that in many zoning ordinances of recent vintage land zoned for agricultural purposes can be devoted only to agricultural and closely related uses.[4]

Exclusive agricultural zoning, unlike agricultural zoning under cumulative ordinances, not only restricts the landowner of agricultural land but confers protection to the farmer by excluding incompatible uses.[5] Such zoning, in theory at least, is a definitive tool for preserving agricultural lands and preventing their conversion to non-agricultural uses. Even if land speculators purchase farmland and take it out of agricultural production, strict enforcement of the zoning code should prevent any development on or changes of the land that would affect its ultimate suitability for agricultural production.

The problems encountered in using exclusive agricultural use zoning as a farmland preservation tool result not from zoning principles but from zoning practice. The farmer himself may find the stringency of the zoning protection economically unacceptable, and he or his vendees may resort to the normal avenues for zoning flexibility—variances, special exceptions, and rezonings—to obtain permission for profitable but ultimately incompatible uses, thus undermining if not defeating the protective goals of such zoning approaches.[6]

al land that want the same higher density zoning that is applied to the rural residential portion. Because the market will sustain only a small share of the total supply farmers everywhere become speculators and eventually through the intrusion of urban uses the region's critical mass of farming activity collapses, leaving thousands of acres of idled or unused farmland. David Berry, The Effects of Urbanization on Agri-cultural Activities, 3 Growth and Change 2–8, (1978).

3. See J. Juergensmeyer & J. Wadley, Florida Zoning—Specific Uses § 29 (1980).

4. See supra § 4.8.

5. See generally David C. Keating, Exclusionary Zoning: In Whose Interests Should the Police Power be Exercised?, 23 Real Est.L.J. 304 (1995).

6. See supra § 5.1.

Since exclusive agricultural use zones are relatively new,[7] little judicial attention has been given to them but most courts which have considered the issue have upheld them.[8]

One case in which the local government's non-exclusive agricultural zoning plan was not upheld provides some judicial guidelines for local governments. In Hopewell Township Board of Supervisors v. Golla,[9] the Supreme Court of Pennsylvania was confronted with a zoning code provision which permitted the owner of a tract of land in an agricultural zone to use the undivided tract as a farm with only one single-family dwelling or to establish as many as five contiguous residential lots of no more than 1 1/2 acres and a single family dwelling on each lot. Plaintiffs did not challenge the agricultural zoning classification but only the reasonableness of the restrictions placed on their own land. The court held that this approach to farmland preservation placed an unreasonably severe limitation on permissible land uses and that it had an arbitrary and discriminatory impact on different landowners since under the ordinance the owner of a small tract of land could devote a larger percentage of his tract to residential development than the owner of a large tract.

The court suggested a cure for the ordinance's defects by stating: "Were the ordinance to permit the dedication of the 1 1/2 acre lot to a single family residence per each X number of acres in the tract, this scheme would have a more equitable effect and would avoid impacting

7. Exclusive agricultural use zoning is used throughout Hawaii and Oregon but in very few other areas. Arthur C. Nelson and James B. Duncan, Growth Management Principles and Practices (1995). Where it is used, the results have been positive as the local, regional, and state economies have sustained an important element of economic diversification (especially with rising international trade in agricultural products) while not impeding growth of other economic sectors. Arthur C. Nelson, Preserving Prime Farmland in the Face of Urbanization, 58 J.Am.Plan.Ass'n 467 (1992).

8. See Joyce v. Portland, 24 Or.App. 689, 546 P.2d 1100 (1976); Gisler v. Madera County, 38 Cal.App.3d 303, 112 Cal.Rptr. 919 (1974); County of Ada v. Henry, 105 Idaho 263, 668 P.2d 994 (1983); Harvard State Bank v. County of McHenry, 251 Ill. App.3d 84, 190 Ill.Dec. 99, 620 N.E.2d 1360 (1993); Wilson v. County of McHenry, 92 Ill.App.3d 997, 48 Ill.Dec. 395, 416 N.E.2d 426 (1981); Caspersen v. Town of Lyme, 139 N.H. 637, 661 A.2d 759, 764 (N.H. 1995); Gardner v. N.J. Pinelands Comm'n, 125 N.J. 193, 593 A.2d 251 (N.J.1991); Still v. Board of County Commissioners, 42 Or. App. 115, 600 P.2d 433 (1979); Reeves v. Yamhill Cty., 132 Or.App. 263, 888 P.2d 79 (1995); Dufour v. Montgomery County Council (Circuit Court for Montgomery County, Md., No. 56964, 1983). See also Zoning for Agricultural Preservation, 36 Land Use Law & Zoning Digest 3 (April 1984). See generally Wright, Some Land Use Issues for the Future, 3 Agric.L.J. 587 (1982); Batie & Looney, Preserving Agricultural Lands: Issues and Answers, 1 Agric. L.J. 600 (1980); W. Toner, Saving Farms and Farmlands: A Community Guide (ASPO Planning Advisory Service Report No. 333) (1978); J. Keene, Agricultural Land Protection: Legal and Constitutional Issues, in R. Coughlin & J. Keene, eds. The Protection of Farmland: A Reference Guidebook for State and Local Government 254 (1981). For a discussion of the problems inherent in distinguishing agriculture uses from other uses in a zoning code, see Hamilton, Freedom to Farm! Understanding the Agricultural Exemption to County Zoning in Iowa, 31 Drake L.Rev. 565 (1982).

9. 499 Pa. 246, 452 A.2d 1337 (1982). The case is analyzed at Berger, Agricultural Zoning Held Invalid, 7 APA Planning & L.Div. Newsletter 10 (May 1983). See also Rosadele Kaufmann, Comment, Agricultural Zoning in Pennsylvania: Will Growth Pressure Prevail?, 91 Dick.L.Rev. 289 (1986).

landowners on an arbitrary basis."[10]

§ 13.9   Agricultural Districts

Agricultural districting is designed to bring about through voluntary compliance and local initiative the same quality of protection for farmland as that afforded by exclusive agricultural zoning. It was pioneered in California,[1] New York,[2] and Virginia.[3] Agricultural landowners whose lands meet specified acreage minimums can voluntarily form special districts.[4] Such status, depending on the exact provisions of the relevant statute, creates a binding agreement between the landowner and local authorities for a specified number of years during which the landowner receives special tax treatment and freedom from eminent domain. The authority of public agencies to install growth—stimulating public services in the area is limited, special assessments against the land are forbidden, and local governments are prohibited from enacting certain regulations of farming practices on the land unless public health and safety factors are involved.[5] If non-agricultural uses are made of the land during the "contract" period, heavy tax penalties are incurred.[6]

10. 499 Pa. 246, 452 A.2d 1337, 1344 (1982). Justice McDermott, dissenting, criticized the majority's setting its own standards rather than accepting the local government's. "There is only so much prime agricultural land in Hopewell Township. Perhaps when the majority's paternal interest recognizes that fact, the Court can represide and reallot the land even closer to its heart's desire." Id. at 1345.

§ 13.9

1. The precursor and inspiration for all agricultural districting acts is said to be California's Land Conservation Act, West's Cal.Govt.Code § 51200–51295, which is known popularly as the Williamson Act. For a recent discussion of this Act and California's Agricultural Land Preservation Act of 1995, see McGurty, The State of Agricultural Land Preservation in California in 1997: Will the Agricultural Land Stewardship Program Solve the Problems Inherent in the Williamson Act?, 7 San Joaquin Ag. L. Rev. 135 (1997). See also, Myers, The Legal Aspects of Agricultural Districting, 55 Ind. L.J. 1, 2 (1979), reprinted in 2 Agric.L.J. 627 (1981). See also, Anne E. Mudge, Impact Fees for Conversion of Agricultural Land: A Resource–Based Development Policy for California's Cities and Counties, 19 Ecology L.Q. 63 (1992).

2. N.Y.—McKinney's Agric. & Mkts. Law §§ 300–307. See John R. Nolon, The Stable Door is Open: New York's Statutes to Protect Farm Land, 67 N.Y.St.B.J. 36.

3. Agricultural and Forestal Districts Act, Va.Code §§ 15.1–1506 to 15.1–1513 (1997). At least three additional states have

enacted agricultural district statutes. See. 505 ILCS 57/1; Iowa Code Ann. § 358A.27; Md. Code, Agric., § 2–501 et seq. For an overview of agricultural districting legislation, see Duncan, Toward a Theory of Broad–Based Planning for the Preservation of Agricultural Land, 24 Nat. Resources J. 51, 96–113 (1984). For comparisons of existing programs, see generally J. Esseks & J. McDonald, Incentives: Agricultural Districting, in R. Coughlin & J. Keene, eds., The Protection of Farmland: A Reference Guidebook for State and Local Government 76 (1981); Geier, Agricultural Districts and Zoning: A State–Local Approach to a National Problem, 8 Ecology L. Q. 655 (1980).

4. Any owner of agricultural land who meets the statutory acreage requirements (in New York the greater of 500 acres or 10% of the land to be included in the district and in Virginia at least 200 acres) may apply to the local governing body that then seeks the opinion of a planning body, holds public hearings, and then adopts, modifies, or rejects the proposal. The details of the New York and Virginia procedure are discussed in Myers, supra note 1.

5. Clayton & Abbitt, Land for Florida Agriculture, 1977 Fla.Food & Resource Econ. (Jan.-Feb.); Lapping, Bevins, & Herbers, Differential Assessment and Other Techniques to Preserve Missouri Farmland, 42 Mo.L.Rev. 369 (1977).

6. In New York, for example, conversion to nonagricultural uses during the contract period results in a penalty equal to five times the tax saved in the last year in

The major advantage and appeal of the agricultural districting approach to farmland preservation lies in its emphasis on voluntary compliance and local initiative. Other strengths, compared to previously and subsequently discussed approaches, include the retention of land ownership by the farmer, the stringent restrictions are voluntary in nature and allow land use without raising taking issue problems, and its emphasis on local control, which thereby at least theoretically makes it responsive to local needs and problems.[7] Given these advantages, the popularity of this approach to farmland preservation is not surprising. By 1978 approximately one-half of the farmland in the state of New York was in agricultural districting.[8]

In spite of this popularity, the approach is not without its problems and disadvantages. The obvious disadvantage is the feature that already has been pointed out as a basis for the concept's appeal—i.e., it is entirely voluntary. Studies indicate that the effectiveness of the approach is limited by the fact that only those lands relatively free from urban fringe development pressures, that is to say, those lands that need protection the least, are placed in districts. Secondly, the special tax treatment, which constitutes the major advantage to the landowner, hampers the revenue raising authority of local governments and provides dubious incentives to retain agricultural district status. Finally, the limitations placed on governmental power in regard to regulation of the land in question and the location of public facilities, may hamper local government comprehensive planning and result in less desirable growth patterns in the long run.

§ 13.10 Clustering, Open Space, Planned Unit Developments, and Minimum Lot Size

One of the most serious dilemmas encountered by owners of agricultural land occurs when adjacent land is developed for residential, commercial or other non-farm uses. Once such development occurs, the farmer usually finds himself subjected to intense economic pressures to convert his farm to non-agricultural use because of the increase in value which results from neighboring development. The farmer also frequently discovers that his land no longer is well-suited to agricultural uses, since the normal odors, noises, and pollutants accompanying many agricultural activities are now nuisances in the eyes of his new neighbors.[1] Cluster zoning, planned unit developments, and open space zoning are land use control techniques designed to alleviate such consequences of development by providing a land buffer on or between the developed land and the neighboring farmland.

which the land benefitted from an agricultural assessment, plus interest. N.Y.—McKinney's Agric. & Mkts.Law § 306.

7. See Geier, Agricultural Districts and Zoning: A State–Local Approach to a National Problem, 1980 Ecology L.Q. 655.

8. Myers, supra note 1.

§ 13.10

1. See infra Chapter 14.

Cluster zoning involves development of a tract of land in order to meet density maximums for the tract as a unit but places improvements on the tract so as to allow the preservation of open space or buffer areas on all or certain borders.[2] As a result, new development need not abut agricultural land, and the development/farming conflict is lessened.[3]

Local governmental use of the cluster concept to provide a buffer between areas of development and of agriculture is relatively simple in the sense that little or no change in basic zoning codes is necessary to allow such an approach. Most courts have recognized the permissibility of such an approach, even pursuant to Euclidean ordinances, since no variation of overall density or of permissible uses occurs. The developer who is required or encouraged to cluster his planned improvements is not usually in a position to assert constitutionally based objections since he is not denied the right to develop the overall density established by the local land use regulation. In fact, developers frequently seek permission to cluster since there often are economies of design and construction to such a development arrangement.[4]

The planned unit development (PUD) is grounded upon the cluster concept but constitutes both a refinement of that concept and a departure from traditional Euclidean zoning approaches. The PUD combines uses within a development so that various housing types—for example, high-rise apartments, townhouses, single family dwellings, and condominiums—co-exist with open spaces, recreational areas, convenience type commercial uses, and business/professional uses.[5]

The use of a PUD for the development of land adjacent to agricultural lands offers various protective aspects. As with clustering, buffer areas that are not built upon can be placed between new improvements and neighboring farmland. Furthermore, unlike clusters, the provision for various commercial, recreational, or business/professional facilities within the PUD means that adjacent farmland is not needed as a location for supportive services that inevitably accompany development. By providing for such nonresidential uses, the PUD offers greater protection for adjacent agricultural land than does simple cluster zoning. Although PUDs frequently receive even greater developer enthusiasm than clusters, local land use control authorities are often less enthusiastic about the PUD since its combination of uses is in conflict with one of the sacred cows of traditional zoning—separation of uses. Additionally, approval for use of PUDs frequently requires the existence of floating zones[6] within the zoning jurisdiction.

Open space zoning is a more drastic way of providing the type of open space or land buffer between new development and neighboring agricultural land that results almost automatically from clusters and

2. See Stroud, The Farm and the City, 9 Fla.Envtl. & Urb.Issues 4 (1981); Pivo, Small, and Wolfe, Rural Cluster Zoning: Survey and Guidelines, Land Use L. & Zoning Dig., vol. 42, No. 9, at 3 (1990).

3. See supra § 4.11.

4. See supra § 7.11–.15.

5. See supra § 7.11.

6. See supra § 4.16.

PUDs. The technique is much simpler, however, since land bordering agricultural areas is designated in the relevant comprehensive plan as being unavailable for development and is zoned for only recreational or other nondevelopment uses. The problem presented by open space zoning is that the economic value of land so zoned is nearly destroyed, thereby entitling the landowner to contest the zoning designation as an unconstitutional taking of property without compensation.[7]

Another related zoning technique frequently advocated as an agricultural lands preservation device is "large lot" zoning. By establishing high minimum lot area requirements such as 1 acre, 5, 10, 15, 18, or, in one case,[8] 160 acres, residential development of rural land is discouraged by increasing the cost of, and thereby decreasing the demand for, such property. Furthermore, if the land is developed, the low density of such developments only slightly affects the continued suitability of adjacent or nearby land for agricultural use. The major disadvantage of using large lot zoning to protect agricultural land is the same encountered with open space zoning: the economic value may be so greatly decreased as to raise the taking issue. The exclusionary effects of large lot requirements provide still another basis for contesting their validity.[9]

§ 13.11 Transferable Development Rights

The application of the transferable development rights (TDR) approach to agricultural land preservation is of relatively recent origin.[1]

7. See supra §§ 10.4–.8.

8. Wilson v. County of McHenry, 92 Ill.App.3d 997, 48 Ill.Dec. 395, 416 N.E.2d 426 (1981).

9. See supra § 6.2. The leading "large lot" zoning cases are Arlington Group v. City of Riverside, 2 F.3d 1156 (9th Cir. 1993); Herrington v. Sonoma County, 834 F.2d 1488 (9th Cir.1987); Ybarra v. Town of Los Altos Hills, 503 F.2d 250 (9th Cir.1974); Steel Hill Dev. v. Town of Sanbornton, 469 F.2d 956 (1st Cir.1972); Pike v. Zoning Board of Appeals of the Town of Hampton, 31 Conn.App. 270, 624 A.2d 909 (Conn.App. 1993); County of Ada v. Henry, 105 Idaho 263, 668 P.2d 994 (1983); Scots Ventures, Inc. v. Hayes Township, 212 Mich.App. 530, 537 N.W.2d 610 (Mich.App.1995); Hay v. Township of Grow, 296 Minn. 1, 206 N.W.2d 19 (1973); Gutoski v. Lane County, 141 Or.App. 265, 917 P.2d 1048 (Or.App. 1996); Oregonians in Action v. Land Conservation & Dev. Comm'n, 121 Or.App. 497, 854 P.2d 1010 (Or.App.1993); Henley v. Zoning Hearing Bd. of West Fallowfield Township, 155 Pa.Cmwlth. 306, 625 A.2d 132 (Pa.Cmwlth.1993).

§ 13.11

1. See Dennis J. McEleney, Using Transferable Development Rights to Preserve Vanishing Landscapes and Land-

marks, 83 Ill.B.J. 634 (1995); D. Merriam & A. Merriam, Bibliography of the Transfer of Development Rights, Council of Planning Librarians Exchange Bibliography No. 1338 (1977); Carmichael, Transferable Development Rights as a Basis for Land Use Control, 2 Fla.St.U.L.Rev. 35 (1974); Costonis, The Chicago Plan: Incentive Zoning and the Preservation of Urban Landmarks, 85 Harv.L.Rev. 574 (1972); Costonis, Development Right Transfer: An Exploratory Essay, 83 Yale L.J. 75 (1973); Merriam, Making TDR Work, 56 N.C.L.Rev. 77 (1978); Schnidman, Transferable Development Rights: An Idea in Search of Implementation, 11 Land & Water L.Rev. 339 (1976); Mere, Transferable Development Rights, An Idea Whose Time Has Come, Fairfax County, Va., Feb. 16, 1974; Tustian, TDR's in Practice: A Case Study of Agriculture Preservation in Montgomery County, Maryland, 1984 Zoning and Planning Law Handbook 223. For a discussion of the TDR approach and an explanation of the PDR (Purchase of Development Rights) scheme, see Duncan, Toward a Theory of Broad Based Planning for the Preservation of Agricultural Land, 24 Nat. Resources J. 61, 113–135 (1984).

The TDR approach designates certain land areas within a given jurisdiction as subject to severe regulations and designates other land areas within the jurisdiction as appropriate for development. Owners of the severely restricted land are allowed to sell their rights to develop, which they cannot exercise because of the land use restrictions, to the owners of land permitted to be developed. The purchasing landowners may be required to purchase the rights of the restricted landowners before they may develop, or the purchase of development rights may authorize them to develop at greater density than otherwise would be permitted.[2]

Although considerable support exists for using the TDR concept as an agricultural lands preservation device, the National Agricultural Lands Study treated the idea rather negatively.[3] In evaluating the usefulness of TDRs, it first should be noted that the statistics used by the NALS are now out of date and actual experience with TDRs is considerably broader and more positive.[4] Furthermore, whatever complexities and difficulties are encountered in regard to implementation of TDR programs, their key potential advantage over virtually all other approaches to agricultural lands preservation is that restricted landowners receive compensation for their losses without the need for expenditure of public funds.[5] The compensation comes from payments made in an open market context by landowners economically benefitted by land use restrictions. In short, TDRs allow payment of compensation without cost to the taxpayer.

Finally, as far as the acceptability of the TDR concept is concerned, the basic principle is a familiar one to farmers. As Professor Torres has observed:[6]

2. TDR's are discussed in detail in § 9.9.

3. "Transfer of development rights (TDR) programs have been instituted by 10 municipalities and two counties, but developers have shown little inclination to participate in them. It is possible that the newer programs, which have been adopted by large suburban counties, may include development locations where the market will support higher densities and where the county government will provide sufficient facilities and public services so that the developers will find it profitable to purchase and transfer rights. But so far, the right combination of factors has not been present." National Agricultural Lands Study, Final Report 61 (1981).

4. See § 9.9. A well-studied TDR regime directed toward farmland preservation is that of Montgomery County, Maryland. Tustian, TDR's in Practice: A Case Study of Agriculture Preservation in Montgomery County, Maryland, 1984 Zoning and Plan-

ning Law Handbook 223. Maryland's program was upheld against a taking challenge in Dufour v. Montgomery County Council, No. 56964 (Cir. Ct. for Montgomery County, Jan. 20, 1983), discussed in 35 Land Use Law 19 (1983). Examples of TDR programs include Collier County, Florida, which in 1974 adopted a TDR plan for its cypress swamp and designated 84 percent of the county's land as a special treatment (SP) zone requiring special permission prior to development. New Jersey has had the most activity with its TDR plan. The 1976 legislature approved $5 million for an agricultural preserve demonstration project. An estimated 10,000 acres will be preserved which, calculated at $500 a preservation acre, is relatively cheap.

5. Bozung, Transferable Development Rights: Compensation for Owners of Restricted Property, 1984 Zoning and Planning Law Handbook 207.

6. Torres, Helping Farmers and Saving Farmland, 37 Okla.L.Rev. 31, 40 (1984).

While in urban areas transferable development rights may be looked upon as a novel land planning device, in farm country the notion that the productive capacity of one area may be severed and transferred to another area is at least as old as the Agricultural Adjustment Act.[7] Depending on the crop being farmed, acreage allotments have traditionally been transferable between farms....

One crop that farmers, especially those farmers in developing areas, hope to harvest is the appreciated non-farm development value of their holdings.... TDRs function much like the transfer of acreage allotments between ... holders of development potential.... Like crops, development potential becomes merely another cash valued commodity.

The judicial reaction to TDR programs is discussed elsewhere in this Hornbook.[8] The initial approval of the TDR concept by the Supreme Court in *Penn Central*[9] has been somewhat clouded by the Supreme Court's decision in Suitum v. Tahoe Regional Planning Agency.[10] Although TDR Programs themselves received favorable comment, the Court left undecided whether the alternate use and value TDRs provide are to be considered in reaching a decision as to whether or not a taking has occurred or only in deciding how much compensation has been paid if a taking is found.[11]

§ 13.12 Conservation Easements

Conservation easements merit special attention as an agricultural lands preservation technique, even though their use is sometimes part of a transferable development rights plan or of the land banking or public and private trusts approach.[1]

---

7. 7 U.S.C.A. § 1281 et seq.

8. See § 9.9.

9. Penn Cent. Transp. Co. v. New York, 438 U.S. 104, 98 S.Ct. 2646, 57 L.Ed.2d 631 (1978), rehearing denied 439 U.S. 883, 99 S.Ct. 226, 58 L.Ed.2d 198 (1978).

10. ___ U.S. ___, 117 S.Ct. 1659, 137 L.Ed.2d 980 (1997).

11. See J. Nicholas, J. Juergensmeyer and B. Leebrick, Transferable Development Rights and Alternatives after *Suitum*, ___ Urb.Law ___ (1998).

§ 13.12

1. For an analysis of conservation easements and a bibliography, see National Trust for Historic Preservation, Information Sheet No. 25, Establishing an Easement Program to Protect Historic, Scenic and National Resources (Washington, D.C. 1980). See also, Melissa Waller Baldwin, Conservation Easements: A Viable Tool for Land Preservation, 32 Land & Water L.R.

89 (1997); Vivian Quinn, Preserving Farmland with Conservation Easements: Public Benefit or Burden?, 24 Real Est.L.J. 274 (1996); Arthur C. Nelson, Economic Critique of Prime Farmland Protection Programs in the United States, 6 Jr. of Rural Studies 114 (1990); Dawson, Compassionate Taxation of Undeveloped Private Land (pt. 11), 3 Zoning & Planning L.Rep. 57 (Sept. 1980); Netherton, Environmental Conservation and Historic Preservation Through Recorded Land Use Agreements, 14 Real Prop.Probate & Trust J. 540 (1979). Barnes, An Alternative to Alternative Farm Valuation: The Conveyance of Conservation Easements to an Agricultural Land Trust, 3 Agric.L.J. 308 (1981); Horne, How an Agricultural Conservation Easement is Negotiated, 2 Farmland 2 (March 1982).

For a discussion of federal conservation easement programs, see Karen A. Jordan, Perpetual Conservation: Accomplishing the Goal Through Preemptive Federal Easement Programs, 43 Case W. Res.L.Rev. 401 (1993); Neil D. Hamilton, Legal Authority

A conservation easement is created when a landowner restricts his rights to develop his own land in ways that would be incompatible with its use as farmland. The landowner burdens his land in the form of a negative restriction, thereby creating a negative easement in favor of other parcels of land or for the benefit of public or private agricultural lands preservation organizations. Unless the negative restriction is in some way limited, it will bind all future owners of the land.

Although such arrangements are generally referred to as conservation or preservation "easements," the same goals can be accomplished from a property law viewpoint through real covenants or equitable servitudes.[2]

Perhaps the greatest advantage to the use of conservation easements is that the farmer remains owner of all interests in the land in question except the right to use the property in a manner inconsistent with the restriction.

One of the best, and thus far most successful, agricultural preservation restriction programs is the program instituted in Massachusetts.[3] Within 7 years, $40 million had been appropriated for the purchase of deed restrictions offered by farmers to the state on a voluntary basis. Over 8,000 acres had already been restricted and purchase of restrictions for nearly 9,000 more acres was pending. The program is especially significant since "Massachusetts has lost nearly three-fourths of its land in farms and one-half of its productive cropland,"[4] in the last forty years. The state officials work closely with a private entity, the Massachusetts Farm and Conservation Lands Trust. The entire program serves as a model to other states.[5]

The institution of comparable programs is proceeding at an impressive pace. At least 34 states have adopted such measures.[6] The federal government has also utilized the theory of voluntary negative easements in its creation of the Conservation Reserve Program. Pursuant to the Program, the Secretary of Agriculture has authority to contract with the owners and operators of specified farmlands to assist them in conserving and improving the soil and water resources on their land.[7]

for Federal Acquisition of Conservation Easements to Provide Agricultural Credit Relief, 35 Drake L.Rev. 477 (1985–86).

2. See infra § 15.6.

3. Mass. Regs. Code tit. 330 § 22. See Connors, The Agricultural Preservation Restriction Program in Massachusetts, ALI–ABA, Land Use Regulation and Litigation 313 (1983).

4. Id.

5. Id.

6. State-by-State Roundup of 1983 Preservation Actions, 4 Am. Farmland 3 (Mar. 1984). See, e.g., Agricultural Land Stewardship Program Act of 1995, Cal.

Agric.Code § 931 (creating state fund which provides grants for acquisition of agricultural conservation easements); Cheryl A. Denton, Conservation Easements in Florida: Do Unsubordinated Mortgages Pose a Threat?, 70 Fla.B.J., April 1996, at 50; Timothy J. Houseal, Comment, Forever a Farm: The Agricultural Conservation Easement in Pennsylvania, 94 Dick.L.Rev. 527 (1990).

7. Conservation Reserve Program, 16 U.S.C.A. § 3831. See also Raymond J. Watson, Jr., Symposium, Changing Structures and Expectations in Agriculture Conservation Reserve Program: What Happens to the Land After the Contracts End?, 14 N. ILL.U.L.Rev. 733 (1994); Neil D. Hamilton, State Initiatives to Supplement the Conser-

§ 13.13 Land Banking and Farmland Trusts

The agricultural lands preservation technique of land banking involves purchase of farmland by governmental or public organizations for the purpose of insuring that the land remains in agricultural production. The use of land banking to control urban land development patterns has long been practiced in Europe,[1] but one of the most ambitious uses of the concept in the agricultural context has occurred in Canada, particularly in the province of Saskatchewan.[2]

In recent years, several American states have expressed interest in the Canadian land bank idea and considered the possible applicability of the concept to this country.[3] To date, however, there has been no widespread acceptance of the idea. Where it has been adopted, it has been used principally as a device by which farmland may be made available to specific groups of individuals rather than as a farmland preservation technique. It is also significant to note that interest in the idea has been more intense at the state or local level and is only very recently finding significant support at the federal level.[4]

The American Law Institute (ALI) Model Land Development Code defines land banking as a "system in which a governmental entity acquires a substantial fraction of the land in a region that is available for future development for the purpose of controlling the future growth of the region.... "[5] The ALI definition requires that: (1) the land being acquired does not become committed to a specific future use at the time of acquisition and (2) the land being acquired is sufficiently large in amount to have a substantial effect on urban growth patterns.

Two aspects of the ALI definition are inapplicable when land banking is used to preserve farmland. First there is a commitment to a specific future use at the time of acquisition—namely, continuation of agricultural uses.

Secondly, the ALI definition presumes government involvement. In many instances in which farmland is "banked" for preservation purposes a government entity is involved. However, land banking for farmland preservation purposes is done on a private as well as a public

---

vation Reserve Program, 37 Drake L.Rev. 251 (1987–88); Margaret R. Grossman, Exercising Eminent Domain Against Protected Agricultural Lands: Taking a Second Look, 30 Vill. L.Rev. 701 (1985).

§ 13.13

1. A. Strong, Land Banking: European Reality, American Prospect (1979). See also David Callies and Malcolm Grant, Paying for Growth and Planning Gain:An Anglo–American Comparison of Development Conditions, Impact Fees, & Development Agreements, 23 Urb. Law 221 (1991); Lapping & Forster, Farmland and Agricultural Policy in Sweden: An Integrated Approach, 7 Int'l Regional Sci.Rev. 3 (1982).

2. Young, The Saskatchewan Land Bank, 40 Saskatchewan L.Rev. 1 (1975). See also, Fitch & Mock, Land Banking, in The Good Earth of America 134 (Harris, ed. 1974); Note, Public Land Banking: A New Praxis for Urban Growth, 23 Case W.Res. L.Rev. 897 (1972). The statutory authority for the Saskatchewan land bank was repealed in 1983.

3. See Carol Kamm, Note, Public Trust, Farmland Protection, and the Connecticut Environmental Protection Act, 23 Conn.L.Rev. 811 (1991).

4. See J. Juergensmeyer & J. Wadley, Agricultural Law § 4.14 (1982).

5. ALI Model Land Development Code Commentary on Art. 6 at 254 (1975).

basis. In fact, the major land banking efforts of agricultural lands preservation advocates are directed to private trusts.[6]

The private land trust is a charitable organization that acquires and holds interests in agricultural land for preservation purposes. To qualify as charitable, the trust must exist for a charitable purpose and operate for the benefit of an indefinite group of persons. Additionally, the trust must satisfy various state laws relating to charitable organizations and numerous federal and state tax laws and regulations in order to qualify for receipt of tax deductible or tax exempt "charitable" donations.

Land trusts need not be organized as "trusts" in the technical legal meaning of the term. In fact, "land trusts" can and do exist as (1) unincorporated associations, (2) charitable trusts, or (3) charitable corporations. The last two of these—charitable trusts and charitable corporations—are clearly the preferable form of organization. The charitable corporation format has been chosen by the most significant agricultural lands trust—the American Farmland Trust (AFT).[7]

§ 13.14 Preferential Assessment and Differential Taxation

The major source of revenue for most local governments is the ad valorem tax levied on real property. In most states, agricultural land is given special treatment regarding ad valorem taxes or "property taxes," as they are often called. The justification given for "special treatment" or the "differential taxation" approach usually combines two arguments.

The first argument is farmland preservation. Agricultural land tax breaks save farmers money, and make agricultural activities more profitable, consequently giving farmers an economic incentive to continue farming. The second justification given for treating farmers differently for property tax purposes is that agricultural activities do not make the demands on governmental services that urban land uses make. Farmers therefore are entitled to tax breaks because they otherwise would be paying more than their fair share of the costs of governmental services. Under this justification, any farmland preservation effects are merely incidental.

6. See John A. McVickar, Land Trusts: A Growing Conservation Institution, 21 Vt. B.J. & L. Digest 33 (1995); Fenner, Land Trusts: An Alternative Method of Preserving Open Space, 33 Vand.L.Rev. 1039 (1980); Rebecca Rice–Osterhoudt, Note, Farmland Preservation in Vermont and the Creative Use of Land Trusts, 11 Vt.L.Rev. 603 (1986); Lapping, Bevins & Herbers, Differential Assessment and Other Techniques to Preserve Missouri's Farmland, 42 Mo. L.Rev. 369 (1977); Large, This Land Is Whose Land? Changing Concepts of Land as Property, 1973 Wis.L.Rev. 1039; McClau-

ghry, A Model State Land Trust Act, 12 Harv.J.Legis. 563 (1975); Renter, Preserving Farm Land Through Zoning and a Community Land Trust, 1971 Land Use Control Ann. 169; Roe, Innovative Techniques to Preserve Rural Land Resources, 5 Envtl. Aff. 419 (1976).

7. The American Farmland Trust was incorporated in 1980 pursuant to the District of Columbia Nonprofit Corporation Act. See American Farmland Trust, Statement of Purpose (1980).

Whatever the justification given, the differential taxation or preferential assessment approach is commonly used. In fact, at least 48 states[1] have statutory and/or constitutional provisions falling under generally accepted definitions of differential taxation or preferential assessment. Not surprisingly, differential taxation is also one of the issues most frequently written about in all of agricultural law.[2] It is also one of the most controversial. The most recent evaluations suggest that differential taxation for ad valorem tax purposes has had little, if any, effect on keeping land in agricultural production. Differential taxation for estate, gift, and inheritance tax purposes is considered much more important and considerably more effective in accomplishing preservation goals.[3] Perhaps the most balanced evaluation of differential taxation programs is that of the National Agricultural Lands Study—Final Report:

> Although many states have used property tax relief as a tool in protecting agricultural land, only a small fraction of farm estates or farms which enjoy the tax benefits of differential assessment meet all the conditions necessary to make this incentive effective. The benefits of reduced taxation, however, are conferred broadly, with no proof required of each recipient that the public policy of protecting farmland is being promoted. For this reason, tax policy is often viewed as a shotgun approach. Furthermore, unless differential assessment programs are combined with agricultural zoning and/or with agreements that restrict the land to agricultural use and/or

---

§ 13.14

1. Real property taxes can account for up to 20 percent of a farmer's net farm income. John C. Keene, Untaxing Open Space, Council on Environmental Quality (1975).

2. For a listing of the citations for the various state statutes and constitutional provisions, see Dunford, A Survey of Property Tax Relief Programs for the Retention of Agricultural and Open Space Lands, 15 Gonz.L.Rev. 675, 696–97 (1980). The editors of a casebook on agricultural law contend that all states except Kansas "have laws that seek to reduce the burden of real property taxes on farmers." K. Meyer, D. Pedersen, N. Thornson & J. Davidson, Agricultural Law: Cases and Materials 853 (1985). See also, Arthur C. Nelson, Economic Critique of Prime Farmland Protection Programs in the United States, 6 Jr. of Rural Studies 114 (1990) (Forty-eight states employ some form of differential assessment of resource land.) Some of the more recent or classic discussions include Gloudemans, Use–Value Farmland Assessments: Theory, Practice and Impact (Int'l Ass'n of Assessing Officers, 1974); J. Wershow, Florida Agricultural Law, at chs. 2 & 3 (1981); Cooke & Power, Preferential Assessment of Agricultural Land, 47 Fla.B.J. 636 (1973); Currier, An Analysis of Differential Taxation as a Method of Maintaining Agricultural and Open Space Land Uses, 30 U.Fla. L.Rev. 832 (1978); Dean, The California Land Conservation Act of 1965 and the Fight to Save California's Prime Agricultural Lands, 30 Hastings L.J. 1859 (1979); Ellingson, Differential Assessment and Local Government Controls to Preserve Agricultural Lands, 20 S.D.L.Rev. 548 (1975); Hady & Sibold, State Programs for the Differential Assessment of Farm and Open Space Land, 256 Agric.Econ.Rep. 6 (U.S.D.A.1974); Sandra A. Hoffman, Note, Farmland and Open Space Preservation in Michigan: An Empirical Analysis, 19 U. Mich. J. L. Ref. 1107 (1986); Buck, Note, Beyond Williamson Act: Alternatives for More Effective Preservation of Agricultural Land, 15 Pac.L.J. 1151 (1984); Survey, Property: Agricultural Use of Land—Cancellation of Contracts, 13 Pac.L.J. 749 (1982); Keene, A Review of Governmental Policies and Techniques for Keeping Farmers Farming, 19 Nat. Resources J. 119 (1989); Stockford, Comment, Property Tax Assessment of Conservation Easements, 17 B.C. Envtl. Aff.L.Rev. 823 (1990).

3. See, e.g., H.R. 520, 104th Cong. (1996) (providing farmers with protection against estate taxes in order to encourage the transfer of farms from generation to generation).

purchase of development rights, there is no assurance that the beneficiaries of tax reduction or abatement will keep their land in agricultural use. Owners may simply enjoy reduced taxes until the time comes when they want to sell. In the case of death taxes, significant tax benefits are made available to large farm estates, even those that are not in serious jeopardy of being converted because of high death taxes.

In isolation, then, differential assessment is largely ineffective in reducing the rate of conversion of agricultural land. It does not discourage the incursion of non-farm uses into stable agricultural areas; it simply enables owners of land under development pressure to postpone the sale of their land until they are ready to retire. The incentives are not keyed into actual need, except in the case of the tax credit programs of Wisconsin and Michigan.

Nevertheless, differential taxation is a valuable component of a comprehensive agricultural land protection program. As a matter of equity, if a program prevents agricultural land from being developed, the owner should pay taxes only on its agricultural use value. Further, benefits such as these may serve as incentives to encourage farmers to participate in integrated agricultural land protection programs.[4]

§ 13.15 Constitutional Limitations on Farmland Protection Programs

The power of state and local governments to use land use planning and control techniques to protect and preserve agricultural lands is based on the police power. It is therefore subject to the same constitutional limitations and requirements that apply to all exercises of the police power.

The issues of constitutional limitation are explored elsewhere in this hornbook.[1] The reader should consider carefully the following interrelated concepts in judging the constitutional validity of farmland preservation programs: (1) the taking issue, (2) the arbitrary, capricious, and unreasonable standard, (3) the requirement of conformity to comprehensive plans, (4) the unlawful delegation of legislative authority issue, and (5) the exclusionary zoning prohibition.[2]

Several aspects of the relationship between the public interest and farming activities suggests that most farmland preservation approaches will survive attacks grounded on complaints that the restrictions consti-

---

4. National Agricultural Lands Study: Final Report 55 (1981). See also Duncan, Toward a Theory of Broad–Based Planning for the Preservation of Agricultural Land, 24 Nat. Resources J. 61, 78–96 (1984); Dunford, A Survey of Property Tax Relief Programs for the Retention of Agricultural and Open Space Lands, 15 Gonzaga L.R. 675 (1980).

§ 13.15

1. See supra Ch. 10.

2. Regarding the taking issue, see § 10.2; arbitrary and capricious conduct, § 10.12; conformity to comprehensive plans, §§ 2.11–.13; unlawful delegation, § 5.3; exclusionary zoning, ch. 6.

tute a "taking." As a general rule, there is no constitutionally protected right to make the "highest and best" use of the land.[3] Thus a restriction denying the owner of the land an opportunity to develop the property to some use that is more economically valuable would not necessarily constitute a talking as long as there was some viable use opportunity left.[4] Further, there is no constitutionally protected right to farm[5] nor is there a proprietary interest in farming per se.[6] Likewise, a jurisdiction can mandate particular conservation measures without affecting a taking.[7]

In that same vein, it has been held that farmers are not a "discrete, insular minority" for purposes of "equal protection" determinations.[8] Thus restrictions that distinguish between the kinds of business entities that can own farms or engage in farming have been considered rationally related to the broad public purpose of keeping farmland in the hands of small, family farms.[9] Indeed, the courts seem to give considerable deference to state interests that promote a popular based agriculture that is proximate to urban areas.[10]

On the other hand, because of the strong federal presence regarding regulation of the agricultural sector, there is potential that there will be conflicts between federal program objectives and those of particular preservation programs or strategies. Federal regulation of agriculture as an industry is grounded in the Commerce Clause of the federal constitution.[11] This raises the possibility that the state programs might be considered preempted by the federal regulation or considered to be an impermissible interference with interstate commerce if the farmland program is too restrictive as to farming practices or opportunities to use the farmland in particular ways. For example, given the flexibility in the current farm program regarding the kinds of farming activities the farmer may engage in, some changes permitted under the federal program may be denied to the farmer under the impact of a local zoning ordinance program where the change might jeopardize the ability of the farm to qualify as a nonconforming use under a zoning code. In such a case, the state program may deter farmers from participating fully in the federal program.

In a somewhat similar vein, some farmers may be deterred from offering their land for enrollment in the Conservation Reserve Program

---

3. City of Miami v. Zorovich, 195 So.2d 31 (Fla.App.1967), cert. den. 201 So.2d 554 (1967): "A zoning ordinance is not invalid merely because it prevents the owner from using the property in the manner which is economically most advantageous. If the rule were otherwise, no zoning could ever stand."

4. Lucas v. South Carolina Coastal Council, 505 U.S. 1003, 112 S.Ct. 2886, 120 L.Ed.2d 798, 112 S.Ct. 2886 (1992).

5. United States v. Garth, 773 F.2d 1469 (5th Cir.1985).

6. Woodbury County Soil Conservation District v. Ortner, 279 N.W.2d 276 (Iowa 1979).

7. United States v. Garth, 773 F.2d 1469 (5th Cir.1985).

8. See, e.g. MSM Farms, Inc. v. Spire, 927 F.2d 330 (8th Cir.1991).

9. Id.

10. Wickard v. Filburn, 317 U.S. 111, 63 S.Ct. 82, 87 L.Ed. 122 (1942).

11. See, generally, Federal Land Bank v. Bott, 240 Kan. 624, 732 P.2d 710 (1987).

(CRP) if they are fearful they may be locked into non-revenue generating conservation practices if the jurisdiction adopts stringent farmland preservation measures while the land is under the contractual agreement of the CRP. Since these contracts run for ten years, farmers in areas where pressure to adopt farmland protection measures is building may be reluctant to keep the land in a conservation use that long if it interferes with their expectation that upon the completion of those contracts, they will not be free to use the land for any lawful purpose, including non-farm use. Indeed, the bid price is generally considered to reflect an agreement between the landowner and the government to only temporarily forego the earning opportunity of the land in exchange for the annual payment.

It is known that ownership changes routinely occur in advance of conversions of the land from farmland use to non-agricultural uses.[12] This is because it is often not the farmers that are the ones developing the property for other uses but those to whom the land is sold. In some instances, binding contractual relationships will be entered into as well regarding the financing or the construction of the improvements. If these arrangements occur prior to the adoption of restrictive farmland preservation ordinances or strategies, not only does this have the potential to disrupt even the best intentioned land use regulatory programs,[13] the parties to those contracts may argue that the farmland preservation restrictions may unconstitutionally impair those relationships.[14]

Most federal and state programs actually seem to work toward most of the same objectives. Conservation programs at the federal level tend to protect open space. Restrictions in the federal banking laws mirror state level restrictions that protect the family farms and prevent unwanted corporate ownership of farmland.[15] Section 2032A of the Internal Revenue Code and state preferential taxation programs seem to pursue the common goal of giving farmers an economic incentive to retain the land in farming.

12. F. Popper, What's the Hidden Factor in Land Use Regulation? Urban Land 4 (Dec. 1978).

13. J. Wadley, Agriculture and Farm Law, § 47.08(1), in Thompson on Real Property (Thomas ed. 1994).

14. See, generally, Federal Land Bank v. Bott, 240 Kan. 624, 732 P.2d 710 (Kan. 1987).

15. See, e.g., Asbury Hospital v. Cass County, 72 N.D. 359, 7 N.W.2d 438 (N.D. 1943), aff'd, 326 U.S. 207, 66 S.Ct. 61, 90 L.Ed. 6 (1945); State v. Liberty National Bank & Trust Co., 427 N.W.2d 307 (N.D. 1988), Allegheny Corp. v. Richardson, 463 N.W.2d 678 (S.D.1990).

Chapter 14

NUISANCES

Analysis

---

§ 14.1 Introduction

Nuisance law is judicial control of land use. In a process sometimes labeled "judicial zoning,"[1] courts use nuisance law to resolve land use disputes by determining which use belongs in the neighborhood and which does not. Developed shortly after the Norman Conquest, nuisance law served for centuries as the primary device to regulate land use between neighbors.[2] As a land use control device, nuisance law has its shortcomings. As judicial zoning, it classifies uses only grossly. Decision making is ad hoc and after the fact, affording little advance notice to persons to invest in land use activities safely. Eventually, comprehensive legislative controls emerged in the belief that more sensitive schemes were needed to accommodate discordant land uses. In general, nuisance law was inadequate to protect the public interest from harmful land use activities, and use of the state's police power, by way of public health measures, environmental controls, building codes, subdivision controls, and zoning, grew.

The spread of comprehensive zoning decreased the use of nuisance law.[3] Nonetheless, it remains important. In the first place, some areas, particularly rural ones, remain unzoned, leaving nuisance law as the sole control available. Furthermore, zoning has raised expectations, and if the local legislative body fails to deal with incompatible development

---

§ 14.1

1. J. H. Beuscher & Jerry W. Morrison, Judicial Zoning Through Recent Nuisance Cases, 1955 Wis.L.Rev. 440, 442.

2. Id.

3. Use of nuisance law reached a zenith in the 1920s and 1930s as landowners invoked it to relieve actual or threatened noxious uses in their neighborhoods. Robert C. Ellickson, Alternatives to Zoning, 40 U.Chi.L.Rev. 681, 721 & n. 15 (1973).

through zoning, persons may turn to the courts for protection through nuisance law.[4] Finally, the Supreme Court has made the common law of nuisance a critical determinant in defining property for the purposes of constitutional protection and the need of government to pay compensation when it regulates land use.[5]

Common law nuisances are classified as public or private nuisances, and as nuisances per se or nuisances in fact (or per accidens). A public nuisance is an unreasonable interference with a right common to the public that impairs the health, safety, morals or comfort of the community. It may, but need not, be conduct proscribed by statute. A public nuisance is usually continuing in nature or produces a long term or permanent effect, and the actor has reason to know of that effect on the common right.[6]

A private nuisance involves a non-trespassory invasion of another's interest in the private use and enjoyment of land. One may be subject to liability for a private nuisance only if one's conduct is the legal cause of the invasion of another's right. The invasion must be intentional and unreasonable, or unintentional and otherwise actionable under rules of negligence, reckless conduct or abnormally dangerous situations.[7] Although theoretically distinct, the difference between public and private nuisances may be of little practical significance. A public nuisance is often also a private nuisance,[8] and courts frequently grant private parties rights to sue under public nuisance doctrine.[9] Remedies, however, may differ.[10]

A nuisance per se is an activity, occupation, or structure that is a nuisance at all times and under any circumstances regardless of location. It is so as a matter of law. A nuisance in fact is an activity, operation or structure that constitutes a nuisance only because of its location, surroundings or manner of operation.

Most nuisances are nuisances in fact because most harm producing activity is lawful somewhere and even socially productive. A halfway house for prisoners, for example, is not a nuisance per se.[11] It might be a nuisance in fact in a residential area if a court finds that its utility does

4. Beuscher & Morrison, supra note 1. See also F. Schnidman, S. Abrams & J. Delaney, Handling the Land Use Case § 7.1.6 (1984); Coquillette, Mosses From an Old Manse: Another Look at Some Historic Property Cases About the Environment, 64 Cornell L.Rev. 761 (1979); Rabin, Nuisance Law: Rethinking Fundamental Assumptions, 63 Va.L.Rev. 1299 (1977).

5. See discussion supra §§ 10.4 and 10.6.

6. Restatement (Second) of Torts § 821B (1976).

7. Id. § 822. See, e.g., Lunda v. Matthews, 46 Or.App. 701, 613 P.2d 63 (1980);

Conlon v. Farmington, 29 Conn.Supp. 230, 280 A.2d 896 (1971).

8. Venuto v. Owens–Corning Fiberglas Corp., 22 Cal.App.3d 116, 99 Cal.Rptr. 350 (1971).

9. See, e.g., West's Ann.Cal.Civ.Proc. Code § 731a (allows suit for damages but precludes injunction against industrial or commercial uses that are permitted by zoning); West's Fla.Stat.Ann. § 60.05(1) (same).

10. See infra §§ 14.3 and 14.5.

11. See Smith v. Gill, 293 Ala. 736, 310 So.2d 214 (1975).

not outweigh the harm to other interests.[12] This principle was recognized as early as the seventeenth century in England. William Aldred's Case[13] was a private nuisance action brought to enjoin the operation of a pig sty next door to the plaintiff's dwelling. The court found the sty to be a nuisance, and that smell and light were protectible interests. This was an early, successful attempt to internalize social costs of certain uses of property, and it demonstrates that courts are vested with the discretion to determine the extent of rights of property that can be protected by court-fashioned remedies.

Over time, changing values and advances in technology have caused some shifting of the rights that inure in property ownership.[14] Whatever the relative values of the competing uses, the initial assignment of legal rights does not determine which use ultimately prevails. By granting one party the legal right to exclude interference by the other, the courts adopt the efficient value-maximizing accommodation of the conflict. In some cases, the costs of transferring the property right are so high that voluntary transfer is not feasible. Placing liability on the party who causes the damage may not be the most efficient solution of the conflict. The common law of nuisance attempts to obtain optimal resource use by assigning property rights to the more valuable use between conflicting land uses.[15]

§ 14.2 Public Nuisances

A public nuisance is an activity that interferes with the rights of the public.[1] This often involves acts that injure the public health or safety, but also includes more intangible injuries to the public morals. Public nuisances encompass such diverse activities as polluting a water supply,[2] operating a race track,[3] running a disorderly saloon,[4] maintaining a structure that creates a traffic hazard,[5] or running a business that generates noxious odors near the center of a city's business district.[6]

The difference between a public and private nuisance is the nature of the interest invaded. A public nuisance invades public rights, and a

---

12. The balancing the utilities doctrine stems from dictum in St. Helens Smelting Co. v. Tipping, 11 Eng.Rep. 1483 (H.L. 1865). Compare with analysis of "sic utere tuo" doctrine in Rocha v. Socony–Vacuum Corp., 54 R.I. 411, 173 A. 627 (1934).

13. William Aldred's Case, 9 Coke 57b, 77 Eng.Rep. 816 (K.B. 1611).

14. See, e.g., Illinois v. Butterfield, 396 F.Supp. 632 (N.D.Ill.1975) (airport noise); Morris v. Ciborowski, 113 N.H. 563, 311 A.2d 296 (1973) (same). See also Prah v. Maretti, 108 Wis.2d 223, 321 N.W.2d 182 (1982) (access to sun for solar heating as protectible property interest).

15. R. Posner, Economic Analysis of the Law 16 (1972). See Coase, The Problem of Social Cost, 3 J.L. & Econ. 1 (1960).

§ 14.2

1. See L. Mark Walker and Dale E. Cottingham, An Abridged Primer on the Law of Public Nuisance, 30 Tulsa L.J. 355 (1994).

2. Nelson v. Swedish Evangelical Lutheran Cemetery Ass'n, 111 Minn. 149, 126 N.W. 723 (1910).

3. Gustafson v. Cotco Enterprises, Inc., 42 Ohio App.2d 45, 328 N.E.2d 409 (1974).

4. Taylor v. State ex rel. Adams, 275 Ala. 430, 155 So.2d 595 (1963).

5. 44 Plaza, Inc. v. Gray–Pac Land Co., 845 S.W.2d 576 (Mo.App.1992).

6. Fort Smith v. Western Hide & Fur Co., 153 Ark. 99, 239 S.W. 724 (1922).

private nuisance invades private property rights. Often conduct is actionable on both grounds. Generally, cases of air pollution and water pollution will be both. If the air pollution harms a limited number of people, and not the public generally, it may be a private nuisance, but it is not a public nuisance.[7] Some conduct can be a public, but not a private, nuisance. Blocking the view of a competitor's business, for example, was held not to be a private nuisance, but, since it was a traffic hazard, it was a public nuisance.[8]

A public nuisance need not, and often does not, involve an invasion of property rights, and therefore, compared with the law of private nuisance, it plays a minor role in land use law. Still, much of today's environmental regulation protecting the air, water, and land from pollution through the exercise of the police power is public nuisance-based.[9] Private parties injured by pollution sometimes turn to public nuisance law for relief seeking perceived benefits in longer statutes of limitations and a more favorable measure of damages.[10]

The state,[11] through its police power, can declare an activity to be a public nuisance that was not a public nuisance at common law,[12] or it may rely on what was a public nuisance at common law.[13] While the legislature can declare what is a public nuisance and the executive can seek to prosecute or enjoin such activities, the question of whether a public nuisance exists in fact is for the courts to determine.[14] Further, government action in the prosecution of a statutory or common law public nuisance is subject to constitutional limitations.[15]

7. Padilla v. Lawrence, 101 N.M. 556, 685 P.2d 964 (1984) (odors were not a public nuisance, but were a private nuisance).

8. 44 Plaza, Inc. v. Gray–Pac Land Co., 845 S.W.2d 576 (Mo.App.1992).

9. See CEEED v. California Coastal Zone Conservation Comm'n, 43 Cal.App.3d 306, 118 Cal.Rptr. 315, 324 (1974). Common law nuisance actions may be preempted by federal law. The Clean Water Act, for example, preempts common law nuisance suits based on the law of the state where the injury occurs in cases of interstate water pollution. International Paper Co. v. Ouellette, 479 U.S. 481, 107 S.Ct. 805, 93 L.Ed.2d 883 (1987).

10. See Walker and Cottingham, supra note 1, discussing primarily Oklahoma law and questioning whether these advantages, if they in fact exist, will be available to private parties through public nuisance suits.

11. In addition, many states have enacted legislation permitting municipalities to define what uses constitute a public nuisance. Vernon's Ann.Texas art. 1175(19); W.Va. Code § 8–12–5(23).

12. Lawton v. Steele, 152 U.S. 133, 14 S.Ct. 499, 38 L.Ed. 385 (1894) (fishing equipment used in violation of state law); Lane v. City of Mount Vernon, 38 N.Y.2d 344, 379 N.Y.S.2d 798, 342 N.E.2d 571 (1976) (removal of structure creating safety hazard). Cf. People v. Lim., 18 Cal.2d 872, 118 P.2d 472 (1941).

13. City of Chicago v. Festival Theatre Corp., 91 Ill.2d 295, 63 Ill.Dec. 421, 438 N.E.2d 159 (1982) (concept of public nuisance is not limited to those activities the legislature has declared public nuisances, finding obscene stage production to be enjoinable); Commonwealth v. MacDonald, 464 Pa. 435, 347 A.2d 290 (1975).

14. Sharon Steel Corp. v. City of Fairmont, 175 W.Va. 479, 334 S.E.2d 616 (1985); City of Bakersfield v. Miller, 46 Cal. Rptr. 661 (Cal.App.1965). As with private nuisances, the existence of a public nuisance frequently turns on the appropriateness of the locale. Commonwealth v. MacDonald, 464 Pa. 435, 347 A.2d 290, 300 (1975).

15. Lawton v. Steele, 152 U.S. 133, 14 S.Ct. 499, 38 L.Ed. 385 (1894); 4M Holding Co. v. Town Bd. of Islip, 81 N.Y.2d 1053, 619 N.E.2d 395, 601 N.Y.S.2d 458 (1993) (removal of burning debris upon 10 days notice not violative of substantive due pro-

§ 14.3 Public Nuisance Remedies

Public nuisances, which historically developed as crimes against the state, may be abated by the state, acting in the public interest.[1] In the absence of statutory provision, compensation need not be made for the destruction or damage of property incurred in abatement.[2] Also, the state can charge the cost of abatement to the responsible party.[3] Most states have enacted criminal statutes declaring that maintenance of a public nuisance is a misdemeanor.[4] While courts early on expressed some reluctance to enjoin public nuisances on the ground that equity did not normally intervene in criminal conduct,[5] today courts generally allow injunctive relief in favor of the state in cases of public nuisances.[6]

While a public nuisance was initially a crime and punishable as such by the state, the common law courts recognized a private cause of action in tort for a private individual who suffers special injuries, different in kind rather than degree from those of the general public.[7] In a private suit, the plaintiff can generally recover damages despite the public character of the nuisance.[8] Injunctive relief in favor of private individuals is usually available in cases of public nuisances (if they show special injury) although equity will not normally enjoin a crime.[9] Where the complained of conduct is both a public and a private nuisance and the primary objective is to stop the conduct, the availability of injunctive relief in a public nuisance suit is attractive since courts will not grant

cess); State, ex rel. Rear Door Bookstore, v. Tenth Dist. Ct. of Appeals, 63 Ohio St.3d 354, 588 N.E.2d 116 (1992) (adult book store closure as public nuisance did not violate First Amendment); Commonwealth v. MacDonald, 464 Pa. 435, 347 A.2d 290 (1975) (prosecution for displaying obscene movies violated First Amendment); State ex rel. Schulman v. City of Cleveland, 8 Ohio Misc. 1, 220 N.E.2d 386 (1966) (demolition of slum property not a taking). In general, see supra Ch. 10.

§ 14.3

1. Copart Indus., Inc. v. Consolidated Edison Co., 41 N.Y.2d 564, 394 N.Y.S.2d 169, 362 N.E.2d 968 (1977). A county or municipality that suffers special injuries to its local interests may also sue to the extent that charter powers, or legislative authorizations, or home rule powers permit. State ex rel. Schneider v. Stewart, 575 S.W.2d 904 (Mo.App.1978); Village of Riverwoods v. Untermyer, 54 Ill.App.3d 816, 369 N.E.2d 1385 (1977); State ex rel. Hoffman v. Swift Co., 127 Kan. 817, 275 P. 176 (1929).

2. Miller v. Schoene, 276 U.S. 272, 48 S.Ct. 246, 72 L.Ed. 568 (1928). See also 6 E. McQuillin, Municipal Corporations § 24.74 (3d ed.rev.1980). But see discussion of Lucas v. South Carolina Coastal Council, 505 U.S. 1003, 112 S.Ct. 2886, 120 L.Ed.2d 798

(1992), supra § 10.6, with respect to Fifth Amendment implications.

3. 4M Holding Co. v. Town Bd. of Islip, 81 N.Y.2d 1053, 619 N.E.2d 395, 601 N.Y.S.2d 458 (1993).

4. See supra § 8.7.

5. See People v. Lim, 18 Cal.2d 872, 118 P.2d 472, 474 (1941).

6. City of Chicago v. Festival Theatre Corp., 91 Ill.2d 295, 63 Ill.Dec. 421, 438 N.E.2d 159 (1982); Marsland v. Pang, 5 Haw.App. 463, 701 P.2d 175 (1985); Town of West Greenwich v. Stepping Stone Enter., Ltd., 122 R.I. 132, 416 A.2d 659 (1979); Black v. Circuit Court of 8th Judicial Circuit Within and for Lawrence County, 78 S.D. 302, 101 N.W.2d 520 (1960).

7. See L. Mark Walker and Dale E. Cottingham, An Abridged Primer on the Law of Public Nuisance, 30 Tulsa L.J. 355 (1994).

8. Proof of substantial injury must be shown. Town of Surfside v. County Line Land Co., 340 So.2d 1287 (Fla.App.1977), cert. denied 352 So.2d 175 (1977); Woods v. Johnson, 241 Cal.App.2d 278, 50 Cal.Rptr. 515 (1966). Cf. Gilmore v. Monroeville, 384 So.2d 1080 (Ala.1980).

9. See case cited supra note 5.

such relief often in a private nuisance suit.[10]

§ 14.4   Private Nuisances

A private nuisance is an unreasonable interference with the use and enjoyment of land. The underlying principle is that one should not use one's property to the injury of the property of another.[1] Factors applied in determining whether a nuisance exists include the use being made of the plaintiff's property, the use being made of the defendant's property, the character of the neighborhood, and the frequency and extent of the injury.[2] Other things considered include the social value of the respective uses, the suitability of the uses to the character of the locality, and the ability of the plaintiff or the defendant to avoid or prevent the harm.[3] As these general statements suggest, nuisance cases are highly fact specific, making it risky to predict the outcome of litigation.

Though none of the above factors is controlling, the principal question is that of locale: is it reasonable for the defendant to be doing what it is doing *where* it is doing it? For that reason, nuisance law is considered judicial zoning, with the court playing the role of the planner, deciding whether the complained of use is proper for the area. Thus, a residential use in a residential area is generally protected against subsequent encroachment by business or industrial interests.[4] Conversely, where an area is not predominately residential, judges tend to permit whatever use they deem appropriate to the area, emphasizing the business necessity or social desirability of the defendant's activity.[5]

Courts also consider potential future development as well as present use to decide whether a particular use is so incompatible as to constitute a nuisance.[6] This concern over future use often conflicts with priority of occupation, but being the first to locate in an area does not preclude a court from deciding that the area is better suited to other types of uses. Land users are in effect charged with foreseeing how an area will develop. A pig farmer who locates on the outskirts of town may have to move when population growth comes his way.[7] A homeowner, who buys

---

10. Spur Industries, Inc. v. Del E. Webb Dev. Co., 108 Ariz. 178, 494 P.2d 700 (1972). See infra § 14.5 for discussion of remedies in private nuisance suits.

§ 14.4

1. Lussier v. San Lorenzo Valley Water Dist., 206 Cal.App.3d 92, 100, 253 Cal.Rptr. 470, 473 (1988).

2. See J. H Beuscher & Jerry W. Morrison, Judicial Zoning Through Recent Nuisance Cases, 1955 Ariz.L.Rev. 440, for discussion of the impact of zoning considerations on judicial decisionmaking in nuisance cases.

3. Restatement (Second) of Torts §§ 826–31 (1976).

4. Schlotfelt v. Vinton Farmers' Supply Co., 252 Iowa 1102, 109 N.W.2d 695 (1961);

Bortz v. Troth, 359 Pa. 326, 59 A.2d 93 (1948). See Freeman, Give and Take: Distributing Local Environmental Control Through Land Use Regulation, 60 Minn. L.Rev. 883, 894–962 (1976). But cf. Essick v. Shillam, 347 Pa. 373, 32 A.2d 416 (1943).

5. Daniel v. Kosh, 173 Va. 352, 4 S.E.2d 381 (1939). Legislation sometimes protects certain uses, such as farming, from threat of nuisance actions. See, e.g., West's Fla.Stat.Ann. § 823.14.

6. See, e.g., Oak Haven Trailer Court, Inc. v. Western Wayne County Conservation Ass'n, 3 Mich.App. 83, 141 N.W.2d 645, affirmed 380 Mich. 526, 158 N.W.2d 463 (1968).

7. Pendoley v. Ferreira, 345 Mass. 309, 187 N.E.2d 142 (1963).

when an area is essentially undeveloped, may be forced to tolerate heavy industry in her neighborhood if the area is now prime for industrial use.[8] While application of that rule may seem harsh, to rule otherwise would preclude development. The "coming to the nuisance" defense that courts sometimes intone, suggests that the first one to arrive fixes forever the character of the area. Yet, some courts do not recognize the defense,[9] and for those that do, it is but a factor to consider.[10]

Typical actionable interferences involve physical discomfort,[11] such as foul odors from a piggery,[12] dust from a cement plant,[13] and noise from a race track.[14] Yet over the years, courts have found that interference with an occupant's peace of mind will sometimes suffice.[15] For example, most courts will enjoin the operation of funeral homes in residential areas based on a psychological injury due to the "constant reminder of death."[16] Other courts have held that mental discomfort and depressed feelings are not actionable.[17] A threat to safety from group homes for the disabled and prisoner halfway houses in residential areas may also suffice to show a nuisance.[18] An injunction against housing for the disabled, however, may raise problems under the federal Fair Housing Act.[19]

Generally, activities that offend aesthetic sensibilities, such as interferences with sight or view, are not considered nuisances.[20] This has

---

8. Bove v. Donner–Hanna Coke Corp., 236 App.Div. 37, 258 N.Y.S. 229 (1932). Whether the plaintiff came to the nuisance or whether the nuisance came to the plaintiff depends on how one construes the facts.

9. Hoffman v. United Iron and Metal Co., 108 Md.App. 117, 671 A.2d 55, 66 n. 11 (1996); Brooks v. Council of Co–Owners, 315 S.C. 474, 445 S.E.2d 630, 632 (1994).

10. Jacques v. Pioneer Plastics, Inc., 676 A.2d 504 (Me.1996); Jerry Harmon Motors, Inc. v. Farmers Union Grain Terminal Ass'n, 337 N.W.2d 427 (N.D.1983) (noting majority and minority views). See also Annot., 42 A.L.R.3d 344, 347 (1972). Right to farm statutes represent codifications of the coming to the nuisance defense. See discussion infra § 14.6.

11. See, e.g., Adams v. Snouffer, 88 Ohio App. 79, 82, 87 N.E.2d 484, 486 (1949); Jordan v. Luippold, 189 Okl. 189, 191, 114 P.2d 917, 918 (1941).

12. Pendoley v. Ferreira, 345 Mass. 309, 187 N.E.2d 142 (1963).

13. Boomer v. Atlantic Cement Co., 26 N.Y.2d 219, 309 N.Y.S.2d 312, 257 N.E.2d 870 (1970), on remand 72 Misc.2d 834, 340 N.Y.S.2d 97 (1972), judg. aff'd 42 A.D.2d 496, 349 N.Y.S.2d 199 (1973).

14. Hooks v. International Speedways, Inc., 263 N.C. 686, 140 S.E.2d 387 (1965).

15. Reynolds Metals v. Yturbide, 258 F.2d 321 (9th Cir.1958), cert. denied 358

U.S. 840, 79 S.Ct. 66, 3 L.Ed.2d 76 (1958). See also, McCastle v. Rollins Envtl. Servs., 514 F.Supp. 936 (M.D.La.1981).

16. Powell v. Taylor, 222 Ark. 896, 263 S.W.2d 906, 907 (1954) (operation of funeral home enjoined in residential area). See generally Annot., 8 A.L.R.4th 324 (1979).

17. McCaw v. Harrison, 259 S.W.2d 457 (Ky.1953). See State ex rel. Cunningham v. Feezell, 218 Tenn. 17, 400 S.W.2d 716 (1966) (discussing majority and minority views).

18. See, e.g., Smith v. Gill, 293 Ala. 736, 310 So.2d 214 (1975) (halfway house for "mental patients" a nuisance); Armory Park Neighborhood Ass'n v. Episcopal Community Servs., 148 Ariz. 1, 712 P.2d 914 (1985) (soup kitchen a public nuisance); Arkansas Release Guidance Found. v. Needler, 252 Ark. 194, 477 S.W.2d 821 (1972) (house for prisoners a nuisance). But see Nicholson v. Connecticut Half–Way House, Inc., 153 Conn. 507, 218 A.2d 383 (1966) (refusal to grant anticipatory injunction).

19. See discussion supra § 4.7 and § 6.8.

20. Fontainebleau Hotel Corp. v. Forty-Five Twenty-five, Inc., 114 So.2d 357 (Fla.App.1959), cert. denied 117 So.2d 842 (1960); Livingston v. Davis, 243 Iowa 21, 50 N.W.2d 592 (1951). Cf. Prah v. Maretti, 108 Wis.2d 223, 321 N.W.2d 182 (1982); Par-

changed somewhat over the years as courts have found that some types of visual blight, such as debris,[21] and wrecked cars,[22] can be the basis for a nuisance finding without regard to the invasion of another human sense.[23] The reluctance of courts to find an aesthetics injury as a sufficient basis for suit is troubling to some who argue that the courts' fear of engaging in subjective determinations of beauty is misplaced. The question, they say, is not beauty, but visual dissonance from the social and cultural character of the neighborhood.[24] A counter concern is the potential infringement of free expression if neighbors can compel conformity to their idea of the way things should look.[25]

An intentional or unintentional invasion of another's interest in the use and enjoyment of property is a basis for liability, regardless of care or skill exercised to avoid injury. Showing that the conduct is negligent is not necessary, reckless or ultrahazardous.[26] An otherwise lawful use may constitute a nuisance if it is part of a general scheme to annoy a neighbor, or if the main purpose of the use is to prevent a neighbor from the enjoyment of her own property.[27]

§ 14.5   Private Nuisance Remedies

Compensatory damages, measured by the character and extent of the injury to the plaintiff's property interest, are always recoverable. Where an interference is permanent, a plaintiff may join claims for both past and prospective injuries in a single cause of action.[1] The general measure of damages is the difference between the fair market value of the property with and without the presence of the nuisance.[2] Otherwise, successive actions must be had for actual, not prospective, losses.[3] Where the nuisance is abatable, the temporary damage awarded is the loss in

---

kersburg Builders Material Co. v. Barrack, 118 W.Va. 608, 191 S.E. 368 (1937). The rule is different in some foreign common law jurisdictions that follow the English doctrine of "ancient lights."

21. Allison v. Smith, 695 P.2d 791 (Colo.App.1984).

22. Foley v. Harris, 223 Va. 20, 286 S.E.2d 186 (1982); Mahoney v. Walter, 157 W.Va. 882, 205 S.E.2d 692 (1974).

23. See Coty v. Ramsey Assoc., 149 Vt. 451, 546 A.2d 196 (1988), noting trend toward acceptance of unsightliness as a factor to consider.

24. See Raymond R. Coletta, The Case for Aesthetic Nuisance: Rethinking Traditional Judicial Attitudes, 48 Ohio St. L.J. 141 (1987); George P. Smith, II, Aesthetic Nuisance: Reeducating the Judiciary, 24 Real Est.L.J. 26 (1995); George P. Smith, II and Griffin W. Fernandez, The Price of Beauty: An Economic Approach to Aesthetic Nuisance, 15 Harv.Envtl.L.Rev. 53 (1991).

25. Galina Krasilovsky, A Sculpture is Worth a Thousand Words: The First Amendment Rights of Homeowners Publicly Displaying Art on Private Property, 20 Colum.-VLA J.L. & Arts 521 (1996).

26. Ryan v. Emmetsburg, 232 Iowa 600, 4 N.W.2d 435 (1942); Morgan v. High Penn. Oil Co., 238 N.C. 185, 77 S.E.2d 682 (1953); Russell Transp. Ltd. v. Ontario Malleable Iron Co., 4 D.L.R. 719 (Ont.High Ct.1952).

27. Hutcherson v. Alexander, 264 Cal. App.2d 126, 70 Cal.Rptr. 366 (1968).

§ 14.5

1. Northern Ind. Pub. Serv. Co. v. Vesey, 210 Ind. 338, 200 N.E. 620 (1936).

2. Weinhold v. Wolff, 555 N.W.2d 454, 465 (Iowa 1996).

3. Ryan v. Emmetsburg, 232 Iowa 600, 4 N.W.2d 435 (1942).

rental value.[4] If a defendant acts with malice, a court may allow punitive damages.[5]

Where the legal remedy is inadequate, a plaintiff may seek an injunction. An injunction is possible where the injury is irreparable, even if the consequential damages are small.[6] Similarly, an injunction is possible where damages would not adequately compensate for the threatened loss or because otherwise there would be a multiplicity of actions at law.[7]

Most courts will balance the relative hardships in deciding whether to enjoin the activity. If the hardship to the defendant is considerable, compared to harm to the plaintiff, the court will deny injunctive relief and award money damages.[8] Boomer v. Atlantic Cement Co.[9] is a leading case involving this remedy. The defendant's cement operation, located near an established residential area, caused dust and ground tremors that disturbed neighboring houses. The court found a nuisance but, after balancing the benefits of the defendant's presence in the community, its investment and the number of people it employed against the damage suffered by the plaintiffs, the court denied the injunctive relief requested by the plaintiffs. Instead, the court awarded permanent damages.

In earlier times, courts issued injunctions as a matter of course when they found a nuisance existed.[10] This is an infrequent occurrence today, however, as economic reality, and perhaps shortsightedness, sets in. The *Boomer* court, for example, simply could not bring itself to enjoin an operation of such immediate financial importance to the community. Short term protection of the local economy may result in long term injury to the community from environmental injury caused the defendant's unenjoined activity. Still, an inflexible rule that an injunction will issue as a matter of course may not work to protect the environment long term. A court subject to such a rule, but fearful of the short term

---

4. Hammond v. City of Warner Robins, 224 Ga.App. 684, 482 S.E.2d 422, 427 (1997). In some cases special damages such as damages from annoyance apart from the loss to the realty, and stigma damages, resulting from the public perception of risk, may be recoverable. Id. Stigma damages represent injury to property located near a facility that has contaminated the land and created uncertainty over whether the contamination will spread. See Anthony Z. Roisman and Gary E. Mason, Nuisance and the Recovery of "Stigma" Damages: Eliminating the Confusion, 26 Envtl.L.Rep. 10070 (Feb.1996).

5. Coty v. Ramsey, Assoc., 149 Vt. 451, 546 A.2d 196 (1988).

6. Hart v. Wagner, 184 Md. 40, 40 A.2d 47 (1944). Cf. Waschak v. Moffat, 379 Pa. 441, 109 A.2d 310 (1954).

7. Hennessy v. Carmony, 50 N.J.Eq. 616, 25 A. 374 (1892).

8. Varjabedian v. Madera, 64 Cal. App.3d 199, 134 Cal.Rptr. 305, affirmed in part and reversed in part on other grounds, 20 Cal.3d 285, 142 Cal.Rptr. 429, 572 P.2d 43 (1977); McKinnon v. Benedict, 38 Wis.2d 607, 157 N.W.2d 665 (1968).

9. 26 N.Y.2d 219, 309 N.Y.S.2d 312, 257 N.E.2d 870 (1970), on remand 72 Misc.2d 834, 340 N.Y.S.2d 97 (1972), judg. aff'd 42 A.D.2d 496, 349 N.Y.S.2d 199 (1973).

10. Hulbert v. California Portland Cement Co., 161 Cal. 239, 118 P. 928 (1911) (where defendant's conduct mandates punitive treatment). See Smith v. Staso Milling Co., 18 F.2d 736 (2d Cir.1927). See generally Riter v. Keokuk Electro–Metals Co., 248 Iowa 710, 82 N.W.2d 151 (1957).

economic consequences of shutting down an industry, may simply not find a nuisance on the merits.[11] When an injunction is issued, a court may make it temporary and conditional where the defendant can reduce or abate the interference by reasonable changes in the conduct of his activities.[12]

Damages and conditional injunctions may be the most efficient remedies for a nuisance. An award of damages against a nuisance serves to internalize the costs and permits the defendant to make his own cost-benefit analysis of preventive measures. Conditional injunctions may facilitate the termination of a nuisance whose harm a plaintiff values greater than recoverable damages only. This situation is most common where the plaintiff is hypersensitive to injury or he has come to the nuisance.[13]

Private nuisance liability requires proof of significant harm.[14] This is problematic for plaintiffs because proof of a connection between plaintiffs' injuries and defendants' acts is often difficult to obtain. Effects of hazardous waste disposal, for example, may not become obvious for many years.[15] A dearth of scientific knowledge of effects of chemicals and other waste products can exacerbate a plaintiff's burden of proof.[16]

Against this problem, public nuisance[17] or combined public and private nuisance[18] actions have been more successful than private nuisance actions alone, in effecting abatement or recovering damages by private parties. In some cases, defendants' activity may be found to pose imminent danger to public health and safety, enjoined, and ordered cleaned up at the defendants' expense.[19]

---

11. According to Professor Ellickson, this is what occurred under New York's pre-*Boomer* rule, when the state followed a pro-injunction rule. Bove v. Donner–Hanna Coke Corp., 236 App.Div. 37, 258 N.Y.S. 229 (1932). See Robert C. Ellickson, Alternatives to Zoning: Covenants, Nuisance Rules, and Fines as Land Use Controls, 40 U.Chic.L.Rev. 681, 720 (1973).

12. McCleery v. Highland Boy Gold Mining Co., 140 F. 951 (C.D.Utah 1904); Yaffe v. Fort Smith, 178 Ark. 406, 10 S.W.2d 886 (1928) (temporary injunction, dissolvable upon payment of damages).

13. Spur Indus., Inc. v. Del E. Webb Dev. Co., 108 Ariz. 178, 494 P.2d 700 (1972).

14. Stockdale v. Agrico Chem. Co., 340 F.Supp. 244 (N.D.Iowa 1972).

15. See, e.g., United States v. Price, 523 F.Supp. 1055 (D.N.J.1981), affirmed 688 F.2d 204 (3d Cir.1982). See generally House Subcomm. on Oversight & Investigations of Comm. on Interstate & Foreign Commerce, Hazardous Waste Disposal, 96th Cong., 1st Sess. (Comm.Print 1979).

16. See, e.g., Miller v. National Cabinet Co., 8 N.Y.2d 277, 204 N.Y.S.2d 129, 168 N.E.2d 811 (1960), remittitur amended 8 N.Y.2d 1025, 206 N.Y.S.2d 795, 170 N.E.2d 214 (1960).

17. City of Philadelphia v. Stepan Chem. Co., 544 F.Supp. 1135 (E.D.Pa.1982); McCastle v. Rollins Envtl. Servs., 514 F.Supp. 936 (M.D.La.1981), class action transferred to state court and injunction affirmed 415 So.2d 515 (La.App.1982).

18. Chappell v. S.C.A. Servs., 540 F.Supp. 1087 (C.D.Ill.1982). This was a class action for damages, following Village of Wilsonville v. S.C.A. Servs., 77 Ill.App.3d 618, 33 Ill.Dec. 163, 396 N.E.2d 552 (1979), affirmed 86 Ill.2d 1, 55 Ill.Dec. 499, 426 N.E.2d 824 (1981), which enjoined SCA's activity and required a cleanup of the site.

19. Wood v. Picillo, 443 A.2d 1244 (R.I. 1982).

§ 14.6 Agricultural Operations as Nuisances: the Right to Farm

Farming and other agricultural operations are frequent targets of public and private nuisance suits brought by residential neighbors. Over the past century, as the population has sprawled into the countryside, the problem has grown. While the plaintiffs have usually been late arrivals to the area, the farmers' use of the defense that the plaintiffs "came to the nuisance"[1] has often not been successful.[2]

As one might expect, many cases involve hog farms and cattle feedlots. When urban growth reaches the farmer's doorstep, courts have found that it is the farmer who must leave to make way for places for people to live. Courts have declared these uses nuisances even though their use of the land conforms to applicable health and safety standards and is otherwise reasonable and consistent with traditional uses in the area.[3] Such farming operations are, in effect, high risk ventures, and the farmer must foresee that he is living on borrowed time. Forseeability is difficult sometimes. In one well known case, Spur Industries, Inc. v. Del E. Webb Development Co.,[4] the court found a cattle feedlot to be a nuisance in a suit brought by a developer who had leapfrogged developable land near Phoenix to acquire cheaper land farther out. The residents of the development, the court found, should not suffer the health risk of living amid the flies and odor of the feedlot. The feedlot operator salvaged something as the court, in an unusual remedy twist, required the developer to indemnify the defendant for the cost of moving its feedlot. In such cases, the farmer's land will likely rise in value as it will now be attractive for residential use.

According to some recent studies,[5] we have lost enormous farmland acreage to urban development, and while we may not run out of land, our most valuable farmland is on the fringe of densely settled urban areas.[6] Recognition of the need to protect against the rapid loss of agricultural land has led to legislative changes. Among a variety of agricultural preservation techniques,[7] a particularly popular one is the abolition of the right to bring a nuisance action against farm operations. In the past two decades, all fifty states adopted "right to farm" statutes[8]

§ 14.6

1. Restatement (Second) of Torts § 840D (1976).

2. As noted supra § 14.4, the "coming to the nuisance" defense is one of several factors balanced by courts. Spencer Creek Pollution Control Ass'n v. Organic Fertilizer Co., 264 Or. 557, 505 P.2d 919 (1973).

3. See, e.g., Pendoley v. Ferreira, 345 Mass. 309, 187 N.E.2d 142 (1963).

4. 108 Ariz. 178, 494 P.2d 700 (1972).

5. Krause & Hair, Trends in Land Use and Competition for Land to Produce Food and Fiber, U.S. Dep't of Agriculture, Perspective on Prime Lands 16 (1975).

6. See The National Agricultural Lands Study (1981) and American Farmland Trust Study (1993). The latter study reports that 5 percent of our farmland represents 56 percent of the food we eat and this 5 percent is on the fringe of urbanized areas.

7. Agricultural preservation is discussed in detail supra Ch. 13.

8. Neil D. Hamilton, A Livestock Producer's Legal Guide to Nuisance, Land Use Control and Environmental Law (1992).

that represent codifications of the "coming to the nuisance" defense.[9]

Most of the statutes provide that agricultural operations that have been in existence longer than one year cannot become either public or private nuisances by virtue of changed conditions in the surrounding area, if they were not nuisances when the agricultural operations began.[10] Some statutes list exceptions to the rule, perhaps to limit judicial erosion.[11] Negligent operations typically are not exempt,[12] and some expressly allow expansion.[13] Inevitably, questions arise as to the kinds of operations that qualify,[14] and whether changes in use qualify for protection.[15] Some states protect all agricultural operations,[16] while others protect operations used for specific purposes, such as production of milk, eggs, or livestock.[17]

Whether right to farm statutes are successful in protecting farm operations is open to question. One study found that they have been less effective than some hoped.[18] On the other hand, if they are successful, society may suffer. Agricultural operations, particularly those that serve the beef, dairy, poultry and pork industries, pose significant environmental risks. The loss of the nuisance action to prevent harmful practices may disserve long term environmental interests. The loss is particularly acute where state adoption and enforcement of meaningful environmental regulations is lacking. Furthermore, if the concern of agricultural preservation is the loss of crop land, the immunity afforded animal operations may be unnecessary.

§ 14.7   Legislative Changes of Common Law Nuisance

The common law of nuisance is subject to legislative change, but such change, in turn, is subject to the same constitutional limitations that apply to any exercise of the police power.[1] As Justice Holmes said,

9. See, e.g., West's Ann.Cal.Civ.Code § 3482.5; West's Fla.Stat.Ann. § 823.14; Neb.Rev.Stat. § 2–401–02–4404. See also supra § 15.2. The question of whether the abrogation of the right to protect one's land from the agricultural nuisance is a taking under the Fifth Amendment is discussed infra § 14.7.

10. Note, Right to Farm Statutes—The Newest Tool in Agricultural Land Preservation, 10 Fla.St.U.L.Rev. 415 (1982). See also Note, Right to Farm in Oregon, 18 Willamette L.J. 153 (1981); Thomas, Defining and Protecting the Right to Farm, 5 Zoning & Planning Law Report 57 (Sept.1982) & 65 (Oct.1982).

11. West's Fla.Stat.Ann. § 823.14.

12. N.D.Code § 42–04–02.

13. S.D.Code § 21–10–25.2 allows reasonable expansion of an operation in terms of acres or animal units without losing protected status.

14. Modern Continental Const. Co., Inc. v. Bldg. Inspector of Natick, 42 Mass. App.Ct. 901, 674 N.E.2d 247 (1997) (slaughterhouse for butchering animals held to be agriculture); Knoff v. American Crystal Sugar Co., 380 N.W.2d 313 (N.D.1986) (a company solely engaged in the preparation and marketing of agricultural products not within the statute's protection).

15. See, e.g., Durham v. Britt, 117 N.C.App. 250, 451 S.E.2d 1 (1994) (change from turkey farm to hog production facility not protected).

16. N.D.Code § 42–04–02.

17. Md.Code, Cts. & Jud.Proc. § 5–308(a). See also Iowa Code Ann. § 172D.2 (livestock) and N.C.Gen.Stat. § 106–701 (agriculture and forestry).

18. See Steven C. Bahls, Preservation of Family Farms–The Way Ahead, 45 Drake L. Rev. 311, 317 (1997).

§ 14.7

1. See supra Ch. 10.

"within constitutional limits not exactly determined, the legislature may change the common law as to nuisances, and may move the line either way, so as to make things nuisances which were not so, or to make things lawful which were nuisances."[2] The constitutional limits arise in two settings. First, the legislature is limited in its ability to legalize a private nuisance, and second, it is said that the police power may not extend to declaring activities nuisances that are not nuisances in fact.[3] In examining these issues, distinguishing between public and private nuisances is important.

A question that arises frequently is whether zoning or other regulatory permission to engage in an activity precludes a finding of nuisance. When a zoning ordinance authorizes a certain use, that use cannot, by definition, constitute a nuisance per se. Courts also generally hold that a permitted use cannot constitute a public nuisance.[4] By statute, for example, California provides that "[n]othing which is done or maintained under the express authority of a statute can be deemed a nuisance,"[5] but the courts interpret the statute narrowly. Mere legislative authorization for use does not excuse the use from being found a nuisance in the manner of its operation.[6] Thus, the general statutory authorization of municipal construction of sewage plants did not protect a plant from suit for producing odors at a level so as to be found a private nuisance.[7] California also precludes injunctive relief by private persons against a use conducted in an appropriate zone that does not employ harmful methods of operation.[8] The statute, however, does not preclude the recovery of damages.[9]

Courts widely hold that a zoning ordinance permitting a use does not immunize the use from being held to be a private nuisance.[10] However, the weight given by a court to the existence of an ordinance affects the question of whether a given use constitutes a private nuisance. The character of the area is an important factor in determining

---

2. Commonwealth v. Parks, 155 Mass. 531, 532, 30 N.E. 174, 174 (1892).

3. City of Scottsbluff v. Winters Creek Canal Co., 155 Neb. 723, 53 N.W.2d 543 (1952).

4. Robinson Brick Co. v. Luthi, 115 Colo. 106, 169 P.2d 171, 174 (1946); Desruisseau v. Isley, 27 Ariz.App. 257, 553 P.2d 1242 (1976); Urie v. Franconia Paper Corp., 107 N.H. 131, 218 A.2d 360 (1966); Commerce Oil Ref. Corp. v. Miner, 281 F.2d 465 (1st Cir.1960). But see National Container Corp. v. State ex rel. Stockton, 138 Fla. 32, 189 So. 4 (1939), holding that an otherwise authorized public nuisance resulting from the manner of use would be subject to abatement.

5. West's Ann.Cal.Civ.Code § 3482.

6. For statutory immunity to exist the action complained of must be authorized in express terms. Hassell v. City of San Francisco, 11 Cal.2d 168, 78 P.2d 1021 (1938).

7. Varjabedian v. City of Madera, 20 Cal.3d 285, 142 Cal.Rptr. 429, 572 P.2d 43 (1977).

8. West's Ann.Cal.Civ.Proc.Code § 731a.

9. West's Ann.Cal.Civ.Proc.Code § 731a.

10. Robinson Brick Co. v. Luthi, 115 Colo. 106, 169 P.2d 171, 174 (1946); Weltshe v. Graf, 323 Mass. 498, 82 N.E.2d 795 (1948); Little Joseph Realty, Inc. v. Town of Babylon, 41 N.Y.2d 738, 363 N.E.2d 1163, 395 N.Y.S.2d 428 (1977); Sweet v. Campbell, 282 N.Y. 146, 25 N.E.2d 963 (1940); DeNucci v. Pezza, 114 R.I. 123, 329 A.2d 807 (1974); Lunda v. Matthews, 46 Or.App. 701, 613 P.2d 63 (1980); Urie v. Franconia Paper Corp., 107 N.H. 131, 218

whether a nuisance in fact exists. Also, the existence of a zoning ordinance permitting or precluding uses is significant in determining the character of the area. Most courts regard proof of the existence of a zoning ordinance to be admissible as evidence of the character of the district and bearing on the question of whether a nuisance exists.[11] While some courts declare the zoning classification to be a persuasive factor, it is not conclusive.[12]

Judicial refusal to allow the legislative body to license a nuisance, as reflected by the above rule,[13] may have constitutional underpinnings. The Court, in Richards v. Washington Terminal Company,[14] discussed the question of legalization of a nuisance. There, a landowner suffering from the operation of an adjoining railroad track and tunnel, sought damages from the railroad in a nuisance action. The Court held that to the extent that the complainant suffered from the gases and dust of the normal operation of the railroad, the injury was non-compensable. Since Congress had authorized the construction, they had legalized the nuisance, and to the extent that the passing of the locomotives indirectly diminished the property's value, it was a burden common to all. There was, however, evidence that the tunnel had been constructed so that a fanning system forced gases and dust from the tunnel onto the plaintiff's land at a single point. The plaintiff could collect damages from the railroad for this "peculiar harm" that he alone suffered. In reaching its decision, the Court in *Richards* stated in dicta that "while the legislature may legalize what otherwise would be a public nuisance, it may not confer immunity from action for a private nuisance of such a character as to amount in effect to a taking of private property for public use."[15] To paraphrase Justice Holmes, the parameters of this limit have not been set.[16] What can be said is that legislative authorization of a nuisance is subject to the same limitations as any other legislative action.

The question can be raised in the context of right to farm statutes discussed above,[17] where some have suggested that legislative abrogation of the neighbor's private nuisance action is a taking of the neighbor's property under the Fifth Amendment.[18] There are problems with the

A.2d 360, 362 (1966); Commerce Oil Ref. Corp. v. Miner, 281 F.2d 465 (1st Cir.1960).

11.	Id.

12.	Desruisseau v. Isley, 27 Ariz.App. 257, 553 P.2d 1242 (1976). The court in Bove v. Donner–Hanna Coke Corp., 236 App.Div. 37, 258 N.Y.S. 229 (1932), suggests that a legislative determination that the area is proper for the use is tantamount to conclusive but the case is likely better read as simply dictating that the one seeking to prove a nuisance has a heavy burden to overcome the presumption created by the zoning ordinance. See Little Joseph Realty, Inc. v. Town of Babylon, 41 N.Y.2d 738, 363 N.E.2d 1163, 395 N.Y.S.2d 428 (1977).

13.	See supra, note 10, this section. See also Acosta v. Jansen, 499 P.2d 631 (Colo.App.1972); Weltshe v. Graf, 323 Mass. 498, 82 N.E.2d 795 (1948).

14.	233 U.S. 546, 34 S.Ct. 654, 58 L.Ed. 1088 (1914).

15.	Id. at 553, 34 S.Ct. at 657.

16.	See quotation in opening paragraph of this section.

17.	See § 14.6.

18.	Weinhold v. Wolff, 555 N.W.2d 454, 465 (Iowa 1996) (lower court found a taking of plaintiff's preexisting nuisance claim, but state supreme court set aside that conclusion by finding the statute did not cut off the cause of action).

suggestion.[19] First, the property owner loses the right to sue, but keeps possession of his or her land. Second, in most instances the diminution in value to the property as a whole will not rise to the level of a taking. The immunity in effect confers an affirmative easement on the farmer to cast pollutants of odors, noise, or dust, as the case may be, on the neighbors land. If this is characterized as a physical invasion, then the prospects in a taking claim look brighter, but it is not clear that a court would so regard it. Finally, the expectations of the plaintiff do not suggest a taking.[20] The person who buys land downwind of a hog farm will be hard pressed to prevail in an arguing that he has a reasonable investment backed expectation to expect clean air. If the farm comes later, the neighbor has a nuisance action since most statutes do not confer the immunity from suit until the passage of one year.

The flip side of the question is whether mere evidence of a violation of a zoning ordinance is a nuisance per se. It is sometimes said that the legislature cannot declare an activity to be a nuisance that is not in fact a nuisance. Yet, it is a common practice of state and local legislatures to declare that the violation of land use regulations, such as zoning ordinances or building and safety codes, constitutes a nuisance. For example, a Michigan enabling statute for municipal zoning provides that " * * * uses violating any provision of local ordinances or regulations * * * are nuisances per se."[21] While the statute eliminates the necessity that a plaintiff establish a nuisance in fact before being entitled to relief,[22] the type of nuisance contemplated is a public nuisance and enforcement by private party requires proof of special damages.[23]

Whatever the legislation may be, it cannot be arbitrary or capricious. It must, in other words, comply with the due process clause.[24] For example, it would be unconstitutional for a legislative body to declare houses in an area to be nuisances, when they were perfectly good houses, but the legislative body wanted them removed so it could acquire the property at less cost for a park. However, if an ordinance is reasonable, government may abate activity declared a statutory nuisance, though without the statutory declaration a court might not find a nuisance in fact.[25] The same result may be reached by courts which nominally require that the activity constitute a nuisance in fact, but defer to the

19. Takings law analysis is found elsewhere in this treatise. See supra Ch. 10. For specific discussion of the right to farm as a taking, see Jacqueline P. Hand, Right-To-Farm Laws: Breaking New Ground in the Preservation of Farmland, 45 U.Pitt.L.Rev. 289, 347 (1984) and Margaret Rosso Grossman and Thomas G. Fischer, Protecting the Right to Farm: Statutory Limits on Nuisance Actions Against the Farmer, 1983 Wis.L.Rev. 95, 141 (1983).

20. Hand, supra note 19, at 347.

21. Mich.Comp.Laws Ann. § 125.294. The statute also provides that "[t]he court shall order such nuisance abated and the

owners * * * shall be adjudged guilty of maintaining a nuisance per se * * *."

22. Bruggeman v. Minster, 42 Mich. App. 177, 201 N.W.2d 344, 345 (1972).

23. Towne v. Harr, 185 Mich.App. 230, 460 N.W.2d 596 (1990).

24. See supra § 10.12.

25. Township of Farmington v. Scott, 374 Mich. 536, 132 N.W.2d 607 (1965) (court held a zoning ordinance precluding a swimming pool supply business in a residential zone to be reasonable and upheld an injunction based on an ordinance declaring nonconforming uses to be nuisances per se).

legislative judgment that the required harm exists.[26] The question is not the label, but whether the state action is rational and fair.

Local governments may be able to pass nuisance prevention ordinances without fully complying with the requirements imposed on zoning enactments in those states that grant broad police powers to local governments.[27] However, if state zoning enabling statutes use broad language in describing the types of land use controls authorized by the statute, an ordinance exercising such type of control may arguably be required to comply with zoning procedures even though it does not purport on its face to be a zoning law.[28] In the absence of statutory guidance, some courts look to the nature and purpose of the specialized measure.[29] If it deals with zoning concepts or its effect is to regulate the use of land, then compliance with zoning procedural safeguards may be necessary.

26. See City of Bakersfield v. Miller, 64 Cal.2d 93, 48 Cal.Rptr. 889, 410 P.2d 393, cert. denied 384 U.S. 988, 86 S.Ct. 1890, 16 L.Ed.2d 1005 (1966).

27. See supra § 3.7.

28. See City of Escondido v. Desert Outdoor Advertising, Inc., 8 Cal.3d 785, 106 Cal.Rptr. 172, 505 P.2d 1012 (1973), cert. denied 414 U.S. 828, 94 S.Ct. 53, 38 L.Ed.2d 62 (1973).

29. See Landmark Land Co. v. City of Denver, 728 P.2d 1281 (Colo.1986); Piper v. Meredith, 110 N.H. 291, 266 A.2d 103 (1970).

Chapter 15

PRIVATE LAND USE CONTROLS

Analysis

I. INTRODUCTION

§ 15.1 Introduction

Prior to the twentieth century, privately created restrictions, along with nuisance law,[1] dominated the control of land use. Public controls, which began at least as early as Elizabethan England,[2] gradually came to the foreground, and now dominate. While overshadowed by zoning, private controls persist and have experienced a resurgence in use in recent years. Private controls complement public controls in two areas: (1) as restrictions in traditional subdivisions and in planned communities to control use more stringently than zoning does, and (2) as methods used by private organizations and government to limit land use for various preservation purposes.

More than thirty million people live in residential communities subject to private restrictions. The use limitations imposed by these restrictions, which may be quite invasive, are enforced by property owners' associations whose powers resemble those of local governments.[3] The desire to protect homeowners from arbitrary controls and the historical canon favoring free land use may lead courts to interpret such provisions narrowly.

Freedom of contract and equity are countervailing concerns. People who buy within privately regulated communities do so voluntarily and either expressly agree to such limits or buy with record notice of preexisting restrictions. There is strong public interest in protecting the expectations of the neighbors who seek to enforce the restrictions, and little equity in favor of those who bought with notice of the restrictions.

Private controls may also adversely affect nonresidents. Such controls have an exclusionary impact, felt particularly by those seeking to live in group homes or in affordable manufactured housing.[4] Gated communities, which may literally wall out the nonresident, may also exclude the public from the use of publicly created resources that lie within the enclave.[5]

It falls to the legislatures and courts to decide whether and when people should be left to live with their own bargains that have turned

---

§ 15.1

1. See supra Chapter 14 for a discussion of nuisance law.

2. See David L. Callies, Robert H. Freilich and Thomas E. Roberts, Cases and Materials on Land Use 2 (2d ed.1994).

3. By the end of the 1980s there were more than 130,000 residential associations housing 30 million persons in the United States. The number of residential communities is increasing by approximately 9,500 annually and is expected to reach 225,000 by the year 2000. See Clayton P. Gillette, Courts, Covenants, and Communities, 61 U.Chic.L.Rev. 1375, n.1 (1994).

4. Ch. 6. supra covers the exclusionary impact of public controls.

5. See Citizens Against Gated Enclaves v. Whitley Heights Civic Ass'n, 23 Cal. App.4th 812, 28 Cal.Rptr.2d 451 (1994). See also David J. Kennedy, Note, Residential Associations as State Actors: Regulating the Impact of Gated Communities on Nonmembers, 105 Yale L.J. 761 (1995).

sour, and whether and when private parties should be able to band together to form communities that exclude others.[6]

Beyond public concern over the severity of private restrictions from the point of view of the affected resident or the excluded nonresident, private restrictions may also conflict with zoning ordinances. Governments also use private controls as alternatives to the exercise of the police power. This is particularly true with the preservation of sensitive lands where government may acquire conservation easements by voluntary purchase, by gift, or by the exercise of the power of eminent domain.

Several forms of controls, either singly or in combination, are available to control land use by private agreement: defeasible estates, easements, and promises respecting the use of the land. We will first examine the devices that may be used, and then turn to the public policy issues.

II. TYPES OF PRIVATE CONTROLS

§ 15.2 Defeasible Estates

All freehold and nonfreehold estates can be made defeasible in three ways: (1) determinable (2) upon condition subsequent or (3) subject to an executory interest. Each type will be illustrated in a land use control context.[1] Nonpossessory interests can also be made defeasible.[2]

A. *Determinable Estates*

If O, owner of Blackacre, conveys that parcel to A "so long as the land is used solely for agricultural purposes, and if the land shall cease to be used for agricultural purposes it shall revert to the grantor or her heirs," O has created a fee simple determinable in A.[3] Since A's interest is less than a fee simple absolute, O retains a future interest called a possibility of reverter. If the holder of the fee simple determinable uses the land for other than agricultural purposes, title to the land automati-

---

6. For general commentary, see Todd Brower, Communities Within the Community: Consent, Constitutionalism, and Other Failures of Legal Theory in Residential Associations, 7 J. Land Use & Envtl.L. 203 (1992); Gregory S. Alexander, Dilemmas of Group Autonomy: Residential Associations and Community, 75 Corn.L.Rev. 1 (1989); A. Dan Tarlock, Private Land Use Controls: What is the Public Interest? Land Use L. & Zoning Dig. 3 (Sept.1989).

§ 15.2

1. See Timothy Jost, The Defeasible Fee and the Birth of the Modern Residential Subdivision, 49 Mo.L.Rev. 695 (1984).

2. See discussion of easements, covenants, and servitudes infra this chapter §§ 15.3–.8.

3. Common phrases held to create a determinable estate are "so long as," "while," "until," and "during such time." Express language of reversion is not necessary according to strict theory that the estate ends automatically upon breach. Like a life estate, it is over when its over. Where an attempt to create the future interest in a third party is declared void, courts generally imply a possibility of reverter in the grantor. Still, without language of reversion, there is greater risk that a fee simple absolute or fee subject to a covenant will be found. See Roger A. Cunningham, William B. Stoebuck, and Dale A. Whitman, The Law of Property 40 (2d ed.1993) and Richard R. Powell and Patrick J. Rohan, 2 Powell on Real Property ¶ 187 (1994).

cally terminates and returns to O or her heirs.[4]

B. Estates Upon Condition Subsequent

If O, owner of Greenacre, conveys that parcel to A "upon the condition that the land is used solely for residential purposes and if the land ever ceases to be so used O, the grantor, or her heirs may re-enter and terminate the estate hereby conveyed," O has created a fee simple upon, or subject to, a condition subsequent in A. O has retained in herself a future interest, which, at early common law, courts called a "right of re-entry." The Restatement of Property needlessly renamed it a "power of termination."[5] Early cases did not require express language of re-entry, but today one who omits a re-entry clause runs a significant risk of a court refusing to find an estate upon condition subsequent.[6]

If A, or a successor in interest, changes the use from residential to any other use, O, or if she is deceased, the person or persons who inherited her right of re-entry, may take possession of the property (re-enter) and thereby terminate the estate of A or his successors.[7]

C. The Distinction Between a Fee Simple Determinable and a Fee Upon Condition Subsequent

Automatic versus nonautomatic termination distinguishes the fee simple determinable from the fee upon condition subsequent. Consider the following examples. O owns two adjoining parcels, Blackacre and Greenacre. She conveys a fee simple determinable estate in Blackacre to A and a fee simple upon condition subsequent in Greenacre to A. The restriction or defeasible event in both is the provision that the land must be used only for residential purposes. A builds a Cheeseburger Paradise restaurant on each parcel. The title to Blackacre automatically reverts to O since A's estate was a fee simple determinable and O retained a possibility of reverter. Since title is O's automatically, continued possession by A is wrongful and the statute of limitations runs from the time of the breach. If O, who may not be aware of the breach, does nothing to oust A, adverse possession could deprive O of title.

In contrast, a change in use of Greenacre does not cause title automatically to return to O. A retains ownership unless and until O exercises her right of re-entry by taking possession and thereby ending A's estate. In the meantime, A's continued possession after the change in use is not wrongful. The statute of limitations will not begin running until O attempts to re-enter.[8]

At early common law the possibility of reverter and the right of re-entry could only pass by inheritance. Today, in most states, both inter-

---

4. The same restriction could be imposed on a life estate or a term of years.

5. Restatement of Property § 45.

6. Cunningham, Stoebuck & Whitman, supra note 3, at 43. Phrases commonly used to create such an estate include "on condition that," "provided that," and "but if." Id. at 42, n.1.

7. Life estates and non-freehold estates also may be made defeasible by being subjected to a condition subsequent.

8. In a few states, the statute of limitations begins running immediately. See Cunningham, Stoebuck & Whitman, Stoebuck, & Whitman, supra note 3, at 51.

ests are also devisable.[9] States differ on the intervivos alienability of these interests.[10]

D. Fee Subject to an Executory Interest

Only the grantor or her estate can retain the possibility of reverter and right of re-entry. At early common law the grantor could not transfer these future interests to, or create them in, a third party. After the Statute of Uses courts allowed a defeasible estate on termination to pass to a third party rather than back to the grantor or her estate.

Consider the following defeasible estate. O conveys Whiteacre to A "provided that A shall use the land solely for residential purposes and if A shall ever use the land for another purpose then title shall pass to B." A has a fee simple subject to an executory limitation and B has a future interest called an executory interest. If the land is ever used for commercial purposes, A's interest is cut off and B has a fee simple absolute. B's executory interest can be created to become possessory automatically.[11]

The Rule Against Perpetuities will invalidate most executory interests following defeasible fees. In the above example, the interest is valid because the condition will be resolved during A's lifetime. If the transfer provides that the land is only to be used for residential purposes, the executory interest in B is invalid since the defeasible event is not tied personally to A but applies equally to A's successors in interest,.[12]

E. The Usefulness of Defeasible Estates as Land Use Control Devices

The inflexibility of defeasible estates makes them poor land use control devices. If they work as they are supposed to, they are, in a sense, too effective.[13] The consequence of violating the land use restriction imposed on the estate is forfeiture of all interest in the land, a drastic result. This feature makes such estates unattractive to most persons seeking land. A well-advised purchaser will normally not acquire title where there is a possibility of a forfeiture remedy for breach of a condition.[14] Furthermore, if the device works, the assertion by the future interest owner of her rights will not necessarily guarantee the continuation of the private restriction. In fact, the contrary may be the case. If the property subjected to a residential use restriction is more valuable for commercial purposes, the future interest holder may make that change in use upon gaining title to the property since the restriction

---

9. In Illinois, an exception, such interests are non-devisable. Ill.-Smith Hurd Ann. ch. 30, ¶ 37b.

10. Cunningham, Stoebuck, & Whitman, supra note 3, at § 3.24.

11. Life estates and non-freehold estates also may be made subject to an executory limitation.

12. See Lawrence W. Waggoner, Estates in Land and Future Interests 201–02 (2d ed.1993). Reversionary interests such as

the possibility of reverter and the right of re-entry are not subject to the Rule Against Perpetuities. Id. at 185.

13. See generally, Goldstein, Rights of Entry and Possibilities of Reverter as Devices to Restrict the Use of Land, 54 Harv. L.Rev. 248 (1940).

14. Quatman v. McCray, 128 Cal. 285, 60 P. 855 (1900).

applied only to the owner of the defeasible estate and not to the owner of the future interest.

In theory, defeasible estates offer a large degree of control, but their usefulness is limited when the object of planning is to impose area-wide controls over the use of land. To the extent that a defeasible estate is intentionally used today it is likely in the charitable context or where the parties desire long-term preservation for a public interest, such as a scenic view. Even then, there are better devices.[15]

History teaches that defeasible estates do not work as designed. When developers used defeasible estates to control land use in the late nineteenth and early twentieth centuries, they proved ineffective. Courts, reluctant to order forfeiture, tended to lean over backwards to avoid finding that a breach had occurred, or used equitable rules of waiver or estoppel to preclude forfeiture.[16]

Defeasible estates also create title nightmares. A title once made defeasible may last forever, and a breach may occur generations after it is imposed when the owners of the future interest are difficult to identify. A number of states solve this problem by extinguishing the future interest following the defeasible estate after the passage of time, typically twenty to thirty years, unless rerecorded.[17]

§ 15.3 Easements

Affirmative and negative easements are widely used in the land development process.[1] An affirmative easement is a nonpossessory right to use land belonging to another person. A negative easement is a restriction placed by the owner on his own land to benefit another person or other land. An example of an affirmative easement is the classic "right of way" pursuant to which A, owner of parcel one, grants to B, owner of adjacent parcel two, the right to cross A's parcel for ingress and egress. An example of a negative easement is a limitation on A's right to build on parcel one to preserve the view from parcel two. Like possessory estates, nonpossessory interests can be made defeasible.[2]

An easement may be appurtenant to the land, that is, created to benefit land owned by the holder of the easement (the dominant estate), or it may be in gross, that is, for the personal benefit of the holder. The burden of an easement appurtenant or an easement in gross passes with the servient land to subsequent transferees.[3] Once an easement is properly created and recorded, express reference to it in successive deeds

---

15. See discussion of easements, covenants, and servitudes infra the balance of this chapter.

16. Jost, supra note 1, at 728.

17. See, e.g., Fla.Stat.Ann. § 689.18 (3) (void after 21 years). See Texaco v. Short, 454 U.S. 516, 102 S.Ct. 781, 70 L.Ed.2d 738 (1982) (upholding Indiana statute that declared unused mineral interests void after passage of 20 years unless rerecorded).

§ 15.3

1. See generally Jon W. Bruce and James W. Ely, Jr., The Law of Easements and Licenses in Land (Rev.ed.1995).

2. See discussion supra § 15.2.

3. See Charles Clark, Covenants and Interests Running with Land 65 et seq. (1947).

is unnecessary. Likewise, the benefit of an easement appurtenant passes with the dominant estate without separate mention in the deed.

The benefit of an easement in gross does not attach to land. In the right of way example above, if B did not own land benefited by the easement, it would be in gross. Easements for railroads and power lines, for example, are generally in gross. In contrast to easements appurtenant, the common law rule is that the benefit of an easement in gross may not be assigned. The trend, however, is to allow assignability, particularly if the benefit is commercial in nature or if the original parties are found to have intended that it be assignable.[4]

Affirmative easements are important in the planning and operation of multi-parcel developments because they grant rights to individual lot owners in common property such as roads and parks, and reserve to the developer rights across lots for utilities. Where a developer sells lots with reference to a plat map that designates areas for roads and recreational common grounds, the purchasers generally acquire affirmative easements in such areas by implication.[5]

An affirmative easement can also be used to protect certain types of development from nuisance suits. Thus, a cement company can create a buffer zone around its operation by acquiring from neighboring lots owners affirmative easements to cast pollutants on their lands.[6] Hog farmers, and others engaging in uses that run the risk of being enjoined as private nuisances, can do the same. Though such easements will confer immunity from suit by the owners of the servient land, the conduct may still be actionable as a public nuisance.[7]

Historical convention has limited the potential effectiveness of negative easements as land use regulation devices. At early common law, English courts limited the subject matter of negative easements to four categories: light, air, drainage of an artificial stream, and lateral support.[8] American courts have been more liberal concerning the use of negative easements to impose restrictions on the use or improvement of property for such purposes as the preservation of view and for residential use restrictions.[9] Still, the historical limitation has hampered reliance on the negative easement. That limitation, coupled with the questions concerning the assignability of easements in gross, led lawyers to look elsewhere to limit land use. They turned to promissory restraints on

---

4. Miller v. Lutheran Conf. & Camp Ass'n, 331 Pa. 241, 200 A.2d 646 (1938). See Note, The Easement in Gross Revisited: Transferability and Divisibility Since 1945, 39 Vand.L.Rev. 109 (1986); Simes, The Assignability of Easements in Gross in American Law, 22 Mich.L.Rev. 521 (1924).

5. See. e.g. Catalano v. Woodward, 617 A.2d 1363 (R.I.1992); Ryder v. Petrea, 243 Va. 421, 416 S.E.2d 686 (1992). See generally Bruce & Ely, supra note 1, at ¶ 4.05.

6. See Boomer v. Atlantic Cement Co., 26 N.Y.2d 219, 309 N.Y.S.2d 312, 257 N.E.2d 870 (1970), where the court found a nuisance from the cement dust cast on neighboring land but ordered the company to pay permanent damages to the owners. The court's judgment effectively created an affirmative easement to conduct a nuisance.

7. See supra Ch.14.

8. See Uriel Reichman, Toward a Unified Concept of Servitudes, 55 S.Cal.L.Rev. 1177, 1260 (1982).

9. See, e.g., Petersen v. Friedman, 162 Cal.App.2d 245, 328 P.2d 264 (1958) (easement of view).

land use and sought to enforce them under the law of real covenants and equitable servitudes. Results have been mixed. While overcoming the limitations on easements, covenants and servitudes encounter other problems.[10] Also, the functional similarity between negative easements and restrictive covenants has led to confusion.[11]

§ 15.4   Promises Respecting Land Use

The use of contracts between landowners to control land use is common. If A owns adjoining parcels and sells one parcel to B, it is common for A and B to agree that their respective pieces of land will be used for residential purposes only. Actions between the contracting parties pose no difficulty. If either party violates the promise, the aggrieved party can collect damages or obtain equitable relief using straightforward contract law principles. Problems arise, however, if A sells his land to C, and C sues B for a violation of the covenant, or if B transfers his interest to D, and A (or C) sues D. Traditional contract principles neither allowed a person to enforce a contract to which he was not a party nor held a person liable for a promise he had not made. A contract unenforceable by and against subsequent owners of the land is not an effective land use control device.

Unable to use contract law,[1] attorneys persuaded judges to use property law, considering the contract between A and B as a modification of the land ownership interests that pass to their successors. In other words, the A–B contract modified the ownership interests of each tract so that transfer of the land from A to C and from B to D impliedly assigned A's contract benefits to C, and B's contract duties to D. Courts balked at first, probably out of a fear that to do so would be a step back to the feudal tenure system, which intertwined land ownership rights and personal obligations. Eventually, however, the courts held that noncontracting parties could enforce, and be bound by, such contracts.

"Covenants that run with the land" is the quaint judicial label for contracts enforceable by and against subsequent landowners under property law. Covenants run in law as "real covenants" or in equity as "equitable servitudes." The elements in law and equity differ slightly and the choice of which to pursue is based on the desired relief. A suit at law to enforce a real covenant is proper to obtain damages, while a suit in equity is the vehicle to obtain injunctive relief.[2]

---

10. See infra §§ 15.6–15.7.

11. See infra § 15.8

§ 15.4

1. These developments preceded the expansion of contract law to include promissory estoppel and third party beneficiary concepts.

2. With the merger of law and equity the distinction should not matter. The ele-ments to recover damages are more onerous than to obtain equitable relief, and if damages are available in an action based in equity the need to worry over the rules of real covenants disappears. That, however, does not appear to be the case. See Roger A. Cunningham, William B. Stoebuck, and Dale A. Whitman, The Law of Property 40, § 8.31 (2d ed.1993).

§ 15.5   Creation of Promises Respecting Land Use

Courts generally view promises respecting land use as interests in land. Normally, they must be in a writing complying with the Statute of Frauds. In the past some courts held that these promises were mere contract rights, not subject to the Statute of Frauds.[1] While some courts might still follow that view, as a practical matter, the promises ought to be in writing. Since the issue rarely arises one might conclude that nearly all such promises are in fact put in writing. If not, the standard exceptions of estoppel and part performance may save an oral promise. Typically, deeds of conveyance contain promises respecting land use, though the owners of the tracts involved may also execute separate instruments containing covenants.[2] When the deeds or instruments are recorded, subsequent purchasers are charged with constructive notice of the restriction.[3]

Equitable servitudes may be created by implication under the doctrine of implied reciprocal servitudes.[4] If a subdivision developer exacts promises from the initial grantees that limit the use of the conveyed lots pursuant to a common plan, the developer will be held to have impliedly subjected its retained land to the same restriction. Whether a common plan existed at the time of the transfers is a question of fact. Evidence of a plan may come from the transfer of restricted land by reference to a recorded plat showing uniform lots. The fact that only some of the deeds contain the covenant is not determinative, but the greater the number of restricted lots and the higher the degree of uniformity in the restrictions imposed, the more likely it is that a common plan will be found to have existed at the outset. A developer's representations or public announcements of intention to create a general scheme may also be used to find a plan.[5] A court may look to the reliance of buyers and to the actual development of the tract to find that a general building plan had been agreed upon.[6]

A subsequent purchaser is bound though no recorded deed contains the restriction.[7] The covenant, after all, is implied, and it runs with the land.[8] While one court hinted that inquiry notice is provided if all the

---

§ 15.5

1. See Roger A. Cunningham, William B. Stoebuck, and Dale A. Whitman, The Law of Property § 8.15 (2d ed.1993).

2. Trustees of Columbia College v. Lynch, 70 N.Y. 440 (1877).

3. There is a difference of opinion on whether one has constructive notice of covenants in collateral chains of title. See Guillette v. Daly Dry Wall, Inc., 367 Mass. 355, 325 N.E.2d 572 (1975) (yes); Witter v. Taggart, 78 N.Y.2d 234, 577 N.E.2d 338, 573 N.Y.S.2d 146 (1991) (no).

4. It is also known as an implied reciprocal negative easement.

5. See, e.g., Gey v. Beck, 390 Pa.Super. 317, 568 A.2d 672 (1990); Chasse v. Town of Candia, 132 N.H. 574, 567 A.2d 999 (1989).

6. Taylor v. Melton, 130 Colo. 280, 274 P.2d 977 (1954).

7. Id. But see Riley v. Bear Creek Planning Committee, 17 Cal.3d 500, 131 Cal. Rptr. 381, 551 P.2d 1213 (1976) (buyer of subdivision lot who takes deed prior to recordation of general plan of mutual restrictions applicable to the entire subdivision is not bound by restrictions, despite actual knowledge of restrictions).

8. See infra § 15.6.

other lots in a development are developed for residential use, it held that there is notice of record of the implied servitude.[9] In effect, one searching title and finding that a grantor in the chain of title transferred other land near the lot whose title is being searched must assume that a reciprocal promise may have arisen by implication. The searcher must then make inquiry as to whether circumstances existed to justify the finding of a common plan.

A few courts refuse to imply servitudes.[10] California, for example, takes the position that a common plan or building scheme requires the express words of the grantor and grantee. Thus, a covenant in a deed must describe the land intended to be benefited and state that the restriction is for the benefit of the described land.[11] While a developer may record a declaration of restrictions, the declaration must describe the whole area to be benefited and affirmatively declare that it is the intent of the subdivider to restrict the various lots for the benefit of the lots described.

Where a general plan or building scheme exists, lot owners may enforce the restrictions among themselves. Generally a prior purchaser may sue a later taker and vice versa.[12] Courts are not always careful to note when the one seeking to enforce a covenant bought her land.[13] Enforcement by subsequent purchasers (those who purchase after the land that is the subject of the action was restricted) poses no problem since these later purchasers own land that the common grantor owned when it imposed the restriction. Those who buy a lot before the subject land is restricted can only sue if they obtained an express or implied promise regarding retained land in their deeds from the common grantor.

In jurisdictions that refuse to imply a reciprocal servitude, enforcement by a prior purchaser will not be available if the common grantor did not expressly restrict its retained land. In such a case, the common grantor is free to convey later lots free of restriction. If, however, the common grantor in fact restricts later lots, the prior purchasers may be able to enforce that later covenant on the grounds that they are intended third party beneficiaries. If evidence of a common plan exists, courts assume that the developer, though not obligated to do so, exacted the later promise for the benefit of those owners to whom it had already sold lots.[14]

---

9. Sanborn v. McLean, 233 Mich. 227, 206 N.W. 496 (1925).

10. See Sprague v. Kimball, 213 Mass. 380, 100 N.E. 622 (1913); Davis v. Robinson, 189 N.C. 589, 127 S.E. 697 (1925).

11. Werner v. Graham, 181 Cal. 174, 183 P. 945 (1919).

12. Boyd v. Park Realty Corp., 137 Md. 36, 111 A. 129 (1920); Snow v. Van Dam, 291 Mass. 477, 197 N.E. 224 (1935).

13. See Thomas E. Roberts, Private Land Use Controls: Enforcement Problems with Real Covenants and Equitable Servitudes in North Carolina, 22 Wake For. L.Rev. 749, 800 (1987).

14. See Snow v. Van Dam, 291 Mass. 477, 197 N.E. 224 (1935). Cf. Malley v. Hanna, 65 N.Y.2d 289, 480 N.E.2d 1068, 491 N.Y.S.2d 286 (1985).

§ 15.6 Real Covenants (Covenants That Run With the Land)

Covenants will run with the land and bind or benefit successors to the estates of the covenanting parties only if (1) the parties intend that the benefit and burden run with the land, (2) the covenant touches or concerns the land, and (3) privity of estate exists. Covenants failing to satisfy these elements are styled personal covenants, and are only enforceable by or against original parties.

A. Intent

To establish that the parties intend that their successors in interest be bound, it is persuasive, but not necessary, to use the words "heirs and assigns." While courts may infer the parties' intent or lack of it from the language of the agreement[1] or from the circumstances surrounding its execution,[2] such evidence may not be necessary. If all other requirements for valid real covenants are met, judges generally presume intent.[3]

B. Touch or Concern

The "touch or concern" test is a bit trickier. Commentators have often decried the inability of courts to articulate a meaningful test for touch or concern. One reason is the failure to ask why a covenant must touch or concern the land other than that an English court said so in 1583. In *Spencer's Case*, the court said that for it to hold an assignee liable for a predecessors's promise, the promise had to touch or concern the land.[4] The court did not say why this was so, or what it meant by the phrase, except to say that the promise could not be collateral. In that case, a lessee's promise to build a wall on the leased premises met the test. Presumably a promise of a lessee to build on other land would be collateral and not run.

Another roadblock in the quest to define touch or concern is the practice of mislabeling the test in the conjunctive as a "touch *and* concern" requirement. Courts widely agree that no requirement of physical touching exists,[5] yet continued repetition of the test as one of "touch and concern" causes courts to ponder what the word "touch" means in the context of covenants. If courts and commentators had stayed with *Spencer's Case* disjunctive "touch or concern"[6] and perhaps dropped the word "touch," they would have had less difficulty in deciding whether a covenant *concerns* land.

§ 15.6

1. Union Trust Co. v. Rosenburg, 171 Md. 409, 189 A. 421 (1937).

2. Clark v. Guy Drews Post of the Am. Legion, 247 Wis. 48, 18 N.W.2d 322 (1945).

3. At early common law, if the covenant related to something not yet in existence (not in esse) such as a party wall *to be built* and maintained, the express words of assignability had to be used. This rule derived from Spencer's Case, 77 Eng.Rep. 72 (Q.B.1583). It is not followed in the United States.

4. Spencer's Case, 5 Co.Rep. 16a, 77 Eng.Rep. 72 (K.B.1583).

5. See Norfleet v. Cromwell, 70 N.C. 634 (1874) (obligation to pay maintenance expenses for canal ran; even though canal did not physically touch the land, it did concern it).

6. Spencer's Case, 5 Co.Rep. 16a, 77 Eng.Rep. 72, 74 (K.B.1583).

Commentators have had as much, if not more, difficulty in stating a test for touch or concern than the courts have had in applying unarticulated assumptions about which covenants sufficiently concern land to run. Without a clear judicial test, several academics have offered formulas.[7] Likely the best is the expectations' test attributable to Judge Clark and Professor Berger: transferees of land should be liable if a reasonable person aware of the covenant would expect to be accountable.[8] One ought not be liable for promises that do not relate to the land even though the promise appears in the chain of title.

Few promises fail the test. Promises to limit the use of land, to maintain land, and to pay rent meet the test.[9] The classroom hypothetical that the covenantor will sing at the covenantee's birthday party every year fails the test, but one is not likely to encounter such promises in deeds. The tentative draft of the Restatement (Third) of Property would eliminate the touch or concern doctrine and rely on the rule that covenants that violate public policy are unenforceable to protect persons from being required to perform unreasonable promises.

Historically, commentators have given much attention to the New York courts' reluctance to find that affirmative covenants to pay money touch or concern. Most other courts have never had difficulty with affirmative covenants.[10] New York overcame its objection in Neponsit Property Owners' Ass'n v. Emigrant Industrial Savings Bank, finding a promise to pay an annual fee to maintain common areas in a subdivision ran with the land.[11] Also, covenants not to use land in competition with businesses on nearby land were viewed as personal by some courts, who took the view that there had to be a physical advantage to land. An economic benefit did not suffice. Courts no longer follow that restrictive view.[12]

The most significant aspect of touch or concern comes in the distinction between running burdens and running benefits. An effort to hold someone who did not make a promise liable for a breach is a running burden question, exemplified by the above hypothetical suit against D.[13] An effort by someone who was not a party to the original contract to seek damages from a breach of the covenant is a running

---

7. One well known, but unhelpful, test is found in Bigelow, The Contents of Covenants in Leases, 12 Mich.L.Rev. 639 (1914), which provides that if a covenantor's legal interest is lessened by the covenant then the burden touches. The test does not say how to determine whether the legal interest is lessened. Of course, if a court says a covenant touches, then the legal interests are lessened. For criticism of the circular Bigelow test, see Jesse Dukeminier and James E. Krier, Property 883 (3d.3d.1993).

8. See Charles Clark, Covenants and Interests Running with Land 65 et seq. (1947) and Lawrence Berger, A Policy Analysis of Promises Respecting the Use of Land, 55 Minn.L.Rev. 167, 208 (1970).

9. See Roger A. Cunningham, William B. Stoebuck, and Dale A. Whitman, The Law of Property 471–475 (2d ed.1993).

10. See Thomas E. Roberts, Private Land Use Controls: Enforcement Problems with Real Covenants and Equitable Servitudes in North Carolina, 22 Wake For. L.Rev. 749, 770 (1987).

11. 278 N.Y. 248, 15 N.E.2d 793 (1938).

12. See Whitinsville Plaza, Inc. v. Kotseas, 378 Mass. 85, 390 N.E.2d 243 (1979).

13. See supra, first paragraph of § 15.4.

benefit question, exemplified by the above suit by C against B. If C is suing D, both running burden and running benefit questions are present.

The test for the burden to run is more onerous than for the benefit to run. In order for the burden of a promise to run to someone who did not make the promise, the touch or concern requirement is twofold: the promise must not only relate to the land of the promisee; it also must relate to land of the promisor. The traditional rule is that if no dominant estate exists, if, in other words the benefit is in gross, the burden will not run.[14] The rule originated as a judicial effort to limit the running covenant doctrine. It has the supposed advantage of promoting alienability by freeing land from control. However, the rule is irrationally underinclusive in achieving this goal, since the burdens of other covenants run. A disadvantage of the rule is that it destroys contract expectations. Consequently, courts and commentators have criticized the anti-in gross rule, and several exceptions to it exist.[15]

The rule that the burden will not run if the benefit is in gross poses a problem for land preservation efforts. Where the goal is to preserve land for agricultural production, for wilderness, for open space, or for historical purposes, courts may see the benefit as in gross. If so, the original promisor can free the land of the restriction by transferring the land to another, rendering the arrangement worthless.

Wise planning dictates consideration of another tool, such as an easement in gross. The difficulty with that choice is that a court may not be willing to characterize an arrangement that looks like a promise as a conveyance.[16] Statutory relief is available in many states that have enacted conservation easement laws that do away with this and other common law limitations on running covenants.[17]

C. *Privity of Estate*

The privity of estate requirement is the major obstacle to the enforcement of covenants at law. Privity of estate is used in two senses: (1) horizontal privity, which relates to the relationship between the original contracting parties, and (2) vertical privity, which relates to succession to the estate of a contracting party.

While a few cases reject the need for horizontal privity of estate between the contracting parties, most require it for the burden to run. There are three definitions of horizontal privity used in running burden cases. The English courts follow the most restrictive view, requiring a tenurial relationship. Less restrictive is the so-called Massachusetts view that requires a mutual and simultaneous interest in the land by both the

---

14. See, e.g., Stegall v. Housing Authority of City of Charlotte, 278 N.C. 95, 178 S.E.2d 824 (1971); Caullett v. Stanley Stilwell & Sons, Inc., 67 N.J.Super. 111, 170 A.2d 52 (1961).

15. See Thomas E. Roberts, Promises Respecting Land Use: Can Benefits be Held in Gross? 51 Mo.L.Rev. 933 (1986).

16. See infra § 15.8

17. See infra § 15.12

promisor and promisee.[18] When courts require horizontal privity in this sense, a relationship between the contracting parties such as that between landlord and tenant or between servient and dominant tenements by way of an easement is necessary for a promise to be enforced against a successor of the covenantor. Most courts find horizontal privity met where there is merely a succession of estate between the parties. This view is sometimes known as grantor-grantee privity. If A owns two lots and transfers one to B, horizontal privity exists by way of the deed from A to B.

If A and B, owning adjacent lots, promise each other to limit the respective uses of their lots, horizontal privity is lacking under all of the views of horizontal privity. Thus, if B sells to C, A cannot enforce the covenant against C at law.[19] To avoid this pitfall, A and B need to use a straw conveyance to create privity.

Horizontal privity is not needed for the benefit to run.[20] If A and B, owning adjacent lots, promise each other to limit the uses of their lots, when B sells to C, C can enforce the benefit of the covenant against A. As the original promisor, A can hardly object.

All courts require vertical privity, but define the relationship differently for the burden and benefit. For the burden to run at law, courts will permit enforcement only against one who succeeds to the entire estate of the promisor. If, after adjoining fee owners A and B enter into a contract, B leases his land to C, vertical privity is lacking. Since C did not take the whole interest of B, C is not liable. For the benefit to run, the transfer of some interest suffices. Thus, C, though merely a lessee, can sue A.

Privity of estate is an anachronistic holdover from days long passed. The explanation for the privity requirement is tied to the concept of the early cases that covenants run not with the land, but "with the estate in land." Thus, there had to be an estate interest pass that could carry the covenant on its journey from one party to another. This arcane concern about which metaphor is the proper one (that of running with an estate in land or that of running with the land itself) interferes with sound policy. A knowledgeable party can create horizontal privity with a straw or avoid vertical privity on the burden side by a technical transfer of a lesser estate. The unwary, of course, fall prey to its trap. While courts should dispense with privity, its potential for harm is modest since one does not need it in equity,[21] the preferred remedy for most beneficiaries.

§ 15.7 Equitable Servitudes

Covenants that cannot be enforced at law because privity is lacking may be enforced in equity as equitable servitudes on the theory that a

18. Morse v. Aldrich, 36 Mass. (19 Pick.) 449 (1837).

19. Johnson v. Myers, 226 Ga. 23, 172 S.E.2d 421 (1970).

20. Restatement of Property § 528; Horn v. Miller, 136 Pa. 640, 20 A. 706 (1890).

21. See infra § 15.7

subsequent grantee who takes with notice of an agreement concerning the use of land cannot equitably refuse to perform. The equitable servitude was created in the leading case of Tulk v. Moxhay,[1] which involved an effort to enjoin construction of a building on Leicester Square in London. Tulk, owner of the square and of land surrounding the square, sold the square to Elms. Elms promised Tulk, among other things, not to build on the square. Moxhay, who acquired the square by mesne conveyances, announced his intent to build on the square. Tulk could not sue Moxhay at law for damages since he did not meet the restrictive view of horizontal privity followed in England (Tulk and Elms were merely grantor-grantee, not landlord-tenant). The chancellor in equity felt unconstrained by the law courts' rules of privity, and on the basis that Moxhay bought with notice of the promise Elms had made, enjoined Moxhay from violating it.

For a covenant to run in equity, a plaintiff must show intent and touch or concern in the same fashion as at law.[2] The only difference between law and equity is the dispensation of privity in the latter. While this is clearly true for horizontal privity and vertical privity on the burden side, the New York Court of Appeals suggested in dicta in the well-known case of Neponsit Property Owners' Ass'n v. Emigrant Industrial Savings Bank[3] that vertical privity might be necessary in equity for the benefit to run. In *Neponsit*, the court allowed a property owners' association to enforce in equity an affirmative covenant requiring the payment of an annual fee for maintenance of common areas in a subdivision. The fact that the plaintiff association was not the grantee of any estate in land from either the developer or the lot owners troubled the court. The court noted that it was uncertain whether it could enforce the covenant in equity despite this lack of vertical privity but it avoided ruling on the issue by finding that the association was acting as the agent of the lot owners. Thus, privity existed in substance if not in form. This injection of uncertainty continues to trouble New York courts,[4] but other authorities agree that vertical privity is not necessary for the benefit to run in equity.[5]

The *Neponsit* court also muddied the waters regarding the running in equity of the burden when the benefit is in gross. The court cited, and briefly discussed, cases holding covenants not to run where they benefit-

---

§ 15.7

1. Tulk v. Moxbay, 41 Eng.Rep. 1143, 2 Phillips 774 (Ch. 1848). See also Trustees of Columbia College v. Lynch, 70 N.Y. 440 (1877).

2. The First Restatement took the position that touch or concern was more relaxed in equity. That view is no longer valid. See Thomas E. Roberts, Promises Respecting Land Use: Can Benefits be Held in Gross? 51 Mo.L.Rev. 933, 938–40 (1986); Roger A. Cunningham, William B. Stoebuck, and Dale A. Whitman, The Law of Property 488 (2d ed.1993).

3. 278 N.Y. 248, 15 N.E.2d 793 (1938).

4. Orange & Rockland Utilities, Inc. v. Philwold Estates, Inc. 52 N.Y.2d 253, 263, 418 N.E.2d 1310, 1314, 437 N.Y.S.2d 291, 295 (1981).

5. 2 American Law of Property § 9.27 (A. Casner ed.1952). While technical privity is not required, a plaintiff must demonstrate that she was intended to be able to enforce the promise, under a third party beneficiary theory, or as agent of those who do own benefited land. See Roberts, supra note 2, at 965–975.

ed no land, as if such was true in the case before the court. It was not. The *Neponsit* covenants were not in gross. The individual lots and the common areas were the benefited land. Since the court allowed the covenant to run, one will occasionally see references to *Neponsit* as exemplifying a rule that "benefits may be held in gross."[6]

The point of confusion lies with failing to distinguish between who can enforce the covenant and whether enforcement benefits any land.[7] *Neponsit* was concerned with who can enforce and, sensibly, the court required that a plaintiff show a connection to the covenant. Officious intermeddlers ought not be able to sue, but a property owners' association is a natural enforcer.[8] *Neponsit* did nothing to detract from the majority rule that the burden will not run if the benefit is in gross.

§ 15.8   Differentiating Restrictive Covenants and Servitudes from Negative Easements

Confusion exists over the difference between negative easements and restrictive covenants. While functionally equivalent in that both limit the use of the servient land and allow no affirmative use, their historical development in separate doctrinal categories may make the label attached to given restrictions determinative of their enforceability. Language of grant or reservation may denote an easement while language of promise may denote a covenant. Professors Bruce and Ely observe that courts treat limitations that apply to the entire servient parcel, such as prohibitions against commercial use, as covenants, and treat limitations on use of only a specific part or particular building of the servient tract, such as a limit on building height or a prohibition against alteration of a building exterior, as negative easements.[1] As they also note, their observation is not a foolproof test since under it a conservation easement would be a covenant.[2]

While differentiation between these two interests is not easy, it is unimportant in the development of residential land where a dominant estate usually exists. Furthermore, if language is to be the controlling test, the restrictions may carry language of both covenant and easements and qualify as both. It is where the interest is in gross that greater problems arise. This occurs in private efforts to control land use for scenic view, agricultural, and historical preservation purposes. If courts treat such interests as easements in gross, they may fall victim to the

---

6. Robert C. Ellickson and A. Dan Tarlock, Land Use Controls: Cases and Materials 624 (1981).

7. See Roberts, supra note 2, at 965–973.

8. McNamee v. Bishop Trust Co., 62 Haw. 397, 616 P.2d 205 (1980); Merrionette Manor Homes Improvement Ass'n v. Heda, 11 Ill.App.2d 186, 136 N.E.2d 556 (1956). A developer may also qualify as an agent of the people to whom it transferred lots. See

this suggestion in Christiansen v. Casey, 613 S.W.2d 906, 912 (Mo.App.1981).

§ 15.8

1. See Jon W. Bruce and James W. Ely, Jr., The Law of Easements and Licenses in Land, ¶ 1.07 (Rev.ed.1995).

2. See Bruce & Ely, supra note 1. See also Gerald Korngold, Privately Held Conservation Servitudes: A Policy Analysis in the Context of in Gross Real Covenants and Easements, 63 Tex.L.Rev. 433 (1984).

common law rule that makes them nonassignable. Thus, if a land conservancy group acquires negative easements in gross limiting the use of land to open space and intends to transfer its rights in the land to a public body, it should not do so unless such easements are clearly assignable in the jurisdiction. To alleviate uncertainty, many states have statutes authorizing assignable conservation easements.[3]

§ 15.9 Modification and Termination

As is true with contracts generally, the acts of the parties may modify or terminate promises respecting land use: through merger by the same person acquiring the dominant and servient estates; through agreement of the parties creating the restriction; or through execution of a release by the dominant owner. However, courts have held a release by the grantor ineffective where a covenant benefits other land than that retained by the grantor and other lot owners insist on enforcing the restriction.[1]

In addition, courts may not enforce a covenant when, due to changed circumstances, enforcement can no longer fulfill the purpose for which the covenant was created and enforcement would be inequitable to the owner of the burdened lot. In the typical case, courts lift restrictions requiring that lots be used for single family residences when the character of the neighborhood has changed so as to render the restriction useless to the benefited land. The cases weigh such factors as the extent of the surrounding commercial uses, increased traffic and noise, hazards to children, and the low value of residential use as opposed to commercial use.[2] For many courts, a showing of increased development external to the protected area is insufficient, if not inapposite; change must come from within. Exterior lots naturally buffer interior lots and presumably a buyer pays a premium reflecting that protection. Though the value of the exterior lot as restricted may plummet due to outside development, a buyer should consider that risk.[3] Some courts, however, do consider external change.[4]

Interior violations may lead to abandonment. In Fink v. Miller,[5] for example, a covenant requiring the use of wood shingles was found to

---

3. See infra § 15.12

§ 15.9

1. See Rick v. West, 34 Misc.2d 1002, 228 N.Y.S.2d 195 (1962). See also Tompkins v. Hale, 172 Misc. 1071, 15 N.Y.S.2d 854 (1939), aff'd 284 N.Y. 675, 30 N.E.2d 721 (1940) (original contract of tenants owning shares in a corporation, formed to take title and operate premises as a cooperative, could not be modified without the unanimous consent of all the parties).

2. See Crimmins v. Simonds, 636 P.2d 478 (Utah 1981); Wolff v. Fallon, 44 Cal.2d 695, 284 P.2d 802 (1955). But cf. Cordogan v. Union National Bank of Elgin, 64 Ill. App.3d 248, 21 Ill.Dec. 18, 380 N.E.2d 1194

(1978) (movant, who created restrictions himself, was unable to remove restrictions without unjustly injuring neighboring properties). See also infra § 15.14 on zoning regulations as evidence of a change in conditions.

3. Elliott v. Jefferson County Fiscal Court, 657 S.W.2d 237 (Ky.1983); Western Land Co. v. Truskolaski, 88 Nev. 200, 495 P.2d 624 (1972).

4. See DeMarco v. Palazzolo, 47 Mich. App. 444, 209 N.W.2d 540 (1973) (discussing split in Michigan authority). See generally, 5 Powell on Real Property § 679[2].

5. 896 P.2d 649 (Utah App.1995).

have been abandoned where twenty-three of the eighty-one homes in the subdivision had noncomplying roofs. The court found the changed circumstances doctrine, requiring a showing that a covenant is valueless, to be inappropriate to a covenant affecting not use of the land, but the selection of building materials. The question said the court was whether the violations were so great that a reasonable person would conclude the restriction had been abandoned.

According to some authorities, a difference may be drawn between enforcement of a covenant in equity and law. If neighborhood transition has reached a point at which the hardship imposed on the burdened estate outweighs the benefits conferred on others, an injunction requiring compliance will not issue. However, nonenforcement in equity does not necessarily mean the covenant no longer exists since a court may allow an action for damages.[6]

Commentators have debated both the wisdom and theoretical justification for the changed circumstances doctrine. If, for example, it is merely an equitable defense then a party cannot raise it in an action at law.[7] Commentators also suggest that freedom of contract principles should lead to enforcement of the covenant despite its lack of value to the land intended to be benefited.[8]

While change in neighborhood conditions may justify the nonenforcement of restrictive covenants, that change will not operate to extinguish a right of reentry for condition broken or a recorded legal easement.[9]

Legislation may terminate private restrictions. Some states by statute have limited the period for which parties may enforce covenants and servitudes.[10] Other states provide that nominal conditions that are of no substantial benefit to the party in whose favor they run are void and unenforceable.[11] Similarly, statutes of limitation may be applied to defeat an attempt to enforce a breach of condition or covenant.[12] Other statutes may declare certain covenants unenforceable on grounds of public policy.[13]

A tax sale of the servient estate will normally not extinguish an

---

6. See Roger A. Cunningham, William B. Stoebuck, and Dale A. Whitman, The Law of Property § 8.20 (2d ed.1993); Case Note, 62 Harv.L.Rev. 1394 (1949) and Restatement of Property § 564 (1944).

7. Cunningham, Stoebuck, and Whitman, supra note 6, at § 8.20.

8. See Richard A. Epstein, Notice and Freedom of Contract in the Law of Servitudes, 55 S.Cal.L.Rev. 1353, 1364 (1982).

9. Waldrop v. Town of Brevard, 233 N.C. 26, 62 S.E.2d 512 (1950).

10. See Mass.Gen.Laws Ann. c. 184, § 23, limiting covenants as well possibilities of reverter and powers of termination to 30

years duration if otherwise unlimited as to time; R.I.Gen.Laws § 34–4–19, limiting rights of reentry and possibilities of reverter to 20 years and covenants and servitudes to 30 years, if otherwise unlimited as to time.

11. See Mich.Comp.Laws Ann. § 554.46. See Kaczynski v. Lindahl, 5 Mich. App. 377, 146 N.W.2d 675 (1966) (prohibition of sale of liquor not nominal).

12. See Wolf v. Hallenbeck, 109 Colo. 70, 123 P.2d 412 (1942); Nearing v. Bridgeport, 137 Conn. 205, 75 A.2d 505 (1950).

13. See infra § 15.11.

appurtenant easement or covenant.[14] This makes sense since the existence of the easement or covenant should diminish the tax value of the servient estate and increase the value of the dominant estate.[15] In many states, statutes expressly provide that easements and covenants survive tax sales.[16]

III. PUBLIC INTEREST IN, AND USE OF, PRIVATE CONTROLS

§ 15.10 Constitutional Limitations

Generally, the constitutional provisions that restrain government in the exercise of the police power will not apply to private covenants due to the absence of state action. However, several caveats are in order. First, a noteworthy exception is that judicial enforcement of racial covenants is state action for the purposes of the Fourteenth Amendment. Second, federal statutes based on the Thirteenth Amendment or the commerce clause apply to private covenants without the need for state action. Third, state constitutions may apply to ban private conduct that is outside the reach of the federal constitution. Fourth, state public policy, enunciated judicially or legislatively, may make private covenants unenforceable.

In Shelley v. Kraemer,[1] the Supreme Court confronted companion cases from Missouri and Michigan where state courts, at the request of white neighbors, had enjoined black purchasers from occupying the homes they had purchased based on violations of racially restrictive covenants. The Court held the state court injunctions were state action for purposes of the Fourteenth Amendment and that the equal protection clause precluded enforcement of the racially restrictive covenants. Two significant questions that arise with respect to the reach of *Shelley* are whether it applies to the enforcement of covenants that discriminate on grounds other than race and whether it applies to property interests other than covenants that discriminate on race.

The Supreme Court has not extended the *Shelley* doctrine beyond racial covenants,[2] and it is improbable that it would do so if the issue were presented to it. In several non-land use cases, the Court has given a

---

14. Engel v. Catucci, 197 F.2d 597 (D.C.Cir.1952); Northwestern Improvement Co. v. Lowry, 104 Mont. 289, 66 P.2d 792 (1937). See generally Jon W. Bruce & James W. Ely, Jr., The Law of Easements and Licenses in Land ¶ 10.11[1] (Rev.ed. 1995).

15. See Bruce & Ely, supra note 14. See also Robert Kratovil, Tax Titles: Extinguishment of Easements, Building Restrictions, and Covenants, 19 Hous.L.Rev. 55 (1981).

16. See, e.g., Ohio Rev.Code Ann. § 5723.12.

§ 15.10

1. 334 U.S. 1, 68 S.Ct. 836, 92 L.Ed. 1161 (1948).

2. See Ross v. Hatfield, 640 F.Supp. 708 (D.Kan.1986) where the court noted that the application of *Shelley* to non-racial covenants was uncertain, but found that even if *Shelley* applied the mere threat of enforcement of a covenant barring satellite dishes was not state action.

restrictive reading to the state action doctrine.[3] The reason is that carried to the extreme, an extension would mean that the judicial enforcement of any private contract would be state action for purposes of the Fourteenth Amendment, eviscerating the state action requirement. The Court does not seem likely to eliminate the distinction between private and public discrimination.

Several state courts, however, have applied *Shelley* to non-racial covenants. In one case, a court found arbitrary enforcement of an adults-only covenant to violate equal protection.[4] State courts have differed over whether a private covenant prohibiting buildings for religious use violates the First Amendment.[5] The Colorado supreme court, without citing *Shelley* or discussing the need for state action, has applied a substantive due process restriction to private covenants regulating architectural design.[6]

The type of property interest at issue may also determine the applicability of *Shelley*. The rights of the covenant beneficiaries in *Shelley* were not self-executing. They needed judicial interference to prevail. However, courts have held *Shelley* inapplicable where possessory title is acquired by automatic reversion to the holder of a possibility of reverter following the breach of a fee simple determinable. In Charlotte Park and Recreation Commission v. Barringer,[7] land for park use was granted to a city pursuant to language held to create a fee simple determinable that nonwhites not be allowed entry. In a declaratory judgment action, the court held that if the city were to breach the condition, title would revert automatically without state court involvement. Since the state courts would not be involved in moving title from one party to another, there was no state action.

3. Flagg Brothers, Inc. v. Brooks, 436 U.S. 149, 98 S.Ct. 1729, 56 L.Ed.2d 185 (1978) (private sale of goods under UCC); Jackson v. Metropolitan Edison Co., 419 U.S. 345, 95 S.Ct. 449, 42 L.Ed.2d 477 (1974) (private utility termination of service).

4. White Egret Condominium, Inc. v. Franklin, 379 So.2d 346 (Fla.1979). See also Riley v. Stoves, 22 Ariz.App. 223, 526 P.2d 747 (1974) (*Shelley* applicable to a challenge against enforcement of a covenant in an adult community that discriminated against children, but covenant found to further a legitimate purpose and thus was not unconstitutionally discriminatory); Shaver v. Hunter, 626 S.W.2d 574 (Tex.App.1981) (*Shelley* deemed applicable but restrictive covenant limiting use to single-family held not to violate equal protection rights of unrelated persons).

5. Ginsberg v. Yeshiva of Far Rockaway, 45 App.Div.2d 334, 358 N.Y.S.2d 477, aff'd, 36 N.Y.2d 706, 325 N.E.2d 876, 366 N.Y.S.2d 418 (1975) (First Amendment not applicable); West Hill Baptist Church v. Abbate 24 Ohio Misc. 66, 261 N.E.2d 196 (1969) (First Amendment applicable).

6. Rhue v. Cheyenne Homes, Inc., 168 Colo. 6, 449 P.2d 361 (1969). See also Linn Valley Lakes Property Owners Ass'n v. Brockway, 250 Kan. 169, 824 P.2d 948 (1992) (enforcement of a restrictive covenant prohibiting the placement of signs on private property not state action prohibited by the First Amendment); McGuire v. Bell, 297 Ark. 282, 761 S.W.2d 904, 911 (1988) (refusing to consider an equal protection argument against the enforcement of a restrictive covenant to prohibit the use of a residence for the mentally disabled).

7. 242 N.C. 311, 88 S.E.2d 114 (1955), cert. denied 350 U.S. 983, 76 S.Ct. 469, 100 L.Ed. 851 (1956). But see Capitol Federal Savings & Loan Ass'n v. Smith, 136 Colo. 265, 316 P.2d 252 (1957), which held that state action was involved regardless of the type of defeasible fee.

Under the *Barringer* rationale, a right of re-entry following a fee simple subject to a condition subsequent is different because title does not vest automatically on breach. The owner must exercise the right of re-entry and, if unable to gain possession voluntarily, would need to secure state court aid. *Shelley* would prelude the court from helping. Use of this arcane distinction between the two types of future interests is lamentable. It is also manipulable in that the language used to create the defeasible fee is often unclear and requires judicial construction. Despite the nicety of the distinction, it did not bother the Supreme Court sufficiently in *Barringer* to accept certiorari.[8]

Another possible avenue to subject private covenants to those constitutional provisions that require state action is the theory used in Marsh v. Alabama,[9] where the Court held that the First Amendment applied to land owned by a company that had assumed virtually all of the responsibilities of a local government. The Court, however, has been strict in applying the *Marsh* company town rule, requiring that the private property be used as the functional equivalent of a local government.[10] For application to a private community this requires that there be a community organization that supplies the full range of services including fire and police protection, schools, utilities, and mail service.[11] Even with the spread of controlled communities, this is not often the case.

Though federal constitutional protection may be lacking, private covenants may violate state constitutional provisions. This may occur either because the state constitution applies to private conduct, or if it requires state action, that the state courts use a less onerous test than the federal one.[12] In New Jersey, for example, the free speech guarantee in the state constitution protects against unreasonably restrictive conduct by private parties.[13] Also, the right of privacy guarantee of the

---

8. See also Evans v. Abney, 396 U.S. 435, 90 S.Ct. 628, 24 L.Ed.2d 634 (1970), where the Court arguably endorsed the distinction by upholding a state court dissolution of a trust that had given land to a city on the basis that it operate it in a racially discriminatory manner. The property reverted to the heirs of the settlor.

9. 326 U.S. 501, 66 S.Ct. 276, 90 L.Ed. 265 (1946). A theory somewhat related to the company town theory is that a symbiotic relationship or close nexus exists between a private community and a town so that state action might be found. See Jackson v. Metropolitan Edison Co., 419 U.S. 345, 95 S.Ct. 449, 42 L.Ed.2d 477 (1974). State v. Kolcz, 114 N.J.Super. 408, 276 A.2d 595 (1971), may reflect application of such a theory.

10. See Hudgens v. National Labor Relations Board, 424 U.S. 507, 96 S.Ct. 1029, 47 L.Ed.2d 196 (1976).

11. See Katharine Rosenberry, The Application of Federal and State Constitu-

tions to Condominiums, Cooperatives, and Planned Developments, 19 Real Prop.Prob. & Trust J. 1, 23 (1984). *Marsh* was used in State v. Kolcz, supra note 9, to force a gated planned retirement community to allow outsiders to exercise First Amendment rights in seeking petition signers. Preceding *Hudgens*, supra note 10, the holding is questionable.

12. See Laguna Publishing Co. v. Golden Rain Foundation of Laguna Hills, 131 Cal.App.3d 816, 182 Cal.Rptr. 813 (1982) (community not a company town under *Marsh*, but state action found under state constitution to provide free speech and press right). See also Park Redlands Covenant Control Committee v. Simon, 181 Cal. App.3d 87, 226 Cal.Rptr. 199 (1986) (municipal insistence on retention of private anti-child covenant created state action for California's right of privacy).

13. Guttenberg Taxpayers and Rentpayers Ass'n v. Galaxy Towers Condominium Ass'n, 297 N.J.Super. 404, 688 A.2d 156 (1996).

California constitution applies to private conduct.[14]

§ 15.11 Legislative and Judicial Public Policy Constraints

A. Federal Statutes

The existence of federal civil rights statutes diminishes the need to find a direct constitutional basis to complain about arbitrary or discriminatory enforcement of private covenants. These statutes apply to private covenants in both racial and non-racial contexts without the need for state action.

The Civil Rights Act of 1866, § 1982 of title 42 of the United States Code provides, in part, that:

> All citizens of the United States shall have the same right as is enjoyed by white citizens * * * to * * * purchase [or] lease * * * real * * * property.[1]

In Jones v. Alfred H. Mayer Company,[2] the Court held the statute constitutional under the Thirteenth Amendment, which has no state action requirement. While *Mayer* dealt with a refusal to sell, the statute also bars an effort to enforce a private racial covenant to block a sale of property. Though the language of the statute refers to the manner of transfer and not use, the Court has held that the right to purchase language of the statute includes the right to be free from race-based private covenants.[3]

While race-based covenants are not used in real estate transactions today,[4] racial discrimination has not disappeared and can be accomplished by discriminatory application of facially neutral covenants. One instance when racial discrimination may occur is where a community association has a right of first refusal to purchase any lot or unit offered for sale. Though the covenant is facially neutral, if the association or a member exercises the right based on the prospective purchaser's color, it will violate § 1982.[5]

While § 1982 is limited in that it applies only to racial discrimination and only protects citizens,[6] the Fair Housing Act is broader. It

---

14. Nahrstedt v. Lakeside Village Condominium Ass'n., 8 Cal.4th 361, 878 P.2d 1275, 33 Cal.Rptr.2d 63 (1994); Hill v. National Collegiate Athletic Assn., Cal.4th 1, 20, 7 Cal.4th 1, 26 Cal.Rptr.2d 834, 865 P.2d 633 (1994); Park Redlands Covenant Control Committee v. Simon, 181 Cal. App.3d 87, 226 Cal.Rptr. 199, 205 (1986).

§ 15.11

1. 42 U.S.C.A. § 1982.

2. 392 U.S. 409, 88 S.Ct. 2186, 20 L.Ed.2d 1189 (1968).

3. Hurd v. Hodge, 334 U.S. 24, 68 S.Ct. 847, 92 L.Ed. 1187 (1948). See also City of Memphis v. Greene, 451 U.S. 100, 120, 101 S.Ct. 1584, 1596, 67 L.Ed.2d 769 (1981).

4. They still appear in older deeds in the chain of title of many properties.

5. See Phillips v. Hunter Trails Community Ass'n, 685 F.2d 184 (7th Cir.1982) (conduct violated the Fair Housing Act as well).

6. The racial "white citizens" language is applied in a historical, not anthropological, context. See Shaare Tefila Congregation v. Cobb, 481 U.S. 615, 107 S.Ct. 2019, 95 L.Ed.2d 594 (1987) (Jews protected by act, since, in 1866 when § 1982 enacted, it was

covers discrimination based on race, color, religion, sex, familial status, national origin, and handicap.[7] The Act also protects "any person." It does not require citizenship. The Act makes it illegal "to refuse to sell or rent * * * or otherwise make unavailable or deny"[8] a dwelling on the basis of the protected categories. That language encompasses "a wide array of housing practices, [including] restrictive covenants."[9] Litigation over restrictive covenants under the Act arises most frequently with respect to efforts by neighbors to block or close down group homes for the mentally retarded[10] or for others protected under the Act's "handicap" provisions.[11] The Fair Housing Act, covered in detail elsewhere in this treatise,[12] also applies to private conduct without state action.[13]

B. State Statutes and Common Law

Private restrictions that are contrary to public policy as expressed by state statute[14] or judicial decision[15] are unenforceable. Several states, for example, have statutes that declare void private covenants that preclude the use of property for group homes or communal living arrangements for disabled persons.[16] Some statutes may only apply prospectively.[17] If the ban applies retroactively, a question that arises is whether legislation can validly terminate preexisting property and contract rights without running afoul of the takings and contract clauses of the constitution. Courts have differed in their responses. While some courts have found or assumed that such a law wrongfully impairs

intended to protect persons from discrimination based on ancestral or ethnic characteristics).

7. Section 1982 has some advantages. It applies to all property transactions, real and personal, not just housing. And, unlike the Fair Housing Act, it has no exemptions.

8. 42 U.S.C.A. § 3604(a).

9. Casa Marie, Inc. v. Superior Court of Puerto Rico, 988 F.2d 252, 256 (1st Cir. 1993).

10. Deep East Texas Regional Mental Health and Mental Retardation Services, 877 S.W.2d 550 (Tex.App.1994); Broadmoor San Clemente Homeowners Ass'n, 25 Cal. App.4th 1, 30 Cal.Rptr.2d 316 (1994); Rhodes v. Palmetto Pathway Homes, Inc., 303 S.C. 308, 400 S.E.2d 484 (1991).

11. Hill v. Community of Damien of Molokai, 121 N.M. 353, 911 P.2d 861 (1996) (AIDS care home); Casa Marie, Inc. v. Superior Court of Puerto Rico, 988 F.2d 252 (1st Cir.1993) (elder care facility).

12. See supra § 4.7 and § 6.8.

13. Williams v. Matthews Co., 499 F.2d 819 (8th Cir.1974) (FHA as applied to racial discrimination based on Thirteenth Amendment); Morgan v. HUD, 985 F.2d 1451 (10th Cir.1993) (FHA and FHAA based on commerce clause).

14. See Hoye v. Shepherds Glen Land Co., 753 S.W.2d 226 (Tex.App.1988) (statute voiding private covenants that allow only wood shingles found not applicable).

15. McMillan v. Iserman, 120 Mich. App. 785, 327 N.W.2d 559 (1982) (covenant excluding group homes contrary to public policy as determined by court).

16. See, e.g., N.C.Gen.Stat. § 168–22. See also Westwood Homeowners Ass'n v. Tenhoff, 155 Ariz. 229, 745 P.2d 976 (Ariz. App.1987) (restrictive covenant void under state developmental disabilities act); Overlook Farms Home Ass'n v. Alternative Living Services, 143 Wis.2d 485, 422 N.W.2d 131 (Wis.App.1988) (retroactive application of statute voiding covenant did not violate contracts clause).

In some states these statutes expressly apply only to zoning ordinances. Mains Farm Homeowners Ass'n v. Worthington, 121 Wash.2d 810, 854 P.2d 1072 (1993) (interpreting Wash.Rev.Code Ann. § 70.128.175 (2)).

17. Barrett v. Lipscomb, 194 Cal. App.3d 1524, 240 Cal.Rptr. 336 (1987) (court refused to read California statute as applying retroactively where it expressly applied to transfers "on" or after January 1, 1979). But see Welsch v. Goswick, 130 Cal. App.3d 398, 181 Cal.Rptr. 703 (1982).

contract rights and constitutes a taking,[18] the view more likely to prevail under current constitutional doctrine is that no taking occurs because the loss of the right to enforce the covenant is but a small part of the landowner's bundle of rights. Furthermore, the loss of the covenant is likely not total since it will usually still be of value to bar other uses, such as commercial uses, not covered by the statute. A similar rationale is used to validate such statutes under the contract clause.[19]

Covenants are also subjected to a reasonableness test. Common law generally imposes the reasonableness limitation, though some states do so by statute.[20] The test in fact, if not in name, is one of substantive due process: a covenant will be invalidated if it is arbitrary or capricious and bears no reasonable relationship to the purposes of the association.[21] In Chateau Village North Condominium Association v. Jordan,[22] for example, the court held a blanket policy against keeping pets arbitrary.[23] In Rhue v. Cheyenne Homes, Inc. the court subjected an architectural compatibility covenant to a test of reasonableness.[24] Examining the reasons given by the review board, the court upheld the refusal to permit a Spanish-style house in an area of ranch style and split level houses.[25] The common law policy against restraints on alienation may also be used to deny enforcement to provisions in condominium and homeowner association bylaws that restrict the ability of members to convey their interest in property.[26]

§ 15.12 Public Use of Private Restrictions for Preservation Purposes

Many preservation interests can be accomplished by private land restrictions. These include land preserved for agricultural use, historical

18. Clem v. Christole, Inc., 548 N.E.2d 1180 (Ind.App.1990), affirmed on contract clause grounds, 582 N.E.2d 780 (Ind.1991).

19. Deep East Texas Regional Mental Health and Mental Retardation Services, 877 S.W.2d 550, 566 (Tex.App.1994) (police power overrides contract); Overlook Farms Home Ass'n v. Alternative Living Services, 143 Wis.2d 485, 422 N.W.2d 131 (Wis.App. 1988); Westwood Homeowners Association v. Tenhoff, 155 Ariz. 229, 745 P.2d 976, 983 (1987).

20. See Vernon's Tex.Prop. Code Ann. § 202.004(a) that provides that a covenant "is presumed reasonable unless the court determines by a preponderance of the evidence that the exercise of discretionary authority was arbitrary, capricious, or discriminatory."

21. See supra § 10.12.

22. 643 P.2d 791 (Colo.App.1982). See also Villas at Hidden Lakes Condominiums Ass'n v. Geupel Const. Co., Inc., 174 Ariz. 72, 847 P.2d 117 (1992) (unreasonable to make late fee charge retroactive); Trieweiler v. Spicher, 254 Mont. 321, 838 P.2d 382

(1992); Makeever v. Lyle, 125 Ariz. 384, 609 P.2d 1084, 1088 (Ariz.App.1980).

23. But see Nahrstedt v. Lakeside Village Condominium Ass'n.,8 Cal.4th 361, 878 P.2d 1275, 33 Cal.Rptr.2d 63 (1994) (covenant against pets valid).

24. Rhue v. Cheyenne Homes, Inc., 168 Colo. 6, 449 P.2d 361 (1969). In passing, the court mentioned due process as a basis for its rule, but offered no explanation as to the state action requirement.

25. See also McHuron v. Grand Teton Lodge Co., 899 P.2d 38 (Wyo.1995).

26. See Northwest Real Estate Co. v. Serio, 156 Md. 229, 144 A. 245 (1929); Mountain Springs Ass'n of New Jersey Inc. v. Wilson, 81 N.J.Super. 564, 196 A.2d 270 (N.J.Super.Ch.1963). But see Gale v. York Center Community Cooperative, Inc., 21 Ill.2d 86, 171 N.E.2d 30 (1960) (covenant proper which allowed the cooperative to redeem a membership within a 12 month period at a price fixed by independent appraisal or negotiation if it found a proposed transfer unacceptable).

sites, environmentally sensitive lands, wilderness, and open space for aesthetic purposes. In recent years, government agencies and private groups have used such restrictions to preserve more than four million acres of land.[1]

Generally, governments may acquire conservation easements by purchase, gift, or by eminent domain.[2] Acquisition of a limited interest, rather than the fee, has the advantage of reducing the cost to the acquirer and of keeping the land in productive, although limited, use. From the government perspective this provides a continued, if diminished, tax revenue. From the private perspective, when the states takes the interest involuntarily by eminent domain, the ability to retain possession and use the property for limited purposes may be of some solace to the condemnee.

While fitting these interests within common law devices such as covenants, equitable servitudes and easements is easy, there is reluctance to do so since each may pose problems of enforcement. The arrangements often employ language of promise, but if styled as a negative covenant or equitable servitude, they will not be enforceable against subsequent transferees of the burdened land if, as often happens, the covenant is in gross. Rejection of the often criticized rule that calls for a dominant estate, or a liberal definition of the dominant estate would overcome the problem.[3] The public interest in preservation ought to counter any concern with the restraint on alienability, but if a dominant estate is needed, it is not a difficult stretch to find that highway land benefits aesthetically by restrictions on adjacent land or that an agreement limiting land to agricultural use benefits other undeveloped land in the community. Still, the specter of the anti-in gross rule is a deterrent. Potential privity problems also arise if the arrangement is treated as a covenant.[4]

A better, but not risk-free, option is to treat the interest as a negative easement in gross. There is no problem with the burden passing to a transferee of the servient estate. Negative easements, however, may be limited in subject matter to the four categories allowed at early common law.[5] There is also the common law rule that may persist in

---

§ 15.12

1. Frederico Cheever, Public Good and Private Magic in the Law of Land Trusts and Conservation Easements: A Happy Present and a Troubled Future, 73 Denv. L.Rev. 1077, 1087 (1996) (citing 1994 study). See also John L. Hollingshead, Conservation Easements: A Flexible Tool for Land Preservation, 3 Envtl.Law. 319 (1997); Melissa W. Baldwin, Conservation Easements: A Viable Tool for Land Preservation, 32 Land & Water L.Rev. 89 (1997); Netherton, Environmental Conservation and Historic Preservation Through Recorded Land Use Agreements, 14 Real Prop., Prob. and Trust J. 340 (1979). For a discussion of the use of restrictive covenants for

historic preservation purposes, see supra § 12.8.

2. Kamrowski v. State, 31 Wis.2d 256, 142 N.W.2d 793 (1966). In a few states, eminent domain for such easements is prohibited. See, e.g., Oregon Rev.Stat. § 271.725 (1). See John W. Bruce & James W. Ely, Jr., The Law of Easements and Licenses in Land ¶ 12.02 (Rev.ed.1995).

3. Thomas E. Roberts, Promises Respecting Land Use: Can Benefits be Held in Gross, 51 Mo.L.Rev. 933, 959–965 (1986).

4. See discussion supra § 15.4.

5. Cheever, supra note 1, at 1080.

some states that the benefit of the easement in gross is not assignable.[6] Thus, if the Nature Conservancy acquires an easement in gross but wishes to transfer enforcement rights to a governmental agency, it could not do so.

The label "conservation easement" has grown to be the most commonly used term, but the enforceability of the arrangement, regardless of labels, may still turn on how a court views the matter in light of the common law rules noted above.[7] To promote use of conservation efforts, several states have passed statutes dispensing with the common law requirements. A North Carolina act, for example, provides that:

> (a) No conservation or preservation agreement shall be unenforceable because of
>
>> (1) Lack of privity of estate or contract, or
>>
>> (2) Lack of benefit to particular land or person, or
>>
>> (3) The assignability of the benefit to another holder as defined in this Article.[8]

Other states have statutes authorizing conservation agreements without regard to how they are named.[9]

§ 15.13 Public Use of Private Restrictions to Complement Zoning

Restrictive covenants may be used by a municipality to complement zoning ordinances and provide individualized treatment to an area for which a zoning change is sought. For example, a municipality may reclassify land to a less restricted use if the applicant for rezoning agrees to special limitations on the use of the rezoned property that are not imposed on other land included in the same classification. The municipality and the landowner will execute and record an agreement complying with the statute of frauds.

The process is not recommended. First, neighbors may challenge it as contract zoning,[1] resulting in a declaration either that the rezoning stands but the covenant is void as ultra vires, or if the covenant is seen as tainting the entire process, that the rezoning itself is void. While a few courts have approved the device as a legitimate manner of exercising the zoning power and achieving flexibility,[2] it may result in uncertainty

6. See list of states adhering to this rule in Hollingshead, supra note 1, at 361, n.41.

7. Bruce & Ely, supra note 2.

8. N.C.Gen.Stat. § 121–38.

9. See, e.g., Alaska Stat. §§ 34.17.030, 17.040(a); Ariz.Rev. Stat. § 33–276; Fla. Stat.Ann. § 704.06(2).

§ 15.13

1. Hartnett v. Austin, 93 So.2d 86 (Fla. 1956); Baylis v. Baltimore, 219 Md. 164, 148

A.2d 429 (1959); V. F. Zahodiakin Eng'r Corp. v. Zoning Bd. of Adjustment of City of Summit, 8 N.J. 386, 86 A.2d 127 (1952). See supra § 5.11 for discussion of contract and conditional zoning.

2. Sylvania Elec. Prod., Inc. v. Newton, 344 Mass. 428, 183 N.E.2d 118 (1962); Bucholz v. Omaha, 174 Neb. 862, 120 N.W.2d 270 (1963); Church v. Town of Islip, 8 N.Y.2d 254, 203 N.Y.S.2d 866, 168 N.E.2d 680 (1960).

about how the land can be used since one looking at the zoning records alone might find no reference to the covenant.[3]

A better approach, if the jurisdiction recognizes conditional zoning as valid, is to put the restriction in the rezoning ordinance. Not only is it discoverable by those examining the records in the zoning office, but the publicity attendant to making it part of the rezoning amendment detracts from the perception of wrongdoing that may arise when the parties bury the restriction in the private land records. If the state has not recognized conditional zoning, there are other ways to achieve flexibility.[4]

A similar process that in form may avoid the contract zoning problem has the developer execute a covenant to the objecting neighbors.[5] The covenant limits use more strictly than the new rezoning classification and should be enforceable by the owner of the neighboring land against the developer and subsequent purchasers.[6] A court, however, might find that silencing the neighbors by purchase is contrary to public policy and therefore unenforceable, or that the covenant tainted the rezoning, resulting in its invalidation.

Where private parties enter into an otherwise valid covenant, a city might be able to enforce the covenant although it was not a party to the covenant by way of third-party beneficiary principles.[7] While the common law might support such a suit, a statute authorizing the suit helps. A Wisconsin statute, for example, allows for public enforcement if a covenant was imposed by demand of the public body, or if the agreement names a public body as a beneficiary of the promise.[8]

A Texas statute provides that municipalities that do not have zoning may sue to enjoin or abate violations of recorded private restrictions.[9] The legislation gives cities like Houston, which do not have zoning, a method for exerting limited police power control over land use. Questions have been raised as to the constitutionality of the Texas act, the most serious being that it represents an unlawful delegation of legislative authority to the nongovernmental parties who created the restriction.[10] Objections have also been raised that the device represents control

3. Haymon v. City of Chattanooga, 513 S.W.2d 185 (Tenn.App.1973) (owners of land entered into a covenant with board of zoning appeals that if the board would rezone the land, the owners would maintain a buffer zone of 200 feet and subsequent owners, without knowledge of the covenant, obtained amendment reducing the buffer zone to 100 feet, the covenant, the ordinance enacted in consideration thereof, and the amending ordinance were void as against public policy); Cederberg v. City of Rockford, 8 Ill.App.3d 984, 291 N.E.2d 249 (1972).

4. See supra § 4.15.

5. See, e.g., Johnson v. Myers, 226 Ga. 23, 172 S.E.2d 421 (1970).

6. But see Johnson v. Myers, 226 Ga. 23, 172 S.E.2d 421 (1970) (covenant not enforceable due to lack of horizontal privity). Of course, horizontal privity can be created by a straw conveyance.

7. See State ex rel Zupancic v. Schimenz, 46 Wis.2d 22, 174 N.W.2d 533 (1970) (covenant expressly provided that the restrictions were for the benefit of the city).

8. Wis.Stat. § 236.293.

9. Vernon's Ann.Tex.Civ.Stat. (§ 230.003), applied in Davis v. City of Houston, 869 S.W.2d 493 (Tex.App.1993).

10. See John C. Allen, Municipal Enforcement of Deed Restrictions: An Alternative to Zoning, 9 Hous.L.Rev. 816 (1972);

without planning and that enforcement of private restrictive covenants without planning or standards can be no better than haphazard.[11]

Restrictive covenants also play a role in public land use planning in that planners may be able to achieve objectives beyond the scope of their regulatory powers by persuading developers to include restrictive covenants in the deeds to property contained in a subdivision. If the government requires the covenants, the contract zoning issued discussed above applies. In instances when the police power is found not to justify certain controls, courts have encouraged landowners to enter into private schemes to achieve their goals.[12]

Redevelopment agencies may impose restrictions on property returned to private uses in the implementation of an urban renewal project. Enforcement problems, however, may arise after the public agency disposes of land that benefits from the restriction. In those jurisdictions that hold that the benefit of a covenant cannot be held in gross, the agency cannot enforce a covenant unless it retains some land that the covenant benefits.[13]

§ 15.14 Conflict Between Private Restrictions and Zoning

Property may be subject to private restrictions and zoning controls that differ in the uses they allow.[1] For example, a prior covenant may restrict property to a residential use while a subsequent zoning ordinance allows a business use.[2] In that event, courts universally hold that the ordinance does not abrogate the restrictive covenant.[3] A would-be violator of a covenant cannot seek refuge behind the permission of zoning authorities. Thus, where a restrictive covenant and zoning ordinance both established thirty foot setbacks and the city granted a

Comment, Houston's Invention of Necessity—An Unconstitutional Substitute for Zoning? 21 Baylor L.Rev. 307 (1969); Municipal Enforcement of Private Restrictive Covenants: An Innovation in Land–Use Control, 44 Texas L.Rev. 741 (1966).

11. Comment, Municipal Enforcement of Private Restrictive Covenants: An Innovation in Land–Use Control, 44 Texas L.Rev. 741 (1966). The author also provides the historical background for Houston's refusal to adopt a zoning ordinance and the resulting necessity for such legislation. But cf. Robert C. Ellickson, Alternatives to Zoning, 40 U.Chi.L.Rev. 681 (1973) (proposing greater reliance on private nuisance actions for damages).

12. National Land And Investment Co. v. Kohn, 419 Pa. 504, 215 A.2d 597 (1965) (declaring invalid a township's efforts to preserve the historical setting of older homes by imposing a four acre minimum lot size, court intimated that the private land-

owners could join together to protect their land through private covenants).

13. See discussion supra § 15.6.

§ 15.14

1. Lawrence Berger, Conflicts Between Zoning Ordinances and Restrictive Covenants: A Problem in Land Use Policy, 43 Neb.L.Rev. 449 (1964). See also Comment, Resolving a Conflict—Ohana Zoning & Private Covenants, 6 U.Haw.L.Rev. 177 (1984).

2. See Dolan v. Brown, 338 Ill. 412, 170 N.E. 425 (1930).

3. McDonald v. Emporia–Lyon Co. Joint Bd. of Zoning App., 10 Kan.App.2d 235, 697 P.2d 69 (1985); Lidke v. Martin, 31 Colo.App. 40, 500 P.2d 1184 (1972); Rofe v. Robinson, 415 Mich. 345, 329 N.W.2d 704 (1982); Singleterry v. City of Albuquerque, 96 N.M. 468, 632 P.2d 345 (1981); City of Gatesville v. Powell, 500 S.W.2d 581 (Tex. Civ.App.1973); Bluett v. County of Cook, 19 Ill.App.2d 172, 153 N.E.2d 305 (1958).

variance from the ordinance, the neighbors could still enforce the set-back through the covenant.[4] A number of courts, while following this general rule, have admitted evidence of the zoning ordinance to show a change in neighborhood conditions has occurred that would render enforcement of the covenant inequitable.[5]

Courts and commentators often say that in the event of conflict between public and private controls, the more restrictive of the two governs.[6] In most cases, however, there is no conflict. When a restrictive covenant requires residential use of the property and the zoning classification is commercial in a cumulative zoning scheme, there is technically no conflict between the private and the public restriction since residential use—as a "higher" use—is permitted in "lower" use zones.

In the case of conflict, where, for example, a lot is privately restricted to residential use but is zoned for exclusive commercial use, the police power will prevail.[7] Some courts have questioned whether a refusal to enforce the covenant would be an unconstitutional impairment of contract rights,[8] but usually the strength of the public purpose behind the zoning law is likely to justify any impairment of contract.[9] A property owner might also argue that a ruling giving effect to the ordinance is a taking of property requiring compensation.[10] The issue has arisen most often with statutes that retroactively void covenants that exclude group homes. The mere fact that covenants are property rights does not establish a regulatory taking. As discussed above, the issue of whether a taking occurs is usually not measured by reference to the loss of a single property right, but by the property as a whole.[11]

§ 15.15 Condemnation

Public agencies frequently acquire less than fee interests in land, such as covenants and easements.[1] They also acquire land burdened by

4. McDonald v. Emporia–Lyon Co. Joint Bd. of Zoning App., 10 Kan.App.2d 235, 697 P.2d 69 (1985).

5. Rofe v. Robinson, 415 Mich. 345, 329 N.W.2d 704 (1982); Key v. McCabe, 54 Cal.2d 736, 8 Cal.Rptr. 425, 356 P.2d 169 (1960); Wolff v. Fallon, 44 Cal.2d 695, 284 P.2d 802 (1955); Martin v. Weinberg, 205 Md. 519, 109 A.2d 576 (1954); Brideau v. Grissom, 369 Mich. 661, 120 N.W.2d 829 (1963); Hysinger v. Mullinax, 204 Tenn. 181, 319 S.W.2d 79 (1958).

6. See cases cited supra note 3.

7. Grubel v. MacLaughlin, 286 F.Supp. 24 (D.Virgin Islands 1968); Restatement of Property § 568 (1944); 8 E. McQuillin, Municipal Corporations § 25.09, at 36 (3rd rev. ed.1965).

8. Rofe v. Robinson, supra note 5, 329 N.W.2d at 708; Mains Farm Homeowners Ass'n v. Worthington, 121 Wash.2d 810, 854 P.2d 1072, 1078.

9. Deep East Texas Regional Mental Health and Mental Retardation Services, 877 S.W.2d 550, 566 (Tex.App.1994) (police power overrides contract); Overlook Farms Home Ass'n v. Alternative Living Services, 143 Wis.2d 485, 422 N.W.2d 131 (Wis.App. 1988); Westwood Homeowners Association v. Tenhoff, 155 Ariz. 229, 745 P.2d 976, 983 (1987). But see Minder v. Martin Luther Home Fdn., 582 N.E.2d 788 (Ind.1991).

10. Burger v. St. Paul, 241 Minn. 285, 64 N.W.2d 73 (1954).

11. See, e.g., Annison v. Hoover, 517 So.2d 420 (La.App.1987) (a takings claim based on loss of covenant by zoning requires showing of destruction of major portion of property's value). See supra Ch. 10.

§ 15.15

1. See generally John L. Hollingshead, Conservation Easements: A Flexible tool or Land Preservation, 3 Envtl.Law. 319 (1997).

such interests in favor of third parties.[2] In either case, whether the agency holds the benefit or burden of the restriction, its rights and duties generally are the same as those of private parties.[3] If the government condemns property burdened by a covenant or easement, generally it must abide by such restriction or condemn it and pay compensation.[4]

2. See infra Ch.16 regarding the acquisition of restricted property by eminent domain.

3. See City of Reno v. Matley, 79 Nev. 49, 378 P.2d 256 (1963).

4. See infra Ch. 16.

Chapter 16

THE POWER OF EMINENT DOMAIN

Analysis

I. INTRODUCTION

§ 16.1 The Power of Eminent Domain

The federal and state governments possess the inherent power, as sovereigns, to take property for public use.[1] Local governments possess no inherent eminent domain power, but they are generally delegated the power by state legislatures.[2] While many courts strictly construe legislative grants of the power to condemn,[3] some state constitutions may confer eminent domain power on municipalities through home rule provisions.[4]

The Fifth Amendment's provision that "private property [shall not] be taken for public use, without just compensation" limits the power of eminent domain. While the Supreme Court did not apply the Fifth Amendment to the states until 1897,[5] by that time state constitutions or judicial concepts of "natural justice" had imposed similar limitations on all state governments.[6]

§ 16.1

1. Cherokee Nation v. Southern Kansas Ry. Co., 135 U.S. 641, 10 S.Ct. 965, 34 L.Ed. 295 (1890); Boise Cascade Corp. v. Board of Forestry, 325 Or. 185, 935 P.2d 411 (1997) (Eminent domain is inherent power of a sovereign state); Gober v. Stubbs, 682 So.2d 430 (Ala.1996).

2. See J. Juergensmeyer and J. Wadley, 1 Florida Land Use and Growth Management Law § 2.02 (1997). See also Richardson v. City and County of Honolulu, 76 Hawai'i 46, 868 P.2d 1193 (1994) (municipality has no inherent power of eminent domain and may exercise only those powers which have been delegated); Sinas v. City of Lansing, 382 Mich. 407, 411, 170 N.W.2d 23, 25 (1969); City of Fargo, Cass County v. Harwood Twp., 256 N.W.2d 694 (N.D.1977). See also 11 McQuillin, Municipal Corporations § 32.12 at 324 (3d ed.1991).

3. Richardson v. City and County of Honolulu, 76 Hawai'i 46, 868 P.2d 1193, 1223 (1994) (strong policy against lightly allowing local governmental bodies to exercise the inherently sovereign power of eminent domain).

4. Matter of Village of Poland to Acquire Certain Real Property, 224 A.D.2d 933, 637 N.Y.S.2d 575 (1996) (constitution delegates state's inherent power of eminent domain to municipalities but only within the bounds of the municipality); City of Carbondale v. Yehling, 96 Ill.2d 495, 499, 71 Ill.Dec. 683, 685 451 N.E.2d 837, 839 (1983); City of Wilmington v. Lord, 340 A.2d 182 (Del.Super.1975).

5. There is some dispute about the history of incorporation of the public use and just compensation clause. In recent years, the Court frequently has cited Chicago, B. & Q.R. Co. v. Chicago, 166 U.S. 226, 239, 17 S.Ct. 581, 585, 41 L.Ed. 979 (1897), as the source of incorporation of the Fifth Amendment.Dolan v. Tigard, 512 U.S. 374, n. 5, 384, 114 S.Ct. 2309, 2316, 129 L.Ed.2d 304 (1994); Hawaii Housing Authority v. Midkiff, 467 U.S. 229, 104 S.Ct. 2321, 81 L.Ed.2d 186 (1984). However, in dissent in *Dolan*, Justice Stevens notes that the 1897 *Chicago, B. & Q. Railroad* case did not mention the Fifth Amendment, but rather was decided on substantive due process grounds. *Dolan*, 512 U.S. 374, 405, 114 S.Ct. 2309, 2326.

6. See Raleigh & Gaston R.R. Co. v. Davis, 19 N.C. 431 (1837).

Eminent domain plays an important role in the implementation of land use planning objectives, particularly in the acquisition of land for urban renewal projects and industrial parks. States also employ eminent domain to acquire historic sites,[7] and to purchase conservation easements for open space, scenic views, and agricultural preservation.[8] The dominant role of eminent domain in land use law, however, is indirect, occurring through excessive exercises of the police power.

§ 16.2 The Eminent Domain Power and the Police Power

Courts and commentators have long debated the relationship between the police power and the power of eminent domain. Many commentators see them as distinct. The police power is a power of regulation while the power of eminent domain, in a narrow sense, is one of the taking, seizing, or conscription of private property for use by the government. Yet, as we discuss in greater detail in Chapter 10,[1] the Supreme Court has read the "taking" language of the Fifth Amendment broadly to hold that exercises of the police power that go "too far" or otherwise impose an unfair burden on a landowner may be treated as exercises of the power of eminent domain.[2] It is these regulatory or constructive takings, rather than direct condemnations, that are of the greatest relevance to land use.

II. PROPERTY, PUBLIC USE AND CONDEMNATION ISSUES

§ 16.3 Compensable Property Rights

The "property" for which compensation must be paid includes personal[1] as well as real property, future[2] as well as present interests, intangible[3] as well as tangible property, and nonpossessory[4] as well as possessory interests.

A. Covenants

Courts have differed over whether compensation must be paid to one who loses the right to enforce the benefit of a covenant or equitable

---

7. See supra § 12.9.

8. See supra § 13.12 and § 15.12.

§ 16.2

1. See supra § 10.4.

2. See supra § 10.5.

§ 16.3

1. United States v. Commodities Trading Corp., 339 U.S. 121, 70 S.Ct. 547, 94 L.Ed. 707 (1950).

2. Stubbs v. United States, 21 F.Supp. 1007 (M.D.N.C.1938) (life tenancy, remainder). But if the future interest is remote and unlikely to vest, only nominal damages may be awarded. See People of Puerto Rico v. United States, 132 F.2d 220 (1st Cir. 1942) and Board of Transp. v. Charlotte Park and Recreation Commission, 38

N.C.App. 708, 248 S.E.2d 909 (1978). But see Ink v. City of Canton, 4 Ohio St.2d 51, 212 N.E.2d 574 (1965) and State v. Independent School Dist. No. 31, 266 Minn. 85, 123 N.W.2d 121 (1963).

3. Ruckelshaus v. Monsanto Company, 467 U.S. 986, 104 S.Ct. 2862, 81 L.Ed.2d 815 (1984) (trade secrets); City of Oakland v. Oakland Raiders, 32 Cal.3d 60, 646 P.2d 835, 183 Cal.Rptr. 673 (1982) (football franchise). The takeover was held to violate the commerce clause in City of Oakland v. Oakland Raiders, 174 Cal.App.3d 414, 220 Cal. Rptr. 153 (1985).

4. City of San Gabriel v. Pacific Electric Railway Co., 129 Cal.App. 460, 18 P.2d 996 (1933) (easement).

servitude.[5] The trend, and likely the majority rule, is that compensation is due on the theory that an equitable servitude is a property right, analogous to an easement, the loss of which must be paid for by the condemning authority.[6] Other courts hold that real covenants and equitable servitudes are merely contractual rights cognizable in equity and do not constitute property interests to be compensated for when taken.[7] These courts reason that it would violate public policy to allow individuals by agreement to inconvenience or burden the governmental exercise of the power of eminent domain.

If one operates from the premise that the law should treat like interests in a like fashion, it should treat covenants like easements. The distinction between easements and covenants is difficult to draw in many instances, and the use of either may serve the same purpose.[8] Since easements are compensable, and since negative easements and negative covenants are often functional equivalents, it is reasonable to treat such covenants in the same manner as we treat easements.

If a state court recognizes the beneficial interest in a covenant or servitude as property, a statute declaring it void is not necessarily a taking. One example is a statute declaring void covenants that bar group homes for the disabled. Certain factors may militate against the finding of a taking. The covenant may still have value since it may be enforceable against other uses. Furthermore, the loss of the right of enforcement may leave other property rights in the benefited lot, which, considered as a whole, lessen the overall impact on the owner to the point that no taking results.[9]

B. Access as a Property Right

Courts recognize a right of access in property abutting a public street.[10] They also generally recognize a right to view, light, and air over that street.[11] The origin of these access rights is unclear. Some suggest

---

5. See supra Ch. 15 for discussion of law of private covenants.

6. Morley v. Jackson Redevelopment Auth., 632 So.2d 1284 (Miss.1994); United States v. Certain Land in City of Augusta, 220 F.Supp. 696 (D.Me.1963); Southern California Edison Co. v. Bourgerie, 9 Cal.3d 169, 107 Cal.Rptr. 76, 507 P.2d 964 (1973). See Annot. 4 A.L.R.3d 1137 (1965).

7. Arkansas State Highway Commission v. McNeill, 238 Ark. 244, 381 S.W.2d 425 (1964); Ryan v. Town of Manalapan, 414 So.2d 193 (Fla.1982); Hospital Serv. Dist. No. 2 v. Dean, 345 So.2d 234 (La.App. 1977); State ex rel. Wells v. Dunbar, 142 W.Va. 332, 95 S.E.2d 457 (1956). See generally Case Note, Restrictive Covenants: Do They Apply to Public Bodies? 10 Fla.St. U.L.Rev. 667 (1983) (outlines majority and minority viewpoints).

8. See supra § 15.8.

9. See discussion supra § 15.14.

10. Brownlow v. O'Donoghue Bros., 276 F. 636 (D.C.Cir.1921); People v. Ricciardi, 23 Cal.2d 390, 144 P.2d 799 (1943).

11. St. Peter's Italian Church Syracuse v. State, 261 App.Div. 96, 24 N.Y.S.2d 759 (1941); State ex rel. Dep't of Highways v. Allison, 372 P.2d 850 (Okl.1962).

Easements of light, air, and access exist only to abutting public streets and not to abutting lands, unless conferred by grant. Thus, in the absence of statute or grant, public acts on other land, which diminish the value of neighboring land by obstructing light and air, does not result in a compensable taking of a property interest in the neighboring land. Rand v. Boston, 164 Mass. 354, 41 N.E. 484 (1895).

the state, in building a highway, intends to create property rights in the abutting property, or that by payment of taxes property owners acquire a property interest.[12] As Professor Stoebuck suggests, it may come down to a sense that it would be unfair to landlock someone by removing access.[13]

If governmental action results in a substantial loss of access, compensation is due.[14] Courts differ as to what constitutes a substantial loss, and cases vary widely among the states.[15] Generally, there is no right to have traffic pass by in any particular place nor is there a right to a commercially advantageous traffic flow.[16] Some courts, however, hold that the landowner has a right of access not only to the immediately abutting street, but also from that street to advantageous intersections and to the general system of streets. Therefore, compensation may be due when the closing of an intersection makes the abutting street a cul de sac.[17]

The interests of an abutting owner in a public way are subject to reasonable interference by police power action without compensation. For example, the public interest in safety and convenience is considered to outweigh the abutting owner's interests when it requires reasonable, temporary obstruction of the way during repairs.[18] Insertion of a median strip can also be done without compensation.[19]

C. Divided Fees

When a fee is divided into several interests all of which are compensable, such as a leasehold and a reversion, courts nonetheless value the property for purposes of eminent domain as an undivided fee. The interest holders then apportion the award according to their respective rights.[20] The rule is applied even though the aggregate value of the separate interests is greater than the value of the property as a whole, unless unusual circumstances justify a departure.[21]

---

12. Or, it may be based on necessity. See Riddle v. State Highway Comm'n, 184 Kan. 603, 339 P.2d 301, 307 (1959).

13. Id. at 736.

14. Rubano v. Dept. of Transp., 656 So.2d 1264 (Fla.1995); William B. Stoebuck, The Property Right of Access Versus the Power of Eminent Domain, 47 Tex.L.Rev. 733 (1969).

15. See Kurt H. Garber ,Note, Eminent Domain: when Does A Temporary Denial of Access Become a Compensable Taking? 25 U. Mem. L. Rev. 271 (1994); Roland F. Chase, Annot., Abutting Owner's Right to Damages for Limitation of Access Caused by Conversion of Conventional Road Into Limited–Access Highway, 42 A.L.R. 3d 13(1996).

16. Rubano v. Dept. of Transp., 656 So.2d 1264, 1267 (Fla.1995).

17. Bacich v. Board of Control, 23 Cal.2d 343, 144 P.2d 818 (1943) (right of access to the next intersecting street in both directions); Village of Winnetka v. Clifford, 201 Ill. 475, 66 N.E. 384 (1903).

18. Farrell v. Rose, 253 N.Y. 73, 170 N.E. 498 (1930).

19. People ex rel. Dep't of Pub. Works v. Ayon, 54 Cal.2d 217, 5 Cal.Rptr. 151, 352 P.2d 519 (1960), cert. denied 364 U.S. 827, 81 S.Ct. 65, 5 L.Ed.2d 55 (1960).

20. City of Ashland v. Price, 318 S.W.2d 861 (Ky.1958). Contra, Boston Chamber of Commerce v. Boston, 217 U.S. 189, 30 S.Ct. 459, 54 L.Ed. 725 (1910) where several interests (fee; easement of light, way, and air; and mortgage) in one piece of property had depressed each other in value.

21. Sowers v. Schaeffer, 155 Ohio St. 454, 99 N.E.2d 313 (1951).

§ 16.4 Public Use

The Fifth Amendment requires compensation for the taking of property for a "public use." While the phrase "public use" suggests physical use by the public, courts have interpreted it broadly to mean public purpose. Accordingly, the Supreme Court has held that any conceivable public purpose qualifies. The term "public use" is, the Court said, "coterminus with the scope of [the] sovereign's police powers."[1]

A. *Taking for a Public Purpose*

Judicial treatment of the public use limitation has taken some twists and turns. It was first interpreted as requiring that the taking further a broadly conceived public good. However, as the scope of governmental activity expanded and the unoccupied lands in both public and private domains dwindled, and as the exercise of the power of eminent domain became more frequent and more burdensome to the private sector, courts began to impose stricter limitations. By the middle of the nineteenth century, if there was no actual use by the public there was some likelihood a court would find no public use.[2] However, courts created exceptions to accommodate uses established in the earlier period, such as the mill acts that authorized a private riparian owner to build a mill dam interfering with a neighbor's riparian rights on payment of compensation for such interference.[3] Further exceptions to meet the country's changing needs were recognized so that the exceptions began to swallow the rule by the end of the nineteenth century. The twentieth century witnessed the virtual demise of the "physical use by the public" test.[4]

The expanded nature of the public use test is perhaps best told in the context of urban renewal where its use was justified first to remove slums, then to prevent blight of developed property, then to remove blight from undeveloped property and finally merely to improve the appearance of neighborhoods. Though urban renewal programs frequently transfer the property they condemn from one private person to another private person, the public use test is still met.[5] The public investment in the renewal property is often more than the resale price of the property, but courts have not regarded that as an improper gift of public property to private persons.

The two leading federal cases are Berman v. Parker[6] and Hawaii Housing Authority v. Midkiff.[7] In *Berman*, the Court upheld a condemnation for urban renewal purposes despite the fact that unblighted property would be taken from one private owner and sold to another. In

---

§ 16.4

1. Hawaii Housing Authority v. Midkiff, 467 U.S. 229, 240, 104 S.Ct. 2321, 2329, 81 L.Ed.2d 186 (1984).

2. Gravelly Ford Canal Co. v. Pope & Talbot Land Co., 36 Cal.App. 556, 178 P. 150 (1918).

3. Head v. Amoskeag Mfg. Co., 113 U.S. 9, 5 S.Ct. 441, 28 L.Ed. 889 (1885).

4. See Comment, The Public Use Limitation on Eminent Domain: An Advance Requiem, 58 Yale L.J. 599 (1949).

5. See Berman v. Parker, 348 U.S. 26, 75 S.Ct. 98, 99 L.Ed. 27 (1954).

6. 348 U.S. 26, 75 S.Ct. 98, 99 L.Ed. 27 (1954).

7. 467 U.S. 229, 104 S.Ct. 2321, 81 L.Ed.2d 186 (1984).

Midkiff, the Court upheld Hawaii's land redistribution program. Land in Hawaii was concentrated in a few owners. To alleviate the evils of oligopolistic land ownership, the Hawaiian legislature created a system of forced sales of the residential property of large landowners.

The *Berman* Court reasoned that the exercise of the power of eminent domain was simply a means to an end. So long as the objective of the action was within the government's police power, the means of implementation did not matter. In *Midkiff*, the Court, relying on *Berman*, put it bluntly: the public use requirement of the Fifth Amendment is "coterminus with the scope of [the] sovereign's police powers,"[8] and any conceivable public purpose suffices. While *Berman* and *Midkiff* both involved instances where the market was not functioning properly, the forceful language of the opinions leaves no reason to think that the eminent domain power is limited to such instances.

Under some state constitutions, the courts may read the public use requirement more narrowly, and the requirement that a taking be "necessary" may be added.[9] In contrast to the United States Supreme Court, which focuses on the reason for the taking rather than an examination of whom actually uses the property, some state courts examine the validity of a condemnation by looking at who may end up in possession. This increases the chances of the taking being disallowed.[10]

Condemnation for parking facilities and for commercial and industrial development has been the subject of controversy in state courts. Governments often seek to solve their parking problems by leasing parking garages constructed on a condemned site to private lessees. A number of courts have found parking projects to be a public use since they relieve congestion and reduce traffic hazards.[11] However, the public character of the use is considered removed when the primary objective is private gain rather than public need.[12] Governmental retention of little control over rates charged and operating rules may evidence an impermissible objective. The existence of too much floor area not associated with parking operations,[13] and the fact that the contract for building the garage and the lease have specifications peculiar to the needs of a particular bidder have been troublesome.[14]

Where government acquires unblighted land for an industrial or commercial enterprise, some state courts have been reluctant to find a

---

8. Id., 467 U.S. at 240, 104 S.Ct. at 2329.

9. See § 16.6 infra on necessity.

10. See, e.g., Karesh v. City Council of City of Charleston, 271 S.C. 339, 247 S.E.2d 342 (1978).

11. City and County of San Francisco v. Ross, 44 Cal.2d 52, 279 P.2d 529 (1955); Larsen v. City and County of San Francisco, 152 Cal.App.2d 355, 313 P.2d 959 (1957); State ex rel. Hawks v. Topeka, 176 Kan. 240, 270 P.2d 270 (1954).

12. City and County of San Francisco v. Ross and Larsen v. City and County of San Francisco, supra, note 11; Opinion of the Justices, 341 Mass. 738, 167 N.E.2d 745 (1960).

13. City and County of San Francisco v. Ross and Larsen v. City and County of San Francisco, supra note 11.

14. Denihan Enterprises v. O'Dwyer, 277 App.Div. 407, 100 N.Y.S.2d 512 (1950), affirmed 302 N.Y. 451, 99 N.E.2d 235 (1951). But see Foltz v. Indianapolis 234 Ind. 656, 130 N.E.2d 650 (1955).

public use. In Hogue v. Port of Seattle,[15] for example, the Port Authority was concerned about the status of the area as a one-industry city and attempted to achieve industrial balance by acquiring land for redevelopment and sale or lease to private industry. The court found that the Authority was condemning fully developed land because it believed it could devote the land to a better economic use and that such a condemnation was not for a public use.[16]

More recent cases allow for such economic planning. In Courtesy Sandwich Shop, Inc. v. Port of New York Authority,[17] the New York court upheld the constitutionality of condemnation of property for what was to become the World Trade Center to centralize New York City's foreign trade facilities. The court found facilitation of the flow of commerce and centralization of all incidental activity to be a public purpose. Thus, the condemnation power extended to property with activities functionally related to that purpose, and included the use of portions of structures otherwise devoted to project purposes for the production of incidental revenue for the expenses of the project.

In a highly controversial action, Detroit condemned a large and thriving neighborhood to transfer the land to General Motors to build a Cadillac factory.[18] The state supreme court upheld the taking, finding that the acquisition of property to bolster the local economy was a public use.

B. *Taking for Private Use*

Although the Constitution does not explicitly prohibit the taking of private property for private use, the Court reads it as doing so implicitly.[19] Even the payment of just compensation will not validate a private taking.[20] The source of the bar on private takings, however, is unclear.[21] In a number of cases, courts seem to assume that it is the Fifth Amendment's taking clause that proscribes private takings[22] but other authority points to the due process clause.[23] The difficulty in relying on

---

15. 54 Wash.2d 799, 341 P.2d 171 (1959).

16. But see, *Midkiff* supra note 8. See also City of Jamestown v. Leevers Supermarkets, Inc., 552 N.W.2d 365 (N.D.1996) (city could only take the property under the state constitution if economic growth was the primary purpose of the condemnation and no finding to that effect had been made and a remand was necessary).

17. 12 N.Y.2d 379, 240 N.Y.S.2d 1, 190 N.E.2d 402 (1963), appeal dismissed 375 U.S. 78, 84 S.Ct. 194, 11 L.Ed.2d 141 (1963), rehearing denied 375 U.S. 960, 84 S.Ct. 440, 11 L.Ed.2d 318 (1963).

18. Poletown Neighborhood Council v. Detroit, 410 Mich. 616, 304 N.W.2d 455 (1981).

19. See Hawaii Housing Authority v. Midkiff, 467 U.S. 229, 104 S.Ct. 2321, 81

L.Ed.2d 186 (1984), on remand 740 F.2d 15 (9th Cir.1984).

20. Thompson v. Consol. Gas Utilities Corp., 300 U.S. 55, 57 S.Ct. 364, 81 L.Ed. 510 (1937).

21. See Julius L. Sackman, 2A Nichols' The Law of Eminent Domain, §§ 7.01[3] to 7.01[5]a (3d rev.ed.1995).

22. Hawaii Housing Authority v. Midkiff, 467 U.S. 229, 104 S.Ct. 2321, 81 L.Ed.2d 186 (1984).

23. Davidson v. New Orleans, 96 U.S. (6 Otto) 97, 102, 24 L.Ed. 616 (1878). See also Calder v. Bull, 3 U.S. (3 Dall.) 386, 388, 1 L.Ed. 648 (1798) (private taking against "all reason and justice.") See discussion in Armendariz v. Penman, 75 F.3d 1311, 1324 (9th Cir.1996).

the Fifth Amendment is its plain language, which does not say that property can only be taken for public use. Rather, it provides that when government takes property for a public use, it must pay just compensation.[24] The source of the wrong is important since procedural differences exist between actions based on the takings clause and on the due process clause.[25]

§ 16.5 Judicial Review of Public Use

The constitutional limitation that a taking must be for a public use creates a justiciable issue, but a legislative declaration of public use generally bears a strong presumption of validity. As for the federal constitution, the Supreme Court has virtually ceded the power of judicial review. As the Court declared in Berman v. Parker[1] in 1954 and reiterated in Hawaii Housing Authority v. Midkiff[2] in 1984, there is a role for the courts but it is an "extremely narrow one. * * * [W]hen the legislature has spoken, the public interest has been declared in terms well-nigh conclusive."[3]

While state courts generally give some deference to legislative determinations of public use,[4] most make their own independent determinations. Some state constitutions declare the question to be a judicial one.[5] Courts that have the power may forcefully exercise it. The Mississippi Supreme Court, for example, holds that when the condemnee raises the issue of public use, the condemning authority has the burden of proof, and vague recitals will not suffice.[6] Some actions are more suspect than others. In Poletown Neighborhood Council v. Detroit,[7] for example, the court said that it would examine "with heightened scrutiny" takings that benefit a specific and identifiable private interest. In that case, however, General Motors was the beneficiary, and the condemnation withstood the court's heightened scrutiny.

24. See Jed Rubenfeld, Usings, 102 Yale L.J. 1077, 1119 (1993); William B. Stoebuck, A General Theory of Eminent Domain, 47 Wash.L.Rev. 553, 591 (1972).

25. Armendariz v. Penman, 75 F.3d 1311, 1324 (9th Cir.1996) (answer determines whether a claimed right is a specifically enumerated right, barring any resort to substantive due process under Graham v. Connor, 490 U.S. 386, 395, 109 S.Ct. 1865, 1871, 104 L.Ed.2d 443 (1989), or whether that right is itself a substantive due process right). In *Armendariz*, the plaintiffs apparently sought to use substantive due process to enable them to file suit in federal court since a Fifth Amendment taking claim would have to be brought in state court. See discussion supra §§ 10.10 and 10.12.

§ 16.5

1. Berman v. Parker, 348 U.S. 26, 75 S.Ct. 98, 99 L.Ed. 27 (1954).

2. Hawaii Housing Authority v. Midkiff, 467 U.S. 229, 104 S.Ct. 2321, 81 L.Ed.2d 186 (1984).

3. Id., 467 U.S. at 239, 104 S.Ct. at 2328.

4. See Dept. of Transp. v. Fortune Federal Savings and Loan Ass'n, 532 So.2d 1267 (Fla.1988).

5. Miss. Const. art.3, § 17; Neb. Const. art 1, § 21. See also Hogue v. Port of Seattle, 54 Wn.2d 799, 341 P.2d 171 (1959), decided under such a constitutional provision.

6. Morley v. Jackson Redevelopment Auth., 632 So.2d 1284 (Miss.1994). See also Burger v. City of Beatrice, 181 Neb. 213, 147 N.W.2d 784 (1967).

7. Poletown Neighborhood Council v. Detroit, 410 Mich. 616, 304 N.W.2d 455 (1981).

§ 16.6 Necessity and Bad Faith

State courts often say that takings must be for a public use *and* be necessary. The requirement of necessity may arise from express constitutional provision[1] or from statutory limitation.[2] In the absence of some such requirement, the concept of a taking being necessary is another way of saying a taking must be for a public use.[3] Condemning land for speculative or future use, for example, may not be a public use because it is presently unnecessary.[4]

In the absence of bad faith, questions of necessity, in the sense of the need for making a given public improvement, for adopting a particular plan for it, or for taking particular property, are considered matters for the discretion of the legislature.[5] In urban renewal, for example, the determination that a particular area is blighted and the definition of project boundaries are likely foreclosed from judicial examination.[6] In states where courts actively review the public use question and put the burden of showing such a use on the condemnor, the burden of proof that the taking is not necessary or is in bad faith is on the condemnee.[7]

Even where claims of fraud, bad faith, or abuse of discretion are judicially determined,[8] success is limited due to a reluctance by courts to second guess the authorities.[9] In Deerfield Park District v. Progress Development Corp.,[10] for example, where the taking was challenged as an

§ 16.6

1. See, e.g., La.Const. Art. 1, § 4; Mich. Const. Art. 13, § 2.

2. See, e.g., West's Ann.Cal.Civ.Proc. Code § 1230.010; Mich.Comp.Laws Ann. § 213.56.

3. See North Carolina State Highway Comm. v. Farm Equipment Co., 281 N.C. 459, 189 S.E.2d 272 (1972). See generally David McCord, 6A Powell on Real Property ¶ 876.18[2][ii][B] (R. Powell and P. Rohan eds.1991).

4. See discussion infra § 16. 7.

5. Note, "Necessity" in Eminent Domain Proceedings: Four Cases, 29 Mont. L.Rev. 69 (1967). A jury determination of necessity may be required by statute or constitution. E.g., Wis. Const. art. 11, § 2 once provided: "No municipal corporation shall take private property for public use, against the consent of the owner, without the necessity thereof being first established by the verdict of a jury."

6. Kaskel v. Impellitteri, 306 N.Y. 73, 115 N.E.2d 659 (1953), cert. denied 347 U.S. 934, 74 S.Ct. 629, 98 L.Ed. 1085 (1954); Davis v. Lubbock, 160 Tex. 38, 326 S.W.2d 699 (1959). In some states, statutes require that a declaration of necessity be adopted by the condemning authority. See West's Ann.Cal.Civ.Proc.Code § 1230.010.

7. Morley v. Jackson Redevelopment Auth., 632 So.2d 1284 (Miss.1994).

8. See, e.g., Mich.Comp.Laws Ann. § 213.56; State ex rel. Sharp v. 0.62033 Acres of Land, 49 Del. 174, 112 A.2d 857 (1955); Kaskel v. Impellitteri, 306 N.Y. 73, 115 N.E.2d 659 (1953), reargument denied, remittitur amended 306 N.Y. 609, 115 N.E.2d 832 (1953), cert. denied 347 U.S. 934, 74 S.Ct. 629, 98 L.Ed. 1085 (1954). Contra, People ex rel. Dept. of Pub. Works v. Chevalier, 52 Cal.2d 299, 340 P.2d 598 (1959). The legislative determination is conclusive under statutes affording conclusive effect to the condemning body's findings of necessity even if fraud, bad faith or abuse of discretion is alleged since to hold otherwise would thwart legislative purpose in making such determinations conclusive and would open the door to endless litigation. Federal courts have long held that "[i]n the absence of bad faith ... if the use is a public one, the necessity for the desired property as part thereof is not a question for judicial determination." Wilson v. United States, 350 F.2d 901, 907 (10th Cir.1965).

9. See, e.g., American Telephone and Telegraph Co. v. Proffitt, 903 S.W.2d 309 (Tenn.App.1995); Moskow v. Boston Redevelopment Authority, 349 Mass. 553, 210 N.E.2d 699 (1965), cert. denied 382 U.S. 983, 86 S.Ct. 558, 15 L.Ed.2d 472 (1966).

10. 26 Ill.2d 296, 186 N.E.2d 360 (1962), cert. denied 372 U.S. 968, 83 S.Ct. 1093, 10 L.Ed.2d 131(1963).

attempt to avoid racially integrated housing, the court refused to prevent the taking unless its sole and exclusive purpose was racially inspired.[11] Even where the land is not used for the public purpose asserted as the justification for its taking or the use is shifted from a public to a private use, the condemnee can only invalidate the previous condemnation by showing collateral and extrinsic fraud,[12] a difficult task.

Some authorities push beyond the limits of judicial tolerance. In Borough of Essex Fells v. Kessler Institute for Rehabilitation, Inc.,[13] bad faith doomed an attempt at acquiring land allegedly for public park purposes. A 68–acre site had been used, and was zoned, for educational purposes for 40 years. Kessler Institute acquired the site and proposed to use it for a rehabilitation facility for sixty persons. This did not sit well with many residents in Essex Fells, who began protests and held rallies to block the issuance of a permit. The town then decided to acquire the site for a public park. Kessler objected, saying the park purpose was a ruse.[14] The history of the battle over the permit lent credence to Kessler's claim. Also, the idea that park land was needed stretched credulity since Essex Fells was well endowed with parks.[15] While the court was reluctant to block the condemnation, noting that eminent domain decisions were within the "exclusive province" of the legislature, it would not tolerate bad faith. If the reason for the acquisition was beyond the law, the power of eminent domain could not be used. That was found to be the case.

§ 16.7 Excess and Future Condemnation

A. *Excess Condemnation: General Considerations*

There are three varieties of excess or future condemnation. A condemnor may seek to acquire more land than is absolutely necessary for an improvement for the purpose of (1) not leaving odd-shaped remnants of land, (2) taking abutting land to impose planning restrictions to protect the public improvement from an inharmonious environment, or (3) taking surplus land to recoup the expense of the project by selling the land at a profit after the completed project enhances the land's value.

As a rule, taking more land or a greater estate than needed is not permitted.[1] Application of the rule requires that a court define the scope

---

11. See § 10.4 supra.

12. Beistline v. San Diego, 256 F.2d 421 (9th Cir.1958), cert. denied 358 U.S. 865, 79 S.Ct. 96, 3 L.Ed.2d 98 (1958).

13. 289 N.J.Super. 329, 673 A.2d 856 (1995).

14. It clearly was. As one town official said " 'we've got to come up with a need the court will allow.' " Id.

15. National standards suggest that a town have from 6.25 to 10.5 acres of park land for each 1000 residents. Essex Fells had 64 acres per 1000 persons. Id.

§ 16.7

1. Silver Bow County v. Hafer, 166 Mont. 330, 532 P.2d 691 (1975); City of Charlotte v. Cook, 125 N.C.App. 205, 479 S.E.2d 503, rev. granted, 281 N.C. 459, 189 S.E.2d 272(1972). See also E. L. Strobin, Annot., Right to Condemn Property in Excess of Needs for a Particular Public Purpose, 6 A.L.R.3d 297 (1966).

of the project. A narrow focus on the land that the public use is to occupy as the land that is necessary will mean that land taken to create a safety or buffer zone for the project will be considered unnecessary. Not all condemnations for such so-called excess lands are invalid, particularly those that involve the remnant and protection purposes noted above. Unfavorable court decisions involving excess condemnation have led to constitutional amendments in some states expressly to authorize certain types of excess condemnation.[2]

B. Remnant Theory

Government may take land under the remnant theory to avoid leaving unusable patches of "blight" that will cause excessive severance damages.[3] California, for example, authorizes the taking of remnants when a city or county condemns land for a street or highway and would have to pay for the part taken plus severance damages in "an amount equal to the fair and reasonable value of the whole parcel."[4] Similarly, condemnors needing only an easement have been allowed to acquire a fee when underlying land is likely to be seriously affected, resulting in large damage awards.[5] Generally, however, the condemnor is limited to taking the minimum estate necessary to carry out the purpose.[6]

C. Protective Theory

Courts may allow the taking of additional property to protect the public improvement that is the primary focus of the condemnation. Thus, a court allowed the acquisition of negative easements on land abutting a highway to prevent structures from blocking views for safety purposes.[7] On the other hand, a court disallowed taking an extra strip of land alongside a strip condemned for a sidewalk.[8] The town asserted the extra land was for safety, but its proof did not hold up. No safety study had been done, and at one point the sidewalk had been narrowed to save some trees. The court found allowing an aesthetic purpose to override safety concerns to contradict the safety justification.

---

2. See People ex rel. Department of Public Works v. Superior Court of Merced County, 68 Cal.2d 206, 436 P.2d 342, 65 Cal.Rptr. 342 (1968) (discussing the now repealed Art. 1, § 14½, West's Cal.Const.). See West's Ann.Cal. Code Civil Proc. § 1240.410, authorizing excess condemnation for remnants. See also Matheson, Excess Condemnation in California: Proposals for Statutory and Constitutional Change, 42 So.Cal.L.Rev. 421 (1969). Note, Excess Condemnation—To take or Not to Take—A Functional Analysis, 15 N.Y.L.F. 119 (1969).

3. People ex rel. Dep't of Pub. Works v. Superior Court, 68 Cal.2d 206, 65 Cal.Rptr. 342, 436 P.2d 342 (1968). See infra § 16.13 regarding severance damages.

4. See West's Ann.Cal.Code Civ.Proc. § 1266. See infra § 16.13.

5. But see City of Charlotte v. Cook, 125 N.C.App. 205, 479 S.E.2d 503, rev. granted, 281 N.C. 459, 189 S.E.2d 272(1972).

6. Silver Bow County v. Hafer, 166 Mont. 330, 532 P.2d 691 (1975); City of Charlotte v. Cook, 125 N.C.App. 205, 479 S.E.2d 503, rev. granted, 281 N.C. 459, 189 S.E.2d 272 (1997).

7. White v. Johnson, 148 S.C. 488, 146 S.E. 411 (1929). See also Dept. of Public Works v. Lagiss, 223 Cal.App.2d 23, 35 Cal. Rptr. 554 (1963) and Culley v. Pearl River Ind. Commission, 234 Miss. 788, 108 So.2d 390 (Miss.1959).

8. City of Troy v. Barnard, 183 Mich. App. 565, 455 N.W.2d 378 (1990).

A condemnation of 200 acres of farmland for an airport was partially invalidated in County of St. Clair v. Faust.[9] Since construction of the airport would destroy 80 acres of wetlands, the Corps of Engineers required wetlands mitigation of an equal amount. The county decided that 85 acres was necessary to meet the mitigation requirements, but the county took an additional 115 acres " 'to create a wetland value * * * commensurate with the wetlands being taken out of use.' " The court found 115 acres of the 200 acres to be grossly in excess of the land needed. The county could take some additional land, but only enough to "reasonably comply with the mitigation requirement."[10]

D. Recoupment Theory

Courts generally disallow excess condemnation for recoupment. Even where specific provisions of state law allow excess condemnation in some situations, they may expressly exclude or be construed by courts as not allowing excess condemnation for recoupment. In City of Cincinnati v. Vester,[11] for example, the court held that excess condemnation for recoupment purposes was not a public use within the meaning of the state excess condemnation constitutional provision and that it violated the due process clause of the Fourteenth Amendment.

E. Condemnation for Future Needs

Acquisition of land in advance of actual need to reduce costs is a variation of excess condemnation. The court in Board of Education v. Baczewski[12] denied a taking for a school site needed thirty years in the future on the ground that such future needs, motivated by economy, did not justify a taking. A court may allow such a taking, within reasonable limitations, however, on the theory that public officials should be permitted to plan for the future.[13]

The use of land banking for a variety of purposes, such as to control growth or preserve agricultural land,[14] runs afoul of cases like Baczewski, but other decisions support land banking. In Commonwealth of Puerto

---

9. 278 Ill.App.3d 152, 214 Ill.Dec. 1018, 662 N.E.2d 584 (1996).

10. Presumably the court did not mean to suggest that a condemnation to preserve wetlands for water resource and flooding protection is not a public use. More likely, putting aside intricacies of Illinois condemnation law, the validity of the amount of land taken in St. Clair was measured by the asserted public purpose, an airport. To build the airport, only 85 acres of wetlands were needed. The county did not attempt to justify its take on broader grounds.

11. 33 F.2d 242 (6th Cir.1929), aff'd on state law grounds in City of Cincinnati v. Vester, 281 U.S. 439, 50 S.Ct. 360, 74 L.Ed. 950 (1930). The Supreme Court affirmed Vester on state grounds, but insofar as the opinion reveals a willingness to scrutinize the purpose of a condemnation under Fifth

or Fourteenth Amendment grounds it is no longer valid in light of the Midkiff decision, discussed supra §§ 16.4 and 16.5.

12. 340 Mich. 265, 65 N.W.2d 810 (1954). See also Rueb v. Oklahoma City, 435 P.2d 139 (Okl.1967) (future hope for need based on speculation insufficient).

13. Carlor Co. v. Miami, 62 So.2d 897 (Fla.1953), cert. denied 346 U.S. 821, 74 S.Ct. 37, 98 L.Ed. 347 (1953); State Road Dept. v. Southland, Inc., 117 So.2d 512 (Fla. 1st D.C.A.1960). D. Shoup & R. Mack, Advance Land Acquisition by Local Governments: Benefit–Cost Analysis as Aid to Policy (1968). Note, Problems of Advance Land Acquisition, 52 Minn.L.Rev. 1175 (1968).

14. See discussion of land banking for agricultural preservation supra § 13.13.

Rico v. Rosso,[15] the court upheld a land banking program. The court reasoned that the taking of land to prevent uncontrolled growth was a public use.[16]

§ 16.8   Condemnation by Private Parties

Under certain circumstances, the legislature may authorize private parties to condemn land. Public service corporations such as power companies and railroads have long held the power to condemn to meet their land needs. Such a corporation must be organized under the authority of the state to serve the public at reasonable rates and without discrimination, and provide a necessity or a convenience that can be provided only if the power of eminent domain is available.[1] More recently, states have given the power to such nonprofit institutions as universities and hospitals. Some states, because of the post-World War II housing shortage, authorized private corporations to exercise the power of eminent domain for redevelopment.[2]

The power to condemn may be delegated even to private uses lacking a public service element because of abnormal local conditions, and to aid trade or agriculture. They include irrigation, drainage, reclamation of wetlands, mills and milldams, mines and mining, lumbering and logging, private roads for landlocked property, and clearing a doubtful title.[3] The private condemnor may have to make a stronger showing of a right of and justification for taking than if it were a public entity. A court might deny such a taking if another remedy less injurious to private property is available.[4]

§ 16.9   Inverse Condemnation

A property owner claiming that a government action or regulation has caused a taking for which compensation is due must commence an action in inverse condemnation.[1] Inverse condemnation is defined as:

> a cause of action against a governmental defendant to recover the value of property which has been taken in fact by the governmental defendant, even though no formal exercise of the power of eminent domain has been attempted by the taking agency.[2]

15. 95 D.P.R. 501 (1967), app. dismissed, 393 U.S. 14, 89 S.Ct. 46, 21 L.Ed.2d 13(1968).

16. See David L. Callies, Commonwealth of Puerto Rico v. Rosso: Land Bankking and the Expanded Concept of Public Use, 2 Prospectus 199 (1968).

§ 16.8

1. Attorney General ex rel. Corporation Com.r. v. Haverhill Gaslight Co., 215 Mass. 394, 101 N.E. 1061 (1913); Minnesota Canal & Power Co. v. Pratt, 101 Minn. 197, 112 N.W. 395 (1907).

2. Robinson & Robinson, A New Era in Public Housing, 1949 Wis.L.Rev. 695.

3. 2 P. Nichols, The Law of Eminent Domain § 7.62 (rev.3d ed. 1983).

4. Linggi v. Garovotti, 45 Cal.2d 20, 286 P.2d 15 (1955).

§ 16.9

1. See supra §§ 10.4 and 10.9.

2. Thornburg v. Port of Portland, 233 Or. 178, 180 n. 1, 376 P.2d 100, 101 n. 1 (1962). See also supra § 10.7 for a more complete discussion of the taking issue including inverse condemnation.

While procedural differences exist among the states as to when an action in inverse condemnation lies, all states are constitutionally obligated to provide such a remedy.[3] Since the Fifth Amendment right is self-executing, an express state statutory vehicle is unnecessary.[4]

In the context of a regulatory taking, it does not matter whether the regulatory authority accused of taking the property has been expressly delegated the power of eminent domain by the state legislature.[5] The grant of the police power includes the possibility that it will be exercised in a manner that effects a taking, and when that occurs the self-executing right to compensation arises.

An action in inverse condemnation may arise in a variety of circumstances. In addition to its use as a remedy for a regulatory taking, it is used by those whose property has been physically invaded by government action. For example, the government may dam a river, flooding upstream land.[6] Overflights by planes also may constitute takings of airspace,[7] and in one case the invasion of noise from an airport operation was found a taking.[8]

Since inverse condemnation arises from the constitution and is not based on a tort theory,[9] the doctrine of governmental tort immunity is avoided.[10] If, however, the governmental act is claimed to have been negligent and the issue is cast as one of governmental tort liability, immunity may bar the action.[11]

III. JUST COMPENSATION

§ 16.10 Fair Market Value

The Fifth Amendment and state constitutional counterparts require that "just compensation" be provided for property taken for public use.

---

3. First English Evangelical Lutheran Church v. County of Los Angeles, 482 U.S. 304, 107 S.Ct. 2378, 96 L.Ed.2d 250 (1987).

4. Zinn v. State, 112 Wis.2d 417, 334 N.W.2d 67 (1983).

5. Boise Cascade Corp. v. Board of Forestry, 325 Or. 185, 935 P.2d 411 (1997); Fountain v. Metropolitan Atlanta Rapid Transit Auth., 678 F.2d 1038 (11th Cir. 1982). See also State, Department of Health v. The Mill, 809 P.2d 434 (Colo.1991) (no action in inverse condemnation under state procedures, but suit available based directly on Fifth Amendment).

6. Pumpelly v. Green Bay & Mississippi Canal Co., 80 U.S. (13 Wall.) 166, 20 L.Ed. 557 (1871).

7. United States v. Causby, 328 U.S. 256, 66 S.Ct. 1062, 90 L.Ed.2d 1206 (1946).

8. Thornburg v. Port of Portland, 233 Or. 178, 376 P.2d 100 (1962). See discussion supra § 4.28.

9. Wolff v. Secretary of South Dakota Game, Fish and Parks Dept., 544 N.W.2d 531 (S.D.1996).

10. Electro-Tech, Inc. v. H.F. Campbell Co., 433 Mich. 57, 445 N.W.2d 61, 77, n. 38 (1989) (obligation to pay just compensation arises under the constitution and not in tort, the immunity doctrine does not insulate the government from liability). See also Barber v. State of Alabama, 703 So.2d 314 (Ala.1997).

11. B Amusement Co. v. United States, 148 Ct.Cl. 337, 180 F.Supp. 386 (1960). In V.T.C. Lines, Inc. v. Harlan for example, 313 S.W.2d 573 (Ky.App.1957), the plaintiff sued for damages to its bus station and garage from emery dust used by the defendant city in sand blasting its swimming pool. The court found no taking, classifying the case as one of negligent acts of city servants while performing governmental functions, for which acts the government is immune.

Compensation is typically provided in cash, but non-monetary compensation may also suffice.[1] Either by constitution, statute or court-made rule,[2] the measure of just compensation for property generally is its fair market value.[3] Market value is defined as the price the property would bring at the time of taking[4] if offered by a willing seller to a willing buyer.[5] Usually a jury determines market value; however, there is no federal constitutional right to a trial by jury in condemnation proceedings.[6]

In determining present market value, courts take into consideration all factors that affect the price that a prudent purchaser would be willing to pay. All uses to which people of prudence would devote the property are to be considered,[7] including its highest and best use as zoned,[8] even though the property is not being used or taken for such use.[9]

There are three typical approaches used in determining fair market value: (1) sales or comparable sales, (2) cost or replacement cost less depreciation, and (3) capitalization of income. A recent arm's length sale of property is the best evidence of market value if not explained away as abnormal.[10] A contract by the owner to sell the property is important evidence, but a condemnee cannot artificially distribute value over different parts of the land in a contract, attributing a higher value to the part to be expropriated to increase compensation for that part.[11] An offer previously made by the condemnor is excluded from evidence[12] since it includes consideration for avoiding litigation, but a recent bona fide offer from a private party is admissible in some states.[13] However, courts often reject evidence of offers as unreliable, indirect, and inaccessible to cross-examination,[14] at least where evidence of actual sales exists. Where sales

---

§ 16.10

1. See infra § 16.11.

2. See Juergensmeyer, Federal Rule of Civil Procedure 71A(h) Land Commissions: The First Fifteen Years, 43 Ind.L.J. 679 (1968).

3. United States v. Miller, 317 U.S. 369, 63 S.Ct. 276, 87 L.Ed. 336 (1943).

4. For the doctrines surrounding the time of assessment, see 3 P. Nichols, The Law of Eminent Domain § 8.5 (rev.3rd ed.1965 & recomp. 1978).

5. Kirby Forest Ind., Inc. v. United States, 467 U.S. 1, 104 S.Ct. 2187, 81 L.Ed.2d 1 (1984); State v. Silver, 92 N.J. 507, 513, 457 A.2d 463, 466 (1983).

6. United States v. Reynolds, 397 U.S. 14, 17, 90 S.Ct. 803, 805, 25 L.Ed.2d 12 (1970). Under Rule 71A (h) of the Federal Rules of Civil Procedure if Congress has not appointed a special tribunal to determine compensation, a party may ask for a jury and is entitled to one unless the court in its discretion decides to appoint a commission to determine compensation.

7. City of Redding v. Diestelhorst, 15 Cal.App.2d 184, 59 P.2d 177 (1936).

8. See infra § 16.12.

9. Olson v. United States, 292 U.S. 246, 54 S.Ct. 704, 78 L.Ed. 1236 (1934); Forest Preserve Dist. v. Lehmann Estate, 388 Ill. 416, 58 N.E.2d 538 (1944).

10. Vanech v. State, 29 A.D.2d 607, 285 N.Y.S.2d 636 (1967); See also, Dasso, Changing Economic Conditions and the Condemnation Value of Real Property, 48 Or.L.Rev. 237 (1969).

11. Municipality of Metropolitan Toronto v. Lowry, 30 D.L.R.2d 1 (Can.Sup.Ct. 1961).

12. Darien & W.R.R. Co. v. McKay, 132 Ga. 672, 64 S.E. 785 (1909).

13. Muller v. Southern Pac. Branch Ry. Co., 83 Cal. 240, 23 P. 265 (1890); City of Chicago v. Lehmann, 262 Ill. 468, 104 N.E. 829 (1914).

14. Brock v. Harlan County, 297 Ky. 113, 179 S.W.2d 202 (1944); State Highway Comm'n v. Triangle Dev. Co., 369 P.2d 864 (Wyo.1962), rehearing denied 371 P.2d 408 (1962).

data are not available for the property, data on similar properties, located close to the acquired property, and recently sold, may be evidence of market value.

Where sale or comparable sales data are not available, cost or replacement cost less depreciation may be the best evidence of market value. Cost may be used for nearly new buildings. Cost is particularly appropriate for valuing a building designed for a particular use such as a church or hospital. If the buildings are old, actual cost is not likely reliable, but replacement cost may be reliable. The cost of replacement with improvements of equal utility is generally the standard, rather than the cost of reproducing an exact. Once the replacement cost of the property is computed, it is then depreciated for wear and tear and functional obsolescence. Various methods of determining depreciation are used, including the regular accounting methods of straight line, declining charges, and sinking fund. However, accounting methods of depreciation are seldom reliable guides to present value. Estimation by an expert on appraisal examination of the premises may be more accurate though expert observations are not easily subject to cross examination. In general, the cost approach lends itself only to valuation of land with improvements. In response to this shortcoming a "development cost approach" may be used.[15]

Capitalization of income is often the best evidence of the value of standard commercial buildings.[16] For example, an apartment building is typically priced in private sales by considering the rental income of the property. Capitalized income is the present worth of future potential benefits of property or the net income which a fully informed person is warranted in assuming the property will produce during its remaining useful life. Yearly projected income is divided by a capitalization rate. The rate depends on the price of money and on an estimate of the security and duration of the income flow. Only profits attributable to the real estate itself can be considered since business profits are avoided as too speculative. An exception is made for rental income, which is considered sufficiently predictable. The net rental value of a building takes into account present rentals in the building, rentals from similar property, the terms of existing leases, and due discount for vacancies or rental losses. Expenses, including interest, taxes, and depreciation, are subtracted from the discounted rental income value to arrive at the net figure.

§ 16.11 Non–Monetary Compensation

There is no federal requirement that the compensation be paid in

15. County of Ramsey v. Miller, 316 N.W.2d 917 (Minn.1982). See also Port Auth. of City of St. Paul v. Englund, 464 N.W.2d 745 (Minn.App.1991).

16. San Diego Metropolitan Transit Development Bd. v. Cushman, 53 Cal. App.4th 918, 62 Cal.Rptr.2d 121 (1997) (income approach based on square foot value of nonexistent improvements was not proper methodology).

money.[1] In the Regional Rail Reorganization Act Cases,[2] the Court said that "[n]o decision of this Court holds that compensation other than money is an inadequate form of compensation under the eminent domain statutes."[3] There are numerous statements over the years that the Court has made to the effect that compensation must be the "full and perfect equivalent in money of the property taken,"[4] but such statements appear in cases where the condemnor was paying money. Compensation other than cash was not the issue. The question of non-monetary compensation is important in the use of transferable development rights, and other innovative programs.[5]

§ 16.12   Governmental Actions and Fair Market Value

Governmental announcement of an intent to condemn property may result in an increase or decrease in value. As a general proposition, these gains and losses are "incidents of ownership" that do not work to the advantage or disadvantage of the property owner in assessing compensation when the condemnation occurs.[1]

A. Pre–Condemnation Increase in Value

The Supreme Court has held that a condemnee is not entitled to the enhanced value that the need of the government for the property has created.[2] Any speculative increase in value due to the probability of taking is excluded from the award.[3]

If a tract of land is taken, neighboring lands may increase in market value due to the proximity of the public improvement erected on the land taken. If the government later decides to take the neighboring lands, it must pay the enhanced market value.[4] However, if the public project included the likely taking of several tracts from the beginning but only some of the tracts are taken initially, the owners of the remaining tracts are not paid the enhanced value of the land ultimately

§ 16.11

1. The issue is discussed in Douglas T. Kendall and James E. Ryan, "Paying" for the Change: Using Eminent Domain to Secure Exactions and Sidestep Nollan and Dolan, 81 Va.L.Rev. 1801, 1837 (1995).

2. 419 U.S. 102, 95 S.Ct. 335, 42 L.Ed.2d 320

3. Id.

4. United States v. Miller, 317 U.S. 369, 63 S.Ct. 276, 87 L.Ed. 336 (1943).

5. See Douglas T. Kendall and James E. Ryan, "Paying" for the Change: Using Eminent Domain to Secure Exactions and Sidestep Nollan and Dolan, 81 Va.L.Rev. 1801 (1995). See § 9.9 regarding TDRs.

§ 16.12

1. "Mere fluctuations in value during the process of governmental decisionmaking, absent extraordinary delay, are 'incidents of ownership. They cannot be considered as a taking in the constitutional sense.'" Agins v. City of Tiburon, 447 U.S. 255, 263, 100 S.Ct. 2138, 2143, 65 L.Ed.2d 106 (1980), quoting Danforth v. United States, 308 U.S. 271, 285, 60 S.Ct. 231, 236, 84 L.Ed. 240 (1939).

2. United States v. Cors, 337 U.S. 325, 69 S.Ct. 1086, 93 L.Ed. 1392 (1949).

3. Id. The dissent points out that in this case the excluded increment in price on the open market had resulted in fact from governmentally created shortage rather than speculation as to taking. Id. at 342, 69 S.Ct. at 1095.

4. United States v. Miller, 317 U.S. 369, 63 S.Ct. 276, 87 L.Ed. 336 (1943), rehearing denied 318 U.S. 798, 63 S.Ct. 557, 87 L.Ed. 1162 (1943).

taken.[5] For example, in United States v. Miller,[6] as a result of a dam project, it was necessary to acquire land to relocate a railroad. The land to be acquired was located in a "boomtown" caused by the construction of the dam. The condemnees were not allowed the benefit of the value added to their property by the previous condemnation of adjacent lands.[7]

It is difficult to separate fluctuations in value attributable to the improvement from those attributable to other causes. It is also difficult to determine when the effect of the improvement began. Designating the authorization date of the project as the date of valuation may exclude the government-created increment.[8] However, this date of valuation may also exclude increments from other sources. In one case, a statute fixing the date of measurement of compensation as that immediately preceding the resolution establishing the necessity of acquiring the property was held to violate the requirement of just compensation.[9] The court held it unjust to exclude all enhancement of the property's value after the date of resolution.

B. Pre–Condemnation Decrease in Value: Condemnation Blight

Owners face two distinct problems of economic loss in the pre-condemnation period. First, news of a planned condemnation may cause the value of the land to be condemned to drop, so that when the condemnation later occurs, the fair market value will be less than it was at the time the plans were announced. Second, the owner may suffer loss of use value during the time period between the announcement of the plans and the actual condemnation. Both situations may be referred to as condemnation blight.[10] Unfortunately, courts are not always careful to distinguish between the two.[11]

With respect to the former situation, the general rule is that the government must pay for the value of the property prior to the announcement of the planned condemnation.[12] This is the counterpoint of

5. Id.

6. Id.

7. Whether a taking is within the original scope of a project is an issue for the court rather than the jury. United States v. Reynolds, 397 U.S. 14, 90 S.Ct. 803, 25 L.Ed.2d 12 (1970).

8. Mann, The Relevant Date for the Assessment of Compensation, 85 Law Q.Rev. 516 (1969).

9. State ex rel. Willey v. Griggs, 89 Ariz. 70, 358 P.2d 174 (1960). See also discussion in Metropolitan Government of Nashville v. Overnite Transp. Co., 919 S.W.2d 598 (Tenn.App.1995).

10. See Gideon Kanner, Condemnation Blight and Inverse Condemnation, SB14 ALI–ABA 377, 384 (1996).

11. See Westgate, Ltd. v. State, 843 S.W.2d 448, 454, n. 4 (1992) and City of Buffalo v. J. W. Clement Co., Inc., 28 N.Y.2d 241, 269 N.E.2d 895, 902, 321 N.Y.S.2d 345, 355 (1971), noting the different rules, and the different results.

12. United States v. Virginia Electric & Power Co., 365 U.S. 624, 81 S.Ct. 784, 5 L.Ed.2d 838 (1961); City of Buffalo v. J. W. Clement Co., Inc., 28 N.Y.2d 241, 269 N.E.2d 895, 321 N.Y.S.2d 345, 358 (1971); City of Cleveland v. Carcione, 118 Ohio App. 525, 190 N.E.2d 52 (1963); City of Cleveland v. Hurwitz, 19 Ohio Misc. 184, 249 N.E.2d 562 (1969).

the rule discussed above regarding value increases that occur after announcement of condemnation plans.[13]

The second type of condemnation blight deals with the effect that the news of a proposed taking will have on the use of the parcel until the condemnation occurs, if in fact it does occur. Frequently, once it becomes known that an area is slated for condemnation, the land is stigmatized and in a state of economic limbo as the condemnation cloud hovers over the land. With rental property, existing tenants may leave and new tenants will be reluctant to lease property that the state may soon take. Expecting their property to be taken, owners may let their buildings deteriorate. They may vacate buildings and vandalism may increase. The land will be difficult to sell and if a purchaser can be found, the purchase price may be lower than the price that they could have obtained before the announcement of the plans to take the land.

In most states, losses sustained during the period between the announcement of the condemnation and the actual condemnation, or the abandonment of the plan, are not compensable.[14] Courts deem such losses "incidents of ownership"[15] that property owners must expect to occur from time to time. However, if the government's delay is unreasonable or its activities otherwise inequitable, a number of courts find compensable takings.[16] Yet, even unreasonable delay will not give rise to a cause of action in some states.[17]

C. *Effect of Zoning on Value*

Fair market value is determined by reference to uses for which the property is zoned.[18] However, where the evidence shows a "reasonable probability" of the removal or imposition of a zoning restriction in the near future, the effect of such probability on the minds of purchasers may be considered,[19] as may the effects on value from other future events.[20] A zoning change that will result from the condemnation itself is not considered. This so-called "project influence doctrine" neutralizes

13. See supra § 16.12 A.

14. Westgate, Ltd. v. State of Texas, 843 S.W.2d 448, 454 (1992); National By-Products, Inc. v. City of Little Rock, 323 Ark. 619, 916 S.W.2d 745 (1996); Auerbach v. Department of Transp., 545 So.2d 514 (Fla.App.1989).

15. Danforth v. United States, 308 U.S. 271, 285, 60 S.Ct. 231, 236, 84 L.Ed. 240 (1939).

16. Kaiser Development Company v. City and County of Honolulu, 913 F.2d 573, 575 (9th Cir.1990); City of Sparks v. Armstrong, 103 Nev. 619, 748 P.2d 7 (1987); Nadler v. City of Mason City, 387 N.W.2d 587 (Iowa 1986); Klopping v. City of Whittier, 8 Cal.3d 39, 104 Cal.Rptr. 1, 500 P.2d 1345 (1972).

17. Westgate, Ltd. v. State of Texas, 843 S.W.2d 448, 454 (1992) (leaving open the question of whether bad faith would be actionable).

18. Town of Paradise Valley v. Young Financial Services, 177 Ariz. 388, 868 P.2d 971, 974 (1993).

19. Id. See also People ex rel. Department of Pub. Works v. Dunn, 46 Cal.2d 639, 297 P.2d 964 (1956). See also Department of Public Works & Bldgs. v. Association of Franciscan Fathers, 44 Ill.App.3d 49, 4 Ill. Dec. 323, 360 N.E.2d 70 (1976), judgment affirmed 69 Ill.2d 308, 13 Ill.Dec. 681, 371 N.E.2d 616 (1977). Michigan State Highway Comm. v. Abood, 83 Mich.App. 612, 269 N.W.2d 247 (1978).

20. Olson v. United States, 292 U.S. 246, 54 S.Ct. 704, 78 L.Ed. 1236 (1934). For the effects of subdivision, see Annot. 26 A.L.R.3d 780 (1969). For effects of restrictive covenants, see Annot. 22 A.L.R.3d 961 (1968).

the effect of the project so that the condemnee is neither helped by an increase in value nor hurt by a decrease due to the condemnation project.[21]

Zoning is sometimes improperly used to lower property values in anticipation of condemnation. For example, in City of Plainfield v. Borough of Middlesex,[22] after property owners and a municipality could not agree as to lands that the owner wanted to sell and the city wished to purchase, the city rezoned the tract for parks, playgrounds and schools. One month later, the municipality declared the acquisition of the land necessary for public use. The court held that the municipality had unlawfully used its power to zone to depreciate the value of the property and limit the possible purchasers to the municipality.[23] Some statutes regulating or forbidding construction in areas to be condemned have been upheld, however.[24]

§ 16.13 Severance Damages

If the state acquires only part of a parcel of land, the owner is entitled to recover for "severance damage" to the remainder not acquired that is directly attributable to the taking or use of the land taken.[1] For the remainder to qualify for damages, generally it must be contiguous to the parcel taken and meet the unities of title and use.[2] These contiguity and unity requirements assure that an owner is compensated for the destruction of the integrity of her land.[3]

If the owner of the taken land has land nearby that might meet these elements, it is generally to the owner's advantage to argue for a broad interpretation of these rules so that damages will be assessed as a partial taking of a larger parcel rather than as a total taking of one parcel. In the former, compensation is awarded for both the taken land and the remainder, but in the latter, compensation is only awarded for the land taken. Nearby land that does not qualify may suffer a diminution in value as a result of the taking, but the loss will not be compensable.[4]

Non-contiguous parcels may qualify if there is a functional unity between them. Thus, where a street separated two parcels, and one was used as a parking lot for the other, a court treated it as a partial taking

---

21. Town of Paradise Valley v. Young Financial Services, 177 Ariz. 388, 868 P.2d 971, 974 (1993), quoting from 4 Nichols' Eminent Domain, § 12.322 (3d ed. 1981).

22. 69 N.J.Super. 136, 173 A.2d 785 (N.J. Super.L.Div.1961).

23. See discussion of illegitimacy of zoning to reduce condemnation costs, supra § 3.21.

24. Hunter v. Adams, 180 Cal.App.2d 511, 4 Cal.Rptr. 776 (1960); Headley v. Rochester, 272 N.Y. 197, 5 N.E.2d 198 (1936). See supra discussion of official maps, § 7.9–.14.

§ 16.13

1. Bauman v. Ross, 167 U.S. 548, 17 S.Ct. 966, 42 L.Ed. 270 (1897); City of Crookston v. Erickson, 244 Minn. 321, 69 N.W.2d 909 (1955).

2. Sharp v. United States, 191 U.S. 341, 24 S.Ct. 114, 48 L.Ed. 211 (1903).

3. Sharp v. United States, 191 U.S. 341, 24 S.Ct. 114, 48 L.Ed. 211 (1903).

4. United States v. 15.65 Acres of Land, 689 F.2d 1329, 1331 (9th Cir.1982).

and awarded severance damages.[5] On the other hand, where several blocks separated a mill and lumberyard, severance damages were denied.[6]

Unity of title does not require that the common owner hold the same estate in each tract. "Substantial unity of ownership" may suffice.[7] In one case, for example, a taking was treated as a partial taking, where one person owned the taken parcel as a tenant by the entirety and owned the remainder with another party as a tenant in common.[8]

Unity of use is said to be the most important element, and it may trump the other elements.[9] Thus, the fact that a street divided two parcels was overshadowed by the fact that they were found to have been used together as an office building and a parking lot.[10] Generally, it is existing use that has been considered relevant to unity of use, but in City of San Diego v. Neumann,[11] the Supreme Court of California held that future use could be considered. The court may award severance damages if the owner of contiguous parcels can show a reasonable probability that the land "will be available for development or use as an integrated economic unit in the reasonably foreseeable future."[12]

The measure of damages for a partial taking may be the market value of the land taken plus the difference before and after in value of the remainder,[13] or the difference between the value of the whole tract before the taking and the value of the remainder afterwards.[14] In determining severance damages, the court may, under the rationale of giving due consideration to all the factors that customarily enter into purchase and sale negotiations, allow the consideration of factors ordinarily excluded from evidence. For example, prospective earning power, evidenced by past earnings, has been considered in determining severance damages though the damage may only be the result of a noncompensable traffic diversion.[15]

5. State of Delaware v. Rittenhouse, 634 A.2d 338 (Del.1993). See also Housing Authority of Newark v. Norfolk Realty, 71 N.J. 314, 364 A.2d 1052 (1976); Spear v. State Highway Bd., 122 Vt. 406, 175 A.2d 511 (1961).

6. City of Oakland v. Pacific Coast Lumber & Mill Co., 171 Cal. 392, 153 P. 705 (1915).

7. City of Winston–Salem v. Yarbrough, 117 N.C.App. 340, 451 S.E.2d 358 (1994).

8. City of Milford v. .2703 Acres of Land, 256 A.2d 759 (Del.Super.1969). See also Stockton v. Ellingwood, 96 Cal.App. 708, 275 P. 228 (1929).

9. Andrews v. City of Greenbelt, 293 Md. 69, 441 A.2d 1064 (1982); Barnes v. North Carolina, 250 N.C. 378, 109 S.E.2d 219 (1959).

10. State of Delaware v. Rittenhouse, 634 A.2d 338 (Del.1993).

11. 6 Cal.4th 738, 863 P.2d 725, 25 Cal.Rptr.2d 480 (1993).

12. Id., 25 Cal.Rptr.2d at 492.

13. City of San Diego v. Neumann, 6 Cal.4th 738, 743, 863 P.2d 725, 728, 25 Cal.Rptr.2d 480, 483 (1993); City of Richardson v. Smith,, 494 S.W.2d 933, 940, n. 4 (1973). For a discussion of the methods of measuring damages in cases of partial taking, see 4 P. Nichols, The Law of Eminent Domain § 14.05 (rev.3rd ed.1995).

14. Under the latter method, the damages are part of the award for the taking. To add the "resulting" damages would double count damages. Commonwealth v. Sherrod, 367 S.W.2d 844 (Ky.1963).

15. Riddle v. State Highway Comm'n, 184 Kan. 603, 339 P.2d 301 (1959).

Compensable damage to the remainder may result in two ways.[16] First, the size of the remaining parcel may make it inappropriate or less valuable for the highest and best use of the whole parcel before the taking. Second, the use of the land taken may negatively affect the value of the remainder. A condemnee is entitled to compensation for damages to the remaining land from the taker's use of land taken but not for damages from the taker's use of other property.[17] As one court has noted, "the application of these rules becomes complex when the injury to the landowner may be said to flow both from the taking and use of but a portion of his property and from the use to which the government puts land taken from a third party neighbor."[18] It has been held that where the land of multiple owners is condemned, one who claims severance damages to a remainder parcel may recover if the land taken from her was both a substantial and indispensable part of the project, and the damages to the remainder are inseparable from those to the land taken.[19]

§ 16.14 Benefits as Setoffs

In cases of a partial taking, the use of the land taken may confer benefits on the remaining land. The Supreme Court has held that government may subtract the value of such benefits from the compensation it must pay.[1] Simply put, the constitution does not require that the condemnee "be placed in any better position than he was before the taking."[2] In contrast to the federal rule, states differ as to whether benefits are to be set off at all, whether they are to be set off against compensation for the partial taking or only against severance damages; and whether general or only special benefits are to be set off.[3]

Special benefits are those enjoyed by the landowner that exceed the general benefit to the public, those that accrue when the public improvement is on privately owned land upon which the government has condemned an easement, and those that result from a physical improvement on the land, e.g., a highway that provides drainage for abutting

16. See Annot., Compensation for Diminution in Value of the Remainder of Property Resulting From Taking or Use of Adjoining Land of Others for the Same Undertaking, 59 A.L.R.3d 488 (1975).

17. Making such a differentiation may be difficult. See Campbell v. United States, 266 U.S. 368, 45 S.Ct. 115, 69 L.Ed. 328 (1924); People ex rel. Dep't of Pub. Works v. Elsmore, 229 Cal.App.2d 809, 40 Cal. Rptr. 613 (1964); Sisters of Charity v. The King, [1922] 2 A.C. 315 (P.C.) (N.S.).

18. United States v. 15.65 Acres of Land, 689 F.2d 1329, 1332 (9ᵗʰ Cir.1982).

19. Id. at 1332.

§ 16.14

1. Bauman v. Ross, 167 U.S. 548, 17 S.Ct. 966, 42 L.Ed. 270 (1897); United States v. Sponenbarger, 308 U.S. 256, 60

S.Ct. 225, 84 L.Ed. 230 (1939). See also City of Van Buren v. United States, 697 F.2d 1058 (Fed.Cir.1983) (finding rule inapplicable).

2. Chiesa v. State of New York, 36 N.Y.2d 21, 29, 324 N.E.2d 329, 334, 364 N.Y.S.2d 848, 855 (1974) (Jasen, J. dissenting from New York view that is contrary to federal view).

3. See Chiesa v. State of New York, 36 N.Y.2d 21, 324 N.E.2d 329, 364 N.Y.S.2d 848 (1974) (listing different positions). See also In re Water Front in City of New York, 190 N.Y. 350, 83 N.E. 299 (1907) (rejecting federal rule). Missouri v. Edelen, 872 S.W.2d 551, 554 (Mo.App.1994) (only special benefits offset); State v. Meyer, 403 S.W.2d 366 (Tex.1966) (no offset).

land.[4] Even in jurisdictions where special benefits are normally setoff, they may not be setoff when the benefit is one that a condemnee's neighbors, whose land is not taken, receive free of charge.[5]

In ordinary highway condemnation cases, a special benefit arises from location on a way to which there is direct access. Nevertheless, in the case of a limited access highway, benefits to both abutting and nonabutting properties are the same, since access afforded to lots not abutting the highway is equal to that afforded the condemnee's land. In the latter instance, the benefits may be treated as general and not offset.[6]

In 1997, reversing long-standing precedent, the California supreme court held that general benefits, as well as special benefits, must be offset. In Los Angeles County Metropolitan Transportation Authority v. Continental Development Corp.,[7] the condemnor took a narrow strip of Continental's land for an elevated light rail line. As a result of the loss of the strip, Continental's office building plans had to be revised, resulting in a potential reduction of future rental value. The condemnor noted that the benefit of having a rail station within a short distance from its building increased the rental value of the building. Thus, it argued that Continental's award should be reduced by the increase in value to the remainder resulting from the publicly-provided improvements. The court, joining a minority of states, agreed that such general benefits should be used to offset any award. The court found the general-special benefit unworkable. It also found that recognition of the general benefit did not deprive the landowner of being fully compensated. It was true that reducing Continental's award would mean that it could not reap a windfall from the taxpayer-provided benefit as some of its neighbors could (those who had no land taken, but who were nonetheless aided by being close to the rail line). The inability of Continental to reap this windfall, however, did not justify making the public pay more for the rail line.

§ 16.15 Noncompensable Damages

A. *Business Losses*

"Just compensation" does not generally require payment for destruction of a business, lost profits, or loss of good will, even though these losses and expenses affect selling price.[1] These elements are

4. See generally Donald G. Hagman, Special Benefits in Road Cases: Myths and Realities, 1964 Institute on Eminent Domain 135; Palmore, Damages Recoverable in a Partial Taking, 21 SW.L.J. 740 (1967); Peacock, The Offset of Benefits Against Losses in Eminent Domain Cases in Texas, 44 Tex.L.Rev. 1564 (1966).

5. Chiesa v. State of New York, 36 N.Y.2d 21, 29, 324 N.E.2d 329, 334, 364 N.Y.S.2d 848, 855 (1974).

6. Territory of Hawaii v. Mendonca, 46 Haw. 83, 126, 375 P.2d 6, 17 (1962).

7. 16 Cal.4th 694, 941 P.2d 809, 66 Cal.Rptr.2d 630 (1997).

§ 16.15

1. Mitchell v. United States, 267 U.S. 341, 45 S.Ct. 293, 69 L.Ed. 644 (1925); Community Redevelopment Agency of City of Los Angeles v. Abrams, 15 Cal.3d 813, 543 P.2d 905, 126 Cal.Rptr. 473 (1975)

considered speculative and personal to the landowner rather than relating to the land, and thus not proper elements of compensation. In theory, it is the land, not the business, that is being condemned.[2]

The policy of noncompensation can work great hardships. For example, in Mitchell v. United States,[3] the United States appropriated land for military use. The land was especially adapted to the owner's business of growing a special grade of corn, and the owners were unable to establish themselves elsewhere. The court denied compensation for destruction of business, reasoning that neither settled rules of law nor statute provided for such compensation.

Such consequences have led some states by statute or case law to provide compensation for business losses, particularly where businesses are destroyed and cannot be relocated.[4] California, for example, enacted Section 1016 of the Uniform Eminent Domain Code, which provides for compensation for loss of goodwill if relocation cannot prevent the loss.[5] In Vermont, business losses are recoverable, but the condemnee must show a "fixed and established" business, and lost profits are not included.[6]

B. Relocation Costs

Generally, the condemnee owner or lessee is also not compensated for expenses in moving personal property,[7] although removal costs may be considered in determining market value, since it is an element bearing on the price a seller would set.[8] Where the property is taken temporarily for a period less than the lessee's outstanding term, removal costs may be considered in the award, not as an independent item of damage, but as bearing on the rental value of the premises.[9] Such costs need not be considered when the whole of the lease is taken, since the

(statute allowing payment for goodwill held not retroactive so as to alter constitutional rule that goodwill not compensable). See generally Sandra L.K.Davidson, Annot., Good Will as Element of Damages for Condemnation of Property on Which Private Business is Conducted, 81 A.L.R.3d 198 (1978).

In Canada there is a right to compensation for loss of good will, In re McCauley & City of Toronto, 18 Ont. 416 (Ch.1889), and for "disturbance," Woods Mfg. Co. v. The King, [1951] 2 D.L.R. 465 (Can.Sup.Ct.), when property is expropriated. See also Klien, Eminent Domain: Judicial Response to the Human Disruption, 46 J.Urban L. 1 (1968).

2. Auraria Businessmen Against Confiscation, Inc. v. Denver Urban Renewal Authority, 183 Colo. 441, 517 P.2d 845, 847 (1974).

3. 267 U.S. 341, 45 S.Ct. 293, 69 L.Ed. 644 (1925).

4. City of Minneapolis v. Schutt, 256 N.W.2d 260 (Minn.1977).

5. West's Ann.Cal.Civ.Proc. § 1263.510. See also; West's Fla.Stat. Ann.§ 73.071(3) (b); Wyo.Stat. § 1–26–713; City of Detroit, v. Michael's Prescriptions, 143 Mich.App. 808, 373 N.W.2d 219 (1985).

6. Pinewood Manor, Inc. v. Vermont Agency of Transp., 164 Vt. 312, 668 A.2d 653 (Vt.1995), applying 19 Vt.Stat.Ann. § 501(2).

7. United States v. 5.42 Acres of Land, 182 F.2d 787 (3d Cir.1950); Housing Authority v. Kosydor, 17 Ill.2d 602, 162 N.E.2d 357 (1959).

8. Harvey Textile Co. v. Hill, 135 Conn. 686, 67 A.2d 851 (1949); State Highway Dep't v. Robinson, 103 Ga.App. 12, 118 S.E.2d 289 (1961).

9. United States v. General Motors Corp., 323 U.S. 373, 65 S.Ct. 357, 89 L.Ed. 311 (1945).

lessee need not return and has no liability for the remainder of the lease.[10]

Relocation expenses may be allowed by statute. The federal Uniform Relocation Assistance and Real Property Acquisition Policies Act of 1970[11] provides for compensation to certain persons displaced as a result of federal projects.[12] State acts are often broader than the federal act. In California, for example, the state relocation law has been interpreted to apply to inverse condemnees.[13]

§ 16.16 Condemnation of Restricted Land

A public body may acquire land by condemnation that is subject to restrictions. It is the general rule that the existence of a restrictive covenant affecting the value of the condemned land should be considered in determining the market value of the property condemned. For example, Staninger v. Jacksonville Expressway Authority[1] held that property restricted to a single family residential use, the highest and best use of which was for business and multi-unit apartment purposes, should be valued in eminent domain at or near its value as restricted.[2] However, Town of Tonawanda v. State[3] held that property was to be valued without consideration of a restriction. The land was owned by a city and acquired from the county for $500 per acre. The deed from the county restricted the property to municipal purposes. The state condemned part of the site at a time when property in the area was selling at $7,000 per acre. Since the county could release the restriction and since replacement property would cost the city the market price for land being sold in the area, the court held the property should be valued as if not restricted.

§ 16.17 Compensation for Regulatory Takings

When government is found to have taken property by regulation, the remedy must be compensation, not injunctive relief.[1] Whether compensation for regulatory takings should track identically the rules developed for compensation for direct exercises of the power of eminent domain or

---

10. United States v. Petty Motor Co., 327 U.S. 372, 66 S.Ct. 596, 90 L.Ed. 729 (1946); United States v. Westinghouse Electric & Manufacturing Co. 339 U.S. 261, 70 S.Ct. 644, 94 L.Ed. 816 (1950).

11. 42 U.S.C.A. §§ 4601 to 4655.

12. See Norfolk Redevelopment & Housing Auth. v. Chesapeake & Potomac Tel. Co., 464 U.S. 30, 104 S.Ct. 304, 78 L.Ed.2d 29 (1983).

13. Beaty v. Imperial Irrigation Dist., 186 Cal.App.3d 897, 231 Cal.Rptr. 128 (1986).

§ 16.16

1. 182 So.2d 483 (Fla.App.1966). See Annot. 22 A.L.R.3d 961 (1968).

2. See also Central Land Co. v. Providence, 15 R.I. 246, 2 A. 553 (1886); State v. Reece, 374 S.W.2d 686 (Tex.Civ.App.1964); Note, 31 U.Pitts.L.Rev. 128 (1969).

3. 50 Misc.2d 3, 269 N.Y.S.2d 181 (Ct. Cl.1966), judgment affirmed 28 A.D.2d 644, 280 N.Y.S.2d 780 (1967). See also Burma Hills Development Co. v. Marr, 285 Ala. 141, 229 So.2d 776 (1969).

§ 16.17

1. The history of the remedy issue in regulatory taking litigation is discussed supra § 10.9.

for takings that result by physical invasion is not settled.[2] The Supreme Court's opinion in First English Evangelical Lutheran Church v. County of Los Angeles,[3] equates the two types of takings for the purposes of determining whether compensation or invalidation is the proper remedy for a regulatory taking, but since no taking was found in that case, no issue as to the calculation of compensation was before the Court.

First English makes it clear that the government defendant, not the plaintiff property owner or the court, decides whether the compensation award is for a permanent taking or a temporary taking. When a court makes the determination in an inverse condemnation action that a regulation has effected a taking, the government can choose to keep the regulation in effect and compensate the owner for a permanent taking. Alternatively, the government can make the taking a temporary one by repealing the offending law. In that event, it must compensate the owner for the loss sustained during the period of time from when the ordinance was applied to the property until it was lifted by the government.[4]

There is no fixed measure of damages used in temporary taking cases.[5] Rental return, which calculates the supposed rent the parties would have negotiated for the period of the take, is probably the most frequently used.[6] Others are option price, where compensation equals the market value of an option to buy the land during the take,[7] interest on lost profits,[8] and before and after valuation.[9]

---

2. See supra § 10.6.

3. 482 U.S. 304, 107 S.Ct. 2378, 96 L.Ed.2d 250 (1987).

4. See supra § 10.9.

5. See Gideon Kanner, Inverse Condemnation of Regulatory Takings, Ch. 14E, in 4 Nichols' Law of Eminent Domain (rev.3d ed.1993).

6. See Yuba Natural Resources, Inc. v. United States, 904 F.2d 1577 (Fed.Cir. 1990); City of Austin v. Teague, 570 S.W.2d 389 (Tex.1978).

7. See Lomarch Corp. v. Mayor of Englewood, 51 N.J. 108, 237 A.2d 881 (1968).

8. Prince George's County v. Blumberg, 44 Md.App. 79, 407 A.2d 1151 (1979).

9. Wheeler v. City of Pleasant Grove, 896 F.2d 1347 (11th Cir.1990). See Barnes, Comment, Just Compensation or Just Damages: The Measure of Damages for Temporary Regulatory Takings in Wheeler v. City of Pleasant Grove, 74 Iowa L.Rev. 1243 (1989).

Appendix

RESEARCHING LAND USE LAW ON WESTLAW

Analysis

Section 1. Introduction

Land Use Planning and Control Law provides a strong base for analyzing even the most complex problems involving land use. Whether your research requires examination of case law, statutes, administrative materials, expert commentary or other materials, West books and Westlaw are excellent sources of information.

To help keep you up-to-date with current developments, Westlaw provides frequently updated databases. With Westlaw, you have unparalleled legal research resources at your fingertips.

Additional Resources

If you have not previously used Westlaw or have questions not covered in this appendix, see the *Westlaw Reference Manual* or call the West Group Reference Attorneys at 1–800–850–WEST (1–800–850–9378). The West Group Reference Attorneys are trained, licensed attorneys, available 24 hours a day to assist you with your Westlaw search questions.

Section 2. Westlaw Databases

Each database on Westlaw is assigned an abbreviation called an *identifier*, which you use to access the database. You can find identifiers for all databases in the online Westlaw Directory and in the print *Westlaw Database Directory*. When you need to know more detailed information about a database, use Scope. Scope contains coverage information, lists of related databases and valuable search tips. To access Scope, click the **Scope** button while in the database.

The following chart lists Westlaw databases that contain information pertaining to land use law. For a complete list of databases relating to land use, see the online Westlaw Directory or the print *Westlaw Database Directory*. Because new information is continually being added to Westlaw, you should also check the Welcome to Westlaw window and the Westlaw Directory for new database information.

Selected Westlaw Databases

Database	Identifier	Coverage
Combined Databases		
Federal & State Case Law	ALLCASES	Begins with 1945
Federal & State Case Law Before 1945	ALLCASES–OLD	1789 1944
Federal Environmental Law Combined Materials	FENV–ALL	Varies by source
Federal Case Law		
Federal Case Law	ALLFEDS	Begins with 1945
Federal Case Law Before 1945	ALLFEDS–OLD	1789 1944
Federal Environmental Law Cases	FENV–CS	Begins with 1789

Database	Identifier	Coverage
Federal Environmental Law Supreme Court Cases	FENV–SCT	Begins with 1790
Federal Environmental Law Courts of Appeals Cases	FENV–CTA	Begins with 1891
Federal Environmental Law District Courts Cases	FENV–DCT	Begins with 1789

Federal Statutes, Regulations and Administrative Materials

Database	Identifier	Coverage
Code of Federal Regulations	CFR	Current data
Federal Register	FR	Begins with July 1980
United States Code Annotated®	USCA	Current data
Environmental Law Reporter Administrative Materials	ELR–ADMIN	Begins with 1971
Federal Environmental Law Administrative Materials	FENV–ADMIN	Varies by agency
Federal Environmental Law Code and Regulations	FENV–CODREG	Varies by source
Federal Environmental Law Code of Federal Regulations	FENV–CFR	Current data
Federal Environmental Law Federal Register	FENV–FR	Begins with July 1980
Federal Environmental Law Final, Temporary, and Proposed Regulations	FENV–REG	Varies by source
Federal Environmental Law U.S. Code Annotated	FENV–USCA	Current data
Gower Federal Service	GFS	Begins with 1970
Department of the Interior Decisions	INTDEC	Begins with 1881
Legislative History U.S. Code, 1948 to Present	LH	Begins with 1948

State Materials

Database	Identifier	Coverage
State Case Law	ALLSTATES	Begins with 1945
State Case Law Before 1945	ALLSTATES–OLD	1821B1944
Individual State Case Law	XX–CS (where XX is a state's two-letter postal abbreviation)	Varies by state
Multistate Environment Cases and Administrative Materials	MENV–ALL	Varies by source
Multistate Environmental Law Cases	MENV–CS (where XX is a state's two-letter postal abbreviation)	Varies by state
Individual State Environmental Law Cases	XXENV–CS (where XX is a state's two-letter postal abbreviation)	Varies by state

Database	Identifier	Coverage
Multistate Real Property Cases	MRP–CS	Varies by state
Individual State Real Property Cases	XXRP–CS (where XX is a state's two-letter postal abbreviation)	Varies by state
Multistate Environmental Law Administrative Decisions	MENV–ADMIN	Varies by state
Individual State Environmental Law Administrative Decisions	XXENV–ADMIN (where XX is a state's two-letter postal abbreviations)	Varies by state
State Administrative Code Multibase (26 states included)	ADC–ALL	Current data
Individual State Administrative Codes (26 states available)	XX–ADC (where XX is a state's two-letter postal abbreviation)	Current data
New York City Charter	NYC–C	Current data
Spokane Municipal Code	SPOKANE–MUN	Current data
State Statutes Annotated	ST–ANN–ALL	Varies by state
Individual State Statutes Annotated	XX–ST–ANN (where XX is a state's two-letter postal abbreviation)	Varies by state
Uniform Laws Annotated®	ULA	Current data

Legal Texts, Periodicals and Restatements

Database	Identifier	Coverage
Texts & Periodicals All Law Reviews, Texts & Bar Journals	TP–ALL	Varies by publication
Andrews Aviation Litigation Reporter	ANAVIALR	Begins with November 1996
Economic Geography	ECGEOGY	Begins with January 1994
Geo Info Systems	GEOINFOS	Begins with November 1994
Journal of Land Use & Environmental Law	JLUEL	Selected coverage begins with 1990 (vol. 6); full coverage begins with 1993 (vol. 9).
Land Economics	LANDECON	Begins with February 1989
Environmental Law Law Reviews, Texts & Bar Journals	ENV–TP	Varies by publication
PLI Real Estate Law and Practice Course Handbook Series	PLI–REAL	Current data
Public Land and Resources Law Review	PUBLRLR	Selected coverage begins with 1982 (vol. 3);

Database	Identifier	Coverage
		full coverage begins with 1993 (vol. 14).
Real Property Law Reviews, Texts & Bar Journals	RP–TP	Varies by publication
Restatement of the Law Property	REST–PROP	Current data

News and Directories

All News	ALLNEWS	Varies by source
Government and Politics News	GOVNEWS	Varies by source
Government Affairs Yellow Book	GOVAFFYB	Current data
Municipal Yellow Book	MUNIYB	Current data
State Yellow Book	STATEYB	Current data
Westlaw Topical Highlights Environmental Law	WTH–ENV	Current data
Westlaw Topical Highlights Real Property	WTH–RP	Current data
West Legal Directory ™ Environmental	WLD–ENV	Current data
West Legal Directory Real Property	WLD–RP	Current data

Section 3. Retrieving a Document with a Citation: Find and Jump

3.1 Find

Find is a Westlaw service that allows you to retrieve a document by entering its citation. Find allows you to retrieve documents from anywhere in Westlaw without accessing or changing databases. Find is available for many documents, including case law (state and federal), the *United States Code Annotated*®, state statutes, administrative materials, and texts and periodicals.

To use Find, simply access the Find service and type the citation. The following list provides some examples:

To Find This Document	Access Find and Type
McMinn v. Town of Oyster Bay, 488 N.E.2d 1240 (N.Y. 1985)	**488 ne2d 1240**
Me. Rev. Stat. Ann. tit. 5, § 3341	**me st t 5 s 3341**
Cal. Code Regs. tit. 14, 13530	**14 ca adc 13530**
12 J. Land Use & Envtl. L. 425	**12 jluel 425**
43 U.S.C.A. § 1712	**43 usca 1712**

For a complete list of publications that can be retrieved with Find and their abbreviations, consult the Find Publications List. Click the **Pubs List** button after accessing Find.

3.2 Jump

Use Jump markers (> or <) to move from one location to another on Westlaw. For example, use Jump markers to go directly from the case, statute or law review article you are viewing to a cited case, statute or article; from a headnote to the corresponding text in the opinion; or from an entry in a statutes index database to the full text of the statute.

Section 4. Natural Language Searching: WIN-Westlaw is Natural

Overview: With WIN, you can retrieve documents by simply describing your issue in plain English. If you are a relatively new Westlaw user, Natural Language searching can make it easier for you to retrieve cases that are on point. If you are an experienced Westlaw user, Natural Language gives you a valuable alternative search method.

When you enter a Natural Language description, Westlaw automatically identifies legal phrases, removes common words and generates variations of terms in your description. Westlaw then searches for the concepts in your description. Concepts may include significant terms, phrases, legal citations or topic and key numbers. Westlaw retrieves the 20 documents that most closely match your description, beginning with the document most likely to match.

4.1 Natural Language Searching

Access a database, such as Multistate Real Property Cases (MRP–CS). If the Terms and Connectors Query Editor is displayed, click the **Search Type** button and choose **Natural Language**. At the Natural Language Description Editor, type a Natural Language description such as the following:

zoning and eminent domain

4.2 Next Command

Westlaw displays the 20 documents that most closely match your description, beginning with the document most likely to match. If you want to view additional documents, click your right mouse button and choose **Next 10 Documents** from the pop-up menu or choose **Next 10 Documents** from the Browse menu.

4.3 Browsing a Natural Language Search Result

Best Mode: To display the best portion (the portion that most closely matches your description) of each document in your search result, click your right mouse button and choose **Next Best** from the pop-up menu or click **Best** f.

Standard Browsing Commands: You can also browse your Natural Language search result using standard Westlaw browsing commands, such as citations list, Locate, page mode and term mode. When you browse your Natural Language search result in term mode, the five portions of each document that are most likely to match your description are displayed.

Section 5. Terms and Connectors Searching

Overview: With Terms and Connectors searching, you enter a query, which consists of key terms from your issue and connectors specifying the relationship between these terms.

Terms and Connectors searching is useful when you want to retrieve a document for which you know specific details, such as the title or the fact situation. Terms and Connectors searching is also useful when you want to retrieve documents relating to a specific issue. If the Natural Language Query Editor is displayed when you access a database, click the **Search Type** button and choose **Term Search**.

5.1 Terms

Plurals and Possessives: Plurals are automatically retrieved when you enter the singular form of a term. This is true for both regular and irregular plurals (e.g., **child** retrieves *children*). If you enter the plural form of a term, you will not retrieve the singular form.

If you enter the nonpossessive form of a term, Westlaw automatically retrieves the possessive form as well. However, if you enter the possessive form, only the possessive form is retrieved.

Automatic Equivalencies: Some terms have alternative forms or equivalencies; for example, *5* and *five* are equivalent terms. Westlaw automatically retrieves equivalent terms. The *Westlaw Reference Manual* contains a list of equivalent terms.

Compound Words and Acronyms: When a compound word is one of your search terms, use a hyphen to retrieve all forms of the word. For example, the term **along-side** retrieves *along-side, alongside* and *along side.*

When using an acronym as a search term, place a period after each of the letters in the acronym to retrieve any of its forms. For example, the term **h.u.d.** retrieves *hud, h.u.d., h u d* and *h. u. d.* Note: The acronym does *not* retrieve *housing and urban development*, so remember to add additional alternative terms to your query such as **housing and urban development**.

Root Expander and Universal Character: When you use the Terms and Connectors search method, placing a root expander (!) at the end of a root term generates all other terms with that root. For example, adding the ! symbol to the root *constitution* in the query

constitution! /s zoning

instructs Westlaw to retrieve such terms as *constitutional, constitutionalism constitutionalization* and *constitutionality.*

The universal character (*) stands for one character and can be inserted in the middle or at the end of a term. For example, the term

withdr*w

will retrieve *withdraw* and *withdrew.* Adding four asterisks to the root *plan*

plan* * **

instructs Westlaw to retrieve all forms of the root with up to four additional characters. Terms like *planner, planned* or *planning* are retrieved by this query. However, terms with more than four letters following the root, such as *plantation* or *planetarium,* are not retrieved. Plurals are always retrieved, even if more than four letters follow the root.

Phrase Searching: To search for a phrase, place it within quotation marks. For example, to search for references to inverse condemnation, type **inverse condemnation**. When you are using the Terms and Connectors search method, you should use phrase searching only if you are certain that the phrase will not appear in any other form.

5.2 Alternative Terms

After selecting the terms for your query, consider which alternative terms are necessary. For example, if you are searching for the term *constitutional*, you might also want to search for the term *unconstitutional*. You should consider both synonyms and antonyms as alternative terms. You can also use the Westlaw thesaurus to add alternative terms to your query.

5.3 Connectors

After selecting terms and alternative terms for your query, use connectors to specify the relationship that should exist between search terms in your retrieved documents. The connectors you can use are described below:

Use:	To retrieve documents with:	Example:
& (and)	both terms	**exclusive & zoning**
or (space)	either term or both terms	**industrial commercial**
/p	search terms in the same paragraph	**uniform! /p classif!**
/s	search terms in the same sentence	**zoning /s ordinance**
+s	the first search term preceding the second within the same sentence	**burden +s prov! proof**
/n	search terms within n terms of each other (where n is a number)	**set-back /3 restrict!**
+n	the first search term preceding the second by n terms (where n is a number)	**planned +3 unit**
	search terms appearing in the same order as in the quotation marks	**economic impact test**
Use:	To exclude documents with:	Example:

Use:	To retrieve documents with:	Example:
%	search terms following the	**zoning /s restrict! ordinance**
(but not)	% symbol	**% taking**

5.4 Restricting Your Search by Field

Overview: Documents in each Westlaw database consist of several segments, or fields. One field may contain the citation, another the title, another the synopsis and so forth. Not all databases contain the same fields. Also, depending on the database, fields with the same name may contain different types of information.

To view a list of fields for a specific database and their contents, see Scope for that database. Note that in some databases not every field is available for every document.

To retrieve only those documents containing your search terms in a specific field, restrict your search to that field. To restrict your search to a specific field, type the field name or abbreviation followed by your search terms enclosed in parentheses. For example, to retrieve a case in the Multistate Real Property Cases database (MRP–CS) entitled *McMinn v. Oyster Bay,* search for your terms in the title field (ti):

ti(mcminn & oyster bay)

The fields discussed below are available in Westlaw databases you might use for researching land use issues.

Digest and Synopsis Fields: The digest (di) and synopsis (sy) fields, added to case law databases by West's attorney-editors, summarize the main points of a case. The synopsis field contains a brief description of a case. The digest field contains the topic and headnote fields and includes the complete hierarchy of concepts used by West's editors to classify the headnotes to specific West digest topics and key numbers. Restricting your search to the synopsis and digest fields limits your result to cases in which your terms are related to a major issue in the case.

Consider restricting your search to one or both of these fields if

● you are searching for common terms or terms with more than one meaning, and you need to narrow your search; or

● you cannot narrow your search by using a smaller database.

For example, to retrieve cases that discuss the relationship between takings and physical invasions, access the State Case Law database (ALLSTATES) and type

sy,di(taking /p physical /5 invasion)

Headnote Field: The headnote field (he) is a part of the digest field, but does not contain topic numbers, hierarchical classification information or key numbers. The headnote field contains only a one-sentence summary for each point of law in a case and any supporting citations given by the author of the opinion. A headnote field restriction is useful when you are searching for specific statutory sections or rule numbers. For example, to retrieve headnotes from federal cases that cite 43 U.S.C.A. § 1712, access the Federal Case Law database (ALLFEDS) and type the following query:

he(43 +s 1712)

Topic Field: The topic field (to) is also a part of the digest field. It contains hierarchical classification information, including the West digest topic names and numbers and the key numbers. You should restrict search terms to the topic field in a case law database if

- a digest field search retrieves too many documents; or
- you want to retrieve cases with digest paragraphs classified under more than one topic.

For example, the topic Zoning and Planning has the topic number 414. To retrieve state cases that discuss the relationship between zoning and property value preservation, access the State Case Law database (ALLSTATES) and type a query like the following:

to(414) /p preserv! /p property /3 value

To retrieve West headnotes classified under more than one topic and key number, search for your terms in the topic field. For example, to search for cases discussing land use planning, which may be classified to Constitutional Law (92), Eminent Domain (148), Health and Environment (199) or Zoning and Planning (414), type a query like the following:

to(land use /p plan**)**

For a complete list of West digest topics and their corresponding topic numbers, access the Key Number service; click the **Key Number Service** button or choose **Key Number Service** from the Services menu.

Prelim and Caption Fields: When searching in a database containing statutes, rules or regulations, restrict your search to the prelim (pr) and caption (ca) fields to retrieve documents in which your terms are important enough to appear in a section name or heading. For example, to retrieve federal regulations regarding land use relating to airports, access the Code of Federal Regulations database (CFR) and type the following:

pr,ca(land use & airport)

5.5 Restricting Your Search by Date

You can use Westlaw to retrieve documents *decided* or *issued* before, after, or on a specified date, as well as within a range of dates. The following sample queries contain date restrictions:

da(aft 1996) & urban /5 sprawl

da(1998) & sy,di(subdivision /p zoning planning)

da(3/12/1998) & eminent domain

You can also search for documents *added to a database* on or after a specified date, as well as within a range of dates. The following sample queries contain added-date restrictions:

ad(aft 1995) & revo! /p zoning /p permit certificat!

ad(aft 2–1–1998 & bef 2–17–1998) & land +2 use control

Section 6. Topic and Key Number Searching

To retrieve cases that address a specific point of law, search using topic and key numbers. If you have an on-point case and want to find additional cases, run a search using the topic and key number from the relevant headnote in an appropriate database to find other cases containing headnotes classified to that topic and key number. For example, to search for all cases containing headnotes classified under topic 414 (Zoning and Planning) and key number 784 (Preliminary injunction), access the Federal & State Case Law database (ALLCASES) and enter the following query:

414k784

For a complete list of West digest topic and key numbers, access the Key Number service; click the **Key Number Service** button or choose **Key Number Service** from the Services menu.

Section 7. Verifying Your Research with Citators

Overview: A citator service is a tool that helps you ensure that your cases are good law; retrieve cases, legislation or articles that cite a case or statute; and verify that the spelling and format of your citations are correct.

For citations not covered by the citator services, including persuasive secondary authority such as restatements and treatises, use a technique called Westlaw as a citator to retrieve cases that cite your authority (see Section 7.3).

7.1 KeyCite

KeyCite is the citation research service from West Group that integrates all the case law on Westlaw. KeyCite helps you trace the history of a case, retrieve a list of all cases and selected secondary sources that cite a case, and track legal issues decided in a case.

KeyCite provides both direct and negative indirect history for any case within the scope of its coverage. The History of the Case window displays a case's direct appellate history and its negative indirect history, which consists of cases outside the direct appellate line that may have a negative impact on its precedential value. The display also includes related references, which are opinions involving the same parties and facts but resolving different issues.

In addition to case history, the Citations to the Case window in KeyCite lists all cases on Westlaw and secondary sources such as law review articles and ALR® annotations that cite the decision. These citing references are added to KeyCite as soon as they are added to Westlaw. All citing cases on Westlaw are included in KeyCite even unpublished opinions.

For citation verification, the KeyCite display provides the case title; parallel citations, including many looseleaf citations; court of decision; docket number; and filing date.

7.2 Shepard's Citations

For case law, Shepard's provides a comprehensive list of cases and other documents that have cited a particular case. Shepard's also includes explanatory analysis to indicate how the citing cases have treated the case, e.g., followed or explained.

For statutes, Shepard's Citations provides a comprehensive list of cases citing a particular statute, as well as information on subsequent legislative action.

7.3 Using Westlaw As a Citator

Using Westlaw as a citator, you can search for documents citing a specific statute, regulation, rule, agency decision or other authority. For example, to retrieve federal cases citing 16 U.S.C.A § 3120, access the Federal Case Law database (ALLFEDS) and type a query like the following:

16 +5 3120

Section 8. Research Examples

8.1 Retrieving Law Review Articles

Recent law review articles are often a good place to begin researching a legal issue because law review articles serve 1) as an excellent introduction to a new topic or review for a stale one, providing terminology to help in query formulation; 2) as a finding tool for pertinent primary authority, such as cases and statutes; and 3) in some instances, as persuasive secondary authority. For example, suppose you need to gain more background information on the constitutionality of zoning ordinances.

Solution

- To retrieve recent law review articles relevant to your issue, access the Journals & Law Reviews database (JLR). Using the Natural Language search method, enter a description like the following:

constitutionality of zoning ordinances

- If you have a citation to an article in a specific publication, use Find to retrieve it. For more information on Find, see Section 3.1 of this appendix. For example, to retrieve the article found at 73 North Dakota Law Review 721, access Find and type

73 nd l rev 721

- If you know the title of an article, but not which journal it appeared in, access the Journals & Law Reviews database (JLR) and search for key terms from the title in the title field. For example, to retrieve the article Commercial Hazardous Waste Projects in Indian Country: An Opportunity for Tribal Economic Development Through Land Use Planning, type the following Terms and Connectors query:

ti(hazardous waste & tribal & land use)

8.2 Retrieving Case Law

Suppose you need to retrieve Texas case law discussing whether governmental takings unreasonably interfere with landowner rights.

Solution

- Access the Texas Cases database (TX–CS). Type a Natural Language description such as the following:

    government taking and landowner rights

- When you know the citation to a specific case, use Find to retrieve it. (For more information on Find, see Section 3.1 of this appendix.) For example, to retrieve *Pennsylvania Coal Co. v. Mahon*, 43 S. Ct. 158 (1922), access Find and type

    43 sct 158

- If you find a topic and key number that is on point, run a search using that topic and key number to retrieve additional cases discussing that point of law. For example, to retrieve cases containing headnotes classified under topic 148 (Eminent Domain) and key number 2(1.2) (Relating to zoning, planning, or land use), type the following query:

    148k2(1.2)

- To retrieve cases written by a particular judge, add a judge field (ju) restriction to your query. For example, to retrieve cases written by Chief Justice Rehnquist that contain headnotes classified under either topic 148 (Eminent Domain) or topic 414 (Zoning and Planning), type the following query:

    ju(rehnquist) & to(148 414)

8.3 Retrieving Statutes

Suppose you need to retrieve Minnesota statutes dealing with agricultural land use.

Solution

- Access the Minnesota Statutes Annotated database (MN–ST–ANN). Search for your terms in the prelim and caption fields using the Terms and Connectors search method:

    pr,ca(agricultur! & land /s use)

- When you know the citation for a specific section of a statute, use Find to retrieve the statute. For example, to retrieve 16 U.S.C.A. § 410y–2, access Find and type

16 usca 410y–2

- To look at surrounding statutory sections, use the Table of Contents service. Select a Jump marker in the prelim or caption field. You can also use Documents in Sequence to retrieve the section following § 410y–2. Click the **Docs in Seq** button.

- When you retrieve a statute on Westlaw, it will contain an Update message if legislation amending or repealing it is available online. To display this legislation, select the Jump marker in the Update message.

8.4 Retrieving Administrative Materials

Suppose you need to review federal administrative materials from agencies such as the Environmental Protection Agency. If you would like information about zoning and the environment, access the Federal Environmental Law Administrative Materials database (FENV–ADMIN) and type

zoning zoned /s environment!

To retrieve all the state administrative codes available on Westlaw that address airport zoning and variances, access the State Administrative Code Multibase (ADC–ALL). Limit your search to code sections that have *zoning, airport* and *variance* in the prelim or caption field (pr,ca) by typing

pr,ca(zoning & variance & airport)

8.5 Using Directories

To retrieve the name, address and telephone number of the zoning administrator in Anaheim, California, access the Municipal Yellow Book database (MUNIYB) and add a citation field (ci) restriction to your query:

ci(anaheim) & zoning /3 administrator

Suppose you would like to consult with an attorney in California who practices in the areas of real estate or land use. Access the West Legal Directory California database (WLD–CA). If you wish to retrieve information about attorneys in the city of Los Angeles, type **los angeles** in the *City* box and **land use real estate** in the *Specific Practice Area* box.

8.6 Using the Citator Services

Suppose one of the cases you retrieve in your case law research is *Pennsylvania Coal Co. v. Mahon*, 43 S. Ct. 158 (1922). You want to determine whether this case is good law and find other cases that have cited this case.

> *Solution:* Use KeyCite to retrieve direct history and negative indirect history for *Pennsylvania Coal Co. v. Mahon*. While viewing the case, click the **KeyCite** button.

To Shepardize the case, click the **Shepard's** button.

8.7 Following Recent Developments

As the land use specialist in your firm, you are expected to keep up with and summarize recent legal developments in this area of the law. How can you do this efficiently?

Solution

One of the easiest ways to stay abreast of recent developments in land use law is by accessing the Westlaw Topical Highlights Real Property (WTH–RP) and Westlaw Topical Highlights Environmental Law (WTH–ENV) databases. The WTH–RP and WTH–ENV databases contain summaries of recent legal developments, including court decisions, and legislative and administrative activities. Some summaries also contain suggested queries that combine the proven power of West's topic and key numbers and West's case headnotes to retrieve additional pertinent cases.

- When you access WTH–RP or WTH–ENV you will automatically retrieve a list of documents added to the database in the last two weeks.

- To read a summary of a document, double-click its entry in the list.

- To view the full text of a document, access Find while viewing its summary.

- To search the WTH–RP database, access the database and choose **New Search** from the Search menu. At the Terms and Connectors Query Editor, type your query. For example, to retrieve information about master plans type:

master +5 plan

Table of Cases

G

Neuberger v. City of Portland, 288 Or. 585, 607 P.2d 722 (Or.1980)—§ **5.9, n. 23.**

Neuberger v. City of Portland, 288 Or. 155, 603 P.2d 771 (Or.1979)—§ **5.9, n. 10.**

Neufeld v. City of Baltimore—§ **10.27, n. 11.**

Newark, City of v. University of Delaware—§ **4.27, n. 8.**

New Brunswick Cellular Telephone Co. v. Old Bridge Tp. Planning Bd.—§ **4.25, n. 17, 30.**

New Burnham Prairie Homes, Inc. v. Village of Burnham—§ **10.12, n. 77;** § **10.13, n. 24;** § **10.24, n. 10.**

New England Legal Foundation v. Costle—§ **11.4, n. 17.**

New Hampshire Motor Transport Ass'n v. Town of Plaistow—§ **4.24, n. 39.**

New Hempstead, N.Y., Village of, United States v.—§ **4.23, n. 19.**

New Jersey v. Baker—§ **4.5, n. 13;** § **4.28, n. 20;** § **10.12, n. 21;** § **10.14, n. 10.**

New Jersey v. Jersey Central Power & Light Co.—§ **4.25, n. 6.**

New Jersey Builders Ass'n v. Bernards Tp., Somerset County—§ **9.8;** § **9.8, n. 61.**

New Jersey Chapter, Am. Institute of Planners v. New Jersey State Bd. of Professional Planners—§ **2.1, n. 5.**

New Jersey, Dept. of Environmental Protection, State of v. United States Environmental Protection Agency—§ **11.4, n. 17.**

New Jersey Shore Builders Ass'n v. Township of Marlboro—§ **7.2, n. 1.**

Newman Signs, Inc. v. Sinner—§ **12.3, n. 35.**

New Orleans, City of v. Board of Com'rs of Orleans Levee Dist.—§ **3.7, n. 5.**

New Orleans, City of v. Coles—§ **5.29, n. 11.**

New Orleans, City of v. Dukes—§ **4.26, n. 11;** § **4.27, n. 15.**

New Orleans, City of v. Hamilton—§ **4.38, n. 17.**

New Orleans, City of v. Impastato—§ **12.7, n. 7.**

New Orleans Public Service, Inc. v. Council of City of New Orleans—§ **10.27, n. 14.**

Newport, City of v. Fact Concerts, Inc.—§ **10.25, n. 9;** § **10.26, n. 6.**

Newport Elec. Corp. v. Town of Portsmouth—§ **4.25, n. 7.**

New Port Largo, Inc. v. Monroe County—§ **10.7, n. 7;** § **10.12, n. 51.**

Newtown Tp. v. Philadelphia Elec. Co.—§ **4.25, n. 15.**

New York, In re City of—§ **3.28, n. 21.**

New York, City of v. F.C.C.—§ **4.25, n. 23.**

New York State Thruway Authority v. Ashley Motor Court, Inc.—§ **12.3, n. 9.**

New York Times Co. v. Sullivan—§ **5.2;** § **5.2, n. 3.**

Nichols v. Tullahoma Open Door, Inc.—§ **4.24, n. 20.**

Nicholson v. Connecticut Half–Way House, Inc.—§ **14.4, n. 18.**

Nigro v. Planning Bd. of Borough of Saddle River—§ **7.12, n. 2.**

Noland, State ex rel. v. St. Louis County—§ **7.8, n. 17.**

Nollan v. California Coastal Com'n—§ **1.4;** § **1.4, n. 9;** § **2.1, n. 6;** § **6.7;** § **6.7, n. 14;** § **7.8;** § **7.8, n. 32;** § **9.8;** § **9.8, n. 34;** § **10.3;** § **10.3, n. 12, 13;** § **10.5, n. 1;** § **10.7, n. 21;** § **10.12, n. 30, 65.**

Noonan v. Zoning Bd. of Review of Town of Barrington—§ **7.6, n. 15.**

Norfleet v. Cromwell—§ **15.6, n. 5.**

Norfolk Redevelopment and Housing Authority v. Chesapeake and Potomac Telephone Co. of Virginia—§ **16.15, n. 12.**

Northbrook, Village of v. Cook County—§ **5.34, n. 27.**

North Carolina v. Joyner—§ **4.39, n. 5, 11.**

North Carolina State Highway Commission v. Farm Equipment Co.—§ **16.6, n. 3.**

Northend Cinema, Inc. v. City of Seattle—§ **4.39, n. 4;** § **10.17, n. 4.**

Northern Illinois Home Builders Ass'n, Inc. v. County of Du Page, 165 Ill.2d 25, 208 Ill.Dec. 328, 649 N.E.2d 384 (Ill.1995)—§ **7.8, n. 27;** § **9.4, n. 19;** § **9.8, n. 30, 44.**

Northern Illinois Home Builders Ass'n, Inc. v. County of Du Page, 251 Ill.App.3d 494, 190 Ill.Dec. 559, 621 N.E.2d 1012 (Ill.App. 2 Dist.1993)—§ **9.8, n. 60.**

Northern Indiana Public Service Co. v. W.J. & M.S. Vesey—§ **14.5, n. 1.**

Northern Transp. Co. v. City of Chicago—§ **12.11, n. 13.**

North Fork Motel, Inc. v. Grigonis—§ **4.2, n. 14.**

North Miami, City of v. Newsome—§ **4.12, n. 4.**

North Muskegon, City of v. Miller—§ **6.9, n. 40.**

N. Pugliese, Inc. v. Palmer Tp. Zoning Hearing Bd.—§ **5.14, n. 14.**

North Shore Unitarian Soc. v. Village of Plandome—§ **4.28, n. 6.**

Northwestern Improvement Co. v. Lowry—§ **15.9, n. 14.**

Northwestern Preparatory School, State v.—§ **4.27, n. 24.**

Northwest Natural Gas Co. v. City of Portland—§ **4.25, n. 11.**

Northwest Real Estate Co. v. Serio—§ **15.11, n. 26.**

Northwood Properties Co. v. Perkins—§ **5.7, n. 4.**

Norwood Builders v. City of Des Plaines—§ **5.35, n. 1;** § **5.38, n. 9.**

Norwood Heights Imp. Ass'n v. Mayor and City Council of Baltimore—§ **4.13, n. 19.**

Nottingham, Town of v. Harvey—§ **2.13, n. 7.**

Nowicki v. Planning and Zoning Bd. of Town of Milford—§ **5.8, n. 5.**

O

Oak Haven Trailer Court, Inc. v. Western Wayne County Conservation Ass'n—§ **14.4, n. 6.**

Oakland, City of v. Oakland Raiders, 174 Cal.App.3d 414, 220 Cal.Rptr. 153 (Cal. App. 1 Dist.1985)—§ **16.3, n. 3.**

Oakland, City of v. Oakland Raiders, 183 Cal.Rptr. 673, 646 P.2d 835 (Cal.1982)—§ **16.3, n. 3.**

Oakland, City of v. Pacific Coast Lumber & Mill Co.—§ **16.13, n. 6.**

Oakland Court v. York Tp.—§ **7.4, n. 1.**

Oak Ridge Care Center, Inc. v. Racine County, Wis.—§ **4.7, n. 9;** § **6.10, n. 2.**

Oakwood at Madison, Inc. v. Madison Tp.—§ **3.18, n. 5.**

O'Brien v. City of Chicago—§ **4.28, n. 7.**

O'Brien v. City of Saint Paul—§ **5.4, n. 9;** § **5.8, n. 5.**

Ocean Acres, Inc. v. State, Dept. of Environmental Protection—§ **7.4, n. 12.**

O'Connor v. City of Moscow—§ **4.2, n. 12.**

Off Shore Rest. Corp. v. Linden—§ **8.3, n. 4.**

Offutt v. Board of Zoning Appeals of Baltimore County—§ **3.16, n. 7;** § **5.8, n. 8.**

Oglesby v. Toledo—§ **5.12, n. 1.**

Ogo Associates v. City of Torrance—§ **9.5, n. 3.**

O'Hara, Appeal of—§ **4.27, n. 23;** § **5.24, n. 8;** § **5.25;** § **5.25, n. 20.**

O'Hare Intern. Bank v. Zoning Bd. of Appeals, City of Park Ridge—§ **5.28, n. 8.**

Ohio v. Kovacs—§ **5.39, n. 10.**

Ohio Civil Rights Com'n v. Dayton Christian Schools, Inc.—§ **10.27, n. 21.**

Oka v. Cole—§ **5.8;** § **5.8, n. 6.**

Oldham County Planning and Zoning Com'n v. Courier Communications Corp.—§ **4.25, n. 28.**

Olson v. United States—§ **16.10, n. 9;** § **16.12, n. 20.**

Olszak v. Town of New Hampton—§ **5.19, n. 16.**

O'Mara v. City Council of Newark—§ **4.38;** § **4.38, n. 7.**

O'Neal, Application of—§ **4.35, n. 6.**

165 Augusta Street, Inc. v. Collins—§ **5.23, n. 2.**

Opendack v. Madding—§ **4.12, n. 7.**

Opinion of the Justices to Senate and House of Representatives—§ **16.4, n. 12.**

Opinion of the Justices to the Senate—§ **12.7, n. 7.**

Orange and Rockland Utilities, Inc. v. Philwold Estates, Inc.—§ **15.7, n. 4.**

Orange Lake Associates, Inc. v. Kirkpatrick—§ **10.26, n. 10.**

Orangetown, Town of v. Magee—§ **5.28, n. 6;** § **10.12, n. 27, 49, 60.**

Oregon v. Troutdale—§ **8.5;** § **8.5, n. 2.**

Oregon City v. Hartke—§ **12.2, n. 4.**

Oregonians In Action v. Land Conservation and Development Com'n—§ **13.10, n. 9.**

Orinda Homeowners Committee v. Board of Sup'rs, Contra Costa County—§ **5.13, n. 6.**

Orion Corp. v. State—§ **5.36, n. 13.**

Ormond Beach, City of v. Volusia County—§ **9.8, n. 13.**

O'Rourke v. City of Tulsa—§ **5.36, n. 18.**

Oshtemo Charter Tp. v. Central Advertising Co.—§ **5.13, n. 5.**

Otto v. Steinhilber—§ **5.16, n. 1, 2;** § **5.19;** § **5.19, n. 3;** § **5.21, n. 3.**

Outdoor Communications, Inc. v. City of Murfreesboro, Tenn.—§ **12.3, n. 30.**

Outdoor Graphics, Inc. v. City of Burlington, Iowa—§ **12.3, n. 32.**

Outdoor Systems, Inc. v. City of Mesa—§ **10.16, n. 11, 21.**

Outerbridge Terminal, Inc. v. City of Perth Amboy—§ **4.23, n. 14, 21.**

Overbrook Farms Club v. Zoning Bd. of Adjustment of City of Philadelphia—§ **4.28, n. 25.**

Overlook Farms Home Ass'n, Inc. v. Alternative Living Services—§ **15.11, n. 16, 19;** § **15.14, n. 9.**

Owen v. City of Independence, Mo.—§ **10.26;** § **10.26, n. 4.**

Oxford House–C v. City of St. Louis—§ **6.8;** § **6.8, n. 28, 37.**

Oxford House, Inc. v. City of Albany—§ **4.7, n. 10.**

P

Pacific County v. Sherwood Pac., Inc.—§ **7.7, n. 12.**

Pacific Gas and Elec. Co. v. State Energy Resources Conservation & Development Com'n—§ **4.25, n. 35.**

Pacific Palisades Ass'n v. City of Huntington Beach—§ **6.9, n. 39.**

Packer v. Hornsby—§ **5.37, n. 21.**

Padilla v. Lawrence—§ **14.2, n. 7.**

Padover v. Township of Farmington—§ **6.2, n. 3.**

Pagels, State ex rel. Schroedel v.—§ **5.28, n. 5.**

Palatine, Ill., Village of, United States v.—§ **6.8, n. 37.**

Palatine Nat. Bank v. Village of Barrington—§ **2.11, n. 5.**

Palermo Land Co., Inc. v. Planning Com'n of Calcasieu Parish—§ **4.24, n. 11;** § **5.12, n. 10, 14.**

Palila v. Hawaii Dept. of Land and Natural Resources—§ **11.16, n. 33.**

Palm Beach County v. Wright, 641 So.2d 50 (Fla.1994)—§ **4.13, n. 26;** § **7.13;** § **7.13, n. 14.**

Q

Z

*

Table of Statutes

NATIONAL ENVIRONMENTAL POLICY ACT

Sec.	This Work Sec.	Note
Tit. II	11.3	
101(a)	11.2	
102	11.2	
102(c)	11.2	

NATIONAL HISTORIC PRESERVATION ACT

Sec.	This Work Sec.	Note
106	12.8	
106	12.8	7
106	12.9	

REHABILITATION ACT

Sec.	This Work Sec.	Note
504	4.7	
504	4.7	7

RIVERS AND HARBORS ACT OF 1899

Sec.	This Work Sec.	Note
10	11.10	
10	11.10	14
10	11.10	15
10	11.11	
10	11.11	1

STANDARD CITY PLANNING ENABLING ACT

Sec.	This Work Sec.	Note
Tit. II	7.2	8
6	2.8	
7	2.8	
14	7.2	10
14	7.6	7
14	7.6	14
14	7.17	16
15	7.17	15
16	7.7	2
18	7.8	

STANDARD STATE ZONING ENABLING ACT

Sec.	This Work Sec.	Note
1	3.13	
1	3.19	
1	4.8	1
1—3	3.6	
2	6.9	7
3	2.10	4
3	3.13	

STANDARD STATE ZONING ENABLING ACT

Sec.	This Work Sec.	Note
3	3.13	2
3	3.13	8
3	3.14	2
3	3.19	
3	5.8	1
3, Comment	5.12	1
7	5.3	
7	5.11	2
7	5.14	1
7	5.22	1
7	5.24	
7	5.26	2
7	5.32	4
7	5.34	
7	5.34	6
7(1)	5.3	
7(1)	5.3	7
7(2)	5.3	
7(3)	5.3	
8	5.34	4
8	5.34	20

STATE STATUTES

ALABAMA CODE

Sec.	This Work Sec.	Note
11–68–5(11)	12.9	9
22–3–100	3.11	5

ALASKA STATUTES

Sec.	This Work Sec.	Note
34.17.030	15.12	9
34.17.040(a)	15.12	9
34.55.004—34.55.046	7.20	6

ARIZONA REVISED STATUTES

Sec.	This Work Sec.	Note
9–461.05(D)	6.6	15
9–500.05	5.31	3
11–826	3.10	2
11–830A	4.34	21
33–276	15.12	9
37–220	10.11	16
37–221	10.11	16
37–222	10.11	16

WEST'S ANNOTATED CALIFORNIA CONSTITUTION

Art.	This Work Sec.	Note
1, § 14 1/2	16.7	2
13, § 8	12.9	1
34	9.3	

WEST'S COLORADO REVISED STATUTES ANNOTATED

Sec.	This Work Sec.	Note
24–65–101 to 24–65–106	3.23	17
24–68–101 to 24–68–106	5.31	3
24–68–105(1)	5.30	10
24–68–105(2)	5.30	15
24–80–1201 to 24–80–1202	12.9	2
30–28–121	3.20	4
31–23–213	7.3	5
6603–21	7.2	3

CONNECTICUT GENERAL STATUTES ANNOTATED

Sec.	This Work Sec.	Note
8–18	7.5	2
8–18	7.5	6
8–30g	6.6	18
20–329a to 20–329m	7.20	6
52–540a	8.7	4

DELAWARE CODE

Tit.	This Work Sec.	Note
10, § 8136—8138	5.2	6
29, § 605	10.11	6
29, § 605(c)	10.11	8

DISTRICT OF COLUMBIA CODE

Sec.	This Work Sec.	Note
5–414	2.13	34

DISTRICT OF COLUMBIA CODE ENCYCLOPEDIA

Sec.	This Work Sec.	Note
5.801 to 5.805	12.9	2

WEST'S FLORIDA STATUTES ANNOTATED

Sec.	This Work Sec.	Note
23.0114(1)	13.7	31
60.05(1)	14.1	9
70.001(2)	10.11	19
70.001(4)	10.10	14
70.001(4)	10.11	22
70.001(5)(a)	10.11	21
70.51	5.2	21
73.071(3)(b)	16.15	5
83.60(2)	8.6	13
161.54—161.56	8.1	12
161.54—161.56	8.2	13
163.225(3)(a)(5)	5.21	8

WEST'S FLORIDA STATUTES ANNOTATED

Sec.	This Work Sec.	Note
163.3177	6.6	17
163.3177(6)(a)	13.7	41
163.3177(6)(e)	13.7	42
163.3177(6)(f)(1)(e)	12.10	15
163.3177(6)(g)	11.13	3
163.3177(10)(h)	9.2	15
163.3178	11.13	3
163.3184	6.6	17
163.3194	2.13	34
163.3194(1)(b)	2.13	9
163.3202	7.3	10
163.3220—163.3243	5.31	3
163.3229	5.31	20
Ch. 186	2.13	13
Ch. 187	13.7	33
187.101(1)	13.7	37
187.101(2)	13.7	34
187.101(3)	13.7	35
187.201	13.7	31
187.201(23)	13.7	38
267.061	12.9	14
286.011	10.13	4
320.8285(5)	6.5	16
337.241(1)	7.13	13
337.243	7.13	15
Ch. 380	2.13	9
Ch. 380	13.7	39
380.04(1)	2.13	9
380.06	2.13	9
380.501—380.515	12.9	2
498.001—498.063	7.20	6
498.001—498.063	7.21	4
553.06	8.1	8
553.19	8.1	8
553.70—553.895	8.6	2
553.71(5)	8.1	7
553.900	8.1	8
663.557	8.1	8
689.18(3)	15.2	17
704.06	12.9	6
704.06(2)	15.12	9
768.28(5)	8.7	16
823.14	14.4	5
823.14	14.6	9
823.14	14.6	11

FLORIDA LOCAL GOVERNMENT COMPREHENSIVE PLANNING ACT

Sec.	This Work Sec.	Note
163.3177(9)	2.13	13

OFFICIAL CODE OF GEORGIA ANNOTATED

Sec.	This Work Sec.	Note
41–1–7	13.3	14

MASSACHUSETTS GENERAL LAWS ANNOTATED

Ch.	This Work Sec.	Note
40A, § 3	4.25	6
40A, § 3	4.25	8
40A, § 6	5.30	7
40A, § 6	5.30	8
40B, §§ 20—23	6.6	14
40C, § 2	3.11	1
41, § 81L	7.5	1
184, § 23	15.9	10
231, § 59H	5.2	6

MASSACHUSETTS ACTS & RESOLVES

Year	This Work Sec.	Note
1989, ch. 716	3.23	17

CODE OF MASSACHUSETTS REGULATIONS

Tit.	This Work Sec.	Note
330, § 22	13.12	3
330, § 22	13.12	4
330, § 22	13.12	5

MICHIGAN CONSTITUTION

Year	This Work Sec.	Note
13, § 2	16.6	1

MICHIGAN COMPILED LAWS ANNOTATED

Sec.	This Work Sec.	Note
5.3395	12.9	6
125.271	3.10	2
125.282	3.10	6
125.294	14.7	21
213.56	16.6	2
213.56	16.6	8
339.2301 et seq.	2.1	2
554.46	15.9	11

MINNESOTA STATUTES ANNOTATED

Sec.	This Work Sec.	Note
83.20–83.42	7.20	6
116B.02	12.1	11
462.12—462.17	3.28	15
462.358, Subd. 2a	5.11	5
462.362	5.40	6
473.861	9.2	12
554.01–554.05	5.2	6

MINNESOTA LAWS

Year	This Work Sec.	Note
1913, Ch. 98, § 1	3.28	11
1913, Ch. 420, § 1—4	3.28	11
1915, Ch. 128	3.28	15
1915, Ch. 128, § 3	3.28	17
1919, Ch. 297	3.28	18

MISSISSIPPI CONSTITUTION

Art.	This Work Sec.	Note
3, § 17	16.5	5

MISSISSIPPI CODE

Sec.	This Work Sec.	Note
17–1–3	10.11	6
49–33–1 to 49–33–17	10.11	28
95–3–29	10.11	6

MISSOURI CONSTITUTION

Art.	This Work Sec.	Note
3, § 48	12.9	1

VERNON'S ANNOTATED MISSOURI STATUTES

Sec.	This Work Sec.	Note
214.040	6.9	60
536.017	10.11	6
536.017	10.11	8
536.018	10.11	6

MONTANA CODE ANNOTATED

Sec.	This Work Sec.	Note
2–9–101 to 2–9–105	8.7	16
42–201	8.6	9
42–202	8.6	9
76–4–1201 to 76–4–1251	7.20	6

NEBRASKA CONSTITUTION

Art.	This Work Sec.	Note
1, § 21	16.5	5

NEBRASKA REVISED STATUTES

Sec.	This Work Sec.	Note
2–401–02–4404	14.6	9
23–114.03	2.13	34

NEW YORK, MCKINNEY'S REAL PROPERTY ACTIONS AND PROCEEDINGS LAW

Sec.	This Work Sec.	Note
769 et seq.	8.6	8

NEW YORK, MCKINNEY'S SOCIAL SERVICES LAW

Sec.	This Work Sec.	Note
143–b	8.6	6

NEW YORK, MCKINNEY'S TOWN LAW

Sec.	This Work Sec.	Note
267–b	5.23	5

NEW YORK, MCKINNEY'S VILLAGE LAW

Sec.	This Work Sec.	Note
7–703	4.18	6

NORTH CAROLINA GENERAL STATUTES

Sec.	This Work Sec.	Note
1–54.1	5.36	27
106–701	14.6	17
121–38	15.12	8
153A–345	5.14	2
160A–364.1	5.32	3
160A–364.1	5.36	27
160A–381	5.33	2
160A–383.1	6.5	17
160A–385.1(e)(2)	5.30	16
160A–400.1	3.11	1
168–22	4.6	3
168–22	15.11	16

NORTH DAKOTA CENTURY CODE

Sec.	This Work Sec.	Note
42–04–02	14.6	12
42–04–02	14.6	16

OHIO REVISED CODE

Sec.	This Work Sec.	Note
303.18	3.12	8
303.25	3.10	2
303.211	4.25	5
519.08	3.12	8
519.211(B)	4.25	29
711.14	3.12	8
1707.01(B)	7.21	2
1707.33(G)	7.21	14
4563.03	3.11	2

OHIO REVISED CODE

Sec.	This Work Sec.	Note
5723.12	15.9	16

OREGON REVISED STATUTES

Sec.	This Work Sec.	Note
30.270	8.7	16
197.010(1)	2.13	34
197.251	2.13	13
197.307	6.6	15
199.410	9.2	11
215.130(5)	4.31	5
221.420	4.25	11
271.725(1)	15.12	2
358.475—358.565	12.9	8

OREGON ADMINISTRATIVE RULES

Rule	This Work Sec.	Note
660–15–000(3)	13.7	29
660–15–000(3)	13.7	30

PENNSYLVANIA STATUTES

Tit.	This Work Sec.	Note
53, § 10201(21)	7.5	5
53, § 10201(21)	7.5	6
53, § 10508(4)	7.4	11
53, § 10508(4)	7.6	9
53, § 10508(4)(ii)	5.30	5
53, § 11006–A(1)	5.38	8
10910.2	5.19	2

PENNSYLVANIA CONSOLIDATED STATUTES ANNOTATED

Tit.	This Work Sec.	Note
102(2)(iv)	4.25	29

RHODE ISLAND GENERAL LAWS

Sec.	This Work Sec.	Note
9–33–1 to 9–33–4	5.2	6
9–33–2(a)	5.2	7
23–19.7–10	5.2	25
34–4–19	15.9	10
45–23–13	7.7	5
45–53	6.6	19

SOUTH CAROLINA CODE

Sec.	This Work Sec.	Note
27–29–10 to 27–29–210	7.20	6
54–23 to 54–35	12.11	10

*

Index

References are to Sections

---

†